R. Wee— 2008

HANDBOOK OF COMPUTATIONAL ECONOMICS
VOLUME 2

HANDBOOKS
IN
ECONOMICS

13

Series Editors

KENNETH J. ARROW
MICHAEL D. INTRILIGATOR

ELSEVIER

AMSTERDAM · BOSTON · HEIDELBERG · LONDON
NEW YORK · OXFORD · PARIS · SAN DIEGO
SAN FRANCISCO · SINGAPORE · SYDNEY · TOKYO

HANDBOOK OF COMPUTATIONAL ECONOMICS

VOLUME 2
AGENT-BASED COMPUTATIONAL ECONOMICS

Edited by

LEIGH TESFATSION
Iowa University

and

KENNETH L. JUDD
Stanford University

ELSEVIER

AMSTERDAM · BOSTON · HEIDELBERG · LONDON
NEW YORK · OXFORD · PARIS · SAN DIEGO
SAN FRANCISCO · SINGAPORE · SYDNEY · TOKYO

North-Holland is an imprint of Elsevier
Radarweg 29, PO Box 211, 1000 AE Amsterdam, The Netherlands
The Boulevard, Langford Lane, Kidlington, Oxford OX5 1GB, UK

First edition 2006

Notice
No responsibility is assumed by the publisher for any injury and/or damage to persons or property as a matter of products liability, negligence or otherwise, or from any use or operation of any methods, products, instructions or ideas contained in the material herein. Because of rapid advances in the medical sciences, in particular, independent verification of diagnoses and drug dosages should be made

Library of Congress Cataloging-in-Publication Data
A catalog record for this book is available from the Library of Congress

British Library Cataloguing in Publication Data
A catalogue record for this book is available from the British Library

ISBN-13: 978-0-444-51253-6
ISBN-10: 0-444-51253-5

ISSN: 0169-7218 (Handbooks in Economics series)
ISSN: 1574-0021 (Handbook of Computational Economics series)

For information on all North-Holland publications
visit our website at books.elsevier.com

Printed and bound in The Netherlands

06 07 08 09 10   10 9 8 7 6 5 4 3 2 1

INTRODUCTION TO THE SERIES

The aim of the *Handbooks in Economics* series is to produce Handbooks for various branches of economics, each of which is a definitive source, reference, and teaching supplement for use by professional researchers and advanced graduate students. Each Handbook provides self-contained surveys of the current state of a branch of economics in the form of chapters prepared by leading specialists on various aspects of this branch of economics. These surveys summarize not only received results but also newer developments, from recent journal articles and discussion papers. Some original material is also included, but the main goal is to provide comprehensive and accessible surveys. The Handbooks are intended to provide not only useful reference volumes for professional collections but also possible supplementary readings for advanced courses for graduate students in economics.

KENNETH J. ARROW and MICHAEL D. INTRILIGATOR

PUBLISHER'S NOTE

For a complete overview of the Handbooks in Economics Series, please refer to the listing at the end of this volume.

CONTENTS OF THE HANDBOOK

PREFACE

Purpose

The explosive growth in computer power over the past several decades offers new tools and opportunities for economists. Volume 1 of the Handbook of Computational Economics [Amman et al. (1996)] surveyed the growing literature on computational methods for solving standard economic models such as Arrow–Debreu–McKenzie general equilibrium models and rational expectations models. This second volume focuses on *Agent-based Computational Economics (ACE)*, a computationally intensive method for developing and exploring new kinds of economic models.

ACE is the computational study of economic processes modeled as dynamic systems of interacting agents who do not necessarily possess perfect rationality and information. Whereas standard economic models tend to stress equilibria, ACE models stress economic processes, local interactions among traders and other economic agents, and out-of-equilibrium dynamics that may or may not lead to equilibria in the long run. Whereas standard economic models require a careful consideration of equilibrium properties, ACE models require detailed specifications of structural conditions, institutional arrangements, and behavioral dispositions.

Although the tools and language may differ, the agendas of standard economics and ACE are thus complementary. For example, many ACE modelers study the processes by which prices are set in decentralized market economies, a problem not considered in standard equilibrium modeling. Moreover, the two modeling approaches share the long-run goal of understanding more fully the dynamic properties of realistically rendered economic systems, an understanding that requires knowledge of potential equilibria *together* with their basins of attraction.

As noted in the preface of Volume 1, there is no clearly defined field that we call Computational Economics. However, the body of ACE research focusing on core topics is now substantial, and it is a good time to take stock of where we are and to communicate this summary to a wider audience of economists.

Moreover, having an ACE handbook at this time also serves an important pedagogical purpose. The ACE approach to economic problems is novel. ACE research requires training in computational modeling skills that few graduate economic programs currently provide, and that relatively few professional economists currently possess. Individuals desiring to take this path will therefore need to have a certain amount of boldness, a willingness to take risks, a willingness to operate outside the boxes outlined by those who have gone before. This ACE Handbook is dedicated to the support and encouragement of these individuals.

Organization

The ACE Handbook is divided into sixteen research reviews, six perspective essays, and a guideline for newcomers to agent-based modeling. These materials cover the following topics.

In the first two chapters, the Editors present overviews of the substantive aims of the ACE literature and the relationship of the ACE methodology to more standard economic modeling. Chapter 16, by L. Tesfatsion, discusses the ACE approach to the study of economic systems and contrasts this approach with more standard equilibrium approaches using a relatively simple two-sector decentralized market economy for concrete illustration. In Chapter 17, K.L. Judd focuses on the problems of determining and communicating the economic content of the results of computationally intensive research, and the trade-offs between standard approaches and computational methods. These two introductory pieces are intended as gateways into the handbook for economists new to ACE modeling.

Chapter 18, by T. Brenner, discusses the key role played in ACE models by learning agents and critically surveys a wide variety of possible agent learning representations. In Chapter 19, J. Duffy examines the potential synergies between experiments conducted with human subjects and experiments conducted with computational agents, with a stress on empirical validation issues.

The determination of agent interaction patterns is a basic foundation for all ACE models. In Chapter 20, A. Wilhite undertakes a series of experiments to explore how bilateral trading and other forms of economic interactions are influenced when conducted within alternative types of networks (e.g., a small-world network). N. Vriend extends this focus in Chapter 21 by considering how ACE researchers have modeled the *endogenous* formation of interaction networks. In the latter models, agents have some degree of choice regarding not only how to behave in any given interaction but also with whom to interact and with what regularity. In Chapter 22, H.P. Young presents and concretely illustrates a rigorous method for analyzing the long-run behavior of systems constituting large numbers of interacting agents with widely differing characteristics.

Financial economics is one of the more active ACE research areas. Chapters 23 and 24 provide extensive surveys of financial market research in which the endogeneous heterogeneity of dynamic investment behavior appears to be critically important for the explanation of observed regularities in financial time series. In Chapter 23, C. Hommes focuses on relatively simple financial market models that are at least partly tractable by analytic methods and that are being used as benchmarks in support of more complex ACE modeling efforts. In contrast, B. LeBaron in Chapter 24 focuses on ACE financial market studies for which the complexity of the models requires the intensive use of computational tools.

Technological change and innovation concern the generation and diffusion of new knowledge, technologies, and products. In Chapter 25, H. Dawid discusses the current and potential contributions of the ACE modeling approach to this difficult topic area. For example, he demonstrates how several empirically established stylized facts regarding technological change and innovation, viewed as puzzles within standard equilibrium modeling, emerge quite naturally in agent-based models.

Organizations are collections of agents who interact with each other within the confines of some formally or informally structured set of rules, and whose activities are guided in part by personal preferences and in part by collective objectives. In Chapter 26, M. Chang and J. Harrington survey a wide variety of organization models, including models of multi-agent firms, multi-plant manufacturers, and retail chains. They develop their chapter around a set of research questions common to the organization literature, comparing and contrasting traditional and agent-based modeling approaches and highlighting new insights afforded by the latter approach.

Over the past thirty years a whole new field of study has blossomed within economics, called *market design*. The normative focus of this field is how institutional rules governing trade can be treated as variables subject to optimization. To date, however, tractability concerns have forced many researchers to restrict attention to equilibrium models in which the strategic options open to traders are severely constrained ex ante.

In Chapter 27, R. Marks first reviews in general terms the manner in which ACE models with strategic learning agents have been used to evaluate market designs from a dynamic perspective. He then highlights ten papers that exemplify recent progress in this topic area, with a particular emphasis on the evaluation of electricity market designs. Chapter 28, by J. Mackie-Mason and M. Wellman, also addresses market design issues. In contrast to Marks, however, the authors focus their attention on automated markets with software trading agents. Their primary concern is the direct use of agent-based tools to achieve a complete effective automation of the various components of market transactions.

A particularly exciting aspect of the ACE methodology is the encouragement and facility it provides for integrative modeling. In keeping with the reasonable Einstein dictum "a scientific theory should be as simple as possible but no simpler," researchers generally tailor their models to the type of issue under study, stressing some features while downplaying or omitting others. But critical model features do not always fall tidily along conventional disciplinary lines.

Chapters 29 and 30 focus on issues of importance to economists for which political concerns are paramount. In Chapter 29, K. Kollman and S. Page critically survey a range of agent-based models developed by economists and political scientists to address collective action problems, pie-splitting problems, electoral competitions, and security and communal stability issues at both the national and sub-national levels. In Chapter 30, M. Janssen and E. Ostrom survey ACE research addressing the governance of systems comprising social and biophysical agents. A key aim of the latter research has been increased understanding of institutional arrangements conducive to the cooperative use of collective ecological resources (e.g., fisheries) in the face of extensive behavioral uncertainty.

In Chapter 31, C. Dibble discusses the potential of computational laboratories for facilitating the design and exploratory analysis of agent-based models with spatial aspects. Illustrative examples include spatial small-world network models, social norm diffusion models, and epidemiology models for the control of infectious diseases.

The next section of the handbook consists of six essays offering perspectives on agent-based modeling. Alphabetically ordered by author, these essays elaborate on the following themes.

W.B. Arthur explains why the movement now under way towards agent-based modeling is not simply an adjunct to neoclassical economics but a major shift to a more general out-of-equilibrium economics. R. Axelrod uses some of his own personal experiences to exemplify how agent-based modeling can help overcome the somewhat arbitrary boundaries between disciplines. J. Epstein argues that the central contribution of agent-based modeling to the scientific enterprise is the facilitation of generative explanation: How can an observed regularity be generated through the autonomous local interactions of heterogeneous boundedly-rational agents?

P. Howitt contends that current economic growth research focuses too exclusively on individual incentives and choice, ignoring critical coordination issues. He advocates the use of agent-based modeling tools as a way of seeing beyond the "individual dots" of an economic system to the overall patterns that emerge from simple interactions among a large number of interacting agents. Following a critique of modern macro theory, A. Leijonhufvud argues that agent-based methods should be used to revive the traditional core of macroeconomics: namely, supply and demand interactions in markets with adaptive boundedly-rational participants. He concludes, in particular, that agent-based methods provide the only means for exploring the self-regulating capabilities of complex dynamic economies, and for advancing our understanding of the adaptive dynamics of actual economies.

In the final perspectives essay, T. Schelling takes the reader back to an airplane trip in the 1960s during which, for amusement, he began experimenting with x's and o's on a penciled-in checkerboard on a piece of paper. His purpose was to see what might result from the repeated location choices of the x and o agents under variously assumed intensities of preference for residing among neighbors of their own type. Out of such musings, the now-famous Schelling City Segregation Model was born.

The handbook concludes with an Appendix by R. Axelrod and L. Tesfatsion offering a general guideline for newcomers to agent-based modeling in the social sciences. The guideline provides a short annotated list of suggested introductory readings.

It also provides pointers to additional readings and software materials to help interested readers get started on their own agent-based research.

LEIGH TESFATSION *
Department of Economics, 260 Heady Hall, Iowa State University, Ames, IA 50011-1070, USA
e-mail: tesfatsi@iastate.edu; url: http://www.econ.iastate.edu/tesfatsi/

KENNETH L. JUDD
Hoover Institution, Stanford, CA 94305, USA
e-mail: judd@hoover.stanford.edu; url: http://bucky.stanford.edu/

Acknowledgements

We are grateful to the General Editors of the Handbooks in Economics Series, Ken Arrow and Mike Intriligator, as well as the Publishing Editor Valerie Teng and Publishing Assistant Pauline Riebeek, for their encouragement and support of this handbook project. We are tremendously in debt to the contributors whose hard work and enthusiasm helped us to bring this project to a successful and just-about-on-time conclusion. Our heartfelt thanks, also, to the many referees who aided these contributors by providing detailed constructive comments at various draft stages. Finally, special thanks to Scotte Page and Howard Oishi for hosting and arranging the ACE Workshop for handbook contributors at the University of Michigan in May 2004.

Reference

Amman, H.M., Kendrick, D.A., Rust, J. (Eds.) (1996). Handbook of Computational Economics. Handbooks in Economics Series, vol. 1. North-Holland, Amsterdam, the Netherlands.

* Corresponding author.

CONTENTS OF VOLUME 2

PART 1

ACE RESEARCH REVIEWS

Chapter 16

AGENT-BASED COMPUTATIONAL ECONOMICS: A CONSTRUCTIVE APPROACH TO ECONOMIC THEORY[*]

LEIGH TESFATSION

Economics Department, Iowa State University, Ames, IA 50011-1070, USA

Contents

[*] Earlier versions of this study have been presented in the Computations in Science Distinguished Lecture Series (University of Chicago, October 2003), at the Post Walrasian Macroeconomics Conference (Middlebury College, May 2004), at the ACE Workshop (University of Michigan, May 2004), and in a Fall 2004 faculty seminar at ISU. For helpful conversations on the topics covered in this paper, thanks in particular to Bob Axelrod, Dave Batten, Facundo Bromberg, Myong-Hun Chang, Dave Colander, Chris Cook, Catherine Dibble, Josh Epstein, Charlie Gieseler, Joe Harrington, Kevin Hoover, Ken Judd, Deddy Koesrindartoto, Blake LeBaron, Abishek Somani, and Nick Vriend.

Handbook of Computational Economics, Volume 2. Edited by Leigh Tesfatsion and Kenneth L. Judd
© 2006 Elsevier B.V.   *All rights reserved*
DOI: 10.1016/S1574-0021(05)02016-2

Abstract

Economies are complicated systems encompassing micro behaviors, interaction patterns, and global regularities. Whether partial or general in scope, studies of economic systems must consider how to handle difficult real-world aspects such as asymmetric information, imperfect competition, strategic interaction, collective learning, and the possibility of multiple equilibria. Recent advances in analytical and computational tools are permitting new approaches to the quantitative study of these aspects. One such approach is *Agent-based Computational Economics (ACE)*, the computational study of economic processes modeled as dynamic systems of interacting agents. This chapter explores the potential advantages and disadvantages of ACE for the study of economic systems. General points are concretely illustrated using an ACE model of a two-sector decentralized market economy. Six issues are highlighted: Constructive understanding of production, pricing, and trade processes; the essential primacy of survival; strategic rivalry and market power; behavioral uncertainty and learning; the role of conventions and organizations; and the complex interactions among structural attributes, institutional arrangements, and behavioral dispositions.

Keywords

agent-based computational economics, complex adaptive systems, endogenous interactions, decentralized market processes, strategic rivalry, behavioral uncertainty, learning, institutions, agent-oriented programming

JEL classification: B4, C6, C7, D4, D5, D6, D8, L1

1. Introduction

Economies are complex dynamic systems. Large numbers of micro agents engage repeatedly in local interactions, giving rise to global regularities such as employment and growth rates, income distributions, market institutions, and social conventions. These global regularities in turn feed back into the determination of local interactions. The result is an intricate system of interdependent feedback loops connecting micro behaviors, interaction patterns, and global regularities.

Economists have grappled with the modeling of economic systems for hundreds of years. Nevertheless, the Walrasian equilibrium model devised by the nineteenth-century French economist Leon Walras (1834–1910) still remains the fundamental paradigm that frames the way many economists think about this issue. Competitive models directly adopt the paradigm. Imperfectly competitive models typically adopt the paradigm as a benchmark of coordination success. Although often critiqued for its excessive abstraction and lack of empirical salience, the paradigm has persisted.

As detailed by Katzner (1989) and Takayama (1985), Walrasian equilibrium in modern-day form is a precisely formulated set of conditions under which feasible allocations of goods and services can be price-supported in an economic system organized on the basis of decentralized markets with private ownership of productive resources. These conditions postulate the existence of a finite number of price-taking profit-maximizing firms who produce goods and services of known type and quality, a finite number of consumers with exogenously determined preferences who maximize their utility of consumption taking prices and dividend payments as given, and a Walrasian Auctioneer (or equivalent clearinghouse construct) that determines prices to ensure each market clears.[1] Assuming consumer nonsatiation, the First Welfare Theorem guarantees that every Walrasian equilibrium allocation is Pareto efficient.

The most salient structural characteristic of Walrasian equilibrium is its strong dependence on the Walrasian Auctioneer pricing mechanism, a coordination device that eliminates the possibility of strategic behavior. All agent interactions are passively mediated through payment systems; face-to-face personal interactions are not permitted. Prices and dividend payments constitute the only links among consumers and firms prior to actual trades. Since consumers take prices and dividend payments as given aspects of their decision problems, outside of their control, their decision problems reduce to simple optimization problems with no perceived dependence on the actions of other agents. A similar observation holds for the decision problems faced by the price-taking firms. The equilibrium values for the linking price and dividend variables are determined by

---

[1] The colorful term "Walrasian Auctioneer" was first introduced by Leijonhufud (1967). He explains the origins of the term as follows (personal correspondence, May 10, 2004): "I had come across this statement by Norbert Weiner, made in the context of explaining Maxwell's Demon to a lay audience, to the effect that 'in the physics of our grandfathers' information was costless. So I anthropomorphized the tâtonnement process to get a Walras's Demon to match Maxwell's."

market clearing conditions imposed through the Walrasian Auctioneer pricing mechanism; they are not determined by the actions of consumers, firms, or any other agency supposed to actually reside within the economy.

Walrasian equilibrium is an elegant affirmative answer to a logically posed issue: can efficient allocations be supported through decentralized market prices? It does not address, and was not meant to address, how production, pricing, and trade actually take place in real-world economies through various forms of procurement processes.

What, specifically, is standardly meant by "procurement processes" in the business world? As discussed at length by Mackie-Mason and Wellman (2006), customers and suppliers must identify what goods and services they wish to buy and sell, in what volume, and at what prices. Potential trade partners must be identified, offers to buy and sell must be prepared and transmitted, and received offers must be compared and evaluated. Specific trade partners must be selected, possibly with further negotiation to determine contract provisions, and transactions and payment processing must be carried out. Finally, customer and supplier relationships involving longer-term commitments must be managed.

Theories always simplify, and substituting equilibrium assumptions for procurement processes is one way to achieve an immensely simplified representation of an economic system. For economic systems known to have a globally stable equilibrium, this simplification might be considered reasonable since procurement processes do not affect the system's long-run behavior. Even in this case, however, the path of adjustment could be of considerable practical concern as a determinant of the speed of convergence. For economic systems without a globally stable equilibrium, procurement processes determine how the dynamics of the system play out over time from any initial starting point.

As carefully detailed by Fisher (1983) and Takayama (1985, Chapters 2–3), economists have not been able to find empirically compelling sufficient conditions guaranteeing existence of Walrasian equilibria, let alone uniqueness, stability, and rapid speed of convergence, even for relatively simple modelings of market economies. For extensions of the Walrasian framework to dynamic open-ended economies, such as overlapping generations economies, multiple equilibria commonly occur and the Pareto efficiency of these equilibria is no longer guaranteed.[2] The explicit consideration of procurement processes would therefore appear to be critically important for understanding how numerous market economies have managed in practice to exhibit reasonably coordinated behavior over time. As eloquently expressed by Fisher (1983, p. 16):

"The theory of value is not satisfactory without a description of the adjustment processes that are applicable to the economy and of the way in which individual

---

[2] See, for example, Pingle and Tesfatsion (1991, 1998a, 1998b). Interestingly, the latter studies illustrate how more explicit attention to procurement processes can produce more optimistic assessments of market performance. The studies show that the First Welfare Theorem can be restored for overlapping generations economies if the passive Walrasian Auctioneer intent only on market clearing is replaced by active private corporate intermediaries intent on the maximization of their shareholders' profits.

agents adjust to disequilibrium. In this sense, stability analysis is of far more than merely technical interest. It is the first step in the reformulation of the theory of value."

A natural way to proceed is to examine what happens in a standard Walrasian model if the Walrasian Auctioneer pricing mechanism is removed and if prices and quantities are instead required to be set entirely through the procurement actions of the firms and consumers themselves. Not surprisingly, this "small" perturbation of the Walrasian model turns out to be anything but small. Even a minimalist attempt to complete the resulting model leads to analytical difficulty or even intractability. As elaborated by numerous commentators, the modeler must now come to grips with challenging issues such as asymmetric information, strategic interaction, expectation formation on the basis of limited information, mutual learning, social norms, transaction costs, externalities, market power, predation, collusion, and the possibility of coordination failure (convergence to a Pareto-dominated equilibrium).[3] The prevalence of market protocols, rationing rules, antitrust legislation, and other types of institutions in real-world economies is now better understood as a potentially critical aspect of procurement, the scaffolding needed to ensure orderly economic process.

Over time, increasingly sophisticated tools are permitting economic modelers to incorporate procurement processes in increasingly compelling ways. Some of these tools involve advances in logical deduction and some involve advances in computational power.[4]

This chapter provides an introductory discussion of a potentially fruitful computational development, *Agent-based Computational Economics (ACE)*. Exploiting the growing capabilities of computers, ACE is the computational study of economic processes modeled as dynamic systems of interacting agents.[5] Here "agent" refers broadly to bundled data and behavioral methods representing an entity constituting part of a computationally constructed world. Examples of possible agents include individuals (e.g., consumers, workers), social groupings (e.g., families, firms, government agencies), institutions (e.g., markets, regulatory systems), biological entities (e.g., crops, livestock, forests), and physical entities (e.g., infrastructure, weather, and geographical regions). Thus, agents can range from active data-gathering decision-makers with

---

[3] See, for example, Akerlof (2002), Albin and Foley (1992), Arrow (1987), Bowles and Gintis (2000), Colander (1996), Feiwel (1985), Hoover (1992), Howitt (1990), Kirman (1997), Klemperer (2002a, 2002b), and Leijonhufvud (1996).

[4] See, for example, Albin (1998), Anderson et al. (1988), Arthur et al. (1997), Axelrod (1997), Brock et al. (1991), Clark (1997), Day and Chen (1993), Durlauf and Young (2001), Gigerenzer and Selten (2001), Gintis (2000), Judd (1998), Krugman (1996), Nelson (1995), Nelson and Winter (1982), Prescott (1996), Roth (2002), Sargent (1993), Schelling (1978), Shubik (1991), Simon (1982), Witt (1993), and Young (1998).

[5] See http://www.econ.iastate.edu/tesfatsi/ace.htm for extensive on-line resources related to ACE, including readings, course materials, software, toolkits, demos, and pointers to individual researchers and research groups. A diverse sampling of ACE research can be found in Leombruni and Richiardi (2004) and in Tesfatsion (2001a, 2001b, 2001c). For surveys and other introductory materials, see Axelrod and Tesfatsion (2006), Batten (2000), Epstein and Axtell (1996), Tesfatsion (2002), and the remaining entries of this handbook.

sophisticated learning capabilities to passive world features with no cognitive functioning. Moreover, agents can be composed of other agents, thus permitting hierarchical constructions. For example, a firm might be composed of workers and managers.[6]

Section 2 explains more fully the basic ACE methodology and discusses the potential advantages and disadvantages of ACE for the study of economic systems. An illustrative ACE model of a relatively simple two-sector decentralized market economy, referred to as the "ACE Trading World," is outlined in Section 3. This model is used in Section 4 to discuss in concrete terms several important but difficult issues associated with procurement processes in real-world economies that ACE is able to address. Concluding remarks are given in Section 5. A detailed discussion of the ACE Trading World is presented in an Appendix A.

2. ACE study of economic systems

A system is typically defined to be *complex* if it exhibits the following two properties [see, e.g., Flake (1998)]:
- The system is composed of interacting units;
- The system exhibits *emergent* properties, that is, properties arising from the interactions of the units that are not properties of the individual units themselves.

Agreement on the definition of a complex *adaptive* system has proved to be more difficult to achieve. The range of possible definitions offered by commentators includes the following three nested characterizations:

DEFINITION 1. A *complex adaptive system* is a complex system that includes *reactive* units, i.e., units capable of exhibiting systematically different attributes in reaction to changed environmental conditions.[7]

---

[6] A person familiar with object-oriented programming (OOP) might wonder why "agent" is used here instead of "object," or "object template" (class), since both agents and objects refer to computational entities that package together data and functionality and support inheritance and composition. Following Jennings (2000) and other agent-oriented programmers, "agent" is used to stress the intended application to problem domains that include entities capable of varying degrees of self-governance and self-directed social interactions. In contrast, OOP has traditionally interpreted objects as passive tools in the service of some specific task. Consider, for example, the following description from the well-known Java text by Eckel (2003, p. 37): "One of the best ways to think about objects is as 'service providers.' Your goal is to produce ... a set of objects that provides the ideal services to solve your problem."

[7] For example, this definition includes simple Darwinian systems for which each unit has a rigidly structured behavioral rule as well as a "fitness" attribute measuring the performance of this unit relative to the average performance of other units in the current unit population. A unit ceases to function if it has sufficiently low fitness; otherwise it reproduces (makes copies of itself) in proportion to its fitness. If the initial unit population exhibits diverse behaviors across units, then the fitness attribute of each unit will change systematically in response to changes in the composition of the unit population.

DEFINITION 2. A *complex adaptive system* is a complex system that includes *goal-directed* units, i.e., units that are reactive and that direct at least some of their reactions towards the achievement of built-in (or evolved) goals.

DEFINITION 3. A *complex adaptive system* is a complex system that includes *planner* units, i.e., units that are goal-directed and that attempt to exert some degree of control over their environment to facilitate achievement of these goals.

The ACE methodology is a culture-dish approach to the study of economic systems viewed as complex adaptive systems in the sense of Definition 1, at a minimum, and often in the stronger sense of Definition 2 or Definition 3. As in a culture-dish laboratory experiment, the ACE modeler starts by computationally constructing an economic world comprising multiple interacting agents (units). The modeler then steps back to observe the development of the world over time.

The agents in an ACE model can include economic entities as well as social, biological, and physical entities (e.g., families, crops, and weather). Each agent is an encapsulated piece of software that includes data together with behavioral methods that act on these data. Some of these data and methods are designated as publicly accessible to all other agents, some are designated as private and hence not accessible by any other agents, and some are designated as protected from access by all but a specified subset of other agents. Agents can communicate with each other through their public and protected methods.

The ACE modeler specifies the initial state of an economic system by specifying each agent's initial data and behavioral methods and the degree of accessibility of these data and methods to other agents. As illustrated in Tables 1–4, an agent's data might include its type attribute (e.g., world, market, firm, consumer), its structural attributes (e.g., geography, design, cost function, utility function), and information about the attributes of other agents (e.g., addresses). An agent's methods can include socially instituted behavioral methods (e.g., antitrust laws, market protocols) as well as private behavioral methods. Examples of the latter include production and pricing strategies, learning algorithms for updating strategies, and methods for changing methods (e.g., methods for switching from one learning algorithm to another). The resulting ACE model must be *dynamically complete*. As illustrated in Table 5, this means the modeled economic system must be able to develop over time solely on the basis of agent interactions, without further interventions from the modeler.

In the real world, all calculations have real cost consequences because they must be carried out by some agency actually residing in the world. ACE modeling forces the modeler to respect this constraint. An ACE model is essentially a collection of algorithms (procedures) that have been encapsulated into the methods of software entities called "agents." Algorithms encapsulated into the methods of a particular agent can only be implemented using the particular information, reasoning tools, time, and physical resources available to that agent. This encapsulation into agents is done in an attempt to

Table 1
A Computational World

---

agent World
{

    Public Access:

        // Public Methods

           The *World Event Schedule*, a system clock permitting World
                inhabitants to time and order their activities (method activations),
                including synchronized activities such as offer posting and trade;
           Protocols governing the ownership of stock shares;
           Protocols governing collusion among firms;
           Protocols governing the insolvency of firms;
           Methods for retrieving stored World data;
           Methods for receiving data.

    Private Access:

        // Private Methods

           Methods for gathering, storing, and sending data.

        // Private Data

           World attributes (e.g., spatial configuration);
           World inhabitants (e.g., markets, firms, consumers);
           Attributes of the World's inhabitants;
           Methods of the World's inhabitants;
           History of World events;
           Address book (communication links);
           Recorded communications.

    }

---

achieve a more transparent and realistic representation of real-world systems involving
multiple distributed entities with limited information and computational capabilities.

    Current ACE research divides roughly into four strands differentiated by objective.[8]
One primary objective is *empirical understanding*: why have particular global regularities evolved and persisted, despite the absence of centralized planning and control? ACE
researchers pursuing this objective seek causal explanations grounded in the repeated interactions of agents operating in realistically rendered worlds. Ideally, the agents should
have the same flexibility of action in their worlds as their corresponding entities have in
the real world. In particular, the cognitive agents should be free to behave in accordance
with their own beliefs, preferences, institutions, and physical circumstances without the
external imposition of equilibrium conditions. The key issue is whether particular types

---

[8] See http://www.econ.iastate.edu/tesfatsi/aapplic.htm for pointers to resource sites for a variety of ACE
research areas.

Table 2
A Computational Market

---

agent Market
{

    Public Access:

// Public Methods

    getWorldEventSchedule(clock time);
    Protocols governing the public posting of supply offers;
    Protocols governing the price discovery process;
    Protocols governing the trading process;
    Methods for retrieving stored Market data;
    Methods for receiving data.

    Private Access:

// Private Methods

    Methods for gathering, storing, and sending data.

// Private Data

    Information about firms (e.g., posted supply offers);
    Information about consumers (e.g., bids);
    Address book (communication links);
    Recorded communications.

}

---

of observed global regularities can be reliably generated from particular types of agent-based worlds, what Epstein and Axtell (1996) refer to as the "generative" approach to science.[9]

A second primary objective is *normative understanding*: how can agent-based models be used as laboratories for the discovery of good economic designs? ACE researchers pursuing this objective are interested in evaluating whether designs proposed for economic policies, institutions, and processes will result in socially desirable system performance over time. The general approach is akin to filling a bucket with water to determine if it leaks. An agent-based world is constructed that captures the salient aspects of an economic system operating under the design. The world is then populated with privately motivated agents with learning capabilities and allowed to develop over time. The key issue is the extent to which the resulting world outcomes are efficient, fair, and orderly, despite attempts by agents to gain individual advantage through strategic behavior.[10]

---

[9] This issue is considered in the handbook entries by Brenner (2006), Dawid (2006), Duffy (2006), Epstein (2006), Hommes (2006), Howitt (2006), LeBaron (2006), and Leijonhufvud (2006).

[10] See, for example, the handbook chapters by Janssen and Ostrom (2006), Mackie-Mason and Wellman (2006), and Marks (2006).

Table 3
A Computational Firm

---

agent Firm
{

 Public Access:

 ## // Public Methods

   getWorldEventSchedule(clock time);
   getWorldProtocol(ownership of stock shares);
   getWorldProtocol(collusion among firms);
   getWorldProtocol(insolvency of firms);
   getMarketProtocol(posting of supply offers);
   getMarketProtocol(trading process);
   Methods for retrieving stored Firm data;
   Methods for receiving data.

 Private Access:

 ## // Private Methods

   Methods for gathering, storing, and sending data;
   Method for selecting my supply offers;
   Method for rationing my customers;
   Method for recording my sales;
   Method for calculating my profits;
   Method for allocating my profits to my shareholders;
   Method for calculating my net worth;
   Methods for changing my methods.

 ## // Private Data

   My money holdings, capacity, total cost function, and net worth;
   Information about the structure of the World;
   Information about World events;
   Address book (communication links);
   Recorded communications.

}

A third primary objective is *qualitative insight and theory generation*: how can economic systems be more fully understood through a systematic examination of their potential dynamical behaviors under alternatively specified initial conditions?[11] Such understanding would help to clarify not only why certain global outcomes have regularly been observed but also why others have not. A quintessential example is the old but still unresolved concern of economists such as Smith (1937), Schumpeter (1934), and Hayek (1948): what are the self-organizing capabilities of decentralized market

---

[11] This question is addressed in the handbook entries by Arthur (2006), Axelrod (2006), Chang and Harrington (2006), Kollman and Page (2006), Schelling (2006), Vriend (2006), Wilhite (2006), and Young (2006).

Table 4
A Computational Consumer

---

agent Consumer
{

    Public Access:

    ### // Public Methods
        getWorldEventSchedule(clock time);
        getWorldProtocol(ownership of stock shares);
        getMarketProtocol(price discovery process);
        getMarketProtocol(trading process);
        Methods for retrieving stored Consumer data;
        Methods for receiving data.

    Private Access:

    ### // Private Methods
        Methods for gathering, storing, and sending data;
        Method for determining my budget constraint;
        Method for determining my demands;
        Method for seeking feasible and desirable supply offers;
        Method for recording my purchases;
        Method for calculating my utility;
        Methods for changing my methods.

    ### // Private Data
        My money holdings, subsistence needs, and utility function;
        Information about the structure of the World;
        Information about World events;
        Address book (communication links);
        Recorded communications.

}

---

economies? For the latter issue, the typical approach is to construct an agent-based world that captures key aspects of decentralized market economies (circular flow, limited information, strategic pricing,...), introduce privately motivated traders with learning capabilities, and let the world develop over time. The key concern is the extent to which coordination of trade activities emerges and persists as the traders collectively learn how to make their production and pricing decisions.[12]

---

[12] An illustrative ACE study of this issue is provided in Section 3, below. Pointers to additional ACE work on this issue can be found at http://www.econ.iastate.edu/tesfatsi/amulmark.htm. There is also an active literature on macroeconomic models with learning (forecasting) agents that maintains price-taking assumptions for firms and consumers and hence rules out any direct strategic interaction effects. See Arifovic (2000) and Evans and Honkapohja (2001) for surveys of some of this work.

Table 5
World Dynamic Activity Flow

main () {	
initWorld();	// *Construct* a world composed of agents
	// (markets, firms, consumers,...).
configWorld();	// *Configure* the world and its constituent
	// agents with methods and data.
For (T = 0,...,TMax) {	// *Enter the World Event Schedule:*
postOffers();	// Firms select supply offers and
	// publicly post them.
seekOffers();	// Consumers seek supply offers in accordance
	// with their needs and preferences.
match();	// Firms and consumers determine trade
	// partners and record transaction costs.
trade();	// Firms and consumers engage in trade
	// interactions and record trade outcomes.
update();	// Firms and consumers update their methods
	// and data based on their search and trade
	// experiences.
}	
}	

A fourth primary objective is *methodological advancement*: how best to provide ACE researchers with the methods and tools they need to undertake the rigorous study of economic systems through controlled computational experiments? To produce compelling analyses, ACE researchers need to model the salient structural, institutional, and behavioral characteristics of economic systems. They need to formulate interesting theoretical propositions about their models, evaluate the logical validity of these propositions by means of carefully crafted experimental designs, and condense and report information from their experiments in a clear and compelling manner. Finally, they need to test their experimentally-generated theories against real-world data. ACE researchers are exploring a variety of ways to meet these requirements ranging from careful consideration of methodological principles to the practical development of programming, visualization, and validation tools.[13]

ACE can be applied to a broad spectrum of economic systems ranging from micro to macro in scope. This application has both advantages and disadvantages relative to more standard modeling approaches.

---

[13] ACE methodological issues are addressed by many of the authors in this handbook. See, in particular, the contributions by Arthur (2006), Axelrod (2006), Brenner (2006), Dibble (2006), Duffy (2006), Epstein (2006), Howitt (2006), Judd (2006), Leijonhufvud (2006), and Schelling (2006).

On the plus side, as in industrial organization theory [Tirole (2003)], agents in ACE models can be represented as interactive goal-directed entities, strategically aware of both competitive and cooperative possibilities with other agents. As in the extensive-form market game work of researchers such as Albin and Foley (1992), Rubinstein and Wolinsky (1990), and Shubik (1991, Chapter 15), market protocols and other institutions constraining agent interactions can constitute important explicit aspects of the modeled economic processes. As in the behavioral game theory work of researchers such as Camerer (2003), agents can *learn*, i.e., change their behavior based on previous experience; and this learning can be calibrated to what actual people are observed to do in real-world or controlled laboratory settings. Moreover, as in work by Gintis (2000) that blends aspects of evolutionary game theory with cultural evolution, the beliefs, preferences, behaviors, and interaction patterns of the agents can vary endogenously over time.

One key departure of ACE modeling from more standard approaches is that events are driven solely by agent interactions once initial conditions have been specified. Thus, rather than focusing on the equilibrium states of a system, the idea is to watch and see if some form of equilibrium develops over time. The objective is to acquire a better understanding of a system's entire phase portrait, i.e., all possible equilibria *together* with corresponding basins of attraction. An advantage of this focus on process rather than on equilibrium is that modeling can proceed even if equilibria are computationally intractable or non-existent.

A second key departure presenting a potential advantage is the increased facility provided by agent-based tools for agents to engage in flexible social communication. This means that agents can communicate with other agents at event-driven times using messages that they, themselves, have adaptively scripted.

However, it is frequently claimed that the most important advantage of ACE modeling relative to more standard modeling approaches is that agent-based tools facilitate the design of agents with relatively more autonomy; see Jennings (2000). Autonomy, for humans, means a capacity for self-governance.[14] What does it mean for computational agents?

Here is how an "autonomous agent" is defined by a leading expert in artificial intelligence, Stan Franklin (1997a):

> "An *autonomous agent* is a system situated within and part of an environment that senses that environment and acts on it, over time, in pursuit of its own agenda and so as to effect what it senses in the future."

Clearly the standard neoclassical budget-constrained consumer who selects a sequence of purchases to maximize her expected lifetime utility could be said to satisfy this definition in some sense. Consequently, the important issue is not whether agent-based tools

---

[14] See the "Personal Autonomy" entry at the Stanford Encyclopedia of Philosophy site, accessible at http://plato.stanford.edu/entries/personal-autonomy/.

permit the modeling of agents with autonomy, per se, but rather the degree to which they usefully facilitate the modeling of agents exhibiting substantially more autonomy than permitted by standard modeling approaches.

What degree of agent autonomy, then, do agent-based tools permit? In any purely mathematical model, including any ACE model in which agents do not have access to "true" random numbers,[15] the actions of an agent are ultimately determined by the conditions of the agent's world at the time of the agent's conception. A fundamental issue, dubbed the First AI Debate by Franklin (1997b, Chapter 5), is whether or not the same holds true for humans. In particular, is Penrose (1989) correct when he eloquently argues there is something fundamentally non-computational about human thought, something that intrinsically prevents the algorithmic representation of human cognitive and social behaviors?

Lacking a definitive answer to this question, ACE researchers argue more pragmatically that agent-based tools facilitate the modeling of cognitive agents with more realistic social and learning capabilities (hence more autonomy) than one finds in traditional *Homo economicus*. As suggested in Tables 3 and 4, these capabilities include: social communication skills; the ability to learn about one's environment from various sources, such as gathered information, past experiences, social mimicry, and deliberate experimentation with new ideas; the ability to form and maintain social interaction patterns (e.g., trade networks); the ability to develop shared perceptions (e.g., commonly accepted market protocols); the ability to alter beliefs and preferences as an outcome of learning; and the ability to exert at least some local control over the timing and type of actions taken within the world in an attempt to satisfy built in (or evolved) needs, drives, and goals. A potentially important aspect of all of these modeled capabilities is that they can be based in part on the *private* internal methods of an agent, i.e., internal processes that are hidden from the view of all other entities residing in the agent's world. This effectively renders an agent both unpredictable and uncontrollable relative to its world.

In addition, as indicated in Tables 3 and 4, an agent can introduce structural changes in its methods over time on the basis of experience. For example, it can have a method for systematically introducing structural changes in its current learning method so that it learns to learn over time. Thus, agents can socially construct distinct persistent personalities.

Agent-based tools also facilitate the modeling of social and biological aspects of economic systems thought to be important for autonomous behavior that go beyond the aspects reflected in Tables 1–5. For example, agents can be represented as embodied (e.g., sighted) entities with the ability to move from place to place in general spatial landscapes. Agents can also be endowed with "genomes" permitting the study of economic systems with genetically-based reproduction and with evolution of biological

---

[15] Agent-based modelers can now replace deterministically generated pseudo-random numbers with random numbers generated by real-world processes such as atmospheric noise and radioactive decay; see, e.g., http://www.random.org. This development has potentially interesting philosophical ramifications.

populations. For extensive discussion and illustration of agent-based models incorporating such features, see Belew and Mitchell (1996), Epstein and Axtell (1996), and Holland (1995).

What are the disadvantages of ACE relative to more standard modeling approaches? One drawback is that ACE modeling requires the construction of *dynamically complete* economic models. That is, starting from initial conditions, the model must permit and fully support the playing out of agent interactions over time without further intervention from the modeler. This completeness requires detailed initial specifications for agent data and methods determining structural attributes, institutional arrangements, and behavioral dispositions. If agent interactions induce sufficiently strong positive feedbacks, small changes in these initial specifications could radically affect the types of outcomes that result. Consequently, intensive experimentation must often be conducted over a wide array of plausible initial specifications for ACE models if robust prediction is to be achieved.[16] Moreover, it is not clear how well ACE models will be able to scale up to provide empirically and practically useful models of large-scale systems with many thousands of agents.

Another drawback is the difficulty of validating ACE model outcomes against empirical data. ACE experiments generate outcome distributions for theoretical economic systems with explicitly articulated microfoundations. Often these outcome distributions have a multi-peaked form suggesting multiple equilibria rather than a central-tendency form permitting simple point predictions. In contrast, the real world is a single time-series realization arising from a poorly understood data generating process. Even if an ACE model were to accurately embody this real-world data generating process, it might be impossible to verify this accuracy using standard statistical procedures. For example, an empirically observed outcome might be a low-probability event lying in a relatively small peak of the outcome distribution for this true data-generating process, or in a thin tail of this distribution.

3. From Walrasian equilibrium to ACE trading

For concrete illustration, this section first presents in summary form a Walrasian equilibrium modeling of a simple two-sector economy with price-taking firms and consumers. The Walrasian Auctioneer pricing mechanism is then removed, resulting in a dynamically incomplete economy. Specifically, the resulting economy has no processes for determining how production and price levels are set, how buyers are to be matched with sellers, and how goods are to be distributed from sellers to buyers in cases in which matching fails to result in market clearing.

One possible way to complete the economy with agent-driven procurement processes is then outlined, resulting in an *ACE Trading World*. The completion is minimal in

---

[16] This point is discussed at some length by Judd (2006).

the sense that only procurement processes essential for re-establishing the underlying circular flow between firms and consumers are considered. As will be elaborated more carefully below, these processes include firm learning methods for production and pricing, firm profit allocation methods, firm rationing methods, and consumer price discovery methods.

In the ACE Trading World, firms that fail to cover their costs risk insolvency and consumers who fail to provide for their subsistence needs face death. Consequently, the adequacy of the procurement processes used by these firms and consumers determines whether they survive and even prosper over time. The critical role played by procurement processes in the ACE Trading World highlights in concrete terms the extraordinarily powerful role played by the Walrasian Auctioneer pricing mechanism in standard Walrasian equilibrium models.

3.1. Walrasian bliss in a hash-and-beans economy

Consider the following Walrasian equilibrium modeling of a simple one-period economy with two production sectors. The economy is populated by a finite number of profit-seeking firms producing hash, a finite number of profit-seeking firms producing beans, and a finite number of consumers who derive utility from the consumption of hash and beans. Each firm has a total cost function expressing its production costs as a function of its output level. Each consumer is endowed with an equal ownership share in each firm as well as an exogenous money income.

At the beginning of the period, each firm has expectations for the price of hash and the price of beans. Conditional on these price expectations, the firm selects a production level to maximize its profits. The solution to this profit-maximizing problem gives the optimal output supply for the firm as a function of its price expectations and its cost function. At the end of the period, all firm profits are distributed back to consumers as dividends in proportion to their ownership shares.

At the beginning of the period, each consumer has expectations regarding the dividends she will receive back from each firm, as well as expectations for the price of hash and the price of beans. Conditional on these expectations, the consumer chooses hash and bean demands to maximize her utility subject to her budget constraint. This budget constraint takes the following form: the expected value of planned expenditures must be less than or equal to expected total income. The solution to this utility maximization problem gives the optimal hash and bean demands for the consumer as a function of her dividend expectations, her price expectations, her tastes (utility function), and her exogenous money income.

DEFINITION. A specific vector e^* comprising each consumer's demands for hash and beans, each firm's supply of hash or beans, nonnegative prices for hash and beans, expected prices for hash and beans, and consumer expected dividends, is said to be a *Walrasian equilibrium* if the following four conditions hold:

(a) *Individual Optimality:* At e^*, all consumer demands are optimal demands conditional on consumer expected prices and consumer expected dividends, and all firm supplies are optimal supplies conditional on firm expected prices.

(b) *Correct Expectations:* At e^*, all expected prices coincide with actual prices, and all expected dividends coincide with actual dividends calculated as consumer shares of actual firm profits.

(c) *Market Clearing:* At e^*, aggregate supply is greater than or equal to aggregate demand in both the market for hash and the market for beans.

(d) *Walras' Law (Strong Form):* At e^*, the total value of excess supply is zero; i.e., the total value of all demands for hash and beans equals the total value of all supplies of hash and beans.

Conditions (c) and (d) together imply that any consumption good in excess supply at e^* must have a zero price. If consumers are nonsatiated at e^*, meaning they would demand more of at least one type of good if their incomes were to increase, their budget constraints must be binding on their purchases at e^*. Given nonsatiation together with conditions (a) and (b), a summation of all consumer budget constraints would then reveal that the total value of excess supply must necessarily be exactly zero at e^*, i.e., Walras' Law in the strong sense of condition (d) necessarily holds. Finally, given consumer nonsatiation together with conditions (a) through (c), the First Welfare Theorem ensures that any hash and bean consumption levels supportable as optimal consumer demands under a Walrasian equilibrium will be a Pareto efficient consumption allocation [see Takayama (1985, Thm. 2.C.1, p. 192)].

3.2. Plucking out the Walrasian Auctioneer

The fulfillment of conditions (b) through (d) in the above definition of Walrasian equilibrium effectively defines the task assigned to the Walrasian Auctioneer. This task has three distinct aspects, assumed costless to achieve. First, all prices must be set at market clearing levels conditional on firm and consumer expectations. Second, all firms must have correct price expectations and all consumers must have correct price and dividend expectations. Third, consumers must be appropriately matched with firms to ensure an efficient set of trades.

To move from Walrasian to agent-based modeling, the Walrasian Auctioneer has to be replaced by agent-driven procurement processes. As discussed at some length in Section 1, this replacement is by no means a small perturbation of the model. Without the Walrasian Auctioneer, the following types of agent-enacted methods are minimally required in order to maintain a circular flow between firms and consumers over time:

Terms of Trade: Firms must determine how their price and production levels will be set.

Seller-Buyer Matching: Firms and consumers must engage in a matching process that puts potential sellers in contact with potential buyers.

Rationing: Firms and consumers must have procedures in place to handle excess demands or supplies arising from the matching process.

Trade: Firms and consumers must carry out actual trades.

Settlement: Firms and consumers must settle their payment obligations.

Shake-Out: Firms that become insolvent and consumers who fail to satisfy their subsistence consumption needs must exit the economy.

Attention thus shifts from firms and consumers optimizing in isolation, conditional on expected prices and dividends, to the interaction patterns occurring among firms and consumers as they attempt to carry out their trading activities.

The *ACE Trading World*, outlined below and detailed in the Appendix, illustrates one possible completion of the hash-and-beans economy with procurement handled by the agents themselves rather than by a Walrasian Auctioneer. The resulting process model is described at each point in time by the configuration of data and methods across all agents. A partial listing of these data and methods is schematically indicated in Tables 1–4. As indicated in Table 5, all outcomes in the ACE Trading World are generated through firm and consumer interactions played out within the constraints imposed by currently prevalent structural conditions and institutional arrangements; market clearing conditions are not imposed. Consequently, in order to survive and even prosper in their world, the firms and consumers must learn to coordinate their behaviors over time in an appropriate manner.

3.3. The ACE Trading World: Outline

Consider an economy that runs during periods $T = 0, 1, \ldots, \text{TMax}$. At the beginning of the initial period $T = 0$ the economy is populated by a finite number of profit-seeking hash firms, a finite number of profit-seeking bean firms, and a finite number of consumers who derive utility from the consumption of hash and beans.

Each firm in period $T = 0$ starts with a nonnegative amount of money and a positive production capacity (size). Each firm has a total cost function that includes amortized fixed costs proportional to its current capacity. Each firm knows the number of hash firms, bean firms, and consumers currently in the economy, and each firm knows that hash and beans are perishable goods that last at most one period. However, no firm has prior knowledge regarding the income levels and utility functions of the consumers or the cost functions and capacities of other firms. Explicit collusion among firms is prohibited by antitrust laws.

Each consumer in period $T = 0$ has a lifetime money endowment profile and a utility function measuring preferences and subsistence needs for hash and beans consumption in each period. Each consumer is also a shareholder who owns an equal fraction of each hash and bean firm. The income of each consumer at the beginning of period $T = 0$ is entirely determined by her money endowment. At the beginning of each subsequent period, each consumer's income is determined in part by her money endowment, in part by her savings from previous periods, and in part by her newly received dividend payments from firms.

At the beginning of each period $T \geq 0$, each firm selects a *supply offer* consisting of a production level and a unit price. Each firm uses a *learning method* to make this selection, conditional on its profit history and its cost attributes. The basic question posed is as follows: Given I have earned particular profits in past periods using particular selected supply offers, how should this affect my selection of a supply offer in the current period? Each firm immediately posts its selected supply offer in an attempt to attract consumers. This posting is carried out simultaneously by all firms, so that no firm has a strategic advantage through asymmetric information.

At the beginning of each period $T \geq 0$, each consumer costlessly acquires complete information about the firms' supply offers as soon as they are posted. Consumers then attempt to ensure their survival and happiness by engaging in a *price discovery process* consisting of successive rounds. During each round, the following sequence of activities is carried out. First, any consumer unable to cover her currently unmet subsistence needs at the currently lowest posted prices immediately exits the price discovery process. Each remaining consumer determines her utility-maximizing demands for hash and beans conditional on her currently unspent income, her currently unmet subsistence needs, and the currently lowest posted hash and bean prices. She then submits her demands to the firms that have posted these lowest prices. Next, the firms receiving these demands attempt to satisfy them, applying if necessary a *rationing method*. Consumers rationed below subsistence need for one of the goods can adjust downward their demand for the remaining good to preserve income for future rounds. Finally, actual trades take place, which concludes the round. Any firms with unsold goods and any rationed consumers with unspent income then proceed into the next round, and the process repeats.

This period-T price-discovery process comes to a halt either when all firms are stocked out or when the unspent income levels of all consumers still participating in the process have been reduced to zero. Consumers who exit or finish this process with positive unmet subsistence needs die at the end of period T. Their unspent money holdings (if any) are then lost to the economy, but their stock shares are distributed equally among all remaining (alive) consumers at the beginning of period $T + 1$. This *stock share redistribution method* ensures that each alive consumer continues to own an equal share of each firm. At the end of each period $T \geq 0$, each firm calculates its period-T profits. A firm incurs positive (negative) profits if it sells (does not sell) enough output at a sufficiently high price to cover its total costs, including its fixed costs. Each firm then calculates its period-T net worth (total assets minus total liabilities). If a firm finds it does not have a positive[17] net worth, it is declared *effectively insolvent* and it must exit the economy. Otherwise, the firm applies a state-conditioned *profit allocation method* to determine how its period-T profits (positive or negative) should be allocated between money (dis)savings, capacity (dis)investment, and (nonnegative) dividend payments to its shareholders.

---

[17] As detailed in the Appendix A, a valuation of each firm's capacity is included in the calculation of its net worth. Consequently, a zero net worth implies a firm has no capacity for production.

In summary, the ACE Trading World incorporates several key structural attributes, institutional arrangements, and behavioral methods whose specification could critically affect model outcomes. These include: initial numbers and capacities of hash and bean firms; initial number of consumers; initial firm money holdings; consumer money endowment profiles; initial firm cost functions; consumer utility functions; market price discovery and trading protocols; world protocols regarding stock ownership, firm collusion, and firm insolvency; firm learning methods; firm rationing methods; and firm profit allocation methods.

The degree to which the ACE Trading World is capable of self-coordination can be experimentally examined by studying the impact of changes in these specifications on micro behaviors, interaction patterns, and global regularities. For example, as detailed in Cook and Tesfatsion (2006), the ACE Trading World is being implemented as a computational laboratory with a graphical user interface. This implementation will permit users to explore systematically the effects of alternative specifications, and to visualize these effects through various types of run-time displays.

3.4. Defining "equilibrium" for the ACE Trading World

Definitions of equilibrium appearing in scientific discourse differ in particulars depending on the system under study. All such definitions, however, would appear to embody the following core idea: a system is in *equilibrium* if all influences acting on the system offset each other so that the system is in an unchanging condition.

It is important to note the absence in this core definition of any conception of uniqueness, optimality, or stability (robustness) with regard to external system disturbances. Once the existence of an equilibrium has been established, one can further explore the particular nature of this equilibrium. Is it unique? Does it exhibit optimality properties in any sense? Is it locally stable with respect to displacements confined to some neighborhood of the equilibrium? If so, what can be said about the size and shape of this "basin of attraction"?

The ACE Trading World is a deterministic system.[18] The state of the system at the beginning of each period T is given by the methods and data of all of the agents currently constituting the system. The methods include all of the processes used by agents in period T to carry out production, pricing, and trade activities, both private behavioral methods and public protocols. These methods are schematically indicated in Tables 1–4 and discussed in detail in Sections A.1–A.7 of the Appendix A. The data include all of the exogenous and period-T predetermined variables for the ACE Trading World; a complete listing of these variables can be found in Section A.8 of the Appendix A.

Let $X(T)$ denote the state of the ACE Trading World at the beginning of period T. By construction, the motion of this state follows a first-order Markov process. That is,

---

[18] Each firm and consumer in the ACE Trading World implementation by Cook and Tesfatsion (2006) has access to its own method for generating "random numbers." However, as usual, these methods are in actuality pseudo-random number generators consisting of systems of deterministic difference equations.

$X(T + 1)$ is determined as a function of the previous state $X(T)$. This function would be extremely difficult to represent in explicit structural form, but it could be done.[19] For expository purposes, let this state process be depicted as

$$X(T + 1) = S(X(T)), \quad T = 0, 1, \ldots, \text{TMax}. \tag{1}$$

If in some period $\bar{T} \geq 0$ all firms were to become insolvent and all consumers were to die for lack of goods sufficient to meet their subsistence needs, the ACE Trading World would exhibit an "unchanging condition" in the sense of an unchanged state,

$$X(T + 1) = X(T) \quad \text{for} \quad T = \bar{T} + 1, \ldots, \text{TMax}. \tag{2}$$

Apart from this dire situation, however, the ACE Trading World has four features that tend to promote continual changes in the data components of $X(T)$: (a) the firms' use of choice probability distributions to select supply offers; (b) firm learning (updating of choice probability distributions); (c) changing firm capacity levels in response to changing profit conditions; and (d) resort by firms and consumers to "coin flips" to resolve indifferent choices. Consequently, although a stationary-state equilibrium in the sense of condition (2) is possible, it is too restrictive to be of great interest.

More interesting than this rarified stationary-state form of balance are conceptions of equilibrium for the ACE Trading World that entail an "unchanging condition" with regard to more global world properties. Some of these possible conceptions are listed below.

- The economy exhibits an *unchanging carrying capacity*, in the sense that it supports an unchanged number of solvent firms and viable consumers over time.
- The economy exhibits *continual market clearing*, in the sense that demand equals supply in the markets for hash and beans over time.
- The economy exhibits an *unchanging structure*, in the sense that the capacity levels (hence fixed costs) of the hash and bean firms are not changing over time.
- The economy exhibits an *unchanging belief pattern*, in the sense that the firms' choice probability distributions for selection of their supply offers are not changing over time.
- The economy exhibits an *unchanging trade network*, in the sense that who is trading with whom, and with what regularity, is not changing over time.
- The economy exhibits a *steady-state growth path*, in the sense that the capacities and production levels of the firms and the consumption levels of the consumers are growing at constant rates over time.

Finally, it is interesting to weaken further these conceptions of equilibria to permit approximate reflections of these various properties. Define an idealized *reference path* for the ACE Trading World to be a collection of state trajectories exhibiting one (or possibly several) of the above-listed global properties. For example, one might consider the set E^* of all state trajectories exhibiting continual market clearing. For any given

---

[19] See Epstein (2006) for a discussion of the recursive function representation of ACE models.

tolerance level τ, define a τ-neighborhood of the reference path E^* to be the collection of all state trajectories whose distance from E^* is within τ for some suitably defined distance measure.[20] Given any initial specification for the ACE Trading World, one can then conduct multiple experimental runs using multiple pseudo-random number seed values to determine the (possibly zero) frequency with which the ACE Trading World enters and remains within this τ-neighborhood.

4. ACE modeling of procurement processes

In real-world economies, rival firms must actively compete for customers in order to survive and prosper. This section focuses on six important issues entailed by this procurement process that ACE frameworks are able to address: namely, constructive understanding; the essential primacy of survival; strategic rivalry and market power; behavioral uncertainty and learning; the role of conventions and organizations; and the complex interactions among structural attributes, institutional arrangements, and behavioral dispositions. The ACE Trading World outlined in Section 3.3 is used to illustrate key points.

4.1. Constructive understanding

If you had to construct firms and consumers capable of surviving and even prospering in a realistically rendered economy, how would you go about it? To express this question in more concrete terms, consider the following exercise similar to the type of exercise undertaken in Section 3.

- Select as your benchmark case an equilibrium modeling of an economy from the economic literature that is clearly and completely presented and that addresses some issue you care about.
- Remove from this economic model every assumption that entails the external imposition of an equilibrium condition (e.g., market clearing assumptions, correct expectations assumptions, and so forth).
- Dynamically complete the economic model by the introduction of production, pricing, and trade processes driven solely by interactions among the agents actually residing within the model. These procurement processes should be both feasible for the agents to carry out under realistic information limitations and appropriate for the types of goods, services, and financial assets that the agents produce and exchange.
- Define an "equilibrium" for the resulting dynamically complete economic model.

---

[20] For example, a state trajectory might be said to be within distance τ of E^* if, for all sufficiently large tested T values, the discrepancy between period-T aggregate demand and period-T aggregate supply is less than τ in absolute value for both hash and beans.

In my experience, economics students are generally intrigued but flummoxed when presented with this type of exercise because it is radically different from the usual economic problems their professors have asked them to consider. In particular, they find it difficult to specify procurement processes driven solely by agent interactions and to define a correspondingly appropriate concept of equilibrium. Yet the key issue is this: If economists cannot rise to this constructive challenge, to what extent can we be said to understand the micro support requirements for actual decentralized market economies and the manner in which such economies might achieve an "unchanging condition"?

4.2. The essential primacy of survival

ACE modeling forces researchers to rise to the constructive challenge posed in Section 4.1. The most immediate, dramatic, and humbling revelation flowing from the ACE modeling of economic systems is the difficulty of constructing economic agents capable of *surviving* over time, let alone prospering.

When firms with fixed costs to cover are responsible for setting their own production and price levels, they risk insolvency. When consumers with physical requirements for food and other essentials must engage in a search process in an attempt to secure these essentials, they risk death. Every other objective pales relative to survival; it is lexicographically prior to almost every other consideration.

The explicit consideration of subsistence needs also has interesting ramifications for the analysis of social welfare. The incorporation of subsistence needs into consumer utility functions induces a fundamental non-concavity in these functions at subsistence levels, i.e., where death occurs. This invalidates many important conclusions drawn from standard utilitarian social welfare analyses, for which concave utility and welfare functions are presumed. For example, a comfortable outcome commonly supported by such analyses is an egalitarian resource distribution. Suppose, however, that consumer utility functions take the form $u_k(x) = 1 - \exp(-[x - \bar{x}_k])$ for $x \geq \bar{x}_k$ and 0 otherwise, where $\bar{x}_k$ is a nonnegative subsistence need. The maximization of a standard utilitarian social welfare function of the form $W(u_1, \ldots, u_K)$ with $dW/du_k > 0$ for each k will then dictate that consumers k with relatively high subsistence needs $\bar{x}_k$ should be permitted to die for the greater benefit of consumers as a whole, even if sufficient resources are available to satisfy the subsistence needs of all consumers (Tesfatsion, 1985, p. 297). In order to ensure survival, a right to subsistence shares must be imposed as an additional constraint on the social welfare maximization problem, thus throwing into question the completeness of utilitarianism as a theory of distributive justice.

Despite these observations, fixed costs and subsistence needs are often assumed to be either absent or unimportant in theoretical models of economic systems.[21] Attention

---

[21] Important exceptions include work by researchers such as Richard Nelson, Roy Radner, Amartya Sen, and Sidney Winter on market survival and famine—see Nelson (1995) and Radner (1998)—and work by Chatterjee and Ravikumar (1999) on endogenous growth models incorporating subsistence requirements.

is focused on economic systems assumed to be operating smoothly at their equilibrium points. Survival is assured as a modeling assumption, not as the outcome of a process of blood, sweat, and tears. Fixed costs and subsistence needs reduce to bells and whistles of no consequence for the model outcomes.

Agent-based modeling tools permit economists to test their ability to construct firms and consumers capable of surviving and prospering in realistically rendered economic environments for which survival is by no means assured.

4.3. Strategic rivalry and market power

In economies organized on the basis of decentralized markets, each firm is necessarily in rivalry with other firms for scarce consumer dollars. The production and price choices of firms are intrinsically linked through consumer budget constraints and preferences. A firm's production and price choices can help attract consumers for its output by making its output relatively cheap, or by making its output relatively abundant and hence free of stock-out risk. In addition, a firm's production and price choices can help to counter the relative preference of consumers for other types of outputs.

For example, in the ACE Trading World each hash firm has to worry about the supply offers (i.e., the production and price choices) of other hash firms. A hash firm might try to set a low price to avoid being undercut by rival hash firms. Alternatively, a hash firm could deliberately price high with an eye to profitably capturing residual hash demand from capacity-constrained lower-price hash firms. A hash firm might also try to use its price as a signal to other hash firms, repeatedly setting a relatively high price in an attempt to induce implicit collusion at this price. The riskiness of these supply offer strategies depends strongly on the microstructure of the market and the learning behaviors of the other hash firms. In particular, the initial money holdings and production capacity of a hash firm limit the degree to which it can afford to experiment with alternative supply offers. Negative profits must be covered by reductions in money holdings or by sale of capacity, hence too many successive periods with negative profits will ultimately force the firm into insolvency.

Also, hash firms as a whole have to worry about setting a market price for hash that is too high relative to the price for beans. Too high a hash price could induce potential hash customers to instead buy beans, thus driving down hash firm profits unnecessarily. Since hash firms do not have prior knowledge of consumer demand functions or of the supply offer strategies of bean firms, they do not have prior knowledge regarding the maximum possible profits they could extract from the market through appropriate supply offers. An additional challenging but realistic complication is that each firm can increase or decrease its production capacity over time in response to its own idiosyncratically changing financial state, hence a hash firm's maximum extractable profits can vary over time even if all other firms have stationary structures and supply offer strategies.

Similarly, each consumer is necessarily in rivalry with other consumers for potentially scarce produced goods. The firms currently offering the lowest prices can suffer stock-outs, hence a consumer formulating her demands conditional on receiving these lowest posted prices has no actual guarantee that her demands will be realized. If a stock-out results in a consumer's demand being rationed below her subsistence needs, preserving income for future purchases to secure these needs becomes a critical survival issue.

For example, as detailed in Section A.7 of the Appendix A, consumers in the current rendition of the ACE Trading World are myopic utility seekers. In each period T they submit hash and bean demands to the firms currently posting the lowest hash and bean prices in an attempt to maximize their period-T utility.[22] If they are then rationed below subsistence needs in one of these goods, they back down their demand for the other good in order to preserve income for future purchases of the rationed good at a possibly higher price. However, consumers do not anticipate and plan in advance for stock-out and rationing contingencies.

It would be interesting to consider alternative specifications of consumer utility-seeking behaviors permitting consumers to display a more sophisticated awareness of the opportunities and risks they face over time. For example, if firms offering the lowest possible prices are frequently stocked out, smart consumers might plan in advance to patronize firms offering slightly higher prices in order to avoid long queue lines and stock-out risk. Alternatively, consumers might engage in a sequential search process, one firm at a time, in which they first attempt to secure their subsistence needs and then revert to utility maximization once these needs are secured. In addition, consumers might deliberately plan to save a portion of their current money income in excess of subsistence needs expenditures as a precautionary measure against uncertain times ahead. It is interesting how naturally one slips back into a consideration of such practical "Keynesian" rules of thumb when procurement processes must be constructively modeled solely in terms of agent interactions.

4.4. Behavioral uncertainty and learning

Substantial progress has been made in understanding how people learn in various social settings captured in laboratory experiments; see, for example, Camerer (2003), Kagel and Roth (1995), and McCabe (2003). In addition, researchers in social psychology, marketing, and other disciplines have accumulated a wealth of empirical evidence on learning in a wide range of natural social settings. Based on these findings, a variety of learning algorithms have been proposed in the economics literature.[23]

Unfortunately, tractability problems have made it difficult for economists to incorporate these insights on learning into their analytical models. In current economic theory it

---

[22] Thus, consumers display an extreme form of "quasi-hyperbolic discounting:" namely, current utility outcomes always have a weight of 1 whereas future utility outcomes always have a weight of 0. Recent experimental evidence appears to support quasi-hyperbolic discounting in the less extreme form $(1, \beta, \beta, \ldots)$ with $0 < \beta < 1$; see Sections 1–4 (pp. 351–365) of Frederick et al. (2002).

[23] See http://www.econ.iastate.edu/tesfatsi/aemind.htm for annotated pointers to some of this research. Detailed surveys of the economics learning literature can be found in Brenner (2006) and Duffy (2006).

is common to see the problem of learning short-circuited by the imposition of a rational expectations assumption. Rational expectations in its weakest form assumes that agents on average make optimal use of their information, in the sense that their subjective expectations coincide on average with objectively true expectations conditional on this information. This weak-form rational expectations assumption is in accordance with a postulate most economists find uncontroversial: namely, that agents continually act to bring their expectations into consistency with their information.[24] Nevertheless, it considerably strengthens this postulate by assuming that agents' expectations *are* consistent with their information. Moreover, economists typically apply rational expectations in an even stronger form requiring optimal usage of information *plus* the inclusion in this information of *all* relevant information about the world.

Whatever specific form it takes, the rational expectations assumption requires uncertainty to be ultimately calculable for all agents in terms of "objectively true" conditional probability distributions as an anchor for the commonality of beliefs. Expectations can differ across agents conditioning on the same information only by noise terms with no systematic relationship to this information, so that these noise terms wash out when average or "representative" expectations are considered. This rules out strategic multiagent situations in which a major source of uncertainty is *behavioral uncertainty*, i.e., uncertainty regarding what actions other agents will take.

For example, firms in the ACE Trading World have no prior knowledge of consumer demand functions or of the cost functions and capacities of other firms. An added complication is that the structure of the ACE Trading World can change endogenously over time if individual firms ever find themselves in profit conditions that induce them to change their capacities and hence their fixed costs. Consequently, firms must operate under a great deal of behavioral and structural uncertainty. Even if each firm were to have complete and correct information about structural conditions, the behavioral uncertainty would remain. This is because structural aspects by no means determine "objectively true" expectations for the supply offer strategies of other firms. Rather, such expectations could be self-referential, depending in part on what one firm expects other firms expect about its own expectations, and so on, resulting in an inherent expectational indeterminacy.

The profit-seeking hash and bean firms in the ACE Trading World therefore face extremely challenging learning problems. Despite profound behavioral and structural uncertainty, they must somehow decide on supply offers in each successive period. These choices require the resolution of a trade-off in each period between two competing objectives:

- **Information Exploitation**: Select production and price levels today so that my current expected profits are as high as possible, given my current information.

---

[24] The strong psychological evidence supporting the prevalence of cognitive dissonance suggests that economists should exercise caution even with regard to this postulate.

- **Information Exploration**: Select production and price levels today in an attempt to learn more about my economic environment, even if this adversely affects my current profits, so that my *future* expected profits can be increased.

The manner in which the firms resolve this trade-off in each successive period determines their long-run fate. Will they survive or become insolvent? If they survive, just how profitable will they be?

Given the importance of learning to firms in the ACE Trading World, a key issue is whether there is any one "best" way for firms to learn. The theoretical literature on multi-agent learning is currently in its infancy and offers little guidance at this point in time. However, the experimental findings reported by ACE researchers to date suggest the answer might well be negative. The main difficulty is the prevalence of two-way feedbacks in multi-agent settings such as the ACE Trading World. The relative performance of a learning method employed by any one particular agent tends to depend heavily on the current behavior of other agents as well as on current structural and institutional conditions. These conditioning factors can, in turn, undergo change in response to actions taken by the agent employing the learning method. Even if a Nash equilibrium in learning strategies were to exist, there is no particular reason to expect that it would be unique or Pareto optimal.

Indeed, it is not even clear what information an ACE Trading World firm should optimally take into account during the course of its learning. For example, as detailed in Section A.4 of the Appendix A, hash and bean firms in the current rendition of the ACE Trading World are assumed to rely on a simple form of reinforcement learning to make their supply offer selections in each period. The information requirements of this learning method are minimal. Each firm keeps track of its own profit history, and each firm uses knowledge of its own cost function in order to exclude consideration of supply offer selections that would result in negative profits for sure. One potentially valuable piece of information ignored by this learning method is the length of the queue lines faced by each firm during the course of the price discovery process. A firm might be able to use the length of its queue lines, in conjunction with its production levels, to obtain excess demand estimates that could be used to better inform both its supply offer selections and its capacity (dis)investment decisions. Another type of information currently ignored by firms is observations on the supply offer selections of other firms.

Could a hash or bean firm necessarily improve its profit performance by making use of additional information either alone or in conjunction with other firms? The experimental findings reported by Axelrod (1997) suggest that transparency can be an important criterion for successful performance in multi-agent settings.[25] A potential

---

[25] In 1979 Robert Axelrod posed an intriguing question: What type of strategy (if any) ensures good individual performance over the long haul when one is engaging in Iterated Prisoner's Dilemma (IPD) game play in round-robin fashion with multiple strangers whose strategies are not known in advance? Axelrod explored this question by conducting an IPD computer tournament with IPD strategies solicited from game experts from all over the world. The winner of this tournament was the *Tit-for-Tat (TFT)* strategy submitted by Anatol Rapoport. The TFT strategy is simply stated: Start by cooperating, then do whatever your rival did in the

downside for a firm attempting to use multiple sources of information to inform its selections is that its actions and intentions might become so opaque to other agents that opportunities for mutually beneficial coordination are lost. In this case the profits of the firm could actually diminish.

On the flip side of this issue, Gode and Sunder (1993) have demonstrated that even highly uninformed *Zero-Intelligence (ZI)* traders can perform well in certain types of market settings. Specifically, Gode and Sunder conducted continuous double-auction experiments with computational traders. They observed that high market efficiency was generally obtained as long as the traders acted within their budget constraints, abided by an auction protocol requiring current bids/offers to be improvements over the currently best bids/offers (p. 122), and satisfied the behavioral assumption that higher-value/lower-cost units were always bid/offered first (p. 122 and footnote 5, p. 131). Gode and Sunder concluded that the high market efficiency they observed in their experiments derived from the structural and institutional aspects of the auction and not from the learning capabilities of the auction traders per se.[26]

Later research has raised some cautions about the generality of these early Gode–Sunder findings; see, e.g., Cliff and Bruten (1997) and Gode and Sunder (1997). For example, Cliff and Bruton consider *Zero-Intelligence-Plus (ZIP)* traders who systematically vary their current bids/offers on the basis of information about the bid/offer levels last accepted in the market. In comparison with Gode–Sunder's original ZI traders, Cliff and Bruten find that the performance of their modestly more informed ZIP traders is significantly closer to the efficient performance of human traders typically observed in human-subject double-auction experiments. Nevertheless, the basic conclusion reached in the original Gode–Sunder work still stands: good market performance should not automatically be attributed to trader learning and rationality.

Finally, timing is another potentially critical aspect of learning. In the current rendition of the ACE Trading World, firms are assumed to update their supply offer selections at the beginning of every period in response to last period's profit outcomes. Moreover, their state-conditioned profit allocation methods dictate that they should undertake capacity investment whenever their profits are positive and their current demand exceeds their current capacity. However, in a decision environment as highly uncertain as the ACE Trading World, some degree of inertia could be beneficial. For example, multiple positive excess demand observations would increase confidence in the wisdom of undergoing a costly capacity expansion.

Intensive experimentation with multi-agent economic models such as the ACE Trading World might help shed additional light on these empirically important learning issues.

---

previous iteration. As stressed by Axelrod (1997), one key reason for the success of TFT in this tournament appears to have been its transparency; other players could easily determine that cooperation with TFT would induce cooperation in turn.

[26] See Duffy (2006) for an extensive discussion of the findings by Gode and Sunder (1993).

4.5. The role of conventions and organizations

In the Walrasian equilibrium model, the fictitious Walrasian Auctioneer pricing mechanism ensures buyers are efficiently matched with sellers at market clearing prices. In the real world, it is the procurement processes implemented by firms, consumers, and other agents actually residing within the world that drive economic outcomes. These procurement processes must allow for a wide range of contingencies in order for economies to function properly.

In particular, buyers and sellers must be able to continue on with their production, pricing, and trade activities even if markets fail to clear. The ACE Trading World illustrates the minimal types of additional scaffolding required to support orderly procurement despite the occurrence of excess supply or demand.

Consider, first, the possibility of excess supply in the ACE Trading World. Excess supply increases a firm's risk of insolvency because the firm's revenues, hence profits, are less than anticipated. In accordance with the market protocol governing the insolvency of firms, a firm must exit the economy when and if it sustains negative profits that wipe out its current money holdings and capacity and leave it with a non-positive net worth. Since amortized fixed costs must be covered in each period regardless of a firm's production level, a decision by a firm to refrain from production is not a safe harbor. Moreover, inventory management is not an effective counter to over-production because goods are perishable.

What firms in the ACE Trading World can do to try to lessen their insolvency risk is to implement state-conditioned profit allocation methods. As illustrated concretely in Section A.3 of the Appendix A, these methods determine how the profits of the firms—whether positive or negative—are to be allocated among money (dis)savings, capacity (dis)investment, and (nonnegative) dividend payments to shareholders. In particular, a profit allocation method permits a firm to tailor its production capacity to its normal demand in order to control the frequency of both stock-outs (missed profit opportunities) and unsold goods (unnecessarily high production costs).

For example, if a firm finds itself in an excess capacity state relative to current demand, it can channel more of any positive profits into money holdings instead of dividend payments or capacity investment, or even sell off capacity if its current demand level is expected to persist. Money holdings provide a way for a firm to store value as a buffer against future adverse revenue shocks. Capacity investment also provides a store of value for the firm, hence a buffer against unanticipated declines in future revenues; but capacity entails a carrying charge through fixed costs. On the downside, a curtailment of dividends represents a curtailment of consumer incomes, which could cause a decline in the future demand for the firm's goods. These competing considerations must all be weighed in the selection of an appropriate profit allocation method.

Consider, next, the possibility that firms in the ACE Trading World experience excess demands for their goods. The firms have to determine their supply offers in each period on the basis of limited information about consumer demands and about the simultaneous supply offers of other firms. Consequently, it is possible that firms posting relatively low prices will find their demand exceeds their supply. A firm facing this contingency must have some way of determining how to ration its limited goods among its current customers.

Each firm in the ACE Trading World is assumed to implement rationing in accordance with its own rationing method. These rationing methods can have a potentially significant effect on the resulting world dynamics. Consumers must consume enough goods in every period in order to meet their subsistence needs. As dictated by the market protocol governing consumer price discovery, consumers in every period search for the lowest posted goods prices in an attempt to meet and even exceed their subsistence needs in accordance with their utility maximization objectives. Consumers who fail to meet their subsistence needs by the end of the period will die.

Suppose, for example, that all firms in the ACE Trading World implement the Random Queue Rationing Method described in Section A.7 of the Appendix A. This rationing method allocates limited goods among current customers through random customer selection, without any regard for differential customer attributes (e.g., differential needs and incomes). Under such a method, lower-income customers with currently unmet subsistence needs could face a significant risk of death; any failure to meet their subsistence needs through the current firm means they will next have to try to meet their needs by patronizing a higher-priced firm. If, instead, firms were to implement rationing methods systematically biased in favor of higher-income customers, the risk of death faced by lower-income customers would become even greater.

Imagine how different the dynamics of the ACE Trading World might be if, in addition to private firms, the world also included non-profit firms constituted as government service agencies specifically and publicly charged with providing priority service to lower-income customers. Nevertheless, even the presence of such agencies might not be sufficient to eliminate subsistence risk for consumers. If the agencies cannot afford to produce (or acquire) enough goods to service all of the subsistence needs of their customers, they will face painfully difficult "life-boat ethics" decisions regarding who will be permitted to live and who will be permitted to die.

Rationing methods are not viewed as critical aspects of procurement in economies with abundant goods and infrequent stock-outs. Nevertheless, as the ACE Trading World suggests, rationing methods could potentially influence the growth paths of economies by affecting the allocation of resources and even life and death itself. An economy's current rationing methods might not appear to matter only because they have mattered so much in the past.

In summary, in order to enable procurement to proceed in the face of excess supply or demand, the ACE Trading World relies on a support system of public and private methods: namely, insolvency protocol, price discovery protocol, profit allocation methods, and rationing methods. The implicit assumption is that all agents accept the outcomes determined in part by these methods. Insolvent firms accept they must exit the economy. Consumers accept that their dividend payments might vary with profit levels, that queue lines will form before the firms posting the lowest prices, and that their actual purchases might in some circumstances be rationed below their planned purchases. Consequently, these methods are in fact *conventions*, i.e., generally accepted practices.

Clearly, however, the ACE Trading World exaggerates the coordination problems faced by firms and consumers in real-world decentralized market economies. Apart from the Walrasian Auctioneer pricing mechanism, Walrasian equilibrium models are free of any organizational structure. Consequently, in trying to retain as much as possible of the basic features of the Walrasian equilibrium model outlined in Section 3.1 apart from equilibrium assumptions, the ACE Trading World is forced to rely on conventions to fill out the needed scaffolding to ensure orderly procurement.

As stressed by Clower and Howitt (1996), Colander (1996), Howitt (2006), and Leijonhufvud (2006), real-world decentralized market economies have evolved a wide variety of organizations to reduce coordination problems. For example, even the humdrum retail store dramatically facilitates orderly buyer–seller exchange through the reduction of transaction and information costs. In the current ACE Trading World, traders can only buy and sell hash and beans through bilateral trades. The coordination problems faced by these traders would be ameliorated if hash and beans could also be purchased through retail grocery stores.

ACE frameworks can incorporate realistically rendered institutional aspects of economies with relative ease. Consequently, ACE researchers are increasingly focusing on the role of conventions and organizations in relation to economic performance.[27]

4.6. Interactions among attributes, institutions, and behaviors

Recall that an agent in an ACE model is an economic, social, biological, or physical entity represented as a bundle of data and methods. An agent's data might include information about the attributes of other agents as well as itself. An agent's methods might include socially instituted codes of conduct (e.g., market protocols and other institutional arrangements) as well as behavioral modes private to the agent. Anyone who has hands-on experience with the construction of ACE models, and hence with the specification of data and methods for multiple agents in a dynamic social setting, is sure to have encountered the following modeling conundrum: everything seems to depend on everything else.

Consider, for example, the complicated feedbacks that arise for firms in the ACE Trading World. The learning methods used by firms to select their supply offers determine in part their profit outcomes, which in turn affect their capacity investment decisions and hence their size and cost attributes. On the other hand, the size and cost attributes of firms affect their feasible supply offer domains, which in turn constrain their learning methods. Similarly complicated feedbacks arise between firms and consumers. The chance that any particular consumer will survive and prosper depends strongly on

---

[27] See the handbook chapters by Chang and Harrington (2006) and Young (2006) for discussions of some of this work.

supply conditions, in particular on the number and types of supply offers posted by firms. In turn, the survival and prosperity of firms depends strongly on demand conditions, and hence on the survival and prosperity of consumers. Moreover, all of these feedbacks among attributes and private behaviors must play out within the constraints imposed by market protocols and other institutional arrangements.

Given these complex interactions, it is generally not possible to conclude for an ACE model that a particular attribute will give an agent an absolute advantage over time, or that a particular method is optimally configured for an agent in an absolute sense. The advantage or optimality accruing to an attribute or method at any given time generally depends strongly on the current configuration of attributes and methods across agents.

In principle, using agent-based tools, a modeler can (if desired) permit any or all agent attributes and methods to vary over time. These variations could be the result of innate or external forces for change, or they could result from deliberate actions undertaken by agents in response to received or acquired data. In short, when in doubt about the exogenous specification of particular attributes or methods, an agent-based modeler could simply relax assumptions to permit endogenous co-development. This raises an interesting nature-nurture modeling issue: namely, which attributes and methods of agents should be viewed as part of their core maintained identities and which attributes and methods should be permitted to vary in response to environmental influences? Moreover, this issue arises at both individual and population levels. How much variation should any one agent be permitted to exhibit over time, and how much variation should be permitted across agents at any one time?

One obvious recourse for ACE researchers is to attempt to calibrate the plasticity of their agents to empirical reality. Empirical evidence strongly indicates that structural attributes, behaviors, and institutional arrangements have indeed co-evolved. For example, McMillan (2002) uses a variety of case studies to argue that markets have both evolved from below and been designed from above, with necessary support from rules, customs, and other institutions that have co-evolved along with the markets. It is both informative and fun to study historically oriented works such as McMillan (2002) in order to better appreciate the extent to which attributes, institutions, and behaviors have undergone significant change over time. Plasticity of biological forms is a major concern of computational biologists (see, e.g., [Belew and Mitchell (1996)]), and computational social scientists might find it both productive and thought-provoking to read some of this literature as well.

Another recourse for ACE researchers is more normative in nature. If certain aspects of the world can be set by design, one can explore through intensive experimentation which designs tend to induce desirable social outcomes when other aspects of the world are permitted to exhibit realistic degrees of plasticity. Alternatively, exploiting the growing power of evolutionary algorithms, one can deliberately induce the co-evolution of forms in "survival of the fittest" tournaments as a means of discovering improved design configurations. For example, Cliff (2003) explores the co-evolution of auction forms and software trader forms for possible use in fully automated Internet markets. This work raises a number of intriguing questions for future research. Have real-world economic institutions specifically evolved to provide robust aggregate performance as a substitute for trader rationality? To what extent do current economic institutions leave room for improvement by design? And to what extent should humans in economic institutions be replaced by computational decision-makers with designed or evolved capabilities?

Finally, given the complex interactions among attributes, institutions, and behaviors, and our growing ability to model these interactions computationally, it seems an appropriate time to reexamine the standards for good economic modeling. As noted by many commentators (e.g., [Clower and Howitt (1996)]), economic theory currently places a great deal of emphasis on the attributes and optimal choice behaviors of individual firms and consumers, downplaying important institutional aspects such as markets and market-making activities. Recently, Mirowski (2004) has argued that this emphasis on "agency" (cognitive decision-makers) should be replaced by an emphasis on markets as evolving computational algorithms. Surely, however, we can do better than either of these polar options alone.

Taking the broad view of "agent" adopted in ACE modeling and in agent-oriented programming in general, institutions and structures as well as cognitive entities can be represented as recognizable and persistent bundles of data and methods that interact within a computationally constructed world. Indeed, as schematically depicted in Tables 1–4, the ACE Trading World includes a world agent, market agents (hash and bean markets), and cognitive agents (firms and consumers). In short, agent-based tools provide tremendous opportunities for economists and other social scientists to increase the depth and breadth of the "representative agents" depicted in their models.

A key outstanding issue is whether this ability to consider more comprehensive and empirically compelling taxonomies of representative agents will ultimately result in better predictive, explanatory, and exploratory models. For example, for the study of decentralized market economies, can the now-standard division of cognitive agents into producers, consumers, and government policy-makers be usefully extended to include brokers, dealers, financial intermediaries, innovative entrepreneurs, and other forms of active market-makers? Similarly, can the traditional division of markets into perfect competition, monopolistic competition, duopoly, oligopoly, and monopoly be usefully replaced with a broader taxonomy that better reflects the rich diversity of actual market forms as surveyed by McMillan (2002)?

5. Concluding remarks

The defining characteristic of ACE models is their constructive grounding in the interactions of agents, broadly defined to include economic, social, biological, and physical entities. The state of a modeled system at each point in time is given by the internal data and methods of the agents that currently constitute the system. Starting from an initially specified system state, the motion of the state through time is determined by endogenously generated agent interactions.

This agent-based dynamical description, cast at a less abstract level than standard equation-based economic models, increases the transparency and clarity of the modeling process. A researcher can proceed directly from empirical observations on the structural conditions, institutional arrangements, and behavioral dispositions of a real-world economic system to a computational modeling of the system. Moreover, the emphasis on process rather than on equilibrium solution techniques helps to ensure that empirical understanding and creative conjecture remain the primary prerequisites for useful model design.

That said, ACE modeling is surely a complement, not a substitute, for analytical and statistical modeling approaches. As seen in the work by Sargent (1993), ACE models can be used to evaluate economic theories developed using these more standard tools. Can agents indeed learn to coordinate on the types of equilibria identified in these theories and, if so, how? If there are multiple possible equilibria, which equilibrium (if any) will turn out to be the dominant attractor, and why? ACE models can also be used to evaluate the robustness of these theories to relaxations of their assumptions, such as common knowledge, rational expectations, and perfect capital markets. A key question in this regard is the extent to which learning, institutions, and evolutionary forces might substitute for the high degree of individual rationality assumed in standard economic theories.

More generally, the use of ACE models could facilitate the development and experimental evaluation of integrated theories that build on theory and data from many different fields of social science. With ACE tools, economists can address growth, distribution, and welfare issues in a comprehensive manner encompassing a wide range of pertinent economic, social, political, and psychological factors. It is particularly intriguing to reexamine the broadly envisioned theories of earlier economists such as Adam Smith (1937), Joseph Schumpeter (1934), John Maynard Keynes (1965), and Friedrich von Hayek (1948), and to consider how these theories might now be more fully addressed in quantitative terms.

Another potentially important aspect of the ACE methodology is pedagogical. As detailed in Dibble (2006), ACE models can be implemented by computational laboratories that facilitate and encourage the systematic experimental exploration of complex economic processes. Students can formulate experimental designs to investigate interesting propositions of their own devising, with immediate feedback and with no original programming required. This permits teachers and students to take an inductive open-ended approach to learning. Exercises can be assigned for which outcomes are not known in advance, giving students an exciting introduction to creative research. The modular form of the underlying computational laboratory software also permits students with programming backgrounds to modify and extend the laboratory features with relative ease.[28]

---

[28] See http://www.econ.iastate.edu/tesfatsi/syl308.htm for an ACE course relying heavily on computational laboratory exercises to involve students creatively in the course materials. Annotated pointers to other ACE-related course preparations can be found at http://www.econ.iastate.edu/tesfatsi/teachsyl.htm.

A number of requirements must be met, however, if the potential of ACE for scientific research is to be realized. ACE researchers need to focus on issues of importance for understanding economic systems. They need to construct models that capture the salient aspects of these issues, and to use these models to formulate clearly articulated theories regarding possible issue resolutions. They need to evaluate these theories systematically by means of multiple controlled experiments with captured seed values to ensure replicability by other researchers using possibly other platforms, and to report summaries of their theoretical findings in a transparent and rigorous form. Finally, they need to test their theoretical findings against real-world data in ways that permit empirically supported theories to cumulate over time, with each researcher's work building appropriately on the work that has gone before.

Meeting all of these requirements is not an easy task. One possible way to facilitate the task is interdisciplinary collaboration. Recent efforts to advance collaborative research have been encouraging. For example, Barreteau (2003) reports favorably on efforts to promote a *companion modeling* approach to critical policy issues such as management of renewable resources. The companion modeling approach is an iterative participatory process involving stakeholders, regulatory agencies, and researchers from multiple disciplines in a repeated looping through a three-stage cycle: field work and data analysis, model design, and computational experiments. Agent-based modeling and role-playing games constitute important aspects of this process. The objective is the management of complex problems through a continuous learning process rather than the delivery of definitive problem solutions.[29]

Realistically, however, communication across disciplinary lines can be difficult, particularly if the individuals attempting the collaboration have little or no cross-disciplinary training. As elaborated by Axelrod and Tesfatsion (2006), economists and other social scientists interested in agent-based modeling should therefore ideally acquire basic programming, statistical, and mathematical skills together with suitable training in their desired application areas. Of these requirements, programming skills remain by far the most problematic for economists because few graduate economic programs currently have computer programming requirements. I would therefore like to conclude with some heart-felt exhortations from the programming trenches.

As a professor of mathematics (as well as economics), I appreciate the beauty of classical mathematics. However, *constructive* mathematics is also beautiful and, in my opinion, the right kind of mathematics for economists and other social scientists. Constructive mathematics differs from classical mathematics in its strict interpretation of the phrase "there exists" to mean "one can construct."[30] Constructive proofs are algorithms that can, in principle, be recast as computer programs. To master a general programming

---

[29] See Janssen and Ostrom (2006) for applications of the companion modeling approach to the study of governance mechanisms for social-ecological systems. Koesrindartoto and Tesfatsion (2004) advocate and pursue a similar approach to the design of wholesale power markets.

[30] See the "Constructive Mathematics" entry at the Stanford Encyclopedia of Philosophy Site, accessible at http://plato.stanford.edu/entries/mathematics-constructive/.

language is to acquire a form of mathematical skill every bit as aesthetically pleasing, powerful, and practical as the differential calculus. Indeed, for economic purposes, computer programming is in some ways more powerful in that it facilitates the modeling of complex interactive processes involving kinks, jumps, and other forms of discreteness imposed or induced by empirical constraints. Consequently, programming frees us to adapt the tool to the problem rather than the problem to the tool. Every graduate economics program should incorporate general programming language requirements. It is time.

Appendix A: The ACE Trading World

This appendix presents a detailed description of the ACE Trading World outlined in Section 3.3. See Cook and Tesfatsion (2006) for a C#/.Net implementation of the ACE Trading World as a computational laboratory with a graphical user interface.

A.1: The economy in the initial period

The ACE Trading World is a discrete-time dynamic economy that runs during periods $T = 0, 1, \ldots,$ TMax. The economy produces two perishable infinitely-divisible goods, hash and beans. At the beginning of the initial period $T = 0$ the economy consists of $J(0)$ hash-producing firms, $N(0)$ bean-producing firms, and $K(0)$ consumers.

Each hash firm j in period $T = 0$ has exogenously given money holdings $\text{Money}_{Hj}(0)$ and an exogenously given hash-production capacity $\text{Cap}_{Hj}(0)$. Hash firms can buy additional hash-production capacity at an exogenously given nominal unit price of ρ_H. Each bean firm n in the initial period $T = 0$ has exogenously given money holdings $\text{Money}_{Bn}(0)$ and an exogenously given bean-production capacity $\text{Cap}_{Bn}(0)$. Bean firms can buy additional bean-production capacity at an exogenously given nominal unit price of ρ_B.

Each consumer k in period $T = 0$ has an exogenously given lifetime money endowment profile $(\text{Endow}_k(T): T = 0, 1, \ldots,$ TMax$)$. Consumer k also has exogenously given subsistence needs for hash and beans, $\bar{h}_k$ and $\bar{b}_k$, which must be met in every period in order to survive. Finally, the utility $U_k(h, b)$ obtained by consumer k from consuming $h \geq \bar{h}_k$ pounds of hash and $b \geq \bar{b}_k$ pounds of beans in any period T is given by

$$U_k(h, b) = (h - \bar{h}_k)^{\alpha_k} \cdot (b - \bar{b}_k)^{[1-\alpha_k]}, \tag{A.1}$$

where the parameter α_k measures consumer k's relative preference for hash versus beans.

A.2: Activity flow for hash firms in period T

At the beginning of each period $T \geq 0$, each hash firm j has money holdings $\text{Money}_{Hj}(T)$ and a hash-production capacity $\text{Cap}_{Hj}(T)$. The amortized fixed costs of hash firm j in period T are proportional to its capacity:

$$\text{FCosts}_{Hj}(T) = f_{Hj} \cdot \text{Cap}_{Hj}(T) + F_{Hj}, \tag{A.2}$$

where f_{Hj} and F_{Hj} are given constants. Each hash firm j selects a feasible (capacity constrained) hash supply $h_j^s(T)$, measured in pounds, together with a per-pound supply price $p_{Hj}(T)$. Hash firm j's total cost of producing $h_j^s(T)$ is

$$\text{TCost}_{Hj}(T) = S_{Hj} \cdot [h_j^s(T)]^2 + R_{Hj} \cdot h_j^s(T) + \text{FCost}_{Hj}(T), \tag{A.3}$$

where S_{Hj} and R_{Hj} are given constants. If hash firm j then actually sells $h_j(T)$ pounds of beans at price $p_{Hj}(T)$ in period T, its (possibly negative) profit level in period T is

$$\text{Profit}_{Hj}(T) = p_{Hj}(T) \cdot h_j(T) - \text{TCost}_{Hj}(T). \tag{A.4}$$

Note that a decision not to produce any hash in period T results in a profit level $-\text{FCosts}_{Hj}(T)$ for hash firm j due to its fixed costs.

At the end of each period $T \geq 0$, each hash firm j calculates its period-T profits $\text{Profit}_{Hj}(T)$ and its period-T net worth

$$\text{NetWorth}_{Hj}(T) = \text{Money}_{Hj}(T) + \rho_H \cdot \text{Cap}_{Hj}(T) + \text{Profit}_{Hj}(T), \tag{A.5}$$

where ρ_H denotes the market price for hash-production capacity. If the net worth of hash firm j is non-positive, the firm is declared *effectively insolvent* and it must immediately exit the economy. If the net worth of hash firm j is positive, then the firm applies the following profit allocation method $A(m_{Hj}, d_{Hj})$ to determine the disposition of its period-T profits among money (dis)savings, capacity (dis)investment, and dividend payments to shareholders.

A.3: Profit allocation method for hash firm j

Capacity investment state: If period-T profits $\text{Profit}_{Hj}(T)$ are *nonnegative* and if actual hash sales $h_j(T)$ are at *maximum capacity* $\text{Cap}_{Hj}(T)$, allocate a portion m_{Hj} of period-T profits towards money holdings and the remaining portion $[1 - m_{Hj}]$ towards capacity investment. Further earmark a portion d_{Hj} of the resulting money holdings as dividend payments to be paid to shareholders at the beginning of period $T + 1$. Thus, in this state, the money holdings, capacity, and dividend payments of hash firm j at the beginning of period $T + 1$ are as follows:

$$\text{Money}_{Hj}(T + 1) = [1 - d_{Hj}] \cdot \big[\text{Money}_{Hj}(T) + m_{Hj} \cdot \text{Profit}_{Hj}(T)\big];$$

$$\text{Cap}_{Hj}(T + 1) = \text{Cap}_{Hj}(T) + \frac{[1 - m_{Hj}] \cdot \text{Profit}_{Hj}(T)}{\rho_H};$$

$$\text{Div}_{Hj}(T + 1) = d_{Hj} \cdot \big[\text{Money}_{Hj}(T) + m_{Hj} \cdot \text{Profit}_{Hj}(T)\big].$$

Precautionary savings state: If period-T profits $\text{Profit}_{Hj}(T)$ are *nonnegative* but actual period-T hash sales $h_j(T)$ are *less* than maximum capacity $\text{Cap}_{Hj}(T)$, allocate all period-T profits to money holdings. Further earmark a portion d_{Hj} of the resulting money holdings as dividend payments to be paid to shareholders at the beginning of period $T+1$. Thus, in this state, the money holdings, capacity, and dividend payments of hash firm j at the beginning of period $T+1$ are as follows:

$$\text{Money}_{Hj}(T+1) = [1 - d_{Hj}] \cdot \left[\text{Money}_{Hj}(T) + \text{Profit}_{Hj}(T)\right];$$
$$\text{Cap}_{Hj}(T+1) = \text{Cap}_{Hj}(T);$$
$$\text{Div}_{Hj}(T+1) = d_{Hj} \cdot \left[\text{Money}_{Hj}(T) + \text{Profit}_{Hj}(T)\right].$$

Contractionary state: If period-T profits $\text{Profit}_{Hj}(T)$ are *negative*, use period-T money holdings to cover as much of these negative profits as possible. If necessary, sell period-T capacity to cover any remaining negative profits. Do not distribute any dividend payments to shareholders at the beginning of period $T+1$. Thus, in this state, the money holdings, capacity, and dividend payments of hash firm j at the beginning of period $T+1$ are as follows. Let $I_{Hj}(T)$ denote the indicator function defined by

$$I_{Hj}(T) = \begin{cases} 1 & \text{if } \text{Money}_{Hj}(T) + \text{Profit}_{Hj}(T) \geq 0; \\ 0 & \text{otherwise.} \end{cases}$$

Then:[31]

$$\text{Money}_{Hj}(T+1) = I_{Hj}(T) \cdot \left[\text{Money}_{Hj}(T) + \text{Profit}_{Hj}(T)\right];$$
$$\text{Cap}_{Hj}(T+1) = \text{Cap}_{Hj}(T) + \left[1 - I_{Hj}(T)\right]$$
$$\cdot \left[\text{Money}_{Hj}(T) + \text{Profit}_{Hj}(T)\right]/\rho_H;$$
$$\text{Div}_{Hj}(T+1) = 0.$$

A.4: Learning for hash firms

Representation of hash firm j's supply offers

A possible supply offer (h, p) for hash firm j at the beginning of any period T consists of a hash production level h and a unit price p. These supply offers can usefully be expressed in an alternative form. By assumption, hash firm j in period T cannot post a negative production level or a production level in excess of its current (positive) capacity

---

[31] The following relationships imply, by construction, that a firm with a positive net worth (A.5) at the end of period T cannot have a non-positive capacity at the beginning of period $T+1$. Consequently, a firm either exits the economy at the end of period T with a non-positive net worth or has a positive capacity at the beginning of period $T+1$.

level $\text{Cap}_{Hj}(T)$. Consequently, a choice of a feasible production level h in period T can alternatively be expressed as a choice to produce a percentage of current capacity:

$$\text{CapPercent}_{Hj}(h, T) = \frac{h}{[\text{Cap}_{Hj}(T)]}. \tag{A.6}$$

By construction, the capacity percentage (A.6) lies between 0 and 1.

Also, given any feasible production level h, a choice of a feasible price p in period T can alternatively be expressed as a choice of a price-cost margin, or *mark-up* for short. This mark-up is defined to be the percentage difference between the price p and the marginal cost of producing h. More precisely, using the total cost function specified for hash firms in Section A.2 above, let $MC_{Hj}(h) = 2S_{Hj}h + R_{Hj}$ denote hash firm j's marginal cost of producing h. Then the mark-up corresponding to any feasible supply offer (h, p) for hash firm j is defined as

$$\text{MarkUp}_{Hj}(h, p) = \frac{p - MC_{Hj}(h)}{p} \quad \text{for } p > 0, \tag{A.7}$$

with $\text{MarkUp}_{Hj}(h, 0) = -1000$. As long as hash firm j never chooses to supply hash either at a zero price or at a price below marginal cost, the mark-up (A.7) will be bounded between 0 and 1 for all of its supply offers.[32] Henceforth, the feasible supply offers of hash firm j in each period $T \geq 0$ will be assumed to take the form (CapPercent, MarkUp).

Hash firm j's learning problem

Hash firm j's learning problem involves two basic decisions: (i) How to select a supply offer in the initial period $T = 0$; and (ii) when and how to *change* a previous supply offer. Assuming it sells all it produces, hash firm j can attempt to secure higher profits by increasing its capacity percentage given its current mark-up, increasing its mark-up given its current capacity percentage, or increasing both its capacity percentage and its mark-up. However, hash firm j must make its supply offers in the face of a high degree of uncertainty about the structure of the economy and the behavior of other agents. Consequently, a danger is that not all produced units will be sold. In this case the revenues of hash firm j could be insufficient to cover its total costs of production. Indeed, overly aggressive experimentation with supply offers could eventually result in forced capacity sales or even insolvency.

Intuitively, then, a cautious approach to learning seems warranted for hash firm j in the ACE Trading World. One such cautious approach is *reinforcement learning (RL)*; see Sutton and Barto (1998). The basic idea underlying RL is that the tendency to implement an action should be strengthened (reinforced) if it produces favorable results and

---

[32] This definition for mark-up coincides with the well-known "Lerner Index" used in industrial organization studies to measure market power in monopolistic and oligopolistic markets; see Tirole (2003, pp. 219–220).

weakened if it produces unfavorable results. Game theorists have begun to explore the use of RL to explain experimental data obtained from human subjects who are learning to play repeated games in laboratory settings involving multiple strategically-interacting players. For example, in Erev and Roth (1998) and Roth and Erev (1995), the authors develop an RL algorithm able to track successfully the intermediate-term behavior of human subjects observed by the authors for a particular test suite of repeated games.

A variation of the Roth–Erev RL algorithm—hereafter referred to as the *VRE learning algorithm*—is one possible learning method that can be specified for firms in the ACE Trading World. A brief outline of this VRE learning algorithm will now be given for an arbitrary hash firm j.

The VRE learning algorithm for hash firm j

Suppose hash firm j can choose from among Z_{Hj} feasible supply offers in each period $T \geq 0$. In the initial period $T = 0$, the initial propensity of hash firm j to choose its ith feasible supply offer is given by a nonnegative *initial propensity* $q_{ji}(0)$, $i = 1, \ldots, Z_{Hj}$. These initial propensities are assumed to be equal valued. That is, it is assumed there exists a constant value $q_{Hj}(0)$ such that

$$q_{ji}(0) = q_{Hj}(0) \quad \text{for all feasible supply offers } i. \tag{A.8}$$

Now consider the beginning of an arbitrary period $T \geq 0$ in which the propensity of hash firm j to choose feasible supply offer i is given by $q_{ji}(T)$. The *choice probability* that hash firm j uses to select a feasible supply offer i in period T is then given by[33]

$$p_{ji}(T) = \frac{\exp(q_{ji}(T)/C_{Hj})}{\sum_{m=1}^{Z_{Hj}} \exp(q_{jm}(T)/C_{Hj})}. \tag{A.9}$$

In (A.9), C_{Hj} is a *cooling parameter* that affects the degree to which hash firm j makes use of propensity values in determining its choice probabilities. As $C_{Hj} \to \infty$, then $p_{ji}(T) \to 1/Z_{Hj}$ for each i, so that in the limit hash firm j pays no attention to propensity values in forming its choice probabilities. On the other hand, as $C_{Hj} \to 0$, the choice probabilities (A.9) become increasingly peaked over the particular supply offers i having the highest propensity values, thereby increasing the probability that these supply offers will be chosen.

At the end of each period $T \geq 0$, the current propensity $q_{ji}(T)$ that hash firm j associates with each feasible supply offer i is updated in accordance with the following rule. Let i' denote the supply offer that was *actually* selected and posted for period T,

---

[33] In the original RL algorithm developed by Erev and Roth (1998) and Roth and Erev (1995), the choice probabilities are defined in terms of relative propensity *levels*. Here, instead, use is made of a "simulated annealing" formulation in terms of *exponentials*. As will be seen below in (A.10), in the current context the propensity values $q_{ji}(T)$ can take on negative values if sufficiently large negative profit outcomes are experienced. The use of exponentials in (A.9) ensures that the choice probabilities $p_{ji}(T)$ remain well defined even in this event.

and let $\text{Profit}_{ji'}(T)$ denote the profits (positive or negative) attained by hash firm j in period T following its actual choice of supply offer i'. Then, for each feasible supply offer i,[34]

$$q_{ji}(T+1) = [1 - r_{Hj}]q_{ji}(T) + \text{Response}_{ji}(T), \tag{A.10}$$

where

$$\text{Response}_{ji}(T) = \begin{cases} [1 - e_{Hj}] \cdot \text{Profit}_{ji'}(T) & \text{if } i = i'; \\ e_{Hj} \cdot q_{ji}(T)/[Z_{Hj} - 1] & \text{if } i \neq i'. \end{cases} \tag{A.11}$$

Equations (A.10) and (A.11) clarify how the settings for the initial propensity values $q_{ji}(0)$ in (A.8) for period $T = 0$ determine initial profit aspiration levels for firm j's supply offer choices i. More generally, for any $T \geq 0$, the propensity $q_{ji'}(T)$ of firm j to choose supply offer i' in period T tends to increase or decrease for period $T + 1$ depending on whether firm j's realized profits from choice of i' in period T are higher or lower than $q_{ji'}(T)$. The introduction of the *recency parameter* r_{Hj} in (A.10) acts as a damper on the growth of the propensities over time. The *experimentation parameter* e_{Hj} in (A.11) permits reinforcement to spill over to some extent from a chosen supply offer to other supply offers to encourage continued experimentation with various supply offers in the early stages of the learning process.

Hash firm j faces a trade-off in each period T between information exploitation and information exploration. The VRE learning algorithm resolves this trade-off by ensuring continual exploration, typically at a declining rate. More precisely, under the VRE learning algorithm, note that hash firm j in period T does *not* necessarily choose a supply offer with the highest accumulated profits to date. Given a suitably small value for e_{Hj}, selected supply offers generating the highest accumulated profits tend to have a relatively higher *probability* of being chosen, but there is always a chance that other supply offers will be chosen instead. This ensures that hash firm j continues to experiment with new supply offers to some degree, even if its choice probability distribution becomes peaked at a particular selected supply offer because of relatively good profit outcomes. This helps to reduce the risk of premature fixation on suboptimal supply offers in the early stages of the decision process when relatively few supply offers have been tried.

In summary, the complete VRE learning algorithm applied to hash firm j is fully characterized once user-specified values are provided for the following five learning parameters: the number Z_{Hj} of feasible supply offers; the initial propensity value $q_{Hj}(0)$

---

[34] As in Nicolaisen et al. (2001), the response function appearing in (A.10) modifies the response function appearing in the original RL algorithm developed by Erev and Roth (1998) and Roth and Erev (1995). The modification is introduced to ensure that learning (updating of choice probabilities) occurs even in response to zero-profit outcomes, which are particularly likely to arise in initial periods when hash firm j is just beginning to experiment with different supply offers and failures to trade tend to be frequent. See Koesrindartoto (2002) for a detailed discussion and experimental exploration of the zero-profit updating problem with the original Roth–Erev learning algorithm. See Nicolaisen et al. (2001) for a detailed motivation, presentation, and experimental application of the modified response function in (A.10).

in (A.8); the cooling parameter C_{Hj} in (A.9); the recency parameter r_{Hj} in (A.10); and the experimentation parameter e_{Hj} in (A.11).

A.5: Activity flow and learning for bean firms

The discussion of basic activity flow and learning for hash firms in Sections A.2–A.4 applies also for the bean firms. All that is needed is a change of subscripts from Hj, H, and j to Bn, B, and n, as well as a change of quantity designations from h to b. See Section A.8 below for a classification of variables for the ACE Trading World that includes the basic exogenous and endogenous variables pertaining to the bean firms.

A.6: Activity flow for consumers in period T

The income $\text{Inc}_k(0)$ of each consumer k at the beginning of period $T = 0$ consists solely of her exogenously given money endowment, $\text{Endow}_k(0)$. The income $\text{Inc}_k(T)$ of each alive consumer k at the beginning of each period $T > 0$ comes from three sources: unintended savings from period $T - 1$; an exogenous money endowment $\text{Endow}_k(T)$; and dividend payments distributed by firms.

More precisely, let $\text{Exp}_k(T - 1)$ denote the total expenditure of consumer k on hash and beans during period $T - 1$, and let the unintended savings of consumer k from period $T - 1$ be denoted by

$$\text{Sav}_k(T) = \text{Inc}_k(T - 1) - \text{Exp}_k(T - 1). \tag{A.12}$$

Let $J(T)$ and $N(T)$ denote the number of effectively solvent hash and bean firms at the beginning of period T, and let $K(T)$ denote the number of alive consumers at the beginning of period T. Then the total income $\text{Inc}_k(T)$ of consumer k at the beginning of period T takes the form

$$\text{Inc}_k(T) = \text{Sav}_k(T) + \text{Endow}_k(T) + \left[\frac{\sum_{j=1}^{J(T)} \text{Div}_{Hj}(T)}{K(T)} \right]$$

$$+ \left[\frac{\sum_{n=1}^{N(T)} \text{Div}_{Bn}(T)}{K(T)} \right]. \tag{A.13}$$

Consumers seek to survive and prosper in period T by participating in the following price-discovery process.

A.7: Consumer price discovery process in period T

The period-T price discovery process begins as soon as each effectively solvent hash and bean firm has publicly posted its period-T supply offer consisting of a production level and a unit price. Any firm that stocks out of goods during the course of the period-T price discovery process immediately has its supply offer removed from posting. Consequently, the lowest posted hash and bean prices either stay the same or rise during the course of the price discovery process; they never fall.

As explained more fully below, the period-T price discovery process consists of a sequence of *rounds*. The process comes to a halt as soon as either all firms are stocked out (hence no posted supply offers remain) or the unspent income levels of all consumers still participating in the process have been reduced to zero (hence no positive demand remains). The total hash and bean amounts actually purchased by each consumer k during the course of the period-T price discovery process are denoted by $h_k(T)$ and $b_k(T)$.

Consumers who exit or finish the period-T price discovery process with positive unmet subsistence needs die at the end of period T. Their unspent money holdings (if any) are then lost to the economy, but their stock shares are distributed equally among all remaining (alive) consumers at the beginning of period $T+1$.

A typical price-discovery round for an arbitrary consumer k

Suppose at least one firm has not stocked out and that the currently unspent portion Inc_k^* of consumer k's period-T income is positive. Let $\bar{h}_k^*$ and $\bar{b}_k^*$ denote consumer k's current *net subsistence needs* for hash and beans, i.e., her basic subsistence needs $\bar{h}_k$ and $\bar{b}_k$ net of any hash and bean purchases she has made in previous rounds of the period-T price discovery process. Finally, let p_H^L denote the *currently lowest* posted price for hash if any hash firms are still posting supply offers, and similarly for p_B^L.

Suppose all hash firms have stocked out but at least one bean firm has not stocked out. If either $\bar{h}_k^* > 0$ or $p_B^L \cdot \bar{b}_k^* > \mathrm{Inc}_k^*$, consumer k exits the price discovery process. Otherwise, consumer k determines her hash and bean demands h_k^d and b_k^d as follows:

$$h_k^d = 0; \qquad b_k^d = \mathrm{Inc}_k^*/p_B^L. \tag{A.14}$$

Conversely, suppose at least one hash firm has not stocked out but all bean firms have stocked out. If either $p_H^L \cdot \bar{h}_k^* > \mathrm{Inc}_k^*$ or $\bar{b}_k^* > 0$, consumer k exits the price discovery process. Otherwise, consumer k determines her hash and bean demands h_k^d and b_k^d as follows:

$$h_k^d = \mathrm{Inc}_k^*/p_H^L; \qquad b_k^d = 0. \tag{A.15}$$

Finally, suppose that at least one hash firm and one bean firm have not stocked out. If the following condition,

$$p_H^L \cdot \bar{h}_k^* + p_B^L \cdot \bar{b}_k^* \leq \mathrm{Inc}_k^*, \tag{A.16}$$

fails to hold, consumer k exits the price discovery process. Otherwise, consumer k chooses demands h_k^d and b_k^d for hash and beans to maximize her utility

$$U_k^*\left(h_k^d, b_k^d\right) = \left(h_k^d - \bar{h}_k^*\right)^{\alpha_k} \cdot \left(b_k^d - \bar{b}_k^*\right)^{[1-\alpha_k]} \tag{A.17}$$

subject to the budget constraint

$$\left[p_H^L \cdot h_k^d + p_B^L \cdot b_k^d\right] \leq \mathrm{Inc}_k^*$$

and the subsistence constraints

$$h_k^d \geq \bar{h}_k^*; \qquad b_k^d \geq \bar{b}_k^*.$$

Since condition (A.16) holds by assumption, the solution to this utility maximization problem yields demands $h_k^d \geq \bar{h}_k^*$ and $b_k^d \geq \bar{b}_k^*$ for hash and beans satisfying the following *demand functions*:

$$h_k^d = [1 - \alpha_k] \cdot \bar{h}_k^* + \alpha_k \cdot [\text{Inc}_k^* - \bar{b}_k^* \cdot p_B^L]/p_H^L; \qquad (A.18)$$

$$b_k^d = \alpha_k \cdot \bar{b}_k^* + [1 - \alpha_k] \cdot [\text{Inc}_k^* - \bar{h}_k^* \cdot p_H^L]/p_B^L. \qquad (A.19)$$

If consumer k's net subsistence need h_k^* (or b_k^*) is negative in value, this indicates that consumer k's purchases of hash (or beans) in previous rounds of the price discovery process have been more than sufficient to cover her basic subsistence needs $\bar{h}_k$ (or $\bar{b}_k$). In this case, one (but not both) of consumer k's current demands h_k^d and b_k^d could be negative.[35] This would indicate that, at the currently lowest posted prices, consumer k would actually prefer to sell some of the hash (or beans) she purchased in previous rounds of the period-T price discovery process. This is not allowed. Consequently, if either of consumer k's initially calculated demands h_k^d and b_k^d in (A.18) and (A.19) is negative, it is assumed that consumer k then resets this demand to 0 and redirects all of her unspent income entirely toward demand for the other good. The demands of consumer k for this round of the price discovery process are thus determined in accordance with the following successive assignment statements:

$$h_k^d = \max\{0, h_k^d\};$$
$$b_k^d = \max\{0, b_k^d\};$$
$$h_k^d = \text{Inc}_k^*/p_H^L \quad \text{if } b_k^d = 0;$$
$$b_k^d = \text{Inc}_k^*/p_B^L \quad \text{if } h_k^d = 0.$$

After consumer k determines her demands h_k^d and b_k^d for hash and beans either from (A.14) or (A.15) in the case of a good stock-out or from the above assignment statements in the case neither good is stocked out, she immediately conveys any positive demands to the hash and/or bean firms who are offering the currently lowest posted prices p_H^L and/or p_B^L. If multiple hash (bean) firms are offering the currently lowest posted hash (bean) price, consumer k randomly decides which of these firms to patronize.

If a hash or bean firm cannot meet its current demand, it implements the following rationing method:

---

[35] Since consumer k's utility function is strictly increasing in hash and bean consumption over her subsistence-constrained budget set, she would never simultaneously choose negative demands for both hash and beans. She would only choose a negative demand for one of these goods if this "sale" permitted a greater positive demand for the other.

Random Queue Rationing Method: Given excess demand for my good, I first randomly order my current customers into a queue line. I then attempt to satisfy each customer's demand in turn, to the fullest extent possible. All rationed amounts offered to consumers must be nonnegative.

If consumer k is offered rationed amounts that do not satisfy fully her demands h_k^d and b_k^d for hash and beans at the currently lowest posted prices p_H^L and p_B^L, her first concern must be her survival. The primary issue is whether she is at least able to cover her net subsistence needs under rationing. If not, she will need to adjust her purchases under rationing to preserve as much income as she can in an attempt to satisfy her net subsistence needs in the next round of the price discovery process.

Thus, consumer k's *actual* purchased amounts in the current round of the price discovery process (as opposed to her demands) are determined by her specific state, as follows.

State I: No rationing. Consumer k satisfies fully her demands h_k^d and b_k^d for hash and beans, i.e., she is not rationed. Her actual purchased amounts are then $h_k = h_k^d$ and $b_k = b_k^d$.

State II: All needs met under rationing. Consumer k is offered hash and beans in rationed amounts $h_k^R \leq h_k^d$ and $b_k^R \leq b_k^d$ that are sufficient to cover her net subsistence needs for both hash and beans, i.e., $h_k^R \geq h_k^*$ and $b_k^R \geq b_k^*$. In this case, her actual purchased amounts are $h_k = h_k^R$ and $b_k = b_k^R$.

State III: One need not met under rationing. Consumer k is offered hash and beans in rationed amounts $h_k^R \leq h_k^d$ and $b_k^R \leq b_k^d$, and exactly one of these amounts is *not* sufficient to cover her net subsistence need. In this case she adjusts down her demand for the *other* good to her net subsistence need (if positive) or to 0 (otherwise) in order to preserve as much income as possible for the next price discovery round. Specifically, if h_k^R is *not* sufficient to cover h_k^*, then b_k^d is adjusted down to $b_k^A = \max\{0, b_k^*\}$ and her actual purchased amounts are $h_k = h_k^R$ and $b_k = b_k^A$. Alternatively, if b_k^R is *not* sufficient to cover b_k^*, then h_k^d is adjusted down to $h_k^A = \max\{0, h_k^*\}$ and her actual purchased amounts are $h_k = h_k^A$ and $b_k = b_k^R$.

State IV: Both needs not met under rationing. Consumer k is offered hash and beans in rationed amounts h_k^R and b_k^R, neither of which is sufficient to cover her net subsistence needs. In this case her actual purchased amounts are $h_k = h_k^R$ and $b_k = b_k^R$.

At the end of the current price discovery round, consumer k updates her unspent income Inc_k^* and her net subsistence needs h_k^* and b_k^* in accordance with the following assignment statements:

$$\text{Inc}_k^* = \text{Inc}_k^* - p_H^L h_k - p_B^L b_k;$$
$$h_k^* = h_k^* - h_k;$$
$$b_k^* = b_k^* - b_k.$$

If $\text{Inc}_k^* = 0$, consumer k exits the price discovery process. Otherwise, she enters into the next price discovery round, which proceeds as described above for the previous price discovery round.

A.8: Classification of variables

NOTE: Only variables persisting at least one time period are listed in the following classification. Locally scoped variables temporarily introduced to carry out method implementations are not included.

Exogenous variables:

Initial economy data:

$$\text{TMax} > 0; \quad J(0) > 0; \quad N(0) > 0; \quad K(0) > 0; \quad \rho_H > 0; \quad \rho_B > 0.$$

Initial firm data: $(j = 1, \ldots, J(0); n = 1, \ldots, N(0))$

$\text{Money}_{Hj}(0) \geq 0; \quad \text{Cap}_{Hj}(0) > 0; \quad q_{Hj}(0);$
$\text{Money}_{Bn}(0) \geq 0; \quad \text{Cap}_{Bn}(0) > 0; \quad q_{Bn}(0);$

$S_{Hj} \geq 0; \quad R_{Hj} > 0; \quad f_{Hj} \geq 0; \quad F_{Hj} \geq 0;$
$0 \leq m_{Hj} \leq 1; \quad 0 \leq d_{Hj} \leq 1; \quad 0 \leq r_{Hj} \leq 1; \quad 0 \leq e_{Hj} \leq 1;$
$Z_{Hj} > 0; \quad C_{Hj} > 0;$
$S_{Bn} \geq 0; \quad R_{Bn} > 0; \quad f_{Bn} \geq 0; \quad F_{Bn} \geq 0;$
$0 \leq m_{Bn} \leq 1; \quad 0 \leq d_{Bn} \leq 1; \quad 0 \leq r_{Bn} \leq 1; \quad 0 \leq e_{Bn} \leq 1;$
$Z_{Bn} > 0; \quad C_{Bn} > 0.$

Initial consumer data: $(k = 1, \ldots, K(0))$

$$\bar{h}_k \geq 0; \ \bar{b}_k \geq 0; \ 0 \leq \alpha_k \leq 1; \ (\text{Endow}_k(T) \geq 0, \quad T = 0, 1, \ldots, \text{TMax}).$$

Period-T endogenous variables: $(T = 0, 1, \ldots, \text{TMax})$

Firm choice variables: $(j = 1, \ldots, J(T); n = 1, \ldots, N(T))$
$h_j^s(T); \quad p_{Hj}(T);$
$b_n^s(T); \quad p_{Bn}(T).$

Other firm variables: $(j = 1, \ldots, J(T); n = 1, \ldots, N(T))$

$\text{FCost}_{Hj}(T); \quad \text{TCost}_{Hj}(T); \quad \text{Profit}_{Hj}(T); \quad \text{NetWorth}_{Hj}(T);$
$J(T+1); \quad \text{Money}_{Hj}(T+1); \quad \text{Cap}_{Hj}(T+1); \quad \text{Div}_{Hj}(T+1);$
$\text{FCost}_{Bn}(T); \quad \text{TCost}_{Bn}(T); \quad \text{Profit}_{Bn}(T); \quad \text{NetWorth}_{Bn}(T);$
$N(T+1); \quad \text{Money}_{Bn}(T+1); \quad \text{Cap}_{Bn}(T+1); \quad \text{Div}_{Bn}(T+1).$

Consumer choice variables: $(k = 1, \ldots, K(T))$

$$h_k^d(T); \quad b_k^d(T).$$

Other consumer variables: $(k = 1, \ldots, K(T))$

$$\mathrm{Inc}_k(T); \quad \mathrm{Sav}_k(T); \quad \mathrm{Exp}_k(T); \quad K(T+1).$$

References

Akerlof, G.A. (2002). "Behavioral macroeconomics and macroeconomic behavior". The American Economic Review 92, 411–433.

Albin, P.S. (1998). Barriers and Bounds to Rationality: Essays on Economic Complexity and Dynamics in Interactive Systems. Princeton University Press, Princeton, NJ.

Albin, P.S., Foley, D. (1992). "Decentralized, dispersed exchange without an auctioneer: A simulation study". Journal of Economic Behavior and Organization 18, 27–51.

Anderson, P.W., Arrow, K.J., Pines, D. (1988). The Economy as an Evolving Complex System, Proceedings Volume V, Santa Fe Institute Studies in the Sciences of Complexity. Addison-Wesley, Reading, MA.

Arifovic, J. (2000). "Evolutionary algorithms in macroeconomic models". Macroeconomic Dynamics 4, 373–414.

Arrow, K.J. (1987). "Oral history I: An interview". In: Feiwel, G.R. (Ed.), Arrow and the Ascent of Modern Economic Theory. New York University Press, NY, pp. 191–242.

Arthur, W.B. (2006). "Out-of-equilibrium economics and agent-based modeling", this handbook.

Arthur, W.B., Durlauf, S.N., Lane, D.A. (Eds.) (1997). The Economy as an Evolving Complex System II, Proceedings Volume XXVII, Santa Fe Institute Studies in the Sciences of Complexity. Addison-Wesley, Reading, MA.

Axelrod, R. (1997). The Complexity of Cooperation: Agent-Based Models of Complexity and Cooperation. Princeton University Press, Princeton, NJ.

Axelrod, R. (2006). "Agent-based modeling as a bridge between disciplines", this handbook.

Axelrod, R., Tesfatsion, L. (2006). "A guide for newcomers to agent-based modeling in the social sciences", this handbook.

Barreteau, O. (2003). "Our companion modeling approach". Journal of Artificial Societies and Social Simulation 6 (1). http://jasss.soc.surrey.ac.uk/6/2/1.html.

Batten, D.F. (2000). Discovering Artificial Economics: How Agents Learn and Economies Evolve. Westview Press, Boulder, Colorado.

Belew, R.K., Mitchell, M. (1996). In: Adaptive Individuals in Evolving Populations: Models and Algorithms, Proceedings Volume XXVI, Santa Fe Institute Studies in the Sciences of Complexity. Addison-Wesley, Reading, MA.

Bowles, S., Gintis, H. (2000). "Walrasian economics in retrospect". Quarterly Journal of Economics 115 (4), 1411–1439.

Brenner, T. (2006). "Agent learning representation: Advice on modeling economic learning", this handbook.

Brock, W.A., Hsieh, D., LeBaron, B. (1991). Nonlinear Dynamics, Chaos, and Instability: Statistical Theory and Economic Evidence. The MIT Press, Cambridge, MA.

Camerer, C. (2003). Behavioral Game Theory: Experiments in Strategic Interaction. Princeton University Press, Princeton, NJ.

Chang, M.-H., Harrington, Jr. J. (2006). "Agent-based models of organizations", this handbook.

Chatterjee, S., Ravikumar, B. (1999). "Minimum consumption requirements: Theoretical and quantitative implications for growth and distribution". Macroeconomic Dynamics 3 (4), 482–505.

Clark, A. (1997). Being There: Putting Brain, Body, and World Together Again. The MIT Press, Cambridge, MA.

Cliff, D. (2003). "Explorations in evolutionary design of online auction market mechanisms". Electronic Commerce Research and Applications 2, 162–175.

Cliff, D., Bruten, J. (1997). "Less than human: Simple adaptive trading agents for continuous double auction markets", Technical Report HP-97-155 (Hewlett Packard Research Laboratories, Bristol, U.K.). http://www.hpl.hp.com/techreports/97/HPL-97-155.html.

Clower, R., Howitt, P. (1996). "Taking markets seriously: Groundwork for a post Walrasian macroeconomics". In: Colander, D. (Ed.), Beyond Microfoundations: Post Walrasian Macroeconomics. Cambridge University Press, Cambridge, MA, pp. 21–37.

Colander, D. (1996). "Overview". In: Colander, D. (Ed.), Beyond Microfoundations: Post Walrasian Macroeconomics. Cambridge University Press, Cambridge, MA, pp. 1–17.

Cook, C., Tesfatsion, L. (2006). "Agent-Based Computational Laboratories for the Experimental Study of Complex Economic Systems", Working Paper, Department of Economics, Iowa State University, Ames, IA, in preparation.

Dawid, H. (2006). "Agent-based models of innovation and technological change", this handbook.

Day, R.H., Chen, P. (Eds.) (1993). Nonlinear Dynamics and Evolutionary Economics. Oxford University Press, Oxford, UK.

Dibble, C. (2006). "Computational laboratories for spatial agent-based models", this handbook.

Duffy, J. (2006). "Agent-based models and human-subject experiments", this handbook.

Durlauf, S.N., Young, H.P. (Eds.) (2001). Social Dynamics. The MIT Press, Cambridge, MA.

Eckel, B. (2003). Thinking in Java, 3rd edn. Prentice Hall, NJ.

Epstein, J. (2006). "Remarks on the foundations of agent-based generative social science", this handbook.

Epstein, J., Axtell, R. (1996). Growing Artificial Societies: Social Science from the Bottom Up. MIT Press/Brookings, MA.

Erev, I., Roth, A.E. (1998). "Predicting how people play games with unique mixed-strategy equilibria". American Economic Review 88, 848–881.

Evans, G.W., Honkapohja, S. (2001). Learning and Expectations in Macroeconomics. Princeton University Press, Princeton, NJ.

Feiwel, G.R. (1985). "Quo vadis macroeconomics? Issues, tensions, and challenges". In: Feiwel, G.R. (Ed.), Issues in Contemporary Macroeconomics and Distribution. State University of New York, Albany, pp. 1–100.

Fisher, F.M. (1983). Disequilibrium Foundations of Equilibrium Economics, Econometric Society Monographs No. 6. Cambridge University Press, Cambridge, UK.

Flake, G.W. (1998). The Computational Beauty of Nature: Computer Explorations of Fractals, Chaos, Complex Systems, and Adaptation. The MIT Press, Cambridge, MA.

Franklin, S. (1997a). "Autonomous agents as embodied AI". Cybernetics and Systems 28, 499–520.

Franklin, S. (1997b). Artificial Minds. The MIT Press, Cambridge, MA.

Frederick, S., Loewenstein, G., O'Donoghue, T. (2002). "Time discounting and time preference: A critical review". Journal of Economic Literature XL (2), 351–401.

Gigerenzer, G., Selten, R. (Eds.) (2001). Bounded Rationality: The Adaptive Toolbox. The MIT Press, Cambridge, MA.

Gintis, H. (2000). Game Theory Evolving. Princeton University Press, Princeton, NJ.

Gode, D.K., Sunder, S. (1993). "Allocative efficiency of markets with zero intelligence traders: Market as a partial substitute for individual rationality". Journal of Political Economy 101, 119–137.

Gode, D.K., Sunder, S. (1997). "What makes markets allocationally efficient?". Quarterly Journal of Economics 112 (2), 603–630.

Hayek, F. (1948). Individualism and the Economic Order. University of Chicago Press, Chicago.

Holland, J.H. (1995). Hidden Order: How Adaptation Builds Complexity. Addison-Wesley, Reading, MA.

Hommes, C. (2006). "Heterogeneous agent models in economics and finance", this handbook.

Hoover, K.D. (1992). The New Classical Macroeconomics: A Skeptical Inquiry. Basil Blackwell, Cambridge, MA.

Howitt, P. (1990). The Keynesian Recovery and Other Essays. The University of Michigan Press, Ann Arbor, MI.

Howitt, P. (2006). "Coordination issues in long-run growth", this handbook.

Janssen, M.A., Ostrom, E. (2006). "Governing social-ecological systems", this handbook.

Jennings, N.R. (2000). "On agent-based software engineering". Artificial Intelligence 17, 277–296.

Judd, K.L. (1998). Numerical Methods in Economics. The MIT Press, Cambridge, MA.

Judd, K.L. (2006). "Computationally intensive analyses in economics", this handbook.

Kagel, J.H., Roth, A.E. (1995). Handbook of Experimental Economics. Princeton University Press, Princeton, NJ.

Katzner, D. (1989). The Walrasian Vision of the Microeconomy: An Elementary Exposition of the Structure of Modern General Equilibrium Theory. University of Michigan Press, Ann Arbor, MI.

Keynes, J.M. (1965). The General Theory of Employment, Interest, and Money (First Harbinger Edition, Harcourt, Brace & World, Inc., New York, NY).

Kirman, A. (1997). "The economy as an interactive system". In: Arthur, W.B., Durlauf, S.N., Lane, D.A. (Eds.), The Economy as an Evolving Complex System II, Proceedings Volume XXVII, Santa Fe Institute Studies in the Sciences of Complexity. Addison-Wesley, Reading, MA, pp. 491–531.

Klemperer, P. (2002a). "What really matters in auction design". Journal of Economic Perspectives 16, 169–189.

Klemperer, P. (2002b). "Using and abusing economic theory", Alfred Marshall Lecture to the European Economic Association, December. http://www.paulklemperer.org/.

Koesrindartoto, D. (2002). "A discrete double auction with artificial adaptive agents: A case study of an electricity market using a double-auction simulator", Economics Working Paper No. 02005, Department of Economics, Iowa State University, Ames, IA. Available at http://deddy.agentbased.net/res.html.

Koesrindartoto, D., Tesfatsion, L. (2004). "Testing the economic reliability of FERC's wholesale power market platform: An agent-based computational economics approach". In: Energy, Environment, and Economics in a New Era, Proceedings of the 24th USAEE/IAEE North American Conference, Washington, DC, July.

Kollman, K., Page, S.E. (2006). "Computational methods and models of politics", this handbook.

Krugman, P. (1996). The Self-Organizing Economy. Blackwell Publishers, Cambridge, UK.

LeBaron, B. (2006). "Agent-based computational finance", this handbook.

Leijonhufud, A. (1967). "Keynes and the Keynesians: A suggested interpretation". American Economic Review 57 (2), 401–410.

Leijonhufvud, A. (1996). "Towards a not-too-rational macroeconomics". In: Colander, D. (Ed.), Beyond Microfoundations: Post Walrasian Macroeconomics. Cambridge University Press, Cambridge, MA, pp. 39–55.

Leijonhufvud, A. (2006). "Agent-based macro", this handbook.

Leombruni, R., Richiardi, M. (Eds.) (2004). Industry and Labor Dynamics: The Agent-Based Computational Economics Approach, Proceedings of the WILD@ACE 2003 Conference. World Scientific Press, Singapore.

Mackie-Mason, J.K., Wellman, M. (2006). "Automated markets and trading agents", this handbook.

Marks, R. (2006). "Market design using agent-based models", this handbook.

McCabe, K. (2003). "Neuroeconomics". In: Nadel, L. (Ed.), Encyclopedia of Cognitive Science. Macmillan Publishing, New York, pp. 294–298.

McMillan, J. (2002). Reinventing the Bazaar: A Natural History of Markets. W.W. Norton & Co., New York, NY.

Mirowski, P. (2004). "Markets come to bits: Evolution, computation, and the future of economic science", Working Paper, Department of Economics and Policy Studies (University of Notre Dame, South Bend, IN).

Nelson, R. (1995). "Recent evolutionary theorizing about economic change". Journal of Economic Literature 33, 48–90.

Nelson, R., Winter, S. (1982). An Evolutionary Theory of Economic Change. Harvard University Press, Cambridge, MA.

Nicolaisen, J., Petrov, V., Tesfatsion, L. (2001). "Market power and efficiency in a computational electricity market with discriminatory double-auction pricing". IEEE Transactions on Evolutionary Computation 5 (5), 504–523.

Penrose, R. (1989). The Emperor's New Mind. Oxford University Press, Oxford, UK.

Pingle, M., Tesfatsion, L. (1991). "Overlapping generations, intermediation, and the First Welfare Theorem". Journal of Economic Behavior and Organization 15, 325–345.

Pingle, M., Tesfatsion, L. (1998a). "Active intermediation in overlapping generations economies with production and unsecured debt". Macroeconomic Dynamics 2, 183–212.

Pingle, M., Tesfatsion, L. (1998b). "Active intermediation in a monetary overlapping generations economy". Journal of Economic Dynamics and Control 22, 1543–1574.

Prescott, E. (1996). "The computational experiment: An econometric tool". Journal of Economic Perspectives 10 (1), 69–86.

Radner, R. (1998). "Economic Survival". In: Jacobs, D., Kalai, E., Kamien, M. (Eds.), Frontiers of Research in Economic Theory. Cambridge University Press, Cambridge, UK, pp. 183–209.

Roth, A.E. (2002). "The economist as engineer: Game theory, experimentation, and computation as tools for design economics". Econometrica 70, 1341–1378.

Roth, A.E., Erev, I. (1995). "Learning in extensive form games: Experimental data and simple dynamic models in the intermediate term". Games and Economic Behavior 8, 164–212.

Rubinstein, A., Wolinsky, A. (1990). "Decentralized trading, strategic behavior, and the Walrasian outcome". Review of Economic Studies 57, 63–78.

Sargent, T.J. (1993). Bounded Rationality in Macroeconomics, The Arne Ryde Memorial Lectures. Clarendon Press, Oxford, UK.

Schelling, T.C. (1978). Micromotives and Macrobehavior. W.W. Norton & Company, New York.

Schelling, T.C. (2006). "Some fun, thirty-five years ago", this handbook.

Shubik, M. (1991). A Game-Theoretic Approach to Political Economy, Fourth Printing. The MIT Press, Cambridge, MA.

Schumpeter, J. (1934). The Theory of Economic Development: An Inquiry into Profits, Capital, Credit, Interest, and the Business Cycle. Translated by Redvers Opie, with a special preface by the author. Harvard University Press, Cambridge, MA.

Simon, H. (1982). The Sciences of the Artificial, 2nd edn. The MIT Press, Cambridge, MA.

Smith, A. (1937). An Inquiry into the Nature and Causes of the Wealth of Nations (Cannan Edition, American Modern Library Series, New York, NY).

Sutton, R.S., Barto, A.G. (1998). Reinforcement Learning: An Introduction. The MIT Press, Cambridge, MA.

Takayama, A. (1985). Mathematical Economics, 2nd Edition. Cambridge University Press, Cambridge, UK.

Tesfatsion, L. (1985). "Fair division with uncertain needs and tastes". Social Choice and Welfare 2, 295–309.

Tesfatsion, L. (Ed.) (2001a). "Special issue on agent-based computational economics". Journal of Economic Dynamics and Control 25 (3–4), 281–654.

Tesfatsion, L. (Ed.) (2001b). "Special issue on agent-based computational economics". Computational Economics 18 (1), 1–135.

Tesfatsion, L. (Ed.) (2001c). "Special issue on the agent-based modeling of evolutionary economic systems". IEEE Transactions on Evolutionary Computation 5 (5), 437–560.

Tesfatsion, L. (2002). "Agent-based computational economics: Growing economies from the bottom up". Artificial Life 8, 55–82.

Tirole, J. (2003). The Theory of Industrial Organization, Fourteenth Printing. The MIT Press, Cambridge, MA.

Vriend, N. (2006). "ACE models of endogenous interactions", this handbook.

Wilhite, A. (2006). "Economic activity on fixed networks", this handbook.

Witt, U. (1993). Evolutionary Economics. Edward Elgar Publishers, Cheltenham, UK.

Young, H.P. (1998). Individual Strategy and Social Structure: An Evolutionary Theory of Institutions. Princeton University Press, Princeton, NJ.

Young, H.P. (2006). "Social dynamics: Theory and applications", this handbook.

Chapter 17

COMPUTATIONALLY INTENSIVE ANALYSES IN ECONOMICS

KENNETH L. JUDD[*]

Hoover Institution, 434 Galvez Mall, Stanford, CA 94305, USA
e-mail: judd@hoover.stanford.edu url: http://bucky.stanford.edu

Contents

[*] I thank Leigh Tesfatsion for helpful comments.

Handbook of Computational Economics, Volume 2. Edited by Leigh Tesfatsion and Kenneth L. Judd
DOI: 10.1016/S1574-0021(05)02017-4

Abstract

Computer technology presents economists with new tools, but also raises novel methodological issues. This essay discusses the challenges faced by computational researchers, and proposes some solutions.

Keywords

computational economics, economic methodology

JEL classification: B49, C60, C63

1. Introduction

The growing power of computers gives economists a new tool to explore and evaluate both old and new economic theories. The essays in this handbook illustrate that potential in many parts of economics, and make clear that they have just scratched the surface of what can be done. The main goal of this handbook is to encourage new work. However, as with any new tool, there are many questions about how to use it wisely and effectively. Important methodological questions need to be addressed before computational tools can achieve their potential for contributing to economic science.

Conventional economics uses computation primarily for two purposes: empirical analysis of data and computing equilibria of conventional models. The primary computational tools for these activities are standard numerical analytic tools for solving optimization problems and nonlinear systems of equations. Agent-based computational economics (ACE) often takes us in new directions that focus on computer models of complex dynamical systems to analyze alternative theories of economic behavior. ACE research is often like theory since it studies the implications of alternative assumptions about economic systems, as described in the description of constructive theory in Tesfatsion (2006). Unfortunately, the complexity that is embraced by ACE research makes it difficult, if not impossible, to use conventional ways for describing theories such as stating and proving theorems, presenting cases with closed-form solutions, and proving comparative statics. Instead, much ACE research uses computer simulations to analyze complex dynamic models.

The computationally intensive approaches to economics research typified in ACE research (as well as some other economics research) presents us with basic questions about how they should be used and what we can learn from their results. Where does simulation of complex dynamic models fit into the general set of economic methodologies? When and how much can we rely on computational findings? What are the criticisms of computationally intensive work? How should we address the challenges raised by critics? This essay will examine these questions and offer some answers[1].

2. Computational tools

Before discussing methodological issues, it is useful to recall why we are here. The key fact is that we now have increasingly powerful computational tools and rapid progress will continue. First, there has been and will almost surely continue to be tremendous progress on improving computer hardware. The progress of the past 40 years has been related to advances in semiconductors. We are all familiar with Moore's law declaring that "chip density doubles every 18 months." Of course, this cannot continue forever

---

[1] This essay updates Judd (1994) and Judd (1997) that also discusses similar questions. I also draw on the suggestions of McFadden (1992).

because the components of a chip cannot be smaller than a molecule. Even optimistic experts argue that this can continue for only another 10–15 years. However, that will likely not be the end of hardware progress. Current research on three-dimensional chips, asynchronous chips, spintronics, optical computing and other technological advances give us good reason to believe that computational speeds will continue to grown exponentially for at least a few more decades. Furthermore, the potential for computational work would explode if we are really lucky and quantum computing achieves just a fraction of its theoretical potential. While this is speculative, it indicates that progress will continue even after the end of Moore's law. While improvements in semiconductor technology have been immeasurably important, we get a better appreciation of historical trends when we remember that the rate of increase in computing speed due to semiconductors in the last half of the 20th century was no greater than improvement in computing speeds achieved in the first half of the 20th century using other technologies. Even if technological advances stopped today, the cost of hardware would continue to fall as we reap the benefits of learning curve effects and increasing returns to scale in the production of computer components. The cumulative impact of this progress will make computation increasingly efficient, cheap, and available to economists.

Second, there has also been significant progress in software engineering with many developments being particularly valuable for ACE modeling. Supercomputing used to mean vector processing, a technique of limited value for ACE modeling. The current strategies in high performance computing exploit massive parallelism and distributed computing. In these environments, many processors of possibly varying power are combined in a network and through communication, sometimes over the Internet, to work together to solve a problem. The value of parallelism depends on the problem. Fortunately, many of the problems discussed in the handbook, particularly those using Monte Carlo simulation, can easily make full use of the computational power of parallel and distributed computing. Of more specific value to ACE modeling has been the work on developing software tools for ACE models, such as the Sugarscape environment discussed in Epstein and Axtell (1996). Here, also, progress will continue and significantly reduce the human cost of doing computationally intensive economics research and make it easier for economists to profitably use ACE modeling.

This is all old news, but it bears repeating when we consider how computation could be used in economics. Some of the ideas I outline below will sound unreasonable and probably are infeasible today given current technology. However, we need to focus on how to proceed in the future, and that discussion should be mindful of the tools we will have then.

3. Weaknesses of standard models

The other reason why economists are turning to ACE modelling is the dissatisfaction with conventional economic models and their frustration with the limitations of standard research paradigms. Of course, all economics research is motivated by some dissatisfaction with the existing theories, and ACE modelling has been applied to many of the same questions, such as how an economic system gets to an equilibrium, that is studied by conventional means. What makes much of the ACE literature different from other research is its methodological novelty. Conventional economic theory, following the style of mathematics in general and real analysis in particular, begins with a set of definitions and assumptions, and proves theorems. The universe of models covered by the definitions is generally infinite. For example, general equilibrium theory begins with the concepts of preference orderings and feasible allocations. Theoretical models often make simplifying assumptions so that they can get clear, substantive results. In basic general equilibrium theory, we assume well-behaved excess demand functions and concave production functions in order to invoke the Brouwer fixed-point theorem. In other cases, such as the CAPM model of asset pricing or oligopoly models with linear demand and marginal cost curves, tractability considerations lead economists to make far more restrictive assumptions in order to get clean solutions. Furthermore, economists often examine simple models in the search for "the" cause of some economic phenomenon, and argue for a parsimonious explanation of their observations. This approach often ignores the possibility that the truth could be multidimensional, and that the multiple dimensions of reality could interact to produce phenomena that no one factor can explain. While we all like parsimony, true parsimony chooses a model as simple as possible without being too simple, and would not force our thinking into a conceptual straightjacket.

We often question the validity of the implications of these models because the elements which are sacrificed in the interest of simplicity are possibly of first-order importance. For many economists, this dissatisfaction with simple models is the main appeal of computational approaches. This dissatisfaction has moved economists in a variety of directions. For example, in public finance, economists often use computation to avoid the single-sector, representative agent models that are commonly used only because of their tractability.

The ACE literature generally aims at other weaknesses of standard models, often focusing on foundational problems instead of, for example, studying models with more goods. The chapters in this handbook study many models for which a computational approach is the only way to attain clear results. The models of social interactions presented in Vriend (2006), Wilhite (2006) and Young (2006) have combinatorial complexities that make it difficult (if not impossible) to attain closed-form solutions. The impact of learning on financial markets, discussed in Hommes (2006) and LeBaron (2006) also requires computational tools, particularly when individuals do not all follow exactly the same learning rules. Multiperson decision making, whether it is on the scale of a firm, as studied in Chang and Harrington (2006), or at the level of politics, as reviewed in Kollman and Page (2006), also involves complex patterns of learning and choices that are difficult to describe precisely without computation.

Many economists dismiss these complexities (along with many other features of real economic life glossed over in conventional models) arguing that they can't matter.

Some will point to convergence theorems and conclude that the convergence problem is "solved" and that factors affecting the convergence process cannot be important "in the long run." Of course, Keynes' observation that "in the long run we are all dead" forcefully reminds us that abstract convergence theorems tell us nothing about what happens at economic time scales. More generally, no matter how good our intuition is, we do not know which features of an economy are important and which are not until we examine them, and do so in a manner that reveals their quantitative importance. That focus on the quantitative properties of complex systems leads us to computationally intensive methods.

4. Criticisms of computationally intensive research

Many economists are dissatisfied with conventional economic models, but have serious doubts about taking a computationally intensive approach to addressing fundamental issues. This is natural since any novel methodology and paradigm will be challenged and scrutinized before it is accepted. Economists using computationally intensive methods need to acknowledge this process and develop responses to the questions and criticisms raised by the status quo. Thinking about these issues will also help us construct more compelling formulations of our ideas.

First, critics point out that computational methods produce only examples, whereas conventional economic theory aims to produce theorems. This is true given the conventional use of the words "examples" and "theorem." The usual theorem in economics, such as existence theorems in general equilibrium theory, will cover an infinite number of possible cases. However, the substantive gap between "examples" and "theorem" is less clear. In fact, isn't "theorem" just a plural of "example"? Theories usually examine a continuum of examples but, in order to attain analytical tractability, that continuum often constitutes a measure zero set of economically plausible and interesting specifications. Assumptions made for reasons of tractability may miss many interesting phenomena. These assumptions may take the form of functional form specifications, such as the linear demand curves we often see in oligopoly theory, or may be qualitative assumptions such as the strong informational assumptions used in rational expectations analyses. While computations examine only a finite set of examples, that set can be taken from a much more robust set of possible specifications, allowing more flexible functional form specifications as well as more complex and realistic assumptions about the distribution of information and evolution of beliefs. The *relevance* and *robustness* of examples is more important than the *number* of examples, and computational methods allow one to examine cases that theory cannot touch. Furthermore, computation can often give us insights when there are no general theorems to be had. Simple general statements are not likely to be globally true, but there may still be patterns that are economically useful, such as statements about what is usually true over empirically plausible parts of the parameter space.

Second, critics point out that numerical results have errors. Again, this is a correct observation for most computational work. For example Monte Carlo simulations have nontrivial sampling error since $N^{-1/2}$ convergence is slow. Many algorithms produce estimates of a bound on the numerical error, but this only reduces the uncertainty. Very few computational techniques produce error bounds along with the results. The presence of numerical errors is another distinction between theorems and computational results. However, these errors can be controlled by the application of sophisticated algorithms and powerful hardware. Careful simulation methods can reduce simulation error by increasing the sample size and by exploiting variance reduction methods. More generally, careful numerical work can reduce numerical errors. The problems of numerical errors in ACE models are no more difficult to handle (and often much easier) than the analogous numerical problems that arise in maximum likelihood estimation and other econometric methods.

Theoretical models may not have errors when they solve particular cases, but they often commit specification errors by focusing on tractable cases. In fact, computational work has an advantage here because numerical errors can be reduced through computation but correcting the specification errors of analytically tractable models is much more difficult. The issue is not whether we have errors, but where we put those errors. The key fact is that economists face a trade-off between the numerical errors in computational work and the specification errors of analytically tractable models. Computationally intensive approaches offer opportunities to examine realistic models, a valuable option even with the numerical errors. As Tukey (1962) put it, "Far better an approximate answer to the right question ... than an exact answer to the wrong question..."

Third, they argue that computational models are black boxes that offer few if any insights. This is an understandable reaction to a single computed example of a model, particularly one with many factors contributing to the result. A single example may show what is possible and an author may come up with an appealing story to explain the result, but one example cannot sort out the relative importance of a model's various components. This is sometimes addressed by sensitivity analysis where a small number of alternative parameterizations are computed and the results are compared; this is essentially a computational version of comparative statics. However, it is unclear how much can be inferred from a few examples. Here, again, is a problem that can be addressed using computation. A few examples may not demonstrate much but a few thousand well chosen examples can be more convincing, and a few million examples may be as compelling as any theorem, as well as being less costly to produce. Of course, this presents us with a different problem: How do we communicate to a reader or listener the lessons learned from thousands of examples? We now turn to that issue.

5. Systematic approaches to computationally intensive research

An important advantage of conventional economic theory is that a theorem is an efficient means of communicating a result: it is a simple but informative statement of a truth about a large set of examples. In contrast, computationally intensive papers in economics often focus on a few examples to show what can happen. Some papers will say "We have examined other cases and found similar results"; this statement may be true but falls far short of what is expected in a "scientific" paper. Readers of any kind of paper, theoretical or computational, want more than a couple of examples and un-supported assertions of generality. Sometimes demands by readers can be unreasonable (examples of which are related in Axelrod (2006)), particularly when the demand for robustness in computational models exceeds the demand for robustness in theoretical models. However, we need to develop tools for addressing reasonable demands.

A computational economist can easily offer up many examples, but it is not obvious how to communicate his findings in a compact and informative manner. For example, space limitations mean that a paper can present only a few graphs of time series gen-erated by simulations of a dynamic process. Tables can summarize results for several cases, but they are often harder to quickly digest than a good graph, and space limita-tions again will limit the amount of information that can be conveyed.

Research that relies on computationally intensive methods needs to find effective ways to communicate its findings, and it needs to develop its own style. It cannot nec-essarily follow what, for example, physicists do. For example, if a physicist wants to simulate the collision of two black holes, he writes down the relevant equations from general relativity, uses the constants of nature that have been precisely estimated by experimentation, and uses astronomical observations to judge what size of black holes he needs to consider. A few examples will suffice for his purposes. Economics is a much less clear mixture of the quantitative and qualitative. We often make qualitative restrictions, such as concave utility, but we do not want to make inflexible functional form assumptions. When we do compute something, we have to make functional form assumptions that we acknowledge are only approximations, and calibrate them with im-precise estimates of parameters of functions that are themselves just approximations to true functions.

In this section, I will discuss some approaches that computationally intensive work may take to address the critical issues.

5.1. Search for counterexamples

While a computer cannot prove a theorem[2], it can help us look for falsifying examples. Suppose we have a model with parameters θ and we have a conjecture that can be expressed as a proposition $P(\theta)$. For the sake of specificity, suppose that the proposition is true if $P(\theta) \geq 0$. For example, suppose are examining one of the asset market models described in Hommes (2006) and want to test a hypothesis about the relation between price volatility and the parameters describing learning rules or agent heterogeneity. In

---

[2] Of course, computers have occasionally proven nontrivial theorems in mathematics, but we are a long way from computer theorem-proving being a common tool in economics.

this case, $P(\theta)$ would be a statement about measures of volatility (some moments or a measure of chaoticity) and θ would include the exogenous parameters. Even if we could not prove the truth of P (that is, the global nonnegativity of $P(\theta)$) we could assess the likelihood of its truth by searching for counterexamples, that is, values of θ such that $P(\theta) < 0$.

Global optimization software could be used for testing $P(\theta)$ by finding the global minimum of $P(\theta)$, and determining if it were ever negative. The choice of global optimization software would depend on the nature of the function $P(\theta)$. If $P(\theta)$ were a rough function, we would have to use methods like genetic algorithms or simulated annealing. If $P(\theta)$ were piecewise continuous, then we would want to combine a global strategy (such as in GA or simulated annealing) with a more conventional optimization method, such as Nelder–Mead, to take the guesses generated by the global strategy and find nearby local optima. If $P(\theta)$ were a smooth, but possibly multimodal, function, we could even combine a Newton-style method with a global strategy. Once we exploit the properties of $P(\theta)$, we could formulate an efficient as well as systematic approach for finding counterexamples.

If we find a counterexample then we will have learned something about the model. Also, the counterexample, or counterexamples, will give insight about when and why a proposition fails to hold. Failure to find a counterexample would not prove the conjecture, but would be strong evidence for its truth. If high-quality global optimization software is used, then this would be even more compelling evidence.

If we do find counterexamples, we would like to find ways to describe when P is true. If we fail to find a counterexample, we may want to consider alternative ways to express the apparent global validity of proposition P. We next turn to methods that help us in those tasks.

5.2. Sampling methods

If we are convinced of a proposition's truth, then we would want to express that in some compact way. Various sampling schemes can be developed for this purpose and produce statements using standard language from statistics or analysis.

Monte Carlo sampling offers one simple procedure. Suppose we want to investigate a set of models where we have imposed a probability measure, μ, over the parameter space θ. Suppose we want to evaluate our proposition $P(\theta)$ over a set $\theta \in \Theta$. We could draw N models at random from Θ according to the measure μ, and use computation to determine the truth of the proposition in those cases. If computation showed that proposition P held in each case, then we could say "We reject the hypothesis that the μ-measure of counterexamples to proposition P exceeds ϵ at the confidence level of $1 - (1 - \epsilon)^N$." Note the crucial role of the randomization; the fact that we randomly drew the cases allows us to use the language of classical statistics.

We could also use Bayesian methods to express "posterior beliefs" after several computations. Let p be the probability that a μ-measure randomly drawn point satisfies proposition P, and suppose that we have a uniform prior belief about the value of p.

Then our posterior belief about p after N draws which satisfy proposition P can be directly computed.

The advantage of Monte Carlo sampling methods is the ease of expression using language from either classical or Bayesian statistics. There is little question about the meaning of these statements since independent draws are easy to implement and well-understood.

Some have told me that they would prefer to use a prespecified, uniform grid of cases for this task instead of random draws. The idea is to examine a set of examples such that each possible case is within some distance δ of one of the cases computed. The uniform grid approach has an advantage over Monte Carlo in that it avoids the clumping and gaps that, due to the Central Limit Theorem, must occur with Monte Carlo sampling. However, uniform grids are inefficient ways of sampling in a multidimensional space. Fortunately, there are quasi-Monte Carlo sampling methods, such as low discrepancy sets, that use far fewer points than the Cartesian grid and accomplish the same goal. With deterministic grids, one cannot use the statistical concept of "confidence levels" to summarize a result. The alternative statement would be based on the maximal size of a ball or cube of counterexamples; that is, if proposition P is true at each point on a grid and the largest ball which can miss each point on the grid is of diameter δ, then δ could be used as a measure of the strength of proposition P.

One advantage of all sampling methods is the ease of implementation. If you can compute $P(\theta)$, then you can execute a sampling method. Sampling methods can efficiently use any computer environment. In particular, because there is little interdependence across different points in a grid, sampling methods can be directly implemented in all distributed computing environments, such as massively parallel supercomputers or grid computing systems. The global optimization approach could also exploit a parallel environment but would require some coordination.

5.3. Regression methods

Instead of trying to prove that $P(\theta)$ is always nonnegative, we may instead try to find the shape of P. Judicious use of computational power can help us here as well. A computational study can compute $P(\theta)$ for a large number θ values, use approximation methods, such as regression, neural nets, or radial basis functions, to express how P depends on the exogenous parameters, θ. The approximation results would then tell us how a model depends on its parameters. If a simple functional form, such a low order polynomial in the components of θ (or $\log \theta$), could fit the data, then the fitting function would cleanly express our findings.

While this looks a lot like statistics, our task would be easier than standard econometrics. First, we can define the set of sample points θ. Econometricians are stuck with the θ's nature gives them. We instead can control the number and distribution of θ's so as to maximize the information we get from our computations. Second, the error in computing $P(\theta)$ can often be controlled much better than an econometrician can control measurement errors. Third, because we have control over the measurement errors, sampling errors and sample size, we can be more flexible in terms of functional form specifications and get more information out of our data. In particular, we could focus on finding functional forms that can compactly express the patterns we find.

There are many ways to accomplish this. The main point is that approximation methods, and data mining in general, could be used to summarize results of a computational study and test hypotheses one has for a model.

5.4. Replication and generalization

We have discussed ways that computational work could be conducted and expressed to produce conclusions that are clear to a reader, and, in some cases, nearly as compelling as a proof. Computational methods have one potentially important advantage over theorem-proving. Suppose that your paper did not examine a case or class of models that some reader cares about. If you have proved a theorem that does not include that case, the reader has to work hard to see what happens for his case, and will usually fail to find the answer unless he has expertise comparable to the author. In contrast, in computational models the reader could just take the computer program you wrote and apply it to the parameter values he wants to examine. If his case is qualitatively different, he could perhaps make modest changes in the (hopefully well-written) code and then run the program. In either case, he can quickly find the answers to his questions in a way that is not possible for theoretical work.

This observation also points out how replication of computational work could be done. Of course, this assumes that the software you use is easily transportable and flexible to use. This is often not true today, partly because there is little incentive to write software that can be used by others. This is a not as bad a problem in empirical work since people often use common data sets and common econometric software. The lack of similar software is holding back the potential of ACE approaches, but that is hopefully only a temporary problem.

5.5. Synergies with conventional theory

The observations above have been of an "us versus them" nature. While this is a useful framework to use when discussing these issues, it is counterproductive for us to view this as a zero-sum contest between two methodologies. The ultimate aim is for computational and theoretical tools to interact in a fruitful manner. We have already seen some examples of this. For example, Arthur (1994) posed the El Farol Problem where customers want to predict the number of people at the El Farol bar because they want to avoid times when it is crowded. Arthur (1994) used computational methods to study the implications of inductive inference by patrons. Motivated by the insights in Arthur (1994), Zambrano (2004) reexamined the problem analytically and arrived at important insights that went beyond both the computational results and the related game theory.

I have laid out several distinctions between conventional theory and the kind of computationally intensive approaches to studying economic models advocated in ACE.

These distinctions will remain in the future even after we have refined our computational tools, and both approaches will be used, each exploiting its own unique strengths. The aim of this essay, as well as much of this handbook, is to highlight the distinct nature of computationally intensive research tools. However, there is no desire that the economics community be divided between computational economists and practitioners of conventional theory. Instead, the hope here is that a clear understanding of alternative methodologies will foster vigorous interactions where each approach benefits from the insights of the other.

6. Conclusion

Any time a new tool is introduced into economics, economists need to decide how best to use it to produce insights about economic problems. Economists who were trained in the literary tradition of classical economics were troubled by the infusion of mathematics in the middle of the 20th century. Likewise, the infusion of computationally intensive approaches will push economists to learn new tools, and raise questions about how best to use them in economic analysis. These questions need to be addressed in a systematic manner. This essay proposes some ideas that could be used more in economics, and I am sure that others will offer suggestions as we think about these issues. The potential usefulness of computational methods is enormous. I am confident that we will find suitable answers if we think carefully about the tradeoffs between conventional approaches and the ACE tools presented in this handbook, and if we make efficient and full use of the computational resources that will become available in the future.

References

Arthur, W.B. (1994). "Bounded rationality and inductive behavior (the El Farol Problem)". American Economic Review Papers and Proceedings 84, 406–411.

Axelrod, R. (2006). "Agent-based modeling as a bridge between disciplines", this handbook.

Chang, M.-H., Harrington, J. Jr. (2006) "Agent-based models of organizations", this handbook.

Epstein, J., Axtell, R. (1996). Growing Artificial Societies: Social Science from the Bottom Up. MIT Press/Brookings, MA.

Hommes, C. (2006). "Heterogeneous agent models in economics and finance", this handbook.

Judd, K.L. (1994). "Comment". In: Sims, C. (Ed.), Advances in Econometrics Sixth World Congress, vol. II. Cambridge University Press, Cambridge, UK, pp. 261–274.

Judd, K.L. (1997). "Computational economics and economic theory: complements or substitutes?". Journal of Economic Dynamics and Control 21, 907–942.

Kollman, K., Page, S.E. (2006). "Computational methods and models of politics", this handbook.

LeBaron, B. (2006). "Agent-based computational finance", this handbook.

McFadden, D. (1992). "Simulation methods for unemployed theorists". Santa Fe Institute Conference.

Tesfatsion, L. (2006). "Agent-based computational economics: A constructive approach to economic theory", this handbook.

Tukey, J.W. (1962). "The future of data analysis". The Annals of Mathematical Statistics 33 (1), 1–67.

Vriend, N. (2006). "ACE models of endogenous interactions", this handbook.

Wilhite, A. (2006). "Economic activity on fixed networks", this handbook.

Young, H.P. (2006). "Social dynamics: Theory and applications", this handbook.

Zambrano, E. (2004). "The interplay between analytics and computation in the study of congestion externalities: The case of the El Farol Problem". Journal of Public Economic Theory 6, 375–395.

Chapter 18

AGENT LEARNING REPRESENTATION:
ADVICE ON MODELLING ECONOMIC LEARNING

THOMAS BRENNER[†]

Max Planck Institute of Economics, Jena, Germany

Contents

† I want to thank John Duffy, Robert Marks, Alex Smajgl, Leigh Tesfatsion and an anonymous referee for helpful comments on earlier drafts of this chapter. The usual disclaimer applies.

Handbook of Computational Economics, Volume 2. Edited by Leigh Tesfatsion and Kenneth L. Judd
DOI: 10.1016/S1574-0021(05)02018-6

Abstract

This chapter presents an overview of the existing learning models in the economic literature. Furthermore, it discusses the choice of models that should be used under various circumstances and how adequate learning models can be chosen in simulation approaches. It gives advice for using the many existing models and selecting the appropriate model for each application.

Keywords

economic learning, modelling

JEL classification: C63, D83

1. Introduction

In the last 20 years the variety of learning models used in economics has increased tremendously. This chapter provides an overview on these learning models. Furthermore, it classifies learning processes and gives tips on choosing amongst the various models.

There are many different ways in which such an overview can be presented and structured. The structure chosen here reflects two considerations: First, the main aim of this chapter is to help agent-based computational economists to choose the adequate learning model in their simulations. In giving such advice, we assume that agent-based computational economists intend to model human behaviour as realistically as possible. Other arguments in the context of choosing learning models are discussed in Section 5.2. However, the question of how real learning processes can be accurately modelled is the central concern of this chapter. As a consequence, the chapter is strongly based on research in psychology because psychologists have established most of the actual knowledge about human learning. Experimental economics has made increasingly larger contributions to this knowledge in recent years (a comprehensive overview is given in Duffy, 2006). Nevertheless, most current knowledge stems from psychology.

Second, most researchers agree that there is no single universal learning model. Different learning processes take place in different situations (see experimental evidence presented in Duffy, 2006). Thus, different learning models have to exist. In order to support agent-based computational economists in choosing a model, the learning situations have to be categorised and separate advice has to be given for each category. Many different categorisations are possible. The categorisation used here was developed earlier on the basis of the psychological literature (see Brenner, 1999). It is based on the assumption that there is a hard-wired learning process that is common among all animals and a flexible learning process that requires features of the human brain. Other categorisations are possible and the specific choice in this overview is motivated and discussed in detail in Section 1.2.

The chapter proceeds as follows: The remaining introductory section gives a short historical overview and presents and discusses the categorisation of learning models used here. Subsequently, for each learning process class, the various models available are presented in Section 2 (non-conscious learning), Section 3 (routine-based learning), and Section 4 (belief learning). Section 5 addresses some basic issues in modelling learning, such as the complexity and validity of learning models, the distinction between individual and population learning, and the calibration of learning models. Furthermore, Section 6 gives detailed advice on how to adequately model the various ways of learning.

1.1. History of modelling learning

This short trip through history will focuses on mathematical learning models used in economics. Nevertheless, it is necessary to start with a short overview of psychological research on learning as the study of learning processes is mainly handled within psychology and many models that are used in economics are based on psychological findings. Furthermore, it was psychologists who developed the first mathematical models of learning.

1.1.1. Psychological research on learning

Psychologists started to study learning processes extensively approximately 100 years ago. At that time, psychology was dominated by the view that processes within the brain cannot be studied and that explanations of behaviour should be based purely on observable variables. Subsequently, psychologists identified two major learning processes: classic conditioning and operant conditioning. So far, classic conditioning has had little impact on economic discussion (an exception can be found in Witt, 2001), although it is still extensively studied in psychology (an overview is given in Mackintosh, 2003). It describes the development of new stimuli and reinforcers on the basis of existing ones and can, therefore, explain change in preferences (see Witt, 2001). Mathematical models for this learning process have so far only been developed within psychology (see Rescorla and Wagner, 1972), while economic literature has focused more on the process of operant conditioning. Most of the empirical studies in psychology on operant conditioning are conducted with animals. A general result that has been found is that actions that lead to rewards occur with a higher frequency in the future, while actions that cause punishment become less frequent. This kind of learning process is nowadays referred to as 'reinforcement learning' in economics. The first mathematical model of this learning process was developed within psychology by Bush and Mosteller (1955).

In the 1950s psychologists started a new line of research into learning processes. They studied the impact of social interaction and observation on learning. The basic argument was that people do not only learn from their own experience but also from the experience of others, meaning that the concept of reinforcement learning was transferred to interactions and observation. However, it was not only assumed that experience was exchanged between individuals but it was also claimed that people are able to understand the similarities and differences between other's and their own situation. Psychologists at that time entered the sphere of cognition and the resulting theory was called a social-cognitive learning theory (with the most prominent work by Bandura, 1977).

Finally, in the last 20 years psychologists have concentrated on the processes of cognitive learning. Cognitive learning, in general, means the development of an understanding of real world processes and interrelations including the development of notions and expressions. Nowadays much research is done on the development of cognitions in children, such as the learning of languages, and logical thinking. However, formulations of the learning processes in the form of equations are absent as the processes are usually described using graphs, accompanied by verbal arguments or logical elements. The main topics centre on the development of structures and the integration of knowledge in the brain. Hence, this research is far removed from the type of decision making usually studied in economics with reference to learning processes.

A recent development is the use of neuro-science in the study of cognitive learning processes (see, e.g., Rumiati and Bekkering, 2003). This research offers new information on the speed of information processing; the interaction between different stimuli that appear simultaneously; the extent to which different parts of the brain are involved in the processing of stimuli and similar aspects of learning. Again this research is, up to this point, of little use for modelling learning processes in economics. However, this may well change in the future.

1.1.2. Learning and optimisation

For a long time learning was a minor issue in economics. When economists started to show some interest in learning, they were mainly concerned with two issues. First, they established a normative learning model that described the optimal learning process, entitled Bayesian learning (see, e.g., Easley and Kiefer, 1988 and Jordan, 1991). Second, they developed models of learning in which behaviour converges towards the optimal behaviour in equilibrium. For quite some time, most economists who studied learning processes were mainly concerned with proving that learning converges towards the optimal behaviour. The first approach of this kind appeared in 1951 (see Brown, 1951). After the proposal of the Nash equilibrium (Nash, 1950) the question arose of how people come to play according to this equilibrium. Brown established a learning model called fictitious play for which Robinson (1951) could show that it converges to Nash equilibrium behaviour (later it was proved that this only holds under certain conditions; see Shapley, 1964).

Many authors who model learning processes still want to show that learning processes converge towards optimisation (examples can be found in Bray, 1982; Yin and Zhu, 1990; Jordan, 1991; Börgers and Sarin, 1997; Dawid, 1997; and Sarin and Vahid, 1999). Often it is even argued that learning models can only be adequate if they converge, at least in the long run, towards optimising behaviour in a stationary situation. However, mainly caused by enormous experimental evidence, this claim is slowly disappearing from the debate. There are increasingly more works that study when and how behaviour predicted by learning models differs from optimal behaviour (see, e.g., Herrnstein and Prelec, 1991; Brenner, 1997; Brenner, 2001; and Brenner and Vriend, 2005).

Nevertheless, economists who model learning processes are still very much divided into two camps: those who prefer learning models that converge towards optimal behaviour and those who are not interested in optimality. In contrast to this, we argue here that finding out under which conditions the various existing models work best is more important (see Börgers, 1996 for a similar argument).

1.1.3. Increasing variety of learning models

In the past few years, there has been a tremendous increase in the number of learning models used in economics. After experimental studies have repeatedly shown that the original economic learning models have been rejected in some experiments (see, e.g.,

Feltovich, 2000), many economists, who modelled learning in economic contexts, developed their own model or their own variation of an existing model. Most of these models are based on introspection, common sense, artificial intelligence approaches or psychological findings. Nearly all of them are in some way or another set up *ad-hoc* without clear scientific justification.

In the meantime some approaches have tried to compare the suitability of different models on the basis of experimental data (see, e.g., Feltovich, 2000; Tang, 2003 and Arifovic and Ledyard, 2000). This topic is addressed and extensively discussed by Duffy (2006).

Independent of this discussion a few learning models have become dominant in economics, while others have been mainly neglected. The most prominent models are Bayesian learning, least-squares learning, as well as the learning direction theory, reinforcement learning, evolutionary algorithms, genetic programming, fictitious play and the learning model by Camerer and Ho. There are different reasons for the dominance of these models, which range from being well-supported by empirical and experimental evidence to converging to optimal behaviour or reducing complexity. We present here more than these prominent models, although it is impossible to present all existing models and modifications of models.

1.2. Classification of learning models

A classification is always as beneficial as it is helpful for practical tasks. We consider here an agent-based computational economist who aims to explain features and dynamics of the economy on the basis of interaction between economic agents. For such an endeavour it is important to know the way in which economic agents behave and the adequate ways to model this behaviour in simulations. The task is to choose a learning model for a planned simulation study. Given the above assumption that the aim is to find the most realistic model, we have to ask what is the right learning model in a given situation.

However, in economic literature on learning this is not the only aim, and not even the most frequent one. Other aims are discussed in Section 5.2.1. Searching for realistic learning models, most information about real learning processes can be found in the psychological literature, thus building the basis for the classification proposed here.

1.2.1. Potential alternative classifications

Alternative ways to classify learning models should not be ignored here. There are at least three other options. First, one might classify learning models according to their origin. This would allow us to distinguish between psychology-based models, rationality-based models, adaptive models, belief learning models, and models inspired by computer science and biology. A classification of all learning models that are discussed here according to such a classification and according to the classification developed below

Table 1
Classification according to the source of the learning models and according to the classification developed below

	Non-conscious learning	Routine-based learning	Belief learning
Psychology-based models	Bush–Mosteller model, parameterised learning automaton	satisficing, melioration, imitation, Roth–Erev model, VID model	stochastic belief learning, rule learning
Rationality-based models			Bayesian learning, least-squares learning
Adaptive models		learning direction theory	
Belief learning models		EWA model	fictitious play
Models from AI and biology		evolutionary algorithms, replicator dynamics, selection-mutation equation	genetic programming, classifier systems neural networks

is given in Table 1. Such a distinction informs the reader about the various sources of learning models, however, it does not help in choosing a model for simulations.

Second, we might classify learning models according to the economic fields in which they are usually applied. For example, macro-economists mainly use Bayesian learning and least-squares learning while reinforcement learning, fictitious play and learning direction theory are prominent among experimental economists. Meanwhile, evolutionary algorithms and genetic programming are frequently used in agent-based computational economics and game theorists seem to prefer fictitious play, replicator dynamics and other adaptive learning models. However, it is unclear why economists in different fields use different learning models. Obviously, economists who use mathematical analysis are restricted in their choice by the requirement of treatable models. The other differences seem to be historical in nature and it could be rather unproductive to support such differences by using them for a classification of learning models.

Third, one might look for existing classifications of learning models in economic literature. However, no classification is available that contains as many different learning models as discussed here. Usually only a few subjectively selected learning models are presented and discussed (see, e.g., Fudenberg and Levine, 1998).

1.2.2. Proposed classification

The classification chosen here is based on the aim to assign realistic learning models to various situations. It is strongly based on psychological knowledge about learning.

It is not clear whether there is a fundamental mechanism within the brain that explains all learning methods. However, since neuro-physiologists and cognitive psychologists have not yet detected such a fundamental mechanism, learning methods can only be developed through empirical observations. Furthermore, it may be technically advantageous not to base all learning processes on one fundamental mechanism. Often it is simpler to describe learning processes on the basis of resulting changes in behaviour than to describe the probably complicated interaction of cognitive processes.

Thus, we are looking for information that helps us decide which learning model is suitable under certain conditions. We ignore the alternative option to search for the best learning model that describes all learning processes and is suitable under every condition. No such model exists, per se, and it is doubtful that there will ever be one.

While looking for a match between adequate learning models and situational characteristics, we are less interested in whether a model has structural attributes facilitating its use in a given situation. We are more interested in whether a learning model describes the relevant processes that occur in reality. Hence, we have to find out if various kinds of learning processes with different features exist in reality and how they occur.

1.2.3. Two ways of learning

Although the psychological literature on learning distinguishes (for historical reasons) between three kinds of learning processes, there are only two fundamentally different ways of learning. First, humans share with other animals a simple way of learning, which is usually called reinforcement learning. This kind of learning seems to be biologically fixed. If an action leads to a negative outcome—a punishment—this action will be avoided in the future. If an action leads to a positive outcome—a reward—it will reoccur. This kind of learning process has been extensively studied in psychology around 100 years ago with different kinds of animals (extensive literature can be found in Thorndike, 1932 and Skinner, 1938). It does not involve any conscious reflection on the situation. Hence, people are not always aware that they are learning.

In addition to reinforcement learning, people are able to reflect on their actions and consequences. We are able to understand the mechanisms that govern our surrounding and life; and we are able to give names to objects and establish causal relations that describe their interaction and nature. Nowadays, this is mainly studied in psychology under the label of learning and is referred to as cognitive learning.

These two kinds of learning are completely different. We argue—without having any empirical proof for this—that reinforcement learning is a mechanism that works in an automatically and continuous fashion. Subsequently, whatever we do is, instantaneously, guided by reinforcement learning. It seems likely that humans are endowed with the same basic mechanisms as animals and therefore learn according to the same hard-wired principles of reinforcement learning.

However, we are able to reflect on our actions and their consequences. This requires active thinking and, therefore, cognitive resources, which are scarce. Hence, we are not able to reflect on all our actions. Imagine if we would have to consider each move of each single muscle. We would not be able to live our life as we do. However, if we think about an action, we are able to overrule the law of reinforcement learning. We argue that the effect of cognitive learning on behaviour is stronger than the effect of reinforcement learning. But, in addition, we argue that we do not have the cognitive capacity to reflect on all our actions and therefore many actions are conducted on the basis of reinforcement learning.

1.2.4. Further distinction of learning processes

While reinforcement learning (or conditioning as it was originally named by psychologists) is well studied and understood, conscious learning processes are more difficult to grasp. Although various learning models exist in psychology, detailed knowledge on the formation of beliefs in the brain are missing.

Hence, there is some temptation to ignore the exact working of the brain and model some basic mechanisms of learning that are well established from empirical and experimental observations. Such models take a mechanistic perspective on learning. People are assumed to learn according to fixed mechanisms or routines. Therefore, we call the learning processes described by these models routine-based learning.

An example is the rule to imitate local people whilst in a foreign country for the first time. In this way one quickly learns about the traditions there and adapts behaviour. However, conscious learning is more than simply imitating the behaviour of others. Conscious learning usually means that we understand why this behaviour is advantageous, maybe how it developed and what are its suitable circumstances. This means that we associate meaning to our observations and build beliefs about relationships and future events. In order to distinguish these processes from simplified routine-based learning, it is defined as associative learning (in accordance with Brenner, 1999) or belief learning in accordance with the term used in the economics literature.

All conscious learning is belief learning because, whenever people reflect upon their situation and learn about appropriate actions, they assign meanings to the gathered information, thus developing beliefs about relationships and future events. Routine-based learning is a simplification of real learning processes that makes life easier for the researcher and is applicable in a number of situations. The correct way would be to model the belief learning process, although the correct way is not always the appropriate way. This holds especially because we have little information about how belief learning processes should be modelled. Nevertheless, while using routine-based learning models, we should keep in mind that they only represent approximations.

2. Modelling non-conscious learning

According to the categorisation proposed here, all learning processes that occur without individuals being aware of them are labelled non-conscious learning. In psychology two such learning processes are identified: classical conditioning and operant conditioning (also called reinforcement learning). As mentioned above, the discussion is restricted here to the process of reinforcement learning as classical conditioning is rarely addressed in economic literature (a discussion of modelling classical conditioning can be found in Brenner, 1999, Ch. 3 and 5). However, it has to be mentioned that if we equate non-conscious learning with reinforcement learning, we depart from the traditional psychological notion of reinforcement learning. In psychology, reinforcement learning was established at a time in which behaviourism was dominant, which meant that models which explicitly considered the internal functioning of the cognitive processes were argued by psychologists to be pure speculation and therefore should be avoided. Hence, they developed models of learning processes that saw decisions as being outcomes of visible processes, i.e. stimulus-response relations. However, these models have not excluded the possibility that there might be cognitive processes in the background that cause visible changes in behaviour. They only hold that these processes should not be explicitly included in the models.

Non-conscious learning, as it is defined here, applies only to those learning processes in which no cognitive reflection takes place. The analogy that we draw here comes from the fact that most psychological studies of conditioning have been based on animal experiments which claim that animals mainly learn non-cognitively. Hence, we argue that reinforcement learning models should be suitable for modelling non-cognitive learning processes in humans. In psychology it is frequently argued that individuals learn according to reinforcement learning if they do not reflect on the situation (see, e.g., Biel and Dahlstrand, 1997).

Reinforcement learning is based on an initial frequency distribution among various possible actions. The origin of this frequency distribution has to be explained by other means, as it has been mainly neglected in the literature. Reinforcement learning means that actions are chosen randomly according to the current frequency distribution. If an action leads to a reward (positive outcome) the frequency of this action in future behaviour is increased. If an action leads to a punishment (negative outcome) the frequency of this action is decreased.

2.1. Existing models

In economics three frequently used models that describe reinforcement learning are the Bush–Mosteller model, the principle of melioration, and the Roth–Erev model. All three models best capture the major characteristic of reinforcement learning: the increase in the frequency of behaviours that lead to relatively better results and the slow disappearance of behaviours if reinforcement is removed. All these models are inspired by psychological research on reinforcement learning. However, as discussed above, non-conscious learning is not the same as reinforcement learning. Therefore, we have to depart from the psychological literature here and assess whether these models actually describe a non-conscious learning process.

The three models do differ in their details. Melioration learning assumes that the learning process is based on the average experience of each behaviour in the past. The

Bush–Mosteller model and the Roth–Erev model assume that the change of behaviour at each point in time is determined by the current outcome together with the previously determined frequency distribution, which are used to determine an updated frequency distribution for current action choice. Hence, while the Bush–Mosteller model and the Roth–Erev model only require the individual to store the actual frequencies of the possible actions, melioration learning requires them to also remember past events. Furthermore, it requires individuals to calculate averages. Herrnstein developed the melioration principle in the light of experimental observations (see Herrnstein, 1970 and Herrnstein and Prelec, 1991). However, given their laboratory settings, such behaviour is probably conscious. Hence, the melioration concept seems to fit better into the modelling of routine-based learning and will be further discussed there. It does not seem to be adequate to model non-conscious learning processes.

Juxtaposing the Bush–Mosteller model and the Roth–Erev model, one may observe that they have the same fundamental structure. The Bush–Mosteller model was set up in 1955 by psychologists according to the psychological knowledge on operant conditioning (see Bush and Mosteller, 1955). It was adapted to economics by Cross about 20 years later (see Cross 1973, 1983). Arthur (1991) generalised the model by allowing for different developments of the learning speed during the learning process. He called his learning model 'parameterized learning automaton'. The two extreme cases that are included in Arthur's model are a constant learning speed and a hyperbolically decreasing learning speed. The former border case is identical to the Bush–Mosteller model. The latter border case later became the original Roth–Erev model. Arthur (1991) developed a very flexible model and discussed the meaning of different learning speeds. However, all these developments did not catch much attention within economics and it is to the merit of Roth and Erev to have reestablished reinforcement learning in economics.

The major difference between the Bush–Mosteller model and the original Roth–Erev model is the speed of learning, which was already discussed by Arthur (1991). In the Bush–Mosteller model the speed of learning remains constant. This means that an individual with a lot of experience in a situation reacts in the same way to a new experience as an individual with no former experience. The original Roth–Erev model assumes that the learning speed converges hyperbolically to zero while experience is collected. Psychological studies describe the aspect of spontaneous recovery (see Thorndike, 1932), which means those actions that have been abandoned because of unpleasant results are quickly taken into the individual's behavioural repertoire again if positive outcomes result from these actions. This spontaneous recovery is captured by the Bush–Mosteller model but not by the original Roth–Erev model. However, Roth and Erev (1995) have modified their original model by including the aspect of forgetting, so that it also captures the process of spontaneous recovery.

A second difference is that the Bush–Mosteller model can also deal with negative payoffs, while the Roth–Erev model and the parameterized learning automaton are only able to use positive payoffs. The original psychological studies show that reinforcement learning has different characteristics for positive (rewarding) and negative (punishing) outcomes. The Bush–Mosteller model is able to capture these effects and accordingly leads to different predictions (see Brenner, 1997). Thus, it is the only learning model that does not contain cognitive elements and is able to reproduce all features of reinforcement learning that have been identified in psychological studies.

As the parameterized learning automaton and the Roth–Erev model are described by Duffy (2006), only the Bush–Mosteller model is described here in detail.

2.2. Bush–Mosteller model

At the beginning of the last century reinforcement learning became a central topic in psychology (cf. the previous section). This eventually led to the development of a mathematical learning model by Bush and Mosteller (1955). Their model is based on the considerations of Estes (1950) who took the first steps towards a mathematical formulation of reinforcement learning. It is based on the idea of representing behaviour by a frequency distribution of behaviour patterns given by a probability vector $\mathbf{p}(t)$ $(= (p(a,t))_{a \in \mathcal{A}})$. This vector assigns a probability $p(a,t)$ $(0 \leq p(a,t) \leq 1$, $\sum_{a \in \mathcal{A}} p(a,t) = 1)$ to each behavioural alternative a $(a \in A)$ at each time t. The term $p(a,t)$ is sometimes called habit strength. The Bush–Mosteller model is a stochastic model that predicts probabilities for the occurrence of behaviour patterns rather than the behaviour pattern itself.

The probability vector $\mathbf{p}(t)$ changes during the learning process according to the theory of reinforcement. Bush and Mosteller distinguished only between rewarding and punishing outcomes, but not within both classes. Cross (1973) further developed the Bush–Mosteller model by answering the question of how to deal with rewards and punishments of different strength. He placed the models into an economic context and so defined the reinforcing character of an event by the utility to which it gives rise. In doing so, he assumed that the impact of an outcome is monotonously increasing in its utility. However, Cross also eliminated the punishing character of events, because in economics it is assumed that utilities can be linearly transformed and negative utilities values can be avoided without a loss of generality as long as they have a finite lower bound. He overlooked that reinforcement learning works in a different manner for those situations in which agents are exposed to punishing outcomes compared to those situations in which they are exposed to rewarding outcomes. Therefore, in reinforcement learning it matters whether punishing or rewarding outcomes motivate learning.

This shortcoming of Cross's version of the Bush–Mosteller model has been overcome by the work of Börgers and Sarin (1997) and Brenner (1997). Only this version of the Bush–Mosteller model, called the generalised Bush–Mosteller model here, is described here (a discussion of all versions can be found in Brenner, 1999, Ch. 3). Reinforcement strengths are defined in such a way that all rewarding outcomes are reflected by positive reinforcement strengths, while all punishing outcomes are reflected by negative reinforcement strengths. Apart from this, the generalised Bush–Mosteller model is identical to the version proposed by Cross. The change in the probability $p(a,t)$ of the individual to realise action a is given by

$$p(a, t + 1) = p(a, t) + \begin{cases} v(\Pi(t)) \cdot (1 - p(a, t)) & \text{if } a = a(t) \\ -v(\Pi(t)) \cdot p(a, t) & \text{if } a \neq a(t) \end{cases} \tag{1}$$

if action $a(t)$ is realised and the resulting reinforcement strength $\Pi(t)$ is positive, and by

$$p(a, t + 1) = p(a, t) + \begin{cases} -v(-\Pi(t)) \cdot p(a, t) & \text{if } a = a(t) \\ v(-\Pi(t)) \cdot \frac{p(a,t)p(a(t),t)}{1-p(a(t),t)} & \text{if } a \neq a(t) \end{cases} \tag{2}$$

if action $a(t)$ is realised and the resulting reinforcement strength $\Pi(t)$ is negative. $v(\Pi)$ is a monotonously increasing function in Π ($\Pi > 0$) with $v(0) = 0$ and $0 \leq v(\Pi) \leq 1$. A reinforcement strength of $\Pi = 0$ can be interpreted as the aspiration level (as done in Börgers and Sarin, 1997).

Usually, a linear formulation $v(\Pi) = v \cdot \Pi$ is used, so that the learning process is described by

$$p(a, t + 1) = p(a, t)$$
$$+ \begin{cases} v \cdot \Pi(t) \cdot (1 - p(a, t)) & \text{if } a = a(t) \wedge \Pi(t) \geq 0 \\ v \cdot \Pi(t) \cdot p(a, t) & \text{if } a = a(t) \wedge \Pi(t) < 0 \\ -v \cdot \Pi(t) \cdot p(a, t) & \text{if } a \neq a(t) \wedge \Pi(t) \geq 0 \\ -v \cdot \Pi(t) \cdot \frac{p(a,t) \cdot p(a(t),t)}{1-p(a(t),t)} & \text{if } a \neq a(t) \wedge \Pi(t) < 0 \end{cases} \tag{3}$$

All versions of the Bush–Mosteller model assume that an outcome has an impact on the frequency distribution $\mathbf{p}(t)$ in the moment of its occurrence only. This means that individuals do not remember previous actions and outcomes. The past is implicitly contained in the frequency distribution $\mathbf{p}(t)$. Learning is assumed to be a Markov process.

This model can only be applied to situations in which individuals have to choose repeatedly between a finite number of alternative behaviours, such as a set of different actions or a number of real-valued actions, e.g., prices. It cannot be applied to situations in which individuals have to choose a value from a set of infinite cardinality, such as an interval of possible prices. Choosing a real value within an interval implies conscious thinking, because the very notion of real value is a cognitive concept and must be consciously learnt.

3. Modelling routine-based learning

It was extensively discussed above that routine-based learning models are approximations for the real conscious learning processes, as they are based on the identification of some simple fundamental principles of learning. These principles are deduced in economic literature either from experimental observations, from ad-hoc reasoning, or from some considerations on optimal learning. They might describe learning quite accurately under certain circumstances. However, they are never able to describe learning in each situation because people are capable of complex reasoning and of understanding the potentially complex environment that they face. Unfortunately, psychologists still have quite a vague comprehension of reasoning and understanding processes. Nevertheless, it is clear that these processes are not simple and that they involve the development of concepts and beliefs (see, e.g. Anderson, 2000).

We define routine-based learning models as those models in which there is a direct connection from the agent's experiences and observations to their behaviour. All models that include beliefs and their development over time are seen as potential candidates for modelling, what is called here, associative or belief learning (they are discussed in the next section). We claim that there will never be a routine-based learning model that accurately describes the conscious learning process in all circumstances.

Nevertheless, under certain circumstances, routine-based learning models may be an adequate and simple description of learning. Several studies have shown that individuals tend to stick to their beliefs even if there is some evidence that falsify them (see, e.g., Luchins, 1942 and Anderson, 2000). Some strands of psychological research have shown that individuals apply simple rather than optimal routines in decision making (see, e.g., Gigerenzer and Selten, 2001).

Although we have to be aware of the restrictions of routine-based learning models, it might be advantageous to search for a routine-based learning model in order to describe behaviour. In this case, the only way to guide this search is empirical and experimental evidence. The aim is not to have a detailed description of the learning process but to find a model that accurately represents the dynamics of these actions.

Various learning models have been put forward in the economics literature that fit into this category. The most frequently used models are represented here; some of them model one aspect of learning, while others combine a number of mechanisms within one model. Furthermore, there are models that describe learning on the individual level, while others describe them on a population level. These issues are discussed in Section 5.2. Here, the most prominent models are presented sequentially.

3.1. Experimentation

The standard form of learning by experimentation is the trial-and-error principle. However, it is not sufficiently specific to be called a model. It requires specification of whether all possible actions are tried, how often they are tried before they can be called an error and what an error means. Therefore, experimentation is usually included in other models as an additional factor. Nowadays, for almost all learning and decision models, some variants exist that include experimentation. Even utility maximisation has been expanded to include these elements, such as errors or individual differences in the evaluation of actions, which are similar to experimentation (see Brenner and Slembeck, 2001 for a detailed presentation). The inclusion of experimentation in other models will be discussed during the presentation of these models below. Here two concepts will be presented that are only based on experimentation: the concept of $S(k)$-equilibria and the learning direction theory.

Experimentation is based on the argument that through choosing different actions individuals can collect information on the consequences of these actions. In the literature it is sometimes argued that there is a trade-off between experimentation and exploitation. This means that an individual can either experiment to obtain further information on the situation or exploit the information collected in the past using this as a basis to choose the best action.

A simple form of this kind of behaviour is the proposed behaviour by Osbourne and Rubinstein (1995). They argued that individuals choose each possible action k times. After this initial phase they choose the action that has led to the highest average payoff whenever they face the same situation. What remains unclear in this approach is the question of how k is determined. This model has also not been tested empirically or experimentally.

More evidence exists in favour of the learning direction theory (see, e.g., Berninghaus and Ehrhart, 1998 and Grosskopf, 2003). The learning direction theory was proposed by Selten (see Selten and Stoecker, 1986 and Selten, 1997). Learning direction theory can only be applied if individuals are confined to choosing from a set of alternatives that can be ordered in a meaningful way, or if, at least, individuals are able to separate the alternatives that increase performance from those which decrease performance each time. Moreover, learning direction theory assumes that individuals are able to identify whether their last action was pitched too high or too low in this order of possible actions. Given these assumptions, learning direction theory states that individuals will change their behaviour in the direction in which they expect their own performance to increase, or stay with the same behaviour. Such a learning procedure has some similarities with gradient methods used in optimisation problems, although in the case of the learning direction theory there does not necessarily have to be something like a potential function. In other words, learning direction theory states that individuals change their behaviour only in a way that increases their payoff. As long as the situation is easy to understand, such a statement is straightforward. So it is no surprise that the theory has been confirmed in many experiments. However, the implications of learning direction theory are rather weak.

3.2. Melioration and experience collection

It is well-known that individuals memorise their experience with certain situations and use this experience to choose an adequate action if they face the situation again. Individuals even transfer experience between different situations that are perceived to be similar. In the psychological literature it is argued that probabilities and values are assigned to outcomes, both determined by previous experience.

In economics, various models have been developed that describe the collection of knowledge about a situation. Some of them are based on statistical considerations about how people should learn in an optimal way. The two most widespread models of this kind are Bayesian learning and least-squares learning. In contrast, some models are built according to how the modeller thinks people learn in reality. These include the models of myopic learning, fictitious play and melioration learning, which is based on experimental findings.

Except for melioration learning, an element that all these models have in common is that individuals not only learn about the results of their actions but also about the probabilities of the actions of other agents or events. Hence, although Bayesian learning, least-squares learning and fictitious play can be used to describe a learning process in which the outcomes of different actions are memorised, they are also able to describe a learning process in which beliefs and hypotheses about the situation are developed. They are suited to describe what is called belief learning here. Therefore, they are discussed in the next section. The only learning model that is only designed to describe the memorising of experience with different actions is melioration learning. However, it should be stated here that we regard also fictitous play as a relevant model for experience collection.

Melioration learning, although it is never related to the model of fictitious play in the literature, is a special case of gradual convergence to fictitious play. Melioration learning was developed to represent reinforcement learning (see Herrnstein, 1970; Vaughan and Herrnstein, 1987; and Herrnstein and Prelec, 1991). However, it is argued here that it is less adequate to model what was called non-conscious learning above. It seems to be more adequate to model the routine-based learning process of experience collection.

The dynamics of melioration learning have been formulated mathematically by Vaughan and Herrnstein (1987). For a case with two possible actions a and $\tilde{a}$, they describe it as a time continuous adjustment process of the form

$$\frac{dp(a,t)}{dt} = v\big(\bar{u}(a,t) - \bar{u}(\tilde{a},t)\big), \tag{4}$$

where $p(a,t)$ denotes the probability of income spent on activity a, $\bar{u}(a)$ denote the average utility from activity a in the past, and $v(\cdot)$ is a monotonously increasing function with $v(0) = 0$.

Vaughan and Herrnstein (1987) neglect cases in which the individuals can choose between more than two alternative actions. Nor do they define the average utilities $\bar{u}(a,t)$ in detail. A discussion of the average utility or payoff is presented by Brenner and Witt (2003). They define $\mathcal{T}_a(t)$ as the set of moments of time in which an individual has realised action a and also has a memory of it at time t. The term $k_a(t)$ denotes the number of these occasions. Consequently the average utility $\bar{u}(a,t)$ is given by

$$\bar{u}(a,t) = \frac{1}{k_a(t)} \cdot \sum_{\tau \in \mathcal{T}_a(t)} u(a,\tau). \tag{5}$$

Brenner and Witt (2003) also claim that it is more adequate to multiply equation (4) by $p(a,t) \cdot (1 - p(a,t))$ instead of the artificial additional condition that the dynamics stop if $p(a,t)$ becomes smaller than zero for at least one action a. Consequently equation (4) can be written as

$$\frac{dp(a,t)}{dt} = p(a,t) \cdot \big(1 - p(a,t)\big) \cdot v\big(\bar{u}(a,t) - \bar{u}(\tilde{a},t)\big). \tag{6}$$

This approach can be easily expanded to a situation in which the individual has more than two options to choose. Let us assume that there is a set $\mathcal{A}$ of alternative actions. Furthermore, let us assume that the function $v(\cdot)$ is linear. Then, the dynamics of melioration learning is given by

$$\frac{dp(a,t)}{dt} = p(a,t) \cdot v \cdot \left(\bar{u}(a,t) - \sum_{\tilde{a} \in \mathcal{A}} p(\tilde{a},t) \cdot \bar{u}(\tilde{a},t) \right). \tag{7}$$

Equation (7) describes a replicator dynamic (compare to equation (13)). At the same time, it also represents a special case of a gradual convergence to fictitious play. The utility or payoff $u(a,t)$ is calculated for each action a on the basis of a finite memory. However, the action that caused the highest payoffs in the past is not immediately chosen. Instead, the behaviour converges towards the choice of the action with the best experience. Through this process, individuals keep experimenting as long as one action does not supersede the others for a relatively long time. Such a model seems to be a good choice for modelling a realistic combination of experience collection and experimentation, but it is nevertheless quite simple. Alternatively, the average payoffs $\bar{u}(a,t)$ might also be calculated as exponentially weighted averages of the past experience according to

$$\bar{u}(a,t) = \frac{1-\beta}{1-\beta^{(t-1)}} \sum_{\tau=0}^{t-1} \beta^{(t-1-\tau)} \cdot u(\tau) \cdot \delta(a(\tau)=a), \tag{8}$$

where $u(\tau)$ is the utility obtained by the individual at time τ, $a(\tau)$ is the action taken at time τ, and $\delta(a(\tau)=a)$ is 1 if $a(\tau)=a$ and otherwise 0. β is a parameter that reflects the time-horizon of the memory.

3.3. Imitation

The process of imitation is often used to describe learning processes in economics. Yet no general model exists that describes imitation. Each author who considers imitation an important aspect makes her own assumptions about the process. Most models of imitation found in economic literature assume that the individuals are able to observe the actions of other individuals and their resulting outcomes. Furthermore, the individuals are assumed to use this information in order to take actions that lead to a better outcome. This contrasts with the recent psychological literature on imitation. There, imitation is seen as an innate process: Children are found to imitate behaviours that have no real advantage. Nevertheless they are also able to concentrate on the crucial features for success and neglect minor aspects as well as learn from unsuccessful behaviour (see Rumiati and Bekkering, 2003 for a condensed overview). However, the psychological research has not produced learning models that could be used in economics.

Therefore, the different models that have been developed in economics are discussed below. These models differ in various characteristics:

- In some models it is claimed that a certain number of individuals are observed, where these are located next to the observer (see, e.g., Eshel et al., 1998) or they are randomly picked from the whole population (see, e.g., Duffy and Feltovich, 1999 and Kirchkamp, 2000). In other models the entire population is observed (see, e.g., Morales, 2002). Because the situation determines how many individuals are observed in reality, the existence of various models is justified.
- Some models calculate the average utility of each action based on observations (see, e.g., Eshel et al., 1998). Other models claim that individuals imitate the one who has obtained the highest utility of those observed (see, e.g., Nowak and May, 1993; Hegselmann, 1996; Vega-Redondo, 1997; and Kirchkamp, 2000). Vega-Redondo adds noise to this assumption. Finally, in some models it is assumed that only one other individual is observed at any time and the payoff or utility obtained by this individual is compared to their own payoff. Then, either a stochastic approach is chosen whereby it is more likely to imitate those with a higher difference between the other's and their own utility (see, e.g., Witt, 1996) or the other individual's behaviour is imitated whenever it has given rise to a higher utility (see Schlag, 1998 for a discussion of these different rules). There is no empirical or experimental study that examines which of these many models is more realistic.

Although the psychological literature offers no mathematical model, it does offer some conceptual help. Imitation learning is discussed in psychology under the label of observational learning (see Bandura, 1977). It is discussed how the attention of people is drawn to the experience made by others and how this experience is transferred to one's own situation. This literature implies that we may treat imitation via the models of experience collection that have been described above. Furthermore, such a modelling would include the process of communication. The above equation (8) can be modified such that it also contains the experience gathered by other individuals. Then, the only question that has to be answered is the question of how much of other individuals' experience is observed and considered in decision making. The answer is context-dependent and has to be found for each situation separately.

A very simple model that combines the routine-based processes of experimentation, experience collection and imitation/communication would consist of two processes: First, an exponentially weighted average of the past experience with each action a is built, including the experience of all N individuals in the population:

$$\bar{u}_i(a, t) = \frac{1 - \beta}{1 - \beta^{(t-1)}} \sum_{\tau=0}^{t-1} \left[\beta^{(t-1-\tau)} \cdot \sum_{j=1}^{N} \sigma(i, j) \cdot u_j(\tau) \cdot \delta(a_j(\tau) = a) \right], \qquad (9)$$

where $u_j(\tau)$ is the utility obtained by individual j at time τ, $a_j(\tau)$ is the action taken by individual j at time τ, and $\sigma(i, j)$ is the weight with which individual i includes the experience of individual j in her own expectation about the future. These weights have to satisfy

$$\sum_{j=1}^{N} \sigma(i, j) = 1 \qquad (10)$$

for each individual i. Besides this, the weights have to be determined specifically for each situation. The change of behaviour can then be modelled by equation (7). The above can however also be used to learn about the circumstances, such as the behaviour of others or any rules of the situation, as it is modelled in fictitious play.

3.4. Satisficing

The concept of satisficing can be found in many learning models in the literature. It was first proposed by Simon (1957). Since then, many models have been proposed that describe learning on the basis of the satisficing principle (for a detailed description of the satisficing principle see Simon, 1987). Many of these models, however, are based on one of the routine-based learning processes above and contain satisficing as an additional aspect.

The satisficing principle is based on the assumption that individuals have an aspiration level. This means that they assign a value z to each situation for the payoff or utility that they expect to obtain. If the actual payoff or utility is above this value they are satisfied, while an outcome below this value dissatisfies them. In order to model satisficing three things have to be specified: 1) the aspiration level, 2) the dependence of behavioural changes on dissatisfaction, and 3) how the new action is chosen if the current one is abandoned because of dissatisfaction.

Aspiration levels have been studied intensively in psychology in the 1940s and 1950s (see, e.g., Festinger, 1942; Thibaut and Kelley, 1959 and Lant, 1992 and Stahl and Haruvy, 2002 for economic studies). From these empirical studies we know that the aspiration level of an individual changes in time. On the one hand, it depends on the outcomes of the individual's own behaviour. These experiences are considered more seriously the more recent they are (see Thibaut and Kelley, 1959). On the other hand, it depends on the performances of others (see Festinger, 1942). Here again the influence of outcomes decreases with increasing time but also depends on the similarity of these people and their situation with one's own position.

In the literature, three kinds of aspiration levels can be found (see Bendor et al., 2001 for an overview). First, some authors assume for simplicity a constant aspiration level z (see, e.g., Day, 1967 and Day and Tinney, 1968). Second, some authors assume an aspiration level $z_i(t)$ of an individual i that adapts towards the payoffs currently obtained by this individual (see, e.g., Witt, 1986; Mezias, 1988; Gilboa and Schmeidler, 1995; Pazgal, 1997; Karandikar et al., 1998; and Börgers and Sarin, 2000). Third, some authors let the experiences of others influence the formation of individual aspirations, as it was proven in psychological studies. This additional impact is called 'social influences' (see, e.g., Dixon, 2000 and Mezias et al., 2002).

The assumption of a constant aspiration level is rare in the recent literature. Therefore, we focus on the two other approaches here. The most common way of modelling (see, e.g., Karandikar et al., 1998 and Börgers and Sarin, 2000) an aspiration level that adapts to the personal experience is based on the equation

$$z(t+1) = \lambda \cdot z(t) + (1-\lambda) \cdot \pi(t). \tag{11}$$

In this equation λ determines how much the new experience influences the aspiration level $z(t)$ and $\pi(t)$ is the payoff obtained by the individual at time t. Alternative models mainly replace the payoff $\pi(t)$ in equation (11) by other variables such as the utility obtained at time t or the maximal or average payoff in the past.

The influence of the experience of other individuals can be included, for example (see Mezias et al., 2002), by introducing a social influence $\pi_{soc}(t)$:

$$z_i(t+1) = \lambda_1 \cdot z_i(t) + \lambda_2 \cdot \left[\pi_i(t) - z_i(t)\right] + \lambda_3 \cdot \pi_{soc}(t), \tag{12}$$

where λ_1, λ_2 and λ_3 determine the strengths of the different influences on the aspiration level and have to add up to one: $\lambda_1 + \lambda_2 + \lambda_3 = 1$. The social influence $\pi_{soc}(t)$ can be defined as the average payoff that other individuals obtain at time t. However, it might also include further social aspects: An individual might put her own aspiration relatively higher or lower to what others reach. Furthermore, other individuals might vary in importance in the formation of the individual's own aspiration.

A further complication is that different assumptions about the reaction to dissatisfaction can be found in the literature. In general it is argued that the probability to change behaviour increases with the degree of dissatisfaction but never reaches one (see Palomino and Vega-Redondo, 1999 and Dixon, 2000). Usually a linear increase in the probability of changing behaviour is assumed (see, e.g., Börgers and Sarin, 2000). However, other forms are possible as well.

Finally, a satisficing model has to specify how the new action is chosen if the current action is abandoned because of dissatisfaction. If there are only two alternative actions, this specification is straight-forward. In the case of more than two alternative actions there are two options. First, one of the other routine-based learning models can be used to determine the new choice. Through this, the satisficing principle can be combined with other concepts. Second, the new choice can be determined randomly.

3.5. Replicator dynamics and selection-mutation equation

The replicator dynamics (see Hofbauer and Sigmund, 1984) is the basis for evolutionary game theory. It originates from biology and simply states that behaviours that are fitter than average occur more frequently and behaviours that are worse than the average occur less frequently. This is mathematically given by

$$\frac{ds(a,t)}{dt} = v(t) \cdot s(a,t)\left[\Pi(a,t) - \langle\Pi(t)\rangle\right], \tag{13}$$

where $v(t)$ denotes the speed of the process, $\Pi(a, t)$ is the average outcome obtained by those individuals that show behaviour a at time t, and $\langle \Pi(t) \rangle = \sum_{a \in \mathcal{A}} s(a, t) \cdot \Pi(a, t)$ is the average outcome in the whole population at time t. The replicator dynamics describes the selection process in biological evolution. There, $v(t)$ is called the selection pressure, meaning the velocity of the elimination of less fit species. $\Pi(a, t)$ is the fitness of the species a at time t.

The selection-mutation equation (see Eigen, 1971), also called Fisher–Eigen equation, also originates from biology. In addition to the selection process that is captured by the replicator dynamics, it also captures the mutation process. The selection-mutation equation can be written as (see Helbing, 1995)

$$\frac{ds(a, t)}{dt} = \sum_{\tilde{a} \in \mathcal{A}} \left[\omega(a|\tilde{a}, t) \cdot s(\tilde{a}, t) - \omega(\tilde{a}|a, t) \cdot s(a, t) \right]$$
$$+ v(t) \cdot s(a, t) \left[\Pi(a, t) - \langle \Pi(t) \rangle \right]. \tag{14}$$

The first term on the right-hand side of equation (14) represents the mutation processes. The mutation matrix $\omega(a|\tilde{a}, t)$ defines the probability of a mutation from genetic variant $\tilde{a}$ to genetic variant a. The mutation matrix has to be chosen according to the biological probabilities of crossovers, mutations and other similar processes. In an economic context it can be chosen according to the probabilities of individuals randomly switching from one choice to another. The second term on the right-hand side of equation (14) corresponds exactly to the replicator dynamics.

The replicator dynamics and selection-mutation equation are mainly used in mathematical analysis of learning processes because they are, in contrast to most other common learning models, analytically treatable. We are not aware of any experimental accuracy test, so little can be said whether they accurately represent learning processes. However, the selection-mutation equation is, at least, a flexible formulation. Defining the mutation matrix $\omega(a|\tilde{a}, t)$ allows the inclusion of various aspects into the model. It is even possible to make this matrix, and thus the experimentation of individuals, dependent on the actual situation (such as the satisfaction of the individuals or their knowledge about potential improvements). However, these possibilities have so far not been examined closely in the literature.

3.6. Evolutionary algorithms

The evolutionary algorithms of Rechenberg and Holland (see Rechenberg, 1973 and Holland, 1975) are based on the same biological basis as the selection-mutation equation. However, equation (14) is not able to exactly represent the dynamics of evolutionary algorithms because the selection process is modelled differently in evolutionary algorithms. Furthermore, evolutionary algorithms explicitly describe the development of each individual and its replacement in the next generation (a detailed description of genetic algorithms can be found in Duffy, 2006; evolutionary strategies are thoroughly described in Beyer, 2001). While the replicator dynamics and the selection-mutation equation dominate mathematical evolutionary game theory, it has become common to use evolutionary algorithms in economic simulations (see Holland and Miller, 1991; Arifovic, 1994; and Dawid, 1996 for some path breaking works). An extensive representation of genetic algorithms and a discussion on the interpretation of these as learning processes can be found in Duffy, 2006. Hence, we take up only two issues here that are rarely considered in computational economics but are important for using evolutionary algorithms to represent economic learning: learning aspects not represented by evolutionary algorithms and the difference between genetic algorithms and evolutionary strategies.

While in computational economics the analogy between genetic algorithms and real learning processes is widely accepted, this does not hold on a more general level where the similarities between biological evolution and cultural evolution, based on learning, are controversially discussed (see, e.g., Maynard Smith, 1982; Hallpike, 1986; Witt, 1991; and Ramstad, 1994). Some differences between biological evolution and learning processes also hold for using genetic algorithms in modelling economic learning. The main difference (for other differences see Brenner, 1998) is that evolutionary algorithms contain a limited type of memory. Past experience is only remembered through the relative share of various actions in the current set of strategies. Consequently, individuals are just as likely to mutate to an action previously tested with very uncomfortable results as to mutate to an action that they have never tried before. In reality and in learning models such as fictitious play and Bayesian learning, people would remember their past experience and would treat the two actions differently.

In the field of technical optimisation, genetic algorithms and evolutionary strategies are still used for different applications, contrastingly, computational economists only use genetic algorithms. The literature does not provide a reason for this neglect of evolutionary strategies. Originally there has been one major difference between the two approaches: evolutionary strategies require the variables that are to be optimised to be real values, while genetic algorithms require a binary coding. This had, of course, some consequences for the modelling of mutations and crossovers. In the case of genetic algorithms mutations are switches of bits in the binary code, while in evolutionary strategies mutations are normally distributed changes in these real values (see Rechenberg, 1973 and Schwefel, 1995). Similarly, crossovers, in the case of genetic algorithms, are the exchange of bits, while crossovers are used in a similar form in evolutionary strategies only if a multi-dimensional variable is to be optimised. However, crossovers in the case of genetic algorithms should also be only used if the bits represent independent features of behaviour. If the bits in a binary string of a genetic algorithm represent the binary coding of a value, crossover might lead to strange results because the crossover of 1000 (representing 8) with 0111 (representing 7) might lead to 1111 (15) and 0000 (0), which is not in line with the interpretation of crossovers as representing communication.

Hence, the coding of variables is the basic difference between genetic algorithms and evolutionary strategies. Therefore, in technical optimisation, which of the two approaches are used depends on which coding is more adequate for the given problem.

In contrast, in economics only genetic algorithms are used and recently authors have started to adapt genetic algorithms to the use of real values instead of the binary coding. It seems as if computational economics are simply throwing away half the available options.

3.7. Combined models: EWA and VID model

There seems to be a natural tendency for researchers to search for general models that describe various processes, which also holds in the learning context. We have seen above that various kinds of learning processes exist and it could be argued that the different models can be combined. Combining different models of routine-based learning can be justified by the argument that each routine-based learning model represents one feature of learning and that all these features are simultaneously given. However, the modelling of routine-based learning was justified by the attempt to focus on one feature to simplify modelling. This justification is lost by combining routine-based learning models. Nevertheless, combined learning models exist and two approaches are presented here: Camerer and Ho's Experience-Weighted Attraction (EWA) model and the Variation-Imitation-Decision (VID) model.

In the EWA model (Camerer and Ho, 1999) it is argued that two fundamental types of learning processes exist: reinforcement learning and belief learning. The model is designed such that it describes these two learning processes as border cases for specific choices of the model parameters. The model is described by two equations that determine the process of updating in the light of new experience:

$$N(t) = \rho \cdot N(t-1) + 1 \tag{15}$$

and

$$A_i^j(t) = \left\{ \phi \cdot N(t-1) \cdot A_i^j(t-1) \right.$$
$$\left. + \left[\delta + (1-\delta) \cdot I\left(s_i^j, s_i(t)\right) \right] \cdot \pi_i\left(s_i^j, s_{-i}(t)\right) \right\} \Big/ N(t). \tag{16}$$

$N(t)$ is called the experience weight and $A_i^j(t)$ is called the attraction of strategy j for individual i. The term $s_i(t)$ denotes the strategy used by individual i at time t, while $s_{-i}(t)$ is a vector that represents the strategies that are chosen by all other individuals, except individual i, at time t. The function $I(s_i^j, s_i(t))$ equals one if $s_i^j = s_i(t)$ holds and equals zero otherwise. The payoff $\pi_i(s_i^j, s_{-i}(t))$ is obtained by individual i if she chooses strategy s_i^j and the behaviour of all others is described by $s_{-i}(t)$. The terms ρ, ϕ, and δ are the parameters of the model. The initial values of $N(t)$ and $A_i^j(t)$ have to be chosen according to considerations about what experience individuals might transfer from other situations.

If $N(0) = 1$ and $\rho = \delta = 0$, the model reduces to the original Roth–Erev model of reinforcement learning. If δ is larger than zero, the experience collection is expanded to actions that are not chosen. Thus, it is assumed that the individual can learn by the observation of events about the adequacy of actions that were not taken. If $\rho = \phi$ and $\delta = 1$, the model reduces to weighted fictitious play. For other parameter values the model presents a mixture of the two learning processes. Finally, the EWA model assumes that people make their choice of action according to a logit formulation. The probability of each strategy j to be taken by individual i is given by

$$P_i^j(t+1) = \frac{e^{\lambda \cdot A_i^j(t)}}{\sum_{k=1}^{m_i} e^{\lambda \cdot A_i^k(t)}}, \tag{17}$$

where λ is a parameter and m_i is the number of possible strategies that individual i can use.

By combining a reinforcement learning model and a belief learning model, the EWA model presents a mixture of non-conscious and conscious learning. Hence, it could be argued that the EWA model is a general learning model.

The VID model combines all the features of learning that have been described above under the heading of routine-based learning: experimentation, experience collection, imitation, and satisficing. Therefore, it presents what has been discussed above: a combination of all main features of conscious learning on the routine level. However, this implies that the VID model is very complex, which reduces its attractiveness. In most situations, the model would contain many aspects that are simply irrelevant. Hence, its adequacy is restricted to addressing some general questions (see, e.g., Brenner, 2001).

A complete description of the model would take too much space here. Therefore, the interested reader is referred to the detailed description by Brenner (1999, Ch. 3). The model assumes that individuals collect information on the outcome of behaviours similar to how it is done in fictitious play. However, this knowledge does not directly influence behaviour. Instead, individuals are assumed to continue displaying the same behaviour if it leads to satisfying outcomes most of the time. Some very rare modifications are assumed without motivation. Besides these, individuals change behaviour only if they are dissatisfied with the previous outcomes of their actions. In this case they choose their next action according to their experience and their observation of others.

The resulting model contains many parameters and is a mixture of various existing models and some psychological findings. It is unclear whether the way in which the model is put together is a realistic one. Many other ways of building such a combined model of routine-based learning are possible. However, we have stated above that routine-based models are not developed in order to describe reality exactly. They are designed to represent certain features of learning processes approximately. In this way, the VID model could be used to show the consequence of combining various learning features.

4. Modelling belief learning

The psychological literature on learning processes is nowadays dominated by cognitive learning process analysis. Neuro-scientific research has added quite some insights to this line of research. However, the class of belief learning does not exactly match what psychologists call cognitive learning. It is rather a subclass of cognitive learning processes.

Nevertheless, the discussion of conscious learning will be based on psychological knowledge. Therefore, we start with an overview on the psychological knowledge on cognitive learning. Then, the models used in economics are explicitly described. We subsume under this category not only the learning models that are called belief learning models in economics, but also the rational learning models as well as many models from artificial intelligence and machine learning. However, despite this large number of available models there is little empirical evidence from experimental economics.

4.1. Psychological findings about cognitive learning

At the beginning of the psychological research into cognitive learning, the main issue was the development of so-called cognitive or mental models or maps (see, e.g., Bruner, 1973; Piaget, 1976; Johnson-Laird, 1983; and Anderson, 2000). They are based on the argument that within the brain a representation of the real world (or at least the part of the real world that is relevant to the individual) is developed. This representation contains subjective knowledge about concepts, connections, causal relationships and so on. The representations in the brain develop according to experience and information obtained from different sources. Still, psychology has not come to one common framework to deal with these processes and many questions are left unanswered. Therefore, we present here one basic concept in order to build some ground for the following discussion. Then, we shall present those insights about cognitive learning that are most relevant to our topic of modelling learning as realistically as possible. These insights will be drawn from different sources. The concept explained here is that of mental models. This term is chosen for examination as it is the only one of the available concepts which has been introduced to economics (Denzau and North, 1994) and has frequently been used thereafter (see, e.g., Gößling, 1996 and Kubon-Gilke 1997).

In psychology the theory of mental models has mainly been influenced by Johnson-Laird (1983). The basic idea is that individuals develop mental models about their surroundings. A detailed model on the development of causal relations according to this theory is provided by Goldvarg and Johnson-Laird (2001). Denzau and North, who have introduced this concept into economics, state that "mental models are the internal representation that individual cognitive systems create to interpret the environment" (Denzau and North, 1994, p. 4). Hence, we can interpret mental models as the sum of all beliefs and knowledge that an individual holds about the world, including the results that different actions will bring about. Mental models are subjective and may not match reality.

Mental models about the working and state of the real world are used to make predictions about the future and the consequences of actions. This, in turn, is the basis for choosing an adequate action. A description of this process should be based on those mechanisms that guide the development of mental models. However, these are difficult to study. From the research into neural networks, we know that these networks are able to reproduce very complex relationships. The structure of the neural network in human brains is more complex than the neural networks that are usually implemented on computers. Hence, people are able to develop extremely complex mental models.

Furthermore, new information is always interpreted and included in the light of existing mental models. The subjective knowledge of an individual is somehow structured in hierarchies (psychologists are still discussing their exact structural appearance). Each new piece of information may change different hierarchical levels. This could cause complex and elaborated mental models. However, experimental studies show that people usually consider only a few levels of a strategic situation (see, e.g., Nagel, 1995 and Stahl, 1998). Hence, most parts of mental models can be assumed to have a rather simple structure.

Mental models contain various elements that are labelled differently by various researchers. In some cases it is helpful to restrict the discussion to specific parts of mental models. Here the categorisation of Anderson (2000) is used. He distinguishes between propositions, schemas and scripts. Propositions represent "what is important about specific things" (Anderson, 2000, p. 55). Schemas sort similar things together and define what they have in common. Scripts are representations of events and sequences of events. Thus, scripts also represent what the individual expects to happen under certain circumstances. Decisions are made on the basis of these expectations and become habits if the same situation is repeatedly faced and the decisions prove to be adequate. Scripts, and thus also expectations, change if a new experience is made. However, people are reluctant to change scripts. They are much faster in processing confirming evidence for the existing scripts than in processing experience that does not fit into the existing scripts and schemas (see, e.g., Kahneman, 2003 and Hebb, 2002 for the neurological basis of this process). Scripts are the elements that are of most interest in the context of belief learning. Some findings that are relevant for modelling belief learning are:

- People typically hold one mental model about reality at any one time (see Dörner, 1999). Sometimes an individual might not be sure about certain issues and may consider different expectations. However, people tend to fix their expectations quickly on the basis of little evidence.
- Scripts, and hence also expectations, change if new knowledge about a situation is gathered (see Anderson, 2000). New knowledge can be obtained by experience, observation or communication.
- Experiments have shown that people do not develop very complex expectations (see Stahl and Wilson, 1994). However, if a situation is repeatedly faced and simple expectations are falsified, people develop more complex expectations (see Brenner and Hennig-Schmidt, 2005).
- People develop scripts quickly without much evidence and tend to stick to scripts without strong opposing evidence (see Dörner, 1999). People have the ability to ignore evidence that contradicts their beliefs.

4.2. Fictitious play

The fictitious play model was developed within the context of games (see Brown, 1951). It assumes that individuals in a game mentally record all previous moves of their opponents. Let us denote each move of their opponents by the vector $\mathbf{a}_{i\_}(t)$ and their own action by $a_i(t)$. The individuals are assumed to remember all previous behaviours of all other individuals. Thus, they are able to calculate the frequency of occurrence for each action profile $\mathbf{a}_{i\_}$. They assume that their opponents' actions will occur with the same probability in the future. Consequently, the expected probability $p(\mathbf{a}_{i\_}, t)$ for each action profile $\mathbf{a}_{i\_}$ realised by the other individuals is given by

$$E(p(\mathbf{a}_{i\_}, t)) = \frac{1}{t} \sum_{\tau=0}^{t-1} \delta(\mathbf{a}_{i\_}(\tau) = \mathbf{a}_{i\_}), \tag{18}$$

where

$$\delta(\mathbf{a}_{i\_}(\tau) = \mathbf{a}_{i\_}) = \begin{cases} 1 & \text{for } \mathbf{a}_{i\_}(\tau) = \mathbf{a}_{i\_} \\ 0 & \text{for } \mathbf{a}_{i\_}(\tau) \neq \mathbf{a}_{i\_} \end{cases}. \tag{19}$$

Furthermore, the individuals have complete knowledge about their payoffs $\Pi_i(a_i, \mathbf{a}_{i\_})$ for each action profile $(a_i, \mathbf{a}_{i\_})$. So they are able to calculate the best response to the expected behaviours of their opponents. To this end, they calculate the expected average payoff

$$E(\Pi_i(a_i, t)) = \sum_{\mathbf{a}_{i\_}} \Pi_i(a_i, \mathbf{a}_{i\_}) \cdot E(p(\mathbf{a}_{i\_}, t)) \tag{20}$$

for each action a_i they are able to realise. Then they choose the action a_i with the highest expected average payoff $E(\Pi_i(a_i, t))$. This action is called the best response to the expectations given by $E(p(\mathbf{a}_{i\_}, t))$.

Of course, the above model is not restricted to learning the behaviour of other players in a game. It can also be applied to any situation in which individuals learn about the frequency of certain events, are able to observe these events after their own action, and know the impact which these events, in combination with their own action, have on their payoff or utility. Hence, the fictitious play model can be easily applied to the learning of beliefs. All that a researcher has to do is to define the set of events and/or causal relations that the individuals build beliefs about.

As modelled above, fictitious play assumes that the likelihood of these events and causal relations is given by a stationary probability distribution. Hence, all the individuals have to do is to approximate this probability distribution by collecting more and more information and calculating appropriate averages. This is done in equation (18). If the real probabilities change, the fictitious play model allows only a very slow adaptation to the new circumstances. The more individuals have already learnt, the less flexible their expectations become. If circumstances continually change, the above fictitious play model is, of course, a rather incompetent learning method.

Moreover the fictitious play model, as it is described above, requires an enormous cognitive capacity because all previous experience has to be remembered and consequently the best response calculated. It is doubtful whether individuals are able to do so.

In recent years, some modifications of the fictitious play model have been presented. These modifications reduce the requirements for the individuals' cognitive capacity. Young (1993) modelled individuals who are only able to remember the last k events. They play the best response based on the average observations in these k rounds. By doing so, the individuals adapt faster to changing circumstances. If k is reduced to one in Young's model, the model of myopic learning is obtained (see, e.g., Ellison, 1993; Kandori et al., 1993 and Samuelson, 1994). However, this extreme again seems to be less realistic.

Another more realistic possibility is to exponentially weigh past experiences (see also the description of the model by Cheung and Friedmand in Duffy, 2006). This means that the latest experience is more important than the experience that occurred further back in the past. For such a model equation (18) has to be replaced by

$$E\big(p(\mathbf{a}_{i_-}, t)\big) = \frac{1 - \beta}{1 - \beta^{(t-1)}} \sum_{\tau=0}^{t-1} \beta^{(t-1-\tau)} \cdot \delta(\mathbf{a}_{i_-}(\tau) = \mathbf{a}_{i_-}), \tag{21}$$

where β is a parameter that determines how fast experience is forgotten.

Some authors have modified the concept of myopic learning by the introduction of errors and occasional adaptation to the best response (see, e.g., Samuelson, 1994) or by the introduction of gradual convergence to the best response behaviour (see, e.g., Crawford, 1995). All this makes the model less demanding with respect to peoples' cognitive capabilities and thus more realistic. Nevertheless, all these versions of fictitious play share the assumption that individuals define a set of events or relationships and keep track of their likelihood.

4.3. Bayesian learning

Although very few economists would claim that people behave optimally, most of economic literature on learning has a connection to optimisation. The oldest and most prominent 'optimal' learning model is Bayesian learning (descriptions and analyses of Bayesian learning can be found in Jordan, 1991; Eichberger et al., 1993; Kalai and Lehrer, 1993; Jordan, 1995; and Bergemann and Välimäki, 1996). Bayesian learning concerns a single learning individual and assumes that the individual establishes a set of hypotheses about the situation she faces. Each hypothesis h makes a probabilistic statement $P(e|h)$ about the occurrence of each event e of a set of events $\mathcal{E}$. This means that hypothesis h implies that event e occurs with probability $P(e|h)$. The set of hypotheses $\mathcal{H}$ has to be complete and complementary, meaning that every possible state of reality has to be represented by one, and only one, hypothesis. At the beginning of the learning process an individual generally assigns the same probability $p(h, 0)$ to each hypothesis $h \in \mathcal{H}$. If the individual has initial information about the situation she faces, the initial probabilities $p(h, 0)$ are different from each other according to this information. $p(h, t)$ denotes the individual estimation of the probability that hypothesis h is correct. In other words, $p(h, t)$ is the belief of the individual in hypothesis h at time t. The sum $\sum_{h \in \mathcal{H}} p(h, t)$ has to equal one.

After each event $e(t)$ the individual updates her presumed probabilities. The updating proceeds as follows (cf. e.g. Easley and Kiefer, 1988 or Jordan, 1991). The individual calculates the probability $P(e(t)|h)$ for each hypothesis h. Subsequently she updates her beliefs according to the following equation:

$$p(h, t+1) = \frac{P(e(t)|h) \cdot p(h, t)}{\sum_{\tilde{h} \in \mathcal{H}} P(e(t)|\tilde{h}) p(\tilde{h}, t)}. \tag{22}$$

By this, the presumed probabilities of hypotheses that predict the occurrence of the observed event with a greater chance increase, while the presumed probabilities of the other hypotheses decrease. The condition $\sum_{h \in \mathcal{H}} p(h, t) = 1$ is maintained while updating the probabilities according to equation (22). After many observed events, the probability $p(h, t)$ should converge to $p(h, t) \approx 1$ for the correct hypothesis about reality, and to $p(h, t) \approx 0$ for all other hypotheses.

Decisions are made according to the following consideration. For each hypothesis h the individual calculates the average utility $\bar{u}(a, t)$ that the action a gives rise to. To this end, she has to assign a utility $u(e, a)$ to each event e and action. $\bar{u}(a)$ is given by

$$\bar{u}(a, t) = \sum_{h \in \mathcal{H}} \sum_{e \in \mathcal{E}} u(e, a) \cdot p(h, t) \cdot P(e|h). \tag{23}$$

The average utility is the expected result from action a. In economics it is called expected utility. As it is learnt adaptively, it is also referred to as adaptive expected utility. Subsequently, the individual decides in such a way that she maximises her expected utility $\bar{u}(a, t)$.

4.4. Least-squares learning

Another learning model that is based on the assumption that people optimise their behaviour is least-squares learning (see Bray, 1982; Marcet and Sargent, 1989; and Bullard and Duffy, 1994). In this model, it is assumed that people make assumptions about the functional dependencies in reality. These dependencies contain, as in regression analysis, a number of parameters. Individuals, it is assumed, intend to learn about the value of these parameters. In order to predict the values of these parameters it is assumed that they proceed statistically. It is further assumed that individuals fit the parameters such that the sum of the squares of the differences between the predicted and the observed values becomes minimal.

If an individual, for example, assumes a linear relationship between $y(t)$ and $\tilde{y}(t)$, the slope parameter β in this linear function can be calculated by

$$\hat{\beta}(t+1) = \frac{\sum_{t'=1}^{t} y(t')\,\tilde{y}(t')}{\sum_{t'=1}^{t-1} y^2(t')}. \tag{24}$$

$\hat{\beta}(t+1)$ is the prediction of β at time $(t+1)$. The formula for linear regression can also be written recursively as follows:

$$\hat{\beta}(t+1) = \hat{\beta}(t) + g(t)\left(\frac{\tilde{y}(t)}{y(t)} - \hat{\beta}(t)\right) \tag{25}$$

and

$$g(t) = \left(\frac{y^2(t)}{y^2(t-1)\,g(t-1)} + 1\right)^{-1}, \tag{26}$$

where $g(t)$ exists only for mathematical reasons and has no economic meaning.

The decision is then made on the basis of the estimated value. In the long run, the algorithm converges to the real value of β if this value is constant (cf. Marcet and Sargent, 1989).

4.5. Genetic programming

Genetic programming has emerged from the concept of genetic algorithms (see Bäck, 1996 for a description of all types of evolutionary algorithms). The basic mechanisms of genetic programming are the same as those of genetic algorithms: selection, reproduction, crossover and mutation. The difference is the unit that is selected and mutated. In the case of genetic algorithms actions or strategies are coded, usually in binary form, and optimised by the algorithm. In the case of genetic programming a formula- or program-like structure is coded and optimised. This formula- or program-like structure can be easily interpreted as a belief about the functioning of the world.

A usual example is the coding of a mathematical formula. For example, the formula $y = 3 \cdot x_1 + 8 \cdot (x_2 - 1)$ would be coded in genetic programming as depicted in Figure 1. It might be assumed that it represents the belief of an individual about the relationship between the variables x_1, x_2 and y. Such a representation allows economic agents to have quite complex beliefs. Furthermore, the beliefs are not restricted at the beginning by the structure of the formula as in the case of fictitious play. Therefore, genetic programming seems to be adequate to describe belief learning (for a similar argument see Chen et al., 2002). If, furthermore, the formula is length restricted, the psychological finding that people tend to think in simple relationships is included in the modelling.

The learning process is modelled in genetic programming by the processes of selection, reproduction, crossover and mutation. At each point in time a number of formulas or programs coded as given in Figure 1 exist. Some of these are selected according to

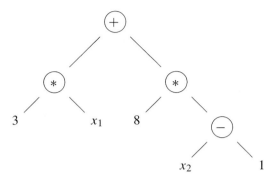

Figure 1. Coding in genetic programming, an example.

the correspondence between their prediction and the observations of the real world (the sum of squares of the errors can be used as in least-squares learning). These selected formulas or programs are reproduced. Then cross-over operations are applied as in genetic algorithms. To this end two formulas or programs are crossed together at a randomly determined node and the two parts connected by this node are exchanged. Finally, the resulting formulas or programs are mutated (for a detailed description see Bäck, 1996).

4.6. Classifier systems

The psychological literature often characterises human beings as classifiers. Humans tend to sort things, events and relationships into classes and act according to their classification. Hence, it seems to be natural to model such classifying behaviour.

Classifier systems seem to be an adequate tool for this purpose (see Holland et al., 1986). The core elements of classifier systems are condition-action rules. These rules state under what conditions specific actions should be taken. Thus, two things have to be codified. First, the set of conditions has to be defined, which is usually, but not necessarily, in binary form. However, it is generally in the form of a string of characteristics: $\{c_1, c_2, \ldots, c_n\}$. The same holds for the actions: $\{a_1, a_2, \ldots, a_p\}$.

A classifier system is characterised at each time by a set of q decision rules R_i ($i = 1, 2, \ldots, q$) of the form $\{c_{i1}, c_{i2}, \ldots, c_{in}\} \rightarrow \{a_{i1}, a_{i2}, \ldots, a_{ip}\}$. In this context each entry in the condition string can be represented by a symbol '#' instead of a number, which implies that the corresponding action is taken independent of the value of this characteristic.

Two values are assigned to each decision rule R_i at each time: its strength, which is determined by its success in the past, and its specificity, which is determined by the number of '#'s in the condition string. If a message $S = \{s_1, s_2, \ldots, s_n\}$ that characterises the current situation is observed, this message is compared to all condition strings. Decision rules with a condition string that matches S compete for being activated. The value

$$B(R_i) = g_1 \cdot (g_2 + g_3 \cdot \text{Specificity}(R_i)) \cdot \text{Strength}(R_i, t)$$

(g_1, g_2 and g_3 are fixed parameters) is calculated for each of these decision rules. The decision rule with the highest value is activated and the respective action taken. The strength of this decision rule is updated according to

$$\text{Strength}(R_i, t + 1) = \text{Strength}(R_i, t) + \text{Payoff}(t) - B(R_i).$$

The specification of classifier systems has so far created mechanisms to identify the most adequate rules out of a given set of rules. However, no new rules evolve. Therefore, the existing decision rules are changed by a second process, which is based on genetic operators. At certain points in time, a certain number of decision rules are eliminated. The probability of each decision rule being eliminated decreases with the actual strength assigned to the rule. To replace the eliminated rules some new rules are created. To this end some existing rules are randomly picked. The probability of each rule to be picked increases with its actual strength. These rules are copied and then slightly modified. Different specifications of these mechanisms exist in the literature (see, e.g., Beltrametti et al., 1997).

4.7. Neural networks

In the last decade, computer technology has developed to such a point that reproducing brain structures on the computer has to some extent become feasible. Hence, it seems to be natural to model human cognitive learning processes by simply rebuilding the brain on the computer. This is done in the field of neural networks.

Many discussions of neural networks can be found in the literature so that it is unnecessary to discuss them at length here (see, e.g., Beltratti et al., 1996). They have been used repeatedly in the recent economic literature to model learning processes (see, e.g., Calderini and Metcalfe, 1998 and Heinemann, 2000). Nevertheless, the prominence of this method of modelling learning processes is still slight. There are two main reasons for this. First, the details of how brain structures are developed and how meaning is created within these networks are not sufficiently known. As a consequence, it is difficult to determine how a neural network that rebuilds the human brain has to be designed. Second, using a neural network, which needs to be quite complex, does not allow us to understand why the modelled agent behaves in a certain way. Using neural networks is akin to a black-box approach. The results of such an approach are difficult to judge as one cannot be sure that the network has been adequately designed.

4.8. Rule learning

Some psychologists have claimed that cognitive learning follows also the rules of reinforcement learning (see, e.g., Kandel and Schwartz, 1982). The only difference is that rules are reinforced instead of actions. This is taken up in the approaches by Erev et al. (1999) and Stahl (2000), the latter calling this process rule learning.

This means that a probability is assigned to each alternative belief or script. Each new experience changes the probabilities according to the mathematical formulation of reinforcement learning. The usual modelling of reinforcement learning implies that if a decision has to be made, a belief is randomly drawn according to the probabilities and the action is taken that is most suitable given this belief. Such a modelling might be adequate if individuals are not consciously aware of their expectations and behave intuitively, but are nevertheless tacitly guided by beliefs and scripts. If individuals are aware of their beliefs it seems unlikely that decisions are made according to one randomly drawn belief each time.

4.9. Stochastic belief learning

A similar approach that takes psychological findings into account is the stochastic belief learning model (see Brenner, 2005). This model differs from rule learning, and also Bayesian and least-squares learning, especially in two features. First, it assumes that not all possible beliefs play a role. Instead, a set of relevant beliefs is defined according to experimental knowledge. Second, it assumes that individuals only consider one belief most of the time. The set of possible beliefs is denoted by $\mathcal{H}$ and each element is denoted by $h \in \mathcal{H}$. The number of different beliefs is denoted by H. The beliefs of each individual i at any time t are given by a set of beliefs $s_i(t) \subset \mathcal{H}$ which is a subset of all possible beliefs. This means that each individual considers at any one time only a few beliefs. The model that is proposed here starts from a situation in which each individual holds exactly one belief, meaning that $s_i(0)$ contains exactly one element denoted by $h_i(0)$ here. The initial beliefs of individuals have to be empirically determined. Usually, beliefs from other situations are transferred. However, so far, there is no available knowledge on this process that would allow us to make predictions about the initial beliefs.

The beliefs are then updated according to incoming information. This information might originate from one's own experience, from observing or communicating with others. The information is only used to update beliefs that are currently considered by an individual. Each belief h in the set $s_i(t)$ is checked against the new information k ($\mathcal{K}$ denotes the set of all possible pieces of information that might be gained). Only two situations are distinguished here: the new information might either contradict or not contradict the belief h.

If none of the beliefs in $s_i(t)$ is contradicted by the new information obtained at time t, the set of beliefs remains unchanged: $s_i(t + 1) = s_i(t)$. For each belief h in the set $s_i(t)$ contradicted by the new information k, it is randomly determined whether this belief disappears from the set $s_i(t + 1)$. According to psychological arguments above, a belief is not automatically eliminated if it is contradicted or proven wrong. People tend to stick to their beliefs even if there is conflicting evidence. Hence, a probability ρ_i is defined for each individual i that determines the likelihood of a belief h to be eliminated in face of information k that contradicts this belief. Hence, ρ_i describes how individual i reacts to new knowledge. The smaller ρ_i, the more individual i sticks to her beliefs.

According to the above process, beliefs could disappear. In contrast, new beliefs appear according to three processes: variation, communication and necessity. First, the model assumes, with a certain likelihood, that individuals consider a new belief by chance. The probability that a new belief is considered by chance is denoted by ν_i. Then, this new belief is added to the set $s_i(t+1)$. Second, an individual might be convinced to consider a belief by others. This can be modelled by assuming that each individual i communicates the beliefs in her set $s_i(t)$ at time t to each other individual j with a certain probability σ_{ij}. σ_{ij} would then describe the probability that at each time t the elements of $s_i(t)$ move into the set $s_j(t+1)$. Third, if a set $s_i(t+1)$ is empty at the end of time t, a new belief has to be taken up. There always has to be at least one element in the set $s_i(t)$ of beliefs, because otherwise the individual is unable to decide about her action.

If, for one of the above three reasons, a new belief is built, this new belief is determined as follows. Each belief h that individual i does not hold so far ($h \in \mathcal{H} \backslash s_i(t)$) is chosen with a probability that is given by

$$P_i(h, t) = \frac{p_i(h, t)}{\sum_{\tilde{h} \in \mathcal{H} \backslash s_i(t)} p_i(\tilde{h}, t)}. \tag{27}$$

This means that the values $p_i(h, t)$ determine the likelihood of each belief h to be considered. The initial values of these probabilities have to be empirically estimated or it has to be assumed that each belief is equally likely.

During the learning process it can be assumed that beliefs that have been considered in the past and are then omitted because of contradicting events are less likely to be reconsidered. Hence, the model assumes that each time a belief h leaves the set $s_i(t)$, the probability for this belief to be reconsidered is updated according to

$$p_i(h, t+1) = \lambda_i p_i(h, t), \tag{28}$$

where λ_i is a parameter that determines how likely individual i reconsiders disconcerned beliefs.

5. Conclusions and recommendations

Each kind of learning process; non-conscious learning, routine-based learning and belief learning; has been discussed separately above. Now, we will return to the general question of choosing a learning model for conducting a computational study.

The use of learning models is often criticised due to the lack of a common model and the ad-hoc choice of specific models. It has been argued above that a common model is unlikely to exist as different learning processes take place in different situations. However, learning models are indeed usually chosen without much justification. This section aims to offer a common platform to justify the use of specific learning models in specific contexts.

The recommendation consists of a two-step process. First, it has to be decided which type of learning should be modelled in the given context. The characteristics of the situation determine whether economic agents learn non-consciously or consciously and whether routine-based modelling is sufficient (Section 5.1).

In a second step, a learning model has to be chosen within the relevant class of learning. There are different ways to choose a learning model and various information sources that can be used (Section 5.2). Here, one specific approach to choose a learning model is taken and the above presented learning models are discussed on the basis of this approach (Section 5.3). However, some degree of freedom remains as the lack of empirical and experimental evidence makes it impossible to precisely recommend one learning model for each learning class. Researchers have to make their final choice according to the specific topic of their study and to some extent according to their own preferences. The whole process of choosing a learning model is summarised in Figure 2.

5.1. Situational characteristics and learning

A very important topic that is rarely discussed in the literature concerns the applicability of learning models in various circumstances. Above, three types of learning have been distinguished: non-conscious learning, routine-based learning and belief learning. Furthermore, it has been argued that basically there are two different learning processes; non-conscious learning and belief learning; while the third type, routine-based learning, presents a simplification of belief learning. Hence, the first question to be answered is when do non-conscious learning and belief learning occur in reality; and the second question addresses when belief learning can be appropriately approximated by routine-based learning models.

5.1.1. Non-conscious versus belief learning

As mentioned above, non-conscious learning seems to be a hard-coded process that takes place in many, if not all, animals. Examples in the economic sphere are affective purchases, tacit knowledge, intuition and routines of interaction within and among firms. In contrast, we will usually not buy a car or a house in an affective way. Humans are able to reflect on their behaviour and build models about the consequences. Such conscious learning seems to be capable of reducing the consequences of non-conscious learning.

As a consequence, non-conscious learning is, in general, mainly relevant if conscious learning does not take place. Conscious learning requires the individual to be aware and reflect upon their behaviour. Therefore, it requires time and cognitive capacity. During a normal day we face an enormous number of decision-making tasks of varying degrees of importance and difficulty. Most decisions are made automatically, without spending a single thought on them. An obvious example is driving a car on the left- or right-hand

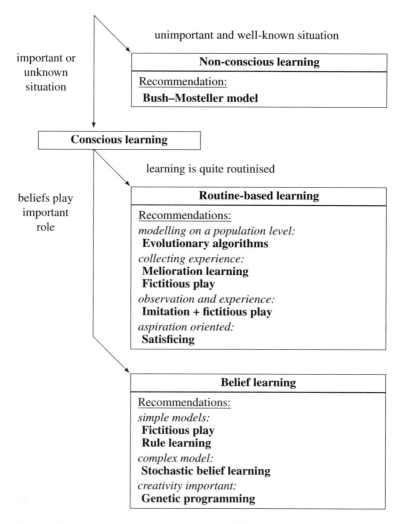

Figure 2. Steps to choose an accurate learning model for representing economic behaviour.

side of the road. In a familiar location this is luckily an unconscious decision. However, many people have experienced this non-conscious behaviour in a foreign country, where people drive on the other side of the road.

Humans seem to be endowed with a mechanism that determines which decisions and behaviours are consciously reflected. This mechanism is not studied in the literature. Hence, we can only speculate about its functioning. Some statements seem to be evident. Conscious reflection on behaviour is restricted by the time available for such contemplation. Furthermore, there are certain motivations that make conscious reflection more likely. Finally, habituation can also occur. All in all, this means that once a situation has been consciously reflected on and a conclusion has been drawn, individuals often repeat the same action without further reflection.

In general we can state that people spend their cognitive time on those behaviours and decisions that they personally find most important to consider. All other actions are the result of non-conscious learning. Various situations provide obvious motives provoking conscious attention:

- In a new situation in which individuals have no established rules to rely on, a cognitive effort is worthwhile as an arbitrary choice may cause poor performance. Nevertheless, in many new situations individuals utilise routines transferred from similar situations. Thus, the expression 'new' has to be handled carefully.
- Dissatisfaction is a strong motivation for dealing with a situation cognitively. When a repeatedly faced situation leads to unsatisfactory outcomes, individuals are motivated to change their behaviour. To this end, they are attentive to the situation and reflect upon it cognitively, in an attempt to improve their performance. In this context the aspiration level plays an important role.
- Certain situations and decisions are regarded as important to the individual for personal reasons, such as personal pride, aesthetic aspirations or the relevance for one's own life. Such specific motivations may explain the large variance of behaviour among individuals.

Except the latter point the above arguments state that attention is directed towards situations in which the outcome is either unsatisfactory or can be anticipated to be unsatisfactory with a high probability. Thus, we claim the following: in general, non-conscious learning is the normal route to behavioural changes. Individuals generally do not pay attention to the repeated situations they face. Paying conscious attention is inspired by unsatisfactory results or their anticipation. Although this assumption is a theoretical abstraction of the factors analysed above, it offers a sound basis for the categorisation of learning processes and for the choice of a learning model to describe the learning process. Whenever a modeller treats a situation that is important or new to the individuals, it is likely that the individual is learning consciously and a conscious learning model should be chosen. If the situation that is modelled is unimportant for the economic agents, it seems adequate to assume that they learn non-consciously and thus, a non-conscious learning model should be chosen.

In reference to the above simplification, however, it must be noted that in the course of a repeated situation faced by an individual, two non-conscious processes should be distinguished. A behaviour may originate and be guided further non-consciously until an unsatisfactory outcome is obtained, or may originate consciously and then be guided further non-consciously. In the case of consciously learnt behaviour, individuals may, as soon as they have found a satisfying behaviour, direct their cognitive attention to other situations. Subsequently, the behaviour becomes subject to non-conscious learning and, as it is repeatedly chosen, this behaviour is confirmed as long as it is reinforcing, i.e., satisfying. If, however, the outcomes prove dissatisfying, conscious attention is usually redirected to the situation.

5.1.2. Routine-based versus belief learning

The choice between the models of the two kinds of conscious learning, routine-based and belief learning, is more difficult. As mentioned above, routine-based learning does not describe a real learning process but is an approximation of belief learning. Hence, the question is not in which situations the two kinds of learning processes occur but when the routine-based approximation sufficiently describes the real learning process.

Models of routine-based learning are usually based on empirical or experimental observations of learning. They reduce the learning process to one or a few main characteristics that can be observed without actually knowing the real processes responsible for the learning process in the brain. Through this, they miss part of the conscious learning process. The missing part could be called the understanding of the situation. Let us consider as an example the process of imitation. If we imitate other people we do not only imitate the behaviour that performs best, we usually also develop a subjective understanding of why they perform best. This includes the possibility to act differently if the situation changes or if the observed agents differ from the own personality.

Nevertheless, in some situations the development of a deeper understanding does not influence behaviour significantly. If, for example, all people sit in front of identical multi-arm bandits and all want to maximise their profits, not much understanding of the situation is needed and people will imitate the choice of the arm that performs best, possibly with some experimentation of other arms. It would be unnecessarily complex to accurately model the processes in the brain in such a situation.

Hence, the question of whether to use a routine-based or belief learning model is related to the discussion between using a complex and realistic model or whether to use a simple, approximating model. In addition, this question is related to the discussion on the validity of models. These questions are taken up in the next section. In the sphere of routine-based models there is quite an amount of supporting evidence available while in the sphere of belief learning, no model has yet been developed that seems completely convincing. Hence, there is a temptation to use routine-based learning models and therefore these are discussed here separately. Nevertheless, whoever uses them should be aware of the fact that they only represent approximations of real learning processes. Furthermore, in the literature various routine-based learning models can be found and it is important to choose the most appropriate one.

5.2. Choosing a learning model

After a modeller has clarified the type of learning process to be modelled, one must choose the model that best describes this kind of learning. Some discussion is needed on how such a choice should be done. This discussion has to deal with several questions, such as the aim of choosing a learning model, the sources of empirical evidence, the complexity of learning models, and the level on which learning is modelled.

5.2.1. Aims in choosing a learning model

There are various approaches in choosing a learning model four of which shall be discussed herein. First, one might search for the model that best describes real learning processes. This can be done on the basis of experimental findings or psychological knowledge. However, sufficient empirical and experimental knowledge is not always available. Nevertheless, we will follow this approach here.

Second, one might look for some learning model that leads to an outcome which corresponds to known stylised facts without worrying about the details of the learning model. Such approaches are often taken in agent-based computational economics and aim to keep the learning model as simple as possible and as complex or realistic as needed to obtain the correct outcome. Such a modelling is helpful to understand the minimum requirements of learning in a given situation. It is also helpful to classify situations with respect to the competences that are required of the economic agents in these situation. However, such an approach does not give information about how people learn. Studying whether certain learning models predict economic dynamics that are in line with our empirical knowledge only allows us to reject some learning models but it does not confirm the others. There might be other learning models that lead to the same predictions. Sometimes this is omitted in the literature.

Third, some researchers search for learning models that converge to equilibrium, since often equilibrium is predicted by the neo-classical theory or other equilibrium concepts. It is not clear what we gain from such approaches. Our economic surrounding permanently fluctuates and learning is rather important because it allows us to react to these changes and not because it converges to an equilibrium. In specific cases, however, an equilibrium might describe the real world adequately and searching for learning models that converge to this equilibrium is what has been described above as the second possible aim.

Fourth, some researchers aim at developing clever or even optimal learning models. One might even compare the performance of learning models in a given situation in order to make statements about how people should learn. Besides the positive aim of agent-based computational economics, there is a normative aim of testing alternative economic structures (see Tesfatsion, 2001) which may be expanded to alternative behaviours. This is a valid aim which is not further considered here. Most of the recent literature on artificial intelligence and machine learning seems to belong to this approach. In general, a tendency has been observed in recent years to borrow methods from other disciplines. These models have become increasingly complex, mixing such features as evolutionary algorithms, classifier systems, fuzzy logic and neural networks. Besides obtaining very competent learning models, some authors seem to believe that the obtained learning models describe real learning without looking at any evidence for this. As discussed above, this does not hold in all cases.

5.2.2. Validity and complexity of learning models

After clarifying that we want to realistically model learning processes, we have to judge how well confirmed learning models have to be before being used in simulations. Clearly it would be preferred that the learning models available are supported by strong empirical evidence. Unfortunately, only a few studies can be found that offer such evidence. We have to live with and use the little evidence that is currently available and hope for more evidence in the future.

There are two sources of this evidence. On the one hand, experimental studies provide us with some information on the suitability of different learning models (see Duffy, 2006). On the other hand, psychological literature also provides us with information about the mechanisms and circumstances involved in learning. We take the position that learning models that are contradicted by experimental findings (in the situation under consideration) or by psychological knowledge should not be used. Given the above aim, this opinion might be confronted with one counter-argument.

Some researchers argue that their study does not mainly aim to identify the implications of a specific learning process. Instead, their main aim is to analyse a certain complex situation and learning is only included to represent the basic dynamics of behaviour. It might be argued that the choice of learning model is not significant under such circumstances. However, this only holds if different learning models predict a similar behaviour. While this is true for some learning models and situations, it is not universally the case. In various situations different learning models predict contrasting behaviours, so that the choice of the learning model might matter tremendously for the study's result.

Nevertheless, some learning models can lead, under numerous circumstances, to quite similar predictions. Furthermore, empirical and experimental evidence on their suitability is often rare, making it difficult to choose. Thus, the first step would be to exclude all models that can be rejected on the basis of psychological knowledge or experimental evidence, then complexity could be used to select among the remaining models. For example, Rapoport et al. (2000) states "that the simplest model should be tried first, and that models postulating higher levels of cognitive sophistication should only be employed as the first one fails".

Hence, in total we have three selection criteria: experimental evidence, psychological knowledge, and simplicity. All three criteria come with advantages and disadvantages that are valued differently by researchers.

Experimental evidence   The primary source for evaluating the existing learning models are empirical and experimental studies. Empirical studies on learning are quite rare. The existing experimental studies that evaluate learning models are presented in Chapter 20 of this book. It was argued previously that the use of learning models that are rejected by experimental evidence should be avoided. However, two remarks are necessary here.

First, there is still the discussion as to what extent laboratory situations can be comparable to real life situations. Experimental situations are usually artificial and often deprived of any context. Therefore, some researchers argue that behaviour is different in these situations. However, it may also be argued that learning models that adequately describe real life learning processes should also suitably describe experimental learning processes, because in both situations the same cognitive apparatus (the brain) is used. Nevertheless, there may well be a difference in learning processes. In this chapter it is argued that different learning processes exist, for example, non-conscious and conscious learning processes. As a consequence, it may be the case that the frequencies with which certain kinds of learning occur in reality and in experiments could differ tremendously. For example, non-conscious learning processes occur frequently in reality because we do not have the time to reflect on all our decisions. Most experiments, in contrast, force the participants to think about their decisions, so that conscious learning processes appear to dominate in experiments. Thus, we argue that the same kinds of learning processes occur in experiments and real life but that their relative importance may differ between the two settings.

This leads to the second remark. All experimental studies include only a limited number of situations and we know that learning processes differ between situations. Results from experimental studies can only be transferred to a situation under the condition that the situations are sufficiently similar. The amount of sufficient similarity is difficult to state, given the lack of experimental studies that attempt to classify situations according to the learning model that fits best (some discussion in this direction is given in Duffy, 2006). Furthermore, the very artificial circumstances often found in experiments must be taken into account.

Nevertheless, we believe that in the long term, experiments will be the major way by which to evaluate the various existing learning models and to support their further development. At the moment there are not many studies of this kind available, so that experimental evidence only offers some help in choosing learning models. Further studies have to be conducted in the future and, most importantly, a classification of situations and a relationship between learning models and situations has to be developed. A primary classification is discussed in this chapter. Checking, refining and revising this classification with the help of experimental studies would tremendously advance the modelling of learning in economics. In addition, these experimental studies should take into account the fact that people differ with respect to their learning processes even in the same situation.

Adequateness of the details of the model   In the psychological literature there is an abundance of knowledge on the details of learning processes. This knowledge can be used to evaluate learning models. However, it might be argued that in economics we are not interested in modelling learning process details. Instead, what we need is a model that effectively describes the resulting behaviour. A model that contradicts psychological findings on the learning process might, nevertheless, predict behaviour correctly. Most of the time agent-based computational economists are only interested in the implications of learning processes for economic processes.

However, as discussed above, evidence about the validity of different model predictions are still rare. Due to the lack of empirical and experimental evidence, adequate representation of the learning process might be a better alternative criterion for learning model evaluation. Detailed models in line with psychological findings could be more trusted than models that contradict psychological findings. However, the inclusion of such details increases the complexity of the model. Hence, there is a trade-off between sufficiently representing all learning details and simplifying the model.

Simplicity of the model   Many economists tend to use simple behavioural models. The neo-classical model of optimisation is a good example. Similarly within the field of economic learning, those models with clear rules and a few parameters have been used most frequently (examples are reinforcement learning, least-squares learning, Bayesian learning and fictitious play). There are good reasons for simplifying learning models.

First, the more parameters a learning model has, an increasing amount of empirical or experimental evidence is necessary to estimate the correct parameters. If there is no sufficient empirical or experimental data, a model with more parameters offers, in general, more vague predictions. Second, simpler models can be more easily interpreted. Third, it is argued that economists are not interested in learning process details, but in their implications for organisation, working and the dynamics of economies. Hence, simple models that capture the basic characteristics of learning processes should suffice.

However, one might also argue in favour of more complex learning models. First, psychological studies suggest that learning processes are complex. The lack of a simple learning model that exactly describes experimental behaviour offers additional evidence for this claim. Second, the progress in computer technology makes it easy to deal with complex models in simulations. Even for very complex learning models simulations can be run with a large variety of parameter values, so that the influence of different parameter values can be studied.

Of course, more complex models require some additional effort. Hence, we have to deal with a trade-off between the effort necessary and the accuracy of the model. There are many economic situations, such as markets, in which the specific set-up of the learning model is not important for the results of the analysis (see Duffy, 2006). However, there are also situations, like a prisoner's dilemma, in which the predictions of different learning models vary tremendously (see Brenner, 2005). Thus, in some situations the loss in suitability by using a simple model may be minor, rendering the use of a more complex model unnecessary. In other situations important details may be lost by using a simple model. We have so far only little knowledge on the various situations which are of the former and the latter type. In situations which have a clear equilibrium point and no contradiction between the individually and socially optimal state, simple models seem to be sufficient. Situations involving strategic thinking and assorted motives seem to be, in general, unsatisfactorily described by simple models.

5.2.3. Individual and population learning

An important aspect of modelling learning processes is the level of modelling. Two options exist: Either the learning process of each individual is modelled explicitly—meaning that at each point in time the situation of each individual is clearly represented in the model—or the implications of the individual learning processes for the behaviour of a population of individuals are modelled—meaning that the model only represents the shares of various situations of individuals in the population at any point in time—(for a discussion of this in the context of genetic algorithms see Vriend, 2000).

Psychological literature deals almost exclusively with individual learning processes, whereas in the economics literature learning models on the individual and population level are used. Again arguments can be put forward in favour of both options, the individual and population level of modelling learning.

The main advantages of modelling learning on a population level is that it simplifies the modelling and one does not have to care about the details of the individual learning process. For example, modelling on the population level and assuming an infinitely large population eliminates the stochastic feature of learning from the analysis. As a consequence, the resulting learning process can be easily treated analytically. An analysis of learning processes on the population level is also often used in experiments. Examining behaviour on the population level permits us to ignore inter-individual differences. Usually learning models on the population level are more straight-forward as only the fundamental dynamics of learning have to be considered. This makes them quite attractive in situations where the modeller is only interested in the implications of learning processes for an economy consisting of many agents.

However, neglecting details and individual differences comes at a risk as learning process details and individual differences may indeed matter. There are situations, such as a market, where the exact characteristics of the learning process of individuals is not important for the resulting dynamics. But, there are also situations in which various learning models lead to assorted predictions, which could lead to wrong predictions. Recognising this risk, individual learning models are favoured especially in simulation approaches where the complexity of the implemented learning processes is irrelevant.

An alternative is the use of sub-populations. This is the division of people into heterogeneous groups, whereby the individual characteristics are homogeneous within the group. This prohibits us to model a situation where each individual is specific but takes into account partial differences between individuals. It presents a compromised way to study the impact of heterogeneous types of people.

In conclusion, the question of whether learning processes should be modelled on an individual or population level cannot be answered here finally. Modelling on the population level simplifies things, whereas modelling on the individual level increases accuracy. The situation that is to be studied determines how accurate an individual learning model is in comparison to a model on the population level. In some situations the gain is small, while in others it is tremendous. Hence, it depends on the situation whether the effort of individual modelling is necessary.

5.2.4. Calibration of learning models

Most learning models contain a number of parameters. Thus, once a researcher has chosen a learning model, the parameters of the model must be adjusted accordingly. This is especially important for simulation approaches, wherein each simulation only one specific choice of parameters can be used. Unfortunately, the empirical and experimental literature on learning processes provides us with little information about the parameters of various learning models. Furthermore, parameters may differ between individuals, which is rarely considered in experimental studies. Comprehensive, or even sufficient parameter information of various learning models is not available.

How one might deal with this problem depends on the research aim. Above, different research aims have been outlined. Here it is assumed that the simulation approach is used to predict real processes or to obtain detailed knowledge about the implications of learning processes. In such a case we argue that a range should be defined for each of the parameters such that the modeller is quite certain that the possible values lie within this range. It is important to note that empirical knowledge can be used to reduce the range. All parameter combinations within these ranges have to be analysed in order to be sure about the model implications. A Monte-Carlo approach is applicable in this case (see Werker and Brenner, 2004 for a detailed discussion of this methodology and Brenner and Murmann, 2003 for an application). If empirical data on learning processes outcomes are available, it can be used in a Bayesian approach to further reduce the parameter ranges or to assign likelihoods to each of the model specifications (see Zellner, 1971 and Werker and Brenner, 2004). Such an approach is very labour-intensive and requires quite an amount of computer time. However, it increases the reliability of the results.

In addition, such a methodology would certainly benefit from further detailed experimental studies that not only compare learning models but also identify the parameters of various learning models that best describe behaviour. Hopefully, more experimental studies of this kind will be conducted in the future.

5.3. Recommendations for the choice of a model

In this section advice is given to computational economists who try to realistically model learning processes. It has been argued above that three considerations are of help in this context: experimental evidence for a model, the psychological knowledge about the details of real learning processes, and the complexity of learning models. Furthermore, it has been argued above that three kinds of learning processes have to be treated separately: non-conscious learning, routine-based learning, and belief learning. The relevant learning models for each of these learning types are discussed in the following.

5.3.1. Recommendations for non-conscious learning

Section 2 discusses three models that could be used to model non-conscious learning. It has been argued that non-conscious learning processes typically do not occur in experiments. Hence, experimental findings on human behaviour should not be used to judge the adequateness of various models in non-conscious learning. The experimental confirmation of the Roth–Erev model (see Roth and Erev, 1995 and Erev and Roth, 1998) has to be interpreted as a confirmation of this model being able to describe the outcomes of cognitive learning, although economic literature interprets this model as representing reinforcement learning. This discrepancy results from the difference between the definition of reinforcement learning as simple model on the level of behaviour—although Roth and Erev include more complex aspects such as experimentation and forgetting—, while non-conscious learning is more rigidly defined here as a learning process people are not aware of.

For non-conscious learning, findings from animal experiments and habit formation knowledge could be adopted. From this literature we know that learning processes slow down under constant circumstances but could be reactivated by environmental changes. Furthermore, we know that people might completely eliminate actions from their repertoire and that rewards (positive outcomes) are treated differently from punishments (negative outcomes) (see Kahneman and Tversky, 1979). Only one of the models presented in Section 2 captures all these features, this being the generalised Bush–Mosteller model. Therefore, it seems to be adequate to use this model. As long as there are no negative outcomes, the parameterized learning automaton and the Roth–Erev model without experimentation also represent all major features. However, they are not able to deal with negative outcomes.

5.3.2. Recommendations for routine-based learning

Choosing a model of routine-based learning is more difficult and ad-hoc because these are approximations that consider only part of the real learning process. The parts of the real learning process that should be included depends on the modelled situation. Two different strategies have to be distinguished: using a general model that includes many or all characteristics of routine-based learning or focusing on one specific feature.

General models   Above various general models are presented: the combined models, the EWA model and the VID model, and evolutionary algorithms which also represent, given their usual interpretation, a combined model. Experimental evidence is available for some of these models. The EWA model is supported by some evidence (see Anderson and Camerer, 2000), while evolutionary algorithms have been repeatedly confirmed (see Duffy, 2006), while the VID model has not yet been experimentally tested.

In comparing the three models in the light of what the psychological literature knows about learning, the VID model is the most accurate. It is developed on the basis of such knowledge. The EWA model combines two models, a reinforcement learning model with a belief learning model. As a consequence, it fails to fit into the classification of learning processes used here and it is not clear whether such a combination does actually occur, although there is separate support for both of these in the psychological literature. Evolutionary algorithms do not match psychological knowledge about learning processes. The cross-over processes are not in line with communication knowledge as well as the interaction and mutation process, which is independent of past experience.

The VID model is obviously the most complex of the three models. Hence, all three models have their shortcomings, so that none of them can be recommended without hesitation. Nevertheless, the use of evolutionary algorithms is favoured here. This recommendation is based on the fact that it might sometimes be helpful to describe the results of a learning process on the population level without much interest in the details of individual learning dynamics. Evolutionary algorithms are well supported by experimental evidence on the population level (see Duffy, 2006). Furthermore, evolutionary algorithms have the interesting feature of being able to deal with very large sets of actions and strategies and even allow the sets of strategies to increase endogenously.

Nevertheless, two points have to be kept in mind while using them. First, Rechenberg and Holland developed their algorithms as means to determine optimal solutions to technical problems. Hence, they are developed to describe an optimising search process and not a learning process. Interpreting their dynamics as individual learning processes seems to be inaccurate, since they contradict psychological knowledge on individual learning processes. Therefore, their use is only recommended on the population level here. Second, the problem of coding actions and strategies should not be neglected while using evolutionary algorithms. Evolutionary strategies and genetic algorithms are two options that mainly differ in their coding. Recoding non-binary values binary and using genetic algorithms thereafter, as it is sometimes done in the literature, seem to be inadequate since it increases the distortion between psychological knowledge on learning and the dynamics of the resulting model.

Separate modelling   All of the above separate routine-based learning models are subject to two limitations. First, they model only one part of the whole learning process. Second, they model the outcome of the underlying learning process, meaning that they only offer an approximation of what actually occurs. There is little knowledge about how suitable this approximation is. Fortunately, there is some experimental evidence in favour of melioriation learning (see Herrnstein, 1970), fictitious play (see Duffy, 2006), satisficing (Stahl and Haruvy, 2002) and some mixed evidence for imitation (Huck et al., 2002 and Bosch-Domenech and Vriend, 2003). There is also various experimental evidence in favour of the learning direction theory (Berninghaus and Ehrhart, 1998 and Grosskopf, 2003). However, this theory has very weak predictions and is, therefore, usually not sufficiently precise for agent-based computational models.

The problem with these models is that they only offer accurate approximations of the real learning processes if the learning part described dominates the learning process. With the help of experiments, knowledge on the dominating parts of learning processes in various situations can be established. However, this has not yet been sufficiently done. It depends on the researcher's good judgement to identify which part of learning dominates the examined situation and to choose the respective model.

Learning by experience is not a central research field in psychology. Since melioration learning and fictitious play are both quite simple learning models and are both supported by experimental evidence, they are recommended here. In the case of imitation psychological literature discusses a cognitive process in which people transfer their observations to their own situation. Therefore an extension of the fictitious play model to include imitation is recommended here, although standard imitation models could also be chosen for simplicity. Satisficing is also less prominently discussed in psychological literature but is supported by experiments. How satisficing should be modelled in detail is less clear.

5.3.3. Recommendations for belief learning

Many different models have been described that are potential candidates for modelling belief learning. If we look for experimental evidence, there is some experimental evidence in favour of fictitious play (see Duffy, 2006), genetic programming (see Chen et al., 2002) and stochastic belief learning (see Brenner, 2005). Rule learning is somewhat supported by experimental evidence in favour of reinforcement learning. However, the models have never been empirically compared and the experimental evidence has never overwhelmingly favoured any model. For example, the study of Nyarko and Schotter (2002) shows that people hold much stronger beliefs than predicted by fictitious play and change them more radically. Brenner (2005) shows that the stochastic belief learning model explains some individuals' behaviour very well while it fails to explain the behaviour of others.

Furthermore, it is difficult to observe what people are thinking while making their decisions, or as (Cheung and Friedman, 1997, p. 49) put it: "experimental learning models must deal with the fact that beliefs are not directly observable". This may change in the future as more and more methods are developed to observe people's beliefs in experiments (see Brenner and Hennig-Schmidt, 2005 for a promising method). So far, we have to deal with the problem that little evidence is available in the context of belief learning.

Neural networks are in line with the knowledge on brain structure. However, we still have no sufficient knowledge to be able to represent the brain. Hence, it is doubted whether neural networks have the correct structure. Rule learning can claim some psychological backing while the stochastic belief learning model is based on currently available psychological knowledge. However, the stochastic belief learning model requires some knowledge on the potential beliefs of individuals that is often not available. In addition, it is more complex than fictitious play and the rule learning model.

Bayesian learning and least-squares learning are not supported by psychological knowledge. Two arguments can be put forward against Bayesian learning. First, people are not able to do the calculations for a proper Bayesian updating. Second, people do not consider a large number of competing expectations or hypothesis at one time. Usually individuals have one specific expectation about reality. Psychologists argue that people tend to fix schemas and scripts very quickly even if little evidence has been collected (see Dörner, 1999) and that they do not change these for more adequate alternatives if they lead to satisficing results (see Luchins, 1942 and Anderson, 2000). Similar to Bayesian learning, least-square learning does not fit the psychological evidence related to cognitive learning. People are simply either not able or not willing to do demanding calculations in most real situations as assumed in least-squares learning.

Genetic programming can be used to describe one individual or a population of agents (see, e.g. Edmunds, 1999 and Chen and Yeh, 2001). Presenting each agent by a population of formulas or programs means that we assume that different beliefs compete in the agent's brain and are simultaneously developed. This contradicts the above psychological finding that people usually only have one mental model at any one time. Presenting a population of agents by a population of formulas or programs implies that agents copy the beliefs of others. It has been stated above that it is difficult to study beliefs because they cannot be observed easily. Hence, it is unclear how agents can perfectly copy beliefs as is assumed in such an approach. In addition, cross-over operations are difficult to interpret. Why do agents exchange part of their beliefs instead of one agent convincing another of her beliefs? The advantage of genetic programming is that it allows the learning process to be very open with respect to the resulting beliefs.

Classifier systems have the interesting feature that they also model the development of a classification of situations. All other available learning models describe the learning process in one given situation. Thus, classifier systems focus on an element of cognitive learning that other learning models ignore: the development and change of schemas. However, this comes at some cost. Classifier systems do not represent beliefs in the same way the other belief learning models do. Instead, classifier systems define simple condition-action rules. They fail to accurately describe the learning of beliefs, which has been declared the central feature of belief learning here.

To sum up, we argue that more research on the modelling of belief learning is necessary. Given the current knowledge, we recommend the models of fictitious play and rule learning as simpler solutions and the stochastic belief learning model if more knowledge about beliefs is available. If the invention of new beliefs by individuals is an important feature of the processes under investigation, genetic programming could be also an option.

For the future we can hope that more empirical and experimental tests are conducted for the various learning models. This would help to develop a clearer picture of the conditions for different learning process to occur and the accurate ways to model them.

References

Anderson, C.M., Camerer, C. (2000). "Experience-weighted attraction learning in sender-receiver signalling games". Economic Theory 16, 689–718.

Anderson, J.R. (2000). Cognitive Psychology and its Implications. Worth Publishers, New York.

Arifovic, J. (1994). "Genetic algorithm learning and the cobweb model". Journal of Economic Dynamics and Control 18, 3–28.

Arifovic, J., Ledyard, J. (2000). "Scaling up learning models in public good games". Journal of Public Economic Theory 6, 203–238.

Arthur, W.B. (1991). "Designing economic agents that act like human agents: a behavioral approach to bounded rationality". The American Economic Review 81, 353–359.

Bäck, T. (1996). Evolutionary Algorithms in Theory and Practice. Oxford University Press, New York.

Bandura, A. (1977). Social Learning Theorie. Prentice-Hall, Englewood Cliffs.

Bendor, J., Mookherjee, D., Ray, D. (2001). "Aspiration-based reinforcement learning in repeated interaction games: an overview". International Game Theory Review 3, 159–174.

Bergemann, D., Välimäki, J. (1996). "Learning and strategic pricing". Econometrica 64, 1125–1149.

Berninghaus, S.K., Ehrhart, K.-M. (1998). "Time horizon and equilibrium selection in tacit coordination games: Experimental Results". Journal of Economic Behavior and Organization 37, 231–248.

Beltrametti, L., Fiorentini, R., Marengo, L., Tamborini, R. (1997). "A learning-to-forcast experiment on the foreign exchange market with a classifier system". Journal of Economic Dynamics and Control 21, 1543–1575.

Beltratti, A., Margarita, S., Terna, P. (1996). Neural Networks for Economic and Financial Modelling. International Thomson Computer Press, London.

Beyer, H.-G. (2001). The Theory of Evolution Strategies. Springer, Berlin.

Biel, A., Dahlstrand, U. (1997). "Habits and the Establishment of Ecological Purchase Behavior". In: Guzmán, G., José, A., Sanz, S. (Eds.), The XXII International Colloquium of Economic Psychology. Promolibro, Valencia, pp. 367–381.

Börgers, T. (1996). "On the relevance of learning and evolution to economic theory". The Economic Journal 106, 1374–1385.

Börgers, T., Sarin, R. (1997). "Learning through reinforcement and replicator dynamics". Journal of Economic Theory 77, 1–16.

Börgers, T., Sarin, R. (2000). "Naive reinforcement learning with endogenous aspirations". International Economic Review 41, 921–950.

Bosch-Domenech, A., Vriend, N.J. (2003). "Imitation of successful behaviour in cournot markets". Economic Journal 113, 495–524.

Bray, M. (1982). "Learning, estimation, and the stability of rational expectations". Journal of Economic Theory 26, 318–339.

Brenner, T. (1997). "Reinforcement learning in 2×2 games and the concept of reinforcably stable strategies", Papers on Economics and Evolution #9703, Max Planck Institute, Jena.

Brenner, T. (1998). "Can evolutionary algorithms describe learning processes?". Journal of Evolutionary Economics 8, 271–283.

Brenner, T. (1999). Modelling Learning in Economics. Edward Elgar, Cheltenham.

Brenner, T. (2001). "Implications of routine-based learning for decision making". European Journal of Economic and Social Systems 15, 131–152.

Brenner, T. (2005). "Stochastic belief learning and the emergence of cooperation", mimeo, Max Planck Institute, Jena.

Brenner, T., Slembeck, T. (2001). "Noisy decision makers—on errors, noise and inconsistencies in economic behaviour", Papers on Economics and Evolution #0107, Max Planck Institute, Jena.

Brenner, T., Murmann, J.P. (2003). "The use of simulations in developing robust knowledge about causal processes: methodological considerations and an application to industrial evolution", Papers on Economics and Evolution #0303, Max Planck Institute, Jena.

Brenner, T., Witt, U. (2003). "Melioration learning in games with constant and frequency-dependent payoffs". Journal of Economic Behavior and Organization 50, 429–448.

Brenner, T., Hennig-Schmidt, H. (2005). "Belief learning in the prisoner's dilemma game—an experimental study of cognitive processes", mimeo, Max Planck Institute, Jena.

Brenner, T., Vriend, N. (2005). "On the behavior of proposers in ultimatum games", Journal of Economic Behavior and Organisation, in preparation.

Brown, G.W. (1951). "Iterative solution of games by fictitious play". In: Activity Analysis of Production and Allocation. John Wiley and Sons, pp. 374–376.

Bruner, J.S. (1973). Beyond the Information Given. Norton, New York.

Bullard, J., Duffy, J. (1994). "Learning in a Large Square Economy", Working Paper 94-013A, Federal Reserve Bank of St. Louis.

Bush, R.R., Mosteller, F. (1955). Stochastic Models for Learning. John Wiley and Sons, New York.

Calderini, M., Metcalfe, S. (1998). "Compound learning, neural nets and the competitive process". Economics of Innovation and New Technology 7, 271–302.

Camerer, C.F., Ho, T. (1999). "Experience-weighted attraction learning in normal form games". Econometrica 67, 827–874.

Chen, S.-H., Yeh, C.-H. (2001). "Evolving traders and the business school with genetic programming: a new architecture of the agent-based artificial stock market". Journal of Economic Dynamics and Control 25, 363–393.

Chen, S.-H., Duffy, J., Yeh, C.-H. (2002). "Equilibrium selection via adaptation: using genetic programming to model learning in a coordination game". The Electronic Journal of Evolutionary Modeling and Economic Dynamics (1002): http://www.e-jemed.org/1002/index.php.

Cheung, Y.-W., Friedman, D. (1997). "Individual learning in normal form games: some laboratory results". Games and Economic Behavior 19, 46–76.

Crawford, V.P. (1995). "Adaptive dynamics in coordination games". Econometrica 63, 103–143.

Cross, J.G. (1973). "A stochastic learning model of economic behavior". Quarterly Journal of Economics 87, 239–266.

Cross, J.G. (1983). A Theory of Adaptive Economic Behavior. Cambridge University Press, Cambridge.

Dawid, H. (1996). "Adaptive Learning by Genetic Algorithms". In: Lecture Notes in Economics and Mathematical Systems, vol. 441. Springer, Berlin.

Dawid, H. (1997). "Learning of equilibria by a population with minimal information". Journal of Economic Behavior and Organization 32, 1–18.

Day, R.H. (1967). "Profits, learning and the convergence of satisficing to marginalism". Quarterly Journal of Economics 81, 302–311.

Day, R.H., Tinney, E.H. (1968). "How to co-operate in business without really trying: a learning model of decentralized decision making". Journal of Political Economy 74, 583–600.

Denzau, A., North, D.C. (1994). "Shared mental models. Ideologies and institutions". Kyklos 47, 3–31.

Dixon, H.D. (2000). "Keeping up with the Joneses: competition and the evolution of collusion". Journal of Economic Behavior and Organization 43, 223–238.

Dörner, D. (1999). Bauplan für eine Seele. Rowohlt, Hamburg.

Duffy, J. (2006). "Agent-based models and human-subject experiments", in this handbook.

Duffy, J., Feltovich, N. (1999). "Does observation of others affect learning in strategic environments? An experimental study". International Journal of Game Theory 28, 131–152.

Easley, D., Kiefer, N.M. (1988). "Controlling a stochastic process with unknown parameters". Econometrica 56, 1045–1064.

Eichberger, J., Haller, H., Milne, F. (1993). "Naive Bayesian learning in 2×2 matrix games". Journal of Economic Behavior and Organization 22, 69–90.

Eigen, M. (1971). "The self-organisation of matter and the evolution of biological macromolecules". Naturwissenschaften 58, 465–523.

Edmunds, B. (1999). "Modelling bounded rationality in agent-based simulations using the evolution of mental models". In: Brenner, T. (Ed.), Computational Techniques for Modelling Learning in Economics. Edward Elgar, Cheltenham, pp. 305–332.

Ellison, G. (1993). "Learning, local interaction, and coordination". Econometrica 61, 1047–1071.

Erev, I., Roth, A.E. (1998). "Predicting how people play games: reinforcement learning in experimental games with unique, mixed strategy equilibria". The American Economic Review 88, 848–881.

Erev, I., Bereby-Meyer, Y., Roth, A.E. (1999). "The effect of adding a constant to all payoffs: experimental investigation, and implications for reinforcement learning models". Journal of Economic Behaviour and Organization 39, 111–128.

Eshel, I., Samuelson, L., Shaked, A. (1998). "Altruists, egoists and hooligans in a local interaction model". American Economic Review 88, 157–179.

Estes, W.K. (1950). "Toward a statistical theory of learning". Psychological Review 57, 94–107.

Feltovich, N. (2000). "Reinforcement-based vs. belief-based learning models in experimental asymmetric-information games". Econometrica 68, 605–641.

Festinger, L. (1942). "Wish, expectation and group standards as factors influencing the level of aspiration". Journal of Abnormal Social Psychology 37, 184–200.

Fudenberg, D., Levine, D.K. (1998). The Theory of Learning in Games. MIT Press, Cambridge.

Gigerenzer, G., Selten, R. (Eds.) (2001). Bounded Rationality: The Adaptive Toolbox. MIT Press, Cambridge.

Gilboa, I., Schmeidler, D. (1995). "Case-based decision theory". Quarterly Journal of Economics 110, 269–288.

Gößling, T. (1996). Entscheidung in Modellen. Hänsel-Hohenhausen Verlag der Deutschen Hochschulschriften, Egelsbach.

Goldvarg, E., Johnson-Laird, P.N. (2001). "Naive causality: a mental model theory of causal meaning and reasoning". Cognitive Science 25, 565–610.

Grosskopf, B. (2003). "Reinforcement and directional learning in the ultimatum game with responder competition". Experimental Economics 6, 141–158.

Hallpike, C.R. (1986). The Principles of Social Evolution. Clarendon Press, Oxford.

Hebb, D.O. (2002). The Organization of Behavior. A Neuropsychological Theory. Lawrence Erlbaum Associates, Mahwa.

Hegselmann, R. (1996). "Social dilemmas in lineland and flatland". In: Liebrand, W.B.G., Messick, D.M. (Eds.), Frontiers in Social Dilemmas Research. Springer, Berlin, pp. 337–361.

Heinemann, M. (2000). "Adaptive learning of rational expectations using neural networks". Journal of Economic Dynamics and Control 24, 1007–1026.

Helbing, D. (1995). Quantitative Sociodynamics. Stochastic Methods and Models of Social Interaction Processes. Kluwer Academic, Boston.

Herrnstein, R.J. (1970). "On the law of effect". Journal of the Experimental Analysis of Behavior 13, 243–266.

Herrnstein, R.J., Prelec, D. (1991). "Melioration: a theory of distributed choice". Journal of Economic Perspectives 5, 137–156.

Hofbauer, J., Sigmund, K. (1984). Evolutionstheorie und dynamische Systeme. Paul Parey, Berlin.

Holland, J.H. (1975). Adaption in Natural and Artificial Systems. University of Michigan Press, Ann Arbor.

Holland, J.H., Miller, J.H. (1991). "Artifical adaptive agents in economic theory". American Economic Review, Papers and Proceedings 81, 365–370.

Holland, J.H., Holyoak, K.J., Nisbett, R.E., Thagard, P.R. (1986). Induction: processes of inference, learning and discovery. MIT Press, Cambridge.

Huck, S., Normann, H.-T., Oechssler, J. (2002). "Stability of the cournot process—experimental evidence". Internation Journal of Game Theory 31, 123–136.

Johnson-Laird, P.N. (1983). Mental Models. Harvard University Press, Cambridge.

Jordan, J.S. (1991). "Bayesian learning in normal form games". Games and Economic Behavior 3, 60–81.

Jordan, J.S. (1995). "Bayesian learning in repeated games". Games and Economic Behavior 9, 8–20.

Kalai, E., Lehrer, E. (1993). "Rational learning leads to Nash equilibrium". Econometrica 61, 1019–1045.

Kahneman, D. (2003). "Maps of bounded rationality: psychology for behavioral economics". The American Economic Review 93, 1449–1475.

Kahneman, D., Tversky, A. (1979). "Prospect theory: an analysis of decision under risk". Econometrica 47, 263–291.

Kandel, E.R., Schwartz, J.H. (1982). "Molecular biology of learning: modulation of transmitter release". Science 218, 433–443.

Kandori, M., Mailath, G.J., Rob, R. (1993). "Learning, mutation, and long run equilibria in games". Econometrica 61, 29–56.

Karandikar, R., Mookherjee, D., Ray, D., Vega-Redondo, F. (1998). "Evolving aspirations and cooperation". Economic Theory 80, 292–331.

Kirchkamp, O. (2000). "Spatial evolution of automata in the prisoner's dilemma". Journal of Economic Behavior and Organization 43, 239–262.

Kubon-Gilke, G. (1997). Verhaltensbindung und die evolution ökonomischer institutionen. Metropolis-Verlag, Marburg.

Lant, T.K. (1992). "Aspiration level adaption: an empirical exploration". Management Science 38, 623–644.

Luchins, A.S. (1942). "Mechanization in problem-solving". Psychological Monographs 54 (248).

Mackintosh, N.J. (2003). "Pavlov and associationism". The Spanish Journal of Psychology 6, 177–184.

Marcet, A., Sargent, T.J. (1989). "Convergence of least squares learning mechanisms in self-referential linear stochastic models". Journal of Economic Theory 48, 337–368.

Maynard Smith, J. (1982). Evolution and the Theory of Games. Cambridge University Press, Cambridge.

Mezias, S.J. (1988). "Aspiration level effects: an empirical investigation". Journal of Economic Behavior and Organization 10, 389–400.

Mezias, S., Chen, Y., Murphy, P. (2002). "Aspiration-level adaptation in an american financial service organization: a field study". Management Science 48, 1285–1300.

Morales, A.J. (2002). "Absolutely expedient imitative behavior". International Journal of Game Theory 31, 475–492.

Nagel, R. (1995). "Unraveling in guessing games: an experimental study". American Economic Review 85, 1313–1326.

Nash, J.F. (1950). "Equilibrium points in n-person games". Proceedings of the National Academy of Sciences (US) 36, 48–49.

Nowak, M.A., May, R.M. (1993). "The spatial dilemmas of evolution". International Journal of Bifurcation and Chaos 3, 35–78.

Nyarko, Y., Schotter, A. (2002). "An experimental study of belief learning using elicited beliefs". Econometrica 70, 971–1005.

Osborne, M.J., Rubinstein, A. (1995). A Course in Game Theory. MIT Press, Cambridge.

Palomino, F., Vega-Redondo, F. (1999). "Convergence of aspiration and (partial) cooperation in the prisoner's dilemma". International Journal of Game Theory 28, 465–488.

Pazgal, A. (1997). "Satisfycing leads to cooperation in mutual interests games". International Journal of Game Theory 26, 439–453.

Piaget, J. (1976). Die Äquilibration der kognitiven Strukturen. Klett, Stuttgart.

Ramstad, Y. (1994). "On the nature of economic evolution". In: Magnusson, L. (Ed.), Evolutionary and Neo-Schumpeterian Approaches to Economics. Kluwer Academic Publishers, Boston.

Rapoport, A., Seale, D., Winter, E. (2000). "An experimental study of coordination and learning in iterated two-market entry games". Economic Theory 16, 661–687.

Rechenberg, I. (1973). Evolutionsstrategie: Optimierung technischer Systeme nach Prinzipien der biologischen Evolution. Frommann-Holzboog Verlag, Stuttgart.

Rescorla, R.A., Wagner, A.R. (1972). "A theory of Pavlovian conditioning: variations in the effectiveness of reinforcement and non-reinforcement". In: Black, A.H., Prokasy, W.F. (Eds.), Classical Conditioning II. Prentice Hall, Englewood Cliffs.

Robinson, J. (1951). "An iterative method of solving a game". Annals of Mathematics 54, 296–301.

Roth, A.E., Erev, I. (1995). "Learning in extensive form games: experimental data and simple dynamic models in the intermediate run". Games and Economic Behavior 6, 164–212.

Rumiati, R.I., Bekkering, H. (2003). "To imitate or not to imitate? How the brain can do it, that is the question!". Brain and Cognition 53, 479–482.

Samuelson, L. (1994). "Stochastic stability in games with alternative best replies". Journal of Economic Theory 64, 35–65.

Sarin, R., Vahid, F. (1999). "Payoff assessments without probabilities: a simple dynamic model of choice". Games and Economic Behavior 28, 294–309.

Schlag, K.H. (1998). "Why imitate, and if so, how? A bounded rational approach to multi-armed bandits". Journal of Economic Theory 78, 130–156.

Schwefel, H.-P. (1995). Evolution and Optimum Seeking. Wiley and Sons, New York.

Selten, R. (1997). "Features of experimentally observed bounded rationality", Discussion Paper No. B-421, University of Bonn.

Selten, R., Stoecker, R. (1986). "End behavior in sequences of finite prisoner's dilemma supergames". Journal of Economic Behavior and Organization 7, 47–70.

Shapley, L.S. (1964). "Some topics in two-person games". In: Dresher, M., Shapley, L., Tucker, A. (Eds.), Advances in Game Theory, pp. 1–28. Annals of Mathematic Studies No. 52, Princeton.

Simon, H.A. (1957). Administrative Behavior. The Macmillan Company, New York.

Simon, H.A. (1987). "Satisficing". In: The New Palgrave Dictionary of Economics, vol. 4. Macmillan Press, London, pp. 243–245.

Skinner, B.F. (1938). The Behavior of Organisms. Appleton, New York.

Stahl, D.O. (1998). "Is step-j thinking an arbitrary modelling restriction or a fact of human nature?". Journal of Economic Behavior and Organisation 37, 33–51.

Stahl, D.O. (2000). "Rule learning in symmetric normal-form games: theory and evidence". Games and Economic Behavior 32, 105–138.

Stahl, D.O., Wilson, P.W. (1994). "Experimental evidence on player's models of other players". Journal of Economic Behavior and Organization 25, 309–327.

Stahl, D.O., Haruvy, E. (2002). "Aspiration-based and reciprocity-based rules of learning dynamics for symmetric normal-form games". Journal of Mathematical Psychology 46, 531–553.

Tang, F.-F. (2003). "A comparative study on learning in a normal form game experiment". Journal of Economic Behavior and Organization 50, 385–390.

Tesfatsion, L. (2001). "Introduction to the special issue on agent-based computational economics". Journal of Economic Dynamics and Control 25, 281–293.

Thibaut, J.W., Kelley, H.H. (1959). The Social Psychology of Groups. Wiley, New York.

Thorndike, E.L. (1932). The Fundamentals of Learning. AMS Press, New York.

Vega-Redondo, F. (1997). "The evolution of Walrasian behavior". Econometrica 65, 375–384.

Vaughan, W., Herrnstein, R.J. (1987). "Stability, Melioration, and Natural Selection". In: Green, L., Kagel, J.H. (Eds.), Advances in Behavioral Economics, vol. 1. Ablex, Norwood.

Vriend, N.J. (2000). "An illustration of the essential difference between individual and social learning, and its consequences for computational analysis". Journal of Economic Dynamics and Control 24, 1–19.

Werker, C., Brenner, T., (2004). "Empirical calibration of simulation models", Papers on Economics and Evolution #0410, Max Planck Institute, Jena.

Witt, U. (1986). "Firms' market behavior under imperfect information and economic natural selection". Journal of Economic Behavior and Organization 7, 265–290.

Witt, U. (1991). "Evolutionary economics—an interpretative survey", Papers on Economics and Evolution #9104, European Study Group for Evolutionary Economics, Freiburg.

Witt, U. (1996). "Bounded rationality, social learning, and viable moral conduct in a prisoners' dilemma". In: Perlman, M., Helmstädter, E. (Eds.), Behavioral Norms, Technological Progress and Economic Dynamics: Studies in Schumpeterian Economics. Michigan University Press, Ann Arbor, pp. 33–49.

Witt, U. (2001). "Learning to consume—a theory of wants and the growth of demand". Journal of Evolutionary Economics 11, 23–36.

Yin, G., Zhu, Y.M. (1990). "On H-valued Robbins–Monro processes". Journal of Multivariate Analysis 34, 116–140.

Young, P. (1993). "The evolution of conventions". Econometrica 61, 57–84.

Zellner, A. (1971). An Introduction to Bayesian Inference in Econometrics. John Wiley, New York.

Chapter 19

AGENT-BASED MODELS AND HUMAN SUBJECT EXPERIMENTS

JOHN DUFFY [*]

Department of Economics, University of Pittsburgh, Pittsburgh, PA 15260, USA
e-mail: jduffy@pitt.edu; url: http://www.pitt.edu/~jduffy/

Contents

[*] I thank Jasmina Arifovic, Thomas Brenner, Sean Crockett, Cars Hommes, Thomas Riechmann, Shyam Sunder, Leigh Tesfatsion and Utku Ünver for helpful comments on earlier drafts.

Handbook of Computational Economics, Volume 2. Edited by Leigh Tesfatsion and Kenneth L. Judd
© 2006 Elsevier B.V.   *All rights reserved*
DOI: 10.1016/S1574-0021(05)02019-8

Abstract

This chapter examines the relationship between agent-based modeling and economic decision-making experiments with human subjects. Both approaches exploit controlled "laboratory" conditions as a means of isolating the sources of aggregate phenomena. Research findings from laboratory studies of human subject behavior have inspired studies using artificial agents in "computational laboratories" and vice versa. In certain cases, both methods have been used to examine the same phenomenon. The focus of this chapter is on the empirical validity of agent-based modeling approaches in terms of explaining data from human subject experiments. We also point out synergies between the two methodologies that have been exploited as well as promising new possibilities.

Keywords

agent-based modeling, human subject experiments

JEL classification: B4, C6, C9

1. Introduction

The advent of fast and cheap computing power has led to the parallel development of two new technologies for doing economic research—the computational and the experimental laboratory. Agent-based modeling using computational laboratories grew out of frustration with the highly centralized, top-down, deductive approach that continues to characterize much of mainstream, neoclassical economic-theorizing.[1] This standard approach favors models where agents do not vary much in their type, beliefs or endowments, and where great effort is devoted to deriving closed-form, analytic solutions and associated comparative static exercises. By contrast, agent-based computational economic (ACE) researchers consider decentralized, dynamic environments with populations of evolving, heterogeneous, boundedly rational agents who interact with one another, typically locally. These models do not usually give rise to closed-form solutions and so results are obtained using simulations. ACE researchers are interested in the aggregate outcomes or norms of behavior that emerge and are sustained over time as the artificial agents make decisions and react to the consequences of those decisions.

Controlled laboratory experimentation with human subjects has a longer history than agent-based modeling as the experimental methodology does not *require* the use of laboratories with networked computers; indeed the experimental methodology predates the development of the personal computer.[2] However, computerization offers several advantages over the "paper-and-pencil" methodology for conducting experiments. These include lower costs, as fewer experimenters are needed, greater accuracy of data collection and greater control of the information and data revealed to subjects. Perhaps most importantly, computerization allows for more replications of an experimental treatment than are possible with paper-and-pencil, and with more replications, experimenters can more accurately assess whether players' behavior changes with experience. For all of these reasons, many human subject experiments are now computerized.

With advances in computing power, the possibility of combining the agent-based computational methodology with the human subject experimental methodology has been explored by a number of researchers, and this combination of methodologies serves as the subject of this survey chapter. Most of the studies combining the two approaches have used the agent-based methodology to understand results obtained from laboratory studies with human subjects; with a few notable exceptions, researchers have not sought to understand findings from agent-based simulations with follow-up experiments involving human subjects. The reasons for this pattern are straightforward. The economic environments explored by experimenters tend to be simpler than those explored by ACE researchers as there are limits to the number of different agent characteristics that one can hope to "induce" in an experimental laboratory and time and budget constraints limit the number of periods or replications of a treatment that can be

---

[1] See, e.g., Axelrod and Tesfatsion (2006) or Batten (2000) for introductions to the ACE methodology.
[2] See, Davis and Holt (1993) and Roth (1995) for histories of the experimental methodology.

considered in a human subject experiment; for instance, one has to worry about human subjects becoming bored! As human subject experiments impose more constraints on what a researcher can do than do agent-based modeling simulations, it seems quite natural that agent-based models would be employed to understand laboratory findings and not the other way around.

There is, however, a second explanation for why the ACE methodology has been used to understand experimental findings with human subjects. Once a human subject experimental design has been computerized, it is a relatively simple matter to replace some or all of the human subjects with "robot" agents. Indeed, one could make the case that some of the earliest ACE researchers were researchers conducting experiments with human subjects. For instance, Roth and Murnighan (1978) had individual human subjects play repeated prisoner's dilemma games of various expected durations against artificial "programmed opponents" in order to more clearly assess the effect of variations in the expected duration of the game on the human subjects' behavior. Similarly, Coursey et al. (1984) and Brown-Kruse (1991) tested contestable market theories with human subjects in the role of sellers and robots in the role of buyers. The robots were programmed to fully reveal their market valuations and were introduced after human subject buyers were found to be playing strategically, in violation of the theory being tested. Gode and Sunder (1993) were the first researchers to "go all the way" and completely replace the human subject buyers and sellers in the experimental laboratory double auction environment with artificial agents, whom they dubbed "zero-intelligence" agents. Their approach, discussed in greater detail below, serves as the starting point for our survey. Subsequently, many researchers have devised a variety of agent-based models in an effort to explain, understand and sometimes to predict behavior in human subject experiments.[3]

Of course, the great majority of ACE researchers, following the lead of Schelling (1978), Axelrod (1984), or Epstein and Axtell (1996), do not feel constrained in any way by the results of human subject experiments or other behavioral research in their ACE modeling exercises. These researchers endow their artificial agents with certain preferences and what they perceive to be simple, adaptive learning rules. As these artificial agents interact with one another and their environment, adaptation takes place at the individual level, or at the population level via relative fitness considerations, or both. The details of how agents adapt are less important than the aggregate outcomes that emerge from repeated interactions among these artificial agents.

ACE researchers contend that these emergent outcomes cannot be deduced without resorting to simulation exercises, and that is the reason to abandon standard neoclassical approaches.[4] But it is not always clear when ACE approaches are preferred over standard, deductive economic theorizing. As Lucas (1986, p. 218) observed,

---

[3] See Mirowski (2002) for an engaging history of the emergence of economics as a "cyborg science," and, in particular, the role played by experimentalists. See also Miller (2002) for a history of experimental analyses of financial markets.

[4] Batten (2000) offers some advice as to when ACE models are appropriate and when old-fashioned analytic methods are preferred.

"It would be useful, though, if we could say something in a general way about the characteristics of social science prediction problems where models emphasizing adaptive aspects of behavior are likely to be successful versus those where the non-adaptive or equilibrium models of economic theory are more promising."

Lucas went on to suggest that experiments with human subjects might serve to resolve such questions, and gave several examples. Of course, economic experiments are not without problems of their own. ACE researchers (e.g., Gode and Sunder, 1993; Chan et al., 1999) have argued that agent-based modeling permits greater control over the preferences and information-processing capabilities of agents than is possible in laboratory experiments, where human subjects often vary in their learning abilities or preferences (e.g. in their attitudes towards risk), despite careful efforts to control some of these differences by experimenters. Further, one can question the external validity of the behavior of the human subjects, who are often inexperienced with the task under examination and who may earn payments that do not accurately approximate "real-world" incentives.[5]

In addition to questioning when the ACE methodology is appropriate, one can also question the external validity of ACE modeling assumptions and simulation findings. Many ACE researchers, following the lead of Epstein and Axtell (1996) adopt the "generative approach" to understanding empirical phenomena. This involves pointing to some empirical phenomenon, for example, skewed wealth distributions, and asking: "can you grow it?" In other words, can you specify a multi-agent complex adaptive system that generates the empirical phenomenon.

While the ability to generate a particular empirical phenomenon via an ACE simulation exercise does represent a certain kind of understanding of the empirical phenomenon, ACE researchers could do more to increase our confidence in this understanding. Indeed, the empirical phenomena under study are often the result of some casual empiricism on the part of the ACE researcher. More precise and careful empirical support, using field data or other observations could be brought to bear in support of a particular phenomenon, but this is not (yet) the standard practice. Further, the processes by which agents in ACE models form expectations, choose actions or otherwise adapt to a changing environment is not typically based on any specific micro evidence; the empirical comparisons that most interest ACE researchers are between the simulated aggregate outcomes and the empirical phenomenon of interest. The shortcomings of such an approach have not gone unnoticed. Simon (1982) for example, writes:

> Armchair speculation about expectations, rational or other, is not a satisfactory substitute for factual knowledge as to how human beings go about anticipating the future, what factors they take into account, and how these factors, rather than others, come within the range of their attention.

---

[5] However, as Smith (1982, p. 930) observes, "... there can be no doubt that control and measurement can be and are much more precise in the laboratory than in the field experiment or in a body of Department of Commerce data."

As I argue in this chapter, data from human subject experiments provide a ready-made source of empirical regularities that can be used to calibrate or test ACE models of individual decision-making and belief or expectation formation. Explaining the aggregate findings of a human subject experiment might also serve as the goal of an agent-based modelling exercise.

The main behavioral principle that ACE researchers use in modeling individual artificial agent behavior is, what Axelrod (1997) has termed, the "keep-it-simple-stupid" (KISS) principle. The rationale behind this folksy maxim is that the phenomena that emerge from simulation exercises should be the result of multi-agent interactions and adaptation, and not because of complex assumptions about individual behavior and/or the presence of "too many" free parameters. Of course, there are many different ways to adhere to the KISS principle. Choosing simple, parsimonious adaptive learning rules that also compare favorably with the behavior of human subjects in controlled laboratory settings would seem to be a highly reasonable selection criterion.

Experimental economists and ACE researchers are natural allies, as both are interested in dynamic, decentralized inductive reasoning processes and both appreciate the importance of heterogeneity in agent types. Further, the economic environments designed for human subject experiments provide an important testbed for agent-based modelers. The results of human subject experiments are useful for evaluating the external validity of agent-based models at the two different levels mentioned above. At the aggregate level, researchers can and have asked whether agent-based models give rise to the same aggregate findings that are obtained in human subject experiments. For instance, do artificial adaptive agents achieve the same outcome or convention that human subjects achieve? Is this outcome an equilibrium outcome in some fully rational, optimizing framework or something different? At the individual level, ACE researchers can and have considered the external validity of the adaptive rules they assign to their artificial agents by comparing the behavior of individual human subjects in laboratory environments with the behavior of individual artificial agents placed in the same environments. Achieving some kind of external validity, at either the aggregate or the individual level, should enable agent-based modelers to feel more confident in their simulation findings. They may then choose to abandon, with even greater justification, the constraints associated with the experimental methodology or those of standard, deductive economic theorizing.

This chapter surveys and critiques three main areas in which agent-based models have been used to study findings from human subject experiments. In the next section, we explore what has been termed the "zero-intelligent" agent approach, which consists of a set of agent-based models with very low rationality constraints. In the following section, we explore a set of agent-based models that employ somewhat more sophisticated individual behaviors, ranging from simple stimulus-response learning to more complicated belief-based learning approaches. Finally, in the last section, we explore agent-based models where individual learning is even more complicated, as in a classifier system, or is controlled by population-wide selection criteria as in genetic algorithms. In all cases, we compare the findings of human subject experiments with those of agent-based simulations.

2. Zero-intelligence agents

The zero-intelligence agent trading model was developed to explain findings from laboratory double auction experiments with human subjects. We therefore begin with a discussion of the double auction environment and laboratory findings.

2.1. The double auction environment

The double auction is one of the most celebrated market institutions, and is widely used in all kinds of markets including stock exchanges and business-to-business e-commerce. The convergence and efficiency properties of the double auction institution have been the subject of intense interest among experimental economists, beginning with the work of Smith (1962), who built on the early work of Chamberlin (1948). Altering Chamberlin's design so that information on bids and asks was centralized as in a stock market, Smith (1962) was able to demonstrate that experimental markets operating under double auction rules yielded prices and trading volumes consistent with competitive equilibrium predictions, despite limited knowledge on the part of participants of the reserve values of other participants.

The double auction markets studied by Smith and subsequently by other experimentalists and ACE researchers can be described using a simple, one-good environment, though multi-good environments are also studied. The single good can be bought and sold over a fixed sequence of trading periods, each of finite length. The N participants are often divided up between buyers or sellers (in some environments agents can play either role). Buyer i has valuation for unit $j = 1, 2, \ldots$ of the good, v_{ij}, where the valuations satisfy the principle of diminishing marginal utility in that $v_{ij} \geq v_{ik}$ for all $j < k$. Similarly, seller i has a cost of selling unit $j = 1, 2, \ldots$ of the good, c_{ij}, which satisfies the principle of increasing marginal cost, $c_{ij} \leq c_{ik}$ for all $j < k$. Sorting the individual valuations from highest to lowest gives us a step-level market demand curve, and sorting the individual costs from lowest to highest gives us a step-level market supply curve. The intersection of these two curves, if there is one, reveals the competitive equilibrium price and quantity. The left panel of Figure 1 taken from Smith (1962), provides an illustration. In this figure, the valuations of the 11 buyers (for a single unit) have been sorted from highest to lowest, and the costs to the 11 sellers (of a single unit) have been sorted from lowest to highest. The equilibrium price is $2.00 and the equilibrium quantity is 6 units bought and sold.

In the experimental double auction markets, subjects are informed as to whether they will be buyers or sellers and they remain in this role for the duration of the session. Buyers are endowed with private values for a certain number of units and sellers are endowed with private costs for a certain number of units. No subject is informed of the

956

J. Duffy

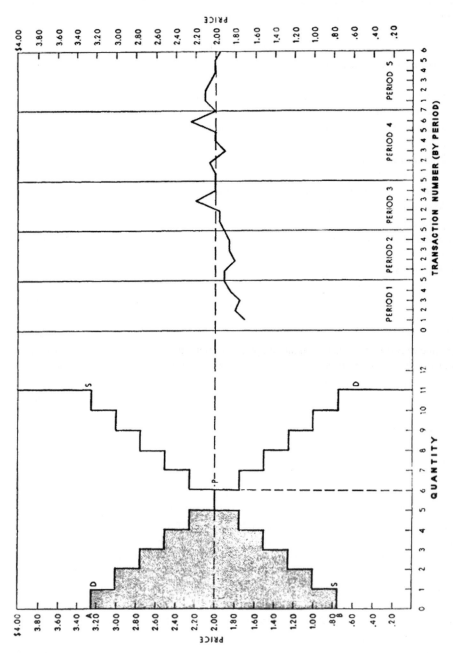

Figure 1. Values and costs induced in an experimental double auction design (left panel) and the path of prices achieved by human subjects (right panel). Source: Smith (1962, Chart 1).

valuations or costs of other participants. Buyers are instructed that their payoff from buying their j^{th} unit is equal to $v_{ij} - p_j$, where p_j is the price the buyer agrees to pay for the jth unit. Similarly, sellers are instructed that their payoff from selling their j^{th} unit at price p_j is equal to $p_j - c_{ij}$. The double auction market rules vary somewhat across studies, but mainly consist of the following simple rules. During a trading period, buyers may post any bid order and sellers may post any ask order at any time. Further, buyers may accept any ask or sellers may accept any bid at any time. If a buyer and seller agree on a price, that unit is exchanged and is no longer available for (re)sale for the duration of the period. The buyer-seller pair earns the profit each realized on their transaction.

In many double auction experiments, the order book is cleared following each transaction, so that buyers and sellers have to resubmit bids and asks. It is also standard practice to assume a closed order book, meaning that subjects can only observe the best bid and ask price at any moment in time. To surplant the current best bid (ask) a buyer (seller) has to submit a bid (ask) that is higher (lower) than the best bid (ask); this is known as the standard bid/ask improvement rule. At all times, the current best bid-ask spread is known to all market participants. The entire history of market transaction prices is also public knowledge.

The striking result from applying these double auction rules in laboratory markets is the rapid convergence to the competitive equilibrium price and quantity. The right panel of Figure 1, shows the path of prices over five trading periods in session 1 of the Smith (1962) study. The first transacted price in period 1 is for \$1.70, the second for \$1.80, etc. Notice that the number of transacted prices in period 1 is 5, which is one short of the competitive equilibrium prediction, and these prices all lie below the competitive equilibrium price of \$2.00. As subjects gain experience over trading periods 2–5, however, the deviations of traded prices and quantities from the competitive equilibrium values steadily decrease. This main finding has been replicated in many subsequent experiments, and continues to hold even with small numbers of buyers and sellers (e.g., 3–5 of each).

2.2. Gode and Sunder's zero-intelligence traders

Gode and Sunder (1993) were interested in assessing the source of this rapid convergence to competitive equilibrium in laboratory double auction markets. They hypothesized that the double auction rules alone might be responsible for the laboratory findings and so they chose to compare the behavior of human subject traders with that of programmed robot traders following simple rules. As these robot players chose bids and asks randomly, over some range, Gode and Sunder chose to label them "zero-intelligence" (or ZI) machine traders. This choice of terminology has stimulated much debate, despite Gode and Sunder's disclaimer that "ZI traders are not intended as descriptive models of individual behavior."

Gode and Sunder's 12 ZI traders were divided up equally into buyers and sellers. In the most basic environment, the buyer's bids and the seller's asks were random draws from a uniform distribution, $U[0, B]$, where the upper bound B, was chosen so as to exceed the highest valuation among all buyers. In particular, Gode and Sunder chose $B = 200$. Buyers' bids and sellers' asks were made without concern for whether the bids or asks were profitable. Gode and Sunder referred to these unconstrained traders as ZI-U traders. In the other, more restrictive environment they considered, buyer i's bid for unit j was a random draw from the uniform distribution, $U[0, v_{ij}]$ and seller i's ask for unit j was random draw from the uniform distribution $U[c_{ij}, B]$. As the traders in this environment were constrained from making unprofitable trades, they were referred to as ZI-C traders.

A trading period consisted of 30 seconds for the ZI traders and 4 minutes for a parallel human subject experiment. Within the 30 second period, the standard double auction rules applied: the best available bid is the one that is currently the highest of all bids submitted since the last transaction, while the best available ask is the one that is currently the lowest of all asks submitted since the last transaction. A transaction occurs if either a new bid is made that equals or exceeds the current-best ask, in which case the transaction occurs at the current-best ask price, or a new ask is made that equals or falls below the current-best bid, in which case the transaction occurs at the current-best bid price. Once a transaction occurs, all unaccepted bids/asks are cleared from the order book and, provided that the period has not ended, the process of bid/ask submission begins anew. Traders were further restricted to buying/selling their j^{th} unit before buying or selling their $j + 1^{th}$ unit. This sequencing restriction is not a double auction trading restriction, and it appears to be quite important to Gode and Sunder's results.[6] Of course, if every agent has a single inframarginal unit to buy or sell (those units to the left of the intersection of demand and supply) and one or more extramarginal units (units to the right of the intersection point), as is often the case in double auction experiments, then there is no sequencing issue.

The results from a simulation run of the ZI-U and ZI-C artificial trading environment and from a human subject experiment with 13 subjects (1 extra buyer) are shown in the three panels of Figure 2. The left panels show the induced demand and supply step-functions and the competitive equilibrium prediction (price = 80, quantity = 24) while the right panels show the path of transaction prices across the 6 trading periods. Gode and Sunder's striking finding is that the transaction price path with the budget constrained ZI-C traders bears some resemblance to the path of prices in the human subject experiment. In particular, prices remain close to the competitive equilibrium price, and within a trading period, the price volatility declines so that prices become even closer to the competitive equilibrium prediction. This finding stands in contrast to the ZI-U environment, where transaction prices are extremely volatile and there is no evidence of convergence to the competitive equilibrium. As the ZI-C or ZI-U agents have no memory regarding past prices, the difference in the simulation findings are entirely due to the difference in trading rules, namely the constraint imposed on ZI-C traders ruling

---

[6] See, e.g., the discussion of Brewer et al. (2002) below.

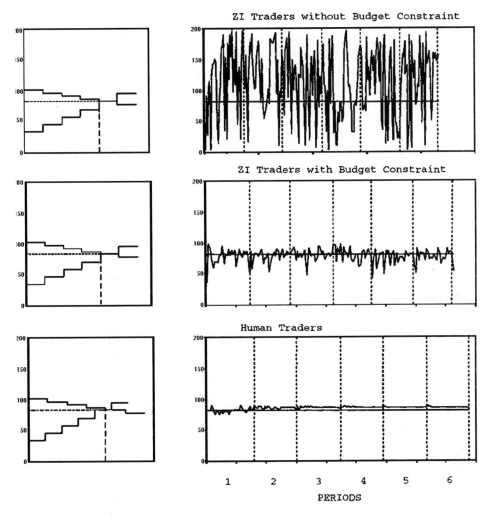

Figure 2. Competitive equilibrium prediction (left) and path of transaction prices (right). Source: Gode and Sunder (1993, figure 1).

out unprofitable trades. The dampened volatility in prices over the course of a trading period arises from the fact that units with the highest valuations or lowest costs tend to be traded earlier in the period, as the range over which ZI-C agents may submit bids or asks for these units is larger than for other units. After these units are traded, the bid and ask ranges of ZI-C agents with units left to trade become increasingly narrow, and consequently, the volatility of transaction prices becomes more damped.

Gode and Sunder also examine the "allocative efficiency" of their simulated and human subject markets, which is defined as the sum of total profit earned over all trading periods divided by the maximum possible profit, which is simply the sum of consumer and producer surplus (e.g., the shaded area in the left panel of Figure 1). They find that with the ZI-U traders, market efficiency averages 78.3 percent, while with ZI-C traders it averages 98.7 percent; the latter figure is slightly higher than the average efficiency achieved by human subjects, 97.6 percent! Gode and Sunder summarized their findings as follows:

> "Our point is that imposing market discipline on random unintelligent behavior is sufficient to raise the efficiency from the baseline level [that attained using ZI-U agents] to almost 100 percent in a double auction. The effect of human motivations and cognitive abilities has a second-order magnitude at best."

One explanation for the high efficiency with the ZI-C agents is provided in Gode and Sunder (1997b). They consider the consequences for allocative efficiency of adding or subtracting various market rules and arrive at some very intuitive conclusions. First, they claim that voluntary exchange by agents who are sophisticated enough to avoid losses is necessary to eliminate one source of inefficiency, namely unprofitable trades. By voluntary exchange, they mean that agents are free to accept or reject offers. The second part of this observation, that agents are sophisticated enough to avoid losses, is the hallmark of the ZI-C agent model, but its empirical validity is not really addressed. We know from experimental auction markets, for example, where private values or costs are induced and subjects have perfect information about these values or costs, that subjects sometimes bid in excess of their private valuations (Kagel et al., 1987). Gode and Sunder (1997a) are careful to note that they "are not trying to accurately model human behavior," (p. 604) but the subtext of their research is that the no unprofitable trades assumption does not presume great sophistication; the traders are "zero-intelligence" but constrained. Perhaps the more restrictive assumption is that agents have perfect information about their valuations and costs and perfect recall about units they have already bought or sold. Absent such certainty, it might be harder to reconcile the assumption of no unprofitable trades with the observation that individuals and firms are sometimes forced to declare bankruptcy.

Other sources of inefficiency are that ZI-C traders fail to achieve any trades, and that extramarginal traders—traders whose valuations and costs lie to the right of the intersection of demand and supply—displace inframarginal traders whose valuations lie to the left of the intersection of demand and supply and who have the potential to realize gains from trade. Gode and Sunder (1997a, 1997b) define an expected efficiency metric based on a simplified model of induced demand and supply and show that inefficiencies arising from failure to trade can be reduced by having multiple rounds of trading. Inefficiencies arising from the displacement of inframarginal traders by extramarginal traders can depend on the "shape" of the extramarginal demand and supply, e.g., whether it is steep or not and on the market rules, e.g., whether bids and asks are ranked and a single market clearing price is determined (as in a call market) or whether decentralized trading is allowed (as in the standard, double auction).

Gode and Sunder (2004) further consider the consequences of nonbinding price ceilings on transaction prices and allocative efficiency in double auctions with ZI-C traders (the analysis of price floors follows a symmetric logic). A nonbinding price ceiling is an upper bound on admissible bid and ask prices that lies above the competitive equilibrium price. If a submitted bid or ask exceeds the price ceiling it is either rejected or reset at the ceiling bound. Since the bound lies above the competitive equilibrium price, theoretically it should not matter. However, in experimental double-auction markets conducted by Isaac and Plott (1981) and Smith and Williams (1981), non-binding price ceilings work to depress transaction prices below the competitive equilibrium level relative to the case where such ceilings are absent. Gode and Sunder (2004) report a similar finding when ZI-C agents are placed in double auction environments with non-binding price ceilings similar to the environments examined in the experimental studies. Gode and Sunder explain their finding by noting that a price ceiling reduces the upper-bound on the bid ask range, and with ZI-C agents, this reduction immediately implies a reduction in the mean transaction price relative to the case without the price ceiling. Further they show that with ZI-C agents, a price ceiling reduces allocative efficiency as well (which is consistent with the experimental evidence) by making it more likely that extramarginal buyers are not outbid by inframarginal buyers, and by excluding extramarginal sellers with costs above the ceiling from playing any role.

Summing up, what Gode and Sunder (1993, 1997a, 1997b, 2004) have shown is that simple trading rules in combination with certain market institutions can generate data on transaction prices and allocative efficiency that approach or exceed those achieved by human actors operating in the same experimental environment. This research finding serves as an important behavioral foundation for the "KISS" principle that is widely adopted in agent-based modeling. However, agent-based modelers are not always as careful as Gode and Sunder to provide external validity (experimental or other evidence) for the simple rules they assign to their artificial agents.

2.3. Reaction and response

Not surprisingly, the Gode and Sunder (1993) paper provoked a reaction, especially by experimenters, who viewed the results as suggesting that market institutions were preeminent and that human rationality/cognition was unimportant. Of course, the various different market institutions are all of human construction, and are continually evolving, so the concern about the *source* of market efficiency (institutional or human behavior) seems misplaced.[7] Nonetheless, there is some experimental literature addressing what human subjects *can* do that Gode and Sunder-type ZI agents cannot.

Van Boening and Wilcox (1996) consider double auction environments where buyers all have the same market valuation for units of the good, and sellers do not have fixed

---

[7] Analogously, there was great outcry in May 1997 when Gary Kasparov, widely considered to be the greatest player in the history of chess, first lost a chess match to a machine nicknamed "Big Blue," even though Big Blue's hardware and algorithms were developed over many years by (human) researchers at IBM.

or marginal costs for various units, but instead have large "avoidable costs"—costs they incur only if they decide to actively engage in exchange. In such environments, seller decisions to enter the market can be fraught with peril since they cannot anticipate the entry decisions of other sellers and consequently, supply, and a seller's average costs (avoidable cost divided by number of units sold) can be highly variable. Van Boening and Wilcox report that the efficiency of human subject traders in the more complex DA-avoidable costs environment is much lower than in the standard DA environment with pure marginal costs, but the efficiency of ZI traders in the DA-avoidable cost market is significantly worse than the human subject traders operating in the same environment.

Brewer et al. (2002) consider a different but similarly challenging variant of the double auction environment, where demand and supply conditions do not change within a trading period as exchanges between buyers and sellers remove units from trade, but where instead, market conditions remain invariant over each (and all) trading periods. This is accomplished by *continually refreshing* the units that all buyers (sellers) are able to buy (sell) following any trades, and Brewer et al. refer to this market environment as one with continuously refreshed supply and demand (CRSD).[8] Recall that the dampened volatility of prices over a trading period in the ZI-C simulations was owing to the greater likelihood that inframarginal units with the lowest marginal cost/highest reservation value would trade earlier than other inframarginal units where the difference between marginal cost and valuation was lower. In the continually refreshed design of Brewer et al. the forces working to dampen price adjustment over the course of a trading period are removed. Hence prices generated by ZI-C traders in the CRSD environment are quite random and exhibit no tendency toward convergence to any competitive equilibrium notion (Brewer et al. consider several). On the other hand, the human subject traders in the CRSD environment have no difficulty converging to the "velocity-based" competitive equilibrium, and are also able to adjust to occasional perturbations to this equilibrium.

Sadrieh (1998) studies the behavior of both human subjects and ZI agents in an "alternating" double-auction market, a discrete-time version of the continuous double-auction market that retains the double auction trading rules. The alternating DA is more conducive to a game-theoretic analysis but differs in some respects from the standard continuous DA in that only one side of the market (buyers or sellers) is active at once, the bids or asks submitted are sealed (made simultaneously), and there is complete information about values, costs and ex post offers of all players. The determination of the opening market side (buyers or sellers) is randomly determined, and then alternates over the course of a trading period. Sadrieh's game-theoretic prediction is that convergence to the competitive equilibrium price would be from above (below) when sellers (buyers) opened the market. By contrast, ZI simulations suggested that convergence to the market price would be from above (below) when the surplus accruing to buyers (sellers) in

---

[8] A motivating example is housing or labor markets without entry or exit of participants. A worker attracted by a firm to fill a job vacancy, leaves another vacancy at his old firm, so that labor demand is effectively constant.

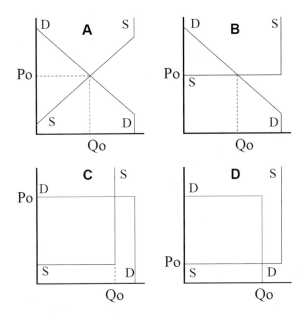

Figure 3. Demand (D) and supply (S) curves for four economies. Source: Cliff and Bruten (1997b).

the competitive equilibrium was relatively larger than that accruing to sellers (buyers). Sadrieh's experimental findings, however, were at odds with both of these predictions; the most typical path for prices in an experimental session involves convergence to the competitive equilibrium from below, regardless of which side opens the market or the relative size of the surpluses. On the other hand, ZI simulations accurately predicted the extent of another of Sadrieh's findings, "the proposer's curse." The curse is that those submitting bids or asks tend to do so at levels that yield them lower profits relative to the competitive equilibrium price; the additional gains go to the players accepting those bids or asks. Sadrieh reports that the frequency of proposer's curse among inexperienced subjects was comparable to that found in ZI simulations, though experienced subjects learned to avoid the curse.

Experimentalists are not the only ones to challenge Gode and Sunder's findings. AI researchers Cliff and Bruten (1997a, 1997b) have examined the sensitivity of Gode and Sunder's findings to the elasticity of supply and demand. In particular they examine DAs with four different types of induced demand and supply curves as shown in Figure 3. Of these four economies, simulations using ZI-C agents converge to the competitive equilibrium price, P_0 and quantity, Q_0 only in economies of type A, the same type that Gode and Sunder consider, and not in economies of type B, C or D. The intuitive reason for this finding (which Cliff and Bruten formalize) is that the probability density function (pdf) for transaction prices (a random variable with ZI agents) is symmetric about the competitive equilibrium price, P_0, only in the case of economy A; in the other economies, the transaction price pdf has P_0 as an upper or lower bound. Since the expected value of a random variable, such as the transaction price, is the "center of gravity" of the pdf, it follows that price convergence with ZI-C agents only occurs in economies of type A. Cliff and Bruten's simulations bear out this conclusion. It remains to be seen how human subject traders would fare in economies such as B, C and D. However, as a purely theoretical exercise, Cliff and Bruten suggest that an alternative algorithm, which they call "zero-intelligence plus" (ZIP), achieves convergence to competitive equilibrium in economies such as B, C, and D more reliably than does Gode and Sunder's ZI approach. By contrast with ZI agents, ZIP agents aim for a particular profit margin on each unit bought or sold, and this profit margin dictates the bid or ask they submit. Each agent's profit margin is adjusted in real time depending on several factors most of which concern properties of the most recent bids, asks and transactions made. Hence ZIP involves some memory though it is limited to the most recent data available. Comparisons of ZIP simulations with some of Smith's aggregate experimental findings are encouraging, though a more detailed analysis of the ZIP mechanism's profit margin adjustment dynamic with experimental data has yet to be performed.

As these critiques make clear, it is relatively easy to construct environments where human subjects outperform ZI agents or environments where ZI agents fail to converge to competitive equilibrium. However the broader point of Gode and Sunder's pioneering work is not that human cognitive skills are unimportant. Rather it is that, in certain market environments, aggregate allocation, price and efficiency outcomes can approach the predictions of models premised on high levels of individual rationality even when individual traders are only minimally rational. Understanding precisely the conditions under which such a mapping can be assured clearly requires parallel experiments with both human and artificial subjects.

2.4. *Other applications of the ZI methodology*

In addition to Cliff and Bruten, several other researchers have begun the process of augmenting the basic ZI methodology in an effort to explain economic phenomena in various environments. The process of carefully building up an agent-based framework from a simple foundation, namely budget-constrained randomness, seems quite sensible, and indeed, is well under way.

Bosch-Doménech and Sunder (2001) expand the Gode and Sunder (1993) double auction environment to the case of m interlinked markets populated by dedicated buyers in market 1, by dedicated sellers in market m, and consisting exclusively of arbitrage traders operating in markets $i = 1, 2, \ldots, m$. In the baseline model, arbitrageurs are prevented from holding any inventory between transactions. They operate in adjacent markets, simultaneously buying units in market $i + 1$ and selling them in market i. As market m is the only one with a positive net supply of the asset, trading necessarily begins there. Absent the possibility of inventories, a transaction in market m instantaneously ripples through the entire economy (the other $m - 1$ markets) so that the good traded quickly ends up in the hands of one of the dedicated buyers in market 1. One interpretation of this set-up is that of a *supply-chain*, consisting of producers in market m, middlemen in markets $m, m - 1, \ldots, 1$ and ultimate consumers in market 1. Bosch-Doménech and Sunder report simulations showing that regardless of whether the number of markets, m is 2, 5 or 10, prices and volume in each market quickly converge to the competitive equilibrium levels obtained by crossing demand in market 1 with supply in market m, and that market efficiency is close to 100%. Bosch-Doménech and Sunder further examine what happens when arbitrageurs can take long or short inventory positions. As the number of short or long positions that arbitrageurs can take is increased, and the number of markets, m, gets large, prices remain very close to the competitive equilibrium prediction in all m markets, but trading volume in the "middle" markets (populated only by arbitrageurs) increases well beyond the competitive equilibrium prediction and market efficiency declines. This finding is an argument for keeping supply chains short (or finding ways to "cut out the middleman"). An experimental test of this prediction remains to be conducted.[9]

Duffy and Ünver (2006) use the ZI methodology to understand asset price bubbles and crashes in laboratory market experiments of the type first examined by Smith et al. (1988). In these laboratory markets there is a single "asset" that is traded in a finite number, T, of trading periods; unlike the previously described double auction experiments, players here can be either buyers or sellers, and so they are referred to as traders. Those holding units of the asset at the end of each trading period are entitled to a random dividend payment per unit, with expected value $\bar{d}$. The fundamental expected market value of a unit of the asset at the start of trading period $t \leqslant T$ is given by $D_t = \bar{d}(T - t + 1) + D_{T+1}$, where D_{T+1} is the final buy-out value per unit of the asset held at the close of period T. All participants' initial endowments of the asset and money have the same expected value, though the allocation of assets and money differs across agents. Consequently, risk neutral traders should be indifferent between engaging in any trades or trading at the fundamental market value which is declining over time. With groups of inexperienced human subjects, the path of the mean transaction price tends to start below the fundamental value in the first trading periods, quickly soaring above this fundamental value in the middle trading periods before finally crashing back to or below fundamental value near to the final trading period T.

Duffy and Ünver show that such asset price bubbles and crashes can arise with ZI agents, who are a little more sophisticated than Gode and Sunder's ZI-C agents—Duffy and Ünver call them "near-zero intelligence agents". In particular, Duffy and Ünver's agents are not constrained from submitting bids or asks in excess of the fundamental market value of the asset as such a constraint would rule out the possibility of bubbles. As in Gode and Sunder (1993) there is an exogenously imposed range for bids and asks given by the interval $[0, \kappa D_t^T]$, where $\kappa > 0$. In addition, bids and asks are not entirely random. The ask of trader i in period t is given by $a_t^i = (1 - \alpha)u_t^i + \alpha \bar{p}_{t-1}$, where u_t^i is a random draw from $[0, \kappa D_t^T]$ and $\bar{p}_{t-1}$ is the mean transaction price from

---

[9] See, however, the related work of Grossklags and Schmidt (2004), who add artificial arbitrage agents to a double auction experiment with human subjects.

the previous trading period; the weight given to the latter, α, if positive, introduces a simple herding effect, and further implies that ask prices must rise over the first few periods. A similar herding rule is used to determine bids. The random component to bids and asks serves to insure that some transactions take place. As in Gode and Sunder (1993) budget constraints are enforced; traders cannot sell units they do not own, nor can traders submit bids in excess of their available cash balances. Finally, to account for the finite horizon, which was known to the human subjects, Duffy and Ünver endow their artificial agents with some *weak foresight*; specifically, the probability that a trader submits a bid (as opposed to an ask) is initially 0.5, and decreases over time, so, over time, there are more asks than bids being submitted reflecting the declining fundamental value of the asset. Standard double auction trading rules are in effect. Duffy and Ünver use a simulated method of moments procedure to calibrate the parameter choices of their model, e.g. κ, α, so as to minimize the mean squared deviations between the price and volume path of their simulated economies and the human subject markets of Smith et al. (1988). They are able to find calibrations that yield asset price bubbles and crashes comparable to those observed in the laboratory experiments and are able to match other, more subtle features of the data as well.

2.5. ZI agents in general equilibrium

The original Gode and Sunder (1993) study follows the Smith (1962) partial equilibrium laboratory design, where market demand and supply are exogenously given. In more recent work, zero-intelligence traders have been placed in general equilibrium settings, with the aim of exploring whether they might achieve competitive equilibrium in such environments. Gode et al. (2000) placed zero-intelligence traders, who could both buy and sell, in a two-good, pure exchange economy (an Edgeworth box). Traders are divided up into two types $i = 1, 2$, that differ only in terms of the parameters of their Cobb–Douglas utility function defined over the two goods and their initial endowments of these two goods. The trading rules for ZI agents in the general equilibrium environment are similar to rules found in the partial equilibrium environment. In particular, in the general equilibrium environment, ZI agents's bids and asks are limited to utility improving allocations. Specifically, each agent of type i begins by calculating the slope of its indifference map at its current endowment point. The slope is calculated in terms of radians, r, where $0 \leqslant r \leqslant \frac{\pi}{2}$; this gives the number of units of good y the trader is willing to give up per unit of good x. Next, the agent picks two random numbers, $b \in [0, r]$ and $a \in [r, \pi/2]$, with the first representing its bid price for units of good y in terms of good x, and the second representing its ask price for units of good y in terms of good x. Finally, the unit of a transaction for simulation purposes involves a discrete step size in the quantity of both goods; otherwise, with an infinitesimal quantity exchanged each period, convergence could take a long time. A consequence of this discrete step size assumption is that an adjustment has to be made to the bid and ask ranges to account for the curvature of the indifference map. Given these trading restrictions, and the double auction rules, market transactions will be limited to lie in the set of Pareto improving re-

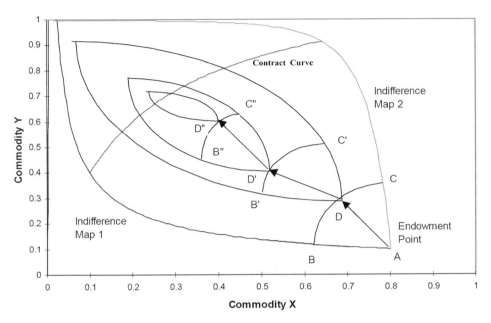

Figure 4. An illustration of the path of ZI transactions in an Edgeworth box. Source: Gode et al. (2000).

allocations, i.e., the area between the two indifference maps. Once an exchange occurs, endowments are updated, and the process described above begins anew.

Figure 4 (taken from Gode et al., 2000) illustrates this process. The initial endowment is at point A, and the indifference maps of the two agent types intersect at this point. The ZI trading restrictions and discrete step size imply that the first transaction occurs along the arc BC. If this first round transaction occurs at, say, point D, this point becomes the new endowment point. The set of feasible trades in the subsequent period lie on the arc B′C′, etc. Given this characterization of ZI trading rules it is clear—even without simulating the system—that this updating process must eventually converge to the contract curve, representing the set of all Pareto optimal allocations, and will then cease, as the bid-ask range shrinks to the null set.[10] And, indeed, this is precisely what Gode et al. (2000) find. Simulations of ZI agents operating according to the rules described above yield limiting allocations that lie on the contract curve, and so these allocations are Pareto optimal. However, these allocations do not necessarily correspond to the competitive equilibrium allocation, the point on the contract curve where the two price-offer

---

[10] One consequence of studying ZI, directed random search processes is that once the environment is specified, actual simulation of the search process may be unnecessary. Still, the value of this approach lies in building the minimal, necessary restrictions on directed random search that achieve the desired outcome. The ZI approach aids in formulating these restrictions, by greatly simplifying agent behavior, allowing the researcher to concentrate on the institutional restrictions.

curves of the two agent types intersect. So, by contrast with the findings in the partial equilibrium framework, ZI-trading rules turn out to be insufficient to guarantee convergence to competitive equilibrium in the two-good general equilibrium environment.

The nonconvergence of the ZI algorithm to competitive equilibrium is further addressed by Crockett, Spear and Sunder (CSS) (Crockett et al., 2004) who provide an answer to the question of "how much additional 'intelligence' is required" for ZI agents to find a competitive equilibrium in a general equilibrium setting with M agents and ℓ commodities. In their environment, ZI agents do not submit bids or asks. Rather a proposed allocation of the ℓ goods across the M agents is repeatedly made, corresponding to a random draw from an epsilon-cube centered at the current endowment point. Agent i compares the utility he gets from the proposed allocation with the utility he receives from the current endowment. If the utility from the proposed allocation is higher, agent i is willing to accept the proposal. If all M agents accept the proposal, the proposed allocation becomes the new endowment point. The random proposal generation process (directed search) then begins anew and continues until no further utility improvements are achieved. At this point the economy has reached a near-Pareto optimum (an allocation that lies approximately in the Pareto set), though not necessarily a competitive equilibrium; this outcome is analogous to the final outcome of the Gode et al. (2000) algorithm. Crockett, Spear and Sunder further assume that once agents have reached this approximate Pareto optimum (PO), they are able to calculate the common, normalized utility gradient at the PO allocation. The ZI agents are then able to determine whether this gradient passes through their initial endowment point (the condition for a competitive equilibrium) or not. If it does not, then, in the PO allocation, some agents are subsidizing other agents. Note that these assumptions endow the ZI agents with some calculation and recall abilities that are not provided (or necessary) in Gode and Sunder's partial equilibrium environment.

Consider for example, the two agent, two-good case. In this case, the normalized utility gradient corresponds to a price line through the tangency point of the two indifference curves (preferences must be convex), representing the relative price of good 2 in units of good 1 at the PO allocation. Suppose that at the end of trading period t, agent i's approximate PO allocation is $\hat{x}_i^t \in R_+^2$. Agent i's gain at this PO allocation can be written as:

$$\lambda_i^t = p^t \left(\hat{x}_i^t - \omega_i \right),$$

where p^t is the price line at the end of period t and $\omega_i \in R_+^2$ is agent i's initial endowment. Agent i is said to be subsidizing the other agent(s) if $\lambda_i < 0$. That is, at $p^t \gg 0$, agent i cannot afford to purchase his initial endowment. Crockett et al.'s innovation is to imagine that if agent i was a 'subsidizer' in trading period t, then in trading period $t + 1$ he agrees to trade for only those allocations, x^{t+1} that increase his utility and that satisfy:

$$0 \geqslant p^t \left(x_i^{t+1} - \omega_i \right) \geqslant \lambda_i^t + v_i,$$

where v_i is a small, positive bound. With this additional constraint in place, the PO allocation achieved at the end of period $t + 1$, $\hat{x}^{t+1}$, is associated with a larger gain for the subsidizing agent i, i.e. $\lambda_i^{t+1} > \lambda_i^t$, so he subsidizes less in period $t + 1$ than in period t. When all i agents' gains satisfy a certain tolerance condition, convergence to a competitive equilibrium is declared. Crockett et al. show that while cycling is a possibility, it can only be a transitory phenomenon. Indeed, they provide a rigorous proof that their algorithm converges to the competitive equilibrium with probability 1.

This subsidization constraint puts to work the Second Welfare theorem—that every Pareto optimum is a competitive equilibrium for some reallocation of initial endowments. Here, of course, the initial endowment is not being reallocated. Instead, agents are learning over time to demand more (i.e. refuse trades that violate the subsidization constraint) if they have been subsidizing other agents in previous periods. The reallocation takes place in the amounts that agents agree to exchange with one another.

The appeal of Crockett et al.'s "ϵ-intelligent" learning algorithm is that it implements competitive equilibrium using only decentralized knowledge on the part of agent i, who only needs to know his own utility function and be able to calculate the normalized utility gradient at the PO allocation attained at the end of the previous period (or more simply, to observe immediate past prices). Using this information, he determines whether or not he was a subsidizer, and if so, he must abide by the subsidization constraint in the following period. The algorithm is simple enough so that one might expect that simulations of it would serve as a kind of lower bound on the speed with which agents actually learn competitive equilibrium in multi-good, multi-agent general equilibrium environments, analogous to Gode and Sunder's (1993) claim for ZI agents operating in the double auction.

Indeed, Crockett (2004) has conducted an experiment with paid human subjects aimed precisely at testing this hypothesis. Crocket's experiment brings the ZI research agenda full circle; his experiment with human subjects is designed to provide external validity for a ZI, agent-based algorithm whereas the original Gode and Sunder (1993) ZI model was developed to better comprehend the ability of human subjects to achieve competitive equilibrium in Smith's double auction model. Crockett's study explores several different experimental treatments that vary in the number of subjects per economy and in the parameters of the CES utility function defined over the two goods. For each subject, a preference function was induced, and subjects were trained in their induced utility function, i.e., how to assess whether a proposed allocation was utility improving. Further, at the end of each trading period, Crocket calculated for subjects the end-of-period-t marginal rate of substitution, p^t, as well as the value of the end-of-period-t allocation, $p^t x_i$, but did not tell subjects what to do with that information, which remained on subjects' screens for the duration of the following period, $t + 1$. Subjects could plot the end-of-period-t price line on their screens to determine whether or not it passed through their beginning-of-period-t endowment point. Thus, subjects had all the information necessary to behave in accordance with the CSS algorithm, that is, they knew what comprised a utility improving trade and they had the information necessary to construct and abide by the subsidization constraint.

970

J. Duffy

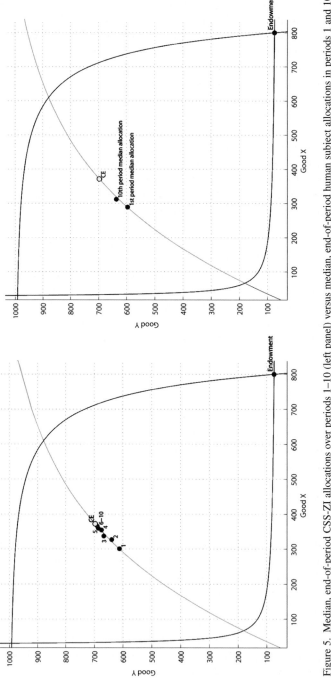

Figure 5. Median, end-of-period CSS-ZI allocations over periods 1–10 (left panel) versus median, end-of-period human subject allocations in periods 1 and 10 (right panel) in an Edgeworth box.

The left panel of Figure 5 presents the median end-of-period allocation of CSS–ZI agents for a particular 2-player CES parameterization, over trading periods 1–10, depicted in an Edgeworth box (the competitive equilibrium is labeled CE). The right panel of Figure 5 presents comparable median end-of-period allocations from one of Crockett's human subject sessions conducted in the same environment. Support for the hypothesis that the CSS-ZI algorithm accurately characterizes the behavior of paid human subjects appears to be mixed. On the one hand, nearly all of the human subjects are able to recognize and adopt utility improving trades, so that end of period allocations typically lie on or very close to the contract curve. And, once the contract curve is achieved, in subsequent periods, the human subjects appear to be moving in the direction of the competitive equilibrium allocation, as evidenced by the change in the median allocation at the end of period 10 relative to the median at the end of period 1 in the right panel of Figure 5. On the other hand, simulations of the CSS–ZI algorithm (left panel of Figure 5) suggest that convergence to the competitive equilibrium should have been achieved by period 6.

The reason for the slow convergence is that most, though not all subjects in Crockett's experiments are not abiding by the subsidization constraint; most are content to simply accept utility improving trades, while a few behave as CSS-ZI agents. The median allocation masks these differences, though the presence of some "CSS-ZI-type" agents moves the median allocation towards the competitive equilibrium. Hence, there is some support for the CSS-ZI algorithm, though convergence to competitive equilibrium by the human subjects is far slower than predicted by the algorithm.

2.6. Summary

The ZI approach is a useful benchmark, agent-based model for assessing the marginal contribution of institutional features and of human cognition in experimental settings. Building up agent-based models starting from zero memory and random action choices seems quite sensible and is in accord with Axelrod's KISS principle. Using ZI as a baseline, the researcher can ask: what is the minimal additional structure or restrictions on agent behavior that are necessary to achieve a certain goal such as near convergence to a competitive equilibrium, or a better fit to human subject data.

Thus far, the ZI methodology has been largely restricted to understanding the process by which agents converge to competitive equilibrium in either the partial equilibrium double auction setting or in simple general equilibrium pure exchange economies. ZI models have achieved some success in characterizing the behavior of human subjects in these same environments. More complicated economic environments, e.g. production economies or labor search models would seem to be natural candidates for further applications of the ZI approach.

The ZI approach is perhaps best suited to competitive environments, where individuals are atomistic and, as a consequence, institutional features together with constraints on unprofitable trades will largely dictate the behavior that emerges. In environments where agents have some strategic power, so that beliefs about the behavior of others become important, the ZI approach is less likely to be a useful modeling strategy. In such environments—typically game-theoretic—somewhat more sophisticated learning algorithms may be called for. We turn our attention to such learning models in the next section.

3. Reinforcement and belief-based models of agent behavior

Whether agents learn or adapt depends on the importance of the problem or choice that agents face. Assuming the problem commands agents' attention, e.g., because payoff differences are sufficiently salient, the *manner* in which agents learn is largely a function of the information they posses and of their cognitive abilities. If agents have little information about their environment and/or they are relatively unsophisticated, then we might expect simple, backward-looking adaptive processes to perform well as characterizations of learning behavior over time. On the other hand, if the environment is informationally rich and/or agents are cognitively sophisticated, we might expect more sophisticated, even forward-looking learning behavior to be the norm.

This distinction leads to two broad sets of learning processes that have appeared in the agent-based literature, which we refer to here as reinforcement and belief learning following Selten (1991). Both learning processes are distinct from the fully rational, deductive reasoning processes that economists assign to the agents who populate their models. The important difference is that both reinforcement and belief learning approaches are decentralized, inductive, real-time, on-line learning algorithms that are unique to each agent's history of play. In this sense, they comprise agent-based models of learning. Our purpose here is to discuss the use of these algorithms in the context of the experimental literature, with the particular aim of evaluating the empirical plausibility of these learning processes.

3.1. Reinforcement learning

The hallmark of "reinforcement," "stimulus–response" or "rote" learning is Thorndike's (1911) 'law of effect': that actions or strategies that have yielded relatively higher (lower) payoffs in the past are more (less) likely to be played in the future. Reinforcement learning involves an inductive discovery of these payoffs; actions that are not chosen initially, are, in the absence of sufficient experimentation, less likely to be played over time, and may in fact, never be played (recognized). Finally, reinforcement learning does not require any information about the play of other participants or even the recognition that the reinforcement learner may be participating in a market or playing a game with others in which strategic considerations might be important. Thus, reinforcement learning involves a very minimal level of rationality that is only somewhat greater than that possessed by ZI agents.

Reinforcement learning has a long history associated with behaviorist psychologists (such as B.F. Skinner), whose views dominated psychology from 1920 through the

1960s, until cognitive approaches gained ascendancy. Models of reinforcement learning first appeared in the mathematical psychology literature, e.g. Bush and Mosteller (1955) and Suppes and Atkinson (1960). Reinforcement learning was not imported into economics however, until very recently, perhaps owing to economists' long-held scepticism toward psychological methods or of limited-rationality heuristics.[11]

Brian Arthur (1991, 1993) was among the first economists to suggest modeling agent behavior using reinforcement-type learning algorithms and to calibrate the parameters of such learning models using data from human subject experiments. In his 1991 paper, Arthur asks whether it is possible to design a learning algorithm that mimics human behavior in a simple N-armed bandit problem. Toward this aim, Arthur used data from an individual-choice, psychology experiment—a 2-armed bandit problem—conducted by Laval Robillard four decades earlier in 1952–3 and reported in Bush and Mosteller (1955) to calibrate his model.[12]

In Arthur's model, an agent assigns initial "strength" s_0^i to each of the $i = 1, 2, \ldots, N$ possible actions. The probability of choosing action i in period t is then $p_t^i = s_t^i / C_t$, where $C_t = \sum_i s_t^i$. Given that action i is chosen in period t, its strength is then updated: $s_t^{i\prime} = s_t^i + \phi_t^i$, where $\phi_t^i \geqslant 0$ is the payoff that action i earned in period t. Finally, all of the strengths, including the updated $s_t^{i\prime}$ are renormalized so as to achieve a prespecified constant value for the sum of strengths in period t: $C_t = Ct^\nu$, where C and ν represent the two learning parameters. When $\nu = 0$ (as in Arthur's calibration) the speed of learning is constant and equal to $1/C$.

Arthur 'calibrated' his learning model to the experimental data by minimizing the sum of squared errors between simulations of the learning model (for different (C, ν) combinations) and the human subject data over all experimental treatments, which amounted to variations in the payoffs to the two arms of the bandit. He showed that regardless of the treatment, the calibrated model tracked the experimental data rather well. In subsequent work, (e.g. the Santa Fe Artificial Stock Market (Arthur et al., 1997) discussed in LeBaron's (LeBaron, 2006) chapter), Arthur and associates appear to have given up on the idea of calibrating *individual* learning rules to experimental data in favor of model calibrations that yield aggregate data that are similar to relevant field data. Of course, for experimental economists, the relevant data remain those generated in the laboratory, and so much of the subsequent development of reinforcement and other types of inductive, individual learning routines in economic settings has been with the aim of exploring experimental data.

Roth and Erev (1995) and Erev and Roth (1998) go beyond Arthur's study of the individual-choice, N-armed bandit problem and examine how well reinforcement learning algorithms track experimental data across various different multi-player games that

---

[11] An even earlier effort, due to Cross (1983), is discussed in Brenner's (Brenner, 2006) chapter.

[12] Regarding the paucity at the time of available experimental data, Arthur (1991, pp. 355–356) wrote: "I would prefer to calibrate on more recent experiments but these have gone out of fashion among psychologists, and no recent more definitive results appear to be available." Of course, economists have recently taken to conducting many such experiments.

have been studied by experimental economists. The reinforcement model that Roth and Erev (1995) develop is similar to Arthur's, but there are some differences and important modifications that have mainly served to improve the fit of the model to experimental data. The general Roth–Erev model can be described as follows.

Suppose there are N actions/pure strategies. In round t, player i has a propensity $q_{ij}(t)$ to play the jth pure strategy (propensities are equivalent to strengths in Arthur's model). Initial (round 1) propensities (among players in the same role) are equal, $q_{ij}(1) = q_{ik}(1)$ for all available strategies j, k, and $\sum_j q_{ij}(1) = S_i(1)$, where $S_i(1)$ is an initial strength parameter, equal to a constant that is the same for all players, $S_i(1) = S(1)$; the higher (lower) is $S(1)$ the slower (faster) is learning.

The probability that agent i plays strategy j in period t is made according to the linear choice rule:

$$p_{ij}(t) = \frac{q_{ij}(t)}{\sum_{j=1}^{n} q_{ij}(t)}.$$

Some researchers prefer to work with the exponential choice rule:

$$p_{ij}(t) = \frac{\exp[\lambda q_{ij}(t)]}{\sum_{j=1}^{n} \exp[\lambda q_{ij}(t)]},$$

where λ is an additional parameter that measures the sensitivity of probabilities to reinforcements. For now, however, we follow Roth and Erev (1995) and focus on the linear choice rule.

Suppose that, in round t, player i plays strategy k and receives a payoff of x. Let $R(x) = x - x_{min}$, where x_{min} is the smallest possible payoff. Then i updates his propensity to play action j according to the rule:

$$q_{ij}(t+1) = (1 - \phi)q_{ij}(t) + E_k(j, R(x)),$$

$$E_k(j, R(x)) = \begin{cases} (1 - \epsilon)R(x) & \text{if } j = k, \\ (\epsilon/(N-1))R(x) & \text{otherwise.} \end{cases}$$

This is a three-parameter learning model, where the parameters are (1) the initial strength parameter, $S(1)$, (2) a forgetting parameter ϕ that gradually reduces the role of past experience, and (3) an experimentation parameter ϵ that allows for some experimentation.[13] Notice that if $\phi = \epsilon = 0$ we have a version of Arthur's model, where the main difference is that the sum of the propensities is not being renormalized in every period to equal a fixed constant. This difference is important, as it implies that as the propensities grow, so too will the denominator in the linear choice rule and the impact of payoffs for the choice of strategies will become attenuated. Thus, one possibility is

---

[13] In certain contexts, the range of strategies over which experimentation is allowed is restricted to those strategies that are local to strategy k; in this case, the parameter ϵ can be regarded also as a 'generalization' parameter, as players generalize from their recent experience to similar strategies.

that certain strategies that earn relatively high payoffs initially get played more often, and over time, there is lock-in to these strategies; alternatively, the "learning curve" is initially steep and then flattens out, properties that are consistent with the experimental psychology literature (Blackburn's (1936) "Power Law of Practice").

The ability of reinforcement learning models to track or predict data from human subject experiments has been the subject of a large and growing literature. Roth and Erev (1995) compare the performance of various versions of their reinforcement learning model with experimental data from three different sequential games: a market game, a best-shot/weakest link game and the ultimatum bargaining game; in all of these games, the unique subgame perfect equilibrium calls for one player to capture all or nearly all of the gains, though the experimental evidence is much more varied, with evidence of convergence to the perfect equilibrium in the case of the market and best-shot games but not in the case of the ultimatum game. Roth and Erev's simulations with their reinforcement learning algorithm yield this same divergent result. Erev and Roth (1998) use simulations of two versions of their reinforcement model (a one parameter version where $\phi = \epsilon = 0$) and the three parameter version to *predict* play in several repeated normal form games where the unique Nash equilibrium is in mixed strategies. They report that the one and three-parameter models are better at predicting experimental data as compared with the Nash equilibrium point predictions, and that the three-parameter model even outperforms a version of fictitious play (discussed in the next section).

Figure 6 provides an illustration of the performance of the three models relative to human subject data from a simple matching pennies experiment conducted by Ochs (1995). This game is of the form

$$
\begin{array}{cc}
 & \textit{Player 2} \\
 & \begin{array}{cc} A2 & B2 \end{array} \\
\textit{Player 1} \quad \begin{array}{c} A1 \\ B1 \end{array} & \begin{array}{cc} x,0 & 0,1 \\ 0,1 & 1,0 \end{array}
\end{array}
$$

where x is a payoff parameter that takes on different values in three treatments ($x = 1$, 4 or 9). The unique mixed strategy equilibrium calls for player 1 to play A1 with probability .5, and player 2 to play A2 with probability $1/(1 + x)$; these Nash equilibrium point predictions are illustrated in the figure, which shows results for the three different versions of the game (according to the value of x). The data shown in Figure 6 are the aggregate frequencies with which the two players play actions A over repeated plays of the game. The first column gives the experimental data, columns 2–3 give the results of the 1 and 3 parameter reinforcement learning models, while column 4 gives the result from a fictitious play-like learning model. The relatively better fit of the three-parameter model is determined on the basis of the deviation of the path of the experimental data from the path of the simulated data. Erev and Roth suggest that the success of reinforcement learning in predicting experimental data over Nash equilibrium point predictions is owing to the inductive, real-time nature of these algorithms as opposed to the deductive approach of game theory, with its assumptions of full rationality and common knowledge.

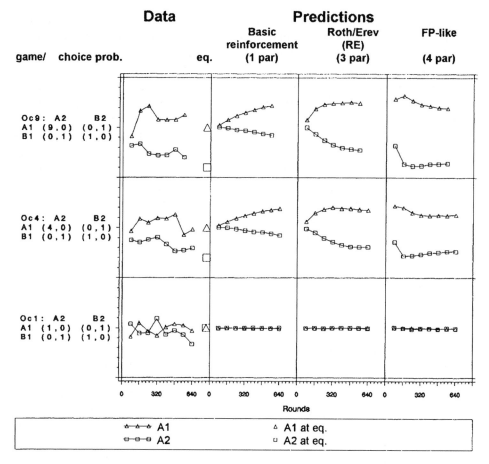

Figure 6. Experimental data from Ochs (1995) and the predictions of the Roth–Erev and fictitious play learning models. Source: Erev and Roth (1998).

Other variants of reinforcement learning have been proposed with the aim of better explaining experimental data. Sarin and Vahid (1999, 2001), for instance, propose a simple deterministic reinforcement-type model where agents have "subjective assessments," $q_j(t)$, for each of the $j = 1, 2, \ldots, N$ possible strategies. As in Roth and Erev's model, an agent's subjective assessment of strategy j gets updated only when strategy j is played: $q_j(t + 1) = (1 - \phi)q_j(t) + \phi\pi_j(t)$, where $\pi_j(t)$ is the payoff to strategy j at time t, and ϕ is the forgetting factor and sole parameter of their model. The main difference between Sarin and Vahid's model and Roth and Erev's is that the strategy an agent chooses at time t in Sarin and Vahid's model is the strategy with the maximum subjective assessment through period $t - 1$. Thus, in Sarin and Vahid's model, agents are acting more like optimizers than in the probabilistic choice framework of

Roth and Erev. Sarin and Vahid show that their one parameter model often performs well and sometimes better than Roth and Erev's 1 or 3-parameter, probabilistic choice reinforcement learning models in the same games that Erev and Roth (1998) explore.

Duffy and Feltovich (1999) modify Roth and Erev's (Roth and Erev, 1995) model to capture the possibility that agents learn not only from their own experience, but also from the experience of other agents. Specifically, they imagine an environment where agent i plays a strategy r and learns his payoff in period t, $\pi_r^i(t)$ but also observes the strategy s played by another player j (of the same type as i) in period t and the payoff that player earned from playing strategy s, $\pi_s^j(t)$. Player i updates his propensity to play strategy r in the same manner as Roth and Erev, (with $\phi = \epsilon = 0$) but also updates his propensity to play strategy s: $q_s^i(t+1) = q_s^i(t) + \beta\pi_s^j(t)$, where $\beta \geqslant 0$ is the weight given to observed payoffs, or "second-hand" experience. Duffy and Feltovich set $\beta = .50$ and simulate behavior in two of the games studied in Roth and Erev (1995), the best-shot game and the ultimatum game. They then test their simulation predictions by conducting an experiment with human subjects; their reinforcement-based model of the effect of observation of others provides a very good prediction of the role that observation of others' actions and payoffs plays in the experiment.

Another modification of reinforcement learning is to suppose that agents have certain "aspiration levels" in payoff terms that they are trying to achieve. This idea has a long history in economics dating back to Simon's (Simon, 1955) notion of satisficing. Aspiration learning has recently been resuscitated in game theory, e.g. by Karandikar et al. (1998) and Börgers and Sarin (2000) among others. Bendor et al. (2001) provide an overview and additional references. The reinforcement learning models discussed above can be viewed as ones where a player's period aspiration level is constant and less than or equal to the minimum payoff a player earns from playing any action in the given strategy set, so that the aspiration level plays no role in learning behavior. More generally, one might imagine that an agent's aspiration level evolves along with the agent's probabilistic choice of strategies (or propensities), and this aspiration level lies above the minimum possible payoff. Thus, in aspiration-based reinforcement learning models, the state space is enlarged to include a player's aspiration level in period t, $a^i(t)$. Suppose player i chooses strategy j in period t yielding a payoff of $\pi_j^i(t)$. If $\pi_j^i(t) \geqslant a^i(t)$, then player i's propensity to play strategy j in subsequent periods is assumed to be (weakly) higher than before; precisely how this is modeled varies somewhat in the literature, but the end result is the same: i's probability of playing strategy j satisfies $p_j^i(t+1) \geqslant p_j^i(t)$. On the other hand, if $\pi_j^i(t) < a^i(t)$, then $p_j^i(t+1) < p_j^i(t)$. Finally, aspirations evolve according to:

$$a_t^i = \lambda a_t^i + (1 - \lambda)\pi_j^i(t),$$

where $\lambda \in (0, 1)$. This adjustment rule captures the idea that aspirations vary with an agent's history of play. The initial aspiration level a_0 as with the initial probabilities for choosing actions, are assumed to be exogenously given. Karandikar et al. (1998) also add a small noise term to the aspiration updating equation representing trembles.

They show, for a class of 2×2 games that includes the prisoner's dilemma, that if these trembles are small, and aspiration updating is slow (λ is close to 1) that in the long-run, both players are cooperating most of the time.

There is some experimental evidence in support of aspiration learning. Bereby-Meyer and Erev (1998) studied behavior in a binary choice game where the probabilities of achieving a 'success' were exogenously fixed at 0.7 for choice 1 and 0.3 for choice 2. In one treatment, subject payoffs were set at 2 for a success and -2 for a failure, while in another treatment, the payoffs were 4 for a success and 0 for a failure, amounting to an addition of 2 to the payoffs in the first case. They found that learning of the optimal choice of strategies (choice 1) was significantly reduced when the payoffs were $(4, 0)$ relative to the case where the payoffs were $(2, -2)$. Erev et al. (1999) explain this result by presenting an adjustable reference point reinforcement learning model. In place of the assumption that $R(x) = x - x_{\min}$ in the Roth–Erev model, they propose that $R(x, t) = x(t) - \rho(t)$, and let the reference point, $\rho(t)$ be a weighted average of the past reference point and current payoffs, where the weights depend on the difference between the payoff and the reference point; if payoffs are highly variable relative to the reference point, learning is slower than if payoffs are less variable; this is simply another version of aspiration learning. They report that this model tracks the difference in the experimental findings rather well.

Huck et al. (2002) find evidence of aspiration learning in a laboratory oligopoly experiment. They test the theoretical proposition that bilateral mergers in oligopoly markets with $n > 2$ firms, homogeneous goods and constant returns to scale are unprofitable; the profit share of the merged firm, $1/n - 1$ is less than the total share of the two firms prior to the merger $2/n$ ($1/n$ each). In the experiment, $n > 2$ subjects make quantity decisions in a Cournot game and midway through a session, two of the subjects combine decision-making as a merged firm. The authors report that, contrary to theory, the subjects in the role of the merged firm produce significantly more output than the other unmerged firms and come close to sustaining total profit levels they would have achieved as unmerged firms. The authors argue that pre-merger aspiration-levels cause merged firms to increase output with the aim of maintaining total profits and the other firms acquiesce by reducing their output. They connect this finding with Cyert and March's (1956) observation that oligopoly firms are guided by "an acceptable-level profit norm" that is a function of market history.

Varieties of reinforcement learning algorithms have become a mainstay of agent-based modeling, perhaps because they accord with Axelrod's KISS principle. Other attractive features are the low level of history-dependent rationality, and relatively few parameters. Examples of the use of reinforcement learning in agent-based models are commonplace. Epstein and Axtell (1996) use several variants of reinforcement learning in their Sugarscape model. Nicolaisen et al. (2001) use Roth–Erev-type reinforcement learning to model buyer and seller price–quantity decisions in a computational model of the wholesale electricity market. Pemantle and Skyrms (2003) use reinforcement learning to study how groups of players play games in endogenously formed social networks. Franke (2003) uses reinforcement learning to study Arthur's (Arthur, 1994) El Farol Bar problem; Kutschinski et al. (2003) use a reinforcement learning model to study buyer search and seller price setting behavior in a competitive market with induced demand and supply schedules. Bendor et al. (2003) use a reinforcement learning model with endogenous aspirations to model voter turn-out. Finally, Erev and Barron (2003) apply reinforcement learning to cognitive strategies, e.g., loss avoidance, hill-climbing, rather than to the direct strategies available to agents in simple, repeated decision problems.

There is also a parallel and much more voluminous literature on reinforcement learning in the machine learning literature. See, e.g., Kaelbling et al. (1996) and Sutton and Barto (1998) for surveys. A popular reinforcement learning model in this literature is Q-learning (Watkins, 1989), which is closely related to Bellman's approach to dynamic programming, but differs from the latter in being much less informationally demanding, e.g. the agent need not know the period payoff or state transition functions. (See, e.g., Mitchell, 1997 for a good introduction the topic.) Q-learning algorithms involve on-line estimation of an evaluation function, denoted $Q(s, a)$, representing the maximum expected discounted sum of future payoffs the agent earns from taking action a in state s. Starting from some random initialization of values, estimation of the Q function occurs in real-time using the history of states and payoffs earned by the agent from action choices in those states. To determine the action chosen, a probabilistic choice rule is used: actions with higher Q-values for the given state s and the current approximation of the Q-function, are more likely to be chosen than actions with lower Q-values. Thus, the main difference between Q-learning and the reinforcement-learning models studied by economists is that Q-learners are learning an *evaluation function* mapping from states to actions, analogous to the policy function of dynamic programming. An advantage of Q-learning over reinforcement learning algorithms studied by economists is that convergence results for Q-learning can be proved under certain assumptions, e.g. for simple Markov-decision processes. Surprisingly, the predictions of Q-learning models have yet to be compared with data from controlled laboratory experiments with human subjects—a good topic for future research.

3.2. Belief-based learning

The primary difference between belief-based learning algorithms and reinforcement learning algorithms is that in belief-learning models, players recognize they are playing a game or participating in a market with other players, and form beliefs about the likely play of these other players. Their choice of strategy is then a best response to their beliefs. By contrast, reinforcement learners do not form beliefs about other players and need not even realize that they are playing a game or participating in a market with others. Belief-based learning models range from naive, Cournot-type learning to slightly more sophisticated "fictitious play," to fully rational, Bayesian learning. Here we discuss the first two types of belief learning models.

Fictitious play was proposed by Brown (1951) as a model of how players form beliefs and best respond to them in two-person zero sum games. Fictitious play was originally proposed as a means of determining the value of a game; indeed, Robinson (1951) shows that fictitious play converges to equilibrium in 2×2 zero sum games, though Shapley shows via a counterexample that this result does not hold in more general games. Subsequently, fictitious play has come to serve as a model of boundedly rational learning: players form beliefs about their opponents based on the historical frequency of their opponent's actions choices and play myopic best responses to these beliefs; the best responses are myopic because agents do not anticipate that their opponent is behaving similarly toward them.

Cheung and Friedman (1997) propose a one-parameter class of learning rules that yields Cournot and fictitious play learning as special cases and thus serves to compactly illustrate the main difference between the two approaches. They suppose there are $i = 1, 2, \ldots, N$ players, each of whom chooses an action a_i from the set of possible actions, A, in each period. Player i's payoff function is $\pi(a_i, s^{-i})$, where s^{-i} is a state vector representing the distribution of action choices chosen by all of i's opponents. It is assumed that each player i discounts past states using a constant discount factor, γ_i, and possesses some initial prior, $s^{-i}(1)$. Player i's belief about the state that will prevail in periods $t = 1, 2, \ldots$ is given by:

$$\hat{s}^{-i}(t+1) = \frac{s^{-i}(t) + \sum_{k=1}^{t-1} \gamma_i^k s^{-i}(t-k)}{1 + \sum_{k=1}^{t-1} \gamma_i^k}.$$

Cournot (naive) belief learning results from setting $\gamma_i = 0$ for all i; in this case, players hold the naive belief that $\hat{s}^{-i}(t+1) = s^{-i}(t)$. Fictitious play belief learning results from setting $\gamma_i = 1$ for all i; in this case, players' beliefs about the current state are simply the average of all past observed states. Weighted average, *adaptive* belief learning results from setting $0 < \gamma_i < 1$.[14] Given beliefs, a player's decision is to choose $a_i \in A$ so as to maximize his expected payoff (i.e., $\max_{a_i \in A} \pi(a_i, \hat{s}^{-i})$).

Consider by way of illustration, the class of 2 player, binary choice games that have been widely studied in the experimental literature. Let the 2×2 payoff matrix be given by $M = (m_{ij})$, and let us assign a '1' to the choice of action 1 and a '0' to the choice of action 2. With a single opponent per period, $s^{-i}(t) \in \{0, 1\}$ and $\hat{s}^{-i}(t) \in [0, 1]$ represents player i's belief about the likelihood that his opponent will play action 1 in period t.[15] Player i evaluates the expected payoff differential from choosing action 1 over action 2:

$$r_{i1} = R(\hat{s}^{-i}(t)) = (1, -1) M (\hat{s}^{-i}(t), 1 - \hat{s}^{-i}(t))'.$$

A deterministic best response in the binary choice game is to choose action 1 if $R(\hat{s}^{-i}(t)) > 0$ and to choose action 2 if $R(\hat{s}^{-i}(t)) < 0$. Some kind of tie-breaking rule is needed for the special case where $R(\hat{s}^{-i}(t)) = 0$. As Fudenberg and Levine

---

[14] Other, less plausible possibilities include $\gamma > 1$, so that the past is given more weight than the present and $\gamma_i < 0$, which implies cycling.

[15] More generally, if player i faces up to $n \leqslant N - 1$ opponents in a binary action game, then $s^{-i}(t) = n^{-1} \sum_{j=1}^{n} I(a_j)$, where $I(j) = 1$ if $a_j = 1$ and $I(a_j) = 0$ otherwise.

(1998) note, fictitious play ($\gamma = 1$) is a form of Bayesian learning in the special case where a player's prior beliefs over the distribution of opponent strategies is Dirichlet.

As was the case under reinforcement learning, researchers examining the predictions of Cournot or fictitious play belief learning have added some kind of noise to the deterministic best response. Boylan and El-Gamal (1993) propose that agents play the deterministic best response with probability $1 - \epsilon$, and any of the available actions $a \in A$ with probability ϵ/A.

Fudenberg and Levine (1998) propose a stochastic approximation to deterministic fictitious play—smooth fictitious play—which can be implemented, as in Cheung and Friedman (1997), through the use of the logistic function:

$$p_{ij}(t) = \frac{1}{1 + e^{-x_i(t)}}, \quad \text{where } x_i(t) = \alpha_i + \beta_i r_{ij}(t),$$

where α_i is an individual specific fixed effect indicating individual i's bias for action j ($\alpha_i = 0$ reveals an unbiased choice) and β_i representing the sensitivity of choices to expected payoff differentials.

These stochastic versions of fictitious play have several advantages over deterministic fictitious play. First, they do not imply that behavior switches dramatically with small changes in the data agents use to form beliefs. Second, insisting that strategies remain probabilistic has certain advantages, e.g., when agents have achieved near convergence to a mixed strategy equilibrium and need to keep their opponent guessing even though the differences in utility from the various actions may be quite small. (See Fudenberg and Levine, 1998 for a further discussion.)

Boylan and El-Gamal (1993) use a Bayesian approach to assess the likelihood that behavior in 9 different matrix game experiments (conducted by other researchers) is consistent with either the noisy-Cournot or the noisy-fictitious play hypothesis. They find that for some games, the Cournot belief hypothesis is favored while for other games the fictitious play hypothesis is favored. Their over all assessment of the relative validity of the two learning hypotheses is that fictitious play describes the experimental data better than Cournot learning.

Cheung and Friedman (1997) estimate their three parameter model (α, β, γ) on data from several different bimatrix games. Median estimates of α, β and γ are all significantly positive; the finding that $\gamma > 0$ rules out the Cournot belief hypothesis. Further they report they can reject the hypothesis that $\gamma = 1$ (fictitious play). Indeed, their estimates of γ always lie between 0 and 1 indicating that subjects' belief updating process is neither Cournot or fictitious play, but is instead approximated best by some adaptive intermediate case.

In addition to asking which belief-based learning model best predicts experimental data, one can also explore the empirical validity of the belief formation process associated with these belief-based models. This can be simply accomplished by asking subjects to state, prior to play of the game, their beliefs about their opponent's play and comparing these stated beliefs with those predicted by belief-based learning models. Nyarko and Schotter (2002) have carried out such an exercise in a simple 2×2 matrix game where the unique Nash equilibrium prediction is in mixed strategies. The two

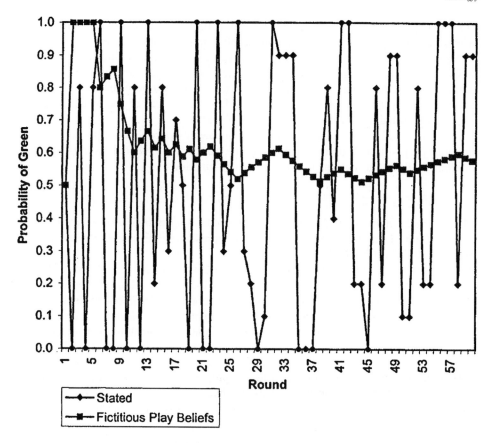

Figure 7.   Stated versus fictitious play beliefs of a typical subject in Nyarko and Schotter's experiment. Source: Nyarko and Schotter (2002, fig. 2).

strategies were labeled Green and Red, and the equilibrium calls on both players to play Green (Red) with probability .4 (.6). Nyarko and Schotter asked subjects to state the probability with which they thought their opponent would play Green prior to the play of each round. Subjects' compensation was determined in part by the accuracy of their stated beliefs and in part by the payoffs they received from playing the game.

Figure 7 plots stated beliefs against those predicted by fictitious play for a "typical subject" in Nyarko and Schotter's experiment. As is apparent, the variance in subject beliefs is much greater than predicted by fictitious play, and the differences do not decrease with experience. A similar difference is found in a comparison of the subjects' beliefs with Cournot beliefs. Nyarko and Schotter further conclude that best responses to subjects' *stated* beliefs provide a better account of the path of actions chosen by subjects than does reinforcement or a hybrid belief-reinforcement model discussed below.

This evidence suggests both that subjects are following some kind of belief-learning process and that a good model of that belief formation process has yet to be developed.

Belief-based learning models also make strong predictions regarding equilibrium selection in environments with multiple, Pareto rankable equilibria. Essentially, belief-based models predict that if the initial conditions lie in the domain of attraction of a particular equilibria under the belief learning dynamic, then, with experience, agents will learn over time to coordinate on that equilibrium, regardless of its efficiency. This hypothesis has been experimentally tested by Van Huyck et al. (1997) and Battalio et al. (2001) in the context of simple coordination games where the domain of attraction of the two symmetric pure strategy equilibria is defined by the best response separatrix. Van Huyck et al. (1997) show that both Cournot and fictitious play learning dynamics predict different equilibrium outcomes depending on initial conditions in a median effort game (involving strategic complementarities), and their experimental findings are remarkably accurate on this score. If the initial condition (median effort) lies in the domain of attraction of the unique, payoff-dominant equilibrium, subjects subsequently coordinate on that equilibrium, otherwise they coordinate on the other symmetric Nash equilibrium. As Van Huyck et al. point out, this behavior is very different from deductive equilibrium selection principles, which might involve, for instance, calculation of all equilibria and selection of the payoff dominant one.

The use of belief-based learning models by economists is not limited to normal form games. Varieties of belief-based learning models have also been used to study bid and ask behavior in the double auction.[16] Gjerstad and Dickhaut (1998) provide a particularly elegant characterization of the DA and propose heuristic rules by which buyers and sellers assess and update the probability that their bids or asks will be accepted, given market history. Using these beliefs together with private information on valuations and costs, individual buyers or sellers propose bids or asks that maximize their (myopic) expected surplus. The main parameter in their model is the length of memory that players use in calculating probabilities. Using a stricter convergence criterion than Gode and Sunder adopt, Gjerstad and Dickhaut show via simulations that their heuristic belief-learning model can more reliably achieve convergence to competitive equilibrium than Gode and Sunder's ZI-C model, and the belief-learning model provides a better fit to the aggregate human subject data as well. Indeed, in their chapter in this handbook, Mackie-Mason and Wellman (2006) argue that this heuristic belief-learning model represents the best agent-based model of the DA. Still, the fit of this belief-learning model to *individual* human subject behavior remains to be examined.

Belief-based learning models are less common in the agent-based literature than are reinforcement learning models, perhaps for the simple reason that belief-based models require that agents possess more memory (e.g. the histories of their opponents). Still, some versions of belief-based learning can be found see, e.g. Kandori et al. (1993), Young (1993, 1998); naive Cournot best response behavior is also found see, e.g. Ellison (1993) or Morris (2000).

---

[16] Early efforts include Friedman (1991) and Easley and Ledyard (1993).

3.3. Comparisons of reinforcement and belief-based learning

A large literature is devoted to testing whether simple reinforcement or more complicated belief-based learning algorithms better characterize experimental data from a wide
variety of different games. In addition to the papers of Roth and Erev and Cheung and
Friedman mentioned above, other papers comparing versions of these two approaches
to learning include Mookherjee and Sopher (1994, 1997), Camerer and Ho (1999),
Feltovich (2000), Salmon (2001), Blume et al. (2002), Stahl (1999) and Haruvy and
Stahl (2004) among others. In making these comparisons, researchers have adopted
some kind of goodness-of-fit metric or made use of an econometric estimator to assess
the fit of various candidate learning models to experimental data.

The findings from this literature are varied, but several conclusions appear to have
wide support. First, the evidence is very strong that either reinforcement or belief-based
learning models are better predictors of human subject behavior than are the static Nash
equilibrium point predictions. This is strong evidence in favor of the bottom-up, inductive reasoning approaches used by ACE researchers as opposed to the top-down,
forward-looking, deductive reasoning of fully rational players that gives rise to those
equilibrium point predictions. Second, in the simple games that experimentalists have
studied, reinforcement and belief-based learning models do not yield predictions that
are all that distinct from one another and so identifying which rule performs well across
a variety of different games leads to murky outcomes that appear sensitive to various
particulars of the datasets or games examined (Feltovich, 2000; Salmon, 2001). Given
the lack of a clear bias in favor of reinforcement or belief-based approaches over a wide
variety of games, a natural approach is to adopt a hybrid model that allows for both
reinforcement and belief-based learning as special cases, as well as mixtures of both.
The hybrid modelling approach is taken e.g., by Camerer and Ho (1999), and discussed
in Brenner's (Brenner, 2006) chapter. While this approach has had some success in
explaining data from human subject experiments (see Camerer, 2003 for an extensive
and detailed assessment), the additional complexity of such models, e.g., more parameters to calibrate, may make this approach less appealing to ACE researchers.[17] Third,
there is some evidence that if subjects' information is restricted to their own histories
of play, that reinforcement learning models perform slightly better than belief-based
learning models that use data on opponent's histories that was unavailable to subjects.
Analogously, in environments where data on opponent's histories was made available,
players appear to condition their expectations, in part, on those histories, in line with
the predictions of belief-based models (Blume et al., 2002). These findings are not so
surprising, and, indeed, simply confirm that players use histories to form expectations.
Finally, there is some evidence that the complexity of the game, the manner in which
players are matched and the length of play are all important factors in the accuracy of
learning models in predicting the play of human subjects.

---

[17] See, however, a simpler, one-parameter version of their model given in Ho et al. (2002).

On the latter point, much of the observed differences in the two approaches to modeling learning may be tied up with the relatively small periods of time over which individual human subject experiments are conducted. While experimentalists often give their subjects repeated experience with a game or decision, concerns about subject boredom or the salience of participation payments severely restrict the length of the time series that can be generated in the laboratory for any individual subject. By contrast, ACE researchers do not feel bound by such considerations, and think nothing of simulating their models out for very long periods of time. Asymptotically, the behavior of reinforcement and belief-based models may not be all that different. Hopkins (2002) shows that both reinforcement learning and stochastic fictitious play can be viewed as noisy versions of replicator dynamics (discussed later in Section 4.1), and that the asymptotic predictions of these two models may be the same; roughly speaking if an equilibrium is locally stable under stochastic fictitious play, then the same holds true under reinforcement learning. Duffy and Hopkins (2005) conduct experiments with a longer than typical number of repetitions under various information conditions in an effort to test this prediction and find that it has some, qualified support. An implication of these findings for ACE researchers is that the kind of learning rule that agents are endowed with may not be of such great importance if the research interest lies in the long-run behavior of the agent-based system.

3.4. Summary

Unlike ZI agent models, reinforcement and belief-based learning models presume that agents have some memory. These models of inductive reasoning have been primarily studied in the context of simple two player games. Reinforcement learners condition their actions on their own histories of play and abide by the principle that actions that have yielded relatively high (low) payoffs in the past are more (less) likely to be played in subsequent periods. Belief-based learning models assume that players have history dependent beliefs over the actions their opponents are likely to play, and they choose actions that are myopic best responses to these beliefs. While there is no guarantee that either type of learning model converges to an equilibrium, these models have nevertheless proven useful in tracking the behavior of human subjects in controlled laboratory settings.

Reinforcement learning models have been widely used in the agent-based literature, perhaps for the simple reason that they require only information on an individual's own history (payoffs and actions). In complex, multi-agent settings, this parsimony of information may be an important consideration in the modeling of agent learning. On the other hand, in settings with just a few agents, and especially in settings where agents interact with one another repeatedly, a belief-based learning approach may be more appropriate. Indeed, the available experimental evidence suggests that agents do condition their actions on both their own history of play and, when available, on information about the play of their opponents. However, the manner in which they do this does not appear to be strictly consistent with either reinforcement or belief-based learning models. Asymptotically, there may be little difference between the two approaches.

4. Evolutionary algorithms as models of agent behavior

In addition to directed random (ZI-agent) searches and individual learning approaches, agent-based researchers have used a variety of different *evolutionary algorithms* to characterize the behavior of populations of heterogenous, interacting, boundedly rational agents facing various economic decisions. Examples include replicator dynamics, genetic algorithms, classifier systems and genetic programming. These evolutionary algorithms differ from the learning processes considered so far in several respects. First, evolutionary algorithms were designed to mimic naturally occurring, biological processes. Not surprisingly, these algorithms can be difficult for social scientists to interpret and for experimentalists to test in the laboratory. Second, these methods are *population-based*, which is to say that the fitness of a particular individual or strategy (the distinction becomes blurred in this literature) is based on its performance relative to a certain population of individuals (or strategies). Thus, these algorithms presume that fitness values across individuals/strategies are readily and immediately available for comparison purposes; in this regard, they can be viewed as the most complex class of algorithms (or least decentralized) in the set of approaches considered in this chapter. Third, as with ZI or reinforcement learning, evolutionary algorithms are not belief-based; players are not aware that they are playing a game against other players and do not act strategically in any way. Fourth, some evolutionary algorithms, e.g., genetic algorithms and genetic programming, are employed in environments where strategies or equilibrium policy functions cannot be characterized analytically. This (alternative) use of evolutionary algorithms is owing to the performance of these algorithms as function optimizers in complex landscapes; indeed, genetic algorithms were developed for precisely this purpose. Finally, evolutionary algorithms may or may not be well-suited to modeling economic decision-making. Evolution is often a slow process and so algorithms that mimic this process tend to work best on an unchanging landscape. However, economic systems are often modeled as state dependent, and may also be subject to temporary shocks or more permanent structural shifts. In such environments, the performance of evolutionary algorithms may be degraded relative to the less volatile (natural) landscapes for which they were developed.

Despite these potential problems and shortcomings, evolutionary algorithms are widely used by agent-based modelers. By contrast with the other agent-based approaches we have discussed, evolutionary algorithms have not been developed or adapted to explain data from economic decision-making experiments. For the most part, the opposite has occurred; agent-based researchers have sought to validate the predictions of evolutionary algorithms by conducting experiments with human subjects placed in the same environments. In certain cases, the experimental environment has been modified to better approximate the evolutionary environment! These comparisons have met with some success, but as I will argue, some difficulties of interpretation remain, for example, the question of the appropriate time-frame for comparisons. It may simply be that evolutionary algorithms cannot be adequately tested using human subject experiments.

4.1. Replicator dynamics

Replicator dynamics comprise the simplest class of evolutionary algorithms that economists have used to model the behavior of populations of players. See Hofbauer and Sigmund (1988, 1998) for a complete treatment. These models presume that the set of strategies (or phenotypes) does not evolve, and that reproduction is asexual. The assumption of a small strategy space is most likely to be satisfied in simple games, and so it is not surprising that replicator dynamics have mainly been employed by game theorists.

To understand how replicator dynamics work, consider a game with N strategies, and let $s(t) \equiv (s_i(t))_{i=1,2,...,N}$ be a vector representing the proportions of the N strategies in the population at time t; $\sum_i s_i(t) = 1$ for all t. The $N \times N$ payoff matrix $M = (m_{ij})$ here represents the payoff earned by each strategy in the population when matched against every other strategy, including itself. For illustration purposes, we focus here in the simplest case where M is symmetric, known as the one-population model. The fitness of strategy i at time t is given by $M_i s(t)$, where M_i denotes the row of the payoff matrix corresponding to strategy i. The idea of assessing how a strategy fares against the entire population of strategies is what Maynard Smith termed "playing the field." The deterministic replicator dynamic posits that strategy i's representation in the population be updated as follows:

$$s_i(t+1) = \frac{s_i(t)M_i s(t)}{s'(t)M s(t)},$$

where the denominator can be interpreted as the average fitness level in the entire population of strategies, including strategy i. The idea of the replicator dynamic is that strategies with above average fitness see their proportion in the population increase while those with below average fitness see their proportion in the population decrease. Further, if $\hat{s}$ is a Nash equilibrium of the symmetric game M, then it is also a fixed point of the replicator dynamic. In the deterministic version of the replicator dynamic, the proportion of certain strategies can go to zero, i.e., extinction is possible. A stochastic version of replicator dynamics due to Foster and Young (1990) eliminates extinction, and can have quite different limiting dynamics than the deterministic version.

Friedman (1996) and Cheung and Friedman (1998) have examined the predictions of replicator dynamics using data from human subject experiments. Friedman studies the predictions of the replicator dynamic for equilibrium stability, and Cheung and Friedman compare replicator dynamic predictions with that of the individual, belief-based, stochastic fictitious play learning algorithm. Most of the games they study are two player, binary choice games with a unique Nash equilibrium in either mixed or pure strategies. In such games, the state, $s(t)' = (s_1(t)), (1 - s_1(t))$, and the replicator dynamic for strategy s_1 is written as:

$$\frac{\Delta s_1(t+1)}{s_1(t)} = \beta \frac{[M_1 s(t) - s(t)'M s(t)]}{s(t)'M s(t)},$$

where $\beta > 0$ represents an adjustment parameter, and $\Delta s_1(t+1) = s_1(t+1) - s_1(t)$. Cheung and Friedman omit the denominator on the right hand side, $s(t)'M s(t)$, which serves as a normalization device ensuring that proportions sum up to one; in the binary choice case this device is unnecessary, and furthermore, Cheung and Friedman report that the unnormalized version fits the data better.

In their experimental design, these authors make some accommodation for the "playing the field" nature of the replicator dynamic; in their "mean matching" treatment, each player is matched against all other players, receiving the average payoff from his choice of action against that of all others. The other matching treatment is the standard, random pairwise matching protocol. While game theory would treat these two environments very differently, with the first corresponding to an n-player repeated game and the second to a two-player, one-shot game, the only difference under the replicator dynamic lies in the greater variance in payoffs that players receive in the random pairwise matching protocol. Friedman and Cheung and Friedman are careful to address issues concerning group size, the length of play of a single game, and of the information that players receive, all of which are important to approximating the environment for which the replicator dynamic was devised.

Cheung and Friedman (1998) use experimental data from the two binary choice games they study to estimate the linear equation:

$$\Delta s_1(t+1)/s_1(t) = \alpha + \beta[M_1 s(t) - s(t)'M s(t)] + \gamma d_t + \epsilon,$$

where $d_t = I(t)[M_1 s(t) - s(t)'M s(t)]$, $I(t) = 1$ if the mean matching treatment was used, and ϵ is an error term. They report that α is typically significantly different from zero, implying a persistent bias from the pure replicator dynamic, and that β is significantly positive as is γ. The latter finding suggests that the mean matching protocol aids in the speed of adjustment relative to random pairings. In a head-to-head comparison of the explanatory power of the replicator dynamic versus an individual, belief learning model—the three parameter weighted fictitious play model of Cheung and Friedman (1997) described in Section 3.2—Cheung and Friedman report that over the two games they study, the belief learning model outperforms the replicator dynamic, where performance is measured by either the root mean squared errors or the mean absolute deviations computed from the three parameter belief-learning or replicator dynamic model.

This finding suggests that there is some value to thinking of human players as playing best responses to beliefs about their opponents' actions rather than thinking of them as playing a game against nature. On the other hand, it is less clear that Cheung and Friedman have successfully implemented the evolutionary game environment germane to the use of replicator dynamics or that such an environment could be implemented in the laboratory, where budget and time constraints limit the number of subjects and replications of a treatment that are possible. Further work reconciling the replicator dynamic with human learning processes is needed.

4.2. Genetic algorithms

Genetic algorithms (GAs) have been widely used by economists to model learning by populations of heterogenous, adaptive agents especially following Sargent's (Sargent, 1993) encouraging assessment and the subsequent use of GAs by his student, Jasmina Arifovic. These algorithms differ from replicator dynamics in that they allow for the development of new strategies or decisions that may not have been included in the initial population. As such, they are efficient sampling methods most appropriate to large decision or strategy spaces.

Indeed, genetic algorithms, originally developed by Holland (1975), are stochastic, directed search algorithms based on principles of population biology.[18] These algorithms have been demonstrated to perform well in large or "rugged" search spaces where classical methods, e.g., grid search or gradient descent, are either inefficient or susceptible to getting stuck at local optima. While there is wide variation in the specific details of genetic algorithms, there are some general principles and procedures that are regarded as relatively standard. First, the researcher must specify the objective function of the genetic algorithm search, the parameter values that will be used to maximize (or minimize) that objective, and the range of admissible parameter values allowed in the search for an optimum. Second, vectors of parameters, representing candidate solutions are encoded as strings of finite length L. The strings are intended to mimic chromosomes, with the individual elements of a string representing genes; hence the name genetic algorithm. In the earliest implementation of genetic algorithms (e.g., Goldberg, 1989), parameters were encoded using the binary $\{0, 1\}$ alphabet, and much of the theory of genetic algorithms as function optimizers is developed for binary encodings. However, more recently, researchers have made use of real-valued, character, or tree encodings in place of traditional binary encodings. Researchers typically work with a population of strings of some fixed size, N. Third, the performance of each string in the population is evaluated using the objective criterion—this is the string's fitness. Fourth, a new generation of N strings is determined using operations that mimic natural selection and naturally occurring biological processes.

The first step in a genetic algorithm, known as selection, is to randomly select N strings from the existing population in such a way that the fitness of the N randomly selected strings is on average higher than the average fitness of the population from which they were chosen. This selection operation can be accomplished in many ways, including the biased roulette wheel selection mechanism originally proposed by Holland, in

---

[18] For a complete treatment of genetic algorithms see, e.g., Goldberg (1989) or Michalewicz (1996). Dawid (1999a) provides a thorough discussion of genetic algorithms as applied to economic problems. See also Sargent (1993) and Judd (1998).

```
g = 0
initialize population of N strings, P(0)
while tolerance criterion remains unmet or g < G
evaluate fitness of strings in P(g)
select N strings for P(g + 1) based on relative fitness
apply crossover to selected strings
apply mutation to recombined strings
evaluate tolerance criterion
g = g + 1
end while
```

Figure 8. Pseudo-code for a genetic algorithm.

which the likelihood of selecting a string is proportional to its relative population-wide fitness or other methods e.g. binary tournaments or rank order lists. The selection operation is intended to mimic Darwinian survival-of-the-fittest. Once a new set of N strings has been selected, these strings undergo two main biological operations that mimic genetic inheritance. The first, crossover, typically involves randomly pairing strings and, with some probability, p_c, randomly cutting the two strings at one or more points and swapping elements. Once crossover is applied to all strings, a second operator, mutation is applied, which involves randomly changing each element in a string with a (small) probability p_m, to some other value; in the case of binary strings, a '0' is flipped to a '1' and vice versa. After these operations are complete, the new generation of N strings is evaluated in fitness terms and the process of choosing a new generation begins again. The genetic algorithm is terminated after a set number of generations, G, or after some tolerance criterion based on the objective function has been satisfied. Some pseudo-code for a genetic algorithm is given in Figure 8.

The main theoretical result for genetic algorithms is known as the schema theorem (Holland, 1975). The idea of a schema can be understood by the addition of a don't care character, *, to the binary alphabet that is typically used to encode strings. A schema is a template characterizing a set of chromosomes. For example, the schema of length 5, (*101*) characterizes the set of chromosomes {(11011), (11010), (01011), (11010)}. The order of a schema is the number of fixed positions; e.g., the order of the schema in our example is 3. The schema theorem (proved, e.g. in Goldberg, 1989) states that low-order, above-average (below-average) schema appear exponentially more often (less often) in subsequent generations of a genetic algorithm. This theorem follows directly from the operation of fitness-proportional selection. These low-order schema are sometimes referred to as "building blocks." Crossover plays the role of introducing new schemata and mutation also contributes to variability while at the same time preventing premature convergence to local optima.

How are the genetic operators to be interpreted when applied to economic systems? Several authors, e.g., Arifovic (1996), Bullard and Duffy (1998), Dawid (1999a), Riechmann (1999, 2001a, 2001b), have offered interpretations. One can think of the individual strings as representing the strategies/decisions of individual agents, so that the GA is made up of many interacting agents. Alternatively, one can imagine there is a single agent with the individual strings of the GA representing different decisions/strategies that agent might adopt. The selection operation is perhaps the easiest to defend; this operator just insures that agents or decisions that have worked well in the past are more likely to be chosen in the future while decisions that have fared poorly are more likely to be discarded. This probabilistic choice of decisions based on relative payoff or fitness success is similar to stochastic reinforcement learning or stochastic replicator dynamics. The turnover of population need not be interpreted so literally as one of birth and death; instead it can be interpreted as a turnover of decisions or ideas among players who are long-lived. The crossover/recombination operator is easiest to interpret if the population of strings is viewed as representing individual agents. In that case, crossover can be thought of as communication between pairs of agents, who exchange bits and piece of ideas, though the population as a whole retains core principles (low-order schema) that have yielded high payoffs in the past. Finally, the mutation operator can be viewed as representing trembles or experimentation.

A further issue concerns the choice of GA parameters: the number of strings, N, the string length, the mutation and crossover parameters, p_c, p_m, etc. Here, the practice has been to adopt parameterizations that computer scientists have found to perform well on test suites of difficult static optimization problems. These optimization problems are not ones that are so applicable to the dynamic settings studied by economists, and so further research into this issue would be of some value.

What about the external validity of simulations using genetic algorithms? Arifovic (1994) was the first to directly compare simulations of a genetic algorithm with the behavior of human subjects in a controlled laboratory experiment.[19] The economic environment studied was a textbook version of Ezekiel's (Ezekiel, 1938) "Cobweb" model of demand and supply for a single good. In this model, market demand in period t is a decreasing, linear function of current period price, p_t, while market supply in period t is an increasing, linear function of the market price that suppliers expected in period $t - 1$ would prevail in period t, $E_{t-1}p_t$; the latter assumption captures the notion that it takes time (one-period) to produce the good, and makes the model dynamic. Arifovic followed experimental researchers, Carlson (1968) and Wellford (1989), who adopted Ezekiel's assumption of naive and homogeneous expectations, i.e. $E_{t-1}p_t = p_{t-1}$ as a benchmark assumption for expectation formation; in that case, the equilibrium is stable (unstable) if the ratio of the slope of the supply curve to the slope of the demand curve, in absolute value, is less than (greater than) unity. Bray and Savin (1986) have shown in a stochastic version of the linear cobweb model that adaptive learners, running regressions of prices on past prices, can learn the equilibrium price level in the stable case but

---

[19] Similarly, Axelrod (1987) sought to determine whether the human-submitted 'tit-for-tat' strategy that won his (Axelrod, 1984) prisoner's dilemma tournament would emerge in a simulation exercise that used a genetic algorithm to evolve strategies (it did).

not in the unstable case.[20] By contrast, a main finding of the experimental studies was that groups of subjects generally converged to a neighborhood of the unique equilibrium regardless of whether that equilibrium was stable or unstable under the naive expectations assumption. However, the variance of quantities or prices was much greater and more persistent in the unstable case as compared with the stable case.

Arifovic represented firms (suppliers) in two ways. In the single-population representation, each firm was represented as one of $N = 30$ strings in a single population. In the multiple population representation, each of the m firms is represented by a different population of 30 strings. In both cases, each string in a population represents a decision as to how much a firm might produce in the current period, $q_i(t) \in [0, \bar{q}]$, absent knowledge of the market price that will prevail. This decision was encoded as a string, of length 30, using a binary alphabet; initial 'bit' values were randomly determined. The fitness criterion used was the firm's current period profit; to evaluate fitness, strings had to be decoded to real quantities. In addition to using the standard genetic algorithm operations of selection, crossover and mutation on the binary strings, Arifovic adopted a fourth operator, which amounted to an augmented, elitist selection criterion which Arifovic called "election." Following crossover and mutation, which yields two new strings from two parent strings, the fitness of the new, offspring strings is evaluated and compared with the fitness of the parent strings; of this group of four strings, the two strings with the highest fitness values are allowed to enter the next generation of candidate solutions. This election operator simply allows the genetic algorithm to converge, asymptotically to a solution; without it, mutations would lead to persistent heterogeneity in the string population in the neighborhood of a solution. In the case of the single population representation, Arifovic reported the average value of $q(t)$ in the population of 30 strings; in the case of the multiple population simulation, Arifovic imagined that each firm randomly chose one of its strings to determine its quantity decision in each period; she then reported the average of these m quantity decisions. In certain simulations, the model parameters were chosen to be the same as in one of Wellford's treatments, including the number of periods, 30, and the number of firms, $m = 5$.

Figure 9 shows results for the unstable parameter case; the left panel shows the average quantity produced (with a 1-standard deviation band) for the human subject experiments and the right panel shows the same for a simulation of the multiple-population version of the genetic algorithm over the same number of periods. Both the human subjects and the genetic algorithm converges to a neighborhood of the equilibrium quantity of 14 though convergence takes longer and is more volatile in this 'unstable case' than in the stable case (not shown). However, the average quantity in the GA simulation appears to get very close to the equilibrium prediction beginning after period 10 while the same cannot be said of the experimental data. However, consistent with the experimental evidence, Arifovic is able to reject the null of no difference between the volatility

---

[20] Hommes (1994) studies the more general case where demand is linear and supply is nonlinear. He provides conditions under which adaptive learning dynamics converge to limit cycles or chaos in the unstable case. Sonnemans et al. (2004) provide experimental evidence in support of Hommes' predictions.

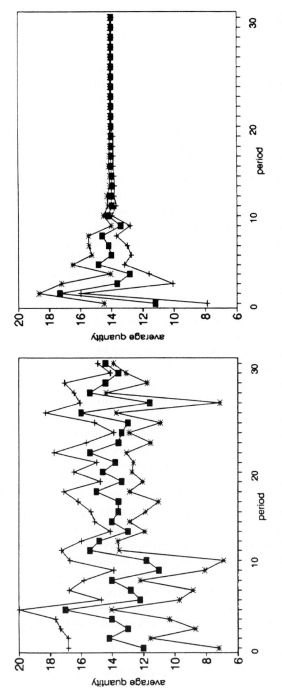

Figure 9. Average quantity in the Cobweb model, unstable case (plus/minus one st. dev.). Left panel: human subject data, right panel: multiple-population GA simulation. Source: Arifovic (1994).

of prices in the stable and unstable cases using the simulation data. These findings provide some support for the reasonableness of genetic algorithms as models of adaptive processes.

Several papers explore GA learning in general equilibrium, overlapping generation models of money, and compare the results with experimental findings. Arifovic (1996) studies exchange rate volatility in a two-country, two-currency, two-period overlapping generations model due to Kareken and Wallace (1981). Details of this model are discussed in LeBaron's (LeBaron, 2006) chapter. Arifovic's main conclusion is that, counter to the theoretical prediction derived under the rational expectations assumption, under genetic algorithm learning, the exchange rate displays persistent volatility, which is due to the persistence of mutation and the election operator.

By contrast, Arifovic (1995) shows that in a single country model, an equilibrium with valued fiat currency and low inflation is asymptotically stable under GA learning with persistent mutation and the election operator in place. The selection by the GA of the stationary, low inflation equilibrium, rather than another high inflation, stationary equilibrium is consistent with the laboratory findings of Marimon and Sunder (1993). Other, homogeneous and non-evolutionary learning algorithms, such as recursive least squares learning, fail to converge to the same low inflation equilibrium (see, e.g., Marcet and Sargent, 1989).

In Arifovic's work, the strings of the GA encode decisions that agents make, e.g., how much to consume in the first period. The GA then works to find the optimal decision, given feasibility and budget constraints. In Marimon and Sunder's (Marimon and Sunder, 1993, 1994) overlapping generation experiments, subjects were not asked to make consumption/savings decisions as pilot studies suggested that subjects had a difficult time solving that kind of intertemporal optimization problem. Instead, Marimon and Sunder asked subjects to provide forecasts of the price level they expected would prevail in the next period. Given a subject's forecast, the computer program solved that subject's optimal consumption/savings allocation and determined market clearing prices. Bullard and Duffy (1999) adopted this same learning-how-to-forecast design in a GA-learning simulation of the environment studied by Arifovic (1995). They imagine that agents have some belief about how prices in period $t + 1$ will be related to prices in period t, and the strings of the GA encode this belief. Given the price forecast, the program optimally determines each agent's consumption/savings decision, along with market clearing prices. Bullard and Duffy (1999) show that this learning-how-to-forecast implementation of GA learning results in findings that are consistent with the experimental evidence of Marimon and Sunder (1994) and also with Arifovic (1995)'s learning-how-to-optimize implementation of GA learning.

Several papers use GAs to understand findings from auction experiments. A difficulty with auctions is that participants frequently fail to win an item or agree to a transaction, so that the fitness of strategies may need to be assessed over a longer period of time than is typical in other applications of GAs.

Andreoni and Miller (1995) use genetic algorithms as a way of studying how close populations of adaptive agents might come to learn equilibrium bid functions in a variety of auction formats: first and second price affiliated-values auctions, first and second price private-values auctions, and common value auctions. The design of their simulation experiments is aligned with that of laboratory experiments with paid human subjects in several dimensions, e.g., the number of bidders in a group and the information available to these bidders. However, their 20 simulation runs of 1000 generations per auction format is more difficult to compare with the 20–30 auctions that human subjects participate in the typical experiment. In Andreoni and Miller's implementation, the genetic algorithm is employed to search over two parameters of a general linear bidding function of the form

$$b(x_i) = \beta_{i1}x_i + \beta_{i2}\epsilon,$$

where x_i is agent (string) i's valuation and ϵ is some distribution parameter that varies according to the knowledge that agents are assumed to have, e.g., whether valuations are private-independent, private-affiliated or common. This functional form nests (to an approximation) all the equilibrium bid functions that are predicted to obtain in the various auction formats. The binary strings of the GA encode the two parameters, β_1 and β_2. For the standard GA implementation, Andreoni and Miller report that the GA simulations come closest to learning the equilibrium bid functions in the affiliated private value, first or second price auction formats and have more difficulty achieving the equilibrium bid functions in the independent-private and common value formats. Consistent with evidence from human subject experiments, e.g. Cox et al. (1982), Kagel and Levin (1986), they find violations of revenue equivalence between first- and second-price auction formats, and they find that smaller groups of 4 rather than 8 bidders are less prone to the winner's curse in common value auctions.

Dawid (1999b) examines genetic algorithm learning in a sealed bid, double auction market. The N buyers' each have some value, v, from consuming a unit of the single good while the N sellers' have some cost, c, of producing a unit of the good, and $1 > v > c > 0$. The strings of the GA encode the buyers' bids and the sellers' asks. In each period, buyer and sellers are randomly paired. If a buyer's bid, p_b, exceeds a sellers' ask, p_a, a transaction occurs at price $p = (p_a + p_b)/2$; otherwise no transaction occurs. Profits are determined in the usual way, $v - p$ for buyers and $p - c$ for sellers, and the fitness of buyer/seller rules and application of genetic operators is assessed every m periods. Dawid shows analytically that the only locally stable equilibria under GA dynamics are those where all buyers (sellers) submit the same bid (ask) in the interval $[v, c]$. In 50 simulation runs where $v = 1$ and $c = 0$, he reports that the most common outcome is a single price equilibrium in a small neighborhood of .5. Interestingly, this finding is quite similar to that observed in an experiment conducted by Valley et al. (2002), where values of v and c are drawn randomly from $[0, 1]$ and after learning these values, pairs of players were allowed to communicate with one another prior to submitting bids/asks. The most common outcome, in cases where gains from trade are possible ($v > c$), was for both buyer and seller to name the same price. While this experimental finding may not be so surprising, the fact that the GA simulation delivers this same finding, without any explicit communication between populations of buyers and sellers, is quite interesting.

Finally, there are several papers comparing GA simulations with experimental findings in labor markets. Pingle and Tesfatsion (2001) examine the impact of varying levels of non-employment benefits on worker–employer matches and on-the-job cooperation using data from both human subject experiments and computational experiments that make use of genetic algorithms. The environment studied is a repeated two-stage game where in the first stage workers decide whether (and for which employer) to work or remain unemployed while employers decide whether to accept these offers or keep a position vacant. At the end of this first stage, unemployed workers and employers with vacancies receive a fixed non-employment benefit while matched workers and employers proceed to the second stage, which involves play of a prisoner's dilemma game, with strategies labeled 'shirk' and 'don't shirk.' The single treatment variable was the size of the non-employment benefit. The human subject experiments revealed that increases in the non-employment benefit both decreased the frequency with which relationships formed, and the frequency of mutual cooperation between worker-employer pairs, though this effect was not monotonic. Further, long-term relationships between the same worker and employer were rare. The computational labor market had four times as many workers and employers as the human subject experiment and was simulated for a much longer period of time: 1000 generations. Each generation consisted of successive trade cycles followed by an evolutionary step that updated strategies; the genetic algorithm operates in the latter stage. A trade cycle consisted of both a matching process, which utilizes a reinforcement learning algorithm to determine the expected utility of potential partners, followed by a work-site interaction among matched players. The work-site interaction was governed by a finite state automaton, and the genetic algorithm was used to search for potentially better work-site rules in the evolution step. Among the findings from simulations of this model are that, consistent with the human subject experiments, the frequency of employment relationships decreases with increases in the non-employment benefit. On the other hand, by contrast with the human subject findings, in the computational experiment, nearly all employers and workers end up in long-term fixed relationships, and either mutual cooperation or mutual defection becomes the norm, depending on initial conditions. The authors suggest that these differences may be owing to differences in the design of the two experiments, in particular the different number of employers and workers in the computational versus the human subject experiments appears to have played an important role in the outcomes, though the different time-frames of analysis may also be a contributing factor.

Ünver (2001a) and Haruvy et al. (2002) use genetic algorithms to model the two-sided, worker-firm matching process in markets for medical intern and federal law clerks and compare these results with human subject experiments. These entry-level labor markets as well as others, have been susceptible to a phenomenon known as unraveling, in which the date at which firms and workers agree to contracts becomes increasingly earlier in time relative to the actual start-date of employment leading to possible inefficiencies in matches due to unavailability of relevant information. Some markets have sought to address this problem by having centralized clearinghouses that match workers with firms. Ünver studies three centralized matching mechanisms used in British medical-intern markets. Of these three, two are still in use, though only one of these two is stable in the Gale and Shapley (1962) sense. Ünver uses a GA to encode and model the evolution of worker-firm strategies under these three mechanisms. Among other findings, he shows that the theoretically unstable, "linear programming" matching protocol may not be susceptible to unraveling under the GA adaptation, which is consistent with the continued use of this mechanism in the field. He is able to corroborate other findings of two-sided matching experiments conducted by Kagel and Roth (2000) and Ünver (2001b) that explore the unraveling in the British medical intern markets.

Haruvy et al. (2002) conduct a parallel experiment with human subjects and with artificial agents modeled using a genetic algorithm with the aim of studying two-sided matching in the market for federal law clerks. Applicants initially decide whether to submit applications to judges of varying qualities, and judges may in turn accept offers. The grades of applicants, affecting the payoff from a match, are only fully revealed later, during a centralized matching process. Matches not made by the end of the first two periods (years) are, in certain treatments, subject to a centralized match in period 3 using a stable matching protocol. In the 'idealized-centralized' treatment, applicants are not required to submit offers prior to the centralized match in order to participate in it, while in the coerced-centralized treatment they are required to submit offers prior to the match. In both cases, offers accepted prior to the centralized match date are binding, consistent with practice in this market, though in the idealized treatment, binding offers can be avoided by waiting for the centralized match. In the human subject experiments, the authors report that many more subjects in the role of applicants and judges wait for the centralized match under the 'idealized-centralized' treatment than do so under the coerced-centralized treatment, and given the additional information that can be obtained by waiting, welfare is higher in the former treatment than in the latter. In genetic algorithm simulations, where the strategies of applicants and judges co-evolve, a similar finding obtains. Haruvy et al. are careful to compare their findings for human subject experiments over the same time-scale used in the genetic algorithm simulations. They then carry out the genetic algorithm simulation exercise much further in time, and find that this difference becomes even more pronounced over time. This seems a reasonable merger of the two technologies they use to understand these matching markets. As they observe (p. 3), "the computations will give us some assurance that our experimental results are not artifacts of slow learning in the laboratory, while experiments will assure us that the behavior produced by the genetic algorithms is in fact similar to human behavior."

The findings from all of these studies provide some support for the reasonableness of genetic algorithms as models of adaptive learning by populations of heterogenous agents. Genetic algorithms appear best suited for large, complex search spaces where it is more efficient to sample from the set of possible actions/strategies than to enumerate all possibilities and consider their relative fitness at every decision step. At the same time, most of the studies treat the genetic algorithm as a kind of black box generator of new-and-improved decisions or strategies, without much regard to the interpretation of genetic operators, or how they compare with actual human decision-making processes. Toward this goal, it would be of interest to consider the marginal contribution of each of the genetic operators in explaining data from human subjects, an exercise akin to adding additional structure to ZI-algorithms or moving from reinforcement to hypothetical reinforcement (belief) learning models.

4.3. Comparisons between genetic algorithm and reinforcement learning

Two papers have compared the performance of genetic algorithm learning and reinforcement learning in terms of explaining data from human subject experiments. Haruvy and Ünver (2003) study matching behavior in procurement-type markets where the matching decision is consequential to both the seller and the buyer. They are interested in the question of whether buyers and sellers achieve a stable outcome, á la Gale and Shapley (1962) and if so, whether the stable matching is optimal for the party who initiates a proposed match (buyers or sellers). As the strategy space in the repeated game they consider is highly complex, and there are multiple stable outcomes, deductive reasoning is not very useful and so they turn to inductive reasoning processes, in particular, reinforcement learning and genetic algorithm learning, to predict what will happen in the experiments they conduct with human subjects. Both the reinforcement and genetic algorithm learning simulations predict that in seller- (buyer-) proposing markets, sellers (buyers) are most likely to achieve the seller- (buyer-) optimal stable outcome, and this prediction is consistent with the experimental findings. Aside from the observation that the two learning models yield the same prediction however, Haruvy and Ünver do not go into a deeper comparison of the performance of the two learning models.

By contrast, Arifovic and Ledyard (2004) look for a clear winner between reinforcement and genetic algorithm learning in the context of a repeated public good game that makes use of a Groves–Ledyard allocation mechanism. As the authors point out, this environment differs from those typically studied by learning researchers in that the strategy space is continuous. They compare the predictions of an "individual evolutionary learning" model (a GA-without-crossover for each individual's strategies) with Roth–Erev-style reinforcement learning and Camerer and Ho's (Camerer and Ho, 1999) hybrid reinforcement-belief learning algorithm in terms of the fit of simulations of these models to the experimental data. To facilitate a comparison, some discretization of the action space is necessary. They report that for two different ways of discretizing the strategy space, reinforcement learning fares substantially worse than the other two learning approaches in that it takes much longer to converge to the Nash equilibrium than does the human subjects. However, the version of reinforcement learning they use is not as general as Roth and Erev allow. For instance, there is no forgetting factor nor is there any spillover in the probability choice updating to nearby strategies. Given the large strategy space considered, it is not so surprising that the genetic algorithm appears to perform best for the reasons noted above. However, before concluding in favor of one approach over others, it would be useful to compare the predictions of evolutionary and reinforcement-type learning models on a broad range of games including those with both continuous and discrete strategy sets.

4.4. Classifier systems

Classifier systems, first proposed by Holland (1986), are inductive, rule-based learning systems that combine reinforcement-type learning over a set of simple logical rules called classifiers, with occasional use of a genetic algorithm search for new classifiers. As with genetic algorithms, there are many variants, but a typical classifier system consists of four parts: 1) a set of if–then decision rules or classifiers, 2) an accounting system for assessing the strength of classifiers and for apportioning credit, 3) an auction system for determining which classifiers are invoked and 4) a genetic algorithm for the introduction of new classifiers. Classifier systems are perhaps best viewed as models of individual learning, akin to expert systems, while genetic algorithms, as typically modeled are often interpreted as models of population or social learning. As Vriend (2000) points out, simulations with classifier systems used to model social learning (mimicry) at the population level can yield outcomes that differ substantially from simulations with classifier systems used to model learning at the level of individual agents, especially in environments where strategic considerations come into play.[21]

The first use of a classifier system (or a genetic algorithm) in an economic application was due to Marimon et al. (1990), who used a classifier system to model behavior in Kiyotaki and Wright's (Kiyotaki and Wright, 1989) model of money as a medium of exchange. That model has equal numbers of three types of agents who produce either good 1, 2 or 3, but who desire to consume another good, e.g. type 1 produces good 2, type 2 produces good 3, and type 3 produces good 1. Each agent may store a single unit of a good at a time, and the goods have different storage costs, with good 1 being the least costly to store and good 3 being the most costly to store. Agents receive utility from consumption of the good they desire in an amount that exceeds the highest storage cost. In each period, agents are randomly paired and decide whether to engage in trade with their match. Trades must be mutually agreed upon by both parties, in which case inventories of the two goods are swapped; otherwise, inventories of goods do not change. Agents earn utility only when they trade for the good they desire; in that case they immediately produce a new unit of their production good. In every period they incur storage costs based on the type of good they hold in inventory. The optimal trading strategy for a type 2 or 3 player is a fundamental, cost-reducing pure strategy in which they agree (refuse) to trade the good they hold in storage for less (more) costly-to-store goods in route to getting the good they desire to consume. On the other hand, depending on parameter values, type 1 players may find it optimal to adopt the fundamental strategy, or a speculative strategy in which they trade their production good 2 for the more costly to store good 3 with the rational expectation that speculating in the more costly to store good 3 will reduce the time it takes to acquire the good they desire, good 1.

---

[21] For a further discussion of this issue see, e.g., Riechmann (2002) and Arifovic and Maschek (2004).

In Marimon et al.'s implementation, there are two classifier systems for every agent, a set of trade and consumption classifiers represented by strings. The trade classifier takes as input the good an agent has in storage and the good that his match has in storage, and provides, as output, a decision (or message) of whether to trade or not. The consumption classifier takes as input the good a player has in storage and provides as output, a decision (message) of whether or not to consume that good. Each classifier has a strength or fitness measure associated with it. In each period, the collection of classifiers that satisfy the current state for an agent, consisting of the good the agent holds in storage and the good in storage of the matched player, bid a fraction of their current strengths in an auction that determines which classifier the agent adopts; the highest bidding classifier of each type is chosen, its bid is deducted from its strength and its decision is implemented. The bid of the winning exchange classifier in the current period is paid to (added to the strength of) the previous period's winning consumption classifier, which determined the current good the agent holds in storage, while the bid of the winning consumption classifier is paid to the current period winning exchange classifier, which determine the good the agent holds in storage. This payment system is what Holland termed a 'bucket brigade' wherein classifiers that are not necessarily active in the current period, but which were critical for activating classifiers that were active can still earn some share of credit and see their strengths improve. The current winning consumption classifier earns the 'external' payoff associated with its decision, which depends on whether the good in storage is the desired good or not. Finally a genetic algorithm is called on, with some decreasing frequency, to generate new classifiers, with the population of parent strings being selected from the population of classifiers according to relative strengths. The set of strings resulting from the genetic operators are assigned the strengths of the parent strings.

In simulations of this system, Marimon et al. report many interesting findings, but the main finding is that speculative trading strategies (e.g. by type 1 players) are not observed in environments where, in equilibrium, they would comprise a unique best response. Marimon et al. comment on this finding by observing that the behavior of the artificial agents, modeled using classifier systems, can be very myopic in the beginning, while it may take time for some optimal strategies, such as speculation, to achieve strengths that will sustain these strategies. They conclude that "the present algorithm seems defective in that it has too little experimentation to support the speculative equilibrium even in the long simulations we have run." [22]

Inspired by Marimon et al.'s simulation findings, Duffy and Ochs (1999, 2002) sought to test the Kiyotaki–Wright model in a laboratory experiment. They made an effort to provide subjects with all the information relevant to making optimal decisions in the theoretical environment. Duffy and Ochs sought to induce a stationary infinite horizon,

---

[22] Subsequent applications of classifier systems in economic applications, include Başçi (1999), Beltrametti et al. (1997) and Vriend (2000). LeBaron's (LeBaron, 2006) chapter discusses the Santa Fe artificial stock market (Arthur et al., 1997) which makes use of a classifier system to model traders' decisions. See Lettau and Uhlig (1999) for a comparison between classifier/rule learning and dynamic programming.

as the theory presumes, by having an indefinite end to a sequence of pairwise trading rounds. Such concerns with implementation of infinite horizons do not typically concern agent-based modelers, as the artificial agents in their models are not typically forward-looking, alleviating concerns about backward induction due to end-game effects. Finally, among the parameterizations they chose was one that was also used by Marimon et al. (1990). Though Duffy and Ochs had only 8 or 10 agents of each of the three types, while Marimon et al. had 50, the findings from the human subject experiments were quite similar to those obtained in the artificial agent simulations using classifier systems. In particular, Duffy and Ochs also find that subjects failed to adopt speculative trading strategies in environments where such strategies comprise an equilibrium best response.[23]

Duffy (2001) considers two alterations of the Kiyotaki–Wright model that might serve to promote the adoption of speculative strategies. In one version, agents whose optimal equilibrium strategy calls for speculation are given more encounters with situations where playing the speculative strategy results in higher expected utility. In the other, two of the three agent types are constrained to playing the strategies that are optimal for them in equilibrium. Duffy adopts a reinforcement learning model which is similar to the exchange classifier of Marimon et al. (1990), automates the consumption classifier and gets rid of the genetic algorithm. A similar model was found to provide a good fit to the experimental data of Duffy and Ochs (1999). Duffy uses this reinforcement model to simulate what will happen in the two alternative environments, and reports that both alternatives speed up the learning of speculative strategies. However, the adoption of speculative strategies is greater in the second alternative, where two thirds of the agent types are constrained to playing optimal strategies. He then conducts an experiment with human subjects designed to test these same alternatives. In the human subject experiment, the model parameters, the number of agents, and other features of the environment are kept as similar as possible to that of the simulated environments to facilitate comparisons. The human subject findings are largely consistent with the artificial agent findings. Duffy stresses that agent-based modeling exercises of this type can be a useful tool for experimental design, and at the same time, the results of human subject experiments might be useful in thinking about how to model the decisions of artificial agents.

4.5. Genetic programming

Another variant of genetic algorithm learning, known as genetic programming, was developed by Koza (1992). In genetic programming, the same genetic operators of the GA are used to search over a population self-executing computer programs represented

---

[23] Brown (1996) conducted an experimental test of the Kiyotaki–Wright that was more narrowly focused on the speculative equilibrium prediction and came to the same conclusion: most subjects failed to adopt the speculative trading strategy.

as decision trees (variable-length strings) in an effort to obtain an optimal functional relationship or program. This type of genetic search is well-suited to finding functional solutions to problems that do not readily yield closed-form solutions. Genetic programming has been mainly used by economists to study financial market phenomena, e.g., to uncover technical trading rules or to discover pricing formulas for financial derivatives. Chen (2002) provides a good survey.

However, the external validity of genetic programming has been assessed through a few comparisons with the results of human subject experiments. Perhaps the best known work is that of Chen and Yeh (1996), who revisit the unstable cobweb model studied by Arifovic (1994) and examined experimentally by Wellford (1989). Chen and Yeh note that it is more general to view agents as learning a *functional relationship* for prices, e.g. $E_{t-1}p_t = f(p_{t-1}, p_{t-2}, \ldots)$ than for them to be learning about what quantity to produce as in Arifovic's (Arifovic, 1994) implementation, as the former approach allows for the possibility that the equilibrium is not a fixed point, e.g., it could be a limit cycle. Chen and Yeh apply a genetic programming algorithm to search over a class of price forecast functions. Essentially the algorithm allows for a wide range of linear and nonlinear functions mapping from observations on as many as 10 past prices to deliver a forecast for period t. These forecast functions determine quantities which subsequently determine actual market prices via the equilibrium market clearing condition. Fitness of individual forecast functions is then assessed, and genetic operations are applied to advance the search for better price forecast functions in a manner analogous to the genetic algorithm search. Chen and Yeh report that for the same unstable parameterization of the model considered by Arifovic and Wellford, (as well as for some even more egregious cases) their genetic programming algorithm has no difficulty yielding price predictions that were very close to the equilibrium price level without the need for an election operator to contain the effects of the mutation operator. The price forecasting functions are initially quite complex and difficult to interpret. However, as convergence to the equilibrium obtains, the price forecasting functions become quite simple, as prices cease to vary so much.[24]

In a quite different application, Duffy and Engle-Warnick (2002) use genetic programming to infer the strategies that human subjects play in a simple bargaining game, given only the actions and histories of the players. This approach, which Koza (1992) termed "symbolic regression", involves evaluation of a population of computer programs in terms of their relative success in mapping from inputs, e.g., players' histories, to output, e.g., player's action choices. An advantage of this approach is that the user does not have to specify the functional form of the strategy model in advance, aside from specifying a set of model primitives; both the form and the coefficients of the computer

---

[24] Chen et al. (2002) use a genetic programming algorithm to reach a similar conclusion in a median effort coordination game studied experimentally by Van Huyck et al. (1994). Chen et al. show that a steady state effort level that is theoretically unstable under a myopic, homogeneous best-response learning dynamic turns out to be stable under the genetic-programming-based learning system in accordance with Van Huyck et al.'s (Van Huyck et al., 1994) finding from human subject experiments.

programs are estimated simultaneously. Using this algorithm, Duffy and Engle-Warnick report that simple threshold strategies characterize the behavior of most of the human subject participants.

4.6. Summary

Evolutionary algorithms, by contrast with ZI and individual learning algorithms, are derived from principles of population biology. While the principle of survival and propagation based on relative fitness is similar to reinforcement learning, fitness assessments in evolutionary algorithms are not made on the basis of an individual agent or strategy's own history, but instead are based on population-wide measures. The biological models from which evolutionary algorithms derive lead to some difficulties of interpretation for social scientists. While some efforts have been made to interpret the operators of evolutionary algorithms, the more common approach has been to treat these algorithms as a kind of black box model of social learning and focus on the similarity between aggregate outcomes in simulations and in human subject experiments.

Two main approaches in evolutionary models have been identified. With the replicator dynamic, the set of strategies or actions must be fully specified at the outset. Such an approach is reasonable in environments where the set of actions or strategies is small. In environments where the search space is larger, a genetic algorithm approach may be preferred. GAs are effective, population-based search algorithms that optimize on the tradeoff between finding new strategies, and exploiting strategies that have worked well in the past.

Comparisons between simulations using evolutionary algorithms and human subject experiments suggest that there is some support for the use of evolutionary algorithms as models of population learning. However, the time-frame and the number of agents used in simulation of evolution algorithms is often quite different from that adopted in human subject experiments.

5. Conclusions and directions for the future

Two parallel computer-based technologies, the experimental and the computational laboratory, have begun to have a major impact on economic research. While top-down, deductive theorizing with fully rational agents remains the standard in economics, the findings of experimentalists and ACE researchers using bottom-up, boundedly rational, inductive models of behavior are attracting increasing attention in the profession, as these models often provide a better fit to experimental (as well as to field) data, and operate without the centralized coordinating devices found in standard theory.

There are difficulties with the external validity of both approaches. Agent-based models have many degrees of freedom, while experimental methods are unable to perfectly induce or control subject behavior, etc. Still, the fact that findings from agent-based models and human subject experiments are often in agreement helps to allay concerns with either approach individually. Can an argument be made for one approach over the other? Analogous to Judd's (Judd, 1997) answer to the question of whether computational economics and economic theory are substitutes or complements, we have seen that agent-based models and humans subject experiments are sometimes nearly perfect substitutes (e.g., zero intelligent agents in certain versions of the double auction market) but are more often complements (e.g., the degree of sophistication in individual learning models can be calibrated based on experimental data).

There are several directions for future research. First, further comparisons of different agent-based models using a variety of experimental data sets are needed. "Horse-races" such as those between reinforcement learning and belief-learning and between belief-learning and replicator dynamics are important for choosing among agent-based modeling approaches. Second, further parallel experiments with human and artificial agents situated in the same environment are needed to better understand the external validity of agent-based models as well as to appropriately calibrate those models. These parallel experiments will necessarily involve more constraints on agent-based modeling exercises than on human subject designs owing to the stricter time and budget constraints of laboratory research. However, if agent-based models can accurately track the behavior of human subjects over the short-time frame of a human subject experiment, that finding would give the ACE researcher some license to carry out simulations of the model over a much longer time-frame, as might be necessary to achieve convergence to an equilibrium. Third, new agent-based models might be developed based on laboratory evidence.

There are at least two possibilities for attacking the latter goal. First, researchers could seek to determine how players go about analyzing the experimental environments in which they are placed. For example, the kind of information subjects consider, their cognitive skills and other characteristics that Costa-Gomes et al. (2001) have termed the players' *strategic sophistication*. Costa-Gomes et al.'s use of the Mouselab software which enables the researcher to capture and study the information that players consider in playing normal form games, as well as Camerer et al.'s (Camerer et al., 1993) use of the Mouselab software to study behavior in extensive form games, is very useful in identifying heterogeneity of player types, and testing cognitive concepts such as backward induction.

A second possibility for designing agent-based models more fully grounded in laboratory evidence is to make greater use of an experimental design known as the strategy method, first proposed by Selten (1967). The strategy method requires subjects to simultaneously specify, prior to the start of a game, the strategies they will play in that game, i.e. their action choice at every information set. Subjects' choices are then made for them based on the strategies they submit.[25] Unlike observing how players make decisions as a game unfolds in real-time and attempting to infer subjects' strategies from their action

[25] The counterpart of the strategy method in the agent-based literature is to hold a tournament á la Axelrod (1984), in which researchers submit computer code (strategies) characterizing the behavior of their gladiatorial-agent models. The tournament organizers then use some matching protocol or test suite

choices, the strategy method provides researchers with all the information necessary to program artificial agent strategies.[26] In more complex environments, it may be necessary to give subjects experience with the game prior to having them submit strategies. For instance, Selten et al. (1997) have subjects play a Cournot duopoly game repeatedly and then ask them to program their strategies. The programmed strategies were then played against one another and the programmers were allowed to alter their strategies based on their performance. The adoption of such an approach might well lead to the development of new adaptive models with a greater claim to the term 'agent-based.'

References

Andreoni, J., Miller, J.H. (1995). "Auctions with artificial adaptive agents". Games and Economic Behavior 58, 211–221.

Arifovic, J. (1994). "Genetic algorithm learning and the cobweb model". Journal of Economic Dynamics and Control 18, 3–28.

Arifovic, J. (1995). "Genetic algorithms and inflationary economies". Journal of Monetary Economics 36, 219–243.

Arifovic, J. (1996). "The behavior of the exchange rate in the genetic algorithm and experimental economies". Journal of Political Economy 104, 510–541.

Arifovic, J., Ledyard, J. (2004). "Scaling up learning models in public good games". Journal of Public Economic Theory 6, 203–238.

Arifovic, J., Maschek, M.K. (2004). "Social vs. individual learning—What makes a difference?", working paper, Simon Fraser University.

Arthur, W.B. (1991). "Designing economic agents that act like human agents: A behavioral approach to bounded rationality". American Economic Review Papers and Proceedings 81, 353–359.

Arthur, W.B. (1993). "On designing economic agents that behave like human agents". Journal of Evolutionary Economics 3, 1–22.

Arthur, W.B. (1994). "Inductive reasoning and bounded rationality". American Economic Review Papers and Proceedings 84, 406–411.

Arthur, W.B., Holland, J.H., LeBaron, B., Palmer, R., Taylor, P. (1997). "Asset pricing under endogenous expectations in an artificial stock market". In: Arthur, W.B., Durlauf, S.N., Lane, D.A. (Eds.), The Economy as an Evolving Complex System II, Proceedings Volume XXVII, Santa Fe Institute Studies in the Science of Complexity. Addison-Wesley, Reading, MA, pp. 15–44.

Axelrod, R. (1984). The Evolution of Cooperation. Basic Books, New York.

of problems/data to determine a winning strategy/program. (See, e.g. the Trading Agent Competition, http://www.sics.se/tac/ or The Turing Tournament, http://turing.ssel.caltech.edu/). However, tournaments, especially the winner-take-all variety, may alter incentives so that the strategies/programs submitted do not reflect decisions agents would make in non-tournament environments, e.g. in random-pairwise interactions. For instance, winner-take-all tournaments might give rise to a higher variance in payoffs than simple random pair-wise interactions. If there is free entry/exit into a tournament (as is typically the case), then one might expect tournament participants to have a higher tolerance for risk than would agents interacting in random pair-wise encounters, so that tournament findings could be misleading for agent-based modelers. Further, tournaments are expensive to run, and are infrequently conducted more than once. By contrast, eliciting strategies from human subjects in non-tournament environments is relatively cheap and can be done repeatedly.

[26] Some researchers believe that the strategy method changes the way players play a game. The experimental evidence on this question is mixed. See, e.g. Brandts and Charness (2000) and Brosig et al. (2003).

Axelrod, R. (1987). "The evolution of strategies in the iterated prisoner's dilemma". In: Davis, L. (Ed.), Genetic Algorithms and Simulated Annealing. Morgan Kaufmann, Los Alamos, CA, pp. 32–41.

Axelrod, R. (1997). The Complexity of Cooperation: Agent-Based Models of Competition and Collaboration. Princeton University Press, Princeton, NJ.

Axelrod, R., Tesfatsion, L. (2006). "A guide for newcomers to agent-based modeling in the social sciences", this handbook.

Başçi, E. (1999). "Learning by imitation". Journal of Economic Dynamics and Control 23, 1569–1585.

Battalio, R., Samuelson, L., Van Huyck, J. (2001). "Optimization incentives and coordination failure in laboratory stag hunt games". Econometrica 69, 749–764.

Batten, D.F. (2000). Discovering Artificial Economics: How Agents Learn and Economies Evolve. Westview Press, Boulder, CO.

Beltrametti, L., et al. (1997). "A learning-to-forecast experiment on the foreign exchange market with a classifier system". Journal of Economic Dynamics and Control 21, 1543–1575.

Bendor, J., Mookherjee, D., Ray, D. (2001). "Aspiration-based reinforcement learning in repeated interaction games: An overview". International Game Theory Review 3, 159–174.

Bendor, J., Diermeir, D., Ting, M. (2003). "A behavioral model of turnout". American Political Science Review 97, 261–280.

Bereby-Meyer, Y., Erev, I. (1998). "On learning to become a successful loser: A comparison of alternative abstractions of learning in the loss domain". Journal of Mathematical Psychology 42, 266–286.

Blume, A., DeJong, D.V., Neumann, G.R., Savin, N.E. (2002). "Learning and communication in sender–receiver games: An econometric investigation". Journal of Applied Econometrics 17, 225–247.

Börgers, T., Sarin, R. (2000). "Naive reinforcement learning with endogenous aspirations". International Economic Review 41, 921–950.

Bosch-Doménech, A., Sunder, S. (2001). "Tracking the invisible hand: Convergence of double auctions to competitive equilibrium". Computational Economics 16, 257–284.

Boylan, R.T., El-Gamal, M.A. (1993). "Fictitious play: A statistical study of multiple economic experiments". Games and Economic Behavior 5, 205–222.

Bray, M.M., Savin, N.E. (1986). "Rational expectations equilibria, learning, and model specification". Econometrica 54, 1129–1160.

Brandts, J., Charness, G. (2000). "Hot vs. cold: Sequential responses and preference stability in experimental games". Experimental Economics 2, 227–238.

Brenner, T. (2006). "Agent learning representation: Advice on modelling economic learning", this handbook.

Brewer, P.J., Huang, M., Nelson, B., Plott, C.R. (2002). "On the behavioral foundations of the law of supply and demand: Human convergence and robot randomness". Experimental Economics 5, 179–208.

Brosig, J., Weimann, J., Yang, C.-L. (2003). "The hot versus cold effect in a simple bargaining experiment". Experimental Economics 6, 75–90.

Brown, G.W. (1951). "Iterative solution of games by fictitious play". In: Koopmans, T. (Ed.), Activity Analysis of Production and Allocation. Wiley, New York, pp. 374–376.

Brown, P. (1996). "Experimental evidence on money as a medium of exchange". Journal of Economic Dynamics and Control 20, 583–600.

Brown-Kruse, J.L. (1991). "Contestability in the presence of an alternative market: An experimental examination". Rand Journal of Economics 22, 136–147.

Bullard, J., Duffy, J. (1998). "A model of learning and emulation with artificial adaptive agents". Journal of Economic Dynamics and Control 22, 179–207.

Bullard, J., Duffy, J. (1999). "Using genetic algorithms to model the evolution of heterogeneous beliefs". Computational Economics 13, 41–60.

Bush, R.R., Mosteller, F. (1955). Stochastic Models for Learning. John Wiley & Sons, New York.

Camerer, C. (2003). Behavioral Game Theory: Experiments in Strategic Interaction. Princeton University Press, Princeton.

Camerer, C., Ho, T.-H. (1999). "Experience-weighted attraction learning in normal form games". Econometrica 67, 827–874.

Camerer, C., Johnson, E., Rymon, T., Sen, S. (1993). "Cognition and framing in sequential bargaining for gains and losses". In: Binmore, K., et al. (Eds.), Frontiers of Game Theory. MIT Press, Cambridge, MA, pp. 27–47.

Carlson, J. (1968). "An invariably stable cobweb model". Review of Economic Studies 35, 360–362.

Chamberlin, E.H. (1948). "An experimental imperfect market". Journal of Political Economy 56, 95–108.

Chan, N.T., LeBaron, B., Lo, A.W., Poggio, T. (1999). "Agent-based models of financial markets: A comparison with experimental markets", working paper.

Chen, S.H. (2002). Genetic Algorithms and Genetic Programming in Computational Finance. Kluwer, Dordrecht.

Chen, S.H., Yeh, C.H. (1996). "Genetic programming learning and the cobweb model". In: Angeline, P.J., Kinnear, K.E. Jr. (Eds.), Advances in Genetic Programming 2. MIT Press, Cambridge, MA, pp. 443–466.

Chen, S.H., Duffy, J., Yeh, C.H. (2002). "Equilibrium selection via adaptation: Using genetic programming to model learning in a coordination game". The Electronic Journal of Evolutionary Modelling and Economic Dynamicshttp://e-jemed.org~article~1002 .

Cheung, Y.-W., Friedman, D. (1997). "Learning in evolutionary games: some laboratory results". Games and Economic Behavior 19, 46–76.

Cheung, Y.-W., Friedman, D. (1998). "A comparison of learning and replicator dynamics using experimental data". Journal of Economic Behavior and Organization 35, 263–280.

Cliff, D., Bruten, J. (1997a). "Minimal-intelligence agents for bargaining behaviors in market-based environments", Technical report HP-97-91, Hewlett–Packard Research Labs, Bristol, England.

Cliff, D., Bruten, J. (1997b). "More than zero intelligence needed for continuous double-auction trading", Hewlett Packard Laboratories Paper HPL-97-157, Bristol, England.

Coursey, D., Issac, R.M., Luke, M., Smith, V.L. (1984). "Market contestability in the presence of sunk (entry) costs". Rand Journal of Economics 15, 69–84.

Costa-Gomes, M., Crawford, V., Broseta, B. (2001). "Cognition and behavior in normal-form games: An experimental study". Econometrica 69, 1193–1235.

Cox, J.C., Roberson, B., Smith, V.L. (1982). "Theory and behavior of single object auctions". In: Smith, V.L. (Ed.), Research in Experimental Economics. JAI Press, Greenwich, CT.

Crockett, S. (2004). "Learning competitive equilibrium in experimental exchange economies", working paper, Carnegie-Mellon University.

Crockett, S., Spear, S., Sunder, S. (2004). "A simple decentralized institution for learning competitive equilibrium", working paper, Carnegie-Mellon and Yale Universities.

Cross, J.G. (1983). A Theory of Adaptive Economic Behavior. Cambridge University Press, Cambridge, UK.

Cyert, R.M., March, J.G. (1956). "Organizational factors in the theory of oligopoly". Quarterly Journal of Economics 70, 44–64.

Davis, D.D., Holt, C.A. (1993). Experimental Economics. Princeton University Press, Princeton.

Dawid, H. (1999a). Adaptive Learning by Genetic Algorithms: Analytical Results and Applications to Economic Models, 2nd revised and enlarged edition. Springer-Verlag, Berlin.

Dawid, H. (1999b). "On the convergence of genetic learning in a double auction market". Journal of Economic Dynamics and Control 23, 1545–1569.

Duffy, J. (2001). "Learning to speculate: Experiments with artificial and real agents". Journal of Economic Dynamics and Control 25, 295–319.

Duffy, J., Feltovich, N. (1999). "Does observation of others affect learning in strategic environments? an experimental study". International Journal of Game Theory 28, 131–152.

Duffy, J., Ochs, J. (1999). "Emergence of money as a medium of exchange: An experimental study". American Economic Review 89, 847–877.

Duffy, J., Engle-Warnick, J. (2002). "Using symbolic regression to infer strategies from experimental data". In: Chen, S.H. (Ed.), Evolutionary Computation in Economics and Finance. Physica-Verlag, New York, pp. 61–82.

Duffy, J., Ochs, J. (2002). "Intrinsically worthless objects as media of exchange: Experimental evidence". International Economic Review 43, 637–673.

Duffy, J., Hopkins, E. (2005). "Learning, information and sorting in market entry games: Theory and evidence". Games and Economic Behavior 51, 31–62.

Duffy, J., Ünver, M.U. (2006). "Asset price bubbles and crashes with near zero-intelligence traders". Economic Theory 27, 537–563.

Ellison, G. (1993). "Learning, local interaction and coordination". Econometrica 61, 1047–1071.

Easley, D., Ledyard, J.O. (1993). "Theories of price formation and exchange in double oral auctions". In: Friedman, D., Rust, J. (Eds.), The Double Auction Market: Institutions Theories, and Evidence, Santa Fe Institute Studies in the Sciences of Complexity, vol. 14. Addison–Wesley, Reading, MA, pp. 63–97.

Epstein, J.M., Axtell, R. (1996). Growing Artificial Societies: Social Science from the Bottom Up. MIT Press, Cambridge, MA.

Erev, I., Roth, A.E. (1998). "Predicting how people play games: Reinforcement learning in experimental games with unique, mixed strategy equilibria". American Economic Review 88, 848–881.

Erev, I., Barron, G. (2003). "On adaptation, maximization and reinforcement learning among cognitive strategies", working paper, Technion and Harvard Universities.

Erev, I., Bereby-Meyer, Y., Roth, A.E. (1999). "The effect of adding a constant to all payoffs: Experimental investigation and implications for reinforcement learning models". Journal of Economic Behavior and Organization 39, 111–128.

Ezekiel, M. (1938). "The cobweb theorem". Quarterly Journal of Economics 52, 255–280.

Feltovich, N. (2000). "Reinforcement-based vs. belief-based learning models in experimental asymmetric information games". Econometrica 68, 605–641.

Franke, R. (2003). "Reinforcement learning in the El Farol model". Journal of Economic Behavior and Organization 51, 367–388.

Friedman (1991). "A simple testable model of double auction markets". Journal of Economic Behavior and Organization 15, 47–70.

Friedman (1996). "Equilibrium in evolutionary games: some experimental results". Economic Journal 106, 1–25.

Foster, D., Young, H.P. (1990). "Stochastic evolutionary game dynamics". Theoretical Population Biology 38, 219–232.

Fudenberg, D., Levine, D.K. (1998). The Theory of Learning in Games. MIT Press, Cambridge, MA.

Gale, D., Shapley, L.S. (1962). "College admissions and the stability of marriage". American Mathematical Monthly 69, 9–15.

Gjerstad, S., Dickhaut, J. (1998). "Price formation in double auctions". Games and Economic Behavior 22, 1–29.

Gode, D.K., Sunder, S. (1993). "Allocative efficiency of markets with zero-intelligence traders: Market as a partial substitute for individual rationality". Journal of Political Economy 101, 119–137.

Gode, D.K., Sunder, S. (1997a). "What makes markets allocationally efficient?". Quarterly Journal of Economics 112, 603–630.

Gode, D.K., Sunder, S. (1997b). "Lower bounds for efficiency of surplus extraction in double auctions". In: Friedman, D., Rust, J. (Eds.), The Double Auction Market: Institutions Theories, and Evidence, Santa Fe Institute Studies in the Sciences of Complexity, vol. 14. Addison–Wesley, Reading, MA, pp. 199–220.

Gode, D.K., Sunder, S. (2004). "Double auction dynamics: structural effects of non-binding price controls". Journal of Economic Dynamics and Control 28, 1707–1731.

Gode, D.K., Spear, S.E., Sunder, S. (2000). "Convergence of double auctions to competitive equilibrium in an Edgeworth box", working paper.

Goldberg, D.E. (1989). Genetic Algorithms in Search, Optimization, and Machine Learning. Addison–Wesley, Reading, MA.

Grossklags, J., Schmidt, C. (2004). "Artificial software agents on thin double auction markets—A human trader experiment", working paper, University of California, Berkeley.

Haruvy, E., Ünver, M.U. (2002). "Equilibrium selection in repeated B2B matching markets", working paper, University of Texas, Dallas and Koç University.

Haruvy, E., Roth, A.E., Ünver, M.U. (2002). "The dynamics of law clerk matching: An experimental and computational investigation of proposals for reform of the market", working paper.

Haruvy, E., Stahl, D.O. (2004). "Deductive versus inductive equilibrium selection: Experimental results". Journal of Economic Behavior and Organization 53, 319–331.

Ho, T.-H., Camerer, C., Chong, J.-K. (2002). "Economic value of EWA lite: A functional theory of learning in games", working paper.

Hofbauer, J., Sigmund, K. (1988). The Theory of Evolution and Dynamical Systems: Mathematical Aspects of Selection. Cambridge University Press, Cambridge, UK.

Hofbauer, J., Sigmund, K. (1998). Evolutionary Games and Population Dynamics. Cambridge University Press, Cambridge, UK.

Holland, J.H. (1975). Adaptation in Natural and Artificial Systems. University of Michigan Press, Ann Arbor, MI.

Holland, J.H. (1986). "Escaping brittleness: The possibilities of general purpose learning algorithms applied to parallel rule-based systems". In: Michalski, R.S., Carbonell, J.G., Mitchell, T.M. (Eds.), Machine Learning: An Artificial Intelligence Approach. Morgan Kaufmann, Los Altos, CA.

Hommes, C.H. (1994). "Dynamics of the cobweb model with adaptive expectations and nonlinear supply and demand". Journal of Economic Behavior and Organization 24, 315–335.

Hopkins, E. (2002). "Two competing models of how agents learn in games". Econometrica 70, 2141–2166.

Huck, S., Konrad, K.A., Müller, W., Normann, H.-T. (2002). "Mergers and the perception of market power", working paper, University College London.

Isaac, R.M., Plott, C.R. (1981). "Price controls and the behavior of auction markets: An experimental evaluation". American Economic Review 71, 448–459.

Judd, K.L. (1997). "Computational economics and economic theory: Substitutes or complements?". Journal of Economic Dynamics and Control 21, 907–942.

Judd, K.L. (1998). Numerical Methods in Economics. MIT Press, Cambridge, MA.

Kaelbling, L.P., Littman, M.L., Moore, A.W. (1996). "Reinforcement learning: A survey". Journal of Artificial Intelligence Research 4, 237–285.

Kagel, J.H., Levin, D. (1986). "The winner's curse and public information in common value auctions". American Economic Review 76, 894–920.

Kagel, J.H., Roth, A.E. (2000). "The dynamics of reorganization in matching markets: A laboratory experiment motivated by a natural experiment". Quarterly Journal of Economics 115, 201–235.

Kagel, J.H., Harstad, R.M., Levin, D. (1987). "Information impact and allocation rules in auctions with affiliated private values: A laboratory study". Econometrica 55, 1275–1304.

Kandori, M., Mailath, G.J., Rob, R. (1993). "Learning, mutation, and long run equilibria in games". Econometrica 61, 29–56.

Karandikar, R., Mookherjee, D., Ray, D., Vega-Redondo, F. (1998). "Evolving aspirations and cooperation". Journal of Economic Theory 80, 292–331.

Kareken, J.H., Wallace, N. (1981). "On the indeterminacy of equilibrium exchange rates". Quarterly Journal of Economics 96, 207–222.

Kiyotaki, N., Wright, R. (1989). "On money as a medium of exchange". Journal of Political Economy 97, 927–954.

Koza, J.R. (1992). Genetic Programming. MIT Press, Cambridge, MA.

Kutschinski, E., Uthmann, T., Polani, D. (2003). "Learning competitive pricing strategies by multi-agent reinforcement learning". Journal of Economic Dynamics and Control 27, 2207–2218.

LeBaron, B. (2006). "Agent-based computational finance", this handbook.

Lettau, M., Uhlig, H. (1999). "Rules of thumb versus dynamic programming". American Economic Review 89, 148–174.

Lucas, R.E. (1986). "Adaptive behavior and economic theory". Journal of Business 59, S401–S426.

Mackie-Mason, J., Wellman, M. (2006). "Automated markets and trading agents", this handbook.

Marcet, A., Sargent, T.J. (1989). "Least-squares learning and the dynamics of hyperflation". In: Barnett, et al. (Eds.), Economic Complexity: Chaos, Sunspots, Bubbles, and Nonlinearity. Cambridge University Press, New York, pp. 119–137.

Marimon, R., Sunder, S. (1993). "Indeterminacy of equilibria in a hyperinflationary world: Experimental evidence". Econometrica 61, 1073–1107.

Marimon, R., Sunder, S. (1994). "Expectations and learning under alternative monetary regimes: An experimental approach". Economic Theory 4, 131–162.

Marimon, R., McGrattan, E., Sargent, T.J. (1990). "Money as a medium of exchange in an economy with artificially intelligent agents". Journal of Economic Dynamics and Control 14, 329–373.

Michalewicz, Z. (1996). Genetic Algorithms + Data Structures = Evolution Programs, 3rd edition. Springer-Verlag, Berlin.

Miller, R.M. (2002). Paving Wall Street: Experimental Economics and the Quest for the Perfect Market. John Wiley, New York.

Mirowski, P. (2002). Machine Dreams: Economics Becomes a Cyborg Science. Cambridge University Press, Cambridge, UK.

Mitchell, T.M. (1997). Machine Learning. McGraw Hill, New York.

Morris, S. (2000). "Contagion". Review of Economic Studies 67, 57–78.

Mookherjee, D., Sopher, B. (1997). "Learning and decision costs in experimental constant sum games". Games and Economic Behavior 19, 97–132.

Mookherjee, D., Sopher, B. (1994). "Learning behavior in an experimental matching pennies game". Games and Economic Behavior 7, 62–91.

Nicolaisen, J., Petrov, V., Tesfatsion, L. (2001). "Market power and efficiency in a computational electricity market with discriminatory double auction pricing". IEEE Transactions on Evolutionary Computation 5, 504–523.

Nyarko, Y., Schotter, A. (2002). "An experimental study of belief learning using elicited beliefs". Econometrica 70, 971–1005.

Ochs, J. (1995). "Games with unique, mixed strategy equilibria: An experimental study". Games and Economic Behavior 10, 202–217.

Pemantle, R., Skyrms, B. (2003). "Network formation by reinforcement learning: The long and medium run", working paper, UC Irivne.

Pingle, M., Tesfatsion, L. (2001). "Non-employment payoffs and the evolution of worker-employer cooperation: Experiments with real and computational agents", Economic Report 55, Iowa State University.

Riechmann, T. (1999). "Learning and behavioral stability—An economic interpretation of genetic algorithms". Journal of Evolutionary Economics 9, 225–242.

Riechmann, T. (2001a). Learning in Economics: Analysis and Application of Genetic Algorithms. Springer-Verlag, Berlin.

Riechmann, T. (2001b). "Genetic algorithm learning and evolutionary games". Journal of Economic Dynamics and Control 25, 1019–1037.

Riechmann, T. (2002). "Cournot or Walras? Agent based learning, Rationality and long run results in oligopoly games", discussion paper, University of Hannover.

Robinson, J. (1951). "An iterative method of solving a game". The Annals of Mathematics 54, 296–301.

Roth, A.E. (1995). "Introduction to experimental economics". In: Kagel, J., Roth, A.E. (Eds.), Handbook of Experimental Economics. Princeton University Press, Princeton, NJ.

Roth, A.E., Murnighan, J.K. (1978). "Equilibrium behavior and repeated play of the prisoner's dilemma". Journal of Mathematical Psychology 17, 189–198.

Roth, A.E., Erev, I. (1995). "Learning in extensive-form games: Experimental data and simple dynamic models in the intermediate term". Games and Economic Behavior 8, 164–212.

Sadrieh, A. (1998). The Alternating Double Auction Market: A Game Theoretic and Experimental Investigation. Lecture Notes in Economics and Mathematical Systems, vol. 466. Springer, Berlin.

Salmon, T.C. (2001). "An evaluation of econometric models of adaptive learning". Econometrica 69, 1597–1628.

Sargent, T.J. (1993). Bounded Rationality in Macroeconomics. Oxford University Press, Oxford.

Sarin, R., Vahid, F. (1999). "Payoff assessments without probabilities: A simple dynamic model of choice". Games and Economic Behavior 28, 294–309.

Sarin, R., Vahid, F. (2001). "Predicting how people play games: A simple dynamic model of choice". Games and Economic Behavior 34, 104–122.

Schelling, T.C. (1978). Micromotives and Macrobehavior. W.W. Norton, New York.

Selten, R. (1967). "Die strategiemethdoe zur erforschung des eingeschränkt rationalen verhaltens im rahmen eines oligopolexperiments". In: Sauermann, H. (Ed.), Beiträge zur Experimentellen Wirtschaftsforschung. J.C.B. Mohr, Tübingen, pp. 136–168.

Selten, R. (1991). "Evolution, learning and economic behavior". Games and Economic Behavior 3, 3–24.

Selten, R., Mitzkewitz, M., Uhlich, G.R. (1997). "Duopoly strategies programmed by experienced players". Econometrica 65, 517–555.

Simon, H.A. (1955). "A behavioral model of rational choice". Quarterly Journal of Economics 69, 99–118.

Simon, H.A. (1982). Models of Bounded Rationality. MIT Press, Cambridge, MA.

Smith, V.L. (1962). "An experimental study of competitive market behavior". Journal of Political Economy 70, 111–137.

Smith, V.L. (1982). "Microeconomic systems as an experimental science". American Economic Review 72, 923–955.

Smith, V.L., Williams, A.W. (1981). "On nonbinding price controls in a competitive market". American Economic Review 71, 467–474.

Smith, V.L., Suchanek, G.L., Williams, A.W. (1988). "Bubbles, crashes, and endogenous expectations in experimental spot asset markets". Econometrica 56, 1119–1151.

Sonnemans, J., Hommes, C., Tuinstra, J., v.d. Velden, H. (2004). "The instability of a heterogeneous cobweb economy: A strategy experiment on expectation formation". Journal of Economic Behavior and Organization 54, 453–481.

Stahl, D. (1999). "A horse race among action-reinforcement learning models", working paper, University of Texas-Austin.

Suppes, P., Atkinson, R. (1960). Markov Learning Models for Multiperson Interactions. Stanford University Press, Stanford.

Sutton, R.S., Barto, A.G. (1998). Reinforcement Learning: An Introduction. MIT Press, Cambridge, MA.

Thorndike, E.L. (1911). Animal Intelligence. Hafner Publishing, New York.

Ünver, M.U. (2001a). "Backward unraveling over time: The evolution of strategic behavior in the entry level British medical labor markets". Journal of Economic Dynamics and Control 25, 1039–1080.

Ünver, M.U. (2001b). "On the survival of some unstable two-sided matching mechanisms: An experimental and computational investigation of the stability hypothesis", working paper, Koç University.

Valley, K., Thompson, L., Gibbons, R., Bazerman, M.H. (2002). "How communication improves efficiency in bargaining games". Games and Economic Behavior 38, 127–155.

Van Boening, M.V., Wilcox, N.T. (1996). "Avoidable cost: Ride a double auction roller coaster". American Economic Review 86, 461–477.

Van Huyck, J.B., Cook, J.P., Battalio, R.C. (1994). "Selection dynamics, asymptotic stability, and adaptive behavior". Journal of Political Economy 102, 975–1005.

Van Huyck, J.B., Cook, J.P., Battalio, R.C. (1997). "Adaptive behavior and coordination failure". Journal of Economic Behavior and Organization 32, 483–503.

Vriend, N.J. (2000). "An illustration of the essential difference between individual and social learning, and its consequences for computational analyses". Journal of Economic Dynamics and Control 24, 1–19.

Watkins, C. (1989). Learning From Delayed Rewards (PhD Dissertation), King's College Cambridge, England.

Wellford, C.P. (1989). "A laboratory analysis of price dynamics and expectations in the cobweb model", Discussion Paper 89-15, Department of Economics, University of Arizona.

Young, P.H. (1993). "The evolution of conventions". Econometrica 61, 57–84.

Young, P.H. (1998). Individual Strategy and Social Structure: An Evolutionary Theory of Institutions. Princeton University Press, Princeton.

Chapter 20

ECONOMIC ACTIVITY ON FIXED NETWORKS

ALLEN WILHITE [*]

Department of Economics and Finance, University of Alabama in Huntsville, Huntsville, AL 35899, USA
e-mail: wilhitea@uah.edu; url: http://cas.uah.edu/wilhitea

Contents

[*] I am indebted to Leigh Tesfatsion, Nick Vriend, David Allen, and an anonymous reader who graciously made several recommendations on earlier drafts. I am also grateful for the feedback given at the *Handbook* workshop held at the Center for the Study of Complex Systems, University of Michigan.

Handbook of Computational Economics, Volume 2. Edited by Leigh Tesfatsion and Kenneth L. Judd
DOI: 10.1016/S1574-0021(05)02020-4

Abstract

A large portion of our economic interactions involves a very small portion of the population. We seem to prefer familiar venues. But the tendency to focus our attention on a few individuals or activities is an attribute that is typically omitted in our characterization of markets. In markets agents seem to interact impersonally and efficiently with countless other faceless agents. This chapter looks into the consequences of including a connection between agents, a tendency to interact with a specific few, in economic decision making. Agents are assumed to occupy the nodes of a network and to interact exclusively with agents to whom they are directly linked. We then study evolution of game strategies and the effectiveness of exchange as the topology of the underlying network is altered. We find that networks matter, that changes in a network's structure can alter the steady-state attributes of an artificial society as well as the dynamics of that system.

Keywords

networks, games on networks, exchange on networks, small worlds, power networks

JEL classification: B4, C63, C7, D5, D83

1. Introduction

For the most part, neoclassical economics views individuals as independent decision makers. People have tastes and preferences and an endowment of resources they employ to maximize their well-being. Agents trade through markets, prices reflect the actions of others, and people tune their decisions to the information broadcast by those prices. Interaction among individuals is institutionalized, impersonal and impartial. This formalization allows a rigor to exist in the field of economics seldom seen in the other social sciences.

But sometimes these impersonal markets are too artificial. Individuals are influenced by more than prices; often they are influenced by others. Typically we turn to game theory in those cases, as it allows us to study how the actions of one individual influence the behavior of another. But even as game theory stresses the interplay between decision makers, it says little about who plays the game. Hearkening back to sociologists who study neighborhoods and peer groups, imitative behavior and learning, economists are beginning to re-explore not only the effects of interaction but also the identity of the agents involved in that interaction. Enter networks. In the last 10 years or so, empirical and theoretical studies have begun to investigate how networks, as structures underlying economic activity, influence behavior. This chapter continues that investigation by examining unchanging, fixed, or stable networks. In reality, truly fixed networks may not exist: institutions and relationships grow, evolve, and eventually fade. But if this evolution is slow relative to the economic activity taking place on the network, the characteristics of the network will have a larger effect on economic decisions than those decisions will have on the network.

Networks become particularly useful when agents primarily interact with only a small part of the population, or in network parlance, when agents interact with their neighbors. There is a familiarity in this: each of us tends to shop at the same stores, interact with the same individuals at work and at play, read the same magazines and newspapers; and even the most gregarious among us limit our conversation to a tiny fraction of the available ears. Surely this narrowing of our attention constrains the flow of information and impacts our economic activities.

Or maybe not. In 1967, Stanley Milgram's famous letter-delivery experiment suggested that even with limited individual interaction, we still manage to connect to distant parts of the world. Even though many economic activities occur locally, they seem to have global reach. What is going on? How do bits of information, goods and services, opinions, and attitudes percolate through a population? These activities are increasingly being explored by placing people on a network, using the network architecture to reflect the many ways individuals can be connected.

All of the traditional tools of economists—theory, empirical testing, and experimentation—have been applied to study the questions raised by networks, but each has its shortcomings. Mathematical theory is confounded by the architecture of many networks; some are too irregular to describe analytically and yet have too much structure to be treated as random and thus statistically regular.[1] Lacking theory, empirical studies are reduced to description and testing ad-hoc hypotheses. Experiments on networks are hampered by their limited time horizon and severe size restrictions. These limitations become especially problematic when certain features of a network emerge only in the presence of many, many nodes, or when features emerge only over time.

Agent-based computational modeling is ideally suited for studying networks and economic activity on networks. ACE researchers can program complex networks with relative ease (but some tedium) and let thousands of agents interact thousands of times on these networks. Virtual experiments can be conducted time and again with the researcher making but a single change in the system and observing the effects of that change. Every decision can be captured and examined. In this way even subtle effects can be revealed with a systematic stream of computations. Of course, agent-based modeling does have shortcomings; it cannot establish proofs, other than existence claims or where a proof is available through exhaustion.

This chapter conducts a string of agent-based, virtual experiments investigating two fundamental economic activities undertaken on a variety of networks. Upon this structure, the literature on static or fixed networks will be draped, and some of the gaps between the existing studies will be filled. By necessity we ignore the infinite variety of networks available for study and instead concentrate on a few that have been singled out as notable and deserving of exploration. We first describe these networks and give a rationale for their selection. We then investigate cooperation by having virtual agents play a series of games on those networks. Finally we consider bilateral trade by letting our agents exchange goods on those same networks. Throughout, we try to keep all other aspects of the experiments unchanged and by comparing results of identical agents on different networks we tickle out some of the effects most readily explained by network structure.

2. Some notable networks

Economists approach networks as reflecting a set of choices, outcomes of interactions between individual decision-makers. Excellent reviews of the analytical literature on the emergence of networks include Jackson (2004), and Goyal (2002) and for an overview of the computational literature on emerging networks see Vriend (2006). Physicists also study networks but appear more interested in their topology, their statistical properties, and how a network with a particular set of attributes might be created in a mechanistic way (see for example Watts, 1999, Newman, 2000, and Barabási, 2002). They appear less interested in the origins of networks and the decisions of individual agents embedded within. But all of these studies focus on a relatively small set of networks, a practice we will follow here.

---

[1] For instance, many of the advances in graph theory rely on random graphs.

As is customary in network studies, we borrow much of our nomenclature from graph theory. We investigate a population of n agents on a network, G, which is an unordered list of the linked pairs of agents $\{i, j\}$ written as $i \sim j$. So the phrase $i \sim j \in G$ means agents i and j are linked in network G. In this chapter, links are *undirected*; that is, if $i \sim j \in G$ then $j \sim i \in G$. All networks are *simple*, in that only one edge connects any linked pair and no link connects a node to itself. The networks are *connected*, meaning any node can be reached from any other node by following a path made up of a finite number of edges. Finally, our edges are *unweighted* in that no edge has any intrinsic value (length or quality) that differs from other edges. Thus the importance of any particular edge derives solely from its location relative to the other edges in the network.

Using this notation and terminology we will define seven specific networks that frame the rest of the study: the *complete* network, the *star*, the *ring*, the *grid*, the *tree*, the *small-world* network, and the scale-free or *power* network. We focus on these seven because they emerge from certain types of behavior, have interesting attributes, and/or reflect networks found in nature. Clearly we omit an infinite variety of other networks, some possessing interesting properties, but this cross-section allows us to address many of the central issues arising in network studies. Our first task is to describe each network and give a brief justification for its inclusion. As a visual aid to the descriptions below, Table 1 provides a sketch of these networks.

2.1. The complete network

In a complete network every node is connected to every other node, that is, $i \sim j \in G$ $\forall i, j, i \neq j$. Although few examples of sizeable, completely-connected networks exist in nature (the telephone system in a developed country is probably close), the abstract simplicity of this network makes it a good starting point. The complete network surfaces as a stable network structure in several studies of network formation. For example, Jackson and Wolinsky (1996) design a model in which agents choose to establish links with other agents because links accrue benefits, but their creation and maintenance is costly. They then define "pairwise stability" as occurring when no pair of agents wishes to establish more links and no individual agent wishes to sever a link. If the costs of establishing and maintaining a link is low relative to the benefits of having such a link, the pairwise stable network is the complete network. Bala and Goyal (2000a, 2000b) study a similar situation where single agents can establish links, and they also find that the complete network is stable.

2.2. The star

The star is a network in which some randomly selected agent, s, is linked to the others, but no other agents are connected; $s \sim j \in G$ $\forall j, s \neq j$. Some have proposed the star network as a representation of the abstract marketplace, with the fictitious Walrasian auctioneer occupying the center. But as Tesfatsion points out in Chapter 16 of this

Table 1
Sketches of seven networks

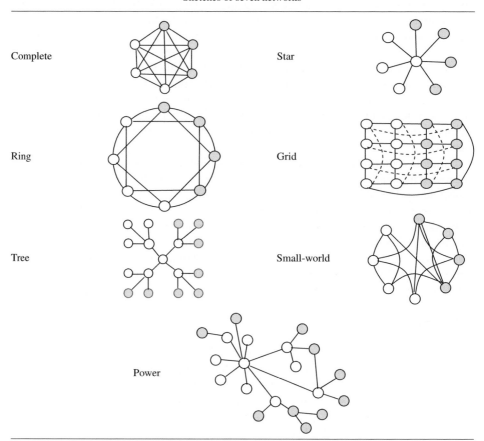

Complete   Star

Ring   Grid

Tree   Small-world

Power

* The shaded nodes illustrate the endowment differences used in Section 4.

Handbook, such simplification glosses over the procurement processes and information systems that are required in practice. Bala and Goyal (2000b) study network reliability (the likelihood that a piece of information traveling over a network's links successfully reaches its intended destination) and network decay (how information degrades as it travels more links). They too use the idea of Nash equilibrium as agents wire and rewire until there is no incentive to continue. Decay leads to efficient and minimally connected networks, like the star, while reliability concerns lead to redundantly wired structures like the complete network. Hendricks et al. (1995) investigate a hypothetical airline trying to optimize its routes. They assume that most of the airline's customers want to fly between two cities out of the group of cities it serves. Given sufficient economies of density, the optimal network is a star. Customers first fly to the center (the hub) and then to their destination.

2.3. The ring

To visualize a ring network, imagine agents sitting around a table, agent i being linked to k neighbors half of which sit to his left and half to his right. Formally,

$$i \sim j \in G \quad \text{if} \begin{cases} j = \{(i-m)+n\} \bmod n \text{ or} \\ j = \{i+m\} \bmod n \end{cases},$$

$$\text{where } m \in \left\{1, 2, \ldots, \frac{k}{2}\right\} \text{ and } k \text{ is an even number.}$$

With the ring we introduce local neighborhood constraints, that is, unlike the complete and star network there is no agent who interacts with everyone else; agents interact only with a fraction of the population. The ring is commonly used as a substrate for network studies because its simple architecture ensures that the graph will be connected even though there are few edges and because it imposes minimal structure on the network (there are no "more central" or "more peripheral" nodes for example). The ring also emerges as a stable network in Bala and Goyal (2000a).

2.4. The grid

Given that economics seems to rely on two-dimensional graphics more than any other social science, it seems natural to include the grid network in our review. A simple grid is a chessboard with nodes residing at the corners of each square. Explicitly, in a grid

$$\text{network: } i \sim j \in G \quad \text{if} \begin{cases} j = \{(i \pm 1)+n\} \bmod n \text{ or} \\ j = \{(i \pm n^{1/2})+n\} \bmod n \end{cases}.$$

The grid also fits our intuitive perception of space; we tend to orientate ourselves in a two-dimensional fashion as we move along the surface of the planet. The applications of a grid network are many: the layout of city blocks, rooms on the floor of a building, and townships in the mid-west and western states. Note that the above formula for the grid eliminates boundary effects by connecting the opposing edges. The resulting three-dimensional form is a torus.

2.5. The tree

A tree is a network in which each node branches off to k other nodes, each of which branches again and so forth. Formally: $i \sim j \in G$ if $i = 1$ and $j = 2 + (0, 1, \ldots, k)$ and if $i > 1$, $j = (ki + v)$, $v \in \{0, 1, \ldots, k-1\}$ where k is the number of edges connecting each node. Tree networks are frequently used to describe hierarchical social systems, mechanical systems, and organizations. For instance, the organization of power in a government, the supply chain for an industry, and the sewage disposal system for a municipality can be represented as tree networks. Radner (1993) studied the processing of information by the administrative staff of a large organization and found the hierarchical network to be the efficient network structure, although it was quite irregular. Trees have some distinguishing characteristics that will be of particular interest in this paper. Trees have minimal overlap between neighborhoods; in fact, no agent's neighbors are neighbors with each other, and not all nodes are created equal in a tree. There are central nodes that on average carry more traffic than other nodes; and periphery nodes located out on the rim that are completely dependent on another node for their link to the rest of the network.

2.6. Small-worlds

Unlike the structures discussed above, the specific topology of small-world and power networks differs from case to case. Consequently physicists and mathematicians have created a variety of metrics to capture their primary attributes. Three commonly discussed measures are: (i) *path-length*, the average minimum number of edges that must be traversed to get from one node to any other node; (ii) *clustering*, the tendency of nodes to clump together (i.e., if nodes i and j are both connected to node k, then in a cluster, nodes i and j are also connected); and (iii) the *degree* of the graph, or the average number of edges connected to each node.[2]

Watts and Strogatz (1998) investigate a small-world network that lies somewhere between a ring network and a random network. Small-worlds have what seems to be an odd pair of attributes: high clustering and short path-lengths. In other words, most of an individual's neighbors are also neighbors of each other, and yet seemingly distant nodes tend to be just a few steps away. Somehow these small, close-knit neighborhoods have global reach. Thirty years after Milgram's (Milgram, 1967) discovery of small-world activity, Watts and Strogatz provided a structure to explain such behavior. Consequently their work triggered a flurry of papers investigating small-world graphs.

Watts and Strogatz (1998) present an elegant way to construct and think about these networks. Starting with a k-ring, each edge is considered for random rewiring with some probability p. A particular connection, $i \sim j$, is rewired by severing that link at j and then randomly selecting a new node, say h, and creating a link $i \sim h$. If the probability of rewiring equals zero, this process leaves the ring undisturbed. If $p = 1$ every edge will be randomly wired, creating a random graph. But in between, $p \in (0, 1)$, intermediate graphs emerge. Watts (1999) shows that for surprisingly small values of p (and thus with relatively few rewired paths), small-world characteristics like short path-lengths between clusters begin to emerge.

Watts and Strogatz (1998), Watts (1999), and Newman (2000) suggest that electric power grids, the neurological network of a worm (*Caenorhabditis elegans*), and the

---

[2] Often it is not a graph's degree that is of most interest, but its degree distribution.

distribution of coauthors in scientific journals appear to be small-world networks. Goyal et al. (2004) also find an emerging small world in economics co-authorship, although they find characteristics of a power network as well. The key ingredient to small-world networks is the bridging of edges or shortcuts that connect otherwise distant clusters. Thus, while most of your acquaintances reside in your cluster of friends, a few are located elsewhere in the network which connects you and everyone in your cluster to the individuals in this distant group. Just a few of these shortcuts drastically reduces the average path-length of the entire system.

2.7. Power networks

Power networks or scale-free networks have a degree distribution that follows a power law.[3] That is, a few nodes possess many, many edges or are of very high degree (commonly called hubs) and at the other extreme many, many nodes have very few edges. Barabási (2002) shows that a power network emerges from the following exercise. Start with small network of any simple configuration. Add new nodes one at a time with each node making k connections to existing nodes. Select the termination nodes through a preferential weighting such that nodes with more edges are more likely to be selected than nodes with fewer edges. The preferential weighting used here follows Albert and Barabási (2002): $P(i \sim j \in G|i) = j_d/n_d$, where j_d is the number of edges reaching node j and n_d is the total number of edges in the entire network. Recent explorations by Albert and Barabási (2002) and Barabási (2002) suggest that the large-scale structures of the internet and the world-wide-web are power networks. This design lends a great deal of resiliency to the web because random attacks that disable nodes have practically no impact on the overall functioning of the network (most nodes have few edges). However, the power law architecture does render a network susceptible to directed attacks; that is, if one explicitly attacks the high-degree hubs, the performance of the web can be degraded quickly.

3. Coordination and cooperation in networks

Suppose the nodes of a network are occupied by economic agents who directly interact with only their neighbors. How does the topology of the network affect the resulting economic decisions? For the most part this question has been ignored until the last few years. There were early pioneers, but among those the stunning insights of Thomas Schelling stand alone. Reading Schelling's (Schelling, 1969, 1971, 1978) studies changes the way one thinks about economics; they offer a simple yet compelling example of how individual actions can lead to unanticipated aggregate behavior.

---

[3] Albert et al. (1999) pioneered this type of network and because the resulting topology has no characteristic node, they called this a scale-free network.

Schelling (1969, 1971) considers agents who wish to have at least one (or sometimes two) of their neighbors sharing a common attribute. He shows that as people act on this mild desire, the population eventually segregates into distinct groups based on that attribute. This segregation occurs even though no one in the population desires segregation or acts in a way to achieve it. Considered in reverse, Schelling shows how flawed it can be to interpret an aggregate result as reflecting individual preferences. Beyond his social insights, his methodology was novel as well. In a sense, these are some of the first agent-based computational models to appear in the social sciences—decades before their time. His elegant studies have intuitive underpinnings, surprising results, and yet are so simple that just about anyone can explore and tinker to build on his work. The balance of this chapter is just such an exercise as we explore how economic activity is affected by network structure.[4]

First consider coordination and cooperation. Coordination and cooperation are essential in society, as the rules, mores, and conventions that guide interaction often become too costly to formally regulate, monitor and enforce. In some cases citizens have strong private incentives to cooperate and the central problem becomes learning what others do and adapting. In other cases cooperation may be more elusive as individuals have private incentives to *not* cooperate even though cooperation raises aggregate welfare.

To investigate the extent to which agents cooperate or coordinate their activities, economists often turn to game theory. This section focuses on games played on a network; that is, the network identifies which players are to be matched for a game. The classic two-person game is conveniently represented by a two-dimensional matrix with payoffs given in each cell as seen in Figure 1. Consider two players, i and j, who can each play one of two strategies, C or D. For example, if agent i plays strategy C against an opponent j playing strategy D, agent i receives a payoff of b and his opponent receives payoff c. Adjusting the payoffs allows us to explore games of coordination as well as games of cooperation. Both games can be embedded into a network and agents can play against their neighbors. The central question becomes whether identical agents located in different networks adopt different strategies.

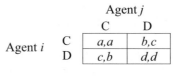

Figure 1.

3.1. Coordination

The game that has received the most scrutiny on networks is a game of coordination. The payoff matrix in Figure 1 describes a game of coordination if we let $a > b$ and

---

[4] I recommend Professor Schelling's recollection of this research in the "perspectives" section of this Handbook (Schelling, 2006).

$d > c$. In this situation each agent can earn a better payoff by playing the same strategy as his opponent, yielding two Nash equilibria, [C,C and D,D]. Notice, however, that payoff a is not necessarily equal to payoff d; thus one of the equilibria may be payoff dominant. When this game is played on a network, the issues typically investigated are: Do societies coordinate, do they find the dominant equilibrium, and how quickly does all this take place?

Ellison (1993) investigates cooperation by comparing local interaction to global decision making. First he randomly matches players in a coordination game and lets the system find its equilibrium. He then places the agents on a ring, restricting their interaction by having them play exclusively with their neighbors. He found, somewhat surprisingly, that the system coordinates its activity more quickly when agents focus on their neighbors. If an agent plays only with his neighbors, the neighborhood, being small, quickly finds the optimal strategy. This quickness replicates throughout the population, and the system converges. Alternatively, randomized play sets agents up with a grab bag of opponents, and it takes longer for agents to learn the prevailing strategy. Ellison and Fudenberg (1993) further consider agents who review the actions of their neighbors and have a tendency to adopt the decision that worked the best. If the returns to each decision incorporate some noise, pure imitation leads to fluctuations in the system, which can take some time to stabilize. But with popularity weighting, meaning the most frequently selected strategy was more likely to be chosen by others, agents find the best alternative more quickly.

Bala and Goyal (2001) look into technological diffusion incorporating the use of historical data and heterogeneous preferences of agents located on a network. They find that if local information is weighted more heavily than global information, different, competing technologies can coexist in a connected network. Bala and Goyal (1998) and Goyal (2002) study agents who play a single strategy with all of their neighbors. After each round of play, agents consider the history of their decisions as well as the complete history of their neighbors' decisions before updating their strategies. At issue is how well agents learn to coordinate their decisions and how network structure affects that learning. First, they create a network in which a particular group of individuals, called the Royal Family, is connected to every other player. This group has enormous influence on the societal outcome, and under most circumstances everyone copies them, even when they make an inferior decision. Bala and Goyal (1998) then contrast that result to results on a line network. In the latter structure society takes longer to coordinate, but becomes more likely to find the optimal solution. In general, Goyal (2002) argues that a network topology that focuses agents locally can improve aggregate learning by restricting the flow of extraneous information.

Morris (2000) uses a coordination game to investigate contagion—the likelihood that a particular strategy spreads to overtake an arbitrary network. He shows that in best response coordination games with a given payoff structure, decisions are more likely to spread the more *cohesive* the neighborhoods and the more *uniform* the network. In a cohesive neighborhood an agent's neighbors tend to be neighbors of one another. Uniformity exists when the neighborhood pattern repeats throughout the network. Cohesiveness encourages all agents in the neighborhood to select the same strategy, while uniformity allows this chosen strategy to spread across the population.

Perhaps the most comprehensive analyses of coordination on a network are those undertaken by Young (1993, 1998), who studies the emergence of societal conventions. He begins with the suggestion that in many situations the hyper-rationality of agents in neoclassical economics is an unreasonable representation of nature. Instead, he considers agents who make sensible decisions, not necessarily optimal ones, and who typically interact with a small portion of the population using the limited information most readily available. Crucial to his work is the evolutionary aspect of games, i.e., while agents are essentially rational, they sometimes neglect to take an action that is warranted or may even take one that is not. Perturbations or mutations such as these allow us to understand how society might sort through multiple equilibria and how it can settle, at least for long periods, on outcomes that are superior.

In many respects, Young formalizes and extends the insights introduced by Schelling. He shows that standard, neoclassical equilibrium solutions to games are frequently the selected conventions of less rational, locally interacting agents. But in addition he shows how there can be punctuated equilibria (systems that tend to stay close to a particular equilibrium for an extended period only to be disrupted to tip into another) and diversity across localities. This diversity across space and time is observed in nature but has resisted explanation. Finally, Young shows that some equilibria are more stable than others and even when individuals react in response to only local signals, they will tend to spend more time near this stochastically stable equilibrium. For greater depths into these issues see Young (2006).

In an examination of the diffusion of innovations through social networks, Young (2002) finds that agents arranged in small, close-knit groups adopt a particular technology more quickly than agents arranged randomly. Burke et al. (2003) studied the practice of physicians choosing one or another treatment by placing hypothetical physicians on a ring network with overlapping neighborhoods. Even when one treatment was superior, their model illustrated how pockets of physicians might choose different approaches, an outcome consistent with empirical evidence of local variation. Similarly, Young and Burke (2001) also present evidence of local diversity in crop-sharing contracts in Illinois even across counties exhibiting relatively uniform productivity of land.

3.2. Cooperation

If individuals have a private incentive not to cooperate, as in a prisoners' dilemma (PD) game, cooperation can be more difficult to attain. The payoff matrix for a conventional prisoner's dilemma game sees $c > a > d > b$ and $2a > (b + c)$. A player has the option to cooperate (C) or not cooperate (or defect, D). Even when individuals have no incentive to cooperate in a single shot PD game, we observe cooperation in experiments and nature. For example, cooperation arises in repeated PD games of uncertain length, and cooperation survives if social success is included in the individuals' utility function, such as when survival of the species benefits an individual by increasing the chances that his genetic code is passed to succeeding generations.

Some suggest that reactive play and learning can also explain the existence of cooperative behavior. Axelrod (1984) has conducted the authoritative analysis of competing strategies in the context of the economics of cooperation. Axelrod takes decision strategies (like TIT for TAT) and has agents play one another in round-robin tournaments. He finds several cooperative strategies can do quite well in repeated play. He also investigates the role of network effects, showing that the success of strategies played on a grid differ from tournament play. For a closer look at Axelrod's study of cooperation see his "perspectives" contribution in this *Handbook* (Axelrod, 2006).

This section probes further into these network differences by comparing play on several different architectures. In the following examples we set up a simple PD game and play it on the seven networks. The specific payoffs (Figure 1) are $a = 4$, $b = 0$, $c = 7$ and $d = 0.1$.[5] Fundamentally we seek to discover how changing the underlying network influences the adoption of a particular strategy. To isolate these effects, we will attempt to keep other attributes of the game constant across the networks. Specifically we shall use the same learning algorithm in all simulations, maintain a constant population size, and replicate the randomly determined initial strategies on every network at time zero. Finally, and central to our discussion, we keep the size of the neighborhood, or the size of the average neighborhood, constant across networks.[6]

Play unfolds as follows. To start, individuals are randomly assigned a strategy, C or D, and they play that strategy in a game with themselves and each of their neighbors.[7] After collecting their payoffs, agents observe their neighbors' strategies and payoffs, and adjust their strategy by copying the strategy of the most successful player in their neighborhood. Using their now updated strategy, agents replay, survey their neighbors again, update, and so forth. Play continues until the aggregate distribution of strategies becomes relatively stable, what we casually call a steady state. That agents imitate winners as opposed to mapping out an optimal strategy is particularly important. Eshel et al. (1998) suggest that people may not think like game theorists or even know they are in a game, but, they write, "people are generally able to form a good estimate of other's payoffs,... and to imitate the behavior of those they observe earning higher profits" (p. 159). In the literature of cooperative play on networks, imitation can take many forms: copying the best average return, copying the best strategy from a sample of neighbors, copying the most frequently used strategy, etc. We have taken one of the simplest approaches; agents copy the most successful player in their neighborhood.

---

[5] As one might expect, the relative size of these payoffs have an enormous impact on the resulting distribution of strategies (see for example Nowak and May, 1992, 1993) but cross-network differences for most (nontrivial) sets of payoffs are persistent.

[6] In the following exercises each agent has four neighbors in a neighborhood of five. Note however, that the complete network and the star have neighborhoods that cannot be replicated in other shapes unless the size of the entire population is limited to five agents.

[7] Nowak and May (1992) suggest self-play captures the idea of family or group play at the node level. As it turns out, the results are not substantially changed if self-play is omitted.

As emphasized by Axtell (2000), the timing of updates can affect the dynamics in an ACE model. Most of the initial studies in cooperation games employed synchronous updating, meaning that every agent updates his strategy after every round of play. Huberman and Glance (1993) explored the opposite extreme by assuming that only a single agent changes his strategy in each period. But this may go too far; it seems unlikely that the vast majority of agents would stick with a losing strategy for so long. Nevertheless, agents may procrastinate due to a conservative bent, a slowness to realize a strategy is losing, or simple laziness. Consequently, Mukherjl et al. (1996) and Nowak et al. (1996) use random updating while Page (1997) and Wilhite (2006) bases updating on an incentive system. The following experiments incorporate two updating routines for every network: synchronous updating in which each agent is allowed to change his strategy each period, and asynchronous or random updating, in which there is a 0.25 chance that any particular agent will change a strategy when such a change is warranted.

Using these rules, we observe an agent-based computational model in which 2500 agents play this PD game on the seven networks of interest. Repeated experiments (fifty trials for each network and updating routine) let us derive typical outcomes for a population starting with an approximate 50/50 split of cooperators and defectors randomly dispersed across the network.

3.2.1. The complete network

In a complete network with synchronous updating everyone becomes a defector after the first round of play as long as at least one agent initially adopts the defection strategy. Consider a network with n individuals, m playing D and $n - m$ playing C. Since every player interacts with every other player, the cooperative agents all earn $4(n - m)$ while the defecting agents earn $7(n - m) + 0.1(m)$. Thus, as long as $m > 0$ cooperators will imitate defectors. The same aggregate result occurs under asynchronous updating although it takes more rounds to get all of the procrastinators to update. In these experiments and reported in Table 2, it takes 27 rounds, on average, for everyone to defect.

3.2.2. The star

In the steady state of the star network with synchronous updating all agents play the same strategy after one round of play: either everyone cooperates or everyone defects. Which strategy dominates depends on the choices made by center player and one other player. Suppose agent s occupies the center of the star and plays strategy D. All players on the rim earn 0 or 0.1 depending on their strategy, while agent s earns $7m + 0.1(n - m)$, where m is the number of cooperators. Consequently all rim players adopt the defection strategy in the second round. On the other hand, if the center agent plays C, he earns $4m$ while the rim defectors earn 7. If $m > 2$ the rim players will copy the center's cooperation strategy. Finally if the center is the only cooperator he switches to defection

Table 2
Proportion of population adopting the cooperative strategy in a prisoners' dilemma game

	Synchronous updating		Asynchronous updating	
	Proportion cooperating	Rounds to steady-state	Proportion cooperating	Rounds to steady-state
Complete	no cooperation	1	no cooperation	27.2 (4.19)
Star	P(all Cs) = ½ P(all Ds) = ½	1	P(all Cs) = ½ P(all Ds) = ½	27.3 (4.10)
Ring	0.967 (.0075)	189.2* (57.45)	0.998 (0.0010)	very large number of rounds
Grid	0.358 (0.071)	no steady state	0.538 (0.071)	no steady state
Tree	P(all Cs) = 0.6 P(all Ds) = 0.4	14.4 (1.12)	0.894 (0.003)	no steady state
Small-world	0.713 (0.021)	150.2* (96.79)	0.700 (0.014)	no steady state
Power	0.947 (0.011)	20.5 (5.22)	0.944 (0.012)	58.4 (13.0)

Top number is the average proportion of cooperators from 50 separate experiments on each network. The second number is the standard deviation of those averages (across experiment variation). Periodic steady states are indicated by *.

immediately. Asynchronous updating leads to the same steady state but again it takes a few rounds for everyone to make the switch.

The complete and star networks yield rather bland results because everyone eventually plays the same strategy. Nature is much richer. Some individuals cooperate, others don't, and still others switch back and forth. One can generate this mixed behavior in a population by imposing utility functions that place value on cooperation, but such an approach raises questions about refutability, making that a less desirable avenue. But as we shall see, a rich mixture of strategies also arises when we alter the underlying topology of the network. We shall also see that in some networks, asynchronous updating not only affects the speed of convergence but can also impact the distribution of strategies in the steady state.

3.2.3. The ring

Consider playing this PD game on a ring with a neighborhood of five individuals. Use the same learning rules, begin with a set of strategies assigned randomly across the network and assume updating is synchronous. The surprising result is that both strategies almost always survive and cooperation does quite well. Society evolves into all defectors only if the initial distribution contains no string with more than three cooperators, and pure cooperation arises only if the initial distribution contains no defectors. Otherwise both strategies survive and cooperators make up the majority of the population. This result was initially put forth by Eshel et al. (1998). Their study used a smaller neighborhood ($k = 2$) and their learning algorithm was different (players adopted the strategy that worked best on average), but this curious result is theirs.

Eshel et al. (1998) provide a proof of their finding making it unnecessary to do so here, but an intuitive explanation of this outcome can help us understand neighborhood effects in the present setting. In a prisoners' dilemma defection dominates any particular game thus it seems likely that defection would spread throughout a ring. It does not. Consider a string of at least four cooperators in a row, hemmed in by defectors, as shown below:

$$\ldots - D - D - D - C - \overbrace{C_i - C_j - C_k - D_l - D_m}^{neighborhood_k} - D - D - D - \ldots$$

Subscripts indicate which agent plays the accompanying strategy and the top brace identifies agent k's neighborhood. Agent k earns a payoff of 12, but he sees agent l earning $2 \times 7 + 3 \times 0.1 = 14.3$ and agent j who earns 16. Thus, his best option is to copy agent j and retain his cooperative strategy. Agent l, currently defecting, sees agents k and m, each earning a payoff less than his own, but he also sees agent j whose payoff of 16 exceeds own. Thus agent l switches to C, and in the following round agent m switches to C, and so forth. Cooperation spreads down the line. A similar situation on the left-hand-side of the cooperators spreads cooperation in that direction. Thus these four initial cooperators spread around the ring. If these four cooperators were the only ones in the initial population they would continue to spread until their strings met on the other side of the ring. What happens?

Suppose things had progressed until a single defector remained.

$$\cdots - C - C - C - C_p - D_q - C_r - C - C - C - C \cdots$$

Now agent q, the last defector, earns $4 \times 7 + 0.1 = 28.1$ which exceeds the payoffs of all the other agents, and in the following round all of his neighbors will adopt his strategy, D. But this creates a string of defectors in which the defectors at ends of the string earn less than one of their cooperative neighbors (as above). Thus, the two end agents switch back to cooperation in the following round, the next two switch in the subsequent round, and we get a three-cycle "blinker" consisting of $(1, 5, 3)$, $(1, 5, 3)$, $\ldots$, defectors as shown here:

round t $\ldots - C - C - C - C_p - D_q - C_r - C - C - C \ldots$ (one defector)

round $t + 1$ $\ldots - C - C - D - D_p - D_q - D_r - D - C - C \ldots$ (five defectors)

round $t + 2$ $\ldots - C - C - C - D_p - D_q - D_r - C - C - C \ldots$ (three defectors)

round $t + 3$ $\ldots - C - C - C - C_p - D_q - C_r - C - C - C \ldots$ (one defector)

Similarly, if a string shrinks to just two defectors, both remaining defectors earn more than all of their cooperative neighbors and defection spreads to their neighbors. Decay then sets in at the ends of the string, it shrinks, and we get another three-cycle blinker $(2, 6, 4), (2, 6, 4), \ldots$.

Unless they exist in a population totally absent of cooperators, defectors can only survive as part of a blinker. Furthermore, at least four cooperators must separate any two blinkers, or else they will connect and the two strings of defectors will become one long string. This longer string would be vulnerable to unraveling at each end until only a single blinker remained.[8] Packing the $(2, 6, 4)$ blinkers to maximize the number of defectors yields a population that contains a minimum of 40% defectors and 60% cooperators, on average. Similar packing of the $(1, 5, 3)$ blinkers yields 33% defectors (see Eshel et al., 1998).

Thus, the ring usually leads to the survival of both strategies with cooperation selected by at least 60% of the population. But typically there are more cooperators than this prescribed minimum. Table 2 presents the results of 50 virtual experiments with a ring topology and 97% of the population cooperates, while the standard deviation is a miniscule 0.0075. Somewhat ironically, the relative difficulty of establishing surviving cooperators leads to their proliferation in the steady state. To survive, cooperators must come in fours (at least), meaning that defectors (at their maximum length) have to be separated by four adjacent cooperators. If two blinkers are separated by less than four cooperators the cooperators die out—become defectors—which connects the two blinkers and creates a long string of defectors vulnerable to unraveling. If it were easier to establish a surviving string of cooperators, say survival required only two cooperative neighbors, the final population would contain fewer cooperators.[9] Intuitively, groups of cooperators chop defectors into strings that shrink into blinkers, the only form in which defectors can survive. More chops, more blinkers, more defectors. The more difficult it is for cooperators to survive, the better they do over time.

Asynchronous updating makes the dynamics of the ring even more curious. Again, strings of defectors unravel at both ends until they shrink into one of the blinkers. But with asynchronous updating these blinkers can move around the ring. Consider the following sequence of events. Suppose cooperation has spread to surround a single defector triggering a $(1, 5, 3)$ blinker centered on agent k:

$$\ldots - C - C - C - C - \overbrace{C_i - C_j - D_k - C_l - C_m}^{neighborhood_k} - C - C - C - \ldots$$

Agent k earns more than all of his neighbors, but with random updating suppose only one of his neighbors, say agent m, decides to change.

$$\ldots - C - C - C - C - \overbrace{C_i - C_j - D_k - C_l - D_m}^{neighborhood_k} - C - C - C - \ldots$$

---

[8] Blinkers could be at different points of their cycle, but the minimum separation must be four cooperators.
[9] In Eshel et al. (1998), for example, only two cooperators were necessary for survival and we would expect 13.75% of the evolved population to be defectors.

In the next round, agent m earns $21.2 = 3 \times 7 + 2 \times 0.1$ which exceeds the earnings of all of his neighbors. Thus, in the next round (if all agents in m's neighborhood happen to update) we would see:

$$\ldots - C - C - C - C - C_i - C_j - \overbrace{D_k - D_l - D_m - D_n - D_o}^{neighborhood_m} - C - C - C - \ldots$$

The $(1, 5, 3)$ blinker has moved from being centered on agent k to being centered on agent m. In subsequent rounds the blinker can shift to the left again, back to the right, or stretch out (at least for a brief period). Still, such strings are susceptible to unraveling and cannot break into two separate strings to establish more blinkers (a break requires a minimum of four cooperators). Consequently, given enough time, a blinker will move around a network and scoop up the other defection blinkers. When such mobile blinkers merge, their subsequent unraveling reduces the aggregate number of defectors. In fact, as $t \to \infty$ only a single, mobile blinker survives.[10]

3.2.4. The grid

Suppose agents are spread out on a grid with a single decision maker occupying each square. To keep these agents' neighborhoods the same size as the neighborhoods on the ring, we limit each agent to four neighbors, those located in the 4 closest squares: one above, one below and one on each side. Consequently, in a grid, none of the agents' neighbors are neighbors with one another.

When these agents play the cooperation game, a single cooperator surrounded by defectors will perish; but two neighboring cooperators will spread. And, a single defector will also spread, leading many agents to adopt the defection strategy. Thus, the pattern of cooperation and defection takes on a complex dynamic. Nowak and May (1992, 1993) first explored this situation for several different neighborhood sizes and payoffs on a two-dimensional grid.

According to Nowak and May (1992), this process of chaotically changing patterns is a dynamic fractal.[11] If the initial distribution of cooperators and defectors is symmetric, this dynamic creates "evolutionary kaleidoscopes" of changing cooperation and defection (a similar pattern of spreading strategies is observed by Axelrod, 1984). Given a finite population, this pattern must eventually repeat, but in our experiments such repetition did not occur after thousands of rounds for our population of 2500 agents. Furthermore, even though each of the fifty simulations starts with a different dispersion of strategies, this chaotic behavior converged to 36% cooperation with a standard deviation across experiments of only 0.071.

Although this system yields a stable distribution of cooperators and defectors, one cannot predict the moves of any individual agent. An agent might adopt one strategy for

[10] A visual display of the spread of defection and cooperation in a ring, grid and small world can be found at http://cas.uah.edu/wilhitea/simsims.html.
[11] A fractal is an object, in this instance a shape, of non-integer dimension (see Flake, 1998).

dozens of rounds of play, switch intermittently between cooperation and defection for awhile, perhaps only to once again stabilize on a single strategy for another extended period. Kirchkamp (2000) extended Nowak and May's studies by introducing more complex strategies, and a longer memory and he found that different strategies survive even though they receive different payoffs.

Huberman and Glance (1993) examined asynchronous updating on the grid and using their payoff matrix cooperation disappeared as a strategy. Nowak et al. (1994) expanded on this by looking at a variety of PD payoff schemes. They found asynchronous up-dating sometimes eliminates cooperation but typically cooperation survives. Using the payoffs defined above, we find that cooperation actually increases with asynchronous updating, from about 36% of the population to almost 54% (see Table 2). In addition, the within-experiment variation was much lower with asynchronous updating. Asyn-chronous updating leads to the establishment of stable cooperative "crosses" in which a complete neighborhood cooperates. The crosses nest together to form blocks of cooper-ative behavior surrounded by strings of defectors. Only the boundaries are susceptible to defection. While these blocks mutate and move around, cooperation remains the ma-jority's choice (for an illustration see footnote 10).

3.2.5. The tree

Our tree network has the same size neighborhood as the grid and ring (except for the furthest reaches, the tips of the branches), but the neighborhoods of an agent's neigh-bors differ. In a tree, none of the agents' neighbors are neighbors with one another, nor do they share neighbors (except the original agent of course). So, the union of agent i's neighbors' neighborhoods is larger than on the grid or ring, and the intersection is smaller; in fact, the intersection contains only agent i.

Defection can spread in such a network as illustrated in Figure 2. Introduce a single defector, D_1, into a tree network of cooperators (someplace other than out on the rim of the tree), and his payoff of 28.1 ($4 \times 7 + 0.1$) exceeds all of his neighbors' earnings and defection spreads (each C' switches to D). In fact, if a single defector is introduced into a network of cooperators, the entire network will quickly adopt the defection strategy. However, isolated defectors on the rim, such as D_2, die out.

Cooperation spreads just as readily if a pair of cooperators starts out as neighbors. Those paired cooperators earn a payoff of 8 which dominates all defectors, who can

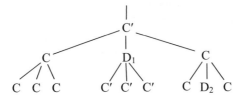

Figure 2.

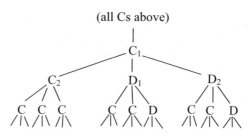

(all Cs above)

Figure 3.

earn at most 7.4.[12] Thus, a single defector will conquer a network of cooperators, but two (neighboring) cooperators will conquer a network of defectors. For this reason, the stable equilibrium strategy in a tree network conforms to one of two states: total cooperation or total defection. Starting with a random allocation of cooperative and defection strategies, we know that the network will eventually converge to one or the other outcome, but which is uncertain.

The dynamics of the tree are surprisingly complex. For example, while a single defector conquers an entire network of cooperators, two defectors do not. Two defectors interfere with one another, reducing each other's payoffs, leaving cooperation as the superior local strategy. Consider Figure 3, in which defectors co-mingle with cooperators and have spread up the tree to this point. Agents D_1 and D_2 have just switched their strategy to defect, and in the next round all cooperators in their neighborhoods, including C_1, will switch to the defection strategy.

At this point the defection strategy will stop spreading. Agent C_1 (now a defector) earns a payoff of $14.3 (= 2 \times 7 + 3 \times 0.1)$, which is less than the payoff of his neighbor playing C_2 so agent C_1 and will switch back to cooperation. In the following round defectors D_1 and D_2 will also switch, and in subsequent rounds the cooperative strategy will eventually wipe out the defectors. Regardless of where the two defectors are initially located, they will eventually meet at a fork and from that point cooperation takes over. One defector conquers a network; two do not.

Cooperators do not face an interference problem because if two cooperators meet they actually increase each other's payoff. However, if three cooperators meet at a fork occupied by a defector, that defector's payoff suddenly increases (because he now can take advantage of all three cooperators) and dominates the cooperative payoff. At that point the momentum shifts and defection takes over.

Thus, two converging defectors interfere and eliminate each other and three converging cooperators stop cooperation. Given a random distribution of initial strategies, a meeting of two defectors more likely occurs than a meeting of three cooperators, and so

---

[12] If two cooperators are neighbors, then by the topology of the tree network no defector shares a neighborhood with both; thus the maximum earnings of any neighboring defector is $(7 + 4 \times 0.1 = 7.4)$.

the steady state more likely takes the form of a cooperative tree. As shown in Table 2, the steady state of the tree consists of all cooperators 60% of the time.

Asynchronous updating has two marked effects on the dynamics in a tree network. First, partial updating dramatically slows things down. As seen in Table 2, the synchronously updated system required only 14 or 15 rounds of decision making to reach the steady state but with asynchronous updating no steady state emerged even after thousands of rounds of play. Second, the lack of synchronicity allows both strategies to survive.

To understand how asynchronous updating induces these changes, reconsider Figure 2 above and focus solely on the neighborhood of the defector D_1. With synchronous updating the next round of play sees all agents indicated by C' switching to the defection strategy. The initial defector's payoff falls dramatically but he retains his defection strategy because all of his neighbors are defecting. But with asynchronous updating some of his neighbors may not switch. Suppose only two of the four agents indicated by C' switch to the defection strategy. Agent D_1 has a payoff of 14.3, but he now has at least one cooperative neighbor earning a payoff of 16 creating an incentive to switch to cooperation. Cooperation offers an even larger payoff if three of the four initial cooperators switch. Now consider all possibilities. With asynchronous updating, one of five changes will occur: exactly 0, 1, 2, 3, or 4 neighbors will update. If none or only one updates, the defector will continue to have the highest payoff and will influence his remaining cooperative neighbors to defect and some will in subsequent rounds. Eventually we will see two, three, or four neighbors switch to defection. Agent D_1 is secure only if all of the cooperators in his neighborhood change at once, which occurs with a probability = 1/256—unlikely but it surely happens. However, for defection to conquer the network this unlikely event has to occur in every neighborhood at just the right time, a probability that becomes vanishingly small as the population gets large. Thus, defection loses its ability to become the dominant strategy.

While asynchronous updating dooms the defection strategy's chances of conquering the network, it also makes defection difficult to eradicate. Again consider agent D_1 in Figure 2 and suppose two of his neighbors have updated and switched to the defection strategy. Agent D_1 will eventually to switch to the cooperative strategy, but in the meantime his newly defecting neighbors will be influencing *their* neighbors to defect. They in turn will eventually be pressured to switch back to cooperation, but their now defecting neighbors will be infecting others still. In this way the defection strategy moves around the tree and manages to avoid its eventual extinction. This activity accounts for the absence of a steady-state. While an unlikely chain of events might still lead to the eradication of defection, none of the experiments conducted here suffered such a fate in tens of thousands of rounds of play.

3.2.6. Small-world networks

Because small-worlds have a ring substructure, the long run distributions of strategies inherit some of the attributes of the ring network. For example, small worlds contain both cooperators and defectors with cooperators making up the majority, and they typically evolve some limit cycle reflecting the presence of "blinkers," groups of defectors that grow and shrink repeatedly. But substantial differences emerge as well. For instance, the pure ring had only two, three-period cycles, the (1, 5, 3) and (2, 6, 4) blinkers. With shortcut edges involved, some of these cycles include more periods, and the coordination of these different-length individual cycles can create very long aggregated cycles. Consequently the periodic, steady-state, aggregate distribution of cooperators versus defectors may repeat itself only after hundreds of rounds of play.

Small-worlds also tend to have fewer cooperators than rings. As summarized in Table 2, 97% of the population cooperates in a ring, but only 70% of the population cooperates in a small world. Shortcuts open the benefits of cooperation to a wider population, limiting its local restraint and more individuals defect to free-ride on this cooperative behavior. By inspecting the experiments visually (one of the advantages of ACE modeling) you can see this difference emerge. First envision a ring with a single group of surviving cooperators (at least four cooperative neighbors). Recall that this cooperation will spread around the ring ending in a single blinker that contains the only surviving defectors. Now contrast that with a ring that has a single shortcut or bridge. As cooperation spreads as it did in the ring, it eventually reaches this bridge. At this point, cooperation splits and one line of cooperators continues its trek around the ring while the other jumps to the other side of the bridge to spread from there. These two distinct lines of cooperators will eventually converge to create two blinkers (instead of the single blinker that would have resulted in a ring). Small worlds thus retain more clusters of defectors than do rings.

As in a ring, incorporating asynchronous updating in a small-world network makes blinkers mobile; they expand and contract irregularly moving around the network soaking up other blinkers. But, unlike the ring, bridges or short cuts can chop a blinker into two surviving groups of defectors (see footnote 10). In these experiments this concurrent fusion and division of blinkers seems to balance out and the aggregate distribution of strategies is changed little, containing about 70% cooperators.[13] Synchronous updating also leads to a more unstable contingent of cooperators that repeats after a long cycle while asynchronous models tend to change less from period to period but wander more erratically over time.

3.2.7. Power networks

Both strategies survive in power networks. Pockets of defectors can persist because small neighborhoods can be surrounded by larger neighborhoods, upstream and downstream. In such a situation, an agent who retains the defection strategy may have some neighbors who keep playing the cooperative strategy because their neighbors are earning a large payoff through cooperation.

---

[13] The determinants of the relative speed of the division and fusion of blinkers include the number of bridges in the small world and the probability of updating. How each affects the eventual distribution of strategies is an open question.

Power networks display an interesting dynamic in the presence of synchronous updating. Cooperation falls in the early rounds, but soon it rallies to quickly become the dominant strategy. There is a phase transition from a state of chaotic, low-cooperation to periodic, high-cooperation. Leigh Tesfatsion (2006) mentions how ACE models sometimes surprise you, bringing forth results that one would not anticipate, yet can make sense on further inspection. This phase transition is such an example. Remember that the power network contains a few nodes of high degree (hubs) which are almost always directly connected to each other. Consequently, even if the network contains only a few cooperators knocking around in its far reaches those cooperators eventually align themselves in such a way to induce one of the hubs to switch to cooperation. His switch induces a switch for most of his neighbors (just as in a star) and the hub's payoff from cooperation soars. This triggers a switch for another, perhaps even larger hub and starts a chain reaction in which all hubs switch to cooperation in just a few rounds. The network dramatically changes from one state in which a minority of the population cooperates to one in which almost everyone cooperates.

Asynchronous updating has minor effects on the aggregate distribution of strategies in a power network, primarily dampening the convergence process. It takes a bit longer to reach its periodic steady state, and the phase transition is smoothed out to a more gradual trend of cooperation.

Reviewing all of the results in Table 2, we see that network structure has dramatic effects on the eventual proportion of agents adopting a cooperative strategy. Further, the impact of asynchronous updating differs across networks, sometimes altering the steady-state distribution of strategies and sometimes altering the dynamics within a network. In both cases network structure—the way we are connected to our neighbors, influences our aggregate decision making.

4. Exchange in networks

But games are not the only game in town. Economic agents frequently engage in non-strategic behavior, like exchange. This section considers exchange when it is shaped by a network. The pure exchange economy created here differs fundamentally from the games played above because agents do not alter their behavior based on a neighbor's behavior. Agents simply exchange if they find it beneficial, and prices are set by an exogenous formula known by all. Thus the economic problem is one of matching voluntary traders. Our primary interest is how the topology of a network affects the efficiency of exchange.

Most of the literature investigating exchange on networks concentrates on the formation of the network, i.e., how traders select partners and the resulting network's attributes. Vriend (1995) advanced one of the first ACE models which studied the self-organization of markets. Following his lead, McFadzean and Tesfatsion (1999), Kranton and Minehart (2001), Dawid (2000), Kirman and Vriend (2001), and Wilhite (2003) have explored a number of additional issues in market-induced network evolution. Vriend (2006) reviews these and related issues in this volume.

But research examining exchange on an existing network remains in its infancy. Bell (1998) compared trade on a ring and a star and found that centralized networks converge more quickly and appeared less prone to spatial price anomalies. Wilhite (2001) examined trade on a complete network, a type of ring, and a small-world and found that the small-world network, while not centralized, still achieved rapid convergence with less search and negotiation costs than the complete network. Other related studies have not explicitly focused on the impact of network topology. For example, Epstein and Axtell (1996) placed the agents in Sugarspace on a grid, but their agents could move; thus their neighborhoods were not fixed as defined in this chapter. However, the *resources* in Sugarspace were spatially fixed and required transportation, consequently Epstein and Axtell also observed spatial price anomalies.

This section explores trade on a network by simplifying to focus on a barter economy with only two goods, g_1 and g_2. These are durable goods in the sense that they suffer no degradation over time. There is no production and there are no imports; thus, the aggregate stock of goods at the beginning of the experiment is the same at the end. These goods have value as intrinsic sources of pleasure and as durable assets usable in exchange. Examples include collectibles such as precious stones, baseball cards, works of art, or antiques. One of the goods, g_2, is infinitely divisible but the other, g_1, must be traded in whole units.[14]

The network trade experiments involve 1000 independent agents, each possessing the same symmetric Cobb–Douglas utility function. Agents are rational, non-strategic, and myopic in that they do not attempt to mislead potential trade partners, or plan for future opportunities. They simply try to improve their current position in each period by engaging in voluntary trade. At the time of an exchange, agents are constrained by their existing wealth, which consists of their current stock of goods 1 and 2. Finally, half of the agents are endowed with an initial allocation of 1500 units of good 1 and 150 units of good 2. The other half of the population has the mirror image, 150 units of good 1 and 1500 units of good 2. These endowments define the entire resource base of society.

Formally, the utility of agent i, U^i, depends on the amount of the two goods, g_1 and g_2, he possesses:

$$U^i = g_1^i g_2^i, \quad i \in \{1, \ldots, 1000\}. \tag{1}$$

Agent i trades as long as the incremental exchange increases U^i. An opportunity for mutually beneficial exchange exists if the marginal rates of substitution of two agents differ. Given the utility function in (1), the *mrs* of agent i is

$$mrs^i = \frac{U'(g_1^i)}{U'(g_2^i)} = \frac{g_2^i}{g_1^i}, \quad i \in \{1, \ldots, 1000\}, \tag{2}$$

where $U'(\cdot)$ is the first derivative of U.

---

[14] Requiring increments of a whole unit of good 1 adds some rigidity (and realism) to the model. The effects of this rigidity were explored by altering the aggregate initial endowment.

Agents are allowed to trade with any agent with whom they are linked, and trade proceeds as follows. A randomly selected agent searches among his neighbors for trading opportunities, picking the one offering the best deal. They establish prices, and trade one unit of good 1 for the stipulated amount of good 2. He then searches and trades again, until four trades are made. Then another agent is selected randomly to search through his neighborhood, set prices and so forth. A complete "round" of trade terminates when 1000 agents (the size of the population) have had the opportunity to initiate trade.[15] Note that, any agent can either buy good 1 (trade g_2 for g_1) or sell good 1 (trade g_1 for g_2). Indeed, in successive rounds a particular agent may buy and later sell the same good.

The exchange price between agent i and agent j, $p_{i,j}$, is set according to the following rule.[16]

$$p_{i,j} = \frac{g_2^i + g_2^j}{g_1^i + g_1^j}, \quad i, j \in \{1, \dots, 1000\}. \tag{3}$$

Equilibrium is defined as a point of rest; trading stops because traders find no deals that improve both parties. Because the market is seeded with equal amounts of g_1 and g_2, the equilibrium price equals one. And since all of the networks are connected, each market eventually reaches this equilibrium price and all agents eventually see their *mrs* approach unity.

Using this simple setup we examine how a network's topology affects trade. To proceed, one of the networks of interest is selected, primed with initial endowments, and agents trade. We explored two alternative methods of distributing the initial endowments: random assignment and directed assignment. At first glance, randomly selecting the agents who start rich in g_1 and those who start rich in g_2 might seem an unbiased way to initialize the system, but a random distribution of the initial goods could hide the very network effects that are of primary interest. For example, if agent i's neighbors just happen to have the goods he wants, networks matter little. Furthermore, in nature, economic commodities generally are not randomly dispersed throughout a system. Instead they clump together around some resource base or spatial anomaly, or they reflect a regional comparative advantage. In general our challenge is not to distribute goods that are already distributed; it is to distribute goods that are not.

Consequently, initial endowments were assigned directly. In this case, the first half of the population received 1500 units of good one and 150 units of good 2 and the rest of the population received the opposite. While this arbitrary allocation is not meant to capture some prevalent distribution found in nature, it does force each network to face the challenge of moving goods from one location to another by trading. A visual image

---

[15] An agent can trade several times in a single round because he may be randomly selected several times in that round, and he may be selected by more than one agent as a trading partner.

[16] In a previous study two other pricing rules, the arithmetic mean and the geometric mean, were explored, but they had little effect on our conclusions. A quick check suggests the same is true here.

Table 3
Trading on networks. Speed of convergence, number of trades and searches

Network type	Number of edges	Rounds of trading	Total trades	Total searches
Complete	500 500	157	468 748	1 568 430 000
		(8.75)	(3314)	(8 741 250)
Star	999	452	481 443	2 257 740
		(2.81)	(2396)	(14 035)
Ring	2000	35 681	45 102 011	142 724 800
		(239.93)	(55 205)	(959 720)
Grid	2000	2515	3 250 932	10 062 000
		(50.45)	(3983)	(201 800)
Tree	999	34 742	2 039 978	138 968 000
		(1548.56)	(155 332)	(6 194 240)
Small-world	2000	3719	3 766 358	14 872 000
		(592.11)	(466 836)	(2 368 440)
Power	2000	422	744 698	1 689 600
		(24.35)	(13 736)	(97 400)

The top number is the average number of rounds, trades or searches to reach equilibrium in fifty trials on each network; the lower number is its standard deviation.

of the initial distribution of goods appears in Table 1 where the shaded nodes represent agents receiving more g_1.

Trade proceeds on the seven networks of interest until the equilibrium price emerges, the agents' *mrs* converges, and no further mutually beneficial exchange opportunities exist. Some networks converge faster, some feature greater amounts of search and negotiation, and others generate more equitable distributions of income or goods.[17] See Table 3 for an overview of these statistics.

Just as one's intuition might suggest, the complete network converges more rapidly than the other structures. When everyone can trade with anyone else, the most profitable exchanges happen in every round and prices quickly converge to their equilibrium. However, the complete network contains the largest number of edges, 250 times more edges than the next, most dense network. So, if edge creation and edge maintenance consume resources, this rapid price convergence is costly. Furthermore, since agents search their entire neighborhood to find the best trading partner, a complete network requires agents to sift through the entire population. Consequently, the complete network's abundance of edges inflates search and negotiation expenses such that it may not be the most efficient way to organize trade.

The star seems to hold promise as an efficient organization because it has a small number of edges and everyone is only two steps away from every other agent. Consistent

---

[17] While agents search and negotiate costlessly in these experiments, in nature they do not. To recognize this potential cost we write as if traders do negotiate at every trading opportunity and just happen to end up at the price as determined in equation (3).

with Bell (1998) we find that the star converges more quickly than most of the other networks and requires less search and negotiation. But there is a catch. The star network generates an extremely uneven income distribution as discussed below. Convergence happens slowly on a ring because goods must be handed from person to person to pass from one side of the ring to the other, much like water moving in an old bucket brigade. In the tree, goods must pass down through the branches and through the single "trunk" node before they can reach the other branches. This slows its convergence considerably. The small-world and the power networks converge more quickly and require less search and negotiation than the grid, ring, or tree. The power network is particularly efficient, clearing markets in fewer rounds and with fewer searches than even the star.[18]

When a network restricts the flow of trade along certain routes, certain positions can gain a spatial advantage. In the above exercise, agents at such crucial nodes could not exploit their position in the sense of allowing or disallowing some individual or group of individuals to trade or to force prices to their advantage. However, those critical nodes still benefit from their location because they offer so many opportunities to trade and each exchange generates some incremental gain. Consequently, agents at these critical nodes can earn much more than others in the network. Table 4 displays a representative income distribution following trade on each network.

Notice the disparity in the star network. The spike represents the wealth of the central agent. Even though he cannot exploit his position by coercing others in the network, he still occupies an advantageous node. Every trade includes him as one of the partners and since every trade is beneficial he acquires more goods. This result brings to mind many historic examples, including how Constantinople accumulated vast wealth when most of Europe's spice merchants routed trade through this territory.[19] The complete network yields a more equitable distribution of goods although the richest individual earns about twice as much as the poorest. Those random agents who were lucky enough to trade early earn a bit more because the best bargains are then available.

The distribution of income in the ring and grid resemble one another, which makes sense. Consider the ring. Given the uneven distribution of initial endowments, the two most critical neighborhoods lie between the agents rich in g_1 and those rich in g_2. Goods must flow through those two regions (which reside directly across from each other on the ring) and so those neighborhoods see more action and earn more profits. This accounts for the peaked earnings in the ring network. A similar results holds for the grid, except the regions separating the two sets of endowments contain several neighborhoods leading to a greater dispersion of wealth.[20]

---

[18] For more on the dynamics of price adjustment in these networks, see the web-site referenced in footnote 10.

[19] Note how the star network's income distribution shifts at the halfway point in the population. This earnings difference is solely a function of the directed assignment of initial endowments and the restriction that good 1 can only be swapped in whole units. That artificially restricts the trades agents can make, which causes the observed difference. If the initial endowments are swapped such that the first half of the population has more of g_2, the second half of the population ends up with the greater earnings.

[20] The skew accompanying the income spikes in the ring and grid are also artifacts of the requirement that g_1 is traded in whole units. Flipping initial endowments flips the skew.

Table 4

Trading on networks. Sample income distributions after trading on each network

Complete:

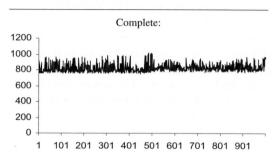

Star:

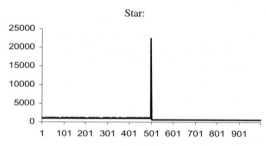

Ring:

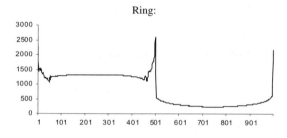

Grid:

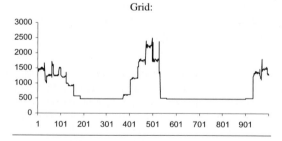

Table 4
(*continued*)

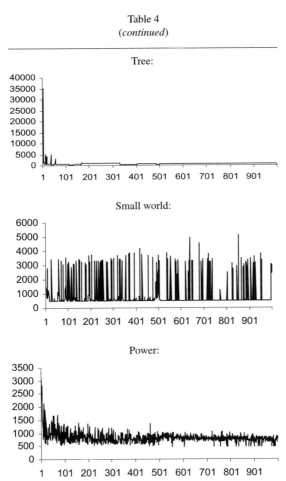

Tree:

Small world:

Power:

The horizontal axis reflects the 1000 agents and the vertical axis measures the level of g_1 held by each agent after trading comes to a halt (recall $g_1 = g_2$ in equilibrium).

The income distribution emerging in a society that trades on a tree network depends critically on the distribution of the initial endowments. If we distribute goods as above, most of the g_2-rich agents reside in two of the four branches. Consequently, trade must flow through the center agents. The resulting distribution reflects great wealth for the center player, a bit less for the next level players (the first nodes off the trunk), and so on. If goods were distributed in another fashion (for instance, if one good was seeded completely around the rim of the tree), the resulting distribution would favor a different sub-group.[21]

---

[21] In that case the critical nodes are those that lay one step upstream of the tips of the branches.

Reviewing Tables 3 and 4, we see that the small-world and power networks quickly allocate goods to reach the equilibrium price and they do not suffer from the undue search costs arising from many edges. These networks also yield a more equitable distribution of income. Hubs in the power networks naturally earn more profits, but the richest agent earns only about seven times the average agent's income, a smaller differential than all but the complete network. We also see variation in small-world networks as the agents with "shortcuts" to regions having the opposite endowment of goods do better than those without such links. But the rich earn only about ten times the poorest agent. Thus, the small world and power networks seem to achieve their increased speed without concentrating earning power into the hands of a few.

5. Conclusions

This chapter has explored the effects of a network's topology on two types of economic activity: strategic coordination and cooperation, and exchange. Given the infancy of economic research on networks, many open questions remain. I expect future network research to focus on more complex topologies. The small-world and power networks appear to be important structures but they have eluded serious study until the last few years and remain largely ignored in economics despite their efficiency, resiliency, and their ability to provide a framework to study some economically important environments. That these two significant creations resided undetected for years makes one wonder what other types of undiscovered network structures exist. Recently Jackson and Rogers (2004) have constructed networks from a search and strategic attachment process that possesses characteristics of both the power and small-world networks. These networks may more readily fit the topology of the world-wide-web by mimicking the clustering of nodes in the web more accurately than the power networks put forth by Albert et al. (1999). Certainly one can envision other hybrid networks. For example, Gastner and Newman (2004) investigate networks that emerge from a cost minimization rule which is "tuned" depending on whether agents are more concerned with minimizing the spatial distance traveled or minimizing the number of edges traversed. They find that grid-like networks emerge when geographic distance matters and power networks emerge when the number of edges matters. In between hybrid networks containing attributes of both arise. The economic properties of these more complex networks deserve our attention.

Networks certainly influence other types of economic activities besides games and pure exchange. For example, Calvó-Armengol and Jackson (2004) present an example of networked labor markets which suggests that an individual's job history depends, in part, on the job history of his acquaintances. Allen (2000) offers a similar explanation for the decision to become an entrepreneur. Kranton and Minehart (2001) look at exchange between buyers and sellers. They find that agents can use networks to pool the risk of uncertainty arising from the stochastic nature of supply and demand, and that under reasonable circumstances non-cooperative actors can successfully establish such networks. Wilhite (2003) suggests that the decreased search and negotiation costs accompanying established trading partners solidifies a network's structure. Tesfatsion (2001) finds that the asymmetric earnings of workers across a contractual network are affected by the relative market power of employers and workers.

In addition, researchers are only beginning to study the effects of weighted edges on economic activity. As networks come to represent more complex structures, we may not treat all links as equals. Some highways are wider, safer, and faster than others, some friends are more cherished, some pundits more respected. Weighted edges offer a simple method by which we can incorporate such differences. We can also represent spatial networks—those that formally incorporate the "distance" between two nodes—by weighting edges. And by weighting edges probabilistically, one can incorporate risk and uncertainty. When edges are given these types of attributes, the shortest route from node A to node B might be different than the fastest route, which could differ from the least costly route, or the most certain route.

Other issues arise when edges are not assumed to be bidirectional as they are in this chapter. Information might flow in only one direction between certain nodes, or an edge might have one weight in one direction and a different weight in the opposite direction (it is harder to swim upstream than down). The information an agent receives might be more reliable than the information he gives out, either by design or by circumstance. Furthermore, the weighting scheme on a network's edges may change over time. Such changes could be internal to the issue being investigated; for example, an edge being used more frequently could become better and stronger, or it could become congested and depreciate from use. Or change could be exogenous to the system; perhaps edges change with the seasons. Dibble (2001) is exploring the effects of technology on edges; for example, technology might shorten the travel time between some nodes and not others.

Network studies offer an intuitive way to incorporate these and many additional attributes governing agent interaction into our thinking. But this complexity also tends to make things more, well, complex. It doesn't take much to render a network's architecture analytically intractable, particularly if the distribution of edges contains a random component or if edges are weighted. But with agent-based computations such complications can be expressed in computer code and then virtual experiments can probe into the finer workings of an architecture. In this manner, the origins of networks can be modeled, their impact on individual decision making can be explored, and their large-scale characteristics can be described statistically. Ultimately network effects can be dissected by economists, turned into research tools, and added to the arsenal of models which help us understand our world.

References

Albert, R., Barabási, A. (2002). "Statistical mechanics of complex networks". Reviews of Modern Physics 74, 47–97.

Albert, R., Jeong, H., Barabási, A. (1999). "Diameter of the World Wide Web". Nature 401, 130–131.

Allen, W.D. (2000). "Social networks and self-employment". The Journal of Socio-Economics 29, 487–501.

Axtell, R. (2000). "Effects of interaction topology and activation regime in several multi-agent systems", working paper (The Brookings Institution).

Axelrod, R. (1984). The Evolution of Cooperation. Basic Books.

Axelrod, R. (2006). "Agent-based modeling as a bridge between disciplines", this handbook.

Bala, V., Goyal, S. (1998). "Learning from neighbours". Review of Economic Studies 65, 595–621.

Bala, V., Goyal, S. (2000a). "A noncooperative model of network formation". Econometrica 68, 1181–1229.

Bala, V., Goyal, S. (2000b). "A strategic analysis of network reliability". Review of Economic Design 5, 205–228.

Bala, V., Goyal, S. (2001). "Conformism and diversity under social learning". Economic Theory 17, 101–120.

Barabási, A. (2002). Linked, The New Science of Networks. Perseus Publishing, Cambridge, MA.

Bell, A.M. (1998). "Bilateral trading on a network: A simulation study", working notes, Artificial Societies and Computational Markets, 31–36.

Burke, M., Gournier, G., Prasad, K. (2003). "Physician social networks and geographical variation in medical care", unpublished typescript (Florida State University).

Calvó-Armengol, A., Jackson, M. (2004). "The effects of social networks on employment and inequality". The American Economic Review 94, 426–454.

Dawid, H. (2000). "On the emergence of exchange and mediation in a production economy". Journal of Economic Behavior and Organization 41, 27–53.

Dibble, K. (2001). "Theory in a complex world: GeoGraph computational laboratories", unpublished dissertation, University of California-Santa Barbara.

Ellison, G. (1993). "Learning, local interaction, and coordination". Econometrica 61, 1047–1071.

Ellison, G., Fudenberg, D. (1993). "Rules of thumb for social learning". Journal of Political Economy 101, 612–643.

Epstein, J., Axtell, R. (1996). Growing Artificial Societies: Social Science from the Bottom Up. Brookings Institute Press, Washington, DC.

Eshel, I., Samuelson, L., Shaked, A. (1998). "Altruists, egoists, and hooligans in a local interaction model". The American Economic Review 88, 157–179.

Flake, G. (1998). The Computational Beauty of Nature. MIT Press, Cambridge, MA.

Gastner, M.T., Newman, M.E.J. (2004). "The spatial structures of networks", arXiv:cond-mat.0407680 v1.

Goyal, S. (2002). "Learning in Networks", unpublished typescript (Queen Mary, University of London, and Econometric Institute).

Goyal, S., van der Leij, M., Moraga-González, J. (2004). "Economics: an emerging small world", discussion paper, Tinbergen Institute, TI 2004-001/1.

Hendricks, K., Piccione, M., Tan, G. (1995). "The economics of hubs: The case of monopoly". Review of Economic Studies 63, 83–100.

Huberman, B.A., Glance, N.S. (1993). "Evolutionary games and computer simulations". Proceedings of the National Academy of Sciences 90, 7716–7718.

Jackson, M. (2004). "A survey of models of network formation: Stability and efficiency". In: Demange, G., Wooders, M. (Eds.), Group Formation in Economics: Networks, Clubs, and Coalitions. Cambridge University Press.

Jackson, M., Wolinsky, A. (1996). "A strategic model of social and economic networks". Journal of Economic Theory 71, 44–74.

Jackson, M., Rogers, B. (2004). "Search and strategic formation of large networks: When and why do we see power laws and small worlds?", working paper, The Division of Humanities and Social Sciences, California Institute of Technology.

Kirchkamp, O. (2000). "Spatial evolution of automata in the prisoners' dilemma". Journal of Economic Behavior and Organization 43, 239–262.

Kirman, A., Vriend, N. (2001). "Evolving market structure: An ACE model of price dispersion and loyalty". Journal of Economic Dynamics & Control 25, 459–502.

Kranton, R., Minehart, D. (2001). "A theory of buyer–seller networks". The American Economic Review 91, 485–508.

McFadzean, D., Tesfatsion, L. (1999). "A C++ platform for the evolution of trade networks". Computational Economics 14, 109–134.

Milgram, S. (1967). "The small-world problem". Psychology Today 2, 60–67.

Morris, S. (2000). "Contagion". Review of Economic Studies 67, 57–78.

Mukherjl, A., Rajan, V., Slagle, J. (1996). "Robustness of cooperation". Nature 379, 125–126.

Newman, M.E.J. (2000). "Models of the small world", arXiv:cond-mat/0001118 v2.

Nowak, M., May, R. (1992). "Evolutionary games and spatial chaos". Nature 359, 826–829.

Nowak, M., May, R. (1993). "The spatial dilemmas of evolution". International Journal of Bifurcation and Chaos 3, 35–78.

Nowak, M., Bonhoeffer, S., May, R. (1994). "More spatial games". International Journal of Bifurcation and Chaos 4, 33–56.

Nowak, M., Bonhoeffer, S., May, R. (1996). "Robustness of cooperation: Reply". Nature 379, 125–126.

Page, S.E. (1997). "On incentives and updating in agent based models". Computational Economics 10, 67–87.

Radner, R. (1993). "The organization of decentralized information processing". Econometrica 62, 1109–1146.

Schelling, T. (1969). "Models of segregation". American Economic Review, Papers and Proceedings 59, 488–493.

Schelling, T. (1971). "Dynamic models of segregation". Journal of Mathematical Sociology 1, 143–186.

Schelling, T. (1978). Micromotives and Macrobehavior. W.W. Norton & Co., Inc., New York.

Schelling, T. (2006). "Some fun, thirty-five years ago", this handbook.

Tesfatsion, L. (2001). "Structure, behavior, and market power in an evolutionary labor markets with adaptive search". Journal of Economic Dynamics and Control 25, 419–457.

Tesfatsion, L. (2006). "Agent-based computational economics: A constructive approach to economic theory", this handbook.

Vriend, N. (1995). "Self-organization of markets: An example of a computational approach". Computational Economics 8, 205–231.

Vriend, N. (2006). "ACE models of endogenous interactions", this handbook.

Watts, D. (1999). Small Worlds. Princeton University Press, Princeton, NJ.

Watts, D., Strogatz, S.H. (1998). "Collective dynamics of 'small-world' networks". Nature 393, 440–442.

Wilhite, A. (2001). "Bilateral trade and 'small-world' networks". Computational Economics 18, 49–64.

Wilhite, A. (2003). "Self-organizing production and exchange". Computational Economics 21, 107–123.

Wilhite, A. (2006). "Protection and social order". Journal of Economic Behavior and Organizations, in press.

Young, H.P. (1993). "The evolution of conventions". Econometrica 61, 57–84.

Young, H.P. (1998). Individual Strategy and Social Structure. Princeton University Press, Princeton, NJ.

Young, H.P. (2002). "The diffusion of innovations in social networks", unpublished typescript (Johns Hopkins University, Brookings Institute, and Santa Fe Institute).

Young, H.P. (2006). "Social dynamics: Theory and applications", this handbook.

Young, H.P., Burke, M.A. (2001). "Competition and custom in economic contracts: A case study of Illinois agriculture". The American Economic Review 91, 559–573.

Chapter 21

ACE MODELS OF ENDOGENOUS INTERACTIONS

NICOLAAS J. VRIEND[*],[†]

Queen Mary, University of London, London, UK
e-mail: n.vriend@qmul.ac.uk; url: http://www.qmul.ac.uk/~ugte173/

Contents

[*] N.J. Vriend, Queen Mary, University of London, Department of Economics, Mile End Road, London E1 4NS, UK.

[†] I would like to thank Bob Axelrod, Josh Epstein, Giorgio Fagiolo, Nobi Hanaki, Marco Janssen, Jerry Silverberg, Leigh Tesfatsion, participants of the ACE Workshop at Michigan, and two referees for helpful discussions, comments and suggestions. The usual disclaimer applies.

Handbook of Computational Economics, Volume 2. Edited by Leigh Tesfatsion and Kenneth L. Judd
DOI: 10.1016/S1574-0021(05)02021-6

Abstract

Various approaches used in Agent-based Computational Economics (ACE) to model endogenously determined interactions between agents are discussed. This concerns models in which agents not only (learn how to) play some (market or other) game, but also (learn to) decide with whom to do that (or not).

Keywords

endogenous interaction, Agent-based Computational Economics (ACE)

JEL classification: C6, C7, D1, D2, D3, D4, D5, D6, D8, L1, M3

1. Introduction

This chapter presents an overview of Agent-based Computational Economics (ACE) models of endogenously determined relationships. This concerns models in which agents not only (learn how to) play some (market or other) game, but also (learn to) decide with whom to do that (or not). Such decisions may depend, for example, on the perceived success of the interactions. These models of endogenous interactions are to be distinguished from models in which the interactions between agents are exogenously determined; for example by the given spatial positions of agents, such as with cellular automata. An alternative way to put this is that in the models with endogenous interactions discussed in this chapter, the speed with which connections can be updated is comparable to (or faster than) the speed with which strategies in some underlying game can be updated, whereas in models with exogenously determined interactions the speed of the network updating is so low that the interaction structure can be taken as given.

The main motivation for studying models of endogenous interactions is that endogeneity is a ubiquitous feature of the reality of social interactions. Therefore, a theory of social interactions must take account of it. Consider, for example, the following quote concerning market organization.

> "*Markets rarely emerge in a vacuum, and potential traders soon discover that they may spend more time, energy, and other resources discovering or making a market than on the trade itself. This predicament is shared equally by currency traders, do-it-yourself realtors, and streetwalkers! Their dilemma, however, seems to have gone largely unnoticed by economists, who simply assume that somehow traders will eventually be apprised of each other's existence—to their mutual benefit or subsequent regret*" (Blin, 1980, p. S193).

Therefore, models of market organization going beyond assumptions of perfectly competitive markets (either considering them as black boxes, or with Walrasian auctioneers or invisible hands pulling the strings), explicitly focusing on the "who interacts with whom?" question seem useful. The endogeneity of interactions is equally ubiquitous in other social domains. As Skyrms and Pemantle (2000) observe:

> "*A child who is being bullied learns either to fight better or to run away. Similarly, a player who obtains unsatisfactory results may choose either to change strategies or to change associates*" (p. 9340).

We will focus on ACE models. The basic idea of ACE modeling is that one computes explicitly (either with paper and pencil, using a computer, or just mentally) the actions and outcomes for each and every individual agent at each relevant moment in time. Modeling individual agents computationally does not pose particular conceptual difficulties to economic theory. After all, as Lucas puts it, doing economics means "*programming robot imitations of people*" (in Klamer, 1984, p. 49). In fact, ACE modeling follows the same methodology of scientific inference as more traditional mathematical modeling in economics, and should be seen as complementary rather than an alternative to such more standard modeling. Both are modeling approaches using equations and deduction. With standard mathematical modeling in economics one typically specifies a certain micropattern (primitives and rules of possible interaction) and then considers a macropattern as an equilibrium of the thus specified model. In this traditional view, if a certain macropattern is not an equilibrium of such a microspecification, then it is not explained. This is what Varian (1984) calls *"recoverability"* (p. 3). The same applies to ACE modeling, where one also focuses on the question whether it is possible to 'recover' regularities known from reality in relatively simple models (abstracting from many aspects of reality), and analyzes how these regularities depend upon parameter choices or modeled mechanisms. Both ACE models and formal, mathematical models are thus models that are in themselves possible explanations for some real phenomena. Whereas the insights offered by mathematical models are typically presented in the form of theorems or propositions, ACE models seem to produce only computational examples. However, as Judd (2006) explains, even in this respect the two approaches are similar because 'theorem' is just a plural of 'example'. Although examples are produced in a somewhat different way in ACE models, there is no fundamental difference in this respect.

The difference between ACE and more traditional mathematical modeling in economics is a matter of the tools and techniques used: mathematical equations and specifications versus computational instructions. This facilitates different microspecifications and different ways to generate macropatterns, which in turn allows for different types of analysis, addressing somewhat different questions. For example, paying more attention to dynamic and non-equilibrium phenomena such as bounded rationality and learning, while maintaining tractability might be easier with ACE models. And as Tesfatsion (2006) explains, this makes ACE similar to constructive rather than classical mathematics.

Sometimes in the literature one can find people comparing the output of an ACE model run on a computer to the data of laboratory experiments with real (human) subjects, as if such a run were a test of some hypotheses, and as if the computer output were data to be explained. Such a view does not seem very helpful. As explained above, an ACE model is a model as much as a more traditional mathematical economics model is. That is, the computer program in itself is the (possible) explanation of some real phenomena. Running an ACE model on a computer (no matter whether this is called a simulation, a computational test-bed, a wind-tunnel experiment, or an artificial petri dish) is *only* a matter of analyzing the model, checking its internal consistency and examining its properties.

The studies presented in this chapter may differ in a number of important aspects from each other. *(i)* In the way connections are formed in a technical sense (e.g., by sending a communication signal, making a trip to a store, being a neighbor, etc.), and whether there are constraints formed by some underlying topology for the connections (e.g., a lattice). *(ii)* The way connections are evaluated and established in an economic sense (e.g., as myopic best-replies, or based on some learning process). *(iii)* The type of game (if any) being played for a given interaction structure or network. *(iv)* The way agents

Table 1
Different ways to model interactions in ACE models

Mechanism	Paper	Section
random		
local		
residential pattern	Schelling (1971)	2.1
resource gradient	Epstein and Axtell (1996)	2.2
predictors	Arthur (1994)	2.3
advertising/patronage	Vriend (1995)	2.4
(threshold) expected payoff	Ashlock et al. (1996)	2.5
arbitrary tags	Riolo (1997)	2.6
trust	Hanaki et al. (2004)	2.7
expected payoff/familiarity	Kirman and Vriend (2001)	2.8
past success rate	Chang and Harrington (2005)	2.9
directed random search	Jackson and Rogers (2004)	2.10

decide upon their strategies in such a game (e.g., as myopic best-replies, or based on some learning process). *(v)* Whether the focus is on the emerging interaction structure, or on the emerging strategies used in the underlying game (e.g. the trade-off between risk- and payoff-dominance in coordination games, or the sustainability of cooperation in prisoner's dilemma games). We will focus on the first two of these dimensions, i.e., on the various ways to model the endogenous interactions themselves.

Table 1 lists a number of different ways used in the ACE literature to model interactions. The first two ways to model interactions are relatively well-known and straightforward. Considering random interactions has been popular in particular in work originating from evolutionary game theory. Local interactions have often been modeled in the form of interactions with nearest neighbors, e.g., on a grid or lattice. Notice that in these first two approaches the interactions are not endogenous. Instead, they are determined through some exogenous random process or through exogenously determined locations of the agents. Therefore, we will focus on the other approaches listed. In all these approaches, the agents themselves decide whether to establish, maintain, or severe a link with some other agent(s), and these decisions are usually somehow related to the perceived success of their interactions. In the remainder of this chapter we present an ACE paper (see Table 1) for each of these ways to model the endogenous determination of interactions.

The overview will focus on the modeling of interactions as such, and will not provide a complete summary of the papers. The prime objective, rather, will be to catalog the ACE ways to model endogenous interactions. We will also not attempt a comparison to find the best (elements of each) approach, but rather we would argue that the choice of model should depend on 'circumstances' to be modeled in a broad sense, and on the purpose of the model. This includes issues such as the cognitive capabilities of the agents and the opportunities to use them (e.g., for interactions that are immediate, a fast and frugal way to guide interactions may be appropriate), the number of agents involved, whether the interactions are face-to-face (allowing for face recognition and use of simple physical cues as signals) or not, whether the interactions are anonymous or not, whether they are repeated or not, and whether trust is an issue or not.

The objective of this chapter is not to attempt to reach a conclusion as to what interaction patterns typically emerge in models with endogenous interactions (e.g., does a fully connected network ever appear?), or whether there are any general differences in this sense between models with endogenous and models with exogenous interactions.[1] On the one hand, it seems much too early for such an attempt. On the other hand, as Wilhite (2006) shows, the relevance of the interaction structure may be different for any different exogenous interaction structure, not to mention the differences among models of endogenous interactions. Similarly, in principle it could be that at some point we will be able to conclude that models with exogenous interactions are satisfactory approximations to the social reality of endogenous interactions. But for the moment any such conclusion would seem premature.

2. Various approaches

2.1. Schelling (1971): residential pattern

Schelling (1971) presents a spatial proximity model of neighborhood segregation. Although Schelling does not actually use any computers, this must be one of the very first ACE models.

There are two versions of this spatial proximity model: a one-dimensional (1D) and a two-dimensional (2D) model. In the 1D model, individual agents are distributed along a line. An agent's position is defined relative to his neighbors only, and agents can always position themselves next to any agent. A given individual's neighborhood is defined as the k nearest neighbors on either side of him. Agents towards the end of the line will have fewer than $2k$ neighbors. Schelling's 2D model concerns a regular lattice with bounds, such as a checkerboard.[2] Each agent occupies one cell of the board, and each cell can be occupied by only one agent at a time. Unlike in the 1D model, there are also some free cells. The neighborhood of an individual agent is the so-called Moore neighborhood. For an agent in the interior of the board this consists of the eight cells directly surrounding his own location, with fewer neighbors for agents at the boundary.

In both versions, Schelling considers a finite number of individual agents, distinguishing two types of individuals. Each individual is concerned only with the number of like and unlike neighbors. More specifically, each agent wants, for example, at most 50% unlike neighbors; otherwise agents are indifferent.

---

[1] For example, Oechssler (1997), Dieckmann (1999), and Mailath et al. (2000) show that for a certain class of coordination games endogeneity of interactions may directly affect the equilibrium selected.

[2] See also Sakoda (1971), which is based on Sakoda (1949), for a very similar model of endogenous interactions.

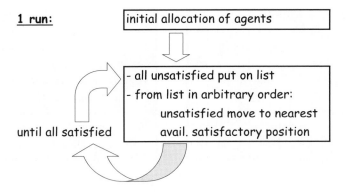

Figure 1. Structure of Schelling (1971).

The time structure of the model is given in Figure 1. The starting configuration is created by randomly distributing equal numbers of agents of each type. The dynamics, then, are an iterative process of agents choosing myopic best-responses to the residential locations chosen by the other agents. At each stage all agents that are not satisfied are put in some arbitrary order. When an agent's turn comes, he moves to the nearest satisfactory position. Since in the 1D version all positions are relative only, he simply inserts himself between two agents (or at either end of the line), and his own departure does not lead to an empty position. In the 2D version, each agent who wants to move has to find an empty location. At the next stage a new list of unsatisfied agents is compiled, and so on. This process continues until no agent wants to move anymore.

The interactions are endogenous in the following sense. Individual agents choose their neighbors on the basis of the current residency pattern (neighborhood ratios of like and unlike agents). As individual agents move, this residency pattern evolves. In fact, there are two kinds of externalities with every move. A leaving agent changes the neighborhood ratios for his old neighbors, while a newly arriving agent modifies the ratios in his new neighborhood. In both cases, these externalities may be positive or negative (depending on the perspective of the agents affected). Agents choose their location directly in (myopic) response to the existing residential pattern right from the start, and there is no learning (e.g., to be forward-looking) in this respect. Notice that there is no further underlying game to be played. The only thing that matters to the agents is with whom they interact, i.e., the proportions of each type in their own neighborhood. In some of the other models we will see that the variable guiding the interactions is some intermediate variable, and the agents can learn how this intermediate variable relates to eventual payoffs.

The random starting state is typically highly integrated. The usual outcome of the dynamic process is a highly segregated state, although nobody actually prefers segregation to integration. Figure 2 gives an example based on Schelling (1971), showing the initial (integrated) and final (segregated) state. Does the endogeneity of the interactions matter? Yes, it is all that matters. Many integrated equilibria exist (see Pancs and

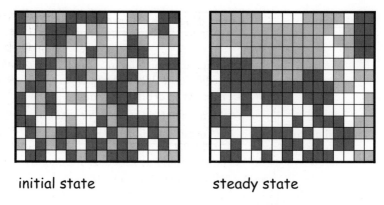

initial state   steady state

Figure 2. Emergence of segregation. Source: based on Schelling (1971).

Vriend, 2003). But externalities of each residential location choice (i.e., the endogenous interaction choice) lead to an unraveling process (i.e., further endogenously determined interactions) resulting eventually in segregation.

2.2. *Epstein and Axtell (1996): resource gradient*

Epstein and Axtell (1996) study a number of different social behavioral phenomena, ranging from simple gathering and consumption, to mating, cultural transmission, combat, trade, credit, and the spreading of diseases.

These phenomena are studied in a so-called 'sugarscape'. This space consists of a lattice in the shape of a torus (i.e., a 2D grid with each edge folded and connected to the opposite edge). At each site, sugar can grow at a given rate up to some maximum (which may differ from site to site). In the basic model, sugar is the only commodity, and individual agents need it to survive, while in the model with trade there is a second commodity, called spice, as well. Each site will generally have some sugar and some spice, and can be occupied by at most one agent at a time, with each agent occupying one cell. When an agent occupies a site, he increases his wealth by accumulating the sugar (and spice) available at that site. Each individual agent has a given metabolic rate, specifying how much sugar per time step is consumed (decreasing the agent's wealth, i.e., sugar holdings), a given maximum age, and lateral vision up to some given limit. In the variant with trade, agents have also a utility function specified, and they have a metabolism for both sugar and spice, needing both to survive. In other variations of the model, the agents may also have their sex, and an array of arbitrary cultural attributes specified. Each agent has at most four neighbors, comprising the agents occupying sites in his von Neumann neighborhood (i.e., the sites laterally adjacent to his own site).

As explained above, Epstein and Axtell study a whole range of behaviors. They do this in a modular setup, in which forms of behavior can be added or taken away as one likes. A typical sequence of events, following the initialization of all individual agents

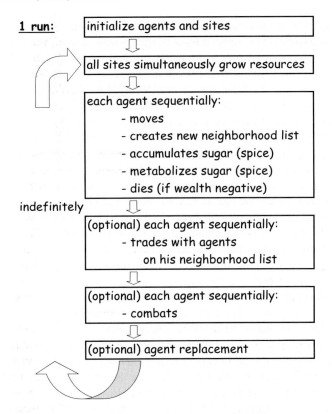

Figure 3. Structure of Epstein and Axtell (1996).

and sites, is given in Figure 3. First, at all sites simultaneously, resources grow at the given rate up to the limit of that site. The agents, then, move sequentially (in random order). Each individual agent checks the sites within his field of vision, moves to the best available location therein (if more than one he selects the nearest), makes a record of his new neighbors (calling this his 'neighborhood'), and increases his wealth by collecting the available sugar, while decreasing his wealth through his metabolism. Agents reaching a negative wealth die. Once these basic modules have finished, the optional trade module can be executed, in which agents may trade sequentially (in random order). A trading agent places all agents on his 'neighborhood' list in random order, and processes this list sequentially, making one transaction (if possible) with each of his neighbors by exchanging sugar for spice (or the other way around). The amounts exchanged depend on their marginal rates of substitution (as defined by the agents' utility functions) such that each trade leads to a welfare improvement of all agents involved, and on a pre-defined bargaining rule. After this, the optional combat module may be used, in which all agents sequentially (in random order) may combat with their neighbors. Finally, the optional agent replacement module may be applied, in which agents who have reached their maximum age, or have died for other reasons (e.g., due to lack of resources or combat), are replaced by new agents with random characteristics.

All interactions are endogenous in the following sense. In all variants of the model, all interactions depend exclusively on the location choices of the agents, and these location choices are guided only by the resource availability, i.e., the distribution of available sugar (and spice) on the landscape. As individual agents move around and harvest sugar (and spice), the pattern of resource availability evolves. As in Schelling (1971), agents choose best-responses to the existing resource pattern right from the start, and there is no learning (e.g., how to react to certain resource patterns). In the basic setup with only consumer-gatherers, there is only indirect interaction between the agents. In the variants studying also other types of behavior (such as sex, trade, and credit), there are direct interactions between the agents as well. These activities take place in 'networks'. But these networks are essentially the (one-step) lagged von Neumann neighborhoods,[3] and these neighborhood choices depend only on the resource availability on vacant sites. For example, in the variant with trade, an agent does not take account of the potential gains from trade on a given location, and agents just trade with whoever turns out to be an accidental new neighbor.

Given the enormous range of behaviors studied in the various modules, we will not try to summarize the results. For each of the modules interesting properties of demographic, economic and other phenomena emerge. What is more, they show that the behaviors of the various modules interact with each other. For example, the outcomes of the economic process are influenced through the demographic dynamics. Given that all interactions are essentially determined through the gradient of the resources in the landscape, the emerging properties are remarkable. Figure 4 gives an example for the model with trade as the only optional module. The figure shows the time series average trading price converging to the "market-clearing" level of 1, which is the emergent property of the model with only bilateral interactions determined through agents myopically following their resource gradient.

2.3. Arthur (1994): predictors

Arthur (1994) examines the importance of inductive reasoning, and illustrates this with the so-called 'El Farol' bar problem.

People like spending some time together in this bar, in particular on Thursday nights with Irish music, unless it is too crowded. More specifically, Arthur (1994) assumes that there is a fixed population of 100 agents, that agents enjoy spending time together in the bar if fewer than 60 people are present, but prefer to stay home if more than 60 show up. Hence, the question in the El Farol problem (and in similar coordination problems) is

---

[3] These networks are formed as follows. When an agent moves in to the nearest best available location within his field of vision, he records his neighbors. Subsequently these neighbors may move on themselves. When, e.g., the trade module is executed, an agent can only initiate trading with those people on his 'neighbor' list.

Mean Price

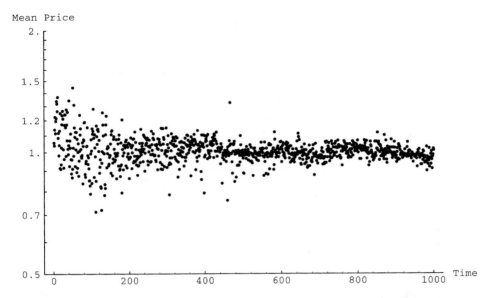

Figure 4. Typical time series for average trade price. Source: Epstein and Axtell (1996).

which agents will interact with each other, and how will they decide to do so (assuming that all agents make up their mind each time independently).

Each individual agent is modeled as follows. An agent has an individualized set of predictors in mind. Each predictor determines the expected number of people attending on the basis of a sample of the past weeks' attendance figures. For example, a predictor could be "the average attendance of the last four weeks", or "the trend in the last eight weeks (bounded by 0, 100)". The agent keeps track of the accuracy of each predictor, using the actual attendance figures.

The time-structure of Arthur (1994) is the following (see Figure 5). The model starts with randomly drawing a set of predictors for each agent individually from an "alphabet soup" of predictors. At the beginning of each period, each agent chooses one of his predictors, the one he currently believes to be the most accurate one. Given the predicted attendance. An agent decides to go to the bar if and only if the predicted number is less than 60. The actual attendance figure determined by all these individual decisions is, then, used to update each agent's belief concerning the accuracy of his attendance predictor.

The interactions are determined endogenously as follows. The individual interaction decisions (whether to go to the bar or not) depend on the past pattern of interactions (attendance figures), as different patterns of past attendances will typically lead to different expected attendance figures and hence different interaction decisions for most given predictors. Through these individual interaction decisions, the pattern of interactions itself evolves, as they will form part of the interaction pattern on which future interactions will be based. What is more, the view of an agent as to how a given pattern

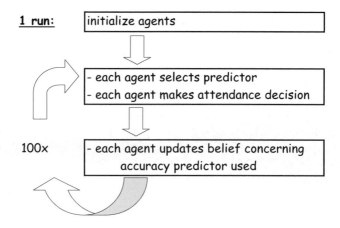

Figure 5. Structure of Arthur (1994).

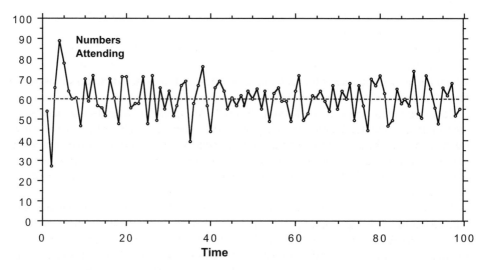

Figure 6. Numbers attending in first 100 weeks. Source: Arthur (1994).

of past attendance figures should lead to an interaction decision itself evolves. That is, the agents learn which predictor to use by updating their beliefs as to how accurate these predictors are, where this accuracy depends on the predictors used by the other agents.

How does the interaction pattern evolve? Figure 6 shows the attendance figures for 100 periods. As we see, it fluctuates around 60% attendance. That is, in each period about 60% of the agents predict attendance below 60%, while another 40% forecast attendance above 60%. Obviously, these predictions cannot be all correct at the same time. Hence, individual choices fluctuate over time as well, not only because the attendance pattern fluctuates, but also because individual agents continue revising the accuracy of their predictors. As Arthur (1994) puts it: *"This is something like a forest whose contours do not change, but whose individual trees do"* (p. 410).

2.4. Vriend (1995): advertising/patronage

Vriend (1995) presents an example of a computational approach to self-organization of markets, in particular buyer-seller networks. The starting point is the idea that market organization depends in a crucial way on knowledge of the identity of some potential trading partners. Such knowledge requires some kind of communication or interaction between the agents. Markets, then, emerge as the result of interacting individual agents pursuing advantageous contacts. The paper analyzes the emerging trading structure of the self-organized markets, the distribution of firm sizes, etc.

Each day, firms produce a certain commodity in advance, without knowing what the demand on the day will be. They may attract the attention of potential customers by sending information signals randomly into the population, directed at nobody in particular (presenting themselves as sellers to the population), and by offering a reliable service. Both production and signaling are costly. Consumers, then, have the choice to either 'shop around' randomly, stay loyal to their current supplier, or follow one of the information signals they received. Consumers want exactly one unit per day (at a given price), and shopping takes place on a first-come first-served basis. Figure 7 shows the structure of the model.

Each individual firm is specified as a set of alternative rules: binary strings, determining a production and an advertising level. The fitness of each rule depends on the actual payoffs generated using that rule, with fitter rules being more likely to be used. This is a form of reinforcement learning. After each block of 50 days, the sets of decision rules used by the individual firms evolve using a genetic algorithm: some rules are eliminated, while others are reproduced, with selection based on the fitness of the rules, applying crossover, and mutation. See also Brenner (2006) and Duffy (2006) on reinforcement learning and genetic algorithms.

Each individual consumer consists of a set of 15 "if ... then..." rules to decide how to shop: the conditions considered relate to the consumer's shopping experience during the previous day (whether he was satisfied, whether he was late and found only empty shelves, or whether he was simply lost in the mist and could not even find a firm selling the commodity), and to his information state (whether he did or did not receive any advertising signals from firms on this day). The possible actions for a consumer to consider are whether to patronize (return to the last firm visited), to visit one of the firms known to be selling this commodity through the advertisement signals, or to try his luck visiting somebody chosen at random. The fitness of each rule depends again on the actual payoffs generated using that rule, and fitter rules are more likely to be used in the future.

The interactions are endogenous in the following senses. The firms decide with how many people to link up through the number of advertising signals they send, and in-

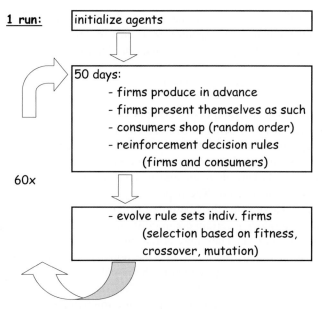

Figure 7. Structure of Vriend (1995).

fluence how many of these interactions are successful through their output decisions. Their views on these decisions evolve as they gain experience about their profitability. This profitability depends also on the shopping behavior of the consumers. These shopping decisions depend on the success of their latest trip and on whether they received advertising signals. These variables may evolve as the result of decisions by the firms and other consumers, and the consumers' view on the importance of these two variables may evolve as well.

What is the dynamic behavior of this model? First, starting from completely random behavior, all agents are relatively quick to learn reasonable behavior (production, signaling and shopping), leading to high efficiency and a good profit margin for the firms, while heterogeneous behavior emerges among consumers and firms. Second, does patronage occur, and what role does it play? As Figure 8 shows, especially 'strict patronage' (i.e., patronage by a satisfied consumer) emerges. That is, consumers quickly learn that in case they had been disappointed by a firm there is much less reason to return to that firm than in case of previous success. Notice that it is strict patronage that leads to the arbitrage of trading opportunities. For suppose some firms offer higher service rates than other firms. Strict patronage would imply that a firm not able to satisfy its clients is likely to loose some of its customers. Given its level of production, that would mean a higher coefficient of customer satisfaction on the next day. On the other hand, a firm satisfying its customers is likely to enlarge its clientele, thus lowering its service rate. Hence, ceteris paribus, strict patronage directly implies arbitrage of trad-

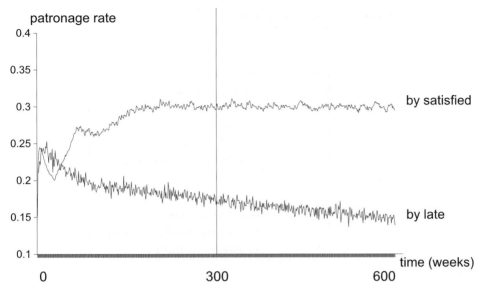

Figure 8. Evolution of patronage rate. Source: Vriend (1995).

ing opportunities, in the sense of the equalization of service rates across firms. Third, does communication matter? Yes, but it is costly and directly related to the endogenous shopping behavior. As can be seen in Figure 2 in Vriend (1995) (showing the costs per unit of sales), the firms, having reached profitable decisions early on, then continue to increase their signaling level steadily, as they are competing with each other to attract the consumers through the advertisement signals, until some constant average level is reached with much lower profits for the firms. Thus, communication matters, although the firms have no (explicit) clue as to why they send such signals. They have no idea what governs shopping behavior. This is illustrated in Figure 11 in Vriend (1995), showing the average signaling level for two versions of the model: the standard version, and a variant in which consumers will always return to a firm after a successful trip (i.e., fixed patronage). Although the firms do not know anything about this, they immediately spot the difference in the value of advertising in the latter setup, avoiding it almost completely, whereas high signaling levels are reached in the standard version.

2.5. Ashlock et al. (1996): (threshold) expected payoff

Ashlock et al. (1996) study the effect of preferential partner selection in an evolutionary study of the prisoner's dilemma game. The Prisoner's Dilemma game studied is a standard two-player simultaneous-move game in which each player can decide to Cooperate or to Defect with the resulting payoffs being as follows: payoffs for mutual cooperation and mutual defection are 3 and 1 respectively, while a unilateral defector gets a payoff of 5, and the sucker payoff equals 0.

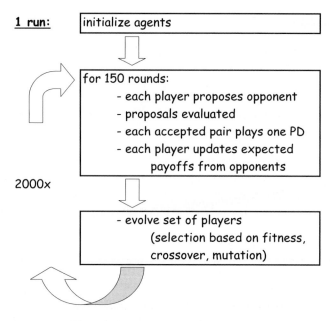

Figure 9. Structure of Ashlock et al. (1996).

Each individual agent is modeled as a finite automaton (Moore machine), represented by a binary string. This string contains two parts. The first part specifies the agent's dynamic game strategy in the iterated prisoner's dilemma. That is, this specifies an agent's action in the first round plus his actions in later rounds, with the latter being dependent on the history of play up to that point. The second part determines the endogenous interactions of the agent (i.e., with whom this agent wants to play the PD game).

The time-structure of the ACE model of Ashlock et al. (1996) is shown in Figure 9. For a given generation of agents, there are 150 rounds. In each round, each agent proposes to one opponent to play one round of the basic Prisoner's Dilemma game. All proposals are evaluated, and each accepted pair plays the game. After 150 rounds, the set of agents is evolved using a genetic algorithm. That is, depending on their performance, some agents are eliminated, while others are reproduced (applying crossover to recombine successful strings and mutation to induce some experimentation). The performance of an agent is measured by his fitness. This fitness equals the sum of payoffs received by an agent divided by the number of payoffs received. An agent receives a payoff either from playing a round of the Prisoner's Dilemma game, or from the refusal of another agent to interact with him (in the latter case the payoff will be 1.0). There is no payoff for an agent if he rejects himself somebody's offer to play. If an agent neither makes nor receives any offers to play in a given round, he receives a wallflower payoff of 1.6. The model considers 2000 generations.

The interactions are made endogenous as follows. Each individual agent keeps track of the payoffs realized with each other individual agent in the population (either from playing or from refusal by the other). An agent updates his assessment of another agent by taking a convex combination of his existing assessment and his very latest experience with that agent. Hence, this assessment is a weighted average of past payoffs, placing more weight on recent interactions. The initial expected payoff is 3 for each agent. When an agent makes a proposal to play the PD game, he will do so only to the best agent in the population, provided this agent is tolerable (see below). An agent receiving offers, on the other hand, will accept all offers from agents that are tolerable. An agent is tolerable if and only if the expected payoff with that agent is greater than a certain threshold. This threshold forms part of the individual agent's string, and evolves in the genetic step, such that threshold levels leading to higher fitness are more likely to be reproduced. The initial thresholds of the individual agents are uniform randomly drawn between 0 and 3.

What does this all imply for the organization of the interactions taking place? Notice that, through their individual threshold levels, the agents care about the payoffs to be expected from other individual agents. First, do agents learn to be picky in this respect? The answer is "yes". The average threshold level increases over time from a level of 1.5 to about 2.1. Second, does being picky matter? Again, the answer is affirmative. The average fitness level increases from a random initial level of 2.25 to a level just above 2.8. In a variant of the model, without allowing for endogenous interactions (which would be the same as having a fixed low threshold level), the average fitness reaches a level of about 2.3. This difference is due to changes in the ways in which agents interact. In particular, the option of refusal gives agents a way to protect themselves from defections without having to defect themselves. As a result, ostracism of defectors occurs endogenously, while parasitic relations are also observed. It is not true in general, however, that higher threshold levels will lead to higher average fitness. There is some risk with caring too much about with whom one will interact. That is, an agent's threshold level might be so high that no agent is acceptable anymore. As a result, only wallflower payoffs are received. Figure 10 illustrates this. The figure shows the frequency distribution over the fitness and threshold levels for all generations over 196 runs. In most cases we observe a high threshold going hand-in-hand with a high average fitness, but there are a good number of generations with a very high threshold and a low fitness. In those generations being too picky led to a breakdown of interactions.

2.6. Riolo (1997): arbitrary tags

Riolo (1997) studies the effects and evolution of tag-mediated selection of partners in populations playing the Iterated Prisoner's Dilemma (IPD) game, analyzing exactly the same basic Prisoner's Dilemma (PD) game as Ashlock et al. (1996).

An individual agent is modeled as a 5-tuple, the first three real-encoded parameters specifying his dynamic game strategy (whether to cooperate or not, conditional on the history of play), and the last two parameters determining the endogenous interactions.

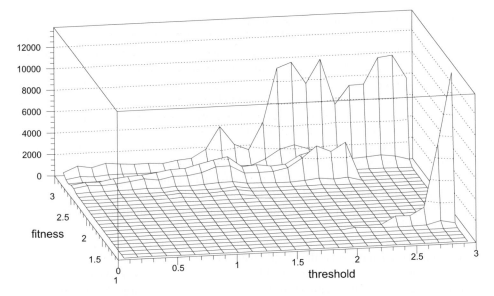

Figure 10. Distribution of threshold and fitness levels. Source: Ashlock et al. (1996).

For a given generation, each agent has to find an opponent ten times. Each success-fully matched pair plays a 4-round IPD game. Once this is all done, the set of agents evolves. That is, some agents are eliminated while others are reproduced, with selection based on the agents' fitness (depending on the payoffs realized), and with noise added to the parameter values to induce some experimentation. Figure 11 shows the structure of the model.

The interactions are made endogenous as follows. Each individual agent i uses some arbitrary tag τ_i in [0, 1]. This tag is some external label or (behavioral) characteristic that can be easily recognized by other agents. One could, for example, think of the tag τ here as a number written on an agent's forehead. When an agent needs to find an opponent, he first selects a possible opponent randomly. He, then, accepts this opponent on the basis of the similarity of their tags: probability (i agrees to play j) $= 1 - |\tau_i - \tau_j|^{b(i)}$, where $|\tau_i - \tau_j|$ measures the absolute distance between the tags of the two agents and $b(i)$ is a parameter in [0, 100] determining the 'pickiness' of agent i. For any given value of $b(i)$, agent i is more likely to interact with others the closer their tags are.[4] The opponent carries out a similar evaluation simultaneously, and they will play the IPD only if both accept to do so. Otherwise an agent will randomly try another possible opponent. There are search costs (to be subtracted from an agent's eventual payoff)

---

[4] The similarity in the tag can be seen as a clue that the players can trust each other as they may have a common understanding of the situation. Thus, somebody might be reluctant to play a game with a person with a weird hairdo who does not wear a tie, unless this player happens to go through life without a decent haircut and a tie himself.

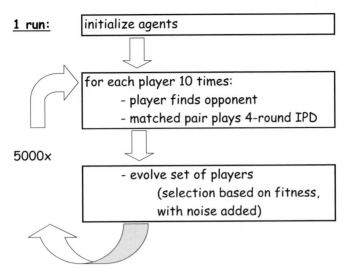

Figure 11. Structure of Riolo (1997).

for each failed attempt to find an opponent. After four failed attempts, an agent will have to play against a randomly chosen opponent, who will have to accept. The tags τ_i are an element of the second part of the 5-tuple specifying an individual agent, and evolve in the 'genetic' step, such that tag values leading to higher fitness are more likely to be reproduced. The other element of the second part of the 5-tuple specifying an individual agent consists of the 'pickiness' parameter b. Notice that a high b implies indifference with respect to tags (the distance does not matter), whereas a low b implies that the agent is very picky (the distance must be very small). The pickiness parameter $b(i)$, being part of the 5-tuple specifying an individual agent, evolves as well in the 'genetic' step, such that values leading to higher fitness are more likely to be reproduced. Notice that selection and reproduction take place at the level of the individual agents (each modeled as a 5-tuple). That is, strategies, tags, and pickiness with respect to tags all evolve together such that successful combinations are more likely to prosper.

Riolo's model has some similarity with models in which agents choose a location in space, and then interact with nearby agents. That is, the abstract tag signal can be seen as a location. Notice, however, that in Riolo's model part of the endogeneity concerns the agents' choices whether or not to care about distance. Such endogeneity seems less natural in space, where the economic importance of the distance is typically exogenously given. One could also imagine an evolving matching function as such, allowing, for example, agents to learn to play only against large distance opponents. Again, this seems more natural with arbitrary tags than in real space.

What are the dynamics of this model to determine endogenous interactions? First, do tags matter? The answer is "yes". As Figure 1 in Riolo (1997) shows, for a given parameter value of $b = 0.02$ for all agents, the use of tags leads to quicker and more stable cooperation (resulting in higher average fitness). It is only without the tags that we observe troughs in fitness levels due to systematic defections. The average fitness with tags fluctuates around the expected payoff for random behavior. Hence, what the tags seem to do is allow the agents to 'escape' from systematic defectors (through the evolving tag values). Second, if the parameter b is no longer exogenously fixed, will agents learn to care about tags (through the pickiness parameter b)? Figure 12 shows that this depends on the (indirect) search costs. The figure shows the evolution of the pickiness parameter b over the generations. If the population starts out caring about tags ($b = 0.01$ initially) and there are no search costs, then the population continues to care about tags (see the — line in Figure 12). But if there are search costs, then the population slides into indifference with respect to tags (o line in Figure 12). If, however, the population starts being relatively indifferent with respect to tags ($b = 2.00$), and there are no search costs, then the population may or may not evolve into one that cares about tags (see □ and △ lines in Figure 12).

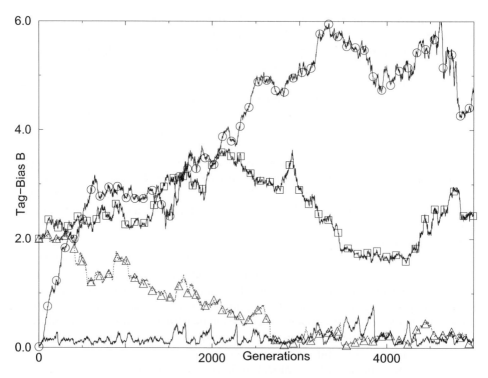

Figure 12. Evolution of tag-bias (pickiness) parameter. Source: Riolo (1997).

2.7. Hanaki et al. (2004): trust

Hanaki et al. (2004) study a repeatedly played one-shot version of a standard Prisoner's Dilemma (PD) game. Just as Ashlock et al. (1996), they start from the observation that defection is the dominant strategy, and ask the question whether cooperation could be sustained with endogenously determined local interactions, with the individual agents choosing their (number of) partners.

Each individual agent can choose a strategy for the one-shot PD and he can revise his links with other agents. The agents are restricted to using the same PD strategy for their entire neighborhood (i.e., all partners they are linked to). An individual agent's payoffs are summed over all his interactions, and there are costs attached to interacting with other agents, with the costs increasing in the number of partners.

The dynamics of the model are given in Figure 13. The model starts with a given number of agents being assigned random actions and beliefs (see below) and without any links between agents. Each period, all agents simultaneously play one round of the PD with all their partners. At the end of each period, with some exogenously given probability, individual agents can update their PD strategy, and with some other exogenously given probability they can update their local network, after which they play another round of the PD. When they update their interaction structure, with some exogenously given probability they either try to severe an existing link or to form a new link, and if this fails they try the opposite action. To choose a PD strategy, each agent copies the most successful strategy in his neighborhood (including his own), where the

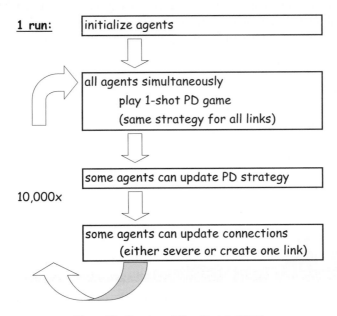

Figure 13. Structure of Hanaki et al. (2004).

measure of success is the sum of all current payoffs. If an agent had no partners before, he randomly chooses to cooperate or defect in the next period.

The interactions are endogenous in the following sense. When looking for a link to severe, an agent chooses one of his existing partners randomly, and terminates the relationship if the net benefit of doing so is positive, myopically assuming other agents will not change behavior and the network remains otherwise unchanged too. No consent is needed. To form a link, on the other hand, consent is needed. Hence, both agents, myopically comparing costs and benefits, need to find positive net marginal payoffs. A potential new partner can be selected either among the partners of his current partners (with the probability of any partner being chosen proportional to the number of shared partners) or be a randomly chosen stranger from the entire population. The probability used to decide between these two routes to a new partner is exogenously fixed. That is, the agents do not learn which route to follow. How to estimate the expected payoff of a new partner? If it is a partner of a partner, this partner will inform the agent about the most recent PD strategy of this new partner. If the potential new partner is a stranger, the initial expected payoff depends on trust, which is effectively the subjective probability that such an agent will cooperate. This trust level itself evolves. That is, it is updated every period such that it is a weighted average of the cooperation levels experienced by the agent (with greater weights for more recent experiences). The experiences that matter in this respect are either (in one version of the model) all others interacted with (including ongoing interactions) or (in another version) only all new partners interacted with. The agents' view on this does not evolve. That is, although the agents update their trust levels, they do not learn on which interactions they should base their trust.

Hanaki et al. (2004) present an extensive analysis for a wide range of parameter values. Figure 14 shows the relative frequency distribution of average cooperation levels

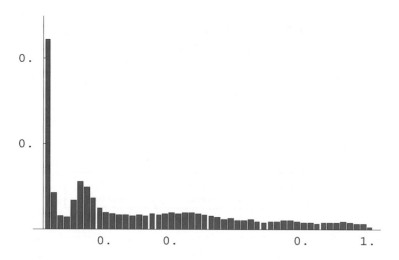

Figure 14. Distribution of average cooperation levels reached. Source: Hanaki et al. (2004).

reached in 10 000 runs of 10 000 periods for a population of 1000 agents, with the other parameter values sampled randomly from pre-specified ranges. As we see, substantial amounts of cooperation can occur. They show that the amount (and volatility) of cooperation relies on networks being sparse (both globally and locally), which is facilitated by high connection costs. In a fully-connected network, where cooperators and defectors interact with the same agents, all agents would quickly learn to defect (which is the dominant strategy). They find that cooperation levels are higher when new partners are chosen at random from the whole population rather than friends of friends. On the one hand, this is due to the fact that relying exclusively on friends to find new partners leads to too high connectivity, and hence collapse of cooperation (see above). On the other hand, the advantage of interacting with strangers is that cooperation can expand. Friends of friends are acceptable only if it is known (through the friends) that they cooperate anyway. But strangers are acceptable depending on the trust of the agent looking for new partners. This trust (based on past experiences) is an imperfect substitute for information. As a result, such agents may seek interaction with current defectors, possibly leading to the recruitment of defectors. If these defectors are relatively isolated, they may immediately be converted (through the payoffs) to cooperation if the cooperating agent initiating the link has enough cooperators in his network. Obviously, this implies that assortive matching is essential, i.e., there must be a limit to this willingness to interact with defectors. The eventual amount of cooperation developed is the net result of these two forces. The balance is due to the endogenous trust level. That is, the amount of expansion is determined endogenously. Imperfectly informed agents are open enough for new contacts while all the time updating their beliefs about their environment.

2.8. Kirman and Vriend (2001): expected payoff/familiarity

Kirman and Vriend (2001) study the evolving structure of an actual market: the wholesale fish market of Marseille. They focus in particular on two stylized facts of that real market: price dispersion and the loyalty of buyers to sellers.

Each day the following sequence of events takes place in this model (see Figure 15). In the morning, before the market opens, the sellers purchase their supply for the day, without knowing the demand they will face during the day. The market, then, opens, and the buyers (who want one unit each of the fish) choose the queue of a seller in the market hall. The sellers handle their queues sequentially, giving each individual buyer a 'take-it-or-leave-it' price (thus, prices are not posted). Once the sellers have handled all queues, the morning session is over. In the afternoon, the market re-opens, allowing unsatisfied buyers from the morning sessions to choose again a queue of a seller. With all queues handled by the sellers, the market closes, and all unsold stocks perish. The buyers, then, re-sell their fish outside the market. The model considers 5000 days.

Each individual seller must decide the quantity to supply, how to handle queues, and which prices to ask during the morning and afternoon sessions. For each decision they use a set of alternative rules. The fitness of each rule depends on the actual payoffs realized when using the rule, and fitter rules are more likely to be used again. An individual

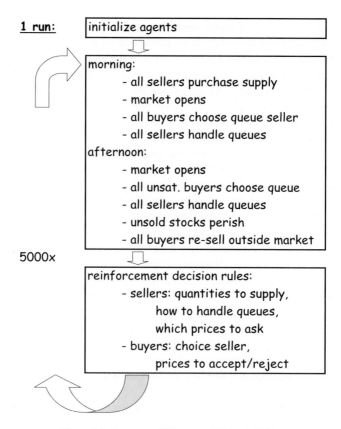

Figure 15. Structure of Kirman and Vriend (2001).

buyer chooses a seller in the morning, and possibly (another) one in the afternoon. Whenever a buyer hears a price, he will need to decide whether to accept or reject the price. For each of these decisions an individual buyer has a set of decision rules at his disposal, being more likely to use the fitter rules, with these fitnesses depending on the payoffs generated by these rules.

The interactions are endogenous as follows. The choice of which seller to visit for the buyers depends directly on the average payoffs a buyer realized with each seller, such that more satisfactory sellers (in the sense of offering a better combination of service and prices) are more likely to be visited by a buyer. When the sellers handle their queues, they can do this in any order they like. That is, they may give precedence to some buyers over other buyers. They do this on the basis of the familiarity of the faces of the buyers in their queue. This familiarity is basically a weighted average of past presences of a buyer in a certain seller's queue, and it evolves directly as the result of the buyer's shopping behavior. What is more, the sellers' view concerning the relevance of this familiarity may evolve. That is, an individual seller can move a more loyal buyer either towards

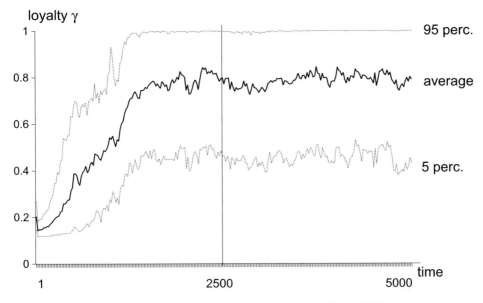

Figure 16. Evolution of loyalty. Source: Kirman and Vriend (2001).

the front or the back of a queue. The probability for a buyer to be served next is a function of a buyer's loyalty, and this function depends on a choice parameter, such that different values of this parameter give either more or less advantage or disadvantage to loyal buyers. The sellers learn which parameter value to use through reinforcement, such that values that led to higher payoffs in the past are more likely to be used again. To decide upon a price to ask from an individual buyer, a seller takes into account the familiarity of the buyer's face too, as well as the remaining stock and remaining queue at that moment. Each seller uses a set of alternative rules linking these two factors to prices, and learns through reinforcement which rule to use.

What kind of interaction pattern does this imply? First, does loyalty emerge? As Figure 16 shows, loyalty does emerge (on average). The loyalty index used is such that it would be 1 if buyers were perfectly loyal, and 0.10 if buyers were not loyal at all. As buyers do not even know the concept loyalty (they just pick a firm each day), and sellers are indifferent with respect to loyalty to start with, why do buyers become loyal? As it turns out, most buyers get a higher average payoff when returning to the same seller the next day than when switching. This occurs mainly through a better service rate of loyal buyers. Why do sellers offer this advantage to loyal buyers? Sellers realize higher gross revenues when dealing with loyal buyers, which is related mainly to a higher acceptance rate. Second, does this familiarity of faces matter? The answer is "yes", and the role it can play with respect to market organization is illustrated nicely by a setup in which there are three types of buyers. The difference between these three types is in the given prices for which they can re-sell outside the market (imagine, e.g., a cheap corner shop versus a posh restaurant). The model explains how 'high' buyers (those that can re-sell for a higher price) do not only pay higher prices than 'low' buyers, but also find higher prices than the latter. This happens notwithstanding the fact that in this model no trader knows about this difference between types of buyers, and no trader can recognize any type of buyer. But different types of buyers notice their different payoffs at the end of each day. This affects their evaluation of their price acceptance/rejection decisions, and their evaluation of the sellers they visited. Hence, this will influence their shopping behavior. These differences in shopping patterns are indirectly picked up by the sellers through the familiarity of buyer faces. In turn, this leads to different treatments in queues and different prices. What is more, differences among sellers emerge. Some sellers learn to specialize in 'high' buyers, some others in 'low' buyers. The latter ask lower prices, experience nevertheless a higher rejection rate, maintain a lower supply/sales ratio, leading to a lower service rate, and put loyal customers towards the end of the queue.

2.9. Chang and Harrington (2005): past success rate

Chang and Harrington (2005) study the issue of discovery and diffusion of knowledge, and the social networks that may thus arise.

They consider a population of individuals, who all have to solve the same given number of separate tasks. A method to solve a given task is described by a sequence of binary bits. Hence, each individual agent's method to solve his entire set of tasks is simply a binary vector of bits. Each individual agent has an optimal, target vector that describes the optimal way to solve all his tasks. Chang and Harrington (2005) assume that individual agents, although they can not simply pick the optimal method themselves, can rank any two method vectors on their Hamming distance from their target vector (which is effectively the number of bits that is different in the two vectors). The individual target vectors may change over time following some pre-specified dynamic process. This implies that there is a persistent need for the individual agents to discover new methods, and for such knowledge to be diffused.

The time-structure is the following (see Figure 17). Having drawn all initial method vectors and target methods randomly, and avoiding any bias in favor of imitation or innovation, or any bias favoring the observation of one individual over another, in each period each individual agent goes through the following sequence: An agent decides whether to innovate (all by himself) or to imitate another agent. If he decides to innovate, then he randomly chooses a method for a randomly chosen task. If, however, he decides to imitate, then he chooses an agent to imitate, and copies the method from this other agent for a randomly chosen task. In both cases (innovation and imitation), the method obtained is actually adopted only if its adoption gets the agent closer to his target vector (using the Hamming distance as measure).

The endogenous interactions are modeled as follows. The structure of interactions depends solely on the success of past interactions. This success depends on the distribution of the vectors of methods adopted by the agents as such, and their state relative to

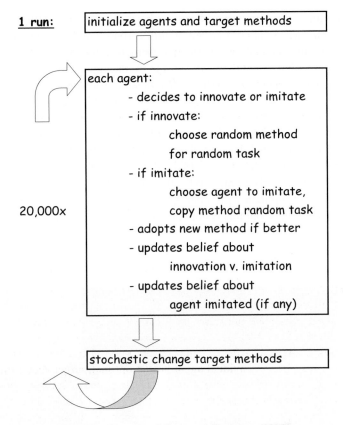

Figure 17. Structure of Chang and Harrington (2005).

the target vector. But the agents do not use any information about this directly. As the agents interact (or not), the distribution of method vectors changes. The agents' view as to whether they should innovate or imitate (and if so, whom) evolves as the agents learn through their own experience. The choice of an agent between imitation and innovation (i.e., whether to interact with others or whether to stay alone) is a probabilistic decision. The decision weight for each depends essentially on the number of successes when choosing that option in the past. In addition, the weights decrease each period through some decay. In case an agent opts for imitation, the choice of the agent to be imitated is made in a similar probabilistic way. The weight for a given agent in the population is increased each time that agent has been imitated successfully, and it decreases through some decay.

Chang and Harrington (2005) focus on the properties of the emerging social networks. In much of their analysis they partition the population into a fixed number of groups to get some persistent similarity in goals, as the dynamics of the target vectors of all agents within a group follow some stochastic process (modeling turbulence in the task environment) such that they stay within certain bounds. The individual agents know nothing about this, and one of the questions is whether they will imitate other agents, and if so to what extent they will learn to imitate agents from their own group or from other groups. The analysis is based on 20 runs of 20 000 periods with 20 individual agents. Figure 18 shows the interaction probabilities for all individual agents for a setup with four fixed groups of five agents. The 20 individual agents are ordered identically on both the horizontal and vertical axis according to their group association. Lighter shades indicate higher probabilities of interaction. Notice that individual agents cannot imitate themselves, which shows up as black diagonal cells. As we see, there are four 5 × 5 blocks that are clearly lighter, indicating that agents learn to interact more with agents within their group than with other agents. Notice that agents within their group are pursuing similar goals, but this is not known to the individual agents. Further analy-

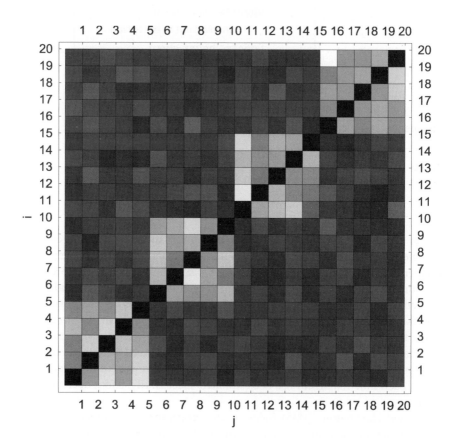

Figure 18. Interaction probabilities between agents i and j. Source: Chang and Harrington (2005).

sis shows that this property is stronger the more groups are similar within and different from other groups.

2.10.   Jackson and Rogers (2004): directed random search

Jackson and Rogers study some abstract network formation process, and in particular the question which processes may lead to power laws and small worlds, properties that have often been observed empirically in large networks. More precisely, they focus on the following three stylized features of such networks: highly clustered connections (which means that two agents linked to a given agent are themselves likely to be linked to each other as well), small maximal distances between nodes (which means that any two nodes in the network can be linked through a short path), and a power law in the upper tail for the distribution of node degrees (which means that there are more nodes with very few or with very many connections than one would expect if links were formed independently).

Jackson and Rogers consider an abstract model of network growth, without any further economic interaction. Figure 19 shows the time-structure of the model. At each time step, one individual agent is added to the network. Before joining the network, the individual agent forms two samples of potential links. First, he creates a uniform randomly chosen sample out of all agents in the current network, and second, he forms another sample chosen uniform randomly out of all agents who are currently directly linked to the agents in his first sample. In the basic setup the net benefit of a link is independently and identically distributed across pairs. Given the two samples of potential links, the new agent myopically chooses any links within those samples providing

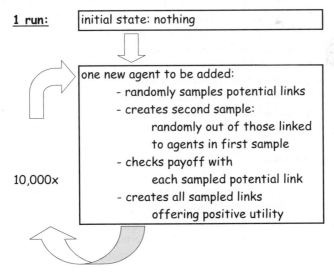

Figure 19. Structure of Jackson and Rogers (2004).

him with positive net utility. Once linked, agents remain linked forever, and no further payoff relevant events occur for these agents.

The links formed are endogenous in the following sense. The choice of agents sampled by a new agent depends on the existing network structure. More precisely, the second sample consisting of partners of the first uniform randomly generated sample of agents is affected directly by the existing network structure. As new agents form links, this network structure evolves. The agents' view on the relevance of certain network structures, however, does not evolve, as the agents do not learn anything. That is, the sizes of the two samples, and the fact to use these two sampling methods are determined exogenously. This is irrelevant in the basic version of the model. Since the net utilities for pairs are independent and identical draws, any sampling method is as good as any other. But as soon as the net utility of connecting to a certain node depends on the existing network structure this is no longer true.

The analysis of this agent-based model of Jackson and Rogers is in part formal mathematical, in part based on mean-field approximations, and in part computational. They show that the model explains high clustering, which does not go to zero as the network grows (unlike a number of alternative network formation processes). This seems due to the search method, as any two nodes linked to by a new agent are likely to have been selected in part because they were linked to each other. The diameters of the networks tend to be small, which seems again related to the directed search method. As search is directed towards nodes with relatively large degree, new links are likely to shorten paths for many existing nodes. Finally, they show that the degree distribution of nodes has a scale-free upper tail. Scale-free means that the 'connectedness' (the distribution of links per node) does not vary with the scale of the network. This can be expressed by a power law as the probability of any given node being connected to k other nodes is $(1/k)^n$, where n is some constant parameter. Figure 20 shows a log–log plot of the complementary cumulative distribution function of node degrees. The solid curve is from a mean-field approximation, and the dotted curve from the computational analysis. The latter is based on a run of 10 000 periods, in which both samples were always of size two, and all agents sampled offer positive net payoffs (which means that they are acceptable links). As we see, the upper tail of the distribution is nearly linear, indicating a scale-free distribution, but the lower tail is not scale-free.

3. Concluding remarks

Although the models discussed cover a wide range of possibilities to model endogenous interactions, we can detect some kind of prototype of modeling endogenous interactions. This prototype seems to consist of up to three elements. *(i)* The interactions are directed (guided) by some variable x, e.g., because the agents are 'picky' with respect to this variable x. *(ii)* This variable x itself evolves directly as a result of the interactions. *(iii)* The agents' view of the relevance of variable x evolves, as they may learn, e.g., how and how much they care about it.

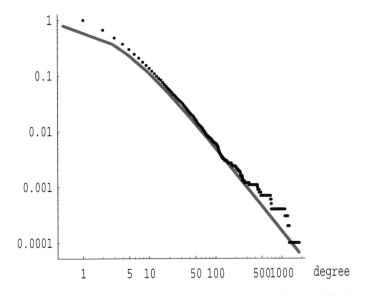

Figure 20. Distribution of node degrees. Source: Jackson and Rogers (2004).

Where can the ACE modeling of endogenous interactions go from here? Obviously the approaches discussed could be improved, and alternatives may be created. It seems in particular interesting if various approaches could be used for the same underlying game or economic situation, to analyze the possible differences in dynamics. In the introduction we argued that the choice of interaction mechanism should depend on the 'circumstances' to be modeled in a broad sense, and on the purpose of the model. But it would seem interesting to add one level of endogeneity to the interaction mechanisms discussed in this chapter, i.e., to let the type of endogenous interaction itself be determined endogenously. This would allow us to study why certain endogenous interaction mechanisms (depending on past payoffs, proximity, familiarity of faces, simple physical cues or tags, trust, advertisements, ...) seem to be relevant for certain types of interactions but not for others.

4. For further reading

Galouye (1964). For a start, consider the following quotes:

> "We can electronically simulate a social environment. We can populate it with subjective analogs—reactional identity units. By manipulating the environment, by prodding the ID units, we can estimate behaviour in hypothetical situations." (p. 7/8).

And:

"... the simulator ... would ... be exploring fully the unpredictable fields of social interaction and human relationships as a means of suggesting a more orderly society, from the bottom up!" (p. 10).

References

Arthur, W.B. (1994). "Inductive reasoning and bounded rationality". American Economic Review, Papers and Proceedings 84, 406–411.

Ashlock, D., Smucker, M.D., Stanley, E.A., Tesfatsion, L. (1996). "Preferential partner selection in an evolutionary study of prisoner's dilemma". BioSystems 37, 99–125.

Blin, J.M. (1980). "Comments on "The Economics of Markets: a Simple Model of the Market-making Process"". Journal of Business 53 (3, Pt. 2), S193–S197.

Brenner, T. (2006). "Agent learning representation: advice on modelling economic learning", this handbook.

Chang, M.-H., Harrington Jr., J.E. (2005). "Discovery and diffusion of knowledge in an endogenous social network". American Journal of Sociology 110, 937–976.

Dieckmann, T. (1999). "The evolution of conventions with mobile players". Journal of Economic Behavior and Organization 38, 93–111.

Duffy, J. (2006). "Agent-based models and human subject experiments", this handbook.

Epstein, J.M., Axtell, R. (1996). Growing Artificial Societies: Social Science from the Bottom Up. Brookings/MIT Press, Washington, DC.

Galouye, D.F. (1964). Counterfeit World. Victor Gollancz, London.

Hanaki, N., Peterhansl, A., Dodds, P.S., Watts, D.J. (2004). "Cooperation in evolving social networks" (mimeo).

Jackson, M.O., Rogers, B.W. (2004). "Search and the strategic formation of large networks: when and why do we see power laws and small worlds?" (mimeo).

Judd, K. (2006). "Computationally intensive analyses in economics", this handbook.

Kirman, A.P., Vriend, N.J. (2001). "Evolving market structure: an ACE model of price dispersion and loyalty". Journal of Economic Dynamics and Control 25 (3/4), 459–502.

Klamer, A. (1984). The New Classical Macroeconomics. Conversations with New Classical Economists and their Opponents. Wheatsheaf, Brighton.

Mailath, G.J., Samuelson, L., Shaked, A. (2000). "Evolution and Endogenous Interactions". In: Pagano, U., Nicita, A. (Eds.), The Evolution of Economic Diversity. Routledge, Siena.

Oechssler, J. (1997). "Decentralization and the coordination problem". Journal of Economic Behavior and Organization 32, 119–135.

Pancs, R., Vriend, N.J. (2003). "Schelling's spatial proximity model of segregation revisited" (Dept. of Economics Working Paper No. 487), Queen Mary, University of London.

Riolo, R.L. (1997). "The effects and evolution of tag-mediated selection of partners in populations playing the iterated prisoner's dilemma". In: Bäck, Th. (Ed.), Proceedings of the 7th International Conference on Genetic Algorithms. Morgan Kaufmann, pp. 378–385.

Sakoda, J.M. (1949). "Minidoka: an analysis of changing patterns of social interaction", unpublished doctoral dissertation, University of California, Berkeley.

Sakoda, J.M. (1971). "The checkerboard model of social interaction". Journal of Mathematical Sociology 1, 119–132.

Schelling, T.C. (1971). "Dynamic models of segregation". Journal of Mathematical Sociology 1 (2), 143–186.

Skyrms, B., Pemantle, R. (2000). "A dynamic model of social network formation". Proceedings of the National Academy of Sciences of the USA 97 (16), 9340–9346.

Tesfatsion, L. (2006). "Agent-based computational economics: a constructive approach to economic theory", this handbook.

Varian, H.R. (1984). Microeconomic Analysis, 2nd edn. Norton, New York.

Vriend, N.J. (1995). "Self-organization of markets: an example of a computational approach". Computational Economics 8 (3), 205–231.
Wilhite, A. (2006). "Economic activity on fixed networks", this handbook.

Chapter 22

SOCIAL DYNAMICS: THEORY AND APPLICATIONS[*]

H. PEYTON YOUNG

Department of Economics, Johns Hopkins University, Baltimore, MD 21218, USA
e-mail: pyoung@jhu.edu; url: http://www.econ.jhu.edu/people/young

University of Oxford

Contents

[*] This article is adapted in part from [Young, H.P. (1998). Individual Strategy and Social Structure: An Evolutionary Theory of Institutions. Princeton University Press, Princeton, NJ], and from H. Peyton Young and Mary A. Burke [Young, H.P., Burke, M.A. (2001). "Competition and custom in economic contracts: a case study of Illinois agriculture". American Economic Review 91, 559–573]. The author thanks Samuel Bowles, Steven Durlauf, Kislaya Prasad, the editors, and several anonymous referees for helpful comments on an earlier draft.

Handbook of Computational Economics, Volume 2. Edited by Leigh Tesfatsion and Kenneth L. Judd
DOI: 10.1016/S1574-0021(05)02022-8

Abstract

Agent-based models typically involve large numbers of interacting individuals with widely differing characteristics, rules of behavior, and sources of information. The dynamics of such systems can be extremely complex due to their high dimensionality. This chapter discusses a general method for rigorously analyzing the long-run behavior of such systems using the theory of large deviations in Markov chains. The theory highlights certain qualitative features that distinguish agent-based models from more conventional types of equilibrium analysis. Among these distinguishing features are: local conformity versus global diversity, punctuated equilibrium, and the persistence of particular states in the presence of random shocks. These ideas are illustrated through a variety of examples, including competition between technologies, models of sorting and segregation, and the evolution of contractual customs.

Keywords

bounded rationality, social norms, Markov chains, random perturbations, stochastic stability, punctuated equilibrium, local conformity, global diversity

JEL classification: C73, D02

1. Adaptive dynamics

Many forms of social and economic behavior evolve from the bottom up: they crystallize from the behavior and beliefs of disparate individuals interacting with each other over time. Language, codes of dress, forms of money and credit, patterns of courtship and marriage, standards of evidence, rules of the road, and economic contracts all have this feature. For the most part no one dictated the form that they have; they emerged through a process of experimentation, historical accident, and the accumulation of precedent. Agent-based models are particularly well suited to studying the dynamics of such processes, since by their nature they involve large numbers of dispersed, heterogeneous actors. In this chapter I shall outline a general framework for analyzing such systems based on theoretical results on large Markov chains, and then show how to apply the theory to concrete situations. Importantly, the theory can be applied without compromising the inherent complexity of the system: agents can be endowed with different characteristics, different levels of rationality, different amounts of information, and different locations.

My starting point is the assumption that agents are boundedly rational but purposeful. They look around them, they gather information, and they act fairly sensibly on the basis of that information.[1] I shall also assume that their choices are not entirely deterministic and predictable, but may be buffeted by random perturbations in the environment, errors of perception, and idiosyncrasies in behavior. Whatever the source, these perturbations play a role similar to mutations in biology by injecting variability into agents' behaviors. Moreover, the presence of perturbations implies that the evolutionary dynamic never settles down completely; it is always in flux. This feature provides a powerful analytical tool for analyzing its long-run behavior. In what follows I shall illustrate this approach through a variety of concrete examples, including competing technologies, neighborhood segregation, and the emergence of contractual norms.[2]

To set the stage, let us consider a classical example: the emergence of money as a medium of exchange.[3] History records the great variety of goods that societies have adopted as money: some used gold or silver, some copper or bronze, others used beads, still others favored cattle. In the early stages of economic development, we can conceive of the choice of currency as growing out of individual decisions that gradually converge on some norm. Once enough people in a society have adopted a particular currency, everyone else wants to follow suit.

At the individual level, this sort of decision problem can be cast as a coordination game. Suppose that there are two choices of currency: gold and silver. At the beginning of a period, each person must decide which currency to carry. During the period, each

---

[1] For a discussion of learning models see the chapters in this volume by Thomas Brenner and John Duffy.

[2] There is a large literature on the evolution of norms, some of which is related to the approach described here. See in particular Ullman-Margalit (1977), Sugden (1986, 1989), Bendor and Swistak (2001), Hechter and Dieter (2001), Skyrms (2004), and Bicchieri (2006).

[3] See for example Menger (1871) and Marimon et al. (1990).

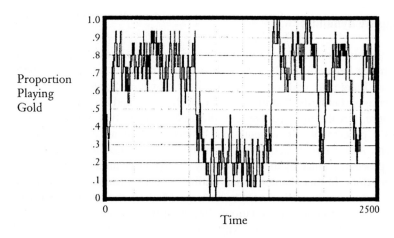

Figure 1. The currency game with equal payoffs, sample size $m = 10$, and $\varepsilon = 0.5$.

person meets various other people in the society at random, and they can trade only if they are both carrying the same currency. Thus the decision problem at the beginning of the period is to choose the currency that one believes will be chosen by a majority of the others.

Schematically we can model the dynamics as follows. Let p^t be the proportion in the population choosing gold at time t, and let $1 - p^t$ be the proportion choosing silver. In period $t + 1$, one person is drawn at random to reconsider his decision. He or she selects a random sample of s other individuals to determine what they are currently doing. Let $\hat{e}^t$ be the sample proportion of those using gold. Assume for the moment that the properties of gold and silver make them equally desirable as currencies. Then the decision maker chooses gold in period $t + 1$ if $\hat{e}^t > 0.5$ and chooses silver if $\hat{e}^t < 0.5$. (If $\hat{e}^t = 0.5$ we shall assume the agent chooses randomly.) All of this happens with high probability, say $1 - \varepsilon$. But with probability $\varepsilon > 0$ a person chooses gold or silver at random, that is, for reasons external to the model.

Qualitatively this process evolves in the following manner. After an initial shakeout, the process converges quite rapidly to a situation in which most people are carrying the same currency—say gold. This norm will very likely stay in place for a considerable period of time. Eventually, however, an accumulation of random shocks will "tip" the process into the silver norm. These tipping incidents are infrequent compared to the periods in which one or the other norm is in place. Moreover, once a tipping incident occurs, the process will tend to adjust quite rapidly to the new norm. This pattern— long periods of stasis punctuated by sudden changes of regime—will be called the *punctuated equilibrium effect*. (The term is used here descriptively; in biology it has a somewhat different meaning.) Figure 1 illustrates this idea for the currency game when the two currencies have equal payoffs.

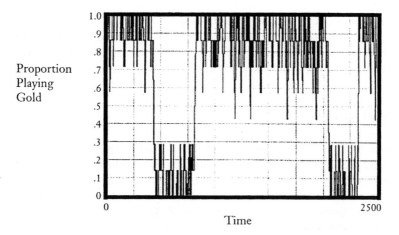

Figure 2. The currency game with asymmetric payoffs, $\alpha = 1/3$, $m = 10$, and $\varepsilon = 0.5$.

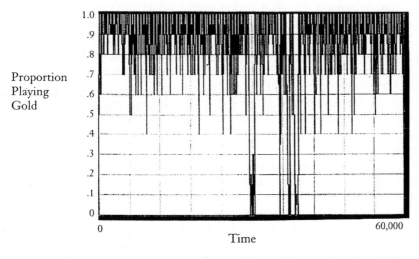

Figure 3. The currency game with asymmetric payoffs, $\alpha = 1/3$, $m = 10$, and $\varepsilon = 0.05$.

Now let us ask what happens when one currency is inherently better than the other. Suppose, for example, that gold is somewhat preferred because it does not tarnish as easily as silver. Then the decision problem at the individual level is to choose gold if $\hat{e}^t > \alpha$, and to choose silver if $\hat{e}^t < \alpha$, where α is a fraction strictly less than one-half. Now the process follows a path that looks like Figure 2. Over the long run there is a bias toward gold, that is, at any given time the society is more likely to have adopted the gold standard than the silver standard. Moreover, the bias becomes *larger* the *smaller* the random perturbations are. Figure 3 shows a characteristic sample path when the noise level is reduced by a factor of ten. Notice that the process is at or near the gold standard a larger fraction of the time, and shifts of regime are more infrequent. These features become more pronounced as the noise level becomes smaller, a fact that can be verified analytically using methods to be discussed in the next section.

2. Stochastic stability

Many agent-based models can be represented as Markov processes of very large dimensionality. A *state* of the system is specified by the location, information, and beliefs of the various actors. The *transition probabilities* are specified by the interaction probabilities among agents and the rules by which they adapt their choices and beliefs to perceived conditions (the learning rules). Let Z denote the set of possible states of such a system, which, though finite, may be extremely large. For every pair of states z, $z' \in Z$, let P be a $|Z| \times |Z|$ matrix such that the component $P_{zz'}$ is the *probability* of moving from state z to state z' in one period. P is the *transition probability matrix* of a finite Markov process. We shall always restrict ourselves to processes that are time-homogeneous, that is, the transition probabilities do not change from one period to the next.

Suppose that the initial state is z^0. For every time $t > 0$, let the random variable $f^t(z|z^0)$ denote the *empirical frequency* with which state z is visited during the first t periods. It can be shown that, as t goes to infinity, $f^t(z|z^0)$ converges almost surely to a limiting frequency distribution. If this distribution depends on the initial state z^0, or on chance events that occur along the way, we shall say that the process is *non-ergodic* or *path-dependent*. If the limiting distribution is uniquely determined independently of z^0, the process is *ergodic*.

There is a simple structural criterion that allows us to say whether or not a process is ergodic.[4] Say that state z' is *accessible* from state z, written $z \to z'$, if there is a positive probability of moving from z to z' in a finite number of periods (including no periods, i.e., z is accessible from z). States z and z' *communicate*, written $z \sim z'$, if each is accessible from the other. Clearly $\sim$ is an equivalence relation, so it partitions the space Z into equivalence classes, which are known as *communication classes*. A *recurrence class* of P is a communication class such that no state outside the class is accessible from any state inside it. It is straightforward to show that every finite Markov chain has at least one recurrence class. A state is *recurrent* if it is contained in one of the recurrence classes; otherwise it is *transient*. In particular, a state is recurrent if and only if, once the process has entered it, the probability of returning to it is one.

A basic result on finite Markov chains is that ergodicity holds if and only if the process has a unique recurrence class. Equivalently, such a process is ergodic if the states can be divided into two disjoint classes A and B such that: there is a positive

---

[4] For a discussion of ergodicity in Markov chains see Karlin and Taylor (1975, Chapter 2).

probability of moving from any state in A to some state in B; there is a positive probability of moving from any state in B to any other state in B; there is zero probability
of moving from any state in B to any state in A. A particular instance occurs when A
is empty and B constitutes the entire state space; in this case the process is said to be
irreducible.

The standard approach to analyzing the asymptotic behavior of a Markov chain is
to solve for the stationary distribution algebraically. Specifically, let μ be a probability
distribution on Z written out as a row vector and consider the system of linear equations

$$\mu P = \mu, \text{ where } \mu \geqslant 0 \quad \text{and} \quad \sum_{z \in Z} \mu(z) = 1. \tag{1}$$

This system always has at least one solution μ, called a *stationary distribution* of the
process P. The solution is unique if and only if P has a unique recurrence class, that is,
if and only if P is ergodic. In this event the empirical frequency distribution converges
almost surely to μ independently of the initial conditions:

$$\lim_{t \to \infty} f^t(z|z^0) = \mu(z). \tag{2}$$

By contrast, if P has more than one recurrence class, the process is path-dependent, and
the initial position—as well as chance events along the way—can influence its long-run
behavior.

Most of the models we shall consider are ergodic; in fact they have another property
that allows us to make even sharper statements about their asymptotic behavior. Given
a finite Markov process P and a state z, let N_z be the set of all positive integers n
such that there is a positive probability of moving from z to z in *exactly* n periods. The
process P is *aperiodic* if, for every z, the greatest common divisor of N_z is unity. If
P is aperiodic and ergodic, not only does its *average* behavior converge to the unique
stationary distribution μ, so does its probabilistic behavior *at each point in time t* when
t is sufficiently large. More precisely, P^t be the t-fold product of P. If the process starts
in an arbitrary state y, then in t periods the probability of being in state z is P_{yz}^t. It can
be shown that, if P is ergodic and aperiodic, then with probability one

$$\forall y, z \in Z, \qquad \lim_{t \to \infty} P_{yz}^t = \mu(z). \tag{3}$$

In particular, the probability of being in a given state z at a *given time t* is essentially
the same as the probability $f^t(z|z^0)$ of being in state z *up through time t* provided that t
is large; furthermore both converge to the stationary distribution $\mu(z)$ independently of
the initial state.

When the state space is very large—as is usually the case with agent-based models—
the stationarity equation (1) is much too cumbersome to solve explicitly. Fortunately
there is an alternative approach, based on the theory of large deviations, that often
permits a good approximation of the stationary distribution without having to solve
equation (1).

Suppose that the Markov process P can be split into two parts: a basic process P^0,
on which is superimposed small trembles or perturbations. An example would be a

model in which agents change their behaviors according to a choice rule that has a small probabilistic component. In this case the basic process is given by the probabilities of interaction among the agents, combined with their *expected* change in behaviors; the perturbations correspond to idiosyncratic aspects of individual-level changes in behavior. (We shall consider a number of concrete examples below.) Under certain regularity conditions, one can identify the states that have high probability when the perturbations are small without solving for the stationary distribution explicitly. These are known as *stochastically stable states*, and correspond to the equilibria that have the greatest persistence or robustness in the presence of random perturbations [Foster and Young (1990)].

3. Technology adoption

We shall first illustrate the approach using a model of technology choice with network externalities, which is similar to the currency model discussed earlier. Consider a population of n individuals. At each point in time every individual owns one of two technologies, A or B, hence the system has 2^n possible states. Both technologies generate positive externalities—the payoff from a given choice increases with the proportion of others who make the same choice. A contemporary example is personal computers: if most people own PCs it is advantageous to own a PC; if most people own Macs it is more desirable to own a Mac. The reason is that the more popular a given model is, the more software will be created for it, and the easier it is to share programs with others.[5]

In each period one individual is chosen at random to make a new choice—say because her current model wears out. She makes her decision by asking s randomly selected people what choices they made, and then choosing a perturbed best response. The payoffs are as follows: if in the random sample k people have chosen A and $s - k$ have chosen B, the payoff to adopting A is ak and the payoff to adopting B is $b(s - k)$. This is equivalent to playing a game against the field in which the row player's payoffs are given by

$$
\begin{array}{ccc}
 & A & B \\
A & a & 0 \\
B & 0 & b
\end{array}
$$

Let us assume that players choose a best response with high probability, but not with certainty. Specifically let us suppose that an individual chooses a best response (given the sample evidence) with probability $1 - \varepsilon$, and chooses an action at random with probability ε. Thus, with low probability the individual does not deliberate about her decision, whereas with high probability she does.

---

[5] For other models of network externalities see Katz and Shapiro (1985, 1986), David (1985), and Arthur (1989).

This is a simple example of a perturbed dynamical process. There is a finite (but large) number of states, and there are well-defined transition probabilities from any state to any other state. Unless the population is very small, however, it is extremely cumbersome to write down the transition matrix and to solve the stationarity equation algebraically. Instead we exploit the fact that the process is perturbed due to the idiosyncratic choices of agents.

If there were no perturbations ($\varepsilon = 0$), the transition probabilities would be calculated as follows. Let the current state consist of m users of A and $n - m$ users of B. At the start of the next period, choose one agent at random and let her draw a sample of size s from the remaining agents. Assume that she chooses a best response to the distribution of A-users and B-users in her sample. The combination of these events determines the probability of transiting to every possible successor state at the end of the period. (Note that the process can only transit to a state that differs from the current state in at most one coordinate, because only one agent reconsiders in each period.) Let P^0 denote the transition probability matrix of the resulting *unperturbed process*. Define a separate process Q in which one agent is drawn at random each period and chooses A or B with equal probability. We can then represent the *perturbed process* (with noise level ε) by the transition matrix $P^\varepsilon = (1 - \varepsilon)P + \varepsilon Q$.

The stationary distribution may now be calculated as follows. First we identify the recurrence classes of P^0. One such class is the absorbing state in which everyone plays A; another is the absorbing state in which everyone plays B. Call these states z^A and z^B respectively. It can be checked that these are the only recurrence classes: from any state the probability is one of eventually landing in one of these two states. Now compute the "path of least resistance" from z^B to z^A and vice versa. Starting from z^B, consider a series of A adoptions (due to perturbations) that lead to a critical or "tipping" state z^*, from which the process can transit to z^A with no further perturbations. This tipping point occurs when there are k^* choices of A, where k^* is the smallest integer satisfying the condition $ak^* \geqslant b(s - k^*)$, that is, $k^* \geqslant bs/(a + b)$. (An agent who draws these k^* individuals in her sample will choose A instead of B.) The probability of this tipping event is approximately $(\varepsilon/2)^{\lceil bs/(a+b) \rceil}$, where in general $\lceil x \rceil$ denotes the least integer greater than or equal to x. Define the *resistance* of the transition $z^B \to z^A$ to be the exponent on ε, that is,

$$r(z^B \to z^A) = \lceil bs/(a + b) \rceil.$$

Similarly, the resistance of the transition $z^A \to z^B$ is

$$r(z^A \to z^B) = \lceil as/(a + b) \rceil.$$

The smaller of these numbers determines the shape of the stationary distribution when ε is small. Specifically, if $r(z^A \to z^B) < r(z^B \to z^A)$ then the stationary distribution puts probability close to 1 on the state z^B. If $r(z^A \to z^B) > r(z^B \to z^A)$, the stationary distribution puts probability close to 1 on the state z^A. It follows that, when the sample size s is sufficiently large, the Pareto efficient technology is favored in the long run:

if $a > b$, society is much more likely to have a large number of A-users than a large number of B-users, and vice versa.

4. Characterizing the stochastically stable states

We now show how this framework can be generalized to a wide variety of agent-based models. Consider a process such that the size of the perturbations can be indexed by a scalar $\varepsilon > 0$, and let P^ε be the associated transition probability matrix. P^ε is called a *regular perturbed Markov process* if P^ε is ergodic for all sufficiently small $\varepsilon > 0$ and P^ε approaches P^0 at an exponentially smooth rate [Young (1993a)]. Specifically, the latter condition means that

$$\forall z, z' \in Z, \qquad \lim_{\varepsilon \to 0^+} P^\varepsilon_{zz'} = P^0_{zz'},$$

and

$$P^\varepsilon_{zz'} > 0 \text{ for some } \varepsilon > 0 \text{ implies } 0 < \lim_{\varepsilon \to 0^+} P^\varepsilon_{zz'}/\varepsilon^{r(z \to z')} < \infty,$$

for some nonnegative real number $r(z \to z')$, which is called the *resistance* of the transition $z \to z'$.

Let P^0 denote the unperturbed process and let its recurrence classes be denoted by $E_1, E_2, \ldots, E_N$. For each pair of distinct recurrence classes E_i and E_j, $i \neq j$, an ij-*path* is defined to be a sequence of distinct states $\zeta = (z_1 \to z_2 \to \cdots \to z_n)$ such that $z_1 \in E_i$ and $z_n \in E_j$. The *resistance* of this path is the sum of the resistances of its edges, that is, $r(\zeta) = r(z_1 \to z_2) + r(z_2 \to z_3) + \cdots + r(z_{n-1} \to z_n)$. Let $\rho_{ij} = \min r(\zeta)$ be the *least resistance* over all ij-paths ζ. Note that ρ_{ij} must be positive for all distinct i and j, because there exists no path of zero resistance between distinct recurrence classes.

Now construct a complete directed graph with N vertices, one for each recurrence class. The vertex corresponding to class E_j will be called "j". The *weight* on the directed edge $i \to j$ is ρ_{ij}. A tree rooted at vertex j, or j-*tree*, is a set of $N - 1$ directed edges such that, from every vertex different from j, there is a unique directed path in the tree to j. The *resistance* of a rooted tree T is the sum of the resistances ρ_{ij} on the $N - 1$ edges that compose it. The *stochastic potential* γ_j of the recurrence class E_j is defined to be the minimum resistance over all trees rooted at j. The following theorem gives a simple criterion for determining the stochastically stable states [Young (1993a, Theorem 4)].

THEOREM 1. *Let P^ε be a regular perturbed Markov process and for each $\varepsilon > 0$ let μ^ε be the unique stationary distribution of P^ε. Then $\lim_{\varepsilon \to 0} \mu^\varepsilon$ exists and the limiting distribution μ^0 is a stationary distribution of P^0. The stochastically stable states (the support of μ^0) are precisely those states contained in the recurrence classes with minimum stochastic potential.*

Figure 4. The currency game with two recurrence classes.

We shall illustrate this result with the preceding example. In this situation there are two recurrence classes, $\{z^A\}$ and $\{z^B\}$, and exactly two rooted trees, as shown in Figure 4.

The tree with least resistance points toward the Pareto dominant equilibrium, and confirms our earlier calculation that this is the stochastically stable outcome.

A more complex example is the following. Consider a technology choice game in which there are three choices of technology—A, B, C—and the payoffs from networking are

	A	B	C
A	5	0	0
B	0	4	0
C	0	0	3

In this case there are three recurrence classes, one for each of the absorbing states z^A, z^B, z^C, and there are nine trees, as shown in Figure 5.

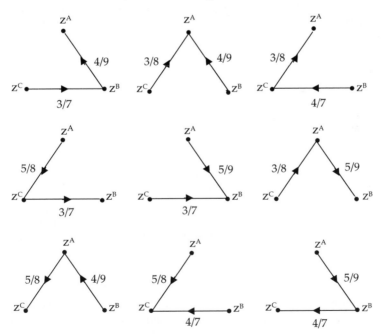

Figure 5. An example with nine rooted trees and three recurrence classes.

The sum of the resistances is minimized for the middle tree in the top row $(3/8 + 4/9$ is the smallest sum among the nine trees). Hence the root of this tree, which corresponds to the state in which everyone adopts technology A, is the stochastically stable state.

5. Efficiency versus stochastic stability

The preceding examples should not lull the reader into believing that evolution invariably selects efficient norms or standards. On the contrary, this state of affairs is quite exceptional, and hinges on the form of the payoff matrix. In this section we discuss the connection between efficiency and stochastic stability when there are two alternatives; a more extended discussion may be found in Young (1993a, 1998).

Assume then that there are two competing technologies, A and B. In the preceding section we assumed that there were gains only from networking with the same technology (the payoff matrix has zeroes off the diagonal). In general, however, there may be positive payoffs from networking with different technologies, and there may also be payoffs that arise from using the technology independently of networking effects. (For example, in the case of computer software there is a payoff from ease of file-sharing with other users, but there is also a payoff from the convenience of the software itself.) To be concrete, suppose that A–A interactions yield a payoff of 4 to each user, A–B interactions yield a payoff of 1 to each user, and the use of A yields a payoff of 1 to the user *in addition to* the networking payoffs. Similarly, suppose that B–B interactions yield a payoff of 1 to each user, B–A interactions also yield a payoff of 1, while using B yields a payoff of 3 in addition to the networking payoffs. The combination of these effects leads to the following total payoff matrix (the entries are the row player's payoffs):

	networking		*own use*		*total payoff*	
	A	B	A	B	A	B
A	4	1	1	1	5	2
B	1	1	3	3	4	4

with $+$ between the networking and own use blocks and $=$ before the total payoff block.

We claim that the efficient outcome is for everyone to adopt A, but the stochastically stable outcome is for everyone to use B. To see why this is so, we need to compute the two resistances $r(z^B \to z^A)$ and $r(z^A \to z^B)$. This involves finding the smallest number, k^*, of mistakes or mutations that are needed to tip the process from z^B to z^A. This is the least integer satisfying the inequality

$$5k^* + 2(s - k^*) \geqslant 4k^* + 4(s - k^*).$$

Subject to rounding this leads to the estimate $r(z^B \to z^A) \approx 2s/3$. Similarly we find that $r(z^A \to z^B) \approx s/3$. Since the latter is smaller, it follows from theorem 1 that (when s is sufficiently large) the stochastically stable state is all-B, which of course is not efficient.

Suppose, more generally, that the payoff matrix is of form

	A	B
A	a	c
B	d	b

When $a > d$ and $b > c$, this is a symmetric coordination game with coordination equilibria (A, A) and (B, B). We say that alternative A is *strictly risk-dominant* if $a - d > b - c$. Similarly, B is *strictly risk-dominant* if the reverse inequality holds. Note that risk dominance is not the same as efficiency, which is determined by the larger of a and b. One implication of the preceding analysis is the following.

THEOREM 2. *Let G be a* 2×2 *symmetric coordination game with a strictly risk-dominant equilibrium. If G is played by a population of n players using samples of size s, then for all sufficiently large s and $n(s \leqslant n/2)$ the unique stochastically stable state is the one in which everyone plays the risk-dominant alternative.*

This result has an interesting implication for the relative "fitness" of competing technologies. Consider again the situation in which each individual's payoff can be decomposed into a payoff from networking and a payoff from own use. We can write this in the following general form:

$$
\begin{array}{ccc}
\text{networking} & \text{own use} & \text{total payoff} \\
\begin{array}{ccc} & \text{A} & \text{B} \\ \text{A} & a & c \\ \text{B} & c & b \end{array} +
\begin{array}{cc} \text{A} & \text{B} \\ a' & a' \\ b' & b' \end{array} =
\begin{array}{cc} \text{A} & \text{B} \\ a+a' & c+a' \\ c+b' & b+b' \end{array}
\end{array} \tag{4}
$$

Assume that $a+a' > c+b'$ and $b+b' > c+a'$, so that both A and B are coordination equilibria. By definition, the risk dominance of A is determined by the inequality

$$(a + a') - (c + b') > (b + b') - (c + a'),$$

that is,

$$a + 2a' > b + 2b'. \tag{5}$$

This has the following implication for the producers of A and B. Suppose that one of the firms—say the A-producer—is contemplating whether to invest in improvements that lead to greater networking transparency with other As, or to greater ease of use. Where should the money be invested to maximize the chance that A will take over the market? The answer is that investment in networking should be chosen only if it increases each user's utility at least *twice* as much as a similar investment in non-networking improvements. For example, suppose that A and B represent two types of cellphones. Suppose that, for a given expenditure, the firm producing A can either improve the clarity of the signal with other A-users, or improve the ease of reading the monitor independently of other users. Say that the first improvement increases the payoff to a given A-user by Δ

per call made to other A's, whereas the second increases it by Δ' per call made to any-one. If everyone in the population were using A, the firm would simply evaluate which is larger: Δ or Δ'. But in a competition for acceptance, the relevant criterion is the larger of Δ or $2\Delta'$. The reason is that Δ results from externalities with other A-users, whereas Δ' does not. To my knowledge this point has not been previously recognized in the literature on network externalities.

6. Application to Schelling's segregation model

We turn now to a more complex example that illustrates the power of the analytical method discussed above. One of the earliest agent-based models in the social science literature is Schelling's illustration of how segregated neighborhoods can emerge spontaneously from decisions by individuals who would in fact prefer to live in integrated settings [Schelling (1971, 1978)]. Here we shall present a variant of Schelling's model that lends itself to the stochastic analysis discussed above; for an extension of the analysis to more complex environments see Zhang (2004a, 2004b).

Assume that the population consists of n individuals, who are of two types: A and B. They cannot change their type, but they can choose where to live. Suppose for simplicity that they are located around a circle as shown in Figure 6. We shall say that an individual is *discontent* if his two immediate neighbors are unlike himself; otherwise he is *content*. An *equilibrium* is a state in which no two individuals want to trade places. In other words, there is no pair of agents such that one (or both) is currently discontent, and both would be content after they trade locations. (If only one agent is discontent beforehand,

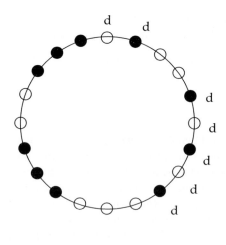

A = ●
B = ○
d = discontent

Figure 6. A disequilibrium state.

we can imagine that he compensates the other to move, so that both are better off after the move than they were before.)

We claim that, if there are at least two agents of each type, then in equilibrium no one is discontent. To see why this is so, suppose to the contrary that an A is surrounded by two B's: ... BAB .... Moving clockwise around the circle, let B^* be the last B-type in the string of Bs who follows this A, and let A^* be the agent who follows B^*:

$$... BAB ... BB^*A^* ...$$

Since there are at least two agents of each type, we can be sure that A^* differs from the original A. But then the original discontent A could switch with B^* (who is content), and both would be content afterwards. Thus we see that the equilibrium configurations consist of those arrangements in which everyone lives next to at least one person of his own type. No one is "isolated." In general there are many different kinds of equilibrium states: some consist of small enclaves of A's and B's scattered around the landscape, while others exhibit full segregation with the A's living on one side of the circle and the B's on the other.

Consider the following adjustment dynamic. In each discrete time period a pair of individuals is selected at random, where all pairs are equally likely to be chosen. Consider such a pair of individuals, say i and j. We shall assume that the probability that they trade depends on their prospective gains from trade. Let us assume that every trade involves moving costs. Thus there can be positive gains from trade only if the partners are of opposite types and at least one of them (say i) was discontent before and is content afterwards. This means that, before the trade, i was surrounded by people of the opposite type, so in fact both i and j are content afterwards. (We shall assume that if j is content before and after the trade, i can compensate j for his moving costs and still leave both better off.) Such Pareto improving trades are said to be *advantageous*; all other trades are *disadvantageous*.

Assume that each advantageous trade occurs with high probability, and that each disadvantageous trade occurs with low probability. Specifically, let us suppose that there exist real numbers $0 < a < b < c$ such that the probability of a disadvantageous trade is ε^a if neither partner's degree of contentment changes (so the losses involve only moving costs), the probability is ε^b if both partners were content before and one is discontent after, and it is ε^c if both were content before and both are discontent after. (These are the only possibilities.) Advantageous trades are assumed to occur with probabilities that approach one as $\varepsilon \to 0$; beyond this we need not specify the probabilities exactly. The resulting perturbed Markov process P^ε is ergodic for every $\varepsilon > 0$, and regular in the sense defined earlier.

To apply the theory, we first need to identify the recurrence classes of the unperturbed process P^0. These obviously include the absorbing (equilibrium) states. We claim that these are in fact the only recurrence classes of P^0. To prove this, consider a state that is not absorbing. It contains at least one discontent individual, say i; without loss of generality we may assume that i is of type A. Going clockwise around the circle, let i' be the next individual of type A. (Recall that there are at least two individuals of each type.) The individual just before i' must be of type B. Call this individual j. If i and j trade places, both will be content afterwards. In any given period there is a positive probability that this pair will in fact be drawn, and that they will trade. The resulting state has fewer discontent individuals. Continuing in this manner, we see that from any non-absorbing state there is a positive probability of transiting to an absorbing state within a finite number of periods. Hence the absorbing states are the only recurrent states.

Denote the set of all absorbing states by Z^0. For any two states z and z' in Z^0, let $r(z, z')$ denote the *least* resistance among all paths from z to z'. The stochastic potential of $z \in Z^0$ is defined to be the resistance of the minimum resistance z-tree on the set of nodes Z^0. By Theorem 1, the stochastically stable states are those with minimum stochastic potential. We claim that these are precisely the *segregated absorbing states*, that is, states in which all the A's are lined up on one side of the circle and all the B's are on the other.

To prove this claim, let $Z^0 = Z^s \cup Z^{ns}$ where Z^s is the set of segregated absorbing states and Z^{ns} is the set of non-segregated absorbing states. We claim that (i) for every $z \in Z^{ns}$, every z-tree has at least one edge with resistance b or c (which by assumption are greater than a); and (ii) for every $z \in Z^s$, there exists a z-tree in which every edge has resistance exactly equal to a. Assume for the moment that (i) and (ii) have been established. In any z-tree there are exactly $|Z^0| - 1$ edges, and the resistance of each edge is *at least* a. It follows from (i) and (ii) that the stochastic potential of every segregated state equals $a|Z^0| - a$, while the stochastic potential of every non-segregated state is at least $a|Z^0| - 2a + b$, which is strictly larger. Theorem 1 therefore implies that the segregated states are precisely the stochastically stable states.

To establish (i), let $z \in Z^{ns}$ be a non-segregated absorbing state. Given any z-tree T, there exists at least one edge in T that is directed from a segregated absorbing state z^s to a non-segregated absorbing state z^{ns}. We claim that any such edge has resistance at least b. The reason is that any trade that breaks up a segregated state must create at least one discontent individual, hence the probability of such a trade is either ε^b or ε^c (see Figure 7). Thus the resistance of the edge from z^s to z^{ns} must be at least b, which establishes (i).

To establish (ii), let $z \in Z^s$ be a segregated absorbing state. From each state $z' \neq z$ we shall construct a sequence of absorbing states $z' = z^1 \to z^2 \to \cdots \to z^k = z$ such that $r(z^{j-1} \to z^j) = a$ for $1 < j \leqslant k$. Call this a $z'z$-path. We shall carry out the construction so that the union of all of the directed edges on all of these paths forms a z-tree. Since each edge has a resistance of a and the tree has $|Z^0| - 1$ edges, the total resistance of the tree is $a|Z^0| - a$ as claimed in (ii).

Suppose first that z' is also segregated, that is, z' consists of a single contiguous A-group and a complementary contiguous B-group. Label the positions on the circle $1, 2, \ldots, n$, in the clockwise sense. Let the first member of the A-group trade places with the first member of the B-group. Since both were content before and after, this trade has probability ε^a. It also results in a new absorbing state, which shifts the A-group and the B-group by one position clockwise around the circle. Hence within n

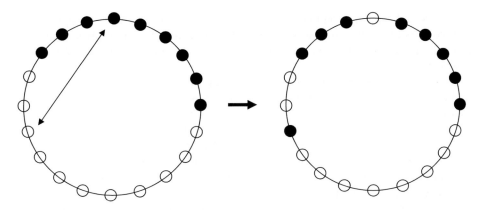

Figure 7. Single disadvantageous trade leading from an equilibrium to a disequilibrium state.

steps we can reach any absorbing state, and in particular we can reach z. Thus we have constructed a sequence of absorbing states that leads from z' to z, where the resistance of each successive pair in the sequence equals a.

Suppose alternatively that z' is not segregated. Moving clockwise from position 1, let **A** denote the first complete group of contiguous As. Let **B** be the next group of Bs, and **A'** the next group of As. Since z' is absorbing, each of these groups contains at least two members. Let the first player in **A** trade places with the first player in **B** (in the clockwise labeling). Since both players were content before and after the trade, its probability is ε^a. This trade also shifts group **A** one position clockwise and reduces by one the number of B players between **A** and **A'**. It either results in a new absorbing state, or else a single B player remains between **A** and **A'**. In the latter case this B player can then trade with the first player in group **A**, and this trade has zero resistance. The result is an absorbing state with fewer distinct groups of As and Bs.

Repeat the process described in the preceding paragraph until all the As are contiguous and all the Bs are contiguous. Then continue as in the earlier part of the argument until we reach the target state z. This construction yields a sequence of absorbing states that begins at z' and ends at z, where the resistance between each successive pair of states is a. The path contains no cycles because the number of distinct groups never increases; indeed with each transition one of the groups shrinks until it is eliminated. Thus the union of these paths forms a z-tree whose total resistance is $a|Z^0| - a$. This concludes the proof that the stochastically stable states are precisely the segregated ones.

7. Local interaction models

Schelling's model is an example of a situation in which agents adapt their behaviors to the actions of their near neighbors. We can easily imagine that the same issue could arise in a model of technological adoption. What happens if people adopt practices or technologies based only on the choices of their immediate neighbors, as opposed to a sample drawn from the population at large? In this section we show how to address this problem using methods from statistical mechanics, an approach pioneered by Blume (1993, 1995).

Consider a group of n agents who are located in a social or geographic space that allows us to talk about their proximity. A very general model of this sort is to suppose that each agent lives at the vertex of a graph. The edges of the graph have weights that indicate the degree of proximity or influence that pertains to each pair of agents. To be specific, let V denote the set of vertices, and let $i \in V$ denote a particular vertex (which is identified with an agent whom we shall also call i). Let $w_{ij} \geqslant 0$ be a weight that measures the proximity of agents i and j in a geographical (or social) sense. We shall assume that this is a symmetric relation, that is, $w_{ij} = w_{ji}$.

Let X be a finite set of available options or choices. The *state* of the process at time t specifies the choice of each agent at that time. A state can therefore be represented as an n-dimensional vector $\mathbf{x}^t \in X^n$, where x_i^t is i's choice at time t. Each individual i gets to reconsider his choice at random times governed by a Poisson random variable ω_i. We shall assume that the random variables ω_i are independent and identically distributed among agents, and that time is scaled so that, on average, there is one revision opportunity per time period at each location. (Allowing differences in the rates of revision opportunities does not change the analysis in any fundamental way.)

In line with our earlier discussion, we shall decompose the utility of each agent i into two parts: the utility of the choice itself (without externalities), and the positive externality from doing what "the Joneses" do. Specifically, let $w_{ij}u(x, y)$ be the *externality payoff* from choosing x at location i when one's neighbor at location j chooses y. Thus $e_i(\mathbf{x}) = \sum_{j \neq i} w_{ij}u(x_i, x_j)$ denotes i's externality payoff in state $\mathbf{x}$. Let $v_i(\mathbf{x})$ denote the utility that i derives from x_i itself without regard to externalities. Assume that i's utility in state $\mathbf{x}$ at time t is given by

$$U_i(\mathbf{x}^t) = v_i(x_i^t) + e_i(\mathbf{x}^t) + \varepsilon_i^t, \tag{6}$$

where ε_i^t is an unobserved utility shock. It is analytically convenient to assume that the ε_i^t are independent and identically distributed according to the extreme value distribution.[6] Suppose that i chooses x_i^t to maximize U_i given that the others' choices at time t are fixed. It can be shown that, from the observer's point of view, i chooses $x_i^t \in X$ according to the logistic distribution

$$P(x_i^t | \mathbf{x}_{-i}^t) = \exp \beta[v_i(x_i^t) + e_i(\mathbf{x}^t)] / \sum_{y_i \in X} \exp \beta[v_i(y_i) + e_i(y_i, \mathbf{x}_{-i}^t)]. \tag{7}$$

---

[6] The random variable z is extreme value distributed if its cumulative distribution function $F(z)$ takes the form $\ln F(z) = -e^{-\beta z}$. This distribution is analytically convenient because it yields a simple closed-form solution for the stationary distribution of the adjustment process; moreover it is standard as a model of discrete choice [McFadden (1974), Blume (1993, 1995), McKelvey and Palfrey (1995), Durlauf (1997), Brock and Durlauf (2001)]. Alternative error distributions can be analyzed using the methods discussed in Section 2.

The resulting stochastic adjustment process can be represented as a finite Markov chain. This process has a unique recurrence class (namely the whole state space) because the choice model implies that any choice will be made with positive probability whenever an agent reconsiders. Hence the process is ergodic and has a unique stationary distribution μ^β on the set of states $\mathbf{X}$. For each $\mathbf{x} \in \mathbf{X}$, $\mu^\beta(\mathbf{x})$ represents the long-run relative frequency with which state $\mathbf{x}$ is visited starting from any initial state.

A noteworthy feature of this set-up is that the stationary distribution can be expressed in a simple closed form. Specifically, define the *potential* of state $\mathbf{x}$ to be

$$\rho(\mathbf{x}) = \sum_{i=1}^{n} v_i(x_i) + (1/2) \sum_{i=1}^{n} e_i(\mathbf{x}). \tag{8}$$

Thus the potential of a state equals the nonexternality payoffs generated by individuals' choices, plus one-half the externalities generated by social interactions. It can be shown that the long-run distribution of the process has the following simple form, known as a Gibbs representation:

$$\mu(\mathbf{x}) = \frac{e^{\beta\rho(\mathbf{x})}}{\sum_{\mathbf{y}} e^{\beta\rho(\mathbf{y})}}. \tag{9}$$

It follows that, when β is large, the probability is close to one that the process will be in a state that maximizes potential, that is, the stochastically stable states are precisely those that maximize $\rho(\mathbf{x})$.

THEOREM 3. *Starting from an arbitrary initial state, the long-run probability of being in any given state $\mathbf{x}$ is proportional to $e^{\beta\rho(\mathbf{x})}$. When β is large, the probability is close to one that the process is in a state $\mathbf{x}$ that maximizes $\rho(\mathbf{x})$.*

We remark that this model can be applied to the technology adoption problem discussed in Section 5. Recall that in this case the choice set consists of just two options, A and B, and the utilities are given by the payoff matrix

$$
\begin{array}{cc}
\textit{networking} & \textit{own use} \\
\begin{array}{ccc}
 & A & B \\
A & a & c \\
B & c & b
\end{array}
+
\begin{array}{cc}
A & B \\
a' & a' \\
b' & b'
\end{array}
\end{array}
=
\begin{array}{c}
\textit{total payoff} \\
\begin{array}{cc}
A & B \\
a+a' & c+a' \\
c+b' & b+b'
\end{array}
\end{array}
$$

Now let us suppose a social structure among the agents that determines who interacts with whom. Specifically, assume that each agent is joined by an edge to s other agents (the graph is regular of degree s), and that the weight on each edge is $1/s$.

Consider any state $\mathbf{x}$, and let $n_{AA}(\mathbf{x})$ be the total number of edges such that the agents at both ends of the edge choose A. Similarly, let $n_{BB}(\mathbf{x})$ be the total number of edges such that the agents at both ends choose B, and let $n_{AB}(\mathbf{x})$ be the total number of edges such that the agent at one end chooses B and the agent at the other end chooses A. Next, let $n_A(\mathbf{x})$ be the number of agents who choose A and let $n_B(\mathbf{x})$ be the number who choose B. Note that $n_A(\mathbf{x}) + n_B(\mathbf{x}) = n$ and $n_{AA}(\mathbf{x}) + n_{BB}(\mathbf{x}) + n_{AB}(\mathbf{x}) = ns/2$. The potential function in (8) can then be written as follows:

$$\rho(\mathbf{x}) = a'n_A(\mathbf{x}) + b'n_B(\mathbf{x}) + (1/s)(an_{AA}(\mathbf{x}) + bn_{BB}(\mathbf{x}) + cn_{AB}(\mathbf{x})). \qquad (10)$$

This is maximized either by the all-A state $\mathbf{x}^A$ or the all-B state $\mathbf{x}^B$. Thus we wish to evaluate which is larger:

$$\rho(\mathbf{x}^A) = a'n + an/2 \quad \text{or} \quad \rho(\mathbf{x}^B) = b'n + bn/2. \qquad (11)$$

This amounts to finding the larger of $a + 2a'$ and $b + 2b'$, which is exactly the risk dominance criterion (see the derivation of (5)). It can be shown, in fact, that risk dominance is the relevant criterion of stochastic stability in a wide variety of binary choice situations [Kandori et al. (1993), Blume (2003)], though this is not always the case when more than two choices are available [Young (1993a)].

8. Contractual norms

The framework outlined above has potential application to any situation in which social norms influence individual agents' decisions. Cases in which this possibility has been discussed include the use of addictive substances, dropping out of school, and criminal behavior [Case and Katz (1991), Crane (1991), Glaeser et al. (1996)]. In this section we apply the theory to yet another domain, the role of social norms in shaping the terms of economic contracts. In particular we show how it can illuminate the pattern of crop-sharing contracts found in contemporary U.S. agriculture [Young and Burke (2001)].[7]

A *share contract* is an arrangement in which a landowner and a tenant farmer split the gross proceeds of the harvest in fixed proportions or shares. The logic of such a contract is that it shares the risk of an uncertain outcome while offering the tenant a rough-and-ready incentive to increase the expected value of that outcome. When contracts are competitively negotiated, one would expect the size of the share to vary in accordance with the mean (and variance) of the expected returns, the risk aversion of the parties, the agent's quality, and other relevant factors. In practice, however, shares seem to cluster around "usual and customary" levels even when there is substantial heterogeneity among principal-agent pairs, and substantial and readily observed differences in the quality of different parcels of land. These contractual customs are pinned to psychologically prominent focal points, such as 1/2–1/2, though other shares—such as 1/3–2/3 and 2/5–3/5—are also common, with the larger share going to the tenant.

A striking feature of the Illinois data is that the above three divisions account for over 98% of all share contracts in the survey, which involved several thousand farms in all parts of the state. An equally striking feature is that the predominant or customary

---

[7] Applications of the theory to the evolution of bargaining norms may be found in Young (1993b) and Young (1998, chapter 9).

shares differ by region: in the northern part of the state the overwhelming majority of share contracts specify $1/2$–$1/2$, whereas in the southern part of the state the most common shares are $1/3$–$2/3$ and $2/5$–$3/5$ [Illinois Cooperative Extension Service (1995)].[8] Thus, on the one hand, uniformity *within* each region exists in spite of the fact that there are substantial and easily observed differences in the soil characteristics and productivities of farms within the region. On the other hand, large differences exist *between* the regions in spite of the fact that there are many farms in both regions that have essentially the same soil productivity, so in principle they should be using the same (or similar) shares. The local interaction model discussed in Section 7 can help us to understand these apparent anomalies.

Let us identify each farm i with the vertex of a graph. Each vertex is joined by edges to its immediate geographical neighbors. For ease of exposition we shall assume that the social influence weights on the edges are all the same. The *soil productivity index* on farm i, s_i, is a number that gives the expected output per acre, measured in dollars, of the soils on that particular farm. (For example, $s_i = 80$ means that total net income on farm i is, on average, \$80 per acre.) The contract on farm i specifies a share x_i for the tenant, and $1 - x_i$ for the landlord, where x_i is a number between zero and one. The tenant's expected income on farm i is therefore $x_i s_i$ times the number of acres on the farm. For expositional convenience let us assume that all farms have the same size, which we may as well suppose is unity. (This does not affect the analysis in any important way.)

Assume that renegotiations occur on each farm according to i.i.d. Poisson random variables, as described in the preceding section. When the time comes to renegotiate on a particular farm, say i, the landlord makes an offer, say x_i. The tenant accepts if and only if his expected return $x_i s_i$ is at least w_i, where w_i is the reservation wage at location i. The expected monetary return to the landlord from such a deal is $v_i(x_i) = (1 - x_i)s_i$.

To model the impact of local custom, suppose that each of i's neighbors exerts the same degree of social influence on i. Specifically, for each state $\mathbf{x}$, let $\delta_{ij}(\mathbf{x}) = 1$ if i and j are neighbors and $x_i = x_j$; otherwise let $\delta_{ij}(\mathbf{x}) = 0$. We assume that i's utility in state $\mathbf{x}$ is $(1 - x_i)s_i + \gamma \sum_j \delta_{ij}(\mathbf{x})$, where γ is a *conformity parameter*. The idea is that, if a landlord offers his tenant a contract that differs from the practices of the neighbors, the tenant will be offended and may retaliate with poorer performance. Hence the landlord's utility for different contracts is affected by the choices of his neighbors. The resulting potential function is

$$\sum_i (1 - x_i)s_i + (\gamma/2) \sum_{i,j} \delta_{ij}(\mathbf{x}). \tag{12}$$

Note that $\sum_i (1 - x_i)s_i$ represents the total *rent to land*, which we shall abbreviate by $r(\mathbf{x})$. The expression $(1/2) \sum_{i,j} \delta_{ij}(\mathbf{x})$ represents the total number of edges (neighbor-pairs) that are coordinated on the same contract in state $\mathbf{x}$, which we shall abbreviate

---

[8] This north–south division corresponds roughly to the southern boundary of the last major glaciation. In both regions, farming techniques are similar and the same crops are grown—mainly corn, soybeans, and wheat. In the north the land tends to be flatter and more productive than in the south, though there is substantial variability within each of the regions.

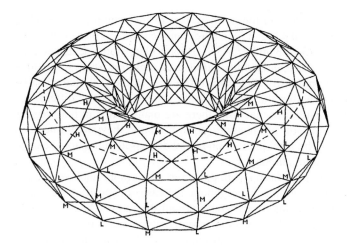

Figure 8. The hypothetical state of Torusota. Each vertex represents a farm, and soil quantities are High (H), Medium (M), or Low (L).

by $e(\mathbf{x})$. We can therefore write

$$\rho(\mathbf{x}) = r(\mathbf{x}) + \gamma e(\mathbf{x}). \tag{13}$$

As in (9) it follows that the stationary distribution, $\mu(\mathbf{x})$, has the Gibbs form

$$\mu(\mathbf{x}) \propto e^{\beta[r(\mathbf{x})+\gamma c(\mathbf{x})]}. \tag{14}$$

It follows that *the log probability of each state* $\mathbf{x}$ *is a linear function of the total rent to land plus the degree of local conformity*. Given specific values of the conformity parameter γ and the response parameter β, we can compute the relative probability of various states of the process, and from this deduce the likelihood of different geographic distributions of contracts. In fact, one can say a fair amount about the qualitative behavior of the process even when one does not know specific values of the parameters.

We illustrate with a concrete example that is meant to capture some of the key features of the Illinois case. Consider the hypothetical state of Torusota shown in Figure 8. In the northern part of the state—above the dashed line—soils are evenly divided between High and Medium quality soils. In the southern part they are evenly divided between Medium and Low quality soils. As in Illinois the soil types are interspersed, but average soil quality is higher in the north than it is in the south. Let n be the number of farms. Each farm is assumed to have exactly eight neighbors, so there are $4n$ edges altogether. Let us restrict the set of contracts to be in multiples of ten percent: $x = 10\%$, $20\%, \ldots, 90\%$. (Contracts in which the tenant receives 0% or 100% are not considered.) For the sake of concreteness, assume that High soils have index 85, Medium soils have index 70, and Low soils have index 60. Let the reservation wage be 32 at all locations.

We wish to determine the states of the process that maximize the potential function $\rho(\mathbf{x})$. The answer depends, of course, on the size of γ, that is, on the tradeoff rate between the desire to conform with community norms and the amount of economic payoff one gives up in order to conform.

Consider first the case where $\gamma = 0$, that is, there are no conformity effects. Maximizing potential is then equivalent to maximizing the total rent to land, subject always to the constraint that labor earns at least its reservation wage on each class of soil. The contracts with this property are 40% on High soil, 50% on Medium soil, and 60% on Low soil. The returns to labor under this arrangement are: 34 on H, 35 on M, and 36 on L. Notice that labor actually earns a small premium over the reservation wage ($w = 32$) on each class of soil. This *quantum premium* is attributable to the discrete nature of the contracts: no landlord can impose a less generous contract (rounded to the nearest 10%) without losing his tenant. Except for the quantum premium, this outcome is the same as would be predicted by a standard market-clearing model, in which labor is paid its reservation wage and all the rent goes to land. We shall call this the *competitive* or *Walrasian* state **w**.

Notice that, in contrast to conventional equilibrium models, our framework actually gives an account of how the state **w** comes about. Suppose that the process begins in some initial state $\mathbf{x}^0$ at time zero. As landlords and tenants renegotiate their contracts, the process gravitates towards the equilibrium state **w** and eventually reaches it with probability one. Moreover, if β is not too small, the process stays close to **w** much of the time, though it will rarely be *exactly* in equilibrium.

These points may be illustrated by simulating the process using an agent-based model. Let there be 100 farms in the North and 100 in the South, and assume a moderate level of noise ($\beta = 0.20$). Starting from a random initial seed, the process was simulated for three levels of conformity: $\gamma = 0$, 3, and 8. Figure 9 shows a typical distribution of contract shares after 1000 periods have elapsed. When $\gamma = 0$ (bottom panel), the contracts are matched quite closely with land quality, and the state is close to the competitive equilibrium. When the level of conformity is somewhat higher (middle panel), the dominant contract in the North is 50%, in the South it is 60%, and there are pockets here and there of other contracts. (This looks quite similar to the Illinois case.) Somewhat surprisingly, however, a further increase in the conformity level (top panel) does not cause the two regional customs to merge into a single global custom; it merely leads to greater uniformity in each of the two regions.

To understand why this is so, let us suppose for the moment that everyone is using the *same* contract x. Since everyone must be earning their reservation wage, x must be at least 60%. (Otherwise southern tenants on low quality soil would earn less than $w = 32$.) Moreover, among all such global customs, $x = 60\%$ maximizes the total rent to land. Hence the 60% custom, which we shall denote by **y**, maximizes potential among all global customs. But it does not maximize potential among all states. To see why this is so, let **z** be the state in which everyone in the North uses the 50% contract, while everyone in the South everyone uses the 60% contract. State **z**'s potential is almost as high as **y**'s potential, because in state **z** the only negative social externalities are suffered by those who live near the north-south boundary. Let us assume that the number of such agents is on the order of $\sqrt{n}$, where n is the total number of farms. Thus the

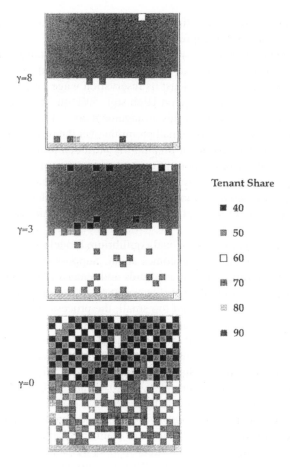

Figure 9. Simulated outcomes of the process for $n = 200$, $\beta = 0.20$.

proportion of farms near the boundary can be made as small as we like by choosing n large enough. But **z** offers a higher land rent than **y** to all the northern farms. To be specific, assume that there are $n/2$ farms in the north, which are evenly divided between High and Medium soils, and that there are $n/2$ farms in the south, which are evenly divided between Medium and Low soils. Then the total income difference between **z** and **y** is $7n/4$ on the Medium soil farms in the north, and $8.5n/4$ on the High soil farms in the north, for a total gain of $31n/8$. It follows that, if γ is large enough, then for all sufficiently large n, the regional custom **z** has higher potential than the global custom **y**.[9]

---

[9] A more detailed calculation shows that **z** uniquely maximizes potential among *all* states whenever γ is sufficiently large and n is sufficiently large relative to γ.

While the details are particular to this example, the logic is quite general. Consider any distribution of soil qualities that is heterogeneous locally, but exhibits substantial shifts in average quality between geographic regions. For intermediate values of conformity γ, it is reasonable to expect that potential will be maximized by a distribution of contracts that is uniform locally, but diverse globally—in other words the distribution is characterized by *regional customs*. Such a state will typically have higher potential than the competitive equilibrium, because the latter involves substantial losses in social utility when land quality is heterogeneous. Such a state will typically also have higher potential than a global custom, because it allows landlords to capture more rent at relatively little loss in social utility, provided that the boundaries between the regions are not too long (i.e., there are relatively few farms on the boundaries).

In effect, these regional customs form a compromise between completely uniform contracts on the one hand, and fully differentiated, competitive contracts on the other. Given the nature of the model, we should not expect perfect uniformity within any given region, nor should we expect *sharp* changes in custom at the boundary. The model suggests instead that there will be occasional departures from custom within regions (due to idiosyncratic influences), and considerable variation near the boundaries. These features are precisely what we see in the distribution of share contracts in Illinois.

9. Conclusion

In this paper I have described a framework for analyzing the asymptotic behavior of a wide variety of agent-based models. In particular, the theory makes quantitative predictions about the long-run probability of various outcomes and thus avoids the hazards of drawing conclusions solely from simulations. (Of course, simulations can still be extremely helpful in understanding the short and medium run dynamics of a process.) I have shown how the theory plays out in specific contexts, including technology adoption, neighborhood segregation, and the evolution of contractual norms. Perhaps the most important aspect of the theory, however, is that it brings into focus certain qualitative features that are common to many agent-based models, but that one does not tend to find in conventional equilibrium types of analysis. The three critical features are: i) local conformity vs. global diversity; ii) punctuated equilibrium; iii) persistence of particular states in the presence of stochastic shocks [Young (1998)].

We can illustrate these concepts by imagining a collection of distinct societies whose members do not interact with each other. Over time, each will develop distinctive institutions to cope with various forms of economic and social coordination—forms of contracts, norms of behavior, property rights, technological standards, and so forth. The solutions that each society finds to these coordination problems will typically take the form of an equilibrium state in an appropriately defined dynamical system. Due to the positive externalities that arise from conforming to the reigning equilibrium, one will tend to find a substantial amount of conformity within a given community. But in separate, noninteracting communities, one may find that the same basic problem is solved in different ways. This is the *local conformity/global diversity effect*. It can apply even within a given society if interactions are sufficiently localized and the externalities are sufficiently strong; Illinois agricultural contracts provide a real-world instance of this phenomenon. A concrete prediction is that two individuals are more likely to exhibit similar behaviors if they come from the same society (or are close in the relevant social network) than if they come from different societies, holding constant all other explanatory variables.

The second qualitative feature of this class of models has to do with the look of the dynamic paths. The theory predicts that the process will tend to exhibit long periods of stasis in which a given equilibrium—or something close to an equilibrium—is in place, punctuated by bursts in which the equilibrium shifts in response to stochastic shocks. In the context of residential segregation Schelling called this the "tipping" phenomenon; here I refer to it as the *punctuated equilibrium effect*.

The third key feature highlighted by the theory is that some equilibrium states are more *persistent* or stable than others. Once established they tend to stay in place for long periods of time because they are robust against stochastic shocks. The methodology outlined allows us to identify these stochastically stable states using the concept of a stochastic potential function. This approach also allows us to make predictions about the long-run behavior of specific dynamical systems, such as segregated outcomes being more stable than integrated ones, and risk dominant technologies being more stable than efficient ones.

I conclude this essay by drawing attention to an important aspect of the theory that we cannot explore in depth here, but that deserves particular recognition, namely, the length of time that it takes for the long-run asymptotic behavior of an evolutionary process to reveal itself. From an empirical point of view it obviously makes a difference if a process takes ten years or a million years to reach its long-run distribution. In the latter case, the short-run dynamics are more important than the long-run asymptotics, and the process may be effectively path dependent even if it is not so from a truly long-run perspective. In practice, however, it is quite difficult to say how long the long run really is. There are several reasons for this. One is that time periods in the model do not correspond to real time intervals; they simply represent markers between distinct events in the model, such as revision decisions by individuals. When the population is large and people interact often, thousands or even millions of such events might be compressed within a short period of real time, such as an hour or a day. Second, the speed of adjustment depends on a number of modeling factors, including the degree of local interaction [Ellison (1993), Young (1998, Chapter 6)], the amount of information that people use to make their decisions, and the extent to which agents' errors are correlated. If agents react only to the behavior of a few neighbors, or they get their information by asking a few friends, or they react similarly to the same conditions, the process can tip from one equilibrium to another in relatively short order. Thus unless we know quite a lot about the topology of interaction and the agents' decision-making processes, estimates of the speed of adjustment could be off by many orders of magnitude.

The theory discussed above identifies those aspects of evolutionary, agent-based models that are critical to determining the speed with which change occurs. The remaining challenge is to bring these theoretical predictions to bear on the forms of social structure that we see in the real world.

References

Arthur, W.B. (1989). "Competing technologies, increasing returns, and lock-in by historical events". Economic Journal 99, 116–131.

Bendor, J., Swistak, P. (2001). "The evolution of norms". American Journal of Sociology 106, 1493–1545.

Bicchieri, C. (2006). The Grammar of Society: The Nature and Dynamics of Social Norms. Cambridge University Press, Cambridge.

Blume, L.E. (1993). "The statistical mechanics of strategic interaction". Games and Economic Behavior 4, 387–424.

Blume, L.E. (1995). "The statistical mechanics of best-response strategy revision". Games and Economic Behavior 11, 111–145.

Blume, L.E. (2003). "How noise matters". Games and Economic Behavior 44, 251–271.

Brock, W.A., Durlauf, S.N. (2001). "Discrete choice with social interactions". Review of Economic Studies 58, 313–323.

Case, A., Katz, L. (1991). "The company you keep: the effects of family and neighborhood on disadvantaged families", National Bureau of Economic Research Working Paper No. 3705.

Crane, J. (1991). "The epidemic theory of ghettos and neighborhood effects on dropping out and teenage childbearing". American Journal of Sociology 96, 1226–1259.

David, P. (1985). "Clio and the economics of QWERTY". American Economic Review 75, 332–337.

Durlauf, S.N. (1997). "Statistical mechanics approaches to socioeconomic behavior". In: Arthur, W.B., Durlauf, S.N., Lane, D. (Eds.), The Economy as a Complex Evolving System, vol. 2. Addison-Wesley, Redwood City, California.

Ellison, G. (1993). "Learning, local interaction, and coordination". Econometrica 61, 1047–1071.

Foster, D., Young, P. (1990). "Stochastic evolutionary game dynamics". Theoretical Population Biology 38, 219–232.

Glaeser, E., Sacerdote, B., Scheinkman, J. (1996). "Crime and social interactions". Quarterly Journal of Economics 111, 507–548.

Hechter, M., Dieter, K. (2001). Social Norms. Russell Sage Foundation, New York.

Illinois Cooperative Extension Service (1995). 1995 Cooperative Extension Service Farm Leasing Survey. Department of Agricultural and Consumer Economics, Cooperative Extension Service, University of Illinois at Urbana-Champaign.

Kandori, M., Mailath, G., Rob, R. (1993). "Learning, mutation, and long-run equilibria in games". Econometrica 61, 29–56.

Karlin, S., Taylor, H.M. (1975). A First Course in Stochastic Processes. Academic Press, New York.

Katz, M., Shapiro, C. (1985). "Network externalities, competition, and compatibility". American Economic Review 75, 424–440.

Katz, M., Shapiro, C. (1986). "Technology adoption in the presence of network externalities". Journal of Political Economy 94, 822–841.

Marimon, R., McGrattan, E., Sargent, T.J. (1990). "Money as a medium of exchange in an economy with artificially intelligent agents". Journal of Economic Dynamics and Control 14, 329–373.

McFadden, D. (1974). "Conditional logit analysis of qualitative choice behavior". In: Zarembka, P. (Ed.), Frontiers Econometrics. Academic Press, New York, pp. 105–142.

McKelvey, R.D., Palfrey, Th.R. (1995). "Quantal response equilibria for normal form games". Games and Economic Behavior 10, 6–38.

Menger, K. (1871). Grundsätze der Volkswirtschaftslehre. W. Braumüller, Vienna. English translation by J. Dingwall and B.F. Hoselitz, under the title Principles of Economics (Free Press, Glencoe, Illinois).

Schelling, Th.C. (1971). "Dynamic models of segregation". Journal of Mathematical Sociology 1, 143–186.

Schelling, Th.C. (1978). Micromotives and Macrobehavior. Norton, New York.

Skyrms, B. (2004). The Stag Hunt and the Evolution of Social Culture. Princeton University Press, Princeton, NJ.

Sugden, R. (1986). The Evolution of Rights, Cooperation, and Welfare. Basil Blackwell, New York.

Sugden, R. (1989). "Spontaneous order". Journal of Economic Perspectives 3, 85–97.

Ullman-Margalit, E. (1977). The Emergence of Norms. Oxford University Press, Oxford UK.

Young, H.P. (1993a). "The evolution of conventions". Econometrica 61 (1), 57–84.

Young, H.P. (1993b). "An evolutionary model of bargaining". Journal of Economic Theory 59 (1), 145–168.

Young, H.P. (1998). Individual Strategy and Social Structure: An Evolutionary Theory of Institutions. Princeton University Press, Princeton NJ.

Young, H.P., Burke, M.A. (2001). "Competition and custom in economic contracts: a case study of Illinois agriculture". American Economic Review 91, 559–573.

Zhang, J. (2004a). "A dynamic model of residential segregation". Journal of Mathematical Sociology 28, 147–170.

Zhang, J. (2004b). "Residential segregation in an all-integrationist world". Journal of Economic Behavior and Organization 54, 533–550.

Chapter 23

HETEROGENEOUS AGENT MODELS IN ECONOMICS AND FINANCE

CARS H. HOMMES[*]

CeNDEF, Department of Quantitative Economics, University of Amsterdam, The Netherlands

Contents

[*] I would like to thank Buz Brock for raising my interest in heterogeneous agent modeling. Our many discussions and joint work over the past decade have greatly influenced the ideas underlying this chapter. An earlier draft of this chapter has been presented at the Handbook workshop at the University of Michican, May 2004 and at the FEE lunch seminar at the University of Amsterdam, November 2004. Detailed comments by Buz Brock, Carl Chiarella, Paul DeGrauwe, Cees Diks, Andrea Gaunersdorfer, Sander van der Hoog, Alan Kirman, Blake LeBaron, Thomas Lux, Sebastiano Manzan, Barkley Rosser, Frank Westerhoff, the Handbook editors Ken Judd and Leigh Tesfatsion, and three anonymous referees on earlier drafts are gratefully acknowledged and greatly improved this chapter. Special thanks are due to Valentyn Panchenko and Peter Heemeijer for programming and simulating several models in this chapter and preparing most of the figures. I also would like to thank Jeffrey Frankel and Kenneth Froot for their permission to reproduce Figure 2. This research has been supported by the Netherlands Organization for Scientific Research (NWO) under a NWO-MaG Pionier grant. None of the above are responsible for errors in this chapter.

Handbook of Computational Economics, Volume 2. Edited by Leigh Tesfatsion and Kenneth L. Judd
DOI: 10.1016/S1574-0021(05)02023-X

Abstract

This chapter surveys work on dynamic heterogeneous agent models (HAMs) in economics and finance. Emphasis is given to simple models that, at least to some extent, are tractable by analytic methods in combination with computational tools. Most of these models are behavioral models with boundedly rational agents using different heuristics or rule of thumb strategies that may not be perfect, but perform reasonably well. Typically these models are highly nonlinear, e.g. due to evolutionary switching between strategies, and exhibit a wide range of dynamical behavior ranging from a unique stable steady state to complex, chaotic dynamics. Aggregation of simple interactions at the micro level may generate sophisticated structure at the macro level. Simple HAMs can explain important observed stylized facts in financial time series, such as excess volatility, high trading volume, temporary bubbles and trend following, sudden crashes and mean reversion, clustered volatility and fat tails in the returns distribution.

Keywords

interacting agents, behavioral economics, evolutionary finance, complex adaptive systems, nonlinear dynamics, numerical simulation

JEL classification: B4, C0, C6, D84, E3, G1, G12

"One of the things that microeconomics teaches you is that individuals are not alike. There is heterogeneity, and probably the most important heterogeneity here is heterogeneity of expectations. If we didn't have heterogeneity, there would be no trade. But developing an analytic model with heterogeneous agents is difficult." (Ken Arrow, In: D. Colander, R.P.F. Holt and J. Barkley Rosser (eds.), *The Changing Face of Economics. Conversations with Cutting Edge Economists.* The University of Michigan Press, Ann Arbor, 2004, p. 301.)

1. Introduction

Economics and finance are witnessing an important paradigm shift, from a representative, rational agent approach towards a behavioral, agent-based approach in which markets are populated with boundedly rational, heterogeneous agents using rule of thumb strategies. In the traditional approach, simple analytically tractable models with a representative, perfectly rational agent have been the main corner stones and mathematics has been the main tool of analysis. The new behavioral approach fits much better with agent-based simulation models and computational and numerical methods have become an important tool of analysis. In the recent literature however, already quite a number of heterogeneous agent models (HAM) have been developed which, at least to some extent, are analytically tractable and for which theoretical results have been obtained supporting numerical simulation results. In this chapter we review a number of *dynamic* HAM in economics and finance. Most of these models are concerned with financial market applications, but some of them deal with different markets, such as commodity good markets. The models reviewed in this chapter may be viewed as simple, stylized versions of the more complicated "artificial markets" and computationally oriented agent-based simulation models reviewed in the chapter of LeBaron (2006) in this handbook. In the analysis of the dynamic HAM discussed in the current chapter one typically uses a mixture of analytic and computational tools.

The new behavioral, heterogeneous agents approach challenges the traditional representative, rational agent framework. It is remarkable however, that many ideas in the behavioral, agent-based approach in fact have quite a long history in economics already dating back to earlier ideas well before the rational expectations and efficient market hypotheses. For example, some of the key elements of the behavioral agent-based models are closely related to Keynes' view that *'expectations matter'*, to Simon's view that economic man is *boundedly rational* and to the view of Kahneman and Tversky in psychology that individual behavior under uncertainty can best be described by simple *heuristics and biases*. Before starting our survey, we briefly discuss these important (and closely related) ideas, which will be recurrent themes in this chapter.

Keynes (1936) argued that investors' sentiment and market psychology play an important role in financial markets, as will be clear from the following famous quote: *'Investment based on genuine long-term expectation is so difficult as to be scarcely practicable. He who attempts it must surely lead much more laborious days and run greater risks than he who tries to guess better than the crowd how the crowd will be-have; and, given equal intelligence, he may make more disastrous mistakes'* (Keynes, 1936, p. 157). According to Keynes, it is hard to compute an objective measure of 'market fundamentals' and, if possible at all, it is costly to gather all relevant information. Another difficulty is that it is not clear what the 'correct' fundamental variables are, and fundamentals can be relevant only when enough traders agree on their role in determining asset prices. Instead of relying on market fundamentals, for an investor it may be easier, less risky and more relevant to make a rule of thumb estimate of the market sentiment. Herbert Simon (1957) emphasized that individuals are limited in their knowledge about their environment and in their computing abilities, and moreover that they face search costs to obtain sophisticated information in order to pursue optimal decision rules. Simon argued that, because of these limitations, *bounded rationality* with agents using simple but reasonable or satisficing rules of thumb for their decisions under uncertainty, is a more accurate and more realistic description of human behavior than perfect rationality with fully optimal decision rules. In the seventies this view was supported by evidence from psychology laboratory experiments of Kahneman and Tversky (1973) and Tversky and Kahneman (1974), showing that in simple decision problems under uncertainty humans do not behave rational, in the sense of maximizing expected utility, but their behavior can be described by *simple heuristics* which may lead to significant *biases*. For a more recent and stimulating discussion of bounded rationality, simple heuristics and biases as opposed to rational behavior we refer to the Nobel Memorial Lectures in Simon (1979) and Kahneman (2003).

In contrast, Milton Friedman has been one of the strongest advocates of a rational agent approach, claiming that the behavior of consumers, firms and investors can be described *as if* they behave rationally. The *Friedman hypothesis* stating that non-rational agents will not survive evolutionary competition and will therefore be driven out of the market has played an important role in this discussion. The following quote from Friedman (1953, p. 175) concerning non-rational speculators is well known: *'People who argue that speculation is generally destabilizing seldom realize that this is largely equivalent to saying that speculators* lose *money, since speculation can be destabilizing in general only if speculators on the average sell when the currency is low in price and buy when it is high'*. In a similar spirit, Alchian (1950) argued that biological evolution and natural selection driven by realized profits may eliminate non-rational, non-optimizing firms and lead to a market where rational, profit maximizing firms dominate. The question whether the Friedman hypothesis holds in a heterogeneous world has played an important role in the development and discussion about HAMs, and we will come back to it several times in this chapter.

Rational behavior has two related but different aspects (e.g. Sargent, 1993). Firstly, a rational decision rule has some micro-economic foundation and is derived from *optimization principles*, such as expected utility or expected profit maximization. Secondly, agents have *rational expectations* (RE) about future events, that is, beliefs are perfectly consistent with realizations and a rational agent does not make systematic forecasting errors. In a rational expectations equilibrium, forecasts of future variables coincide with the mathematical conditional expectations, given all relevant information. Rational expectations provides an elegant and parsimonious way to exclude 'ad hoc' forecasting rules and market psychology from economic modeling. Since its introduction in the sixties by Muth (1961) and its popularization in economics by Lucas (1971), the rational expectations hypothesis (REH) has become the dominating expectation formation paradigm in economics.

Another important issue in the discussion of rational versus boundedly rational behavior is concerned with *market efficiency*, as e.g. emphasized by Fama (1965). If markets were not efficient, then there would be unexploited profit opportunities, that would be exploited by rational arbitrage traders. Rational traders would buy (sell) an underpriced (overpriced) asset, thus driving its price back to the correct, fundamental value. In an efficient market, there can be *no forecastable structure* in asset returns, since any such structure would be exploited by rational arbitrageurs and therefore disappear.

In the seventies and eighties the representative agent, rational expectations and efficient market hypotheses became the dominating paradigm in economics and finance. In the late eighties and nineties however, HAMs and bounded rationality became increasingly popular. The following developments contributed to this change:

1. In a world where all agents are rational and it is common knowledge that all agents are rational, there will be *no trade*. A trader with superior private information can not benefit from his information, because other rational traders anticipate that he must e.g. have positive information about an asset and will therefore not sell the asset to him. Several *no trade theorems* have been obtained (Milgrom and Stokey, 1982; see Fudenberg and Tirole (1991, especially Section 14.3.3) for a discussion). No trade theorems are in sharp contrast with the high daily trading volume observed in real markets, such as the stock market and the foreign exchange market. This tremendous trading volume reinforces the idea of heterogeneous expectations and the idea that it takes differences of opinion among market participants to trade.

2. In the early eighties, Shiller (1981, 1989) and LeRoy and Porter (1981) claimed that stock prices exhibit *excess volatility*, that is, movements in stock prices are much larger than movements in underlying economic fundamentals. Statistical tests for excess volatility were developed, but the power of these tests turned out to be low and the issue is still heavily debated. The stock market crash in October 1987 reinforced the idea of excess volatility and the crash appeared to be difficult to explain by a representative, rational agent model. Another important empirical observation has been the strong appreciation followed by a strong depreciation of the dollar in the mid eighties, which seemed to be unrelated to economic fundamentals as stressed by Frankel and Froot (1986). Cutler et al. (1989) showed that the days of the largest aggregate stock market movements in the S&P500 index, 1941–1987, do not coincide with the days of the most important fundamental news and vice versa. These empirical observations have played an important role in the increasing popularity of non-rational, heterogeneous agent explanations of asset price movements.

3. Following earlier ideas of Simon, in the nineties and since more and more econo-mists have come to question the unrealistically strong rationality assumptions concerning perfect information about the environment and unlimited computing abilities. In particular, in a *heterogeneous* world a rational agent has to know the beliefs of *all* other, *non-rational* agents, which seems highly unrealistic as empha-sized e.g. in Arthur (1995) and Hommes (2001). These developments contributed to a rapidly growing interest in *bounded rationality* in the 1990s, see for exam-ple the survey by Sargent (1993). A boundedly rational agent forms expectations based upon *observable* quantities and adapts his forecasting rule as additional observations become available. *Adaptive learning* may converge to a rational ex-pectations equilibrium or it may converge to an "approximate rational expectations equilibrium", where there is at least some degree of consistency between expec-tations and realizations (see Evans and Honkapohja (2001) for an extensive and modern treatment of adaptive learning in macroeconomics).

4. A problem with behavioral economics and bounded rationality is that it leaves *"many degrees of freedom"*. Any HAM with bounded rationality must provide a plausible story that there is at least some reasonable consistency between beliefs and realizations and how agents select from a large class of possible forecasting and trading strategies. One plausible story is an *evolutionary approach*, advocated by Nelson and Winter (1973, 1974, 1982), where agents or firms select from a class of simple, behavioral strategies according to their relative performance, e.g. as measured by relative profitability and how much this strategy is used by others. The evolutionary approach plays an important role in this chapter.

5. New developments in mathematics, physics and computer science in *nonlinear dynamics*, *chaos* and *complex systems* motivated economists to apply these tools. Economic applications of nonlinear dynamics are surveyed in Brock et al. (1991), Day (1994), Lorenz (1993) and Medio (1992). The Santa Fe conference proceed-ings Anderson et al. (1988) and Arthur et al. (1997a) contain contributions in which the economy is viewed as a *complex evolving system*, see also Arthur (2006) and the collection of papers in Rosser (2004a). Nonlinear dynamics, chaos, and complex systems have important consequences for the validity of the REH. In a simple (linear) stable economy with a unique steady state path, it seems natural that agents can learn to have rational expectations, at least in the long run. A repre-sentative, perfectly rational agent model nicely fits into a linear view of a globally stable and predictable economy. But how could agents have rational expectations or perfect foresight in a complex, nonlinear world, with prices and quantities mov-ing irregularly on a strange attractor? A boundedly rational world view with agents using simple forecasting strategies, perhaps not perfect but at least approximately right, seems more appropriate within a complex, nonlinear world; see e.g. Brock and Hommes (1997b). Applications of tools from nonlinear dynamics and com-plex systems theory have stimulated much work in HAM, which are almost always highly nonlinear, adaptive systems.

6. Laboratory experiments have shown that individuals often do not behave rationally. We already mentioned the work by Kahneman and Tversky, showing that individuals tend to use heuristics and biases in making decisions under uncertainty. In a stimulating and influential paper, Smith et al. (1988) showed the occurrence of bubbles in *asset pricing laboratory experiments*; see also the survey in Sunder (1995). These bubbles occur despite the fact that participants had sufficient information to compute the fundamental value of the asset. This type of laboratory experiments reinforced theoretical work on HAMs with non-rational agents. See also the chapter of Duffy (2006) on the relationship between laboratory experiments and agent-based modeling.

7. Evidence from *survey data* on exchange rate expectations of financial specialists, e.g. by Frankel and Froot (1987a, 1987b, 1990a, 1990b), Allen and Taylor (1990), Ito (1990) and Taylor and Allen (1992), showed that financial practitioners use different trading and forecasting strategies. A consistent finding from survey data is that at short horizons investors tend to use extrapolative chartists' trading rules, whereas at longer horizons investors tend to use mean reverting fundamentalists' trading rules. Frankel and Froot (1987b, p. 264) conclude the following from their survey data analysis: *"It may be that each respondent is thinking to himself or herself, "I know that in the long run the exchange rate must return to the equilibrium level dictated by fundamentals. But in the short run I will ride the current trend a little longer. I only have to be careful to watch for the turning point and to get out of the market before everyone else does"."* For a long time academic work has been skeptical concerning the usefulness of technical trading. Brock et al. (1992) tested 26 simple, frequently used technical trading rules (e.g. moving average and trading range breaks) on the Dow Jones index in the period 1897–1986 and showed that they can generate significantly positive returns, suggesting extra structure above and beyond the EMH benchmark. Dacorogna et al. (1995) show that trading models with different time horizons and risk profiles can be profitable when applied to high frequency exchange rate data. Both the work on survey data, the fact that technical trading is used extensively among practitioners and empirical work suggesting the potential success of technical trading have stimulated much work on HAMs with chartists versus fundamentalists.

8. Finally, the fact that computational tools became widely available in the late eighties and the nineties has enormously stimulated the development and numerical simulation analysis of behavioral HAMs with boundedly rational agents, both in research and in teaching. The current Handbook provides the best proof of this fact, see in particular the chapters of Judd (2006) and Tesfatsion (2006).

There is already too much work on HAMs to provide a comprehensive review in this chapter. We focus on stylized dynamic HAMs using some simple examples to illustrate and discuss what we believe to be important characteristics of HAMs. A long list of references is provided to help guide the interested reader through the already extensive literature. The chapter of LeBaron (2006) contains an overview of larger, computational HAMs as well as many more references to the literature. This chapter is organized as follows. Section 2 discusses some early HAMs with chartists and fundamentalists and work on survey data analysis of expectations of financial experts. Section 3 relates the work on HAMs to behavioral finance. Section 4 presents examples of disequilibrium HAMs, where the interaction of agents leads to complex market dynamics such as cycles or chaotic fluctuations. Section 5 discusses stochastic interacting agent systems and work on social interactions. Section 6 discusses simple financial market HAMs with herding behavior, able to generate important stylized facts such as clustered volatility. Section 7 discusses models where sophisticated agents using advanced but costly strategies compete against simple agents using cheap rule of thumb strategies. Section 8 discusses an asset pricing model with heterogeneous beliefs with endogenous evolutionary switching of strategies. Section 9 summarizes and discusses some future perspectives.

2. Fundamentalists and chartists

In many HAMs two important types of agents are distinguished, *fundamentalists* and *chartists*. Fundamentalists base their expectations about future asset prices and their trading strategies upon market fundamentals and economic factors, such as dividends, earnings, macroeconomic growth, unemployment rates, etc. They tend to invest in assets that are undervalued, that is, whose prices are below a benchmark fundamental value, and sell assets that are overvalued, that is, whose prices are above the market fundamental value. In contrast, chartists or technical analysts do not take market fundamentals into account but instead base their expectations about future asset prices and their trading strategies upon observed historical patterns in past prices. Technical analysts try to extrapolate observed price patterns, such as trends, and exploit these patterns in their investment decisions. A well known example of a technical trading rule is the *moving average* trading rule, buying (selling) an asset when a short run moving average crosses a long run moving average from below (above).

This section discusses some early work emphasizing the importance of fundamentalists and chartists. Subsection 2.1 discusses one of the first financial HAMs with fundamentalists and chartists, due to Zeeman (1974). Subsection 2.2 discusses work on survey data on expectations of Frankel and Froot (1986, 1987a, 1987b, 1990a, 1990b) and Allen and Taylor (1990), showing the importance of chartists trading rules among financial practitioners. Finally, Subsection 2.3 discusses another early model with fundamentalists and chartists discussed in a series of papers by Frankel and Froot (1986, 1987a, 1987b, 1990a, 1990b), which have stimulated much subsequent work in this area.

2.1. An early example

One of the first HAMs for the stock market (or for exchange rates) can be found in Zeeman (1974). This model is an application of the *cusp catastrophe with a slow feedback flow*. Zeeman's purpose was to offer a qualitative description of the observed stylized fact of temporary bull and bear markets. The model is highly stylized and lacks any micro foundations, but nevertheless it contains a number of important, behavioral elements that have also been used in recent heterogeneous agents modeling.

The model contains two types of traders, fundamentalists and chartists. Fundamentalists know the 'true' value of the stock and buy (sell) when the price is below (above) that value. Chartists are trend followers, buying when price rises and selling when price falls. There are three variables J, F and C. J denotes the rate of change of a stock market index or of an exchange rate. $J = 0$ represents a static market, whereas $J > 0$ ($J < 0$) represents a bull (bear) market. C denotes the proportion of the market held by chartists, i.e. the proportion of speculative money in the market, and F denotes the excess demand for stock by fundamentalists. Zeeman assumes that J responds to C and F much faster than C and F respond to J. Stated differently, J is a fast variable (a state variable) and C and F are slow variables (control variables or slowly changing parameters).

Zeeman postulates seven hypotheses based upon observed qualitative features of the stock exchange and the behavior of speculators (chartists) and value investors (fundamentalists). Using Thom's classification theorem, Zeeman then shows that the simplest generic mathematical model that can be derived from these hypotheses is the cusp catastrophe model with a slow feedback flow. Figure 1 shows the surface S satisfying

$$J^3 - (C - C_0) - F = 0. \tag{1}$$

The surface S represents the equilibria of the system.[1] The projection of S onto the (C, F)-plane yields the cusp region, bounded by two fold curves tangent to each other in the cusp point. For (C, F) outside the cusp region, S is single sheeted and the model has a unique (stable) steady state. Inside the cusp region, S is 3-sheeted, the middle sheet representing an unstable equilibrium and the other two sheets stable equilibria. The system converges quickly to the attractor surface S and then slowly moves along the surface. For example, consider a situation where the system is in a bull market at the upper sheet of S. In a bull market the proportion of chartists increases, because they 'follow the trend', thus accelerating a further increase of the stock index. At some point however fundamentalists start selling stocks, because they judge that the market has become overvalued, causing the growth of the index to decrease. The excess demand F of fundamentalists decreases and the system moves along the upper sheet of S in the direction of the point B, causing a crash and a rapid decline of the stock prices until the system reaches the lower sheet of S. During this bear market, at some point fundamentalists start buying stocks again, because they believe that the stock is undervalued, causing a decrease in the proportion of chartists and an increase of the market index. As the index rises, the proportion of chartists increases again, accelerating the rise in stock prices leading to a new bull market. Zeeman's model thus explains a switching between bull and bear markets, as indicated by the arrows in Figure 1, derived from behavioral assumptions about chartists and fundamentalists.

---

[1] Notice that, since J denotes the rate of change, these equilibria are not steady states, but rather equilibria with constant growth rate.

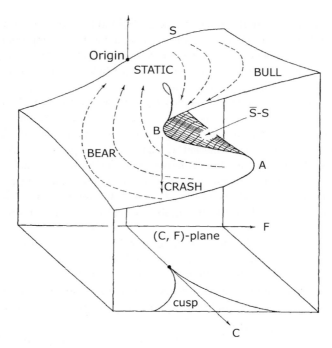

Figure 1. The cusp catastrophe surface of equilibria. The state variable J is the rate of change of the stock index, whereas the control variables F and C represent excess demand of fundamentalists and the proportion of chartists. For clarity the (C, F)-plane has not been drawn through the origin, but below the surface. Reprinted with permission from *Journal of Mathematical Economics*, Vol. 1, No. 1, 1974, E.C. Zeeman, The unstable behavior of stock exchange, Figure 3, p. 46.

Catastrophe theory became quite popular in the early seventies, but was heavily criticized as being a "science fad" in the late seventies and eighties, for example in Zahler and Sussmann (1977). Rosser (2004b) contains an interesting recent discussion and reappraisal of mathematical methods from catastrophe theory and of Zeeman's model. Guastello (1995, pp. 292–297) studied the 1987 market crash using Zeeman's model, whereas recently Rheinlaender and Steinkamp (2004) introduced a stochastic version of Zeeman's model using random dynamical systems theory.

2.2. Survey data on expectations

In the late eighties and early nineties, a number of authors including Frankel and Froot (1987a, 1987b, 1990a, 1990b), Shiller (1987), Allen and Taylor (1990) and Taylor and Allen (1992) conducted questionnaires among financial practitioners to obtain detailed information about investors' expectations. This survey data work has been an important source of inspiration for the development of HAMs. More recent survey based evidence includes Cheung et al. (1999), Lui and Mole (1999) and Menkhoff (1997, 1998).

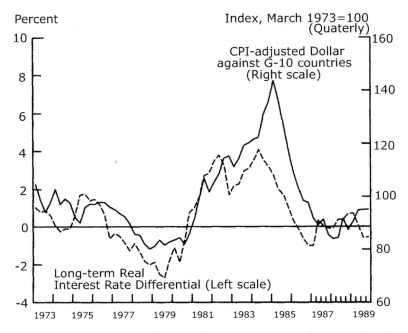

Figure 2. Time series of the real value of the dollar against a weighted average of the currencies of the foreign G-10 countries plus Switzerland (bold graph) and the time series of the real interest differential between the US and a weighted average of the foreign country rates (dotted graph) in the eighties. Reprinted with permission from *American Economic Review*, Vol. 80, No. 2, AEA Papers and Proceedings, Frankel, J.A. and Froot, K.A., The rationality of the foreign exchange rate. Chartists, fundamentalists and trading in the foreign exchange market, Figure 1, p. 181.

In their series of papers in the mid eighties and early nineties, Frankel and Froot studied the large movements of the US dollar exchange rate in the eighties and in particular they investigated the question whether investors' expectations may have amplified those movements. Frankel and Froot (1990a) contains a detailed description of this research; a short, but stimulating discussion is also given in Frankel and Froot (1990b). Figure 2 shows a time series of the real value of the dollar against a weighted average of the currencies of the foreign G-10 countries plus Switzerland and the time series of the real interest differential between the US and a weighted average of the foreign country rates in the eighties. Frankel and Froot (1990b, p. 181) note the following:

"At times, the path of the dollar has departed from what would be expected on the basis of macroeconomic fundamentals. The most dramatic episode is the period from June 1984 to February 1985. The dollar appreciated another 20 percent over this interval, even though the real interest differential had already begun to fall. The other observable factors that are suggested in standard macroeconomic models (money growth rates, real growth rates, the trade deficit) at this time were also moving in the wrong direction to explain the dollar rise."

Indeed it seems difficult to believe that a rational theory could explain such an increase of 20% of the equilibrium real exchange rate within 9 months and that this rapid rise would then be reversed within the next month. Instead Frankel and Froot (1990b, p. 182) argue that "*the appreciation may have been an example of a speculative bubble—that it was not determined by economic fundamentals, but rather was the outcome of self-confirming market expectations.*" Frankel and Froot use survey data on exchange rate expectations to test this hypothesis.[2]

Frankel and Froot (1987a, 1987b, 1990a, 1990b) use three different sources for their survey data on exchange rate expectations of financial specialists, bankers and currency traders. Some of the surveys go back to 1976 and include telephone interviews. The time horizon of the exchange rate expectations vary from 1 week to 12 months. An important finding is that respondents' short-term expectations are quite different from their long-term expectations. Frankel and Froot estimate three simple, standard models for expectations, namely extrapolative expectations, regressive (or mean reverting) expectations and adaptive expectations. The *extrapolative expectations* model assigns a weight g to the lagged spot rate and a weight $(1 - g)$ to the current spot rate, that is, the expected spot rate is given by

$$s_{t+1}^e = (1 - g)s_t + gs_{t-1}, \tag{2}$$

where s_t is the log of the current spot rate, or equivalently

$$\Delta s_{t+1}^e = -g\Delta s_t, \tag{3}$$

where Δs_{t+1}^e is the expected change of the (log) spot rate and Δs_t the last realized change. For short-term horizons (1 week, 2 weeks, 1 month) significantly negative values of g (ranging from -0.13 to -0.05) are obtained, characteristic of *destabilizing* or *bandwagon* expectations for which a current appreciation generates self-sustaining expectations of future appreciations. In contrast, at longer-term horizons of 6–12 months, significantly positive values of g (ranging from 0.07 to 0.38) are obtained characteristic of *stabilizing* expectations, where a trend is expected to reverse.

The *regressive* or *mean-reverting expectations* model is a weighted average between the current (log) spot rate and the (log) long-run equilibrium spot rate $\bar{s}_t$, that is

$$s_{t+1}^e = (1 - v)s_t + v\bar{s}_t, \tag{4}$$

or in terms of expected depreciation

$$\Delta s_{t+1}^e = v(\bar{s}_t - s_t). \tag{5}$$

---

[2] Another rational explanation of the large fluctuations in the exchange rate is a time varying risk premium. Froot and Frankel (1989) show however that the bias in the forward discount, i.e. the log difference of the forward exchange rate and the spot rate, cannot be explained by rational expectations and a (time varying) risk premium, but may be attributable to systematic expectational errors.

If the weight v is positive (negative), then investors expect the exchange rate to move towards (away from) the long run equilibrium value. A negative weight v is characteristic of *destabilizing* or *explosive* expectations, while a positive weight v is characteristic of *stabilizing* expectations. Again, at short-term horizons (1 week, 2 weeks, 1 month) significantly negative values of v (ranging from -0.03 to -0.08) are obtained, whereas at longer-term horizons of 6–12 months significantly positive values of v (ranging from 0.06 to 0.17) are obtained. Similar results are also found for the case of adaptive expectations. Frankel and Froot (1990a, pp. 98–101) conclude that

> "*... short-term and long-term expectation behave very differently from one another. In terms of the distinction between fundamentalists and chartists views, we associate the longer-term expectations, which are consistently stabilizing, with the fundamentalists, and the shorter term forecasts, which seem to have a destabilizing nature, with the chartists expectations. Within each of the above tables, it is as if there are actually two models of expectations operating, one at each end of the forecasting horizons, and a blend in between. Under this view, respondents use some weighted average of the chartist and fundamentalist forecasts in formulating their expectations for the value of the dollar at a given future date, with weights depending on how far off that date is.*"

This conclusion is in line with other questionnaire surveys of Allen and Taylor (1990) and Taylor and Allen (1992), conducted on behalf of the Bank of England, among chief foreign exchange dealers in London. Taylor and Allen (1992, p. 304) conclude:

> *... at least 90 per cent of the respondents place some weight on this form of non-fundamental analysis when forming views at one or more time horizons. There is also a skew towards reliance on technical, as opposed to fundamentalist, analysis at shorter horizons, which becomes steadily reversed as the length of horizon considered is increased. A very high proportion of chief dealers view technical and fundamental analysis as complementary forms of analysis and a substantial proportion suggest that technical advice may be self-fulfilling.*

Finally, Table 1 is reproduced from Frankel and Froot (1990b) showing how the relative importance of fundamentalist and technical analysis shifts over time. The table shows that in 1978 most of the forecasting services (19 vs. 3) relied on fundamental analysis, whereas in 1985 the situations has been reversed (5 vs. 15). Frankel and Froot (1990b, pp. 184–185) conclude the following:

> "*... it may indeed be the case that shifts over time in the weight that is given to different forecasting techniques are a source of changes in the demand for dollars, and that large exchange rate movements may take place with little basis in macroeconomic fundamentals.*"

Table 1

From Frankel and Froot (1990b, p. 184, Table 2); source: Euromoney, August issues. Total = number of services surveyed; Chart. = number who reported using technical analysis; Fund. = number who reported using fundamentals models; and Both = number reporting a combination of the two. When a forecasting firm offers more than one service, each is counted separately.

	Techniques used by forecasting services			
Year	Total	Chart.	Fund.	Both
1978	23	3	19	0
1981	13	1	11	0
1983	11	8	1	1
1984	13	9	0	2
1985	24	15	5	3
1988	31	18	7	6

2.3. An exchange rate model

Their work on questionnaire surveys among financial practitioners motivated Frankel and Froot (1986, 1990a 1990b) to develop a heterogeneous agent model for exchange rates with time varying weights of forecasting strategies, which has stimulated much subsequent research in the field. Their exchange rate model contains three classes of agents: fundamentalists, chartists and portfolio managers. Fundamentalists think of the exchange rate according to a model—e.g. the overshooting model—that would be exactly correct if there were no chartists in the market. Chartists do not have fundamentals in their information set; instead they use autoregressive time series models—e.g. simple extrapolation—having only past exchange rates in the information set. Finally portfolio managers, the actors who actually buy and sell foreign assets, form their expectations as a weighted average of the predictions of fundamentalists and chartists. Portfolio managers update the weights over time in a rational, Bayesian manner, according to whether the fundamentalists or the chartists have recently been doing a better job of forecasting. Thus each of the three is acting rationally subject to certain constraints. The model departs from the orthodoxy in that the agents could do better, in expected value terms, if they knew the complete model. The departure is a general model of exchange rate determination

$$s_t = c\Delta s_{t+1}^m + z_t, \quad c \geq 0, \tag{6}$$

where s_t is the log of the spot exchange rate, Δs_{t+1}^m is the rate of depreciation expected by the market, i.e. by the portfolio managers, and z_t, represents market fundamentals. Portfolio managers use a *weighted average of the expectations of fundamentalists and chartist*:

$$\Delta s_{t+1}^m = \omega_t \Delta s_{t+1}^f + (1 - \omega_t)\Delta s_{t+1}^c, \quad 0 \leq \omega_t \leq 1. \tag{7}$$

Fundamentalists' forecast are given by

$$\Delta s_{t+1}^f = v(\bar{s} - s_t), \tag{8}$$

where $\bar{s}$ is the fundamental exchange rate and v is the speed of adjustment. For simplicity, Frankel and Froot (1990b) assume that the 'chartists' believe that the exchange rate follows a random walk, that is,

$$\Delta s_{t+1}^c = 0. \tag{9}$$

Portfolio managers' expected change of exchange rates (7) then simplifies to

$$\Delta s_{t+1}^m = \omega_t v(\bar{s} - s_t). \tag{10}$$

The weight ω_t attached to fundamentalists views by portfolio managers evolves according to

$$\Delta \omega_t = \delta(\widehat{\omega}_{t-1} - \omega_{t-1}), \quad 0 \leq \delta \leq 1, \tag{11}$$

where $\widehat{\omega}_{t-1}$ is defined as the weight, computed ex post, that would have perfectly predicted the realized change in the spot rate, that is, $\widehat{\omega}_{t-1}$ is defined by the equation

$$\Delta s_t = \widehat{\omega}_{t-1} v(\bar{s} - s_{t-1}). \tag{12}$$

Equations (11) and (12) together determine the change of weights that portfolio managers give to fundamentalist's views:

$$\Delta \omega_t = \delta \left(\frac{\Delta s_t}{v(\bar{s} - s_{t-1})} - \omega_{t-1} \right), \tag{13}$$

where the coefficient δ measures the speed of adaption. Portfolio managers thus adapt the weight given to the fundamentalist forecast in the direction of the weight that would have yielded a perfect forecast.

Frankel and Froot (1990a) take a continuous time limit and obtain differential equations for $\omega(t)$ and $s(t)$. Since the fundamental steady state may be unstable, the model is extended by adding an endogenous stabilizing fundamental force, due to current account imbalance when the exchange rate moves too far away from the fundamental. Simulations of the extended model show that the exchange rate may exhibit a temporary bubble, during which fundamentalists weight is driven to zero, with a rapidly increasing exchange rate, but at some point when the exchange rate has moved too far away from its fundamental value external deficits turn the trend and portfolio managers start giving more weight again to fundamentalists forecast, accelerating the depreciation. Frankel and Froot (1990a, p. 113) note that *"Ironically, fundamentalists are initially driven out of the market as the dollar appreciates*, even though they are ultimately right about its return to $\bar{s}$."

In the model the three types of agents, portfolio managers, chartists and fundamentalists are not fully rational. In defending their approach against the Friedman hypothesis that speculative, destabilizing investors will be driven out of the market by smart, stabilizing investors, Frankel and Froot (1986, pp. 35–36) use a bounded rationality defense for their model [emphasis added]:

*"All this comes at what might seem a high cost: portfolio managers behave ir-rationally in that they do not use the entire model in formulating their exchange rate forecasts. But another interpretation of this behavior is possible in that port-*folio managers are actually doing the best they can in a confusing world. *Within this framework they cannot have been more rational; abandoning fundamental-ism more quickly would not solve the problem in the sense that their expectations would not be validated by the resulting spot process in the long run. In trying to learn about the world after a regime change, our portfolio managers use con-vex combinations of models which are already available to them and which have worked in the past. In this context, rationality is the rather strong presumption that one of the prior models is correct. It is hard to imagine how agents, after a regime change, would know the correct model."*

3. Noise traders and behavioral finance

The work on HAMs discussed in this chapter is closely related to recent ideas from *behavioral finance*. In their recent survey, Barberis and Thaler (2003, p. 1052) state: *behavioral finance argues that some financial phenomena can plausibly be understood using models in which some agents are not fully rational.* Behavioral finance has two building blocks. The first is *limits to arbitrage*, meaning that it can be difficult and risky for rational arbitrageurs to correct mispricing caused by non-rational traders, be-cause the mispricing may get worse in the short run when a majority of traders adopts a trend following strategy. The second building block is *market psychology*, an attempt to characterize which heuristics and biases play a role in financial markets. The finan-cial market HAMs discussed in the current chapter fit within behavioral finance in that they provide tractable, parsimoniously parameterized models capturing key features in behavioral finance.

In the HAMs with fundamentalists versus chartists discussed in Section 2, none of the two trader types is fully rational, because none of the two takes into account the presence of the other. Would not, as the Friedman hypothesis suggests, a fully rational trader perform better and drive out all other trader types? In this section we discuss two early models due to DeLong et al. (1990a, 1990b). This approach has been called the *noise trader approach* and has e.g. been nicely summarized in Shleifer and Summers (1990). Another early, related HAM with "smart money" versus "ordinary" traders has been introduced by Shiller (1984). In these models there are two types of investors: *ra-tional arbitrageurs* and *noise traders*. Arbitrageurs—also called *smart money* traders or *rational speculators*—are investors who form fully rational expectations about security returns. In contrast, "noise traders", a term due to Kyle (1985) and Black (1986),— sometimes also called *liquidity traders*—are investors whose changes in asset demand are not caused by news about economic fundamentals but rather by non-fundamental considerations such as changes in expectations or market sentiment.

3.1. Rational versus noise traders

In DeLong et al. (1990a) there are two types of traders, noise traders and sophisticated, rational traders. There are two assets, a safe asset paying a fixed dividend r in each period, and a risky asset paying an uncertain dividend

$$r + \epsilon_t, \tag{14}$$

where ϵ_t is IID, normally distributed with mean 0 and variance σ_ϵ^2. The price of the unsafe asset in period t is denoted by p_t.

Noise traders incorrectly believe that they have special information about the future price of the risky asset. For example, they use signals from technical analysts, stock brokers or economic consultants and irrationally believe that these signals carry information and select their portfolios based upon these incorrect beliefs. For sophisticated traders it is optimal to exploit noise traders misperceptions. Sophisticated traders buy (sell) when noise traders depress (push up) prices. This contrarian trading strategy pushes prices in the direction of the fundamental value, but not completely.

For both trader types, demand for the risky asset is derived from expected utility maximization of constant absolute risk aversion (CARA) utility of tomorrow's wealth,

$$\lambda_t^R = \frac{r + E_t p_{t+1} - (1+r)p_t}{2\gamma(\sigma_{p_{t+1}}^2 + \sigma_\epsilon^2)}, \tag{15}$$

$$\lambda_t^N = \frac{r + E_t p_{t+1} - (1+r)p_t}{2\gamma(\sigma_{p_{t+1}}^2 + \sigma_\epsilon^2)} + \frac{\rho_t}{2\gamma(\sigma_{p_{t+1}}^2 + \sigma_\epsilon^2)}, \tag{16}$$

where γ is the coefficient of absolute risk aversion, $E_t[p_{t+1}]$ is the expected price at date $t + 1$ conditional on information up to time t, $\sigma_{p_{t+1}}^2$ is the expected one period variance of p_{t+1} and ρ_t is the *misperception* of the expected price for tomorrow by the noise trader. Notice that the only difference in the demand of rational and noise traders is the second term in (16), due to the misperception ρ_t of the noise traders of next periods price of the risky asset. The misperception of noise traders is an *exogenously given* IID normally distributed random variable with mean ρ^* and variance σ_ρ^2.

There is a fixed fraction μ of noise traders and a fraction $1 - \mu$ of rational, sophisticated traders. Market equilibrium requires that aggregate demand equals fixed supply normalized to 1, yielding the equilibrium price

$$p_t = \frac{1}{1+r}\left[r + E_t p_{t+1} - 2\gamma\left(\sigma_{p_{t+1}}^2 + \sigma_\epsilon^2\right) + \mu\rho_t\right]. \tag{17}$$

DeLong et al. (1990a) only consider steady state equilibria satisfying the pricing rule

$$p_t = 1 + \frac{\mu\rho^*}{r} + \frac{\mu(\rho_t - \rho^*)}{1+r} - \frac{(2\gamma)}{r}\left[\sigma_\epsilon^2 + \frac{\mu^2\sigma_\rho^2}{(1+r)^2}\right]. \tag{18}$$

The last three terms show the impact of noise traders on the price of the risky asset. Notice that, when the distribution of the misperception ρ_t of the noise traders converges to a point mass at $\rho^* = 0$, the price of the risky asset converges to its fundamental value $1 - (2\gamma\sigma_\epsilon^2/r)$. The second term on the RHS of (18) captures the fluctuations in prices due to the average misperception ρ^* of noise traders. The higher the average misperception of noise traders, the higher the asset price in equilibrium. The third term on the RHS of (18) captures the fluctuations in prices due to the variation $\rho_t - \rho^*$ in misperception of noise traders. When noise traders in period t are more bullish (bearish) than on average, the asset price increases (decreases). The final term on the RHS of (18) captures both *fundamental risk* and *noise trader risk*. A higher variance σ_ϵ^2, or a higher fraction μ of noise traders or a higher variance σ_ρ^2 of noise traders' misperceptions all increase the risk premium to hold the risky asset and thus lower the asset price.

An important question is which type of traders, sophisticated or noise traders, earn relative higher returns. DeLong et al. (1990a) compute the (unconditional) *expected difference of return* between noise traders and sophisticated traders to be

$$E[\Delta R_t] = \rho^* - \frac{(\rho^*)^2 + \sigma_\rho^2}{2\gamma\left[\frac{\mu\sigma_\rho^2}{(1+r)^2} + \frac{\sigma_\epsilon^2}{\mu}\right]}. \tag{19}$$

From this expression it follows that for the noise traders to earn higher expected returns. the mean misperception ρ^* of returns must be positive. It is also clear, due to the dominating quadratic term in ρ^*, that for high values of ρ^* the expected difference in returns will become negative. However, for intermediate degrees of average bullishness ρ^* noise traders earn higher expected returns than sophisticated traders. Furthermore, the larger is the value of γ, that is, the more risk averse traders are, the larger is the range of ρ^*-values for which noise traders earn higher expected returns.

Imitation of beliefs

The arguments above show that when the fractions of both types are fixed, noise traders may earn higher expected returns suggesting that they may be able to survive in the long run. DeLong et al. (1990a) also discuss a dynamic version of the model with time varying fractions. Strategy selection is based upon the *relative performance* of the two strategies. Letting μ_t be the fraction of noise traders and R_t^N and R_t^S be the realized return of noise traders and sophisticated traders, the fraction of noise traders changes according to

$$\mu_{t+1} = \max\{0, \min[1, \mu_t + \alpha(R_t^N - R_t^S)]\}, \tag{20}$$

where $\alpha > 0$ is the rate at which investors become noise traders. According to (20) the strategy that has performed better, according to realized returns, attracts more followers, and such a rule may be interpreted as an *imitation* rule. It should be noted that this HAM with sophisticated agents and time varying fractions can only be solved for small values of α, because sophisticated agents have to calculate the effect of the realization of returns on the fractions of noise traders and sophisticated traders in the next period.

For α sufficiently small realized returns can be calculated under the approximation that the fraction of noise traders remains the same.

For α small, the expected return difference between noise traders and sophisticated traders is obtained from (19) by replacing μ by μ_t:

$$E[\Delta R_t] = \rho^* - \frac{(\rho^*)^2 + \sigma_\rho^2}{2\gamma\left[\frac{\mu_t \sigma_\rho^2}{(1+r)^2} + \frac{\sigma_\epsilon^2}{\mu_t}\right]}. \tag{21}$$

The fraction of noise traders will increase (decrease) as long as the difference in expected returns (21) is positive (negative). A steady state fraction μ^* must satisfy either

$$E[\Delta R_t] = 0, \tag{22}$$

or $\mu^* = 0$ or $\mu^* = 1$. A straightforward computation shows that the number of steady states μ^* depends upon the parameter condition

$$\sigma_\epsilon^2 > \frac{(1+r)^2(\rho^* + \sigma_\rho^2)^2}{16\gamma^2(\rho^*)^2\sigma_\rho^2}. \tag{23}$$

The dynamics of the fraction of noise traders, in the limit as the speed of adjustment α tends to 0, has the following properties:

- If (23) is satisfied, then there are no steady states μ^* satisfying (22); noise traders always earn higher expected return and drive out sophisticated rational traders, that is, the noise trader share μ_t tends to 1;
- If (23) is not satisfied, then (22) has (at least one) positive real root(s); the smallest $\mu_L^* > 0$ is stable and thus a positive share of noise traders always survives in the market; if $\mu_L \geq 1$, then noise traders drive out sophisticated rational traders.

The fact that noise traders may survive in the long run, is only true if selection of trading strategies is based upon *realized returns*, and it can be argued that this contradicts traders' objective of maximizing expected utility. Since sophisticated investors maximize true expected utility, any other trading strategy that earns a higher mean return must have a variance sufficiently higher to make it non-optimal, that is, it must have sufficiently higher risk. When strategy selection is based upon *realized utility* instead of realized return, noise traders can not survive in the long run, because on average realized utility of sophisticated traders is higher than realized utility of noise traders. DeLong et al. (1990a, p. 724) however argue that a wealth based performance rule such as realized returns may be more relevant for real markets: "*... we find it plausible that many investors attribute the higher returns of an investment strategy to the market timing skills of its practitioners and not to its greater risk. This consideration may be particular important when we ask whether individuals change their own investment strategies that have just earned them a high return. When people imitate investment strategies, they appear to focus on standard metrics such as returns relative to market averages and do not correct for ex ante risk. As long as enough investors use the pseudo signal of realized returns to choose their own investment strategy, noise traders will persist*". Realized returns are also important simply because those who make them become wealthier and get more weight in the market. The noise trader model thus contradicts the Friedman hypothesis.

3.2. Informed arbitrage versus positive feedback trading

DeLong et al. (1990b) consider a different model where noise traders are replaced by *positive feedback traders*. The purpose of the model is to show that, in contrast to the Friedman hypothesis, in the presence of positive feedback traders, rational speculation can be *destabilizing*. The model only has four periods (0, 1, 2 and 3) and two assets, cash and stock. The stock is liquidated and pays an uncertain dividend $\Phi + \theta$ in period 3, when investors consume all their wealth. θ is normally distributed with mean 0, and no information about θ is revealed. Φ can take three different values, $-\phi$, 0 or ϕ; the value of Φ becomes public in period 2, and a signal ϵ about Φ is released in period 1.

There are three types of investors. *Positive feedback traders*, whose asset demand depends upon the latest observed price change, *informed rational speculators* who maximize utility of period 3 consumption using private information and *passive investors* whose asset demand depends only on the asset price relative to its fundamental price and who only have access to public information. In period 2, the value of Φ is revealed to both the informed rational investors and the passive investors. In period 1 a signal about period 2 fundamental news Φ is given, but only the informed rational investors have access to this private information. The fractions of the three types are constant over time. The fraction of positive feedback traders is normalized to 1, the fraction of rational informed speculators is μ and the fraction of passive investors is $1 - \mu$. The sum of the last two types is held constant in order to keep the risk-bearing capacity of the market constant. An increase in μ is therefore an increase in the proportion of rational investors who receive information and exploit short run price dynamics, holding the risk-bearing capacity of the market constant.

The structure of the model is summarized in Table 2. Informed rational speculators are perfectly rational in the sense that they form their demand optimally from mean-variance maximization given private information and taking into account the other type of investors in the market. Demand of passive investors is assumed to be negatively related to the price deviation from the fundamental. Finally, the demand of feedback traders is determined by the most recently observed past price change.[3]

In period 1, the rational informed investors receive a signal $\epsilon \in \{-\phi, 0, \phi\}$. We focus on the situation where this signal is positive, i.e. $\epsilon = \phi > 0$. We consider two cases, one where the signal is *noiseless* and a second case where the signal, $\epsilon = \phi$ is *imperfectly informative* and $\Phi = \phi$ or $\Phi = 0$ each with probability $1/2$. The equilibrium prices in periods 0, 1, 2 and 3 can be computed by solving the model backwards, and

---

[3] As pointed out in DeLong et al. (1990b, p. 385, footnote 6) it is the responsiveness of feedback traders to *past* price changes and not the responsiveness to current price changes that leads to the possibility of destabilizing rational speculation.

Table 2

As in DeLong et al. (1990b, p. 385). Demand of different investor types and information for different investor types. β and α are the slope of the demand curves of positive feedback traders and passive investors. p_0, p_1, p_2 and p_3 are asset equilibrium prices in the corresponding periods.

Structure of the model				
Period	Event	Total demand of		
		Positive feedback traders	Passive investors	Informed rational speculators
0	None, benchmark period	0	0	optimal choice $(= 0)$
1	Speculators receive signal ϵ of period 2 fundamental shock	0	$-\alpha p_1$	optimal choice
2	Passive investors learn Φ	$\beta(p_1 - p_0)$	$-\alpha(p_2 - \Phi)$	optimal choice
3	Liquidation of stock dividend $\Phi + \theta$ revealed publically	$\beta(p_2 - p_1)$	$-\alpha(p_3 - (\Phi + \theta))$	optimal choice

they are graphically represented in Figure 3. Period 0 forms a reference period and the initial price is set to the fundamental price 0, i.e. $p_0 = 0$. When there are no rational informed speculators (i.e. $\mu = 0$), the equilibrium price jumps from 0 in period 1 to ϕ in period 2, when private information becomes public. When there are rational informed traders in the market, arbitrage pushes up the equilibrium prices p_1 and p_2 in periods 1 and 2, in both the noiseless and noisy signal cases. This effect is amplified by the presence of positive feedback trading leading to equilibrium prices far above fundamental prices reflecting private information in period 1 and public information in period 2. The conclusion is that, in contrast to the Friedman hypothesis, *in the presence of positive feedback traders, rational speculation can be destabilizing*. The model thus explains overreaction to news about economic fundamentals, caused by rational informed speculators taking into account the presence of feedback traders.

In the models of DeLong et al. (1990a, 1990b) the behavior of noise traders is exogenously given, and the other group, the sophisticated (informed) traders, take the presence of noise traders into account and respond perfectly rational to their erroneous behavior. In a way, this requires even more rationality than in a RE-model, because in a heterogeneous market a rational agent must anticipate the beliefs of all other, *non-rational* traders. More recently, behavioral finance HAMs have been developed where two (or more) different groups of *boundedly rational* traders interact. A recent example is Hong and Stein (1999), who consider a model with *newswatchers* versus *momentum* traders. Newswatchers make forecasts based on private information without conditioning on past prices, whereas momentum traders' forecasts are based on the most recent price change. These type of behavioral finance models can explain im-

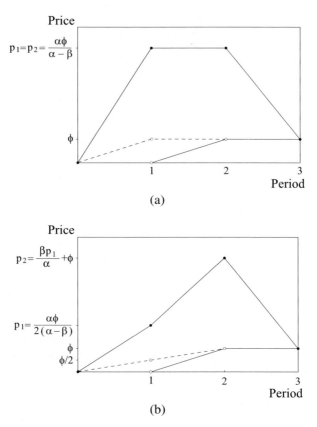

Figure 3. As in DeLong et al. (1990b, p. 390). Equilibrium prices with a noiseless signal (a) and a noisy signal (b) ϵ for rational informed traders. Without rational informed traders in the market (circles, lower graphs) the equilibrium price jumps from 0 in period 1 to ϕ in period 2 when the positive, private information becomes public. In the absence of feedback traders, arbitrage of rational informed traders pushes up the equilibrium prices p_1 to a fundamental value ϕ when the signal is perfect ((a), dotted line) resp. a fundamental value $\phi/2$ (when all agents are informed, i.e. $\mu = 1$) when the signal is imperfect ((b), dotted line). In the presence of feedback traders rational speculation by informed traders causes the equilibrium prices (black dots, upper graphs) to overshoot the fundamental price by a large amount. α is the slope of the demand curve of the passive and informed rational traders; β is the responsiveness of positive feedback traders to past price changes.

portant stylized facts, which can not be explained by a perfectly rational agent EMH model, such as excess volatility, positive correlations of returns at short horizons and negative correlation of returns at long horizons. It also provides an explanation for the risk premium puzzle: because of noise trader risk, the difference between average returns on stocks and bonds—the risk premium—is higher than the fundamental risk. We refer the reader to the recent survey by Barberis and Thaler (2003) and their many references.

4. Complex dynamics

In the seventies and the eighties, due to the discovery of *deterministic chaos*, it became widely known that simple nonlinear deterministic laws of motion can generate seemingly unpredictable, chaotic fluctuations; see e.g. Medio and Lines (2001) for a mathematical introduction. Dynamic HAMs are often highly nonlinear, for example due to the fact that the weights or the fractions of the different trader types are time dependent. HAMs can therefore generate complicated, chaotic fluctuations for a broad range of parameter settings. Chaotic models offer the possibility to describe erratic, unpredictable movements in asset prices by a simple, nonlinear 'law of motion', and this possibility has stimulated much research in this area. In particular, a chaotic HAM with chaotic asset price fluctuations around a benchmark fundamental may explain excess volatility. In a non-linear, chaotic market system arbitrage trading is difficult and risky, because such a system is difficult to predict, especially when it is buffeted with (small) noise representing e.g. news about economic fundamentals. In this section, we review some nonlinear HAMs exhibiting periodic and chaotic asset price fluctuations.

In the models in Subsections 4.1 and 4.2 the price setting mechanism is not the classical Walrasian market clearing framework, but rather a market maker who sets prices according to aggregate excess demand. Subsection 4.1 discusses a continuous time model due to Beja and Goldman (1980) and Chiarella (1992), allowing for limit cycles, whereas Subsection 4.2 discusses a discrete time model due to Day and Huang (1990), exhibiting chaotic asset price fluctuations, and a market maker model due to Farmer (2002) and Farmer and Joshi (2002). Finally, Subsection 4.3 discusses an exchange rate model with fundamentalists and chartists of DeGrauwe et al. (1993), with the weights of both trader types changing endogenously over time.

4.1. An early disequilibrium model with speculators

Beja and Goldman (1980) were among the first to consider a dynamic HAM with a stylized representation of the market institution by a *market maker* who adjusts prices according to aggregate excess demand. They argue that a real asset market does not operate as a perfect Walrasian market, but that a price formation process admitting a finite adjustment speed that allows for transactions at disequilibrium prices is a more accurate description. In their model traders try to exploit these market imperfections and, at least partly, act on their perception of the current price trend.

Movements in the asset price p are driven by aggregate excess demand with a finite adjustment speed, i.e. the price change is given by

$$\frac{dp}{dt} = D_t^f + D_t^c, \tag{24}$$

where D_t^f and D_t^c represent excess demand of fundamentalists and chartists respectively. Let $w(t)$ denote the (exogenously generated) fundamental price that clears fundamental demand at time t. Fundamental excess demand is assumed to be a linear function of the form

$$D_t^f = a(w(t) - p(t)), \quad a > 0, \tag{25}$$

where the coefficient a measures the relative impact of fundamental demand upon price movements.

Let $\psi(t)$ be the chartists' assessment of the current price trend, and $g(t)$ the (exogenously given) return on alternative securities (e.g. $\psi(t)$ could represent the return on stocks and $g(t)$ the return on bonds). Chartists' excess demand is a linear function of the expected return differential $\psi(t) - g(t)$, that is,

$$D_t^c = b(\psi(t) - g(t)), \quad b > 0, \tag{26}$$

where the coefficient b measures the relative impact of speculator's demand upon price movements. According to (24)–(26), aggregate price change is given by

$$\frac{dp}{dt} = a[w(t) - p(t)] + b[\psi(t) - g(t)] + e(t), \tag{27}$$

where $e(t)$ denotes an additional noise term. Speculators use an adaptive process for trend estimation

$$\frac{d\psi}{dt} = c\left[\frac{dp}{dt} - \psi(t)\right], \quad c > 0, \tag{28}$$

where c is the adaption speed. The trend estimate ψ is thus adjusted upwards (downwards) when the current price change is higher (lower) than expected.

A stability analysis of the 2-D linear system of differential equations (27) and (28) shows that the system is stable if and only if $a > c(b - 1)$. Hence, if the impact a of fundamental demand is sufficiently large or if the impact b of speculative demand is low ($b < 1$), then the market will be stable. However, when the market impact b of speculative demand becomes large and/or when the adaption speed c with which speculators adapt their perceived price trend becomes large, the system becomes unstable with exploding price oscillations. This simple, behavioral model thus shows that, under a market maker scenario, speculative trading may destabilize prices.

Chiarella (1992) considers a nonlinear generalization of the model, where linear chartists' excess demand (26) is replaced by a *nonlinear* function $h(\cdot)$ of the expected return differential $\psi(t) - g(t)$, that is,

$$D_t^c = h(\psi(t) - g(t)). \tag{29}$$

The function h is nonlinear, increasing and S-shaped. More precisely, h satisfies (i) $h'(x) > 0$, (ii) $h(0) = 0$, (iii) there exists x^* such that $h''(x) < 0 \; (> 0)$ for all $x > x^* \; (x < x^*)$, and (iv) $\lim_{x \to \pm\infty} h'(x) = 0$. Although Chiarella (1992) does not provide a micro-foundation for this aggregate excess demand function of chartists, he does provide behavioral arguments why such a demand function may be reasonable. For example, each chartist may seek to allocate a fixed amount of wealth between speculative risky assets and riskless bonds so as to maximize intertemporal utility of consumption.

The demand for the risky asset is then proportional to the difference in expected return $\psi - g$, but is also bounded above and bounded below due to wealth constraints. For a chartist, the individual demand function would then be piecewise linear, and adding many such individual demand functions together leads approximately to an S-shaped increasing aggregate excess demand function.

Chiarella (1992) focuses on the simplest case where the fundamental price and the return on alternative investments are constant, $w(t) \equiv w$ and $g(t) \equiv g$. The dynamics of the nonlinear model is then described by the 2-D system of differential equations

$$\frac{dp}{dt} = a\big[w - p(t)\big] + h\big(\psi(t) - g\big), \tag{30}$$

$$\frac{d\psi}{dt} = c\left[\frac{dp}{dt} - \psi(t)\right]. \tag{31}$$

The nonlinear system has a unique steady state $(p^*, \psi^*) = (w + h(-g)/a, 0)$. The local stability analysis yields the same results as in Beja and Goldman (1980): a large market impact of speculative demand (i.e. a large $h'(-g)$) and/or a high adaption speed c with which speculators adapt their perceived price trend *destabilizes* the system. Moreover, Chiarella (1992) shows that in the unstable case, a (unique) *stable limit cycle* exists along which price and trend estimation of chartist fluctuate over time. The limit cycle and the corresponding time series are illustrated in Figure 4.

4.2. Market maker models

Another early, stimulating and influential model with price setting by a market maker has been introduced by Day and Huang (1990). The model is in discrete time and it is one of the first models exhibiting complicated, chaotic asset price fluctuations around a benchmark fundamental price, qualitatively similar to real stock market fluctuations, with bull markets suddenly interrupted by market crashes.

There are three types of investors, α-investors, β-investors and market makers. The α-investors base their investment decision upon a sophisticated estimate of the long run investment value u in relation to the current price and on an estimate of the chance for capital gains and losses. The α-investors thus base their investment decision on a combination of (long run) economic fundamentals, such as dividends, earnings, growth, etc., and an estimate about the probability that an investment opportunity may disappear in the near future. The excess demand, D_t^α, by α-investors as a function of the market price p_t is given by

$$\begin{aligned} D_t^\alpha &= a(u - p_t)f(p_t) \quad \text{if } p \in [m, M], \\ \alpha(p) &= 0 \qquad\qquad\quad \text{if } p < m \text{ or } p > M, \end{aligned} \tag{32}$$

where u is the (constant) long-run investment value expected by the α-investors, a measures the relative strength of their investment demand, and $f(p)$ is a bimodal probability density with peaks near the extreme values m and M. The α-investors believe that, when

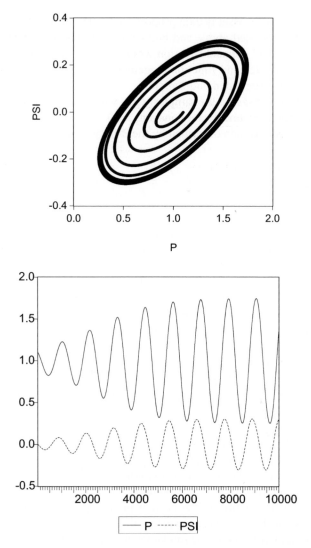

Figure 4. Limit cycle and time series of price (p) and perceived price trend (ψ) by chartists. When the perceived price trend is positive, the price change is reinforced by the speculators. The function $h(x) = \text{Tanh}(\lambda x)$, with $\lambda = 2$, and other parameters are $a = 0.5$, $w \equiv 1$, $g = 0$ and $c = 0.5$.

p_t is close to the topping price M, the probability of loosing a capital gain and experiencing a capital loss is high, and if p_t is close to the bottoming price m, the probability of missing a capital gain by failing to buy is high.

The β-investors are less sophisticated than the α-investors. Their investment decision is based upon a simple extrapolative rule of their expected investment value,

$u^s_{t+1} = p_t + \sigma(p_t - v)$, where v is the (constant) fundamental value of the asset. The β-investors thus believe that the investment value of the asset can be extrapolated from past deviations from the fundamental value. Excess demand of β-investors is given by

$$D^{\beta}_t = \delta\left(u^s_{t+1} - p_t\right) = b(p_t - v), \tag{33}$$

with $b = \delta\sigma$. Hence, β-investors buy (sell) when the price is above (below) its perceived fundamental value. In contrast to the α-investors, β-investors do not take into account an estimate of the probability of investment opportunities in the near future.

The third trader type are *market makers* who mediate transactions on the market out of equilibrium by providing liquidity. The market maker sets a price and supplies stock out of his inventory when there is excess demand and accumulates stock to his inventory when there is excess supply. Aggregate excess demand of α- and β-investors is given by

$$ED(p_t) = D^{\alpha}_t + D^{\beta}_t, \tag{34}$$

and the change of the market makers' inventory V_t of stock is

$$V_{t+1} - V_t = -ED(p_t). \tag{35}$$

Prices are set by the market maker according to the price adjustment rule

$$p_{t+1} = g(p_t) := p_t + \lambda ED(p_t), \quad \lambda > 0, \tag{36}$$

where the parameter λ is the *speed of adjustment*. This price adjustment rule is similar to the classical price tâtonnement process. Day and Huang (1990) argue that the price adjustment rule is determined by the market institution, and that the market maker should be viewed as a stylized version of the specialist at the New York Stock Exchange.

When the probability distribution $f(p)$ is bimodal, the price adjustment function g in (36) is a non-monotonic 1-D mapping. Day and Huang (1990) consider a simple example $f(p) = (p - m + \epsilon)^{-d_1}(M + \epsilon - p)^{-d_2}$, for $m \leq p \leq M$ and $f(p) = 0$ otherwise, whose graph is illustrated in Figure 5. They show that for suitable values of the parameters, stock prices exhibit chaotic fluctuations.

In these simulations, the fundamental value v and the long run investment value u are both constant and equal to 0.5. Stock prices switch irregularly between bull markets with prices rising above the fundamental and bear markets with prices dropping below the fundamental value. Prices are driven up (or down) by trend extrapolating β-investors, until they get close to their topping (or bottoming) price where the excess demand of α-investors sharply decreases (increases) causing the bull (bear) market to end. The β-investors (who may be compared with noise traders) 'follow market prices like sheep' thus making the market for α-investors (or better informed investors) whose behavior is exactly opposite. Day and Huang (1990, p. 307) also note that "*the market makers must buy high from investors and sell low to them, but the damage to their position can be offset by investments on their own account and by their fees for conducting the market*".

More recently, Farmer (2002) and Farmer and Joshi (2002) have derived a similar price setting rule, which they call the *market impact function*. In their model, there are

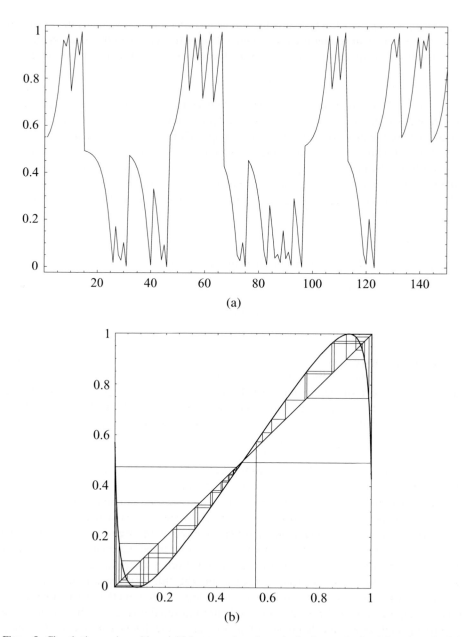

(a)

(b)

Figure 5. Chaotic time series, with an initial state p_0 just above the fundamental price 0.5, and graph of the 1-D map (36). Stock prices switch irregularly between bull and bear markets, as explained in the graphical analysis for initial state $p_0 = 0.55$ (b). Parameters: $m = 0$, $M = 1$, $d_1 = d_2 = 0.5$, $\epsilon = 0.0097$, $u = v = 0.5$, $a = 0.2$, $b = 0.88$ and $\lambda = 1$.

N directional traders who buy or sell a single risky asset by placing market orders, which are always filled. Typically, the buy and sell orders of the directional traders do not match, but the excess demand or excess supply is taken up from or added to the inventory of a *market maker*, who increases (decreases) the price when there is net excess demand (supply). The market impact function is the algorithm used by the market maker to set prices. To be more concrete, let $x_t^i = x^i(P_{t-1}, P_{t-2}, \ldots, I_{t-1})$ be the position of directional trader i at time t, where x^i represents the trading strategy or decision rule of agent i depending on past prices $P_{t-1}, P_{t-2}, \ldots$ and exogenous information I_{t-1}. The net order ω_t^i of directional trader i is given by

$$\omega_t^i = x_t^i - x_{t-1}^i. \tag{37}$$

The aggregate net order is then

$$\omega = \sum_{i=1}^{N} \omega^i. \tag{38}$$

The market maker adjust prices according to

$$P_{t+1} = P_t \phi(\omega), \tag{39}$$

with ϕ an increasing function and $\phi(0) = 1$. Taking logs a linear approximation yields

$$\log P_{t+1} - \log P_t \approx \frac{\omega}{\mu}, \tag{40}$$

where the parameter μ normalizes the order size and is called *liquidity*. The function ϕ is referred to as the *log linear market impact function*. Writing $p_t = \log P_t$ and adding a noise term ϵ_t (e.g. representing noise traders), the (log) price dynamics is given by

$$p_{t+1} = p_t + \frac{1}{\mu} \sum_{i=1}^{N} \omega^i(p_t, p_{t-1}, \ldots, I_t) + \epsilon_t. \tag{41}$$

Notice that this price updating rule is essentially the same as the market maker price adjustment rule in Beja and Goldman (1980), Day and Huang (1990) and Chiarella (1992), as discussed above, except that p_t now represents log price instead of price. The liquidity parameter μ in (41) is inversely related to the speed of adjustment λ in (36). Farmer (2002) and Farmer and Joshi (2002) consider different types of directional traders, either using value investment strategies (or fundamental trading strategies) based upon the perceived value of the asset or using chartists, trend following trading strategies based upon past prices. They show that trend following strategies induce short run positive autocorrelations in returns, whereas value trading induces negative autocorrelations. Furthermore, they present a simple HAM with value investors versus trendfollowers, where autocorrelations of returns are close to zero and other stylized facts observed in financial time series, such as noise amplification, excess volatility, excess kurtosis and clustered volatility, are also matched.

4.3. A chaotic exchange rate model

DeGrauwe et al. (1993) introduce an equilibrium exchange rate model with fundamentalists and chartists, following earlier work of Frankel and Froot (1986, 1990a). It is
one of the first HAMs where the weights of the two investor types is determined *endogenously* and fluctuates over time. The basic equation determining the exchange rate
is

$$s_t = X_t \big(E_t[s_{t+1}] \big)^b, \tag{42}$$

where s_t is the exchange rate in period t, X_t is an exogenous variable representing the
underlying economic fundamental driving the exchange rate, $E_t[s_{t+1}]$ is next period's
expected exchange rate and the parameter b is a discount factor, $0 < b < 1$.

The aggregate change in the expected future exchange rate consists of two components, a forecast made by chartists and a forecast made by fundamentalists:

$$E_t[s_{t+1}]/s_{t-1} = \big(E_{ct}[s_{t+1}]/s_{t-1} \big)^{m_t} \big(E_{ft}[s_{t+1}]/s_{t-1} \big)^{1-m_t}, \quad 0 \le m_t \le 1, \tag{43}$$

where $E_t[s_{t+1}]$ is the aggregate market forecast for next period's exchange rate made at
date t, $E_{ct}[s_{t+1}]$ and $E_{ft}[s_{t+1}]$ are the forecasts made by chartists and fundamentalists,
and m_t and $1 - m_t$ are the *weights* given to chartists and fundamentalists respectively.

Fundamentalists believe that the exchange rate returns towards its fundamental value
s_t^* at rate α, $0 \le \alpha \le 1$, that is,

$$E_{ft}[s_{t+1}]/s_{t-1} = \big(s_{t-1}^*/s_{t-1} \big)^\alpha, \tag{44}$$

where $s_t^* = X_t^{1/(1-b)}$ is the *steady state* equilibrium exchange rate s_t^* obtained
from (42). Chartists look for patterns in past exchange rates and their forecast is

$$E_{ct}[s_{t+1}] = f(s_{t-1}, s_{t-2}, \ldots, s_{t-N}), \tag{45}$$

where N is the maximum lag used. DeGrauwe et al. (1993) mainly focus on moving
average rules for chartists of the form

$$\frac{E_{ct}[s_{t+1}]}{s_{t-1}} = \left(\frac{SMA(s_{t-1})}{LMA(s_{t-1})} \right)^{2\gamma}, \quad \gamma > 0 \tag{46}$$

where $SMA(s_{t-1})$ and $LMA(s_{t-1})$ are short run and long run moving averages. According to (46), when the short run moving average is above (below) the long run moving
average, chartists expect a future increase (decline) of the exchange rate. This type of
technical trading rule is employed frequently by financial practitioners. The parameter
γ measures the rate at which chartists extrapolate the past into the future. DeGrauwe et
al. (1993) mainly focus on the simplest moving average rules, with a one-period change
short run rule

$$SMA(s_{t-1}) = \frac{s_{t-1}}{s_{t-2}}, \tag{47}$$

and a simple two-period moving average for the long run, i.e.

$$LMA(s_{t-1}) = \left(\frac{s_{t-1}}{s_{t-2}}\right)^{0.5} \left(\frac{s_{t-2}}{s_{t-3}}\right)^{0.5}. \tag{48}$$

Using the short run and long run moving averages (47) and (48), the chartists expected change of the exchange rate (46) becomes

$$\frac{E_{ct}[s_{t+1}]}{s_{t-1}} = \left(\frac{s_{t-1}}{s_{t-2}}\right)^{\gamma} \left(\frac{s_{t-3}}{s_{t-2}}\right)^{\gamma}. \tag{49}$$

We now turn to the *endogenous* determination of the weight m_t of chartists. DeGrauwe et al. (1993) postulate the following weighting function:

$$m_t = \frac{1}{1 + \beta(s_{t-1} - s_{t-1}^*)^2}, \quad \beta > 0. \tag{50}$$

DeGrauwe et al. (1993, pp. 75–76) present the following behavioral motivation. There is uncertainty about the fundamental exchange rate equilibrium and fundamentalists have heterogeneous expectations about its true value. When the exchange rate is at its fundamental equilibrium value, $s_{t-1} = s_{t-1}^*$, half of the fundamentalists will find that the market rate is too low, and the other half will find it too high compared to their own estimate. Assuming that all fundamentalists have the same degree of risk aversion and the same wealth, the amount of foreign exchange bought by the first half equals the amount sold by the second half. Hence, when the exchange rate equals its fundamental value, fundamentalists do not influence the market and the market expectation will be completely dominated by chartists ($m_t = 1$). When the exchange rate deviates from its fundamental equilibrium value, the weight of fundamentalists increases, at a rate measured by the parameter β. The endogenous switching mechanism (50) for the weights of chartists and fundamentalists acts as a *"far from the fundamental equilibrium stabilizing force"* on exchange rates. The more the exchange rate deviates from its fundamental equilibrium, the higher the weight of fundamentalists and the stronger the exchange rate will be pushed back towards its fundamental equilibrium value.

In the simplest case, with the fundamental $X_t \equiv 1$ normalized to 1, and one-period short run and two-period long run moving averages, the model can be written as

$$s_t = s_{t-1}^{\phi_1} s_{t-2}^{\phi_2} s_{t-3}^{\phi_3}, \tag{51}$$

$$m_t = \frac{1}{1 + \beta(s_{t-1} - 1)^2}, \tag{52}$$

with $\phi_1 = b[1 + \gamma m_t - \alpha(1 - m_t)]$, $\phi_2 = -2b\gamma m_t$ and $\phi_3 = b\gamma m_t$. The unique fundamental steady state is $(s^*, m^*) = (1, 1)$. The model exhibits rich dynamical behavior ranging from a stable steady state to (quasi-)periodic as well as chaotic dynamics. In particular, when the parameter γ, measuring the rate at which chartists extrapolate a trend, is sufficiently large, the fundamental steady state becomes unstable and chaotic exchange rate fluctuations around the fundamental equilibrium rate arise, as illustrated in Figure 6. In the next sections we discuss HAMs with switching between trading strategies driven by evolutionary selection and social interactions.

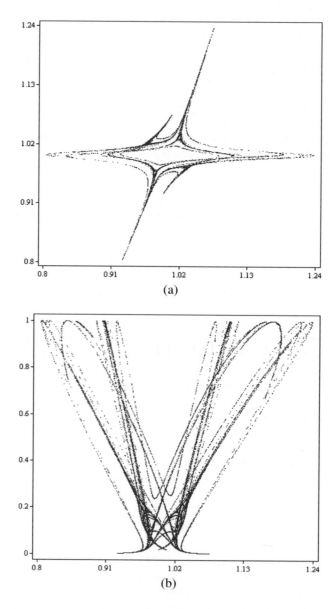

Figure 6. Strange attractor in the (s_t, s_{t-1}) (a) and (s_t, m_t) (b) phase space and corresponding chaotic time series of the exchange rate s_t (c) and the weight of chartists m_t (d). Parameters: $b = 0.95$, $\alpha = 0.65$, $\gamma = 3$ and $\beta = 10000$.

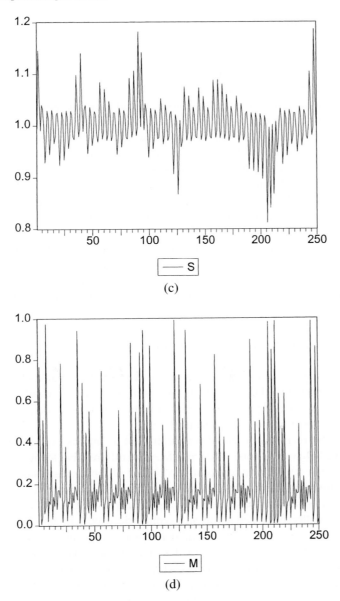

(c)

(d)

Figure 6. (*continued.*)

5. Interacting agents

In this section we discuss models in which individual agents interact stochastically. At
first sight one may think that, due to a law of large numbers, stochastic interactions
average out and can not affect aggregate variables. However, this is not the case. Even
weak (local) interactions among individuals may lead to strong dependencies and cause
large movements at the aggregate level. Aggregation of simple interactions at the micro level may generate sophisticated behavior and structure at the macro level. An early
model with interaction effects has been introduced by Föllmer (1974), who considers an
exchange economy with random preferences with a probability law depending upon the
agents' environment. Using results on interacting particle systems in physics, Föllmer
(1974) shows that even short range interaction may propagate through the economy and
lead to aggregate uncertainty causing a breakdown of price equilibria. In this section we
discuss work on local interactions by Kirman (1991, 1993) and work on social interactions by Brock and Durlauf (2001a, 2001b).[4] These papers have been quite influential
and stimulated much work in this area. For surveys on interacting agent models see, for
example, Brock (1993) and Kirman (1999); see also the papers on path dependence in
Arthur (1994) and the collection of articles in Gallegati and Kirman (1999) and Delli
Gatti et al. (2000).

5.1. An exchange rate model with local interactions

This section discusses an exchange rate model with fundamentalists and chartists introduced by Kirman (1991). The model consists of two parts: an equilibrium model of
foreign exchange rate and a model of opinion formation as described by the stochastic
model of recruitment proposed by Kirman (1993).

The stochastic recruitment model was motivated by an observed puzzle in biology
concerning the behavior of ants. When ants face two different but identical food sources,
surprisingly often the majority concentrates on one of the food sources, say with 80%
of the population on one food source and only 20% of the populations on the other.
Moreover, after some time these proportions suddenly switch. Ants facing a symmetric
situation, thus collectively behave in an asymmetric way. Kirman (1993) proposed a
simple and elegant dynamic stochastic model explaining this observed asymmetric, aggregate behavior. The model offers an explanation for the behavior of ants, but here we
follow Kirman's discussion of the model within a financial market framework. There
is a fixed number of N agents. Agents must form an opinion about next period's price
p_{t+1} of a risky asset and can choose between two opinions, optimistic and pessimistic.
The expectations of agents are affected by random meetings with other agents. The state
of the system is determined by the number k of agents holding say the optimistic view,

---

[4] Related continuous time diffusion models of stock prices with stochastic interacting agents have been
pioneered by Föllmer and Schweizer (1993) and Föllmer (1994).

with $k \in \{0, 1, 2, \ldots, N\}$. Two agents meet at random. The first agent is converted to the second agent's view with probability $(1 - \delta)$. There is also a small probability ϵ that the first agent will change his opinion independently. This (small) ϵ-probability is necessary, in order to prevent the system to get stuck in the absorbing extreme states $k = 0$ or $k = N$. The state k then evolves according to

$$k \to k + 1, \text{ with probability } P(k, k + 1) = \left(1 - \frac{k}{N}\right)\left(\epsilon + (1 - \delta)\frac{k}{N - 1}\right),$$

$$k \to k - 1, \text{ with probability } P(k, k - 1) = \frac{k}{N}\left(\epsilon + (1 - \delta)\frac{N - k}{N - 1}\right), \tag{53}$$

$$k \to k, \text{ with probability } P(k, k) = 1 - P(k, k + 1) - P(k, k - 1).$$

The stochastic process (53) is a simple Markov chain. Kirman investigates the equilibrium distribution $\mu(k)$ of (53), and shows that the form of the equilibrium distribution $\mu(k)$ depends on the relative magnitude of the parameters δ and ϵ:

- if $\epsilon < (1 - \delta)/(N - 1)$, then the equilibrium distribution is bimodal, with a minimum at $k/N \approx 0.5$ and maxima at the extremes $k = 0$ and $k = N$;
- if $\epsilon = (1 - \delta)/(N - 1)$, then the equilibrium distribution is uniform;
- if $\epsilon > (1 - \delta)/(N - 1)$, then the equilibrium distribution is unimodal with a maximum at $k/N \approx 0.5$.

Note that this result does not depend on the size of the probabilities δ or ϵ itself, but rather on their relative magnitudes. When the probability ϵ of self-conversion is low compared to the probability $(1 - \delta)$ of being converted by the other trader, the limiting distribution is bimodal with maxima at the extremes. In that case, a typical time series of the state k is highly persistent and spends little time close to its average $k = 0.5$, but much more time close to the extremes $k = 0$ and $k = N$, as illustrated in Figure 7. This equilibrium distribution thus explains the asymmetric 80%–20% distribution of ants and its occasional flipping to a 20%–80% distribution and vice versa.

Kirman (1991) considers an exchange rate model where the fractions of chartists and fundamentalists are driven by the stochastic model for opinion formation. The exchange rate equilibrium model is similar to the model of Frankel and Froot (1986), but Kirman (1991) provides a micro-foundation of asset demand. Agents can choose to invest in a risk free domestic currency paying a fixed interest rate r or in a risky foreign currency paying an uncertain (stochastic) dividend y_{t+1} in period $t + 1$, assumed to be IID with mean $\bar{y}$. Agent type i maximizes expected utility from a mean-variance utility function $U^i(W_{t+1}^i) = E_i[W_{t+1}^i] - \mu^i V_i[W_{t+1}^i]$, where E_i and V_i denote agent type i's belief about conditional expectation and conditional variance of tomorrow's wealth W_{t+1}^i and $2\mu_i$ represents risk aversion. Agent type i's demand for foreign currency is then given by

$$d_t^i = \frac{s_{i,t+1}^e + \bar{y} - (1 + r)s_t}{2\alpha\mu^i}, \tag{54}$$

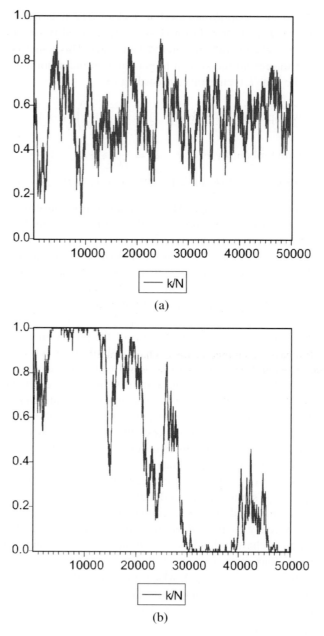

Figure 7. Fractions k/N of optimistic types, for $N = 100$, $\delta = 0.01$ and $\epsilon = 0.05$ (a) resp. $\epsilon = 0.002$ (b). In the latter case (b) the equilibrium distribution is bimodal with peaks at 0 and 1 and the time series is highly persistent and spends relatively much time close to the extremes. In the other case (a) the fraction stays relatively close to 0.5, i.e. to a symmetric distribution of the two types, most of the time.

where $s^e_{i,t+1}$ represents agent type i's expectation about the exchange rate s_{t+1}, $\bar{y}$ is the mean of the IID dividend process and $\alpha = V[s_{t+1} + y_{t+1}]$. In the case of homogeneous, rational expectations, the fundamental value of the exchange rate is given by

$$s^* = \frac{\bar{y} - 2\alpha\mu_i X_t}{r}, \tag{55}$$

where X_t is the supply of foreign exchange. In the heterogeneous agents case of fundamentalists versus chartists, with fractions n_t resp. $1 - n_t$, market equilibrium yields

$$n_t d^f_t + (1 - n_t)d^c_t = X_t. \tag{56}$$

The expectations of fundamentalists and chartists about next period's exchange rate s_{t+1} are given by[5]

$$s^e_{f,t+1} = s_{t-1} + v(s^* - s_{t-1}), \quad 0 \le v \le 1, \quad \text{fundamentalists}, \tag{57}$$

$$s^e_{c,t+1} = s_{t-1} + g(s_{t-1} - s_{t-2}), \quad g > 0, \quad \text{chartists}. \tag{58}$$

Fundamentalists believe that the exchange rate will move back towards its fundamental value s^*, or equivalently, their expected change of the exchange rate is proportional to the observed distance to the fundamental. In the special case $v = 1$ fundamentalists expect the exchange rate to jump to its fundamental value s^* immediately, whereas the other extreme case $v = 0$ corresponds to naive expectations where fundamentalists expect the exchange rate to follow a random walk. Chartists extrapolate in a simple linear way and forecast the change of the exchange rate to be proportional to the latest observed change; Kirman focuses on the case $g = 1$.

Substituting the expectation rules (57) and (58) in the market equilibrium equation (56) and solving for the equilibrium exchange rate yields the difference equation

$$(1+r)s_t = \left[1 - vn_t + g(1 - n_t)\right]s_{t-1} - g(1 - n_t)s_{t-2} + \bar{y} - 2\alpha\mu^i X_t. \tag{59}$$

In deviations $x_t = s_t - s^*$ from the fundamental benchmark this simplifies to

$$(1+r)x_t = \left[1 - vn_t + g(1 - n_t)\right]x_{t-1} - g(1 - n_t)s_{t-2}. \tag{60}$$

Kirman's exchange rate model with fundamentalists versus chartists is thus given by (60) with the fraction $n_t = k_t/N$ evolving according to the (exogenously given) Markov chain (53).[6] It is easily verified that when all agents are fundamentalists, i.e.

---

[5] We choose a specification where s_{t-1} is the most recent observation used in the forecasts of s_{t+1}. Kirman discusses a specification where s_t is used as the most recent observation to forecast s_{t+1}, but in that case the HAM generates exploding exchange rate paths. As Kirman (1991, p. 364) notes when expectations are based on earlier observations (such as s_{t-1}) the HAM allows for symmetric bubbles, both rising and falling. The approach chosen here is similar to the asset pricing model of Brock and Hommes (1998), as discussed in Section 8, and the forecasting rules (57) and (58) are the same as in Gaunersdorfer and Hommes (2006).

[6] Kirman (1991, pp. 359–360) describes a slightly more complicated way of determining the fractions of the two types. Agents try to assess the majority opinion, but observe $n_t = k_t/N$ with noise. If agent i's observation $q_{it} = n_t + \epsilon_{it} \ge 1/2$ ($< 1/2$), then he acts as a fundamentalist (chartist).

$n_t \equiv 1$, (60) yields

$$x_t = \frac{1-v}{1+r} x_{t-1}, \tag{61}$$

which is a *stable* linear system with eigenvalue $\lambda = (1-v)/(1+r)$. In the other extreme case when all agents are chartists, i.e. $n_t \equiv 0$, (60) reduces to

$$x_t = \frac{1+g}{1+r} x_{t-1} - \frac{g}{1+r} x_{t-2}. \tag{62}$$

For $g = 1$ (62) has a pair of stable complex eigenvalues. Notice however that, if the time period of the model is one day, the daily domestic interest rate r is very close to 0 so that these complex eigenvalues are in fact close to a unit root $+1$. These complex roots become unstable when g increases beyond $1 + r$, that is, when chartists expect the change in exchange rates to be larger than the risk free gross return.

In periods when the market is dominated by fundamentalists, the exchange rate s_t is stable and is pushed towards its fundamental value s^*. In contrast, when the market is dominated by chartists, the exchange rate is driven by a stable, but near unit root process for $g = 1$ or an unstable process when $g > 1 + r$. A typical example of simulated time series of the exchange rate and the fraction of fundamentalists is illustrated in Figure 8. The fraction n_t of fundamentalists is driven by the stochastic recruitment model with the same parameters as in Figure 7b and is therefore highly persistent, switching between two different phases where one of the two groups dominates the market. When chartists (fundamentalists) dominate the market, i.e. when n_t is close to 0 (1), volatility of the exchange rate fluctuations is high (low). This HAM therefore captures, at least qualitatively, the phenomenon of volatility clustering, with exchange rates switching irregularly between phases of high and low volatility. Kirman and Teyssière (2002) discuss stylized facts, such as clustered volatility and long memory, generated by the model in more detail. Section 6 of this chapter also discusses stylized facts generated by HAMs. A related model with interaction through a random communication structure has been introduced by Cont and Bouchaud (2000); see also the survey of Kirman (1999).

5.2. Social interactions

Social interaction among individuals refers to a situation where the utility or payoff of an individual agent depends directly upon the choices of other individuals in their reference group, in addition to the dependence which occurs through the intermediation of markets. When the spillovers are positive, i.e. when the payoff is higher if others behave similarly, social interactions induce a tendency for conformity among members of the reference group. Social interactions may explain large cross-group variations, when different groups conform to alternative, self-reinforcing behavior. In the absence of a coordination mechanism social interactions can lead to multiple equilibria. Social interactions may cause a large social multiplier, meaning that small changes in private utility may cause large changes at the aggregate level.

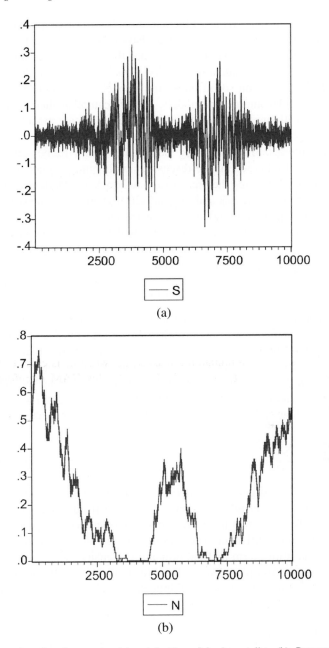

Figure 8. Time series of exchange rates (a) and fraction of fundamentalists (b). Parameters: $N = 100$, $\epsilon = 0.002$, $\delta = 0.01$, $r = 0.01$, $v = 0.5$ and $g = 0.8$. Exchange rates switch irregularly between phases of high volatility when the market is dominated by chartists and low volatility when the market is dominated by fundamentalists.

Schelling (1971) introduced one of the first models with some form of social interaction. He considered a model where individuals have preferences over their neighborhood of racial composition and showed that, even when these preferences are relatively weak, it may lead to pronounced residual segregation. Brock and Durlauf (2001a, 2001b) have written excellent surveys on social interaction models in economics and developed a general class of social interaction models. A key feature of their models, following Brock (1993) and Blume (1993), is the use of discrete choice models with interaction effects. Their approach leads to analytically tractable models that can be used in estimating social interaction effects using the discrete choice framework of Manski and McFadden (1981). In this section we discuss a simple binary choice model with social interactions, closely following the presentation in Brock and Durlauf (2001a); the interested reader is referred to Brock and Durlauf (2001b) and their references for detailed discussions of more general social interactions models.

Each individual of a population of N agents makes a binary choice $\omega_i \in \{-1, +1\}$. Let $\omega_{-i} = (\omega_1, \ldots, \omega_{i-1}, \omega_{i+1}, \ldots, \omega_I)$ denote the choices of all agents other than i. Individual utility derived from choice ω_i consists of three components:

$$V(\omega_i) = u(\omega_i) + S\big(\omega_i, \mu_i^e(\omega_{-i})\big) + \epsilon(\omega_i). \tag{63}$$

Here $u(\omega_i)$ represents *private utility* associated with choice ω_i, $S(\omega_i, \mu_i^e(\omega_{-i}))$ represents *social utility* depending upon choice ω_i of individual i as well as upon the conditional probability measure $\mu_i^e(\omega_{-i})$ agent i places on the choice of other agents and $\epsilon(\omega_i)$ is an idiosyncratic random utility term IID distributed across agents. Instead of a general dependence of social utility on the conditional probability measure $\mu_i^e(\omega_{-i})$, it is often assumed that social utility depends upon agent i's expectation $\bar{m}_i^e$ of other individual choices j given by the average of subjective expected values $m_{i,j}^e$, i.e.

$$\bar{m}_i^e = \frac{1}{N-1} \sum_{j \neq i} m_{i,j}^e. \tag{64}$$

We focus on the case of *global interaction*, where the average (64) is taken over the entire population, i.e. over all individuals j different from i. One may also consider *local interaction* by restricting the average over the reference group of an individual i.

Brock and Durlauf (2001a) focus on simple and tractable parametric representations of both the social utility term and the probability density of the random utility term. Assuming constant cross partial derivatives leads to two functional forms for social utility. The first form is given as a multiplicative interaction between individual and expected average choices, that is,

$$S\big(\omega_i, \bar{m}_i^e\big) = J\omega_i \bar{m}_i^e. \tag{65}$$

This form is referred to as *proportional spillover*, because the percentage change in individual utility from a change in the mean choice level is constant. The second parametrization of social utility with constant partial derivatives captures the pure conformity effect as considered by Bernheim (1994), and is given by

$$S(\omega_i, \bar{m}_i^e) = -\frac{J}{2}(\omega_i - \bar{m}_i^e)^2. \tag{66}$$

Notice that this form penalizes choices far from the mean more strongly than the proportional spillover case. Using the fact that $\omega_i^2 = 1$, (66) can be rewritten as

$$-\frac{J}{2}(\omega_i - \bar{m}_i^e)^2 = J\omega_i\bar{m}_i^e - \frac{J}{2}(1 + (\bar{m}_i^e)^2). \tag{67}$$

This shows that (65) and (66) only differ in levels, but coincide on the terms including individual choices. Therefore, these two different parametrizations of social utility lead to the same discrete choice probabilities as discussed below. In what follows we focus on the proportional spillover specification for social utility in (65).

A standard way to obtain a convenient parametrization for the choice probabilities is to assume that the random utility terms $\epsilon(-1)$ and $\epsilon(1)$ in (63) are independent and extreme-value distributed, so that the difference in errors are logistically distributed,

$$\text{Prob}\{\epsilon(-1) - \epsilon(1) \le x\} = \frac{1}{1 + \exp(-\beta x)}, \quad \beta \ge 0. \tag{68}$$

Under this assumption the probability for individual choices is given by the logit model probability

$$\text{Prob}\{\omega_i\} = \frac{\exp(\beta[u(\omega_i) + J\omega_i\bar{m}_i^e])}{\sum_{v_i \in \{-1,1\}} \exp(\beta[u(v_i) + Jv_i\bar{m}_i^e])}. \tag{69}$$

The parameter β is called the *intensity of choice* and it is inversely related to the level of random utility $\epsilon(\omega_i)$. In the extreme case $\beta = \infty$ the random utility term will vanish and all agents will choose the alternative with highest utility. In the other extreme case $\beta = 0$ the effect of the random utility term will dominate both individual and social utility and each alternative will be chosen with probability $1/2$.

Since the errors $\epsilon(\omega_i)$ are independent across agents, the joint probability distribution over all choices is given by

$$\text{Prob}\{\omega\} = \frac{\exp(\beta[\sum_{i=1}^{N}(u(\omega_i) + J\omega_i\bar{m}_i^e)])}{\sum_{v_1 \in \{-1,1\}} \cdots \sum_{v_N \in \{-1,1\}} \exp(\beta[\sum_{i=1}^{N} u(v_i) + Jv_i\bar{m}_i^e])}. \tag{70}$$

This probability structure is equivalent to the so-called mean field version of the Curie–Weiss model of statistical mechanics, see e.g. Brock and Durlauf (2001b) for further discussion.

For the binary choice model the private utility function can be replaced by a linear private utility function $\tilde{u}(\omega_i) = h\omega_i + k$, with h and k chosen such that $h + k = u(1)$ and $-h + k = u(-1)$. This linearization is possible since the linear functions coincide with the original private utility function on the support of the binary choices (but this trick does not work when more than two choices are possible). Notice that the parameter $h = (u(1) - u(-1))/2$, i.e. h is proportional to the difference in private utility between the two alternatives. Using this linearization and reintroducing expectations of individual choices in (64), the expected value of individual choice ω_i is given by

$$E[\omega_i]$$

$$= 1 \cdot \frac{\exp(\beta h + \beta J (N-1)^{-1} \sum_{j \neq i} m_{i,j}^e)}{\exp(\beta h + \beta J (N-1)^{-1} \sum_{j \neq i} m_{i,j}^e) + \exp(-\beta h - \beta J (N-1)^{-1} \sum_{j \neq i} m_{i,j}^e)}$$

$$(-1) \cdot \frac{\exp(-\beta h - \beta J (N-1)^{-1} \sum_{j \neq i} m_{i,j}^e)}{\exp(\beta h + \beta J (N-1)^{-1} \sum_{j \neq i} m_{i,j}^e) + \exp(-\beta h - \beta J (N-1)^{-1} \sum_{j \neq i} m_{i,j}^e)}$$

$$= \text{Tanh}(\beta h + \beta J (N-1)^{-1} \sum_{j \neq i} m_{i,j}^e). \tag{71}$$

Brock and Durlauf (2001a) now impose a self-consistent equilibrium or rational expectations equilibrium condition $m_{i,j}^e = E[\omega_j]$ for all i, j. A *rational expectations* or *self-consistent* equilibrium must satisfy

$$E[\omega_i] = \text{Tanh}\left(\beta h + \beta J (N-1)^{-1} \sum_{j \neq i} E[\omega_j]\right). \tag{72}$$

By symmetry it follows that $E[\omega_i] = E[\omega_j]$, for all i, j, hence a self-consistent, rational expectations equilibrium average choice level m^* must satisfy

$$m^* = \text{Tanh}(\beta h + \beta J m^*). \tag{73}$$

Brock and Durlauf (2001a) show that a rational expectations equilibrium always exists and, depending upon the parameters, multiple equilibria may exist. More precisely:

- if $\beta J < 1$, then (73) has a unique solution;
- if $\beta J > 1$ and $h = 0$, then (73) has three solutions: 0, one positive solution m^+ and one negative solution m^-;
- if $\beta J > 1$ and $h \neq 0$, then there exists a threshold H (depending on βJ) such that
  - for $|\beta h| < H$, (73) has three solutions, one of which has the same sign as h, and the others possessing opposite signs;
  - for $|\beta h| > H$, (73) has a unique solution with the same sign as h.

Notice that the possibility of multiple equilibria depends on the intensity of choice β, the strength of social interactions J and the difference h in private utility between the two choices. In particular, for each β and J when the difference h is large enough, the equilibrium is unique. Multiplicity of equilibria is most likely when the difference in private utility among alternatives is small and the choice intensity and/or social interaction are strong.

Brock and Durlauf (2001a) also briefly discuss dynamic stability of the steady states of expected choice levels under the assumption of myopic expectations, that is, agents use last period's choice level m_{t-1} as their expectation of others' individual choices. In that case, the dynamic version of (73) becomes

$$m_t = \text{Tanh}(\beta h + \beta J m_{t-1}). \tag{74}$$

Since $f(m) = \text{Tanh}(\beta h + \beta J m)$ is an increasing function of m, it follows easily that
(i) if (74) has a unique steady state, then it is globally stable, and (ii) if (74) has three
steady states, then the middle one is locally unstable, whereas the smallest and largest
steady states both are locally stable. In the case of multiple steady states, the system
thus settles down in one of its extremes, where a vast majority of individuals choose
one strategy or the other. A large social multiplier exists in such circumstances, that is,
small differences in individual utility may lead to large changes at the aggregate level.

6. Heterogeneity and important stylized facts

An important motivation for HAMs has been to explain the stylized facts observed in
financial market data. An immediate advantage of a HAM compared to a representative
rational agent model is that heterogeneity easily generates large trading volume consistent with empirical observations. Other important stylized facts of financial time series
at the daily frequency that have motivated much work on HAMs are: (i) asset prices
follow a near unit root process, (ii) asset returns are unpredictable with almost no autocorrelations, (iii) the returns distribution has fat tails, and (iv) financial returns exhibit
long range volatility clustering, i.e. slow decay of autocorrelations of squared returns
and absolute returns. Facts (i) and (ii) are consistent with a random walk model with
a representative rational agent. However, for example, Cutler et al. (1989) have shown
that a substantial fraction of stock market fluctuations can *not* be explained by macroeconomic news and that large moves in stock prices are difficult to link with news about
major economic or other events. Therefore, a rational agent model has difficulty in explaining fact (iii). One of the most important empirical stylized facts observed in many
financial time series is *clustered volatility*, that is, asset price fluctuations are characterized by phases of high volatility interspersed with phases of low volatility. Mandelbrot
(1963) was the first to observe this phenomenon. In time series econometrics the class
of (generalized) autoregressive conditional hetereroskedastic (G)ARCH-models, pioneered by Engle (1982), has become very popular to describe volatility clustering.
However, since news about economic fundamentals do *not* seem to arrive in clusters
of high and low volatility, there is no satisfactory representative rational agent explanation of this phenomenon.

   In this section we discuss the HAM introduced in Lux (1995, 1998) and Lux and
Marchesi (1999, 2000), which has been successful in explaining the stylized facts (i)–
(iv) simultaneously. In particular, clustered volatility arises through the *interaction* and
switching between fundamental and chartist trading strategies. Other HAMs explaining
these stylized facts include Brock and LeBaron (1996), Arthur et al. (1997a, 1997b),
Youssefmir and Huberman (1997), LeBaron et al. (1999), Farmer and Joshi (2002),
Kirman and Teyssière (2002), Hommes (2002), Iori (2002), Giardina and Bouchaud
(2003) and Gaunersdorfer and Hommes (2006).

6.1. Socio-economic dynamics of speculative markets

The model of Lux (1995, 1998) and Lux and Marchesi (1999, 2000) describes an asset market with a fixed number N of speculative traders, divided in two groups, *fundamentalists* and *chartists*. Fundamentalists' trading is based upon the fundamental price: they sell (buy) when the price is above (below) the fundamental value. Chartists or technical analysts pursue a combination of *imitative* and *trend following* strategies. At time t, there are n_t^c technical analysts and n_t^f fundamentalists in the market, $n_t^c + n_t^f = N$. The chartists are subdivided into two subgroups: at time t, n_t^+ of them are *optimistic* (bullish) and n_t^- are *pessimistic* (bearish), $n_t^+ + n_t^- = n_t^c$. The number of fundamentalists and (optimistic and pessimistic) chartists changes over time, but to keep the notation simple, we suppress the time index below. The model contains three elements: (1) chartists switching between optimistic and pessimistic beliefs; (2) traders switching between a chartist and a fundamental trading strategy, and (3) a price adjustment process based upon aggregate excess demand.

Contagion behavior of chartists

Chartists switch between an optimistic and a pessimistic mood, depending upon the majority opinion and upon the prevailing price trend. The first element, the contagion behavior, can be motivated as in Keynes' beauty contest that traders try to forecast 'what average opinion expects average opinion to be'. This element is similar in spirit to Kirman's model of opinion formation and Brock and Durlauf's social interaction effects, as discussed in Section 5. An *opinion index*, representing the average opinion among non-fundamentalist traders, is defined as

$$x = \frac{n^+ - n^-}{n^c}, \quad x \in [-1, +1]. \tag{75}$$

Obviously, $x = 0$ corresponds to the balanced situation where the number of optimists equals the number of pessimists, whereas $x = +1$ (resp. $x = -1$) corresponds to the extreme case where all chartists are optimists (resp. pessimists). It is also useful to define the proportion of chartist traders as

$$z = \frac{n^c}{N}, \quad z \in [0, +1]. \tag{76}$$

The probabilities for chartists' switching between pessimistic and optimistic depend upon the opinion index x and the price trend (in continuous time) $\dot{p} = dp/dt$. Let

$$U_1 = \alpha_1 x + \alpha_2 \frac{\dot{p}}{v_1}, \quad \alpha_1, \alpha_2 > 0, \tag{77}$$

where the parameters α_1 and α_2 measure the sensitivity of traders to the opinion index (i.e. the behavior of others) resp. their sensitivity to price changes. The switching probabilities are formalized following the synergetics literature, originally developed in physics for interacting particle systems (e.g. Haken (1983)). The probabilities π^{+-} and π^{-+} that chartists switch from pessimistic to optimistic and vice-versa are given by

$$\pi^{+-}(x) = v_1 \frac{n^c}{N} e^{U_1}, \quad \pi^{-+}(x) = v_1 \frac{n^c}{N} e^{-U_1}, \quad v_1 > 0. \tag{78}$$

The parameter v_1 measures the frequency of this type of transition, while the term n^c/N represents the probability for a chartist to meet a chartist.

Switching between chartists and fundamentalists

Agents can also switch between chartists and fundamentalists strategies. These switches are driven by expected or realized excess profits. For chartists, realized excess profit per unit is given by $(y + dp/dt)/p - r$, where y are (constant) nominal dividends of the asset and r is the average (risk adjusted) real return from other investments. It is assumed that $y/p^f = r$, so that at the steady state fundamental price the return from the asset will equal the average return on other investments.

Fundamentalists believe that the asset price will revert back to its fundamental value p^f, and therefore will buy (sell) the asset when its price is below (above) the fundamental value. Fundamentalists expected excess profit is then given by $s|(p - p^f)/p|$. The parameter $s > 0$ may be interpreted as a discount factor, since these are expected excess profits realized only when the price has returned to its fundamental value. Let

$$U_{2,1} = \alpha_3 \left(\frac{y + \dot{p}/v_2}{p} - R - s \left| \frac{p - p^f}{p} \right| \right), \tag{79}$$

$$U_{2,2} = \alpha_3 \left(R - \frac{y + \dot{p}/v_2}{p} - s \left| \frac{p - p^f}{p} \right| \right), \tag{80}$$

where α_3 measures the sensitivity of traders to differences in profits. The probabilities to switch from fundamentalists to optimistic chartist, from optimistic chartist to fundamentalists, from fundamentalist to pessimistic chartist resp. from pessimistic chartist to fundamentalists are given by:

$$\pi^{+f} = v_2 \frac{n^+}{N} e^{U_{2,1}}, \quad \pi^{f+} = v_2 \frac{n^f}{N} e^{-U_{2,1}}, \tag{81}$$

$$\pi^{-f} = v_2 \frac{n^-}{N} e^{U_{2,2}}, \quad \pi^{f-} = v_2 \frac{n^f}{N} e^{-U_{2,2}}, \tag{82}$$

where $v_2 > 0$ is a parameter measuring the frequency of this type of transition. Notice the inclusion of the terms n^f/N, n^+/N, n^-/N in the probabilities (81) and (82), representing the probabilities for a fundamentalist to meet an optimistic chartist, etc. U_1, $U_{2,1}$ and $U_{2,2}$ in fact play the role of a *fitness measure* determining the switching probabilities, similar to Brock and Hommes (1997a, 1997b, 1998).[7] There is an asymmetry in the fitness measure for chartists and fundamentalists however, since chartists' switching is driven by *realized* profits, whereas fundamentalists' switching is driven by *expected* arbitrage profits which will not be realized until the price has reversed to its fundamental value. Goodhart (1988) pointed out that this asymmetry may bias traders towards chartist strategies. The asymmetry also reflects 'limits to arbitrage' of fundamentalists.

Price formation

Price changes are determined by a *market maker* according to aggregate excess demand of chartists and fundamentalists (cf. Section 4). A chartist buys (sells) a fixed amount t^c of the asset per period when he is optimistic (pessimistic). Using the opinion index x in (75) and the proportion of chartists z in (76), excess demand by chartists is

$$ED^c = \left(n^+ - n^-\right)t^c = xzNt^c \equiv xzT^c, \quad T^c \equiv Nt^c, \tag{83}$$

where T^c denotes the maximum trading volume of chartists. Fundamentalists buy (sell) when the asset price is below (above) its fundamental value, and their excess demand is

$$\begin{aligned} ED^f &= n^f \gamma\left(p^f - p\right) = (1 - z)N\gamma\left(p^f - p\right) \\ &\equiv (1 - z)T^f\left(p^f - p\right), \quad T^f \equiv N\gamma, \end{aligned} \tag{84}$$

where $\gamma > 0$ measures the reaction speed of fundamentalists to price deviations from the fundamental and T^f is a measure of the trading volume of fundamentalists.

A market maker adjusts prices according to aggregate excess demand by

$$\frac{dp}{dt} = \beta\left[ED^c + ED^f\right] = \beta\left[xzT^c + (1 - z)T^f\left(p^f - p\right)\right], \tag{85}$$

where β denotes the speed of adjustment.

In their numerical simulations, Lux and Marchesi (1999, 2000) use a stochastic process for the market maker price adjustment. The market maker is assumed to adjust the price to the next higher (lower) possible value (one cent say) within the next time increment with a certain probability depending upon aggregate excess demand. It is also assumed that there are some *noise traders* or *liquidity traders* in the market whose asset demand is random, or alternatively excess demand is observed by the market maker with some imprecision, captured by a noise term μ, normally distributed with standard deviation σ_μ. The transition probabilities for an increase or decrease of the price by an amount $\Delta p = \pm 0.01$ are then given by

$$\begin{aligned} \pi^{\uparrow p} &= \min\{\max\{0, \beta(ED + \mu)\}, 1\}, \\ \pi^{\downarrow p} &= \min\{-\min\{0, \beta(ED + \mu)\}, 1\}. \end{aligned} \tag{86}$$

---

[7] Obviously, these probabilities need to be restricted to the unit interval $[0, 1]$. Note that if one normalizes the expressions for π^{+-} and π^{-+} in (78), π^{+f} and π^{f+} in (81), resp. π^{-f} and π^{f-} in (82) by dividing by their sum, expressions similar to the discrete choice or logit model probabilities used in Brock and Hommes (1997a, 1997b, 1998) are obtained (see Sections 7 and 8).

6.2. Dynamical behavior and time series properties

A formal analysis of this kind of stochastic interacting agent system is possible using the so-called *master equation* for the time evolution of the probability distribution in order to derive differential equations describing a first order approximation of the dynamics of the first moment, i.e. the mean, of the stochastic variables. This approach originates from elementary particle systems in physics and has been followed in the synergetics literature (e.g. Haken (1983)) and its applications to social science (e.g. Weidlich and Haag (1983)); see also Aoki (2002, 1994) and references therein for a more detailed treatment and (macro)economic applications. For the current stochastic system the set of differential equations has been derived in Lux (1995, 1998).[8] The change in the opinion index is governed by:[9]

$$
\begin{aligned}
\frac{dx}{dt} &= \left(\frac{dn^+}{dt} - \frac{dn^-}{dt}\right)\Big/ n^c - \left(n/(n^c)^2\right)\frac{dn^c}{dt} \\
&= z\big[(1-x)\pi^{+-} - (1+x)\pi^{-+}\big] \\
&\quad + 0.5(1-z)(1-x^2)\left(\pi^{+f} - \pi^{f+} + \pi^{f-} - \pi^{-f}\right), \\
&= 2zv_1\big[\mathrm{Tanh}(U_1) - x\big]\mathrm{Cosh}(U_1) \\
&\quad + (1-z)(1-x^2)v_2\big[\mathrm{Sinh}(U_{2,1}) - \mathrm{Sinh}(U_{2,2})\big],
\end{aligned}
\tag{87}
$$

while the change of the proportion of chartists is governed by

$$
\begin{aligned}
\frac{dz}{dt} &= \frac{dn^c}{dt}\Big/ N \\
&= 0.5(1-z)z(1+x)\left(\pi^{+f} - \pi^{f+}\right) + 0.5(1-z)z(1-x)\left(\pi^{-f} - \pi^{f-}\right), \\
&= (1-z)z(1+x)v_2\mathrm{Sinh}(U_{2,1}) + (1-z)z(1-x)v_2\mathrm{Sinh}(U_{2,2}).
\end{aligned}
\tag{88}
$$

Equations (85), (87) and (88) constitute a highly nonlinear 3-D system of differential equations. The system has three types of *steady states*:
  (i) $x^* = 0$, $p^* = p^f$, with arbitrary $0 \le z \le 1$,
  (ii) $x^* = 0$, $z^* = 1$, with arbitrary p, and
  (iii) $z^* = 0$, $p^* = p^f$, with arbitrary $-1 \le x \le +1$.
The most important steady states are of type (i), with the price at its fundamental value, a balanced proportion between optimists and pessimists and an arbitrary proportion of chartists; there exists a continuum of steady states of type (i). At type (ii) steady states the market is completely dominated by chartists, with balanced proportion between optimists and pessimists, and an arbitrary price level. Type (iii) steady states correspond to

---

[8] Lux (1997) uses the master equation approach to derive an approximate system of differential equations describing the dynamical behavior of the first *two* moments, the mean and the co-variances, of the stochastic variables.

[9] Recall that $\mathrm{Sinh}(y) = (e^y - e^{-y})/2$, $\mathrm{Cosh}(y) = (e^y + e^{-y})/2$ and $\mathrm{Tanh}(y) = \mathrm{Sinh}(y)/\mathrm{Cosh}(y)$.

the other extreme where the market is completely dominated by fundamentalists, with the price at its fundamental value. These extreme cases (ii) and (iii) act as absorbing states of the system. In the numerical simulations of Lux and Marchesi (1999, 2000) these absorbing states are avoided by additional borderline conditions.

Concerning the *(in)stability* of steady state type (i) it should first be noted that, since for any $0 \leq z \leq 1$ such a steady state exists, the corresponding Jacobian matrix of the mean value differential equation system has a zero root, or equivalently, the corresponding discrete system has a unit root. For the stochastic system one thus expects that the proportion of chartists z follows a path close to a random walk, especially when the price is close to the fundamental and the proportions of optimists and pessimists are balanced. Lux (1997) and Lux and Marchesi (2000) provide precise (in)stability conditions of steady states of type (i), which can be summarized as follows. When the parameters α_1, α_2 and α_3 measuring traders sensitivity w.r.t. the opinion index, price changes and profits are larger than some critical value, all steady states of type (i) are repelling. When these sensitivity parameters are below their critical value, the (in)stability depends upon the corresponding proportion z^* of chartists; when this proportion z^* exceeds a critical value, the steady state becomes repelling.

Figure 9 shows simulated time series of the model as well as autocorrelations of returns, squared returns and absolute returns.[10] In this simulation, the price stays fairly close to its fundamental value most of the time, because for these parameter values the steady states of type (i) are *not* unstable.[11] Prices follow a near unit root process and financial returns are unpredictable with little autocorrelations (except some small negative autocorrelations at the first lag). Autocorrelations of squared returns and absolute returns are positive and decay slowly, showing long range volatility clustering. The high volatility phase is due to noise amplification through the interactions of agents at the micro-level and coincides with a large proportion of chartists in the market whose opinion is more or less balanced. Returns also exhibit fat tails and Lux and Marchesi (1999, 2000) show that the tail of the returns distribution follows a power law.

Lux and Marchesi (1999, 2000) note that these results are fairly robust w.r.t. choices of the parameters. However, Egenter et al. (1999) show that a puzzling 'finite size effect' occurs, that is volatility clustering tends to disappear when the number of agents N tends to infinity. This finite size effect seems to be due to some law of large numbers. As N becomes large, the random fluctuations in the opinion index become smaller and the population of chartists remains close to being balanced. As a result, the market becomes dominated by fundamentalists and price changes are mainly driven by fundamentals. Nevertheless, this type of HAM matches some important stylized facts remarkably well. In the last 5 years, physicists have done quite a lot of work in finance in particular looking for *scaling laws* in financial market data. The power law decay of the returns

---

[10] I would like to thank Thomas Lux and Timur Yusupov for providing these simulations.

[11] The Jacobian matrix of the steady state has a unit root due to existence of a continuum of steady states. Lux (1997, 1998) shows that, for different parameter values the steady state becomes repelling and stable periodic cycles and chaos can occur. In the unstable case, prices persistently deviate from the fundamental value.

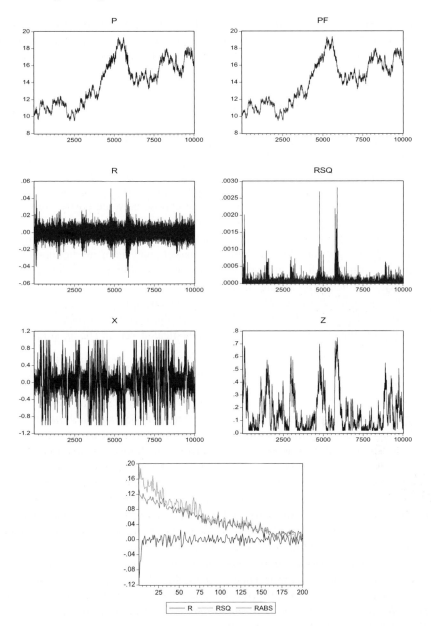

Figure 9. Time series of prices (top left), fundamental price (top right), returns (second panel, left), squared returns (second panel, right), opinion index (third panel, left), fraction of chartists (third panel, right) and autocorrelation patterns (bottom panel) of returns, squared returns and absolute returns. Parameters: $N = 500$, $v_1 = 3$, $v_2 = 2$, $\beta = 6$, $T_c(\equiv Nt_c) = 10$, $T_f(\equiv N\gamma) = 5$, $\alpha_1 = 0.6$, $\alpha_2 = 0.2$, $\alpha_1 = 0.5$, $p_f = 10$, $y = 0.004$, $R = 0.0004$, $s = 0.75$ and $\sigma_\mu = 0.05$.

distribution and of autocorrelations of squared returns are examples of such a scaling law. For a discussion and overviews of this literature see e.g. Farmer (1999), Mantegna and Stanley (2000), Bouchaud (2001), Cont (2001) and Mandelbrot (2001a, 2001b).

7. Costly sophisticated versus cheap simple rules

Herbert Simon (1957) already stressed information gathering and processing costs as an obstacle to fully rational, optimal behavior. Agents must either face search and information gathering costs in using sophisticated, optimal rules or may choose to employ free and easily available simple rules of thumb that perform "reasonably well". In this section we discuss HAMs where agents can choose between costly, sophisticated strategies and simple, but cheap rules of thumb. Simple strategies include naive expectations, adaptive expectations, trend extrapolation, simple technical trading rules, etc. Sophisticated strategies are e.g. fundamental market analysis or predictions of macro economic quantities such as growth, inflation or unemployment, which usually require costly information gathering. In Subsection 7.1 we briefly discuss some early, stimulating examples due to Conlisk (1980), Evans and Ramey (1992) and Sethi and Franke (1995), whereas Subsection 7.2 discusses the model of Brock and Hommes (1997a) of endogenous selection of costly, sophisticated versus cheap, simple expectations rules.

7.1. Examples

An interesting and early dynamic model with *costly optimizers versus cheap imitators* has been introduced by Conlisk (1980). There are two types of agents, rational optimizers and simple imitators, who try to minimize a quadratic loss function depending upon their choice and an exogenously generated stochastic state of the economy. Optimizers pay a cost for their optimal strategy, to cover the cost of analyzing the decision problem at hand, searching the market or preparing or reading consumer reports, etc. Non-optimizers' behavior is imitative and they adapt their behavior in the direction of last period's observed average optimal choice. Non-optimizers "will make mistakes, but avoid the costs of avoiding mistakes". The mix between the two types evolves over time according to the relative average performance of the two strategies. Conlisk (1980) shows that if the average loss for imitators exceeds the costs for optimizers, imitators can not survive and in the long run optimizers completely dominate the economy. Stated differently, *"Imitation can have no redeeming merit when optimization is cheap enough"* (Conlisk, 1980, p. 282). In contrast, if the cost of optimizing is substantial imitators will not disappear but can survive, and both optimizers and imitators will coexist in the long run. Note that in this model the state of the economy evolves according to an *exogenous* stochastic process and is *not* affected by the behavior of the optimizers and imitators.

Evans and Ramey (1992) consider a dynamic macroeconomic model where calculation of rational expectations is costly. Agents have preferences over expectational errors and calculation costs, and in each period choose optimally whether or not to calculate expectations at costs C or keep the same expectation at no costs. The strategy choice is coupled endogenously to the market dynamics. Evans and Ramey discuss the possibility of different types of equilibria. In a *calculation equilibrium* agents start close enough to a REE, it is optimal to never calculate and the system stays close to the REE. Two stage equilibria are characterized by the system starting off far from REE, so that all agents choose to calculate until the point where the system is close enough to REE and it becomes optimal for all agents to switch to 'never calculate'. Sethi and Franke (1995) consider a macroeconomic model with *evolutionary dynamics* and endogenous switching between naive agents using costless adaptive expectations and sophisticated agents using costly rational expectations. Dynamics of output are driven by exogenous shocks to production costs. Strategy fractions are updated according to the relative success of the strategies. Naive agents generally persist in the market, especially when optimization is costly. Both in Evans and Ramey (1992) and Sethi and Franke (1995) market dynamics and strategy selection are endogenously coupled and the state of the economy and the population of strategies co-evolve over time. These examples however are *globally stable*: in the absence of any exogenous random shocks to the economy, both dynamic models converge to a globally stable steady state with all agents using the simple, freely available strategy.

7.2. Rational versus naive expectations

Brock and Hommes (1997a), henceforth BH97a, introduce a model of endogenous, evolutionary selection of heterogeneous expectations rules. In particular, BH97a consider evolutionary switching between a costly sophisticated forecasting strategy, such as rational expectations, versus a free, simple rule of thumb strategy such as naive expectations. They introduce the concept of *Adaptive Rational Equilibrium Dynamics (ARED)*, an endogenous coupling between market equilibrium dynamics and evolutionary selection of expectations rules. The ARED describes evolutionary dynamics among competing prediction strategies, in which the state of the economy and the distribution of agents over different expectation rules co-evolve over time.

Agents can choose between H different (prediction) strategies and update their choice over time. Strategies that have been more successful in the recent past are selected more often than less successful strategies. More precisely, the fraction n_{ht} of traders using strategy h are updated according to an evolutionary *fitness measure* or *performance measure*, such as (a weighted sum of) past realized profits. All fitness measures are publically available (e.g. published in newspapers), but subject to noise e.g. due to measurement error or non-observable characteristics. Fitness of strategy h is given by a random utility model

$$\tilde{U}_{ht} = U_{ht} + \epsilon_{ht}, \tag{89}$$

where U_{ht} is the *deterministic part* of the fitness measure and ϵ_{ht} represents the noise in the observed fitness of strategy h at date t. Assuming that the noise ϵ_{ht} is IID across types and drawn from a double exponential distribution, in the limit as the number of agents goes to infinity, the probability that an agent chooses strategy h is given by the well known *multinomial logit model* or 'Gibbs' probabilities

$$n_{ht} = \frac{\exp(\beta U_{ht})}{Z_t}, \quad Z_t = \sum_{h=1}^{H} \exp(\beta U_{ht}), \tag{90}$$

where Z_t is a normalization factor for the fractions n_{ht} to add up to 1. Manski and Mc-Fadden (1981) and Anderson et al. (1993) give an extensive overview and discussion of discrete choice models, in particular the multinomial logit model, and their applications in economics. The crucial feature of (90) is that the higher the fitness of trading strategy h, the more agents will select strategy h. The *intensity of choice* parameter $\beta > 0$ in (90) measures how sensitive agents are to selecting the optimal prediction strategy. This intensity of choice β is inversely related to the variance of the noise ϵ_{ht}. The extreme case $\beta = 0$ corresponds to noise with infinite variance, so that differences in fitness cannot be observed and all fractions (90) will be equal to $1/H$. The other extreme case $\beta = \infty$ corresponds to the case without noise, so that the deterministic part of the fitness is observed perfectly and in each period, *all* agents choose the optimal forecast. An increase in the intensity of choice β represents an increase in the degree of rationality w.r.t. evolutionary selection of strategies.[12]

BH97a employ the classical cobweb framework to study a HAM with two prediction strategies, costly rational versus free naive expectations. A related, artificial cobweb economy with genetic algorithms learning is studied by Arifovic (1994). The cobweb model describes fluctuations of equilibrium prices in a market for a non-storable consumption good. The good takes one period to produce, so that producers must form price expectations one period ahead. Applications of the cobweb model mainly concern agricultural markets, such as the classical examples of cycles in hog or corn prices. Supply $S(p_t^e)$ is a function of producer's next period expected price, p_t^e and is derived from expected profit maximization, that is, $S(p_t^e) = \text{argmax}_{q_t}\{p_t^e q_t - c(q_t)\} = (c')^{-1}(p_t^e)$, where $c(\cdot)$ is the cost function. BH97a assume a quadratic cost function $c(q) = q^2/(2s)$, so that the supply curve is linear, $S(p_t^e) = sp_t^e$, $s > 0$. Consumer demand is linearly decreasing in the market price p_t and given by $D(p_t) = a - dp_t$, $d > 0$.[13]

---

[12] The probabilities (90) are also used in game theory, in quantal response equilibria introduced by McKelvey and Palfrey (1995), where $\beta = \infty$ corresponds to a Nash equilibrium. Blume (1993) also uses the same type of probabilities in a game theoretic setting and argues that $\beta = \infty$ corresponds to the noise free case where all weight is given to best response(s). Nadal et al. (1998) argue that the logit probabilities (90) can be derived as an optimal response in an exploration-exploitation trade off. They derive (90) from maximizing a linear combination of past profit and new information (using entropy as a measure), with β being the weight given to past profit.

[13] Goeree and Hommes (2000) extend the analysis of the cobweb model with rational versus naive expectations to the case of nonlinear (but monotonic) supply and demand.

Producers can choose between two different forecasting rules. They can either buy a sophisticated, rational expectations (perfect foresight) forecast at positive per period information cost $C \geq 0$, or freely obtain the simple, naive forecast. The two forecasting rules are thus $p_{1,t}^e = p_t$ and $p_{2,t}^e = p_{t-1}$. Market equilibrium in the cobweb model with rational versus naive expectations and linear demand and supply is given by

$$a - dp_t = n_{1,t-1}sp_{1,t}^e + n_{2,t-1}sp_{2,t} = n_{t-1}^R sp_t + n_{t-1}^N sp_{t-1}, \tag{91}$$

where $n_{1,t-1} = n_{t-1}^R$ and $n_{2,t-1} = n_{t-1}^N$ are the fractions of producers using the rational respectively naive predictor, at the beginning of period t. Notice that producers using RE have perfect foresight, and therefore must have perfect knowledge about the market equilibrium equation (91), including past prices as well as the fractions of both groups. Consequently, rational agents have perfect knowledge about the beliefs of all other agents. The difference C between the per period information costs for rational and naive expectations represents an extra effort cost producers incur over time when acquiring this perfect knowledge. Solving (91) explicitly for the market equilibrium price yields

$$p_t = \frac{a - n_{t-1}^N sp_{t-1}}{d + n_{t-1}^R s}. \tag{92}$$

When all agents have rational expectations, $p_t \equiv p^* = a/(d + s)$, for all $t \geq 1$, that is, the price jumps immediately to its steady state value p^* where demand and supply intersect. When all agents have naive expectations (92) reduces to the linear difference equation $p_t = (a - sp_{t-1})/d$, leading to the familiar up and down price oscillations around the steady state p^*. Price oscillations under naive expectations are stable (unstable) under the familiar 'cobweb theorem' condition $s/d < 1$ ($s/d > 1$).

To complete the model, the fractions of traders using either rational or naive expectations must be specified. As discussed above, these fractions are updated according to a publically available evolutionary fitness measure associated to each predictor. BH97a focus on the case with the most recent realized net profit as the performance measure for predictor selection.[14] For the rational resp. the naive forecasting strategies with linear supply, the realized profits in period t are given by

$$\pi_t^R = p_t S(p_t) - c\big(S(p_t)\big) = \frac{s}{2}p_t^2, \tag{93}$$

$$\pi_t^N = p_t S(p_{t-1}) - c\big(S(p_{t-1})\big) = \frac{s}{2}p_{t-1}(2p_t - p_{t-1}). \tag{94}$$

---

[14] The case where the performance measure is realized net profit of the most recent past period, leads to a two-dimensional dynamical system. The more general case, with a weighted sum of past net realized profits as the fitness measure, leads to higher dimensional systems, which are not as analytically tractable as the two-dimensional case. In this more general higher dimensional case however, numerical simulations suggest similar dynamic behavior.

Notice that the *net* realized profit for rational expectations is given by $\pi_t^R - C$, where C is the per period information cost that has to be paid for obtaining the perfect forecast. The fractions of the two groups are determined by the logit discrete choice model probabilities, as discussed above. The fraction of agents using the rational expectations predictor in period t equals

$$n_t^R = \frac{\exp(\beta(\pi_t^R - C))}{\exp(\beta(\pi_t^R - C)) + \exp(\beta \pi_t^N)}, \tag{95}$$

and the fraction of agents choosing the naive predictor in period t is

$$n_t^N = 1 - n_t^R. \tag{96}$$

A key feature of this evolutionary predictor selection is that agents are boundedly rational, in the sense that most agents use the predictor that has the highest fitness. From (95) and (96) we have that $n_t^R > n_t^N$ whenever $\pi_t^R - C > \pi_t^N$, although the optimal predictor is not chosen with probability one. The *intensity of choice*, i.e. the parameter β, measures how fast producers switch between the two prediction strategies. For $\beta = 0$, both fractions are fixed over time and equal to $1/2$. In the other extreme case $\beta = \infty$ (the *neoclassical limit*) *all* producers choose the optimal predictor in each period.

The timing of predictor selection in (95) is important. In (92) the old fractions n_{t-1}^R and n_{t-1}^N determine the new equilibrium price p_t. This new equilibrium price p_t is used in the fitness measures (93) and (94) for predictor choice and the new fractions n_t^R and n_t^N are updated according to (95) and (96). These new fractions in turn determine the next equilibrium price p_{t+1}, etc. Equilibrium prices and fractions thus co-evolve over time. BH97a called the coupling between the equilibrium price dynamics and adaptive predictor selection an *Adaptive Rational Equilibrium Dynamics (ARED)* model.

The model has a unique steady state $(p^*, n^*) = (a/(d+s), 1/(1+\exp(\beta C/2)))$, with p^* the price where demand and supply intersect. When there are no costs for rational expectations ($C = 0$), at the steady state the fractions of the two types are exactly balanced. In contrast, for positive information costs for rational expectations ($C > 0$), $n^* < 0.5$, so that at the steady state most agents use the naive forecasting rule. This makes sense, because at the steady state both forecasting rules yield exactly the same forecast, and most agents then prefer the cheap, naive forecast.

If the familiar cobweb stability condition $s/d < 1$ is satisfied, implying that the model is stable under naive expectations, then the heterogeneous cobweb model with rational versus naive expectations has a globally stable steady state, for all β. Prices will then always converge to p^*, and the fraction of rational agents converges to n^*. More interesting dynamics occur when the cobweb model is unstable under naive expectations.

Assume that the market is *unstable under naive expectations*, that is, $s/d > 1$:
1. without information costs ($C = 0$), the steady state is globally stable for all β;
2. with positive information costs ($C > 0$), there is a critical value β_1 such that the steady state is (globally) stable for $0 \leq \beta < \beta_1$ and unstable for $\beta > \beta_1$. At $\beta = \beta_1$ a *period doubling bifurcation* occurs and a stable 2-cycle is created;

3. as β increases from 0 to $+\infty$ a *rational route to randomness* occurs, that is, a bifurcation route from a stable steady state to a strange attractor occurs and chaotic price fluctuations arise.

Figure 10 shows an example of a strange attractor, with corresponding chaotic time series of prices p_t and fractions n_t^R of rational producers. Numerical simulations suggest that for (almost) all initial states (p_0, m_0) the orbit converges to this strange attractor. For a high intensity of choice price fluctuations are characterized by an irregular switching between a stable phase, with prices close to the steady state, and an unstable phase with fluctuating prices, as illustrated in Figure 10. There is a strikingly simple *economic intuition* explaining this switching behavior when the intensity of choice is large. Suppose we take an initial state close to the (locally unstable) steady state. Most agents will use the cheap, naive forecasting rule, because it does not pay to buy a costly, sophisticated forecasting rule that yields an almost identical forecast. With most agents using the cheap, naive predictor prices diverge from the steady state, start fluctuating, and net realized profits from the naive predictor decrease. At some point, it becomes profitable to buy the rational expectations forecast, and when the intensity of choice to switch predictors is high, most agents will then switch to rational expectations. As a result, prices are driven back close to the steady state, and the story repeats. Irregular, chaotic price fluctuations thus result from a (boundedly) rational choice between cheap 'free riding' and costly sophisticated prediction.[15]

Price fluctuations in this simple evolutionary system are thus characterized by an irregular switching between a low volatility phase with prices close to the fundamental steady state and a high volatility phase with large amplitude price fluctuations. The evolutionary system has a locally destabilizing force due to cheap free riding and a far from the steady state stabilizing force of sophisticated prediction. In this simple evolutionary system, in contrast to the Friedman hypothesis, simple and sophisticated types co-exist in the long run with their fractions fluctuating over time. Due to information gathering costs, rational agents can not drive out naive agents.

Several extensions of the BH97a framework have been considered recently. Branch (2002) investigates the cobweb model with three (rational, adaptive and naive) expectation rules, and Lasselle et al. (2005) investigate the case of rational versus adaptive expectations. The same evolutionary framework is applied to an overlapping generations monetary economy by Brock and de Fontnouvelle (2000) and to a Cagan type monetary model by Chiarella and Khomin (1999). Branch and McGough (2004) investigate the cobweb model with evolutionary replicator dynamics and obtain similar results; Droste et al. (2002) investigate evolutionary replicator dynamics in a Cournot duopoly model with a Nash rule versus a best reply rule. Branch and Evans (2005) consider a HAM where agents can choose between a number of misspecified econometric models, with a dual learning process of agents learning the model parameters

---

[15] Brock and Hommes (1997a) show that for a large intensity of choice, the ARED-cobweb model is close to having a so-called homoclinic orbit, a notion already introduced by Poincaré around 1890, and one of the key features of a chaotic system; see Hommes (2005) for a recent, more detailed discussion.

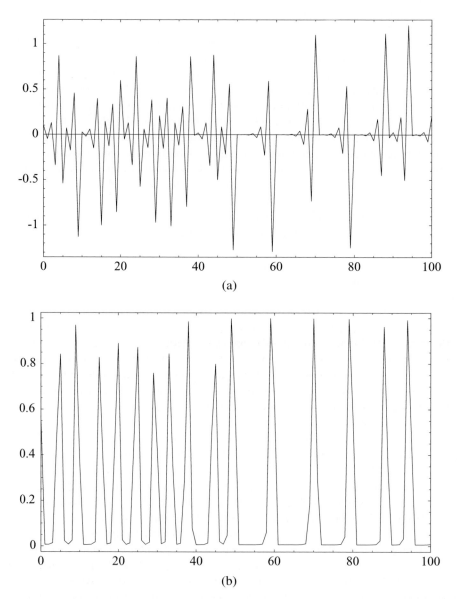

Figure 10. Chaotic time series of price *deviations* from the steady state (a) and fractions of rational agents (b) and the corresponding strange attractor in the (x, n^R)-phase space (c), where $x = p - p^*$ is the deviation from the steady state price. Parameters are: $\beta = 5$, $a = 10$, $d = 0.5$, $s = 1.35$ and $C = 1$.

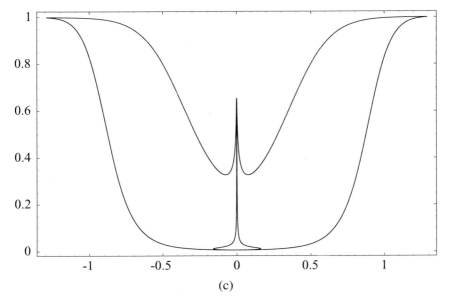

(c)

Figure 10. (*continued.*)

by ordinary least squares (OLS) and strategy fractions updated according to relative performance. De Fontnouvelle (2000) applies the ARED to a financial market model, where agents can choose to buy information about future dividends with high precision, or obtain information with low precision for free. Another recent contribution along these lines is Goldbaum (2005). In the next subsection we discuss an application of the BH97a evolutionary framework to an asset pricing model.

8. An asset pricing model with heterogeneous beliefs

In this section we discuss *Adaptive Belief Systems (ABS)* as introduced by Brock and Hommes (1998), henceforth BH98, a financial market application of the evolutionary selection of expectation rules introduced by Brock and Hommes (1997a). An ABS is in fact a standard discounted value asset pricing model derived from mean-variance maximization, extended to the case of *heterogeneous beliefs*. Agents are boundedly rational and select a forecasting or investment strategy based upon its recent, relative performance. An ABS may be seen as a stylized, to some extent analytically tractable, version of more complicated artificial markets and is in fact similar to the SFI model of Arthur et al. (1997b) and LeBaron et al. (1999) (see also the chapter of LeBaron). A convenient feature of an ABS is that it can be formulated in terms of deviations from a benchmark fundamental and therefore an ABS can be used in experimental and empirical testing of deviations from the RE benchmark.

8.1. The model

Agents can either invest in a risk free asset or in a risky asset. The risk free asset is perfectly elastically supplied and pays a fixed rate of return r; the risky asset (e.g. a stock or a stock market index) pays an uncertain dividend. Let p_t be the price per share (ex-dividend) of the risky asset at time t, and let y_t be the stochastic dividend process of the risky asset. Agents are myopic mean-variance maximizers so that the demand z_{ht} per trader of type h for the risky asset is given by

$$z_{ht} = \frac{E_{ht}[\mathbf{p}_{t+1} + \mathbf{y}_{t+1} - (1+r)p_t]}{a V_{ht}[\mathbf{p}_{t+1} + \mathbf{y}_{t+1} - (1+r)p_t]} = \frac{E_{ht}[\mathbf{p}_{t+1} + \mathbf{y}_{t+1} - (1+r)p_t]}{a\sigma^2}. \tag{97}$$

E_{ht} and V_{ht} denote the 'beliefs' or forecasts of trader type h about conditional expectation and conditional variance of excess return $\mathbf{p}_{t+1} + \mathbf{y}_{t+1} - (1+r)p_t$ and a is the risk aversion parameter. Bold face variables denote random variables at date $t+1$. For analytical tractability, the conditional variance $V_{ht} = \sigma^2$ is assumed to be equal and constant for all types.[16] Let z^s denote the supply of outside risky shares per investor, assumed to be constant, and let n_{ht} denote the fraction of type h at date t. When there are H different trader types, equilibrium of demand and supply yields

$$\sum_{h=1}^{H} n_{ht} \frac{E_{ht}[\mathbf{p}_{t+1} + \mathbf{y}_{t+1} - (1+r)p_t]}{a\sigma^2} = z^s. \tag{98}$$

BH98 focus on the special case of zero supply of outside shares, i.e. $z^s = 0$, for which the Walrasian market clearing price satisfies[17]

$$(1+r)p_t = \sum_{h=1}^{H} n_{ht} E_{ht}[\mathbf{p}_{t+1} + \mathbf{y}_{t+1}]. \tag{99}$$

It is well known that in a *homogeneous* world where all agents have rational expectations, the asset price is completely determined by economic fundamentals and given by the discounted sum of expected future dividends:

$$p_t^* = \sum_{k=1}^{\infty} \frac{E_t[\mathbf{y}_{t+k}]}{(1+r)^k}. \tag{100}$$

In general, the properties of the *fundamental price* p_t^* depend upon the stochastic dividend process y_t. In the special case of an IID dividend process y_t, with constant mean

---

[16] Gaunersdorfer (2000) investigates the case with time varying beliefs about variances and Chiarella and He (2002) study heterogeneous risk aversion.

[17] Brock (1997) motivates this special case by introducing a risk adjusted dividend $y_{t+1}^{\#} = y_{t+1} - a\sigma^2 z^s$, and after dropping the superscript "#" obtains the market equilibrium equation (99).

$E[y_t] = \bar{y}$, the fundamental price is constant and given by[18]

$$p^* = \sum_{k=1}^{\infty} \frac{\bar{y}}{(1+r)^k} = \frac{\bar{y}}{r}. \tag{101}$$

Heterogeneous beliefs

We now discuss traders' expectations about future prices and dividends. As discussed above, beliefs about the conditional variance $V_{ht} = \sigma^2$, for all h, t, are assumed to be equal and constant for all types. Beliefs about future dividends are assumed to be the same for all trader types and equal to the true conditional expectation, that is, $E_{ht}[y_{t+1}] = E_t[y_{t+1}]$, for all h, t; in the special case of IID dividends this simplifies to $E_{ht}[y_{t+1}] = \bar{y}$. All traders are thus able to derive the fundamental price p_t^* in (100) that would prevail in a perfectly rational world. Traders nevertheless believe that in a heterogeneous world prices may *deviate* from their fundamental value p_t^*. It is convenient to introduce the *deviation* from the fundamental price:

$$x_t = p_t - p_t^*. \tag{102}$$

Beliefs about the future price of the risky asset are of the form

$$E_{ht}[\mathbf{p}_{t+1}] = E_t[\mathbf{p}_{t+1}^*] + f_h(x_{t-1}, \ldots, x_{t-L}), \quad \text{for all } h, t. \tag{103}$$

Each forecasting rule f_h represents a *model of the market* (e.g. a technical trading rule) according to which type h believes that prices will deviate from the fundamental price. We use the short hand notation $f_{ht} = f_h(x_{t-1}, \ldots, x_{t-L})$.

An important and convenient consequence of these assumptions concerning traders' beliefs is that the heterogeneous agent market equilibrium equation (99) can be reformulated in deviations from the benchmark fundamental as

$$(1+r)x_t = \sum_{h=1}^{H} n_{ht} E_{ht}[\mathbf{x}_{t+1}] = \sum_{h=1}^{H} n_{ht} f_{ht}. \tag{104}$$

In this general setup, the benchmark rational expectations asset pricing model is *nested* as a special case, with all forecasting strategies $f_h \equiv 0$. In this way, the adaptive belief systems can be used in empirical and experimental testing whether asset prices deviate significantly from a benchmark fundamental.

Evolutionary selection of strategies

The evolutionary part of the model, describing how beliefs are updated over time, follows the endogenous selection of forecasting rules introduced by Brock and Hommes

---

[18] Brock and Hommes (1997b), for example, discuss a non-stationary example, where the dividend process is a geometric random walk; see also Hommes (2002).

(1997a) as discussed in Subsection 7.2. The fractions n_{ht} of trader types are given by the *multinomial logit probabilities* of a discrete choice:

$$n_{ht} = \frac{\exp(\beta U_{h,t-1})}{Z_{t-1}}, \quad Z_{t-1} = \sum_{h=1}^{H} \exp(\beta U_{h,t-1}). \tag{105}$$

$U_{h,t-1}$ is the fitness measure of strategy h evaluated at the beginning of period t. A natural candidate for evolutionary fitness is (accumulated) *realized profits*, given by

$$U_{ht} = (p_t + y_t - Rp_{t-1}) \frac{E_{h,t-1}[\mathbf{p}_t + \mathbf{y}_t - Rp_{t-1}]}{a\sigma^2} + wU_{h,t-1}, \tag{106}$$

where $R = 1 + r$ is the gross risk free rate of return and $0 \leq w \leq 1$ is a *memory* parameter measuring how fast past realized profits are discounted for strategy selection.[19] We will focus on the simplest case with no memory, i.e. $w = 0$, so that fitness U_{ht} equals the most recently observed realized profit. Fitness can now be rewritten in deviations from the fundamental as

$$U_{ht} = (x_t - Rx_{t-1}) \left(\frac{f_{h,t-1} - Rx_{t-1}}{a\sigma^2} \right). \tag{107}$$

8.2. Few-type examples

BH98 have investigated evolutionary competition between *simple linear* forecasting rules with only *one lag*, i.e.[20]

$$f_{ht} = g_h x_{t-1} + b_h, \tag{108}$$

where g_h is a *trend* parameter and b_h a *bias* parameter. It can be argued that, for a forecasting rule to have any impact in real markets, it has to be simple. For a complicated forecasting rule it seems unlikely that enough traders will coordinate on that particular rule so that it affects market equilibrium prices. Notice that for $g_h = b_h = 0$ the linear forecasting rule (108) reduces to the forecast of *fundamentalists*, i.e. $f_{ht} \equiv 0$, believing that the market price will be equal to the fundamental price p^*, or equivalently that the deviation x from the fundamental will be 0. Notice also that the forecasting rule (108) uses x_{t-1} (or p_{t-1}) as the most recently observed deviation (or price) to forecast x_{t+1} (or p_{t+1}), because the market equilibrium equation (98) has not revealed the equilibrium

---

[19] We focus on the case where there are no differences in the costs for the strategies.

[20] Brock and Hommes (1998, pp. 1246–1248) also discuss a 2-type example with a costly rational expectations or *perfect foresight* forecasting rule $f_{ht} = x_{t+1}$ versus pure trend followers, and show that the fundamental steady state may become unstable and multiple, non-fundamental steady states may arise. Global dynamics in such an example are difficult to handle, because the system is only *implicitly defined*. Such implicitly defined evolutionary systems cannot be solved explicitly and often they are not even well-defined. See also Arthur (1995) and Hommes (2001) for a discussion of a fully rational agent type within a heterogeneous agents setting.

price p_t yet when forecasts for p_{t+1} are formed. A convenient feature of this setup is that the market equilibrium price p_t is always uniquely defined at all dates t.

This section presents two simple examples of ABS, an example with three and an example with four competing *linear* forecasting rules (108). The ABS becomes (in deviations from the fundamental):

$$(1+r)x_t = \sum_{h=1}^{H} n_{ht}(g_h x_{t-1} + b_h) + \epsilon_t, \tag{109}$$

$$n_{h,t} = \frac{\exp(\beta U_{h,t-1})}{\sum_{h=1}^{H} \exp(\beta U_{h,t-1})}, \tag{110}$$

$$U_{h,t-1} = (x_{t-1} - Rx_{t-2})\left(\frac{g_h x_{t-3} + b_h - Rx_{t-2}}{a\sigma^2}\right), \tag{111}$$

where ϵ_t is a small noise term representing uncertainty about economic fundamentals, e.g. random outside supply of the risky asset. The timing of the coupling between the market equilibrium equation (109) and the evolutionary selection of strategies (110) is important. The market equilibrium price p_t (or deviation x_t from the fundamental) in (109) depends upon the fractions n_{ht}. The notation in (110) stresses the fact that these fractions n_{ht} depend upon *past* fitnesses $U_{h,t-1}$, which in turn depend upon past prices p_{t-1} (or deviations x_{t-1}) in periods $t-1$ and further in the past. After the equilibrium price p_t (or the deviation x_t) has been revealed by the market, it will be used in evolutionary updating of beliefs and determining the new fractions $n_{h,t+1}$. These new fractions $n_{h,t+1}$ will then determine a new equilibrium price p_{t+1} (or deviation x_{t+1}), etc. In the ABS, market equilibrium prices and fractions of different trading strategies thus co-evolve over time.

Fundamentalists versus opposite biases

The first example of an ABS has *three* trader types, fundamentalists and two purely *biased* belief, optimists and pessimists expecting a constant price above or below the fundamental price:

$f_{1t} = 0$		fundamentalists,	(112)
$f_{2t} = b$	$b > 0,$	positive bias (optimists),	(113)
$f_{3t} = -b$	$-b < 0,$	negative bias (pessimists).	(114)

For low values of the intensity of choice β, the 3-type evolutionary system is stable and the asset price converges to its fundamental value. However, as the intensity of choice increases the fundamental steady becomes unstable due to a *Hopf* bifurcation and the dynamics of the ABS is characterized by cycles around the unstable steady state. This example shows that, even when there are *no* information costs for fundamentalists, they cannot drive out other trader types with opposite biased beliefs. In the evolutionary ABS with high intensity of choice, fundamentalists and biased traders co-exist with their fractions varying over time and asset prices fluctuating around the unstable fundamental steady state. Moreover, Brock and Hommes (1998, p. 1259, lemma 9) show that as the intensity of choice tends to infinity the ABS converges to a (globally) stable cycle of period 4. Average profits along this 4-cycle are equal for all three trader types. Hence, if the initial wealth is equal for all three types, then in this evolutionary system in the long run accumulated wealth will be equal for all three types. This example suggests that the Friedman argument that smart fundamental traders will drive out simple habitual rules of speculative traders is not true in general.

Fundamentalists versus trend and bias

The second example of an ABS is an example with *four* trader types, with linear forecasting rules (108) with parameters $g_1 = 0$, $b_1 = 0$; $g_2 = 0.9$, $b_2 = 0.2$; $g_3 = 0.9$, $b_3 = -0.2$ and $g_4 = 1 + r = 1.01$, $b_4 = 0$. The first type are fundamentalists again and the other three types follow a simple linear forecasting rule with one lag. The dynamical behavior is illustrated in Figure 11. For low values of the intensity of choice, the 4-type ABS is stable and the asset price converges to its fundamental value. As the intensity of choice increases, as in the previous three type example, the fundamental steady becomes unstable due to a *Hopf* bifurcation and a stable invariant circle around the unstable fundamental steady state arises, with periodic or quasi-periodic fluctuations. As the intensity of choice further increases, the invariant circle breaks into a strange attractor with chaotic fluctuations. In the evolutionary ABS fundamentalists and chartists co-exist with fractions varying over time and prices moving chaotically around the unstable fundamental steady state.

   This 4-type example shows that when traders are driven by short run profits, even when there are *no* information costs, fundamentalists cannot drive out other simple trend following strategies and fail to stabilize price fluctuations towards its fundamental value. As in the three type case, the opposite biases create cyclic behavior, but apparently trend following strategies turn these cycles into unpredictable chaotic fluctuations.

   The (noisy) chaotic price fluctuations are characterized by irregular switching between phases of close-to-the-EMH-fundamental-price fluctuations, phases of 'optimism' with prices following an upward trend, and phases of 'pessimism', with (small) sudden market crashes, as illustrated in Figure 11. In fact, in the ABS prices are characterized by an evolutionary switching between the fundamental value and temporary speculative bubbles. In the purely deterministic chaotic case, the start and the direction of the temporary bubbles seem hard to predict. However, once a bubble has started, in the deterministic case, the burst of the bubble seems to be predictable in most of the cases. In the presence of small noise however, as illustrated in Figure 11 (top right), the start, the direction as well as the time of burst of the bubble all seem hard to predict.

   In the deterministic chaotic as well as the noisy chaotic case, the autocorrelations of returns are close to zero, so there is little linear predictability in this model. In order to investigate the (un)predictability of this market model in more detail, we employ a

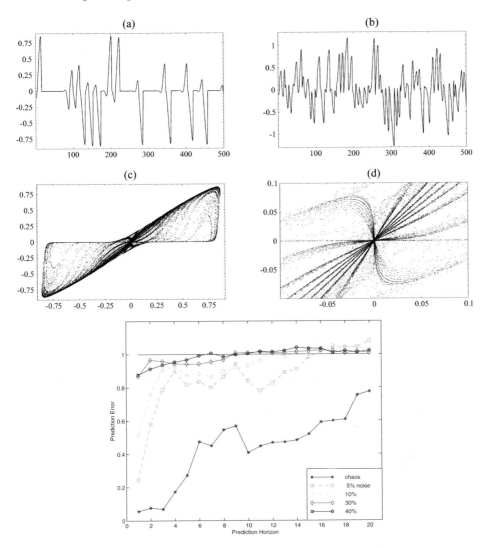

Figure 11. Chaotic (top left) and noisy chaotic (top right) time series of asset prices (deviations from fundamental value) in ABS with four trader types. Strange attractor (middle left) and enlargement of strange attractor (middle right). Belief parameters are: $g_1 = 0$, $b_1 = 0$; $g_2 = 0.9$, $b_2 = 0.2$; $g_3 = 0.9$, $b_3 = -0.2$ and $g_4 = 1 + r = 1.01$, $b_4 = 0$; other parameters are $r = 0.01$, $\beta = 90.5$ and $w = 0$. The bottom shows forecasting errors for the nearest neighbor method applied to noisy chaotic returns series, for different noise levels (see the text). All returns series have close to zero autocorrelations at all lags. The benchmark case of prediction by the mean 0 is represented by the horizontal line at the normalized prediction error 1. Nearest neighbor forecasting applied to the purely deterministic chaotic series leads to much smaller forecasting errors (lowest graph). A noise level of say 10% means that the ratio of the variance of the noise term ϵ_t in (109) and the variance of the deterministic price series is 1/10. As the noise level slowly increases, the graphs are shifted upwards. Small dynamic noise thus quickly deteriorates forecasting performance.

so called *nearest neighbor forecasting method* to predict the returns, at lags 1 to 20, for the purely chaotic as well as for several noisy chaotic time series, as illustrated in Figure 11.[21] Nearest neighbor forecasting looks for past patterns close to the most recent pattern, and then yields as the prediction the average value following all nearby past patterns. It follows essentially from Takens' embedding theorem that this method yields good forecasts for deterministic chaotic systems. Figure 11 shows that as the noise level increases, the forecasting performance of the nearest neighbor method quickly deteriorates. Hence, in our simple nonlinear evolutionary ABS with noise it is hard to make good forecasts of future returns. The market is close to being efficient in the sense that there is "no easy free lunch". However, the market is inefficient in the sense that prices exhibit persistent deviations from fundamental value, due to self-fulfilling temporary speculative bubbles driven by short run profit opportunities.

Recently several modifications of ABS have been studied. In BH98a the demand for the risky asset is derived from a constant absolute risk aversion (CARA) utility function. Chiarella and He (2001) consider the case with constant relative risk aversion (CRRA) utility, so that investors' relative wealth affects asset demand and realized asset price, and study wealth and asset price dynamics in such a heterogeneous agents framework.[22] Anufriev and Bottazzi (2005) characterize the type of equilibria and their stability in a HAM with CRRA utility and an arbitrary number of agents. Chiarella et al. (2002, 2006) use CRRA utility in an ABS with a market maker price setting rule Chiarella and He (2003). Hommes et al. (2005a) investigate an ABS with a market maker price setting rule, and find similar dynamical behavior as in the case of a Walrasian market clearing price. Chang (2005) studies the effects of social interactions in an ABS with a Walrasian market clearing price. DeGrauwe and Grimaldi (2005a, 2005b) recently applied the ABS framework to exchange rate modeling. A related stochastic model with heterogeneous agents and endogenous strategy switching similar to the ABS has recently been introduced in Föllmer et al. (2005). Scheinkman and Xiong (2004) review related stochastic financial models with heterogeneous beliefs and short sale constraints.

8.3. Many trader types

In most HAMs discussed in this chapter the number of trader types is small, restricted to two, three or four. Analytical tractability can only be obtained at the cost of restriction to just a few types. Brock et al. (2005), henceforth BHW05, have recently developed a theoretical framework to study evolutionary markets with *many* different trader types. They introduce the notion of *Large Type Limit (LTL)*, a simple, low dimensional approximation of an evolutionary market with many trader types. BHW05 develop the

---

[21] See e.g. Kantz and Schreiber (1997) for an extensive treatment of nonlinear time series analysis and forecasting techniques such as nearest neighbors. I would like to thank Sebastiano Manzan for providing the nearest neighbor forecasting plot.

[22] In the artificial market of Levy et al. (1994), asset demand is also derived from CRRA utility.

notion of LTL within a fairly general market clearing setting, but here we focus on its application to the asset pricing model.

Recall that in the asset market with H different trader types, the equilibrium price (104), in deviations x_t from the fundamental benchmark, is given by

$$x_t = \frac{1}{1+r} \sum_{h=1}^{H} n_{ht} f_{ht}. \tag{115}$$

Using the *multinomial logit* probabilities (105) for the fractions n_{ht} we get

$$x_t = \frac{1}{1+r} \frac{\sum_{h=1}^{H} e^{\beta U_{h,t-1}} f_{ht}}{\sum_{h=1}^{H} e^{\beta U_{h,t-1}}}. \tag{116}$$

The equilibrium equation (116) determines the evolution of the *system with H trader types*—this information is coded in the *evolution map* $\phi_H(\mathbf{x}, \lambda, \theta)$:

$$\phi_H(\mathbf{x}, \lambda, \theta) = \frac{1}{1+r} \frac{\sum_{h=1}^{H} e^{\beta U(\mathbf{x}, \lambda, \theta_h)} f(\mathbf{x}, \lambda, \theta_h)}{\sum_{h=1}^{H} e^{\beta U(\mathbf{x}, \lambda, \theta_h)}}, \tag{117}$$

where $\mathbf{x} = (x_{t-1}, x_{t-2}, \ldots)$ is a vector of lagged deviations from the fundamental, λ is a structural parameter vector (e.g. the risk free interest rate r, the risk aversion parameter a, the intensity of choice β, etc.) and the *belief variable* θ_h is now a multidimensional *stochastic* variable which characterizes belief h. At the beginning of the market, a large number H of beliefs is sampled from a general distribution of beliefs. For example, all forecasting rules may be drawn from a linear class with L lags,

$$f_t(\theta_0) = \theta_{00} + \theta_{01} x_{t-1} + \theta_{02} x_{t-2} + \cdots + \theta_{0L} x_{t-L}, \tag{118}$$

with $\theta_{0h}, h = 0, \ldots, L$, drawn from a multivariate normal distribution.

The evolution map ϕ_H in (117) determines the dynamical system corresponding to an *asset market with H different belief types*. When the number of trader types H is large, this dynamical system contains a large number of stochastic variables $\theta = (\theta_1, \ldots, \theta_H)$, where the θ_h are IID, with *distribution function* F_μ. The distribution function of the stochastic belief variable θ_h depends on a multi-dimensional parameter μ, called the *belief parameter*. This setup allows to vary the population out of which the individual beliefs are sampled at the beginning of the market.

Observe that both the denominator and the numerator of the evolution map ϕ_H in (117) may be divided by the number of trader types H and thus may be seen as sample means. The evolution map ψ of the large type limit is then simply obtained by *replacing sample means in the evolution map ϕ_H by population means*:

$$\psi(\mathbf{x}, \lambda, \mu) = \frac{1}{1+r} \frac{E_\mu[e^{\beta U(\mathbf{x},\lambda,\theta_0)} f(\mathbf{x}, \lambda, \theta_0)]}{E_\mu[e^{\beta U(\mathbf{x},\lambda,\theta_0)}]}$$

$$= \frac{1}{1+r} \frac{\int e^{\beta U(\mathbf{x},\lambda,\theta_0)} f(\mathbf{x}, \lambda, \theta_0) dv_\mu}{\int e^{\beta U(\mathbf{x},\lambda,\theta_0)} dv_\mu}. \tag{119}$$

Here θ_0 is a stochastic variable which is distributed in the same way as the θ_h, with distribution function F_μ. The *structural* parameter vectors λ of the evolution map ϕ_H and of the LTL evolution map ψ coincide. However, whereas the evolution map ϕ_H in (117) of the heterogeneous agent system contains H randomly drawn multi-dimensional stochastic variables θ_h, the LTL evolution map ψ in (119) only contains the *belief parameter* vector μ describing the joint probability distribution. Taking a large type limit thus leads to a huge reduction in stochastic belief variables.

BHW05 prove an LTL-theorem, saying that, as the number H of trader types tends to infinity, the H-type evolution map ϕ converges almost surely to the LTL-map ψ. The LTL theorem implies that the corresponding LTL dynamical system is a good approximation of the dynamical behavior in a heterogeneous asset market when the number of belief types H is large. In particular, all *generic* and *persistent* dynamic properties will be preserved with high probability. For example, if the LTL-map exhibits a bifurcation route to chaos for one of the structural parameters, then, if the number of trader types H is large, the H-type system also exhibits such a bifurcation route to chaos with high probability.

For example, in the case of linear forecasting rules (118) with three lags ($L = 3$), the corresponding LTL becomes a 5-D nonlinear system given by

$$(1+r)x_t = \mu_0 + \mu_1 x_{t-1} + \mu_2 x_{t-2} + \mu_3 x_{t-3}$$
$$+ \eta(x_{t-1} - Rx_{t-2} + a\sigma^2 z^s)$$
$$\times (\sigma_0^2 + \sigma_1^2 x_{t-1} x_{t-3} + \sigma_2^2 x_{t-2} x_{t-4} + \sigma_3^2 x_{t-3} x_{t-5}), \tag{120}$$

where $\eta = \beta/(a\sigma^2)$. BHW05 show that a bifurcation route to chaos, with asset prices fluctuating around the unstable fundamental steady state, occurs when η increases. This shows that a *rational route to randomness* can occur in an asset market with many different trader types, when traders become increasingly sensitive to differences in fitness (i.e. an increase in the intensity of choice β) or traders become less risk averse (i.e. a decrease of the coefficient of risk aversion a). In a many trader types evolutionary world fundamentalists will in general not drive out all other types and asset prices need not converge to their fundamental value.

Recently Diks and van der Weide (2003, 2005) have generalized the notion of LTL and introduced so-called *Continuous Belief Systems* (*CBS*), where the beliefs of traders are distributed according to a continuous density function. The beliefs distribution function and the equilibrium prices co-evolve over time. Assuming a suitable performance measure, e.g. quadratic in the belief parameter θ, the evolution of the distribution of beliefs is determined by the evolution of the first two moments, and analytical expressions for the change of the mean and the variance over time can be obtained. The LTL theory discussed here as well as its extensions can be used to form a bridge between an analytical approach and the literature on evolutionary artificial market simulation models reviewed in the chapter of LeBaron (2006) and LeBaron (2000).

9. Concluding remarks and future perspective

The work on heterogeneous agent modeling within the new paradigm of behavioral economics, behavioral finance and bounded rationality is rapidly expanding. This chapter has reviewed HAMs emphasizing models that, at least to some extent, are analytically tractable. The development and analysis of these models requires a combination of analytical and computational tools. The review shows a development from very simple, early models in the seventies and the eighties based on somewhat ad hoc assumptions (e.g. ad hoc demand or supply functions, fixed fractions using the different strategies) to more sophisticated models in the nineties based on micro foundations (e.g. local interactions, social utility, asset demand derived from myopic mean-variance maximization) with switching between different strategies according to an evolutionary fitness measure based upon recent realized performance and social interaction effects. Markets are viewed as *complex adaptive systems*, with the evolutionary selection of expectations rules or trading strategies endogenously coupled to the market (dis-)equilibrium dynamics. Prices, trading volume and the population of beliefs and strategies co-evolve over time. In this behavioral world the "wilderness of bounded rationality" is disciplined by parsimony and simplicity of strategies and their relative performance as measured by recent profits, forecasting errors and social utility. Aggregation of interactions of individuals at the micro-level may explain structure and stylized facts at the macro-level.

Dynamic HAMs are highly nonlinear systems, generating a wide range of dynamical behaviors, ranging from simple convergence to a stable steady state to very irregular and unpredictable fluctuations which are highly sensitive to noise. Sophisticated traders, such as fundamentalists or rational arbitrageurs typically act as a *stabilizing force*, pushing prices in the directions of the RE fundamental value. Technical traders, such as feedback traders, trend extrapolators and contrarians typically act as a *destabilizing force*, pushing prices away from the fundamental. When the proportion of chartists believing in a trend exceeds some critical value, the price trend becomes reinforced and the belief becomes self-fulfilling causing prices to deviate from fundamentals. Nonlinear interaction between fundamental traders and chartists can lead to deviations from the fundamental price in the short run, when price trends are reinforced due to technical trading, and mean reversion in the long run, when more agents switch back to fundamental strategies when the deviation from fundamental price becomes too large. Asset prices switch irregularly between temporary bull and bear markets, and are very unpredictable and highly sensitive to noise. Fractions of the different trading strategies fluctuate over time and simple technical trading rules can survive evolutionary competition, and on average chartists may earn profits comparable to the profits earned by fundamentalists or value traders. In financial market applications, simple HAMs can mimic important stylized facts, such as persistence in asset prices, unpredictability of returns at daily horizon, mean reversion at long horizons, excess volatility, clustered volatility and fat tails in asset returns. These models also generate high and persistent trading volume in sharp contrast to no trade theorems in RE models. High trading volume is mainly caused by differences in beliefs. Volatility in asset prices is driven by news about economic fundamentals, which is amplified due to the interaction of different trading strategies. Self-fulfilling trend following investment strategies may cause persistent deviations from fundamental values.

Much more work in this area remains to be done and of the many open issues that remain we can only mention a few. We have seen examples of HAMs where non-rational, non-fundamental traders survive competition in the market. Under which conditions is this true? This important question has also been addressed from a theoretical perspective in the recent *evolutionary finance* literature. Blume and Easley (1992, 2002) have shown that in a general equilibrium setting, when markets are incomplete, rational agents are not always able to drive out non-rational traders. Sandroni (2000) shows that in a complete market, agents who do not make accurate predictions are driven out of the market by agents who make accurate predictions.[23] Evstigneev et al. (2002), Hens and Schenk-Hoppé (2005) and Amir et al. (2005) investigate market selection of portfolio rules and investment strategies in asset markets. Applying the theory of random dynamical systems they show that in an incomplete market with short lived assets a unique evolutionary stable strategy distributing wealth according to expected relative payoffs accumulates all wealth. It is an open question whether this result holds for infinite lived assets. It is also an open question whether the Brock and Hommes type of instability will survive in a general equilibrium framework with consumption.

Another important issue is how *memory* in the fitness measure affects stability of evolutionary adaptive systems and survival of technical trading (see Brock and Hommes, 1999). This question is related to heterogeneity in investors' *time horizon*, both their planning and their evaluation horizon. In a computational framework this problem has been addressed by LeBaron (2002), but simple, analytically tractable models are not available yet. Most dynamic HAMs focus on a market with one risk free and one risky asset, and little attention has been paid to multi risky asset markets. Westerhoff (2004) recently considered multi-asset markets, where chartists can switch their investments

---

[23] There is an important difference between Sandroni (2000) and e.g. the approach of Brock and Hommes (1997a, 1998). Sandroni assumes heterogeneity in expectations about future states of the world, generated by an exogenous stochastic process. These beliefs affect asset prices, but do *not* affect realized states of the world, so that agents with correct beliefs have a comparative advantage in realized utility and asset prices converge to RE prices. In contrast, Brock and Hommes assume correct beliefs about dividends for all agents, but heterogeneous beliefs about prices. These beliefs endogenously affect realized prices. For example, optimistic traders may then survive in the market when enough traders share their optimism, causing the asset price to increase above its RE fundamental value and giving optimists a relatively high return on their investment decision.

between different markets for risky assets. The interaction between the different markets causes complex asset price dynamics, with different markets exhibiting co-movements as well as clustered volatility and fat tails of asset returns. In another recent paper, Böhm and Wenzelburger (2005) apply random dynamical systems to investigate the performance of efficient portfolios in a multi-asset market with heterogeneous investors. A final important question concerns futures or derivative markets. In a homogeneous, rational agent world futures markets are stabilizing because agents can hedge risk and thus force prices closer to their fundamental values. But what happens in a heterogeneous world with boundedly rational agents? Are futures markets stabilizing because risk can be hedged, or will boundedly rational agents take larger positions and destabilize markets?

Expectations play a key role in dynamic HAMs. It is remarkable that relatively little work in laboratory experiments and survey data analysis has focused on dynamic selection of expectation strategies. We mention three recent contributions, and emphasize that much more work needs to be done; see also the chapter of Duffy (2006) for an extensive discussion of the relationship between human subject laboratory experiments and agent-based modeling. Branch (2004) uses survey data on inflation expectations of households to estimate a version of the dynamic HAM of Brock and Hommes (1997a, 1997b), with naive expectations, adaptive expectations and a VAR-forecasting rule. The dynamic HAM fits the survey data best (better than the corresponding homogeneous agent models) with time varying proportions of the three expectations types inversely related to each predictor's MSE. Adam (2005) presents an experimental monetary sticky price economy in which output and inflation depend on expected future inflation. Participants are asked to forecast inflation for about 50 periods, and the average expectation determines next period's output and inflation. In the experimental sessions, output and inflation display considerable persistence and regular cyclical patterns. Such behavior emerges because subjects inflation expectations fail to be captured by rational expectations functions, but instead are well described by simple forecast functions using only one period lagged output and inflation as explanatory variables. Hommes et al. (2005b) conduct laboratory experiments, where individuals are asked to forecast an asset price for 50 periods, with realized prices determined endogenously in the laboratory by the Brock–Hommes (Brock and Hommes, 1998) asset pricing model with feedback from individual forecasts. In this simple stationary environment, in most cases the asset price does *not* converge to its fundamental value. Agents learn to coordinate on a common, simple prediction rule, e.g. a simple linear trend following rule, and asset prices oscillate around the fundamental value exhibiting short run bubbles and long run mean reversion.

Although there are already quite a number of HAMs, only few attempts have been made to estimate a HAM on economic or financial data. An early attempt has been made by Shiller (1984), who presents a HAM with smart money traders, having rational expectations, versus ordinary investors (whose behavior is in fact not modeled at all). Shiller estimates the fraction of smart money investors over the period 1900–1983, and finds considerable fluctuations of the fraction over a range between 0 and 50%. More recently, Baak (1999) and Chavas (2000) estimate HAMs on hog and beef market data, and found evidence for the heterogeneity of expectations. For the beef market Chavas (2000) finds that about 47% of the beef producers behave naively (using only the last price in their forecast), 18% of the beef producers behaves rationally, whereas 35% behaves quasi-rationally (i.e. use a univariate autoregressive time series model of prices in forecasting). Winker and Gilli (2001) and Gilli and Winker (2003) estimate the model of Kirman (1991, 1993) (see Subsection 5.1) with fundamentalists and chartists, using the daily DM–US$ exchange rates 1991–2000. Their estimated parameter values correspond to a bimodal distribution of agents, and Gilli and Winker (2003, p. 310) conclude that "*. . . the foreign exchange market can be better characterized by switching moods of the investors than by assuming that the mix of fundamentalists and chartists remains rather stable over time*". Westerhoff and Reitz (2003) also estimate an HAM with fundamentalists and chartists to exchange rates and find considerable fluctuations of the market impact of fundamentalists. In a recent paper, Boswijk et al. (2005) use yearly data of the S&P500 index, 1890–2003, to estimate a version of the Brock and Hommes (1998) asset pricing model with two types of strategies and switching of strategies driven by short run profits. Their estimation yields two different regimes, one stable mean-reverting and one unstable trending regime. Fractions of the two types change considerably over time, and especially in the nineties, the fraction of trend followers becomes large, suggesting that the strong rise in stock prices in the nineties has been exaggerated by trend extrapolation driven by short run profits. All these empirical papers suggest that heterogeneity is important in explaining the data, but much more work is needed to investigate the robustness of this empirical finding.

Much of the work on HAMs is computational and theoretically oriented, but little work has been done on policy implications. The most important difference with a representative rational agent framework is perhaps that in a heterogeneous boundedly rational world, asset price fluctuations exhibit excess volatility. If this is indeed the case, it has important policy implications e.g. concerning the debate on whether a Tobin tax on financial transactions is desirable. In an interesting recent paper, Westerhoff and Dieci (2005) use a HAM to investigate the effectiveness of a Tobin tax. Investors can invest in two different speculative asset markets. If a Tobin tax is imposed on one market, it is stabilized while the other market is destabilized; if a tax is imposed on both markets, price fluctuations in both markets decrease. Another example of a policy oriented paper is Westerhoff (2004), who investigates the effectiveness of trading brakes in a HAM. Although much more work is needed to be conclusive on these important issues, these are interesting results illustrating how HAMs can be used to investigate policy issues in future work.

The paradigm of agent-based, behavioral economics, behavioral finance and bounded rationality is rapidly expanding. Heterogeneity is likely to play a key role in this approach, and agent-based computational HAMs deserve high priority in future work. Will an analytical approach survive within more computational oriented research in the 21st century? Computational models are becoming increasingly important and have the advantage that many aspects at the micro level and details of the interaction among agents can be modeled and simulated on a computer. But a problem with large computer simulation models is that there are *too many degrees of freedom* and *too many parameters*. For example, in a computational model often there are many places where noise enters the model at the micro-level, which makes it very difficult to assess the main causes of observed stylized facts at the aggregate, macro level. The search for a (large) computational agent-based HAM capturing the stylized facts as closely as possible deserves high priority. But at the same time one would like to find the *simplest* behavioral HAM (e.g. in terms of number of parameters and variables), with a plausible behavioral story at the micro level, that still captures the most important stylized facts observed at the aggregate level. The simplest HAM can then be used to estimate behavioral heterogeneity in laboratory experimental and/or empirical time series data. Simple and parsimonious HAMs can thus help to discipline the wilderness of agent-based modeling.

References

Adam, K. (2005). "Experimental evidence on the persistence of output and inflation", working paper, European Central Bank, January 2005.

Alchian, A.A. (1950). "Uncertainty, evolution, and economic theory". Journal of Political Economy 58, 211–221.

Allen, H., Taylor, M.P. (1990). "Charts, noise and fundamentals in the London foreign exchanche market". Economic Journal 100 (400), 49–59.

Amir, R., Evstigneev, I.V., Hens, T., Schenk-Hoppé, K.R. (2005). "Market selection and survival of investment strategies". Journal of Mathematical Economics 41, 105–122.

Anderson, P.W., Arrow, K.J., Pines, D. (Eds.) (1988). The Economy as an Evolving Complex System II. Addison-Wesley, Reading, MA.

Anderson, S., de Palma, A., Thisse, J. (1993). Discrete Choice Theory of Product Differentiation. MIT Press, Cambridge.

Anufriev, M., Bottazzi (2005). "Price and wealth dynamics in a speculative market with an arbitrary number of generic technical traders", L.E.M. Working Paper, no. 2005-06, Pisa.

Aoki, M. (1994). "New macroeconomic modeling approaches. Hierarchical dynamics and mean-field approximation". Journal of Economic Dynamics and Control 18, 865–877.

Aoki, M. (2002). Modeling Aggregate Behavior and Fluctuations in Economics. Stochastic Views of Interacting Agents. Cambridge University Press, Cambridge.

Arifovic, J. (1994). "Genetic algorithm learning and the cobweb model". Journal of Economic Dynamics and Control 18, 3–28.

Arthur, W.B. (1994). Increasing Returns and Path Dependence in the Economy. University of Michigan Press, Ann Arbor.

Arthur, W.B. (1995). "Complexity in economic and financial markets". Complexity 1, 20–25.

Arthur, W.B. (2006). "Out-of-equilibrium economics and agent-based modeling", this handbook.

Arthur, W.B., Durlauf, S.N., Lane, D.A. (Eds.) (1997a). The Economy as an Evolving Complex System II. Addison-Wesley, Reading, MA.

Arthur, W.B., Holland, J.H., LeBaron, B., Palmer, R., Tayler, P. (1997b). "Asset pricing under endogenous expectations in an artificial stock market". In: Arthur, W., Lane, D., Durlauf, S. (Eds.), The Economy as an Evolving Complex System II. Addison-Wesley, pp. 15–44.

Baak, S.J. (1999). "Tests for bounded rationality with a linear dynamic model distorted by heterogeneous expectations". Journal of Economic Dynamics and Control 23, 1517–1543.

Barberis, N., Thaler, R. (2003). "A survey of behavioral finance". In: Constantinidis, G.M., Harris, M., Stulz, R. (Eds.), Handbook of the Economics of Finance. Elsevier, pp. 1051–1121.

Beja, A., Goldman, M.B. (1980). "On the dynamic behavior of prices in disequilibrium". Journal of Finance 35, 235–248.

Bernheim, D. (1994). "A theory of conformity". Journal of Political Economy 5 (102), 841–877.

Black, F. (1986). "Noise". Journal of Finance 41, 529–543.

Blume, L. (1993). "The statistical mechanics of strategic interaction". Games and Economic Behavior 5, 387–424.

Blume, L., Easley, D. (1992). "Evolution and market behavior". Journal of Economic Theory 58, 9–40.

Blume, L., Easley, D. (2002). "If You're So Smart, Why Aren't You Rich? Belief Selection in Complete and Incomplete Markets", Cowles Foundation Discussion Paper No. 1319, July 2002.

Böhm, V., Wenzelburger, J. (2005). "On the performance of efficient portfolios". Journal of Economic Dynamics and Control 29, 721–740.

Boswijk, H.P., Hommes, C.H., Manzan, S. (2005). "Behavioral heterogeneity in stock prices", CeNDEF Working Paper 05-12, University of Amsterdam.

Bouchaud, J.P. (2001). "Power laws in economics and finance: some ideas from physics". Quantitative Finance 1, 105–112.

Branch, W.A. (2002). "Local convergence properties of a cobweb model with rationally heterogeneous expectations". Journal of Economic Dynamics and Control 27, 63–85.

Branch, W.A. (2004). "The theory of rationally heterogeneous expectations: evidence from survey data on inflation expectations". Economic Journal 114, 592–621.

Branch, W.A., McGough, B. (2004). "Replicator dynamics in a cobweb model with rationally heterogeneous agents", working paper, October 2004.

Branch, W.A., Evans, G.W. (2005). "Intrinsic heterogeneity in expectation formation", Journal of Economic Theory 2005, in press.

Brock, W.A. (1993). "Pathways to randomness in the economy: emergent nonlinearity and chaos in economics and finance". Estudios Económicos 8, 3–55.

Brock, W.A. (1997). "Asset price behavior in complex environments". In: Arthur, W.B., Durlauf, S.N., Lane, D.A. (Eds.), The Economy as an Evolving Complex System II. Addison-Wesley, Reading, MA, pp. 385–423.

Brock, W.A., LeBaron (1996). "A structural model for stock return volatility and trading volume". Review of Economics and Statistics 78, 94–110.

Brock, W.A., Hommes, C.H. (1997a). "A rational route to randomness". Econometrica 65, 1059–1095.

Brock, W.A., Hommes, C.H. (1997b). "Models of complexity in economics and finance". In: Hey, C., et al. (Eds.), System Dynamics in Economic and Financial Models. Wiley Publ., pp. 3–41.

Brock, W.A., Hommes, C.H. (1998). "Heterogeneous beliefs and routes to chaos in a simple asset pricing model". Journal of Economic Dynamics and Control 22, 1235–1274.

Brock, W.A., Hommes, C.H. (1999). "Rational animal spirits". In: Herings, P.J.J., van der Laan, G., Talman, A.J.J. (Eds.), The Theory of Markets. North-Holland, Amsterdam, pp. 109–137.

Brock, W.A., de Fontnouvelle, P. (2000). "Expectational diversity in monetary economics". Journal of Economic Dynamics and Control 24, 725–759.

Brock, W.A., Durlauf, S.N. (2001a). "Discrete choice with social interactions". Review of Economic Studies 68, 235–260.

Brock, W.A., Durlauf, S.N. (2001b). "Interactions-based models". In: Heckman, J.J., Leamer, E. (Eds.), Handbook of Econometrics, vol. 5, pp. 3297–3380.

Brock, W.A., Hsieh, D., LeBaron, B. (1991). Nonlinear Dynamics, Chaos and Instability: Statistical Theory and Economic Evidence. MIT Press, Cambridge, London.

Brock, W.A., Lakonishok, J., LeBaron, B. (1992). "Simple technical trading rules and the stochastic properties of stock returns". Journal of Finance 47, 1731–1764.

Brock, W.A., Hommes, C.H., Wagener, F.O.O. (2005). "Evolutionary dynamics in markets with many trader types". Journal of Mathematical Economics 41, 7–42.

Chang, S. (2005). "A simple asset pricing model with social interactions and heterogeneous beliefs", working paper, Wayne State University.

Chavas, J.P. (2000). "On information and market dynamics: the case of the U.S. beef market". Journal of Economic Dynamics and Control 24, 833–853.

Cheung, Y., Chinn, M., Marsh, I. (1999). "How do UK-based foreign exchange dealers think their markets operates?", CEPR Discussion Paper 2230.

Chiarella, C. (1992). "The dynamics of speculative behaviour". Annals of Operations Research 37, 101–123.

Chiarella, C., Khomin, P. (1999). "Adaptively evolving expectations in models of monetary dynamics—The fundamentalists forward looking—". Annals of Operations Research 89, 21–34.

Chiarella, C., He, X. (2001). "Asset price and wealth dynamics under heterogeneous expectations". Quantitative Finance 1, 509–526.

Chiarella, C., He, X. (2002). "Heterogeneous beliefs, risk and learning in a simple asset pricing model". Computational Economics 19, 95–132.

Chiarella, C., He, X. (2003). "Heterogeneous beliefs, risk and learning in a simple asset pricing model with a market maker". Macroeconomic Dynamics 7, 503–536.

Chiarella, C., Dieci, R., Gardini, L. (2002). "Speculative behaviour and complex asset price dynamics: a global analysis". Journal of Economic Behavior & Organization 49, 173–197.

Chiarella, C., Dieci, R., Gardini, L. (2006). "Asset price and wealth dynamics in a financial market with heterogeneous agents", Journal of Economic Dynamics and Control, in press.

Conlisk, J. (1980). "Costly optimizers versus cheap imitators". Journal of Economic Behavior & Organization 1, 275–293.

Cont, R. (2001). "Empirical properties of asset returns: stylized facts and statistical issues". Quantitative Finance 1, 223–236.

Cont, R., Bouchaud, J.-P. (2000). "Herd behavior and aggregate fluctuations in financial markets". Macroeconomic Dynamics 4, 170–196.

Cutler, D.M., Poterba, J.M., Summers, L.H. (1989). "What moves stock prices?". Journal of Portfolio Management 15, 4–12.

Dacorogna, M.M., Müller, U.A., Jost, C., Pictet, O.V., Olsen, R.B., Ward, J.R. (1995). "Heterogeneous real-time trading strategies in the foreign exchange market". European Journal of Finance 1, 383–403.

Day, R.H. (1994). An Introduction to Dynamical Systems and Market Mechanisms. Complex Economic Dynamics, vol. I. MIT Press, Cambridge.

Day, R.H., Huang, W. (1990). "Bulls, bears and market sheep". Journal of Economic Behavior & Organization 14, 299–329.

DeGrauwe, P., Grimaldi, M. (2005a). "Heterogeneity of agents, transaction costs and the exchange rate", Journal of Economic Dynamics and Control, in press.

DeGrauwe, P., Grimaldi, M. (2005b). "Exchange rate puzzles: A tale of switching attractors", European Economic Review, in press.

DeGrauwe, P., Dewachter, H., Embrechts, M. (1993). Exchange Rate Theory. Chaotic Models of Foreign Exchange Markets. Blackwell.

DeLong, J.B., Shleifer, A., Summers, L.H., Waldmann, R.J. (1990a). "Noise trader risk in financial markets". Journal of Political Economy 98, 703–738.

DeLong, J.B., Shleifer, A., Summers, L.H., Waldmann, R.J. (1990b). "Positive feedback investment strategies and destabilizing rational speculation". Journal of Finance 45, 379–395.

Delli Gatti, D., Gallegati, M., Kirman, A. (Eds.) (2000). Interaction and Market Structure. Essays on Heterogeneity in Economics. Lecture Notes in Economics and Mathematical Systems, vol. 484. Springer Verlag, Berlin.

Diks, C.G.H., van der Weide, R. (2003). "Heterogeneity as a natural source of randomness", CeNDEF Working paper 03-05, University of Amsterdam.

Diks, C.G.H., van der Weide, R. (2005). "Herding, a-synchronous updating and heterogeneity in memory in a CBS". Journal of Economic Dynamics and Control 29, 741–763.

Droste, E., Hommes, C., Tuinstra, J. (2002). "Endogenous fluctuations under evolutionary pressure in Cournot competition". Games and Economic Behavior 40, 232–269.

Duffy, J. (2006). "Agent-based models and human–subject experiments", this handbook.

Egenter, E., Lux, T., Stauffer, D. (1999). "Finite-size effects in Monte Carlo simulations of two stock market models". Physica A 268, 250–256.

Engle, R.F. (1982). "Autoregressive conditional heteroscedasticity with estimates of the variance of United Kingdom inflation". Econometrica 50, 987–1007.

Evans, G.W., Ramey, G. (1992). "Expectation calculation and macroeconomic dynamics". American Economic Review 82, 207–224.

Evans, G.W., Honkapohja, S. (2001). Learning and Expectations in Macroeconomics. Princeton University Press, Princeton.

Evstigneev, I., Hens, T., Schenk-Hoppé, K.R. (2002). "Market selection of financial trading strategies: global stability". Mathematical Finance 12, 329–339.

Fama, E.F. (1965). "The behavior of stock market prices". Journal of Business 38, 34–105.

Farmer, J.D. (1999). "Physicists attempt to scale the ivory towers of finance". Computing in Science & Engineering (Nov./Dec.), 26–39.

Farmer, J.D. (2002). "Market force, ecology, and evolution". Industrial and Corporate Change 11, 895–953.

Farmer, J.D., Joshi, S. (2002). "The price dynamics of common trading strategies". Journal of Economic Behavior & Organization 49, 149–171.

Föllmer, H. (1974). "Random economies with many interacting agents". Journal of Mathematical Economics 1, 51–62.

Föllmer, H. (1994). "Stock price fluctuations as a diffusion in a random environment". Philosophical Transactions: Physical Sciences and Engineering, Mathematical Models in Finance 347 (1684), 471–482.

Föllmer, H., Schweizer, M. (1993). "A microeconomic approach to diffusion models for stock prices". Mathematical Finance 3, 1–23.

Föllmer, H., Horst, U., Kirman, A. (2005). "Equilibria in financial markets with heterogeneous agents: a probabilistic perspective". Journal of Mathematical Economics 41, 123–155.

de Fontnouvelle, P. (2000). "Information dynamics in financial markets". Macroeconomic Dynamics 4, 139–169.

Frankel, J.A., Froot, K.A. (1986). "Understanding the US dollar in the eighties: the expectations of chartists and fundamentalists". Economic Record 1 (2), 24–38. Also published as NBER working paper No. 0957, December 1987, special issue.

Frankel, J.A., Froot, K.A. (1987a). "Using survey data to test standard propositions regarding exchange rate expectations". American Economic Review 77, 133–153.

Frankel, J.A., Froot, K.A. (1987b). "Short-term and long-term expectations of the yen/dollar exchange rate: evidence from survey data". Journal of the Japanese and International Economies 1, 249–274. Also published as NBER working paper 2216, April 1987.

Frankel, J.A., Froot, K.A. (1990a). "Chartists, fundamentalists and the demand for dollars". In: Courakis, A.S., Taylor, M.P. (Eds.), Private behaviour and government policy in interdependent economies. Oxford University Press, New York, pp. 73–126. Also published as NBER Working Paper No. r1655, October 1991.

Frankel, J.A., Froot, K.A. (1990b). "The rationality of the foreign exchange rate. Chartists, fundamentalists and trading in the foreign exchange market". American Economic Review, AEA Papers and Proceedings 80 (2), 181–185.

Friedman, M. (1953). "The case of flexible exchange rates". In: Essays in Positive Economics. University of Chicago Press.

Froot, K.A., Frankel, J.A. (1989). "Forward discount bias: is it an exchange rate premium?". Quarterly Journal of Economics 104, 139–161.

Fudenberg, D., Tirole, J. (1991). Game Theory. MIT Press, Cambridge.

Gallegati, M., Kirman, A. (Eds.) (1999). Beyond the Representative Agent. Edward Elgar, Northampton.

Gaunersdorfer, A. (2000). "Endogenous fluctuations in a simple asset pricing model with heterogeneous beliefs". Journal of Economic Dynamics and Control 24, 799–831.

Gaunersdorfer, A., Hommes, C.H. (2006). "A nonlinear structural model for volatility clustering", CeNDEF working paper, University of Amsterdam. In: Kirman, A., Teyssière, G. (Eds.), Microeconomic Models for Long Memory in Economics, in press.

Giardina, I., Bouchaud, J.-P. (2003). "Bubbles, crashes and intermittency in agent based market models". European Physics Journal B 31, 421–437.

Gilli, M., Winker, P. (2003). "A global optimization heuristic for estimating agent based models". Computational Statistics & Data Analysis 42, 299–312.

Goeree, J.K., Hommes, C.H. (2000). "Heterogeneous beliefs and the non-linear cobweb model". Journal of Economic Dynamics and Control 24, 761–798.

Goldbaum, D. (2005). "Market efficiency and learning in an endogenously unstable environment". Journal of Economic Dynamics and Control 29, 953–978.

Goodhart, C. (1988). "The foreign exchange market: a random walk with a dragging anchor". Economica 55, 437–460.

Guastello, S.J. (1995). Chaos, Catastrophe, and Human Affairs: Applications of Nonlinear Dynamics to Work, Organizations, and Social Evolution. Lawrence Erlbaum Associates, Mahwah.

Haken, H. (1983). Synergetics: An Introduction, 3rd edn. Springer, Berlin.

Hens, T., Schenk-Hoppé, K.R. (2005). "Evolutionary stability of portfolio rules in incomplete markets". Journal of Mathematical Economics 41, 43–66.

Hommes, C.H. (2001). "Financial markets as nonlinear adaptive evolutionary systems". Quantitative Finance 1, 149–167.

Hommes, C.H. (2002). "Modeling the stylized facts in finance through simple nonlinear adaptive systems". Proceedings of the National Academy of Sciences 99, 7221–7228.

Hommes, C.H. (2005). "Heterogeneous agents models: two simple examples". In: Lines, M. (Ed.), Nonlinear Dynamical Systems in Economics. CISM Courses and Lectures, vol. 476. Springer, pp. 131–164.

Hommes, C.H., Huang, H., Wang, D. (2005a). "A robust rational route to randomness in a simple asset pricing model". Journal of Economic Dynamics and Control 29, 1043–1072.

Hommes, C.H., Sonnemans, J., Tuinstra, J., van de Velden, H. (2005b). "Coordination of expectations in asset pricing experiments". Review of Financial Studies 18, 955–980.

Hong, H., Stein, J. (1999). "A unified theory of underreaction, momentum trading and overreaction in asset markets". Journal of Finance 55, 265–295.

Iori, G. (2002). "A microsimulation of traders activity in the stock market: the role of heterogeneity, agents' interactions and trade frictions". Journal of Economic Behavior & Organization 49, 269–285.

Ito, K. (1990). "Foreign exchange rate expectations". American Economic Review 80, 434–449.

Judd, K.L. (2006). "Computationally intensive analyses in economics", this handbook.

Kahneman, D. (2003). "Maps of bounded rationality: psychology for behavioral economics". American Economic Review 93, 1449–1475.

Kahneman, D., Tversky, A. (1973). "On the psychology of prediction". Psychological Review 80, 237–251.

Kantz, H., Schreiber, T. (1997). Nonlinear Time Series Analysis. Cambridge University Press, Cambridge.

Keynes, J.M. (1936). The General Theory of Unemployment, Interest and Money. Harcourt, Brace and World, New York.

Kirman, A. (1991). "Epidemics of opinion and speculative bubbles in financial markets". In: Taylor, M. (Ed.), Money and Financial Markets. Macmillan.

Kirman, A. (1993). "Ants, rationality and recruitment". Quarterly Journal of Economics 108, 137–156.

Kirman, A. (1999). "Aggregate activity and economic organisation". Revue Européene des Sciences Sociales XXXVII (113), 189–230.

Kirman, A., Teyssière, G. (2002). "Microeconomic models for long memory in the volatility of financial time series". Studies in Nonlinear Dynamics & Econometrics 5 (4), 281–302.

Kyle, A.S. (1985). "Continuous auctions and insider trading". Econometrica 47, 1315–1336.

Lasselle, L., Svizzero, S., Tisdell, C. (2005). "Stability and cycles in a cobweb model with heterogeneous expectations". Macroeconomic Dynamics 9, 630–650.

LeBaron, B. (2000). "Agent based computational finance: suggested readings and early research". Journal of Economic Dynamics and Control 24, 679–702.

LeBaron, B. (2002). "Short-memory traders and their impact on group learning in financial markets". Proceedings of the National Academy of Sciences 99 (Suppl. 3), 7201–7206.

LeBaron, B. (2006). "Agent-based computational finance", this handbook.

LeBaron, B., Arthur, W.B., Palmer, R. (1999). "Time series properties of an artificial stock market". Journal of Economic Dynamics and Control 23, 1487–1516.

LeRoy, S.F., Porter, R.D. (1981). "The present-value relation: tests based on implied variance bounds". Econometrica 49, 555–574.

Levy, M., Levy, H., Solomon, S. (1994). "A microscopic model of the stock market". Economics Letters 45, 103–111.

Lorenz, H.W. (1993). Nonlinear Dynamical Economics and Chaotic Motion, 2nd, revised and enlarged edition. Springer-Verlag, Berlin.

Lucas, R.E. (1971). "Econometric testing of the natural rate hypothesis". In: Eckstein, O. (Ed.), The Econometrics of Price Determination Conference. Board of Governors of the Federal Reserve System and Social Science Research Council.

Lui, Y., Mole, D. (1999). "The use of fundamental and technical analysis by foreign exchange dealers: Hong Kong evidence". Journal of International Money and Finance 17, 535–545.

Lux, T. (1995). "Herd behavior, bubbles and crashes". The Economic Journal 105, 881–896.

Lux, T. (1997). "Time variation of second moments from a noise trader/infection model". Journal of Economic Dynamics and Control 22, 1–38.

Lux, T. (1998). "The socio-economic dynamics of speculative markets: interacting agents, chaos, and the fat tails of return distribution". Journal of Economic Behavior & Organization 33, 143–165.

Lux, T., Marchesi, M. (1999). "Scaling and criticality in a stochastic multi-agent model of a financial market". Nature 397, 498–500.

Lux, T., Marchesi, M. (2000). "Volatility clustering in financial markets: a micro-simulation of interacting agents". International Journal of Theoretical and Applied Finance 3, 675–702.

Mandelbrot, B. (1963). "The variation of certain speculative prices". Journal of Business 36, 394–419.

Mandelbrot, B. (2001a). "Scaling in financial prices: I. Tails and dependence". Quantitative Finance 1, 113–123.

Mandelbrot, B. (2001b). "Scaling in financial prices: II. Multifractals and the star equation". Quantitative Finance 1, 124–130.

Mantegna, R.N., Stanley, H.E. (2000). An Introduction to Econophysics. Correlations and Complexity in Finance. Cambridge University Press, Cambridge.

Manski, C., McFadden, D. (Eds.) (1981). Structural Analysis of Discrete Data with Econometric Applications. MIT Press, Cambridge, MA.

McKelvey, R.D., Palfrey, T.R. (1995). "Quantal response equilibria in normal form games". Games and Economic Behavior 10, 6–38.

Medio, A. (1992). Chaotic Dynamics. Theory and Applications to Economics. Cambridge University Press, Cambridge.

Medio, A., Lines, M. (2001). Non-linear Dynamics. A Primer. Cambridge University Press.

Menkhoff, L. (1997). "Examining the use of technical currency analysis". International Journal of Finance and Economics 2, 307–318.

Menkhoff, L. (1998). "The noise trading approach—Questionnaire evidence from foreign exchange". Journal of International Money and Finance 17, 547–564.

Milgrom, P., Stokey, N. (1982). "Information, trade and common knowledge". Journal of Economic Theory 26, 17–27.

Muth, J.F. (1961). "Rational expectations and the theory of price movements". Econometrica 29, 315–335.

Nadal, J.-P., Weisbuch, G., Chenevez, O., Kirman, A. (1998). "A formal approach to market organization: choice functions, mean field approximation and maximum entropy principle". In: Lesourne, J., Orlean, A. (Eds.), Advances in Self-organization and Evolutionary Economics. Economica, London, pp. 149–159.

Nelson, R.R., Winter, S. (1973). "Toward and evolutionary theory of economic capabilities". American Economic Review 63, 440–449.

Nelson, R.R., Winter, S. (1974). "Neoclassical vs. evolutionary theories of economic growth". Economic Journal 84, 886–905.

Nelson, R.R., Winter, S. (1982). An Evolutionary Theory of Economic Change. Harvard University Press, Cambridge, Mass.

Rheinlaender, T., Steinkamp, M. (2004). "A stochastic version of Zeeman's market model". Studies in Nonlinear Dynamics & Econometrics 8 (4). Article 4.

Rosser, J.B. (2004a). Complexity in Economics: The International Library of Critical Writings in Economics 174. Edward Elgar, Aldergate. 3 volumes.

Rosser, J.B. (2004b). "The rise and fall of catastrophe theory applications in economics: was the baby thrown out with the bath water?", Working Paper, James Madison University, September 2004.

Sandroni, A. (2000). "Do markets favor agents able to make accurate predictions?". Econometrica 68, 1303–1341.

Sargent, T.J. (1993). Bounded Rationality in Macroeconomics. Clarendon Press, Oxford.

Schelling, T. (1971). "Dynamic models of segregation". Journal of Mathematical Sociology 1, 143–186.

Scheinkman, J.A., Xiong, W. (2004). "Heterogeneous beliefs, speculation and trading in financial markets". In: Paris–Princeton Lectures in Mathematical Finance 2003. In: Carmona, R.A., et al. (Eds.), Lecture Notes in Mathematics, vol. 1847. Springer Verlag, Berlin, pp. 217–250.

Sethi, R., Franke, R. (1995). "Behavioural heterogeneity under evolutionary pressure: macroeconomic implications of costly optimization". Economic Journal 105, 583–600.

Shiller, R.J. (1981). "Do stock prices move too much to be justified by subsequent changes in dividends?". American Economic Review 71, 421–436.

Shiller, R.J. (1984). "Stock prices and social dynamics". Brookings Papers in Economic Activity 2, 457–510.

Shiller, R.J. (1987). "Investor behavior in the October 1987 stock market crash: survey evidence", NBER working paper No. 2446, November 1987, published in: Shiller, R.J., Market Volatility, MIT Press, Cambridge, 1989, chapter 23.

Shiller, R.J. (1989). Market Volatility. MIT Press, Cambridge.

Shleifer, A., Summers, L.H. (1990). "The noise trader approach to finance". Journal of Economic Perspectives 4 (2), 19–33.

Simon, H.A. (1957). Models of Man. Wiley, New York, NY.

Simon, H.A. (1979). "Rational decision making in business organizations". American Economic Review 69, 493–513.

Smith, V., Suchanek, G.L., Williams, A.W. (1988). "Bubbles, crashes and endogenous expectations in experimental spot asset markets". Econometrica 56, 1119–1151.

Sunder, S. (1995). "Experimental asset markets: a survey". In: Kagel, J., Roth, A. (Eds.), Handbook of Experimental Economics. Princeton University Press. chapter 6.

Taylor, M.P., Allen, H. (1992). "The use of technical analysis in the foreign exchange market". Journal of International Money and Finance 11, 304–314.

Tesfatsion, L. (2006). "Agent-based computational economics: a constructive approach to economic theory", this handbook.

Tversky, A., Kahneman, D. (1974). "Judgment under uncertainty: heuristics and biases". Science 185, 1124–1131.

Weidlich, W., Haag, G. (1983). Concepts and Models of a Quantitative Sociology. Springer, Berlin.

Westerhoff, F.H. (2004). "Multi-asset market dynamics". Macroeconomic Dynamics 8, 596–616.

Westerhoff, F.H., Reitz, S. (2003). "Nonlinearities and cyclical behavior: the role of chartists and fundamentalists". Studies in Nonlinear Dynamics & Econometrics 7 (4). Article 3.

Westerhoff, F.H., Dieci, R. (2005). "The effectiveness of Keynes–Tobin transaction taxes when heterogeneous agents can trade in different markets: a behavioral finance approach", Journal of Economic Dynamics and Control, in press.

Winker, P., Gilli, M. (2001). "Indirect estimation of the parameters of agent based models of financial markets", FAME Research Paper No. 38, University of Geneva, November 2001.

Youssefmir, M., Huberman, B.A. (1997). "Clustered volatility in multi agent dynamics". Journal of Economic Behavior & Organization 32, 101–118.

Zahler, R., Sussmann, H.J. (1977). "Claims and accomplishments of applied catastrophe theory". Nature 269 (10), 759–763.

Zeeman, E.C. (1974). "The unstable behavior of stock exchange". Journal of Mathematical Economics 1, 39–49.

Chapter 24

AGENT-BASED COMPUTATIONAL FINANCE

BLAKE LEBARON[*]

International Business School, Brandeis University, Waltham, MA 02454-9110, USA
e-mail: blebaron@brandeis.edu url: http://www.brandeis.edu/~blebaron

Contents

[*] The author is also a research associate at the National Bureau of Economic Research. The author is grateful to many people who have made comments on earlier drafts. These include W.A. Brock, Cars Hommes, Robert Marks, Leigh Tesfatsion, Frank Westerhoff, and two anonymous referees.

Handbook of Computational Economics, Volume 2. Edited by Leigh Tesfatsion and Kenneth L. Judd
DOI: 10.1016/S1574-0021(05)02024-1

Abstract

This chapter surveys research on agent-based models used in finance. It will concentrate on models where the use of computational tools is critical for the process of crafting models which give insights into the importance and dynamics of investor heterogeneity in many financial settings.

Keywords

learning, evolutionary finance, financial time series, asset pricing, efficient markets, behavioral finance, market microstructure, genetic algorithms, neural networks, artificial financial markets, evolutionary computation

JEL classification: C6, D8, E2, F3, G0

1. Introduction

In the mid to later part of the 20th century, finance witnessed a revolution. The advent of the efficient markets hypothesis, the capital asset pricing model, and the Black/Scholes options pricing formula put the field on a new, solid scientific foundation. This world was built on the assumption that asset markets were powerful computational engines, and were able to aggregate and process the beliefs and demands of traders, leaving in prices the full set of properly processed information currently available. At the core of asset pricing, efficient market theories give a clean and compelling picture of the world which is as appealing to financial economists as it is potentially unappealing to financial practitioners.[1] It is interesting to note that these foundations came with a very important computational dimension. The early availability of large machine-readable data sets, and the computational power to analyze them, laid the critical foundation for this new financial rigor.[2] In agent-based computational models the computer is once again at the center of a change in thinking about financial markets. This time it is helping to pursue a world view in which agents may differ in many ways, not just in their information, but in their ability to process information, their attitudes toward risk, and in many other dimensions.

Models in the realm of agent-based computational finance view financial markets as interacting groups of learning, boundedly-rational agents. The computer may or may not be a necessary tool to understand the dynamics of these markets. This survey will concentrate on the cases where analytic solutions would be impossible, and computational tools are necessary.[3] It is important to distinguish agent-based models from other more general heterogeneous agent models in finance, since the latter have been part of the field for some time.[4] In agent-based financial markets, dynamic heterogeneity is critical. This heterogeneity is represented by a distribution of agents, or wealth, across either a fixed or changing set of strategies. In principle, optimizing agents would respond optimally to this distribution of other agent strategies, but in general, this state space is far too complicated to begin to calculate an optimal strategy, forcing some form of bounded rationality on both agents and the modeler. It is important to note that in these worlds bounded rationality is driven by the complexity of the state space more than the perceived limitations of individual agents. It is also important to remember that the simplified rules of thumb used by agents do not suggest that the exercise is forcing some sort of simplified solution on the dynamics of the steady state or the model, or is presupposing that markets are not well represented by equilibrium rational stories.

---

[1] This view is not far off the more general perspective on information dissemination in the economy as a whole put forth in Hayek (1945).

[2] A good early collection of work from this era is Cootner (1964).

[3] The survey by Hommes (2006) covers the more analytic heterogeneous agent models. Also, the recent book by Levy et al. (2000) provides another survey of recent work in the field.

[4] See Tesfatsion (2006) for more extensive definitions of agent-based approaches in economics.

However, it is stressing that rules of thumb need to be built from a foundation of simple adaptive behaviors.

Financial markets are particularly appealing applications for agent-based methods for several reasons. First, the key debates in finance about market efficiency and rationality are still unresolved. Second, financial time series contain many curious puzzles that are not well understood. Third, financial markets provide a wealth of pricing and volume data that can be analyzed. Fourth, when considering evolution, financial markets provide a good approximation to a crude fitness measure through wealth or return performance. Finally, there are strong connections to relevant experimental results that in some cases operate at the same time scales as actual financial markets.

Academic finance has debated the issue of market efficiency for some time. The concept of market efficiency has a strong theoretical and empirical backing which should not be ignored.[5] On the theoretical side, the argument is that traders with less than rational strategies will disappear, and if prices contain any predictable components either in their own past series, or connected to fundamentals, the remaining rational investors will reduce these to zero. This is very close to the evolutionary arguments put forth in both Alchian (1950) and Friedman (1953) for the evolution of firms and rational behavior in general. This powerful idea still holds sway in much of the academic financial world, and can be seen in papers such as Rubenstein (2001). As appealing as this idea is, it is interesting to note that there never really has been a truly accepted dynamical process describing how market efficiency comes about. The second foundation for efficient market theories, supported by much of the early empirical work on financial markets, is that markets are much more unpredictable than the world of the financial practitioner suggests.[6] In this early literature, the random walk model appeared to be a pretty good approximation for the movements of stock prices, and it can be argued that the same holds true today. We know that markets are probably not completely unpredictable, but they still are very difficult to forecast.[7]

The early ideas of efficient markets were made more formal as modern tools of dynamic optimization were brought to bear on these problems.[8] This led to an even stronger representation for financial markets, the representative agent.[9] This model formally connects asset prices to the beliefs of a single aggregate individual who can then be linked to various state variables of the macroeconomy.

The theoretical parts of efficient markets ideas have been attacked for quite some time. One of the most important questions for market efficiency comes from Grossman

---

[5] The field has been surveyed many places, but the classic surveys remain Fama (1970) and Fama (1991).

[6] Examples are in Cootner (1964) and Fama (1970).

[7] It is also important to note that the radical idea that randomness was a good model for financial prices goes back to the beginning of the 20th century in Bachelier (1900).

[8] See, for example, Merton (1971), Breedon (1979), and Lucas (1978).

[9] Constantinides (1989) is a good example describing the assumptions necessary to get a representative consumer in many cases. Also, Kirman (1992) critically assesses the use of representative agents in many economic contexts.

and Stiglitz (1980). Here, agents have the choice of purchasing an information signal on a financial asset. In a perfectly efficient world with a small cost on the signal, no one would have an incentive to buy the signal. However, if no one bought the signal, how did the market get informationally efficient in the first place? It is interesting to note that many of the papers mentioned here, and in Hommes (2006), are based on the paradoxical structure of this model. More recently, the literature on noise trading, e.g., [DeLong et al. (1990)], introduced the important idea that risk averse rational types may not be able to "take over" the dynamics from less rational strategies, since they trade less aggressively because they are sensitive to the risk induced by the other traders. We will see that this concept plays an important role in many of the computational models considered here.

The attacks on the empirical side of market efficiency have been more controversial. During the 1980's and 1990's evidence began appearing indicating weaknesses with the efficient market hypothesis and related equilibrium theories. There was evidence of predictability at long horizons as in Campbell and Shiller (1988), and at shorter horizons as in Lo and MacKinlay (1988). Old prediction methods which had been previously discredited began to appear again. An example of this was the use of moving average technical analysis rules as in Brock et al. (1992). Also, connections between financial markets and macro dynamics were called into question by papers such as Mehra and Prescott (1988) and Hansen and Singleton (1983). Finally, the single factor CAPM model was shown to be insufficient in Fama and French (1992). Predictability alone did not mean the efficient market was dead. Indeed, in his later survey Fama (1991) is well aware that some studies had found some market predictability, but he correctly reminds us that predictability alone does not necessarily mean that markets are inefficient since profitable strategies may be bearing higher risk.[10]

Beyond simple predictability, there is a large range of empirical financial puzzles which remain difficult to explain using traditional asset pricing models. Among these are the overall level of volatility and long swings around fundamentals.[11] Also, the equity premium, which measures the difference between the real return on risky and riskless assets, is difficult to explain.[12] This feature is directly connected to the failure of macro time series to connect well to financial markets. Series such as consumption are not volatile enough, and do not comove with markets in a way that can justify the magnitudes of risk premia observed in financial series. There have been many attempts to address these issues in the academic finance literature, and these wont be surveyed here.[13]

---

[10] A good recent survey on this literature is Campbell (2000); see also, the textbook by Campbell et al. (1996).

[11] Shiller (2003) is a good recent survey on this.

[12] This one feature has generated an extensive literature which is surveyed in Kocherlakota (1996) and more recently in Mehra (2003).

[13] Two recent models attempting to address many of these features are Campbell and Cochrane (1999) and Bansal and Yaron (2004).

Beyond these puzzles there are a set of facts that are still not well explained by any existing model. Trading volume is probably the most important. Financial markets generally exhibit large amounts of trading volume, and it is difficult to imagine that this can be driven by any situation not involving continuing disagreement between individuals. Beyond the level of volume, there are also some interesting dynamic effects which include persistence and cross correlations with returns and market volatility.[14] Also, volume has recently been shown to be a long-memory process with persistence extending out many periods [see, e.g., Lobato and Velasco (2000)]. At this time no convincing mechanisms exist for any of these features.

Equally puzzling, but more extensively studied, the persistence of volatility is another major feature that lacks an accepted explanation. While the direction of stock returns is generally unpredictable, their magnitudes are often very predictable.[15] Stock markets repeatedly switch between periods of relative calm and periods of relative turmoil. This feature remains one of the most robust, and curious, in all of finance. Although much is known about the structure of volatility persistence, little is known about its causes.[16] Similar to volume persistence, it is also a potential long-memory process.[17] Beyond simple persistence there are some more complicated issues in the dynamics of volume and volatility.[18]

Closely related to volume and volatility persistence is the issue of fat tails, or excess kurtosis. At frequencies of less than one month the unconditional returns of financial series are not normally distributed. They usually display a distribution with too many observations near the mean, too few in the mid range, and again, too many in the extreme left and right tails. This feature has puzzled financial economists since it was discovered by Mandelbrot (1963). Recently, it has gained more attention since practical problems of risk management critically depend on tail probabilities. Precisely tuned complex derivative portfolios need very good estimates of potential tail losses. Return distributions eventually get close to normal as the time horizon is increased. At the annual frequency, the normal distribution is not a bad approximation. Fat tails are not entirely independent of volatility persistence. The unconditional distributions of most volatility persistent processes are fat tailed, even when their conditional distributions are Gaussian. Beyond the frequency of large moves there is a continuing debate about the exact shape of the tails of return distributions. It is possible that these may be described by power laws.[19]

---

[14] Many of these are documented in Gallant et al. (1992) and Gallant et al. (1993).

[15] This has been well known since Mandelbrot (1963), and has led to a large industry of models for fitting and testing volatility dynamics. See Bollerslev et al. (1995) for a survey.

[16] One of the few examples of theoretical models generating persistent volatility is McQueen and Vorkink (2004).

[17] See Ding et al. (1993), Andersen et al. (2003), and also Baillie et al. (1996).

[18] These include connections between volatility and volume to return autocorrelations, LeBaron (1992) and Campbell et al. (1993), and temporal asymmetries in volatility documented in Dacorogna et al. (2001). Also, there are general indications that volatility tends to lead volume, but not vice versa, Fung and Patterson (1999).

[19] Good surveys on power laws in finance are Cont (2001), Dacorogna et al. (2001), Mantegna and Stanley (1999), and Lux et al. (2002). Power laws are difficult to formally test empirically. However, Solow et al.

One of the reasons for this wide range of puzzles is another justification for finance being a good agent-based test bed. Financial data are generally plentiful, accurate, and available on many different aspects of financial market functions. Good time series of up to forty years are available on prices and volume. Series of lengths up to one hundred years are available for lower frequencies, and for certain securities. Over the past twenty years, extremely high frequency data has become available. These series often record every trade or every order entering a financial market, and sometimes include some information as to the identity of traders. Therefore, researchers have a detailed picture of exactly how the market is unfolding, and the exact dynamics of trade clearing. Also, series are available that show detailed holdings of institutions, such as mutual funds, and that record the flows coming in and out of these funds. For individuals a few series have been used that reveal the trades of investors' accounts at various brokerage firms.[20] This gives an amazing level of detail about the behavior of individuals which will be useful in the construction and validation of agent-based models. Finally, experimental data are available that can be used to line up and calibrate agent behavior. Several of the models covered here have already done this, and more examples of using experiments are given in Duffy (2006). Finance experiments are particularly appealing since they often can be done at time scales that are reasonable for the real data. It is more credible that you can simulate a day of trading in the laboratory, than to simulate someone's entire life cycle.

To summarize, financial markets are particularly well suited for agent-based explorations. They are large well-organized markets for trading securities which can be easily compared. Currently, the established theoretical structure of market efficiency and rational expectations is being questioned. There is a long list of empirical features that traditional approaches have not been able to match. Agent-based approaches provide an intriguing possibility for solving some of these puzzles.[21] Finally, financial markets are rich in data sets that can be used for testing and calibrating agent-based models. High quality data are available at many frequencies, and in many different forms.

The remainder of this chapter will summarize recent work on agent-based computational models in finance. The next section introduces some of the computational tools and design issues that are important in building markets. Section 3 covers artificial market models that attempt to recreate an entire market. Section 4 covers a few other types of markets which do not fit into the earlier categories. Section 5 covers some on-going debates and criticisms of agent-based markets, and Section 6 concludes and suggests questions for the future.

(2003) is one framework for attempting to build a test of power law behavior. LeBaron (2001c) provides an example showing how visual tests of power laws can be deceiving.

[20] Barber and Odean (2000) is example of this research.

[21] There are other explanations that may yet prove to be important. These come from the area of behavioral finance which allows for deviations from strict rationality, and emphasizes the presence of certain key psychological biases which have been experimentally documented. See Hirshleifer (2001) and Barberis and Thaler (2002) for recent surveys on this literature.

2. Design questions

In constructing an agent-based financial market the researcher is faced with a large number of basic design questions that must be answered. Unfortunately, there is often little guidance on which direction to follow. This section briefly overviews most of these questions which will be seen again as the setup of different markets is covered in later parts of this survey.

Probably the most important question is the design of the economic environment itself. What types of securities will be traded? Will there be some kind of fundamental value, and how does this move? Is there an attempt to model a large subset of the macro economy or just a very specific financial market? As in any economic modeling situation these are not easy questions. In the case of agent-based models they are often more complicated, since the accepted knowledge of how to craft good and interesting worlds of heterogeneous agents is still not something economists are very good at. It is not clear that the knowledge base for building representative agent macro economies will necessarily carry over into the agent-based world. This design question is probably the most important, and the most difficult to give guidance on.

2.1. Preferences

Agent preferences are an important decision that must be made. Questions about preference types are critical. Should they be simple mean/variance preferences, or standard constant relative risk aversion form? Also, myopic versus intertemporal preferences is another issue. The latter brings in more realism at a cost of additional complexity in the learning process. It is also possible that certain behavioral features, such as loss aversion, should be included. Finally, there may be an argument in certain cases to avoid preferences altogether, and to concentrate simply on the evolution of specific behavioral rules. The use of well-defined preferences is the most comfortable for most economists. Their use facilitates comparisons with other standard models, and they allow for some welfare comparisons in different situations. Most applications to date have stayed with myopic preferences since the added complexity of moving to an intertemporal framework is significant. It involves learning dynamic policy functions in a world which already may be ill-defined.

2.2. Price determination

Many models considered here focus on the fundamental problem of price formation, and the method for determining prices is critical. As we will see, many methods are used, but most fall into one of four categories. The first mechanism uses a slow price adjustment process where the market is never really in equilibrium. An early example of this is Day and Huang (1990). In this case a market-maker announces a price, and agents submit demands to buy and sell at this price. The orders are then summed; if there is an excess demand the price is increased, and if there is an excess supply the price is decreased. The price is often changed as a fixed proportion of the excess demand as in equation (1).

$$p_{t+1} = p_t + \alpha(D(p_t) - S(p_t)). \tag{1}$$

An advantage and disadvantage of this is that the market is never in equilibrium. This might be reasonable for the adaptively evolving situations that are being considered. However, it also may be a problem, since, depending on α, these markets may spend a lot of time far from prices that are close to clearing the market. Another issue is how is excess demand handled? Are excess demanders supplied from some inventory, or is rationing used?

A second market mechanism is to clear the market in each period either numerically, or through some theoretical simplifications that allow for an easy analytic solution to the temporary market clearing price. Two examples of this method are Brock and Hommes (1998) and Arthur et al. (1997). This method reverses the costs and benefits of the previous method. The benefit is that the prices are clearing markets, and there is no issue of rationing, or market-maker inventories that need to be dealt with. There are two critical problems for this type of market. It may impose too much market clearing, and it may not well represent the continuous trading situation of a financial market. Also, it is often more difficult to implement. It either involves a computationally costly procedure of numerically clearing the market, or a simplification of the demands of agents to yield an analytically tractable price.[22]

These two pricing mechanisms take opposite extremes in terms of market clearing. Two other mechanisms fall somewhere in between. The most realistic mechanism from a market microstructure perspective is to actually simulate a true order book where agents post offers to buy and sell stock. Orders are then crossed using some well-defined procedure. Examples of this are Chiarella and Iori (2002) and Farmer et al. (2005). This method is very realistic and allows detailed analysis of trading mechanisms. Its only drawback is that these same institutional details need to be built into both the market architecture, and the learning specifications of agents. Any market that hopes to simulate realistic market microstructure behavior should follow this procedure.

The final market mechanism that can be used is to assume that agents bump into each other randomly and trade if it benefits them. This is closest to a random field sort of approach as in Albin and Foley (1992). A finance example of this is Beltratti and Margarita (1992). This mechanism may have some connections to floor trading as used in the Chicago futures and options exchanges. It might also be a good representation for informal markets such as foreign exchange trading where, until recently, a lot of trade was conducted over the telephone. It would appear realistic for situations where

---

[22] A close relation to this method is to assume that prices are a function of the aggregation of expectations as in Kirman (1991) and De Grauwe et al. (1993). Although trades don't actually take place, these papers do provide a clean mechanism for determining the current period price, and they can concentrate on agent expectation formation.

no formal trading markets have been established. However, it may not be very natural in places where trading institutions are well defined, and function to help buyers meet sellers in a less-than-random fashion.

2.3. Evolution and learning

Much of the agent-based literature has used tools taken from the artificial intelligence literature to model learning. One of these is the Genetic Algorithm (or GA), which is a key component in many, but not all, agent-based financial markets.[23] It is viewed by some as a power tool for modeling learning and adaptation. It is an alternative to more traditional learning approaches such as Bayesian learning and adaptive linear models. It is also controversial in that it is not clear that this is a good mechanism for replicating the learning process that goes on inside market participants' heads.

The most common application of the GA is as a simple optimization technique used in various problem solving situations. It is one of several optimization tools that are useful in situations where traditional hill climbing methods can fail, such as multi-peaked objectives, or nondifferentiable objective functions, possibly with discrete input variables. Although in this context the behavior of the GA is still not completely understood, this is a far simpler setting than the multi-agent models that will be considered in this survey. Many beginning researchers view the GA as a kind of black box, and simply follow previous work in setup and structure.[24] This approach is probably a mistake. It is important to think more about evolutionary computation in general than about the particular pieces of the GA. The general field of evolutionary computation includes other methods such as evolutionary programming, and evolutionary strategies, and genetic programming. For the consumer of these techniques distinctions are somewhat unnecessary, and parts of different methods should be used when the problem warrants it.[25]

Setting up an evolutionary learning framework requires several preliminary steps. First, the mapping from behavioral rules into a genetic structure is important. In some contexts this might involve simply combining real-valued parameters into a vector of parameters, or in some instances it might involve coding real values as strings of zeros and ones. It also may involve taking a complex representation such as a neural network and mapping it into some simpler object. One needs to end up with some type of object that represents behavior and can be easily manipulated by evolutionary operators.

In most evolutionary methods there will be a population of the previously mentioned solutions. In the individual optimization setting the information contained in the population is crucial to aiding in the search for solutions. Attached to each solution or rule is a fitness value. This is essentially the objective function for this potential solution. In the traditional optimization setting this isn't a problem since it is most likely a well-defined

---

[23] More information on genetic algorithms along with many other learning algorithms is presented in Brenner (2006) and Duffy (2006).

[24] Goldberg (1989) is the classic book for early GA adopters.

[25] A nice balanced overview of all these methods is Fogel (1995).

function of the given parameters. This gets more difficult in multi-agent settings where the question of optimality may be less well defined. Given a fitness value, the population can now be ranked. The computer simulates evolution by removing some set of low fitness solutions. The fraction of the population removed is an important design parameter to be decided. Setting this too high may cause the population to converge too quickly to a suboptimal solution. Setting it too low may make selection weak, and the GA may converge far too slowly.

In financial settings agents and strategies can be evolved using either wealth, or utility-based fitness. In the case of wealth, evolution of the agents themselves might be unnecessary since agents gaining more wealth will have a larger impact on prices. Utility is another possible fitness measure. Agents can be evaluated based on ex post utility achieved. Rules or trading strategies are often evolved and evaluated. The simplest criterion is to use a forecast-based measure such as mean squared error, or mean absolute error, and to promote rules that minimize this. Forecasts are then converted into asset demands using preferences. This is a very transparent route, and it is possible to evaluate and compare agents based on their forecasting performance. This also aligns with the bulk of the learning literature in macroeconomics, which often concentrates on forecast evaluation.

A second route is to ignore forecasts altogether and to deal directly with asset demands and strategies. The strategies are then evolved based on their impact on agents' utilities. This may be more difficult than considering forecast errors, but it eliminates an extra step in converting forecasts to demands and is a little cleaner from a decision-theoretic standpoint. In some cases this also avoids the need to estimate variances and other higher moments since risk would be taken into account. Finally, it is important to remember that all these fitness measures will most likely be measured with noise. Furthermore, it is not clear that the time series used to estimate them are stationary. Agents may end up choosing different lengths of history, or memory, in their rule evaluations, which can translate into interesting dynamics. In a nonstationary world, there is no a priori argument for any particular history length. This greatly complicates the evolutionary process, and distances these problems from those often considered in the evolutionary computation literature.

2.4. Information representation

One of the biggest problems in market design is how information is presented to the agents, and how they process it. Theoretically, this is the daunting task of converting large amounts of time series information from several series into a concise plan for trading. To handle this researchers are often forced to predefine a set of information variables as well as the functional structure used to convert these into trading strategies. A second problem is how information is revealed about securities. Are there special signals visible only to certain agents? Are there costly information variables? How frequent are information releases? Unfortunately, there are no easy answers to these questions.

This is another area where technology is often taken from the artificial intelligence literature. In Arthur et al. (1997) a method known as a classifier system is used, which will be described later in this chapter and in Brenner (2006) and Duffy (2006). In Beltratti and Margarita (1992) and LeBaron (2001b) neural networks are used to represent trading strategies. However, strategies can be as simple as a vector of parameters as in Lettau (1997).

2.5. Social learning

How agents learn from each other is another important design question. This is often known as "social learning", and has been the subject of much discussion in the agent-based modeling community.[26] At one extreme, agents may operate completely on their own, learning rules over time, and only reacting with others through common price and information variables. However, in financial settings it may be useful to try to implement some form of communication across agents, or even to transfer rule-based information across individuals from generation to generation. How this information transfer is handled may be critical in market dynamics; these information correlations cause eventual strategy correlations, which can translate into large price movements and other features suggestive of a breakdown in the law of large numbers.

2.6. Benchmarks

The final design issue is the creation of useful benchmark comparisons. It is very important to have a set of parameters for which the dynamics of the market is well understood. This demonstrates certain features in terms of learning dynamics and trading. An important benchmark might be the convergence to a well defined rational expectations equilibrium for certain parameters. The existence of such a benchmark further strengthens the believability of a computational market. Parameter sensitivities can reveal critical factors in a simulation that lead a market towards or away from an equilibrium. Finally, the dynamics of the learning process may be just as interesting in a neighborhood of an equilibrium as far away from an equilibrium. To make this distinction the definition of a benchmark is essential.

3. Artificial financial markets

It is easy to get lost in the many different types of models used in agent-based financial markets. Several approaches are used, and it is often difficult to distinguish one model from the next. This survey will take an initial stand on trying to categorize the many models that exist in a hope that this will help new researchers to better sort out what is

---

[26] See Vriend (2000) for a description and examples.

going in the field. At such an early stage, it is still possible that some may argue about how markets are being categorized, or that some markets belong in multiple categories, or that the categories themselves are wrong. Most of the earliest models were intended to create an entire functioning financial market. They were often referred to as "artificial financial markets." The next several subsections deal with different parts of this literature.

3.1. Few-type models

Most of the earliest artificial financial markets carefully analyze a small number of strategies that are used by agents to trade a risky asset. The advantage of a small set of strategies comes in tractability, and in many cases these models are more analytic than computational. Many of these models follow the early lead of Frankel and Froot (1988), Kirman (1991), and De Grauwe et al. (1993). In these papers it is assumed that there is a population of traders following two different types of strategies, labeled "technical" and "fundamental." Technical traders are generally responsive to past moves in prices, while fundamental traders make decisions based on some perceived fundamental value. The relative numbers in the populations usually respond to past performance of the given strategies. The simplicity of these models makes them an important base case for the more complicated computational models which will be discussed later. Most of these models are analytic, but several with small strategy sets still require computational techniques to get their dynamics. These will be discussed here.[27]

One of the earliest few-type financial market models was developed by Figlewski (1978). This market model examines the impact of shifting wealth across differentially-informed agents in a simple asset pricing framework. In this market agents possess a critical piece of information which might be unrealistic when considering real financial markets. It is assumed that they know the wealth level of the other type of agent in the market. This is critical in forming price expectations across the two types. There is an efficient market benchmark, and many of the simulation runs converge to this. Certain sets of parameters do not perform well in terms of convergence. Among these is the case where one set of agents has better information in terms of signal variance. In this case the simulated variance in the market is 14 percent larger than the efficient market benchmark. Actually, the simulations show that overall market efficiency might be reduced by the addition of traders with inferior information. Though this paper contains little information on the dynamics of prices and trades, it is still an important early reminder on how wealth dynamics affect the convergence to an efficient market.

Kim and Markowitz (1989) are interested in the problem of market instability, and the impact that computerized strategies such as portfolio insurance may have had on the

---

[27] Other important early papers in this area which are discussed in Hommes (2006) are Beja and Goldman (1980), Brock and Hommes (1998), Chiarella (1992), Cont and Bouchaud (2000), Day and Huang (1990), Lux (1997), and Zeeman (1974).

crash of 1987. Portfolio insurance strategies attempt to put a floor on the value of a portfolio through the use of a dynamic trading strategy. As the market falls, investors move holdings to cash to stop their losses. It is obvious that a market with many traders using portfolio insurance strategies can be very unstable. Since the strategy is well defined, this allows for a simple computational test bed to assess their impact. The authors find that price volatility, trading volume, and the size of extreme price changes is increased as the fraction of portfolio insurance traders increases.

3.2. Model dynamics under learning

The papers described in this section are more computational than those mentioned previously. In most cases the small sets of tractable trading rules are replaced with larger sets of strategies, which are usually represented using various computational techniques. These will be referred to as many-type models. This first section concentrates on applications where the economic environment is well understood and where there is often a simple homogeneous rational expectations equilibrium which gives a useful benchmark comparison.

Lettau (1997) provides a good example of a computational model of this type. He implements a financial market model with a set of heterogeneous learning agents, that is simple, transparent, and easy to implement. The model is a portfolio choice environment where investors must decide what fraction of wealth to put in a risky asset. There is also a risk-free asset paying zero interest. The world is a repeated two-period model with myopic preferences based only on wealth in the second period. The risky asset has an exogenously given price and pays a random dividend, d, which follows a normal distribution. The second period wealth of agents is given by,

$$w = s(d - p),\tag{2}$$

and their preferences are assumed to exhibit constant absolute risk aversion which can be parameterized as in,

$$U(w) = -e^{-\gamma w}.\tag{3}$$

This is clearly a very simplified market. No attempt is made to look at the feedback from agents' demands to returns on the risky asset. There is no consumption, and wealth is not linked to agents' impact on asset prices, or evolution. However, it is a very straightforward test of learning in a financial market.

Given the normally distributed dividend process, there is a well-known optimal solution to the portfolio problem given by,

$$s^* = \alpha^*(\bar{d} - p),\tag{4}$$

$$\alpha^* = \frac{1}{\gamma \sigma_d^2},\tag{5}$$

where σ_d^2 is the variance of the random dividend payout. The main exercise in Lettau's paper is to see if and when agents are able to learn this optimal portfolio strategy using a genetic algorithm. In general, agents' policy functions could take the form of

$$s = s(\bar{d}, p),\tag{6}$$

but Lettau simplifies this by using the optimal linear functional form for agent i,

$$s_i = \alpha_i(\bar{d} - p).\tag{7}$$

This gives the agents a head start on the portfolio problem, but they still need to learn the optimal α.[28]

The market is run for S periods with new independent draws of the dividend for each period. Each agent continues to use the portfolio determined by α_i, which remains fixed. At the end of each block of S the genetic algorithm (GA) is run, and the set of agent parameters is redrawn. Agents are parameterized with a bitstring encoding given by

$$\alpha_i = MIN + (MAX - MIN)\frac{\sum_{j=1}^{L}\mu_{j,i}2^{j-1}}{2^L - 1},\tag{8}$$

where $\mu_{j,i}$ is the bitstring for the strategy of agent i. The GA first gets a fitness value for each agent estimated over the S periods using

$$V_i = \sum_{s=1}^{S} U(w_{i,s}).\tag{9}$$

This sets the fitness to the ex post estimated expected utility over the sample. A new population is chosen using a technique known as "fitness proportional" selection. Each agent is assigned a probability using

$$p_i = \frac{1/V_i}{\sum_{j=1}^{J}(1/V_j)}.\tag{10}$$

Then a new population of length J is drawn from the old, with probability p_i assigned to each type. This new population is now the basis for the crossover and mutation operators in the GA. Each new rule is crossed with another rule chosen at random according to a fixed crossover probability. Crossover chooses a midpoint in each of the two bitstrings, and then combines the first substring of one rule, with the second substring of another rule. This new set of rules is then mutated, where each bit is flipped according to a fixed probability. In Lettau's framework the mutation rate is slowly decayed over time, so that eventually mutation probabilities go to zero. This is a form of cooling down the learning rate as time progresses. After mutation, the new population is ready to go back to purchasing the risky asset for another S periods before the GA is run again.

Lettau's results show that in various specifications the GA can learn the optimal parameter for the portfolio policy, nevertheless, there are some important caveats. First,

---

[28] A more complicated functional form is tried, but the only change is that convergence is slowed down by the need to learn more parameters.

the specification of S is crucial. For example, Lettau ran experiments for which the optimal value of α was $\alpha^* = 1.0$. With $S = 150$, he found that the experimentally-determined value of α in his agent population was 1.023. However, for $S = 25$ this average population α increased to 1.12, substantially different from the optimal value. It is not surprising that sample size matters, but this is a fact that can often be forgotten in more complicated setups where this choice is not as transparent. Also, Lettau's estimated α values are all biased above the optimal value. The intuition for this is clear for the case where $S = 1$. Ex post it is optimal for S to be 0 or 1 depending only on the draw of d. Lettau sets the mean, $\bar{d}$, to a positive value, so that, on average, it will be better to hold the risky asset. This leads to an upward bias for the smaller values of S. In larger samples this bias dissipates as agents are better able to learn about the advantages of the diversified optimal strategy. This small bias is an important reminder that learning diversified strategies can be difficult.

This is a very stylized and simplified agent-based market. There is no attempt to model the price formation process at all. Therefore, this cannot be viewed as an attempt to model an actual financial market, in which the dependence between today's price and traders' strategies is the most critical aspect of the agent-based modeling approach. However, it is a very clean and straightforward setup and hence a good learning tool. Also, the biases and sample size issues that it brings up will also pertain to many of the much more complicated models that will be considered later.[29]

In Arifovic (1996) a richer more extensive model is constructed. Once again, the model stays close to a well-defined theoretical framework while extending the framework to include learning agents. The model that is used is the foreign exchange model of Kareken and Wallace (1981). This is a two-country, two-period, overlapping generations model. Agents have income and consumption in both periods of their lives. Agents' only means for saving income from the first to the second period of their lives is through either country's currency.

Agents maximize a two-period log utility function subject to their budget constraints as in,

$$\max_{c_{t,t}, c_{t,t+1}} \log c_{t,t} + \log c_{t,t+1}$$

$$\text{st. } c_{t,t} \leq w_1 - \frac{m_{1,t}}{p_{1,t}} - \frac{m_{2,t}}{p_{2,t}}$$

$$c_{t,t+1} \leq w_2 + \frac{m_{1,t}}{p_{1,t+1}} + \frac{m_{2,t}}{p_{2,t+1}}.$$

$m_{1,t}$ and $m_{2,t}$ denote the money holdings of agents in the two currencies. There is only one consumption good, which has a price in each currency. The exchange rate is given by

$$e_t = \frac{p_{1,t}}{p_{2,t}}. \tag{11}$$

---

[29] Another simple example of this can be found in Benink and Bossaerts (2001).

Given this setup, all agents care about in terms of money holdings are the relative returns of the two currencies. In an equilibrium where both currencies are held, these returns must be equal.

$$R_t = \frac{p_{1,t}}{p_{1,t+1}} = \frac{p_{2,t}}{p_{2,t+1}}. \tag{12}$$

It is also easy to show that the agents' maximization problem yields the following demand for savings:

$$s_t = \frac{m_{1,t}}{p_{1,t}} + \frac{m_{2,t}}{p_{2,t}} = \frac{1}{2}\left(w_1 - w_2\frac{1}{R_t}\right). \tag{13}$$

The model has a fundamental indeterminacy in that, if there exists one price series and an exchange rate paring that constitutes an equilibrium, then there will exist infinitely many such equilibria. One of the interesting issues that Arifovic is exploring is whether the GA learning mechanism will converge to a single exchange rate. Sargent (1993) explored this same question; he found that certain learning algorithms converge, but the final exchange rate depends on the starting value.

The multi-agent model is set up with a population of agents in each generation. Agents are represented with a bitstring which represents both their first period consumption decision, and the fraction of their savings to put into currency 1. A bitstring of length 30 is divided as 20 binary bits for consumption in period 1, and 10 for the fraction of savings put into currency 1. These two values completely determine a period 1 agent's behavior through life. The price level in this model is determined endogenously. The agent bitstrings determine their desired real savings in each currency, which gives the aggregate demand for real balances in the two currencies. Nominal currency supplies are given, so this determines the price level in each currency. This setup avoids some of the complexities that appear in other papers in finding prices.

The evolution of strategies is similar to Lettau (1997). The fitness of a strategy is determined by its ex post utility, and a new population is drawn using fitness proportional selection. Agents are paired, and a crossover operator is applied to each pair with a given probability generating two new children. When crossover is not used, the children are direct copies of the parents. These children are then mutated by flipping bits with a certain probability. The fitness of the new rules is then estimated by implementing them on the previous round of prices and returns. At this point all four of the children and parents are grouped together, and the fittest two of this set are put into the next generation's population. This is known as the *election operator*, which was first used in Arifovic (1994). It is designed to make sure that evolution continues to progress to higher fitness levels.

Arifovic analyzes the dynamics of this market for various parameter values. The results show that the first-period consumption level converges to a stable value close to the optimum. However, the exchange rate continues to move over time, never settling to any constant value. There is an interesting interpretation for this dynamic price process. In the equilibrium the return on the two assets is the same, so the learning agents are indifferent between holding the two currencies. Groups of agents move to holding one currency or another, the exchange rate moves around as they shift demands between currencies. In a model such as this, it is clear that a constant exchange rate equilibrium can only be maintained through some mechanism that shuts down learning and exploration in the model. Arifovic also shows that similar features are obtained in experimental markets.[30]

Routledge (2001) also critically examines what happens when leaning agents are introduced into a well-known model. He implements GA learning in a version of the heterogeneous information model of Grossman and Stiglitz (1980). This is a repeated version of a model where agents can purchase a costly signal about a future dividend payout of a stock. Learning takes place as agents try to convert the noisy signal into a forecast of future dividends. Agents who decide not to purchase the signal must use the current price to infer the future dividend payout. Individual agent representations encode not just the decision on whether to purchase the signal but also the linear forecast parameters which convert the signal into a conditional expectation of the future dividend payout.

Grossman and Stiglitz (1980) show that there is an equilibrium in which a certain fraction of agents will purchase the signal. Routledge (2001) shows that this can be supported in the GA learning environment. However, there are also sets of parameters for which the original equilibrium proves to be unstable. The dynamics of this instability are very interesting. There is instability and exploration going on around the equilibrium, and by chance a few more-informed agents may enter the market. The change in market proportions of informed versus uninformed agents means that the current linear forecast parameters are now wrong. In particular, the uninformed need to learn how to interpret the price with fewer of their type around. Unfortunately, as the number of uniformed agents falls, the ability of their population to learn decreases due to small sample size. Typically the end result is convergence to a situation in which all agents are informed.[31]

3.3. Emergence and many-type models

The next set of artificial market models moves farther from testing specific models and more towards understanding which types of strategies will appear in a dynamic trading environment. All have at their core a philosophy of building a kind of dynamic ecology of trading strategies and of examining their coevolution over time. This methodology attempts to determine which strategies will survive, and which will fail. Also, one observes which strategies will emerge from a random soup of starting strategies, and which are capable of self-reinforcing themselves, so that survival is possible. They also attempt to perform a very direct exploration into the dynamics of market efficiency. If

---

[30] These results are discussed in Duffy (2006).
[31] Routledge (1999) presents similar results in an analytic framework.

the market moves into a state where certain inefficiencies appear, then the hope is that the evolutionary process will find new strategies to capitalize on this. The objective is to explore a market that may not be efficient in the textbook sense, but is struggling toward informational efficiency.

The Santa Fe Artificial Stock Market, SF-ASM, is one of the earliest in this set of models. It is described in Arthur et al. (1997), and also in LeBaron et al. (1999).[32] The basic objective of the SF-ASM is to understand the behavior of an environment of evolving trader behavior, where prediction strategies compete against each other. Part of this objective is to find if and when the market converges to a tractable rational expectations equilibrium. A second part is to explore the dynamics of the computational model for the cases in which convergence does not occur, and to compare these to results from real financial time series.

The basic economic structure of the market draws heavily on existing market setups such as Bray (1982) and Grossman and Stiglitz (1980). The traders have one-period myopic preferences of future wealth with constant absolute risk aversion (CARA) utility functions. There are two assets that agents trade in the market, a risky stock paying a random dividend, d_t, and a risk-free bond paying a constant interest rate, r. The dividend follows an autoregressive process as in,

$$d_t = \bar{d} + \rho(d_{t-1} - \bar{d}) + \epsilon_t, \tag{14}$$

where ϵ_t is Gaussian, independent, and identically distributed, and $\rho = 0.95$ for all experiments. It is well known that, assuming CARA utility functions, and Gaussian distributions for dividends and prices, the demand for holding shares of the risky asset by agent i is given by,

$$s_{t,i} = \frac{E_{t,i}(p_{t+1} + d_{t+1}) - p_t(1+r)}{\gamma \sigma^2_{t,i,p+d}}, \tag{15}$$

where p_t is the price of the risky asset at t, $\sigma^2_{t,i,p+d}$ is the conditional variance of $p + d$ at time t for agent i, γ is the coefficient of absolute risk aversion, and $E_{t,i}$ is the expectation for agent i at time t. Assuming a fixed number of agents, N, and a number of shares equal to the number of agents gives,

$$N = \sum_{i=1}^{N} s_i, \tag{16}$$

which closes the model.

The SF-ASM includes an important benchmark for comparison. There exists a linear homogeneous rational expectations equilibrium in which all traders agree on the model

---

[32] There is also an earlier version of the SFI market which is described in Palmer et al. (1994). This market has one crucial difference with the later market in that it implements an excess demand price adjustment mechanism. The later version uses a form of market clearing.

for forecasting prices and dividends. In the equilibrium it is easy to show that the price is a linear function of the dividend,

$$p_t = b + ad_t, \tag{17}$$

where d_t is the only state variable. The parameters a and b can be easily derived from the underlying parameters of the model by simply substituting the pricing function back into the demand function and setting it equal to 1, which is the equilibrium holding of shares for each agent.

The most important part of the SF-ASM is its implementation of learning and forecasting. This is done with a classifier forecasting system, which is a modification of Holland's condition-action classifier [Holland (1975), Holland et al. (1986)]. It maps current state information into a conditional forecast of future prices and dividends.[33] Traders build their own individual forecasts of future prices and dividends by matching specific forecasting rules to current market conditions. In the classifier system traders can use, or ignore, any part of a predefined set of current information in their forecasts. In the SF-ASM classifiers are used to select between different forecasts that are conditioned on certain pieces of market information. Information is coded into bitstrings, and each bit is connected to different ranges for various indicators. The information bits are classified either as fundamental or technical. Fundamental bits refer to the current price relative to the current dividend level. Technical bits are trend following indicators that refer to the current price relative to a moving average of past prices.[34] A classifier forecasting rule is matched to a specified vector of these conditions, and corresponds to a linear price-dividend forecast of the form

$$E_{t,i}(p_{t+1} + d_{t+1}) = a_j(p_t + d_t) + b_j. \tag{18}$$

The classifier selects the appropriate real-valued pair, (a_j, b_j). Therefore, the classifier selects a piecewise linear forecasting rule which is then used in the demand relationship (15). It is important to note that given the linear structure of the forecasting rule and the rational expectations equilibrium in (17), neither fundamental nor technical bits would provide additional information if the market were in the equilibrium.

At the end of each period, each trader with probability p engages in a learning process to update his current set of forecasting rules for the next period and with probability $(1 - p)$ leaves his current set of forecasting rules unchanged. The probability, p, is an important model parameter that determines the average number of periods between learning for each trader as a function $K = K(p)$. This K is referred to as the "learning rate." Learning takes place with a modified genetic algorithm (GA) designed to handle both the real and binary components of the rule sets. The worst performing 15 percent

---

[33] Classifiers are not used extensively in economic modeling. Examples of other studies using classifiers are Marimon et al. (1990) and Lettau and Uhlig (1999). See Brenner (2006) and Duffy (2006) for more discussion.
[34] The bits code these based on conditions. An individual bit would refer to the test $p_t/ma_t > 1$. If this is true the bit is set to 1, and if it is false it is set to 0.

of the rules are dropped out of an agent's rule set, and are replaced by new rules. New rules are generated using a genetic algorithm with uniform crossover and mutation. For the bitstring part of the rules, crossover chooses two fit rules as parents, and takes bits from each parent's rule string at random.[35] Mutation involves changing the individual bits at random. Crossover also is implemented on the real components of the forecasting rules too. This is one of the earlier applications of a real-valued crossover operator in finance.

One of the objectives of the SF-ASM was to examine the dynamics of learning, and to explore its likelihood of convergence to an efficient market equilibrium. Experiments are performed for two values of the learning rate. A slow-learning experiment sets the average time between runs of the GA to $K = 1000$, and a fast-learning experiment sets the average time between runs to $K = 250$. In the first case, the market converges to the benchmark rational expectations equilibrium, where all agents agree on how to process the fundamental dividend information. They also ignore all other information. In the fast-learning experiments, $K = 250$, a very different outcome occurs. The market does not appear to converge, and it shows several indications of interesting features in the stock return time series.[36] Among these are nonnormal return distributions, or "fat tails", persistent volatility, and larger amounts of trading volume than for the slow learning case. All of these are elements of the empirical puzzles mentioned in the early sections of this chapter. Though the SF-ASM does a good job in replicating these facts qualitatively, no attempt is made to quantitatively line them up with actual financial data. Indeed, the SF-ASM never even clearly states what it considers to be the frequency of the returns series that it generates, or whether the underlying dividend process is realistic.

The SF-ASM has formed a platform for other explorations. Joshi et al. (2000) explore the interactions between the technical and fundamental traders. They find that the use of technical trading bits is a dominant strategy in the market. If all other traders are using technical bits, then it would be in the interest of new agents to use them too. Also, if all other agents are using fundamental bits only, then it is optimal for the new agent to add technical bits as well. This strongly suggests that trend-following behavior may be difficult to remove from a market. The most sophisticated addition to the SFI classifiers is in Tay and Linn (2001), who replace the classifiers with a fuzzy logic system.

The SF-ASM market has generated much interest since its software is now publicly available. It was originally written in the programming language C, then objective-C, and finally ported to the Swarm system. Johnson (2002) gives an overview and critique of the software from a design perspective, and Badegruber (2003) provides an extensive replication and reliability study. It is fair to summarize that the software is not easy to read or use. Much of this stems from its long history on several different platforms. Also,

---

[35] Selection is by tournament selection. This means that, for every rule that is needed, two are picked at random and the strongest is taken.

[36] This parameter sensitivity is closely related to the changes observed in Brock and Hommes (1998) as the intensity of choice parameter is changed.

it began before objective languages were popular, and was only adapted to objective form in its later versions. It was not built to be an objective piece of code from the start.

Another important software replication issue arising from work with the SF-ASM is presented in Polhill et al. (2005). These authors show that the precise trajectory dynamics in the SF-ASM can be altered by making mathematically irrelevant changes in the code. For example one might change,

$$d = \frac{a+b}{c} \tag{19}$$

to

$$d = \frac{a}{c} + \frac{b}{c}. \tag{20}$$

Although these two equations are the same, they generate different code in the compiler. This change appears to have no impact on the general results, but it does impact the exact replication of trajectories. Runs using the two different forms will eventually diverge. This is an interesting reminder about the importance of nonlinearities inside these large systems, and on the difficulties in replicating exact trajectories across different computing platforms. While general statistical properties and features should be maintained, exact replications may be an elusive goal.

In addition to software critiques of the SF-ASM, there are also important design issues to consider. Many of these are covered in LeBaron (2005). Qualitatively, the classifier system has proved to be a very complicated and unwieldy way to model and understand the market dynamics. Many parameters are needed to define the operation of the classifier, and it not clear which of these is important. Also, the implementation of the classifier is often criticized. Ehrentreich (2002) addresses the GA and its impact on the classifier bitstrings. His claim is that the original SF-ASM GA mutation operator was biased, and he implements a new operator that he claims is unbiased. In his modified market bitstrings contains fewer 1's and 0's which connect forecasts to information bits. Also, the emergence of technical trading rules does not occur. This is an interesting modification, but the entire classifier system makes it difficult to judge what is unbiased in terms of mutation. There is a generalizer system which periodically removes bits in the classifier from rules that haven't been used recently. This puts a downward pressure on bit-setting in the Ehrentreich (2002) system. Second, it is not clear whether one has to have an unbiased mutation operator in terms of bitstrings. One could view a biased operator as putting many possible conditional rules out in public view, and then it is the agents' choice to ignore them. The traders are designed to ignore useless rules since the forecast performance of these rules will be inferior to the others. Disagreements about the "right" mechanism here indicate why the classifier system is difficult to implement and completely understand. One major question about the classifier that is left unanswered is how important the definition of the bitstring is to the dynamics of the market. These bit information values are obviously pre-loaded. Finally, another important critique is that by assuming CARA utility functions, the SF-ASM ignores the wealth dynamics of agents. In other words, it is not the case that wealthier agents have a greater impact on prices in the SF-ASM.

If the general goal of the financial markets in this section is to see strategies form out of a general set of functional building blocks with little structure entered initially by the designer, then the model of Chen and Yeh (2001) is probably the best model directly addressing this problem. These authors use a computational methodology known as genetic programming to model agent learning. They allow traders to evolve actual predictor functions for financial forecasting.[37]

The economic setup in Chen and Yeh (2001) is similar to the SF-ASM except that the price adjustment occurs in response to excess demands as in Palmer et al. (1994). Also, demands are based on the forecast of future prices and dividends. This is where genetic programming learning is implemented. The forecast takes the form of

$$E_{i,t}(p_{t+1} + d_{t+1}) = (p_t + d_t)(1 + \theta_1 \tanh(\theta_2 f_{i,t})), \tag{21}$$

where $f_{i,t}$ is evolved using genetic programming. It takes as inputs $p_{t-j} + d_{t-j}$ for $j = 1, 2, \ldots, 10$.

A second important innovation is the use of a common pool of rules, which the authors refer to as a "business school." This allows for some strategy learning to occur across agents in a very natural way.[38] The rules in the common pool are evolved according to forecast accuracy. Traders then decide to update their own strategies based on current performance. They draw rules from the common pool, comparing their performance with their current rules. If the new rule is better they switch, but if they are unsuccessful after several tries, they quit and stay with their current rule.

Simulations of this financial market display some features of actual return time series. They exhibit fat tails, and visually they do not settle down to any price level. However, there are several features that disagree with the actual data. For example, there is a large level of positive skew. Also, the linearly filtered return series are independent, which indicates there may be no persistent effects in volatility. Another interesting feature that the authors test for is a unit root in the price series. The standard tests cannot reject a unit root. This is a little curious since the dividend process is stationary. It is probably sensible that in the long run prices should not diverge too far from the fundamental, and should therefore also be stationary.

Another financial market model is the Genoa artificial market, Raberto et al. (2001). In the original version of their market model the authors used random-order selection, meaning that buy and sell limit orders are generated at random by traders. Traders first determine whether they are a buyer or seller at random, and then place a limit buy or sell order determined by their budget constraints. These limit prices in each case are

---

[37] Genetic programing is discussed in Brenner (2006) and Duffy (2006). There have been some implementations of this technology on actual data as in Neely et al. (1997) and Allen and Karjalainen (1998). The origins of genetic programming go back to Koza (1992).

[38] This is the recurring theme of individual versus social learning; see Vriend (2000).

generated as random variables. In contrast to the previous markets, these traders are generally fairly unsophisticated. As in the study by Cont and Bouchaud (2000) they exhibit a kind of herding behavior. Buyers and sellers group into larger dependent sets, which then move together.

The Genoa artificial stock market has an interesting market-clearing property. The limit orders are all collected after a short period has gone by, and then the market is cleared by crossing the supply and demand curves given by the current limit orders. The market-clearing price is then used to clear all of the trades that can be executed on the limit order book. This interesting batch-order book market is very simple and direct. Similar to the other models discussed earlier, the Genoa market generates uncorrelated returns, fat tailed return distributions, and persistent price volatility.

The financial market model presented in Beltratti and Margarita (1992) and in Beltratti et al. (1996) is quite different from the other markets described here. It is again searching for an emergent pattern in the trading behavior of adaptive agents. However, unlike the previous models, this one has no organized central trading institution. Agents trade in a completely disaggregated fashion in a market where they randomly bump into potential trading partners. This is similar to structures such as Albin and Foley (1992).

The traders build a forecast of what they think the stock is worth using past information and an artificial neural network. The network builds a forecast of the following form,

$$E_{i,t}(p + t + 1) = f(p_{i,j,t-1}, \Delta p_{i,j,t-1}, \pi_{t-1}, \Delta \pi_{t-1}), \qquad (22)$$

where π_{t-1} is the average transaction price at time $t - 1$ across all traders, $p_{i,j,t-1}$ is the last price execution that the trader received, and Δx refers to the one-period change in x. This is an interesting function because it implies the traders are using both local and global information. When two traders meet, they compare their price forecasts. The trader with the larger forecasted price then purchases 1 share from the trader with the smaller forecasted price. The trade is executed at the simple average of the two prices. The market keeps track of the average execution price across the random pairings, and this is included in the information sets of the traders. After a day of trading, traders are allowed to update the weights of their neural networks in a direction that they perceive will improve forecast accuracy.

Beltratti et al. (1996) present many experiments with this basic structure. One of the more interesting explorations tackles the problem of heterogeneous agents with differing levels of complexity. This is covered in Beltratti and Margarita (1992). The population consists of different neural network structures. Trader sophistication is represented by more complicated neural networks. The more complicated structure comes at a given complexity cost, c, that is paid directly by the traders. The simulations show the eventual heterogeneous population depends critically on the value of c. For low levels of c, traders purchase the extra network complexity, and for high levels of c, they eventually only use the simple networks. There is an interesting mid-range of c values where both types of strategies are able to coexist.

In all of the papers reviewed so far, the traders are assumed to behave competitively. That is, they view themselves as having no price impact, and they believe there is little information to be gained by observing other individual's trades. Chakrabarti and Roll (1999) is an interesting exception to this. These authors model an information acquisition process where agents observe other large traders in the market and adjust their own beliefs based on the observed actions of others. This is in the spirit of other sequential trading models such as Welch (1992).

The individual traders receive a signal each period, and they also observe the trades of others. Their own trading strategies are based on optimally forecasting the final payment of the security using Bayesian updating from their initial priors. Though the individual strategies are analytically defined, the final dynamics of the market as a whole requires a computational experiment. The authors employ a novel approach to explore the impact of many different parameters. They run many simulations at randomly chosen parameter values, and record various results. To analyze all this data, they run multiple linear regressions on the parameter values, to observe their impact on empirical market outcomes. This may seem like a lengthy and indirect method to understand parameter sensitivity, but it may be important when there are many parameters, and when the interactions between parameters are not well understood.

The authors analyze many properties of the market, including price volatility, and price prediction error (or tracking). An interesting result is that, when signal diversity increases, price volatility increases, but the price is also a better forecast of future value. This implies that increased trading activity can lead both to greater price movements and to better learning and information-sharing through price signals. This should remind policy makers that simple measures of volatility alone may not always be a good measure of market quality. Other interesting results include the fact that a more diffuse prior on the value of the stock can lead to better learning in the market. This is because, when the traders have less belief in their initial information, they have a greater incentive to glean knowledge from the better informed market as a whole. The authors' model allows for another interesting experiment. One of the parameters of their model is the threshold level at which a trade between two agents is noticed by other traders. Trades which are smaller than this threshold level go unnoticed, but the larger trades are observed. The authors find that reducing this threshold reduces price volatility and increases forecast accuracy. This is again suggests that, in the end, the learning processes in this sequential market are effective although not perfect.

3.4. Calibration

The markets discussed in this section emphasize the replication of many of the empirical puzzles that were mentioned at the beginning of this chapter. In each case the agent-based model itself is less important than the replication of various empirical results from financial market time series.

3.4.1. Memory and return autocorrelations

Levy et al. (1994) presents a financial market model with outcomes emerging from agent strategies.[39] Similar to the market models covered above, these outcomes depend on the presence of many different heterogeneous agent types. However, the traders in Levy et al. (1994) do not form complicated strategies and predictors. Traders maximize a one-period myopic utility function exhibiting constant relative risk aversion rather than constant absolute risk aversion. This technical change is important in that now agents' impact on prices depend on their relative wealth levels.

The economic foundations of the model are similar to other agent-based financial markets. There is a risk-free asset which pays a constant interest rate. There is a risky stock paying a random dividend that follows a multiplicative random walk,

$$d_{t+1} = d_t(1 + z_{t+1}), \tag{23}$$

where z_t is drawn from a well-defined distribution designed to roughly replicate actual dividend growth.

The market consists of several types of traders. There are fundamental traders who possess a model for pricing the stock based on the dividend fundamental. They use this to predict the future price, and to then set their optimal portfolio fraction accordingly. A second, and more important, type for this model uses past information only to determine its current portfolio. This trader looks at the past m periods of returns, and finds what fraction of stock and bond holdings would have been optimal over this period. This is a kind of memory length for traders. It allows for some to believe that only a short period of the past is necessary for forecasting, and others to a believe a much longer series is necessary. The short-memory types represent a kind of short-term trader who is only interested in the latest fads and who believes the older returns data are irrelevant.[40] The memory length history of past returns is used to make a portfolio recommendation for the next period. There is often a population of these traders with many different memory lengths.

The authors progressively add richer sets of the heterogeneous memory traders who trade alongside the fundamental traders. For sets with only one, or two memory types, the stock price dynamics clearly reflect the memory length, in that distinct cycles are observed. However, when a full spectrum of these traders is added, the prices show no perceptible cycles, and display very realistic features. The returns show relatively large positive autocorrelations at shorter horizons and negative autocorrelations at longer horizons. The authors suggest that this is representative of actual markets, where it has been shown that stock returns demonstrate small positive autocorrelation over short horizons, but negative autocorrelation over longer horizons.[41] Many empirical aspects

---

[39] This model is presented in the book, Levy et al. (2000), which also contains useful summaries of many other agent-based markets.

[40] See Mitra (2005) and Sargent (1999) for analysis of short memory, mis-specified forecasting models.

[41] See Hirshleifer (2001) for summaries of these empirical results.

of the model are explored, including large amounts of trading volume, and its positive correlation with volatility. The market also is capable of endogenously generating market crashes. The authors are also very concerned with the coexistence of both the fundamental strategy, and the finite-memory strategies. They give some examples showing the two types can coexist with neither one evolutionarily driving the other out.[42]

The model has been criticized recently by Zschischang and Lux (2001). These authors claim that some of the original results are sensitive to the initial conditions in the simulation. They further indicate that the results may be sensitive to the number of agents in the simulation. This critique is interesting, but it was done for a set of only three different memory lengths of traders, 10, 141, 256. It remains to be seen if it has implications over more general distributions of memory length.

3.4.2. Volatility

One of the most interesting empirical features that various financial market models try to replicate is the persistence of asset price volatility. While stock returns themselves are relatively uncorrelated, the squares or absolute values of returns are autocorrelated, reflecting a tendency for markets to move from periods of relative quiet to more turbulent periods. Significant positive autocorrelations for absolute stock returns continue out a year or more, and decay at a rate which is slower than exponential. This slow decay rate cannot be captured by traditional time series models, and may indicate the presence of fractional integration in volatility.[43] The mere fact that volatility is persistent is puzzling enough, but the fact that it may be fractionally integrated presents a high hurdle for agent-based financial markets to hit in terms of empirical replications.

The model of Iori (2002) is interesting both in its structure and in its ability to fit these facts. The model is based on the spatial spread of information across traders.[44] In this model each trader i in each period t receives a signal $Y_{i,t}$ that combines information about the decisions of this trader's local neighbors. For example,

$$Y_{i,t} = \sum_{(i,j)} J_{i,j} S_{j,t} + A v_{i,t}, \tag{24}$$

where $S_{j,t}$ are the decisions of other traders in the neighborhood of i, and $J_{i,j}$ controls the weighting and the neighborhood size, and $v_{i,t}$ is a noise term. $J_{i,j}$ declines as the distance between i and j increases. This signal is an input into a trader i's final decision

---

[42] Levy et al. (2000) begin to explore some simple multi asset models. Their goal is to begin to understand how well the predictions of the Capital Asset Pricing Model hold up in heterogeneous agent situations. Their early findings are supportive of the CAPM, but the model only allows heterogeneity to enter in a limited way, through mean expectations.

[43] See Baillie et al. (1996) for an example of a fractionally integrated volatility process. Also, see LeBaron (2001c) for further discussion of fractional integration in stock return series.

[44] Other examples of this type of model are discussed by Hommes (2006). These examples include Cont and Bouchaud (2000) and Stauffer and Sornette (1999).

to purchase or sell one share of the stock. The interesting part of this decision is that agents are assumed to have a range of inaction on the signal. For $-w_t < Y_{i,t} < w_t$ there is no trade by agent i, and $S_{i,t} = 0$. When the signal is less than $-w_t$, the agent sells one unit, $S_{i,t} = -1$, and when the signal is greater than w_t the agent buys one unit, $S_{i,t} = 1$.

It is clear that the decisions of trader i in turn feed into the signals of other traders. The traders' belief formation and demand processes are iterated several times until there is convergence. Then the demands to buy and sell shares are calculated as the number of positive and negative values of $S_{i,t}$, respectively, and are recorded as D_t and Z_t. There is a market-maker who covers the order imbalance and who adjusts the price using

$$p_{t+1} = p_t \left(\frac{D_t}{Z_t} \right)^\alpha. \tag{25}$$

Stock returns are measured as the log difference of this price series, and the volatility is estimated with the absolute values of these returns. The model generates returns that are nearly uncorrelated, but the volatility series generates a very persistent autocorrelation pattern which is similar to actual asset return data. Further, the model is also able to display the strong positive correlation between trading volume and volatility that is observed in the data. It also appears that the thresholding of the signals is critical for volatility clustering to occur.

Kirman and Teyssiere (2001) develop another model capable of generating very persistent return volatility. It is a modified version of Kirman (1991) which is described more extensively in Hommes (2006). This model is a form of the earlier-mentioned few-type models in which agents follow a finite set of well-defined portfolio rules. These are defined as technical and fundamental, and the traders shift back and forth between these according to an epidemiological process of contagion. The authors perform extensive tests on the properties of returns generated by the model, and show good qualitative agreement with actual foreign exchange series in terms of long range persistence in volatility.

3.4.3. Macro fundamentals

Several papers have taken the step of trying to tie markets to actual market fundamentals. In Farmer and Joshi (2002) the authors use U.S. aggregate real dividends interpolated to daily frequencies as a fundamental input into market with heterogeneous value investors and trend followers. Their financial market model generates reasonable long swings away from the fundamental pricing as well as uncorrelated daily returns. It also generates most of the important empirical features described in previous sections, including, fat tails, volatility persistence, and trading volume persistence. The model also offers interesting tractability since it is built from a foundation of realistic trading strategies.

LeBaron (2001a, 2002a) performs some extensive calibration exercises. These exercises are based on an agent-based model presented in LeBaron (2001b). This model combines several features of the models mentioned previously. It uses a neural network structure to represent trader portfolio strategies. In this model traders do not build forecasts. The neural network maps past information directly into a recommended portfolio holding directly, and thus avoids the intermediate step of mapping a forecast into a portfolio policy. It also avoids having to estimate the return variance using a separate volatility equation. Traders are defined by heterogeneous memory lengths as in Levy et al. (1994). Some traders evaluate strategies using a short past history of returns, while others use longer histories. Also, the preferences for the agents are constant relative risk aversion, so agents with more wealth control a larger fraction of the market. The strategy population evolves separately from the traders; the traders choose strategies perceived to be optimal based on time series with lengths corresponding to the traders' memory lengths. This has some similarities to the social learning mechanisms in Chen and Yeh (2001). The strategies are evolved using a modified genetic algorithm designed to respect the neural network architecture. Finally, the economic structure is similar to many of the financial market models reviewed above in that there are only two traded assets, a risky asset and a risk-free asset. The risky asset pays a well-defined stochastic dividend following a geometric random walk with drift and volatility calibrated to match aggregate U.S. dividends. The time period in the model is set to 1 week.

The model is compared with values drawn from the S&P 500, and it is able to replicate a large range of features quantitatively. These range from simple statistics, such as means and variances of returns, to the more complicated dynamic features of volatility persistence, and volatility/volume cross correlations.[45] These results appears to be connected to the presence of short-memory traders. Eliminating the latter group leads the market to converge to a well-defined rational expectations equilibrium. Other modifications are shown to improve learning and to induce the market to converge. Among these are slowing down the rate at which agents switch rules, and having them switch strategies only when a new strategy beats the current one by a certain threshold [LeBaron (2002b)]. Both of these operate to slow down the learning process, which one would think would make things worse.

The strategies used in this market are emergent in that they are not prewired into the model. It is interesting to note that the learning process does evolve as the market progresses. LeBaron (2001a) shows that in the early stages of the market, predictability is quite high. Regressions of returns on simple lagged returns can yield R-squared values as high as 0.7. These patterns are quickly learned by agents, however, and this unrealistically high predictability is greatly reduced. It is also interesting that the dividend–price ratio remains a consistently good predictor in many different time periods, which is consistent with results from real financial data.

Bullard and Duffy (2001) introduce learning into a more traditional macroeconomic framework for asset prices. The model is a multiperiod overlapping generations setup

---

[45] An interesting feature is that the model replicates the tendency for volatility to lead trading volume. This is consistent with results in Gallant et al. (1993).

with a constant returns to scale aggregate production technology. Also, important is the fact that the government issues money in the economy at a constant growth rate that is greater than the growth rate of the economy. Therefore, the forecasting of inflation and real returns becomes an important problem for agents in this economy. They forecast future price levels using a recursive regression framework. This learning mechanism yields excess volatility in the asset market. The authors perform a search over their parameter space using a genetic algorithm to find parameters generating results similar to actual data. They find parameter values that are able to give them reasonable volatility in asset returns along with a low volatility in per capita consumption growth. For the most part, the parameter values that generate these results are consistent with U.S. macroeconomic data.

3.4.4. Other calibration examples

This section briefly summarizes several other calibration examples which try to line up with interesting data sets, and scrutinize time series generated by agent-based financial markets. Arifovic and Masson (1999) implement an agent-based model of foreign exchange currency crises which is aligned with empirical results from foreign exchange crises periods. Another model examining foreign exchange markets is Marey (2004) which uses foreign exchange survey forecasts to calibrate agent behavior. Finally, several papers such as Chen et al. (2001) and Arifovic and Gencay (2000) perform detailed tests on the nonlinear properties of the time series output from various agent-based financial markets. They find evidence similar to that from actual markets.

3.5. Estimation and validation

While many market models have been calibrated to financial time series, very few computational models have attempted to actually fit parameters to data in a direct estimation procedure. Obviously, in most computational models this will be a costly procedure in terms of computer time. A recent exception to this is Winker and Gilli (2001) where the authors estimate parameters in the Kirman (1991) model. They search over two parameters in the model with an objective of fitting two features of actual financial returns, kurtosis, and the first order volatility coefficient in an ARCH(1) specification. Since the search space and objective are relatively simple, this paper provides the most detailed view into the sensitivity of the results to various parameter specifications.

Estimation of few-type models has been a much more common activity, and has already yielded some interesting early results. The simpler structure of these models permits their conversion into tractable, albeit nonlinear, time series structures. Vigfusson (1997) is one of the first papers to estimate one of these models. The framework is based on a model by Frankel and Froot (1988) for studying exchange rate movements, which was mentioned in Section 3.1 and is also covered by Hommes (2006). The model is implemented empirically as a Markov switching model, as in Engel and Hamilton (1990), where the two states correspond to fundamental and chartist regimes. Exchange rate predictions are generated as a weighted average of the two different regimes, where the weights are given by conditional probabilities of the two states. Some general support is given to the different conditional forecasts in different states of the world, but some of the results are mixed. Ahrens and Reitz (2005) is a more recent test of a Markov switching model. They find better evidence in favor of the model with chartists and fundamentalists, and they also test several different specifications for the chartist regime. They see an interesting connection between volatility and the types of traders, and many of these results appear robust across different subsamples. They also document an interesting result that volatility is larger during the fundamental regime. This result is interesting, but a little difficult to explain.

Westerhoff and Reitz (2003) and Reitz and Westerhoff (2004) fit a nonlinear threshold model of a financial market to various time series. This model is also inspired by the few-type models with chartists and fundamentalists trading in a market. The model results are generally supportive of the transition between the two different types of trading strategies. They find different market dynamics depending on how close the price is to fundamental value. These are an interesting first test of heterogeneous trader behavior. More extensive tests will be necessary to judge the general robustness of this modeling framework.

A common concern about all agent-based computational modeling is validation. The usual criticism leveled at agent-based financial markets is that there are too many degrees of freedom. Researchers are able not just to move freely through large parameter spaces, but can also change entire internal mechanisms at their discretion in the attempt to fit sets of stylized facts. Anyone using agent-based financial markets must acknowledge that there is some truth to these criticisms. However, these comments should not stop all experimentation. Furthermore, there are directions in which the field is moving that will give these markets a more solid foundation.

Some steps that researchers can take to ameliorate these problems include replicating difficult empirical features, putting parameters under evolutionary control, and using results from experimental markets. The first of these suggestions involves making sure that an agent-based financial market fits facts which are not well replicated by standard models. Examples of this would be empirical features such as the long range persistence of volume and volatility in financial time series. This requirement sets a higher standard for empirical replication, and also pushes the envelope in terms of our understanding about which mechanisms may be at work in financial markets.[46] The second suggestion is to put as many parameters as possible in the market under evolutionary control. An example of this change is reflected in the differences between markets such as the SF-ASM, and LeBaron (2001b). In the first case fixed learning rates for all traders implicitly give them a common perspective on how much past data is allowed into fitness evaluation. It turns out that this parameter is crucial to the behavior of the market. In the

[46] An extension of this is to concentrate model fitting on extreme event periods in the market as in Ecemis et al. (2005).

second case, traders with different perspectives on the past compete against each other. If there were an optimal memory length of past data to use, this would dominate the market in terms of wealth. Thus the setting of this effective value of this parameter is reflected in the wealth distribution of traders in the model, and is part of the evolutionary dynamics. The final suggestion would be to use results from experimental economics to build better, and more realistic learning dynamics in the artificial financial markets. This seems like a promising procedure, but as yet there are not that many examples of it.[47]

4. Other markets

This sections covers several financial market models which are different from those considered above. Among these are markets which consider detailed trading institutions and learning market makers, and also models which consider the coevolution of strategies and financial securities.

Most of the markets considered up to now have abstracted away from actual trading institutions. This is somewhat of a puzzle in the agent-based finance world, since a bottom up approach would appear to call for starting from the basics of how trades are executed. Most models build stylized economic structures that avoid the institutional details of trading. However, research has begun appearing which implements more realistic trading systems.[48] Market design and market microstructure questions appear to be well suited for agent-based approaches. First, large amounts of data are available. Second, there are critical policy questions which clearly need to be tested in an environment with heterogeneous, adaptive strategies. Since some of this area is covered in other handbook chapters, the descriptions of models here will be relatively brief.

It is interesting that Rieck (1994), one of the earliest agent-based financial market studies, specifies the trading process in detail. Rieck (1994) looks at the evolution of trading strategies with a simple order-book trading mechanism. His model has many similarities to some of the emergence papers mentioned in the previous sections in that the coevolution of strategies is the crucial issue of interest. Also, strategies are evolved using evolutionary techniques, but these are applied to functional forms that are designed to replicate actual trading strategies. His results show that fundamental strategies are not able to take over the market and drive the price to the fundamental value. Rieck (1994)'s findings suggest that many results obtained in agent-based financial market

---

[47] Duffy (2006) surveys agent-based models and experimental work. There are several examples given there of agent-based learning mechanisms which fit experimental data. Whether such mechanisms could be taken into settings that are more complicated that the human experimental settings is an interesting and open question.

[48] This area of financial research overlaps with work on market design which is covered more extensively in Mackie-Mason and Wellman (2006) and Marks (2006).

models without detailed specifications for trading strategies could be replicated using more empirically-based micro trading mechanisms.[49]

Much simpler models have been implemented using an order-book trading mechanism with the goal of replicating empirical features of actual market data. One example of this is Chiarella and Iori (2002). This is a few-type model with technical, fundamental, and noise traders placing orders in an electronic order book system. They show that the interaction of these three types generates realistic price series, and trading activity. Just how much agent complication is necessary to replicate high frequency features in financial time series is a question which is addressed in Farmer et al. (2005). This is not exactly an agent-based market since order flow is completely random and there is no individual trading agent per se. Random order flow is calibrated to the actual order flow for several different stocks on the London Stock Exchange. This flow is then fed into a market clearing mechanism with a standard electronic order book. The types of incoming orders, limit or market, are determined randomly and calibrated to the actual order flow from the data. Even though traders in this model have no learning capabilities, the authors are able to show that the outcomes of their model replicate many feature from actual price history data sets. As in the work by Gode and Sunder (1993) on "zero intelligence traders," these results help us to understand which empirical regularities are the result of learning behavior, and which are simply a feature of the trading institution.[50]

One of the most well documented features in intra-day data is the U-shaped pattern in bid ask spreads which are wide at the opening of trading, narrow during the day, and again widen before the close. There are also similar patterns in the volatility of spreads, return volatility, and trading volume as well. Chakrabarti (1999) seeks to replicate these features in a microstructure trading model that uses an agent-based framework for foreign exchange dealers. Dealers receive random order flow through the day which gives them information about the aggregate order flow, and the eventual value of the foreign currency they are dealing in. This information is augmented by quotes they receive from other dealers during the intra-day trading period. Dealers are risk averse and are concerned about variances of their positions during the day, and also on the positions they hold overnight. The reservation prices for these dealers are determined in a Bayesian learning framework. Each dealer determines an optimal selling (ask) and buying (bid) price at each time step. The spread between these is the return that compensates the dealer for risk in the inventory position. Trade takes place in a random matching process of the dealers. They trade when a calling dealer's bid is greater than the responding dealer's ask, or when the calling dealer's ask is less than the responding dealer's bid. Dealers use information from the other dealer spreads to update their own beliefs about order flow as they move through the day. As trading proceeds, all traders' information

---

[49] Yang (2002) replicates many of the SF-ASM results with a microstructure foundation.

[50] A very early example of this type of research on random order flow is Cohen et al. (1983). Another recent research direction has been to link electronic trading agents to live data feeds coming off of actual markets. In the Penn-Lehman Trading Project, Kearns and Ortiz (2003), the survival of different strategies can be monitored as they interact with live market data.

improves, and order flow uncertainty falls. This leads to smaller spreads from the morning into the day. As the day reaches the close, the impact of overnight risk takes over for the dealers and spreads rise again.

The model is simulated for a wide range of parameters values. The author chooses 729 unique parameter value combinations, performs simulation runs for each combination off parameters values and records their results as separate observations. Parameter sensitivity is then determined using least squared regressions. The results show a general presence of the U-shaped spreads of return volatility over the simulated trading days, and these results are robust across many of the tested parameter combinations. An interesting general result is that there is more unexplained variation in the afternoon variables. The author conjectures that this indicates the importance of path dependence of the prices and trades executed through the day. Finally, the nonlinear impact of the parameter values on the results is explored. In most cases there are significant nonlinear effects in both quadratic and cross terms. This suggests a very complex relationship connecting the underlying information and preference parameters to final market outcomes.

Most financial markets depend critically on the behavior of a market maker, or dealer, who brings liquidity and continuity to a real time trading market. Several agent-based models explore the behavior of dealers. Gu (1995) takes the model of Day and Huang (1990) and explores changing the market maker behavior built into the model. This analysis includes estimating the market maker profitability under different parameters. The results show that a profit-maximizing specialist may be interested in generating some amount of extra market churning. The specialist's objectives will not align with price variance minimization which could be construed as the maintenance of an orderly market. Westerhoff (2003c) also explores the impact of inventory restrictions in a setup with an implied market maker. The market maker price adjustment reactions differ depending on the current inventory position along with current excess demands. The market maker is assumed to make greater price adjustments when these two variables are of the same sign. Increasing this adjustment level leads to increased volatility. Although interesting, this result does depend critically on very specific behavioral assumptions made for the market maker.[51]

Most of the papers considered in this survey could loosely be considered part of the investment side of finance. There is no consideration for the issuance of securities by firms, or the design and evolution of securities themselves. A recent exception is Noe et al. (2003) which represents the first paper to consider corporate finance issues in an agent-based framework. The authors are interested in the problem of which securities firms will issue to raise investment capital, and how investors learn to price these securities. Firms need to issue securities that maximize their profits, but cannot do this

[51] A related paper is Chan and Shelton (2001) which models a dealer learning optimal behavior when faced with a random order flow. Further research in the area of market design includes papers examining tick sizes (Darley et al., 2000 and Yeh, 2003), order book versus dealer markets (Audet et al., 2001), and price limits, trading taxes, and central bank intervention (Westerhoff, 2003a, 2003b, 2003d).

independent of investors' pricing strategies. On the other hand, investors must learn how to price and evaluate the securities issued by firms, but they can only do this for securities they have seen in the past. The importance of this coevolutionary process of firm and investor learning turns out to be critical in the authors' model.

In Noe et al. (2003) a firm has an investment project that needs to be financed, and there are two potential investors. The firm can chose from a fixed set of six different securities that it can issue. These include standard debt and equity securities, along with some more complex ones. The latter include convertible and subordinated debt, as well as something known as a "do-or-die" security. In each case the security represents a well-defined contract for splitting the payout to the firm's risky project between the firm and the two investors. Both the firm and investors encode their strategies as bitstrings for use with a GA. The firm maintains a pool of 80 potential security issue decisions which is a vector of numbers (binary coded) between one and six corresponding to the six types of securities. The firm will chose one of these at random each period. The fitness of a strategy is updated with the realized cash flow received by the firm after the investment project has been completed and the investors have been paid. Evolution takes place by replacing all the rules that encode the least profitable strategies with rules that encode the most profitable strategy. Then a mutation operator is applied to all rules.

The investors are encoded as bitstrings. The two investors maintain a price table that indicates the price that they will pay for each possible security. The investor has a table of 80 possible pricing strategies for each security. In each round, each investor choses a pricing strategy at random from the appropriate security table after the firm has decided on the security that it will issue.[52] The security goes to the highest bidder in each round. The profitability of the strategy from the investor's perspective is recorded, and the populations are adjusted with a selection procedure in which the 10 worst strategies are replaced by the 10 best. At this point the GA is applied to the population with crossover, mutation, and the election operator.

The authors then run this simulation for many rounds and in many different design situations. One of the most interesting results comes from the choice of securities. Experiments are performed that try to separate out the joint learning processes. Firms play against a fixed set of investors who know the appropriate pricing functions. In this situation equity and subordinated debt dominate the market, and straight debt is rarely used in stark contrast to the real world. When learning is allowed for both parties, debt moves to becoming the most commonly used security, with subordinated debt next, and equity third. This shows the importance of the coevolutionary learning dynamic. In this world the preponderance of debt may have more to do with the ability of firms to learn how to price this relatively simple security, and the ensuing positive feedback this has on the issuance decision. Several other results from the model are also interesting. Investors tend to systematically underprice the securities in all cases. Also, the situation where the firm is not able to raise sufficient investment funds actually occurs more often with two-sided learning than investor-only learning.

---

[52] As in the earlier GA papers there is a binary-to-real mapping that determines the real valued price.

The results in this paper will eventually need to be explored under different learning specifications and investment structures, but it is an interesting first attempt to use agent-based models in the field of corporate finance. The coevolution of agent behavior along with the institutions that guide this behavior is interesting both for finance and for economics in general.

One final agent-based model which is often compared to financial markets is the minority game.[53] This is a repeated game in which agents must chose one of two doors, left or right. If the minority of agents choses left this group wins, and if the minority chose right this group wins. The connection to finance is through the notion of contrarian strategies, where it is best to move against the herd. Connecting this model to finance is a controversial subject since its basic version does not have a natural role for prices. Also, it would appear that the contrary nature of the minority game is somewhat forced, and in real financial markets it may be better to follow the herd for a short period of time. An interesting application of the minority game to financial data is Johnson et al. (2001). In this model the authors convert a financial series into a binary string depending on whether the price rises or falls. The agents play the game for many periods, watching the real financial time series as the input into their rule selection process. The agents are then allowed to continue playing the game after the price series is shut off, and the continued model dynamics are used in a kind of out of sample forecasting context. They are able to produce some small forecasting gains in some high frequency data. It remains to be seen how robust and reliable these numbers are, but this is an interesting test of the minority game model on real data.[54]

5. Cautions and criticisms

Agent-based markets have been criticized from many different angles. The most common criticism is that the models have far too many parameters, and the impact of many of these parameters is not well understood. This issue has already been discussed in the section on calibration. However, beyond simple parameter questions, these models have made use of a wide selection of the available computational tools and methods. Table 1 gives a short overview of the design structures of some of the agent-based financial market models described in this paper. This is far from being an all inclusive list, since many of the models described in this chapter would not fit well into the criteria for the list. This emphasizes what should have become clear from the earlier sections: agent-based

---

[53] There are several early implementations of this model. These include Arthur (1994), and Challet and Zhang (1997). However, early versions of similar models can be found in Schelling (1978). See Jefferies et al. (2000) for a recent survey. Interested readers should go to the website for the minority game at http://www.unifr.ch/econophysics/minority/.

[54] Another agent-based model indirectly related to finance is the resource allocation setup in Youssefmir and Huberman (1997).

Table 1
Model structures

Authors	Preferences	Price determination	Evolution, fitness	Strategy representation
Arifovic (1996)	CRRA	Market clearing	GA, utility	Real parameters
Arthur et al. (1997)	CARA	Market clearing	GA, forecast	Classifier
Beltratti and Margarita (1992)	CRRA	Random matching	Hill climbing, forecast	Neural network
Bullard and Duffy (2001)	CRRA	Market clearing	OLS, forecast	Real parameters
Chen and Yeh (2001)	CARA	Price adjustment	GP, forecast	GP functions
Chiarella and Iori (2002)	None	Order book	None, none	Real parameters
Farmer and Joshi (2002)	None	Price adjustment	None, none	Real parameters
LeBaron (2001b)	CRRA	Market clearing	GA, utility	Neural network
Lettau (1997)	CARA	Exogenous	GA, utility	Real parameters
Levy et al. (1994)	CRRA	Market clearing	None, utility	Real parameters
Raberto et al. (2001)	None	Order book	None, none	Real parameters
Routledge (2001)	CARA	Market clearing	GA, utility	Real parameters
Tay and Linn (2001)	CARA	Market clearing	GA, forecast	Fuzzy logic

This is a short description of some of the multi-agent computational models considered here along with their design structures described in Section 2. Preferences describe the types of preferences used by agents. Price determination describes the method for determining asset prices. Evolution refers to which computational evolution mechanisms, if any, are used. Fitness is the fitness measure used to evolve strategies, and to determine agent strategy choices. Strategy representation is the way strategies are stored in the computer. Often this is a predefined functional form, and the representation is simply a vector of real parameters. GA stands for the genetic algorithm. CARA and CRRA are constant absolute risk aversion, and constant relative risk aversion, respectively.

financial models have been built using many different features and designs. This is natural for a field at this early stage, but it has made comparisons across market platforms difficult. Unlike analytic models, there are still relatively few general principles that one can confidently apply to the construction of different agent-based market models. This is a problem, but the situation should improve as the field evolves.

Another important issue that is brought up is the stability of a given agent-based model's results to the addition of new trading strategies. Specifically, are there strategies that would smoke out obvious patterns in the data and change the dynamics? Agent-based models are trying to continuously defend against this with the continuously learning agents, but something outside the learning structure is possible. An initial defense of this is that most markets generate very little autocorrelation and therefore yield no obvious arbitrage opportunities for new trading strategies to exploit. However, there is a possibility that more complex nonlinear strategies could detect such opportunities. Arifovic (2001) is an example testing this sort of issue, and finds that the more complicated agents do not do better in her simulated market environment. This problem is still one of the most important for agent-based modelers to worry about, and no one should feel immune to this criticism.

Another very common and pertinent criticism is that most agent-based financial market models assume a small number of assets. Often agents trade only one risky asset, and one risk-free asset alone.[55] It is certainly true that, with all of the new methodological tools in use in these models, it was important to start with the simplifying case of one risky and one risk-free asset. However, this simplification may eliminate many interesting features. The criticisms of models with a single representative agent may carry over equally well to models with a single representative risky asset. Questions naturally arise about calibrating to aggregate dividends, and exactly what this calibration means, since aggregate dividends are not paid by any single stock. Also, recent events such as the technology bubble of the 1990s remind us that bubbles are often very sector dependent. Finally, when thinking about trading volume, it is really necessary to have a multi-asset world where traders are allowed to move back and forth between stocks. The single asset market puts an extreme restriction on the amount of trading volume that can be generated in a simulated market. Another related problem is that, even though most agent-based markets have two assets, they actually shut down pricing in one market. In many cases the risk-free rate is fixed, hence the market is not a general equilibrium model. This is problematic in that explaining the level and volatility of the risk-free asset itself has been another asset pricing puzzle. Getting the risk-free rate to be as low and stable as it is in actual macro data is not easy, and most agent-based models simply avoid this problem completely. Endogenously opening multiple markets for trading is still a difficult problem, but it needs to be addressed at some point. Once researchers are more confident they have mastered agent-based modeling tools, they will probably tackle multi-asset market modeling more frequently.

Egenter et al. (1999) address another interesting question for agent-based modelers to consider. What happens as the number of agents is increased? They have performed some tests on models that can be studied analytically, and they find that the dynamics can change dramatically as the number of agents becomes large. What initially looks like random behavior for small numbers of agents can become increasingly predictable as the number of agents becomes very large. Is it possible that many of the nice features that many models display are artifacts of the limitation to relatively small numbers of traders imposed by computer modeling? This is a very important question. One response to this question is that assuming an infinite number of agents might not be realistic in some settings. There may be real-world market situations in which the thinness of the market is an important and critical issue for the determination of the market's dynamics. This issue will definitely be an important one for the field to tackle in the future.

Almost all of the agents that are modeled and discussed in this survey operate inductively. They adopt rules and forecasts which have performed well in the recent past, and they adjust these rules and forecasts to perform better in the future. The early spirit of agent-based models is clearly to push away from more traditional deductive styles

---

[55] Two recent exceptions to this are Chiarella et al. (2004) and Westerhoff (2004). Also, Levy et al. (2000) perform some experiments in multi-asset settings with options.

of learning and towards more inductive styles of learning. However, it is often asked if there still may be a role for some form of deductive reasoning. Is it going too far to think of agents simply looking for patterns in the past and using behaviors that have worked in the past? Can they be allowed to do some form of deductive reasoning? Can they learn commonly held theories in finance, such as present value analysis, or the Black-Scholes option pricing formula? An interesting question is whether an agent-based model can be constructed that allows for a little deductive reasoning while keeping the general inductive spirit of simple rules of thumb.

A final problem, often ignored, is timing. Almost all agent-based models need to make explicit assumptions about the timing of decisions, information, and trade. Of course, any asset pricing model needs to make these choices, but in analytic settings more events can be assumed to take place simultaneously. In the computer this sequence of events often needs to be spelled out. The degree to which results depend on arbitrary timing decisions is definitely important. One example that has been discussed here is the delayed price adjustment approach, where prices are adjusted based on current excess demand in the market. It is important to note that in a world of evolving strategies, this timing may have a large impact since the strategies themselves adapt to the specific timing and trading structures. It will be interesting to see if agent-based financial models start permitting actions to take place more asynchronously, and if this has an impact on any of the early results.

6. Conclusions

This paper has given an overview of the current state of research in agent-based computational finance along with some ideas concerning the design and construction of working simulations. It is important to note that this is a very young field, and it still shows the kind of open-ended exploratory nature of such an endeavor. However, several crucial trends are starting to appear.

First, the models are beginning to divide into several different types. These range from the few-type models covered in Section 3.1, in which traders are assumed to choose from among relatively small fixed sets of trading strategies, to the many-type models covered in Sections 3.2 and 3.3 in which traders choose from among large and possibly evolving sets of trading strategies. The few-type models offer an important dimension of tractability relative to the many-type models, and they often provide definitive connections between parameters and results which might not be seen or noticed in the more complex frameworks, so it is easy to see their appeal. However, a key reason for doing computer modeling is that the use of more sophisticated trading strategies in many-type models needs to be understood as well. There are two basic reasons for this. First, many-type models take emergence very seriously in that they do not bias toward any particular strategy loaded ex ante by the researcher. The strategies that end up being used are those that appear and persist inside a learning structure. They therefore partially answer a criticism of the few-type models that their specification of trading strategies is ad hoc. Second, they use the computer and the learning algorithms to continuously search the time series record to smoke out new trading opportunities. This is something that is not present in the few-type models. The obvious limitation is that their ability to seek out and take advantage of any inefficiencies that may appear depends critically on the data representations and implementations of the learning algorithms. Few-type and many-type models clearly each have both strengths and weaknesses that users should take into account.

Agent-based modelers are also starting to move from the more stylized earlier financial market models toward models incorporating explicit market microstructure. The latter try to model very explicitly the actual mechanisms of trade that are being used in the market as opposed to building a stylized trading framework. These microstructure oriented models are well designed to answer questions concerning the construction and design of these same trading mechanisms. In some of these markets it is the institutions that are at the center of the investigation, and the agents are just a mechanism for testing their behavior. Some of the policy questions addressed in this work are much more sharply defined than in other agent-based models. An example of this would be the explorations into decimalization on markets, or the implementation of price limits. From a policy perspective this would seem to be a very natural place for the field to move as it matures.

Up to this point very little reference has been made to the growing literature on behavioral finance. It is important to define where agent-based financial markets sit relative to this larger field. First, they are clearly behavioral models themselves, since the agents are boundedly rational and follow simple rules of thumb. This is a key characteristic of any behavioral model, and agent-based models have this characteristic. Where agent-based financial market models have diverged to date from behavioral finance models is their typical presumption that agent preferences have relatively standard representations. Typically, no attempt is made to model common behavioral biases such as loss aversion or hyperbolic discounting. This is not because agent-based models cannot handle these behavioral aspects. Rather, it has just seemed sensible in this early stage of the field to refrain from adding too many more complications to models which are already very complicated. It is important to note that agent-based technologies are well suited for testing behavioral theories. They can answer two key questions that should be asked of any behavioral structure. First, how well do behavioral biases hold up under aggregation; and second, which types of biases will survive in a coevolutionary struggle against others. Therefore, the connections between agent-based approaches and behavioral approaches will probably become more intertwined as both fields progress.

Whether computational or not, all of the models mentioned in this survey share a common tie to ideas from nonlinear dynamics and chaos. The relationship between model structure and noise in nonlinear systems can be very complicated, and these markets share this feature. In many cases the markets operate as noise magnifiers, taking a small amount of input noise, or underlying fundamental risk, and increasing its level to a much larger observed macro value. Noise can also help to stabilize a nonlinear system by keeping it off unstable trajectories. As is well known, nonlinear systems can also be difficult to forecast, and most of the markets described here share this feature. Unfortunately, this may also make them difficult to estimate using traditional econometric tools. Agent-based modelers should be aware of these nonlinear issues, and take them into account when evaluating market simulations.

Financial markets are an important challenge for agent-based computational modelers. Financial markets may be one of the important early areas where agent-based methods show their worth, for two basic reasons. First, the area has many open questions that more standard modeling approaches have not been able to resolve. Second there is a large amount of financial data available for testing. It will be interesting to see if, sometime in the future, financial economists eventually replace the stylized theories of equilibrium market dynamics with a more realistic picture of the continuing struggle of learning and adapting agents who push markets in the direction of efficiency, even though they never quite reach this goal.

References

Ahrens, R., Reitz, S. (2005). "Heterogeneous expectations in the foreign exchange market: Evidence from daily DM/US dollar exchange rates". Journal of Evolutionary Economics 15, 65–82.

Albin, P.S., Foley, D.K. (1992). "Decentralized, dispersed exchange without and auctioneer: A simulation study". Journal of Economic Behavior and Organization 18 (1), 27–52.

Alchian, A. (1950). "Uncertainty, evolution, and economic theory". Journal of Political Economy 58, 211–221.

Allen, F., Karjalainen, R. (1998). "Evolution of trading rules in financial markets". Journal of Financial Economics 51, 245–271.

Andersen, T.G., Bollerslev, T., Diebold, F.X., Labys, P. (2003). "Modeling and forecasting realized volatility". Econometrica 71, 529–626.

Arifovic, J. (1994). "Genetic algorithm learning and the cobweb model". Journal of Economic Dynamics and Control 18, 3–28.

Arifovic, J. (1996). "The behavior of the exchange rate in the genetic algorithm and experimental economies". Journal of Political Economy 104, 510–541.

Arifovic, J. (2001). "Performance of rational and boundedly rational agents in a model with persistent exchange rate volatility". Macroeconomic Dynamics 5, 204–224.

Arifovic, J., Masson, P. (1999). "Heterogeneity and evolution of expectations in a model of currency crisis", Technical report, Simon Fraser University, Vancouver, BC, Canada.

Arifovic, J., Gencay, R. (2000). "Statistical properties of genetic learning in a model of exchange rate". Journal of Economic Dynamics and Control 24, 981–1005.

Arthur, W.B. (1994). "Inductive reasoning and bounded rationality". American Economic Review 84, 406–411.

Arthur, W.B., Holland, J., LeBaron, B., Palmer, R., Tayler, P. (1997). "Asset pricing under endogenous expectations in an artificial stock market". In: Arthur, W.B., Durlauf, S., Lane, D. (Eds.), The Economy as an Evolving Complex System II. Addison-Wesley, Reading, MA, pp. 15–44.

Audet, N., Gravelle, T., Yang, J. (2001). "Optimal market structure: Does one shoe fit all?", Technical report, Bank of Canada, Ottawa, CA.

Bachelier, L. (1900). "Theorie de la speculation", PhD thesis, Ecole Normale Superieure, Paris, France.

Badegruber, T. (2003). "Agent-based computational economics: New aspects in learning speed and convergence in the Santa Fe artificial stock market", PhD thesis, Universitat Graz, Graz, Austria.

Baillie, R.T., Bollerslev, T., Mikkelsen, H.-O. (1996). "Fractionally integrated generalized autoregressive conditional heteroskedasticity". Journal of Econometrics 74, 3–30.

Bansal, R., Yaron, A. (2004). "Risks for the long run: A potential resolution of asset pricing puzzles". Journal of Finance 59, 1481–1509.

Barber, B., Odean, T. (2000). "Trading is hazardous to your wealth: The common stock investment performance of individual investors". Journal of Finance 55, 773–806.

Barberis, N., Thaler, R. (2002). "A survey of behavioral finance". In: Constantinides, G., Harris, M., Stulz, R. (Eds.), Handbook of Economics and Finance. North-Holland.

Beja, A., Goldman, M.B. (1980). "On the dynamic behavior of prices in disequilibrium". Journal of Finance 35, 235–248.

Beltratti, A., Margarita, S. (1992). "Evolution of trading strategies among heterogeneous artificial economic agents". In: Meyer, J.A., Roitblat, H.L., Wilson, S.W. (Eds.), From Animals to Animats 2. MIT Press, Cambridge, MA.

Beltratti, A., Margarita, S., Terna, P. (1996). Neural Networks for Economic and Financial Modeling. International Thomson Computer Press, London, UK.

Benink, H., Bossaerts, P. (2001). "An exploration of neo-Austrian theory applied to financial markets". Journal of Finance 56 (3), 1011–1027.

Bollerslev, T., Engle, R.F., Nelson, D.B. (1995). "ARCH models". In: Handbook of Econometrics, vol. 4. North-Holland, New York, NY.

Bray, M. (1982). "Learning, estimation, and the stability of rational expectations". Journal of Economic Theory 26, 318–339.

Breedon, D. (1979). "An intertemporal asset pricing model with stochastic consumption and investment". Journal of Financial Economics 7, 265–296.

Brenner, T. (2006). "Agent learning representation: Advice on modeling economic learning". In: Tesfatsion, L., Judd, K.L. (Eds.), Handbook of Computational Economics. Elsevier.

Brock, W.A., Hommes, C.H. (1998). "Heterogeneous beliefs and routes to chaos in a simple asset pricing model". Journal of Economic Dynamics and Control 22 (89), 1235–1274.

Brock, W.A., Lakonishok, J., LeBaron, B. (1992). "Simple technical trading rules and the stochastic properties of stock returns". Journal of Finance 47, 1731–1764.

Bullard, J., Duffy, J. (2001). "Learning and excess volatility". Macroeconomic Dynamics 5, 272–302.

Campbell, J., Grossman, S.J., Wang, J. (1993). "Trading volume and serial correlation in stock returns". Quarterly Journal of Economics 108, 905–940.

Campbell, J.Y. (2000). "Asset pricing at the millennium". Journal of Finance 55, 1515–1568.

Campbell, J.Y., Shiller, R. (1988). "The dividend–price ratio and expectations of future dividends and discount factors". Review of Financial Studies 1, 195–227.

Campbell, J.Y., Cochrane, J.H. (1999). "By force of habit: A consumption-based explanation of aggregate stock market behavior". Journal of Political Economy 107, 205–251.

Campbell, J.Y., Lo, A.W., MacKinlay, A.C. (1996). The Econometrics of Financial Markets. Princeton University Press, Princeton, NJ.

Chakrabarti, R. (1999). "Just another day in the inter-bank foreign exchange market". Journal of Financial Economics 56 (1), 29–64.

Chakrabarti, R., Roll, R. (1999). "Learning from others, reacting and market quality". Journal of Financial Markets 2, 153–178.

Challet, D., Zhang, Y.C. (1997). "Emergence of cooperation and organization in an evolutionary game". Physica A 246, 407.

Chan, N.T., Shelton, C. (2001). "An electronic market-maker", Technical report, MIT, Cambridge, MA.

Chen, S.H., Yeh, C.H. (2001). "Evolving traders and the business school with genetic programming: A new architecture of the agent-based artificial stock market". Journal of Economic Dynamics and Control 25, 363–394.

Chen, S., Lux, T., Marchesi, M. (2001). "Testing for non-linear structure in an artificial financial market". Journal of Economic Behavior and Organization 46, 327–342.

Chiarella, C. (1992). "The dynamics of speculative behaviour". Annals of Operations Research 37, 101–123.

Chiarella, C., Iori, G. (2002). "A simulation analysis of the microstructure of double auction markets". Quantitative Finance 2, 346–353.

Chiarella, C., Dieci, R., Gardini, L. (2004). "Diversification and dynamics of asset prices under heterogeneous beliefs", Technical report, University of Technology, Sydney, Australia.

Cohen, K.J., Maier, S.F., Schwartz, R.A., Whitcomb, D.K. (1983). "A simulation model of stock exchange trading". Simulation 41, 181–191.

Constantinides, G.M. (1989). "Theory of valuation: Overview and recent developments". In: Bhattacharya, S., Constantinides, G.M. (Eds.), Theory of Valuation: Frontiers of Modern Financial Theory. Rowman and Littlefield, Totowa, New Jersey, pp. 1–24.

Cont, R. (2001). "Empirical properties of asset returns: stylized facts and statistical issues". Quantitative Finance 1, 223–236.

Cont, R., Bouchaud, J.P. (2000). "Herd behavior and aggregate fluctuations in financial markets". Macroeconomic Dynamics 4, 170–196.

Cootner, P. (Ed.) (1964). The Random Character of Stock Market Prices. MIT Press, Cambridge.

Dacorogna, M.M., Gencay, R., Muller, U.A., Olsen, R.B., Pictet, O.V. (2001). An Introduction to High-Frequency Finance. Academic Press, San Diego, CA.

Darley, V., Outkin, A., Plate, T., Gao, F. (2000). "Sixteenths or pennies? Observations from a simulation of the Nasdaq stock market", Technical report, Santa Fe Institute.

Day, R.H., Huang, W.H. (1990). "Bulls, bears, and market sheep". Journal of Economic Behavior and Organization 14, 299–330.

De Grauwe, P., Dewachter, H., Embrechts, M. (1993). Exchange Rate Theory: Chaotic Models of Foreign Exchange Markets. Blackwell, Oxford.

DeLong, J.B., Shleifer, A., Summers, L.H., Waldmann, R. (1990). "Noise trader risk in financial markets". Journal of Political Economy 98, 703–738.

Ding, Z., Granger, C., Engle, R.F. (1993). "A long memory property of stock market returns and a new model". Journal of Empirical Finance 1, 83–106.

Duffy, J. (2006). "Agent-based models and human subject experiments". In: Tesfatsion, L., Judd, K.L. (Eds.), Handbook of Computational Economics. Elsevier.

Ecemis, I., Bonabeau, E., Ashburn, T. (2005). "Interactive estimation of agent-based financial markets models: Modularity and learning". In: Proceedings Genetic Evolutionary Computation Conference 2005. ACM Press, pp. 1897–1904.

Egenter, E., Lux, T., Stauffer, D. (1999). "Finite-size effects in monte-carlo simulations of two stock market models". Physica A 268, 250–256.

Ehrentreich, N. (2002). "The Santa Fe artificial stock market re-examined: suggested corrections", Betriebswirtschaftliche Diskussionsbeiträge 45/02, Martin Luther University Halle-Wittenberg.

Engel, C., Hamilton, J.D. (1990). "Long swings in the dollar: Are they in the data and do markets know it?". American Economic Review 80, 689–713.

Fama, E.F. (1970). "Efficient capital markets: A review of theory and empirical work". Journal of Finance 25, 383–417.

Fama, E.F. (1991). "Efficient capital markets: II". Journal of Finance 45, 1575–1617.

Fama, E.F., French, K.R. (1992). "The cross-section of expected stock returns". Journal of Finance 47, 427–465.

Farmer, J.D., Joshi, S. (2002). "The price dynamics of common trading strategies". Journal of Economic Behavior and Organization 49, 149–171.

Farmer, J.D., Patelli, P., Zovko, I. (2005). "The predictive power of zero intelligence models in financial markets". Proceedings of the National Academy of Sciences of the United States of America 102, 2254–2259.

Figlewski, S. (1978). "Market efficiency in a market with heterogeneous information". Journal of Political Economy 86 (4), 581–597.

Fogel, D.B. (1995). Evolutionary Computation: Toward a New Philosophy of Machine Intelligence. IEEE Press, Piscataway, NJ.

Frankel, J.A., Froot, K.A. (1988). "Explaining the demand for dollars: International rates of return and the expectations of chartists and fundamentalists". In: Chambers, R., Paarlberg, P. (Eds.), Agriculture, Macro-economics, and the Exchange Rate. Westview Press, Boulder, CO.

Friedman, M. (1953). "The case for flexible exchange rates". In: Essays in positive economics. University of Chicago Press, Chicago, IL.

Fung, H.G., Patterson, G.A. (1999). "The dynamic relationship of volatility, volume, and market depth in currency futures markets". Journal of International Financial Markets, Institutions and Money 17, 33–59.

Gallant, A.R., Rossi, P.E., Tauchen, G. (1992). "Stock prices and volume". The Review of Financial Studies 5, 199–242.

Gallant, A.R., Rossi, P.E., Tauchen, G. (1993). "Nonlinear dynamic structures". Econometrica 61, 871–908.

Gode, D.K., Sunder, S. (1993). "Allocative efficiency of markets with zero intelligence traders". Journal of Political Economy 101, 119–137.

Goldberg, D.E. (1989). Genetic Algorithms in Search, Optimization and Machine Learning. Addison Wesley, Reading, MA.

Grossman, S., Stiglitz, J. (1980). "On the impossibility of informationally efficient markets". American Economic Review 70, 393–408.

Gu, M. (1995). "Market mediating behavior: An economic analysis of the security exchange specialists". Journal of Economic Behavior and Organization 27, 237–256.

Hansen, L., Singleton, K. (1983). "Stochastic consumption, risk aversion, and the temporal behavior of asset returns". Journal of Political Economy 91, 249–265.

Hayek, F.A. (1945). "The use of knowledge in society". American Economic Review 35 (4), 519–530.

Hirshleifer, D. (2001). "Investor psychology and asset pricing". Journal of Finance 56 (4), 1533–1597.

Holland, J.H. (1975). Adaptation in Natural and Artificial Systems. University of Michigan Press, Ann Arbor, MI.

Holland, J.H., Holyoak, K.J., Nisbett, R.E. (1986). Induction. MIT Press, Cambridge, MA.

Hommes, C.H. (2006). "Heterogeneous agent models in economics and finance". In: Tesfatsion, L., Judd, K.L. (Eds.), Handbook of Computational Economics. Elsevier.

Iori, G. (2002). "A microsimulation of traders activities in the stock market: The role of heterogeneity, agents, interactions and trade frictions". Journal of Economic Behavior and Organization 49, 269–285.

Jefferies, P., Hart, M., Hui, P.M., Johnson, N.F. (2000). "From market games to real-world markets", Technical report, Physics Deptartment, Oxford University, Oxford, UK.

Johnson, N.F., Lamper, D., Jefferies, P., Hart, M.L., Howison, S. (2001). "Application of multi-agent games to the prediction of financial time-series". Physica A 299, 222–227.

Johnson, P. (2002). "What I learned from the artificial stock market". Social Science Computer Review 20 (2), 174–196.

Joshi, S., Parker, J., Bedau, M.A. (2000). "Technical trading creates a prisoner's dilema: Results from an agent-based model". In: Computational Finance 99. MIT Press, Cambridge, MA, pp. 465–479.

Kareken, J., Wallace, N. (1981). "On the indeterminacy of equilibrium exchange rates". Quarterly Journal of Economics 96, 207–222.

Kearns, M., Ortiz, L. (2003). "The Penn-Lehman automated trading project". IEEE Intelligent Systems (November/December), 22–31.

Kim, G., Markowitz, H. (1989). "Investment rules, margin, and market volatility". Journal of Portfolio Management 16 (1), 45–52.

Kirman, A.P. (1991). "Epidemics of opinion and speculative bubbles in financial markets". In: Taylor, M. (Ed.), Money and Financial Markets. Macmillan, London.

Kirman, A.P. (1992). "Whom or what does the representative individual represent?". Journal of Economic Perspectives 6, 117–136.

Kirman, A.P., Teyssiere, G. (2001). "Microeconomic models for long-memory in the volatility of financial time series". Studies in Nonlinear Dynamics and Econometrics 5, 281–302.

Kocherlakota, N. (1996). "The equity premium: It's still a puzzle". Journal of Economic Literature 34 (1), 42–71.

Koza, J.R. (1992). Genetic Programming: On the Programming of Computers by Natural Selection. MIT Press, Cambridge, MA.

LeBaron, B. (1992). "Some relations between volatility and serial correlations in stock market returns". Journal of Business 65 (2), 199–219.

LeBaron, B. (2001a). "Empirical regularities from interacting long and short memory investors in an agent based stock market". IEEE Transactions on Evolutionary Computation 5, 442–455.

LeBaron, B. (2001b). "Evolution and time horizons in an agent based stock market". Macroeconomic Dynamics 5 (2), 225–254.

LeBaron, B. (2001c). "Stochastic volatility as a simple generator of apparent financial power laws and long memory". Quantitative Finance 1, 621–631.

LeBaron, B. (2002a). "Calibrating an agent-based financial market", Technical report, International Business School, Brandeis University, Waltham, MA.

LeBaron, B. (2002b). "Short-memory traders and their impact on group learning in financial markets". Proceedings of the National Academy of Science: Colloquium 99 (Suppl. 3), 7201–7206.

LeBaron, B. (2005). "Building the "Santa Fe artificial stock market". In: Luna, F., Perrone, A. (Eds.), Agent-based Theory, Languages, and Experiments. Routledge Publishing. In press.

LeBaron, B., Arthur, W.B., Palmer, R. (1999). "Time series properties of an artificial stock market". Journal of Economic Dynamics and Control 23, 1487–1516.

Lettau, M. (1997). "Explaining the facts with adaptive agents: The case of mutual fund flows". Journal of Economic Dynamics and Control 21, 1117–1148.

Lettau, M., Uhlig, H. (1999). "Rules of thumb versus dynamic programming". American Economic Review 89, 148–174.

Levy, M., Levy, H., Solomon, S. (1994). "A microscopic model of the stock market: cycles, booms, and crashes". Economics Letters 45, 103–111.

Levy, M., Levy, H., Solomon, S. (2000). Microscopic Simulation of Financial Markets. Academic Press, New York, NY.

Lo, A.W., MacKinlay, A.C. (1988). "Stock prices do not follow random walks: Evidence from a simple specification test". Review of Financial Studies 1, 41–66.

Lobato, I., Velasco, C. (2000). "Long memory in stock-market trading volume". Journal of Business and Economic Statistics 18, 410–426.

Lucas, R.E.J. (1978). "Asset prices in an exchange economy". Econometrica 46, 1429–1445.

Lux, T. (1997). "Time variation of second moments from a noise trader/infection model". Journal of Economic Dynamics and Control 22, 1–38.

Lux, T. (2002). "Financial power laws: Empirical evidence, models and mechanisms", Technical report, University of Kiel, Kiel, Germany.

Mackie-Mason, J.K., Wellman, M.P. (2006). "Automated markets and trading agents". In: Tesfatsion, L., Judd, K.L. (Eds.), Handbook of Computational Economics. Elsevier.

Mandelbrot, B.B. (1963). "The variation of certain speculative prices". Journal of Business 36, 394–419.

Mantegna, R.N., Stanley, H.E. (1999). An introduction to econophysics: Correlations and compexity in Finance. Cambridge University Press, Cambridge, UK.

Marey, P.S. (2004). "Exchange rate expectations: controlled experiments with artificial traders". Journal of International Money and Finance 23, 283–304.

Marimon, R., McGrattan, E., Sargent, T.J. (1990). "Money as a medium of exchange in an economy with artificially intelligent agents". Journal of Economic Dynamics and Control 14, 329–373.

Marks, R. (2006). "Market design". In: Tesfatsion, L., Judd, K.L. (Eds.), Handbook of Computational Economics. Elsevier.

McQueen, G., Vorkink, K. (2004). "Whence GARCH? A preference-based explanation for conditional volatility". Review of Financial Studies 17, 915–949.

Mehra, R. (2003). "The equity premium: Why is it a puzzle?". Financial Analysts Journal (January/February), 54–69.

Mehra, R., Prescott, E.C. (1988). "The equity risk premium: A solution?". Journal of Monetary Economics 22, 133–136.

Merton, R. (1971). "Optimum consumption and portfolio rules in a continuous-time model". Journal of Economic Theory 3, 373–413.

Mitra, K. (2005). "Is more data better?". Journal of Economic Behavior and Organization 56, 263–272.

Neely, C., Weller, P., Dittmar, R. (1997). "Is technical analysis in the foreign exchange market profitable? A genetic programming approach". Journal of Financial and Quantitative Analysis 32, 405–426.

Noe, T., Rebello, M., Wang, J. (2003). "Corporate financing: An artificial agent-based analysis". Journal of Finance 63, 943–973.

Palmer, R., Arthur, W.B., Holland, J.H., LeBaron, B., Tayler, P. (1994). "Artificial economic life: A simple model of a stock market". Physica D 75, 264–274.

Polhill, J.G., Izquierdo, L.R., Gotts, N.M. (2005). "The ghost in the Model (and other effects of floating point arithmetic)". Journal of Artificial Societies and Social Simulation 8.

Raberto, M., Cincotti, S., Focardi, S.M., Marchesi, M. (2001). "Agent-based simulation of a financial market". Physica A 299, 319–327.

Reitz, S., Westerhoff, F. (2004). "Commodity price cycles and heterogeneous speculators: A STAR-GARCH model", Technical report, University of Osnabruck, Dept. of Economics, Osnabruck, Germany.

Rieck, C. (1994). "Evolutionary simulation of asset trading strategies". In: Hillebrand, E., Stender, J. (Eds.), Many-Agent Simulation and Artificial Life. IOS Press.

Routledge, B.R. (1999). "Adaptive learning in financial markets". Review of Financial Studies 12, 1165–1202.

Routledge, B.R. (2001). "Genetic algorithm learning to choose and use information". Macroeconomic Dynamics 5, 303–325.

Rubenstein, M. (2001). "Rational markets: Yes or no? The affirmative case". Financial Analyst Journal 17, 15–29.

Sargent, T. (1993). Bounded Rationality in Macroeconomics. Oxford University Press, Oxford, UK.

Sargent, T. (1999). The Conquest of American Inflation. Princeton University Press, Princeton, NJ.

Schelling, T. (1978). Micromotives and Macrobehavior. Norton, New York, NY.

Shiller, R.J. (2003). "From efficient market theory to behavioral finance". Journal of Economic Perspectives 17, 83–104.

Solow, A., Costello, C., Ward, M. (2003). "Testing the power law model for discrete size data". The American Naturalist 162 (5), 685–689.

Stauffer, D., Sornette, D. (1999). "Self-organized percolation model for stock market fluctuations". Physica A 271, 496–506.

Tay, N.S.P., Linn, S.C. (2001). "Fuzzy inductive reasoning, expectation formation and the behavior of security prices". Journal of Economic Dynamics and Control 25, 321–362.

Tesfatsion, L. (2006). "Agent-based computational economics: A constructive approach to economic theory". In: Tesfatsion, L., Judd, K.L. (Eds.), Handbook of Computational Economics. Elsevier.

Vigfusson, R. (1997). "Switching between chartists and fundamentalists: A Markov regime-switching approach". International Journal of Finance and Economics 2, 291–305.

Vriend, N. (2000). "An illustration of the essential difference between individual and social learning, and its consequences for computational analysis". Journal of Economic Dynamics and Control 24, 1–19.

Welch, I. (1992). "Sequential sales, learning, and cascades". The Journal of Finance 47, 695–732.

Westerhoff, F. (2003a). "Central bank intervention and feedback traders". International Financial Market, Institutions, and Money 13, 419–427.

Westerhoff, F. (2003b). "Heterogeneous traders and the Tobin tax". Journal of Evolutionary Economics 13, 53–70.

Westerhoff, F. (2003c). "Market-maker, inventory control and foreign exchange dynamics". Quantitative Finance 3, 363–369.

Westerhoff, F. (2003d). "Speculative markets and the effectiveness of price limits". Journal of Economic Dynamics and Control 28, 493–508.

Westerhoff, F. (2004). "Multi-asset market dynamics", Macroeconomic Dynamics. Forthcoming.

Westerhoff, F.H., Reitz, S. (2003). "Nonlinearities and cyclical behavior: The role of chartists and fundamentalists". Studies in Nonlinear Dynamics and Econometrics 7.

Winker, P., Gilli, M. (2001). "Indirect estimation of the parameters of agent based models of financial markets", Technical Report 38, FAME.

Yang, J. (2002). "Agent-based modelling and market microstructure", PhD thesis, Concordia University, Montreal, Canada.

Yeh, C.H. (2003). "Tick size and market performance", Technical report, Yuan Ze University, Chungli, Taiwan.

Youssefmir, M., Huberman, B.A. (1997). "Clustered volatility in multiagent dynamics". Journal of Economic Behavior and Organization 32, 101–118.

Zeeman, E. (1974). "On the unstable behavior of stock exchanges". Journal of Mathematical Economics 1, 39–49.

Zschischang, E., Lux, T. (2001). "Some new results on the Levy, Levy, and Solomon microscopic stock market model". Physica A 291, 563–573.

Chapter 25

AGENT-BASED MODELS OF INNOVATION AND TECHNOLOGICAL CHANGE

HERBERT DAWID[*]

Department of Business Administration and Economics and Institute of Mathematical Economics, Bielefeld University, Bielefeld, Germany
e-mail: hdawid@wiwi.uni-bielefeld.de
url: http://www.wiwi.uni-bielefeld.de/~dawid/Mitarbeiter/hdawid.html

Contents

[*] I am grateful to Giovanni Dosi, Giorgio Fagiolo, Ken Judd, Leigh Tesfatsion, Klaus Wersching and five anonymous referees for very helpful comments and suggestions.

Handbook of Computational Economics, Volume 2. Edited by Leigh Tesfatsion and Kenneth L. Judd
© 2006 Elsevier B.V. *All rights reserved*
DOI: 10.1016/S1574-0021(05)02025-3

Abstract

This chapter discusses the potential of the agent-based computational economics approach for the analysis of processes of innovation and technological change. It is argued that, on the one hand, several genuine properties of innovation processes make the possibilities offered by agent-based modelling particularly appealing in this field, and that, on the other hand, agent-based models have been quite successful in explaining sets of empirical stylized facts, which are not well accounted for by existing representative-agent equilibrium models. An extensive survey of agent-based computational research dealing with issues of innovation and technological change is given and the contribution of these studies is discussed. Furthermore a few pointers towards potential directions of future research are given.

Keywords

agent-based computational economics, innovation, technological change, evolutionary economics

JEL classification: C6, O3, O4

1. Introduction

Innovation and technological change[1] is today generally seen as one of the driving forces if not **the** driving force of economic growth in industrialized countries (see e.g. Maddison (1991) or Freeman (1994)). Whereas this aspect of economic activity has for a long time been largely neglected in mainstream economics, its importance has by now been recognized and a large rather diversified literature has evolved focusing on different aspects of technological change. Based on the fast growing empirical literature on this issue a rich set of well accepted facts concerning technological change have been established. Concepts of incremental/radical innovations or technological paradigms and trajectories have been developed to capture patterns holding across sectors. Typical patterns of industry evolution and the general importance and structure of knowledge accumulation processes have been established. Also, the existence of heterogeneity in employed technology and firm size within many industries as well as a large degree of sector specificity of patterns of technological change has been observed. The reader is referred to Dosi (1988), Dosi et al. (1997), Freeman (1994), Klepper (1997), Kline and Rosenberg (1986), Malerba (1992), Pavitt (1984, 1999), Rosenberg (1994) for extensive discussions of empirical findings about technological change. Likewise, the set of modelling approaches and tools that have been used to gain theory-based insights about origins and effects of innovation and technological change is very wide including dynamic equilibrium analysis, static and dynamic games, theory of complex systems or evolutionary theorizing. Overviews over different strands of theory-oriented literature can be found e.g. in Dosi et al. (1988), Grossman and Helpman (1994), Hall (1994), Nelson and Winter (2002), Stoneman (1995), Sutton (1997) or van Cayseele (1998).

The aim of this chapter is to highlight and discuss the past and potential future role of the agent-based computational economics (ACE)[2] approach in the important endeavor to gain a better understanding of technological change. Two main arguments will be put forward to make the point that agent-based models might indeed contribute significantly to this literature. First, as will be argued below, predictions of standard equilibrium models do not provide satisfying explanations for several of the empirically established stylized facts which however emerge quite naturally in agent-based models. Second, the combination of very genuine properties of innovation processes call for a modelling approach that goes beyond the paradigm of a Bayesian representative-agent with full rationality and it seems to me that the possibilities of ACE modelling are well suited to incorporate these properties. The genuine properties I have in mind are: (i) the dynamic structure of the process(es); (ii) the special nature of 'knowledge', arguably the most important input factor for the 'production' of innovation; (iii) the strong substantive

---

[1] Throughout this chapter the term 'technological change' will be interpreted in a wide sense to subsume processes leading to generation and diffusion of new knowledge, technologies and products.

[2] No general introduction to the field of ACE is given in this chapter. See e.g. Tesfatsion (2006a) or Tesfatsion (2006b) in this handbook for such an introduction.

uncertainty involved; (iv) the importance of heterogeneity between firms with respect
to knowledge, employed technology and innovation strategy for technological change.

Let us briefly discuss these four points. (i) The dynamic aspects of the process of
innovation and technological change have been stressed at least since the seminal work
of Schumpeter (1934, first published 1911 in German language). Technological change
does not only lead to an increase in overall factor productivity but also has significant
effects on the way the market and industry structure evolves over time. Schumpeter's
trilogy of invention-innovation-diffusion already indicates that the innovation process
per se has a time structure which should be taken into account. In particular, the speed
of diffusion has important implications for the expected returns to innovation on one
hand and for the evolution of the market structure on the other hand. The way innovations diffuse are industry specific and such processes typically involve path dependency
and dynamic externalities. Also the other two stages in the trilogy involve truly dynamic
processes. Investment decisions about innovation projects are typically not made once
and for all but are continuously updated over time. This is necessary due to the substantive uncertainty involved in predicting markets and technological developments as well
as the accumulation of own knowledge (see the comments below)[3].

(ii) The success of innovative activities of a firm does not only depend on its current
investment but also to a large extent on the size and structure of the knowledge base
the firm has accumulated. The stock of knowledge of a firm is not uniform and has a
lot of structure[4]. For example distinctions should be made between explicit and tacit
knowledge as well as between general knowledge and specific skills. A large body of
empirical evidence has demonstrated that the knowledge base (Dosi, 1988) needed for
successful inventions and innovations has to be gradually accumulated over time. Several mechanisms have been identified to gain such knowledge, among them in-house
R&D, informal transfer of knowledge between companies (spillovers) or learning by
doing. In all cases the effect of current actions depends crucially on past experience
and therefore the entire process of knowledge accumulation has to be considered when
studying innovative activities. Studying accumulation of knowledge is however quite
different from studying accumulation of physical capital. Knowledge can only to a certain extent be traded on a market. It is often embodied in individuals and groups of
people ('tacit knowledge'; see Polanyi, 1966), can almost without cost be duplicated
by its owners and has a tendency to flow through several local and global channels of
diffusion. Studying such flows means dealing also with issues of local interaction and
communication network formation. Incorporation of explicit knowledge accumulation

---

[3] Also within the literature dealing with fully rational Bayesian decision makers the importance of the dynamic resolution of uncertainty in innovation projects has been acknowledged leading to the application of a
real-option approach for such decision problems (see e.g. Grenadier and Weiss, 1997 or Smit and Trigeorgis,
1997).

[4] Loasby (1999) provides an excellent discussion of the nature of knowledge and cognition and its role in
economic interactions and development.

processes and non-market interactions between firms into an equilibrium model of technological change might in principle be possible, but this would most probably destroy any analytical tractability and to my knowledge has not been attempted yet.[5]

(iii) The level of uncertainty associated with innovations depends on the type of industry and the type of innovation we are dealing with. Typically a distinction is made between incremental innovations, where minor extensions to existing processes or products are introduced without leaving the current paradigm, and radical innovations which try to open new markets or to employ a new technique or organizational structure for the production of a good. Building beliefs about future returns of an attempt to develop a radical innovation is a very challenging task (see Freeman and Perez, 1988). There is uncertainty not only about the technical aspects (feasibility, reliability, cost issues) but also about market reaction. Whether an innovation turns out to be a market-flop, a solid profit earner or the founder of a new market depends on numerous factors and is ex ante hard to see[6].

More generally, any economic agent operating in an environment influenced by innovations is subject to 'strong substantive uncertainty' (Dosi and Egidi, 1991) in the sense that it is impossible to foresee the content of inventions to be made in the future (otherwise it would not be a new invention) and therefore to anticipate all possible directions of future technological development. Put more formally, the current mental model of the agent cannot include all possible future contingencies. Accordingly, a standard Bayesian approach, which has to assume that the agent ex ante knows the set of all possible future states of the world, is not appropriate to capture the essence of the uncertainty involved with innovation processes. Or, as Fremman and Soete (1997) put it: '*The uncertainty surrounding innovation means that among alternative investment possibilities innovation projects are unusually dependent on 'animal spirits*'. [p. 251]. Furthermore, it has been argued in Dosi and Egidi (1991) that 'procedural uncertainty' referring to the inability of an agent to find the optimal solution in a choice problem—either due to her limited capabilities or due to actual problems of computability—is also of particular importance in many tasks associated with innovation and technological change (see also Dosi et al., 2003). It seems that a rule-based model of the decision making

---

[5] A recent example of a dynamic equilibrium model which explicitly takes into account the heterogeneity of knowledge stocks and spillovers is Eeckhout and Jovanovic (2002). Here spillovers work on a one-dimensional stock variable representing *an aggregate of physical and human capital*. The stock of a firm is updated based on the part of the population distribution above the own stock using a weighted average rule. The interaction leading to exchange of knowledge is not explicitly modelled but the weighting function is estimated using stock market data. As usual in equilibrium the (physical-human) capital stock of all firms grows at a uniform rate.

[6] Beardsley and Mansfield (1978) show, based on 1960–1969 data from a multi-billion dollar corporation, that (discounted future) profitability forecasts for new products were wrong by a factor larger than 2 in more than 60% of the cases, although the study was not restricted to radical innovations. Even 5 years after development of new products forecasts were off by a factor larger than 2 in more than 15% of the cases. See also e.g. Cooper and Kleinschmidt (1995), Hultink et al. (1994) or Fremman and Soete (1997) for more recent discussions of the issue.

process which, on the one hand, makes constraints on computability explicit and, on the other hand, restricts usable information to what is available to the agent at a certain point in time, rather than assuming an ex-ante knowledge about the set of all possible future contingencies, is better able to capture decision making under strong substantive and procedural uncertainty than dynamic optimization models with Bayesian updating or even perfect foresight.

(iv) Finally, the study of processes and effects of innovation requires particular consideration of the heterogeneity between firms in a market. Different types of heterogeneity should be distinguished. I will mention here three types of heterogeneities relevant for understanding technological change, but this is certainly no complete list. First, it has been shown that the basic approach towards innovative activities—e.g. whether to focus efforts on product or process innovation, on incremental or radical innovation or even completely on imitation and reverse engineering—is in many instances quite heterogeneous even within one industry (e.g. Malerba and Orsenigo, 1996). Second, heterogeneity and complementarity of the knowledge held by different firms in an industry is an important factor in facilitating the generation of new knowledge through spillovers as well as in the exploration of the potential avenues of technological development. Third, heterogeneity is not only an important pre-requisite for the emergence of technological change, it is also a necessary implication of innovative activities. The whole point of innovating for firms is to distinguish themselves from the competitors in the market according to production technique or product range, thereby generating heterogeneities. Innovation incentives depend on (potential) heterogeneities between firms. So, whereas heterogeneity of agents is an important property in any market interaction, consideration of heterogeneities of firm characteristics, strategies, technologies and products seems essential if the goal is to understand the processes governing technological change. It is well established by now that in general aggregate behavior stemming from heterogeneous agents cannot be properly reproduced by using a representative agent instead (see e.g. Kirman, 1992) and therefore these heterogeneities should be properly represented in the models used to analyze technological change.

Summarizing the brief discussion of properties (i)–(iv) we conclude that when considering the process of technological change in an industry, we are looking at a highly decentralized dynamic search process under strong substantive and procedural uncertainty, where numerous heterogeneous agents search in parallel for new products/processes, but are interlinked through market and non-market interactions. So already from the purely theoretical perspective that a micro-founded economic model, even if highly stylized, should capture the essential effects influencing the phenomenon under examination, the possibilities offered by agent-based computational models are appealing. The modelling of the dynamic interaction between individuals who might be heterogenous in several dimensions and whose decisions are determined by evolving decision rules can be readily realized using ACE models.

Whereas my discussion so far has focused on the issue of realism of the assumptions underlying a model, there is a second argument of at least the same importance for the use of an ACE approach in this field, namely that of the explanatory power of the model. This is particularly true, if we compare the ACE modelling with neoclassical equilibrium analysis. The problems of neoclassical models to explain and reproduce important stylized facts about innovation, technological change and industry evolution have been discussed among other places in Dosi et al. (1995, 1997), Sutton (1997) or Klepper and Simmons (1997). Here, no extensive discussion of this issue is possible. I restrict myself to sketching a few of the empirically supported observations which are at odds with or at least not satisfactorily explained by a neoclassical approach, particularly if we consider several of these facts jointly (for more details on these 'stylized facts' see the references given above, Silverberg and Verspagen (2005a) and a special issue of *Industrial and Corporate Change* (Vol. 6, No. 1, 1997)).

- In almost all industries a relatively stable skewed firm size distribution can be observed, i.e. there is persistent co-existence of plants and firms of different sizes.
- Persistent heterogeneities between firms with respect to employed technology, productivity and profits rather than convergence to a common rate of return can be observed in many industries.
- In general, there is a positive correlation between entry and exit rates of firms across industries. Industry profitability does not seem to have a major effect on entry and exit rates.
- Patterns of industry evolution and demographics vary considerably from industry to industry. On the other hand, there are strong similarities of these patterns across countries in the same technological classes. In particular, the knowledge conditions shaping the technological regime underlying an industry have substantial influence on the observed pattern.
- The arrival of major innovations appears to be stochastic, but clustering of major innovations in a given time interval is stronger than one would expect under a uniform distribution.

As will be demonstrated in Subsections 3.4 and 3.5, quite a few of these observed patterns can be rather robustly reproduced using ACE models. This is particularly encouraging since these patterns are in no way explicitly incorporated into these models, but are *emergent properties* of the aggregate behavior in complex models, which in many cases are built upon rich micro foundations incorporating at least some of the key features of the processes involved in actual technological change. This highlights another important feature of ACE models: namely, that due to its reliance on computer simulations, this approach can easily link the interplay of individual innovation strategies, market structure and micro effects to the development of industry-wide or even economy-wide variables like average factor productivity, number of firms or economic growth. The emergence of regular macro patterns based on decentralized uncoordinated micro interaction is an important general feature of agent-based models. The fact that ACE models are well able to reproduce actual aggregate behavior under given economic conditions becomes particularly relevant if ACE models are used to predict and evaluate the effects of policy measures that might change the industry or market environment (see e.g. Kwasnicki, 1998 or Pyka and Grebel, 2006 for more extensive discussions of the potential of agent-based modelling in evolutionary economics).

Despite the apparent merit of the agent-based simulation approach for the analysis of a wide range of issues in the economics of innovation and technological change, the amount of relevant ACE-based work in this area is not huge. A large fraction of this work has been conducted in the tradition of the evolutionary economics approach pioneered by Nelson and Winter (1982). However, the amount of work in this area substantially increased during the last few years where also several issues outside the scope of evolutionary analyses were addressed. This chapter will give an overview over the issues addressed in the different types of ACE studies in this area and highlight some examples of the kinds of models which were developed to do this. The presentation will be organized around the two main arguments for the use of ACE models in the domain of the economics of innovation which were discussed in this introduction. I will first illustrate the different ways ACE researchers have tried to address each of the four discussed specific properties of technical change processes in their models.[7] Afterwards, I will discuss a number of ACE models which have been successful in reproducing stylized patterns of industry evolution and economic growth. Although there will be some coverage of ACE models of economic growth, the overall focus of the chapter is on the micro foundations and industry level behavior rather than on economic growth. A more extensive discussion of the potential of ACE models for the analysis of economic growth from a broader perspective can be found in the chapter by Howitt (2006) in this handbook. It is also important to point out a few topics what will *not* be covered in this chapter in spite of their relevance for the understanding of economic change. I will not discuss issues associated with organizational change (this is at least partly covered in the chapter by Chang and Harrington, 2006 in this handbook). I will only touch upon the important relationship between organizational and technological change and the crucial role of organizational structure of a firm for the success of its innovative activities. Also, there will be little discussion of networks emergence and information diffusion models although such models are of obvious relevance for the understanding of several aspects of the process of technological change (e.g. knowledge spillovers, speed of diffusion of new technologies). Models of this kind are discussed in the chapters by Vriend (2006) and Wilhite (2006) in this handbook. See also Cohendet et al. (1998) for a collection of surveys and papers dealing with this issue.

The plan for the remainder of this chapter is the following. In Section 2 the evolutionary approach is briefly discussed and in Section 3 I survey some of the existing

---

[7] Actually, I will explicitly deal only with the importance of knowledge, the effect of the strong uncertainty and issues of heterogeneity. By their very nature ACE models incorporate the dynamic nature of innovation and technological change and therefore this point is not separately addressed. It should be noted however that many game-theoretic results characterizing innovation incentives in different market environments rely on static models. Among many others Dasgupta and Stiglitz (1980), D'Aspremont and Jaquemin (1988), Bester and Petrakis (1993), Qiu (1997). Although using vastly simplified settings these papers make interesting points about strategic effects that might influence the firms choice of innovation efforts. A static setting indeed seems to be a useful way to clearly identify some of these effects, although it should also be considered in how far the obtained insights transfer to a dynamic world.

literature[8] where ACE models have been developed to address issues of innovation and technological change. In Section 4 I will briefly discuss whether my statements in this introduction concerning the potential of ACE research in this domain can be justified based on the work surveyed in Section 3. I conclude with Section 5, where a few challenges and promising topics for future work are highlighted.

2. The evolutionary approach

The dynamic process of technological change has been extensively analyzed in the field of evolutionary economics. The range of work which is subsumed under the label evolutionary economics is quite broad and heterogenous. According to Boulding (1991) *'evolutionary economics is simply an attempt to look at an economic system, whether of the whole world or of its parts as continuing process in space and time.'* Clearly the notion of some kind of 'selection' process which determines the direction of the dynamics is a key concept for most of the studies in this field which also provides the bridge to theories of biological evolution. The idea that behavior of economic decision makers might be determined by a selection process rather than by the application of optimization calculus is not new (see e.g. Alchian, 1950) and has even been used by neoclassical economists to make the 'as if' argument in defense of the assumption of perfect rationality of economic decision makers (Friedman, 1953)[9]. Schumpeter is generally seen as the pioneering figure in the field since he was one of the first to stress the importance of innovation for economic growth and rejected the idea of 'convergence' in favor of viewing the economy as an ever-changing system. Although he rejected the simple application of biological selection metaphors to economic systems, his ideas about technological competition characterized by the interplay of entrepreneurs advancing technology by introducing innovations (thereby earning additional transitory profits) and imitators aiming to adopt them certainly describe a type of selection and diffusion mechanism. The early contributors were however rather isolated and it is fair to say that 'modern' evolutionary economics gained momentum only about 30 years ago. Since then it has been a very active field of research.

2.1. General characteristics of the evolutionary approach

Branches within evolutionary economics have relied on approaches heavily influenced by models of natural evolution to study what kind of behavior emerges in the long

---

[8] The actual selection of papers which are included in this literature review is of course strongly influenced by the available information and the personal bias of the author. I apologize to all authors whose work is not or not properly represented in this chapter.

[9] It should be stressed that the 'as if' argument is flawed for several reasons. The main reason being that it either implicitly assumes global stability of the state, where everyone uses the optimal decision rule, with respect to the underlying evolutionary dynamics—which holds in only few special cases—or implicitly assumes that the initial condition of the system happens to be in the basin of attraction of such an optimal state.

run in a population whose members are engaged in some kind of repeated direct interaction. The huge literature on evolutionary game theory falls into this category (see e.g. Weibull, 1995). Like Schumpeterian and neo-Schumpeterian work this approach is based on population thinking and scepticism towards too strong rationality assumptions about economic agents. Contrary to the Schumpeterian approach the focus is however typically on questions of dynamic equilibrium selection for a given strategy set rather than on the exploration of actual innovation dynamics. More relevant in our context is the branch of literature that interprets the process of technological change as an evolutionary process and thereby applies evolutionary ideas to gain insights into industry dynamics and in particular into the co-evolution of technology and industry structure. Much of this literature was inspired by the seminal work of Nelson and Winter (1982) and accepts computer simulations as a useful and suitable tool to study the properties of the considered dynamic process.[10] Accordingly, the evolutionary approach has been underlying a large fraction of the agent-based work on innovation and technological change. Before I briefly discuss the simulation models examined by Nelson and Winter (1982) I would like to point out some of the arguments and observations concerning technological change made in the evolutionary economics literature which highlight the merit of agent-based modelling in this field. More extensive recent discussions of the evolutionary approach can be found in Dopfer (2001), Dosi and Winter (2002), Fagerberg (2003), Nelson (1995), Nelson and Winter (2002), Witt (2001) or Ziman (2000).

Evolutionary processes in their most general form might be characterized by three main stages: (i) generation of variety by means of individual innovations; (ii) selection based on some measure of 'success'; (iii) reduction of variety due to diffusion and adaptation. The interpretation of the three stages for biological evolution is straightforward but this is less so if we are concerned with the evolution of economic systems. In each of these three stages individuals make important decisions but in an evolutionary view the subject of analysis is not the individual but rather the entire population. The question which company is introducing a certain new technology is of less concern than the question when such a new technology will be first developed in the entire population. Obviously, there are crucial feedbacks between the individual and the population level. Population characteristics are the aggregate of individual decisions, but it is also important to realize that individual decisions in all three stages are in general determined by population characteristics. So, an evolutionary approach always calls for 'population thinking' and highlights the importance of an integrated analysis of the micro and the population level (sometimes called meso level) as well as the feedbacks between the two. The complexity of this endeavor is obvious and calls for simulation methods. This is even more so if one considers the importance of variety (or heterogeneity) for

---

[10] Some of the work on industrial evolution and growth has relied on analytical tools and findings from evolutionary biology like results on replicator dynamics or Fisher's theorem of natural selection (e.g. Silverberg et al., 1988; Metcalfe, 1988).

the understanding of evolutionary processes. The interplay between the generation of variety in the first stage and the reduction of variety by some kind of selection is the fuel of the evolutionary process, which comes to a halt once the population becomes homogenous. Therefore, the explicit consideration of heterogeneity in a population of economic agents is indeed a natural implication of an evolutionary approach.

Another aspect of the evolutionary approach which has contributed to the popularity of agent-based simulation models in this field is the way decision-making processes within the firm are seen. Particularly for work influenced by Nelson and Winter (1982), organizational routines are at the center-stage of these considerations. This view stresses procedural rationality as the key concept for understanding firm's decision-making rather than the neoclassical perfect rationality assumption. Nelson and Winter (1982)[11] argue that firms develop over time routines to deal with situations they are frequently facing. This process is based on feedback learning rather than on perfect foresight or complex optimization arguments. The decision-making process of a firm is characterized by the set of its developed routines and therefore routines have an important role as the organizational memory. Hence, this view on the decision-making process of firms incorporates in a natural way 'behavioral continuity' of firms, which seems to be an important property of actual decision-making in many real world firms (some empirical evidence is cited in Nelson and Winter, 2002).

This behavioral foundation of evolutionary economics has led to a focus on models where decision-making processes are represented in an explicit procedural way rather than by relying on abstract optimization calculus. Such a shift of focus makes agent-based models a natural choice, since they easily allow the incorporation of decision processes relying on sets or even hierarchies of rules (e.g. using classifier systems), whereas such attempts are typically cumbersome in pure analytical formulations and in general do not allow for general mathematical characterizations.

2.2. The analysis of Nelson and Winter (1982)

In this subsection I will briefly discuss a few selected parts of the book by Nelson and Winter (1982). The reasons to do this are twofold. First, the way the analysis is carried out in this book has been quite influential for the way simulation studies of industrial dynamics were motivated, set-up and performed afterwards. Second, quite a few of the agent-based models reviewed in Section 3 are more or less directly based on the models presented in this book.

In part IV of their book Nelson and Winter develop an evolutionary model of economic growth. There are two input factors, labor and physical capital, and firms are characterized by the current values of the input coefficients for both factors and the capital stock. Firms can improve the values of the input coefficients by local search

---

[11] Nelson and Winter build upon previous work, most notably that by Cyert and March (1963) and Simon (1959).

and imitation. There is a fixed supply of labor and wages are determined endogenously based on the aggregate demand for labor. Gross investment is determined by gross profits. Nelson and Winter argue that an evolutionary model of economic growth should be based on plausible micro foundations and at the same time should be able to explain patterns of aggregate variables like outputs and factors prices. They calibrate their model using data reported in Solow (1957) and show that this very simple evolutionary growth model is able to qualitatively reproduce dynamic patters of key variables for Solow's data. The focus on the reproduction of 'stylized facts' using micro-founded dynamic models stressed in this exercise has been a main theme of subsequent evolutionary research on industrial dynamics and growth.

In part V of the book a more complex model of Schumpeterian competition and industry evolution is considered. Firms produce with constant returns to scale a single homogeneous good. Every period each firm is using its capital stock in order to produce output according to its current productivity level. By investing in imitation or process innovation, firms can increase their probability to have a successful imitation or innovation draw. Success means that the draw leads to the adoption of the highest current productivity level in the industry or the development of a new technique whose productivity is random and might be above or below the current best practice (but is only chosen if it is above the firms' current productivity)[12]. A firm is characterized by its fraction of profits invested for imitation and innovation and by its investment function, which determines desired expansion or contraction of capital based on observed price-cost margin, market-share, profit and the physical depreciation rate. Since the entire capital stock is always employed in production, the investment function is crucial for the determination of the production quantities of the firm.

In all sets of simulations these characteristics of firms are fixed over time. However, there are initial heterogeneities between firms with respect to their innovation strategies. In particular, it is assumed that the industry is a mix of imitators (investing only in imitative R&D) and innovators (investing in imitative and innovative R&D). The different paces of capital accumulation and exit of single firms therefore lead to selection effects of behavior on the industry level. The analysis of the simulation runs focuses on the long run outcomes (after 100 periods) of industry evolution with respect to the distribution of productivity, the degree of industry concentration and the relative performance of innovators and imitators. In a first step these long run outcomes are compared for a science-based industry across scenarios characterized by different degrees of initial concentration. It turns out that average productivity is larger for more concentrated industries but no strict positive relationship between concentration and cumulative expenditures on innovative R&D can be observed. Innovators are on average

---

[12] Nelson and Winter distinguish the cases of 'cumulative' and 'science-based' technological advance. Whereas in the first case the expected productivity of a new technology equals the firms current productivity, for science-based industries the expectation of the productivity of a new technology equals an exogenously given parameter called 'latent productivity'. Latent productivity is supposed to represent the technological possibilities created outside the industry (public research labs, universities) and grows at a given rate.

less profitable than imitators but some still survive in the industry. In a second step Nelson and Winter analyze the impact of several industry characteristics (aggressiveness of investment policies, difficulty of imitation, rate of latent productivity growth, variability of innovation outcomes) on the degree of long run concentration. The simulations show that among these factors the aggressiveness of investment policies is most crucial for determining the long run industry concentration. More aggressive investment behavior leads to higher concentration. Also the direction of the impact of the other considered factors is quite intuitive but less pronounced.

The model and the analysis of Nelson and Winter (1982) is extended in Winter (1984). Two main changes with respect to the model are introduced: (i) the innovation strategies are adaptive, firms increase or decrease spending for innovative and imitative R&D based on the past average success of these activities; (ii) if return on capital in the industry is high, additional firms might enter the industry. The focus of the analysis is on the comparison of two technological regimes, the entrepreneurial and the routinized regime, which loosely correspond to the different descriptions of the innovation process in Schumpeter's early writings and in his later work. The main difference between the regimes is that in the entrepreneurial regime a larger number of innovation attempts is made outside the industry but the probability of success for a single innovation attempt is smaller. The parameters are chosen such that these two effects are balanced and the expected number of potential entrants, who have succeeded with an innovation, are identical in both regimes. The simulations show quite distinct patterns of industry evolution under the two regimes. In particular, the routinized regime results in much smoother dynamics for the best practice-technology in the industry, in a higher degree of concentration and in higher R&D expenses in the long run. These observed qualitative differences match well with Schumpeter's description of industry evolution before and after the 'industrialization' of R&D.

These pioneering simulation studies of the interplay of industry evolution and technological change already nicely highlight some of the merits of the agent-based approach for the study of innovation dynamics. Firms are rule-based autonomous agents that differ not only with respect to capital stock and employed technology but also with respect to their production and innovation strategy. The interplay between the dynamics of industry concentration and the dynamics of productivity distribution generates feedback effects with non-trivial implications for the long run outcome. The consideration of different scenarios characterized by different constellations of technological parameters (difficulty of imitation) or strategy characteristics (aggressiveness of investment policies) allows a modeller to evaluate how sensitive results depend on the 'type' of the industry considered. The possibility of such 'laboratory experiments' are indeed an important feature of ACE modelling (see e.g. Tesfatsion, 2006a). On the other hand, certain aspects are highly simplified in the original Nelson and Winter model and, due to the large impact this work has had on subsequent research in this direction, this holds in a similar way for quite a bit of work in the evolutionary tradition to be reviewed in the next section. I will mention three points here: (i) the assumption that firms never adapt their decision rules[13]; (ii) the lack of any explicit-structure governing interactions between firms and the shape of externalities[14]; (iii) the representation of the process of technological change leaves a large black box between the inflowing funds and the resulting productivity increase. Innovation probabilities only depend on current investments, there is no accumulation of research investment and also no explicit role for knowledge accumulation at the firm[15]. The mechanistic nature of the innovation process also leaves no room for considering the direction of the innovative activities of the individual firm (and the direction of technological change as a whole) and the timing of the *introduction* of innovations. Additional structure at the firm level is needed to address such issues.

3. Agent-based models of technological change

In this section I will discuss a number of ACE studies dealing with different aspects of innovation and technological change. The presentation is organized according to the main themes discussed in the introduction. I will first focus again on the four important properties of technological change processes discussed in the introduction. For each of the properties (ii)–(iv)[16] I will discuss examples of ACE models addressing this issue. In Subsection 3.5 I will then shift focus to the power of ACE models to reproduce stylized facts and discuss the success of agent-based growth models in this respect. The final subsection of Section 3 will then be dedicated to a stream of research where detailed models of the evolution of specific industries are developed using an agent-based approach.

3.1. Knowledge accumulation, knowledge structure and spillovers

The success of innovative activities of a firm does not only depend on its current investment but also to a large extent on the size and structure of the knowledge base the firm has accumulated. The stock of knowledge of a firm is not uniform and has a lot of structure. For example, distinctions should be made between explicit and tacit knowledge as well as between general knowledge and specific skills. There is vast empirical evidence (see e.g. Griliches, 1992; Geroski, 1996) for the relevance of technological spillovers

---

[13] Of course this point does not hold for the extension of the model in Winter (1984). An extension of Nelson and Winter's model of Schumpeterian competition, where firms can adapt their R&D strategy was recently considered in Yildizoglu (2002).

[14] See however Jonard and Yildizoglu (1998) for a formulation of the Nelson and Winter model in a spatial setting.

[15] For cumulative industries the current productivity of the firm might however be seen as a proxy for the knowledge stock of the firm at the time of its most recent innovation.

[16] All ACE models discussed are dynamic, so no separate discussion of models incorporating property (i) ('dynamics') is provided.

representing knowledge flows between firms or individuals. Cohen and Levinthal (1989) have provided empirical evidence that the extent of spillovers flowing into a firm depends on the firms own R&D efforts. Rosenberg (1990) argues that different types of research efforts have to be distinguished in this respect and particularly that *basic* research capability is essential to enable absorption of knowledge generated elsewhere. Existing analytical approaches and also papers using the Nelson and Winter framework typically do not consider the dynamic accumulation of a *structured* knowledge base of firms competing in a market. Knowledge accumulation is treated either implicitly, by assuming that all current knowledge is embodied in the technology currently used, or by considering a simple R&D stock variable which is increased by investments over time[17].

Using agent-based simulations allows a modeller to add some of the empirically relevant structure to the standard models of knowledge accumulation and spillovers. Cantner and Pyka (1998) consider a dynamic heterogenous oligopoly model, where firms allocate their R&D expenditures between investment in an R&D capital stock and the increase of their absorptive capacity. Firms might carry out product and process innovations where the probability for a successful innovation of a firm depends on its R&D capital stock and on the size of spillovers. It is assumed that the size of the spillovers flowing into a firm depends on the accumulated absorptive capacity of the firm, on the variance of the unit costs (for process innovations), respectively product quality (for product innovations) and on the relative position of the firm in the industry with respect to process respectively product technology. Motivated by empirical observations, a bell shaped relationship is used. Spillovers are small for firms close to the frontier of industry technology and for firms too far behind but large for firms whose gap to the frontier is in an intermediate range. Both the bell-shaped spillover function and the fact that the size of spillovers depends on the heterogeneity of the technologies used in the population stresses the point that received information only increases knowledge if it is complementary to the firm's current knowledge. This point is often ignored in models of technological spillovers.

The authors run simulations for scenarios where all firms have identical fixed R&D quotas but differ with respect to the share of investments used for building absorptive capacity (the decision rules of all firms are fixed over time). Comparing the firms profits, Cantner and Pyka find that initially the firm with zero minimal investment for building absorptive capacity is most profitable, but if potential spillovers are large this is only a transient phenomenon. In such a scenario firms who accumulated absorptive capacity eventually become more profitable than firms solely relying on the own R&D stock. The

---

[17] There are a few exceptions like Jovanovic and Nyarko (1996), who develop a Bayesian model of learning by doing and technology choice which explicitly takes into account that agents develop expertise specific to their current technology and also deals with spillover effects. However, they treat competition only in a very rudimentary way. Cassiman et al. (2002) analyze a static dominant firm model where the firm allocates R&D investments between basic and applied research.

long run profitability of building absorptive capacity is however jeopardized if appropriability conditions are relatively high and cross effects between the different markets are relatively low.

Similar in spirit is the work of Ballot and Taymaz (1997) who analyze an extensive micro-macro simulation model based on a model of the Swedish economy by Eliason (1991). Firms in their model can, through training, build stocks of specific skills enabling them to increase productivity and stocks of general knowledge which increase the probability for successful radical innovations. One of their numerous interesting findings is that there is a positive statistical relationship between a firms' early investment in general knowledge and the profit rate, while, with the exception of a few periods, there is always a negative relationship between a firm's specific human capital and the profit rate. Their conclusion is that R&D investments should be preceded by a buildup of general knowledge since *innovators with a strong knowledge base fare better in the long run* [p. 455]. Also in this paper the firms' strategies allocating resources between the different types of training are fixed over time. An extension where the strategies are updated via a classifier system has been considered in Ballot and Taymaz (1999) but the focus there is on growth issues and it is not reported how far the findings concerning knowledge accumulation change with adaptive strategies.

In their work on innovation networks Gilbert et al. (2000, 2001) have developed a way to model knowledge and capabilities of a firm in substantially more detail. The model is part of a general simulation platform which is intended to be used to simulate and reproduce the evolution of innovation networks in various real world industries. The knowledge base of an agent here is represented by a 'kene' which is a collection of triples, each triple giving a technological capability, a corresponding specific ability and a cardinal value describing the agent's level of expertise for this specific ability. Agents develop innovation hypotheses by randomly selecting a set of triplets from their kene. This selection is supposed to capture the current research direction of the agent. The abilities and levels of expertise involved in this hypothesis determines the financial reward which might be gained by this innovation. To capture learning by doing effects the levels of expertise for abilities involved in the current research direction are increased, whereas the expertise for abilities not currently needed are decreased and might eventually vanish. If the financial reward of an innovation hypothesis is above a certain threshold the hypothesis is considered a success and launched as an actual innovation. The concrete interpretation of technological capabilities, specific abilities and the way financial rewards from innovations are determined depends on the properties of the industry that are examined. A general feature of the map determining financial rewards is, however, that it changes with the launch of an innovation in such a way that launching an exact copy of the innovation does not pay, whereas a successful innovation increases the attractiveness of points in its neighborhood.

Agents might change their kenes through their own costly R&D where both incremental research, modifying abilities and expertise within the set of capabilities chosen for its innovation hypothesis, and radical changes, where new capabilities are added, are possible. Agents might also change their knowledge base by cooperating with a partner.

In such a case the (capability, ability, expertise) triplets from each agent's kene is added to the partner's kene. The expertise level is given by the max of the two partners for abilities which were present in both kenes and set to one for all abilities which were not previously present in an agent's kene. Partners might decide to start a network, which is a persistent connection and can be extended to more than two partners. Network members share results of their research and always have identical innovation hypotheses, dividing the reward if a successful innovation is launched.

This way of representing the knowledge base allows a modeller to study the accumulation of knowledge in the industry in a very structured way. One can not only study the increase in amount of knowledge but also identify patterns of knowledge accumulation, for example whether knowledge is accumulated uniformly across the space spanned by capabilities and abilities or whether concentration on one or maybe a few key capabilities can be observed. Also, since in this approach the exchange of knowledge is modelled explicitly, spillovers only occur if partners with complementary abilities and expertise exchange knowledge. Hence, this seems to be a very promising approach to further examine in more detail the building of knowledge bases needed for innovations in industries.

3.2. Dealing with substantive uncertainty: design of innovations, search in the technology landscape and prediction of market response

As discussed in the introduction, the substantive uncertainty associated with innovation processes raises several issues. First, in a world where a firm is not able to conceive all possible outcomes of an innovation project and is even less able to generate the payoff distributions resulting from different innovation strategies, the question of *how* to search for new products and processes is far from obvious. Associated issues then are how different type of search strategies for innovations compare to each other from the firm's perspective and how their interplay influences shape and speed of technological change, industry development and growth. Second, closely related to these issues is the question how firms can develop models to predict market reaction to the introduction of new products and to estimate the expected returns generated by innovations.

In the analytical neoclassical innovation literature the problem of finding the optimal search strategy is in many instances not addressed at all. Typically it is either assumed that R&D expenditures transform in a deterministic or stochastic way into cost reductions (among many others e.g. Dasgupta and Stiglitz, 1980; D'Aspremont and Jacquemin, 1988; Kortum, 1997), quality improvements (e.g. Grossman and Helpman, 1991; Aghion and Howitt, 1992; Bonanno and Haworth, 1998) or horizontal differentiation of the new product from the rest (e.g. Lin and Saggi, 2002). If the dynamic nature of the innovation process is explicitly considered, like in the patent-race literature, it is usually assumed that there are exogenously given innovation steps the firms are aiming for (see e.g. Reinganum, 1989; Beath et al., 1995). A few papers on technological change have incorporated search theoretic considerations into equilibrium models (see e.g. Bental and Peled, 1996; Kortum, 1997) and in Section 4 I will briefly discuss the basic differences between these studies and the ACE work surveyed in this subsection.

The agent-based approach allows a modeller to explicitly address the issues related to substantive uncertainty of innovations and search on technology and product landscapes. The existing literature aiming in this direction is not huge but a few agent-based models have been developed to study in more detail the process of designing and searching for innovations as well as the interplay of this search process with the industry dynamics and the evolution of consumer preferences[18]. Cooper (2000) makes the point that firms are trying to solve certain design problems when carrying out R&D and that in reality these design problems are typically 'ill-structured' and hard to solve. He considers the example of designing a pin-joined frame with certain properties and minimal mass in order to compare the learning curves if firms try to develop the design in isolation with the learning curves under social learning. Each firm searches the design space (represented by the set of all binary strings of a certain length describing key parameters of the design) employing a simulated annealing algorithm. In the case of social learning, in addition each firm every period collects design bits from a given number of other firms selected by roulette wheel selection and puts them together as a potential new design. This design is adopted if it outperforms the current design of the firm. Cooper shows that social learning speeds up the process of finding better designs and that partial imitation, where firms combine design bits from several firms on average, leads to faster learning than a scenario where firms simply adopt the design of one top performer. The reason for this finding is that with partial imitation (corresponding to something like crossover in Genetic Algorithms (see Dawid, 1999) a lock-in of the industry at suboptimal designs is avoided. Unfortunately, individual incentives are not assigned with these considerations, since firms individually can gain by relying on simple imitation of the best performer rather than on partial imitation.

Since in Cooper's model the evaluation of designs is entirely based on their technical characteristics, it is reasonable to assume that new designs which have not yet been adopted can be compared to existing designs. If the evaluation of designs depends on their success in the market, however, such a comparison is only possible if the firm has a way to estimate the success of a new design in the market. Firms have to build an 'internal model' to be able to estimate the profitability of new designs in the market and, as stressed in Section 1, this is a very challenging task. Internal models have to be developed based on past experience. Birchenhall (1995) points out that this means that there is co-evolution of a population of potential new designs and of the models needed to evaluate them[19]. He models such a situation using two co-evolving genetic algorithms.

---

[18] Models of search in complex technology spaces without explicit considerations of involved firms or markets have been provided for example by Ebeling et al. (2000) and Silverberg and Verspagen (2005a).

[19] There are also several ACE-type market studies where firms are not able to perfectly understand the (time-invariant) demand structure but update and select innovation strategies based on exogenously fixed evaluation models (e.g. Kwasnicki and Kwasnicka, 1992; Adner and Levinthal, 2001; Dawid and Reimann, 2004). Since the focus of these studies is neither on the way search in the technology landscape is performed nor on internal model building, I do not discuss them in detail here.

In the GA governing the search for a new technological design a new design created by mutation and/or crossover is only adopted if it is more profitable than the current technology of the firm according to at least one of estimation functions present in the second population (actually the second population consists of encoded parameters for a parameterized evaluation function). The fitness of strings in the second population, which represent evaluation models, is determined by the evaluation errors of these models in the past. It is shown that the use of such evolved internal models for selection of designs to be implemented substantially increases the performance of the firm compared to a case where any new developed design is implemented. A similar point has also been made by Yildizoglu (2001) who inserts firms which develop an internal model of the market into a slightly adapted version of Nelson and Winter's model of Schumpeterian competition.

Natter et al. (2001) consider the co-evolution of several internal models within a firm in a rather detailed model addressing issues of organization and learning related to the new product development process. A market with monopolistic competition structure is considered, where each firm consists of a marketing and a production agent. The production agent builds an internal model about the relationship between the production processes and resulting product features as well as about the relationship between the production process and costs. The marketing agent has to develop a model of the relationship between product features and the attractiveness of the features in the market. Agents build these internal models by training artificial neural networks. Using these internal models the agents have to decide on the type of production process to be implemented. Different organizational forms are compared (sequential or team-based structures) where life-cycle returns are used to evaluate performance. Among other insights, the simulations show that team-based structures are superior to sequential decision-making and highlight the need to adjust incentive schemes to the organizational structure chosen.

Dawid and Reimann (2004) provide a systematic study of the effect of the interaction of different approaches for predicting the success of product innovations in an oligopolistic market[20]. An industry is considered where several horizontally and vertically differentiated products are offered. Consumers have Chamberlinian love-of-variety-preferences, where the utility gained from consumption of a good is influenced by the current attractiveness of this product. The attractiveness parameter of a product changes over time according to a stochastic process resembling the shape of a life cycle. The expected maximal attractiveness depends on the effort which has been invested by the innovating firm in the corresponding product innovation process. Since consumers face a budget constraint, the actual demand for a product depends on its relative attractiveness compared to the other products offered, which yields endogenously determined demand life-cycles for the products. Each firm might offer a whole range of products.

---

[20] An empirical study analyzing simple decision heuristics for making such predictions can be found in Astebro and Elhedhli (2003).

Each period a firm can extend its product range either by adding a product to its range, that is new to the firm but already exists in the market, or by introducing a product innovation which is new to the market. If a new product is taken to the market the consumers utility function is extended accordingly, where the expected value of the attractiveness parameter depends on accumulated investments for this product development. At the same time, a firm might decide to drop one or more products from its range. Additionally, firms have to make output, investment and investment allocation decisions.

The focus of Dawid and Reimann (2004) is on the interplay of different firms' strategies for the evaluation of existing and potential new sub-markets. The evaluation of a sub-market is based on current profits on this sub-market, the current growth rate and the anticipated long run potential of the sub-market. The weights assigned by a firm to each of these three factors is seen as part of the firm's strategy parameters. Using extensive simulations followed by statistical tests, Dawid and Reimann (2004) show that individual incentives induce firms to put the larger weight on market growth compared to profit, where this effect is particularly strong if the horizontal differentiation between products is strong. This means that, in a scenario where firms adapt their evaluation strategies over time, the firms in the industry become more and more oriented towards sub-markets with high growth rates, which are typically markets for recently introduced innovations. However, if all firms use evaluation strategies which put higher weight on current profits, average industry profits increase. These findings demonstrate that, in a complex uncertain environment, dynamic adaptation of internal evaluation models of new products might itself induce inefficiencies with respect to the introduction and adoption of innovations.

In the industry model of Dawid and Reimann (2004, 2005) the endogeneous product life-cycles are driven by the fact that the offered product range has some influence on aggregate demand, but there is no micro-founded representation of the demand side. A more explicit consideration of the interplay between the design of product innovations and the evolution of demand is provided in Windrum and Birchenhall (1998). They consider the search for designs of innovative products as a search problem on a shifting rather than a fixed landscape. In their agent-based model consumer preferences co-evolve with the product designs offered by the producers. The search for designs of producers is modelled via an algorithm similar to a genetic algorithm. Furthermore, there is a fixed and finite set of possible consumer types where the frequency of each type varies depending on how effectively different consumer types have been served by the offered supply. The model reproduces patterns of decreasing (product) innovation activities over the life-cycle, which is typically observed in real-world industries. Furthermore, in this industry typically several co-existing product designs survive which are interpreted as different niche-markets. The authors argue that this finding—although contradicting the dominant design hypothesis—is consistent with observable patterns in numerous industries and that the dominant design hypothesis should rather be seen as a special case of the more general phenomenon of niche-formation.

Before I move on to the discussion of models focusing on the effects and importance of ex-ante heterogeneity of strategies, I want to mention that several of the agent-based growth models also incorporate interesting and rather explicit models of technological search. I will discuss these in Subsection 3.4.

3.3. The importance of the heterogeneity of innovation strategies

Heterogeneity of behavior of agents is a prevalent phenomenon in almost any economic setting. As has been stressed in Section 1, this is particularly true in the context of innovations. In the framework of neoclassical analysis heterogeneity of behavior can be explained by heterogeneities of agent characteristics or initial endowments. Yet even in a symmetric equilibrium among agents with symmetric characteristics, heterogeneous behavior can emerge if the equilibrium involves mixed strategies. Heterogeneity of *strategies* in a neoclassical world with symmetric agents can however only arise if an asymmetric equilibrium exists. Several analytical studies dealing with innovation have in such a way explained heterogeneity of innovation strategies (e.g. Gersbach and Schmutzler, 2003). In an agent-based approach, where the complexity and substantive uncertainty associated with a firm's maximization problem is taken into account, and strategies are rule-based rather than derived as the solution of a tractable well-posed optimization problem, it is quite natural to deal with heterogeneity of strategies. Several of the models discussed so far, including Nelson and Winters model of Schumpeterian competition, incorporate heterogeneity of strategies not induced by differences in endowments. The point of this subsection is therefore not to survey agent-based models of technological change which feature heterogenous behavior—almost any ACE model does—but to stress that several agent-based studies in this domain have explicitly focused on the effects of strategy heterogeneity from a firm and an industry perspective. They have shown that heterogeneity of innovation strategies in not only induced by individual incentives of firms but also has significant positive effects on the overall evolution of the industry.

Dawid et al. (2001) address the question at the firm level. Using a simplified version of the model in Dawid and Reimann (2004, 2005) described above, they study the question how much inertia firms should show when switching from an established product to a new one, and under which circumstances firms should primarily rely on imitation of existing designs for product innovation or try to develop their own innovative designs. Among other findings, the paper shows that, ceteris paribus, it is advantageous for a firm to deviate with respect to the imitation-innovation weighting from the average industry strategy. Put differently, in any state of the industry with uniform innovation strategies, firms have incentives to deviate, thus generating strategy heterogeneity.

The effect of strategy diversity on overall industry performance is pointed out by Llerena and Oltra (2002). They consider a setup which is based on the Nelson and Winter model but extends significantly the description of the innovation process. Firms' innovation probabilities depend on the stock of accumulated knowledge rather than only on current investment. There are two types of firms characterized by different ways to acquire knowledge and generate innovations. The cumulative firms build their stock of knowledge by own R&D and generate innovations internally. The non-cumulative firms invest in building up their absorptive capacity in order to exploit the knowledge generated externally. Accordingly, the average productivity of a new technology of a cumulative firm is given by its own current productivity, whereas for a non-cumulative firm the productivity is centered around the market share-weighted average industry productivity. Loosely speaking, the two types might be labelled as innovators and imitators. Firms are not allowed to change their innovation strategy, but there is endogenous exit and entry of firms and therefore the number of firms of the two types in the population varies over time. Llerena and Oltra show that, in industries where both types co-exist, the technological evolution is superior (higher average productivity) to homogeneous industries. Typically such a heterogenous industry ends up in a state with a few large cumulative firms plus a fringe of many small non-cumulative ones.

Similar results concerning the importance of strategy diversity have also been obtained in several other agent-based papers on industry dynamics and economic change. Chiaromonte and Dosi (1993) consider an evolutionary agent-based growth model and compare simulation results where technological competence and *parameters of decision rules* are heterogenous with scenarios where these parameters are homogenous with unchanged means. They report that homogenous parameter settings lead to significantly less technical progress and lower long-term aggregate income. Ballot and Taymaz (1997, 1999), which I briefly reviewed in Subsection 3.1, consider the interplay between four different types of decision rules in their micro-to-macro model and show that heterogeneity of rules is not only self-sustained but that the absence of strategy diversity reduces total output and the level of technology attained. Ballot and Taymaz' work also makes clear that ex-ante given strategy-diversity, where firms cannot adapt strategies later on, is not sufficient to yield high productivity levels. Crucial for dynamic efficiency is the interplay of heterogeneity and strategy selection by the firms, so these findings are very much in the spirit of an evolutionary approach.

3.4. Micro-founded models of economic growth

The main goal of my survey of innovation-related ACE-work in Subsections 3.1–3.3 is to highlight how ACE researchers have incorporated important aspects of innovation processes, which have been largely neglected in analytical papers, into their models. Guided by the focus on three of the four important aspects of innovation processes, which I discussed in the introduction, I have reviewed the modelling choices made in order to deal with these issues, the research questions asked, and some insights obtained. Hence my basic approach in these subsections was that of an economic theorist who uses rather abstract models to gain insights into general economic phenomena[21]. In the introduction I have argued that the second main advantage of ACE modelling in the domain of innovation and industrial dynamics, besides the capability to incorporate a

---

[21] To avoid any misunderstanding, I like to stress that quite a few of the papers reviewed in Sections 3.1–3.3 show that results obtained in the used simulation model match well with empirical stylized facts.

larger number of important aspects of the innovation process into the analysis, is the good ability of ACE models to reproduce empirically observed stylized facts. The focus of the literature survey in the following two subsections will be on this aspect. In the remainder of this section I briefly discuss some influential evolutionary growth models with an agent-based flavor. The reader is referred to Silverberg and Verspagen (2005b) or Windrum (2004) for a more extensive coverage of this field.

Starting with Nelson and Winters' evolutionary growth model, a main concern of evolutionary and ACE-minded scholars working on economic growth has been to build models where well known stylized facts about economic growth emerge as aggregate properties from realistic assumptions about economic interactions at the micro level. An influential series of papers in this respect has been published by Silverberg and Verspagen (1994, 1995, 1996), who develop an agent-based growth model with rich economic structure. The model takes into account several stylized facts about technological change and growth, among them the co-existence of diverse concurrent technologies (a vintage capital approach), the exploration vs. exploitation tradeoff of innovation efforts, the importance of innovation diffusion speed and the characteristics of knowledge. A firm's innovation strategy is characterized by its R&D quota, determining which portion of profit is used for R&D. Firms are heterogenous with respect to this strategy, which is adapted over time by imitation (proportional to market share) and mutation. Several key points are made in Silverberg and Verspagen (1994). The trajectory of the average R&D quota ends up fluctuating around a positive 'evolutionary equilibrium' which, at least for linear innovation functions, is independent from initial conditions. Hence, there are endogenously generated positive long-run growth rates. The evolution of the rate of technical change is characterized by a long period of slow increase followed by a sudden 'takeoff' where the rate of technological change jumps up and then keeps fluctuating at this high level. The takeoff is also associated with a sharp decrease in market concentration. This observation makes nicely the point that the connection between R&D activity and market concentration might be characterized by co-evolution rather than by causal relationships in either direction (as suggested in many models rooted in the industrial organization tradition). Silverberg and Verspagen (1996) stick to the same basic setup with the single difference that the innovation strategy of a firm is determined by two parameters, where the first determines which portion of profits and the second which portion of total output is invested in R&D. It turns out that in the long run for most firms in the population the value of the first parameter is close to zero whereas the value of the second parameter is positive. The authors argue that profits are more volatile than output and accordingly this result can be seen as an indicator that firms with strongly fluctuating R&D expenditures have lower survival chances than those with relatively stable investment streams. A comparison of the data generated by the model with R&D expenditures in four US and Japanese industries is made and it is demonstrated that the results of the model seem to be consistent with the empirical data not only qualitatively but also with respect to the range of the observed values.

In Silverberg and Verspagen (1995) the model of Silverberg and Verspagen (1994) is extended to a framework with two countries and it is demonstrated that complex patterns of technological convergence and divergence between the countries are generated. The authors argue that the data generated by their model matches well several characteristics observable in OECD data. In particular they show that, like in the OECD data, the power spectrum of the coefficient of variation of per capita GDP is an almost linear function with negative slope.

Another string of agent-based evolutionary growth models has been developed in Chiaromonte and Dosi (1993), Chiaromonte et al. (1993) and Dosi et al. (1994). Several differences to the Silverberg-Verspagen models should be pointed out. There is no vintage capital, but there are two sectors, one sector producing capital goods and the other consumption goods, where production coefficients in both sectors might change over time yielding dynamics in a two-dimensional technology space. Furthermore, firms do not adapt innovation strategies over time. Rather, they follow ex-ante determined behavioral rules with in general heterogenous strategy parameters. Although the papers differ a bit in the details of the micro-foundation of the analyzed models, they all also incorporate technological change through innovation and imitation, where the innovation process incorporates the basic distinction between incremental and radical innovations and the diffusion of technologies is modelled explicitly as a time-consuming process. Dynamics are open-ended since there is an ever-growing set of notional, only partly explored technological opportunities. Market interaction is modelled in reduced form, where in each sector market share in a given period is determined by a firm's relative 'competitiveness', which depends on the price charged by the firm, the demand for its product and—in the capital good sector—also on the productivity of labor. Chiaromonte and Dosi (1993) provide only results for a few individual runs of the model but argue that the simulations generate plausible time series for income and labor productivity. Furthermore, it is demonstrated that persistent heterogeneities in market share and labor productivity emerge among consumption good producers, quite in accordance with empirical observations. The main message of the paper is the importance of persistent heterogeneity of behavioral rules and employed technology for the rate of growth. Chiaromonte et al. (1993) use the same model but focus on how price and wage adjustments affect growth performance. In Dosi et al. (1994) a multi-country model of similar type is analyzed and again it is argued, that in spite of its relatively simple structure, the model reproduces several stylized facts such as persistent inter-firm asymmetries in productivities and profits, persistence in aggregate fluctuations of per capita income within a country, and increasing differentiation in level and rate of growth of per-capita income between countries. These are indeed emergent properties of the model since there are no country-wide externalities and since institutional design, parameter settings and so forth are identical across countries.

An even richer agent-based growth model reproducing a large set of empirical findings has been proposed by Fagiolo and Dosi (2003). In this model several of the micro-aspects of the innovation process discussed in Subsections 3.1–3.3 are incorporated. They consider a finite population of agents exploring an unlimited two-dimensional lattice which represents the technology space. Each agent every period produces a certain output which depends on a productivity parameter of her current technology and (in an increasing way) on the number of other agents employing the same technology. Agents in this economy every period are in one of three possible 'modes': (i) 'Mining', i.e. producing using their current technology; (ii) 'Imitating', i.e. moving on the technology landscape towards some other technology which is already in use by some other agents. Such moves are triggered by signals about other technologies received by the agent, where the strength of the signal depends on the productivity of the technology and its (technological) distance from the agent's current technology. (iii) 'Exploring', i.e. moving around randomly in the technology space until a new feasible technology is discovered, where only a subset of the points on the lattice corresponds to a feasible technology. If an explorer discovers a new feasible technology the productivity parameter of the new technology is determined stochastically, where the mean increases with the distance from the origin and accumulated skills of the explorer. While an agent moves around exploring or imitating she cannot produce. There is no market interaction in this model[22] and the characteristics of the employed technologies translate directly to output and, on the aggregate level, to GDP. The model generates plausible outcomes on several levels. On a technology level the model produces clusters of agents at different co-existing technologies of comparable productivity where the adoption curves of technologies have the typical S-shape. Over time the clusters move slowly towards more and more productive technologies. This persistent movement generates positive GDP growth, and the authors identify conditions under which (persistently fluctuating) exponential growth can be obtained. Using a much richer set of simulation data and more sophisticated techniques compared to the ones employed in the analyses discussed so far in this subsection, the authors also demonstrate that their artificial GDP time series share several well established statistical properties of real-world GDP data. In particular, there are persistent fluctuations, where autocorrelation of growth rates is significantly positive for small lags and decreases towards zero as the lag increases. Also, it is pointed out by the authors that, in spite of the fact that there is sustained growth, growth rates do not increase with the population size and therefore their model does not exhibit scale effects.

3.5. Industry studies and 'history-friendly' models

The previous section has demonstrated the ability of agent-based growth models to combine a strong micro-foundation with the reproduction of a number of stylized facts about economic growth. Models in the evolutionary tradition have also been used to gain micro-founded insights into the structure of industry evolution and to account for stylized facts in that respect. Klepper (1996) proposes an analytically tractable industry life cycle model which is able to explain several stylized facts including the positive correlation of entry and exit rates, the existence of industry shake-out phenomena and the shift

---

[22] For a model in a similar spirit which includes market interaction see Kwasnicki (2001).

of producers efforts from product to process innovation during the life-cycle[23]. Furthermore, evolutionary industry models by Dosi et al. (1995) and Winter et al. (2000, 2003) reproduce stylized facts concerning the skewed firm size distribution in many industries, the long lasting co-existence of firms with different efficiency in production, the long-term advantages of early entrants and the importance of the technological 'regime' in an industry for the characteristics of the industry's evolution. However, these models are only in a wider sense agent-based since the focus is on the analysis of the evolution of industry-level distributions and interactions between agents and individual decisions rules are only considered in very reduced form. Nevertheless, these models reinforce the conclusion obtained from some of the agent-based growth models that several of the stylized facts on the industry level emerge quite naturally from industry models based on an explicit consideration of the dynamic interaction of heterogenous rule-based firms.

However, the argument could be made that some of the models presented in this section, although very sophisticated in structure, are formulated in such an abstract setting that the modeller has enough freedom to adapt the underlying assumptions to generate certain stylized facts. Hence, these models (similarly to traditional formal economic theory) highlight which mechanisms are **potential** explanations for observed phenomena. In order to be more confident about capturing **actual** causalities in given concrete industries it might be necessary to link the building blocks of the model more closely to empirical observations in that given industry. Using similar arguments, Malerba et al. (1999, 2001a) argue for the need of a new generation of evolutionary economic models they call 'history friendly' models. These models should be developed based on detailed consideration of characteristics of the industry as known to an empirically-oriented scholar in the field. Furthermore, they should be capable of reproducing the main facts in the historic development of the industry. The idea is to start with verbal descriptions of the actual structure of an industry and then to translate the verbal arguments into a formal model. Given the complexity of the topic under consideration, we will see that the resulting model typically has the structure of a dynamic agent-based simulation model.

Before describing a history friendly model in more detail, I want to mention that an early simulation study in similar spirit was presented by Grabowski and Vernon (1987). They build a dynamic model of the pharmaceutical industry, where specifications of model relationships and parameters are based on empirical data describing the industry. The model abstracts from a micro-founded representation of described relationships, relying rather on observed statistical relationships. The model is used to evaluate and compare the effects on the innovation rate of changes in patent duration and in the duration of the regulatory review process which has to be finished before a new drug can

---

[23] Explanations of at least some of the empirically observable regularities of industry life cycles within dynamic equilibrium models have been given by Ericson and Pakes (1995), Hopenhayn (1992), Jovanovic (1982), and Jovanovic and MacDonald (1994).

be introduced to the market. The simulations imply that these two policy-determined variables have strong influence on the rate of innovation. The positive effect of a reduction of regulatory approval time by a year approximately matches the effect of a patent duration increase by five years.

The new generation of history-friendly models gives a much more detailed description of firm and behavior compared to the approach of Grabowski and Vernon (1987). As an example I will here describe in some detail the history-friendly model of the computer industry developed in Malerba et al. (1999, 2001b) and afterwards mention a few other recent industry studies based on a similar approach.

Malerba et al. (1999, 2001b) include many of the issues discussed in the previous subsections, such as the gradual buildup of technical competence, direction of search and advance of innovations, the importance of the distance of a firm from the technological frontier for its costs of innovation, the influence of supply on consumer preferences and demand, the importance of diffusion of information about new technologies and the implications of firms diversification decisions. The chosen specifications are motivated by empirical observations in the computer industry. The model is supposed to capture main phenomena observed in the transition of the computer industry from transistor to microprocessor technology and the associated emergence of the market for PCs in addition to the original mainframe market. In particular, the authors try to explain the empirical observation that a dominant firm emerges in the original market using 'old' technology and then quickly adopts the 'new' technology and keeps its strong position in the original market. However, this dominant firm is not able to gain a similar strong position in an emerging new market (PC market). The products in the model are characterized by two attributes 'cheapness' and 'performance'. It is also assumed that there are two types of consumers, where one type ('big firms') puts more weight on performance whereas the second type ('small users') is more interested in cheapness. The first type of consumers form the mainframe market whereas consumers in the PC market are of the second type. Both types have minimal demands for both attributes which a supplying firm has to meet in order to enter the corresponding market. A given technology puts certain limits on how much of the two attributes can be delivered by a product. The microprocessor technology extends the limit in both directions, where the potential improvement with respect to cheapness is more substantial. In the initial period a certain number of firms start with the transistor technology, and after a given number of periods a new bunch of firms starts developing products using the new microprocessor technology. Firms invest constant fractions of profits into R&D and advertising and prices are determined by simple markup rules. Firms two main decisions, first, to adopt the new technology and, second, to diversify into the new market, are represented in a very simple fashion. Firms perceive the new technology with some probability which depends positively on the technological level of the firm in the old technology and the current advancement of the best-practice firm in the new technology. Once the new technology is perceived, the firm adopts it as soon as it is able to cover the associated costs. Based on observations in the computer industry, diversification in this model means that a spin-off firm is created, which inherits parts of the budget and the technical and advertising competence of the parent firm but positions in a spot in the attribute space oriented towards the new market.

Malerba et al. (1999) show that under certain parameter constellations the qualitative empirical observations described above are indeed reproduced by the model (history-replication). Deviating from such parameter constellations yields 'history-divergent runs'. In particular, it is shown that if the number of entrants goes down (e.g. due to smaller initial budgets) the mainframe firms do not switch to the microprocessor technology and the PC market never takes off. The authors argue that, based on this observation, the lack of venture capital in Europe and Japan might be seen as a reason for the inability of firms in these regions to take advantage of the new technological and market opportunities in the computer industry. In Malerba et al. (2001b) the descriptive analysis is complemented by an evaluation of industrial policy measures using this model. In particular, the effect of antitrust measures which break up a dominant firm a given period after it has reached 75% market share, and different measures aimed at facilitating market entry of small firms are considered. The main conclusion from these experiments is that large and focused policy interventions would have been needed to significantly change the pattern of market development that has been observed in this industry.

The model developed here is very elaborated in its attempt to put together a large number of stylized facts about development of technology and demand in a specific industry in a manageable and transparent model. One possible concern could be a kind of 'over-fitting' of the model. It seems that some modelling choices might have been influenced by the concrete set of historical stylized facts the authors intended to reproduce. To carry out an 'out of sample' test of the model, if at all possible, takes time; we will have to see how well future industry developments can be explained. Also, following the tradition of formal evolutionary modelling, the representation of firm behavior is very simple, relying on fixed-percentage investment rules and simple probabilistic rules for technology perception and diversification. Whereas firms' actions vary over time, their strategies are assumed to be fixed. In particular, for the evaluation of the effect of policy interventions, it might be important to take into account the reaction of firms' strategies to given measures. Combining more flexible representation of firm strategies with the 'history-friendly' approach therefore seems to be a challenging but hopefully rewarding task.

Following the successful application of the 'history friendly' approach to the computer industry, Malerba and Orsenigo (2002) have developed a simulation model of the pharmaceutical industry along similar lines. Pyka and Saviotti (2000) develop an agent-based simulation model of biotechnology-based sectors in order to study the emergence of innovation networks in such industries.

4. Discussion

I have started this chapter by arguing that there are two main reasons why agent-based models should be particularly useful for the analysis of processes of innovation and technological change. First, several of the crucial defining aspects of the process of innovation and technological change are readily incorporated in ACE models but can hardly be captured in neoclassical equilibrium analyses. Second, ACE models seem to be able to reproduce a number of stylized facts in this domain which are not well accounted for by existing analytical work.

I believe that the survey of ACE work in Section 3 reinforces this view. Although we are certainly talking about a field of research in its infancy with a large variety of addressed research topics and employed approaches, some general insights emerge from the surveyed body of work. It has been shown that a structured model of the knowledge base allows concrete statements about the effect of the allocation of investments between general and specific knowledge build-up and of the structure of knowledge exchange between individuals and firms on firm success and industry development. Considering that also economic policy makers pay more and more attention to the importance of the structure of the knowledge base for technological change and growth[24], these are certainly relevant issues. ACE studies further have highlighted the importance of the interplay of (potentially heterogeneous) individual approaches of firms towards the search for new products and processes and the estimation of market response to innovations. A conclusion emerging from a number of ACE studies with quite diverse setups is that heterogeneity of innovation strategies has a positive effect on the speed of technological change, a theme not present in mainstream theoretical analyses. For some of the covered issues, it can be argued that these questions could in principle also be posed in an intertemporal equilibrium setting—for example the effect of heterogeneity of strategies could be addressed by comparing the speed of technological change under symmetric and asymmetric intertemporal equilibria in a dynamic industry model. Even if one might have concerns about the underlying assumptions, this could serve as a useful benchmark analysis shedding additional light on the mechanisms underlying this effect. However, analytical tractability is a severe problem as soon as asymmetric dynamic equilibria are considered and hence general analytical results might be infeasible.

For other issues, like the analysis of search and prediction strategies under substantive uncertainty, an equilibrium analysis relying on the Bayesian optimization framework does not even allow a modeller to properly formulate the relevant question. For sake of illustration, let us briefly compare the ACE approaches to technological search reviewed in Subsection 3.2 with a well received equilibrium approach, like the search theoretic

---

[24] See for example the extensive literature on regional and national innovation systems (e.g., Nelson, 1993; Freeman, 1995; Lundvall et al., 2002) or the 'European Innovation Scoreboard' project of the European Union (http://trendchart.cordis.lu/).

model of technological change by Kortum (1997). In Kortum's approach there is a continuum of individuals, where a certain fraction is engaged in research and accumulates over time a research stock. There is also a continuum of goods, where independence of search across different goods is assumed. This allows the author to basically analyze the search for new production techniques for one 'representative' good. The common research stock is available to all researchers and determines the frequency at which new ideas about production techniques arrive. If a new idea for a production technique arrives, the corresponding labor productivity parameter is drawn from a random distribution, which is positively influenced by the common research stock. The mappings determining the frequency of new ideas and the distribution of productivity parameters given a certain research stock are common knowledge and the actual productivity of a new technique is perfectly revealed to the innovator once he has this new idea. Innovators can patent their new idea restricting their competitors to the second best technique, and due to the chosen demand structure it is always optimal for them to set prices such that all competitors are shut out. So, overall we have a scenario where a set of ex-ante identical potential innovators employ some identical but not explicitly specified search strategy to generate process innovations for a continuum of goods. Potential innovators have no proprietary knowledge and the type of technique they use for producing the other goods has no influence on their ability to generate good new techniques. For each product at each point of time all the output is produced by the same technique. All potential innovators share the same correct expectations about the (discounted infinite horizon) future return of engaging in research today. Although all these features are not consistent with most empirical observations, the model is quite successful in explaining empirical observations about the time evolution of research employment, patenting and total factor productivity in the US. Nevertheless, it seems to me that a search theoretic approach of this kind can provide less insight about the type of search problem a potential real world innovator faces, and the effect different type of search strategies have on technological change, in comparison with a micro-founded agent-based model.

To get to my second main argument (reproduction of stylized facts), I will now point out a few features of the *results* of the surveyed agent-based evolutionary growth models, which in my eyes make them attractive alternatives to the growing literature on new growth theory (NGT) (see Aghion and Howitt, 1998; Grossman and Helpman, 1994), which shares the desire of these models to provide micro-founded explanations for economic growth. This should be considered *in addition* to the discussion about the appropriateness of the use of representative firms carrying out infinite horizon optimization, and the use of non-structured knowledge variables and technology spaces in models dealing with technological change. An important point in this respect is that, contrary to the evolutionary growth models discussed above, NGT models predict some balanced growth rate, but provide no endogenous explanation of the empirically observable persistent fluctuations. Other issues where evolutionary studies provide empirically plausible results but NGT models are silent or generate implausible predictions are the co-existence of several technologies employed in an industry for the production of the same good, the co-existence of firms of different size, the endogenous generation of persistent cross-country differences in growth rates, the endogenous generation of changing growth episodes, and take-off phenomena. Furthermore, as pointed out in Subsection 3.4, evolutionary growth models do not exhibit a positive effect of population size on the growth rate. Such a scale effect, which is at odds with much of 20th century data on economic growth, is however present in the most influential early NGT models, in particular Aghion and Howitt (1992), Grossman and Helpman (1991) and Romer (1990). New growth models developed later have avoided this problem and exhibit scale effects only with respect to per capita GDP but not with respect to growth rates (see Jones, 1999).

The discussion in the previous two paragraphs highlights another point often made by evolutionary and ACE scholars: namely, that ACE models are in principle able to incorporate many realistic features of interaction and behavior on the micro level, and simultaneously produce plausible time series on all different levels, rather than being tailored to explain only a few specific phenomena. Although this is certainly an advantage of this approach, the literature survey above shows that many ACE models in the field focus on some aspect of the process of technological change and rely on agent-based models where large parts of the economic system are represented in a highly stylized way. Is this a 'waste' of the versatile powerful method at hand? In my opinion certainly not. The use of an agent-based approach does not avoid the need to carefully design a model under the trade-off between a proper representation of the relevant effects and the ability to generate and interpret meaningful results. As pointed out above, ACE modelling allows a modeller to simultaneously incorporate many important aspects of the process of innovation and technological change into a formal model, but this does not mean that all of them should necessarily be there. Which of the aspects are actually relevant depends on the underlying research agenda.

Having already briefly discussed whether some of the research questions raised in ACE studies could also be addressed using equilibrium analysis, I close this section by pointing out that ACE scholars have so far pretty much ignored many traditional major topics of theoretical research in the field. These issues include the relationship between mode of competition and innovation, the optimal R&D strategy in patent races or the optimal relationship between length and scope of patents[25]. It seems to me that analyses of these issues in a dynamic heterogenous agent setting could provide interesting complementary insights to the existing theoretical findings.

5. Outlook

An important aspect of the overall ACE research agenda is the provision of micro-founded explanations for meso-level and macro-level phenomena. Quite a bit has been

---

[25] A preliminary exploration of the effect of patents in the framework of the Nelson and Winter (1982) model is carried out in Vallee and Yildizoglu (2004).

done in this respect also with respect to the analysis of innovation and technological change, but obviously there is still much more to do.

The process of technological change and the associated economic processes are extremely rich and many aspects have so far been only lightly touched or even completely ignored in the literature. Accordingly, there is a plethora of potential directions to pursue and certainly no 'natural' trajectory for the field to follow. On a general level, a promising extension of the current approaches might be to try to link the industry development with closely linked parts of the economy which are up to now typically considered as exogenous in the economics of innovation. I would like to give two brief pointers towards issues in this respect[26]. The first pointer is to study in more detail the co-evolution of innovations and demand. The marketing literature provides models of the impact of product pre-announcements and final product positioning on consumer demand with empirical foundation. Putting together an agent-based demand side[27] based on such models with an agent-based dynamic industry model should allow a modeller to capture more realistically the properties of the 'search on a shifting landscape' associated particularly with product innovation. Another challenge is to couple the description of innovation and industry dynamics with developments in the labor market. The role of knowledge for the rate of innovation is by now well accepted but the innovation literature is relatively silent about how exactly a workforce which has the necessary competence is built and knowledge is transferred through the labor market. A proper understanding of the processes governing such a buildup might need to consider private household decisions concerning investment in knowledge acquisition as well as those of firms. There is a significant empirical literature studying the effect of technological change on the demand for different skill levels on the labor market (see e.g. Pianta, 2000). On the other hand, the innovation strategy of a firm and its success depends heavily on the ability of the firm to recruit the 'right' workforce. Therefore there seems to be a feedback between innovative activities and labor market conditions. Developing agent based models which combine the two sides is a challenging but also promising task[28].

To a large degree the agent-based work in this field has been descriptive rather than normative, but it seems that recently more attention has been paid to the potential of this approach for normative analysis on the level of the individual firm, of the market (see Marks, 2006) and of public policy (e.g. Berger, 2001). The agent-based approach has

---

[26] To avoid any misunderstanding, I am not claiming that no work addressing these issues has been carried out, but there is very little in terms of published papers.

[27] There is some agent-based work dealing with the coupling of innovations and demand dynamics, see Aversi et al. (1999).

[28] Some work aiming in this direction exists. The model of Ballot and Taymaz (1997) discussed in Subsection 3.1 has an explicit representation of the labor market, but no specific knowledge is embodied in the employees and hence no knowledge is transferred through the labor market. Fagiolo et al. (2004) consider an agent-based labor market model incorporating technical change. The model of the process of technical change is however quite mechanistic and simple without considering firm's decision concerning R&D and innovation.

large potential to provide guidance with respect to good (if not optimal) firm strategies and public policies. This potential has been shown in concrete case studies in several areas besides the economics of innovation. The recently developed 'history-friendly' models suggest that this approach can also be successfully applied to think about concrete industrial and innovation policy measures. However, to be able to derive robust and convincing policy recommendations from ACE models, important issues concerning model validation and calibration as well as robustness testing of simulation results should be addressed in a systematic way. Recent contributions to the ACE literature have shown increasing awareness of these issues. Many researchers in the field now try to provide statistical evidence that reported qualitative findings are significant in a statistical sense and robust with respect to parameter variations. Also, with respect to model building, validation, and calibration, several concrete approaches have been proposed recently in addition to the history friendly approach discussed in this chapter (e.g. Moss, 2002; Duffy, 2006; Werker and Brenner, 2004). Hence, it should be expected that we will not only see more insightful descriptive agent-based work on technological change but also a growing use of this technique for the design and evaluation of individual firm strategies and of economic policy measures.

References

Adner, R., Levinthal, D. (2001). "Demand heterogeneity and technology evolution: implications for product and process innovation". Management Science 47, 611–628.

Aghion, P., Howitt, P. (1992). "A model of growth through creative destruction". Econometrica 60, 323–351.

Aghion, P., Howitt, P. (1998). Endogenous Growth Theory. MIT Press, Cambridge, MA.

Alchian, A. (1950). "Uncertainty, evolution, and economic theory". Journal of Political Economy 58, 211–222.

Astebro, T., Elhedhli, S. (2003). "The effectiveness of simple decision heuristics: a case study of experts' forecasts of the commercial success of early-stage ventures", working paper, University of Toronto.

Aversi, R., Dosi, G., Fagiolo, G., Meacci, M., Olivetti, C. (1999). "Demand dynamics with socially evolving preferences". Industrial and Corporate Change 8, 353–408.

Ballot, G., Taymaz, E. (1997). "The dynamics of firms in a micro-to-macro model: The role of training, learning and innovation". Journal of Evolutionary Economics 7, 435–457.

Ballot, G., Taymaz, E. (1999). "Technological change, learning and macro-economic coordination: An evolutionary model". Journal of Artificial Societies and Social Simulation 2. http://www.soc.surrey.ac.uk/JAstrophys.Space.Sci.S/2/2/3.html.

Beardsley, G., Mansfield, E. (1978). "A Note on the accuracy of industrial forecasts of the profitability of new products and processes". Journal of Business 51, 127–135.

Beath, J., Katsoulacos, Y., Ulph, D. (1995). "Game-theoretic approaches to the modelling of technological change". In: Stoneman, P. (Ed.), Handbook of the Economics of Innovation and Technological Change. Blackwell, Oxford, pp. 132–181.

Bental, B., Peled, D. (1996). "The accumulation of wealth and the cyclical generation of new technologies: a seach theoretic approach". International Economic Review 37, 687–718.

Berger, T. (2001). "Agent-based spatial models applied to agriculture: a simulation tool for technology diffusion, resource use changes and policy analysis". Agricultural Economics 25, 245–260.

Bester, H., Petrakis, E. (1993). "The incentives for cost reduction in a differentiated industry". International Journal of Industrial Organization 11, 519–534.

Birchenhall, C. (1995). "Modular technical change and genetic algorithms". Computational Economics 8, 233–253.

Bonanno, G., Haworth, B. (1998). "Intensity of competition and the choice between product and process innovation". International Journal of Industrial Organization 16, 495–510.

Boulding, K.E. (1991). "What is evolutionary economics?". Journal of Evolutionary Economics 1, 9–17.

Cantner, U., Pyka, A. (1998). "Absorbing technological spillovers: simulations in an evolutionary framework". Industrial and Corporate Change 7, 369–397.

Cassiman, B.C., Perez-Castillo, D., Veugelers, R. (2002). "Endogenizing know-how flows through the nature of R&D investments". International Journal of Industrial Organization 20, 775–799.

Chang, M.-H., Harrington, J.E. (2006). "Agent-based models of organizations", this handbook.

Chiaromonte, F., Dosi, G. (1993). "Heterogeneity, competition and macroeconomic dynamics". Structural Change and Economic Dynamics 4, 39–63.

Chiaromonte, F., Dosi, G., Orsenigo, L. (1993). "Innovative learning and institutions in the process of development: on the foundations of growth regimes". In: Thompson, R. (Ed.), Learning and Technological Change. MacMillan Press, pp. 117–149.

Cohen, W., Levinthal, D.A. (1989). "Innovation and learning: the two faces of R&D". Economic Journal 99, 569–596.

Cohendet, P., Llerena, P., Stahn, H., Umbauer, G. (1998). The Economics of Networks: Interaction and Behaviours. Springer, Berlin.

Cooper, B. (2000). "Modelling research and development: how do firms solve design problems?". Journal of Evolutionary Economics 10, 395–413.

Cooper, R.G., Kleinschmidt, E.J. (1995). "New product performance keys to success, profitability and cycle time reduction". Journal of Marketing Management 11, 315–337.

Cyert, R.M., March, J.G. (1963). A Behavioral Theory of the Firm. Prentice Hall, Englewood Cliffs.

Dasgupta, P., Stiglitz, J. (1980). "Industrial structure and the nature of innovative activity". The Economic Journal 90, 266–293.

D'Aspremont, C., Jacquemin, A. (1988). "Cooperative and noncooperative R&D in duopoly with spillovers". American Economic Review 78, 1133–1137.

Dawid, H. (1999). Adaptive Learning by Genetic Algorithms, Analytical Results and Applications to Economic Models. Springer, Berlin.

Dawid, H., Reimann, M. (2004). "Evaluating market attractiveness: individual incentives vs. industrial profitability". Computational Economics 24, 321–355.

Dawid, H., Reimann, M. (2005). "Diversification: a road to inefficiency in product innovations?", Working Paper, University of Bielefeld.

Dawid, H., Reimann, M., Bullnheimer, B. (2001). "To innovate or not to innovate?". IEEE Transactions on Evolutionary Computation 5, 471–481.

Dopfer, K. (2001). "Evolutionary economics—framework for analysis". In: Dopfer, K. (Ed.), Evolutionary Economics Program and Scope. Kluwer, Amsterdam, pp. 1–44.

Dosi, G. (1988). "Sources, procedures and microeconomic effects of innovation". Journal of Economic Literature XXVI, 1120–1171.

Dosi, G., Egidi, M. (1991). "Substantive and procedural uncertainty". Journal of Evolutionary Economics 1, 145–168.

Dosi, G., Winter, S. (2002). "Interpreting economic change: evolution, structures and games". In: Augier, M., March, J.G. (Eds.), The Economics of Choice, Change and Organization. Edward Elgar, Cheltenham, pp. 337–353.

Dosi, G., Fremann, C., Nelson, R.R., Silverberg, G., Soete, L. (Eds.) (1988). Technical Change and Economic Theory. Francis Pinter, London.

Dosi, G., Fabiani, S., Aversi, R., Meacci, M. (1994). "The dynamics of international differentiation: a multi-country evolutionary model". Industrial and Corporate Change 3, 225–242.

Dosi, G., Marsili, O., Orsenigo, L., Salvatore, R. (1995). "Learning, market selection and the evolution of industrial structures". Small Business Economics 7, 411–436.

Dosi, G., Malerba, F., Marsili, O., Orsenigo, L. (1997). "Industrial structure and dynamics: evidence, interpretations and puzzles". Industrial and Corporate Change 6, 3–24.

Dosi, G., Marengo, L., Fagiolo, G. (2003). "Learning in evolutionary environments", LEM working paper 2003/20, Laboratory of Economics and Management, Sant' Anna School of Advanced Studies, Pisa.

Duffy, J. (2006). "Agent-based models and human subject experiments", this handbook.

Ebeling, W., Molgedey, L., Reimann, A. (2000). "Stochastic urn models of innovation and search dynamics". Physica A 287, 599–612.

Eeckhout, J., Jovanovic, B. (2002). "Knowledge spillovers and inequality". American Economic Review 92, 1290–1307.

Eliason, G. (1991). "Modelling the experimentally organized economy". Journal of Economic Behavior and Organization 16, 163–182.

Ericson, R., Pakes, A. (1995). "Markov-perfect industry dynamics: a framework for empirical work". Review of Economic Studies 62, 53–82.

Fagerberg, J. (2003). "Schumpeter and the revival of evolutionary economics: an appraisal of the literature". Journal of Evolutionary Economics 13, 125–159.

Fagiolo, G., Dosi, G. (2003). "Exploitation, exploration and innovation in a model of endogenous growth with locally interacting agents". Structural Change and Economic Dynamics 14, 237–273.

Fagiolo, G., Dosi, G., Gabriele, R. (2004). "Matching, bargaining and wage-setting in an evolutionary model of labor market and output dynamics". Advances in Complex Systems 7, 1–30.

Freeman, C. (1994). "The economics of technical change". Cambridge Journal of Economics 18, 463–514.

Freeman, C. (1995). "The 'National System of Innovation' in historical perspective". Cambridge Journal of Economics 19, 5–24.

Freeman, C., Perez, C. (1988). "Structural crises of adjustment, business cycles and investment behaviour". In: Dosi, G., Freeman, C., Nelson, R., Silverberg, G., Soete, L. (Eds.), Technical Change and Economic Theory. Pinter, London, pp. 38–66.

Fremman, C., Soete, L. (1997). The Economics of Industrial Innovation. MIT Press, Cambridge, MA.

Friedman, M. (1953). "The methodology of positive economics". In: Friedman, M. (Ed.), Essay in Positive Economics. University of Chicago Press, Chicago, pp. 3–43.

Geroski, P. (1996). "Do spillovers undermine incentives to innovate?". In: Dowrick, S. (Ed.), Economic Approaches to Innovation. Edward Elgar, Aldershot, pp. 76–97.

Gersbach, H., Schmutzler, A. (2003). "Endogenous spillovers and incentives to innovate". Economic Theory 21, 59–79.

Gilbert, N., Pyka, A., Ropella, G.E.P. (2000). "The development of a generic innovation network simulation platform", SEIN Project Paper No. 8, The SEIN Project, University of Surrey.

Gilbert, N., Pyka, A., Ahrweiler, P. (2001). "Innovation networks-a simulation approach". Journal of Artificial Societies and Social Simulation 4. http://www.soc.surrey.ac.uk/JAstrophys.Space.Sci.S/4/3/8.html.

Grabowski, H.G., Vernon, J.M. (1987). "Pioneers, imitators, and generics—a simulation model of schumpeterian competition". Quarterly Journal of Economics 102, 491–525.

Grenadier, S., Weiss, A. (1997). "Investment in technological innovations: an option pricing approach". Journal of Financial Economics 44, 397–416.

Griliches, Z. (1992). "The search for R&D spillovers". Scandinavian Journal of Economics 94 (Suppl.), 29–47.

Grossman, G.M., Helpman, E. (1991). Innovation and Growth in the Global Economy. MIT Press, Cambridge, MA.

Grossman, G.M., Helpman, E. (1994). "Endogenous innovation in the theory of growth". Journal of Economic Perspectives 8, 23–44.

Hall, P. (1994). Innovation, Economics & Evolution. Harvester, London.

Hopenhayn, H.A. (1992). "Entry, exit and firm dynamics in long run equilibrium". Econometrica 60, 1127–1150.

Howitt, P. (2006). "Coordination issues in long-run growth", this handbook.

Hultink, E.J., Griffin, A., Hart, S., Robben, H.J.S. (1994). "Launch decisions and new product success: an empirical comparison of consumer and industrial products". Journal of Product Innovation Management 17, 5–23.

Jonard, N., Yildizoglu, M. (1998). "Technological diversity in an evolutionary industry model with localized learning and network externalities". Structural Change and Economic Dynamics 9, 35–53.

Jones, C. (1999). "Growth: with or without scale effects?". American Economic Review 89, 139–144.

Jovanovic, B. (1982). "Selection and evolution of industry". Econometrica 50, 649–670.

Jovanovic, B., MacDonald, G.M. (1994). "The life cycle of a competitive industry". Journal of Political Economy 102, 322–347.

Jovanovic, B., Nyarko, Y. (1996). "Learning by doing and the choice of technology". Econometrica 64, 1299–1310.

Kirman, A.P. (1992). "Whom or what does the representative individual represent?". Journal of Economic Perspectives 6, 117–136.

Klepper, S. (1996). "Entry, exit, growth, and innovation over the product life cycle". American Economic Review 86, 562–583.

Klepper, S. (1997). "Industry life cycles". Industrial and Corporate Change 6, 145–181.

Klepper, S., Simmons, K. (1997). "Technological extinctions of industrial firms: an enquiry into their nature and causes". Industrial and Corporate Change 6, 379–460.

Kline, S.J., Rosenberg, N. (1986). "An overview of innovation". In: Landau, R., Rosenberg, N. (Eds.), The Positive Sum Strategy: Harnessing Technology for Economic Growth. National Academy Press, Washington, pp. 275–305.

Kortum, S. (1997). "Research, patenting, and technological change". Econometrica 65, 1389–1419.

Kwasnicki, W. (1998). "Simulation methodology in evolutionary economics". In: Schweitzer, F., Silverberg, G. (Eds.), Evolution and Self-Organization in Economics. Duncker & Humbold, Berlin, pp. 161–186.

Kwasnicki, W. (2001). "Firms decision making process in an evolutionary model of industrial dynamics". Advances in Complex Systems 1, 1–25.

Kwasnicki, W., Kwasnicka, H. (1992). "Market, innovation, competition: an evolutionary model of industrial dynamics". Journal of Economic Behavior and Organization 19, 343–368.

Lin, P., Saggi, K. (2002). "Product differentiation, process R&D, and the nature of market competition". European Economic Review 46, 201–211.

Llerena, P., Oltra, V. (2002). "Diversity of innovative strategy as a source of technological performance". Structural Change and Economic Dynamics 13, 179–201.

Loasby, B.J. (1999). Knowledge, Institutions and Evolution in Economics. Routledge, London.

Lundvall, B.A., Johnson, B., Andersen, E.S., Dalum, B. (2002). "National systems of production, innovation and comepetence building". Research Policy 31, 213–231.

Maddison, A. (1991). Dynamic Forces in Capitalist Development: A Long-Run Comparative View. Oxford University Press, Oxford.

Malerba, F. (1992). "Learning by firms and incremental technical change". The Economic Journal 102, 845–859.

Malerba, F., Orsenigo, L. (1996). "The dynamics and evolution of industries". Industrial and Corporate Change 5, 51–87.

Malerba, F., Orsenigo, L. (2002). "Innovation and market structure in the dynamics of the pharmaceutical industry and biotechnology: towards a history-friendly model". Industrial and Corporate Change 11, 667–703.

Malerba, F., Nelson, R., Orsenigo, L., Winter, S. (1999). "History-friendly models of industry evolution: the computer industry". Industrial and Corporate Change 8, 3–40.

Malerba, F., Nelson, R., Orsenigo, L., Winter, S. (2001a). "History-friendly models: an overview of the case of the computer industry". Journal of Artificial Societies and Social Simulation 4. http://www.soc.surrey.ac.uk/JAstrophys.Space.Sci.S/4/3/6.html.

Malerba, F., Nelson, R., Orsenigo, L., Winter, S. (2001b). "Competition and industrial policies in a 'history-friendly' model of the evolution of the computer industry". International Journal of Industrial Organization 19, 635–664.

Marks, R. (2006). "Market design", this handbook.

Metcalfe, J.S. (1988). Evolutionary Economics and Creative Destruction. Routledge, London.

Moss, S. (2002). Policy analysis from first principles. Proceedings of the US National Academy of Sciences 99, 7267–7274.

Natter, M., Mild, A., Feuerstein, M., Dorffner, G., Taudes, A. (2001). "The effect of incentive schemes and organizational arrangements on the new product development process". Management Science 47, 1029–1045.

Nelson, R.R. (Ed.) (1993). National Systems of Innovation: A Comparative Study. Oxford University Press, Oxford.

Nelson, R.R. (1995). "Recent evolutionary theorizing about economic change". Journal of Economic Literature 33, 48–90.

Nelson, R.R., Winter, S.G. (1982). An Evolutionary Theory of Economic Change. Belknap, Cambridge, MA.

Nelson, R.R., Winter, S.G. (2002). "Evolutionary theorizing in economics". Journal of Economic Perspectives 16, 23–46.

Pavitt, K. (1984). "Sectoral patterns of technical change: towards a taxonomy and a theory". Research Policy 13, 343–373.

Pavitt, K. (1999). Technology, Management and Systems of Innovation. Edward Elgar, Cheltenham, UK.

Pianta, M. (2000). "The employment impact of product and process innovations". In: Vivarelli, M., Pianta, M. (Eds.), The Employment Impact of Innovation: Evidence and Policy. Routledge, London, pp. 77–95.

Polanyi, M. (1966). The Tacit Dimension. Anchor Books, New York.

Pyka, A., Saviotti, P. (2000). "Innovation networks in the biotechnology-based sectors", SEIN Project Paper No. 7, The SEIN Project, University of Surrey.

Pyka, A., Grebel, T. (2006). "Agent-based modelling—a methodology for the analysis of qualitative development processes". In: Lombardi, M., Squazzoni, F. (Eds.), Saggi di Economia Evolutiva. Franco Angeli, Milan, Italy, in press.

Qiu, L.D. (1997). "On the dynamic efficiency of Bertrand and Cournot equilibria". Journal of Economic Theory 75, 213–229.

Reinganum, J. (1989). "The timing of innovation: research, development and diffusion". In: Schmalensee, R., Willig, R.D. (Eds.), Handbook of Industrial Organization. North-Holland, Amsterdam, pp. 849–908.

Romer, P. (1990). "Endogenous technological change". Journal of Political Economy 98, S71–S102.

Rosenberg, N. (1990). "Why do firms do basic research, (with their own money)?". Research Policy 19, 165–174.

Rosenberg, N. (1994). Exploring the Black Box: Technology, Economics and History. Cambridge University Press, Cambridge.

Schumpeter, J. (1934). The Theory of Economic Development. Harvard University Press, Cambridge.

Silverberg, G., Verspagen, B. (1994). "Collective learning, innovation and growth in a boundedly rational, evolutionary world". Journal of Evolutionary Economics 4, 207–226.

Silverberg, G., Verspagen, B. (1995). "An evolutionary model of long term cyclical variations of catching up and falling behind". Journal of Evolutionary Economics 5, 209–227.

Silverberg, G., Verspagen, B. (1996). "From the artificial to the endogenous: modeling evolutionary adaptation and economic growth". In: Helmstädter, E., Perlman, M. (Eds.), Behavioral Norms, Technological Progress, and Economic Dynamics. The University of Michigan Press, Ann Arbor, pp. 331–354.

Silverberg, G., Verspagen, B. (2005a). "A percolation model of innovation in complex technology spaces". Journal of Economic Dynamics and Control 29, 225–244.

Silverberg, G., Verspagen, B. (2005b). "Evolutionary theorizing on economic growth". In: Dopfer, K. (Ed.), The Evolutionary Foundations of Economics. Cambridge University Press, Cambridge, MA, pp. 506–539.

Silverberg, G., Dosi, G., Orsenigo, L. (1988). "Innovation, diversity and diffusion: a self-organization model". Economic Journal 98, 1032–1054.

Simon, H.A. (1959). "Theories of decision making in economics". American Economic Review 49, 253–283.

Smit, H.T.J., Trigeorgis, L. (1997). "R&D option strategies", working paper, University of Chicago.

Solow, R.M. (1957). "Technical change and aggragate produciton function". Review of Economics and Statistics 39, 312–320.

Stoneman, P. (Ed.) (1995). Handbook of the Economics of Innovation and Technological Change. Blackwell, Oxford.

Sutton, J. (1997). "Gibrat's legacy". Journal of Economic Literature XXXV, 40–59.

Tesfatsion, L. (2006a). "Agent-based computational economics". In: Luna, F., Perrone, A., Terna, P. (Eds.), Agent-Based Theories, Languages, and Practices. Routledge, London, in press.

Tesfatsion, L. (2006b). "Agent-based computational economics: A constructive approach to economic theory", this handbook.

Vallee, T., Yildizoglu, M. (2004). "Social and technological efficiency of patent systems", Cahier No. 2004-11, GRES, Universite Montesquieu-Bordeaux 4.

Van Cayseele, P.J.G. (1998). "Market structure and innovation: a survey of the last twenty years". De Economist 146, 391–417.

Vriend, N. (2006). "ACE Models of endogenous interactions", this handbook.

Weibull, J. (1995). Evolutionary Game Theory. MIT Press, Cambridge, MA.

Werker, C., Brenner, T. (2004). "Empirical calibration of simulation models", Papers on Economics and Evolution #0410, Max Planck Instiute for Research into Economic Systems, Jena.

Wilhite, A.W. (2006). "Economic activity on fixed networks", this handbook.

Windrum, P. (2004). "Neo-Schumpeterian simulation models", MERIT-Infonomics Research Memorandum 2004-002, Maastricht University.

Windrum, P., Birchenhall, C. (1998). "Is product life cycle theory a special case? Dominant designs and the emergence of market niches through coevolutionary-learning". Structural Change and Economic Dynamics 9, 109–134.

Winter, S.G. (1984). "Schumpeterian competition in alternative technological regimes". Journal of Economic Behavior and Organization 5, 287–320.

Winter, S.G., Kaniowski, Y.M., Dosi, G. (2000). "Modelling industrial dynamics with innovative entrants". Structural Change and Economic Dynamics 11, 255–293.

Winter, S.G., Kaniowski, Y.M., Dosi, G. (2003). "A baseline model of industry evolution". Journal of Evolutionary Economics 13, 355–383.

Witt, U. (2001). "Evolutionary economics—an interpretative survey". In: Dopfer, K. (Ed.), Evolutionary Economics: Program and Scope. Kluwer, Amsterdam, pp. 45–88.

Yildizoglu, M. (2001). "Connecting adaptive behavior and expectations in models of innovation: the potential role of artificial neural networks". European Journal of Economic and Social Systems 15, 203–220.

Yildizoglu, M. (2002). "Competing R&D strategies in an evolutionary industry model". Computational Economics 19, 51–65.

Ziman, J. (Ed.) (2000). Technological Innovation as an Evolutionary Process. Cambridge University Press, Cambridge, UK.

Chapter 26

AGENT-BASED MODELS OF ORGANIZATIONS[*]

MYONG-HUN CHANG[†]

Department of Economics, Cleveland State University, Cleveland, OH 44115, USA
e-mail: m.chang@csuohio.edu; url: http://academic.csuohio.edu/changm

JOSEPH E. HARRINGTON JR.

Department of Economics, Johns Hopkins University, Baltimore, MD 21218, USA
e-mail: joe.harrington@jhu.edu; url: http://www.econ.jhu/people/harrington

Contents

[*] The issues addressed in Section 5.1 are closely related to the concerns of [Janssen, M.A., Ostrom, E. (2005). "Governing social-ecological systems", this handbook].

[†] The authors gratefully acknowledge the comments of Rich Burton, Josh Epstein, Vijay Mathur, Scott Page, Jan Rivkin, Nicolaj Siggelkow, Leigh Tesfatsion, and two anonymous economic theorists.

Handbook of Computational Economics, Volume 2. Edited by Leigh Tesfatsion and Kenneth L. Judd
DOI: 10.1016/S1574-0021(05)02026-5

Abstract

The agent-based approach views an organization as a collection of agents, interacting with one another in their pursuit of assigned tasks. The performance of an organization in this framework is determined by the formal and informal structures of interactions among agents, which define the lines of communication, allocation of information processing tasks, distribution of decision-making authorities, and the provision of incentives. This chapter provides a synthesis of various agent-based models of organizations and surveys some of the new insights that are being delivered. The ultimate goal is to introduce the agent-based approach to economists in a methodological manner and provide a broader and less idiosyncratic perspective to those who are already engaging in this line of work. The chapter is organized around the set of research questions that are common to this literature: (1) What are the determinants of organizational behavior and performance? (2) How does organizational structure influence performance?

---

[1] The issues addressed in this section are closely related to the concerns of Janssen and Ostrom (2006).

(3) How do the skills and traits of agents matter and how do they interact with structure? (4) How do the characteristics of the environment—including its stability, complexity, and competitiveness—influence the appropriate allocation of authority and information? (5) How is the behavior and performance influenced when an organization is coevolving with other organizations from which it can learn? (6) Can an organization evolve its way to a better structure?

Keywords

agent-based models, organizations, organizational structure, organizational search, organizational learning, complexity, exploration, exploitation, centralization, decentralization, coordination, information processing, hierarchy, networks, coevolution, organizational norms, endogenous hierarchies

JEL classification: B4, C6, D2, D7, D8, M5

1. Introduction

An organization is a collection of agents that interact and produce some form of output. Formal organizations—such as corporations and governments—are typically constructed for an explicit purpose though this purpose needn't be shared by all organizational members. An entrepreneur who creates a firm may do so in order to generate personal wealth but the worker she hires may have very different goals. As opposed to more amorphous collections of agents such as friendship networks and societies at large, organizations have a formal structure to them (though informal structures typically emerge as well) with the prototypical example being a corporation's organizational chart. This structure serves to define lines of communication and the distribution of decision-making. Organizations are also distinguished by their well-defined boundaries as reflected in a clear delineation as to who is and who is not a member. This boundary serves to make organizations a natural unit of selection; for example, corporations are formed and liquidated though they can also morph into something different through activities like mergers.

The primary task of organization theory is to understand how organizations behave and to identify and describe the determinants of organizational performance.[2] To take an *agent-based* approach means not having to assign an objective to an organization and instead modelling the agents that comprise it with explicit attention to how decisions are made and how the interaction of these decisions produce organizational output. The smallest decision-making unit is then required to be smaller than the organization itself. The anthropomorphic view associated with the theory of the firm—firms are profit-maximizers—is not an agent-based model. Though neoclassical economics has many agent-based models of organizations, including agency theory and team theory, these models are generally quite restrictive in terms of the assumptions placed on agent behavior, the number and heterogeneity of agents, the richness of the interaction among agents, and the features of the environment. These restrictions are forced upon scholars by virtue of the limited power of analytical methods. To derive universal results ("proving" them) requires limiting the size of one's universe (the class of models). While some structures are relatively simple in their real form (for example, many auctions), organizations are inherently complex; they are their own brand of society, plagued with conflicting interests while dealing with multi-faceted problems amidst a coevolving environment. Proving universal results is only achieved at the cost of severely restricting the richness of the setting.

A *computational* agent-based model uses the power of computing to "solve" a model. A model is written down, parameter values are specified, random variables are realized, and, according to agents' behavioral rules, agent output is produced. Organizational output comes from the specified mapping from the environment and agents' actions

---

[2] A thoughtful statement as to what is an organization and what organization theory is about can be found in Aldrich (1999).

into the output space. At the end of vast CPU time, the simulation output can yield results that are rich and insightful but ultimately are a collection of examples, perhaps many examples—thousands of periods, hundreds of runs, dozens of parameter configurations—but still noticeably finite. In deploying numerical methods, the presumption is that the model is unsolvable by the human mind (in practice, not necessarily in principle). If the use of computing power is not to reflect laziness or ineptness on the modeler's part, a computational agent-based model must then have some minimum level of complexity—whether due to agent heterogeneity, the structure of interactions among agents, a poorly behaved environment, dynamics, or some other feature. A legitimate computational agent-based model is then not simply one that is solved by a computer but rather one for which it is necessary that it be solved by a computer.[3]

Organization theory is traditionally of two varieties: (i) broad, institutionally rich, and vague while using informal arguments articulated in a narrative; and (ii) narrow, simplistic, and mathematically precise while using formal logic articulated in a set of assumptions, a statement of a theorem, and a proof. The appeal of computational modelling is that it achieves middle ground in that it has the precision of (ii) and the ability to handle a rich set of features as with (i). It trades off the universality of results of (ii) for a richer model while maintaining rigor and formality. This trade-off is generally judged to be a good one when it comes to modelling a complex entity such as an organization.

In writing this chapter, the hope is to describe to the reader the central research questions addressed, synthesize the models and methods deployed, and survey some of the new insight being delivered. Given the incipiency of this literature, what we will not provide is a coherent set of results because such has not yet emerged. Work on computational agent-based models of organizations is very much in the exploratory phase with highly varied approaches to pursuing a broad range of questions. Our objective is to introduce it to economists in a methodological manner and provide a broader and less idiosyncratic perspective to those who are already engaging in this type of work.

Before launching into specific models, let us offer a quick review of some of the questions addressed by research so that these can frame the reader's mind. What are the determinants of organizational behavior and performance? How does organizational structure influence performance? How do the skills and traits of agents matter and how do they interact with structure? What determines whether more skilled agents and a more decentralized structure are complements or substitutes? What is the proper balance of exploration and exploitation? How do the characteristics of the environment—including its stability, complexity, and competitiveness—influence the appropriate allocation of authority and information? How is behavior and performance influenced when an organization is coevolving with other organizations from which it can learn? Can an organization evolve its way to a better structure?

---

[3] Not all computational models of organizations are agent-based; Carroll and Harrison (1998) being an example. Their formulation begins not with a specification of agents but rather a system of equations describing hiring, socialization, and turnover.

1.1. Related literatures

There are a number of closely related literatures that will not be covered here. A more complete treatment of agent-based models of organizations would discuss the extensive literature in neoclassical economics on organizations.[4] These models are rich in their modelling of incentives but mired in poverty when it comes to modelling agent heterogeneity, the cognitive limitations of agents, organizational structure, and the coevolving nature of a population of organizations. A second related literature is on networks, for implicit in any non-degenerate model of an organization is a network which describes how agents communicate and influence each other. As there are two other chapters in this handbook devoted to networks (Vriend, 2006; Wilhite, 2006), we will generally exclude such work other than that which is specifically designed to understand organizations. Thirdly is work on distributed artificial intelligence which develops better ways to solve problems through the distribution of tasks among agents.[5] While some of these models have something meaningful to say regarding the questions of this chapter, the ultimate objective is quite different. For example, as the objective is developing more efficient solutions rather than better explaining organizations, it is common to assume agents' goals coincide with the organizational goal. Finally, there is the line of work best referred to as organizational engineering. This research develops a relatively literal description of an organization which can then be calibrated and simulated to provide quantitative answers to policy questions. As a result, the models are not designed to provide qualitative insight and have different objectives from the work that is reviewed here. At the risk of unfairly over-generalizing, organizational engineering models are designed for prediction, not explanation.

As to other review articles, the Introduction to Lomi and Larsen (2001) offers a most enlightening historical perspective that draws on many scholarly antecedents. The review article closest to what we are doing here is Carley and Gasser (1999) though they give emphasis to organizational engineering. Sorensen (2002) provides a nice review of organizational models based on the *NK*-approach (Kauffman, 1993) and cellular automata. One of the best papers that discusses the general topic of complexity and how it relates to issues in organization theory is Carroll and Burton (2000). Collections of papers dealing with computational organization theory (not just agent-based modelling) include Baum and Singh (1994), Carley and Prietula (1994), Cohen and Sproull (1996), Prietula et al. (1998), and Lomi and Larsen (2001). Also see Baum (2002) for general work on organizations with several entries dealing with computational modelling.

1.2. Roadmap and a guide for neoclassical economists

A synthesis of the central features of computational agent-based models of organizations is provided in Section 2. The literature itself is partitioned according to the

---

[4] Holmstrom and Tirole (1989), Milgrom and Roberts (1992), and Prendergast (1999) offer good general treatments.

[5] See, for example, Durfee (1999) and Mackie-Mason and Wellman (2006).

basic task with which an organization is faced. Section 3 focuses on models for which organizations search and learn; it represents the most well-developed body of work. Section 4 looks into modelling the processing of information which is, roughly speaking, a production function for organizational decision-making. Thus far, models are a bit mechanical and the literature is not as developed. While these two research strands make up the bulk of the literature, other issues are tackled and Section 5 describes the best work on some of the more important organizational issues not covered in Sections 3 and 4. A critical appraisal is provided in Section 6 where we also identify some lines for future work.

For the neoclassical economist largely unfamiliar with computational agent-based modelling, we recommend focusing on Sections 2 and 3. Section 2 introduces many concepts and elements of this modelling approach and, in its final subsection, contrasts neoclassical and computational agent-based models and suggests why a neoclassical economist should be interested in these methods. The search and learning literature reviewed in Section 3 is the closest in style to that conducted by neoclassical economists and, in addition, we take the opportunity to begin synthesizing existing results and contrasting the associated insight with what one would get using a neoclassical approach. We ask: What do we learn from the computational agent-based approach that we would not have learned from using the neoclassical approach?

2. How to model an organization

> How can intelligence emerge from nonintelligence? To answer that, we'll show that you can build a mind from many little parts, each mindless by itself. ... These we'll call agents. Each mental agent by itself can only do some simple thing that needs no mind or thought at all. Yet when we join these agents in societies—in certain very special ways—this leads to true intelligence. [Marvin Minsky, *The Society of Mind* (1986), p. 17.]

The typical neoclassical description of a firm—the organization that has drawn the most attention within economics—is as a profit-maximizing entity. Being a single-agent formulation, it represents a rather uninteresting model of an organization.[6] Similarly, there are models in the agent-based literature, such as the early work of Levinthal (1997), that model an organization as a single agent adaptively learning. However, to be a meaningful agent-based model of an organization, an agent must be "smaller" than the organization itself. But then, how does organizational behavior emerge from a collection of agents making choices? Just as Marvin Minsky asks how mindless components can form a mind and produce intelligence, we ask how agents—representing human

---

[6] Though no economist would see the theory of the firm as a model of an organization, this misses the point. The theory of the firm is used to make predictions about corporations which *are* organizations.

actors—can form an organization and produce output beyond the capacity of any individual agent.

This section is divided into five parts. The first part reviews the concept of an agent. An agent represents the smallest decision-making unit of an organization. Next we turn to examining the various dimensions of an organization; what transforms a collection of agents into an organization? The third section describes the environment into which an organization is placed and the task with which it is presented. The fourth section offers a brief discussion on computationally implementing an agent-based organizational model. In the final section, this approach is contrasted with the more standard approach in economics.

2.1. Agents

There are many definitions of an "agent" in the agent-based literature. An agent is said to be purposeful, autonomous, adaptive, and so on. While these terms serve to convey a sense of what the researcher is after, they only shift the question of "what is an agent?" to "what does it mean to be purposeful? autonomous? adaptive?" Perhaps the best we can do is to describe our intent—what is this thing called an agent suppose to represent?—and what we actually do—how is an agent instantiated? In almost all models of organizations, an agent represents a flesh-and-blood human.[7] Being purposeful may mean adjusting behavior to improve some measure of well-being; being autonomous may mean choosing actions even if they are in conflict with an organizational goal; being adaptive may mean modifying behavior in response to past experiences. Though the terms are vague, the way in which they are implemented has substantive content.

The neoclassical approach in economics to modelling agents takes preferences and beliefs as primitives. Typically, an agent is endowed with a utility function and, given beliefs over that which is unknown to the agent, acts to maximize expected utility or, in an intertemporal setting, the expectation of the discounted sum of utility. When an agent is making choices in a multi-agent context and what is best depends on what others do—and this certainly describes an organization—this approach is augmented with the (Bayes–Nash) equilibrium assumption that each agent understands how other agents behave. This doesn't necessarily mean that agents know exactly what others will do but they do know other agents' decision rules—how private information maps into actions. Agents have complete understanding though may lack complete information.

In contrast to the assumption of a hyper-rational agent, it is standard in the computational agent-based literature to assume agents are boundedly rational. The most concise statement of this modelling approach is that agents engage in adaptive search subject to various cognitive constraints (and not just informational constraints). These models

---

[7] This needn't be the case for, in actual organizations, agents can be software such as expert systems or automated bidding rules at auctions.

may continue to deploy the optimization framework though assuming myopic optimization and that beliefs are empirically-based rather than the product of understanding what is optimal behavior for others. Agents observe but do not necessarily theorize. For example, a common specification is that an agent engages in hill-climbing as it adopts a new alternative when doing so yields higher current performance than the previously selected action (Chang and Harrington, 2000). Or the optimization framework may be entirely discarded as preferences and beliefs are replaced with behavioral rules cast as primitives. For example, in information processing models, an agent receives data and is endowed with a rule that converts it into a lower-dimensional message sent to the next agent in line (Carley, 1992; Barr and Saraceno, 2002).

Within this bounded rationality framework, models often provide a parameter by which one can "tune" the cognitive skills of an agent. When rules adapt to experience, a key parameter is how much experience an agent has as well as the size of memory (Carley, 1992). In the context of information dissemination, the likelihood that an agent observes an innovation reflects a level of skill (DeCanio and Watkins, 1998). For hill-climbing algorithms, agents may only evaluate alternatives imperfectly—less skilled agents may have noisier evaluations (Chang and Harrington, 1997)—or are constrained in the set of alternatives—more skilled agents are able to consider options in a wider neighborhood around their current practices (Kollman et al., 2000). A novel and promising approach is to assume that an agent has a "model" of how actions map into performance but where the model is of lower dimensionality than reality (Gavetti and Levinthal, 2000).

2.2. Organizations

Let us now turn to the issue of what transforms a collection of agents into an organization. Our discussion is organized along three questions. Who comprises an organization? How are agents connected to produce organizational output? And, how are agents motivated?

An organization is comprised of multiple agents and indeed one common question in the literature is how the number of agents influences organizational performance. But more than pure numbers is relevant, especially when agents are heterogeneous. There is an architecture to organizations, which we will elaborate upon momentarily, which raises questions of how agents are distributed across various units and how agents are matched to tasks. Given the often significant role to agent heterogeneity in computational agent-based models, it is surprising that there is little research exploring how agents with different skills are distributed across the different levels of an organization. This is an area begging for work.

Organizational structure is another one of those terms that has defied a common definition. A broad but useful one refers to it as "those aspects of the pattern of behavior in an organization that are relatively stable and that change only slowly" (March and Simon, 1958, p. 170). Under the rubric of organizational structure, we will place three dimensions. First, there is the allocation of information. This refers to how information moves between the environment and the organization—which agents receive data from the environment—and how it moves within the organization—who reports to whom. This may have a fairly stable component to it, as might be described by the rules of communication laid out in an organizational chart. Such well-defined flows are a common feature of information processing models (Miller, 2001). However, just as people create dirt paths in a park by veering from the sidewalk, information can flow outside of mandated channels. There is then an endogenous feature to how information is distributed.[8] For example, Chang and Harrington (2000) allow an upper level manager to observe a new practice and then decide whether to communicate it to lower level agents.

A second element to organizational structure is the allocation of authority—who makes the decisions—associated with which are two critical facets: modularity and decentralization. An organization may have to perform many sub-tasks in solving a problem and a key structural issue is how these sub-tasks are combined into distinct modules which are then re-integrated to produce an organizational solution. The degree to which a problem can be efficaciously modularized depends on the nature of the task (what is referred to as decomposability, which we discuss later). Two classic structures that represent alternative modular forms are the *M-form*—where all of the sub-tasks associated with a particular product line are combined—and the *U-form*—where all similar sub-tasks are combined (for example, the marketing divisions for all product lines are in the same module). With this allocation of tasks, there is still the issue of which agents ultimately make the decisions. In the context of a hierarchy—which describes most organizations—to what degree is authority centralized in higher levels? Is authority matched with who has the best information? Here we are referring to formal authority which, as noted by Aghion and Tirole (1997), may differ from real authority. If an agent with decision-making authority relies heavily on the information provided by other agents then the real authority (or power) may lie with those providing the information. The allocation of information and real authority are thus intertwined.

A third element of structure is the least well-defined: organizational norms and culture. Though there are probably as many definitions of culture as scholars who have sought to define it, we'll put forth the one of Sathe (1985): "Culture is a set of shared assumptions regarding how the world works (beliefs) and what ideals are desirable (values)." Agent behavior is somehow influenced by an organization's past and this past is embodied in what is called norms or culture. Of particular interest is modelling the associated feedback dynamic—norms, being determined by past behavior, influence current behavior which then serves to define future norms. This is a driving force in March (1991).

The final element to organizations to be covered is agent motivation. Agents may be modelled as having preferences—for example, they desire income and dislike exerting effort—but how that translates into behavior depends on an organization's incentive

---

[8] This type of model is more fully explored in Vriend (2006).

scheme for rewarding and punishing.[9] The compensation scheme for corporate managers may drive them to seek higher organizational profit, while the scheme for division managers may be tied to division profit (so as to induce high effort) which can then create a conflict of interests. Conflict may also arise when an organization uses promotion or bonuses based on relative performance to encourage effort.[10] An important element to any conception of an organization is the degree of such conflicts and how it varies within and across levels. By contrast, models of distributed problem solving in AI assume agents have a coherence of goals. More realistic models of organizations recognize that conflict of interest is an endemic feature of actual organizations.

An organization has an output—say, a set of practices—and delivers some measure of performance. Performance may be measured by profit (or some analogous criterion) or may involve specifying a particular target (for example, the global optimum) and then measuring performance by the frequency with which an organization reaches it or, if eventually it'll always reach it, the average time it takes to do so. While most organizations are designed with a particular objective in mind (the objective of the entrepreneur), it doesn't follow that organizational behavior is consistent with that or any other objective. An organization's members may have different goals than those of the entrepreneur. Fortunately, an agent-based model needn't answer the dicey question of "what is an organization's utility function" as it is sufficient to instantiate agents and let organizational behavior emerge from the interaction of agents amongst themselves and with the environment. By building an organization from the ground-up, we can avoid taking an anthropomorphic view to complex entities such as organizations.

2.3. Environments

An organization resides in an environment and is faced with a problem (or task) and constraints to be faced in trying to solve it. The problem may be choosing a political platform, if it is a political party, or producing and selling a product, if it is a firm. Problems vary in terms of their difficulty. A problem may be more difficult because it requires more information. It may be more difficult because there are interactions between various choice variables which makes it less likely that one can search, dimension by dimension, for a multi-dimensional solution. Relatedly, it may be more difficult because directed search is infeasible or ineffective. Knowing where to go from one's current position to achieve higher performance can greatly ease search. Such directed search may be infeasible because there is no metric on the solution space; there is no notion of two solutions being close. Even if there is a metric, the relationship between

[9] Many computational agent-based models of organizations are not explicit about the form of the incentive scheme but, if one makes standard assumptions about agents' preferences, there is often an obvious implicit specification.

[10] Though these forces haven't been modelled in the agent-based literature, there has been some computational work elsewhere (Harrington, 1998, 1999).

performance and actions may not be well-behaved in that the components of the gradient may quickly change sign and admit many optima. This means that hill-climbing algorithms can get stuck on lousy local optima and it isn't clear where to look for better ones.[11]

Related to the issue of difficulty is the extent to which a problem is decomposable. A problem is said to be decomposable if there exists a way in which to partition it into sub-problems such that the concatenation of the solutions to the sub-problems is a solution to the original problem. Such problems are easier and quicker to solve as it means solving a collection of simpler (lower dimensional) problems in parallel. Furthermore, how a problem decomposes suggests a "natural" organizational structure, an issue explored in Ethiraj and Levinthal (2002).

An organization's problem may also have a dynamic component to it. In solving a single task in real time, the best solution may evolve with changes in the environment. A less stable environment makes the problem more difficult as the organization is pursuing a moving target. Or an organization may face a series of problems. Is the same problem being faced repeatedly or are the problems distinct and, if so, how are they related? As long as the problems retain some similarity, the solution to one will provide clues for another, thereby creating opportunities to learn.

A more distinctive feature of an organization's environment is the presence of other entities that are also solving problems; there may be a pool of organizations coevolving. Other organizations may influence an organization's current performance—consider a setting in which they compete (Barr and Saraceno, 2002)—or influence future performance when they can learn from each other (Miller, 2001) or exchange personnel (Axtell, 1999). There may be other adapting agents such as consumers—Chang and Harrington (2003) allow consumers to search at the same time that firms are adapting their practices—or lobbyists (if the organizations are governments). In providing an endogenous source of change in an organization's environment, coevolution can provide rich and non-trivial dynamics.

2.4. Implementation of an agent-based model of an organization

Having identified many of the components that go into an agent-based model of an organization, how does one implement it computationally? As space constraints prevent a comprehensive answer, let us focus on two broad and essential elements to implementation: *agent processes* and *super-agent processes*. In a computational model, an agent is instantiated as a mapping from inputs into outputs. Input includes information from outside the organization (from customers, input suppliers, competitors, etc.) and information from inside the organization (subordinates, peers, superiors); it takes the form of processed information, new ideas, actions. The ensuing output may be a concrete

---

[11] Page (1996) provides a rigorous investigation into what it means for a problem to be more difficult from the perspective of search algorithms.

action or a message to other agents. The important point is that many of the elements of an organization—communication network, hierarchy, incentive schemes, and the like—are embedded in an agent's mapping. When one writes a code that specifies that agent i observes some data and makes a recommendation to agent h who, after also receiving a recommendation from agent j, chooses between these alternatives, one is making assumptions about the allocation of information (i and j receive information from the environment while h does not) and the allocation of authority (h has authority while i and j do not). The particular form of this mapping similarly depends on organizational features such as the form of compensation and norms (peer pressure, standard operating practices, etc.) as well as agent-specific traits including preferences, beliefs, and cognitive skills. This mapping may evolve over time due to learning but also because the identity of an agent changes as a result of personnel turnover. In sum, an organization is implicit in the modelling of agents' mappings. What emerges from the interaction among agents and the environment is organizational behavior.

Lying on top of these agent processes are super-agent processes which systematically influence an organization but are not embodied in agents' mappings. Super-agent processes are commonly used to endogenize organizational structure. This may mean using a genetic algorithm defined over a population of organizations which creates new organizational designs and weeds out poorly performing ones (Miller, 2001).[12] Or one might model the adaptation of organizational design through a hill-climbing algorithm (Ethiraj and Levinthal, 2002) or simulated annealing (Carley and Svoboda, 1996). These super-agent processes provide a black box mechanism to substitute for modelling the agents who actually make these decisions. For example, a CEO typically decides on organizational structure, creditors decide whether to force an organization to exit, and entrepreneurs decide whether to create a new organization. As modelling all agents is often too daunting a task, super-agent processes represent a parsimonious way in which to encompass these other forces.

2.5. How does agent-based computational economics differ from neoclassical economics?

The objective of this section is to summarize the essential differences between agent-based computational economics (or ACE) and neoclassical economics (or NCE). In so doing, we will argue why economists ought to be interested in ACE.

The first essential difference is that agent behavior is characterized by *adaptive search* in ACE, which departs from the assumption in NCE that agent behavior is optimal (for some preferences and beliefs). In short, NCE describes "what is best," while ACE

---

[12] The role of selection is particularly interesting because part of what makes a collection of agents an "organization" is that it is a unit of selection. Corporations are created and fail; governments are put in power and overthrown. By comparison, general societies are more amorphous and thus less natural a unit of selection. Indeed, conquerers can be assimilated in which case which society has really prevailed? While the same might be said of firms—consider hostile takeovers—it is not as compelling.

describes "what is better." With ACE, learning is based more on experience than understanding, more on retrospection rather than foresight. Furthermore, imperfections to agent behavior are modelled very differently. With NCE, imperfections are due to incomplete information. Consistent with the bounded rationality approach, cognitive limitations are central to ACE which means that what information is possessed may not be fully processed. This distinction between optimal behavior and adaptive search has a considerable impact on the logic of the model and the ensuing insight that is produced. This will come out in Section 3 when we examine a particular class of ACE models.

The next two distinctive elements of ACE emanate from the methods used in solving the model. Results are proven with NCE, while they are numerically derived for a particular parameter specification with ACE. Computational implementation has implications for both modelling and analysis.

The second essential difference is the way in which agents' environments are modelled. The forte of expert NCE modelers is constructing a well-behaved environment in the sense of, for example, having a unique optimum or equilibrium and allowing comparative statics to be signed. In other words, building a plausible model that can be mentally solved. With ACE, there are much fewer constraints of this sort since the model is solved numerically. This allows for *complex environments* which are richer with more descriptive realism. Without as many modelling constraints, a researcher is more apt to be able to make the primitive assumptions thought to be most appropriate and let the environment be what it will be. Complexity is not shunned but rather embraced when it is a property of the environment that actual agents and organizations face. In short, ACE allows for richer environments than does the NCE approach and, furthermore, makes complexity a trait of the environment whose role is to be explored. Indeed, research reveals that qualitative results can vary significantly with environmental complexity.

The third essential difference is in the mode of analysis. Dynamic models in the NCE tradition typically focus on the long-run, whether a steady-state or a stationary distribution. Behavior is characterized when all has settled—the environment has calmed down (in actuality or in expectation) and the system has converged to some form of equilibrium. A primary virtue of the ACE approach is that, by running simulations, it can describe *medium-run dynamics*. By medium-run dynamics we mean that some learning and adaptation has taken place but the system is not close to stabilizing. Not only are medium-run dynamics important if one wants to understand the transitional impact of various policies but, if convergence to equilibrium is slow (or if there is no convergence at all), it may be the time scale of greatest relevance.

These three identifying traits of ACE—adaptive search with cognitive constraints, complex environments, and medium-run dynamics—are quite complementary in that a complex environment makes optimal behavior more problematic an assumption and, furthermore, it is more appropriate to describe the system using medium-run dynamics rather than a long-run equilibrium.

In light of these unique features, economists should be interested in ACE because it offers a new set of modelling and analytical tools which, in many instances, are quite complementary to that of NCE. First, a computational agent-based approach can be used when the environment is inherently complex and poorly behaved (multiple optima, non-quasi-concave, coevolution among agents, etc.) so that analytical methods are likely to fail and the assumption of game-theoretic equilibrium is particularly problematic as a characterization of behavior. Rather than making heroic assumptions on behavior and the environment in order to ensure the model can be mentally solved, one can use ACE methods. Second, ACE can characterize medium-run dynamics, a long neglected element of NCE in spite of its importance. Third, ACE methods can be used to explore not just traditional NCE issues—such as the role of organizational structure—but also previously ignored issues such as the role of environmental complexity and the cognitive limitations of organizational members. Complexity may differ across economic settings because of the production process and the extent of complementarities among an organization's activities. For example, greater connectedness among agents due to innovations in information technology may mean a better global optimum but also a more complex environment in terms of more local optima. Cognitive limitations may differ across organizations because of education, training, and how effectively an organization "selects" smarter people. Also, the extent to which cognitive skills matter will vary across positions within an organization; such skills are less important for tasks that can be routinized and more important for those that are continually subject to novelty. These new tools and issues are capable of providing new insight into organizations, as we'll show in this chapter.

Free your mind. [Morpheus to Neo from *The Matrix*.]

A challenge to a neoclassical economist in reading this chapter will be the unorthodox logic of these models. The optimization framework produces a certain logic which can be quite distinct from that due to adaptive search. The canonical ACE environment is one in which an agent is searching on a landscape with multiple optima. Changes—such as with respect to organizational structure—may actually result in a lower global optimum but nevertheless enhance performance because search may not always find the global optimum or medium-run dynamics may generally not be near the global optimum. For example, a change which throws the organization into the basin of attraction for a better optimum can enhance performance even though it may be deleterious in the short-run. The logic of these models rests not just on how the landscape is affected in terms of its highest point but on a broader range of landscape properties which impact how search is conducted. With NCE, what matters are the set of optima or equilibria; with ACE, the entire landscape can matter because at issue is how likely adaptive search can take an organization from one point of the space to another. The path matters and not just the destination.

... a straight line may be the shortest distance between two points, but it is by no means the most interesting. [The Doctor from "The Time Monster" episode of *Doctor Who*.]

3. Search and learning

[T]he assumption that business behavior is ideally rational and prompt, and also that in principle it is the same with all firms, works tolerably well only within the precincts of tried experience and familiar motive. It breaks down as soon as we leave those precincts and allow the business community under study to be faced by—not simply new situations, which also occur as soon as external factors unexpectedly intrude—but by new possibilities of business action which are as yet untried and about which the most complete command of routine teaches nothing. [Joseph A. Schumpeter, *Business Cycles: A Theoretical, Historical, and Statistical Analysis of the Capitalist Process* (1939), p. 98.]

In this section, we take the perspective that a primary task of an organization is to constantly search for and adopt routines that improve (though do not necessarily maximize) performance. This *search-and-learn* perspective of a firm, as an alternative to the neoclassical approach, is central to the evolutionary theory of the firm where firms are "modeled as simply having, at any given time, certain capabilities and decision rules [which are] modified as a result of both deliberate problem-solving efforts and random events" (Nelson and Winter, 1982, p. 4).[13]

As formulated by Schumpeter and Nelson and Winter, a firm is represented by a single agent—an entrepreneur carrying out search and making performance-enhancing adoption decisions for the entire enterprise. The agent-based approach to modelling organizations takes this one step further. It recognizes that the bounded rationality on the part of a single decision maker, faced with a large and complex routine space, makes an organizational search strategy utilizing multiple agents compelling. The main objective of this research program is understanding how a firm's performance is influenced by the way in which parallel search is carried out among multiple agents.[14] This typically takes the form of managers of various departments independently searching for better routines. Furthermore, if we make the reasonable assumption that there is no single individual who is instantaneously and costlessly informed of all new knowledge in the organization, it then becomes crucial for effective organizational decision-making that there be collocation of the uncovered information and the right to act on that information. This collocation may occur at the top, thereby requiring knowledge to be pulled up the hierarchy, or at lower-level units, thereby requiring decision rights to be pushed down (Jensen and Meckling, 1995).

As Hayek (1945) stated so forcefully, the assumption of bounded rationality puts an upper limit on the effectiveness with which the central authority can process and act on

---

[13] One of the earliest computational papers on organizational search is Levinthal and March (1981).

[14] Burton and Obel (1980) is one of the pioneering efforts in using a computational model to understand the effect of organizational form. The authors compare the M-form and U-form as a function of the degree of decomposability in production technology; see Section 2.2 for definitions of these structural forms. Their model anticipated many of the crucial elements of organizational modeling considered in more recent papers reviewed in this chapter.

the large set of information sent up by an organization's lower levels. Pushing against this limit are two beneficial roles that the centralized authority structure may play in formal organizations. First, it can act as a conduit for *knowledge transfer*. Depending on the circumstances surrounding the local units, a piece of information uncovered by one may prove to be of value to other units. The global exploitation of a local discovery realizes an immediate static gain—as a useful routine is shared—but, as we will later explain, there may also be dynamic implications in that mutual learning can influence what units adopt in the future. While an informal social learning mechanism may be capable of facilitating these static and dynamic processes, upper level management can have an important role to play in this regard. Second, centralization can help disparate units to work together by providing *coordination*. To the extent that an action taken by one unit may interact with the productivity of various actions of other units, superior organizational performance may require upper management to intervene and constrain the choices made by these units. Our discussion will focus on how various organizational forms influence these aspects of multi-unit search.

This section is organized as follows. Section 3.1 begins with a description of how an organization's search space is modelled. There are two general approaches: the *NK model* (which is imported from biology) and the *economic model* (which is built upon economic primitives). We then briefly discuss the cognitive requirements for a search unit exploring such landscapes as well as their implications for multi-agent search. The relevant literature is then divided into two broad classes. One class has all of the units of an organization engaged in similar operations and striving to solve similar (though perhaps not identical) problems. This is covered in Section 3.2. Examples include retail chains and multi-plant manufacturers. The second class, which is reviewed in Section 3.3, has the organizational problem segmented into distinct and dissimilar sub-problems which are distributed among the units who separately engage in search. The typical *U*-form organization is an example. The evolution of organizational designs is covered in Section 3.4. Finally, Section 3.5 distills some of the new insight and contrasts it with what a neoclassical economic approach delivers.

3.1. Modelling search

Two approaches have been taken in modelling the search space faced by an organization. One approach is to assume the space of routines, over which an organization is searching, is a highly structured space; typically, it is a subset of Euclidean space with a metric that allows one to measure how "close" two routines are. Given this search space, a mapping from it to the real line is constructed which assigns performance to each routine. How this mapping is constructed varies significantly between the *NK* model and the economic model. A second approach involves less structure as its primitive is a probability distribution over the performance (say, profit) attached to an idea. Examples utilizing this approach are March (1991) and Chang and Harrington (1997). As the dominant approach is the first one, we will focus exclusively on it with the exception of discussing March (1991) in Section 5.2 due to its unique analysis of the evolution of organizational norms.

Agent-based models of organizational search characterize an organization by a fixed number of attributes. The search space for an organizational unit, frequently called a *landscape*, is defined on Euclidean space in which each attribute of an organization is represented by a dimension of the space and a final dimension indicates the performance of the organization. The organization's attributes are indexed by the set $S \equiv \{1, 2, \ldots, N\}$. For each attribute, there exists a fixed number of possible options which we will refer to as "practices" and which Nelson and Winter (1982) call "routines." The practice of the organization in attribute $j \in S$ takes values in a non-empty set $Z_j \subseteq \Re$, where $\Re$ is the set of all real numbers. Letting $A \equiv Z_1 \times \cdots \times Z_N$, a vector defined in A then completely describes the organization's practices. There is a metric $d : A \times A \rightarrow \Re$ which measures how "close" practices are to one another. Finally, to each vector of practices, there corresponds a level of performance for the organization as described by $v : A \rightarrow \Re$. The search spaces in the *NK* model and the economic model, to be discussed below, are two special cases of this general model.

A key factor in the organization's search process is the exact shape of the landscape. Figure 1 shows two possible search landscapes for an organization which has two attributes with 15 possible practices for each. Figure 1a captures a smooth landscape having a unique local (and thereby global) optimum, while Figure 1b captures a rugged landscape with many local optima. The shape of the landscape is typically determined by the way the organization's various attributes interact with one another. How the interaction pattern affects the extent of ruggedness is discussed below for both the *NK* model and the economic model.

3.1.1. NK model

Even though the *NK* model was initially conceived by Kauffman (1993) for understanding biological systems, it has been extensively applied in many other domains including computational organization theory. An organization is conceptualized as a system of activities. It makes decisions concerning N activities where each activity can take on two states, 0 or 1, so that, referring back to the general model, $A = \{0, 1\}^N$. A particular configuration of activity is then described by a binary vector of length N. The distance between two such vectors, $\underline{x} \equiv (x_1, \ldots, x_N)$ and $\underline{y} \equiv (y_1, \ldots, y_N)$, is captured by the Hamming distance:

$$d(\underline{x}, \underline{y}) = \sum_{i=1}^{N} |x_i - y_i|; \tag{1}$$

that is, the number of dimensions for which the vectors differ. As part of the *NK* model, the mapping v from the activity vector to the level of performance is a primitive. v is set to depend on the performance contributions that these activities make individually, where the contribution of each activity depends on the interactions among a subset of

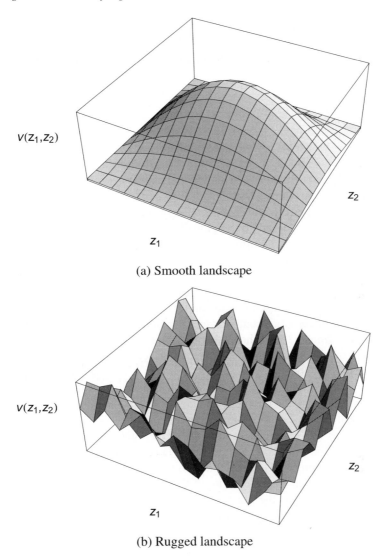

(a) Smooth landscape

(b) Rugged landscape

Figure 1. Search landscapes.

activities. The degree of interdependence among activities is captured by a parameter K which is the number of other activities that directly affect the contribution of a given activity. In its original formulation, these K activities are randomly selected from S for each activity.

To be more concrete, let $v_i(x_i, x_i^1, \ldots, x_i^K)$ denote the contribution of activity i to the organization's performance where its dependence on activity i, x_i, and the K activities to which it is coupled, $(x_i^1, \ldots, x_i^K)$, is made explicit. It is common to assume that the value attached to v_i is randomly drawn from [0, 1] according to a uniform distribution for each possible vector $(x_i, x_i^1, \ldots, x_i^K)$. The overall organizational performance is then

$$v(\underline{x}) = \left(\frac{1}{N}\right) \sum_{i=1}^{N} v_i\left(x_i, x_i^1, \ldots, x_i^K\right). \tag{2}$$

Normalization by N enables performance comparisons when N is changed.

The interaction parameter, K, controls the difficulty of the search problem by making the value of the contribution of an activity dependent upon K other activities. When $K = 0$, the activities are completely independent so that changing the state of one activity does not affect the performance contribution of the remaining $N - 1$ activities. The landscape is then single-peaked so the globally optimal vector of activities is also the unique local optimum. That is, improving v_i by changing x_i must raise the organization's performance since the contribution of the other activities is unaffected by x_i. The other extreme is when $K = N - 1$ so that a change in the state of an activity changes the performance contributions of *all* other activities. This typically results in numerous local optima for $v(\cdot)$ due to the complementarity among activities. That is, changing any one of a collection of activities could lower v but simultaneously changing all activities could raise v. Kauffman (1993) shows that the number of local optima increases in K.

Rather than specify the coupled or interacting activities to be randomly selected, many organizational models using the *NK* framework choose the interaction pattern so as to explore how different architectures influence performance. For those purposes, it is convenient to capture the interdependencies in an *adjacency matrix* (Ghemawat and Levinthal, 2000). Figure 2 shows four such matrices for $N = 6$ in which the degree of interdependence as well as the exact structure of the interdependence differ. If the performance contribution of the jth activity (row j) is affected by the chosen activity in the ith activity (column i) then the element in the matrix corresponding to row j and column i has an 'x'. This is always true of the principal diagonal as the contribution of an activity depends upon the practice chosen for that activity. Figure 2a is an adjacency matrix for an organization in which $K = 0$ so that the activities are completely independent. Figure 2b is when $K = 5$ and each activity is influenced by every other activity in S. Figure 2c captures a special case of $K = 2$, where the interdependencies are restricted to non-overlapping strict subsets of S; the activities in $\{1, 2, 3\}$ influence one another, while those in $\{4, 5, 6\}$ influence one another. Figure 2d is another case of $K = 2$, though there is no obvious systematic structure in comparison to the other matrices. This is what would be typical if the interactions were random.

3.1.2. Economic model

The essence of the *NK* model is to build a generic landscape through a random construction process. In contrast, the economic model builds it systematically from a set

(a) Independence $(K = 0)$

	1	2	3	4	5	6
1	x					
2		x				
3			x			
4				x		
5					x	
6						x

(b) Full Interaction $(K = 5)$

	1	2	3	4	5	6
1	x	x	x	x	x	x
2	x	x	x	x	x	x
3	x	x	x	x	x	x
4	x	x	x	x	x	x
5	x	x	x	x	x	x
6	x	x	x	x	x	x

(c) Block-Diagonal $(K = 2)$

	1	2	3	4	5	6
1	x	x	x			
2	x	x	x			
3	x	x	x			
4				x	x	x
5				x	x	x
6				x	x	x

(d) Random Interaction $(K = 2)$

	1	2	3	4	5	6
1	x	x			x	
2	x	x		x		
3		x	x			x
4	x				x	x
5		x			x	x
6	x		x			x

Figure 2. Adjacency matrix $(N = 6)$.

of economic primitives. By way of example, let us describe the specification in Chang and Harrington (2000). Consider an organization—such as a retail chain—that consists of a corporate headquarters (HQ) and $M \geq 2$ units (such as stores). In this section, we will focus on constructing the landscape for only one of the stores and defer the discussion of the overall organizational search problem. As in the NK model, there exist N activities to a store's operation. For each activity there are R possible practices so that $A = \{1, \ldots, R\}^N$. A store is then characterized by a vector of N operating practices $(z_1, \ldots, z_N) \in A$, where $z_i \in \{1, \ldots, R\}$ is the store's practice for the ith dimension. These practices influence the appeal of the store to consumers. The distance between any two vectors of practices, $\underline{x}$ and $\underline{y}$, is measured by Euclidean distance:

$$d(\underline{x}, \underline{y}) = \sqrt{\sum_{i=1}^{N}(x_i - y_i)^2}. \tag{3}$$

Each consumer has an ideal vector of store practices which is an element of $\{1, \ldots, R\}^N$. The net surplus to a consumer of type $\underline{w} \equiv (w_1, w_2, \ldots, w_N)$ from buying q units at a price of p from the unit is specified to be

$$\left[\Gamma - \sqrt{\sum_{i=1}^{N}(z_i - w_i)^2}\right]^{\gamma} \cdot q^{\beta} - pq.$$

It is assumed that $\beta \in (0, 1)$, $\gamma \geq 1$, and $\Gamma - \sqrt{\sum_{i=1}^{N}(z_i - w_i)^2} > 1$. Having q take its utility-maximizing value, a consumer's demand is

$$(\beta/p)^{\frac{1}{1-\beta}}\left[\Gamma - \sqrt{\sum_{i=1}^{N}(z_i - w_i)^2}\right]^{\frac{\gamma}{1-\beta}}.$$

The set of consumers in a market is represented by a cdf F defined on the space of consumer types, $\{1, \ldots, R\}^N$, and is allowed to vary across markets so that the environment a store faces varies across stores. In Chang and Harrington (2000), additional structure is placed upon F as a consumer's type is assumed to lie in $\{(1, \ldots, 1), \ldots, (R, \ldots, R)\}$ so that it can be represented by a scalar. This captures the idea that a consumer's preferences over the various dimensions are correlated so that, for example, a consumer who prefers value 3 for dimension 1 is likely to prefer value 3 for the other dimensions. The set of consumers in the market is represented by a triangular density function defined on $\{1, \ldots, R\}$.[15]

Using the derived demand for a consumer and specifying the optimal price of c/β, a store's profit is:

$$v(\underline{z}) \equiv \left[\left(\frac{c}{\beta}\right) - c\right]\left(\frac{\beta^2}{c}\right)^{\frac{1}{1-\beta}} \int \left[\Gamma - \sqrt{\sum_{i=1}^{N}(z_i - w_i)^2}\right]^{\frac{\gamma}{1-\beta}} dF(\underline{w}). \qquad (4)$$

The crucial property here is that a store's profit is decreasing in the distance between its practices and those desired by its customers. For a given store, the profit function defined above then represents its performance landscape over which it searches for better combinations of practices. As in the NK model, an important property of the landscape structure is its ruggedness. Here, the number of local optima can be shown to increase in γ, the consumers' sensitivity to store practices, as well as the degree of preference complementarity (Chang and Harrington, 2004). Unlike the NK model, for which the level of complexity is directly specified by the interaction parameter K, the economic model allows the complexity in a decision problem to result from more fundamental economic primitives.

3.1.3. Modelling search by a single agent

The potential for multi-agent search to outperform single-agent search on a per-agent basis derives from its capacity to overcome the bounded rationality of individual agents through sharing and coordination in the search process. Two forms of bounded rationality stand out in these models: a lack of information about the search space (landscape), and a constraint on the considered set of alternatives to the status quo.

---

[15] Chang and Harrington (2004) relax the assumption of a perfect correlation in a consumer's preferences over dimensions and examine how the degree of preference complementarity affects the relationship between an organization's structure and its performance.

If a unit has full information about the mapping from practices to performance then search is irrelevant as the organization can simply identify and adopt the practice vector that corresponds to the global peak. Almost all agent-based models instead take the view that agents are largely uninformed and assume the other extreme—nothing is known about the shape of the landscape—so that agents must resort to blind search using some form of hill-climbing algorithm. The myopic but adaptive search on the landscape entails considering a practice vector that is different in several dimensions from the organization's current one—the change may involve as few as one and as many as all dimensions.

This forces us to confront the second form of bounded rationality. To what extent is the organization capable of considering different changes? Is it capable of contemplating a major change in its operation which involves changing practices in all dimensions? Or, is it constrained to considering only minor modifications? The ruggedness of the landscape—which is determined by K in the NK model and partially determined by γ in the economic model—turns out to affect the efficacy of search. When the landscape is smooth and single-peaked, constraining the breadth of change that an organization considers has no impact on the optimum eventually attained—as any hill-climbing algorithm will find the global optimum—though it will influence the speed of convergence and thus intermediate-run performance. This form of bounded rationality does make a difference, however, when the landscape is rugged. While an organization capable of carrying out transformations involving all dimensions will still eventually attain the global optimum,[16] an organization which is only capable of considering changes involving a small subset of the dimensions may become trapped on an inferior local optimum.

Central to the search-and-learn perspective of organizational theory is this dynamic interaction between a boundedly rational search unit and the structure of its search space, which serves to restrict the set of search paths and outcomes that the unit is capable of achieving. The organization as a multi-agent search mechanism can overcome such restrictions through the sharing of their discoveries and internal coordination.[17]

3.2. Organizational search with units solving similar problems

Examples of organizations in which various units are solving similar problems include retail chains, multi-plant manufacturers, and manufacturers producing a line of related products. Such a situation is modelled by endowing each unit with a performance landscape over which it searches. All of the landscapes are defined over the same space

---

[16] It should be noted, however, that it may take a very long time for the organization to find such a global optimum by chance when N is relatively large.

[17] Both Levinthal (1997) and Rivkin (2000) consider the impact of this interaction on the Darwinian selection process in a population of firms climbing an NK landscape. Levinthal (1997) examines how successful firms with tightly coupled systems (high K) find adaptation difficult in the face of environmental change, while Rivkin (2000) allows imitation among firms and focuses on how tight coupling protects a successful firm from potential imitators. It should be noted that both papers are restricted to single-agent models of an organization.

of activities and similarity between units' problems is reflected in the similarity of the landscape, that is, how activities map into performance. Given that units are searching over similar landscapes, the possibility of knowledge transfer among units is significant. The main organizational issue here is how inter-unit learning can be promoted through an appropriate organizational structure.

3.2.1. Kollman et al. 2000

Recognizing the possibility of multiple searches as the central benefit from decentralization, Kollman et al. (2000), hereafter KMP, consider four factors affecting the magnitude of this benefit: (1) difficulty of the problem; (2) sophistication in search; (3) heterogeneity among unit preferences; and (4) organizational size. Extending the NK model into the multi-unit organizational setting, KMP endow each unit with an NK search space which is common for all units (including the central authority).[18] Search involves myopic hill-climbing on a fixed landscape. The objective is to investigate the efficacy of a multi-unit organization in searching for solutions in parallel by exploiting units' search capacities and combining the revealed information to the benefit of the entire organization.

Four types of organizational forms (or search rules) are considered: (1) full centralization in which search is carried out solely by the central authority and the best policy found is mandated for all units—hence, this is equivalent to single agent search; (2) full decentralization in which each unit searches independently and makes its own adoption decision (so that there is no inter-unit spillovers of knowledge); (3) partial decentralization with "best adoption" which means that each unit searches on its own but, after a fixed number of search periods, the central authority mandates the best policy discovered; and (4) partial decentralization with "incremental adoption" which means that each unit searches on its own for a given length of time and then the central authority forces the units to change policies incrementally (attribute by attribute) toward the best known current policy so that, ultimately, all units have the same policy.[19] The potential trade-off between centralization and decentralization is that the former may draw from a better distribution while the latter has multiple units searching. Under each of these organizational rules, KMP examines the impact on the organization's performance of the four previously mentioned factors.

A focus of their analysis is to understand the relationship between the complexity of the environment—measured by K in the NK formulation—and the cognitive constraints of the organization's units which are represented by the maximum number of

---

[18] The central authority in this setting is just another unit carrying out the search for the organization, though it may have superior search capability.

[19] In this case, the target policy—that is, the "best-to-date" policy—could change along the adoption process, since the organization-wide switching of unit policies takes place one attribute at a time. This is to be contrasted to the "best adoption" rule under which all units immediately adopt the best policy in its entirety, while discarding everything that they have found individually through local search.

dimensions, denoted z, along which a new idea can depart from the status quo policy. To begin, the benefits from decentralization are always positive under the best adoption rule when the units are as capable as the central authority. There is also an interaction between problem difficulty and the benefits of decentralized search because the greatest advantage occurs with a moderate level of difficulty. Even a single unit can do very well when problems are simple, so having more units searching in this case is of little value. When problems are very hard, each unit tends to get stuck on a local optimum of similar value (as the peaks become more numerous with more similar values as K increases) so once again organizational structure doesn't matter. It is when the problem is of moderate difficulty that the additional search under decentralization makes a substantive difference.

In comparing the two partial decentralization rules, KMP find that the incremental adoption rule always outperforms the best adoption rule. This is due to the fact that the units are allowed to keep in place what has worked for them, while simultaneously allowed to try what has worked elsewhere in the organization. This blending of diverse local solutions proves superior to the alternative of requiring all but one unit to discard the knowledge they accumulated. This comparative advantage of incremental adoption is found to be non-monotonic in the difficulty of the problem. When K is low, the probability of any one unit finding the global optimum is relatively high and, therefore, the advantage of incremental adoption is minimal. And, when K is high, there are many local optima which tend to be uncorrelated so that blending them together has little value and, like any random change, generally proves deleterious. In other words, the activities identified as worthwhile by one unit (that is, are at or close to a local optimum) are unlikely to be of much value to another unit that is targeting a different optimum because these different optima could be vastly distant from one another. Once again, it is for moderately difficult problems that incremental adoption does significantly better than best adoption. Finding the global optimum is then not easy, and information associated with one local optimum is still of value to units that are at another local optimum as it may allow them to move to yet better local optima.

3.2.2. Chang and Harrington (2000)

The focus of this work is to explore the relationship between organizational structure— specifically, the degree of centralization—and firm performance. The case of a single chain with multiple local stores is analyzed in Chang and Harrington (2000). The model is then extended in Chang and Harrington (2003) to allow for competing chains and searching consumers, thereby enabling an investigation of the coevolutionary dynamics among organizations, units within an organization, and consumers in heterogeneous markets.

Chang and Harrington (2000) consider a retail chain consisting of M stores, each with a performance (profit) landscape defined by equation (4). The heterogeneity in the markets that the stores serve is captured by differences in the distributions of consumer types. Organizational profit is the simple sum of its stores' profits. While stores' landscapes may be similar, they are independent in that a choice made by one store does not affect the profit earned by another store. However, as explained below, inter-unit learning creates a dynamic and endogenous linkage among stores' search paths and profits.

Search over the profit landscape takes place through an iteration of myopic one-step hill-climbing, where a new idea is represented as a point in store practice space. In each period, each store possesses a vector of current practices and generates one idea where an idea is created by randomly selecting a dimension from $\{1, \ldots, N\}$ and assigning to it a randomly selected element from $\{1, \ldots, R\}$. If it is adopted then the store's practice in the specified dimension is changed to the new value.

Two organizational forms are considered in this setting. In the decentralized organization, a store manager evaluates his own idea and the ideas adopted by other stores in the current period. A store manager sequentially evaluates these ideas and adopts an idea if it raises *store* profit. Hence, each store manager searches over his store's landscape and has the authority to implement any useful ideas. This is equivalent to KMP's full decentralization, except that inter-unit learning is voluntary. In a centralized organization, a store manager once again generates an idea and considers whether, if adopted, it would raise store profit. If so, the idea is passed to *HQ*. If not, the idea is discarded. With this set of ideas, *HQ* sequentially evaluates them in a myopic manner, mandating a practice throughout the chain if doing so raises *chain* profit, and otherwise discarding the idea. Thus, uniformity of practices is a feature of centralization in this model. *HQ* then searches over its landscape which is based on chain profit, and it alone has the authority to implement ideas.

Measuring performance by average chain profit, the main insight of this study is that centralization can outperform decentralization. This occurs when markets are sufficiently similar, the horizon is sufficiently short, and consumer preferences are sufficiently sensitive to store practices relative to price. Given that markets are heterogeneous, the benefit of decentralization is clear—it allows each store manager to tailor practices to its market. So, how can a centralized structure generate higher profit? It turns out there is an implicit cost to decentralization. By adjusting practices to one's own consumers in a decentralized chain, stores' practices tend to drift apart. As a result, a new practice adopted by one store is increasingly unlikely to be compatible with the current practices of other stores. In essence, stores come to target distinct consumers (by targeting distinct local optima) and what works for one type of consumer doesn't tend to work for another type of consumer in light of preference complementarities. Inter-store learning is then less under decentralization and this is detrimental to the rate of improvement in store practices. The virtue of a centralized structure is that it enhances inter-store learning by keeping stores close in store practice space so that they are targeting similar consumers. With these two countervailing effects, a centralized structure outperforms as long as markets are not too different. The value to enhanced inter-unit learning is greatest when stores are farther from local optima and for this reason centralization does particularly well in the short-run. In the long-run, decentralization is typically superior because the uniformity of practices under centralization prevents the global optimum being achieved since the global optimum has different practices in different markets.

Finally, centralization also outperforms when consumers are sufficiently sensitive to store practices (γ is high). This result is related to the property that the ruggedness of the landscape increases in γ. As the number of local optima rises, stores in different markets (and thereby different landscapes) are more likely to share some common local optima. This enhances opportunities for inter-store learning and the analysis shows that this is best exploited by a centralized organization.[20]

A changing environment is encompassed by allowing the population of consumer types to shift probabilistically. Measuring performance by steady-state chain profit, centralization is more likely to outperform when market fluctuations are sufficiently large. Recall the earlier result in the static environment that centralization is favored in the short run because stores are farther away from local optima, in which case inter-store learning is especially valuable. As increased fluctuations in market environments shake the landscapes more vigorously, they act to push stores further away from local optima. Thus, a constantly fluctuating environment requires the firm to perpetually learn at a high rate, which then sets the stage for the short-term superiority of centralization to become a long-term advantage. Quite contrary to the received wisdom that volatility in markets requires greater decentralization, Chang and Harrington (2000) find it is the centralized organization that is more effective in responding to change.

3.2.3. Chang and Harrington (2003)

A more challenging issue is to consider how market structure interacts with organizational structure to influence the dynamic performance of chains. Does increased competition make centralization more or less desirable? To address this issue, Chang and Harrington (2003) modify the previous model by allowing for competition and consumer search. There are L chains and M markets with each chain having a store in each market. Within each market, there is a fixed population of consumers that engage in search by moving among stores. At any point in time, a consumer in a given market (served by L stores) has a favorite store and buys from it with probability $1 - Q$. With probability Q the consumer experiments by randomly selecting another store and buying from it. If the resulting surplus for the consumer is higher than what the consumer received most recently from the favorite store then this new store becomes the consumer's favorite store. If not, then the consumer's favorite store remains unchanged and, in the next period, the process is repeated. Q regulates the extent of experimentation. If $Q = 0$ then there is no competition as consumers are permanently loyal, while $Q = (L - 1)/L$ implies no loyalty. The organizational structures are as before. A store evaluates the profit attached to adopting a new idea using its current base of consumers—those that are currently buying from it. In a centralized organization, HQ evaluates ideas using a measure of profit based on the current sets of consumers at its stores.

---

[20] The robustness of these results with respect to the shape of the landscape is explored in Chang and Harrington (2004).

A key result is that centralization is more attractive when there is a larger number of competing chains and may even outperform in the long-run. The basis for this finding is an implicit increasing returns mechanism when competing organizations are coevolving with consumers. To understand this result, recall that centralization does particularly well in the short-run. Thus, early on a centralized chain is developing better practices and thereby attracting more customers than a decentralized chain. In the one-chain model, decentralization would eventually outperform, but that needn't be true when consumers are searching. This early advantage from centralization establishes a customer base which tends to include the most prevalent consumer types in the market, and it is this customer base which is used to evaluate the profitability of new ideas. A centralized organization then tends to adopt practices well-suited for the prevalent consumer types, which results in their retention and the attraction of more of those types and which makes the chain even more inclined to adopt ideas suiting their preferences, and so forth. In this way, an early advantage of centralization—coming from enhanced inter-store learning—is fed into a feedback loop to maintain an advantage in the long run. As a result, a decentralized chain may not be able to catch up because it is adopting ideas for a less prevalent niche of consumers. In other words, the rate at which a chain climbs a landscape (by coming up with better practices for its current customers) influences the shape of its future landscape (by affecting the set of loyal customers). A centralized chain climbs its landscape faster and this results in its future landscape being more attractive. Coevolutionary dynamics among firms and consumers produce a powerful increasing returns mechanism.[21]

3.3. Organizational search with units solving different problems

The previous section is applicable when the organization is divided into units solving similar problems such as selling a particular product line to consumers (retail chains) or producing a particular product line (multi-plant manufacturers). Such organizations are examples of the M-form, but let us now consider the U-form organization. The organization's various activities are allocated among functional departments such as Accounting, Finance, Sales, Purchasing, Production, and so on. A new practice adopted in Sales is unlikely to be applicable to the operation carried out in Finance—they are engaged in entirely different types of operations and thereby solving quite distinct problems. However, it *will* have an impact on the effectiveness of the overall operation of Finance when the value of certain financial practices depends on sales practices; that is, there is a complementarity between them. These organizational issues can be modelled by specifying the firm as a system of N activities in the context of the NK model but with the feature that these N activities are allocated to various departments for specialized search occurring in parallel. For instance, half of the activities may be put under

---

[21] As an example of how analytical and computational methods are complementary, this issue is explored analytically in Harrington and Chang (2005) as they consider a highly stripped-down version of Chang and Harrington (2003).

the control of department *A* while the remaining activities may be under the control of department *B*, with each department attempting to find the optimal configuration of decisions over the activities it controls according to some evaluation criterion. As the departments are then searching over distinct non-overlapping set of activities, there is no prospect for inter-unit learning. Rather, the issue is how to structure the organization so that the gains of parallel search can be had while balancing it with the need to coordinate search in light of how these activities interact.

3.3.1. Rivkin and Siggelkow (2003)

A long line of scholars studying complex organizations have observed that there are many interdependencies among elements of design such as the allocation of decisions, incentives, and information flows. Rivkin and Siggelkow (2003) offer as one source of such interdependencies two conflicting needs of a multi-unit organization that are central to the search-and-learn perspective. First, to be successful, an organization must search broadly for good actions (exploration). Second, it must also stabilize around good actions once discovered (exploitation). An effective organization balances search and stability. The authors focus on three prominent elements of organizational design in exploring how they interact to influence this delicate balance: (1) a central authority that may choose to review the proposals sent up from subordinates; (2) an incentive system that influences the degree to which managers act parochially for the good of their departments or for the good of the overall firm; and (3) the decomposition of an organization's decisions into distinct departments. Their focus is on how these design elements interact with one another to determine organizational performance through the balancing of search and stability and how that relationship depends on the interdependent structure of activities as dictated by the problem and on the limits on the cognitive ability of managers.

Their simulation considers a hierarchy with a CEO and two subordinate managers, A and B. The firm engages in multi-agent search which takes place on performance landscapes generated by the *NK* model. An organization has $N = 6$ decision attributes and part of its design is how they are allocated among the two managers. Manager A has responsibility for a subset S_A of these attributes and manager B for the complementary subset S_B. In each period, each subordinate manager reconsiders the actions assigned to its attributes by comparing the current configuration to some fixed number α of alternatives, so that α reflects the cognitive capacity of a subordinate manager. These α alternatives are ranked by a manager on the basis of an evaluation criterion which is a weighted average of the performance of his department and of the other department.

Initially, it is supposed that $S_A = \{1, 2, 3\}$ and $S_B = \{4, 5, 6\}$. Denoting by $\delta \in [0, 1]$ the degree to which Manager A cares about the other department's performance, the evaluation criterion for Managers A and B, respectively, are

$$v^A = \frac{v_1 + v_2 + v_3 + \delta(v_4 + v_5 + v_6)}{6},$$

$$v^B = \frac{\delta(v_1 + v_2 + v_3) + v_4 + v_5 + v_6}{6},$$

where recall that v_i is the contribution of the ith activity to total organization performance. If $\delta = 0$, a manager only cares about his own department, while if $\delta = 1$ he cares about firm profit. δ then controls the degree to which managers' incentives are aligned with those of the organization.

Finally, the form of vertical hierarchy and the ability of the CEO affect the organizational search process. From the status quo and the α alternatives, a manager sends up the best P proposals to the CEO where "best" is according to the manager's preferences. There are two types of CEO's: rubberstamping (decentralization) and active (centralization). The first type always approves all proposals sent up by both managers so that, effectively, an organization with a rubberstamping CEO is decentralized since the real authority lies with the department managers. The active CEO, on the other hand, selects β proposals from all combinations of the submitted proposals and implements the one that generates the highest firm profit (so $\delta = 1$ for the active CEO). Thus, β captures the cognitive capacity of the CEO. Since an active CEO has the final authority, we will refer to this as the *centralized organization*.

In sum, there are five different factors that affect the organizational search process and, consequently, performance: the grouping of activities into departments, the amount of information sent up to senior management (P), the allocation of authority (centralization/active CEO vs. decentralization/rubberstamping CEO), the extent to which managers care about firm as opposed to department performance (δ), and the cognitive abilities of the department managers (α) and the CEO (β).

There is found to be a significant interaction between the allocation of authority and the complexity of the environment (as measured by K). When the complexity is low ($K = 0$), the benefit of centralization is non-existent since the lack of interdependencies means there is no need for coordination while, at the same time, there is a cost due to slower adaptation. In such a case, short-run performance is lower under centralization. When complexity is moderate, centralizing authority in the CEO is shown to enhance performance as the interdependence among activities makes coordination critical. But then for highly complex environments (high K), it is better to push authority back down to the managers. Centralization suffers from the problem that an active CEO is always moving the organization to points of higher firm profit and, when K is high, there are many bad local optima. As a result, the organization is typically getting stuck at a point of low performance. In essence, centralization results in excessive stability. In contrast, a decentralized organization—by giving authority to department managers who care more about their own department's profit—may periodically result in organizational performance deteriorating which, when it causes movement into a basin of attraction for a better optimum, can enhance long-run performance. This weakness to centralization can not be mitigated by increasing the skill of the CEO (as measured by

β), but only by increasing the information flow, P. In sum, centralization is undesirable when interactions are pervasive and the CEO gets little information from below.

The skills and incentives of the subordinate managers have some subtle and surprising effects. In a complex environment, highly skilled managers can be harmful in a decentralized organization. By considering alternatives that are far away from their current position, a highly skilled manager may undermine the improvement efforts of other managers. The organization can suffer from excessive instability as it dances around the landscape without making much progress. Centralizing authority in the CEO provides useful coordination. An active CEO and skilled department managers are then complements, not substitutes. Managerial incentives that are more closely aligned with the interests of the firm are complementary to centralization as well. When managers are parochial (low δ), many of their suggestions are turned down in a centralized organization because the CEO uses a different criterion in evaluating them. Hence, the organization doesn't make much progress. This is contrary to the usual argument which is that, if managers have the right incentives, why does one need an active CEO? Here, the problem is that departmental managers have partial information and control and one needs the coordination that centralization delivers.

The above results are obtained for landscapes created using the usual random interaction *NK* model. Rivkin and Siggelkow (2003) also considers the interdependence between decomposition and the allocation of authority. With decomposable interactions—as represented by the block-diagonal adjacency matrix in Figure 2c—centralizing authority is irrelevant since department managers are solving independent problems. There is no need for coordination. Superior performance can, however, come from the combination of imperfect decomposition—there is some interdependence across departments—and an active, well-informed CEO. For instance, given a block-diagonal matrix (Figure 2c), performance is higher when an active CEO is combined with $(S_A, S_B) = (\{1, 2, 6\}, \{3, 4, 5\})$ than with $(S_A, S_B) = (\{1, 2, 3\}, \{4, 5, 6\})$. At work is the balancing of search and stability. Some overlap expands the range of search as each manager proposes options that change the landscape faced by another department. This may serve to move the organization to a different basin and, in some cases, result in it homing in on a superior local optimum.

3.3.2. Siggelkow and Levinthal (2003)

Using a model similar to the preceding one, Siggelkow and Levinthal (2003) examine the division of task and specialized search under three different organizational forms: centralization, decentralization, and reintegration. In the centralized firm, decisions are made only at the level of the firm as a whole, whereas a decentralized organization is disaggregated into a number of departments in which decisions are made independently. A reintegrated organization initially has a decentralized structure and then switches to centralization after a fixed number of periods (typically, 25 periods). A key variable is the degree and pattern of interactions among various activities as specified by an adjacency matrix. The decision problem for the organization is decomposable if the activities can be grouped so that all interactions are contained within each group and thus there are no cross-group interdependencies. The block-diagonal adjacency matrix in Figure 2c is a decomposable system. On the other hand, the decision problem is non-decomposable if there is no way to group the activities so as to eliminate all cross-group interdependencies; see, for example, the matrix in Figure 2d.

The simulation entails creating $10\,000$ landscapes using the NK model with $N = 6$. The three organizational forms are compared in terms of their performance (averaged over the $10\,000$ landscapes) under conditions of both non-decomposability and decomposability of the decision problems. Firms carry out myopic local search and they only consider changing one activity at a time. The centralized firm evaluates an idea on the basis of firm profit: $v = (v_1 + v_2 + v_3 + v_4 + v_5 + v_6)/6$. The decentralized firm is assumed to have two departments, A and B, with department A controlling activities $\{1, 2, 3\}$ and department B controlling $\{4, 5, 6\}$. In each period, each department comes up with an idea which it then evaluates on the basis of the profit contribution of those activities that are under its exclusive control. This means that the evaluation criteria used by departments A and B are $v^A = (v_1 + v_2 + v_3)/3$ and $v^B = (v_4 + v_5 + v_6)/3$, respectively. In evaluating an idea, a department takes the other department's current choices as given.

In a decomposable environment with a block-diagonal interaction structure (Figure 2c), they find that the decentralized firm outperforms the centralized firm in the short-run. This result is directly due to the asymmetric number of draws that are allowed under these two forms: the decentralized firm gets two draws per period (one for each department), while the centralized firm gets only one. As there is no interaction between the activities of the two departments, there is no mitigating benefit from centralization. The average levels of performance under these two forms do converge in the long run, however. The reintegrated firm's performance is nearly identical to that of the decentralized firm.

The results are quite different when the organization searches in a non-decomposable environment. Assuming a random interaction structure with $K = 2$, the advantage of having more draws under decentralization is offset by the coordination benefit attained under centralization due to the presence of cross-departmental interdependencies. More interesting is the performance of the reintegrated firm. Prior to reintegration, the performance is, of course, the same as that of a decentralized firm. After the departments are integrated, performance not only improves but it eventually outperforms the centralized firm. The problem with the organization when it is centralized is that it is apt to get stuck early on at an inferior local optimum, similar to the active CEO structure in Rivkin and Siggelkow (2003). This is less likely with the reintegrated firm as it is initially decentralized. Once centralization occurs, it is more likely to be in the basin of a better optimum which it can take advantage of now that coordination can occur. The lesson is that superior performance may be had by a temporal blending of different organizational forms.

Those simulations assume the organization starts its search from a random point on the landscape. An alternative exercise is to suppose there is an environmental shock after the firms have achieved some steady-state. Siggelkow and Levinthal (2003) position a firm at Hamming distance d from the global optimum—implying that the firms were at the global optimum *ex ante* and then were thrown off it by a shock of magnitude d. In this setting, the question is how effectively a firm can *climb back* to the global optimum. Centralization outperforms reintegration for sufficiently low values of d, while reintegration outperforms centralization for sufficiently high values of d. The appropriate organizational form then depends on the size of the shock. The intuition is that a centralized firm has a relatively high probability of getting locked onto nearby local optima which makes it less suitable for large shocks but quite desirable for small shocks since the firm is likely to start in the basin of attraction for a good optimum (recall that the firm started at the global optimum). By comparison, reintegration initially pursues a decentralized form and thus can better handle large shocks. The general lesson is that an organization should be centralized at a steady-state but should temporarily decentralize when there is a large change in its environment.

The preceding results suggest that there may be merit to grouping activities so that there is some cross-departmental interdependence even when the decision problem is decomposable. Suppose the interaction structure is characterized by the adjacency matrix in Figure 2c. An obvious grouping of activities would be to have department A in charge of $\{1, 2, 3\}$ and department B in charge of $\{4, 5, 6\}$, thereby eliminating any interaction between the activities controlled by these two managers. However, such a structure underperforms one which is eventually of that form but during the early periods has A controlling $\{1, 4, 5\}$ and B controlling $\{2, 3, 6\}$. Quite interestingly, the temporarily scrambled firm is superior to the "ideally" decomposed firm because cross-departmental interdependence avoids excessive stability.

3.4. Evolving an organizational structure

Thus far the focus has been on comparing the performance of different elements of organizational design. This begs the question of whether upper level management of an organization, which is endowed with a sub-optimal design, can effectively alter design elements so as to achieve a superior structure. What makes this a non-trivial problem is the presence of interdependence among component tasks, which is representative of any complex system, be it social, biological, or technological. The significance of this problem is well illustrated by Herbert Simon in the context of organizations:

> The basic idea is that the several components in any complex system will perform particular subfunctions that contribute to the overall function. ... To design such a complex structure, one powerful technique is to discover viable ways of decomposing it into semi-independent components corresponding to its many functional parts. The design of each component can then be carried out with some degree of independence of the design of others... There is no reason to expect that the decomposition of the complete design into functional components will be unique... Much of classical organization theory in fact was concerned precisely with this issue of

alternative decompositions of a collection of interrelated tasks. [Herbert A. Simon, *The Sciences of the Artificial* (1996), p. 128.]

In a decomposable system such as the one in Figure 2c, the obvious division of tasks would entail assigning activities $\{1, 2, 3\}$ to one department and $\{4, 5, 6\}$ to another. As there is no interdependence between the sets of activities of these two departments, the optimal solution they arrive at independently will form the optimal solution for the entire organization. Alternatively, systems may have inherent "near decomposability" where they can be decomposed into a collection of subsystems with the property that the components within a subsystem interact more strongly than the components belonging to different subsystems, but with a certain degree of interdependence remaining between the subsystems. In such situations, the problem solvers facing computational constraints will be motivated to decompose the problem into subproblems in order to benefit from parallel processing, while recognizing that the problem may not be decomposable.

3.4.1. Ethiraj and Levinthal (2002)

Define an organization's "true architecture" to be a description giving the correct number of the organization's modules and a correct assignment of functions to the respective modules as dictated by the characteristics of the problem. Ethiraj and Levinthal (2002) set out to identify the relationship between two key design elements—decomposability and hierarchy—and an organization's ability to *discover* its true architecture.

They consider the following four structural types: (1) hierarchical and nearly decomposable; (2) non-hierarchical and nearly decomposable; (3) hierarchical and non-decomposable; and (4) non-hierarchical and non-decomposable. Figure 3 presents the adjacency matrices of the systems that belong to each one of these categories when $N = 9$ and there are three non-overlapping modules labelled a, b, and c. Figure 3a is nearly decomposable and hierarchical as $b1$ in module b is influenced by $a3$ in module a and $c1$ in module c is affected by $b3$ in module b but module c does not influence modules b or a and module b does not influence module a. Hence, the inter-module interdependencies are unidirectional. Figure 3b is nearly decomposable and non-hierarchical in that modules a and b are mutually interdependent (through $b1$ and $a3$), while modules b and c are mutually interdependent (through $c1$ and $b3$). Figure 3c is a non-decomposable but hierarchical system as there is a tight coupling between modules in that all components of modules b (c) are influenced by all components of module a (b) and are unidirectional. Finally, a non-decomposable and non-hierarchical system is captured in Figure 3d, where all modules are tightly and mutually coupled with one another. For each of these four structures, search for the true architecture occurs through three operations: splitting, combining, and re-allocation. *Splitting* of modules involves breaking up existing departments into two or more new departments. *Combining* is the opposite of splitting in that it involves integrating two or more departments. *Re-allocation* is when the organization reassigns functions from one unit to another.

Suppose the module designer observes the presence or absence of interactions among attributes within the module as the result of a change in an attribute. All attributes for

(a)
Hierarchical and
Nearly Decomposable

	a1	a2	a3	b1	b2	b3	c1	c2	c3
a1	x	x	x						
a2	x	x	x						
a3	x	x	x						
b1			x	x	x	x			
b2				x	x	x			
b3				x	x	x			
c1						x	x	x	x
c2							x	x	x
c3							x	x	x

(b)
Non-Hierarchical and
Nearly Decomposable

	a1	a2	a3	b1	b2	b3	c1	c2	c3
a1	x	x	x						
a2	x	x	x						
a3	x	x	x	x					
b1			x	x	x	x			
b2				x	x	x			
b3				x	x	x	x		
c1						x	x	x	x
c2							x	x	x
c3							x	x	x

(c)
Hierarchical and
Non-Decomposable

	a1	a2	a3	b1	b2	b3	c1	c2	c3
a1	x	x	x						
a2	x	x	x						
a3	x	x	x						
b1	x	x	x	x	x	x			
b2	x	x	x	x	x	x			
b3	x	x	x	x	x	x			
c1				x	x	x	x	x	x
c2				x	x	x	x	x	x
c3				x	x	x	x	x	x

(d)
Non-Hierarchical and
Non-Decomposable

	a1	a2	a3	b1	b2	b3	c1	c2	c3
a1	x	x	x	x					
a2	x	x	x	x	x				
a3	x	x	x	x	x	x			
b1	x	x	x	x	x	x	x		
b2		x	x	x	x	x	x	x	
b3			x	x	x	x	x	x	x
c1				x	x	x	x	x	x
c2					x	x	x	x	x
c3						x	x	x	x

Figure 3. Adjacency matrix ($N = 9$).

which their contribution to performance is unaffected by this change are identified as not belonging to the module that includes the original attribute. All such attributes are either transferred to a randomly chosen different module (if they constitute less than half the total number of attributes in the current module) or are split into a new module (otherwise). If the change of the given attribute does not affect any other attributes within the module, then the attribute is viewed as not belonging to that module. In this case it is transferred to another randomly chosen module. In each period, the module designers also consider combining each module with another module by randomly selecting two modules and evaluating the impact of attribute changes in both modules. The modules are combined if changes in each module affect the other and remain separate otherwise.

Each module engages in one-step offline search based on local module performance. This occurs in parallel. When considering a population of systems in order to explore recombination of systems or substitution of modules, they select two systems at random and then select two functionally equivalent modules at random for recombination. The lower performing module is replaced with the higher performing module. Finally, in the multi-systems analysis, the selection mechanism used is the roulette wheel algorithm, where the probability that a system is selected equals its performance level divided by the sum of the performance of all systems in the population at that time.

Consider a system with N attributes for which the true architecture has M modules with each module having an equal number of attributes. The initial design of the system is random and thus is likely to have the wrong number of modules, modules with the wrong attributes, and modules with different numbers of attributes. The performance measure is the number of periods its takes for the system to converge to the true architecture.

The simulation exercise is based on 100 experiments, where each experiment involves a randomly selected landscape and initial design and entails each of the four archetypes being run. The simulations show that an organization always discovers the true structure when the system is hierarchical, even when it is non-decomposable. But when it is non-hierarchical, an organization never manages to reach a stable state. The violation of both principles—hierarchy and decomposability—is seriously detrimental to discovering the right structure. These results suggest that the search rule for discovering the true system structure is robust when there is a strong interaction within modules and there is a hierarchical precedence structure underlying between-module interactions.

3.5. What do we learn from a computational agent-based approach?

The primary issue explored in agent-based models of organizational search and learning is the role of organizational structure and, more specifically, how a centralizing authority can influence performance by coordinating certain activities. In this section, we want to review what we've learned about when an organization should be centralized, highlight the role played by the unique features of ACE models identified in Section 2, contrast this insight with what a NCE analysis would produce, and make the case for ACE.

One important insight is that decentralization can be advantageous even when complementarities suggest that coordination is valuable. Consider an organization in which there are interdependencies across units. If each unit evaluates a new practice based upon what it generates in terms of unit performance, then decentralized search can lead to lower organizational performance due to externalities across units. A NCE analysis would suggest that centralization is beneficial because it internalizes these externalities by evaluating the impact of a new practice in terms of organizational profit. In contrast, Rivkin and Siggelkow (2003) show using an ACE model that centralization can perform worse because it results in excessive coordination. Once a centralized organization is in the basin of attraction of a particular local optimum, it steadily marches towards it and, as a result, it never learns whether there are other more attractive optima. Under decentralization, individual units—each of which is engaging in hill-climbing using the unit's performance—can inadvertently result in organizational performance declining. Though detrimental in the short-run, it may serve to throw the organization into the basin of a different and potentially better optimum. Put differently, the high level of coordination achieved under centralization leads to excessive stability. Though stability is desirable once a good optimum is reached, it can be harmful while learning because it closes off alternatives. In the context of adaptive search—as opposed to optimal selection of organizational practices—coordination can be excessive. Second best arguments are rampant within ACE models and this is one example—the limitations of adaptive search may mean that fully internalizing externalities across agents can be detrimental, an intuition quite contrary to what would emerge from an NCE analysis.

A second important insight is that centrally mandated uniform practices can be valuable even when units face heterogeneous environments. Consider an organization in which there are no interdependencies across units. Each unit is in a different environment and organizational performance is the simple sum of the units' performances. An NCE analysis would suggest that decentralization is preferable as it allows practices to be tailored to the environment. However, Chang and Harrington (2000) show that a decentralized organization creates dynamic externalities related to knowledge transfer which impact adaptive search. Since units are solving similar problems, what one learns and adopts may prove useful to other units. Under decentralization, units fail to internalize the following externality: when a unit adopts a new practice that moves them away from other units, those other units can expect to learn less from it. A centralized organization serves a coordinating function by keeping units' practices close to one another, and this enhances knowledge transfer. Note that this result is produced by medium-run dynamics. In the long run the organization will typically achieve its global optimum and, since the global optimum is lower when constrained to uniform practices, decentralization outperforms in the long-run.

A unique feature of ACE models mentioned in Section 2 is the complexity of the environment, and this indeed played a central role in the preceding analysis. Complexity is measured by the ruggedness of the landscape. A more rugged landscape means more optima, in which case it becomes easier to get stuck on poor optima. Chang and Harrington (2000) show that a more complex environment makes knowledge transfer more important as it is more difficult for a unit, learning on its own, to succeed. This implies that more complexity means centralization is more likely to be preferred. In Kollman et al. (2000), organizational form matters only when environments are moderately complex. In Rivkin and Siggelkow (2003), the potential advantage to the enhanced coordination from centralization increases with complexity (which is associated with more inter-dependencies) but the chances of getting stuck at a bad optimum also increases with complexity. When the environment is moderately complex, the first effect dominates so that centralization performs better but, when the environment is very complex, the second effect dominates so decentralization outperforms.

The above discussion reveals that ACE delivers different insight than would an NCE analysis. Furthermore, in reviewing NCE research on organizations, the forces at work are quite distinct. In one class of NCE models, organizational structure affects the in-centives of lower-level agents to produce useful information for higher levels. In Aghion and Tirole (1997), decentralization promotes lower-level agents' incentives to invest in acquiring information—as their decision is less likely to be overruled (and there is little value to investing in information if the information doesn't make a difference)—but at the cost of them pursuing their own interests which are distinct from the interests of the organization. In Dessein (2002), the problem is that lower-level agents may distort the information that they pass along to higher levels. A second class of models focuses on how organizational structure influences monitoring, wages, and the incentives for agents to work hard. In Qian (1994), a more hierarchical organization (which means more lev-els and each manager has fewer agents to monitor below him) enhances monitoring and lower wages but is less productive. Maskin et al. (2000) compare the M-form and U-form with respect to their productivity in monitoring when pay is based on relative performance. The emphasis, the forces, and the insight of these organizational models are then quite different from ACE organizational models. While ultimately these alter-native approaches may compete, thus far their analyses are complementary.

4. Information processing

Economists have also often failed to relate administrative coordination to the the-ory of the firm. For example, far more economies result from the careful coor-dination of flow through the processes of production and distribution than from increasing the size of producing or distributing units in terms of capital facilities or number of workers. Any theory of the firm that defines the enterprise merely as a factory or even a number of factories, and therefore fails to take into account the role of administrative coordination, is far removed from reality. [Alfred Chan-dler, *The Visible Hand: The Managerial Revolution in American Business* (1977), p. 490.]

As reviewed in the previous section, search and learning models of organizations have agents receive new ideas, evaluate them, and then decide what to do—whether to discard them, pass them along to a superior, or implement them (depending on the allocation of authority). An implicit assumption is that the evaluation process is costless and instantaneous. This is a striking departure from reality. It can take resources, time, and expertise to evaluate new information and then make a decision. This section considers the costs of processing information. An organization takes input from the environment ("data") and performs operations on it prior to making a decision. Information processing is costly because, for example, it requires hiring agents and it imposes delay in reaching a decision under the constraint of avoiding information overload. Though all models of organization involve information processing to some degree, we have reserved this terminology for those models where the cost of processing is explicitly modelled and is a primary force determining organizational performance.

The organization is faced with a task which, if it were to be handled by a single agent, would translate into long delays and inaccuracies due to processing and memory constraints. A more efficacious structure involves distributed problem-solving—multiple agents solving sub-problems and then putting these sub-solutions together to produce a solution for the original problem. We'll address the following questions: What is the best size and structure of an organization? What is the best way in which to allocate sub-problems, organize information flows, and more broadly connect agents so as to lead to fast and accurate solutions? Should the organization be "flat" so that many agents are handling data? Should it be decentralized like a team or centralized like a hierarchy? How many levels should the hierarchy have and should communication channels cut across levels so high-level personnel connect with many levels? In addressing these questions, research has considered two sets of factors: first, the characteristics of agents with respect to their cognitive skills and accumulated knowledge; and second, the characteristics of the environment in terms of its complexity, stability, and decomposability.

We begin in Section 4.1 with the canonical model of an information processing organization and an exploration of its generic properties—properties that hold for most networks, not just optimal ones. The impact of organizational structure on performance when agents have the capacity to learn is investigated in Section 4.2, while organizational design endogenously evolves in the models reviewed in Section 4.3. We conclude with a critical discussion in Section 4.4.

4.1. Generic properties of information processing networks

Radner (1993) describes the canonical information processing problem faced by an organization.[22] The organization is a network of agents (or information processors or nodes) which are endowed with a fixed ability to process incoming data and a limited capacity for doing so. For example, data might be a series of integers, the processor has the ability to multiply them together, and its capacity limits it to handling seven numbers. The architecture defines how information is distributed and tasks are assigned. In

---

[22] Also see Van Zandt (1999) and, for early work on modelling an organization as a network, Dow (1990).

this canonical model, information enters the lowest level where it is processed and sent through the network for further processing. Once processing is completed, an output (that is, an organizational decision) emerges. The basic line of inquiry investigates the relationship between size and structure of the network and performance, which is measured by the speed with which a problem is solved. More nodes in the network (or more agents in the organization) provide more processing power—which may be particularly critical when agents have limited capacity—but at the potential cost of more delay as information has to traverse a longer path. Under certain conditions, it is shown that the most efficient network is a particular type of hierarchy.

4.1.1. Miller (2001)

This canonical problem is explored in Miller (2001) with an eye to learning generic properties of networks. He considers randomly generated networks with the hope of identifying "order for free" without the expense of optimality. The organization faces a series of associative (and thereby decomposable) problems. The organization receives data in the form of a series of integers and the task is to generate their sum. Each agent has the ability to sum two numbers. With this class of problems, and given the assumptions placed on agents, accuracy is assured and the performance of an organization is measured by the delay in generating a solution. As the associative nature of the problem means that the sequence with which it is solved is irrelevant, such problems are ripe for distributed problem solving.

An organization is a network of nodes with each node being a processor and representing an agent. Figure 4 shows all of the possible (non-redundant) networks associated with five bits of information, (a, b, c, d, e), where each bit is handled by exactly one agent. For example, a single-agent organization has all five bits coming into that agent who must progressively sum them by adding a to b, then adding the solution to c, and so forth, until the solution is derived after four operations and four periods. In comparison, there is a three-agent network (denoted #12) in which one agent sums three bits, another sums two bits, and a third sums the sub-solutions. The first two agents are referred to as child agents to the last one, who is the parent agent. Note that this network takes fewer periods to derive a solution but at the cost of more agents.

Faced with a sequence of problems, an agent is not allowed to work on the next problem until its output is retrieved by the next agent in the network. An agent can be in one of three states: (i) inactive; (ii) active and unfinished; and (iii) active and finished, in which case it can, if called upon, convey its solution to its parent agent. An agent must decide on what problem to work, whether any sub-solutions from child agents can be incorporated, and whether more processing is required on the current problem. When an inactive agent is activated, it either tries to draw a child agent's solution or data from the queue. An agent remains active until processing is completed and the sub-solution is taken by the parent agent.

For the purpose of identifying generic properties, Miller considers random networks constructed as follows. A number of nodes is randomly chosen from between 1 and 50.

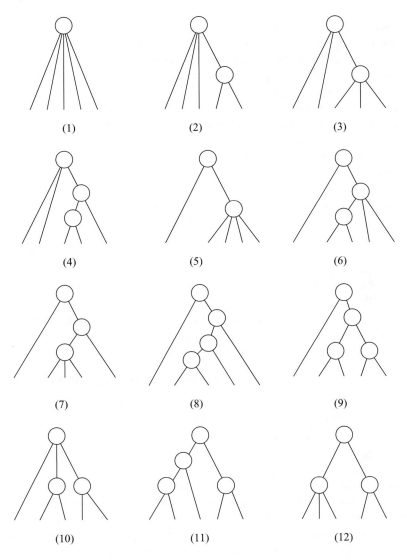

Figure 4. Networks with 5 bits of information.

The organization is iteratively constructed starting with a single node to which a child is added. One of those nodes is randomly selected and a child is added to it. This continues until the network has the specified number of nodes. Finally, all terminal nodes are connected to the data queue and an interior node is connected with probability 1/2.

To explore the significance of synchronization of agents in distributively solving a problem, Miller (2001) compares the performance of networks where nodes are randomly activated with one in which there is "ordered firing" so that child nodes are activated before parent nodes. Some interesting properties arise when exploring how performance is related to organizational size, as measured by the number of nodes. When firing is synchronized, performance mildly increases with size while, with random firing, performance appears to be maximized at an intermediate number of nodes. This suggests that, to sustain larger organizations, synchronization among agents is critical. Also noteworthy is that the variation in performance across random networks is greater for small organizations. The possible explanation is that they are more susceptible to bad design causing bottlenecks, which creates delay as agents wait for sub-solutions from other agents. In contrast, the denser web of connections when there are more nodes allows information to flow more freely, which serves to make the particular architecture less important.

4.2. Organizations with adaptive/learning agents

Now consider an organization that faces what Carley (1992) calls a quasi-repetitive task. In each period a problem arises as an *iid* selection from a finite set, which provides two types of opportunities for the organization to learn. First, if the cardinality of the set of problems is not large relative to the number of periods, the organization is likely to face a problem repeatedly so they can learn from past mistakes. Second, the problems may be related, in which case the solution to one problem provides information pertinent to solving other problems. The challenge is to learn the latent function generating the problems. For an organization to take advantage of these opportunities, agents must be endowed with a capacity to learn. Exploring how the ability to learn influences the relationship between organizational structure and performance is a central issue.

4.2.1. Carley (1992)

Suppose an organization faces a sequence of binary classification problems. For example, suppose that a new project arrives each period and the organization has to decide whether it is *profitable* or *unprofitable*. It receives information on the project that takes the form of an element of $\{0, 1\}^N$. There is a true (fixed and deterministic) latent mapping from $\{0, 1\}^N$ into $\{profitable, unprofitable\}$ which assigns the status of *profitable* when a majority of the bits take the value 1. Each drawn problem assigns equal probability to a bit being a 0 or 1. Based on the information, the organization must decide whether or not to conclude it is *profitable*.

In contrast to the rich set of organizational structures allowed by Miller (2001), here just two organizational forms are considered, hierarchy and team. A hierarchy comprises three levels where the lowest level has nine agents (referred to as analysts) who receive the data. The data consisting of N bits are partitioned into nine sub-vectors with each analyst receiving one of them. In response to observing an element from $\{0, 1\}^{N/9}$, an analyst puts forth a recommendation, either *profitable* or *unprofitable*, to an agent (manager) at the next level. There are three managers and each receives recommendations from three analysts. At the top is a single agent (CEO) who receives recommendations from the three managers and makes a final evaluation regarding profitability of the project. A team is also comprised of nine analysts but has just one level. Each analyst makes a recommendation in response to their input, and the organizational decision is based on majority rule. Though the number of decision makers varies between the two organizational forms, the number of agents receiving information about the problem is the same.

Agents engage in experiential learning about the latent mapping between $\{0, 1\}^N$ and {*profitable,unprofitable*}. After the organization makes its decision, all agents observe the true state of the project. Each agent keeps track of how information relates to the true state. For example, an analyst keeps a running tab of how many times a project was *profitable* for each observed input from $\{0, 1\}^{N/9}$. Similarly, managers and the CEO keep track of how many times a project was *profitable* for each observed element from {*profitable,unprofitable*}^{3}. The specified behavioral rule is that an agent reports *profitable* (*unprofitable*) in response to his information when the fraction of times that the true state was *profitable* (*unprofitable*) for that given information exceeds 50%. When it is exactly 50%, the agent randomizes.

The task varies in terms of complexity and decomposability. Complexity is measured by the length of the data vector. More data means more problems, with less opportunity to see a particular problem repetitively, and also a bigger set of possible mappings to sort among. A problem is referred to as *decomposable consensual* when all analysts are given the same sub-problem.[23] For example, the task 110110110 is decomposable consensual to three analysts. Since the more frequent bit value for each analyst is also the more frequent bit value for all N bits, in principle an individual analyst can come to correctly identify a project's true state based only on his own $N/9$ bits of data. By contrast, a non-decomposable task is when the accuracy of an individual's prediction is dependent upon information possessed by others. For example, the task 111010000 is nondecomposable to three analysts as one analyst receives 111, a second receives 010, and the third receives 000. This information is insufficient to determine whether 1 is in the majority and thus that the project is *profitable*.

One of the unique and interesting features of this model is personnel turnover. According to a Poisson process, an agent may be replaced with a new agent.[24] Analysts can be replaced with someone who has no experience ("novice"), someone who has experience with 500 sub-problems generated by the same stochastic process ("good fit"), and someone who has experience with 500 sub-problems in an organization with a slightly different problem-generating process ("poor fit"). Managers can also be replaced, although their replacements are restricted to be novices. Given that agents are learning,

---

[23] The modifier "consensual" is added because this task is more restrictive than the standard definition of decomposability (see Section 2). A problem can be decomposable but not involve identical sub-problems.

[24] Here, turnover is exogenous though in other models it is endogenous. An agent may decide to leave, as in Axtell (1999), and managers may decide whether to hire someone, as in Glance et al. (1997).

replacing experienced agents with possibly less experienced ones obviously deteriorates performance. Less clear is what type of organizational structure better handles such disruptions.

In contrast to Miller (2001), the organization is not necessarily given enough data to correctly solve the problem. Thus, performance is measured by the accuracy of solutions. The average percentage of correct assessments in the final 200 of 2500 periods measures long-run performance, while the average number of periods it takes to reach 60% accuracy serves as a measure of the speed of learning. As there are only two true states and the organization is endowed with no experience, it is initially guessing and so starts with 50% accuracy.

For either organizational type, performance is greater with a less complex task and when the task is decomposable. Teams learn significantly faster than hierarchies (though an important exception is noted below). A key force at work here is information loss. Analysts convert information defined on a space with $2^{N/9}$ elements into a signal from a two-element space. In the hierarchy, managers take information defined on an eight-element space (the three possible recommendations from those at the next lower level) to a two-element space. On these grounds, one expects teams to perform better because there is less information loss; it occurs twice for a hierarchy but only once for a team. However, when turnover is sufficiently high, hierarchies perform better for both decomposable and nondecomposable tasks. It is unclear whether this is due to hierarchies being less sensitive to the recommendation of a single rogue analyst or to their managers having more experience.

4.2.2. Barr and Saraceno (2002)

A similar exercise to that of Carley (1992) is performed in Barr and Saraceno (2002) though a distinctive feature of their approach is to model the organization as an artificial neural network (ANN). The organization's task is to identify the latent relationship between information that lies in $\{0, 1\}^{10}$ and the true state that lies in $\{0, 1, \ldots, 1023\}$ (as the latent function converts 10 binary digits to its equivalent number in base 10). The organization is an ANN with three layers (see Figure 5). The input layer is comprised of ten input nodes, each of which receives one of the ten bits of data. The next (hidden) layer is made up of n nodes—which can be interpreted as the lowest level in the organization with each node being an agent. Each of these agents takes a weighted sum of the data from the input layer and transforms it into an output. These n outputs then go to the top level where they are weighted and summed to produce the organization's output. This output is a prediction of the true state.

On a broad level, learning is equivalent to that in Carley (1992) though the specifics differ both because of the type of function being learned and the use of an ANN. The state of the organization is represented by the weights that each node in the low level uses to produce output for the high level and the weights that the high level uses to produce organizational output. Initially, these weights are randomly selected. After receiving data, the organization produces an output, denoted $\widehat{y}$, and then agents observe

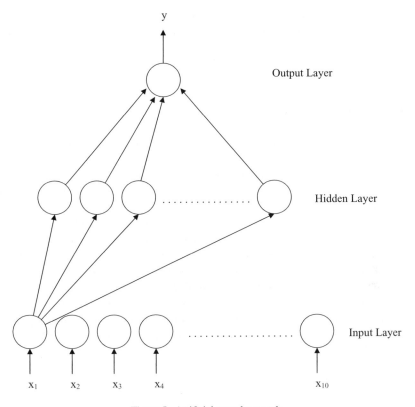

Figure 5. Artificial neural network.

the realization of the latent function, y. Each agent calculates the gradient of the mean squared error, $(1/2)(y - \hat{y})^2$, with respect to their weights and incrementally adjusts them in the direction that reduces mean squared error, taking other agents' weights as fixed.

While Carley (1992) fixes organizational size and varies structure, here structure is fixed at the two-level hierarchy and the role of size, as measured by the number of low-level agents, is explored. Interestingly, a bigger organization is not necessarily better. The reason lies in two types of prediction error. Approximation error is associated with the limited capacity of an ANN to represent a latent function. By expanding the space of approximating functions, more agents reduce approximation error. Of course, better fit also depends on the efficiency with which the coefficients (weights) of the ANN are estimated. The authors refer to this as estimation error and it measures how badly the ANN performs relative to maximal performance for a given size. The trade-off is that a larger organization reduces approximation error but, with more agents and thus more weights to be estimated, estimation error can rise. Clearly, with enough data, a bigger organization means better predictions; but, as in the real world, the simulations have only a limited number of problems from which to learn. Small firms are interpreted as having a simpler class of functions—they don't need many problems to get low estimation error—while large firms have a richer class of functions—they are slow to learn but may ultimately have a more sophisticated solution.

An organization is faced with a set of feasible problems, each of which is a random draw from $\{0, 1\}^{10}$. The complexity of the environment is measured by the size of that feasible set, which numbers at most ten. Stability is measured by the probability that an element of the feasible set is replaced with a fresh draw from $\{0, 1\}^{10}$. This random event occurs each period.[25] Performance depends on the accuracy of an organization's solution and, more specifically, equals the inverse of the squared error less the cost of the network. Network cost is composed of a cost per agent plus the cost of delay, which is linear in the number of operations performed on data. Larger firms experience greater network costs but may have less error.

Optimal firm size is typically found to be an interior solution, reflecting the trade-off from a bigger organization: less approximation error, more estimation error, and a higher network cost. The most interesting results concern the interaction between stability and complexity. When complexity is high, the optimal number of agents is lower when the environment is less stable. With the set of problems to be learned changing at a faster rate, agents have to adapt their weights more frequently, and this is done less effectively when there are more weights to adjust. When instead complexity is low, optimal firm size is higher in unstable environments than in a near-stable environment. With low complexity, there are only two problems to be learned and this doesn't require many agents. As stability falls, the set of examples is changing at a faster rate and having more agents allows the organization to adapt faster. More broadly, these results seem to suggest a rising marginal cost to the number of agents. With only a few problems to be learned, the organization is initially small so that reduced stability is best handled by adding agents. However, if there are a lot of problems, then the organization is already large and adding agents in response to less stability means having to adjust far too many weights. It is preferable to reduce the number of agents, thereby trading off lower estimation error for higher approximation error.

4.2.3. Barr and Saraceno (2005)

In an ensuing paper, the authors make a modelling advance that is innovative from both a computational and economic perspective. They allow two ANNs—each representing a firm—to coevolve in a competitive market situation. The situation is the classic symmetric Cournot game in which two firms make simultaneous quantity choices. The demand function is linear and its two parameters follow an *iid* stochastic process. The task before a firm is to learn its optimal quantity where the data it receives pertain

---

[25] Unfortunately, the model is designed so that a less complex environment implies a more stable one, which means any comparative statics with respect to complexity confounds these two effects.

to the unknown demand parameters. Learning is modelled as in Barr and Saraceno (2002). A firm chooses a quantity then learns *ex post* what would have been the profit-maximizing quantity. Learning occurs in the face of an exogenously stochastic demand function and an endogenously stochastic quantity for the other firm.

In comparison with Barr and Saraceno (2002), the environment is stable and there is no network cost so performance equals profit. Given the absence of network costs, the only reason not to have more agents is greater estimation error. The coevolving system always converges to Nash equilibrium; that is, each firm's quantity converges to that which maximizes its profit. As this occurs for each realization of the demand parameters, firms are learning how the signals map into the true state of demand. Further analysis shows that average profit is initially increasing in a firm's own network size but, due to estimation error, is eventually decreasing. More interesting is that a firm's performance is initially increasing in the other firm's network size. We conjecture the reason is that a smaller rival learns slower, which means it takes longer for its quantity to settle down. This would translate into a more volatile environment for a firm and serve to lower its profit. Interestingly, it may be in the best interests of a firm that its competitor be sophisticated.

4.3. Adaptation and evolution of organizational structure

In performing comparative statics to explore the impact of organizational size and structure on performance, a critical question is begged: To what extent can an organization find and adopt better structures? When dealing with complex entities such as an organization's architecture, it isn't sufficient to characterize optimal structure and presume an organization somehow finds it. Actual organizations are endowed with a structure and find large-scale change difficult. It is then worthwhile to know whether incremental changes can lead to superior designs. In addition, models of the previous section consider a very limited set of structures. By instead specifying a large class of organizations and a flexible dynamic for moving among them, new structures can emerge that are truly novel. To address these issues, we review Carley and Svoboda (1996), where simulated annealing searches for better organizations. We also return to discussing Miller (2001), who utilizes the forces of selection and adaptation through a genetic algorithm (GA). The driving question is, how effectively can an organization evolve to efficacious structures and what do those structures look like?

4.3.1. Carley and Svoboda (1996)

With some minor modifications, Carley and Svoboda (1996) adapt the organizational model of adaptive agents of Carley (1992) by appending an organizational design dynamic to it. Thus, structure is adapting at the same time that agents are learning. A key feature of this type of model is the class of organizations over which search occurs. An organizational structure is defined by the number of agents, which agents receive data, and how agents are connected. The set of feasible organizations is limited to those with at most three levels (where each level can only report to the next higher level), at most fifteen agents on each level, and at most nine pieces of information on a task. In the event that the highest level has more than one agent, those agents use majority rule to determine the organization's choice with an equality of votes being broken through randomization.

Upon this space of organizations, a dynamic is applied which constructs a new feasible organization through four operations: (i) firing (the elimination of agents); (ii) hiring (the addition of agents); (iii) re-tasking (a link to the data queue is redirected from one agent to another); and (iv) reassigning (a link between two agents is changed so that an agent reports to a new agent). Faced with a new design, the process by which it is adopted is modelled using simulated annealing. First, an offline experiment is performed whereby the organization's performance (as measured by the accuracy of the organization's decisions) is projected out for 100 tasks under this new design. If this performance exceeds the performance of the existing design then the new design is adopted. If performance is lower—and here lies a singular feature of simulated annealing—it is adopted with positive probability where this probability decreases with the existing design's performance during the preceding 500 periods (where there is one task each period) and also exogenously declines every 200 tasks.[26] The minimum time between new design adoptions is 100 periods. The initial organizational structure is randomly selected and there is a training period of 500 periods before the design dynamic is turned on.

As a theoretical benchmark, the optimal design is to have a one level organization with nine agents, each receiving one of the nine bits of info, and making their decision by majority rule. Simulated annealing never finds it. Compared to random organizations, the organizations that emerge after 20 000 periods have noticeably more agents on average, a lower span of control (the average number of links to a higher level agent), and fewer links to the data queue though none of these differences are statistically significant.[27] Though the results of the analysis are ambiguous, the approach represents a pioneering step in modelling the evolution of organizational structure.

4.3.2. Miller (2001)

Finally, let us return to Miller (2001) whose work on randomly generated organizations was reviewed earlier. Recall that the task is associative and thereby decomposable. As all solutions are accurate, the performance criterion is speed. Using a genetic algorithm (GA), a population of fifty randomly created organizations coevolve.[28] In each generation, there is a sequence of problems that each of the fifty organizations solves. Two

---

[26] The purpose of this feature is to try to keep the organization from getting stuck on bad local optima. By accepting performance-deteriorating designs, the organization might get kicked into the basin of attraction for a better local optimum.

[27] They actually run two experiments and the results referred to here are for the case of "dual learning."

[28] Also see Bruderer and Singh (1996) for an early use of a GA in organization theory. For more detailed discussions of GA learning, see Brenner (2006) and Duffy (2006).

organizations are then randomly selected and replaced with two copies of the one with greater speed. This operation is performed fifty times with replacement. These organizations are then randomly paired to engage in two genetic operations—crossover and mutation. For crossover, a node (other than one that is attached to the data queue) is randomly selected from each organization and the subtree beginning with each node (that is, the node and all of its children) are exchanged. Each organization also has a chance of mutating, which means a change in links. A single run has fifty generations and the output for analysis is the best organization after fifty generations. Results are based on an average over fifty runs. Miller (2001) considers the four possible cases associated with random versus ordered firing and single versus multiple problems.

To begin, is a GA outperforming random search? For comparison purposes, random search means starting with a set of randomly generated organizations (comparable in number to what the GA handles over its fifty generations) and choosing the best performer. GA is also identifying a best performer but uses crossover and mutation as well. For the case of ordered firing and a single problem, the GA impressively reduces speed by 25% compared to random search. For the other three cases, the reduction is considerably more modest at 2%. Still, the GA is creating better structures.

Whether the organization is trying to solve a single problem or a sequence of problems, results show that synchronizing the activation of agents sustains larger organizations with more levels. For a single problem, a GA produces, on average, an organization with 34 agents and eight levels under ordered firing while organizations are quite small under random firing with only three agents and less than two levels. Adding agents allows more processing to be done but at the cost that information has to travel through more levels. This can create delay, which makes ordered firing critical in keeping it under control. The superior performance of larger organizations is even stronger with multiple problems (and ordered firing) as the average size of 48 is pushing the upper bound of 50 agents. The range of size is 43 to 50 for the 50 runs (with a standard deviation of 1.9) which further suggests that to be a top performer requires being big. In contrast, for the case of a single problem, the range is vastly greater; it runs from 7 to 50 with a standard deviation of 14.2. When an organization has a light workload, a wide range of structures can perform well; when pushed harder, it becomes crucial to be larger so problems can be effectively handled without much delay.

In conclusion, a challenge for analysis is developing informative summary statistics for emergent structures. Miller (2001) goes to considerable lengths by also reporting mean path length, highest level attached to the queue, and maximum number of nodes at a level. Still, it's hard to see from these measures what the architecture looks like. One suspects it wouldn't "look like" a typical corporation. Having meaningful summary statistics for designs is essential for drawing insight and comparing results across studies. Indeed, two studies could produce organizations with a comparable number of nodes and levels but result in quite different structures. This is a challenge for future work.

4.4. Summary

Contrary to the models of search and learning in Section 3, the models explored in this section focus on organizational size as a critical factor in connection with an organization as an information processing network. Generally, more agents available to process information acts to improve predictions and produce better decisions. The analysis of Carley and Svoboda (1996) and Miller (2001) both find that their adaptive design dynamics produce organizations with more agents. This advantage to size is more acute when the task is more complex, as the organization needs the additional processing power that comes from more agents. But bigger is not universally better. This is obvious when one assumes there is a cost to more nodes in a network, but as shown in Barr and Saraceno (2002, 2005), more agents to "train" may slow down an organization's rate of learning. While the long-run efficiency of a network is increasing with the number of agents, smaller organizations can outperform in the intermediate run. This advantage from fewer agents is particularly relevant for a less stable environment where perpetual training occurs.

A second but more tentative piece of insight is that while bigger is typically better, organizational structure and coordination among agents may be more critical for bigger organizations. Miller (2001) finds that, when lower-level agents are activated prior to higher-level agents, the best performing organizations are vastly larger than when activation is random. Synchronization is then critical for taking advantage of larger size. This relationship between size and structure requires further examination.

In conclusion, research on information processing is trying to develop a "production function" for organizational decision-making, a difficult and challenging problem. Though significant progress has not yet occurred, the modelling approaches have been rich, novel, and provocative.

5. Effort, norms, and endogenous hierarchies

While the vast majority of computational agent-based models of organizations focuses on search and information processing, there are many other organizational issues tackled. Here, we provide some of the best of this other work and in doing so touch on issues of effort and shirking, norms, and endogenizing organizational structure.

5.1. Effort and the commons problem in organizations[29]

[H]ardly a competent workman can be found in a large establishment... who does not devote a considerable part of his time to studying just how slow he can work and still convince his employer that he is going at a good pace. [Frederick W. Taylor, *The Principles of Scientific Management* (1919), p. 21.]

---

[29] The issues addressed in this section are closely related to the concerns of Janssen and Ostrom (2006).

The models of organization considered thus far have assumed that the efforts required of agents—be it associated with production, innovation, or information processing—are achieved costlessly. Of course, effort is, in practice, costly and, more importantly, poses the organizational challenge of inducing agents to work hard. Organizations suffer from the "tragedy of commons" (Hardin, 1968) whereby agents shirk from a collective perspective. The essential problem here arises from the possibility that an agent may have to *share* the returns to his costly effort with other agents in the organization. While all agents would be better off if all were to exert effort, shirking with the intention to free-ride may turn out to be the dominant strategy for each individual agent. As an individual's share of the returns to his/her effort is likely to depend on the number of other agents in the firm, the incentive to shirk tends to be affected by firm size. This intuition plays an important role in the ensuing analysis.

5.1.1. Axtell (1999)

Consider a population of (non-competing) firms with workers being able to partially control their exposure to the intra-firm commons problem by switching firms or even starting their own firm. As the mobility of the workers implies that the size of the existing firm can change, it has implications for the extent to which workers will free-ride. A central focus of Axtell (1999) is on the dynamics of a population of firms whose number and size are endogenous.

A firm having $M \geq 2$ workers engages in production through the joint efforts of its members. Let $e_i \in [0, 1]$ denote worker i's level of effort and $E \equiv \sum_{i=1}^{M} e_i$ be the total effort of the firm. The firm's value, $V(E)$, takes the following form: $V(E) = aE + bE^\beta$ with $a, b > 0$ and $\beta > 1$. Assume an egalitarian sharing rule so that each worker receives exactly $V(E)/M$. Denote by $U_i(e_i, E_{-i}; M)$ the utility of worker i in a firm of M workers, where he supplies e_i and everyone else supplies $E_{-i}(\equiv E - e_i)$. Workers are assumed to have Cobb–Douglas preferences for income and leisure such that

$$U_i(e_i, E_{-i}; M) = \left(\frac{V(e_i + E_{-i})}{M} \right)^{\theta_i} (1 - e_i)^{1-\theta_i}, \tag{5}$$

where θ_i is worker i's relative weight for income over leisure (which equals $1 - e_i$). Preferences are heterogeneous in the population as θ_i is an independent draw from a uniform distribution on $[0, 1]$.

To characterize the population of firms, let $J(t)$ be the number of firms operating at t and $M^j(t)$ denote the size of firm $j \in \{1, \dots, J(t)\}$. $e_i^j(t)$ and $E^j(t)$ represent, respectively, the effort exerted by worker i in firm j and the total effort level of firm j. The initial configuration for the computational experiment assumes a population of N workers and N single-worker firms.

In any given period, a fixed number of workers are randomly selected to alter their behavior. Workers are myopic optimizers in that, in period t, each chooses effort to maximize period t utility under the assumption that the period t total effort of the other members equals what it was in the previous period, which is denoted $E_{-i}^j(t - 1)$ for firm j, and the number of its workers is the same as previously, which is $M^j(t-1)$. In this case, i was a member of firm j in $t-1$. If he remains at firm j, then worker i's optimal effort level, $\widehat{e}_i^j(t)$, is

$$\widehat{e}_i^j(t) = \arg\max_e U_i\left(e, E_{-i}^j(t-1); M^j(t-1)\right). \tag{6}$$

This gives expected utility from remaining at firm j.

Alternatively, worker i can join another firm or start up a new firm (which will, at least initially, consist only of himself). As regards the former option, worker i is (randomly) endowed with a network of ν_i other workers and can consider joining the firms to which they were members at $t-1$. The baseline simulation assumes $\nu_i = 2\ \forall i$. For each of these alternatives, the worker computes the maximal utility level using the procedure described in (6). Out of the (at most) $\nu_i + 2$ firm-options, a worker chooses the one yielding the highest expected utility.

Simulations show that the stochastic process by which firms are created, expand, and contract never settles down. Furthermore, there is considerable intertemporal fluctuations in the number of firms, average firm size (as measured by the number of workers), and average effort. Though average firm size is only four, firms can grow to be much larger. The basic forces are that, as firm size grows, increasing returns to total effort enhances marginal productivity—thereby making it more attractive for a worker to join the firm and thus leads to growth—but the free-riding problem is exacerbated with more employees—which serves to contract firm size. Firms expand when they offer a high value per worker as it induces workers to join. Now recall that a worker's optimal effort is based on the *previous* period's firm size and effort. Thus, a firm that currently has a high value per worker will experience a high inflow of new workers and, furthermore, this will continue to result in a high value per worker because each of those workers base their effort on a smaller sized firm so there is less free-riding than is appropriate for a firm of that size. This serves to attract yet more workers to join and, as long as the flow of workers into the firm remains high, increasing returns in total effort stays ahead of the intensifying free-riding problem. In this manner, a firm can experience sharp growth but it is also why it cannot maintain large size because once the flow of new workers subsides (which is sure to occur since there is a finite population of workers) then free-riding becomes the dominant force; value per worker declines and this leads to a rapid exodus of workers. Firms grow but then, like the bursting of a Ponzi scheme, eventually collapse. The model is parsimonious as a rich set of dynamics is generated by three factors: increasing returns, free-riding, and worker mobility.

Though focusing on a different set of issues, the work of Axtell (1999) has a predecessor in Glance et al. (1997). The latter authors model two organizational dilemmas: the lack of accountability in large organizations with the free-riding that ensues, as is in Axtell (1999), and the risk associated with training workers who are mobile. An organization realizes the benefits from training employees only if they remain with the organization but, once trained, a worker may leave to join another organization. Towards encompassing this latter issue, Glance et al. (1997) enrich the flat organizations of Axtell (1999) by assuming each firm has a manager whose role is to decide whether to train workers and whether to add workers. A worker can join a firm only upon invitation by its manager. Both of these distinctions result in the model of firms confirming closer to reality than in Axtell (1999).

In an early model of the commons problem in a team production setting, Alchian and Demsetz (1972) proposed a top-down organizational solution to free-riding. The firm is hierarchical with salaried workers and a capitalist who is motivated to monitor worker effort by virtue of being the residual claimant of firm profit. In contrast, Glance et al. (1997) and Axtell (1999) take a bottom-up approach to the issue by assuming that the workers themselves can independently control their exposure to the commons problem by moving from one firm to another and that they also share in the firm's profit. Augmenting these models with the mechanism of Alchian and Demsetz (1972) would move these models in a useful and realistic direction. In particular, firm size is greatly limited in these models because of the intensity of the free-riding problem. Allowing multiple layers with each layer monitoring the one below them could allow for larger firms and perhaps even persistently large firms, which is a feature of the data (see, for example, Mueller, 1986) but not a property of the model.

5.2. Organizational norms

> At one point during his investigations, [consultant] Sym-Smith asked [Sears managers] how controversy was handled at the upper level of Sears. He was told that there was no controversy. Senior Searsmen were trained from their corporate infancy to participate in a veritable cult of contrived harmony and consensus. [Donald R. Katz, *The Big Store: Inside the Crisis and Revolution at Sears* (1987), p. 28.]

As discussed earlier in the context of organizational search and learning, the long-run performance of an organization depends crucially on the way it balances exploration with exploitation. There are two issues central to this trade-off. First, exploitation at the organizational level relies upon diversity at the agent-level; there must be someone who knows something special in order for the rest of the organization to learn something new and possibly useful. When agents engage in independent innovation, diversity is naturally generated, thereby providing the raw material for exploitation by the organization. However, the very process of global exploitation reduces the degree of diversity—replacing ideas with what are considered to be superior ones—so that eventually improvements in organizational performance disappear.

The second issue is how the global exploitation of local knowledge gets carried out in the organization. We've considered exploitation being done under centralization (for example, the top-down mandate of a superior practice) as well as decentralization (for example, agents share information and individually decide on whether to adopt an idea). March (1991) considers a particular form of decentralized learning in which the agents learn from organizational norms—"accepted wisdom" as to the proper way in which to do things—but where the norms themselves evolve as they are shaped by the behavior of the more successful agents within the organization. The coevolutionary dynamics between organizational norms and agent behavior drive performance by influencing the extent of diversity in the population and, therefore, the delicate balance between exploration and exploitation.

5.2.1. March (1991)

Consider an organization facing an external reality that takes values from $\{-1, 1\}$ on m dimensions. The external reality is known only to the modeler and is assumed to be fixed for the initial set of analyses. The organization has n agents who in each period hold beliefs about the external reality. Agents' beliefs on each dimension lie in $\{-1, 0, 1\}$ as does the organizational norm (or code). These beliefs coevolve and only indirectly connect to external reality. In any period, if the code is 0 for a particular dimension, then agents do not modify their beliefs about that dimension. It is as if the code has nothing to prescribe for that dimension. If instead the code is -1 or 1 and differs from an agent's belief, then the belief of that agent switches with probability p_1 to what the code dictates. It is natural to interpret p_1 as a measure of socialization since it controls the degree to which an agent is influenced by organizational norms. As agents learn from the code, the code itself evolves to conform to the beliefs of those agents whose beliefs are closer to external reality than that of the code. To be specific, if the code differs from the majority view of those agents whose beliefs (over all dimensions) are closer to reality, then the code remains unchanged with probability $(1 - p_2)^k$ where k is the difference between the number of agents whose beliefs differ from the code and the number with the same belief. p_2 then controls how effectively the code responds to the beliefs of the "best" agents.

The performance of the organization is measured by two levels of knowledge: the accuracy of the organizational code (which is the proportion of the organizational code that matches reality) and the average accuracy of the organization's members (which is the average proportion of individual beliefs that match reality). As agents and the code influence each other, they converge over time. An equilibrium is reached when the organizational code and the individuals share common beliefs over all m dimensions. At that point, no further learning is possible though these beliefs need not match up with external reality.

Given the mutual learning dynamics between an organization's members and its norms, slower socialization (that is, a lower value for p_1) enhances the equilibrium level of knowledge. Furthermore, there is an interesting interaction between socialization and the adaptivity of the organizational code (as measured by p_2). When socialization is slow, an increase in code adaptivity raises the average level of knowledge; when socialization is fast, a more adaptive code reduces knowledge. The equilibrium knowledge level is maximized when norms respond quickly and the population is comprised of slow-adjusting agents. The key to understanding these results is to recognize from where the raw material for learning is coming. In that agents and the organizational code learn from each other to the extent that their beliefs differ, what drives mutual learning is *sustained* diversity in beliefs. Rapid socialization causes agents' beliefs to converge to the organizational code before the code has been able to match the beliefs of the agents whose beliefs are most accurate. In contrast, slow socialization coupled with a rapidly learning code maintains a sufficient amount of diversity in the population during the code's adaptation. This augments the spreading of correct beliefs throughout the organization, with these correct beliefs ultimately becoming embedded in the code.

Just as diversity of beliefs is conducive to knowledge accumulation, so is heterogeneity in learning rates among agents. For the same average rate of learning, a mix of fast and slow learners leads to more aggregate knowledge than a homogeneous group. The slow learners provide the raw material that the organization needs to adapt in the long run, while the fast learners take advantage of the code capitalizing on this diversity; they perform the exploitation function. Providing a dilemma for organizations, the individual performance of slow learners is worse than that of fast learners, as reflected in the inaccuracy of their beliefs, which means that fast learning can be good for the agent but bad for the organization.

A similar set of forces comes into play when personnel turnover and environmental turbulence are introduced. Suppose that, in each period, an agent is replaced with probability p_3 by a new agent with a fresh set of beliefs. When socialization is slow, an increase in p_3 decreases the average level of knowledge as these new agents replace accurate beliefs with randomly selected ones. However, when socialization is rapid, long-run knowledge is maximized with a moderate rate of personnel turnover as it serves to introduce diverse beliefs and thus to prevent premature fixation on homogeneous (but incorrect) beliefs. The impact of environmental turbulence is examined by stochastically shifting external reality. If the rate of environmental change is such that the population reaches an equilibrium before effectively responding to the turbulence, organizational performance tends to degrade as the homogeneous population lacks the raw material to respond to a changing reality. Once again, personnel turnover can enhance knowledge by injecting new beliefs into the organization.

In evaluating this model, it clearly lacks the richness of structure of the previous models reviewed. Learning is occurring in an unstructured space, thus the model does not deliver the type of insight obtained when there is the additional structure of a landscape. Also, the focus on beliefs without an explicit specification of how they map into performance omits an essential step in the norm-formation process. All these weaknesses aside, the paper makes a singular contribution in providing a plausible and parsimonious feedback mechanism for the determination of organizational norms.

5.3. Growing an organization

If you don't zero in on bureaucracy every so often, you will naturally build in layers. You never set out to add bureaucracy. You just get it. [David Glass, CEO of Wal-Mart, quoted in Sam Walton with John Huey, *Sam Walton: Made in America* 1992, p. 232.]

Thus far, the primary approach to studying organizational structure has been to exogenously specify various structures—in terms of the communication network and the allocation of information and decision-making—and to compare their performance. While these models are bottom-up to the extent that organizational behavior is the product of the interactions of individual agents' acting according to their decision rules, they are top-down in terms of organizational structure, as it is pre-specified by the modeler. Though organizational structure is endogenized in such work as Carley and Svoboda (1996), DeCanio et al. (2000), Miller (2001), and Ethiraj and Levinthal (2002), this is done by specifying a super-agent process as reflected in, for example, applying a genetic algorithm on a population of organizations. It fails to produce organizational structure from the bottom-up by having it be the product of the decisions of individual agents within the organization. This all-important task—using the bottom-up approach of agent-based models to generate the structure of an organization—is initially attempted in Epstein (2003). Though, as we'll later argue, the model has features running counter to real organizations, it is a novel and thought-provoking initial salvo on this challenging fundamental problem.

5.3.1. Epstein (2003)

In this model, individual agents in the organization endogenously generate internal hierarchy in response to their environment. The environment for the organization is represented by a flow of "opportunities" that are met by the available pool of labor (agents). The central organizational problem is how to allocate the fixed pool of labor within the organization so as to most effectively respond to these opportunities.

The type of task faced by the organization is visually summarized in Figure 6. There is a fixed number N of sites (where $N = 8$ in Figure 6), each of which may receive a profit opportunity. One might imagine a site corresponds to a geographic or product market and an opportunity is demand to be met. The baseline organization consists of a fixed number of workers and level-1 managers. Each worker is assigned to a market site and the organization earns profit when a worker is at a site when it receives an opportunity. Using Epstein's colorful terminology, a worker "intercepts" an opportunity if present when one arrives and a "penetration" occurs when an opportunity arrives without a worker there to intercept it. In Figure 6, the firm has five workers who are positioned at sites 1, 3, 4, 7, and 8 and there are four level-1 managers, each being in charge of two adjacent sites. Opportunities are coming into sites 1, 2, 4, 5, 6, and 7 with the workers at sites 1, 4, and 7 positioned to intercept. The opportunities coming into sites 2, 5, and 6, on the other hand, are wasted and represent penetrations. Finally, the workers at sites 3 and 8 are idle for lack of opportunities. Penetrations and idle workers are monitored by level-1 managers. For instance, the level-1 manager in charge of sites 1 and 2 recognizes the need for a worker to meet the opportunity at site 2. Concurrently, the level-1 manager in charge of sites 3 and 4 recognizes that the worker at site 3 is underutilized. Clearly, an appropriate move for the organization is to shift the worker from site 3 to site 2.

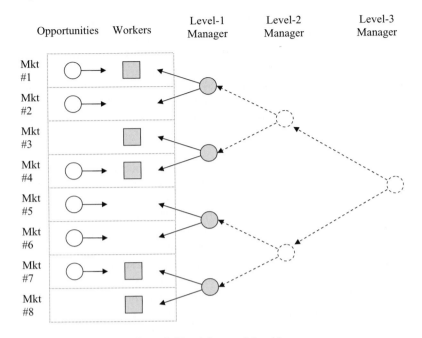

Figure 6. Epstein's essential problem.

The organizational problem in this model is to efficiently allocate its workforce. However, workers cannot, by themselves, move among sites but may be reallocated by upper management. Epstein considers two approaches to solve the allocation problem, though only the hierarchy approach will concern us here.[30] This approach has managers creating higher level managers to solve the allocation problem. In the example above, a level-1 manager would "activate" a level-2 manager who would be in control of the four sites (two sites each from the two subordinate managers) and thus have the capacity to move workers among those sites. For instance, the level-1 manager controlling sites 1 and 2 can activate a level-2 manager who has control over sites 1 through 4 and who can thus observe and respond to the excess demand at site 2 and the excess supply at site 3. Being in charge of sites 1 through 4, he has the authority to shift the worker in site 3 to site 2 and balance the demand and supply of the workers for the sites that are under his control.

A manager's decision rule for activating an upper level manager is defined by three parameters: two penetration threshold values, denoted $T_{\min}$ and $T_{\max}$, and a finite memory of length m. Given the number of penetrations recorded in their memory, a level-k

---

[30] Indeed, the primary objective of the paper is to characterize the optimal solution—hierarchy or a trade mechanism—and how it depends on the organization's objective. Our interest is more in terms of it as a modelling approach to endogenizing hierarchies.

manager computes the average number of penetrations per period, P, over the 2^k market sites he controls. If $P \geq T_{\max}$ then, with some upward inertia, a manager of level $k + 1$ is created. If $P < T_{\min}$ then, with some downward inertia, the manager cedes authority to managers at level $k - 1$. This inertia captures the reluctance of a manager to relinquish control. There is no change in the current hierarchical structure when $T_{\min} \leq P < T_{\max}$. The threshold values can vary across levels, though they are specified to be the same within a managerial level. Given a pattern of opportunities arriving at these sites over time, the baseline organization can endogenously grow its hierarchy to as many as $\log_2 N$ levels.

Suppose the flow of opportunities is continual and concentrated on a set of sites for which there are, initially, no workers. The hierarchy mechanism creates additional managerial layers to handle this misallocation as long as the penetration thresholds and the upward inertia parameter are set sufficiently low. The emergent hierarchy, even after the workers have been properly allocated to effectively intercept all incoming opportunities, tends to remain in place when the downward inertia of the top managerial level is sufficiently high. When downward inertia is instead low at all management layers, then the generated hierarchy quickly dissolves after successfully reallocating labor. The flexibility with which the organization restructures itself internally—both to effectively reallocate labor and then to dismantle itself when no longer needed—depends on the inertia embedded in agents' decision rules as well as the thresholds for inducing a change in structure.

As a theory of organizational structure, Epstein (2003) offers a rich and novel approach to organizations but it has a critical feature which runs counter to our understanding of real organizations.[31] In this model, managerial layers emerge from below, as managers create levels above them to coordinate the behavior of what were originally independent divisions. To begin, in most organizations (such as corporations and governments), there is always a manager at the top who, at least in principle, can reallocate resources as desired. More importantly, managers only have authority over reorganizing what lies beneath them in the hierarchy so that, as a result, new managerial layers are created from above. A commonly purported motivation for adding middle level managers is that upper managers perceive themselves as overburdened and thus distribute tasks and authority to newly created managerial levels. In Epstein's model, organizational structure is created in a direction running counter to reality.

In spite of this weakness, Epstein (2003) is a provocative study. Epstein lays down an important issue for future research—to model the internal organizational pressures that create a need for a new organizational structure and the process by which change is realized. This would represent the acme of agent-based models of organizations; it closes the circle in that an organization can re-invent itself through the decisions of the organization's members.

---

[31] In fairness, Epstein (2003) states that the model is not intended to represent any existing organization.

6. Critique of the past and directions for the future

You don't want to learn a science in its early stages. . . . You have to think about. . . your mind as a resource to conserve, and if you fill it up with infantile garbage it might cost you something later. There might be right theories that you will be unable to understand five years later because you have so many misconceptions. You have to form the habit of not wanting to have been right for very long. If I still believe something after five years, I doubt it. [Marvin Minsky quoted in Stewart Brand, *The Media Lab: Inventing the Future at M.I.T.* (1987), pp. 103–104.]

Recent research in the computational agent-based literature has provided a new and fresh perspective to exploring organizations. There is real promise that theory can produce precise results while encompassing the rich institutional features of corporations, governments, political parties, and other organizations. But if we are to effectively traverse the learning curve associated with this new modelling approach, we must maintain a healthy level of skepticism. Research builds its own momentum as assumptions initially considered problematic are routinized, arbitrary modelling conveniences become entrenched and leave unexplored the sensitivity of results to them, and standards for acceptable work form when methods are rudimentary. As March (1991) discovered, stability during an intense learning phrase can be quite deleterious. We are at such a point and it is wise that we be on guard against acquiring bad habits. Towards this end, we'll make three methodological points in this section and conclude with a few suggested directions for research.

The first point is that, while there is always a disconnect between our models and what they are intended to represent, this can be a more serious issue with computational agent-based models. This concern does not come from modelling simplicity—indeed, the models are quite rich compared to their predecessors—but rather that insufficient attention may be given to relating a model to reality. Many of the modelling components—artificial neural networks, simulated annealing, genetic algorithms, and the like—were originally developed for very different purposes and some work has used them without adequately explaining how these theoretical constructs map into real-world entities and processes. For example, what is the correspondence between the components of an artificial neural network and the components of a firm? Is it appropriate to interpret a node as a person? If not, what additional structure would make a node a reasonable representation of a person? What is the correspondence between a genetic algorithm and the process of imitation and innovation conducted within and between organizations? Is crossover a descriptively accurate model of some organizational process? Before "off-the-shelf" modules are deployed in modelling organizations, the researcher should map it to what is being modelled. Doing so will not only lead to more confidence in the model but is likely to suggest useful modifications.

One of the reasons that neoclassical economists resist bounded rationality is that there are so many ways to model it, and often which is selected is arbitrary. This is a legitimate concern, although it should not deter one from engaging in such work. Indeed, the equilibrium assumption—an agent "understands" the world around him in the sense of, for example, knowing the behavioral rules used by other agents—is as *ad hoc* as most assumptions of boundedly rational agents in that, in most instances, it is not based on empirical evidence and often no credible story can be told to make the assumption convincing. (The appeal of the equilibrium assumption is not its empirical validity but rather its power in generating precise results and its accordance with the faith of many neoclassical economists in equilibrating processes.) This leads to our second point. Given there are many ways in which to model bounded rationality, a feature to the broad research program should be assessing the robustness of insight to the particular way bounded rationality is instantiated in agents and how the tasks facing agents are represented. In finding a solution, does it make a difference whether an organization is modelled as an artificial neural network or as a collection of myopic hill-climbing agents? Do results depend on the organization solving a decomposable problem or a binary classification problem or minimizing a distance function? Does it make a difference whether organizational structure evolves as represented by simulated annealing or a genetic algorithm? Rather than consider one particular task, it may be more useful to allow for a variety of tasks, exploring how the optimal organizational structure depends on the task and identifying those structures that perform reasonably well for an assortment of tasks.

The third point to make about this literature is that results can be inadequately explained. This is partly due to models being too complex and researchers forgetting that parsimony is a virtue, not a weakness emanating from a lack of computing power. Indeed, the poignancy of Einstein's well-known apothegm—"Everything should be as simple as possible, but not simpler."—is nowhere greater than with agent-based computational modelling.[32] As the power of computing allows us to solve models of increasing complexity, there is a natural tendency to complicate. This is a mistake. Even with Moore's Law sailing at full mast, computing constraints continue to make our models gross simplifications of what we are trying to understand. The deliverable of formal models remains what it has always been—insight. A model that is so complex that its implications elude explanation is a model that has not altered our understanding.[33]

Complexity aside, a more disturbing feature of this work is the sometimes perceived lack of necessity to carefully explain results. An attractive feature of a mathematical proof is that it provides a paper trail that can be used to explain results. Though computational results are also the product of logical operations, there is a tendency to think that if the model cannot be solved analytically then there is little point to trying to carefully sort out how output is produced. Anyone who has worked with computational models knows that results can be the product of arbitrary assumptions of convenience or coding

---

[32] Indeed, some work in the computational agent-based literature seems to be guided by the axiom: "Make it simple enough to be computable and complex enough to be incomprehensible."

[33] It is in this light that we decry "emergent phenomena" when it is meant to refer to results unanticipatable by virtue of a model's complexity. If one could not, upon proper reflection, anticipate the possibility of some results then it is hard to see how one can *ex post* explain them and, if one cannot explain them, in what sense do we understand more.

errors, which makes it all the more critical that they be adequately explained. Though computational work may not leave an analogous paper trail, it can offer a way in which to "test" an explanation. If one conjectures that a result is due to a particular force, then it may be possible to "turn off" that force. If the result persists then one's conjecture is wrong; if the result goes away then the "evidence" is consistent with that explanation. Furthermore, explanation is not only essential to gaining insight but also to assessing robustness. Convincingly arguing that the forces driving the results are not peculiar to those examples is the way in which to develop confidence that the insight uncovered is broadly applicable. The bottom line is that researchers must apply the same standards for explaining results that are used in the assumption-proof-theorem tradition.[34]

Given research on organizations using a computational agent-based approach is in its incipiency, there are multitudes of research directions. Rather than propose specific lines, which would only serve to scratch the surface and deplete what minuscule scholarly wealth the authors possess, let us instead provide three general directions for research.

One direction is to take bounded rationality another step further. While agents are modelled as being limited in their decision-making capacity, they are often assumed to have an unrealistic amount of information, either before or after acting. A common assumption in rugged landscape models is that an agent observes *ex ante* the true performance associated with an idea and, based on that information, decides whether or not to adopt it. In some cases, this can be plausibly motivated by imagining that the idea is temporarily implemented with (noiseless) performance being observed. Learning is then occurring offline. If, however, there is noise, then learning will have to occur in real time—an organization may need to continue the experiment for a non-trivial length of time in order to get a sufficiently informative signal. Before even experimenting with an idea, it will want to make an assessment of its potential but then the agent must have a "model" so as to make such a judgment. That is a feature lacking in most agent-based models (Gavetti and Levinthal, 2000, being an exception). Depending on how one models the evolution of an agent's model of the landscape, biased and not just noisy evaluations could emerge.

An analogously strong assumption is made in many information-processing models, which is that agents learn *ex post* what was the true state; an organization receives data, makes a choice, observes the outcome, and is able to infer from the outcome what would have been the right choice. In practice, the true state is rarely observed and, while performance may be observed, it provides noisy information regarding what would have been the best decision. In addition, when there are more than a few members, organizational performance is a highly uninformative signal of what an agent outside of the upper-most levels should have done. Agents need to know about their "local" performance rather than the global performance of the organization. Models have to come

---

[34] This comment was distinctly improved by a stimulating dinner conversation between one of the authors and Patrick Rey in Siena, Italy.

to grips with how an organization measures an individual agent's contribution to total performance.

A second direction is to bring in more structure. Thus far, models have been too generic. The results generated by models of search and learning are extensions or applications of insight regarding search on rugged landscapes. If we're to move beyond that, we need to impose more structure so that a variable is not some faceless dimension but concretely corresponds to an actual practice. This would allow one to explore not only how many dimensions should be centralized but also *which* dimensions should be centralized. What determines whether, say, marketing is controlled by the corporate office or a product manager? What determines which dimensions a store manager controls rather than assistant managers? An important step is to further pursue the approach of building a landscape from economic primitives by modelling specific functions—pricing, product selection, training practices, marketing, inventory policy, etc. Such an approach could open up an entirely new set of questions and make these models more powerful both in explaining organizational behavior and serving a normative role for organizations.

More structure is also needed in information processing models where, thus far, agents are excessively simple-minded and too heavily "programmed," even by the standards of the computational agent-based literature. Endowing them with preferences and giving them choices—such as how much effort to exert and what information to pass onto the next node in the network—is vital for the distance between models and reality to lessen.

At present, organization theory is partitioned into the neoclassical economics approach and the agent-based computational approach and "ne'er the twain shall meet." It is obvious that these two research lines should not be moving independently. Each has its virtues—computational work provides a rich modelling of organizational structure and how agents interact while neoclassical work is sophisticated in its modelling of incentives—and a superior theory of organizations is to be had if the two can be integrated. This challenge is the third direction.

References

Aghion, P., Tirole, J. (1997). "Formal and real authority in organizations". Journal of Political Economy 105, 1–29.
Alchian, A., Demsetz, H. (1972). "Production, information costs, and economic organization". American Economic Review 62, 777–795.
Aldrich, H. (1999). Organizations Evolving. Sage Publications, London.
Axtell, R. (1999). "The emergence of firms in a population of agents: local increasing returns, unstable Nash equilibria, and power law size distributions", CSED working paper No. 3, Brookings Institution.
Barr, J., Saraceno, F. (2002). "A computational theory of the firm". Journal of Economic Behavior and Organization 49, 345–361.
Barr, J., Saraceno, F. (2005). "Cournot competition, organization and learning". Journal of Economic Dynamics and Control 29, 277–295.
Baum, J.A.C. (Ed.) (2002). The Blackwell Companion to Organizations. Blackwell Publishers, Oxford.

Baum, J.A.C., Singh, J.V. (Eds.) (1994). Evolutionary Dynamics of Organizations. Oxford University Press, New York.

Brand, S. (1987). The Media Lab: Inventing the Future at M.I.T. Viking, New York.

Brenner, T. (2006). "Agent learning representation: advice on modelling economic learning", this handbook.

Bruderer, E., Singh, J.V. (1996). "Organizational evolution, learning, and selection: a genetic-algorithm-based model". Academy Management Journal 39, 1322–1349.

Burton, R.M., Obel, B. (1980). "A computer simulation test of the M-form hypothesis". Administrative Science Quarterly 25, 457–466.

Carley, K.M. (1992). "Organizational learning and personnel turnover". Organization Science 3, 20–46.

Carley, K.M., Prietula, M.J. (Eds.) (1994). Computational Organization Theory. Lawrence Erlbaum Associates, Hillsdale, NJ.

Carley, K.M., Svoboda, D.M. (1996). "Modeling organizational adaptation as a simulated annealing process". Sociological Methods & Research 25, 138–168.

Carley, K.M., Gasser, L. (1999). "Computational organization theory". In: Weiss, G. (Ed.), Multiagent Systems: A Modern Approach to Distributed Artificial Intelligence. The MIT Press, Cambridge, MA.

Carroll, G.R., Harrison, J.R. (1998). "Organizational demography and culture: insights from a formal model and simulation". Administrative Science Quarterly 43, 637–667.

Carroll, T., Burton, R.M. (2000). "Organizations and complexity: searching for the edge of chaos". Computational and Mathematical Organization Theory 6, 319–337.

Chandler, A.D. Jr. (1977). The Visible Hand: The Managerial Revolution in American Business. Belknap Press of Harvard University Press, Cambridge, MA.

Chang, M.-H., Harrington, J.E. Jr. (1997). "Organizational structure and firm innovation in a retail chain". Computational and Mathematical Organization Theory 3, 267–288.

Chang, M.-H., Harrington, J.E. Jr. (2000). "Centralization vs. decentralization in a multi-unit organization: a computational model of a retail chain as a multi-agent adaptive system". Management Science 46, 1427–1440.

Chang, M.-H., Harrington, J.E. Jr. (2003). "Multi-market competition, consumer search, and the organizational structure of multi-unit firms". Management Science 49, 541–552.

Chang, M.-H., Harrington, J.E. Jr. (2004). "Organization of innovation in a multi-unit firm: coordinating adaptive search on multiple rugged landscapes". In: Barnett, W., Deissenberg, C., Feichtinger, G. (Eds.), Economic Complexity: Non-linear Dynamics, Multi-agents Economies, and Learning, ISETE, vol. 14. Elsevier, Amsterdam, pp. 189–214.

Cohen, M.D., Sproull, L.S. (Eds.) (1996). Organizational Learning. Sage Publications, Thousand Oaks, CA.

DeCanio, S.J., Watkins, W.E. (1998). "Information processing and organizational structure". Journal of Economic Behavior and Organization 36, 275–294.

DeCanio, S.J., Dibble, C., Amir-Atefi, K. (2000). "The importance of organizational structure for the adoption of innovations". Management Science 46, 1285–1299.

Dessein, W. (2002). "Authority and communication in organizations". Review of Economic Studies 69, 811–838.

Dow, G.K. (1990). "The organization as an adaptive network". Journal of Economic Behavior and Organization 14, 159–185.

Duffy, J. (2006). "Agent-based models and human subject experiments", this handbook.

Durfee, E.H. (1999). "Distributed problem solving and planning". In: Weiss, G. (Ed.), Multiagent Systems: A Modern Approach to Distributed Artificial Intelligence. The MIT Press, Cambridge, MA.

Epstein, J.M. (2003). "Growing adaptive organizations: an agent-based computational approach", The Santa Fe Institute, working paper 03-05-029 [forthcoming in: Epstein, J.M. (2005). Generative Social Science: Studies in Agent-Based Computational Modeling. Princeton University Press, Princeton, NJ].

Ethiraj, S.K., Levinthal, D. (2002). "Search for architecture in complex worlds: an evolutionary perspective on modularity and the emergence of dominant designs", Wharton School, University of Pennsylvania, pdf copy.

Gavetti, G., Levinthal, D. (2000). "Looking forward and looking backward: cognitive and experiential search". Administrative Science Quarterly 45, 113–137.

Ghemawat, P., Levinthal, D. (2000). "Choice structures and business strategy", The Wharton School, University of Pennsylvania, pdf copy.

Glance, N.S., Hogg, T., Huberman, B.A. (1997). "Training and turnover in the evolution of organizations". Organization Science 8, 84–96.

Hardin, G. (1968). "The tragedy of the commons". Science 162, 1243–1248.

Harrington, J.E. Jr. (1998). "The social selection of flexible and rigid agents". American Economic Review 88, 63–82.

Harrington, J.E. Jr. (1999). "Rigidity of social systems". Journal of Political Economy 107, 40–64.

Harrington, J.E. Jr., Chang, M.-H. (2005). "Coevolution of firms and consumers and the implications for market dominance". Journal of Economic Dynamics and Control 29, 245–276.

Hayek, F.A. (1945). "The use of knowledge in society". American Economic Review 35, 1–18.

Holmstrom, B.R., Tirole, J. (1989). "The theory of the firm". In: Schmalensee, R., Willig, R.D. (Eds.), Handbook of Industrial Organization, vol. I. Elsevier, Amsterdam.

Jensen, M.C., Meckling, W.H. (1995). "Specific and general knowledge, and organizational structure". Journal of Applied Corporate Finance 8, 4–18.

Janssen, M.A., Ostrom, E. (2006). "Governing social-ecological systems", this handbook.

Katz, D.R. (1987). The Big Store: Inside the Crisis and Revolution at Sears. Penguin Books, New York.

Kauffman, S. (1993). The Origins of Order. Oxford University Press, New York.

Kollman, K., Miller, J.H., Page, S.E. (2000). "Decentralization and the search for policy solutions". Journal of Law, Economics, and Organization 16, 102–128.

Levinthal, D.A. (1997). "Adaptation on rugged landscapes". Management Science 43, 934–950.

Levinthal, D., March, J.G. (1981). "A model of adaptive organizational search". Journal of Economic Behavior and Organization 2, 307–333.

Lomi, A., Larsen, E.R. (Eds.) (2001). Dynamics of Organizations: Computational Modeling and Organization Theories. AAAI Press/The MIT Press, Menlo Park, CA.

Mackie-Mason, J., Wellman, M. (2006). "Automated markets and trading agents", this handbook.

March, J.G. (1991). "Exploration and exploitation in organizational learning". Organization Science 2, 71–87.

March, J.G., Simon, H.A. (1958). Organizations. Wiley, New York.

Maskin, E., Qian, Y., Xu, C. (2000). "Incentives, information, and organizational form". Review of Economic Studies 67, 359–378.

Milgrom, P., Roberts, J. (1992). "Economics, Organization and Management". Prentice Hall, Englewood Cliffs, NJ.

Miller, J.H. (2001). "Evolving information processing organizations". In: Lomi, A., Larsen, E.R. (Eds.), Dynamics of Organizations: Computational Modeling and Organization Theories. AAAI Press/The MIT Press, Menlo Park, CA.

Minsky, M. (1986). The Society of Mind. Simon and Schuster, New York.

Mueller, D. (1986). Profits in the Long Run. Cambridge University Press, Cambridge.

Nelson, R.R., Winter, S.G. (1982). An Evolutionary Theory of Economic Change. The Belknap Press of Harvard University Press, Cambridge, MA.

Page, S.E. (1996). "Two measures of difficulty". Economic Theory 8, 321–346.

Prendergast, C. (1999). "The provision of incentives in firms". Journal of Economic Literature 37, 7–63.

Prietula, M.J., Carley, K.M., Gasser, L. (Eds.) (1998). Simulating Organizations: Computational Models of Institutions and Groups. The MIT Press, Cambridge, MA.

Qian, Y. (1994). "Incentives and loss of control in an optimal hierarchy". Review of Economic Studies 61, 527–544.

Radner, R. (1993). "The organization of decentralized information processing". Econometrica 61, 1109–1146.

Rivkin, J. (2000). "Imitation of complex strategies". Management Science 46, 824–844.

Rivkin, J., Siggelkow, N. (2003). "Balancing search and stability: interdependencies among elements of organizational design". Management Science 49, 290–311.

Sathe, V. (1985). Culture and Related Corporate Realities: Text, Cases, and Readings on Organizational Entry, Establishment, and Change. R.D. Irwin, Homewood, IL.

Schumpeter, J.A. (1939). Business Cycles: A Theoretical, Historical, and Statistical Analysis of the Capitalist Process, Vol. I. McGraw-Hill, New York.

Siggelkow, N., Levinthal, D.A. (2003). "Temporarily divide to conquer: centralized, decentralized, and reintegrated organizational approaches to exploration and adaptation". Organization Science 14, 650–669.

Simon, H.A. (1996). The Sciences of the Artificial. MIT Press, Cambridge, MA.

Sorensen, O. (2002). "Interorganizational complexity and computation". In: Baum, J. (Ed.), The Blackwell Companion to Organizations. Blackwell, Oxford.

Taylor, F.W. (1919). The Principles of Scientific Management. Harper and Brothers Publishers, New York. [Original edition, 1911].

Van Zandt, T. (1999). "Real-time decentralized information processing as a model of organizations with boundedly rational agents". Review of Economic Studies 66, 633–658.

Vriend, N. (2006). "ACE models of endogenous interactions", this handbook.

Walton, S., Huey, J. (1992). Sam Walton: Made in America. Doubleday, New York.

Wilhite, A. (2006). "Economic activity on fixed networks", this handbook.

Chapter 27

MARKET DESIGN USING AGENT-BASED MODELS

ROBERT MARKS

Australian Graduate School of Management, The Universities of Sydney and New South Wales, Sydney, NSW 2052, Australia
e-mail: bobm@agsm.edu.au; url: http://www.agsm.edu.au/~bobm

Contents

Handbook of Computational Economics, Volume 2. Edited by Leigh Tesfatsion and Kenneth L. Judd
© 2006 Elsevier B.V. All rights reserved
DOI: 10.1016/S1574-0021(05)02027-7

Abstract

This chapter explores the state of the emerging practice of designing markets by the use of agent-based modeling, with special reference to electricity markets and computerized (on-line) markets, perhaps including real-life electronic agents as well as human traders. The paper first reviews the use of evolutionary and agent-based techniques of analyzing market behaviors and market mechanisms, and economic models of learning, comparing genetic algorithms with reinforcement learning. Ideal design would be direct optimization of an objective function, but in practice the complexity of markets and traders' behavior prevents this, except in special circumstances. Instead, iterative analysis, subject to design criteria trade-offs, using autonomous self-interested agents, mimics the bottom-up evolution of historical market mechanisms by trial and error. The chapter highlights ten papers that exemplify recent progress in agent-based evolutionary analysis and design of markets in silico, using electricity markets and on-line double auctions as illustrations. A monopoly sealed-bid auction is examined in the tenth paper, and a new auction mechanism is evolved and analyzed. The chapter concludes that, as modeling the learning and behavior of traders improves, and as the software and hardware available for modeling and analysis improves, the techniques will provide ever greater insights into improving the designs of existing markets, and facilitating the design of new markets.

Keywords

market, analysis, design, auctions, learning, electricity, on-line

JEL classification: C150, C630, C790, D440, D490

1. Introduction

Institutional arrangements for exchange—markets—have emerged and evolved over the millennia since—and perhaps as a consequence of—specialization of labor, which can be intensive (making something "better" than others do, absolutely or relatively) or extensive (taking the risk of fetching an item, not locally available, from afar). "Trade" first meant exchange of foreign-produced goods for domestic goods, a form of barter, which is made more efficient with the emergence of money—numeraire, store of wealth, and medium of exchange, in the textbooks' trio.

Many different market institutions have evolved, well described in John McMillan's book, *Reinventing the Bazaar* (McMillan, 2002). The development of economics, in one view, has been the outcome of reflecting on, describing, and analyzing various markets, from the market-town's weekly bazaar to the complex financial markets for exchanging risk. One form of market institution is the auction, and only over the past forty-odd years, with the development of the tools of game theory, has formal analysis of auctions begun.

1.1. Designer markets

As engineers say, after analysis comes synthesis—design. Designing markets is a new discipline. At least five examples of designed market can be identified: simulated stock markets; emission markets; auctions for electro-magnetic spectrum; electricity markets; and on-line, e-commerce markets:

1. First, the markets for new financial instruments, derivatives, that were created and traded after Black, Scholes, and Merton solved the seventy-year-old problem of pricing options. Previously, financial traders understood that options were valuable, but not how to value them exactly. More recently, there has been research into the rules and micro-structure of stock markets, continuous double-auction trading, through the use of simulated markets. See LeBaron (2006) for further discussion of this research.

2. Second, the markets for pollution emissions, usually sulphur dioxide and carbon dioxide. The realization that the emissions from industrial processes in particular, and the emission of anthropogenic chemicals into the environment in general, were, at least potentially, altering the biosphere for the worse was followed only after a lag with the awareness by policy makers that market mechanisms could be harnessed to control such emissions, generally more efficiently than could other mechanisms.

3. Third, the auctions for electro-magnetic spectrum. The simultaneous ascending-bid auctions that have recently been designed for selling bands of local spectrum to be used for new communications technologies did not arise without some hiccups. Perhaps as an offshoot of the privatization of government assets and activities in the 1980s in many countries, the use of auctions to choose the new owners and to value these assets slowly replaced so-called "beauty contests," in which subject to

certain technical requirements licenses were virtually given away. But these new auction mechanisms at first did not allow for the complementary nature of bands in different localities. Only after intensive efforts by economists advising, first, governments, and, second, bidding companies did the successful "3G" auctions occur [Milgrom (2004)].

4. Fourth, the markets for the exchange of electricity. Again, as a consequence of the twin political aims of privatizing government-owned electricity utilities and of improving the efficiency of electricity generation and distribution systems (perhaps by separating ownership of generators and distributors), while reducing the bureaucratic weight of regulation even on privately owned utilities, there has in many jurisdictions been a move away from centralized engineering-dominated means of allocating electricity load across generators and distribution networks to using market mechanisms of various kinds. Electricity cannot (easily or cheaply) be stored, a characteristic which, with some engineering issues, has meant that previously existing market mechanisms were not appropriate. Instead, several types of new market mechanisms have been introduced.[1]

5. Fifth, on-line markets. With the growth of the use and extent of the Internet over the past eight years, and the dot-com boom, with buying and selling on-line, opportunities for designing on-line markets de novo, as opposed to trying to emulate existing face-to-face markets, have arisen. In the last few years these opportunities have given rise to much work by computer scientists, as well as economists. Indeed, there is a productive research intersection of the two disciplines, as revealed in some of the papers discussed below.

The use of game theoretic methods to analyze market design is related to the use of these techniques to analyze another kind of interaction, those governed by contracts. Contract design is another area where agent-based modeling might be used, but negotiation and design of contracts by use of computer simulation and agent-based modeling is only now emerging from its infancy.[2]

As examples of the use of agent-based models in market design, this chapter will examine the use of such models in designing the fourth type of market, that for electricity, and the fifth, for on-line trading, which is also examined in MacKie-Mason and Wellman (2006). The first, for emissions abatement, is covered by Janssen and Ostrom (2006).[3] The second is covered by the chapter by LeBaron (2006), and referred to further below. The chapter by Duffy (2006) provides evidence of validation of artificial ("designed") agents and the behavior of human subjects in experiments, as discussed below.

---

[1] Despite the debacle of the California blackouts of 2000, it is increasingly clear that it was not the underlying market design per se at fault, rather it was its implementation and the consequences of lobbying by vested interests: the retail price was regulated, while the unregulated wholesale price sky-rocketed as a consequence of market manipulation, which had the effect of squeezing the retail electricity companies, such as Pacific Gas & Electricity [Sweeney (2002)].

[2] A good starting point is Jennings et al. (2001).

[3] Agent-based models have also been used in other environmental settings: Hailu and Schilizzi (2004).

Before reviewing the use of agent-based simulation models in market design, we contrast analysis with design, closed-form calculations with simulation in both analysis and design, non-agent-based simulation with agent-based simulation of analysis and design, and finally different models of learning and adaptation in agent-based simulation models.

2. Analysis, design, and simulation

Before design must come analysis. Simulation allows analysis of systems that are too complex to analyze using traditional, closed-form techniques. Once we understand through analysis how the elements of the phenomenon of concern work together, we can ask the question of how to improve its operation: how better to design it.

2.1. Analysis

In the world of analytical, closed-form solutions, there is a certain logic to the progress of research. A phenomenon is observed; a need for explanation and understanding is identified; a model is built, incorporating simplifying assumptions; the model is manipulated to obtain necessary and sufficient results, traditionally concerned with existence, uniqueness, and stability of an equilibrium, and perhaps possible improvement in the operation of the system is identified, if it is a human-made system. The former part of the progress is analysis, the latter synthesis, or design, to improve some characteristic of the system or its operation. Successful analyses are published, indexed, and referenced, to be used and modified by future analysts and designers.

A common understanding of this process in general, but particularly the process of model-building and deducing the system's behavior and outcomes, means that, by and large, later researchers can stand on the shoulders of earlier researchers. With today's on-line indexing services, it is even easier to find antecedent papers, to relax an assumption or two, and to attempt to solve the ensuing model, which might (or might not) be a closer approximation to reality, or result in a better design.

This process, I believe, is driven in particular directions by the mathematical tractability of particular types of model, and the relative intractability of others. (If this reminds us of the joke about the economist searching for his car keys under the street-light, instead of in the darkness around his car, it might not be coincidental.)

2.2. Simulation and analysis

The advantage of using simulation techniques is that they provide us with light where the analytical techniques cast little or none, in our metaphorical search, so we are no longer restricted to working with models which we hope will prove tractable to our analytical tools. As computing tools (both hardware and software) have grown more powerful and user-friendly, research using simulation techniques has blossomed. Analysis of observed phenomena has not been a driving motivation of the research of computer scientists—yet they have a fifty-year history of design and invention, which continues apace (although they have from time to time looked for analogies to the natural world, neural nets mimic in some sense the brain, and Genetic Algorithms (GA) were inspired by natural selection with sexual reproduction). Over thirty year ago it was possible for Donald Knuth to write an encyclopedic study of *The Art of Computer Programming* in three volumes [Knuth (1968–1973)], but such a task would be daunting now.[4]

Moreover, as they attempt to implement automated on-line markets, computer scientists have discovered economists' work on auctions, spurred by applications of game theory to study these traditional market institutions, and to develop new, designer markets, given the opportunities of the modern technology.

The focus in this section will be on analysis, rather than design. This is because, as we discuss in Section 3.1 below, direct design or optimization requires a degree of understanding of the mapping from the design space to the performance space which has not yet been developed. Indeed, given the complexity of market phenomena, direct design might never be possible, as Edmonds and Bryson (2003) remind us. Instead, searching the design space will be an iterative process of analyzing the performance of a specific model, modifying the model in the light of this analysis, and analyzing the modified model, until the designer is happy with the performance of the multi-modified model against various criteria.

2.3. Evolutionary simulation techniques

To the evolutionary biologist, the design is the genotype, and the performance is the phenotype. Evolution can be characterized as a dynamic search in a population for genotypes that result in better phenotypes, where that mapping too is ill-defined. It might not be surprising, therefore, that the development of agent-based methods of optimization and simulation began with techniques that mimic aspects of natural selection. Holland's 1976 Genetic Algorithm (GA) (Holland, 1992) was used as a new kind of optimizing tool for problems intractable to calculus-based tools. The GA tests and scores individual solutions in a population of possible solutions, and, based on the "fitness" score of each, selects pairs of "parents" for a new "offspring" generation of possible solutions. This artificial reproduction uses the genetic operations of "crossover" and "mutation" (analogous to mimicry of existing solutions and to exploration of new regimes of the solution space) on the parents. Testing, selection, and generation of a new population results in the emergence of never-worse best solutions. GA has been widely used as an optimizer, a directed form of trial and error that obviates exhaustive testing of all possibilities.

But using the GA as an optimizer in this way—focusing on the single best solution (an individual)—throws away the population's emerged characteristics qua population.

---

[4] Apparently, Knuth has been undertaking a fourth volume, since TeX and METAFONT were put to bed [Knuth (1979)].

A line of research then began with Axelrod's (Axelrod, 1987) simulation of individuals playing the Iterated Prisoner's Dilemma (IPD). It used the population of individuals—stimulus–response automata, where the stimulus was the state of the interaction, and the response was the next action of the player—to consider not only the emergence of new strategic automata, but also to examine the stability of the population against "invasion" by a new strategy.

Axelrod, a political scientist, was interested in combinations of strategies that exhibited the emergence of cooperation [see Axelrod (2006)], a manifestation of the Folk Theorem of repeated games [Fudenberg and Maskin (1986)]. But since the IPD can be thought of as a simple model of a repeated Bertrand duopoly, his work soon gained the attention of economists, who had found the analytical characterizations of equilibria in oligopolistic competition incomplete, not least in the paucity of out-of-equilibrium characterizations of the dynamics of the interaction. That is, the intermediate behavior of a dynamic interaction, a game, might be more important than its asymptotic properties.[5]

When the players face identical payoff sets and choose from identical action sets, a single population is satisfactory, since the GA processes (selection, crossover, and mutation) which model learning among the individuals and between generations of the population are focused on the same end: faced with the same state of the interaction, either of the players would behave identically, and fitness is average (or discounted) profit.

But when modeling oligopolistic players who have distinct payoff sets (because of distinct costs, facing distinct demands, and perhaps with distinct action sets), a single population of agents means that the GA processes are faced with a fitness "landscape" [Kauffman (1995)] that is not only possibly rugged, but also shifting (as each agent wears a distinct sellers hat, as it were). In this case, separate populations of sellers is absolutely necessary.

The GA was developed and pioneered by computer scientists and engineers who were intent on solving optimization problems exhibiting rugged landscapes. Although it was at first used only where these were static, where the landscape did not change as the process of genetic "learning" took place, it also turned out to be well suited to simulating and solving problems where the environment was changing. When the individual agents modeled by the GA are competing against each other, the GA is modeling the process of co-evolution.[6] GAs were originally used as means of seeking optimal solutions to static problems; Marks (1989) and others adapted them to seek solutions of co-evolutionary strategic problems, such as the IPD and oligopolies with asymmetric players, where the fitness of an agent depends on the state of the whole population of agents: state-dependent fitness [Riechmann (2001)]. Sargent (1993) surveys studies using adaptive algorithms (including the GA) to model macro-economic phenomena with learning agents, but not explicitly agent-based models.

---

[5] Just how to characterize out-of-equilibrium behavior (or bounded rationality, for that matter) remains an open question. See Arthur (2006).

[6] This process was mistakenly called boot-strapping by Marks (1989), in the first published research into co-evolution of rivals' strategies in oligopolies.

Chattoe (1998) argues that GA applications in economics confuse the role of the GA as instrumental in searching the solution space and its role as a description of firms' decision-making and individual learning. Dawid (1999) has argued that, despite its foundation in computer science, the GA is good at modeling the ways in which populations of economic actors can learn. Indeed, Curzon Price (1997) spoke of the GA as providing a stream of hypothetical scenarios within the firm, even if not all are acted upon. Duffy (2006) provides an extensive review of the descriptive role of GAs in economic models, and concludes that the findings from many studies "provide some support for the reasonableness of GAs as models of adaptive learning by populations of heterogeneous agents."

When applied to economic systems, the GA operators have been interpreted several ways. Each individual string can represent either an individual agent or one possible decision of a single agent. The selection operator ensures that past performance is reflected in future choices: well (badly) performing decisions are more (less) likely to be chosen in the future. Each new generations of strings might be new individual decision-makers, or it might be new ideas or heuristics among long-lived players.

With few exceptions, the models of analysis and design that we discuss below are evolutionary in nature—"dynamic models in which successful agents and activities gradually increase their share of the economy at the expense of less successful agents and activities" [Conlisk (1996)]—whether explicitly so (as with GAs) or implicitly.

2.4. Learning

The populations in the first applications of GAs were seen as trial solutions to arguments that would optimize the function in question (usually highly non-linear and discontinuous). Later applications, however, treated the populations as comprised of agents rather than numbers. Individual agents were immutable, but in each generation the population of agents would change, under selective pressure. This is implicit learning and adaptation.[7] Just how learning and adaptation are modeled can clearly affect the model's behavior.

Agent-based modeling has since modeled learning as explicit. Arthur (1991, 1993) was the first economist to support modeling agent behavior using reinforcement-learning (RL) algorithms and to calibrate the parameters of such learning models using data from human-subject experiments.[8] In RL models, how an actor chooses to behave later is a function of the outcomes he has experienced earlier, in part as a consequence

---

[7] "Implicit" in that the individual agents do not change at all, but succeeding populations embody improvements ("learning") in the manner of response. Wood (2005) points out that psychological experiments have shown that for human subjects learning can be adaptive, but that adaptation does not necessarily imply learning, the long-term rewriting of memory.

[8] Brenner (2006, Section 2.1) recounts how Arthur generalized the Bush and Mosteller (1955) model, also used by Cross (1973, 1983).

of his earlier choices [the Thorndike effect, Thorndike (1911)].[9] At first, Arthur was interested in calibrating *individual* learning to experimental data, but later he and his associates [Arthur et al. (1997)] "model calibrations that yield aggregate data that are similar to relevant field data" [Duffy (2006)].

Roth and Erev (1995) and Erev and Roth (1998) ask how well RL algorithms track experimental data across various multi-player games. Their general RL model, which improves the fit of the model to human–subject experimental data, includes Arthur's earlier model as a subset, as seen below.

The general Roth–Erev model of reinforcement learning can be characterized as follows: Suppose there are N actions/pure strategies. In round t player i has a propensity $q_{ij}(t)$ to play the jth pure strategy, where propensities are equivalent to strengths in Arthur's model. Initial propensities are equal, $q_{ij}(1) = q_{ik}(1)$ for all available strategies j, k, and $\sum_j q_{ij}(1) = S_i(1)$, where $S_i(1)$ is an initial strength parameter, equal to a constant that is the same for all players, $S_i(1) = S(1)$; the rate of learning is proportional to the size of $S(1)$:

$$\sum_j q_{ij}(1) = S_i(1) = S(1) \quad \text{for all } i. \tag{1}$$

The probability that agent i plays strategy j in period t is made according to the linear choice rule:

$$p_{ij}(t) = \frac{q_{ij}(t)}{\sum_{k=1}^{N} q_{ik}(t)}. \tag{2}$$

Suppose that, in round t, player i plays strategy k and receives payoff of x. Let $R(x) = x - x_{\min}$, where $x_{\min}$ is the smallest possible payoff. Then player i updates his propensity to play action j according to the rule:

$$q_{ij}(t+1) = (1 - \phi)q_{ij}(t) + E_k(j, R(x)), \tag{3}$$

where

$$E_k(j, R(x)) = \begin{cases} (1 - \epsilon)R(x), & \text{if } j = k; \\ \frac{\epsilon}{N-1}R(x), & \text{otherwise.} \end{cases} \tag{4}$$

This is a three-parameter model, where the parameters are: the initial-strength parameter, $S(1)$; a recency parameter ϕ that gradually reduces the power of past experiences to influence future actions; and an experimentation parameter ϵ, which can be localized for similar strategies, or be made more intrepid.

---

[9] Recent psychological research is questioning Thorndike's Law of Effect: the more specific and immediate the feedback, the greater the effect on learning. The Law is a reasonable description of human behavior in a simple world (of decision-making), but is not so good in a complex, stochastic world (of exploration and problem-solving) [Wood (2005)].

If $\phi = \epsilon = 0$ then the model becomes a version of Arthur's model, but without re-normalization of the sum of propensities in every period. The model without re-normalization reflects a learning curve that flattens with experience over time.

Duffy (2006) and Brenner (2006) discuss, among others, four types of RL models: the Arthur–Roth–Erev model mentioned above; Q-learning, which optimizes long-term payoffs, rather than immediate payoffs [Watkins and Dayan (1992)]; multi-agent Q-learning [Hu and Wellman (1998)]; and Adaptive Play [Young (1998)]. Below we discuss several papers that use these models, including a useful modification of the Roth–Erev model summarized above in equations (1)–(4).

Selten [Selten and Stoecker (1986), Selten (1998)] has devised a much simpler learning mechanism, directed learning. This is based on the notion that ex-post rationality is the strongest influence in adaptive behavior. It requires an ordering over the set of possible actions, and models players learning to do better by probabilistically altering their actions in the direction that would have led to higher payoffs had these actions been chosen earlier, and never altering their actions in a direction that would have lowered their payoffs [Brenner (2006)]. For instance, Hailu and Schilizzi (2004) model bidders' learning in auctions: if a bidder won the previous auction, then choose an equi-probable mixed action of the same bid or one ten percent higher for the next auction; if the bidder did not win in the previous auction, then choose an equi-probable mixed action of the same bid or one ten percent lower, with prior upper and lower limits to legitimate bids. They find that the efficiency benefits of one-shot auctions dissipate with repetition and learning.

Vriend (2000) draws the distinction between the social learning of the GA (whereby the individuals in the population have learned from their parents, through selection and crossover, and so there is the possibility of good "genes" spreading through society over several populations) and the individual learning of non-GA agent-based models (with explicit learning incorporated into the structures of the artificial, adaptive agents).[10] Both sorts of models, and both sorts of learning, have been termed "agent-based" models.

The learning in reinforcement-based models and in the extant GA models is inductive: that is, future actions are based on past experience, with no attempt to anticipate and reason back, in a truly deductive, strategic fashion. Belief-based learning, however, incorporates recognition by the players that they are interacting with other players. They thus form beliefs about the likely actions of these other players. "Their choice of strategy is then a best response to their beliefs", [Duffy (2006), Section 3.2]. "By contrast, reinforcement learners do not form beliefs about other players, and need not even realize that they are playing a game or participating in a market with others." Almost all the research we review models inductive learning, but two papers which use anticipatory, belief-based learning are reviewed in Section 3.4 below.

---

[10] Strictly speaking, individual learning can also be modeled using classifier systems, closely related to the GA [Holland (1992)].

2.5. From analysis to design

As remarked by Roth (1991) in an earlier paper on market design, three approaches are suitable for the iterative process of market design: first, traditional closed-form game-theoretic analysis, as discussed above; second, human–subject experiments; and, third, computational exploration of different designs. Indeed, if the design criteria are clearly defined, some of the recent techniques of simulation and optimization developed by computer scientists and computational economists can be used to search for optimal market designs, directly and indirectly.

Market performance may depend on the degree of "intelligence" or "rationality" of the agents buying and selling, which has led to computer experiments in which trading occurs between artificial agents of limited or bounded rationality, as discussed further below. As Walia et al. (2003) remark, if a market design with agents of low degree of "intelligence" is found to be sufficient for a specific level of market performance, then we might expect that agents with a higher level of intelligence, or agents whose rationality is less bounded, will, through their decisions to buy and sell, inadvertently create for themselves a market that is working efficiently.

But this is not necessarily the case: for instance, a market design could have a loophole—obscure to stupid agents—that makes it completely degenerate. Even without loopholes, smarter agents might find strategic ploys that reduce efficiency, or might spend more effort (wasted, from a social efficiency perspective) on counter-speculation.[11] This is confirmed by Arifovic (2001), who finds that more complicated agents do not necessarily do better in her simulated market environment.

Of course, historical market institutions have in general not simply been imposed from above (so-called top-down design) but have also emerged from the bottom up as a consequence of a multitude of actions and interactions of the myriad traders [McMillan (2002)]. Although the omnipotent programmer can experiment with different market forms and different kinds of boundedly rational agents to discover sufficient combinations of each for specific behavior of the market, evolutionary computation raises the possibility of bottom-up design, or emergence of market design through simulation.

This in turn raises the issue of whether agent-based experiments are being used as a model of human behavior (where analysis is followed by design, given the behavior of the agents and the emergent aggregate outcomes)—in which case it is an empirical question as to how boundedly rational the agents should be to best model human agents [Duffy (2006)]—or whether the agent-based experiments are an end in themselves, because on-line it is possible to use agents ("buy-bots, sell-bots") to buy and sell, without the errors that human agents are heir to.

These alternatives raise two issues [Tesfatsion (2002, p. 19)]: First, to what extent are the learning processes of human participants in real-world markets mal-adapted to market institutions? Perhaps the use of agent-based optimization tools could improve

---

[11] I thank an anonymous referee for pointing this out.

human market behavior, as is already seen, for instance, in eBay auctions, when bidders use software to enhance their chances of being the high bidder at the deadline.

Second, to what extent have existing market protocols (or market designs) evolved or been designed to avoid the need for any great rationality on the part of market participants? Gode and Sunder (1993) and others seek to answer this question for financial markets, but their results may, under certain conditions, be valid for other markets. These issues are explored at greater length in the chapters by LeBaron (2006) and Duffy (2006).

When there are several criteria by which the desirability of a designer market might be judged, trade-offs are necessary, and in the case of the GA, which needs one measure of each agent's fitness, such trade-offs must be explicit beforehand. See Section 3.2 below.

3. Market design

Design is a process of building directed by the pre-specified design objectives, if not by an explicit how-to plan. Unfortunately, specifying objectives does not always immediately delineate exactly how the model building should occur: these objectives are specified in a performance space (or behavior space) and the building occurs in a design space. The mapping from the designed structure to the desired performance may not be clear.

In the case of evolution, the design would occur in the genome space, while the behavior or performance occurs in the phenome space. In the case of designer markets, policy-makers have been using theory, experiments with human subjects, and computer simulations (experiments) to reduce the risk that the mapping from design (structure and rules) to behavior of the economic actors (the performance of the system) is incompletely understood, and so that there are fewer surprises.

Where the mapping is sufficiently well understood, and where closed-form analytic solution is tractable, it should be possible to describe not only sufficiency—if the market has this structure, and the rules of trading are such and such and the traders are given this information, then this performance and behavior will follow, at least in general form—but also necessity—if you want this performance and behavior, then this is the only set (or sets) of designs (combinations of structure and rules) that will produce it.

Without a closed-form analytical solution, but instead with human experiments or with computer simulations, necessity is in general out of reach, and we must make do with sufficiency. (Note that this is not always the case: James Watson and Francis Crick [Watson and Crick (1953)] used a form of simulation to determine the structure of DNA, with their metal rods and brass atoms, but the experimental results from the work of others had so constrained the degrees of freedom in the space of possible structures that they knew when they had simulated the structure correctly. Model-building ("stereochemical arguments" in Watson and Crick's 1953 phrase) could not clinch the structure until greater congruence between the model and the observed structure of the actual molecule was shown to exist, as the future Nobel laureates emphasized in their 1953 paper. And any negative results would have meant returning to the drawing board, or in this case the brass rods and sheet metal. See Marks (2003) for further discussion of this pioneering simulation.)

MacKie-Mason and Wellman (2006) present a Marketplace Design Framework, which delineates the three fundamental steps that constitute a transaction: first, the connection (searching for and discovering the opportunity to engage in a market interaction); second, the deal (negotiating and agreeing to terms); and, third, the exchange (executing a transaction). They define a "marketplace system" as consisting of agents and the market mechanism through which they interact, all embedded in an environment of social institutions (language, laws, etc.). Their market mechanism is the set of "rules, practices, and social structures of a social choice process, specifying, first, permissible actions" (including messages), and, second, market-based exchange transactions as outcomes of a function of agent messages. If there is some entity, apart from the participating agents, that manages any inter-agent communication and implements the mechanism rules, then the market mechanism is mediated.

MacKie-Mason and Wellman note that, as a consequence of this characterization of a marketplace, there are at least two design decisions: first, the design of the market mechanism, which might be decomposed into the design of mechanisms for, successively, the connection, the deal, and the exchange phases of a transaction; and, second, design of agents to interact with the market mechanism, whether existing or newly designed. They define an agent as an "autonomous decision-making locus in a system of multiple decision-making entities"; an agent has "type" attributes, such as preferences, beliefs, intentions, and capabilities. There will be a form of consistency between the agents' behavior, beliefs, and preferences, consistent with some principle of rationality. In this chapter, the focus is on design of MacKie-Mason and Wellman's market mechanism, specifically, the deal negotiation task. As with most of the existing literature, this chapter focuses on market mechanisms that govern the settlement from allowable actions.

Mechanisms specify, first, the agents' concerns that are recognized, and, second, rules mapping actions into allocation outcomes. A rule might specify which actions are permissible, or the procedure for choosing a settlement of agents' concerns based on observable actions. For instance, auctions, MacKie-Mason and Wellman point out, include rules governing allowable actions, and rules governing settlement.

To be effective, design of the market mechanism must be measured, and will usually consist of a constrained optimization, even if not explicitly or directly. "No external subsidies" or "maintain horizontal equity" are two possible constraints given by MacKie-Mason and Wellman. We explore others below.

The general design problem has become designing a market mechanism that includes defining a set of concerns over which agents can interact, specifying rules of permissible actions, and rules for mapping from actions to settlement and outcomes.

3.1. Complexity of design

Edmonds and Bryson (2003) speak of the syntactic complexity of design. This is the lack of a clear mapping from design to behavior: the only way to know the system's outcomes is to run the system and observe the emerging performance. Analysis is not able to predict the outcome. They are speaking of multi-agent computer systems, but could be speaking of standard double auctions in continuous time, which have not yet been solved analytically. Simon (1981) put it this way: "... it is typical of many kinds of design problems that the inner system consists of components whose fundamental laws of behavior... are well known. The difficulty of the design problem often resides in predicting how an assemblage of such components will behave."

One reason why analytical methods of analysis might fail is that the mapping from initial conditions of structure and rules to behavior and performance is not smooth or continuous, and, as such, is not amenable to calculus-based tools. The rugged nature of this landscape is its complexity, a complexity that is multiplied if it too is changing, perhaps as a function of the strategic complexity that occurs if the design has also to account for the interacting agents' patterns of behavior changing as a result: the biologist's *co-evolution*.

It is partly because of these complexities that direct design of markets is hardly ever attempted. Another reason is the possibility of conflicts among several design trade-offs.

3.2. Design trade-offs

Where there are several design criteria, the possibility arises of trade-offs between the criteria. For instance, if a firm has market power, it can maximize its seller revenue, but at the cost of market efficiency, as measured by the sum of seller (or producer) surplus and buyer (or consumer) surplus. Or it might be possible to improve the fairness of a market outcome, but at the cost of market efficiency. As we shall see below, to use computer simulation such trade-offs must be explicit. It might be possible to use a version of Simon's [Simon (1981)] satisficing, whereby so long as the other criteria are met (above some target level), the remaining criterion is used to rank designs. Or different criteria could be weighted to derive a single, scalar maximand.

Possible criteria for judging the design of a single-auction market might include [Phelps et al. (2002a, 2005)]: first, maximizing seller revenue: this has been one of the main criteria in the design of the spectrum auctions, most famously the 3G auctions [Milgrom (2004)]; second, maximizing market allocative efficiency: from a policy viewpoint and not a seller viewpoint this is a desirable attribute of a marketplace system; third, discouraging collusion, as a means to attaining the first and second criteria; fourth, discouraging predatory behavior, which will also help to maximize efficiency; fifth, discouraging entry-deterring behavior, again as a means of maximizing seller revenue (in a single (selling) auction the greater the number of potential bidders, the greater the seller revenue); sixth, budget balance: no third-party payments or subsidies for a deal to be reached; seventh, individual rationality: the expected net benefit to each participant from the market mechanism should be no less than the best alternative; and eighth, strategy-proofness: participants should not be able to gain from non-truth-telling behavior.

Myerson and Satterthwaite (1983) derived an impossibility result that demonstrates that no double-sided auction mechanism with discriminatory pricing[12] can be simultaneously efficient, budget-balanced, and individually rational.

Talukdar (2002) emphasized that before the market can be designed (solved), the design problem must be well posed, that is, complete, feasible (all constraints can be satisfied), and rich (allows for innovative and desirable solutions). To be complete, the design problem must contain: first, the attributes to be used in characterizing behavior of the market; second, the decision variables to be used to characterize the structure; third, the goals to be attained (desired behaviors, laws, regulations); and, fourth, a computable mapping of decision variables into goals (does each point in decision space meet the goals?). This fourth requirement is achieved for complex design problems by iterative analysis, which can be achieved using agent-based simulation tools and agent-based verification tools, since such tools are open and modular.

LeBaron (2006), in examining the use of agent-based models of financial markets, discusses seven basic design questions for his models, which translate across to more general models. First, the economic environment itself needs to be resolved: What will be traded? Second, how are agents' preferences to be modeled? What particular functional forms will be used, such as mean–variance, constant absolute risk aversion, myopic or inter-temporal? Or will specific behavioral rules simply be evaluated directly? Third, market clearing and price formation need to be modeled. Fourth, the fitness of the model must be evaluated. For example, should wealth or utility be used? And should the evolving behavioral rules to which fitness measures are applied be forecasts, demands, or some other type of action? Fifth, how is information to be processed and revealed? Sixth, how does learning occur? Is it social or is it individual? Seventh, how is benchmarking to be undertaken? While these questions relate to the models used to design markets, they may also reflect on the design criteria for the final designer markets.

3.3. Moving from closed-form equilibria

Traditionally for the last sixty years, economists have sought closed-form solutions to understanding the performance of economic institutions. Economic actors have been assumed to be perfectly rational, with the means to solve for equilibria outcomes in complex situations. Economists have sought to characterize the equilibria of economic interactions in terms of their existence, uniqueness, and stability, under this assumption. When the interactions among economic actors are strategic, the equilibria become Nash equilibria.

---

[12] In discriminatory-price auctions (sometimes known as "pay-as-bid" auctions), distinct trades in the same auction round occur at distinct prices; in uniform-price auctions, all trades in any given auction round occur at the same price.

But in an operating, real-time actual market, it turns out that we are not interested just in equilibrium characterization: continual shocks might never allow the system to approach, let alone reach, the equilibrium. And, moreover, it turns out in a repeated interaction that almost any individually rational outcome for each player can be supported as an equilibrium (the Folk Theorem of repeated games). This is particularly so for interactions which have the general character of the IPD.

Consequently, there are at least two reasons why market design has moved away from traditional closed-form solutions: first, because of tractability: it has been very difficult, despite advances made in recent years, to obtain solutions to the design of some markets, such as continuous double auctions (CDAs); and, second, we should like to characterize out-of-equilibrium behavior, and especially the dynamic behavior of an operating market with fluctuating demand, and perhaps varying numbers of sellers, with unpredictable, varying costs.

A third reason for considering other techniques of analysis is that the assumption of perfect rationality and unlimited computational ability on the part of human traders is unrealistic, and not borne out by laboratory experiments with human subjects. Instead, using computer models of trading agents, we should like to model economic actors in markets as "boundedly rational." This might mean bounded computational ability, or bounded memory, or bounded perception [Marks (1998)].[13]

There is a fourth reason for wanting to move from closed-form solutions, even where they are available: to model learning. There are two reasons to include learning in any models used to design markets: First, individuals and organizations learn. Human players learn (perhaps with the added incentive of the prospect of bankruptcy if they do not learn from their mistakes), which means that a model without learning is not as realistic as one incorporating learning. Bunn and Oliveira (2003) note that many researchers [including Erev and Roth (1998)] have shown that learning models predict people's behavior better than do Nash equilibria.

Moreover, learning can help to eliminate many otherwise legitimate Nash equilibria from further contention. Indeed, evolutionary (or learning) game theory has been seen as a solution to the multiplicity of Nash equilibria that occur in closed-form game-theoretic solutions: a priori, all are possible, but to see which are likely in reality, see how players learn and choose amongst them.

3.4. Explicit use of agents

It is possible to design without the use of agents: given a market with demand and supply schedules, economic efficiency is maximized at the output level where marginal value

---

[13] Rubinstein (1998) elaborates on some of these bounds. Conlisk (1996) gives four reasons for incorporating bounded rationality into economic models: empirical evidence of limits to human cognition; successful performance of economic models embodying bounded rationality (including some surveyed here); sometimes unconvincing arguments in favor of unbounded rationality; and the costs of deliberation.

equals the marginal unit cost, no matter how the social surplus is divided between buyers and sellers. But such direct design (optimization) requires a well defined problem. With several design trade-offs and the possible emergence of unforeseen performance in the system, agent-based analysis and design, in which the market system can be modeled as "evolving systems of autonomous, interacting agents with learning capabilities" [Koesrindartoto and Tesfatsion (2004)], is increasingly employed.

LeBaron (2006) places some weight on how actual trading occurs: the institutions under which trading is executed. He argues that agent-based models are well suited to examining market design and micro-structure questions because, first, they can produce a large amount of data, and, second, they allow testing of market design in a heterogeneous, adaptive environment.

Audet et al. (2002) report an agent-based study of micro-structure (order books v. dealers), while Bottazzi et al. (2003) examine tick sizes (and unexpectedly determines that smaller tick sizes do not necessarily improve the market's efficiency). Chan and Shelton (2001) examine how a model behaves with different RL mechanisms, all of which enable the optimum policy function for a market-making broker to be found.

Belief-based learning has been used to study market design: Gjerstad and Dickhaut (1998) propose heuristic rules by which buyers and sellers in a double auction will assess and update their probabilities that their bids (offers to buy) and asks (offers to sell) will be accepted, given market history. "Using these beliefs together with private information on valuations and costs, individual buyers or sellers propose bids or asks that maximize their (myopic) expected surplus" [Duffy (2006)]. The main parameter of their model is the length of memory that players use in calculating probabilities. Their model, with stricter convergence criteria than Gode and Sunder (1993) adopt, more reliably converges to competitive equilibrium, and the anticipatory, belief-based learning model provides a better fit to *aggregate* human-subject data as well. Gjerstad (2004) coins the phrase "heuristic belief learning" to describe this version of belief learning, and shows that what he calls "pace," the timing of the bid, is pivotal.

GA strings can be used to encode decisions that agents make (e.g., how much to consume, what price to charge, etc.) and the GA works to find the optimal decision, given feasibility and other constraints. This is how Marks et al. (1995), Arifovic (1994), Midgley et al. (1997) modeled the interactions. Duffy (2006) calls this learning-how-to-optimize.

An alternative is to use the strings as encoding beliefs about how prices will change from period to period. This learning-how-to-forecast model [Duffy (2006)] was first used by Bullard and Duffy (1999). It was introduced in order to calibrate the GA model with human-subject experiments of overlapping-generation decision models. Duffy (2006) explains that subjects found it easier to forecast future prices than to decide on inter-temporal consumption/saving decisions. Given the price forecasts, the GA algorithm solved that individual's optimal consumption/savings allocations and determined the market-clearing prices at future dates.

3.5. The design economist

Recently, software engineers have been *designing* systems of exchange, of markets. Their designs—of distributed computing systems, and on-line trading in real time— have begun to borrow from economists' insights into how traditional face-to-face markets have evolved to operate. They have also [Phelps et al. (2002a)] begun to realize that the equilibrium characterizations of mathematical economics do not always provide the answers they need in designing their on-line markets, which will be in disequilibrium almost always if trading in real time. That is, the adjustments of the operation of the markets to the current equilibrium (or attractor) will almost never happen fast enough to reach equilibrium, especially when the location of the attractor is continuously changing.

The shortcomings of these results from equilibrium analyses of economic mechanisms have been underlined by Roth (2000, 2002) in two papers that begin to point the way forward for market design, with the economist as engineer. Indeed, Roth makes the point that, as engineers have learned to borrow from the insights of physics, the design economist can use insights not only from equilibrium mathematical economics, but also from computer science.

When, however, these insights are curtailed, perhaps by the tractability of closed-form analytical methods, both economists and software engineers have been using simulation in analysis, to obtain sufficient, but rarely necessary, conditions. Simulation has occurred using GAs, numerical solutions, and explicit agent-based models. Iterative analysis has been used as a means of designing systems.

LeBaron (2006), in his conclusion, lists some criticisms of the agent-based approach to modeling financial markets. Some (such as too few assets considered, questions of timing ignored) are more specific to the models he examines, but several are relevant to more general market models: too many parameters; questions about the stability of trading to the introduction of new trading strategies; sensitivity to the number of agents trading; over-reliance on inductive models of agents, which respond to past rules and forecasts; and not enough on deductive models which might learn commonly held beliefs about how markets work. These are issues that have been addressed in the two areas of market design that we now consider: electricity markets and automated markets.

4. Electricity market design

In 1998 the U.S. Federal Energy Regulatory Commission (FERC) Chairman, James Hoecker [Hoecker (1998)], said: "Arguably, a well-constructed computer model could improve the accuracy of our competitive analysis in at least two ways: by explicitly representing economic interactions between suppliers and loads at various locations on the transmission network; and by accounting for the actual transmission flows that result from power transactions." He warned, however, that: "Consistency of data sources and consistent application of those data is an attraction, but such techniques require time, education, and consistent refinement. Moreover, adequate data may not be available. I hope the benefits will be worth our trouble and investment. Our economists are trying to get a handle on precisely that equation."

Other economists, engineers, and computer scientists had already been at work on this issue for some years, when Mr Hoecker spoke. Applications of agent-based modeling to electricity market analysis and design occurred independently in several research centers. The application of genetic algorithms to, first, oligopolies [Marks (1989)], and then to macro-economic models [Arifovic (1994)], has more recently been followed by its use in analyzing the behavior of new markets for electricity generation and transmission, most recently as a means of designing electricity markets.

4.1. Electricity market design trade-offs

As a consequence of the California blackouts of 2000, market efficiency has been joined by several other criteria for the design of electricity markets. The FERC (2003) White Paper discusses four primary objectives for wholesale electricity market design: reliable service (no blackouts or brownouts); fair and open access to the transmission grid at reasonable prices; effective price signals to provide incentives for appropriate investment in generation and transmission capacity; and effective procedures for market oversight and mitigation of exercise of market power.[14] Koesrindartoto and Tesfatsion (2004) speak of "efficient, orderly, and fair" market outcomes.

Cramton (2003) discusses issues of electricity market design, in general, and the mitigation of market power in particular. He also emphasizes that the market designer must understand the preferences and constraints of the market participants, in order to keep the design as simple as possible, but not too simple.[15] The greater the number of dimensions for measuring the performance of market designs, the greater the relative attractiveness of simulation as a design tool: as discussed above, closed-form analysis—with its promise of the derivation of necessary conditions—becomes ever more elusive.

4.2. Academic engineers

In 1992, a pioneering paper by Verkama et al. (1992) at the Helsinki University of Technology argued that the two disparate areas of oligopoly theory and distributed artificial intelligence (DAI) could learn from each other, since each was concerned with modeling the interaction of autonomous, self-interested, interacting agents. Using object-oriented programming, they had developed a test-bed for examining agents' interactions under various initial conditions. They acknowledged that "very general results are difficult to

---

[14] Nicolaisen et al. (2001) distinguish the exercise of structural market power that occurs when the buyers and sellers ask and bid their true reservation values, from the exercise of strategic market power that occurs when opportunistic bids or asks are made.

[15] Wilson (2002) surveys the experiences of electricity market designs in the U.S. and beyond at a much greater level of detail than has yet been seen even in simulation studies.

come by with simulations and computer experiments" (p. 157), but argued that such approaches allow the exploration of market evolution, with entry and exit, learning, and reputation effects. They even suggested that the market itself could be modeled as an agent, the first suggestion in the literature that the design of markets could be modeled and analyzed, necessary antecedents for market design using agents.

Verkama et al. (1992) do not cite any works in evolutionary computation, but two years later, after presentation at a workshop in computational organization theory, they [Verkama et al. (1994)] cited Arthur (1991, 1993), Holland and Miller (1991), and Lane (1993a, 1993b). The linkages between two previously independent lines of research had been made.[16] In the 1994 paper, as well as object-oriented programming, they mention inter alia genetic algorithms and learning automata, and the need for agents to mimic human behavior in simulation models of strategic interaction (their "reactive behavior"). The test-bed itself had evolved: in their Multi-Agent Reactions Testbed agents can inherit properties from previous generations and add new features, in order to explore the interactions of different decision rules, and the market structure and rules of engagement.

In 1994 Räsänen et al. (1994) introduced an object-oriented model of electricity demand-side load, the first application of such techniques to electricity market modeling, although the use of inherited characteristics was not to allow the objects to evolve or learn, but rather to aid the programmer in modeling changed load. A year later, however, Hämäläinen and Parantainen (1995) introduced a new "agent-based modeling framework" for analyzing electricity markets by using agents to model the demand-side load.

4.2.1. Hämäläinen et al. (1997) model both sides of the market

Two years later Hämäläinen et al. (1997) went much further, with agents representing both sides of the electricity market—consumers and producers—with bounded reasoning capabilities and bounded reactions. Specifically, they use a two-hierarchy, multi-agent system to model a von Stackelberg market, where the leader (the seller) anticipates and reasons back to set a price for electricity which maximizes the overall market efficiency, given the responses of the followers (the buyers, who use electricity for space-heating). Agents can be modeled as: sufficiently rational to determine their best response dynamics; or as boundedly rational (and so not always succeeding

---

[16] In a private communication Hämäläinen (2004) explains: "The origins of my interest go very far back. We had been working on game theory, coordination and resource economics, and to me as an engineer it was a natural idea to see what could be achieved by a computational analysis of economic systems. One of the first computational analyses was [a 1978] paper on the role of information in decentralized macro-economic stabilization. Later, coordination ideas grew in my head when I was working on fishery models [in 1986 and 1990]. This was followed by incentive and coordination work: Verkama et al. (1992). At the time of the emergence of our interest in energy economics the Finnish market had not yet been deregulated, but this took place during our research project on real-time pricing of electricity. For a period this kind of research was not considered interesting as markets were the hot topic."

in determining the best response, perhaps because of limited comparisons of possible actions); or as constrained in their reactions from one period to the next; or with asynchronous reactions.

The electricity price can vary hourly, and the electricity producer, announcing prices 24 hours ahead, can attempt to control consumption in order to smoothly costly load peaks. Each consumer takes account of the heat-storage capacity of its dwelling and the outside temperature. The consumer's payoff is the difference between the utility from consumption and the cost of the energy. The producer's cost function reflects the increasing (quadratic) marginal cost of production.

Using their Power Agents software for simulation of electricity markets, the authors gain insight into a market in which consumers could have their homes heated by a computerized agent-based heating system which would respond to changing electricity tariffs in order to maximize the system goals. It is not clear which form of bounded rationality they use. They have not adopted GAs or other computer science techniques referred to in the 1994 paper. This has been left to others.

Meanwhile, at Carnegie Mellon University, Talukdar and Ramesh (1992) suggested software to manage electricity generation when the operating environment (market) could change rapidly. Their asynchronous and autonomous agents represent one of the first examples of a multi-agent system in the electricity literature. Krishna and Ramesh (1998) extend the idea to developing "intelligent software agents" to help generators to negotiate with potential coalition partners; they point to the possibility of such agents replacing human players in computerized electricity exchanges.

4.2.2. Talukdar (2002) models customers holding down the wholesale price

Talukdar (2002) continues to use artificial agents as members of his asynchronous teams, sometimes borrowing from the GA models, most recently to simulate and verify the trades that occur in repeated markets, such as electricity markets, as part of the market design process. His focus is on centralized auctions, without electricity storage facilities, where sellers have multiple blocks of energy to sell, and customers can adjust their demands and can automatically learn. He asks: What structures (load-adjustment facilities) do customers need so they can use automatic learning to hold the monopolistic price to reasonable levels?

His agents are simple: they are not intended to simulate human behavior; rather, the dynamics of the repeated markets are probed using the emergent behaviors (which can be quite complex) of simple agents. He finds that sellers with multiple generating units can learn which units to withhold and that total profits rise by a fifth over a thousand periods, with prices and profits almost at centralized (monopolistic) levels, under several (static) demand characterizations. He then allows buyers to learn too. They aim, first, to minimize cost, and, second, to minimize energy deviation. Over 1400 periods they learn to reduce the price to less than a third of the monopolistic price. But with the same quantity sold, the sellers' profits fall below 30% of the monopolist's profits.

Meanwhile, at Iowa State University, a group of electrical engineers led by Gerald Sheblé had started in 1994 to examine the operation and design of electricity markets. Maifeld and Sheblé (1996) use a GA for solving the unit-commitment scheduling problem in electricity markets.[17] They referred to no earlier work by economists, but Richter and Sheblé (1998) referred to unpublished work by LeBaron and by Tesfatsion, and used a GA to learn (evolve) bidding strategies in an electricity market as generators and distributors buy and sell power via double auctions. Amongst other things this model can be used to explore how bidding behavior affects overall market performance. Richter et al. (1999) extended their previous work on bidding strategies in double auctions for trading electricity competitively. They used adaptive automaton strategies: tested in an auction simulator, the automata learn using a GA. The paper examined high-profit strategies and also modeled certain types of trading behaviors.

4.2.3. Lane et al. (2000) use GAs for double auctions

Lane et al. (2000) broadened the scope of the research: they modeled the traders in an electricity market as adaptive agents learning with the help of a GA in a discriminatory-price k-double auction [Satterthwaite and Williams (1989, 1993)], and, perhaps influenced by Tesfatsion's economics research, calculated the degrees of market power for various combinations of relative capacity and production costs.

They use the EPRI[18] Market Simulator, which simulates a double auction between buyers and sellers on a graph, where the edges are the capacity-constrained transmission lines and the buyers and sellers are at the nodes. The auction is performed in rounds or generations; buyers and sellers are matched in each round and the price of their contract is given by $kb + (1 - k)a$, where bid $b \geq$ ask a, and $0 \leq k \leq 1$; here $k = 0.5$. Learning is via a GA with binary strings. The GA treats buyers and sellers separately, and takes the risk-neutral traders' profits as their fitnesses.

The benchmarking simulation assumes price-taking agents. The buyers' profits and sellers' profits in a competitive equilibrium and in the auction simulation are determined (respectively, $PBCE, PSCE, PBA, PSA$), and an index of market power (MPI) is calculated:

$$MPI = \frac{(PBA + PSA) - (PBCE + PSCE)}{PBCE + PSCE}.$$ (5)

The simulated market has three sellers and three buyers (homogeneous, and unconstrained in their total demand, in order to allow sellers to play strategically). There are three scenarios for capacity constraints on sellers, increasingly unequal, and three scenarios for relative costs of the largest producer. Will this market converge to a near-competitive equilibrium? Will the largest seller exhibit price leadership and the exercise of market power?

---

[17] Unit commitment is the problem of determining the optimal set of generating units within a power system to be used up to a week ahead.

[18] The Electric Power Research Institute, Palo Alto, CA.

Analysis of *MPI* averaged over 100 runs for each of the 3×3 treatments indicates that neither marginal cost nor market share has a significant effect on the large seller's exercise of market power, and on average total available surplus is evenly distributed among buyers and sellers. The authors identify an anomaly: relatively more expensive sellers gain market power, the opposite of what theory would suggest.

Why? The authors suggest four aspects of their model: limited numbers of buyers and sellers; the GA allows indirect exchange of information among sellers and among buyers through the genetic operators; a seller's (buyer's) ask (offer) price is its marginal cost (revenue) plus (minus) a real number derived from its bit-string; and calculation of profits in the auction (relative the averaged transaction price) is different from such calculation in competitive equilibrium (relative to the uniform market price). There is a rapid loss of genetic diversity, and each of the three sellers (buyers) will be tacitly working to solve the same maximization problem.

The authors argue that a GA is inappropriate when there are few agents, and conclude that another search method which incorporates memory and self-learning would be better. They do not mention the possibility of a GA with separate populations for the six distinct agents. Would such a model give results closer to those suggested by theory? I believe so.

With the increased use of markets to help allocate the generation and distribution of electricity in several countries, this concern with using models of electricity markets to examine the exercise of market power is an obvious extension of the simulations, and reflects the shift from analysis of the traders' actions to analysis of the markets' performance, a necessary step for market design.

4.2.4. MacGill and Kaye (1999) simulate for system efficiency

Meanwhile, engineers at the University of New South Wales [MacGill and Kaye (1999), MacGill (2004)] were exploring a decentralized coordination framework to maximize the market efficiency of the power-system operation, not through the operation of Smith's invisible hand as each resource competes to maximize its own return, but via a decentralized framework in which each resource is operated to achieve overall system objectives. The authors use a so-called "dual evolutionary approach," which uses a (non-binary coding) version of the GA, but not explicitly with autonomous, self-interested agents. Their model contained explicit intertemporal links for actions and payoffs (such as energy storage in, for example, pumped storage dams) across periods, and the dual evolutionary programming model, rather than optimizing on trajectories (the "primal" approach), uses as its variables the incremental benefit-to-go functions (the "dual"), which means that detailed knowledge of the resources models is not required.

They are able to solve for two-storage networks, with ramp rates, leakage, and stochastic supply (with photo-voltaics and hydro). A surprising result, when they allow strategic actions by players, is that the surplus of the sole strategic player is lower than its surplus without strategic actions. Is this a consequence of their modeling agents' fitness not as their individual surpluses but as the system's goals? They also find that the total system surplus falls with strategic actions, and the surplus on the load side falls most, as one might expect from theory.

Cau and Anderson (2002) used GAs to examine co-evolutionary behavior of agents in markets for electricity, where such agents were modeled as autonomous, self-interested players [see also Cau (2003)]. In particular they were interested in exploring the conditions of the players and of the market under which tacit collusion occurred. Since collusion leads to inefficiencies, from a policy-maker's viewpoint a market structure which discourages the emergence of learned tacit collusion is a good design, even if discouraging the exercise of market power is not an explicit goal of market design.

The number of engineering studies of electricity supply and distribution networks that employ agent-based (or "multi-agent") simulations of some sort or other continues to grow, as reflected in published papers in the IEEE journals, transactions, and proceedings.

4.3. Economists

4.3.1. Curzon Price (1997) models electricity markets

In 1997 an economist at University College London, Curzon Price (1997), presented simulation models of simple electricity pools, in which he used the GA as a means of simulating the repetition of two rival sellers. He saw competition in electricity markets, often across jurisdictional borders, as a field in which the "underlying economic models are often quite simple," but the real-world phenomena "complicated and richly detailed in important ways" (1997, p. 220), and hence suitable for simulation.

Curzon Price derived two models, each a simplification of the England and Wales electricity market, where the pool price is equal to the bid of the last producer required to satisfy demand, a uniform-price auction. The first model assumes that neither producer can supply the whole market, but that together their capacity exceeds demand. With price as the only choice variable, this model has two pure- and one mixed-strategy Nash equilibria. He was able to derive the pure-strategy equilibria, but not clearly the mixed-strategy equilibrium, even when he set the initial population proportions to the mixed-strategy proportions. For levels of GA crossover above 6% he found that the equilibrium mix could not be sustained. He concluded that, with an underlying situation of residual monopoly, the electricity pool rules would not lead to competitive prices, a finding of great significance to the market design.

His second model included the two producers' choice of capacities as well as prices. The first model was modified: if either producer could satisfy the entire market, then the lowest bid would be chosen. Players offered both price and quantity bids, the quantity offered incurring a cost whether or not the capacity was used. His analysis yielded three regimes: one where the high bidder is a residual monopolist; one where the low bidder can satisfy the demand; and one where there is excess demand because the higher bid is too high. The equilibrium strategies found by the GA can be characterized as similar to the first model without capacity as a strategic variable: one producer offering the lowest capacity possible and bidding it at the maximum price, and the other producer offering the highest residual quantity at a low price. The firms evolve their capacities to avoid Bertrand (marginal cost) outcomes.

Curzon Price's work was directly descended from Axelrod's (Axelrod, 1987) work with GAs and IPDs, Marks' (Marks, 1992) work on oligopolistic behavior, and other economists' use of GAs, such as Andreoni and Miller's (Andreoni and Miller, 1995) exploration of auctions using the GA to model the co-evolution of artificial adaptive agents. Andreoni and Miller found that their model of adaptive learning was consistent with the main results from laboratory experiments, and that—significantly for the purpose at hand—various auction designs ("institutions") display very different adaptive dynamics. Curzon Price suggested that plausible behavioral elements could be included in the simulations.

Iowa State University has been a fertile place for cross-disciplinary research in agent-based modeling of electricity markets. As well as Sheblé in engineering, it is home to Tesfatsion in economics. Two of the most widely cited papers on the application have emerged from her research group. These we now discuss.

4.3.2. Nicolaisen et al. (2000) search for market power

Nicolaisen et al. (2000) used a GA agent-based model of a discriminatory-price clearinghouse[19] k-double auction electricity market [Klemperer (2002)] to examine the exercise of market power (as deviations from competitive equilibrium values of prices and quantities). They used the EPRI Power Market [see Lane et al. (2000), above], where each agent simultaneously submitted a single price-quantity bid or ask. Buyers and sellers are matched to maximize total profit, using $k = 0.5$ again. Each agent's fitness is proportional to its profit in the last round: only the last round's bid or ask is remembered. The linear revenue and cost functions ensure that bids and asks are at the capacity quantities. Bids (asks) are bound between [marginal revenue $-$ \$40, marginal revenue] (marginal cost). Two definitions: first, the relative concentration of sellers NS to buyers NB, $RCON = NS/NB$; and, second, the relative capacity of buyers to sellers, $RCAP = (NB/NS) \times (CB/CS)$, where CB (CS) is the maximum quantity of electrical energy that each buyer (seller) can resell (generate) in a retail market. Six buyers and six sellers compete, with 3×3 treatments of three values of $RCON$ and three values of $RCAP$.

The authors derived sellers' market power, $MPS = (PSA - PSCE)/PSCE$, and buyers' market power, $MPB = (PBA - PBCE)/PBCE$. They found no evidence that MPB is negatively related to $RCAP$, or that MPS is positively related to $RCAP$, either in aggregate or individually, contrary to expectations from theory.

---

[19] A clearinghouse (or call) market is one in which all traders place offers before the market is cleared; they can have discriminatory or uniform prices. A continuous market is one in which trades are executed as new offers arrive; prices are thus discriminatory.

How could this be explained? As Tesfatsion (2005) notes, the measures of concentration and capacity (*RCON* and *RCAP*) are structural characteristics of the market. As is standard in the industrial organization literature, they are calculated before any experiments have been run, and hence before the analyst knows which traders are inframarginal (and so will actually engage in trade) and which are extramarginal (and so will not engage in any trades). Because they do not trade, the bids/asks of extramarginal traders will have no affect on market power outcomes. As a result, by varying the numbers and capacities of the extramarginal traders, the concentration and capacity measures can be made arbitrarily large or small while keeping the market power measure constant. Consequently, so long as the extramarginal/inframarginal decision for each trader is endogenous [as in Nicolaisen et al. (2000)], no systematic relationship among *RCON*, *RCAP*, and market power outcomes will be seen.

In Nicolaisen et al. (2000), trading agents were quite boundedly rational, with only one round of memory. Moreover, the GA was given only two populations (one for buyers and one for sellers), whereas the treatments meant that agents with different marginal costs and revenues faced different concentrations and capacities: the GA was not modeling this heterogeneity. Furthermore, the social learning process (mimicry of other buyers or other sellers) of the GA meant that any comparative advantages in strategies (as a consequence of different firm structures) soon spread to the rest of the population of players and became dissipated, as Vriend (2000) discussed. Moreover, social learning means that firms that would rightly decline to trade (the extramarginals) may now engage in opportunistic trades (and become inframarginal), thus potentially lowering market efficiency. The paper cites earlier work by Lane and by Richter, both at Iowa State.

4.3.3. Nicolaisen et al. (2001) use reinforcement learning

Following from their 2000 study (see above), Nicolaisen et al. (2001) altered their model by using a form of learning that, unlike the GA, did not impose strategic homogeneity on structurally distinct buyers and sellers. As well as mimicry, individual learning would be permitted. The model used the EPRI Power Model again, suitably modified, with the same 3×3 treatments of *RCON* and *RCAP*, the same six buyers and sellers, as characterized by their (private) marginal revenues and costs, respectively.

But in an attempt to obtain results on market power that were closer to those from standard theory, Nicolaisen et al. (2001) used reinforcement learning [a modification of Erev and Roth (1998)] instead of GA learning to allow individual learning and to prevent any comparative advantage in strategies being dissipated among the artificial agents. They point out that there are two shortcomings of the Roth–Erev model (see equations (1)–(4) above). First, there might be degeneracy of its parameters: when the experimentation parameter $\epsilon = (N - 1)/N$, there is no updating of the choice parameter. Second, if there are zero profits, then the choice probabilities are not upgraded, because a trader's current propensity values are reduced proportionately. Lack of probability updating in response to zero profits can result in a substantial loss of market efficiency as traders struggle to learn how to make profitable price offers.

Nicolaisen et al. (2001) present a simple modification of the Roth–Erev RL algorithm that addresses both of these issues while maintaining consistency with the learning principles in the original formulation. The update function $E(.)$ in equation (4) was replaced by the following modified function:

$$E_k(j, R(x)) = \begin{cases} (1 - \epsilon)R(x), & \text{if } j = k; \\ \frac{\epsilon}{N-1}q_{jk}, & \text{otherwise.} \end{cases} \qquad (6)$$

In effect, this modification introduces a differentiated value for the recency parameter ϕ for selected versus non-selected actions, while also omitting the profit term in the updating equation for propensities corresponding to non-selected actions. The recency parameter for non-selected actions falls from ϕ to $\phi^* = \phi - \epsilon/(N - 1)$. As Nicolaisen et al. (2001) put it, "The choice probabilities corresponding to action choices resulting in zero-profit outcomes tend to decrease relative to other choice probabilities while the choice probabilities corresponding to action choices resulting in positive profit outcomes tend to increase." Otherwise the paper's model was similar to the earlier work [Nicolaisen et al. (2000)]: a clearinghouse k-double auction with discriminatory pricing, and $k = 0.5$.

The nine treatments were each tested three times, using different settings for the three parameters of the modified Roth–Erev (MRE) model of equations (1)–(3) and (6): the scaling parameter $S(1)$, a recency parameter ϕ, and an experimentation parameter ϵ. For the first two tests, the parameter values were chosen to facilitate the emergence for each trader of a dominant price offer with a relatively large choice probability, by the final auction round in each run. The third test used the parameter values obtained by Erev and Roth (1998) by best overall fit of their RL algorithm (equations (1)–(4)) to experimental data from twelve distinct types of games run with human subjects: $S(1) = 9.00$, $\phi = 0.10$, $\epsilon = 0.20$.

Under all treatments, the presence of active buyers and sellers reduces the ability of structurally disadvantaged traders to exercise strategic market power, that is, to use strategic pricing to overcome the structural market-power biases inherent in the discriminatory-pricing protocol. Moreover, traders' ability to exercise strategic market power is further limited by the threat of entry of extramarginal traders, as discussed in Section 4.3.2 above.

Nicolaisen et al. (2001) obtained generally high market efficiency (defined as $EA = (PBA + PSA)/(PBCE + PSCE)$) under all treatments. Notably, as seen in the earlier study (above) by Nicolaisen et al. (2000), market efficiency was relatively low when the traders used the inappropriate form of social mimicry embodied in GA learning. The later results from Nicolaisen et al. (2001) suggest that the market efficiency of double auctions operating under a discriminatory pricing rule is reliably high when buyers and sellers refrain from inappropriate learning behavior or bad judgment [Tesfatsion (2005)]. These results confirm Vriend's (Vriend, 2000) argument that market efficiency is not robust with respect to a switch from individual learning (here MRE) to social learning (here GA).

In asking whether the market design ensured efficient, fair, and orderly market outcomes over time despite repeated attempts by traders to game the design for their own personal advantage, Nicolaisen et al. (2001) were clearly focused on market design. The paper cited Bower and Bunn (2001) and Lane et al. (2000).

One of the most successful academic economists to use agent-based techniques to analyze electricity markets is Bunn with his associates at the London Business School. As well as publishing in the economics literature, he has also published in the energy and regulatory literature, and his models have been calibrated against historical data. In Bunn and Oliveira (2001), we read: "The development of a detailed simulation platform representing the agents, the markets, and the market-clearing mechanisms, together with reinforcement learning to facilitate profit-seeking behavior by the agents, can, in principle, provide a computational framework to overcome the limitations of the analytical approaches." That is, such a platform could be used to design a market.[20]

Following the deregulation and privatization of the electricity generation sector in Britain, Bunn and Day (1998) proposed using agent-based simulation of electricity power pools to analyze the short- and longer-term behavior of the generators, as they learned, partly to see whether high prices might be the result of implicit collusion.

Bower and Bunn (2000, 2001) developed a simulation model of the wholesale electricity market in England and Wales as a means of systematically testing the potential impact of alternative trading arrangements on market prices, specifically uniform- versus discriminatory-price auctions, thus undertaking a form of market design. Generators were represented as autonomous, adaptive, computer-generated agents, which progressively learned better profit-maximizing bidding behavior, by developing their own trading strategies, in order to explore and exploit the capacity and technical constraints of plant, market demand, and different market-clearing and settlement arrangements. Their agents used simple internal decision rules that allowed them to discover and learn strategic solutions which satisfied their profit and market-share objectives over time. These rules constituted what is essentially a naïve RL algorithm, and the behavior of the simulated market is thus almost entirely emergent. The agents knew everything about their own portfolio of plants, bids, output levels, and profits, but nothing about other agents or the state of the market. Their ability to capture and retain data was limited, they had no powers of strategic reasoning, and hence they exhibited a high degree of bounded rationality. The agents were modeled as data arrays in Excel 97 and manipulated with Visual Basic. Bower and Bun concluded that the discriminatory auction results in higher

---

[20] In a private communication, Bunn (2004) remembered that his interest in using agent-based models followed from a new Ph.D. candidate with a computer science background who suggested using Object-Oriented Programming [Gamma et al. (1995)], such as Java, as a better platform for simulating the electricity market than Systems Dynamics [Forrester (1961)]. As we see below, OOP leads to agent-based models relatively easily.

market prices than does the uniform-price auction. The papers did not cite any earlier work on agent-based modeling.

This research did not capture the interaction between the bilateral trading and the balancing market, nor did it incorporate any sophistication in the agents' learning abilities. Bunn and Oliveira (2001), however, describe a model with agents whose learning was inspired by the fitness function and selection mechanisms used in GAs. They argue that, by keeping the probabilities of exploration and exploitation independent of the expected reward from following a particular bidding strategy, their GA model should be trapped at local equilibria less often than would agents using a naïve RL algorithm, such as Erev and Roth (1998), especially in non-stationary environments. Their new simulation platform was a much more detailed representation: it actively modeled the demand side and the interactions between two different markets, as well as the settlement process; and it took into account the daily dynamic constraints and different marginal costs for each generation technology. It referenced two earlier works from the GA simulation literature: LeBaron et al. (1999) and Nicolaisen et al. (2000).

Bower et al. (2001) applied a similar agent-based model to the German electricity market, specifically examining the effects on peak prices of consolidation, and the potential for the exercise of market power by the dominant generators. The references in this paper included Hämäläinen (1996) and Curzon Price (1997).

4.3.4. Bunn and Oliveira (2003) help design a new wholesale market

Bunn and Oliveira (2003) use agent-based simulation in a coordination game to analyze the possibility of market power abuse in a competitive electricity market. The model builds on the work in Bunn and Oliveira (2001), but does not allow the agents to learn as they did in the earlier, GA-based model, in order to retain more transparency in understanding their actions. Instead, the model uses reinforcement learning. The aims of the authors were not to evaluate the market structure but rather to see whether market conditions were sufficient to allow the exercise of market power by a certain player. The paper referenced Nicolaisen et al. (2001).

The authors used agent-based simulation in a coordination game to analyze the possibility of market power (structural or strategic, as measured by higher prices and profitability than competitive outcomes) being exercised in a competitive electricity market: the policy issue was to help answer the question of whether two specific generators could influence wholesale electricity prices.

They extended Bun and Oliveira's (Bunn and Oliveira, 2001) New Electricity Trading Arrangements simulation platform. Their agents can be modeled as having the capacity to learn, and represented generating companies (possibly owning several plants with different generation philosophies) and buyers in the wholesale market who then supply end-use consumers. Agents use a RL algorithm to improve their performance: each agent evaluates the profit earned, and then derives new policies to bid or offer, given its strategic objectives of profit maximization and market exposure.

The authors were not interested in whether a particular market design, or structure, resulted in a competitive equilibrium; rather, whether a particular player, by its conduct, finds it profitable to act (choosing its offer price and strategically withholding capacity) in order to increase wholesale electricity prices.

They derive a simplified analytical model of the market: two generators in a stylized discriminatory-price Bertrand game with capacity constraints, from which they derive several propositions, which are then tested in the simulation of a more realistic model of the electricity industry. They used the eight largest generators in the England and Wales electricity market in 2000, splitting each generator's capacity into three categories, based on the degree of flexibility and running times of each technology (nuclear, large coal and combined-cycle gas turbines, and the rest). The simulated industry had 80 gensets, owned by 24 generators, who sell power to 13 suppliers. Four daily demand profiles were used. After initial learning by the agents, they found that the evolution of prices settled by about 50 iterations (trading days), and results were averaged over the last 10 days (of 50).

They simulated six different strategies for one and (or) both of the generators whose behavior was under scrutiny, under six different scenarios, each of which was repeated twice, with small differences. Average prices of the six strategies (under the 12 simulations) were higher than the marginal costs (even with full capacity available). This indicated structural market power caused by the industry structure, exacerbated by strategic market power (such as deliberately withholding capacity).

In order to evaluate the capacity of the two generators to manipulate market prices through capacity withholding, they compared different simulations using t-statistics (for pooled samples), a result of the complexities introduced by multiple equilibria and the effects of agents' learning. The two can act as price makers, but only when they both simultaneously withdraw capacity from the market can they profit from price manipulation.

They argued that the agent-based simulation technique enabled substantial insights to be gained before the new wholesale electricity market was introduced, and enabled the modeling of complex adaptive behavior in an environment with possible multiple equilibria, with heterogeneous agents and price uncertainty.

4.4. Recent non-academic research centers

It is the mark of a successful research method that its use has spread beyond the academy into government agencies (as foreshadowed eight years ago by the head of the FERC) and commercial research organizations and companies. The agent-based analysis and design of electricity markets is a successful research method. We briefly mention the latest centers of research into electricity market design using agent-based models: EPRI and the Lawrence Berkeley National Laboratory; Argonne National Laboratory; and Hewlett-Packard. [Koesrindartoto and Tesfatsion (2004) discuss other centers.]

The Argonne National Laboratory has developed the Electricity Markets Complex Adaptive Systems (EMCAS) model, which incorporates agent learning and adaptation based on performance and changing conditions [North et al. (2001, 2002)]. There are user-specified market rules affecting the behavior of individual agents as well as the system. Earlier work at Argonne [North (2000)] was based on the SWARM agent-based modeling platform [Burkhart et al. (2000)]. Although EMCAS is based on the RePast open-source agent-based simulation platform [Collier and Sallach (2001)] and uses GA learning for certain agents, it is a proprietary system. EMCAS is designed to determine the state or states to which the market will gravitate, and the transients involved in getting there. Customer agents represent electricity users and company agents represent electricity suppliers. In EMCAS, each company agent seeks to maximize its individual corporate utility, not overall social utility, as it interacts with other agents and with the Independent System Operator (ISO) or Regional Transmission Organization (RTO) agent. EMCAS operates at six interdependent time scales: from real-time dispatch; to planning day-ahead; week-ahead; month-ahead; year-ahead; and in the medium-to-long term (2–10 years). The authors are aware that as well as allowing alternative company strategies to be simulated, EMCAS allows market rules to be tested: iterative market design.

Meanwhile, Harp et al. (2000) developed a proof-of-concept software tool, SEPIA (simulator for electric power industry agents), an agent-based simulation platform for modeling and exploring a complex adaptive system, the electric power industry. It used two kinds of learning algorithms: Q-learning [Watkins and Dayan (1992)], a version of reinforcement learning; and genetic classifier systems. SEPIA was hosted at Honeywell, and was under-written by EPRI. [See Amin (2002) for further discussion.]

EPRI has used agent-based models to explore market design: Entriken and Wan (2005) describe experiments using computer-based agents to simulate the impact of the California Independent System Operator's proposed Automatic Mitigation Procedure (AMP) on market behavior. These computer agents play the role of market participants seeking to maximize their profits as they formulate bids under a number of scenarios over a simple, two-node market at various levels of demand and transfer capability, with and without the AMP in force. The study demonstrates that agent-based simulation is a useful tool for analyzing existing and proposed design features of electricity markets. One aim was to eliminate the need for human laboratory subjects, and they configured the computer agents in an attempt to eliminate experimental bias. The researchers modeled demand players as price takers: they always bid their willingness-to-pay. Suppliers used an identical strategy of aggressive profit maximization. By comparing their bid prices with the market-clearing price, suppliers could determine whether they were marginal, in which case they used a very simple naïve rule for rent capture: they tested the margin by raising their bid prices. Agents were given the opportunity to learn, although the exact learning algorithm is not described.

5. Computer trading and on-line markets

As mentioned above, inspired by natural phenomena, computer scientists invented various forms of evolutionary programs, such as Holland's GA. They had for some time also been interested in DAI and object-oriented programs, which allow parallel processing to speed solution of the simulation models. This use of multi-agent systems resulted in a special issue of the *Journal of Artificial Intelligence*, edited by Boutilier et al. (1997), on the Economic principles of multi-agent systems, which attempted to introduce computer scientists to the work of economists and game theorists in modeling the interactions of few and many economic actors in markets.

Note that, as they design computerized trading systems, computer scientists have also become interested in the means by which explicit communication between agents might facilitate the operation of these virtual markets. Economists analyzing oligopolistic markets and auctions using agent-based models have denied their agents the possibility of explicit communication: under the various antitrust regimes such communication would probably be illegal. Instead, any communication must be arm's-length signaling by means of prices chosen in previous rounds, if common knowledge.

As well as developing algorithms to pursue simulations of market interactions, computer scientists have also been pioneers in the task of parameterizing auction design space [Wurman et al. (2001)]. This achieves two things: it allows a standard way to describe auction rules, for human beings or for software agents; and, more importantly for the purpose at hand, parameterization of the design space of auctions is necessary to allow direct agent-based design of markets in general and auctions in particular to proceed. A further motivation is to aid the development of auctioneer programs, perhaps on-line.

At IBM, Walsh et al. (2002) used replicator dynamics [Weibull (1995)] to model learning in a multi-agent system to analyze the dynamics and equilibria of two market types for which a full game-theoretic analysis is intractable: automated dynamic pricing, where sellers compete; and automated bidding in the CDA. Unlike GA learning, replicator dynamics cannot generate new strategies or rules: it can only alter the likelihoods of strategies and rules existing at the start of the simulation [Duffy (2006)]. The authors are explicit about the need to obtain clear understanding of the workings of such mechanisms through analysis before design is possible: efficiency and stability are two design criteria mentioned.

5.1. "Evolutionary mechanism design" at Liverpool

A group at the University of Liverpool have been developing techniques of what they dub "evolutionary mechanism design" to examine not just buyer and seller behavior, but auctioneer behavior too, that is, how the transaction price is (or might be) derived in double auctions. Specifically, they took the wholesale electricity market of Nicolaisen et al. (2001) almost intact, with one change: they moved from a clearinghouse double auction to a CDA, using the open-source "4-heap" algorithm [Wurman et al. (1998)].

As a CDA, there was discriminatory pricing, and Myerson and Satterthwaite's [Myerson and Satterthwaite (1983)] impossibility theorem holds.

In the first of a series of papers, Phelps et al. (2002a) sought to co-evolve the buyers, the sellers, and the auctioneer. That is, they viewed the market as the outcome of some evolutionary process involving these three types of actors. They identified two possible techniques for computer-aided auction design based on evolutionary computing: Koza's (1993) genetic programming (GP) and the MRE RL algorithm as formalized [in equations (1)–(3) and (6) above.

The authors first used the same best-fit MRE parameters and the same 3×3 treatment of *RCON* and *RCAP* as in Nicolaisen et al. (2001). They were able to replicate Nicolaisen et al.'s results for market power and for mean market efficiency (close to 100%). But market efficiency was more volatile than in Nicolaisen et al. (2001), perhaps because of the change from clearinghouse to CDA.

The authors then switched to assuming that each trader used GP instead of MRE reinforcement learning to search for a pricing strategy. Each agent's fitness was a function of its profits. Separate populations allowed the emergence of collusive strategies between self-interested traders. Could high-efficiency outcomes be sustained in this model? The answer was no: After 2000 generations, market efficiency stabilized at the relatively low level of 74%.

The final section of the paper added a seventh population, that of auctioneers, again using GP to search a space of pricing rules that included both uniform-pricing and discriminatory-pricing versions of the k-double auction. The auctioneer's fitness was proportional to the total profits earned in the market.

The simulation results showed that the adaptive auction was able to significantly improve its mean *EA*: to 94.5% and stability after only 500 generations, with the same 3×3 treatment of *RCON* and *RCAP* as above. In each of the 9 cases the evolved pricing rule was a linear function of either b or a, the two prices, but not both. When $NS = NB$, the price is determined by a, suggesting that sellers control the market whatever the values of *RCAP*. They cited Curzon Price (1997).

In a succeeding paper, Phelps et al. (2002b) use an objective function which is a weighted sum of *MPB*, *MPS*, and *EA*, each suitably normalized. They restrict search of the mechanism design space to the question: What is the best k-double-auction rule? Are there alternatives that perform as well or better when agents play strategies derived from a cognitive model of strategic interacting: the MRE?

They first simulated the same wholesale electricity market for a range of k values, using stochastic sampling, and found that $k \approx 0.5$ gave good performances. Then they used GP to search the larger space of arbitrary pricing rules, from b and a prices in the CDA. They derived several pages of "completely impenetrable" Lisp-based arithmetical expressions, which only became clear when plotted: effectively the discriminatory-price k-CDA with $k = 0.5$, apart from a small variation when a is small, or $a = b$. So $k = 0.5$ is reasonable.

A third paper [Phelps et al. (2003)] extended the earlier work to examine the strategy-proofness of k. It found that $k = 0.5$ is close to strategy-proof. A fourth paper [Phelps et al. (2005)] uses a "heuristic-strategy" approach and replicator dynamics [Duffy (2006)] to compare the clearinghouse double auction with the CDA, in terms of strategy-proofness and *EA* efficiency. It concluded that although the CDA is, on average, slightly less efficient, it can handle higher flows of transactions.

To summarize the significance of these papers: Agent-based market models have used two kinds of learning: social evolutionary learning algorithms, such as Holland's GAs or Koza's GP; and versions of individual reinforcement learning, such as the Roth–Erev model and modifications. On the one hand, Nicolaisen et al. (2001) argue that the social learning implicit in the GA together with the endogenous extramarginal/inframarginal decision militates against the emergence high market efficiency in agent-based models, while a version of Roth–Erev is sufficient for its emergence. On the other hand, Phelps et al. (2002a) believe that a GP model of learning in electricity markets is a better model in which to design the auction by including the auction rules in the search space of the GP algorithm, as well as including the buyers' and sellers' strategies. It remains a challenge to reconcile the power of evolutionary algorithms in searching a complex design space for agents' strategies and auction rules with the greater realism (but less effective exploration and exploitation of the design space) of models using individual reinforcement learning.

Design of markets might occur with simultaneous "design" of trading agents, a line of research pursued with GA learning at Hewlett-Packard by Cliff (2001, 2002a, 2002b, 2003a)[21] on CDAs and by Byde (2002) on sealed-bid auctions. Two weakness of Cliff (2001) are that, one, it uses a single population for many heterogeneous agents, and, two, the fitness function selects only for globally desirable outcomes, not individually desirable ones. This might be of interest when the designer market will not be a venue for human traders (or their organizations), but rather will be a venue for the designer trading agents (the "buy-bots" and "sell-bots"). This situation has become a possibility with the growth of the Internet. The use of artificial trading agents in business-to-business wholesale trading and in allocations internal to the company or organization is where one might expect such agents to appear most naturally.

5.2. Byde (2002) evolves a new form of sealed-bid single auction

The emphasis of the mechanism-design research in this chapter has been almost exclusively on double auctions. Yet, the single (or monopolist) auction is also of great interest, especially the new, spectrum auction. Byde (2002) examines the design of the sealed-bid single auction, using automated agents as bidders. The agents learn via a

---

[21] On his web page, Cliff (2003b) explains how he came to develop computer traders—his ZIP (Zero Intelligence Plus) traders—that researchers at IBM found outperformed human traders [Das et al. (2001)]. "The wonderful results in the IBM paper, and the success of using the GA to get better ZIPs, led me to think about using a GA to design new marketplaces that are specialized for trading agents." [See Cliff (2002a), et seq.] See the chapter by Duffy (2006) for an extensive discussion of Zero-Intelligence traders.

GA, and the objective is to maximize seller revenue, while not ignoring buyers' von-Neumann–Morgenstern utilities under different designs. Each bidding agent's valuation of the item for sale is some function of the signals received by all bidders.

Byde defines a w-price auction as a generalization of first- and second-price auctions: let $w = (w_1, w_2, \ldots, w_n)$ be a vector of n non-negative real numbers. A w-price auction is a sealed-bid auction in which the highest bidder wins the item, and pays

$$\frac{\sum_{j=1}^{N} w_j bid_j}{\sum_{j=1}^{N} w_j}, \tag{7}$$

where N is the minimum of n and the number of bidders, and $bid_1, bid_2, \ldots$ are the bids ordered from highest to lowest. Byde used the GA to examine a one-dimensional sub-space of w-price auctions: those of the type where the vector $w = (1 - w_2, w_2)$. When $w_2 = 0$, this is a standard first-price auction; when $w_2 = 1$, this is a second-price (Vickrey) auction; and when $0 < w_2 < 1$, the payout is $(1 - w_2)bid_1 + w_2 bid_2$, a non-standard sealed-bid auction.

The space of agent preferences and environmental variables searched allowed Byde to examine exceptions to the Revenue Equivalence Theorem [Milgrom (2004)]: variable numbers of bidders, risk preferences, correlated signals, and degrees of commonality of values. Using a GA, he simulated a population of bidding agents which bid as a function of the signal each received, and played the game many times with stochastic sampling. He noted that each agent's fitness is relative to other agents (although, with a single population, he was not strictly co-evolving agents), which can lead to strategic behavior, such as bidding above one's signal if low, in order to reduce the winner's surplus. The game was repeated, not once-off, modeling bidders who come to know each others' behaviors.

With risk-neutral bidders, independent signals, and a fixed number of bidders, Byde benchmarked the Revenue Equivalence Theorem: there is no seller revenue advantage to any particular w_2. With risk-averse agents cet. par., first-price ($w_2 = 0$) gave highest seller revenue; with correlated signals cet. par., second-price ($w_2 = 1$) gave highest. He then found that "under several classes of non-pathological conditions (e.g. bidders were risk-averse, and unaware of how many players they would face in a given auction), there existed sealed-bid mechanisms expected to return significantly higher revenue to the auctioneer than either the first- or second-price sealed-bid mechanisms," specifically a payout where $w_2 = 0.3$, or $= 0.7$ under other conditions. He noted that since agents' average expected utility seems insensitive to w_2, sellers could design sealed-bid auctions to maximize their revenue without much buyer resistance. Byde's paper directs the market engineer to a new family of designs for sealed-bid auctions, and a new way to examine their performance in silico, before committing to real-world construction.

6. Conclusion

The practical design of markets—mechanism design—using the tool of agent-based simulation is emerging from its infancy. On the one hand, there are mechanisms, such as monopoly auctions, that have been in use since antiquity [McMillan (2002, p. 69)] without much self-conscious design effort. On the other, recent advances in theory and computation have allowed analysis and design to derive new or better mechanisms. The iterative analysis of electricity markets with agent-based models is now just ten years old, and the work on automated markets is even more recent. Only recently have there been attempts to use such models, after parameterizations of auctions, to directly design markets, including electricity markets, as we have seen. Indeed, direct market-design modeling attempts have only occurred in the last several years. Clearly, we have further to travel down this road, as Roth's (Roth, 2002) notion of the design economist emerges from the work of many modelers, in economics, engineering, and computer science.

In this chapter, we have discussed the meaning of market design, its challenges, and the use of agent-based simulation models to achieve it, examining in detail published research in two of the five designer markets we introduced in Section 1 above, as examples of design by simulation.

We have discussed, first, analyzing electricity markets; second, attempting to design such markets directly; and, third, designing new markets for on-line and automated transactions. We have also mentioned in passing design issues in financial markets. It has been impractical to mention all or even most modeling efforts in the literature, and we have focused on the pioneering efforts and the most successful efforts so far. Nonetheless, the future development of the field of agent-based market design will flourish, as evidenced by the large numbers of researchers in different disciplines across the Internet now involved in advancing our knowledge and understanding.

Acknowledgements

I acknowledge help in writing this chapter from the editors, and from Raimo Hämäläinen, Derek Bunn, Peter McBurney, Bob Wilson, Paul Klemperer, Simon Parsons, Enrico Gerding, Eddie Anderson, Thai Cau, Steve Phelps, Carol McCormack, Robert Wood, and my fellow contributors at the *Handbook* Workshop at the University of Michigan, May, 2004. Three anonymous referees were very helpful with their comments.

References

Amin, M. (2002). "Restructuring the electric enterprise: simulating the evolution of the electric power industry with intelligent adaptive agents". In: Faruqui, A., Eakin, K. (Eds.), Market Analysis and Resource Management. Kluwer, Dordrecht. Chapter 3.

Andreoni, J., Miller, J.H. (1995). "Auctions with artificial adaptive agents". Games and Economic Behavior 10, 38–64.

Arifovic, J. (1994). "Genetic algorithm learning and the cobweb model". Journal of Economic Dynamics and Control 18, 3–28.

Arifovic, J. (2001). "Performance of rational and boundedly rational agents in a model with persistent exchange rate volatility". Macroeconomic Dynamics 5, 204–224.

Arthur, W.B. (1991). "Designing economic agents that act like human agents: a behavioral approach to bounded rationality". American Economic Review 81, 353–359.

Arthur, W.B. (1993). "On designing economic agents that behave like human agents". Journal of Evolutionary Economics 3, 1–22.

Arthur, W.B. (2006). "Out-of-equilibrium economics and agent-based modeling", this handbook.

Arthur, W.B., Holland, J., LeBaron, B., Palmer, R., Tayler, P. (1997). "Asset pricing under endogenous expectations in an artificial stock market". In: Arthur, W.B., Durlauf, S., Lane, D. (Eds.), The Economy as an Evolving Complex System II. Addison-Wesley, Reading, MA, pp. 15–44.

Audet, N., Gravelle, T., Yang, J. (2002). "Alternative trading systems: does one shoe fit all?", working paper 2002-33 (Bank of Canada, Ottawa).

Axelrod, R. (1987). "The evolution of strategies in the iterated Prisoner's Dilemma". In: Davis, L. (Ed.), Genetic Algorithms and Simulated Annealing. Pittman, London, pp. 32–41.

Axelrod, R. (2006). "Agent-based modeling as a bridge between disciplines", this handbook.

Bottazzi, G., Dosi, G., Rebesco, I. (2003). "Institutional architectures and behavioural ecologies in the dynamics of financial markets: a preliminary investigation", Technical Report, Laboratory of Economics and Management, Sant' Anna School of Advanced Studies, Pisa, Italy.

Boutilier, C., Shoham, Y., Wellman, M.P. (1997). "Economic principles of multi-agent systems". Journal of Artificial Intelligence 94 (1–2), 1–6. Editorial.

Bower, J., Bunn, D.W. (2000). "Model-based comparison of pool and bilateral markets for electricity". Energy Journal 21 (3), 1–29.

Bower, J., Bunn, D.W. (2001). "Experimental analysis of the efficiency of uniform-price versus discriminatory auctions in the England and Wales electricity market". Journal of Economic Dynamics and Control 25 (3–4), 561–592.

Bower, J., Bunn, D.W., Wattendrup, C. (2001). "A model-based analysis of strategic consolidation in the German electricity industry". Energy Policy 29, 987–1005.

Brenner, T. (2006). "Agent learning representation", this handbook.

Bullard, J., Duffy, J. (1999). "Using genetic algorithms to model the evolution of heterogeneous beliefs". Computational Economics 13 (1), 41–60.

Bunn, D.W. (2004). Personal communication.

Bunn, D.W., Day, C.J. (1998). "Agent-based simulation of electric power pools: a comparison with the supply function equilibrium approach". In: Technology's Critical Role in Energy and Environmental Markets, Proceedings of the 19th Annual North American Conference of the United States Association for Energy Economics and the International Association for Energy Economics, 18–21 October 1998, Albuquerque, New Mexico. IAEE/USAEE, Cleveland.

Bunn, D.W., Oliveira, F.S. (2001). "Agent-based simulation: an application to the New Electricity Trading Arrangements of England and Wales". IEEE Transactions on Evolutionary Computation 5 (5), 493–503.

Bunn, D.W., Oliveira, F.S. (2003). "Evaluating individual market power in electricity markets via agent-based simulation". Annals of Operations Research 121, 57–77.

Burkhart, R., Askenazi, M., Minar, N. (2000). "Swarm Release Documentation", available as http://www.santafe.edu/projects/swarm/swarmdocs/set/set.html. Accessed 25 November 2004.

Bush, R.R., Mosteller, F. (1955). Stochastic Models for Learning. Wiley, New York.

Byde, A. (2002). "Applying evolutionary game theory to auction mechanism design", Hewlett-Packard Technical Report HPL-2002-321.

Cau, T.D.H. (2003). "Analyzing tacit collusion in oligopolistic electricity markets using a co-evolutionary approach", PhD dissertation, Australian Graduate School of Management, University of New South Wales.

Cau, T.D.H., Anderson, E.J. (2002). "A co-evolutionary approach to modeling the behavior of participants in competitive electricity markets". In: Proceedings of the Power Engineering Society Summer Meeting. IEEE Society Press, Piscataway, NJ, pp. 1534–1540.

Chan, N.T., Shelton, C. (2001). "An electronic market-maker", Artificial Intelligence Lab, M.I.T., AI Memo 2001-005, April.

Chattoe, E. (1998). "Just how (un)realistic are evolutionary algorithms as representations of social processes?". Journal of Artificial Societies and Social Simulation 1 (3). http://www.soc.surrey.ac.uk/JASSS/1/3/2.html.

Cliff, D. (2001). "Evolutionary optimization of parameter sets for adaptive software-agent traders in continuous double auction markets", Hewlett-Packard Technical Report HPL-2001-99.

Cliff, D. (2002a). "Evolution of market mechanism through a continuous space of auction-types". In: Proceedings of the 2002 Congress on Evolutionary Computation, (CEC '02) Honolulu. IEEE Society Press, Piscataway, NJ, pp. 2029–2034.

Cliff, D. (2002b). "Evolution of market mechanism through a continuous space of auction-types II: Two-sided auction mechanisms evolve in response to market shocks", Hewlett-Packard Technical Report HPL-2002-128.

Cliff, D. (2003a). "Explorations in evolutionary design of online auction market mechanisms". Electronic Commerce Research and Applications 2 (2), 162–175.

Cliff, D. (2003b). "Artificial trading agents for online auction marketplaces", http://www.hpl.hp.com/personal/dave_cliff/traders.htm. Accessed 15 July 2004.

Collier, N., Sallach, D. (2001). "RePast". Available at http://repast.sourceforge.net.

Conlisk, J. (1996). "Why bounded rationality?". Journal of Economic Literature 34, 669–700.

Cramton, P. (2003). "Electricity market design: the good, the bad, and the ugly". In: Proceedings of the 36th Hawaii International Conference on System Sciences. IEEE Society Press, Piscataway, NJ.

Cross, J.G. (1973). "A stochastic learning modle of economic behavior". Quarterly Journal of Economics 87, 239–266.

Cross, J.G. (1983). A Theory of Adaptive Economic Behavior. Cambridge University Press, Cambridge.

Curzon Price, T. (1997). "Using co-evolutionary programming to simulate strategic behavior in markets". Journal of Evolutionary Economics 7 (3), 219–254.

Das, R., Hanson, J.E., Kephart, J.O., Tesauro, G. (2001). "Agent-human interactions in the continuous double auction". In: Nebel, B. (Ed.), Proceedings of the 17th International Joint Conferences on Artificial Intelligence (IJCAI), Seattle. Morgan Kaufmann, San Francisco, pp. 1169–1187.

Dawid, H. (1999). Adaptive Learning By Genetic Algorithms: Analytical Results and Applications to Economic Models, 2nd edn. Springer, Berlin.

Duffy, J. (2006). "Agent-based models and human-subject experiments", this handbook.

Edmonds, B., Bryson, J.J. (2003). "Beyond the design stance: the intention of agent-based engineering", Centre for Policy Modelling, CPM Report No.: CPM-03-126. http://cfpm.org/papers/btds.pdf.

Entriken, R., Wan, S. (2005). "Agent-based simulation of an Automatic Mitigation Procedure". In: Proceedings of the 38th Hawaii International Conference on System Sciences. IEEE Society Press, Piscataway, NJ.

Erev, I., Roth, A.E. (1998). "Predicting how people play games: reinforcement learning in experimental games with unique mixed strategy equilibria". American Economic Review 88 (4), 848–881.

FERC (2003). "Notice of White Paper", U.S. Federal Energy Regulatory Commission Docket No. RM01-12-000, April 28.

Forrester, J.W. (1961). Industrial Dynamics. M.I.T. Press, Cambridge.

Fudenberg, D., Maskin, E. (1986). "The Folk Theorem in repeated games with discounting or incomplete information". Econometrica 54, 533–554.

Gamma, E., Helm, R., Johnson, R., Vlissides, J. (1995). Design Patterns: Elements of Reusable Object-Oriented Software. Addison-Wesley, Reading, MA.

Gjerstad, S. (2004). "The impact of bargaining pace in double auction dynamics", Department of Economics, University of Arizona.

Gjerstad, S., Dickhaut, J. (1998). "Price formation in double auctions". Games and Economic Behavior 22, 1–29.

Gode, D., Sunder, S. (1993). "Allocation efficiency of markets with Zero Intelligence traders: market as a partial substitute for individual rationality". Journal of Political Economy 101, 119–137.

Hailu, A., Schilizzi, S. (2004). "Are auctions more efficient than fixed price schemes when bidders learn?". Australian Journal of Management 29, 147–168.

Hämäläinen, R.P. (1996). "Agent-based modeling of the electricity distribution system". In: Hamza, M.H. (Ed.), Modelling, Identification and Control, Proceedings the 15th International Association of Science and Technology for Development (IASTED) International Conference, February 19–21, Innsbruck. ACTA Press, Calgary, pp. 344–346.

Hämäläinen, R.P. (2004). Personal communication.

Hämäläinen, R.P., Kettunen, E., Ehtamo, H. (1997). "Game modelling and coordination processes for two-level multi-agent systems". In: Hamza, M.H. (Ed.), Modelling, Identification and Control, Proceedings of the 16th IASTED International Conference, February 17–19, Innsbruck. ACTA Press, Calgary, pp. 234–240.

Hämäläinen, R.P., Parantainen, J. (1995). "Load analysis by agent-based simulation of the electricity distribution system". In: Proceedings of the 2nd International Federation of Automatic Control (IFAC) Symposium on Control of Power Plants and Power Systems SIPOWER95, Cancun, Mexico, December 6–8, 1995. Elsevier, Oxford, pp. 213–217.

Harp, S.A., Brignone, A., Wollenberg, B.F., Samad, T. (2000). "SEPIA: a Simulator for Electric Power Industry Agents". IEEE Control Systems Magazine 20 (4), 53–69.

Hoecker, J. (1998). "Keeping electric restructuring moving forward" (Feb. 3, 1998) (11th Annual Utility M&A Symposium, New York), quoted in: E.P. Kahn, "Numerical techniques for analyzing market power in electricity", The Electricity Journal 34–43, July.

Holland, J.H. (1992). Adaptation in Natural and Artificial Systems: An Introductory Analysis with Applications to Biology, Control, and Artificial Intelligence, 2nd edn. M.I.T. Press, Cambridge.

Holland, J.H., Miller, J.H. (1991). "Artificial adaptive agents in economic theory". American Economic Review 81 (2), 365–370.

Hu, J., Wellman, M.P. (1998). "Multiagent reinforcement learning: theoretical framework and an algorithm". In: Proceedings of the Fifteenth International Conference on Machine Learning. Morgan Kaufmann, San Francisco, pp. 242–250.

Janssen, M.A., Ostrom, E. (2006). "Governing socio-ecological systems", this handbook.

Jennings, N.R., Faratin, P., Lomuscio, A.R., Parsons, S., Sierra, C., Wooldridge, M. (2001). "Automated negotiation: prospects, methods, and challenges". International Journal of Group Decision and Negotiation 10 (2), 199–215.

Kauffman, S.A. (1995). At Home in the Universe: The Search for the Laws of Self-Organization and Complexity. Oxford University Press, New York.

Klemperer, P. (2002). "What really matters in auction design". Journal of Economic Perspectives 16 (1), 169–189.

Knuth, D.E. (1968–1973). The Art of Computer Programming. Addison-Wesley, Reading, MA.

Knuth, D.E. (1979). TeX and METAFONT: New Directions in Typesetting. Digital Press, Bedford, MA.

Koesrindartoto, D., Tesfatsion, L. (2004). "Testing the reliability of FERC's Wholesale Power Market Platform: an agent-based computational economics approach". In: Energy, Environment and Economics in a New Era, Proceedings of the 24th Annual North American Conference of the United States Association for Energy Economics and the International Association for Energy Economics, 8–10 July 2004, Washington, DC. IAEE/USAEE, Cleveland.

Koza, J.R. (1993). Genetic Programming: On the Programming of Computers by Means of Natural Selection. M.I.T. Press, Cambridge.

Krishna, V., Ramesh, V.C. (1998). "Intelligent agents in negotiations in market games, Part 2, Application". IEEE Transactions on Power Systems 13 (3), 1109–1114.

Lane, D.A. (1993a). "Artificial worlds and economics, part I". Journal of Evolutionary Economics 3, 89–107.

Lane, D.A. (1993b). "Artificial worlds and economics, part II". Journal of Evolutionary Economics 3, 177–197.

Lane, D., Kroujiline, A., Petrov, V., Sheblé, G. (2000). "Electricity market power: marginal cost and relative capacity effects". In: Alzala, A. (Ed.), Proceedings of the 2000 Congress on Evolutionary Computation. IEEE Society Press, Piscataway, NJ, pp. 1048–1054.

LeBaron, B. (2006). "Agent-based computational finance", this handbook.

LeBaron, B., Arthur, W.B., Palmer, R. (1999). "Time series properties of an artificial stock market". Journal of Economic Dynamics and Control 23 (9–10), 1487–1516.

Maifeld, T., Sheblé, G. (1996). "Genetic-based unit commitment". IEEE Transactions on Power Systems 11 (3), 1359.

MacGill, I.F. (2004), "Exploring spot electricity market operation through agent-based simulation and evolutionary programming", Canberra: CSIRO Agent-Based Modeling Seminar, February.

MacGill, I.F., Kaye, R.J. (1999). "Decentralized coordination of power system operation using dual evolutionary programming". IEEE Transactions on Power Systems 14 (1), 112–119.

MacKie-Mason, J.K., Wellman, M.P. (2006). "Automated markets and trading agents", this handbook.

Marks, R.E. (1989). "Breeding optimal strategies: optimal behavior for oligopolists". In: Schaffer, J.D. (Ed.), Proceedings of the Third International Conference on Genetic Algorithms, George Mason University, June 4–7, 1989. Morgan Kaufmann Publishers, San Mateo, CA, pp. 198–207.

Marks, R.E. (1992). "Breeding hybrid strategies: optimal behaviour for oligopolists". Journal of Evolutionary Economics 2, 17–38.

Marks, R.E. (1998). "Evolved perception and behaviour in oligopolies". Journal of Economic Dynamics and Control 22 (8–9), 1209–1233.

Marks, R.E. (2003). "Models rule". Australian Journal of Management 28 (1), i–ii. Editorial.

Marks, R.E., Midgley, D.F., Cooper, L.G. (1995). "Adaptive behavior in an oligopoly". In: Biethahn, J., Nissen, V. (Eds.), Evolutionary Algorithms in Management Applications. Springer, Berlin, pp. 225–239.

McMillan, J. (2002). Reinventing the Bazaar: A Natural History of Markets. Norton, New York.

Midgley, D.F., Marks, R.E., Cooper, L.G. (1997). "Breeding competitive strategies". Management Science 43 (3), 257–275.

Milgrom, P. (2004). Putting Auction Theory to Work. Cambridge University Press, Cambridge.

Myerson, R.B., Satterthwaite, M.A. (1983). "Efficient mechanisms for bilateral trading". Journal of Economic Theory 29, 265–281.

Nicolaisen, J., Smith, M., Petrov, V., Tesfatsion, L. (2000). "Concentration and capacity effects on electricity market power". In: Alzala, A. (Ed.), Proceedings of the 2000 Congress on Evolutionary Computation. IEEE Society Press, Piscataway, NJ, pp. 1041–1047.

Nicolaisen, J., Petrov, V., Tesfatsion, L. (2001). "Market power and efficiency in a computational electricity market with discriminatory double-auction pricing". IEEE Transactions on Evolutionary Computation 5 (5), 504–523.

North, M.J. (2000). "SMART II: The Spot Market Agent Research Tool Version 2.0". In: Proceedings of SwarmFest 2000. Swarm Development Group, Logan, Utah, pp. 9–13.

North, M.J., Macal, C., Cirillo, R., Conzelmann, G., Koritarov, V., Thimmapuram, P., Veselka, T. (2001). "Multi-agent social and organizational modeling of electric power and natural gas markets". Computational & Mathematical Organization Theory 7 (4), 331–337.

North, M., Conzelmann, G., Koritarov, V., Macal, C., Thimmapuram, P., Veselka, T. (2002). "E-Laboratories: agent-based modeling of electricity markets". In: Proceedings of the 2002 American Power Conference. PennWell, Tulsa, Okla.

Phelps, S., McBurney, P., Parsons, S., Sklar, E. (2002a). "Co-evolutionary auction mechanism design: a preliminary report". In: Padget, J.A., Shehory, O., Parkes, D.C., Sadeh, N.M., Walsh, W.E. (Eds.), Lecture Notes In Computer Science: Revised Papers from the Workshop on Agent-Mediated Electronic Commerce IV: Designing Mechanisms and Systems. Springer, Berlin, pp. 123–142.

Phelps, S., Parsons, S., Sklar, E., McBurney, P. (2002b). "Applying multi-objective evolutionary computing to auction mechanism design", University of Liverpool Computer Science Technical Report ULCS-02-031.

Phelps, S., McBurney, P., Sklar, E., Parsons, S. (2003). "Using genetic programming to optimise pricing rules for a double auction market". In: Proceedings of the Workshop on Agents for Electronic Commerce, Pittsburgh, PA.

Phelps, S., Parsons, S., McBurney, P. (2005). "Automated trading agents versus virtual humans: an evolutionary game-theoretic comparison of two double-auction market designs". In: Faratin, P., Rodriguez-Aguilar,

J.A. (Eds.), Agent-Mediated Electronic Commerce VI: Theories for and Engineering of Distributed Mechanisms and Systems. In: Lecture Notes in Computer Science. Springer, Berlin.

Räsänen, M., Hämäläinen, R.P., Ruusunen, J. (1994). "Visual interactive modelling in electricity load analysis". In: Hamza, M.H. (Ed.), Modelling, Identification and Control, Proceedings the 13th International Association of Science and Technology for Development (IASTED) International Conference, Grindelwald, Switzerland, Feb. 21–23. ACTA Press, Calgary, pp. 339–342.

Richter, C.W., Sheblé, G. (1998). "Genetic algorithm evolution of utility bidding strategies for the competitive marketplace". IEEE Transactions on Power Systems 13 (1), 256–261.

Richter, C.W. Jr., Sheblé, G.B., Ashlock, D. (1999). "Comprehensive bidding strategies with genetic programming/finite state automata". IEEE Transactions on Power Systems 14 (4), 1207–1212.

Riechmann, T. (2001). "Genetic algorithm learning and evolutionary games". Journal of Economic Dynamics and Control 25, 1019–1037.

Roth, A.E. (1991). "Game theory as a part of empirical economics". Economic Journal 101 (401), 107–114.

Roth, A.E. (2000). "Game theory as a tool for market design". In: Patrone, F., García-Jurado, I., Tijs, S. (Eds.), Game Practice: Contributions from Applied Game Theory. Kluwer, Dordrecht, pp. 7–18.

Roth, A.E. (2002). "The economist as engineer: game theory, experimentation, and computation as tools for design economics". Econometrica 70 (4), 1341–1378.

Roth, A.E., Erev, I. (1995). "Learning in extensive form games: experimental data and simple dynamic models in the intermediate term". Games and Economic Behavior 8, 848–881.

Rubinstein, A. (1998). Modeling Bounded Rationality. M.I.T. Press, Cambridge.

Sargent, T.J. (1993). Bounded Rationality in Macroeconomics. Oxford University Press, New York.

Satterthwaite, M.A., Williams, S.R. (1989). "Bilateral trade with the sealed bid k-double auction: existence and efficiency". Journal of Economic Theory 48, 107–133.

Satterthwaite, M.A., Williams, S.R. (1993). "The Bayesian theory of the k-double auction". In: Friedman, D., Rust, J. (Eds.), The Double Auction Market: Institutions, Theories, and Evidence. Addison-Wesley, Reading, MA, pp. 99–123.

Selten, R. (1998). "Features of experimentally observed bounded rationality". European Economic Review 42, 413–436.

Selten, R., Stoecker, R. (1986). "End behavior in sequences of finite Prisoner's Dilemma supergames". Journal of Economic Behavior and Organization 7, 47–70.

Simon, H. (1981). The Sciences of the Artificial, 2nd edn. M.I.T. Press, Cambridge.

Sweeney, J.L. (2002). The California Electricity Crisis. Hoover Institution Press, Stanford.

Talukdar, S. (2002). "Agent-based market testing", DOE Transmission Reliability Research Review, Washington, DC, December 10.

Talukdar, S., Ramesh, V.C. (1992). "A-teams for real-time operations". International Journal of Electrical Power & Energy Systems 14 (2–3), 138–143.

Tesfatsion, L. (2002). "Agent-based computational economics: growing economies from the bottom up". Artificial Life 8 (1), 55–82.

Tesfatsion, L. (2005). Personal communication.

Thorndike, E.L. (1911). Animal Intelligence: Experimental Studies. Macmillan, New York.

Verkama, M., Hämäläinen, R.P., Ehtamo, H. (1992). "Multi-agent interaction processes: from oligopoly theory to decentralized artificial intelligence". Group Decision and Negotiation 1 (2), 137–159.

Verkama, M., Hämäläinen, R.P., Ehtamo, H. (1994). "Modeling and computational analysis of reactive behavior in organizations". In: Carley, K.M., Prietula, M.J. (Eds.), Computational Organization Theory. Lawrence Erlbaum Assoc., Hillsdale, NJ, pp. 161–177.

Vriend, N. (2000). "An illustration of the essential difference between individual and social learning and its consequences for computational analyses". Journal of Economic Dynamics and Control 24, 1–19.

Walia, V., Byde, A., Cliff, D. (2003). "Evolving market design in zero-intelligence trader markets". In: Proceedings of the IEEE International Conference on E-Commerce, 2003 (CEC '03). IEEE Society Press, Piscataway, NJ, pp. 157–164.

Walsh, W.E., Das, R., Tesauro, G., Kephart, J.O. (2002). "Analyzing complex strategic interactions in multi-agent systems". In: Gmytrasiwicz, P.J., Parsons, S. (Eds.), Game Theoretic and Decision Theoretic Agents, American Association for Artificial Intelligence Technical Report WS-02-06. AAAI Press, Menlo Park, CA, pp. 109–118.

Watkins, C.J.C.H., Dayan, P. (1992). "Q-learning". Machine Learning 8, 279–292.

Watson, J.D., Crick, F.H.C. (1953). "Molecular structure of nucleic acids: a structure of deoxyribose nucleic acid". Nature 4356, 737–738.

Weibull, J.W. (1995). Evolutionary Game Theory. M.I.T. Press, Cambridge.

Wilson, R. (2002). "Architecture of power markets". Econometrica 70 (4), 1299–1340.

Wood, R.E. (2005). Personal communication.

Wurman, P.R., Walsh, W.E., Wellman, M.P. (1998). "Flexible double auctions for electronic commerce: theory and implementation". Decision Support Systems 24, 17–27.

Wurman, P.R., Wellman, M.P., Walsh, W.E. (2001). "A parameterization of the auction design space". Games and Economic Behavior 35, 304–338.

Young, H.P. (1998). Individual Strategy and Social Structure: An Evolutionary Theory of Institutions. Princeton University Press, Princeton.

Chapter 28

AUTOMATED MARKETS AND TRADING AGENTS

JEFFREY K. MACKIE-MASON AND MICHAEL P. WELLMAN

University of Michigan, Ann Arbor, MI 48109, USA
e-mails: jmm@umich.edu; wellman@umich.edu
url: http://www-personal.umich.edu/~jmm/; url: http://ai.eecs.umich.edu/people/wellman/

Contents

Handbook of Computational Economics, Volume 2. Edited by Leigh Tesfatsion and Kenneth L. Judd
© 2006 Elsevier B.V.   All rights reserved
DOI: 10.1016/S1574-0021(05)02028-9

Abstract

Computer automation has the potential, just starting to be realized, of transforming the design and operation of markets, and the behaviors of agents trading in them. We discuss the possibilities for automating markets, presenting a broad conceptual framework covering resource allocation as well as enabling marketplace services such as search and transaction execution. One of the most intriguing opportunities is provided by markets implementing computationally sophisticated negotiation mechanisms, for example combinatorial auctions. An important theme that emerges from the literature is the centrality of design decisions about matching the domain of goods over which a mechanism operates to the domain over which agents have preferences. When the match is imperfect (as is almost inevitable), the market game induced by the mechanism is analytically intractable, and the literature provides an incomplete characterization of rational bidding policies. A review of the literature suggests that much of our existing knowledge comes from computational simulations, including controlled studies of abstract market designs (e.g., simultaneous ascending auctions), and research tournaments comparing agent strategies in a variety of market scenarios. An empirical game-theoretic methodology combines the advantages of simulation, agent-based modeling, and statistical and game-theoretic analysis.

Keywords

computational markets, automated markets, trading agents, mechanism design

JEL classification: C63, C72, D40, D44

1. Introduction

Many digitally mediated activities present participants with complex strategic decisions, involving significant interaction with other agents. The strategic dimension of electronic commerce, for instance, is obvious, not just for negotiation and trading, but also for ancillary commerce operations such as matchmaking, resource finding, advertising, recommendation, contracting, and executing transactions. All of these are increasingly subject to automation as part of online marketplaces [Wellman (2004)]. Other digital realms, not necessarily viewed as commerce per se, nevertheless involve pivotal strategic relationships. Examples include peer-to-peer resource sharing [Golle et al. (2001); Cox and Noble (2003)], formation of coalitions, teams, or affinity groups [Brooks and Durfee (2003); Sandholm and Lesser (1997); Tambe (1997)], scientific sharing of large-scale instrumentation and other infrastructure [Finholt and Olson (1997); Finholt (2003)], and coordination of activity within organizations [Malone (1987); Pynadath and Tambe (2002)].

There are a variety of possible benefits from automating markets. One is cost saving from automating some functions of existing non-computational markets. For example, search automation reduces the cost of finding goods and potential trading partners. Micropayment systems offer the hope—not yet fully realized—of enabling large volumes of remote, low-value transactions by reducing the execution overhead. Another benefit is the ability to extend markets in time and geographic scope by conducting them over networks. For example, eBay's main innovation is not in the form of its markets, but in its ability to make markets that bridge time and space.

The greatest disruptive potential may lie in the opportunity to deploy market mechanisms that are simply infeasible to operate without computer automation. Creating previously missing markets enables gains from trade, and the creation of new products and services, with first-order effects on social welfare. Such mechanisms were dubbed "smart markets", apparently by Vernon Smith. For example, a multi-airport landing slot allocation policy might require the solution of a constrained integer program as a function of bid messages from participating agents. Such policies are well beyond the capabilities of non-automated market mediators; in some applications they take CPU days to solve even with current hardware. The emergence of cheap, high-speed computation created excitement among market designers, because without automated computation many interesting allocation mechanisms were infeasible for problems with real-world scale.

We study issues in the design of automated markets with software agents: how to automate effectively various components of market transactions? We emphasize design issues impinging on strategy, and strategic behavior particular to the market setting. Our chapter complements Marks (2006), who focuses on the use of agent-based computational techniques as a *tool* for use in (not necessarily computational) market design. Thus, Marks emphasizes positive analysis: how we can use agent-based models to evaluate performance of various market designs. We adopt this perspective briefly in

Section 5, where we describe a computational game methodology for analyzing agent strategies and computational market designs.

Given our focus on design, much of the contribution of our chapter to agent-based computational economics (ACE) is to the development of infrastructure. For ACE modelers to study the implications of various market designs and agent strategies they need to be able to implement computational representations that are correct, interesting, and tractable.

To assist in these endeavors, we first present, in Section 2, a conceptual market design framework. After graphically characterizing the design space for marketplace systems, we present a brief specification of a formal model that encompasses many of the interesting problems for market and agent design. The model provides a structured framework for organizing the literature review in the rest of the chapter.

Section 3 covers the largest body of material. We discuss design issues and implementation research for mechanisms that provide the three different types of market transaction services we identified in our conceptual framework: discovery, negotiation (what is usually, narrowly, called "the market"), and execution. We devote disproportionate attention to negotiation or deal-making market mechanisms, reflecting the relative attention economists in general give to each of the three stages.

In Section 4 we focus on the other major area for design: trading agents, who interact through the market mechanisms discussed in Section 3. We consider both theoretical and practical problems of designing strategies needed to make economically-intelligent trading agents. We present a case study based on a several-year history of trading agent competitions that have attracted substantial attention.

We close the chapter by presenting an emerging computational agent-based methodology for empirical game-theoretic analysis. This method has been developed to address a fundamental problem in the design of both trading agent strategies and the market mechanisms through which they interact: optimal strategies for complex (realistic) markets are analytically intractable. We consider empirical game-theoretic analysis a promising approach for systematic investigation of agent strategies, and then for the evaluation of market mechanism performance when agents follow successful strategies. These agent-based methods offer one way to close the loop between the over-simplified theoretical models of agents and market, and the practical problems that designers must solve to implement realistic markets.

2. Marketplace design framework

Markets allocate resources through a series of *transactions*, each an exchange of goods and services expressed in terms of an underlying monetary system. We find it useful to organize the life cycle of a transaction into three stages, representing the fundamental steps that parties must go through in order to conduct trade.

1. **Connecting**: the search for and discovery of an opportunity to engage in a market interaction.

Figure 1. The fundamental steps of a market transaction.

2. **Dealing**: the negotiation of terms.
3. **Exchanging**: the execution of the terms of an agreed transaction.

These steps are illustrated in Figure 1. Of course, the boundaries between steps are not sharp, and these activities may be repeated, partially concluded, retracted, or interleaved along the way to a complete commercial transaction. Nevertheless, keeping in mind the three steps is useful as a way to categorize particular resource allocation services, which tend to focus on one or the other.

Rarely are all of these tasks automated. Only some agents may be automated, and even then perhaps only partially. Some of the market functions (say, finding connections, or negotiating deals) may be automated, but not others. Therefore, it is not very useful to discuss automation of an entire system as a single problem. In this chapter we consider the components separately, reflecting the complexity of the problem and the division of labor in the research literature.

2.1. Marketplace systems

To organize our discussion, we present and discuss a schematic representation of the overall design problem.[1] In Figure 2 we embed a marketplace system in an environment of social institutions (e.g., language, laws, etc.). The marketplace system itself consists of agents and the market mechanism through which they interact. The market mechanism can be roughly subdivided into structures, practices, and rules for the tasks of connecting, dealing, and exchanging. We now offer more precise definitions of the central concepts, and provide a formal framework within which we analyze them.

Marketplace system The *agents* who participate in the resource allocation problem, together with the *market mechanisms* through which they interact.

Mechanism The rules, practices and social structures of a social choice process, specifying (1) permissible actions (often limited to messages, expressible as a communication protocol) and (2) outcomes as a function of agent actions. A mechanism is *mediated* if there is some entity, distinct from the participants, that manages the communication and implements the mechanism rules.

---

[1] The descriptive terms we use do not have standard definitions, so we need to establish our own for these purposes. For example, some use "market" to refer to what we call a marketplace system. But others use "market" just for the practices and structures for making deals, excluding the participating agents and the other activities (such as connecting) from the term.

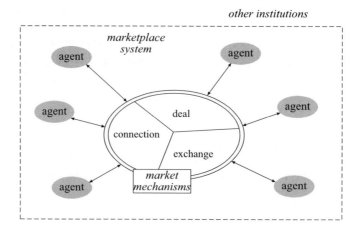

Figure 2. Schematic for a marketplace system.

Market mechanism A mechanism for which the possible ultimate outcomes comprise market-based exchange transactions.

Agent An autonomous decision-making locus in a system of multiple decision-making entities.[2] An agent has "type" attributes such as preferences, beliefs, intentions, and capabilities. Type information is generally considered private, not inherently accessible to others. For purposes of analysis, we may attribute to agents particular decision-making rules, or more generally, assume that they conform to some *decision rule*, specifying a form of consistency between the agent's behavior, beliefs and preferences. Such attributions may appeal to classical notions of rationality, as well as alternative bounded or otherwise nonstandard coherence criteria.

Our characterization of a marketplace system indicates that there is not just one design problem, but several. The first is design of the market mechanism, for use by human (undesigned), or computational (designed) agents. The market mechanism may be decomposed into several design subproblems: for example, mechanisms typically are designed separately for the connection, deal and exchange phases of a transaction. The second top-level problem is design of agents to interact (perhaps with human assistance) with existing market mechanisms, or with new mechanisms designed by others. In some situations one might be in a position to design an entire marketplace system, though we consider this unusual.

In this chapter, we focus on market mechanism design in Section 3, devoting most of our attention to the deal negotiation task. We also provide a brief discussion of automating the connecting and exchanging functions. We address agent design in Section 4.

---

[2] For purposes of framing the general design problem, we apply the term *agent* generically to humans, computational processes, or organizations as long as they exhibit agent characteristics.

2.2. Formal model

We present a formal model of a marketplace system to focus attention on the important design issues that we review the rest of the chapter. The formal representation is not essential to understand the rest of the chapter, but it provides a concise organization of the main themes. This representation also implicitly suggests (we do not provide extensive references) the links between the topics we cover and the more theoretical literature on mechanism design that we do not review in detail.

Marketplaces can be designed for transactions in goods, services, tasks, plans or other resources and activities. For simplicity, we will refer to these state variables as *goods*, and represent them as a vector of quantities that takes values from a domain X. Given N total agents, an *allocation* is an assignment of a matrix $\vec{x} \in X^N$ to agents $i \in \{1, \ldots, N\}$, with the individual allocation vector to each agent denoted by $\vec{x}_i \in X$.

A market mechanism specifies (1) the goods it recognizes, and (2) rules for determining allocation outcomes. There are typically two types of rules: those specifying a set of permissible actions (strategies), $s_i \in S_i$ for each agent i, and procedures for choosing an allocation based on the observable actions. We denote a mechanism by $\gamma = (s_1, \ldots, s_N, g(\cdot))$, where g maps the set of actions into allocations, $g : S_1 \times \cdots \times S_N \to X^N$. We denote the allocation this mechanism makes to a specific agent by $g_i(\vec{s}) = \vec{x}_i$. An example of the rules governing allowable strategies is the set of bidding rules in an ascending auction (for example, bids must be over single lots, and must exceed the previous bid by at least some specified increment). An example of an allocation rule is the English auction rule for unitary objects (the high bidder wins the object, and pays her announced bid).

When a market mechanism is designed, the designer presumably wishes to fulfill some objective subject to various constraints. Let θ be the information state across all agents, defined on the Cartesian product of the individual information spaces Θ_i. Typically the objective can be expressed as a function (often called a *social choice function*) that maps from the information state of the agents to a preferred allocation, as $f : \Theta_1 \times \cdots \times \Theta_N \to X^N$. However, since elements of the θ_i are private to the agents, and thus not directly accessible to the designer, the ability to achieve this objective depends on the extent to which agents choose to reveal this information, and the cost to the mediator of inducing revelation. Further, the space of possible mechanisms may be constrained by additional social restrictions such as "no external subsidies", or "maintain horizontal equity", which taken together restrict the set of allocations to some permissible space, $f(\vec{\theta}) \in F$.

Agents are distinguished by their possession of *private information* and *autonomy*. We let θ_i denote agent i's private information, which can be taken to include all of the agent's relevant knowledge of or beliefs about states of the world. This information is private in the sense that other agents j do not generally have access to all of the information in the set θ_i. An agent is autonomous if it exhibits *preferences* over allocations, and chooses actions according to some *decision rule*. Assume that i's preferences can be represented by a real-valued function $u_i(\vec{x}_i, \theta_i)$, called agent i's *utility* for a given allocation $\vec{x}_i$ given its private information, which has the property that $u_i(\vec{x}_i', \theta_i) > u_i(\vec{x}_i, \theta_i)$ exactly when i prefers allocation $\vec{x}_i'$ to $\vec{x}_i$.

An autonomous agent maps its preferences into actions according to decisions that follow from its decision rule. For example, the canonical decision rule assumed by economists for non-strategic settings is that an agent will select feasible actions that maximize its (expected) utility. In strategic settings, one commonly assumed decision rule is that an agent will choose a dominant strategy if one exists. This decision rule is not complete, because it does not specify what to do when no dominant strategy exists. There are many more complete decision rules commonly studied in the literature. For example, every finite game of (incomplete) information has a set of agent strategies that form a mixed perfect (Bayesian) Nash equilibrium [Fudenberg and Tirole (1991)].[3] A corresponding decision rule is that an agent will play a strategy from the Bayes-Nash set. Unfortunately, this decision rule offers a choice for every (finite) problem, but may still be incomplete because there may be multiple equilibria, and then it is necessary to specify *which* Bayes-Nash strategy to play. A particular computational implementation of the agent's decision rule may or may not involve explicit optimization of u_i, or explicit models of beliefs and preferences [Russell and Norvig (2003)].

This formal description of a marketplace system highlights many of the problems that must be addressed by the designer of an automated system. One crucial thing to remember when reading the literature, and when engaging in computational marketplace design, is that some features will be explicitly designed while others will be unspecified (and thus taken as found in the environment in which the system is applied). The performance of the system is likely to depend at least as crucially on the features that are not designed as those that are.

We defined a role for goods, mechanisms and agents. We now use the model to illustrate with just a few examples the design issues for these features in turn.

2.2.1. Design and goods

One issue for the designer is which goods the system will recognize, and in particular whether the domain of the goods a market mechanism allocates corresponds to the domain of the goods over which agents have preferences. For example, externality problems (such as pollution) have long been characterized as problems of "missing markets" for certain goods. Some computational markets are designed specifically to enable allocations of goods that matter to agents but which are not generally traded in spontaneous (undesigned) markets (see, e.g., Ledyard and Szakaly (1994)). The issue of which goods to transact is central to the interest in combinatorial mechanisms, which we discuss below in Section 3.2.2.

---

[3] A Nash equilibrium is one in which each agent is playing a strategy that is a best response to the strategies of the others: that is, all strategies are mutual best responses. Bayes-Nash equilibrium means that when information is incomplete, players update their beliefs as new information arrives in the game according to Bayes' Rule, and then play Nash strategies with respect to their expectations.

2.2.2. Designing market mechanisms

An important issue for automated market designers is to decide which of the several market mechanism features to design, and which to leave unspecified. Recall from Figure 2 that market transactions require mechanisms for mediating the functions of connecting, dealing and exchanging. Much of the market mechanism literature focuses on the dealing function: the determination of terms of trade and the assignment of allocations. Even when there is attention to mechanisms for the other functions, the most common approach is to define for each function as a separate entity; thus in Section 3 we discuss separately design for each. However, ignoring interactions between the mechanisms may result in inefficiencies and failures. We expect that as automated market design matures we will see increasing attention to mechanisms that integrate more of these several necessary functions.

Recall also (see Figure 2) that a marketplace system operates in the context of a problem environment, consisting of technological and institutional constraints. Other institutions are features of the environment that restrict the set of possible mechanism designs. In this chapter we treat other institutions and technology as given, and immutable by the designer; e.g., laws, common languages, government structures, CPU capabilities. The institutions restrict feasible mechanisms to some space, Γ. The design problem is to configure a feasible mechanism $\gamma \in \Gamma$—that is, to define a set of goods over which agents can deal, rules specifying permissible actions, and rules mapping actions to allocations—that implements the constrained social choice function $f(\vec{\theta}) \in F$. Designers of computational markets thus need to either implicitly or explicitly make assumptions about laws, languages and other social institutions necessary to support transactions.

2.2.3. Designing agents

We defined agents by their information, preferences and decision rules. Each raises important design considerations. For example, to predict the performance of a particular mechanism the designer must make assumptions about the decision rule the agents will follow when interacting with the mechanism, which in turn depends on assumptions about agent information and preferences. When building automated agents themselves, the designer must deal with information acquisition, storage and processing problems (for example, to compute Bayesian updates or other predictions of relevant events). Designers must endow agents with feasible algorithms to implement their decision rules, which is no small matter in some settings. For example, in many market mechanisms—such as the ubiquitous multiple simultaneous ascending auctions—it is generally computationally infeasible to determine Bayes-Nash strategies. We discuss this problem and a method for analyzing agent strategies for intractable mechanisms in Section 5.

2.3. Possibilities and impossibilities

It is often difficult in complex problem environments to find a mechanism that implements the desired objective while satisfying even a few, seemingly reasonable constraints on the social choice functions that it implements. Indeed, in very general classes of problems, no such mechanisms of any sort exist. A considerable body of design theory characterized the space of social choice functions that are possible; this literature provides crucial guidance for the design of computational markets.

For example, suppose the marketplace designer wants a system that will satisfy the following rather weak requirements (we use $f_i(\vec{\theta})$ to denote the subset of allocation $f(\vec{\theta})$ received by agent i):

1. *Ex-post efficiency* (Pareto optimality): For no profile $\vec{\theta} = \{\theta_1, \ldots, \theta_N\} \in \Theta_1 \times \cdots \times \Theta_N$ is there an $\vec{x} \in X$ such that $u_i(x_i, \theta_i) \geq u_i(f_i(\vec{\theta}), \theta_i)$ for all i, and $u_i(x_i, \theta_i) > u_i(f_i(\vec{\theta}), \theta_i)$ for some i. That is, there is no alternative outcome in which at least one agent would be better off, and no agent would be worse off.

2. *Ex-interim participatory efficiency* (individual rationality): Suppose agent i begins with an endowment of goods, $\omega_i \in \Omega_i$, which it keeps if it refrains from participating in the mechanism. Then $u_i(f_i(\vec{\theta}), \theta_i) \geq u_i(\omega_i, \theta_i)$ for every i. That is, agents must be willing to voluntarily participate given the rules of the mechanism and their private knowledge about their own situation (before the final allocation is revealed).

3. *No subsidies*: The mechanism does not require any external injection of resources (e.g., payments to agents) that are not obtainable through the allocation of endowments $\Omega_1 \times \cdots \times \Omega_N \to X$.

Myerson and Satterthwaite (1983) showed that in general for a bilateral exchange problem there is *no* mechanism that satisfies (1)–(3) (if agents are assumed to use a Bayes-Nash strategy as their decision rule).[4]

Given this strong impossibility result, designers must choose ways in which to relax the design requirements. Three typical approaches are to (1) assume (or impose if under designer control) agent preferences that are more tightly restricted in the space of rational preferences; (2) assume or impose that agent decision rules are restricted more narrowly; or (3) relax some of the social choice constraints on an acceptable mechanism.

Two of the more important constructive results are the Vickrey-Clarke-Groves (VCG) family of social efficiency maximizing mechanisms and the Maskin-Riley revenue maximizing mechanism. In VCG (discussed in more detail in Section 3.2.2, below), agent preferences are restricted to those that can be expressed as quasilinear utility functions, and the "no subsidies" constraint is abandoned. The Maskin and Riley (1989) mechanism limits the space of goods, and replaces ex-post efficiency with revenue maximization (that is, the social choice function depends on the preferences of only one agent, the seller).

---

[4] A bit more precisely, the result holds for at least bilateral trade between agents each of whom is autonomous and self-interested, has private information about its own value, satisfies Bayes-Nash rationality, and for whom the support for those valuations overlap.

3. Automating market mechanisms

We organize our review on the design of computational market mechanisms to follow the three stages in our diagram of the canonical transaction problem: discovery, negotiation and execution (see Figure 1).

We focus primarily on computational mechanisms for *negotiation*, or making the deal, which is the second of the three steps. This focus largely reflects the bias in the economics field, which is most relevant for the audience of this book. However, we think it is important to recognize the plethora of ancillary services that must also be provided to support trading. Each is potentially subject to automation as well. As agent-based computational systems mature, we hope to see increasing attention to the design of mechanisms for connecting and exchanging. These are relatively open-ended problems, with services often provided by third parties outside the scope of a particular marketplace, as well as within the marketplace itself.

In the first subsection we provide a brief overview of some discovery facilities to illustrate some of the opportunities provided by the online medium, as well as requirements for operating a successful marketplace. In the second and longest subsection we discuss in some detail research on the design of computational mechanisms for deal negotiation (the "market" to many, though we use the term more expansively to describe all three functions). In the third subsection we survey briefly a few systems to facilitate transaction execution. The need for additional attention to discovery and execution as problems of market design should become evident.

3.1. *Connecting: discovery services*

At a bare minimum, marketplaces must support discovery to the extent of enabling users to navigate the opportunities available at a site. More powerful discovery services might include electronic catalogs, keyword-based or hierarchical search facilities, and the like. The world-wide web precipitated a resurgence in the application of information retrieval techniques [Belew (2000)], especially those based on keyword queries over large textual corpora.

Going beyond generic search, industry groups proposed a variety of standards for describing and accessing goods and services across organizations. Examples include languages extending XML with commerce-specific constructs [Hofreiter et al. (2002)], and protocols and registration infrastructure supporting web services [Curbera et al. (2002)]. Some recent proposals suggested using *semantic web* [Berners-Lee et al. (2001)] techniques to provide matchmaking services based on inference over richer representations of goods and services offered and demanded [Di Noia et al. (2004), Li and Horrocks (2004)].

The task of discovering commerce opportunities inspired several innovative approaches that go beyond matching of descriptions to gather and disseminate information relevant to comparing and evaluating commerce opportunities. Here we merely enumerate some of the important service categories:

3.1.1. Recommendation

[Resnick and Varian (1997), Schafer et al. (2001)]. Automatic recommender systems suggest commerce opportunities (typically products and services to consumers) based on prior user actions and a model of user preferences. Often this model is derived from cross-similarities among activity profiles across a collection of users, in which case it is termed *collaborative filtering* [Resnick et al., 1994; Hill et al., 1995; Riedl and Konstan, 2002]. A familiar example of collaborative filtering is Amazon.com's "customers who bought" feature.

3.1.2. Reputation

When unfamiliar parties consider a transaction with each other, third-party information bearing on their reliability can be instrumental in establishing sufficient trust to proceed. In particular, for person-to-person marketplaces, the majority of exchanges represent one-time interactions between a particular buyer and seller.

Reputation systems [Dellarocas (2003), Resnick et al. (2002)] fill this need by aggregating and disseminating subjective reports on transaction results across a trading community. One of the most prominent examples of a reputation system is eBay's "Feedback Forum" [Cohen (2002), Resnick and Zeckhauser (2002)], which some credit significantly for eBay's ability to achieve a critical-mass network of traders.

3.1.3. Comparison shopping

The ability to obtain deal information from a particular marketplaces suggests an opportunity to collect and compare offerings across multiple marketplaces. The emergence on the web of *price comparison services* followed soon on the heels of the proliferation of searchable retail web sites. One early example was BargainFinder [Krulwich (1996)], which compared prices for music CDs available across nine retail web sites. The University of Washington ShopBot [Doorenbos et al. (1997)] demonstrated the ability to automatically learn how to search various sites, exploiting known information about products and regularity of retail site organization. Subsequent research systems emphasized issues such as adaptivity to user preferences [Menczer et al. (2002)]. Today's shopping engines employ direct data feeds from product vendors, and provide standard interfaces with typically price-based product rankings.

3.1.4. Auction aggregation

The usefulness of comparison shopping for fixed-price offerings suggested that similar techniques might be applicable to auction sites. Such information services might be even more valuable in a dynamically priced setting, as there is typically greater inherent uncertainty about the prevailing terms. The problem is also more challenging, however, as auction listings are often idiosyncratic, thus making it difficult to recognize all correspondences. Nevertheless, several auction aggregation services (BidFind, Auc-tionRover, and others) launched in the late 1990s. Concentration in the online auction industry and resistance from auction sites has combined with the difficulty of delivering reliable information to limit the usefulness of such services, however, and relatively few are operating today.

3.2. Dealing: negotiation mechanisms

Negotiations are the major component of many computational market institutions (see Figure 2), and probably the component that received the most research attention. We use the word "negotiation" to refer to any process through which potential traders come to agreement on the terms of a deal. This includes a range of practices, from two agents haggling over price in a bazaar to a standard retail transaction in which the selling agent posts a fixed price and the buying agent says either "yes" or "no".

Computational negotiation mechanisms often involve a mediator: an entity that collects offer messages from the potential traders, and facilitates the mapping of those messages into an outcome. Well-known non-computational examples include an auctioneer and a market maker on a stock exchange floor. Auction web sites such as eBay are the best known examples of mediation in computational markets. In general a mediator may have a stake in the outcome (e.g., as party to transactions, or through commissions), in which case it also plays the role of an agent. However, to sharpen the distinction we maintain a strict separation between the agent and mediator roles, modeling the latter as following a fixed policy determined by the mechanism designer. For example, an eBay auction is mediated by the process that receives and validates bids, following the specified eBay rules for showing the current high bid, and determining the final winner and price.

In this section we discuss research on the design of mediated computational negotiation mechanisms. We start with a review of designs (and some implementations) for a smorgåsbord of domain-specific applications, ranging from computer file systems to energy markets to belief aggregation. We describe the main goals, assumptions and some results, without attempting to be comprehensive or exhaustive. We selected applications areas because they are significant in the historical development of thought in this area, or because they received intensive research attention in recent years.

We then turn to the large body of recent work that focuses on mostly technical questions arising from the design of an important class of computational markets: combinatorial mechanisms. We give extra attention to this particular area of the market design theory literature because it emerged from important real market design applications (most notably public spectrum auctions), it attracted the attention of many top researchers in both economics and computer science, and it represents an important area at the current leading edge of research. Further, many of the problems that arise in other settings are similar to those in combinatorial markets, so it is a good representative for other bodies of literature we have insufficient space to review.

3.2.1. Smart markets for domain-specific applications

There are many computational markets in use. Most research, with some exceptions, concerned designs that have not (yet) been implemented. One important exception has been a recent surge in matching markets for solving various social problems. The best known is the medical resident matching market in the U.S. [Roth and Peranson (1999)]. Related field work is underway, though not yet complete, for markets to match pairs of potential kidney donors [Roth et al. (2005)] and to match students to public schools [Abdulkadiroglu et al. (2005)]. More often, due to the high cost of implementing test markets, empirical research to evaluate performance is carried out through human subject laboratory experiments on stylized instances of the designs, or through numerical computer simulations.

In the remainder of this section we discuss a number of computational negotiation mechanisms—only some of which have been implemented in the field—designed for specific domains. We call these "smart markets", following Vernon Smith [McCabe et al. (1991)], because nearly all of these mechanisms involve a nontrivial computation on submitted offer messages to determine the outcome. Thus, we do not discuss the negotiation mechanisms that underlie markets such as eBay, because they are simple enough to not require any special computational capabilities. Indeed, such negotiation mechanisms are notable for mimicking non-computational auctions and other market forms that have been common for centuries.[5] Instead, we focus on negotiation mechanisms that for the most part are infeasible to operate without computer automation.

3.2.1.1. Allocating computational and communication network resources

Given that computer scientists directly confront allocation problems involving computational resources (e.g., sharing bandwidth, CPU cycles, file space), it is perhaps unsurprising that much research in computational market mechanisms has targeted such problems. This reflexive phenomenon has been important for development of the research community. Over time, a number gravitated towards principles from economics: the discipline most focused on the analysis of resource allocation questions. More or less contemporaneously, economists interested in computationally-intensive mechanisms began picking up ideas from computational science. Mechanism design for network and computational resources became an early meeting ground for economists and computer scientists, and much of the research began to exhibit cross-disciplinary approaches, often supported by cross-disciplinary collaboration. These early efforts resulted in important learning about the interaction between incentives theory and computational method that informed much of the more recent negotiation design research in other domains.

Several computer scientists in the 1980s focused on the possibility of applying market-mediated transactions to allocate computational resources.[6] These projects drew

---

[5] Other features of eBay and similar online auctions, such as search facilities and reputation management, *do* make innovative use of computational and communication technology.

[6] Ironically, an early market for time-sharing computer resources was implemented at Harvard without computational support, with bids and schedules posted by hand on a bulletin board [Sutherland (1968)].

attention to the problem of defining the goods over which a computational market negotiates. There are many levels of abstraction and aggregation at which computing resources and services could be specified; to create an automated market it is necessary to explicitly specify the set of goods. Among these early studies were investigations of the problems of specifying markets for file space [Kurose and Simha (1989)], communications channels [Kurose and Simha (1986)], and CPU loads [Ferguson et al. (1988)].

In a novel approach to allocating scarce computing resources, Brewer (1999) proposes a "computation procuring clock auction" which addresses the challenge at the level of a market for problem solutions, rather than a market for problem-solving resources. In Brewer's mechanism a mediator poses a computationally costly problem and agents offer approximate solutions. Thus, the computational market effectively creates a decentralized "computer" out of the participating agents. At any instant the market displays the current best solution to the problem of interest. Agents can then submit improved solutions; they are paid some fraction of the improvement in the objective function. The auction ends when a defined interval passes without new solution submissions. Brewer obtained positive results in human subject experiments, using a complex train schedule from another smart market as the problem to be solved.

The academic research Internet rapidly grew and made the transition to the commercial Internet in the early 1990s. For several years, usage (traffic) doubled approximately annually, outstripping (physical and technical) increases in the network. Congestion became a significant problem, and engineers were concerned that with continued growth the Internet would collapse. From these conditions emerged a quite large literature on designing computational markets for allocating bandwidth. The early work focused on characterizing the economics of bandwidth congestion and the potential benefits from a designed market [Cocchi et al. (1993), Shenker (1994), MacKie-Mason and Varian (1994a, 1995a)]. Congestion is an externality: that is, a given user putting a load on the network does not directly bear the cost of additional congestion experienced by others. Thus in general the allocation of bandwidth resources by a market will be inefficient unless the market is specifically designed to internalize the congestion externality.

Internet traffic is transported using packet-switching; by contrast, voice networks switch circuits. MacKie-Mason and Varian (1994a, 1995b, 1996) explored the implications of the Internet's architecture for good market design, and proposed a mechanism designed specifically for packet networks that would allocate congested bandwidth to packets. Their mechanism charges a positive price for packets when there is congestion (and zero otherwise), respects agents' autonomy and private information, and obtains an efficient allocation despite the congestion externality. This mechanism is a smart market that necessarily depends on a high degree of automation to process agent messages, determine the allocation, and implement the allocation. This computational market is a Generalized Vickrey Auction [MacKie-Mason and Varian (1994b)], which is a feasible instance of a Vickrey-Clark-Groves (VCG) mechanism designed specifically to handle externalities. This is the first proposal for a VCG mechanism we have found for computational markets; the later literature on combinatorial markets extensively explores VCG mechanisms, as we discuss below.

Other mechanisms proposed for congestion priority allocation include [Cocchi et al. (1993), Gupta et al. (1996), Korilis et al. (1995)]. These and the Generalized Vickrey Auction have various difficulties with the matching of the domain of allocations offered in the market to the domain of agent preferences. Some proposed mechanisms are specific to allocating packets, but generally users have preferences defined over sessions or flows with many (sometimes many thousand) packets. Further, all of these proposals were for static allocation markets, but user preferences generally encompass schedule and other time dependencies.

Well over one hundred papers were published about computational markets for network bandwidth in the ensuing decade. One important topic addressed early was the design of markets to allocate multiple qualities of service (rather than merely congestion priority); see, e.g., [Cocchi et al. (1991), Shenker (1995), MacKie-Mason et al. (1996b)]. Mechanisms were designed for networks with virtual circuits [MacKie-Mason et al. (1996a), Thomas et al. (2002), Kelly et al. (1998)].[7] Others developed computational mechanisms for cost-sharing network services that generate joint costs, such as multi-casting [Moulin and Shenker (2001), Feigenbaum et al. (2001)]. Chen (2003) tested some of these mechanisms with human subjects. Some work addressed additional problems that arise in markets for network services that support mobile users [Mullen and Breese (1998)]. Recent work in "distributed algorithmic mechanism design" obtains results for a mechanism to assign interdomain routing that is constrained to be backwards compatible with existing Internet communication protocols [Feigenbaum et al. (2005)].

Recently there has been renewed interest in computational markets for other computational resources. In particular, in the late 1990s several authors explored markets for CPU resources. This research responded to the observation that most CPU cycles available from desktop computers and workstations are unused. For a price, computer owners might be willing to let others run programs on their machines. Researchers explored market designs for CPU markets on networks of workstations [Amir et al. (2000), Gagliano et al. (1995), Waldspurger et al. (1992)], as well as the broader Internet [Amir et al. (1998), Regev and Nisan (1998)]. Recent work introduced market models for peer-to-peer [Gupta and Somani (2004), Cox and Noble (2003)] and grid computing [Wolski et al. (2001)].

The other significant strand of computational market design for computational resources focused on providing file system services. Specific applications include markets for distributed databases [Stonebraker et al. (1996)]; Web servers and web caching [Karaul et al. (1998), Kelly et al. (1999, 2006)]; and data replication [Anastadiadi et al. (1998)].

---

[7] Virtual circuits are a blend of packet- and circuit-switching technology of which asynchronous transfer mode (ATM) is the best known example.

3.2.1.2. Energy markets Computational mechanisms have been employed for electric generation in England, California, France, New England, and other locations. In an important study, given the paucity of empirical evaluations of implemented markets, Wolfram (1998) studies the behavior of (non-automated) bidders in the automated daily generating capacity auction in England. This is a multi-unit uniform-price mechanism; Wolfram finds that bidders strategically manipulate their bids in accordance with theoretical predictions about this mechanism design, resulting in less than optimal social efficiency. Cameron and Cramton (1999) analyze some of the institutional details of market implementations in California, and their implication for efficiency. Nicolaisen et al. (2001) develop a simulation model of electricity markets, relating efficiency and market power to mechanism microstructure. Ygge and Akkermans (1996) design a computational market mechanism for power load management, where agents representing individual devices present demands, responding competitively to price changes. See Marks (2006) for an extended discussion of agent-based simulation models applied to energy markets.

A joint market for natural gas supplies and transportation was designed and evaluated with human subject experiments by McCabe et al. (1989). The market calls for sealed, one-shot bids. Wholesale buyers and wellhead producers submit location-specific offers, and pipeline owners submit link-specific capacity offers. The smart market solves a linear programming problem for the network, sets uniform prices and assigns a consistent allocation of gas and transport that maximizes social surplus (given the constraints of the market design). In experiments the market achieved 90% or higher efficiency, and marginal bids were approximately truthful (thus fulfilling a price discovery role). However, inframarginal bids were substantially below truth values, and the authors point out that the theoretical literature predicts an equilibrium for this market that is not truth-revealing and thus is less than fully efficient.

3.2.1.3. Scheduling Resource allocation with time contingencies is known as a *scheduling* problem. There is a huge research literature on the centralized solution of scheduling problems. A simple keyword search yields over 1500 references, covering many varieties of scheduling problems distinguished by constraints, objectives, and information available. Recently a few authors have started to develop market solutions to scheduling problems, addressing the decentralized structure of many scheduling environments.

In traditional scheduling problems, agents submit their bids for time-indexed resources in advance, the mediator applies the mechanism allocation function, and the schedule is announced, then implemented [Nisan and Ronen (2001)]. Time dependencies almost always lead to complementarities in preferences; Wellman et al. (2001a) analytically compare three designs along a spectrum of matching the domain of allocations to the domain of preferences (separate markets, restricted package markets, and a fully combinatorial VCG mechanism). Train scheduling is one application for which specific markets have been designed and tested (with human subject experiments) [Brewer and Plott (1996, 2002)].

Another interesting category for computational markets contains *online* scheduling problems: the inputs arrive sequentially, and allocations are made dynamically, before all of the inputs are known. At any given moment there is a set of jobs that want to use the resource. One difference from offline scheduling is that some or all of the resource may already be in use, facing the mediator with a decision whether to pre-empt a running task. Another difference is that new bids for service may arrive in the future, creating an option cost of committing current resources to current job requests.

Online scheduling problems highlight a problem caused by uncertainty. The economic objective in an online problem usually involves some sort of expected value maximization. In deterministic problems, it is relatively straightforward to evaluate the performance of a particular allocation rule given the agents' (static) private information. With uncertainty, the outcome also depends on the future evolution of these state variables. Some of these stochastic processes themselves may be endogenous to the problem: for example, the arrival of new requests may depend on the current allocation decisions by the mediator. This only complicates what is already typically an intractable (NP-hard) optimization problem.

Due to the complexity, there are few results on markets that maximize expected value for online scheduling problems. The smart markets proposed typically implement heuristic allocation rules, for instance pre-empting a currently running job if a new request has an estimated expected value greater than some threshold. Two recent contributions provide some hope for traditional mechanism designs (that maximize a social objective function) in online scheduling problems. Friedman and Parkes (2003) define a class of problems for which a "delayed Vickrey-Clarke-Groves mechanism" has a dominant strategy equilibrium. Parkes and Singh (2003) show that an online mechanism design problem can be formulated and solved as a Markov Decision Process (MDP) problem, and they define a mechanism in which there is an approximately efficient (though computationally intractable) Bayes-Nash equilibrium.

Most of the online scheduling literature has avoided the complexity problems by focusing on minimax optimization, that is, reaching lower bounds for worst case performance. Two teams established that the best ratio achievable for worst case online scheduling performance (in centralized (non-strategic) problems) relative to full-information (offline) scheduling is $(1 + \sqrt{k})^2$, where k is the maximum ratio between the value per time unit of any two jobs [Baruah et al., 1992; Koren and Shasha, 1995]. These authors also provide algorithms that reach these bounds. Two recent approaches construct market solutions for strategic agents. In one the worst case ratio is increased to only $((1 + \sqrt{k})^2 + 1)$ [Porter (2004)]; the other addresses a somewhat different question, but also provides constructive results [Hajiaghayi et al. (2004)].

3.2.1.4. Belief discovery and aggregation   One of the benefits of market allocations is the discovery of value information. Of particular interest, markets for securities whose value depends on the future realization of a random variable will aggregate beliefs about the outcome, and thus provide a predictor. For example, it has long been known that well-functioning financial markets provide excellent predictors of the underlying asset values [Forsythe and Lundholm (1990), Plott and Sunder (1988)]. Forsythe et al. (1992) implemented and studied the long-running Iowa Electronic Market, in which agents bid for securities that pay off on the results of political events (e.g., presidential primaries) and other well-defined events such as corporate earnings announcements. This market has routinely forecast political outcomes more accurately than professional polling organizations.

Standard financial markets introduce independent auctions for each security, which presents scaling problems when there are a large number of uncertain propositions. Pennock and Wellman (2000) establish conditions under which probabilistic dependence structure can or cannot reduce the number of securities needed for an operationally complete market. Hanson (2003) addresses the problem by defining a hybrid between pure markets and the evaluation methods sometimes used to score probability assessors. His *market scoring rules* exhibit properties of a market when there exists sufficient activity, reverting to the properties of scoring rules in cases of low liquidity. This market was implemented as a DARPA experiment to aggregate public information relevant to national security concerns [Polk et al. (2003)], but days before trading began it was halted due to political uproar. Inspired by market scoring rules, Pennock (2004) introduced a dynamic pari-mutuel market for information aggregation that exhibits guaranteed liquidity, no risk to the mediator, and continuous updating of information.

3.2.2. Combinatorial markets

3.2.2.1. Problems with complementarities
Complementarities in demand are one of the more common causes, at least in the research literature, for the complexity that calls for smart markets. Goods are complements when acquisition of one increases demand for the other. In such a case, an agent's willingness to pay for one good will depend on whether or not the other can also be obtained. Many problems have this feature. For example, a take-off slot is worth little if the airline cannot also secure a landing slot. One hour of job-shop time may be worth zero if the firm cannot obtain the second hour necessary to complete the job. Fast delivery of the first packet in a file or email delivery is worth little if the remaining packets are delayed.

When goods are complements, a standard competitive price equilibrium may not exist [Bikhchandani and Mamer (1997)].[8] Even when one does, standard price-formation protocols are not guaranteed to find it [Scarf (1973)]. The fundamental problem is that when markets operate by separately forming prices for each good, agents cannot directly express information concerning value complementarities. Using the language from our conceptual framework, the domain of goods allocated by the mechanism does not match the domain of goods over which agents have preferences. For example, consider two

---

[8] A "standard" competitive price equilibrium is a vector of unit prices and corresponding feasible allocation such that each agent receives the quantities it desires taking these prices as given.

simultaneous sealed-bid auctions, one each for goods A and B. An agent who jointly values the goods at \$3, but who values each separately at \$0, might be willing to pay \$1 for good A if it can also purchase good B for no more than \$2, but not otherwise. However, in this auction market the agent can bid for A at \$1, but cannot ensure that if it wins it can simultaneously purchase B for \$2 or less.

A direct response to this mismatch between the agent's preference domain and mechanism's allocation domain is to design mechanisms that allocate a domain of goods better aligned with the domain of agent preferences. Many authors pursue this through the design of combinatorial mechanisms.

Aligning the scopes of mechanism allocations and agent preferences does not, it turns out, solve the design problem. There are two types of difficulties. First, as shown by Myerson and Satterthwaite (1983), for a surprisingly broad set of problems, it is impossible to design mechanisms that satisfy minimally desirable constraint sets. Then, though all else equal some combinatorial mechanisms may outperform non-combinatorial options, the problem remains of choosing among the possible second-best combinatorial mechanisms, which may be unbounded in number. The second difficulty is that all else is not equal: when we take into account the computational and other costs of combinatorial mechanisms, non-combinatorial mechanisms may better achieve the designer's objective. We shall discuss these two problems, and then some highlights of the literature that developed around them.

The first problem is that in a broad class of problems there exists no Bayesian-Nash mechanism that is efficient, individually rational, and budget balanced (see Section 2), but generally two of these can be satisfied at the expense of the third. Therefore, designers typically choose which property to sacrifice, and then try to limit loss on that dimension. As an alternative, a designer might give up one of these criteria but offer a mechanism that satisfies the other two plus some other desiderata. Thus, the intuition to design combinatorial mechanisms when agents exhibit complementary preferences is only the first search step through a vast design space: the quality of a design depends in a strong way on the designer's objective and desired constraints. There may be many or zero combinatorial mechanisms that are best.

The second problem is that mechanisms implemented for actual use inevitably incur transaction, computation, and cognitive costs that are often ignored in theoretical analyses. Computational costs include most directly the complexity of solving combinatorial optimization problems, but also the communication complexity of transmitting offers over many possible bundles. Cognitive costs include the burden of constructing offers over such bundles. Transaction costs include delays, coordination effort, and other costs of addressing multi-dimensional allocation domains in a single overarching mechanism. These implementation costs create standard economic tradeoffs (largely ignored by mechanism design economists) between the advantages of combinatorial mechanisms and their inherent diseconomies of scope. The potential benefits of aligning mechanism allocation domains with agent preference domains, along with the computational challenges, motivated a surge in mechanism design research by computer scientists [Dash et al. (2003), Nisan and Ronen (2001), Papadimitriou (2001), Rosenschein and Zlotkin

(1994)]. This line of work has begun to address some of these additional costs, however we are unaware of any work that presents a reasonably complete and explicit model of the overall design tradeoffs.

3.2.2.2. Combinatorial market design   A combinatorial auction specifies rules for permissible messages that express values over combinations of goods, and an allocation function over these messages that assigns combinations. See de Vries and Vohra (2003) for a good survey; Cramton et al. (2006) collect articles by many of the leading researchers on this topic, presenting an in-depth review of technical issues. We can only briefly introduce this huge literature. We highlight crucial issues for computational market design and open research questions.

Combinatorial mechanisms are motivated in part by the Arrow-Debreu theorem, which establishes that if markets span the complete domain of agent preferences, a competitive equilibrium exists and is efficient [Arrow (1964), Debreu (1954)]. However, a full set of Arrow-Debreu markets, including markets for all bundles of interest to agents, is not sufficient for two reasons. First, when preferences exhibit complementarities, the conditions of the Arrow-Debreu theorem are not met and a competitive equilibrium may not exist [Bikhchandani and Mamer (1997)]. Second, designers are often concerned with strategic (non-competitive) situations as well. The most important motivation for computational market design when agents are strategic is a result due to Vickrey, Clarke, and Groves: a direct revelation mechanism that guarantees an efficient, individually rational allocation [Vickrey (1961), Clarke (1971), Groves (1973)]. In a direct revelation mechanism, agents announce to the mediator their preferences over allocations; in the VCG family of mechanisms, the scope of allocations is the same as the scope of agent preferences. For our discussion of combinatorial mechanisms we focus on VCG-based mechanisms.[9]

Based on the number of papers solving implementation design problems for VCG mechanisms, it might appear that researchers view the VCG as an ideal form. In general, it is not. First, VCG does not overcome the Myerson and Satterthwaite (1983) impossibility result: a VCG mechanism that is guaranteed to be efficient and individually rational will not in general be budget balanced. Indeed, in bad cases, for N agents the VCG can require a subsidy on the order of $N - 1$ times the total surplus of the final allocation.[10] Second, although individual rationality and efficiency is a plausible

---

[9] VCG mechanisms maximize Marshallian social welfare, which is the unweighted sum of surpluses (value net of any payments) for all buying and selling agents, measured in some common unit such as dollars. Another common design goal is to maximize the seller's revenue. Most of the points we make about VCG mechanisms are qualitatively true for revenue-maximizing mechanisms as well, though of course the details are different. The literature on revenue maximizing mechanisms over complementary goods is much less developed than that for VCG mechanisms.

[10] Roughly speaking, the VCG pays to each agent the value of the surplus that the agent's value creates by its participation in the final allocation. Consider a problem in which the participation of all agents is necessary for any positive value to be created (a coordination, or joint production problem). In this case, if a total value of S is created, the VCG pays NS in total, of which only S is financed by the surplus created through the allocation.

set of minimally desirable criteria, other criteria may be desirable for some allocation problems. For example, VCG payments are typically "discriminatory": different agents likely make (or receive) different payments for the same allocation. In some settings social norms or other goals may impose a non-discriminatory constraint.[11] Third, there are substantial concerns about the computational feasibility of VCG mechanisms in moderately complex problems. The practical problems proved to be so numerous, and thus far, sufficiently intractable, that almost no VCGs are implemented in observed practice. We now discuss these feasibility concerns.

One computational design issue is the *winner determination* problem: how to compute the allocation function $g(S_1, S_2, \ldots, S_N)$ (see Section 2.2)? For a general combinatorial problem, the VCG computation requires $N - 1$ separate solutions of an NP-hard set-packing problem [Rothkopf et al. (1998)]. Known algorithms for NP-hard problems have worst-case exponential runtimes: the computational cost effectively doubles with each additional good.[12] One line of research focused on developing algorithms with good average-case performance on representative problem classes [Leyton-Brown (2003), Sandholm and Suri (2003)]. A second logical approach is to find an algorithm that is guaranteed to find an *approximate* solution to the VCG allocation in polynomial time. However, Nisan and Ronen (2000) demonstrate that approximate (non-optimal) but polynomial (computationally feasible) VCG-based mechanisms that are truthful have arbitrarily bad performance in the worst case. Yet a third approach is to impose sufficient restrictions on agent rationality (or permissible strategies) to enable mechanisms that implement the VCG outcomes exactly with feasible computations [Parkes and Ungar (2002)]. Another line of research studied problems in which there is a structure on the space of goods that provides sufficient simplification to make the winner determination problem tractable [Rothkopf et al. (1998), Wellman et al. (2001a)].

A symmetric problem is that of *preference elicitation*: extracting value information from agents without imposing an undue or infeasible burden. Given a fully combinatorial allocation space, agents must determine and express an exponential number of valuations. For example, with only 30 distinct goods, there are $2^{30} - 1$ (over a billion) possible bundles for which to bid.

A number of authors investigate the communication complexity of various resource allocation mechanisms. For a convex economy, the Walrasian mechanism is the unique individually rational mechanism that is informationally efficient (minimizes the dimensionality of the message space necessary to verify a Pareto efficient allocation) [Jordan

---

[11] Much has been written over the years about the social ethics of discriminatory prices. In practice they are common: for example, students generally pay less for movie tickets than do their professors. Nonetheless, non-discriminatory pricing is sometimes imposed, particularly for public projects. For example, in designing a computational market for the provision of evaluations, such as product reviews, Avery et al. (1999) require that the same action (timing of an evaluation) must be paid the same price.

[12] For example, the FCC simultaneously auctioned 1472 licenses in one 1996 auction. The total number of possible combinations to consider in a fully combinatorial allocation function would have been $2^{1472} - 1$.

(1982), Hurwicz (1960), Mount and Reiter (1974)].[13] Among other things, for an economy to be convex preferences must be sub-additive (which rules out complementarities between goods), and continuous (which rules out integer constraints), and thus many interesting problems cannot be treated as convex. Unfortunately, the results are somewhat negative for non-convex economies. Nisan and Segal (2006) show that any efficient mechanism must communicate at least as much information as a full revelation of one agent's preferences, which will in general be exponential when agents have preferences over combinations of goods. They further prove that even approximately efficient allocations are hard: To guarantee an improvement over the approximation represented by selling all of the items as a single bundle requires communication that is exponentially increasing in the number of goods. This is true in a worst-case analysis, and also in expectation for at least some probability distributions over agent valuations.

Although the preference elicitation problem is provably hard, a number of authors have worked on pragmatic approaches to making it manageable for some problems. For example, some researchers address this problem by designing iterative, or *progressive* combinatorial auctions [Ausubel and Milgrom (2002), Parkes (1999), Parkes and Ungar (2000), Wurman and Wellman (2000)], in which agents are expected to bid on each iteration only on bundles that appear best given the current information. Recently, some proposed methods based on explicit queries [Conen and Sandholm (2002)], where agents are asked their values for particular bundles based on the auction's defined query policy for its current state. There are a variety of related approaches to the elicitation problem [e.g., Faratin and de Walle (2002), Conen and Sandholm (2001), Parkes (2005)]. One is to develop bidding languages that are natural and concise for human agents [Boutilier and Hoos (2001)].

A different approach is to identify special problem classes that require less complete expressions of preferences. For example, Bikhchandani et al. (2002) focus on settings in which "agents are substitutes": the contribution to problem value of a group of agents is more than the sum of their individual contributions. In such cases, agents can describe their preference over a smaller number of bundles, and communication and computation are polynomial (requiring the solution of two linear programs). Another class of examples are problems in which valuations satisfy the gross substitutes property [Kelso and Crawford (1982)]: a Walrasian equilibrium exists [Gul and Stacchetti (1999)] and it can be found with polynomial communication [Nisan and Segal (2006)].[14]

Another pragmatic concern for VCG mechanisms (as well as many others) is their susceptibility to the often unenforceable assumption that agents do not collude. In our conceptual framework this assumption is represented by limiting communications to the links between agents and the mediator (see Figure 2). Specifying mechanism rules that

---

[13] A *Walrasian* mechanism is one that yields a competitive equilibrium; see footnote 8.

[14] Two goods are *gross substitutes* when the Marshallian demand for one increases as the price of the other increases. The Marshallian demand is the "ordinary" demand; that is, it reflects how a consumer's demand changes with price changes, without any income compensation to hold the consumer's level of overall utility constant. See, e.g., Mas-Colell et al. (1995).

forbid collusion does not necessarily prevent it. VCG mechanisms perform arbitrarily badly when agents can collude [Ausubel and Milgrom (2002)]. A related concern is their vulnerability to "false name" bids (one agent splitting package bids between multiple pseudonyms to change the allocation or associated payments) [Sakurai et al. (1999)].

Despite the known problems with combinatorial mechanisms, they have been tested in a number of laboratory experiments in which the space of goods was small enough for the computations to remain tractable. For example, Rassenti et al. (1982) developed a sealed-bid combinatorial auction to allocate airport runway time slots. Their specification of goods allowed for agents to express preferences over packages of multiple slots to accommodate complementarities (for example, needing a landing slot to combine with every take-off slot). They implemented an algorithm to determine the allocation that maximized system surplus, then awarded packages at prices guaranteed to be no more than the amounts bid. They tested this smart market negotiation mechanism in a laboratory setting with cash-motivated human subjects, where it obtained about 10% higher efficiency than a mechanism of independent auctions for each slot.

NASA funded a team of Caltech economists to study various computational market designs to allocate payload space, power, and other resources for commercial experiments in the space station program. Banks et al. (1989) report on several designs and human subject experimental tests of their performance. As in Rassenti et al. (1982), the designs were driven by the specification of the goods over which negotiations were defined. They addressed problems with multiple resources (space, power), uncertainties in demand and supply (for example, some shuttle launches are cancelled), unresponsive supply (no inventories and fixed capacities), and demand indivisibilities. They tested two smart market negotiation mechanisms: one an iterative approximation to a Vickrey-Clarke-Groves mechanism, and the second a simpler iterative package bidding process. Traditional markets averaged only 66% efficiency; the iterative VCG averaged 78%, and the package bidding mechanism averaged 81% efficiency.

Another Caltech experiment tested a combinatorial design for the FCC spectrum auctions [Bykowsky et al. (2000)]. The FCC did not use combinatorial markets for its spectrum auctions despite the well-known complementarities, due to concerns with computational costs and bidding strategy issues.[15]

Combinatorial mechanisms directly address the problem we have identified many times in this chapter: the performance of negotiation mechanisms will depend crucially on the quality of the match between the mechanism's domain of goods and the domain of agent preferences. To date few combinatorial mechanisms have been implemented, but the very active research on each of the design problems we identify offers hope that this approach to computational negotiation will become more usable in the future.

---

[15] We discuss the FCC auctions further in Section 4.3.2 below, when we address agent bidding strategies for simultaneous ascending auctions.

3.3. Exchanging: transaction services

Once a deal is negotiated, it remains for the parties to execute the agreed-upon exchange. Many online marketplaces support transaction services to some extent, recognizing that integrating "back-end" functions—such as logistics, fulfillment, and settlement—can reduce overall transaction costs and enhance the overall value of a marketplace [Woods (2002)].

A critical component of market-based exchange, of course, is *payment*, the actual transfer of money as part of an overall transaction. The online medium enables the automation of payment in new ways, and indeed, the 1990s saw the introduction of many novel *electronic payment mechanisms* [O'Mahony et al. (1997)], offering a variety of interesting features [MacKie-Mason and White (1997)], including many not available in conventional financial clearing systems. For example, some of the schemes supported anonymity [Chaum (1992)], micropayments [Manasse (1995)], or atomic exchange of digital goods with payment [Sirbu and Tygar (1995)].

As it turned out, none of the innovative electronic payment mechanisms really caught on. There are several plausible explanations [Crocker (1999)], including inconvenience of special-purpose software, network effects (i.e., the need to achieve a critical mass of buyers and sellers), the rise of advertising-supported Internet content, and decreases in credit-card processing fees. Nevertheless, some new payment services proved complementary with marketplace functions, and thrived. The most well-known example is PayPal, which became extremely popular among buyers and sellers in person-to-person auctions, who benefited greatly from simple third-party payment services. PayPal's rapid ascension was in large part due to an effective "viral marketing" launch strategy, in which one could send money to any individual, who would then be enticed to open an account [Jackson (2004)]. PayPal is still not economical for micropayments, however, and new schemes—most notably, Peppercoin [Micali and Rivest (2002)]—have emerged aiming to provide such services.

4. Automating market participants

Part of automating markets is automating the behavior of participants in those markets. Of course, computerized trading has been a reality almost as long as we have had computers. What is relatively new is the proliferation of electronic markets on networks, and their potential to dramatically expand the opportunities for automating trading functions in a broad variety of domains. Conversely, automating traders can shape the automation of markets, for example, by rendering feasible some market designs too complex for manual traders.

As in most realms of computerization, there is no sharp line between automated and non-automated trading. Virtually all trading in financial markets is mediated by computers at some stage of the process, and the same is true by definition for markets that themselves operate electronically. Consider the communication flow of the generic

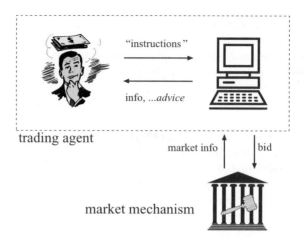

Figure 3. The trading agent interacts with a market mechanism by submitting bids in response to market information. The process can be automated to varying degrees, depending on the role of the computer in the process of translating instructions and market information.

trading system diagrammed in Figure 3. The human trader issues "instructions" to the computer, resulting in bids submitted to the market. The instructions may be direct, for example, "buy 100 shares XYZ at \$20", in which case the computer is merely serving a communication interface function, and the trading is essentially manual. To the extent instructions are indirect, such as "balance my portfolio", or "liquidate my holdings in sector S in an orderly manner", we would characterize the trading as automated to a correspondingly greater degree. Similarly, to the extent the computer processes the market information for presentation to the human—summarizing, identifying patterns, even recommending specific trading actions—we would have to credit the machine with a share of the overall decision process.

The upshot is that automated trading exists on a continuum, and it is futile to attempt a precise binary classification of human and computer trading activity. We merely observe that the computer's role is often significant, and growing over time in sophistication and complexity. Of course, the trading is ultimately on behalf of humans (or organizations operated by and for humans), and so the humans will continue to exert ultimate control and influence over their *trading agents*. As the machines prove increasingly worthy of trust in their competence to execute decreasingly direct instructions, it is inevitable that a significant fraction of trading activity will become fully automated for all practical purposes.

Recognizing that overall trading activity is the product of manual and automated components, we henceforth apply the term "trading agent" to the combined entity interacting with the market, enclosed by the dashed box in Figure 3.

The phenomenon of automated trading raises several interesting questions.

- How should trading agents behave? How can we design effective strategies for a range of environments? How can we construct agents capable of incorporating new information and objectives, and adapting to changing circumstances?
- How will automated traders change the character and behavior of markets? Will additional stabilization, security, or other safety-related mechanisms be required?
- How can we design markets to cater to or exploit the capabilities of automated trading agents?

In the sections below we address these questions, in the course of surveying some significant threads in trading agent research. Our focus is on works that study the behavior or potential of trading agents themselves, as opposed to efforts that use computational agents as a way to model human trading behavior. The latter is the domain of much research in agent-based computational economics, addressed in several other chapters of this handbook.

4.1. Program trading

As noted above, automation of trading in financial markets is a well-established practice. The term "program trading" (or "programmed trading") is sometimes applied generically to any initiation of trade activity based on procedural rules (typically implemented by computer programs), but more frequently refers to a particular form of trading based on *index arbitrage* [Brennan and Schwartz (1990)] or other standard portfolio trading strategies. Index-arbitrage programs monitor the price of index futures contracts (e.g., for the Standard & Poor's 500), as well as the basket of underlying securities, and trigger trades whenever the futures price deviates from the underlying price by some pre-specified threshold dependent on the interest rate. Academic interest in program trading focused on the effect of this activity on price volatility, including much investigation of its relation to the October 1987 stock market crash [Baldauf and Santoni (1991)].

The New York Stock Exchange (NYSE) requires its members to report trades involving fifteen or more stocks with aggregate value of a million dollars or more. This definition is designed to capture the common pattern of program trading for index or other derivative-based arbitrage, portfolio insurance, and other portfolio-based actions. According to NYSE, such trades account for a large fraction of overall volume: 51.2%, for a typical example, in the last week of January 2005. Of this, 11.4% was attributed to index arbitrage specifically.

It is of course possible to implement any systematic trading strategy in a computer program, and many such programs have been marketed to investors as "black-box" or "gray-box" trading systems (so-called because their specific trading rules are secret or only partially revealed). As the availability of financial market data via the Internet has increased, so have the offerings of software packages providing analysis and monitoring tools, some providing interfaces for user-specified trading rules. Whereas it is doubtful that retail investors can profit substantially through such means, major brokerages reportedly devoted significant resources to computational modeling and automated trading strategies for internal use by their trading units. For proprietary reasons, little is publicly known about the nature and extent of these computerized trading activities. Bass (1999) presents an unusually forthcoming story of the Prediction Company's efforts in automated trading, but even this account stops short of technical and strategic precision.

4.2. Market interfaces

Automated agents interact with electronic markets according to standardized interfaces. Program trading in financial markets is facilitated by ECNs (electronic crossing networks) such as Island and Instinet, which support specified network protocols for submitting stock orders. The Small Order Execution System provides an analogous standard interface to Nasdaq market makers.

Online marketplaces inherently provide a window to automated traders, as a side effect of supporting standard web protocols. For example, eBay cannot necessarily distinguish a bid submitted by a human user through a browser from one generated by a program constructing the same web posting. Users have taken advantage of this opportunity, for example by employing programs to submit bids at prespecified times, typically seconds before the scheduled auction close. This practice, called *sniping*, is quite common on eBay, and can be supported by several auction-theoretic arguments [Roth and Ockenfels (2002)]. Services such as eSnipe also provide rudimentary facilities to condition bids on auction events, such as the success or failure of related bids in specified auction groups.

Definition of a market interface is part of the overall task of market design. Bidding rules comprise a dimension of market design space, governing the language of allowable bids as well as the policy for admitting bids over time [Wurman et al. (2001)]. Choice of a bidding language often entails addressing rich tradeoffs, for example in the complexity of bidding or evaluating bids [Nisan (2000)]. In some cases, a designer might intentionally restrict bidding rules in order to simplify the interface implementation or to bias toward simple negotiation strategies [Cranor and Resnick (2000)].

To fully support automated trading, market interfaces would provide machine-readable specification of bidding rules, as well as other market policies. This would facilitate deployment and testing of mechanisms, promote transparency, and ultimately support automatic adaptation of trading strategies. Although sufficiently flexible and formal standards for specifying markets are not yet available, special-purpose languages for specifying auctions [Lochner and Wellman (2004)] and reasoning about negotiation protocols [Guerin and Pitt (2002)] constitute steps in this direction.

4.3. Agent strategies

How a trading agent should behave depends, of course, on the market mechanism and other agents in its environment. Studies of trading agent strategy typically focus on a particular environment; there have been few attempts thus far to distill general cross-cutting principles. In this section we examine research on strategies for two canonical market environments: individual continuous double auctions and collections of simultaneous auctions. In Section 4.4 we consider a more complex market game combining several different market mechanisms.

4.3.1. Continuous double auction strategies

One of the most basic trading scenarios is an abstract market based on the continuous double auction (CDA) mechanism [Friedman (1993)]. The CDA is a simple and well-studied auction institution, employed commonly in commodity and financial markets. The "double" in its name refers to the fact that both buyers and sellers submit bids, and it is "continuous" in the sense that the market clears instantaneously on receipt of compatible bids.[16]

The CDA has also been widely employed in experimental economic studies, and notably in an open research competition conducted at a Santa Fe Institute workshop in 1990 [Friedman and Rust (1993), Rust et al. (1994)]. The winning trader in this competition held back until most of the other agents revealed their valuations through bidding behavior, then "stole the deal" by sniping at an advantageous price. Agents employing more elaborate reasoning failed to make such sophistication pay off. This is consistent with observations that even extremely naive strategies—exhibiting what Gode and Sunder (1993) dubbed "zero intelligence" (ZI)—achieve virtually efficient outcomes in this environment. Such results suggested a strong limit on the potential returns to positive smarts.

Over the last fifteen years, CDA markets served as a basis for many further studies of artificial trading agents. The simplicity and familiarity of the abstract CDA framework presents some distinct advantages as the basis for trading agent research. These include ease of explanation and simulation, low barriers to entry, consensus understanding of market rules, predictability of behavior, opportunity to build on prior work (on design of both mechanism and agents), and analyzability of outcomes. Given the ubiquity of the CDA institution, there is even a potential to incorporate real-world market data of various kinds.

Cliff (1998) provides an extensive bibliography covering much of this work, including his own evolutionary studies of "ZI plus" agents. One particularly influential trading strategy was proposed by Gjerstad and Dickhaut (1998), later revised and termed the "heuristic belief learning" (HBL) model [Gjerstad (2004)]. An HBL agent maintains a belief state over acceptance of hypothetical buy or sell offers, constructed from historical observed frequencies. It then constructs optimal offers with respect to these beliefs and its underlying valuations. The timing of bid generation is stochastic, controlled by

---

[16] In the computer science literature "continuous" mechanisms are usually called "on-line"; we discussed some theoretical results for on-line scheduling market design in Section 3.2.1, above.

a *pace* parameter, which may depend on absolute time and the agent's current position. Gjerstad (2004) demonstrates that pace is a pivotal strategic variable, and that indeed there is surprisingly large potential advantage to strategic dynamic behavior despite the eventual convergence to competitive prices and allocations.

In extensive simulated trials, Tesauro and Das (2001) found that a modified version of HBL outperformed a range of other strategies, including ZI, ZI plus, and the sniping strategy that won the original Santa Fe tournament. The strategy also compared favorably with human traders [Das et al. (2001)].

Because CDAs or close variants are widely employed in financial markets, models from the finance literature that account for details of the trading mechanism, or *market microstructure* [Garman (1976)], are also highly relevant to trading agent strategy.[17] Much of this literature addresses the trading problem from a market maker's perspective, explaining price spreads and the potential for dealer profit by way of transaction costs and inventory management, information asymmetries, or strategic opportunities [O'Hara (1995)].

Availability of real-time market information has recently begun to enable higher-fidelity modeling of financial trading environments. The Penn Exchange Simulator [Kearns and Ortiz (2003)] merges bids from automated trading agents with actual limit-order streams, providing realistic volume and volatility patterns, whether or not these would emerge naturally from the artificial agent strategies. Competitions based on this simulator enabled comparison of a wide variety of CDA bidding policies [Sherstov and Stone (2004)], including some that may use information from the entire order book [Kearns and Ortiz (2003)].

4.3.2. Simultaneous ascending auction strategies

A *simultaneous ascending auction* (SAA) allocates a set of M related goods among N agents via separate English auctions for each good. Each auction may undergo multiple rounds of bidding. At any given time, the *bid price* on good m is β_m, defined to be the highest agent bid $\max_{1 \le j \le N} \{b_j^m\}$ received thus far, or zero if there have been no bids. To be admissible, a new bid must meet the bid price plus a bid increment (which we take to be one w.l.o.g.), $b_j^m \ge \beta_m + 1$. If an auction receives multiple admissible bids in a given round, it admits the highest (breaking ties arbitrarily). An auction is *quiescent* when a round passes with no new admissible bids.

The auctions proceed concurrently. When all are simultaneously quiescent, the auctions close and allocate their respective goods per the last admitted bids. Because no good is committed until all are, an agent's bidding strategy in one auction cannot be contingent on the outcome for another. Thus, an agent j desiring a bundle of goods inherently runs the risk—if it bids at all—that it will purchase some but not all goods

---

[17] Agent-based finance models, as discussed by Hommes (2006) and LeBaron (2006), are primarily directed at explaining aggregate behavior, but may also prove useful for strategic studies.

in the bundle. This is the well-known *exposure problem*, and arises whenever agents have complementarities among goods allocated through separate markets. The exposure problem is perhaps the pivotal strategic issue in SAAs.

As noted above, dealing with complementarities was a prime motivation for the development and exploration of combinatorial auctions in recent years. Although such mechanisms may provide an effective solution in many cases, there are often significant barriers to their application. Most significantly, conducting a combinatorial auction requires the existence of a competent authority to coordinate the allocation of interdependent resources, and incurs costs and delays associated with such coordination. It is a simple fact that today we see many markets operating separately, despite apparent strong complementarities for their respective goods. Whereas automation will very likely increase the prevalence of combinatorial markets, we expect that the issue of trading in separate dependent markets will remain for the foreseeable future.

Perhaps the most natural baseline for SAAs is a strategy called *straightforward bidding* (SB).[18] A straightforward bidder takes a vector of *perceived prices* for the goods as given, and bids those prices for the bundle of goods that would maximize the agent's surplus if it were to win all of its bids at those prices.

Let $v_j(X)$ denote the value to agent j of obtaining the set of goods X. Given that it obtains X at prices $\vec{p}$, the agent's *surplus* is its value less the amount paid, $\sigma(X, \vec{p}) = v_j(X) - \sum_{m \in X} p_m$. When agent j is winning the set of goods X_{-1} in the previous bidding round, we define the current perceived prices to be $\hat{p}_m = \beta_m$ for $m \in X_{-1}$, and $\hat{p}_m = \beta_m + 1$ otherwise. Then, under SB, agent j bids $b_j^m = \hat{p}_m$ for $m \in X^*$ such that $X^* = \arg\max_X \sigma(X, \vec{p})$.

The straightforward bidding strategy is quite simple, involving no anticipation of other agents' strategies. For the single-unit problem, such anticipation is unnecessary, as the agent would not wish to change its bid even after observing what the other agents did [Bikhchandani and Mamer (1997)]. This is called the *no regret* property [Hart and Mas-Colell (2000)], and means that from the agent's perspective, no bidding policy would have been a better response to the other agents' bids.

For a *single-unit value function*, the value of a set of goods is just that of its most valuable included singleton. When all agents have single-unit value, and value every good equally, the situation is equivalent to a problem in which all buyers have an inelastic demand for a single unit of a homogeneous commodity. For this problem, Peters and Severinov (2006) showed that straightforward bidding is a perfect Bayesian equilibrium. Up to a discretization error, the allocations from SAAs are efficient when agents follow straightforward bidding. It can also be shown [Bertsekas (1992), Wellman et al. (2001a)] that the final price vector will differ from the minimum unique equilibrium price by at most $\kappa \equiv \min(M, N)$. The value of the allocation, defined to be the sum of the bidder surpluses, will differ from the optimal by at most $\kappa(1 + \kappa)$.

---

[18] We adopt the terminology introduced by Milgrom (2000). The same strategy concept is also referred to as "myopic best response", or "myopically optimal", or even "myoptimal" [Kephart et al. (1998)].

Unfortunately, the very nice properties for straightforward bidding with single-unit value do not carry over to multiple-unit problems. Indeed, the resulting price vector can differ from the minimum equilibrium price vector, and the allocation value can differ from the optimal, by arbitrarily large amounts [Wellman et al. (2001a)]. However, whereas the case against SB is quite clear, auction theory [Krishna (2002)] to date has relatively little to say about how one *should* bid in simultaneous markets with complementarities. In fact, determining an optimal strategy even when it is known that other agents are playing SB turns out to be an unsolved and surprisingly difficult problem, sensitive to the smallest details of preference distributions [Reeves et al. (2005)].

Our gap in knowledge about SAA strategy is especially striking given the ubiquity of simultaneous auctions in economically significant settings. Indeed, markets for interdependent goods operating simultaneously and independently represents the normal or default state of affairs. Even for some markets that are expressly designed, most famously the US FCC spectrum auctions starting in the mid-1990s [McAfee and McMillan (1996)], a variant of the SAA is deliberately adopted, despite awareness of strategic complications [Milgrom (2000)]. Simulation studies of scenarios based on the FCC auctions shed light on some strategic issues [Csirik et al. (2001)], as have accounts of some of the strategists involved [Cramton (1995), Weber (1997)], but the general game is still too complex to admit definitive strategic recommendations.

In our own work, we explored SAA strategies in the context of a simple market-based scheduling scenario [MacKie-Mason et al. (2004), Reeves et al. (2005)]. In the scheduling game, agents need to complete a job requiring a specified duration of resource, by acquiring the resource over individual time slots. The value for completing a job depends on when it is finished. Complementarities arise whenever jobs require more than a single time slot.

We investigated a family of possible strategies for this game, employing an empirical methodology discussed in some detail in Section 5 below. Our basic approach was to start with SB as a baseline, and evaluate parametric variations through extensive simulation and analysis. In particular, we considered two extensions of SB designed to mitigate the exposure problem. First, we modify SB to account for sunk costs to some degree, recognizing that goods an agent is already winning will pose no marginal costs if other agents do not submit additional bids. The strategy is implemented in terms of a "sunk awareness" parameter ranging over [0,1], with zero treating all winning bids as sunk costs and one corresponding to unmodified SB. Perhaps it should not be surprising that the equilibrium settings of this parameter are quite sensitive to the distribution of agent job characteristics (length, deadline values). We identified qualitatively distinct equilibria corresponding to different job distributions.

The second alternative we considered attempts to explicitly predict the closing prices for each slot, and selects bundles based on these price predictions [MacKie-Mason et al. (2004)]. Our overall finding is that this approach is quite effective compared to SB or employing a global sunk-awareness parameter. Performance, of course, depends on the prediction vector employed by the agent, as well as the distribution of job characteristics. Since prices are observable, however, it is perhaps plausible to glean the prediction vectors directly from experience (real or simulated). The structure of the prediction methods surviving in equilibrium appear relatively robust to changing the agent job distributions.

4.4. Case study: trading agent competition

Inspired by success of Santa Fe double auction tournament and other research competitions, a community of trading-agent researchers established an annual competition event designed to focus effort on a common problem, thus enabling researchers to compare techniques and build on each others' ideas [Wellman et al. (2001b)]. Working on a shared problem coordinates attention on particular issues (among the many of interest in the trading domain), and facilitates communication of methods and results by fixing a set of assumptions and other environment settings.

The multi-year Trading Agent Competition (TAC) series offers the further prospect of learning from shared experience over time. As a case study of trading agent research, we examine the experience of the first four years of TAC, and some of the research results spawned from that activity. The first TAC was held in 2000, followed by annual sequels, each attracting approximately twenty participant teams. In 2003, TAC introduced a second game, in the domain of supply chain management [Arunachalam and Sadeh (2005)], which also produced significant interest and research activity. In this case study we focus on the original travel-shopping market game.

4.4.1. TAC travel-shopping rules

The TAC travel-shopping market game presents a travel-shopping task, where traders assemble flights, hotels, and entertainment into trips for a set of eight probabilistically generated clients. Clients are described by their preferred arrival and departure days, the premium they are willing to pay to stay at the nicer hotel, and their respective values for three different types of entertainment events. The agents' objective is to maximize the value of trips for their clients, net of expenditures in the markets for travel goods. The three categories of goods are exchanged through distinct market mechanisms.

Flights. A feasible trip includes round-trip air, which consists of an inflight day i and outflight day j, $1 \leq i < j \leq 5$. Flights in and out each day are sold independently, at prices determined by a stochastic process. The initial price for each flight is distributed uniformly, following a random walk thereafter with an increasingly upward bias.

Hotels. Feasible trips must also include a room in one of the two hotels for each night of the client's stay. There are 16 rooms available in each hotel each night, and these are sold through ascending 16th-price auctions. Agents submit bids for various quantities, specifying the price offered for each additional unit. Each minute, the hotel auctions issue *quotes*, indicating the 16th- (*ASK*) and 17th-highest (*BID*) prices among the currently active unit offers. To ensure ascending prices, hotel bidders are subject to a "beat-the-quote" rule [Wurman et al. (2001)], requiring that any new bid offer to purchase at least one unit at a price of $ASK + 1$, and at least as many units at $ASK + 1$ as the agent was previously winning at *ASK*. Also each minute, starting at minute four, one of the hotel auctions is selected at random to close, with the others remaining active and open for bids. When the auction closes, the units are allocated to the 16 highest offers, with all bidders paying the price of the lowest winning offer.

Entertainment. Agents receive an initial random allocation of entertainment tickets (indexed by type and day), which they may allocate to their own clients or sell to other agents through CDAs. The entertainment auctions issue *BID* and *ASK* quotes representing the highest outstanding buy and lowest sell offer, respectively, and remain open for buying and selling throughout the 12-minute game duration.

A feasible client trip is defined by inflight and outflight days, rooms in the same hotel for all nights in the interim, and a set of entertainment tickets. The client's utility for this trip is given by a constant base value, minus penalties for deviating from preferred dates, plus (if applicable) bonuses for staying in the premium hotel and attending entertainment. At the end of a game instance, the TAC server calculates the optimal allocation of trips to clients for each agent, given final holdings of flights, hotels, and entertainment. The agent's game score is its total client trip utility, minus net expenditures in the TAC auctions.

4.4.2. TAC experience

As we can see, the TAC travel-shopping game scenario presents a challenging trading problem, involving multiple interdependent goods allocated over time, through three distinct market mechanisms. Flights are sold through take-it-or-leave-it offers, hotels through multiunit SAAs (with stochastic termination), and entertainment through CDAs. Each of these poses open strategic problems.

The TAC record is well documented, including accounts of particular tournaments [Wellman et al. (2001b, 2003b), Lanzi and Strada (2002), Eriksson and Janson (2002)], and summary descriptions of competing agents [Greenwald and Stone (2001), Greenwald (2003)]. We also investigated behavior across years [Wellman et al. (2003a)], finding that over time the allocation of travel resources in TAC play has become increasingly efficient. Since the TAC market appears to be quite competitive (as discussed below), this provides indirect evidence of general progress in agent performance.

One of the first findings to emerge from TAC was simply that a diverse set of research groups (ranging from individual students or employees to teams of senior researchers) were capable of constructing competent agents to play a complex game. By and large, most participants recognized the key strategic issues, and solved relevant subproblems accurately. For example, two key subproblems identified and solved by many participants were determining the optimal allocation of a given set of goods to clients, and evaluating the marginal utility of a particular good [Greenwald and Boyan (2001), Stone et al. (2001)]. Techniques for such core problems are generally disclosed by participants after the competition, and often incorporated and extended by other entrants in the next year's event.

In some cases, work on challenging TAC problems spurred research on techniques applicable much more generally in automated reasoning and decision making. For example, Stone et al. (2003) extended boosting techniques from machine learning to estimate conditional densities, driven by the pivotal TAC problem of estimating future hotel prices given current and historical price information, as well as other features.

Sophisticated learning of price distributions was undoubtedly a major ingredient in the success of ATTac-2001, which finished in a virtual two-way tie for first place in the 2001 TAC tournament. Its precise monitoring and reaction to prices was in stark contrast with the other first-place agent, livingagents [Fritschi and Dorer (2002)], which implemented a comparatively simple strategy of predicting optimal trips at the beginning and then taking hotel prices however they turned out. That such open-loop behavior could work so well was initially surprising. Indeed, if all agents played the livingagents strategy, hotel prices would skyrocket to unprofitable levels. But in the actual tournament, stabilizing agents like ATTac-2001 were the norm, effectively removing the risk to blind price-taking behavior.

An interesting lesson from this 2001 outcome was that interactions among the strategies are indeed important in TAC. The success of price-taking in the finalist pool also suggests that the market was fairly competitive. In the 2002 tournament, Walverine [Cheng et al. (2005)] took the competitiveness assumption seriously, modeling the TAC hotel market as a perfectly competitive system. Specifically, Walverine derived the Walrasian equilibrium for hotel prices given the initial flight prices and expected demand based on the known distribution of client preferences. This proved to be quite accurate as an initial prediction for hotel prices, performing on par with the sophisticated machine learning method employed by ATTac-2001 [Stone et al. (2003)], and significantly better than all other approaches in the TAC-02 finals [Wellman et al. (2004)]. This is perhaps surprising, given that Walverine was the only agent that did not employ historical data in its prediction method. Subsequent analysis indicated that a key determinant of success was taking into account the effect of flight prices on clients' choices of travel dates (and therefore hotel demands on different days). This relationship was pivotal in Walverine's competitive equilibrium analysis, and was empirically learned by ATTac-2001 as well as kavayaH [Putchala et al. (2002)], which predicted prices based on a neural-network model.

Predictions are of course uncertain, and TAC participants have identified several approaches to using probability distribution information in their bidding strategies. ATTac-2001 made decisions based on sampling from the price distribution, but its developers found in subsequent experiments that deciding directly based on distribution means was more effective [Stone et al. (2003)]. Similar results in the context of other agents were reported by the developers of RoxyBot and Walverine. Greenwald and Boyan (2004) performed a careful study of the general problem of bidding under uncertainty, comparing the problem as it arises in TAC to simpler models of purely sequential and simultaneous auctions. Hotel auctions in TAC are a hybrid, as agents bid simultaneously in all of them, after which one closes, and the agents have an opportunity to revise bids in the rest based on the results. Their study found that TAC hotel auctions strategically resemble simultaneous more than sequential auctions, which suggests that insights from research on SAAs (Section 4.3.2) may prove applicable to this problem.

Overall, success in TAC requires putting together solutions to the several subproblems comprising the game. The top scorer in the 2002 tournament was whitebear, whose developers tuned to victory through a process of extensive simulation experiments, performed systematically over a set of key control parameters [Vetsikas and Selman (2003)]. The 2003 tournament proved to be the tightest competition yet, with less than 100 points separating the top five agents: ATTac-2001, PackaTAC, whitebear, Thalis, and UMBCTAC.

5. A computational reasoning methodology for analyzing mechanisms and strategies

To conduct descriptive and explanatory research, economists traditionally rely heavily on the specification of stylized models that abstract from many real-world details in order to obtain formal results. One of our themes is that less formalism is reasonable when economics is practiced as a normative science applied to the design of computational markets and agents. Implementation details, problem complexity, and context matter in a fundamental way.

Direct application of analytic (usually game) theory quickly becomes infeasible as problem complexity grows, as reflected (informally) in size of strategy space, number of agents, degree of incomplete and imperfect information, and dynamism. Despite recent advances in game computation [Koller et al. (1996), McKelvey and McLennan (1996), Kearns et al. (2001), Porter et al. (2004)], even moderate size coupled with uncertainty and dynamics suffices to place modest but interesting market designs beyond the range of currently available solution methods.[19] As one well-known example, consider the FCC spectrum auctions. These multi-billion dollar auctions were designed by some of the best auction theory researchers alive, and major bidders hired most of the rest of the top auction researchers to help them devise strategies. Yet neither the market or agent strategy designers were able to analytically solve the game induced by the auction rules.[20] The outlook is more bleak for the numerous other markets that are at least as complex but less rich with potential gains from analytical solution.

When analytic methods are infeasible, what other tools are available for market and agent designers? One standard method is to statistically study quasi-experimental evidence from real-world market implementations to test generalizable hypotheses. Of

---

[19] Although the theoretical complexity of various game-computation problems [Conitzer and Sandholm (2003), Papadimitriou (2001)] is to some extent unsettled, the practical unsolvability of many games of interest—now and for the foreseeable future—is an uncontroversial proposition.

[20] Nor, apparently, did the designers anticipate and prevent certain collusive strategies; see, e.g., Weber (1997).

course, for computational market design there are few implementations in the field, especially if we wish to test new ideas. In this case, a variant is to design markets based on heuristics when theory is not complete, implement them in the field, and test their performance. This process, unfortunately is both slow and extremely expensive.

A related approach that has been used from the earliest days of computational market design is to test implementations in human subject laboratory experiments. Some of the earliest computational market designers were also among the pioneers of experimental lab methods in economics; in particular, the economists at the University of Arizona [Smith (1962)] and the California Institute of Technology [Plott (1986)]. This coincidence is not terribly surprising: to test any market, including non-computational, in a lab setting, researchers quickly found it expedient to build computational markets so that the experiment interface and instrumentation could be automated. However, although laboratory experiments are often more practical than field trials, they are still expensive. Further, mechanism and strategy complexity is limited by reliance on non-expert human participants.

We describe an emerging methodology that uses computational experiments to systematically investigate agent strategies and the performance of market mechanisms. The method begins with an explicit formulation of the resource allocation problem, and proceeds through at least five distinct tasks (we elaborate on these and provide references in the ensuing subsections):

1. **Specify a computational mechanism** (or several). Designs can be generated from innovation to existing forms, creative speculation, or through directed search (say, with a genetic program [Cliff (2003), Phelps et al. (2002)]).
2. **Generate candidate strategies.** As with mechanisms, candidate strategies can be generated in several ways. One promising idea is to search systematically or randomly through some encoding of strategy space. Another is to specify a strategy family parameterized to address important tradeoffs, perhaps based on a previously studied strategy. In any case, it is necessary to reduce dimensionality by restricting the strategy space, in order to employ numeric analysis methods.
3. **Estimate the "empirical game".** Simulation and sampling converts the extensive form game of incomplete information into a normal form with expected payoffs associated with each possible strategy profile.
4. **Solve the empirical game.** Methods such as replicator dynamics exploit symmetry or other available structure to efficiently solve large games for their equilibria.
5. **Analyze the results.** Attempt to extract generalizable regularities, and employ sensitivity analysis to drive further sampling and search.

These methods are emerging in the work of several authors [Reeves et al. (2005), MacKie-Mason et al. (2004), Armantier et al. (2005), Kephart and Greenwald (2002), Walsh et al. (2002)]. They are related in some respects to the generative social science methods used elsewhere in agent-based research [Epstein (2006)].

In the remainder of this section we discuss most of the main steps in this methodology. We do not devote any further attention to the first step of specifying a mechanism: this was the subject of Section 3 (especially Section 3.2).

5.1. Generate candidate strategies

One important source of intractability in market mechanisms is the enormousness of the strategy space. For example, in the market-based scheduling problem we studied, agent strategies include all functions from preferences (job length and deadline values) and price-quote histories to current-round bid vectors. The strategy domain includes all preferences ($(M + 1)$-dimensional, when there are M time slots), plus all price-quote histories up to the current time T (MT-dimensional). Partial or full combinatorial mechanisms have even higher dimensionality. Exploring all possible mappings from an $M(T + 1)$ to an M dimensional space is clearly not feasible. The traditional approach is to impose a rationality assumption (usually Bayes-Nash) and solve analytically for optimal strategies, but as we noted above the problem is not tractable for most complex mechanisms.

To render computational analysis feasible, the researcher restricts the strategy space to a manageable set. Typically, the researcher will specify a few "interesting" strategies, generated by intuition or experience, and analyze their performance against each other. Selten et al. (1997) implement a strategy generation method first proposed by Selten in 1967: humans play strategies in a laboratory setting to gain experience with the game and the mechanism, and then program those strategies so the researchers could analyze them further. In a similar vein, Axelrod (1984) solicited programmed strategies. Another approach is to implement a directed search strategy, such as a genetic algorithm, to select candidates from the full strategy space [Miller (1988), Koza (1991), Ünver (2001)].

A different approach for identifying such strategies that we explored is to specify a reasonable skeletal structure augmented with control parameters addressing key tradeoffs, and then to vary the parameters. For example, as discussed in Section 4.3.2, straightforward bidding (SB) is a natural candidate for a baseline strategy in any simultaneous ascending auction situation [Milgrom (2000)]. An SB agent determines which subset of goods (including the null set) would be most profitable at currently available prices, and places incremental bids on those it is not currently winning. For our scheduling problem we considered variants of SB that admit deviations from its myopic behavior. One variant was to introduce a "sunk awareness" parameter to account for exposure risk when an agent is already high bidder on some but not all slots it needs to complete its package [Reeves et al. (2005)]. Parameters need not be limited to scalar quantities. We recently investigated bidding strategies that use explicit price prediction [MacKie-Mason et al. (2004)], similar to many of the trading agents in the TAC competition (see Section 4.4). The parameters in this case may be vectors of expected prices, full belief distributions, or more generally, methods for price prediction that may be plugged in to the broader bidding strategy.

Although sometimes for a different purpose, many investigations of bidding agents include simulations of what are essentially restricted strategy profiles [Csirik et al. (2001), Goldman et al. (2001), Wellman et al. (2003a, 2005), Stone et al. (2001, 2003), Vetsikas and Selman (2003)].

5.2. Estimate the "empirical game"

Given a restricted set of candidate strategies, the cross-product of these sets across agents induces a space of *strategy profiles*, defining a restricted game. The payoff to each agent in a given profile is defined as the expected payoff for playing its corresponding strategy, where expectations are taken with respect to the distribution over the agents' private information, and any other stochastic factors.

For shorthand, refer to the joint probability function over these random variables as the *type distribution*. Given a specification of the type distribution, the expected payoffs with respect to this distribution can be estimated via sampling. The researcher draws randomly from the type distribution, and simulates play for a given profile. In the limit, the sample average payoff vector will approach the true expected payoffs for this profile if the mild conditions hold to support a weak law of large numbers. We refer to the mapping of strategy profiles to their estimated payoff vectors as an *empirical game*. This mapping has also been termed a *heuristic strategy payoff matrix* [Walsh et al. (2003)].

For example, we investigated a task-allocation problem in an information-collection domain [Cheng et al. (2003)]. The game has five agents, and we restricted the agents to choose among three available strategies (A, B, C). The game is symmetric, which means that each agent receives the same payoff from a given strategy when it faces a given profile of strategies played by the other agents (in payoff matrix terms, the matrix is symmetric). Agent types represent resources and tasks assigned in a particular game instance. Figure 4 depicts the empirical game matrix. We constructed similar empiri-

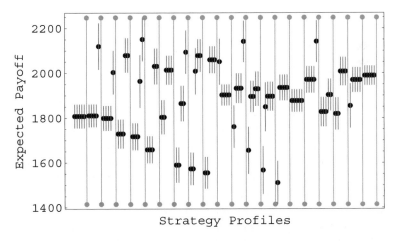

Figure 4. Payoff matrix for symmetric game with five agents choosing from strategies A,B,C. Each column corresponds to a strategy profile: {A,A,A,A,A} through {C,C,C,C,C} in lexicographic order. The jth dot within a column represents the mean payoff for the jth strategy in the profile. This payoff matrix is based on over 200 games simulated for each of the 21 distinct profiles. The error bars denote 95% confidence intervals.

cal games for many other scenarios, including several configurations of the scheduling problem, with varying numbers of agents and strategies.

5.3. Solve the empirical game

With a normal form expression of the empirical game, the next step is to solve for one or more of the Nash equilibria. Because it is based on a restricted strategy set, a Nash equilibrium of the empirical game—termed a *constrained strategic equilibrium* (CSE) [Armantier et al. (2005)]—does not correspond to an equilibrium of the full original game (even ignoring sampling error). Moreover, because the strategies already dictate how agents choose their actions based on private information, the CSE is not even a Bayes-Nash equilibrium (BNE) of the game where agents may play any of the strategies conditional on this private information. For this reason, Walsh et al. (2003) refer to the derived solution profile as an *ex ante* Nash equilibrium. In the limit as we relax strategy restrictions, a CSE converges to a BNE [Armantier et al. (2005)].

There are a variety of tools for finding a CSE in the restricted empirical game. The state-of-the-art solver for finite games is GAMBIT [McKelvey et al. (1992)]. But GAMBIT fails to exploit key structure in many games, such as symmetry. Converting the compact, symmetric representation of a payoff matrix into the more general form often renders the problem of finding equilibria intractable. For example, we have had GAMBIT fail on games with five agents choosing among five strategies. For this reason, we used two other solution methods that do exploit symmetry, described below.

In his original exposition of the concept, Nash (1950) suggested an evolutionary interpretation of the Nash equilibrium. We used the related replicator dynamics formalism [Taylor and Jonker (1978), Schuster and Sigmund (1983)] in service of computing equilibria. Friedman (1991) proves that if the probabilities in a mixed strategy are cast as proportions of a large population of agents playing the corresponding pure strategies, then an agent population that reaches a fixed point with respect to the replicator dynamics will be a symmetric mixed-strategy Nash equilibrium. This definition suggests an evolutionary algorithm in which population proportions are iteratively updated in successive generations.

We illustrate this evolutionary process in Figure 5 for a version of our scheduling game [MacKie-Mason et al. (2004)]. In this particular example, agents in a five-player game are drawn from a population in which the indicated fractions play one of five strategies from the set labeled by {16, 17, 18, 19, 20}. These strategy labels refer to a parameter we call "sunk awareness"; when zero the strategy treats all winning bids as sunk costs, and when the parameter is one the strategy completely ignores sunk costs. In the figure, the population is converging to the mixed strategy of playing strategy 16 with probability 0.745, and 17 with probability 0.255. In our experience the replicator dynamics method converges quickly, however the theory only guarantees convergence to a Nash equilibrium as the number of generations approaches infinity. We are unaware of any literature that systematically analyzed the performance of this method for solving matrix form games.

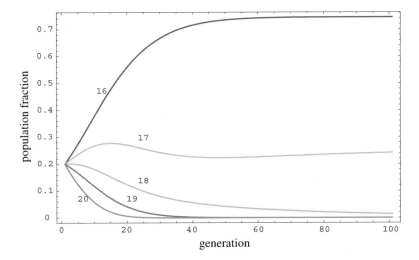

Figure 5. Replicator dynamics for a five-strategy version of a scheduling market.

Another solution method for symmetric games characterizes (symmetric) Nash equilibrium as the global minimum of a function mapping mixed strategies to the reals. For our experiments, we used an adaptation of a Nelder and Mead (1965) nonlinear function minimizer developed by Walsh et al. (2002).

Although, in part by exploiting symmetry and using replicator dynamics, we have been able to solve moderately large games faster and more successfully than GAMBIT, the problem is still computationally burdensome. The number of strategy profiles in a game with N agents and S strategies is the binomial coefficient $\binom{N+S-1}{N}$. For example, we recently studied a problem with five agents and 53 possible strategies, which has over four million unique strategy profiles to evaluate and hand to a game solving tool to find the equilibrium strategy set [Osepayshvili et al. (2005)]. We have not come close to estimating empirically all of the cells in the payoff matrix.

5.4. Analyze the results

Once an equilibrium strategy set is obtained, all of the usual analyses can be performed (subject to the caveat that the equilibria hold with respect to a restricted set of permissible strategies). For example, the equilibrium strategies can be analyzed to discover critical features that explain their strategic robustness, or to measure their performance under various conditions. Or, the equilibrium set can be calculated for each of several candidate mechanisms, and then the performance of the mechanisms compared under equilibrium play as part of the design loop to obtain better mechanisms.

As we noted above, fully solving a large game may be infeasible. However, partial empirical data offers opportunities for analysis as well. For example, in our game with five agents and 53 possible strategies, we have empirically evaluated only 4916 of the more than four million possible strategy profiles (and that only for a single assumed preference distribution). However, we have been able to establish that a particular strategy, s^*, forms a pure symmetric Nash equilibrium when all five agents play it. We did this by selectively estimating the payoff submatrix for 53 profiles: one with all agents playing s^*, and 52 with four agents playing s^* and one agent unilaterally deviating to an alternate strategy. None of the deviations was successful, so all-s^* is a Nash equilibrium [Osepayshvili et al. (2005)].

5.5. Discussion

The automation of markets and agents that trade in them opens up many new opportunities in market design and deployment. It also raises many new issues for strategic analysis: extending attention to challenging new market environments, and accounting for the wide strategic options available to computational agents. It may seem ironic (particularly for a chapter in the Handbook of Agent-Based Computational Economics) that we conclude by sketching a methodology that uses agent-based simulations in service of game-theoretic analysis. Indeed, many of the works in the agent-based economic literature [Tesfatsion (2006)] aim expressly to overcome the limitations of overly stylized analyses of markets abstracted from their microstructure. We share this aim, but emphasize the possibility of addressing issues of model fidelity without necessarily discarding the underlying theoretical framework. Computational modeling will likely prove just as valuable in service of game-theoretic analyses, as it can be as an alternative.

Acknowledgements

The authors gratefully acknowledge the helpful suggestions made by the editors, by five hard-working, generous, but anonymous reviewers, and by the other authors in this volume and additional participants at a book workshop in May 2004 at which we presented a first draft. This work was supported in part by grants CSS-9988715 and IIS-0414710 from the National Science Foundation.

References

Abdulkadiroglu, A., Pathak, P., Roth, A., Sönmez, T. (2005). "The Boston public school match". American Economic Review Papers and Proceedings 95 (2), 368–371.
Amir, Y., Awerbuch, B., Borgstrom, R.S. (1998). "The Java market: Transforming the Internet into a metacomputer", Technical Report CNDS-98-2, The Johns Hopkins University.
Amir, Y., Awerbuch, B., Barak, A., Borgstrom, R.S., Keren, A. (2000). "An opportunity cost approach for job assignment in a scalable computing cluster". IEEE Transactions on Parallel and Distributed Systems 11, 760–768.
Anastadiadi, A., Kapidakis, S., Nikolaou, C., Sairamesh, J. (1998). "A computational economy for dynamic load balancing and data replication", in: First International Conference on Information and Computation Economies, Charleston, SC, 166–180.

Armantier, O., Florens, J.-P., Richard, J.-F. (2005). "Approximation of Bayesian Nash equilibrium", Technical report, University of Pittsburgh.

Arrow, K. (1964). "On the role of securities in the optimal allocation of risk bearing". Review of Economic Studies 31 (2), 91–96.

Arunachalam, R., Sadeh, N.M. (2005). "The supply chain trading agent competition". Electronic Commerce Research and Applications 4, 63–81.

Ausubel, L., Milgrom, P. (2002). "Ascending auctions with package bidding". Frontiers of Theoretical Economics 1 (1). Article 1.

Avery, C., Resnick, P., Zeckhauser, R. (1999). "The market for evaluations". American Economic Review 89, 564–584.

Axelrod, R. (1984). The Evolution of Cooperation. Basic, New York.

Baldauf, B., Santoni, G.J. (1991). "Stock-price volatility: Some evidence from an ARCH model". Journal of Futures Markets 11, 191–200.

Banks, J.S., Ledyard, J.O., Porter, D.P. (1989). "Allocating uncertain and unresponsive resources: An experimental approach". RAND Journal of Economics 20, 1–25.

Baruah, S., Koren, G., Mao, D., Mishra, B., Raghunathan, A., Rosier, L., Shasha, D., Wang, F. (1992). "On the competitiveness of on-line real-time task scheduling". Real-Time Systems 4 (2), 125–144.

Bass, T.A. (1999). The Predictors. Henry Holt and Company.

Belew, R.K. (2000). Finding Out About. Cambridge University Press.

Berners-Lee, T., Hendler, J., Lassila, O. (2001). "The semantic web". Scientific American 284 (5), 34–43.

Bertsekas, D.P. (1992). "Auction algorithms for network flow problems: A tutorial introduction". Computational Optimization and Applications 1, 7–66.

Bikhchandani, S., Mamer, J.W. (1997). "Competitive equilibrium in an exchange economy with indivisibilities". Journal of Economic Theory 74, 385–413.

Bikhchandani, S., de Vries, S., Schummer, J., Vohra, R.V. (2002). "Linear programming and Vickrey auctions". In: Mathematics of the Internet: E-Auction and Markets. In: IMA Volumes in Mathematics and its Applications, vol. 127. Springer, pp. 75–116.

Boutilier, C., Hoos, H.H. (2001). "Bidding languages for combinatorial auctions", in: Proceedings of the Seventeenth International Joint Conference on Artificial Intelligence (IJCAI-01), Seattle, Wash, 1211–1217.

Brennan, M.J., Schwartz, E.S. (1990). "Arbitrage in stock index futures". Journal of Business 63, S7–S31.

Brewer, P.J. (1999). "Decentralized computation procurement and computational robustness in a smart market". Economic Theory 13 (1), 41–92.

Brewer, P.J., Plott, C.R. (1996). "A binary conflict ascending price (Bicap) mechanisms for the decentralized allocation of the right to use railroad tracks". International Journal of Industrial Organization 14 (6), 857–886.

Brewer, P.J., Plott, C.R. (2002). "A decentralized, smart market solution to a class of back-haul transportation problems: Concept and experimental test beds". Interfaces 32 (5), 13–36.

Brooks, C.H., Durfee, E.H. (2003). "Congregation formation in multiagent systems". Autonomous Agents and Multi-Agent Systems 7, 145–170.

Bykowsky, M.M., Cull, R.J., Ledyard, J.O. (2000). "Mutually destructive bidding: The FCC auction design problem". Journal of Regulatory Economics 17, 205–228.

Cameron, L., Cramton, P. (1999). "The role of the ISO in U.S. electricity markets: A review of restructuring in California and PJM". Electricity Journal 12 (3), 71–81.

Chaum, D. (1992). "Achieving electronic privacy". Scientific American 267 (2), 96–101.

Chen, Y. (2003). "An experimental study of the serial and average cost pricing mechanisms". Journal of Public Economics 87 (9–10), 2305–2335.

Cheng, S.-F., Wellman, M.P., Perry, D.G. (2003). "Market-based resource allocation for information-collection scenarios", in: IJCAI-03 Workshop on Multi-Agent for Mass User Support, Acapulco.

Cheng, S.-F., Leung, E., Lochner, K.M., O'Malley, K., Reeves, D.M., Schvartzman, L.J., Wellman, M.P. (2005). "Walverine: A Walrasian trading agent". Decision Support Systems 39, 169–184.

Clarke, E. (1971). "Multipart pricing of public goods". Public Choice 8, 19–33.

Cliff, D. (1998). "Evolving parameter sets for adaptive trading agents in continuous double-auction markets", in: Agents-98 Workshop on Artificial Societies and Computational Markets, Minneapolis, MN, 38–47.

Cliff, D. (2003). "Explorations in evolutionary design of online auction market mechanisms". Electronic Commerce Research and Applications 2, 162–175.

Cocchi, R., Estrin, D., Shenker, S.J., Zhang, L. (1991). "A study of priority pricing in multiple service class networks", in: ACM SIGCOMM, 123–130.

Cocchi, R., Estrin, D., Shenker, S.J., Zhang, L. (1993). "Pricing in computer networks: Motivation, formulation and example". IEEE Transactions on Networking 1 (6), 614–627.

Cohen, A. (2002). The Perfect Store: Inside eBay. Little, Brown, and Company.

Conen, W., Sandholm, T. (2001). "Minimal preference elicitation in combinatorial auctions", in: IJCAI-2001 Workshop on Economic Agents, Models, and Mechanisms, Seattle, WA, 71–80.

Conen, W., Sandholm, T. (2002). "Partial-revelation VCG mechanisms for combinatorial auctions", in: Eighteenth National Conference on Artificial Intelligence, Edmonton, 367–372.

Conitzer, V., Sandholm, T. (2003). "Complexity results about Nash equilibria", in: Eighteenth International Joint Conference on Artificial Intelligence, Acapulco, Mexico, 765–771.

Cox, L.P., Noble, B.D. (2003). "Samsara: Honor among thieves in peer-to-peer storage", in: Nineteenth ACM Symposium on Operating Systems Principles, Bolton Landing, NY.

Cramton, P. (1995). "Money out of thin air: The nationwide narrowband PCS auction". Journal of Economics and Management Strategy 4, 267–343.

Cramton, P., Shoham, Y., Steinberg, R. (Eds.) (2006). Combinatorial Auctions. MIT Press.

Cranor, L.F., Resnick, P. (2000). "Protocols for automated negotiations with buyer anonymity and seller reputations". Netnomics 2, 1–23.

Crocker, S. (1999). "The siren song of Internet micropayments". iMP: The Magazine on Information Impacts.

Csirik, J.A., Littman, M.L., Singh, S., Stone, P. (2001). "FAucS: An FCC spectrum auction simulator for autonomous bidding agents". In: Second International Workshop on Electronic Commerce. In: Lecture Notes in Computer Science, vol. 2232. Springer-Verlag, pp. 139–151.

Curbera, F., Duftler, M., Khalaf, R., Nagy, W., Mukhi, N., Weerawarana, S. (2002). "Unraveling the web services web: An introduction to SOAP, WSDL, and UDDI". IEEE Internet Computing 6, 86–93.

Das, R., Hanson, J.E., Kephart, J.O., Tesauro, G. (2001). "Agent-human interactions in the continuous double auction", in: Seventeenth International Joint Conference on Artificial Intelligence, Seattle, WA, 1169–1176.

Dash, R.K., Jennings, N.R., Parkes, D.C. (2003). "Computational-mechanism design: A call to arms". IEEE Intelligent Systems 18 (6), 40–47.

de Vries, S., Vohra, R. (2003). "Combinatorial auctions: A survey". INFORMS Journal on Computing 15 (3), 284–309.

Debreu, G. (1954). "Valuation equilibrium and Pareto optimum". Proceedings of the National Academy of Sciences U.S.A. 40, 588–592.

Dellarocas, C. (2003). "The digitization of word-of-mouth: Promise and challenges of online reputation mechanisms". Management Science 49, 1407–1424.

Di Noia, T., Di Sciascio, E., Donini, F.M., Mongiello, M. (2004). "A system for principled matchmaking in an electronic marketplace". International Journal of Electronic Commerce 8, 9–37.

Doorenbos, R.B., Etzioni, O., Weld, D.S. (1997). "A scalable comparison-shopping agent for the world-wide web", in: First International Conference on Autonomous Agents, 39–48.

Epstein, J.M. (2006). "Remarks on the foundations of agent-based generative social science", this Handbook.

Eriksson, J., Janson, S. (2002). "The Trading Agent Competition: TAC 2002". ERCIM News, 51.

Faratin, P., de Walle, B.V. (2002). "Agent preference relations: Strict, equivalent and incomparables". In: First International Joint Conference on Autonomous Agents and Multi-Agent Systems. AAAI Press, Bologna, Italy, pp. 1317–1324.

Feigenbaum, J., Papadimitriou, C., Shenker, S. (2001). "Sharing the cost of multicast transmissions". Journal of Computer and System Sciences 63, 21–41.

Feigenbaum, J., Papadimitriou, C., Sami, R., Shenker, S. (2005). "A BGP-based mechanism for lowest-cost routing". Distributed Computing 18, 61–72.

Ferguson, D., Yemini, Y., Nikolaou, C. (1988). "Microeconomic algorithms for load balancing in distributed computer systems", in: Eighth International Conference on Distributed Computing Systems, 491–499.

Finholt, T.A. (2003). "Collaboratories as a new form of scientific organization". Economics of Innovation and New Technology 12, 5–25.

Finholt, T.A., Olson, G.M. (1997). "From laboratories to collaboratories: A new organizational form for scientific collaboration". Psychological Science 8, 28–36.

Forsythe, R., Lundholm, R. (1990). "Information aggregation in an experimental market". Econometrica 58 (2), 309–347.

Forsythe, R., Nelson, F., Neumann, G.R., Wright, J. (1992). "Anatomy of an experimental political stock market". American Economic Review 82 (5), 1142–1161.

Friedman, D. (1991). "Evolutionary games in economics". Econometrica 59 (3), 637–666.

Friedman, D. (1993). "The double auction market institution: A survey". In: Friedman, D., Rust, J. (Eds.), The Double Action Market. Addison-Wesley, pp. 3–25.

Friedman, D., Rust, J. (Eds.) (1993). The Double Auction Market. Addison-Wesley.

Friedman, E., Parkes, D. (2003). "Pricing WiFi at Starbucks: Issues in online mechanism design". In: Fourth Conf. on Electronic Commerce. ACM.

Fritschi, C., Dorer, K. (2002). "Agent-oriented software engineering for successful TAC participation", in: First International Joint Conference on Autonomous Agents and Multi-Agent Systems, Bologna.

Fudenberg, D., Tirole, J. (1991). "Perfect Bayesian equilibrium and sequential equilibrium". Journal of Economic Theory 53, 236–260.

Gagliano, R., Fraser, M., Schaefer, M. (1995). "Auction allocation of computing reserves". Communications of the ACM 38 (6), 88–99.

Garman, M.B. (1976). "Market microstructure". Journal of Financial Economics 3, 257–275.

Gjerstad, S. (2004). "The impact of bargaining pace on double auction dynamics", Technical report, University of Arizona.

Gjerstad, S., Dickhaut, J. (1998). "Price formation in double auctions". Games and Economic Behavior 22, 1–29.

Gode, D.K., Sunder, S. (1993). "Allocative efficiency of markets with zero-intelligence traders: Market as a partial substitute for individual rationality". Journal of Political Economy 101, 119–137.

Goldman, C.V., Kraus, S., Shehory, O. (2001). "Equilibria strategies for selecting sellers and satisfying buyers". In: Klusch, M., Zambonelli, F. (Eds.), Cooperative Information Agents V. In: Lecture Notes in Artificial Intelligence, vol. 2182. Springer-Verlag, pp. 166–177.

Golle, P., Leyton-Brown, K., Mironov, I., Lillibridge, M. (2001). "Incentives for sharing in peer-to-peer networks". In: Second International Workshop on Electronic Commerce. In: Lecture Notes in Computer Science, vol. 2232. Springer-Verlag.

Greenwald, A. (2003). "The 2002 trading agent competition: An overview of agent strategies". AI Magazine 24 (1), 83–91.

Greenwald, A., Boyan, J. (2001). "Bidding algorithms for simultaneous auctions: A case study", in: Third ACM Conference on Electronic Commerce, Tampa, FL, 115–124.

Greenwald, A., Stone, P. (2001). "The First International Trading Agent Competition: Autonomous bidding agents". IEEE Internet Computing 5, 52–60.

Greenwald, A., Boyan, J. (2004). "Bidding under uncertainty: Theory and experiments", in: Twentieth Conference on Uncertainty in Artificial Intelligence, Banff, 209–216.

Groves, T. (1973). "Incentives in teams". Econometrica 41, 617–631.

Guerin, F., Pitt, J. (2002). "Guaranteeing properties for e-commerce systems". In: Agent-Mediated Electronic Commerce IV. In: Lecture Notes in Computer Science, vol. 2153. Springer-Verlag, pp. 253–272.

Gul, F., Stacchetti, E. (1999). "Walrasian equilibrium with gross substitutes". Journal of Economic Theory 87, 95–124.

Gupta, R., Somani, A.K. (2004). "CompuP2P: An architecture for sharing of compute power in peer-to-peer networks with selfish nodes", in: Second Workshop on the Economics of Peer-to-Peer Systems, Cambridge, MA.

Gupta, A., Stahl, D.O., Whinston, A.B. (1996). "An economic approach to network computing with priority classes". Journal of Organizational Computing and Electronic Commerce 6, 71–95.

Hajiaghayi, M.T., Kleinberg, R., Parkes, D.C. (2004). "Adaptive limited-supply online auctions", in: Fifth ACM Conference on Electronic Commerce, 71–80.

Hanson, R. (2003). "Combinatorial information market design". Information Systems Frontiers 5 (1), 107–119.

Hart, S., Mas-Colell, A. (2000). "A simple adaptive procedure leading to correlated equilibrium". Econometrica 68, 1127–1150.

Hill, W., Stead, L., Rosenstein, M., Furnas, G. (1995). "Recommending and evaluating choices in a virtual community of use". In: Conference on Human Factors in Computing Systems. ACM, Denver, pp. 194–201.

Hofreiter, B., Huemer, C., Klas, W. (2002). "ebXML: Status, research issues, and obstacles", in: Twelfth International Workshop on Research Issues in Data Engineering, San José, CA, 7–16.

Hommes, C. (2006). "Heterogeneous agent models in economics and finance", this Handbook.

Hurwicz, L. (1960). "Optimality and informational efficiency in resource allocation processes". In: Arrow, K., Karlin, S., Suppes, P. (Eds.), Mathematical Methods in the Social Sciences. Stanford University Press, Stanford, CA, pp. 27–46.

Jackson, E.M. (2004). The PayPal Wars. World Ahead Publishing.

Jordan, J.S. (1982). "The competitive allocation process is informationally efficient uniquely". Journal of Economic Theory 28 (1), 1–18.

Karaul, M., Korilis, Y.A., Orda, A. (1998). "A market-based architecture for management of geographically dispersed, replicated web servers", in: First International Conference on Information and Computation Economies, Charleston, SC, 158–165.

Kearns, M., Ortiz, L. (2003). "The Penn-Lehman automated trading project". IEEE Intelligent Systems 18 (6), 22–31.

Kearns, M., Littman, M.L., Singh, S. (2001). "Graphical models for game theory", in: Seventeenth Conference on Uncertainty in Artificial Intelligence, Seattle, 253–260.

Kelly, F., Maulloo, A., Tan, D. (1998). "Rate control in communication networks: shadow prices, proportional fairness and stability". Journal of the Operational Research Society 49, 237–252.

Kelly, T.P., Chan, Y.M., Jamin, S., MacKie-Mason, J.K. (1999). "Biased replacement policies for web caches: Differential quality-of-service and aggregate user value", in: Fourth International Web Caching Workshop, San Diego, CA.

Kelly, T.P., Jamin, S., MacKie-Mason, J.K. (2006). "Variable QoS from shared web caches: User centered design and value-sensitive replacement". In: McKnight, L. (Ed.), Internet Service Quality Economics. MIT Press. In press.

Kelso Jr., A.S., Crawford, V.P. (1982). "Job matching, coalition formation and gross substitutes". Econometrica 50, 1483–1504.

Kephart, J.O., Greenwald, A.R. (2002). "Shopbot economics". Autonomous Agents and Multiagent Systems 5, 255–287.

Kephart, J.O., Hanson, J.E., Sairamesh, J. (1998). "Price and niche wars in a free-market economy of software agents". Artificial Life 4, 1–23.

Koller, D., Megiddo, N., von Stengel, B. (1996). "Efficient computation of equilibria for extensive two-person games". Games and Economic Behavior 14, 247–259.

Koren, G., Shasha, D. (1995). "D-over: An optimal on-line scheduling algorithm for overloaded uniprocessor real-time systems". SIAM Journal on Computing 24 (2), 318–339.

Korilis, Y.A., Lazar, A.A., Orda, A. (1995). "Architecting noncooperative networks". IEEE Journal on Selected Areas in Communications 13 (7), 1241–1251.

Koza, J.R. (1991). "Evolution and co-evolution of computer programs to control independently-acting agents". In: Proceedings of the First International Conference on Simulation of Adaptive Behavior: From Animals to Animats. MIT Press, Cambridge, MA, pp. 366–375.

Krishna, V. (2002). Auction Theory. Academic Press.

Krulwich, B.T. (1996). "The BargainFinder agent: Comparison price shopping on the Internet". In: Williams, J. (Ed.), Bots and Other Internet Beasties. Sams Publishing, pp. 257–263.

Kurose, J.F., Simha, R. (1986). "A microeconomic approach to optimal file allocation", in: Sixth International Conference on Distributed Computing Systems, 28–35.

Kurose, J.F., Simha, R. (1989). "A microeconomic approach to optimal resource allocation in distributed systems". IEEE Transactions on Computers 38 (5), 705–717.

Lanzi, P.L., Strada, A. (2002). "A statistical analysis of the trading agent competition 2001". SIGecom Exchanges 3 (2), 1–8.

LeBaron, B. (2006). "Agent-based computational finance", this Handbook.

Ledyard, J., Szakaly, K. (1994). "Designing organizations for trading pollution rights". Journal of Economic Behavior and Organization 25, 167–196.

Leyton-Brown, K. (2003). "Resource allocation in competitive multiagent systems", PhD thesis, Stanford University.

Li, L., Horrocks, I. (2004). "A software framework for matchmaking based on semantic web technology". International Journal of Electronic Commerce 8, 39–60.

Lochner, K.M., Wellman, M.P. (2004). "Rule-based specification of auction mechanisms", in: Third International Joint Conference on Autonomous Agents and Multi-Agent Systems, New York, 818–825.

MacKie-Mason, J.K., Varian, H.R. (1994a). "Economic FAQs about the Internet". Journal of Economic Perspectives 8, 75–96.

MacKie-Mason, J.K., Varian, H.R. (1994b). "Generalized Vickrey auctions", working paper, University of Michigan.

MacKie-Mason, J.K., Varian, H.R. (1995a). "Pricing congestible network resources". IEEE Journal on Selected Areas of Communications 13 (7), 1141–1149.

MacKie-Mason, J.K., Varian, H.R. (1995b). "Pricing the Internet". In: Kahin, B., Keller, J. (Eds.), Public Access to the Internet. MIT Press, pp. 269–314.

MacKie-Mason, J.K., Varian, H.R. (1996). "Some economics of the Internet". In: Sichel, W. (Ed.), Networks, Infrastructure and the New Task for Regulation. University of Michigan Press, Ann Arbor, MI.

MacKie-Mason, J.K., White, K. (1997). "Evaluating and selecting digital payment mechanisms". In: Rosston, G.L., Waterman, D. (Eds.), Interconnection and the Internet: Selected Papers from the 24th Annual Telecommunications Policy Research Conference. Lawrence Erlbaum.

MacKie-Mason, J.K., Murphy, J., Murphy, L. (1996a). "Feedback and efficiency in ATM networks". In: International Conference on Communications, vol. 2. IEEE, pp. 1045–1049.

MacKie-Mason, J.K., Murphy, J., Murphy, L. (1996b). "The role of responsive pricing in the internet". In: Baily, J., McKnight, L. (Eds.), Internet Economics. MIT Press, Cambridge, pp. 279–304.

MacKie-Mason, J.K., Osepayshvili, A., Reeves, D.M., Wellman, M.P. (2004). "Price prediction strategies for market-based scheduling", in: Fourteenth International Conference on Automated Planning and Scheduling, Whistler, BC, 244–252.

Malone, T.W. (1987). "Modeling coordination in organizations and markets". Management Science 33, 1317–1332.

Manasse, M.S. (1995). "The Millicent protocols for electronic commerce", in: First USENIX Workshop on Electronic Commerce, New York, 117–123.

Marks, R. (2006). "Market design", this Handbook.

Mas-Colell, A., Whinston, M.D., Green, J.R. (1995). Microeconomic Theory. Oxford University Press, New York.

Maskin, E., Riley, J. (1989). "Optimal multi-unit auctions". In: Hahn, F. (Ed.), The Economics of Missing Markets, Information, and Games. Clarendon Press, Oxford, pp. 312–335. Chapter 14.

McAfee, R.P., McMillan, J. (1996). "Analyzing the airwaves auction". Journal of Economic Perspectives 10 (1), 159–175.

McCabe, K.A., Rassenti, S.J., Smith, V.L. (1989). "Designing 'smart' computer-assisted markets: An experimental auction for gas networks". European Journal of Political Economy 5, 259–283.

McCabe, K.A., Rassenti, S.J., Smith, V.L. (1991). "Smart computer-assisted markets". Science 254, 534–538.

McKelvey, R.D., McLennan, A. (1996). "Computation of equilibria in finite games". In: Handbook of Computational Economics. Elsevier.

McKelvey, R.D., McLennan, A., Turocy, T. (1992). Gambit Game Theory Analysis Software and Tools.

Menczer, F., Street, W.N., Monge, A.E. (2002). "Adaptive assistants for customized e-shopping". IEEE Intelligent Systems 17, 12–19.

Micali, S., Rivest, R.L. (2002). "Micropayments revisited". In: Cryptographer's Track at the RSA Conference. In: Lecture Notes in Computer Science, vol. 2271. Springer-Verlag, Heidelberg, pp. 149–163.

Milgrom, P. (2000). "Putting auction theory to work: The simultaneous ascending auction". Journal of Political Economy 108, 245–272.

Miller, J.H. (1988). "The evolution of automata in the repeated prisoners dilemma", in: Two Essays on the Economics of Imperfect Information, Ph.D. dissertation, University of Michigan, Ann Arbor.

Moulin, H., Shenker, S. (2001). "Strategyproof sharing of submodular access costs: Budget balance versus efficiency". Economic Theory 18, 511–533.

Mount, K., Reiter, S. (1974). "The informational size of message spaces". Journal of Economic Theory 8, 161–192.

Mullen, T., Breese J. (1998). "Experiments in designing computational economies for mobile users", in: First International Conference on Information and Computation Economies, Charleston, SC, 19–27.

Myerson, R., Satterthwaite, M. (1983). "Efficient mechanisms for bilateral trading". Journal of Economic Theory 29, 265–281.

Nash, J. (1950). Non-cooperative Games. Dept. of Mathematics, Princeton University.

Nelder, J.A., Mead, R. (1965). "A simplex method for function minimization". Computer Journal 7, 308–313.

Nicolaisen, J., Petrov, V., Tesfatsion, L. (2001). "Market power and efficiency in a computational electricity market with discriminatory double-auction pricing". IEEE Transactions on Evolutionary Computation 5, 504–523.

Nisan, N. (2000). "Bidding and allocation in combinatorial auctions", in: Second ACM Conference on Electronic Commerce, Minneapolis, MN, 1–12.

Nisan, N., Ronen, A. (2000). "Computationally feasible VCG mechanisms", in: Second ACM Conference on Electronic Commerce, Minneapolis, MN, 242–252.

Nisan, N., Ronen, A. (2001). "Algorithmic mechanism design". Games and Economic Behavior 35, 166–196.

Nisan, N., Segal, I. (2006). "The communication requirements of efficient allocations and supporting prices", Journal of Economic Theory, in press.

O'Hara, M. (1995). Market Microstructure Theory. Blackwell.

O'Mahony, D., Peirce, M., Tewari, H. (1997). Electronic Payment Systems. Artech House.

Osepayshvili, A., Wellman, M.P., Reeves, D., MacKie-Mason, J.K. (2005). "Self-confirming price prediction for bidding in simultaneous ascending auctions". In: Uncertainty in Artificial Intelligence, Edinburgh.

Papadimitriou, C.H. (2001). "Algorithms, games, and the Internet", in: Thirty-Third Annual ACM Symposium on the Theory of Computing, Hersonissos, Greece, 749–753.

Parkes, D.C. (1999). "iBundle: An efficient ascending price bundle auction", in: ACM Conference on Electronic Commerce, 148–157.

Parkes, D.C. (2005). "Auction design with costly preference elicitation". Annals of Mathematics and ACM 44, 269–302.

Parkes, D.C., Singh, S. (2003). "An MDP-based approach to online mechanism design". In: 17th Annual Conf. on Neural Information Processing Systems.

Parkes, D.C., Ungar, L.H. (2000). "Iterative combinatorial auctions: Theory and practice". In: Seventeenth National Conference on Artificial Intelligence, pp. 74–81.

Parkes, D.C., Ungar, L.H. (2002). "An ascending-price generalized Vickrey auction", manuscript, Harvard University.

Pennock, D.M. (2004). "A dynamic pari-mutuel market for hedging, wagering, and information aggregation", in: Fifth ACM Conference on Electronic Commerce, 170–179.

Pennock, D.M., Wellman, M.P. (2000). "Compact securities markets for Pareto optimal reallocation of risk", in: Sixteenth Conference on Uncertainty in Artificial Intelligence, Stanford, 481–488.

Peters, M., Severinov, S. (2006). "Internet auctions with many traders". Journal of Economic Theory, in press.

Phelps, S., Parsons, S., McBurney, P., Sklar, E. (2002). "Co-evolution of auction mechanisms and trading strategies: Towards a novel approach to microeconomic design", in: GECCO-02 Workshop on Evolutionary Computation in Multi-Agent Systems, 65–72.

Plott, C.R. (1986). "Laboratory experiments in economics: The implications of posted-price institutions". Science 232, 732–738.

Plott, C.R., Sunder, S. (1988). "Rational expectations and the aggregation of diverse information in laboratory security markets". Econometrica 56 (5), 1085–1118.

Polk, C., Hanson, R., Ledyard, J., Ishikida, T. (2003). "Policy analysis market: An electronic commerce application of a combinatorial information market", in: Fourth ACM Conference on Electronic Commerce, San Diego, CA, 272–273.

Porter, R. (2004). "Mechanism design for online real-time scheduling", in: Fifth ACM Conference on Electronic Commerce, New York, 61–70.

Porter, R., Nudelman, E., Shoham, Y. (2004). "Simple search methods for finding a Nash equilibrium", in: Nineteenth National Conference on Artificial Intelligence, San Jose, CA.

Putchala, R.P., Morris, V.N., Kazhanchi, R., Raman, L., Shekhar, S. (2002). "kavayaH: A trading agent developed for TAC-02", technical report, Oracle India.

Pynadath, D.V., Tambe, M. (2002). "The communicative multiagent team decision problem: Analyzing teamwork theories and models". Journal of Artificial Intelligence Research 16, 389–423.

Rassenti, S.J., Smith, V.L., Bulfin, R.L. (1982). "A combinatorial auction mechanism for airport time slot allocation". Bell Journal of Economics 13, 402–417.

Reeves, D.M., Wellman, M.P., MacKie-Mason, J.K., Osepayshvili, A. (2005). "Exploring bidding strategies for market-based scheduling". Decision Support Systems 39, 67–85.

Regev, O., Nisan, N. (1998). "The POPCORN market: An online market for computational resources", in: First International Conference on Information and Computation Economies, Charleston, SC, 148–157.

Resnick, P., Varian, H.R. (1997). "Recommender systems". Communications of the ACM 40 (3), 56–58.

Resnick, P., Zeckhauser, R. (2002). "Trust among strangers in Internet transactions: Empirical analysis of eBay's reputation system". In: Baye, M.R. (Ed.), The Economics of the Internet and E-Commerce, Advances in Applied Microeconomics, vol. 11. Elsevier Science.

Resnick, P., Iacovou, N., Suchak, M., Bergstrom, P., Riedl, J. (1994). "Grouplens: An open architecture for collaborative filtering of netnews". In: CSCW '94: Conference on Computer Supported Coorperative Work. ACM, Chapel Hill., pp. 175–186.

Resnick, P., Zeckhauser, R., Friedman, E., Kuwabara, K. (2002). "Reputation systems". Communications of the ACM 43 (12), 45–48.

Riedl, J., Konstan, J.A. (2002). Word of Mouse: The Marketing Power of Collaborative Filtering. Warner Books.

Rosenschein, J.S., Zlotkin, G. (1994). Rules of Encounter: Designing Conventions for Automated Negotiation Among Computers. MIT Press.

Roth, A.E., Peranson, E. (1999). "The redesign of the matching market for American physicians: Some engineering aspects of economic design". American Economic Review 89, 748–780.

Roth, A.E., Ockenfels, A. (2002). "Last-minute bidding and the rules for ending second-price auctions: Evidence from eBay and Amazon auctions on the Internet". American Economic Review 92, 1093–1103.

Roth, A., Sönmez, T., Unver, U. (2005). "A kidney exchange clearinghouse in New England". American Economic Review Papers and Proceedings.

Rothkopf, M.H., Pekeč, A., Harstad, R.M. (1998). "Computationally manageable combinatorial auctions". Management Science 44, 1131–1147.

Russell, S., Norvig, P. (2003). Artificial Intelligence: A Modern Approach, 2nd edn. Prentice Hall.

Rust, J., Miller, J.H., Palmer, R. (1994). "Characterizing effective trading strategies: Insights from a computerized double auction tournament". Journal of Economic Dynamics and Control 18, 61–96.

Sakurai, Y., Yokoo, M., Matsubara, S. (1999). "A limitation of the generalized Vickrey auction in electronic commerce: Robustness against false-name bids", in: Sixteenth National Conference on Artificial Intelligence, Orlando, FL, 86–92.

Sandholm, T.W., Lesser, V.R. (1997). "Coalitions among computationally bounded agents". Artificial Intelligence 94, 99–137.

Sandholm, T., Suri, S. (2003). "BOB: Improved winner determination in combinatorial auctions and generalizations". Artificial Intelligence 145, 33–58.

Scarf, H. (1973). The Computation of Economic Equilibria Cowles Foundation Monograph No. 24. Yale University Press, New Haven.

Schafer, J.B., Konstan, J.A., Riedl, J. (2001). "E-commerce recommendation applications". Data Mining and Knowledge Discovery 5, 115–153.

Schuster, P., Sigmund, K. (1983). "Replicator dynamics". Journal of Theoretical Biology 100, 533–538.

Selten, R., Mitzkewitz, M., Uhlich, G.R. (1997). "Duopoly strategies programmed by experienced players". Econometrica 65 (3), 517–555.

Shenker, S. (1994). "Making greed work in networks: A game-theoretic analysis of switch service disciplines", in: ACM SIGCOMM, 47–57.

Shenker, S. (1995). "Service models and pricing policies for an integrated services Internet". In: Kahin, B., Keller, J. (Eds.), Public Access to the Internet. MIT Press, pp. 315–337.

Sherstov, A., Stone, P. (2004). "Three automated stock-trading agents: A comparative study", in: AAMAS-04 Workshop on Agent-Mediated Electronic Commerce, New York.

Sirbu, M., Tygar, J.D. (1995). "NetBill: An Internet commerce system optimized for network delivered services". IEEE Personal Communications 2 (4), 34–39.

Smith, V.L. (1962). "An experimental study of competitive market behavior". Journal of Political Economy 70, 111–137.

Stone, P., Littman, M.L., Singh, S., Kearns, M. (2001). "ATTac-2000: An adaptive autonomous bidding agent". Journal of Artificial Intelligence Research 15, 189–206.

Stone, P., Schapire, R.E., Littman, M.L., Csirik, J.A., McAllester, D. (2003). "Decision-theoretic bidding based on learned density models in simultaneous, interacting auctions". Journal of Artificial Intelligence Research 19, 209–242.

Stonebraker, M., Aoki, P.M., Litwin, W., Pfeffer, A., Sah, A., Sidell, J., Staelin, C., Yu, A. (1996). "Mariposa: A wide-area distributed database system". VLDB Journal 5, 48–63.

Sutherland, I.E. (1968). "A futures market in computer time". Communications of the ACM 11 (6), 449–451.

Tambe, M. (1997). "Towards flexible teamwork". Journal of Artificial Intelligence Research 7, 83–124.

Taylor, P., Jonker, L. (1978). "Evolutionary stable strategies and game dynamics". Mathematical Biosciences 40, 145–156.

Tesauro, G., Das, R. (2001). "High-performance bidding agents for the continuous double auction", in: Third ACM Conference on Electronic Commerce, Tampa, FL, 206–209.

Tesfatsion, L. (2006). "Agent-based computational economics", this Handbook.

Thomas, P., Teneketzis, D., MacKie-Mason, J.K. (2002). "A market-based approach to optimal resource allocation in integrated-services connection-oriented networks". Operations Research 50, 603–616.

Ünver, U. (2001). "Backward unraveling over time: The evolution of strategic behavior in the entry-level British medical labor markets". Journal of Economic Dynamics and Control 25 (6–7), 1039–1080.

Vetsikas, I.A., Selman, B. (2003). "A principled study of the design tradeoffs for autonomous trading agents", in: Second International Joint Conference on Autonomous Agents and Multiagent Systems, Melbourne, Australia, 473-480.

Vickrey, W. (1961). "Counterspeculation, auctions, and competitive sealed tenders". Journal of Finance 16, 8–37.

Waldspurger, C.A., Hogg, T., Huberman, B.A., Kephart, J.O., Stornetta, S. (1992). "Spawn: A distributed computational economy". IEEE Transactions on Software Engineering 18 (2), 103–117.

Walsh, W.E., Das, R., Tesauro, G., Kephart, J.O. (2002). "Analyzing complex strategic interactions in multiagent systems", in: AAAI-02 Workshop on Game-Theoretic and Decision-Theoretic Agents, Edmonton.

Walsh, W.E., Parkes, D., Das, R. (2003). "Choosing samples to compute heuristic-strategy nash equilibrium", in: AAMAS-03 Workshop on Agent-Mediated Electronic Commerce, Melbourne, Australia.

Weber, R.J. (1997). "Making more from less: Strategic demand reduction in the FCC spectrum auctions". Journal of Economics and Management Strategy 6, 529–548.

Wellman, M.P. (2004). "Online marketplaces". In: Singh, M. (Ed.), Practical Handbook of Internet Computing. CRC Press.

Wellman, M.P., Walsh, W.E., Wurman, P.R., MacKie-Mason, J.K. (2001a). "Auction protocols for decentralized scheduling". Games and Economic Behavior 35, 271–303.

Wellman, M.P., Wurman, P.R., O'Malley, K., Bangera, R., Lin, S.-D., Reeves, D., Walsh, W.E. (2001b). "Designing the market game for a trading agent competition". IEEE Internet Computing 5, 43–51.

Wellman, M.P., Cheng, S.-F., Reeves, D.M., Lochner, K.M. (2003a). "Trading agents competing: Performance, progress, and market effectiveness". IEEE Intelligent Systems 18 (6), 48–53.

Wellman, M.P., Greenwald, A., Stone, P., Wurman, P.R. (2003b). "The 2001 trading agent competition". Electronic Markets 13, 4–12.

Wellman, M.P., Reeves, D.M., Lochner, K.M., Vorobeychik, Y. (2004). "Price prediction in a trading agent competition". Journal of Artificial Intelligence Research 21, 19–36.

Wellman, M.P., Estelle, J., Singh, S., Vorobeychik, Y., Kiekintveld, C., Soni, V. (2005). "Strategic interactions in a supply chain game". Computational Intelligence 21, 1–26.

Wolfram, C. (1998). "Strategic bidding in a multi-unit auction: An empirical analysis of bids to supply electricity in England and Wales". RAND Journal of Economics 29, 703–725.

Wolski, R., Plank, J.S., Brevik, J., Bryan, T. (2001). "Analyzing market-based resource allocation strategies for the computational grid". International Journal of High Performance Computing Applications 15, 258–281.

Woods, W.W.A. (2002). B2B Exchanges 2.0. ISI Publications, Bermuda.

Wurman, P.R., Wellman, M.P. (2000). "AkBA: A progressive, anonymous-price combinatorial auction", in: Second ACM Conference on Electronic Commerce, Minneapolis, MN, 21–29.

Wurman, P.R., Wellman, M.P., Walsh, W.E. (2001). "A parametrization of the auction design space". Games and Economic Behavior 35, 304–338.

Ygge, F., Akkermans, H. (1996). "Power load management as a computational market", in: Second International Conference on Multiagent Systems, Kyoto, 393–400.

Chapter 29

COMPUTATIONAL METHODS AND MODELS OF POLITICS

KEN KOLLMAN[*]

Department of Political Science, University of Michigan, USA
e-mail: kkollman@umick.edu

SCOTT E. PAGE

Departments of Political Science and Economics, University of Michigan, USA
e-mail: spage@umich.edu

Contents

[*] The authors would like to thank Bob Axelrod, Jenna Bednar, Joe Harrington, and Leigh Tesfatsion for helpful comments on earlier drafts of this chapter.

Handbook of Computational Economics, Volume 2. Edited by Leigh Tesfatsion and Kenneth L. Judd
DOI: 10.1016/S1574-0021(05)02029-0

Abstract

In this chapter, we assess recent contributions of computational models to the study of politics. We focus primarily on agent-based models developed by economists and political scientists. These models address collective action problems, questions related to institutional design and performance, issues in international relations, and electoral competition. In our view, complex systems and computational techniques will have a large and growing impact on research on politics in the near future. This optimism follows from the observation that the concepts used in computational methodology in general and agent-based models in particular resonate deeply within political science because of the domains of study in the discipline and because early findings from agent-based models align with widely known empirical regularities in the political world. In the process of making our arguments, we survey a portion of the growing literature within political science.

Keywords

agent based models, political economy, spatial voting, collective action, complexity

JEL classification: D72, D74, H72

1. Introduction

In this chapter, we assess recent contributions of computational models to the study of politics. We focus primarily on agent-based models developed by economists and political scientists. These models address collective action problems, questions related to institutional design and performance, issues in international relations, and the study of competition in elections.

In order to place in context the research contributions discussed in this chapter, it is important to begin with a description of political science as an academic and scientific discipline. Modern political science is very broad, much broader than economics, both in terms of methodological approaches and in terms of the questions addressed. Despite this breadth, the set of methodologies used in political science does not contain the set used in economics. There are marked differences. As this is a volume on economics, these differences may not be apparent to all readers, and thus, we begin by describing the key subjects, approaches, and methods that animate contemporary political science.

As we discuss below, political scientists address three fundamental problems: collective action, the allocation of finite resources, and the determination of boundaries and secure spaces. These problems (especially the first two) have direct analogues to problems regularly studied in economics. Indeed, there is considerable overlap and cross-fertilization between the disciplines, especially in the field of political economy.

We discuss the implications of the fact that political scientists as a whole place much more emphasis on description and less emphasis on optimal design. Relative to economics, political science devotes more attention to history, case studies, and cross-national differences. And finally, political scientists show a greater willingness to engage the question of whether people are fundamentally self-interested or act in the interest of groups or collectivities.

We also discuss the methodological diversity of the discipline. Political science is open to far more methodologies than economics. In principle, this should make it easier for researchers attempting to integrate computational techniques into the discipline. However, at the same time computational techniques were being introduced into mainstream political science, there was a backlash of sorts against formal modeling, which has likely slowed the growth in use of these methods.

As will become evident, we are optimistic that complex systems and computational techniques will have a large and growing impact on research on politics in the near future. This optimism follows from the observation that the concepts used in computational methodology in general and agent-based models in particular resonate deeply within political science because of the domains of study in the discipline and because early findings from agent-based models align with widely known empirical regularities in the political world. In the process of making our arguments, we survey a portion of the growing literature within the discipline. We conclude with a discussion of fruitful research agendas that are already under way, and suggest some prospects for further progress.

2. Core questions motivating political scientists

The topics covered in political science research journals include the study of consti-
tutions, public decision-making institutions, philosophical issues on the relationship
between governments and individuals, courts and legal systems, race and ethnicity,
economic growth and institutional structure, urban politics, public opinion, mass participation, lobbying, elections and voting, and cultural difference. Amidst this topical
diversity, three major sets of questions cut across these topics and form the substantive
bases of modern political science:

    (i) How, when, and if individuals work together to accomplish common tasks, other-
        wise referred to as collective action for the purposes of, among other things, the
        production of public goods, the selection of leaders, and the determination of rules
        of behavior.

    (ii) How governments, organizations, or societies divide up resources and who ben-
        efits from the division. Let us call this "pie-splitting."

    (iii) How and when do groups and political units form, creating new identities or
        new legal entities. This includes both the origins of conflicts of interest and the
        study of how and when countries or sub-national groups decide to exit from the
        everyday, legal institutions of conflict resolution to threaten or engage in violent
        action. Let us call this "security and communal stability."

For any given domain of politics, all three questions can be important. For instance,
electoral campaigns for national office concern who gets what (pie splitting), what public goods the government should provide (collective action), and how to define and then
defend a country's interests (security and communal stability).

The disciplinary emphasis on collective as opposed to decentralized pie-splitting
links the first two questions within political science. Political (i.e. non-market) institutions almost by definition require coordinated collective action to function. For example,
federal systems, like the United States, involve collective participation by the subunits
to decide on policies (as in the U.S. Senate) as well as dividing up of resources to states
and regions. The pie is not always split fairly across geographic areas as electoral incentives of national leaders may lead them to provide benefits to different populations.

The discipline of economics places some emphasis on both of these two questions
as well. Market allocations are of course of fundamental concern to economists, but
as a general rule, political scientists focus more on non-market institutions that split
pies–organizations, governments, courts, legislatures, electoral systems. They put less
emphasis on market-based mechanisms than do economists. A major reason for the
difference is the simple fact that governments tend to intervene when markets fail. While
economics can be thought of as the study of how and when markets work, part of politics
is the study of how to allocate resources when either markets fail to work or they result
in distributions that people find unpalatable.

The third set of questions is central to political science. Defining the boundaries between political units, between organized groups, and between electoral, legislative, or
judicial coalitions is fundamental to political processes. The international system of

nation-states at any moment in time is a consequence of wars, diplomatic agreements, and declarations of both independence and subservience by national and ethnic groups. Political scientists devote much attention to how the various boundaries are determined and potentially change over time, and whether some kinds of political pressures lead to instability and violence.

Moreover, the option for persons, groups, or countries to "exit" from legitimate institutions makes it difficult for researchers to contain all that happens in politics into simple models of specific institutional settings. In political settings, nations or groups can opt out of a structured institutional environment (a well defined "game", if you will).

An act of war, rebellion, or terrorism can be thought of as abandoning current institutional arrangements. There are two ways to characterize these actions within models. One can consider war as a type of punishment in an institution-free repeated game setting, or one can consider violence as destroying the game itself, not something typically allowed in most game theoretic models of institutions. At the end of the war, it is not necessarily the case that the countries or groups go back to playing the same game. In some political settings, the option exists to eliminate your opponent. One country may take over another country and impose a new set of laws and institutions, or interactions among groups or regions can cease altogether after violence ends.

3. Different practices in comparison with economics

The many overlapping interests across the two disciplines, economics and political science, have resulted in substantial cross-fertilization of ideas and tools. Researchers in both disciplines model, estimate, and compare levels of efficiency, equity, growth and robustness across places and eras. Political economy, a field blending insights from both disciplines, has flourished in recent years. These similarities notwithstanding, on the whole the two disciplines are quite different. To paint in very broad strokes, economics is more technical and probes deeper empirically and theoretically into topics, while political science is richer and broader.

In comparison with economists, political scientists tend to devote less attention to the study of idealized mechanisms for the distribution of resources and more attention describing how existing mechanisms perform. A consequence of this different emphasis is that relatively less effort is spent in political science proposing mechanisms for improving the efficiency of social institutions. Put differently, political science devotes less attention to the "engineering" part of social science than does economics. Rather, the practice of political science places more attention on what has been and what is.

Political science also emphasizes more than economics cross-cultural and cross-national differences. While it is true that economics departments include scholars who focus on particular regions and countries, regional economics does not occupy as central a place in its discipline as does comparative political science. Moreover, the type of analysis done in political science is more nuanced and certainly broader in scope. While development and growth economists typically focus on variations in performance measures—rates of growth, inequality, and education levels—political scientists more often immerse themselves in understanding broader sets of concepts, including the culture of the countries they study. They consider, among other things, the lifestyles, beliefs, family structures, political participation, levels of trust, and religious practices.

An important reason for this emphasis on cross-cultural and cross-country variation is that the data demand it. Countries can have similar formal social, political and economic institutions, and yet the operation of those institutions can vary dramatically. For instance, Canada and India have the same electoral systems and systems of government, yet the nature of political competition, the relationships between levels of government, and the types of polices adopted by both countries have been vastly different. Argentina copied the United States constitution almost exactly. How political institutions have operated within those rules varies substantially across the two countries. Survey courses of comparative politics which cover many countries, the kind of courses taught at the undergraduate level, emphasize that, even though countries exhibit similarities in formal institutions, variation over time and across countries is the norm. Thus, as political scientists seek to discover and explain the empirical patterns in pie-splitting and collective action that emerge across countries or regions they incorporate not only institutional factors in their explanations. They also pay close attention to historical trajectories and cultural differences.

It is also the case that political scientists more openly grapple with the assumption of self interest. Granted, the rebirth of behavioralism has led economists to examine not only biases in behavior but also to question the self interest assumption (Camerer, 2003). And granted, some of that research demonstrates that in some contexts people act altruistically. But those experiments have not led economists to abandon the assumption of self interest. And for good reason. Economists mostly study situations for which an assumption of self interest makes sense. When a person buys a house or groceries, they create few externalities, other than pecuniary ones, so they might as well act in their self interest.

The three questions at the heart of political science, however—collective action, pie-splitting, and security and communal stability—all involve decisions and outcomes that create externalities. And in each case, there may be reasons for individuals to act in the collective interest rather than in their narrow self interest. In fact, many of the experiments that reveal altruism involve variants of the divide the dollar games and collective action games, corresponding to two of the core problems for political science.

Not surprisingly, political scientists have long been interested in the degree to which people act in their self interest, in their group's interest, or in what they perceive to be the collective interest of some large polity. From studies of voting (do people vote with their pocketbooks?) to studies of family structure (do people take in elderly relatives?), to studies of trust among neighbors (are people willing to lend money to friends?), research demonstrates what appear to be systematic differences across countries in the extent to which people are individually and collectively motivated. Whether people act in their self interest or are willing to act in the collective interest influences how institutions perform. The invisible hand at the core of economics implies that self interest and collective interest align. When providing for a public good, splitting a pie, or fighting wars, as everyone knows all too well, those interests may not align. In comparing the two disciplines, on balance political scientists are confronted more often with situations where the contrast between self-interest and group interest is evident.

4. Methodological diversity

Political science is a diverse and lively academic discipline. It is not uncommon for political science faculties to include scholars of ancient and modern political philosophy, area studies specialists who cover Russian and Chinese politics, students of the Supreme Court, experts on cultural change or diplomatic history, formal mathematical and statistical modelers using the latest techniques from econometrics or game theory to understand public opinion, elections, or legislative behavior, and researchers using the experimental techniques from psychology to understand mass political demonstrations. As we have mentioned several times, the discipline prizes empirical work and historical work, but it is decidedly not the case that the bulk of research is thick description. Many, if not most, political scientists are interested in discovering general understandings that translate across time and region. Nevertheless, there is a shared belief that such an understanding benefits from having solid accounts of what has happened and is happening across time and space so that such theories can be substantiated.

The upshot is that political scientists as a group will look at a single problem, process, or puzzle through many lenses. Voting behavior is analyzed with formal mathematical models, large N studies, small n in-depth surveys, controlled experiments, and historical analysis. Given this back-drop, computational models will never be seen as providing any definitive answers but as contributing to a general understanding formed through multiple methods. This is not a shortcoming of the approach—the same can be said of mathematical models—but a comment on the discipline (De Marchi, 2005).

Political scientists have made numerous methodological contributions to the social and behavioral sciences, including advances in survey research, spatial analysis of social processes, and models of collective decision-making, organizations and organizational decision-making. Yet the discipline also owes methodological debts to other disciplines, including, of course, economics. Researchers have borrowed theoretical concepts, statistical and experimental techniques, game-theoretic solution concepts, mathematical and behavioral axioms, and research design templates from across the social, natural, and even physical sciences. Given the broad scope of inquiry necessary to understand political systems and processes, perhaps this methodological diversity is inevitable and desirable.

In the best of scenarios, a diversity of approaches, methods, and areas of interest makes for interesting and productive seminars, faculty meetings, and professional conferences. The same diversity that can seed the cross fertilization of ideas, however, can lead to tension. In recent years, political science has delved into what have at times been heated controversies over the value of historical research, rational choice modeling (what some have called economic hegemony), and psychological experiments. A focal moment in this discipline-wide debate was the circulation of an e-mail document by "Mr. Perestroika" in 2000, and then a follow-up letter signed by hundreds of professional political scientists that same year demanding an end to hegemonic economic-type methods and the opening of journals to a wider assortment of methodologies. Much more commonly than does economics, political science tolerates and even accommodates on a regular basis internal debates over methodology, the appropriate fundamental assumptions of human behavior and cognition, and the social value of abstract theorizing.

Within this context—methodological pluralism and a portion of the discipline resenting the accretion of dominant methodologies from economics—complex systems approaches have become more prominent and accepted in political science in the last ten years. By and large, the techniques and approaches used did not originate within political science, though clearly some political scientists have been at the forefront of some areas of computational modeling. The techniques were largely borrowed from other disciplines. In this case, the providers were physicists, computer scientists, economists, theoretical biologists, and even persons now called complexologists. At the same time the reactions to complex systems have been complicated.

The Perestroika letter and its resulting movement within the discipline were partly a backlash against abstract (particularly mathematical) modeling in recent years. The complaints about modeling are themselves varied. Some political scientists call for more direct empirical grounding in theoretical models, and wish for more realism in the concepts used. This complaint sometimes pairs with another one: that highly technical work focuses attention on trivial, technical problems at the expense of important political problems. Some object in particular to rational choice assumptions as unrealistic. Others complain about attempts to "scientize" what are highly contingent and time-dependent processes in the political world. Others question the validity of much of the data being collected and analyzed.

Of course, several of these complaints can extend to computational models as well. Complex systems research, while not necessarily based on rational choice assumptions, deals with abstract, technical models, often without direct empirical implications. The methodological debates within political science, while they signal a colorful and sometimes tolerant discipline, might have come at an unfortunate time for computational and complex systems approaches.

We think this would be unfortunate if true, because computational techniques can potentially build a bridge within political science between those who value the rigor of modeling and those who see the explanatory power of particular contextual details. Complex systems approaches in the social sciences typically allow for historical contingency, more complicated interactions of diverse agents, and adaptation of preferences and agent-types. Looking to the future, we see reasons to be optimistic that these approaches will gain increasing respect, prestige and usage, largely because many of the core concepts that define and characterize the computational agenda resonate among political scientists (Johnson, 1999).

5. Resonance within political science

As we have discussed, political scientists study collective action, pie-splitting, and security and communal stability. The political systems within which these activities occur also exhibit characteristics that are similar to those found in other systems of interest to researchers in complex systems.

Consider the following seven terms, referring to concepts fundamental to complex systems and agent based modeling: *adaptation, difference, externalities, path dependence, geography, networks*, and *emergence* (Page, 2000). These concepts all map to empirical features of political systems.

In other words, political systems and complex adaptive systems appear similar in many respects. This resonance between the methodology of complex adaptive systems and the reality of politics provides strong support for an increased mingling of computational techniques and approaches within mainstream political science.

5.1. Adaptation

By adaptation, we mean selective pressures and learning (Axelrod and Cohen, 2000). Both forms of adaptation occur in political systems. They often occur simultaneously and at different time scales. A politician who does not learn fast enough loses his or her job in the next election. Institutions also learn and get selected for and against based on their performance. The study of selection and learning holds a prominent place in political science. Lindbloom's (Lindbloom, 1959) seminal article on government agencies is entitled, "The Science of Muddling Through." His follow-up two decades later (Lindbloom, 1979) was entitled, "Still Muddling, Not Through Yet."

Political science PhD students tend to read a lot of history and case studies of particular events or institutions, in addition to receiving basic statistical and game theoretic training. Naturally, this differs from the training of economics PhD students, who devote much more time to mathematics and the intricacies of studying quantitative data. A reasonable defense of political science training is that the study of politics requires an appreciation of the complexity of particular circumstances, because contexts change rapidly, and decision-makers rarely face the same competitive situation more than once. Moreover, in many political settings, the range of tactics or strategies available to decision-makers can be immense, and the number of potential influences on the consequences of decisions can be far beyond what decision-makers can comprehend.

In combination, the relative lack of repeated, highly correlated decision-making environments and the vast strategy spaces confronting decision-makers makes politics a fertile ground for studying adaptive behavior. Game theoretic models of battlefield decisions on where to allocate troops (Colonel Blotto Games, for instance) and on which policy platforms to propose in electoral campaigns, typically do not have pure strategy equilibria even if it is assumed that there is complete information.

The idea that behavior adapts over time rather than being chosen by rational actors has implications for the study of social systems, including voting and elections

(Bendor et al., 2003a). Some have already used agent-based models to argue that fighting among agents, with some dying off, leads to selection towards altruists (Cederman, 1997; Bowles et al., 2003). The research identifies a fundamental tension present in many political situations, one that in the abstract is a basic collective action problem, but with a steep discount factor. Self interest can help an agent to survive in the short run, while relying on notions of collective interest helps the group of agents survive in the long run (Miller, 1996).

If there are frequent interactions that lead to extermination, such as wars or election results that wipe out competitors, group selection perhaps can lead to an increase in collectively-interested behavior. Thus, the collective-based incentives that we see in some societies may in fact have evolved over time given the propensity of dangerous conflict. As we discuss later in more detail, Harrington (1998) has shown that actors within organizations can adapt over time as hierarchical structures weed out certain types of potential leaders in ways that affect organizational performance.

5.2. Difference

At a descriptive level, political scientists often begin with the basic fact of difference. There are deep and consequential differences across population groups and across countries. Even within a country, groups differ by their levels and types of political participation. It is not enough to know different resource endowments, underlying preferences, or institutional rules. Cultural differences abound, and culture interacts in complicated ways with other differences that influence the success or failure of policies and reforms. As we discuss in more detail below, complex systems research, with its emphasis on interactions among agents, can help in understanding the emergence of cultural differences that are hard to explain with more traditional economic methods that focus on preferences and information.

In understanding the mechanisms of politics, the two opposing forces, splitting and unifying, are always present. Individuals with different characteristics, preferences, and information have to conduct pie-splitting. At the same time, nothing of consequence can happen in most political settings without coalitions of diverse individuals, organizations, or countries, putting aside their differences to accomplish collective action.

Two important classes of traditional models in political science concern coalition formation among diverse individuals. Game theoretic bargaining models, such as those proposed by Baron and Ferejohn (1989) and by Harrington (1990)—both are variants of the Rubinstein bargaining model—help us to understand how coalitions might form within majority-rule legislatures to decide how to divide up a fixed pie. Agenda-setting agents make proposals and try to win majority support with a legislature. Variations in institutional rules can then be shown to affect how the pie is split. Being able to make the first proposal conveys an advantage. Allowing legislators to propose amendments can increase equality.

Spatial voting models, in a similar fashion, depict political parties or candidates as offering campaign platforms to try to win the votes of diverse citizens (Downs, 1957;

Enelow and Hinich, 1984). The parties or candidates that attract a coalition of voters around their platforms sufficient enough to win elections can choose how to divide the governmental pie.

Potential differences across individuals in these models are depicted as dimensions, where each political issue or each policy domain is its own dimension. For both classes of models, there exists the well-known problem of a lack of a core allocation in multiple dimensions. This means that if players are selfish, there typically is no collective decision or allocation of resources in multiple dimensions that cannot be blocked by some coalition of players. In bargaining models, tight agenda-control can avoid the problem of winning coalitions fragmenting with each new proposal. And in spatial voting models, with multiple dimensions, only by introducing uncertainty among agents or by fixing some party's or candidate's behavior artificially can we tie down pure strategy equilibria (Kollman et al., 1998; De Marchi, 1999).

Yet in real politics, coalitions and party ideologies are far more durable than these traditional models would generally predict. Agent-based models can help to understand this durability. The models help us pay careful attention to the limited cognition of political competitors and the consequences of repeated interactions with other people who live nearby and share similar cultures.

Difference can also lead to fighting. As we discuss later, Bhavnani and Backer (2000) model ethnic conflict using computational methods. Ethnic conflict naturally lends itself to dynamic, computational models because it is not a one-shot event, but a series of reactions and counter-reactions that result in patterns of activity over time.

Political scientists also care about difference as representation. When putting together a cabinet, a committee, or a court, a leader is often under tremendous pressure to choose members who represent various identity groups (by gender, race, ethnicity, and so on). Most arguments in favor of such diverse representation are based primarily on norms of fairness. Yet, as some complex systems research has shown (Hong and Page, 2001), diversity may also lead to better collective decisions.

5.3. Externalities

In economics, it is widely known that markets can fail because of unpriced externalities. Indeed, much of political science concerns the allocation of goods and services when markets do not work as intended, and specifically, how governments decide to manage externalities. Governments, at least in principle, ought to adopt policies to try to mitigate negative externalities and promote positive externalities. Government may also deliberately take actions intended to create positive externalities, such as building infrastructure and establishing the rule of law. Government actions have pronounced boundary effects: encouraging growth by protecting and encouraging industries; providing for schools, parks, roads, prisons, and welfare systems; and ensuring public peace by maintaining a military.

The scope of externalities can influence the performance of political institutions. Lacy and Niou (1998), for example, have shown how certain voting systems can perform poorly when decisions have externalities, and Kollman et al. (2000) have shown that whether to decentralize or centralize decisions on policies in a federal system may depend upon the level of external effects among decisions. More externalities make for harder problems. Organizations, governments, or people facing harder problems may benefit from more sophisticated search techniques to find solutions (Page, 1996).

When the trading of goods only affects buyers and sellers, in principle any trade increases total happiness or utility: both sets of participants are better off and no one else is affected. Since total happiness probably has a maximum (due to resource or technological constraints), the trading system must stop and reach an equilibrium. In graduate economics textbooks, this process is often modeled with a Lyapunov function. With externalities, total happiness does not have to increase with each trade, so the trading process may not reach an equilibrium. If North Korea trades with a member of the former Soviet Union for nuclear fuel, both trading partners have improved their utility, but the rest of the world is worse off. Aggregate utility need not rise with some kinds of trading among nations. Furthermore, trades can beget further trades as total happiness flows up and down over time. The system can churn endlessly rather than settle.

Many political systems appear to be constantly churning and not settling into an equilibrium. (See Janssen and Ostrom, 2006 "Governing Social-Ecological Systems", this Handbook.) Admittedly, the alliance formation process that occurs in the international arena and the coalition formation process in electoral or legislative politics are more durable that one might predict in the absence of some kind of institutional structure, as discussed above, but it would be a stretch to say that participants in either domain attain a steady-state. Agent-based models can provide insight into both the dynamics of social interactions with externalities and the reasons some systems settle into equilibria and other systems do not (Jackson, 2003; Cederman, 1997).

Political scientists and economists both try to understand when it is better to use market solutions to solve problems of negative externalities and when it is better to centralize decision-making and solve those problems politically. Agent-based modeling techniques, by allowing for the exploration of different kinds of externalities affecting diverse agents interacting in space and in time, can help in making such decisions.

5.4. Path dependence

Path dependence refers to the idea that the particular way events unfold over time shapes future outcomes, and that systems exhibit feedback leading outcomes toward a strict subset of all possible steady-state or equilibrium outcomes. Political scientists have long acknowledged such path dependence in explaining specific institutional and cultural features of societies.

Sequential decisions can be path dependent. Consider, for example, how this matters for urban and regional development. In the splitting up of the pie in a federated system, giving a region a slice in the form of an airport, military base, or public works project can create positive and negative externalities. These externalities shape future decisions on splitting the next pie, so that governments may want to continue to invest or cease such investments in a region, depending on the nature of the externalities. (See Arthur, 2006 "Out of Equilibrium Economics and Agent-Based Modeling", this Handbook.)

Institutional development can be path dependent. As Pierson (2000) has argued, the operations of political institutions lead to public attitudes and preferences among the population that in turn pressure government leaders to shape reforms of those institutions and to create new ones. Governmental programs, such as social security or educational loans, create constituencies among voters that severely limit the options available to public officials in budgeting and in administrative operations (Jackson, 2003). Over time, many governmental programs can outlive their usefulness but they survive because their histories have created constituencies that monitor closely government action.

Beliefs, values, and understandings support this path dependence. In international relations or in ethnic conflict, for instance, the past can shape present outcomes long after it seems rational for decision-makers to invoke the past in predicting the future behavior of adversaries. Tensions across national and ethnic boundaries often have their origins in events that transpired generations ago. In Ireland and in Serbia, for example, battles won or lost many centuries ago appear as focal events in generating collective action among ordinary Irish and Serbs. The collective actions then shape contemporary negotiations over splitting pies and establishing security and stability. History matters and lingers in ways that are hard to imagine in most systems that economists study, such as industrial or financial markets (Page, 2006).

5.5. Geography

Geography has become increasingly important in some fields of economics, such as in the study of city formation and location. It has long been important in political science, especially in the study of international relations, urban politics, and voting and elections. Besides the fact that wars and diplomatic disputes are often about the protection or acquisition of land, geography seems to have broader consequences in politics. People living near each other interact and influence each other on a regular basis, and differences can emerge among population groups based on little more than geographic proximity. Animosity can grow between groups that otherwise have similar political preferences simply because they live in different areas.

Geographic correlation of induced preferences over policies in democracies may be largely due to electoral districting rules. In all but a handful of countries, representatives are allocated by geographic districts or regions, and thus candidates or parties structure their campaigns around geography. They promise particular populations living in specific areas pieces of the pie to win their votes.

Geography has the effect of reducing the number of potential coalitions in a democracy or in an international dispute down to manageable numbers. Consider the potential number of coalitions of the members of the U.S. Senate or the U.S. House of Representatives. In the former case, the potential set of majority coalitions is 100 choose 51, or over a million billion, while for the latter it is 435 choose 218, substantially bigger than a billion billion. Yet throughout American history, coalitions within the Congress have always had enduring geographic bases, over and above shared policy preferences that exist across widely spread population groups.

In international relations, the fact that wars are usually over land has the (hardly redeeming) characteristic of enabling coalitions to become manageable. The number of sides in wars has nearly always been two (Jervis, 1997). When Germany invaded its erstwhile ally the Soviet Union in 1941, it unified the Allies and the Soviets instead of creating a three-sided war, even though there were huge differences between the main Allied countries and the Soviets. It was not geographic proximity in this case, but the fact that the two new allied sides were poised to squeeze Germany from east and west. The aggregation of diverse preferences is central to the study of politics, and geography offers a convenient way for leaders to unify people, organizations, or countries, around common goals.

Agent-based models from political science have analyzed the dynamics of interactions and coalition formation not just in time but in space (Cederman, 1997; Lustick and Miodownik, 2000). Researchers can depict interactions of agents as occurring on a grid that has geographic features of proximity and the observable spread of something—agents, culture, characteristics, empires, political control—over space. (See Dibble, 2006 "Agent-Based Computational Laboratories", this Handbook.)

5.6. Networks

The idea that information can spread through networks in unexpected but consequential ways has long been understood by social scientists, including political scientists. Just as people tend to get jobs through weak ties, they also obtain political information through friends of friends. Moreover, there has been a long-standing interest in how these networks are connected and who has power within those networks. This includes research on the topology of networks, such as the research by Padgett and Ansell (1993) on the Medici family in Italy. (See Vriend, 2006 "ACE Models of Endogenous Interactions", and Wilhite, 2006 "Economic Activity on Fixed Networks", both in this Handbook.)

Within political science, there has been a great deal of research on social capital. Putnam's research (Putnam, 2000) concludes that social capital in the United States is declining, with negative consequences. Tilly (1998) provides data indicating that a systematic lack of social capital for one group can lead to long term inequality relative to other groups with higher social capital. For Putnam, a lack of social capital can lead to less pie to split; for Tilly, network connections may explain how the pie is split.

In our times, the link of networks to security and stability seems obvious, though it was not twenty years ago. Terrorist networks are now one of the greatest threats to domestic and international security and stability. Threats are no longer restricted to state-sponsored militaries. Naturally, there is growing interest in network structures that cross national boundaries and that rely on religious motivations to work.

Research on networks in political science is still primarily empirical and descriptive. At present, efforts are more toward documenting the operations of the networks rather than trying to understand theoretically the structural implications of those networks. There are reasons to be optimistic that computational techniques can help researchers lead the way in understanding both beneficial and insidious networks in the politics. The recent work by Huckfeldt et al. (2004) discussed below on political participation demonstrates the power of computational techniques to study social networks.

5.7. Emergence

Emergence refers to surprising aggregate phenomena that result from the micro level actions of agents (Axelrod et al., 1995). Gliders can emerge in the "game of life", and prices can emerge in complex markets. Segregation can emerge in Schelling's (Schelling, 1978) tipping model, and criticality emerges in sand pile models. Emergence can even be formally defined as a logical or statistical property that occurs at a higher level than the component units.

Since political scientists observe cultural differences across space and time, the notion of emergence resonates in the discipline. (See Axelrod (2006), "Agent-based Modeling as a Bridge Between Disciplines", this Handbook.) As an indication, the studies by Axelrod on the emergence of cooperation (Axelrod, 1984) and the emergence of norms (Axelrod, 1986) have been very influential. Empirically, macro-level characteristics of societies can change over time, sometimes gradually and sometimes dramatically. For example, societies vary substantially in their levels of trust and individualism displayed in surveys and in experiments (Inglehart, 1997). If asked if they trust other people, over two-thirds of Scandinavians will reply that they do. Fewer than a fifth of Turkish people do. Some countries have seen increases in measures of trust, something often attributed to economic growth. Economic growth itself has an emergent quality that is hard to predict in advance, and can occur in a relatively short period of time, as observed in several East Asian economies, and in Ireland in the 1980s and 1990s. (See Howitt, 2006 "Coordination Issues in Long-Run Growth", this Handbook.)

Most political scientists agree that cultural differences exist and are meaningful, but there is less agreement on where these cultural differences come from, and the role of institutions in forming and transforming culture. Putnam et al. (1993) attributes the profound differences between the trusting, economically well-off Northern Italians and the less trusting, less well-off Southern Italians to the "mists of the dark ages", or the historical legacies of centuries-old practices.

We have reasons to believe that complex systems and agent-based modeling are well suited to construct valuable models of culture. There has already been computational research on where and how cultural differences emerge (Axelrod, 1997; Bowles et al., 2003, and Bednar and Page, 2006). This research examines three different aspects of culture: within group homogeneity, altruism, and behavioral consistency; all three programs hint at the enormous potential for future work. Some political scientists, especially from the area studies tradition, believe that each region or country is exceptional, and that because people of different regions interpret the world differently and act differently, comparative work across cultural contexts obscures the uniqueness of each setting and leads to false inferences about the causes of varying outcomes. Computational models can help us understand how unique kinds of behavior emerge in specific contexts (Epstein, 2003).

For political scientists, fieldwork to study the local context will continue to be valuable. In fact, they may be even more so as it becomes possible to link more tightly the results of models on the emergence of those cultural contexts with data collected in the field.

6. The state of research

In reviewing current research on computational methods in political science and political economy, not surprisingly we observe diverse approaches and purposes. If we cast our net broadly, to capture all computational modeling, including numerical estimations of equilibria from game theory (see, for example, Baron and Herron, 2003), calculations of all possible coalitions in large groups (see, for example, Laver and Benoit, 2003), or Monte Carlo simulations of social processes using empirically-derived estimators, then the amount of published work is quite large. For purposes of this handbook, however, it is most useful to cast our net somewhat narrower, to focus on agent-based computational models.

Political scientists have used computer simulation and computational modeling in various guises for many decades. Guetzkow (1963) simulated the international system using complicated computer models in the 1960s. Computational versions of Axelrod's prisoner's dilemma tournament (Axelrod, 1984) were summarized in publications more than 20 years ago. The use of computation to explore domains of interest to political scientists has grown tremendously. A list of the computational versions of the repeated prisoner's dilemma would alone fill a chapter of this handbook.

In this brief summary of the research, we focus on those papers or books that address what we previously identified as the core concerns of political scientists: collective choices and production of public goods; pie splitting; and cohesion and conflict. However, as will be seen below, many of the models we summarize address more than one of these concerns, and thus it is difficult to categorize the models cleanly. Nevertheless, to generalize over the following summary, the models of electoral competition and institutional comparisons tend to focus on issues of collective choice, the models of adaptive agents within organizations and complex environments tend to focus on issues of pie-splitting, and the models of identity tend to focus on issues of cohesion and conflict.

6.1. Models of electoral competition

The study of elections is central to political science. A great deal of research is devoted to the analysis of party position-taking and voter behavior. By some depictions, in U.S. presidential elections, the candidates compete within vast multi-dimensional issue spaces and voters are bombarded with diverse and often conflicting information from a variety of sources. The resulting system of positioning, advertising, and voting among diverse kinds of actors lends itself to agent-based modeling.

We consider electoral models in some detail to provide a vivid example of how computational models can add value to the study of politics. The model that is most widely used to study candidate behavior is called the spatial model, as policies and voter ideal points are represented as vectors. Voters vote for the party or candidate closest to them in the space of possible positions. This was first proposed by Hotelling (1929) as a model of economic spatial competition in one dimension. Downs (1957) applied this model to candidate positioning with the result that in two-candidate competition, the candidates converge to the median voter's position.

For nearly fifty years spatial models of electoral competition have been prominent fixtures in political science journals or on bookshelves. Subsequent to Downs, Plott (1967) proved that in higher dimensions, unless voter ideal points satisfied radial symmetry (an extremely strong condition), any policy position could be defeated. This ruled out pure strategy equilibria in predicting candidate behavior. The lack of a pure strategy equilibrium can be overcome by introducing uncertainty by candidates, but the informational assumptions in such models are still quite strong. Candidates have to know the distribution over votes for all pairs of positions. Building upon the logic in Plott's result, McKelvey (1976) then showed that the top cycle set, the set of positions that defeat any other position, equals the entire set. This is typically taken to mean that there is no equilibrium policy position in a multidimensional voting model where majority rule is the means of deciding among policies.

Yet the McKelvey result is often interpreted incorrectly. Some have concluded that the result means electoral democracy in general leads to chaos (Riker, 1982). In fact, the McKelvey result is a theorem about what kind of preference aggregation is possible under majority rule. It does not tell us what happens under specific institutions (other than majority rule) or given a specific set of behavioral assumptions about rational actors. The latter consideration was considered by Kramer (1977) who showed that if an incumbent party remains fixed while the challenger party seeks a position to defeat the incumbent, and parties want to maximize their vote total, over a sequence of elections policies would converge to the min max set, the set of policies that lose by a minimal amount. This would seem to lend some stability to electoral outcomes. Unfortunately, once the min max set is reached, the winning policy can then jump back out of the set in a future period. Kramer's result does not, therefore, imply stability.

Viewed in summary, the Plott, McKelvey, and Kramer results made some scholars question whether democratic procedures could aggregate preference information in a coherent way. The multidimensional results have also led theorists and empiricists to rely on more manageable one-dimensional models. A single-dimensional model of competition, while useful for some purposes, is by some considered too simplistic to capture many aspects of electoral competition, such as the trade-offs voters make across issue dimensions in evaluating candidates or parties.

To draw an analogy to economics, suppose that economists discovered in mathematical models with rational consumers and firms that supply equaled demand if there were a single market but not if there were more than one market attracting the dollars of consumers. If economists then collectively decided that there was really only one market and that this was the only kind of model worth studying, we would be disappointed that constraints on modeling were leading us away from studying more complex aspects of the real economy. In fact, in standard economic models, two markets work as efficiently as one. (To be fair, economists are not faultless either. They assume that a million markets also behave like a single market, a conjecture that certainly cannot be true.)

The contribution of computational models to the elections literature takes three forms. First, scholars have asked the basic computational question: how hard would it be to find a sequence of policies that led through a series of votes from one policy to a second arbitrary policy? More formally, given a policy x and a policy y, how difficult is finding policies $x_1, x_2, \ldots x_n$ such that $x_1 = x$, $x_n = y$, and x_{i-1} loses in a democratic election to x_i for each $i = 1 \ldots n$? Bartholdi et al. (1989) show that manipulating a plurality voting system is computationally hard. They show that if there are C candidates and V voters, then the difficulty of manipulating a voting system by adding or deleting candidates is NP hard in $C * V$, the number of candidates times the number of voters. This result points toward a more nuanced interpretation of McKelvey's result. Even if the top cycle set is the entire set, the ability of someone to manipulate outcomes may well be limited by computational constraints. We might think of McKelvey as showing what is possible and the later results of Bartholdi, Tovey, and Trick as describing what is plausible.

Moreover, if anything, these findings understate the difficulty of the task because these researchers assume sincere voting (voting for the most preferred outcome in the choice set) by everyone. With sophisticated voting (voting for the option that maximizes one's utility given one's knowledge of others' behavior) or a blend of sophisticated and sincere voting, predicting the outcomes of various configurations of candidates might itself be even more difficult computationally than even Bartholdi, Tovey, and Trick describe.

The second computational contribution to this literature relies on agent-based models of elections. These papers relax the assumption that parties choose their platforms optimally. Instead, the parties adapt platforms using search strategies that range from quite simple to rather sophisticated. In an early paper, Kollman, Miller, and Page (Kollman et al., 1992) show that adaptive parties in a multidimensional environment tend to converge to central regions of the policy space.

In the basic KMP model, voters have ideal points in an N-dimensional policy space. Candidates or parties choose policies in that space. A voter chooses to vote for whichever party's platform is closer to her ideal point. Unlike in the standard spatial model, parties are constrained in their movements and in the information they have. In the KMP model, parties can only move locally, in the neighborhood of their current policy platform.

In one version of the KMP model, a party's decision about where to move is dictated by polling results. A party with a policy $(y_1, y_2, \ldots y_n)$ tests a neighboring policy $(\hat{y}_1, \hat{y}_2, \ldots \hat{y}_n)$. If that new policy gets more votes against the opponent in a poll than does the old policy, then the party moves to $(\hat{y}_1, \hat{y}_2, \ldots \hat{y}_n)$. In another version of the model, parties toss out an initial set of policies in the neighborhood of their current policies and choose the best among those. In yet another, the parties use a genetic algorithm to evolve policies. (See Brenner, 2006 "Agent Learning Representation: Advice on Modeling Agent-based Learning", and Duffy, 2006 "Agent-based Models and Human Subjects Experiments", both in this Handbook, for detailed discussion of genetic algorithms.)

Regardless of the policy formation rule, the qualitative results remain unchanged: parties tend to choose policies near the center of the policy space. Once both parties locate there, they make small changes hoping to build winning coalitions of voters. One result that depends upon the learning rule was the time it took the parties to locate the center of the policy space. This depended on the relationship between the sophistication of the policy search algorithm and the size of the policy space.

The convergence of the parties' platforms depended on other parts of the model. In later work KMP (Kollman et al., 1998) reveal a relationship between the nature of voter preferences and policy convergence. They use the metaphor of an "electoral landscape" as a way to describe the adaptive environment that a political party faces. In their use of the concept, higher points on the landscape mean more voter support. They find that voter preferences help determine whether electoral landscapes are relatively flat or relatively rugged. This matters because with flat landscapes, parties have difficulty finding more popular, winning policies through adaptation. With more pointed landscapes and steep slopes, parties can easily find pathways to high ground. In contrast, if modelers assume optimizing parties, as is standard in traditional spatial models, the notion of landscapes is irrelevant. The slope of the payoff function does not matter with optimizing parties because the parties can find the optima immediately and do not need to find pathways there. Thus, the computational approach with adaptive parties can highlight a linkage between voters' preferences and rates of party convergence by focusing on *how* parties adapt toward more popular policy positions.

The near-convergence result from the computational model suggests a reconsideration of the importance of a lack of a formal equilibrium in the multiple-issue domain. Does the equilibrium really matter that much if it is just a benchmark? Given optimizing agents and certain additional regularity conditions, a market has an equilibrium that is efficient. But agent-based models of markets do not necessarily go right to that equilibrium. Instead, they often bounce around in the neighborhood of the efficient allocation. Two-party competition in multiple dimensions does not have a pure strategy equilibrium in the absence of institutional or information constraints, but in agent-based, adaptive models candidates tend to bounce around in the neighborhood of the policies that give the highest utility. If modern social science relied on agent-based models with adaptive, purposeful, but not hyper-rational agents, and not on equilibrium notions, then perhaps social scientists would not be led to think that markets work and electoral democracy does not. Instead, perhaps the two kinds of systems for aggregating preferences would look about equally effective at carrying out their respective tasks.

In addition to convergence results, KMP also find that incumbents, who are assumed to be fixed in the policy space, often win elections. This occurs because challengers may not adapt well enough to locate winning policy positions. These challengers were not stupid. The difficulty in beating an incumbent results from the fact that the challenging candidate who has just been defeated often has many possible policy changes that improve its vote total but there is no-clear direction on which changes will lead to winning. Moreover, the elections are depicted are zero sum games. If one candidate is at a multi-dimensional peak, then the other is stuck in a multi-dimensional hole. Positioned in this hole, any path leads upward, toward more votes, but only a few of these paths may lead to a platform that wins the election (Tovey, 1991).

These computational models of elections not only generate intuitively appealing results, they display a kind of realism lacking in some game theoretic models that assume perfect optimizing behavior. In the adaptive models, parties take polls and respond to the polling information by moving locally in policy space. Parties attain office with moderate platforms. And the parties occasionally, but only occasionally, re-aligne themselves, changing the blocks of voters to whom they appeal. This is similar to real politics, such as when most African-Americans switched their allegiances from the Republican Party to the Democratic Party over the latter half of the 20th Century because of the changes in party position-taking.

The initial KMP models were somewhat primitive. There have been extensions and variations by other authors that include interest groups and adaptive voters. De Marchi (2003), for instance, considers a two-dimensional issue space. As before, the parties respond to polls of voters on issues. His models depart from the more basic KMP model in their assumptions about voter information and sophistication. In the KMP model, voters know the parties' policy positions exactly. De Marchi's assumptions incorporate widely accepted research findings on the distribution of information among mass electorates. Including empirically supportable assumptions of informational diversity among voters lends realism to his computational models and offers the potential for empirical testing as well as calibration.

In the first of De Marchi's models, some voters have sophisticated ideologies and therefore are consistent in their survey responses to pollsters. Other voters are not ideologically "constrained", and their poll responses across issue dimensions are highly variable. He finds that the responsiveness of the adaptive parties to the voters is sensitive to the instability of voters' answers to pollsters about their favorite policy positions, and not so much to the levels of ideological sophistication.

In the second model, voters vary in the amount of information they have. He finds that less voter information leads to an even greater incumbency advantage compared with the case of more voter information. Incumbents' platforms are better known so incumbents do better. De Marchi also explores competition over which issues candidates choose to highlight. Candidates can emphasize certain issues at the expense of others. Here again, we get an incumbency advantage. Incumbents tend to have more money, and therefore can highlight issues upon which they have an electoral advantage.

In light of the fact that adaptive parties tend to converge in more than one dimension, there are single-dimensional political models with adaptive agents. In one such model, Jackson (2003) proposes a single-dimensional dynamic model of two-party electoral competition where both parties and voters adapt. The parties adapt to the position of the median voter in trying to win elections, while simultaneously the position of the median voter adapts to the positions of the parties. Voters change policy positions because they develop partisan attachments to the parties and are influenced by the policy positions of the parties. The computer in this case solves a system of five equations that depicts the changing policy positions of the parties, the changing position of the median voter, and the changing levels of party loyalty present among the voters. Jackson finds that for reasonable ranges of parameter values, the model does settle into equilibrium party positions, but only after a lengthy time period. Under various conditions, the fortunes of the parties, and their policy positions, fluctuate over time, with alternating stretches of one party dominance followed by collapse and the emergence of the other party as the dominant force. This again is similar to real election results in American history, where there have been long stretches of one-party dominance, followed by abrupt change.

In a recent paper, Laver (2005) proposes an innovative computational model of party competition and then tests its implications using electoral data from Ireland. The model includes parties with different kinds of strategies and different motivations. Some parties in the model, for example, change their policy positions to mimic the largest party, and then move in the direction of the maximal gradient. Other parties retain their founding policy positions and move incrementally in search of more votes. Laver studies competition with diverse kinds of parties with different motivations, and suggests that his model captures the essence of many multi-party systems, such as those in many European countries. Some parties seek to maximize votes while others seek to retain their ideological identities. He calibrates his simulations using real data from Irish elections, making assumptions about the strategies of the various Irish parties. He is able to create simulated results that resemble historical changes in parties' support in Ireland.

6.2. Institutional comparisons

Institutions enable groups to decide over public goods, but they also enable collective decisions over pie-splitting—who gets what, where and when, and how, to paraphrase the definition of politics given by Harold Lasswell (1958), a famous political scientist from the 1950s. (See Janssen and Ostrom, 2006 "Governing Social-Ecological Systems", this Handbook.)

A small but growing literature is devoted to comparisons of political institutions using computational models. We think this area of research is particularly promising. For example, McGann et al. (2002) study voting behavior under three different electoral rules using a computational model. In the model, candidates are randomly selected from the population to run for office and their policy platforms are depicted as falling on a one-dimensional scale. Citizens vote sincerely for the candidate closest to them. McGann et al. evaluate results from many simulations of voting behavior under plurality, run-off, and sequential elimination voting rules, and measure how closely the winner in each election approximates the median voter or is the Condorcet winner among the candidates.

In this model, candidates or citizens are not adapting in a complex environment, in contrast to most agent-based models. Instead the computer is able to replicate various instantiations of specific kinds of voting behavior under different institutional rules. The researchers find that winners are more often than not representative of modes in the distribution of voters instead of medians, and that the run-off and sequential elimination rules reward the Condorcet winner more often than plurality rules.

Hayes and Richards (2003) rely on computational methods to analyze economic behavior in the context of different kinds of exchange rate regimes by governments. In their model, buyers and sellers of foreign currencies who can profit by predicting future exchange rates attempt to learn the true nature of the monetary regime by observing changes in the money supply. The currency traders use Bayesian reasoning to learn whether the regime is contractionary or expansionist, although the agents receive noisy information generated by the stochastic environment. The model indicates, surprisingly, that politically-dependent central banks may benefit traders because learning the nature of the regime becomes easier. A dependent central bank produces politically motivated policies, and therefore traders can ascribe less of the variance in the money supply to stochastic variables than they can in the case of an independent central bank. They compare the results of their computational model to real data from Britain and Germany. The trajectories of excess returns from both countries differ in ways predicted by the model.

As these papers suggest, computational models allow scholars to capture explicit differences in institutions and to consider the implications of those differences. Another advantage of computational models is that they allow for multiple institutions to be considered simultaneously. As an example, Kollman et al. (1997) embed their spatial voting model with adaptive parties in a Tiebout framework. In the model, citizens are free to move between locations based upon the locations' offerings of public goods. Those public goods are decided by voting among the citizens at the locations.

The results of this model were surprising. Poorly performing rules for voting—those that produced the least stable policies within locations—did the best in the Tiebout setting. Thus, the instability of majority rule voting, the lack of equilibrium that everyone considers a weakness, turns out to be a strength when Tiebout effects are included. After analyzing the results of the computational model, the reason becomes apparent. Stability of electoral outcomes is correlated with the homogeneity of preferences. If people in a location all want the same thing, the parties offer that. If people have diverse preferences, the parties wander in policy space. This policy instability leads to more sorting. If people have not yet sorted into homogeneous preference groups, then the policies continue to cycle. If the people have sorted into groups with homogeneous preferences, then the system stabilizes.

The key insight is that, if instability of the entire system decreases as utility increases, then the system stabilizes at good outcomes. Bad outcomes get disturbed by the local instability, leading the system to search for better policies in locations and better distributions of citizens across locations. This results in a search that is even better than simulated annealing. In simulated annealing, the amount of instability decreases with time. In the Tiebout model, the amount of instability decreases with total utility.

There is a further point related to the future of the spatial modeling literature. In political institutions, voters cast ballots for candidates who then comprise a legislature. Within that legislature, there are rules for how votes get aggregated. The candidates, when making appeals to voters, propose policies. These policies generate outcomes over which the voters have preferences. Voters, candidates, parties, legislatures—political systems are linked at several levels that ultimately result in policy outcomes of great importance. Many game theoretic models of politics tend to focus on a single level, such as the relationship between voters and election outcomes, the relationship between legislative composition and coalition formation, or the relationship between coalitions and policy choices. Some game theoretic models include voters who take into account the composition of the legislature, but it is very difficult to model the full linkage that includes whether policies lead to good outcomes and learning about the policy space among the various actors. Agent-based models and computational equilibrium models may allow richer institutional analyses of linked levels of conflict and organized behavior among people deciding over public goods. (See Chang and Harrington, 2006 "Agent-based Models of Organizations", this Handbook.)

6.3. Individuals or agents adapting in complex political environments

The computational literatures on electoral competition and on institutional analysis complement a relatively large literature that considers adaptive individuals and organizations in political systems. We discuss four general classes of research here: general models of political organizations; models of information transmission in political networks; models of violence (non-lattice based); and models of electoral settings. Within each, we highlight a handful of prominent papers.

The Tiebout model by Kollman et al. (1997) analyzes multiple institutional forces occurring simultaneously. Several organizational models consider structural features of an environment or organization and ask how those features influence behavior of agents. Harrington (2003), for example, examines a series of models of competition within hierarchies. In one paper, he proposes a model of agents competing for promotion in a hierarchical society or organization. We can think of these as politicians rising to positions of prominence. In the political story told to motivate the model, candidates pair off against each other at each level of the hierarchy. The winner goes on to compete again, while the loser leaves the population of competitors.

There are two types of candidates in the Harrington model, those who adapt to their environment and those who are rigid and do not adapt. The policies that the agents propose correspond to unidimensional issue positions. The rigid types are ideologues. They will not switch their positions to match current public opinion. Given the assumptions of the model, the number of survivors gets smaller as competitors ascend up the hierarchy of political offices. Harrington analyzes which kinds of agents (or candidates) survive to higher office when the exogenous environment changes over time. In particular, he traces the proportion of rigid (as opposed to flexible) agents in the top level of the hierarchy as competition unfolds and the population of surviving politicians evolves. Thus, the Harrington model can be thought of as a model of pie-splitting in two senses. First, the agents are proposing a particular way to split the pie. Second, there are only a limited number of positions at the top of the hierarchy.

Intuitively, we might expect the rigid agents to lose more often. However, in his model, voters have lexicographic preferences. They prefer someone who takes their preferred position; but if both candidates propose the same policy, the voter prefers a candidate who has consistently favored the policy. Thus, as they move up the hierarchy, the flexible agents get exposed and will lose to a rigid agent provided the rigid agent advocates the policy currently in fashion. Under some conditions, Harrington shows that the rigid agents, and not the flexible agents, win out.

The Harrington paper considers politicians who evolve in a complex system. A natural question to ask is what attributes of voters might emerge. In a series of papers, Bendor et al. (2003a, 2003b) explore how the aspiration levels of agents evolve over time. They find surprising emergent outcomes in the aggregate. In one paper (Bendor et al., 2003a), they propose a model of citizens deciding whether to vote when it is costly to do so. Voters have aspiration levels that respond to whether they voted and the election outcome, and they decide whether to vote based on how their expected utility compares to aspiration levels. Instead of focusing on free-riding, as with most voter turnout models, this research examines the dynamics of voter turnout as aspiration levels evolve over time, and whether that turnout settles into an equilibrium level. The computational experiments allow for different scenarios, such as specifying the cost of voting and the number of voters. They find that turnout does equilibrate at empirically observable levels—ranging from 30% to 70% in two-party systems—and those levels are lower as the number of voters increases and the cost of voting increases.

In another paper (Bendor et al., 2003b), agents pair off and play one of a number of well-known games, such as stag hunt, chicken, or prisoner's dilemma. However, instead of assuming optimization by agents, they assume that agents "satisfice" according to an aspiration level. An agent's aspiration level adjusts in response to payoffs from previous games. Thus, the agents adapt their decision rules according to their experience. With this simple model, the authors can examine a large number of questions, such as the amount of cooperation induced by agents with adaptive aspirations and the sensitivity of players' strategies to initial conditions (e.g., the initial aspiration levels). Among the many results in their paper, they find that cooperation in games like prisoner's dilemma can occur even in one-shot settings. They also show by including trembles that the games have unique limiting distributions, a valuable "existence" result that allows for empirical applications of the model.

In a recent book, Huckfeldt et al. (2004) summarize a study of how individuals talk politics within social networks. The authors begin with the following stylized facts that might seem contradictory. People are easily influenced by their friends and acquaintances on politics. People interact with many others over the course of a relevant period prior to an election. Diversity of political attitudes exists within electorates, even among people who interact with each other on a regular basis and who even talk about politics with each other. Given how easily people are influenced, how does the diversity happen? Why do societies fail to converge on uniform opinions?

The authors demonstrate empirically, first, that individuals talk about politics within social networks, and that diversity exists even among loose social networks. The authors suggest that the social networks are the key mechanisms that lead to diversity of opinions within an electorate. To understand these social networks, the authors describe a simple agent-based model, based on the culture model by Axelrod (1997) discussed below. In brief, agents with political attitudes interact and can influence each other, and one can trace the spread of attitudes across the social system. In the first version of this model, all agents eventually agree on the same political attitudes. In contradiction to their empirical findings, there is no diversity of opinion after a relatively short period of time within the model. They test several simple solutions, such as introducing rigid agents who do not change, and various parameter changes that make sense.

Eventually, they introduce different, more realistic changes to the model. Most importantly, they give agents different layers of friends and acquaintances, where the probability of being influenced depends on how close the other agent is to you. As they examine the runs of this model, they see that social networks begin to emerge, and over time diversity exists in the societies. The social networks cling to opinions that differ from other social networks, and the entire population exhibits both an intra-group homogeneity but an across-group heterogeneity. It looks a lot like the empirical data. The basic insight, which is similar to others from the research summarized below, is that social systems can exhibit a balance of influence and social cohesion that leads to clumping of people into like-minded social groupings. Moving the parameters of choice, interaction, or influence too much in one direction or the other in the model can lead to complete homogeneity.

Bhavnani and Backer (2000) analyze the spread of genocide using a computational model. In the model, there are two groups of agents, and each agent has a different propensity to violence based on the number of others participating, and a different level of hatred toward the other group. The agents interact and influence each other. The model begins with a signal sent to one or the other group, or both, that violence has broken out. Then agents react to the news and to the behavior of other agents. They discover two sets of findings. In some instances, violence between the groups can occur sporadically and intensely, with many killed. In other instances, violence occurs at a moderate level at a constant rate. Which outcome occurs depends on the initial conditions: the distribution of propensities, of inter-ethnic hatred, and of frequencies of interactions between the groups.

6.4. The spread of collective identities or authority structures

As in other fields, in political science agent-based models have been used to analyze the spread of characteristics across a lattice, when the agents on the lattice interact and influence each other. Sometimes those characteristics are the component descriptors of a location on the lattice. Other times, those characteristics are the boundaries of political units or social networks.

As for the former type of model, Axelrod (1997) models the spread of culture by creating a $N \times m$ lattice of sites—interpreted in one version as villages—where two sites interact with probability in proportion to their cultural similarity. If sites interact, then with a given probability one site takes on some of the cultural characteristics of the other. He finds that the social system usually settles into a relatively small number of cultural zones, defined as homogeneous groups of sites forming a contiguous set on the lattice. Moreover, the number of cultural zones that exist either in equilibrium or after a very large number of interactions varies with the size of the lattice, the number of cultural characteristics, and the number of possible types of culture.

In a similar vein, Lustick and Miodownik (2000), model a process of deliberation among citizens trying to decide on a common course of action. A prominent topic for research within political science and law has been on the value of having groups of people discussing current events or political issues before deciding how to answer opinion polls, vote, or choose a particular action for the collective. Some think that deliberation leads to wiser or more considered decision-making (Fishkin, 1997), while others are deeply skeptical (Lupia, 2002).

The Agent-Based Argument Repertoire (ABAR) model developed by Lustick is a two-dimensional lattice with agents in locations on the lattice interacting with neighbors and influencing them. Lustick and Miodownik (2000) use this model to simulate democratic deliberation. There are two types of agents on the lattice, ordinary citizens and opinion leaders. All agents in the model interact with only their neighbors, but opinion leaders have larger neighborhoods. A citizen is called upon to propose an argument (a way of interpreting the problem at hand), and others in the neighborhood are differentially influenced by that argument, depending on their types. Through interactions, neighbors with some probability reduce their levels of disagreement with each other, but may increase it with other groups on the lattice.

In one version of the model, Lustick and Miodownik vary the number of different arguments available in the population, the number of opinion leaders relative to ordinary citizens, and the size of the opinion leaders' neighborhoods. They then track the overall level of disagreement in the population on the lattice. They find a trade-off in the deliberative process between engendering less disagreement and more common stances on proposed solutions, and diversity in the population. That is, under certain conditions, the population comes to agreement but has little diversity and not much flexibility to adapt to new information, and under other conditions the population remains divided, but diverse and flexible.

In a paper using similar methodology but tackling a different set of questions, Lustick et al. (2004), simulate the changing identities of agents on a two-dimensional lattice and how the emergence of identity patterns might encourage secession. One possible identity, if agglomerated in sufficient weight in one geographic region, will encourage agents to push for secession from the entire group of agents. Lustick, et al. examine different parameter ranges to examine what can cause more or less sentiment for secession. For instance, one kind of identity that can emerge in the population is the propensity for agents to share power with minorities, and this is varied to understand how it interacts with other identities to mitigate or possibly encourage secession by those minorities. They find that increased power-sharing sentiments among the population as a whole leads to greater numbers of minorities arising, with fewer number of secessionist movements proportional to the number of minorities. However, secessionism can still arise even under tolerant regimes.

For the second kind of model, where characteristics that change on the lattice are political boundaries or networks of trusting agents, several studies deserve mention here. Macey and Skvoretz (1998) analyze the evolution of trust and cooperation among agents engaging in one-shot prisoner's dilemma games. As in the earlier Axelrod models of iterated prisoner's dilemma games and dynamic population changes, the authors depict agents as having strategies that can evolve over time as they interact with other agents, using a genetic algorithm to simulate the evolution of strategies. Payoffs to an agent in the Macey and Skvoretz model do not depend on prospects for repeated play with the same opponent, but rather on the standard cooperation and defect choices in a one-shot setting and also on the possibility of refusing to play at all. They track the propensity of agents to cooperate as one increases the payoff for refusing to play, and as one embeds agents into smaller and smaller communities. It turns out that, in this model, embeddedness in small communities is the key linchpin to increasing cooperation among strangers in one-shot PD games.

In several articles and a book, Cederman (1997, 2002, 2003) reports a series of results using a network model (projected onto a lattice) of political units that can choose to cooperate or fight each other. His basic interest is in understanding the emergence of new political boundaries, thus simulating the spread of empires or the enlargement of countries. Each political unit exists as a location on a two-dimensional lattice. With some probability, one location, following a fight if it takes place, can 'swallow" the other to integrate together into a larger political unit.

Cederman's core model has many facets. He varies parameters such as the propensity of units to attack each other, the costs of defending oneself, and the size of the grid. His main variables of interest are the number and size of the political units over time. In Cederman (2003), for example, he finds that territories expand and wars take place in distributions that correspond to empirical patterns discovered many decades ago in international relations. Empirically, the size of wars and the number of casualties in those wars approximate a power law distribution when plotted against their frequency. This relationship also emerges from Cederman's simulations, with the parameters of that power law determined by the initialized parameters in the computational experiments.

Cederman interprets many of his results that accord with data on inter-state conflicts as vindicating an agent-based modeling approach. He notes that agent-based modeling can provide distributions of outcomes in international relations, not simply point predictions about specific events.

Several researchers have analyzed models of civic violence using interacting agent-based models. Epstein (2002) proposes a model with two types of agents, ordinary persons and cops, who live on a lattice. Ordinary persons decide in each time period whether to rebel or not, and they can influence each other. Cops decide whether or not to arrest rebellious persons. There are various renditions of the model, including one where two different population groups might fight each other as a form of rebellion. Epstein examines the rebelliousness of persons as their grievance levels increase relative to the number of cops, and as the behavior of the cops change. He finds that over time rebelliousness comes in waves (like punctuated equilibria), with the size and frequency of the waves varying with parameters in some intuitive and some nonintuitive ways.

7. Conclusion

In taking stock of the contributions of agent-based modeling to the study of politics so far, we conclude that though small in number, the papers and models have been high in quality and growing in their impact. We also detect an increase in interest among political scientists of all disciplinary stripes from formal theorists to empiricists to historians. At our most optimistic, we might even claim, with others, that complex systems research might prove to be a glue that can hold some disparate parts of the discipline together. Computational methods may offer a bridge between the side of political science with scientific aspirations, including those researchers with preferences for, or openness to, rigorous theories, falsifiable propositions, and systematic data collection, and the side of political science that forces us to confront contextual details that provide vital information about cross-national and cross-cultural differences (Kollman et al., 2003).

Computational models can perform this role because of what they are well disposed to capture: systems with adaptive structures but not deterministic structure, and systems with diverse agents who interact over time on a geographic space. Political systems contain diverse actors who pass information among each other through complicated networks. Conflict within political systems is often highly dimensional, and outcomes appear to be path dependent. Some outcomes in political systems emerge into stable equilibria, but much of what emergences is complex and nonlinear.

The separate components of complex systems research resonate within political science—adaptation, difference, externalities, path dependence, geography, networks, and emergence—but so does the complete picture. One might argue, as Jervis (1997) has in reference to the importance of complexity studies in international relations, that most of the linear and equilibrium features of political systems are now understood, and that we should turn to these latest techniques to grapple with what is left, the complex. Major events in the political world are often unpredictable. By definition, terrorist acts can only be predictable in a statistical sense. The implications of events are often impossible to foresee from simple models. As Neil Harrison (2004) writes: "The reality of world politics is more complex than dreamt of in most theories."

In addition to enabling political science to enlarge the domain of possible questions, agent-based models may allow the discipline to accommodate some of the conflicting claims made by rational choice modelers and scholars who advocate thick description. Rational choice theory allows us to capture important basic causal forces, but models based on game theory are limited in helping us understand how history, culture, information networks, and collective-interested behavior also matter. Agent-based-models may enable us to advance the discipline by bridging formal modeling and thick description given the dual capacity of these models to capture the richness of history and the theoretical sturdiness of logically consistent aggregation.

References

Arthur, W.B. (2006). "Out of equilibrium economics and agent-based modeling", this handbook.

Axelrod, R. (1984). The Evolution of Cooperation. Basic Books, New York.

Axelrod, R. (1986). "An evolutionary approach to norms". American Political Science Review 80, 1095–1111.

Axelrod, R. (1997). The Complexity of Cooperation. Princeton University Press, Princeton.

Axelrod, R. (2006). "Agent-based modeling as a bridge between disciplines", this handbook.

Axelrod, R., Cohen, M. (2000). Harnessing Complexity: Organizational Implications of a Scientific Frontier. Free Press.

Axelrod, R., Mitchell, W., Thomas, R., Bennett, D.S., Bruderer, E. (1995). "Coalition formation in standard-setting alliances". Management Science 41, 1493–1508.

Baron, D.P., Ferejohn, J.A. (1989). "Bargaining in Legislatures". American Political Science Review 89, 1181–1206.

Baron, D., Herron, M. (2003). "A dynamic model of multidimensional collective choices". In: Kollman, K., Miller, J., Page, S. (Eds.), Computational Models in Political Economy. MIT Press, Cambridge, MA.

Bartholdi, J., Tovey, C., Trick, M. (1989). "Voting schemes for which it can be difficult to tell who won the election". Social Choice and Welfare 6, 157–166.

Bhavnani, R., Backer, D. (2000). "Localized ethnic conflict and genocide: accounting for differences in Rwanda and Burundi". Journal of Conflict Resolution 44, 283–307.

Bednar, J. Page, S. (2006). "Can game(s) theory explain culture?", Rationality and Society, in preparation.

Bendor, J., Diermeier, D., Ting, M. (2003a). "A behavioral model of turnout". American Political Science Review 97, 261–280.

Bendor, J., Diermeier, D., Ting, M. (2003b). "Recovering behavioralism". In: Kollman, K., Miller, J., Page, S. (Eds.), Computational Models in Political Economy. MIT Press, Cambridge, MA.

Bowles, S., Gintis, H., Boyd, R., Fehr, E. (2003). "Explaining altruistic behavior in humans". Evolution and Human Behavior 24, 153–172.

Brenner, T. (2006). "Agent learning representation: advice on modeling agent-based learning", this handbook.

Camerer, C. (2003). Behavioral Game Theory: Experiments in Strategic Interaction. Princeton University Press, Princeton, NJ.

Cederman, L.-E. (1997). Emergent Actors: How States and Nations Develop and Dissolve. Princeton University Press, Princeton, NJ.

Cederman, L.-E. (2002). "Endogenizing geopolitical boundaries with agent-based modeling". Proceedings of the National Academy of Sciences 99, 7296–7303.

Cederman, L.-E. (2003). "Modeling the size of wars: from billiard balls to sandpiles". American Political Science Review 97, 135–150.

Chang, M.-H., Harrington, J.E. (2006). "Agent-based models of organizations", this handbook.

De Marchi, S. (1999). "Adaptive models and electoral instability". Journal of Theoretical Politics 11 (3), 393–419.

De Marchi, S. (2003). "A Computational Model of Voter Sophistication, Ideology and Candidate Position-taking". In: Kollman, K., Miller, J., Page, S. (Eds.), Computational Models in Political Economy. MIT Press, Cambridge, MA.

De Marchi, S. (2005). Lifting the Curse of Dimensionality: Computational Modeling in the Social Sciences. Cambridge University Press, New York.

Dibble, C. (2006). "Agent-based computational laboratories", this handbook.

Downs, A. (1957). Economic Theory of Democracy. Harper and Row, New York.

Duffy, J. (2006). "Agent-based models and human subjects experiments", this handbook.

Enelow, J., Hinich, M. (1984). Spatial Theory of Voting. Cambridge University Press, New York.

Epstein, J. (2002). "Modeling civil violence: an agent-based computational approach". Proceedings of the National Academy of Sciences 99 (5), 7243–7250.

Epstein, J. (2003). Generative Social Science. Princeton University Press, Princeton, NJ.

Fishkin, J. (1997). Voice of the People. Yale University Press, New Haven, CT.

Guetzkow, H. (1963). Simulation in International Relations. Prentice Hall, Englewood Cliffs, NJ.

Harrington, J. (1990). "Power of the proposal-maker in model of endogenous agenda formation". Public Choice 64, 1–20.

Harrington, J. (2003). "Rigidity and flexibility in social systems". In: Kollman, K., Miller, J., Page, S. (Eds.), Computational Models in Political Economy. MIT Press, Cambridge, MA.

Harrington, J. (1998). "The social selection of flexible and rigid agents". American Economic Review 88 (5), 63–82.

Harrison, N. (Ed.) (2004). Complexity in World Politics: Concepts, Methods, and Policy Effects. State University of New York Press, Albany, NY.

Hayes, J., Richards, D. (2003). "Learning, central bank independence, and the politics of excess foreign returns". In: Kollman, K., Miller, J., Page, S. (Eds.), Computational Models in Political Economy. MIT Press, Cambridge, MA.

Hong, L., Page, S. (2001). "Problem solving by teams of heterogeneous agents". Journal of Economic Theory 97, 123–163.

Hotelling, H. (1929). "Stability in competition". The Economic Journal 39, 41–57.

Howitt, P. (2006). "Coordination issues in long-run growth", this handbook.

Huckfeldt, R., Johnson, P., Sprague, J. (2004). Political Disagreement. Cambridge University Press, New York.

Inglehart, R. (1997). Modernization and Post Modernization. Princeton University Press, Princeton, NJ.

Jackson, J. (2003). "A computational theory of electoral competition". In: Kollman, K., Miller, J., Page, S. (Eds.), Computational Models in Political Economy. MIT Press, Cambridge, MA.

Janssen, M., Ostrom, E. (2006). "Governing social-ecological systems", this handbook.

Johnson, P. (1999). "Simulation modeling in political science". American Behavioral Scientist 42 (8), 1509–1530.

Jervis, R. (1997). System Effects: Complexity in Political and Social Life. Princeton University Press, Princeton, NJ.

Kollman, K., Miller, J., Page, S. (1992). "Adaptive parties in spatial elections". American Political Science Review 86, 929–937.

Kollman, K., Miller, J., Page, S. (1997). "Political institutions and sorting in a Tiebout model". American Economic Review 87, 977–992.

Kollman, K., Miller, J., Page, S. (1998). "Political parties and electoral landscapes". British Journal of Political Science 28, 139–158.

Kollman, K., Miller, J., Page, S. (2000). "Decentralization and the search for policy solutions". Journal of Law, Economics, and Organization 16, 102–128.

Kollman, K., Miller, J., Page, S. (Eds.) (2003). Computational Models of Political Economy. MIT Press, Cambridge, MA.

Kramer, G. (1977). "A dynamical model of political equilibrium". Journal of Economic Theory 12, 472–482.

Lacy, D., Niou, E. (1998). "Elections in double-member districts with nonseparable voter preferences". Journal of Theoretical Politics 10, 89–110.

Lasswell, H. (1958). Politics: Who Gets What, When, How. Meridian Books, New York.

Laver, M. (2005). "Policy and the dynamics of political competition". American Political Science Review 99, 263–281.

Laver, M., Benoit, K. (2003). The Evolution of Policy-Seeking Political Competition Between Elections. Trinity College, Dublin.

Lindbloom, C. (1959). "The science of muddling through". Public Administration Review 19, 79–88.

Lindbloom, C. (1979). "Still muddling, not yet through". Public Administration Review 39, 517–526.

Lupia, A. (2002). "Deliberation disconnected". Law and Contemporary Problems 65, 135–150.

Lustick, I., Miodownik, D. (2000). "Deliberative democracy and public discourse: the agent-based argument repertoire model". Complexity 5, 13–30.

Lustick, I.S., Miodownik, D., Eidelson, R.J. (2004). "Secessionism in multicultural states: does sharing power prevent or encourage it?". American Political Science Review 98, 209–230.

Macey, M., Skvoretz, J. (1998). "The evolution of trust and cooperation between strangers: a computational model". American Sociological Review 63, 638–660.

McGann, A., Koetzle, W., Grofman, B. (2002). "How an ideologically concentrated minority can trump a dispersed majority: non-median voter results plurality, run-off and sequential elimination elections". American Journal of Political Science 46, 134–148.

McKelvey, R.D. (1976). "Intransitivities in multidimensional voting models and some implications for agenda control". Journal of Economic Theory 12, 472–482.

Miller, J. (1996). "The coevolution of automata in the repeated prisoner's dilemma". Journal of Economic Behavior and Organizations 29, 87–113.

Padgett, J., Ansell, Ch. (1993). "Robust action and the rise of the Medici 1400–1434". American Journal of Sociology 98, 1259–1319.

Page, S. (1996). "Two measures of difficulty". Economic Theory 8, 321–346.

Page, S.X. (2000). "Computational economics from A to Z". Complexity 5, 35–40.

Page, S. (2006). "Essay: path dependence", Quarterly Journal of Political Science, in preparation.

Pierson, P. (2000). "Increasing returns, path dependency, and the study of politics". American Political Science Review 94, 251–267.

Plott, Ch. (1967). "A notion of equilibrium and its possibility under majority rule". American Economic Review 57, 787–806.

Putnam, R. (2000). Bowling Alone. Simon and Shuster, New York.

Putnam, R., Leonardi, R., Nanetti, R. (1993). Making Democracy Work. Princeton University Press, Princeton, NJ.

Riker, W. (1982). Liberalism Against Populism. Freeman, San Francisco.

Schelling, Th. (1978). Micromotives and Macrobehavior. Norton, New York.

Tilly, Ch. (1998). Durable Inequality. University of California Press, Berkeley.

Tovey, C. (1991). "The instability of instability", Technical Report NPSOR 91-15. Department of Operations Research, Naval Post Graduate School, Monterey, CA.

Wilhite, A.W. (2006). "Economic activity on fixed networks", this handbook.

Vriend, N.J. (2006). "ACE models of endogenous interactions", this handbook.

Chapter 30

GOVERNING SOCIAL-ECOLOGICAL SYSTEMS

MARCO A. JANSSEN[*]

School of Human Evolution and Social Change, and Department of Computer Science and Engineerin,
Arizona State University, Box 872402, Tempe, AZ 85287-2402, USA
e-mail: Marco.Janssen@asu.edu; url: http://www.public.asu.edu/~majansse/

ELINOR OSTROM

Department of Political Science, Workshop in Political Theory and Policy Analysis, Center for the Study of
Institutions, Population, and Environmental Change, Indiana University, Bloomington, IN 47408, USA
e-mail: ostrom@indiana.edu; url: http://www.indiana.edu/~iupolsci/bio_ostrom.html

Contents

[*] We gratefully acknowledge support from the Center for the Study of Institutions, Population, and Environmental Change at Indiana University through National Science Foundation grants SBR9521918 and SES0083511. We also want to thank the participants of the conference for the Handbook of Computational Economics, Vol II: Agent-Based Computational Economics, Ann Arbor, Michigan, May 21–23, 2004, as well as Marty Anderies, David Batten, François Bousquet, Matt Hoffmann, and several anonymous referees for their feedback on an earlier version of this chapter. We thank Leigh Tesfatsion for her careful reading of the manuscript and the editorial suggestions, and Joanna Broderick and Patty Lezotte for the editorial help in various stages of this project.

Handbook of Computational Economics, Volume 2. Edited by Leigh Tesfatsion and Kenneth L. Judd
DOI: 10.1016/S1574-0021(05)02030-7

Abstract

Social-ecological systems are complex adaptive systems where social and biophysical agents are interacting at multiple temporal and spatial scales. The main challenge for the study of governance of social-ecological systems is improving our understanding of the conditions under which cooperative solutions are sustained, how social actors can make robust decisions in the face of uncertainty and how the topology of interactions between social and biophysical actors affect governance. We review the contributions of agent-based modeling to these challenges for theoretical studies, studies which combines models with laboratory experiments and applications of practical case studies.

Empirical studies from laboratory experiments and field work have challenged the predictions of the conventional model of the selfish rational agent for common pool resources and public-good games. Agent-based models have been used to test alternative models of decision-making which are more in line with the empirical record. Those models include bounded rationality, other regarding preferences and heterogeneity among the attributes of agents. Uncertainty and incomplete knowledge are directly related to the study of governance of social-ecological systems. Agent-based models have been developed to explore the consequences of incomplete knowledge and to identify adaptive responses that limited the undesirable consequences of uncertainties. Finally, the studies on the topology of agent interactions mainly focus on land use change, in which models of decision-making are combined with geographical information systems.

Conventional approaches in environmental economics do not explicitly include non-convex dynamics of ecosystems, non-random interactions of agents, incomplete understanding, and empirically based models of behavior in collective action. Although agent-based modeling for social-ecological systems is in its infancy, it addresses the above features explicitly and is therefore potentially useful to address the current challenges in the study of governance of social-ecological systems.

Keywords

social-ecological systems, agent-based computational models, commons dilemma, cooperation, non-convex ecosystem dynamics

JEL classification: C70, C90, D70, D80, H41, Q20, Q30, Q57

1. Introduction

For millennia, human activities have affected their environment. In ancient times, the use of fire and tools enabled humans to learn to live outside their original environment—the savannah of eastern Africa. The development of agriculture about ten thousand years ago, and industrialization during the last two hundred years, have generated massive population increases and intense uses of natural resources. Now, we live on a human-dominated planet. Human activities have transformed the land surface, altered the major biogeochemical cycles, and added or removed species in most of Earth's ecosystems (Vitousek et al., 1997).

This chapter reviews the efforts by many scholars to use agent-based computational models to study the governance of social-ecological systems. This field is truly inter-disciplinary. It will be difficult, if not impossible, therefore to restrict our focus solely to economics. Although economics will be our starting point, we will include studies from other disciplines. To facilitate communication across disciplines we will use an organizing framework in the second section of this chapter. To structure our chapter, we identify three main challenges for the study of the interactions between human activities and ecosystems.

- What conditions enhance the likelihood of cooperative solutions to the massive number of social dilemmas that confront social-ecological systems? This relates to the problem of preventing overharvesting of common-pool resources such as fish stocks, forests, and fresh water.
- How do economic agents make effective and robust decisions given the fundamental uncertainty of the complex dynamics of the social-ecological system?
- How can the topology of interactions among actors be explicitly included in the analysis of the first two questions given the importance of interactions to an understanding of natural resource dynamics?

The aim of this chapter is to show the contribution of agent-based computational economics to these challenges. We emphasize the linkages between field research, laboratory experiments, and agent-based modeling. Pure analytical models have proved to be essential tools for analyzing highly competitive markets and other settings with strong selection pressures (Ruttan, 2003). When trying to understand how and why individuals engage in collective action, however, analytical models have not proved as useful. In the field and in the experimental laboratory, we have observed many settings in which individuals overcome the incentives to free ride, increase the levels of inter-personal trust, produce public goods, and manage common-pool resources sustainably (Bromley et al., 1992; Gibson et al., 2000a; National Research Council, 2002; Ostrom and Walker, 2003; Dietz et al., 2003). Candidate theories for explaining these surprising empirical results are too complex to be usefully pursued using only analytical techniques. To understand these phenomena agent-based modeling has become an essential tool complementing empirical methods. Other chapters in this volume (Brenner, 2006; Duffy, 2006) also address the combination of laboratory experiments and agent-based modeling. Their contribution focuses more on learning models, while our focus is on public goods and common-pool resource experiments using several models of human decision-making. It is important to realize that every method used to study social-ecological systems has its methodological problems. We will therefore emphasis in this chapter the plurality of approaches, which may unravel the complexity of the systems when findings are consistent with all the types of approaches used.

The studies reviewed in this chapter differ from those most frequently addressed by environmental economists. Conventional economic theory predicts that when agents have free access to a common-pool resource they will consume ecosystem services to the point where private costs equal the benefits, whereas externalities are imposed on the rest of the community. This can lead to the well-known tragedy of the commons (Hardin, 1968). Traditionally, economists study the management of ecosystems in terms of harvesting ecosystem services from renewable resources. Substantial progress has been made during the last 30 years. Prior to 1970, models were mainly static, such as the seminal work on renewable resource harvesting by Gordon (1954). During the 1970s, the trend shifted toward dynamic systems for the economics of renewable resources. The resulting optimization problem was addressed by dynamic programming, game theory, and equilibrium analysis (Clark, 1990; Dasgupta and Heal, 1979; Mäler, 1974). Irreversibility and uncertainty have been addressed since the early 1970s (Arrow and Fisher, 1974; Henry, 1974) and remain among the main foci of environmental economics (e.g., Chichilnisky, 2000). Recently, economists have started to include non-convexities of ecosystems into their analysis of optimal management of ecosystems (Dasgupta and Mäler, 2003; Janssen et al., 2004).

In simple models in mainstream environmental economics, a representative agent is presumed to have perfect knowledge (or knowledge on the probabilities of outcomes) and to maximize utility of consumption for an infinite time horizon. Such an approach results in interesting insights. Representing agents as maximizing known utility functions is, however, of limited use when systems are characterized by non-convex dynamics, structural uncertainty, heterogeneity among agents, multi-attribute utility, and spatial heterogeneity. Evidence is accumulating that social-ecological systems frequently do have complex, non-linear dynamics. This affects the type of governance that may lead to sustainable outcomes (Scheffer et al., 2001). Initial steps has been taken to include such non-linear dynamics in environmental economics (Dasgupta and Mäler, 2003). Furthermore, increasing evidence exists that agents are able to self-govern some types of common-pool resources without external governmental intervention but do not always succeed (Bromley et al., 1992; Ostrom, 1990; National Research Council, 2002; Ostrom et al., 1994). The question is how to analyze ecosystem management problems with spatially explicit, non-convex dynamics influenced by multiple stakeholders with divergent interests and who consume different types of ecosystem services. We need new tools. Agent-based modeling is a promising tool for the analysis of these complex problems (Janssen, 2002a).

Several developments outside environmental economics during the last thirty years have influenced the current state of agent-based modeling of social-ecological systems. We will briefly discuss some of these developments. Since the early 1970s, scholars from system dynamics have developed and used integrated models of humans and their environment (Ford, 1999). Prime examples are the World 2 and 3 models of Forrester (1971) and Meadows et al. (1972, 1974). The World 2 and 3 models simulated the long-term interactions between population, industrial and agricultural production, resource use, pollution and food supply at an aggregated global level. A core finding was that continuing early 1970s' trends would lead to an overshoot and collapse in terms of population and economic development. The World 2 and 3 models were highly criticized for the subjectivity of the assumptions and the lack of rationality of the decision-making actors within the model (Cole et al., 1973; Nordhaus, 1973). In fact, the actors, economic sectors on a global level, reacted in a predetermined way.

The first type of agent-based model for governing social-ecological systems that we were able to trace in the literature is Bossel and Strobel (1978). They developed a model to address two lacunae in the World 2 and 3 models—namely, their failure to account for cognitive processes and their usual neglect of normative criteria and changes in these criteria. In fact, the Bossel and Strobel model is of a cognitive agent interacting with the global system. Their agent bases its decisions on the state of the global system, using indicators, so-called system's orientors, like existence needs, security, freedom of action, adaptivity, and effectiveness. This agent receives information about the state of the system and decides to change priorities or aspirations, which affect the investment decisions of the agent. Inclusion of these "intelligent" agents prevents the preprogrammed "pollution crisis" from occurring. It also leads to policies producing very satisfactory overall results, provided the planning horizon and the control sensitivity are sufficiently large. The current field of integrated modeling of humans and the environment still faces similar problems, uncertainty, subjective assumptions and lack of behavioral models, to those of the initial models (Janssen and de Vries, 1999). Core questions remain regarding how to deal with uncertainty and subjective assumptions and how to include human dimensions.

Another field that contributed to the development of agent-based modeling of social-ecological systems is individual-based modeling in ecology, which really took off in the late 1980s (Huston et al., 1988). Individual-based modeling refers to simulation models that treat individuals as unique and discrete entities who have at least one property, in addition to age, that changes during the life cycle, e.g. weight, rank in a social hierarchy, etc. Often motivated by pragmatic reasons, individual-based models are used to study systematically the behavior of organisms in complex (spatially explicit) environments (Grimm, 1999).

In the artificial intelligence field since the late 1980s, scholars developed tools for natural resource management (Coulson et al., 1987). Well known are geographic information systems and expert systems, but also a number of models have been developed that included intelligent agents interacting with their complex environment (Anderson and Evans, 1994). An interesting early example is the PHOENIX model on fire management (Cohen et al., 1989). The model simulates a forest fire and the actions of intelligent agents, representing bulldozers and airplanes. The model is an event-driven simulation model, meaning that the agents perform real-time tasks based on events that happen in their local environment. Every five simulated minutes of the model, the agents are synchronized to allow coordination among the agents. The model is aimed at evaluating fire-fighting plans in various scenarios.

Bousquet et al. (1994) developed an objected-oriented model of natural resource management of fisheries in the central Niger delta. Based on fieldwork, an artificial world was created where different scenarios of rules of when and where to fish in a wetland area were analyzed for this impact on long term viability of the natural resources. The existence of space-sharing rules was found to be essential to avoid overfishing.

Deadman and Gimblett (1994) constructed a system that handles the complexity of goal-oriented autonomous human agents seeking recreational opportunities in natural environments. The model simulates the behavior of three types of visitors and their interactions in an event-driven GIS environment of a park environment using intelligent agents: hikers; bikers; and visitors transported in tour vehicles. The results of hiker interactions with other users have been used to provide feedback about the implications for alternative recreation management planning.

Complexity science is still another foundation for the study of the governance of complex social-ecological systems. Social-ecological systems can be viewed as complex adaptive systems—systems in which the components, and the structure of interactions between the components, adapt over time to internal and external disturbances (Holland, 1992a). Order in complex systems is emergent as opposed to predetermined. The system's history is irreversible, and future behavior is path dependant. The system's future is often unpredictable due to the non-linearity of many basic causal relationships. The variables that affect performance are both fast and slow moving. If information about slow-moving variables is not recorded for a long period of time, substantial surprises can occur when a slow-moving variable reaches some threshold. In social-ecological systems, the key components are individuals and institutions. With institutions we refer to the formal and informal rules that shape human interactions. Individuals may change their relations with other individuals, their strategies, and the rules they are using. In fact, individual strategies and institutional rules interact and co-evolve, frequently in unpredictable ways. For example, the peasants who were starting to drain the peat mires on a local level more than 1000 years ago in the precursor of the Netherlands did not foresee the large-scale consequences in the few hundred years on the larger-scale landscape (lowering of the surface by about 2 cm a year), leading to new institutions (like waterboards), and different practices (livestock instead of agriculture).

From this perspective, the question arises of how to govern social-ecological systems. In systems that are indeed complex, one needs to understand processes of organization and reorganization including collapse and the likely processes that happen after collapse. Does a system have one and only one equilibrium to which it returns after a major shock and temporary collapse? Are there multiple equilibria with different characteristics? How easy is it for a system to flip from a desirable equilibrium to an undesirable one? These are crucial questions.

The complex adaptive systems perspective provides us the view of individuals within a variety of situations structured by the biophysical world, the institutional rules, and the community in which they interact. Within ongoing structures, individuals search out perceived advantageous strategies given the set of costs and benefits that exist and the strategies that others adopt. Boundedly rational individuals trying to do as well as they can in uncertain situations continuously tinker with their strategies, including trying to change the rules that affect particular situations. They may look for loopholes in the law, particularly if they think others are doing the same. They may check out the level of enforcement by occasionally breaking rules. Those who have responsibility for changing the rules of an institution also experiment with new rules and try to learn from others why other institutional arrangements appear to work better than their own.

Agent-based models are a suitable methodology to study these complex social-ecological systems in a formal manner for the following reasons:

- Agent decisions are based on internal decision rules; this fits very well with the increasing insights from experimental social science that humans use various types of heuristics in different situations (Gigerenzer et al., 1999; Gigerenzer and Selten, 2001).
- The explicit inclusion of agent interactions helps to integrate the increasing insight of the importance of communication in managing social dilemmas (Ostrom et al., 1994; Ahn et al. 2003, 2004).
- Agent-based modeling shares similarities with models used in ecology, such as individual-based models, system theory, and the inclusion of space. Therefore, agent-based modeling facilitates collaborative efforts of ecologists and social scientists.
- Agent-based models are suitable for modeling complex adaptive systems, in which the interactions of individual units lead to larger-scale phenomena.
- Agent-based modeling makes it possible to address the problem of scale explicitly (Gibson et al., 2000b).

The perspective of social-ecological systems as complex adaptive systems provides us a useful stepping stone for using agent-based modeling for the study of social-ecological systems. In the next section we discuss a general framework of social-ecological systems that we will use as a guideline to discuss the work done in this field.

2. A framework for social-ecological systems

The social-ecological systems (SESs) to be examined in the rest of this chapter are (1) systems composed of both biophysical and social components, (2) where individuals self-consciously invest time and effort in developing forms of physical and institutional infrastructure that affect the way the system functions over time in coping with (3) diverse external disturbances and internal problems, and (4) that are embedded in a network of relationships among smaller and larger components. In other words, humans have designed *some parts* but not all of the overall SES. In most instances, the design has evolved over time as feedback generated information about how the SES was operating

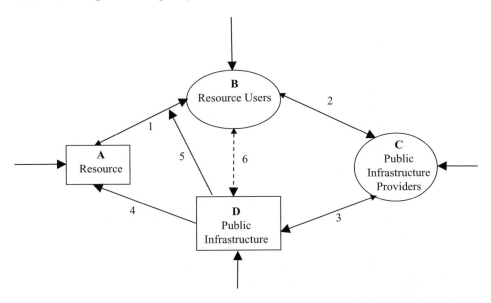

Figure 1. A conceptual model of a social-ecological system. Source: Anderies et al. (2004).

and participants in various positions try to improve the operation of the system—at least from their perspective.

We adopt the general framework proposed by Anderies et al. (2004) that identifies the relevant parts of a social-ecological system and how they are linked. In Figure 1, the elements of such a framework are presented. Given that most multi-level SESs are very complex, we start by focusing first on a single-level SES. We identify four "entities" that are normally involved in SESs utilized by groups of individuals over time. Two of these entities are composed of humans. First are the resource users (*B* in Figure 1), who are the population of those harvesting from the resource (*A* in Figure 1). Second are the public infrastructure providers (*C* in Figure 1), who receive monetary taxes or contributed labor and make policies regarding how to invest these resources in the construction, operation and maintenance of a public infrastructure. A substantial overlap may exist among the individuals in *B* and in *C* or they may be entirely different individuals depending on the structure of the social system governing and managing the SES.

The public infrastructure (*D* in Figure 1) combines two forms of capital: human-made capital (physical capital) and institutional capital (see Ostrom and Ahn, 2003; Costanza et al., 2001). The physical capital includes a variety of engineered works, for example the headworks and canals of an irrigation system and the constructed highways of a transportation system. The institutional capital includes the rules actually used by those governing, managing and using the system that create opportunities and constraints in the action-outcome linkages available to participants.

The resource (A in Figure 1) is most frequently a biophysical system or a form of natural capital that has been transformed for use by B through the efforts of C to invest in D. We will focus on common-pool resources where it is difficult to exclude potential beneficiaries from receiving the costs or benefits of governance strategies, and where the resource flows withdrawn from the resource system subtract from the availability of resource flows for other users (Ostrom et al., 1994). If one is going to examine robustness or resilience, one needs to include external disturbances (*incoming arrows* on Figure 1), which can include biophysical disruptions (Linkages 7) including floods, earthquakes, landslides, and climate change which impact on A and D or socioeconomic changes (Linkages 8) including population increases, changes in economic opportunities, depressions or inflations, and major political changes that impact on B, C and D.

A social-ecological system can be challenged in two ways: (1) by external disturbances; and (2) by fluctuations within internal entities and the links between them. The internal fluctuations may result from the strategic interactions among the resource users and among the participants in the process of providing the public infrastructure. Further, strategic interactions exist among resource users regarding the harvesting rate from the resource (Linkage 1 on Figure 1), the linkages among resource users and the public infrastructure providers (Linkage 2 on Figure 1), the public infrastructure providers and the investments made in the infrastructure (Linkage 3), and potentially, the linkage between resource users and the public infrastructure (Linkage 6). Further, the linkages among the ecological entities (Linkages 1, 4 and 5) are also sources of fluctuations that may challenge the robustness of the overall SES at any particular point in time.

The simplest example of a social-ecological system consistent with the framework is a small group of actors with relatively homogeneous interests who are in both positions B and C. Without a medium of exchange other than labor and goods, cooperation must be undertaken by direct interactions and transparent means. Such a system might be a small irrigation system where farmers who own relatively similar plots of land meet regularly to discuss how many days to work on maintenance and how to allocate the water (see Tang, 1992; Lam, 1998; Ostrom, 1992). A social-ecological system becomes more complex when task specialization occurs and most actors are either resource users or public infrastructure providers. This might create incentives for rent seeking, corruption, and mismanagement due to incomplete or competing knowledge systems. So the internal stability might become less robust when a system becomes more diverse and specialized.

External threats may affect the various components and links within the SES. Natural events, human induced impacts, and accidents can disrupt the resource system. External sources may change the preferences of resource users as a consequence of new information and inward and outward migration of people. The abilities to perform by public infrastructure providers can be affected due to changes in higher level regulations, and by the emergence or decline of local champions, those individuals who make a difference in making things happen. Finally, the public infrastructure can itself be affected by natural events and accidents (physical infrastructure) and changes in higher level regulations (institutional rules). These external disturbances interdependently affect the activities within the social-ecological system. In fact, there might be interactions across scales that make SES's become more or less robust to internal and external challenges.

This general framework lets us rephrase the three puzzles identified in the introduction. The first set of questions addresses social dilemmas: What kind of institutional frameworks lead to robust governance of social-ecological systems? What is the influence of the ecological dynamics? What kind of information do resource users and public infrastructure providers exchange? What are conflicting and compromising interactions between the different agents involved? What is the effect of different levels of spatial and temporal scale? How do institutional rules evolve?

The second type of question addresses uncertainty: What information do resource users and public infrastructure providers have, and what is the asymmetry of this information? How do resource users learn, and how do their learning processes differ from how public infrastructure providers learn? How do different mental models of agents affect the use and governance of the resource? Finally, social and biological agents interact in a spatially explicit landscape formulated as maps or networks. How does spatial heterogeneity affect the functioning of social-ecological systems? How does information spread among nodes in a network? Who talks with whom, when and about what, and how does this affect resource management?

We will now discuss each of the three areas and dig in more deeply to discuss theoretical and applied agent-based models, and the relation of laboratory experiments with agent-based modeling.

3. Social dilemmas

A key theoretical and empirical puzzle in all of the social sciences is how individuals overcome the strong temptation not to cooperate in social dilemmas, in which individual contributions exceed individual returns, and instead attempt to achieve joint benefits through cooperation (Axelrod, 2006). Both sets of human actors identified in Figure 1 face multiple social dilemmas. Resources users (B) face common-pool resource dilemmas that can, if unresolved, lead to serious over-harvesting and potentially the destruction of the resource. As one New England fisher recently put it, "I have no incentive to conserve the fishery, because any fish I leave is just going to be picked up by the next guy" (cited in Tierney, 2000, p. 38). Some users may develop trust (Ostrom and Walker, 2003) and/or strong reciprocity even when they have heterogeneous interests (Bowles and Gintis, 2004). Without some agreed-upon and enforced rules, however, resources users may simply race each other to use up the resource. Public infrastructure providers (C) also face social dilemmas in their effort to develop effective institutions (a public good) or efficient infrastructure (usually another common-pool resource). Simply authorizing some individuals to govern a resource does not guarantee that they will overcome the temptations to engage in rent-seeking, to accept bribes, or simply to avoid investing in costly information acquisition.

Cooperation in social dilemmas can be easily explained when the social agents are genetically related (Frank, 1998) and/or interact repeatedly over a long indeterminate time (Kreps et al., 1982). The question of why non-related social agents cooperate relates to a number of important issues in ecological economics, especially to the question of designing effective institutional configurations for common-pool resources and public goods. Schlager (2004) reviews the extensive empirical cases where local communities have developed institutions to deal with social dilemmas. These examples demonstrate that people have the capacity to organize themselves to achieve much higher outcomes than predicted by conventional economic theory. Capacity is not, however, sufficient to ensure that resources are governed sustainably.

Empirical research stimulated in large part by a mid-1980s Committee of the National Research Council (National Research Council, 1986) and synthesized by a more recent committee (National Research Council, 2002) has demonstrated that no form of governance is guaranteed to change the strong incentives of the pervasive social dilemmas faced by resource users and public infrastructure providers so as to generate long-term sustainability. Governing resources successfully is always a struggle (Dietz et al., 2003). Empirical findings suggest that successful, adaptive governance of natural resources requires: (1) generating substantial information about stocks, flows, and processes within the resource (the arrows in Figure 1); (2) dealing with conflict that arises among multiple users and uses of a resource; (3) inducing rule compliance among all participants so that each has confidence that the others are not cheating; (4) providing effective physical and institutional infrastructure (C in Figure 1); and (5) preparing for the inevitable changes that occur due to external disturbances as well as internal changes in resource and human dynamics (Dietz et al., 2003). A recent empirical study of over 200 forests located in Africa, Latin America, Asia, and the United States provides strong evidence that regular rule enforcement is more important in achieving sustainable forest conditions than the form of organization governing a forest, the level of social capital existing among users, or the level of dependence of users on a forest (Gibson et al., 2005).

3.1. Theoretical models

Field research has thus generated substantial evidence that, contrary to earlier economic theory, no optimal form of governance exists that can be imposed on all SESs with the expectation that resource users and public infrastructure providers will accept the system and make it work. On the other hand, field research has also shown that resource users and public infrastructure providers have devised an ingenious array of rule configurations that work effectively in specific ecological and social settings. Thus, there is a lot for theory to explain!

As discussed in more detail by Dibble (2006), Axelrod (2006), Young (2006), and Kollman and Page (2006), agent-based models are being intensely used to derive a better theoretical understanding of the conditions that lead social agents to cooperate. Axelrod (1984, 1987) pioneered in this field with his iterated prisoner's dilemma (IPD) tournaments and with his simulation of the evolution of strategies using genetic algorithms. This led to a vast number of human–subject experiments (summarized in Davis and Holt, 1993; Colman, 1995) and agent-based models on variations of the IPD game focused on the effects of partner choice, tags, reputation symbols, spatial interactions, noise, probabilistic choice, and so forth (see Gotts et al., 2003). Multiple theoretical efforts have been made to provide a coherent, analytical framework for explaining the repeated finding that cooperation levels in social dilemmas are frequently above the zero contribution level predicted by non-cooperative game theory (see Boyd and Richerson, 1992; Bowles, 1998; Gintis, 2000; Camerer, 2003).

Axelrod (1986) was among the first to tackle how norms supporting cooperative strategies, that were not the strategies leading to a Nash equilibrium, could be sustained over time. He posited that individuals could adopt norms—meaning that they usually acted in a particular way and were often punished if they were not seen to be acting in this manner. He posited that some individuals also developed a norm to punish those who defected in social dilemmas as well as the concept of a meta norm—a norm that "one must punish those who did not punish a defection" Axelrod (1986, p. 1109). With punishment norms backing cooperative norms, and the meta norm of punishing those who did not punish defectors, Axelrod was able to develop an evolutionary theory of cooperation consistent with evidence from the field.

Recent evolutionary models by Kameda et al. (2003) have developed these ideas even further. In a formal analysis of a set of simplified strategies, these authors explore the viability of a "communal sharing strategy" which cooperates when in the role of resource acquisition and imposes sanctions on others if they engage in non-sharing behavior. They establish that the communal-sharing strategy is a unique evolutionarily stable strategy that blocks any other strategy from successfully invading for a wide range of parameters. Kameda et al. also undertook a simulation of the performance of multiple strategies when ten players are involved and their strategies could evolve over time. Here they observed that free riding could become the dominate strategy over multiple generations due to the problem of second-order free riding in regard to norm enforcement. When they added an "intolerant" norm enforcer who is willing to bear extra costs for excluding others who are second-order free riders on the enforcement of cooperative norms, simulated ten-person games tended to sustain cooperative sharing over very large number of generations. In field settings of robust SESs, one does tend to find some members of self-organized groups who are "fired up" about the need for everyone to follow the rules and norms they have evolved over time. Some groups rotate the role of being the local enforcer among their membership, so no one has to bear the cost of monitoring and enforcing at all times, while each of them is "super-charged" with the responsibility for local monitoring on a rotating basis.

Many of the specific rules that empirical researchers have observed in the field have puzzled theorists. In addition to rotating enforcement responsibilities, elaborate turn-taking rules have, for example, been observed in robust institutions related to harvesting fish from inshore fisheries (see Berkes, 1986) and obtaining water from farmer-governed irrigation systems (Ostrom, 1992). Even subjects in repeated common-pool resource experiments with opportunities to engage in face-to-face communication have devised rotation systems enabling one set of subjects to gain more in one round and less in the next (Ostrom et al., 1994). A recent paper by Lau and Mui (2003) has now provided a strong game-theoretic analysis of how such complex rules can be sustained in a repeated environment characterized by asymmetric payoffs in any one period.

Let us now turn to agent-based models of cooperation. Thébaud and Locatelli (2001), for example, developed an agent-based model to address a puzzle initially proposed by Sugden (1989). Sugden observed the emergence of property-right rules of those who gather driftwood after a storm on the Yorkshire coast. Whoever found an item first could take it and gather it into piles. By placing two stones on the top of each pile, the gatherer could mark his property. If a pile had not been removed after two more high tides, the ownership rights terminated. Thébaud and Locatelli were able to generate the emergence of piles, whose existence varied with the range of vision (could the agent steal without being caught?) and the threshold of the size of the pile before it is considered private property (lower threshold makes it easier to generate private piles). Another aspect that was found important is the imitation rule. Agents compare their wood pile with others they encounter and, if the observed pile is larger than their own (including the wood they are currently carrying), they adopt the strategy of its owner with regard to the property rule.

Another set of papers discusses the effect of different models of human behavior on the management of common resources. Jager et al. (2000) discuss the harvesting by a population of agents of a fish stock and a gold mine (whose pollutants negatively affect the carrying capacity of the fish population). They tested two types of models of behavior. In the first model, the agents considered all possible actions. In the second, agents used heuristics mimicking repetition, deliberation, social comparison, and imitation. Which heuristic was active at a certain moment in time depended on the level of satisfaction and uncertainty. Jager et al. (2000) show that constant deliberation over all possible options leads to a faster decline of the resources, and an uneven transition from fishing to gold digging. Several social psychology-based agent-based models on the collective use of common resources have especially focused on including the effects of resource uncertainty (Jager et al., 2002; Mosler and Brucks, 2002). Jager et al. (2002), for example, show that overharvesting is more severe in periods of uncertainty, which is consistent with laboratory experimental and field evidence. Due to the use of agent-based models, Jager et al. were able to pin-point three different behavioral processes that may contribute to this overuse. Another relevant paper is by Janssen and Ostrom (2005), who study the conditions that are needed for a population of agents to voluntarily restrict their own behavior to avoid collapse of the resource in the longer term. They show that when agents are able to evolve mutual trust relationships, a proposed rule on restricted use of the resource will be accepted because the agents trust each other to follow the rules.

3.2. *Laboratory experiments related to the governance of social-ecological systems*

Behavioral game theory has been instrumental in testing the effects of alternative models of decision-making on social dilemmas (see, for example, Erev and Roth, 1998; Camerer and Ho, 1999; Camerer, 2003; Duffy, 2006). With regard to the governance of social-ecological systems, the study of public goods and common-pool resources are important. The standard linear public-good provision experiment can be characterized by the number of individuals (N), the marginal per capita return (r), the number of repetitions (T), and the initial endowment of token money for each player (ω). An experimental linear public-good provision game involves a free-rider problem if $r < 1$ and $N \times r > 1$. Suppose, in a given round, individual i contributes x_i of ω for the provision of the public good. The subject's payoff (π_i) is:

$$\pi_i = \omega - x_i + r \sum_{j=1}^{N} x_j.$$

The equilibrium prediction, assuming individuals maximize own monetary payoffs, is that the public good will not be provided at all.

For the common-pool resource experiments with a quadratic production function, the experiments are formulated in the following way. The initial resource endowment ω of each participant consists of a given set of tokens that the participant needs to allocate between two markets: Market 1, which has a fixed return; and Market 2, which functions as a collective resource and which has a return determined in part by the actions of the other participants in the experiment. Each participant i chooses to invest a portion x_i of his/her endowment of ω in the common resource Market 2, and the remaining portion $\omega - x_i$ is then invested in Market 1. The payoff function as used in Ostrom et al. (1994) is:

$$u_i(\mathbf{x}) = \begin{array}{ll} 0.05 \cdot e & \text{if } x_i = 0 \\ 0.05 \cdot (\omega - x_i) + \left(x_i / \sum x_i\right) \cdot F\left(\sum x_i\right) & \text{if } x_i > 0 \end{array}$$

where

$$F\left(\sum x_i\right) = \left(23 \cdot \sum_{i=1}^{8} x_i - 0.25 \cdot \left(\sum_{i=1}^{8} x_i\right)^2\right) / 100.$$

According to this formula, the payoff of someone investing all ω tokens in market one $(x_i = 0)$ is $0.05 \times \omega$, thus 0.5 tokens. The return is like a fixed wage paid according to the hours invested. Investing a part or all of the tokens in market two $(x_i > 0)$ yields an outcome that depends on the investments of the other players. If the players behave according to the non-cooperative game theory, they would derive the Nash equilibrium, where each player maximizes payoff given the strategies chosen by the other players.

A series of laboratory experiments during the last twenty years have shown that subjects do invest in public goods and are able to govern common-pool resources more sustainably than predicted by theory (Isaac et al., 1984, 1985, 1994; Isaac and Walker,

1988; Marwell and Ames, 1979, 1980, 1981; Ostrom et al., 1994). Depending on the return rate from investments in the public good, the initial contribution rate remains the same or decreases with the number of rounds. Laboratory experiments have consistently shown that communication is a crucial factor for achieving cooperative behavior (Sally, 1995; Brosig, 2002).

In the common-pool resources, the average harvest approaches the Nash equilibrium when no communication or sanctioning is allowed, but decreases to a cooperative level when participants do communicate (cheap talk) or are able to penalize (impose costs on) those who harvest more than agreed upon. The ability of participants to determine their own monitoring and sanctioning system is critical for sustaining efficient cooperative behavior (Ostrom et al., 1994).

3.3. Agent-based models of laboratory experiments

Since the behavior of subjects is not consistent with predictions using a rational choice model of individual behavior, an important question is what types of models of human behavior explain the observations. A recent development is the use of agent-based models to test alternative models that replicate the patterns of the subjects in the laboratory experiments. Peter Deadman (1999) defined agents who chose a certain strategy and could update these strategies in an environment that is similar to the common pool experiments run at Indiana University (Ostrom et al., 1994). He modeled their updating process to be based on the expected and experienced performance of strategies in previous rounds. The types of strategies he used were based on exit interviews conducted after a session of common-pool resource experiments had ended (Ostrom et al., 1994).

One strategy attempts to maximize the individual return received in each round by comparing investments in Market 2 in previous rounds with the resulting returns. If returns on tokens are increasing, then more tokens are placed in Market 2. If returns on tokens invested in Market 2 are decreasing, then fewer tokens are placed in Market 2. Another strategy mentioned by subjects is to compare average returns between Market 1 and Market 2, increasing the tokens allocated to the market that performs better. The last type of strategy directly compares an individual agent's investment with the investments of the group as a whole. The agent-based model showed similar fluctuations in aggregated token investment levels in Market 2 as in the laboratory experiments reported in (Ostrom et al., 1994).

Deadman et al. (2000) introduce communication between agents in their agent-based model. During communication, agents are assumed to pool their experience in regard to the various strategies they have used. In this way, all agents derive a similar map of which strategies work well. As in the laboratory experiments where communication was allowed, investment levels moved closer to the optimal level of full cooperation.

Like Deadman (1999), Jager and Janssen (2002) used agent-based models to provide a possible explanation of observed patterns in common-pool experiments without communication. The agents in Jager and Janssen are based on a meta-theoretical framework of psychological theories. An agent is assumed to have different type of needs, including subsistence, identity and exploration. Depending on whether the needs of the agent are satisfied or not, and whether the agent is uncertain or not, an agent uses one of four decision rules: deliberation; social comparison; repetition; and imitation. An unsatisfied agent spends more cognitive energy (e.g., deliberation or social comparison) than a satisfied agent (who relies more on repetition and imitation). An uncertain agent uses information from other agents (social comparison or imitation) instead of relying on individual information (deliberation or repetition). The difference between social comparison and imitation is that during social comparison an agent checks whether copying the strategy of another agent leads to an expected improvement of the utility.

Jager and Janssen found that agent-based models of individual behavior in common-pool resource settings needed to include

- social value orientation,
- preferences one has for a particular distribution of outcomes for oneself and others,
- satisfying behavior,
- exploratory behavior when payoffs of an agent remain the same for a number of rounds, and
- heterogeneity of needs among the agents.

All five individual characteristics are needed in the analysis to derive token investment patterns at the group level similar to those resulting in the human–subject experiments. The investment patterns were evaluated by taking into account the average investment level, the differences between the agents in a group, and the changes of investment levels across rounds.

Castillo (2002) investigates the decision rules individuals used during field experiments of common-pool resources conducted by Cardenas among coastal communities in the Colombian Caribbean Sea (Cardenas et al., 2000). The model is based on the theory of collective action of Ostrom (1998) and implemented from a systems dynamics perspective. As in previous studies, Castillo simulates the experiments describing the actions of individual agents. By using response functions, Castillo is able to estimate the theoretical framework of Ostrom (1998) without describing the mechanisms of reputation, trust, and reciprocity explicitly.

We are aware of two additional papers that use agent-based model to understand the behavior of agents in public-good experiments. Iwasaki et al. (2003) examined a reinforcement learning model to explain patterns of behavior observed in their threshold public-good experiments. In such an experiment, a minimum threshold of investments in the public good must be contributed before the public good is provided. Their model of reinforcement learning was only partly able to explain the observed data. It did reproduce cooperative patterns, but was not able to reproduce non-cooperative patterns.

Janssen and Ahn (2005) compare the empirical performance of two decision making models to explain the outcomes in a large set of public-good experiments without communication (Isaac and Walker, 1988; Isaac et al., 1994), namely, the experienced weighted attraction learning model of Camerer and Ho (1999), and the best-response model with signaling based on Isaac et al. (1994). In contrast with the previous studies,

Janssen and Ahn focus on the problems on parameter calibration and the evaluation of the model performance on individual and group level statistics. Both models outperform the selfish rational actor model as an explanation of observed behavior. Furthermore, the learning model was found to give the best performance using the individual level calibration, while the best response model was found to calibrate best at the group level. The essential elements of the model that enhances its performance is the inclusion of other regarding preferences and satisficing behavior, similar to Jager and Janssen (2002) for common-pool resources.

The strategy method, where human subjects develop strategies based on their experience in laboratory experiments, is an interesting method which links agent-based models and experiments (Selten et al., 1997). Keser and Gardner (1999) apply the strategy method to common-pool resources. Their common-pool resource game consisted of a constituent game played for twenty periods. Sixteen students, all experienced in game theory, were recruited to play the game over the course of six weeks. In the first phase of the experiment, they played the common-pool resource game on-line three times. In the second phase of the experiment, the tournament phase, they designed strategies which, after implementation as agents, were then played against each other. As for human subjects, a Nash equilibrium was found at the aggregate level, but at the individual level, fewer than 5% of subjects played in accordance with the game equilibrium prediction.

Combining agent-based modeling and laboratory experiments of complex dynamic social dilemmas has just started (see Duffy, 2006 for a more general discussion on agent-based modeling and laboratory experiments). The current publications demonstrate considerable potential to test alternative theories of human behavior. Huge methodological challenges still exist, however, in regard to parameter estimation and model comparison. For example, Salmon (2001) showed that identification of the correct learning models using econometrics techniques leads to potential problems. Salmon generated experimental data by simulation of normal-form games using a number of learning models so that he could test four different econometric approaches in their accuracy of distinguishing the individual models by which the data was generated. Wilcox (2003) did a similar experiment to test the implication of the assumption of homogeneity of the subjects. If the agent population is heterogeneous in parameter values, serious problems in accuracy of parameter estimation are created.

Model selection is an important line of research in cognitive science (Pitt and Myung, 2002). Various approaches have been developed to test models in regard to goodness of fit and generalizability. These approaches penalize models with increasing complexity. Approaches based on maximum likelihood depend on the assumption that the observations are statistically independent. This is not the case when multiple actors interact over time in experiments with public goods and common-pool resources. Interdependence in a complicated fashion definitely exists when communication, monitoring, and sanctioning are allowed.

3.4. Applications to social-ecological systems

An early application of agent-based modeling to study the coordination among resource users is the study of the irrigation systems of Bali (Lansing and Kremer, 1993). The irrigators have to solve a complex coordination problem (Lansing, 1991). On one hand, control of pests is most effective when all rice fields in a watershed have the same schedule of planting rice. On the other hand, the terraces are hydrologically interdependent, with long and fragile systems of tunnels, canals, and aqueducts. To balance the need for coordinated fallow periods and use of water, a complex calendar system has been developed that details what actions should be done on each specific date in each organized group of farmers—called a *subak*. These actions are related to offerings to temples, ranging from the little temples at the rice terrace level to the temples at the regional level and all the way up to the temple of the high priest Jero Gde, the human representative of the Goddess of the Temple of the Crater Lake. Crater Lake feeds the groundwater system, which is the main source of water for irrigating in the entire watershed. These offerings were collected as a counter gift for the use of water that belonged to the gods.

The function and power of the water temples were invisible to the planners involved in promoting the Green Revolution during the 1960s. They regarded agriculture as a purely technical process. Farmers were forced to switch to the miracle rice varieties, which were predicted to lead to three harvests a year, instead of the two of the traditional varieties. Farmers were stimulated by governmental programs that subsidized the use of fertilizers and pesticides. After the governmental incentive program was started, the farmers continued performing their rituals, but they no longer coincided with the timing of rice-farming activities. Soon after the introduction of the miracle rice, a plague of plant-hoppers caused huge damage to the rice crop. A new variety was introduced, but then a new pest plague hit the farmers. Furthermore, there were problems of water shortage.

During the 1980s, an increasing number of farmers wanted to switch back to the old system, but the engineers interpreted this as religious conservatism and resistance to change. It was Lansing (1991) who unraveled the function of the water temples, and was able to convince the financers of the Green Revolution project on Bali that the irrigation was best coordinated at the level of the subaks with their water temples. Lansing built an agent-based model of the interactions of subak management strategies and the ecosystem, and the local adaptation of subaks to strategies of neighboring subaks, and showed that for different levels of coordination, from farmer level up to central control, the temple level was the level of scale where decisions could be made to maximize the production of rice (see also Lansing and Kremer, 1993). He also showed how the coordination might have been evolved as a result of local interactions (Lansing, 2000).

In Lansing and Miller (2003), a simple game-theoretic model is used to provide a compact explanation for many of the most salient features observed in the system. While externalities caused by either water scarcity or pests in isolation would be expected to cause a serious failure in the system, they find that the ecology of the rice farming system links these two externalities in such a way that cooperation, rather than chaos, results. The reason for this, depending on the underlying ecological parameters in the system, is that regimes exist in which the farmers would like to coordinate their cropping patterns (in particular, have identical fallow periods) so as to control pest populations. In other regimes, coordination is not an equilibrium, even though coordinated farming would result in greater aggregate crop output. Lansing and Miller identified two indirect mechanisms by which the system can reach cooperation. The first is to have the upstream farmers share their water with the downstream farmers. The second is that increases in pest damage can drive the system into a coordinated equilibrium, enhancing aggregate output. The Balinese rice temples would have played a facilitating role in deriving coordination in this complex system. In an earlier game-theoretical paper, Ostrom (1996) also examined how differences between head-end and tail-end farmers could be the foundation for extensive mutually productive coordination in the maintenance of irrigation infrastructure.

Bousquet and his colleagues (Bousquet et al., 1998) developed a modeling platform, CORMAS, dedicated to the study of common-pool resources through agent-based modeling. They have performed many applications and work together with local stakeholders, often in Africa and Asia, to develop agent-based models for practical natural resource management problems.[1] Barreteau and Bousquet (2000), for example, study the underutilization of irrigated systems in the Senegal River Valley in North Senegal. An agent-based model was developed to simulate an archetypal irrigation system. The agents represent farmers, credit access, and water allocation groups. The processes represented deal with the circulation of water and credit and with interactions about their allocation and access to them. The model was used in role-playing experiments to test its potential as a negotiation support tool and to test the model with the agents they try to simulate (Barreteau et al., 2001). The use of a role-playing game was found very useful for testing the model and interacting with local stakeholders. This led Bousquet et al. (2002) to the idea of *companion modeling*, which interactively combines agent-based modeling and role-playing games and uses the latter to acquire knowledge, build and validate the agent-based model, and use the model in the decision-making process. This has been applied to a number of case studies, as reviewed in Bousquet et al. (2002). We come back to role-playing games later in this chapter.

Rouchier et al. (2001) discuss a coordination problem of nomad herdsmen securing their access to the rangelands in Cameroon. Herdsmen who need the grass and water from the villages negotiate with village leaders to get access to the land of the farmers. The herdsmen choose which leaders to approach. Those leaders may reject offers if they are lower than a minimum acceptance level. Herdsmen need to sell some of their animals to derive the resources to pay the fee. Three types of choice processes are simulated: (1) herdsmen make offers to place their animals on random spots; (2) they make offers

---

[1] See http://cormas.cirad.fr.

for the cheapest spots; or (3) they make offers to the villages with the best friendship relations that take into account past refusals of offers. Rouchier et al. found that choices based on costs lead to the lowest number of animals that the simulated system could sustain, because considerable resources are lost by negotiation and refusals when all herdsmen try to enter cheapest village. Since the herdsmen do not learn in this model, they continue losing productivity by aggregating around the same village every time period. Other applications of the CORMAS group include collaborative forest management in East Kalimantan in Indonesia (Purnomo et al., 2003) and the management of livestock effluents in Réunion, France (Farolfi et al., 2002).

3.5. What have we learned?

In regard to the governance of common-pool resources, agent-based modeling has been able to draw on a foundation of extensive fieldwork and laboratory experiments as well as extending our theoretical understanding of cooperation in social dilemma settings. Since both forms of empirical research had already challenged the capacity of simple, analytical theory based on non-cooperative game theory to explain empirical results, the field was ripe for the use of agent-based models. We have learned from agent-based models of the processes linking resource users, public infrastructure providers, and their resources and infrastructures that much of the data reported by field researchers is consistent with a complex, adaptive systems view of social dilemmas.

From the combination of research methods examining factors enhancing levels of cooperation, we have learned that devising rules that allocate benefits to resource users in a legitimate, fair, and enforceable way is essential to overcome incentives to free ride. Rarely can external authorities devise rules that are well tailored to a local ecology and culture and also invest substantial resources in monitoring patterns of resource use and sanctioning those who do not follow rules. Thus, the repeated finding that individuals can devise agreed-upon norms for governing a resource that they themselves can monitor and enforce has changed our scientific understanding of these processes. Unfortunately, public policies have all too frequently relied on simple panaceas that either recommend government, private property, or decentralized governance of SESs. We have strong evidence that simplistic solutions that are imposed by external agencies on resource users rarely work (National Research Council, 2002; Dietz et al., 2003). And, fortunately, we now have methods—agent-based models—that facilitate the analysis of complex SESs by stakeholders and officials. No longer do we need to throw up our hands in despair because the system is so complex! We do, however, need to continue a sense of modesty. Even with agent-based models of complex SESs, we rarely can prescribe "the" optimal solution for any complex setting. Those involved have to learn over time by experimenting with local ideas, with what they can learn from others and with ideas from the literature describing what has worked well in other settings.

4. Dealing with uncertainty

Understanding of the processes of social-ecological systems is incomplete and is likely to remain incomplete. Given the persistent uncertainty facing resource users and public infrastructure providers in the field, researchers need to incorporate uncertainty explicitly in their analyses (Ludwig et al., 1993). Agent-based models can address uncertainty by analyzing the consequences of how people make decisions under uncertainty and by assessing the impact of different types of hypotheses about these processes in social-ecological systems.

Models of human decision-making under uncertainty have traditionally been approached from a probabilistic standpoint: human performance was compared to probabilistic prescriptions. Any divergence was interpreted as a deviation from the optimal behavior. Laboratory experiments of human decision-making, however, show that frequently people do not make decisions under uncertainty that are consistent with the probabilistic perspective (Kahneman and Tversky, 1979). Further, many decision problems cannot be characterized by a closed set of probabilities (Ludwig et al., 1993).

If agents do not have complete knowledge of a complex ecological system, how do their mental models of the system affect their actions? How can they learn to derive a more accurate mental representation? These questions refer to the general problem in agent-based modeling that agents do not have perfect knowledge of the system. They make their decisions based on the perceptions they have of the problem. These perceptions do not have to include correct representations of reality and may vary among agents. The focus in this section is on the uncertainty of agents about the ecological dynamics.

4.1. Theoretical models

An important source of uncertainty in the governance of social-ecological systems is the fundamental uncertainty of the functioning of the biophysical system. One of the uses of agent-based models is to explore the consequences of agents who have incomplete perceptions of reality. Different perceptions of reality can be visualized by different perspectives of stability (Figure 2). According to the equilibrium perspective, systems are in equilibrium. External effects can push the system briefly out of equilibrium, but it automatically returns to the previous equilibrium situation. This perspective corresponds very well with the Newtonian-modeling paradigm. The perspective of stability can be represented graphically as a ball at the bottom of a valley (Figure 2c). Perturbations only temporarily knock the ball away from the bottom of the valley. An implicit assumption of this perspective is that systems have the capacity to dampening all kinds of disturbances.

An alternative perspective is the obverse: namely, the perspective of instability. Systems are assumed to be very sensitive to disturbances. Every disturbance can lead to a catastrophe. Applied to environmental issues, the perspective of instability explains why some people argue that human activities are not supposed to disturb the natural

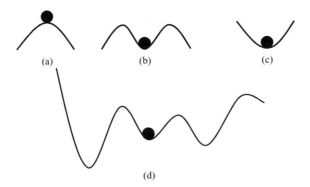

Figure 2. Perspectives of nature: (a) nature is unstable; (b) nature is stable within limits; (c) nature is stable; (d) nature has different stability domains (after Janssen, 2002b).

system. Any degree of pollution or increase of extractions can lead to a collapse of the system. This perspective can be visualized by a ball on a peak (Figure 2a). Any perturbation can cause the ball to roll down the slope. A third perspective is in-between the perspectives of stability and instability: namely, a system is assumed to be stable within limits. When the system is managed well, the system can absorb small perturbations. This perspective can be visualized as a ball in a valley between two peaks (Figure 2b).

A more advanced framework is to consider multiple stable states (Scheffer et al., 2001). As depicted in Figure 2d, this perspective can be represented as a number of peaks and valleys. The ball is resting in a valley and is able to absorb a certain degree of disturbance. However, a severe disturbance can push the ball over a peak such that it will rest in another valley, an alternative equilibrium. Examples of these multiple states are lakes that can flip from an oligotropic state to a eutrophic state due to inputs of phosphates, and rangelands that can flip from a productive cattle-grazing system into unproductive rangeland dominated by woody vegetation, triggered by variability in rainfall.

A perspective of systems that is more advanced, and lies in line with the complex adaptive system modeling paradigm, is the perspective of resilience. The perspective of resilience not only considers the balls moving up and down the peaks and valleys, but also considers possible movements of the peaks and valleys themselves. In this evolutionary picture, stability domains can shrink, and disturbances that previously could be absorbed might now dislodge the system. This view has important implications for managing systems. In the previously discussed perspective, systems could be known perfectly. Surprises could lead to changes of management, because the balls move into another valley; but, in principle, management is simply a matter of controlling the system. From the perspective of an evolving 'landscape,' however, one has to manage a system in the face of fundamental uncertainty about the functioning of the system. One continually needs to observe the system in order to respond adequately. Moreover, small human-induced perturbations are recommended in order to learn from the system over time.

Various concepts called worldviews are designed to classify different perceptions of reality. Michael Thompson and his colleagues give a general description of perspectives on natural and human systems and social relations in their Cultural Theory (Thompson et al., 1990). This theory was used during the 1990s to classify different types of institutional designs in relation to global environmental change. Cultural Theory is even used in various mathematical models, when suitable, because it includes perspectives on human and natural systems that claim generality and includes the determinism of explaining the rationality of each perspective. Cultural Theory combines anthropological and ecological insights, and results in multiple types of culture.

The three main worldviews in Cultural Theory are:

- Hierarchists assume that nature is stable in most circumstances but can collapse if it crosses the limits of its capacity. Therefore, central control is advocated as a management style.
- Egalitarians assume that nature is highly unstable and that the least human intervention could lead to its complete collapse. A preventive management style is preferred.
- Individualists assume that nature provides an abundance of resources and believe it is stable with human interventions. A responsive management style is advocated.

Human-induced climate change is a topic surrounded with many uncertainties and is therefore an excellent example to illustrate how worldviews can be quantified to simulate alternative futures based on different perceptions of reality. Such an analysis was made by Janssen and de Vries (1998), who developed three versions of a simple model of a social-ecological system based on alternative assumptions about climate sensitivity, technological change, mitigation costs, and damage costs due to climate change. Egalitarians, for example, assume high climate sensitivity, high damage costs, low technological development, and low mitigation costs. For management styles, they assume different strategies for investments and reductions of emissions of carbon dioxide. The individualist, for example, assumes a strategy that maximizes economic growth and assumes emissions are reduced only if a certain threshold of economic damage is exceeded.

Suppose the agents in a model world are all hierarchists, all egalitarians, or all individualists. If agents are assumed to have perfect knowledge of their world, their utopia can be simulated. If their worldview is incorrect and they still apply their preferred management style, their dystopia can be simulated. An example is presented in Figures 3a and 3b. In the egalitarian utopia, emissions of carbon dioxide will be reduced to zero within a few decades, leading to a modest temperature change. However, if the individualistic worldview manages a world that actually operates according to the egalitarian worldview, emissions increase until climate change causes such an economic disaster that an emission reduction policy is unavoidable.

By introducing a population of agents with heterogeneous worldviews, a complex adaptive system is produced. It is assumed that the better an agent's worldview ex-

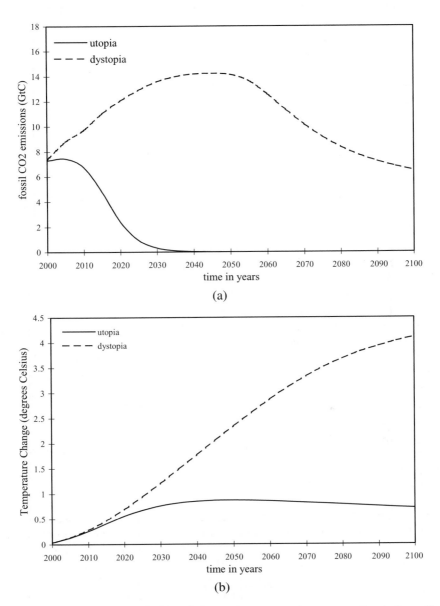

Figure 3. (a, b) Expected carbon dioxide emissions and temperature increase according to the egalitarian utopia an a possible dystopia (individualistic management style in an unstable global system). (c, d) Expected carbon dioxide emissions and temperature increase according to different views on the functioning of the global system. (Based on Janssen and de Vries, 1998).

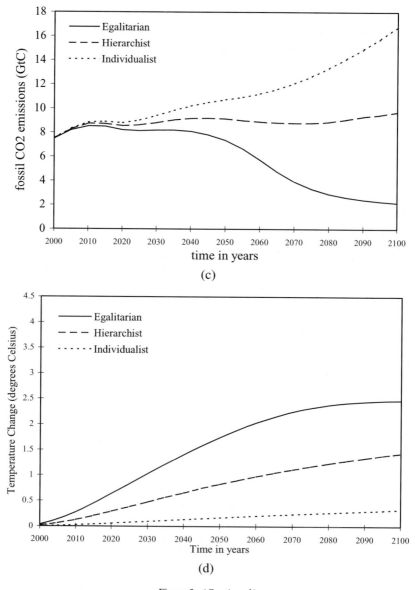

Figure 3. (*Continued.*)

plains the world's observed behavior, the greater is the chance that it will be stable.
A genetic algorithm is used to simulate a battle between perspectives (Holland, 1992b).
The better a worldview explains observations, the more it is likely to be followed by a
larger proportion of the population. They simulate a learning process where agents may

adjust their mental models when they are surprised by observations, and may make adjustments in their decisions according to their new perceptions of the problem. Agents tolerate some level of error, however, before they change their worldviews. The initial distribution of worldviews is therefore important for the long-term evolution of the social-ecological system. On aggregate, worldviews tend to change to the worldview that explain the observations in the most convincing way. Suppose that reality is one of the three possible worlds, and an agent obtains information over time that causes it to adjust (or not) its perspective on the problem of climate change. Three sets of projections are derived in which agents adapt to climate change (Figures 3c and 3d). Prior to year 2040, the observed climate change does not lead to domination of one of the worldviews. After 2040, the climate signal becomes clear enough that one of the worldviews begins to dominate. In the event of the world functioning according to the egalitarian worldview, the emissions growth stabilizes in the coming decades and decreases to a level below half of the present amount of emissions. However, this reduction cannot avoid a global mean temperature increase of about 2.5°C in the coming century.

The explicit inclusion of subjective perceptions of reality has led to a rich variety of possible futures. This approach has also been applied to lake management (Carpenter et al., 1999a, 1999b; Janssen and Carpenter, 1999; Janssen, 2001; Peterson et al., 2003) and rangeland management (Janssen et al., 2000). Lakes are a favorite ecosystem for the study of social-ecological systems, because the multiple stable states are well studied and simple, empirically based models are available (Carpenter et al., 1999b). The typical lake model focuses on phosphorus pollution. Phosphorus flows from agriculture to upland soils, and then on to surface waters where it cycles between water and sediments. The lake ecosystem has multiple locally stable equilibria and moves among basins of attraction depending on the history of pollutant inputs. Lakes are often classified as oligotrophic or eutrophic depending on their productivity. Oligotrophic lakes are characterised by low nutrient inputs, low to moderate levels of plant production, relatively clear water, and relatively high economic value of ecosystem services. Eutrophic lakes have high nutrient inputs, high plant production, murky water with problems including anoxia and toxicity, and relatively low value of ecosystem services. When mitigating eutrophication, lakes can respond differently to reduced phosphorus inputs, which is mainly related to recycling of phosphorus from sediments to the overlying water.

In Carpenter et al. (1999a), an agent-based model is developed in which agents form expectations about ecosystem dynamics, markets, and/or the actions of managers, and they choose levels of pollutant inputs accordingly. Agents have heterogeneous beliefs and/or access to information. Their aggregate behavior determines the total rate of pollutant input. As the ecosystem changes, agents update their beliefs and expectations about the world they co-create. They modify their actions accordingly. For a wide range of scenarios, Carpenter et al. observe irregular oscillations among ecosystem states and patterns of agent behavior. These oscillations resemble some features of the resilience of complex adaptive social-ecological systems. Janssen and Carpenter (1999) applied the same framework of worldviews as used in Janssen and de Vries (1998) to the management of lakes. The agents learn and adapt to unexpected changes in the state of the lake, and a mix of perspectives is required to manage the resilience of the system. Although low levels of phosphorus in the lake will not be reached, the lake is prevented from flipping to catastrophically high phosphorus levels.

The agents are always learning, but never get it exactly right. They come close enough, however, to sustain the social-ecological system. In Janssen (2001), the agents were enriched with a mix of various cognitive processes, such as imitation, deliberation, and repetitive behavior, in their decisions about how much phosphorus to use. Analyses with the model showed that the dominating type of cognitive processing was a relevant factor in the response to uncertainty and policy measures. When agents are easily unsatisfied with their economic performance, it leads to a more intensive use of phosphorus and to higher levels of phosphorus in the lake. Simulated farmers used phosphorus more intensively in situations with high natural variability. A tax on phosphorus had little effect on the behavior of the farmers when they felt uncertain and were easily satisfied.

Peterson et al. (2003) describe the management of a lake as a learning process. The agents consider two management models of the lake, one for an oligotrophic lake and the other for a eutrophic lake. As agents observe the lake varying from year to year, they estimate how well each of the two management models is supported by the observed data. Management policies maximize the expected net present value of the lake. Even under optimistic assumptions about environmental variation, learning ability, and management control, conventional decision theory and optimal control approaches fail to stabilize ecological dynamics. Rather, these methods drive ecosystems into cycles of collapse and recovery.

Weisbuch and Duchateau-Nguyen (1998) study fisheries where fishers do not have complete understanding of the underlying (logistic) resource dynamics. Historical information about catches, capital amounts, and the fraction of the income used for consumption, are used by the agents to predict future catches. Incremental learning is used to update the weights on the various sources of information. The agents were able to learn to manage the system and could cope with sudden shocks to the system.

In the rangeland model of Janssen et al. (2000), agents do not learn but may go bankrupt, leave the system, and be replaced by a random, new pastoralist. The agents have incomplete understanding of the complex rangeland system. They tend to overgraze their property by putting too many sheep on their land, and suppress fire too much so woody shrubs can start dominating. Janssen et al. analyzed the consequence of different government regulations on the evolution of types of agents. Agents who evolve under a regime of limited grazing do not have a proper understanding of the dynamics of the system. Agents who evolve without regulations, experience the whole spectrum of possible events. In the latter case, many properties are unproductive for a longer period, but those agents who evolve have a good understanding of the system. This example shows the importance of exploring the possible dynamics of a regime and the effects of precautionary policies to avoid overuse of the resource.

Bodin and Norberg (2005) examine the principal impact of information sharing in (social) networks of artificial natural resource managers capable of experimenting, simple information processing, and decision-making. All managers adaptively manage their own local ecological resources. All properties are close to a threshold at which the ecological system flips into an unproductive state. Aggregate properties of the coupled social-ecological system are analyzed in relation to different network structures. Bodin and Norberg find that the network structures have a profound effect on the system's behavior. Networks of low- to moderate-link densities significantly increase the sustainability of the ecological resource. However, networks of high-link densities contribute to a highly synchronized behavior of the managers, which causes occasional large-scale ecological crises between meta-stable periods of high production. It is demonstrated that in a coupled social-ecological system the system-wide state transition occurs not because the ecological system flips into the undesired state, but because the managers loose their capacity to reorganize back to the desired state.

4.2. Laboratory experiments

We will discuss the work of scholars who test different types of heuristics to explain experimental observation of decision-making in different situations (Gigerenzer et al., 1999). In a similar vein, we will analyze the comparative analysis of quantitative learning models on experimental data of subjects learning to find good solutions for allocation problems in complex environments (Rieskamp et al., 2003). For a broader discussion on agent-based models, laboratory experiments, and learning we refer to Brenner (2006) and Duffy (2006) in this volume.

Gigerenzer et al. (1999) argue that humans use fast and frugal heuristics to make satisfying decisions about a set of alternatives that respect the limitations of human time and knowledge. Complexity and uncertainty of the environment have led in the evolution of the brain to smart solutions that are "ecologically rational." The authors discuss a large number of experiments in which they test simple heuristics such as one-reason decision-making (e.g., "take the last," "take the best"), elimination heuristics, or recognition heuristics. A drawback of this research program, so far, is that the decision-making experiments are very simple, like what city has the largest population, compared to the more dynamic decision environments with social interactions as is characteristic of social-ecological systems.

Rieskamp et al. (2003) used experiments to compare two learning models related to long-term decisions made under uncertainty. One learning model is reinforcement learning, a global search model that assumes that decisions are made probabilistically based on the experience aggregated across all past decisions. The other learning model is hill-climbing, a local search model that assumes a new decision is made by comparing the preceding decision with the most successful decision up to that point. One application of their model is explaining the decisions made by resource users about diverse strategies of land use. In the laboratory experiment, participants were asked to allocate three financial assets in a repeated session of two hundred rounds. The optimal allocation was often not found, but a learning effect was still measurable. Rieskamp et al. (2003) conclude that the hill-climbing model best describes their observations.

Goldstone and Ashpole (2004) performed experiments where a large number of human participants interacted in real time within a shared virtual world. Two resource pools were created with different rates of replenishment. The participants' task was to obtain as many resource tokens as possible during an experiment. Besides variation in the rate at which consumed tokens were replaced, Goldstone and Ashpole manipulated whether agents could see each other and the entire token distribution, or had their vision restricted to tokens in their own location. The optimal solution for participants is to distribute themselves in proportion to the distribution of resources. The human subjects did not to distribute themselves in this optimal fashion. Rather, they systematically allocated themselves more to the relative scarce resource, leading to an underutilization of the resources. Furthermore, especially when the vision of the subjects was restricted, oscillations in the harvesting rates of the resources across time were observed. Perceived underutilization of a resource resulted in an influx of agents to that resource. This sudden influx, in turn, resulted in an excess of agents, which then led to a trend for agents to depart from the resource region. Thus, uncertainty about the availability of resources increased instability of the distribution of the subjects, which itself enhanced uncertainty.

4.3. Applications

In the spirit of adaptive management (Holling, 1978), various researchers develop their agent-based models together with the stakeholders of the problem. Like the participatory modeling approach, such as practiced in systems dynamics (e.g., Costanza and Ruth, 1998), they use the model as a tool in the mediation process with stakeholders and as a way for the stakeholders to learn strategies that might solve the dilemmas they face in complex environments. In Bousquet et al.'s (Bousquet et al., 2002) companion modeling, the role-playing games are meant to reveal some aspects of social relationships by allowing the direct observation of interactions among players, the stakeholders. Barreteau et al. (2003) argue that such role-playing games are good communication tools among stakeholders, but it is difficult to reproduce the results. Systematic comparison of the results is difficult since many factors are uncontrolled. When players play again, they may change the context of the game due to their learning experience in the previous experiment.

In Etienne et al. (2003), for example, an agent-based model was developed to simulate strategies of natural resource management in the Causse Méjan, a limestone plateau in southern France dominated by a rare grassland-dominated ecosystem endangered by pine invasion. To facilitate discussion of alternative long-term management strategies for the sheep farms and the woodlands, contrasting perspectives on land resources from foresters, farmers, and rangers of the National Park of Cévennes were designed at different spatial scales. A series of exercises with different stakeholder groups was performed to confront the consequences of their viewpoints, and that of the other stakeholders. As a result of this iterative process it was possible to select a set of feasible scenarios stemming from the current actors' perceptions and practices and to suggest alternative sylvopastoral management based on innovative practices. D'Aquino et al. (2003) describe their project on irrigation systems in Senegal. Since 1997 they have experimented at an operational level (2500 km^2) in the Senegal River valley with agent-based modeling intertwined with role-playing games. Their self-design approach is aimed to include as much as possible the knowledge of the local participants. This development of methodology may contribute to additional tools of resource users and public infrastructure providers to self-govern their common resources.

Pahl-Wostl (2002) discusses a similar development that she calls participatory agent-based social simulation. This modeling technique inputs social processes into integrated models that are developed in participatory settings. Hare and Pahl-Wostl (2002) illustrate in a Swiss case study how card-sorting can be used to categorize stakeholders to inform the design of agent-based models.

An interesting application of learning models to natural resource management is the work of Dreyfus-Leon on fisheries. Dreyfus-Leon (1999) presents a basic model to mimic the search behavior of fishers. It is built on two neural networks to cope with two separate decision-making processes in fishing activities. One neural network deals with decisions to stay in current fishing grounds or move to new ones. The other is constructed for the purpose of finding prey within the fishing grounds. Reinforcement learning is used to derive expectations of catches from previous neural network-based decisions. Feedback about catches is used to update the weights of the neural networks. Some similarities with the behavior of real fishers were found: the concentrated local search once a prey has been located to increase the probability of remaining near a prey patch and the straightforward movement to other fishing grounds. Also, they prefer areas near the port when conditions in different fishing grounds are similar or when there is high uncertainty in their world.

The observed behavior of the artificial fisher in uncertain scenarios can be described as a risk-aversion attitude. In Dreyfus-Leon and Kleiber (2001), the model of fishers' behavior was applied to yellow-fin tuna fishing in the eastern Pacific Ocean. In contrast to Dreyfus-Leon (1999)—where the schools of fish were located at fixed points—in this study, movements of schools of fish were simulated with artificial neural networks, based on relative habitat comfort. Like Dreyfus-Leon (1999), the individual fishing vessels were represented with artificial neural networks. The tuna vessels searched for the tuna schools during a fishing trip. An interesting Turing experiment was performed to test the performance of the model by asking experts, fishers, and tuna researchers to identify which tracks were simulated and which were real. The experts were not able to provide the correct answer more frequently than random choice. This provided the modelers some confidence in their results. Two scenarios were considered in the analysis: one with no fishing regulation and another with an area closure during the last quarter of the year. In the scenario without regulation, fishing effort was allocated, particularly in higher levels nearer the coast and where high concentrations of tuna were detected. In the scenario with regulation, redistribution of effort was uneven but increased in neighboring areas or in areas relatively near the closure zone. Decrease in effort was evident only in the closed area. Effort redistribution when regulations were implemented is not well understood, but this modeling approach can help fishery managers to envisage some regulation effects in the fishery.

4.4. What have we learned?

Uncertainty and limited knowledge about ecological processes are crucial elements in the study of social-ecological systems. Agent-based modeling provides us a tool to test the consequences of the limitations of knowledge of various actors in decision-making processes on the governance of natural resources. Theoretical models focused on mental models match very well the applications that use role-playing games and the participatory approach. These applications provide stakeholders instruments to test the consequences of different perceptions of the systems, which enable them to identify compromises and conflicts. The participatory use of models, such as systems-dynamics, already existed. Agent-based models enable researchers to be more explicit about the behavioral and spatial aspects of social-ecological systems.

The experimental work related to natural resource management and uncertainty relates primarily to heuristics and learning models. In that respect there is a mismatch with the theoretical and applied agent-based models. A considerable challenge remains to develop experimental work to test the consequences of various mental models for the management of natural resources.

5. Topology of interactions

The importance of non-random and non-uniform topologies of interactions between agents can be an important reason to use agent-based models. As discussed by Dibble (2006), Wilhite (2006), and Vriend (2006), the role of the structure of interactions has been found important in various areas of agent-based computational economics. In this chapter we mainly focus on exogenous structures of interactions, especially as they are caused by ecological processes. In fact, when we include space, many questions arise related to the structure of interactions.

Explicit inclusion of space in the analysis of environmental economic problems leads to the questions of how to allocate a scarce amount of space, how to manage land given uncertainty of the dynamics of the system, how to deal with spatial externalities and resulting spatial conflicts, and how information spreads in a spatially explicit system. The area of land-use and land-cover change addresses these issues, and agent-based modeling has been applied in this area. Agent-based modeling for land-use and land-cover change combines a cellular model representing the landscape of interest with an agent-based model that represents decision-making entities (Parker et al., 2003). Due to the digitalization of land-use/cover data, i.e. remotely sensed imagery, and the development of geographic information systems, cellular maps can be derived for analysis.

Since the 1980s, cellular automata have been used to model land use/cover over time (Couclelis, 1985). Human decision-making was taken implicitly into account in the transition rules, but not expressed explicitly. Sometimes the cells represent the unit of decision-making. In most applications, however, the unit of decision-making and the cell are not the same. The desire to include more comprehensive decision rules, and the mismatch between spatial units and units of decision-making, led to the use of agent-based modeling for land-use and land-cover change. By including agents, one can express ownership explicitly, as the property about which an agent can make decisions. An agent can make decisions on the land use in a number of cells—for example, by allocating cells to derive a portfolio of crops.

Another rapid development is the study of the structure of networks (Watts and Strogatz, 1998; Barabasi and Albert, 1999). Since agent-based models are characterized by the interactions of agents, it is important to understand the consequences of the effects of different network structures on the collective behavior in social-ecological systems. We will review some of this literature from the perspective of governing social-ecological systems.

5.1. Theoretical models

In a number of examples, Axtell (2000) shows that changes in the interaction topology can have important consequences for the outcomes in agent-based simulations, since the topology affects the speed at which information is processed among agents. For example, having X interactions in each time step, or on *average*, may lead to different aggregated results, depending on the nonlinear behavior of the agent-based model. In a similar vein, Flache and Hegselmann (2001) investigated the sensitivity of two main processes in social science, migration dynamics and influence dynamics, to different spatial relationships among the agents. They concluded that most of the insights are robust to alternative spatial patterns, but some interesting differences do exist. Irregular grids, for example, result in path-dependent processes, leading to lock-ins of certain patterns.

Within the theoretical studies of social dilemmas, the paper of Nowak and May (1992) simulated the study of social dilemmas in a spatial context. In their study, agents play a Prisoner's Dilemma game with their nearby neighbors in a rectangular cellular automata environment. The players defect or cooperate, and update their strategy each round, by imitating the strategy with the highest payoff in their neighborhood. The deterministic model led to spatially chaotic patterns of cooperation and defection. Thus, without memory, patterns of cooperation can be derived in a spatial context.

We will not review the comprehensive literature on spatial games here, but focus on public-good games because of their relevance for natural resource management. Hauert and colleagues study the evolution of cooperation in spatial public-good games (Hauert et al., 2002; Brandt et al., 2003; Hauert and Szabo, 2003). They show that when agents are able to leave a game, defectors, cooperators, and non-players co-exist in a dynamic environment (Hauert et al., 2002). The possibility of costly punishment of defectors significantly increases the level of cooperation (Brandt et al., 2003). Hauert and Szabo (2003) tested the consequence of different geometries of interactions. Cooperation is higher on honeycomb versus square interactions. Also, larger neighborhoods, and thus larger groups who share the pubic good, reduce the level of cooperation.

5.2. Laboratory experiments

Laboratory experiments with regard to the importance of the structure of interactions are rare, especially with respect to the governance of social-ecological systems. This may change in the near future since new laboratories for experimental studies have been established at the University of Rhode Island and Indiana University. Both laboratories will focus on spatially explicit experiments with human subjects.

An interesting set of experiments that is of particular interest for this chapter seeks to understand how information from other agents affects decision-making. Kameda and Nakanishi (2002, 2003) performed experiments to analyze the consequences when human subjects had the choice to solicit information on the choices of other participants in the experiment. The experiment was called "Where is the rabbit?" and simulated a fluctuating uncertain environment in a laboratory setting. In this game, participants were asked to judge in which of two nests a rabbit was currently located based on stochastic information. Participants played the game for a total of sixty rounds. They were instructed that the rabbit (environment) had a tendency to stay in the same nest over time, but this tendency was not perfect: The rabbit might change its location between any two consecutive rounds with a probability of 20%. Thus, the location of the rabbit in a given round corresponded to the current state of the fluctuating environment. In one half of the experiments, subjects did not derive information from the choices of other participants. In the other half of the experiments, subjects in six-person groups derived information of three others (randomly chosen) in their group. In both cases, the subject could derive information about the location of the rabbit by a costly information search. Kameda and Nakanishi showed that the subjects who were able to derive information from others in their group derived a higher payoff than those who could only learn individually. A simulation was developed that mimicked the observed findings.

5.3. Applications

Balmann (1997) studied structural change in agricultural activities. He developed a model that was based on a number of individually acting farms located at different points in an agricultural region. Like a cellular automaton, the region was subdivided into a number of spatially ordered plots. The farms competed for these plots and competed in different markets. Farms were allowed to engage in different production possibilities and could use several investment alternatives. They optimized their activities with respect to their objective function by considering their expectations, financial state, and existing assets. The model was applied to a hypothetical region and studied how agricultural development was path dependent. In Balmann et al. (2002), an application of the model is presented with data from a region in Germany. The model consists of approximately 2600 farms, distinguishing twelve farm types, as observed in the data. In their application of the model, heterogeneity among the agents resulted in diversity of adjustment costs to policy interventions. The model provides insights into the distribution and dynamics of the impacts of policy changes on incomes.

Building on the work of Balmann (1997), Berger (2001) developed an agent-based model for an agricultural region in Chile. The farm-household decision-making was represented as a linear programming problem solved for each simulated year. Berger analyzed the adoption of new export-oriented agricultural activities using a network-threshold framework (Valente, 1995). Empirical studies provided the foundation for the type of networks and the heterogeneity of threshold values. The analysis showed that a governmental policy to stimulate export-oriented agricultural activities was effective to double the income from agriculture in a twenty-year period, compared to a stabilization of the income level if the policy intervention was not implemented.

Deffuant et al. (2002) present another agent-based model of innovation among farmers. Their model is based on an in-depth survey and interviews with farmers in various locations in Europe. The empirical model presented about Allier, France, tried to understand how organic farming was diffused. A positive attitude toward organic farming was necessary but not sufficient to get adoption started. Positive information in the press stimulated farmers to exchange opinions, and stimulated adoption of organic farming.

Allen and McGlade (1987) developed a spatially explicit model of fishers. These fishers could have different strategies, based on the information available to them, such as fishing only at the location from which they expected the highest catch, or moving around randomly. Inclusion of stochastic behavior for some fishers was necessary to discover the location of fish stocks and to maintain the fish industry.

Hoffmann et al. (2002) present a pilot study of land-use change in south-central Indiana, USA. This part of the state was primarily forested prior to the arrival of settlers from Europe in the early 1800s. These settlers cleared substantial areas of land for agricultural production (crops and pasture) and for forest products used for construction materials. The process of clearing land continued until the early 1900s, at which time areas marginal for agricultural production were gradually abandoned, resulting in a pattern of forest regrowth in areas of low agricultural suitability. The agents (private landowners) made decisions regarding their portfolio of land-use products that affected their utility. The utility depended on components such as income from timber, income from farming, and aesthetic enjoyment of the forests. Using scenarios of prices for agricultural commodities, Hoffmann et al. were able to reproduce land-cover dynamics in line with observed stylized facts (agriculture on the flat land, reforestation on the slopes).

Evans and Kelley (2004) tested an elaborated version of the Hoffmann et al. model on Indian Creek Township, located in southwest Monroe County, Indiana. This area is approximately 10×10 km, with private landholders as the primary actors in the landscape. Indian Creek Township is characterized by a series of rolling hills with bottomland areas suitable for agricultural production interspersed between ridges/hills that are largely forested. Landowners are a mix of households that derive a portion of their household income from extraction practices (agriculture, farming, haying, timber harvesting) and other households that derive all their income from non-farm activities. Evans and Kelley analyzed the consequences of using different scales of modeling the decisions of the private landowners. The best fit of the calibrated model was derived at the highest resolution, and declined non-monotonically with scale. The authors argue that agent-based models of land use need to be analyzed at different levels of scale.

Parker and Meretsky (2004) focus on externalities of land use, and their affect on land-use composition and pattern. Their model was used to analyze interactions between urban use and agricultural use, and how externalities of the use of the property affected spatial patterns if agents made rational decisions to maximize their utility. The assumption was that when agents adopt NIMBY (not in my back yard) strategies related to urban activities, inefficient urban sprawl results.

Brown et al. (2005) present a model of urban sprawl applied to Washtenaw County, Michigan, USA. The agents entering the county weigh aesthetics, distance to the service center, and neighborhood density to make decisions about where to live. In addition to their empirical landscape, Brown et al. used artificial landscapes to test the ability of the model to predict certain spatial patterns generated by a known model. It was not always possible to predict settlement patterns with the model, illustrating the difficulty of getting a good fit in spatially explicit models. Nevertheless, they were able to derive good fits with *aggregated* spatial metrics.

The study areas of Brown et al. (2005) and Evans and Kelley (2004) are similar in some aspects (agents are households making decisions on a detailed, real landscape), but differ in others (urban vs. rural, residential choice vs. allocation of land-use activities). It is important to note the difference between the two modeling approaches as applied. Brown et al. developed an extremely stylized model. By keeping it as simple as possible, they were able to explore the parameter space in a comprehensive way. The agents and decision-making processes in the Evans and Kelley model were more sophisticated, and the model was calibrated on the observed detailed pattern of land-cover changes. Both approaches are defended as being more appropriate to understanding the underlying processes. More work definitely needs to be done to define the right type of model for the research question at stake.

5.4. What have we learned?

Agent-based models offer various new aspects to spatially explicit modeling. By explicitly including decision-making processes we may be able to test the consequences of various behavioral theories on spatial processes, such as land-use change and urban sprawl. We recognize a lacuna in the availability of laboratory experiments that may inform the choice of behavioral theories, but new laboratories at Indiana University and the University of Rhode Island are currently conducting such experiments.

Spatially explicit processes in landscapes and networks of interactions are important to investigate, since agent-based models are defined by the topology of interactions among agents. Much more work needs to be done to address how the structures of interactions and networks affect aggregated outcomes.

6. Challenges ahead

The use of agent-based computational modeling to understand the governance of social-ecological systems is rapidly developing. We identify a number of challenges for the coming years that are fundamental to the further development of this field.

- Throughout this chapter we have discussed theoretical and applied models in relation to laboratory experiments. Such a triangular approach is an exception within most research groups. We stress the importance of using multiple methods to analyze a common set of puzzles. No one method guarantees the right answer. When similar answers are derived from methodological triangulation, we can have more confidence in our findings.
- The Internet provides us new opportunities to study social-ecological systems from an agent perspective. Users need to make decisions in a complex, interlinked environment. Most of the information used during this process can be recorded. This leads to interesting opportunities to perform experiments in cyberspace, such as the experiment of Dodds et al. (2003) to identify social networks at a global scale.
- Significant progress has been achieved to understand the evolution of strategies and norms in collective-action situations, given a fixed set of commonly understood rules. What is currently lacking is a formal model of the process of rule change and the evolution of institutional rules, although some initial models have been developed (Janssen, 2005; Janssen and Ostrom, 2005).
- During the last few years considerable progress has been achieved in understanding the structure of networks. This has also been explored by those who are interested in the governance of social-ecological systems. An interesting development is the formal modeling of co-evolving networks, such as the work of Börner et al. (2004) in information science. From the perspective of social-ecological systems, it would be interesting to explore the co-evolution of social and ecological networks.
- Agent-based models often have a tendency to become complicated and detailed, which reduces the ability for rigorous analysis of the model. How to find a balance between detail and simplicity is an important question. Therefore, evaluation techniques for the balance between complexity of the model and explanation of the empirical phenomena need to be developed. In a broader sense, we need to develop appropriate methodologies for model testing, model selection, and model validation (Durlauf, 2003).

7. Discussion and conclusions

The governance of social-ecological systems has been dominated during the last century by a top-down control paradigm. Concepts and tools from environmental economics generate the maximum sustainable yield of fish stocks, the optimal time to harvest forests, and the optimal allocation of water in irrigation systems. Empirical studies have shown that such a top-down perspective is often ill-suited and can stimulate unsustainable use of the resource. Empirical studies also have shown that complex, nested governance systems operating at multiple levels can govern similarly complex ecological systems at multiple scales more efficiently than single, large units lacking knowledge of many specific structures and processes. Social-ecological systems are complex, adaptive systems in which heterogeneity, multiple scales, multiple domains of attraction, surprise, and fundamental uncertainty of the functioning of the ecosystem need to be explicitly considered. Agent-based modeling may provide new tools to address important questions of how to govern our common resources now that we have a better appreciation of the complexity of social-ecological systems and the multiple dilemmas facing resource users and public infrastructure providers at multiple scales. However, the development of agent-based modeling is in its infancy. Whatever the future may bring, agent-based models need to be used as one of the tools in a pluralistic toolbox of concepts, frameworks, and methods in understanding and improving the governance of social-ecological systems.

References

Ahn, T.K., Ostrom, E., Walker, J.M. (2003). "Heterogeneous preferences and collective action". Public Choice 117 (3–4), 295–314.

Ahn, T.K., Janssen, M.A., Ostrom, E. (2004). "Signals, symbols and human cooperation". In: Sussman, R.W., Chapman, A.R. (Eds.), Origins and Nature of Sociality. Aldine De Gruyter, New York, pp. 122–139.

Allen, P.M., McGlade, J.M. (1987). "Modelling complex human systems: a fisheries example". European Journal of Operational Research 31, 147–167.

Anderies, J.M., Janssen, M., Ostrom, E. (2004). "A framework to analyze the robustness of social-ecological systems from an institutional perspective". Ecology and Society 9 (1), 18. Online: http://www.ecologyandsociety.org/vol9/iss1/art18.

Anderson, J., Evans, M. (1994). "Intelligent agent modeling for natural resource management". Mathematical and Computer Modelling 20 (8), 100–119.

Arrow, K.J., Fisher, A.C. (1974). "Environmental preservation, uncertainty, and irreversibility". Quarterly Journal of Economics 88, 312–319.

Axelrod, R. (1984). The Evolution of Cooperation. Basic Books, New York.

Axelrod, R. (1986). "An evolutionary approach to norms". American Political Science Review 80, 1095–1111.

Axelrod, R. (1987). "The evolution of strategies in the iterated Prisoners' Dilemma". In: Davis, L. (Ed.), Genetic Algorithms and Simulated Annealing. Morgan Kaufmann, Los Altos, CA.

Axelrod, R. (2006). "Agent-based modeling as a bridge between disciplines", this handbook.

Axtell, R. (2000). "Effect of interaction topology and activation regime in several multi-agent systems", Santa Fe Institute Working Papers 00-07-039.

Balmann, A. (1997). "Farm-based modelling of regional structural change". European Review of Agricultural Economics 25 (1), 85–108.

Balmann, A., Happe, K., Kellermann, K., Kleingarn, A. (2002). "Adjustment costs of agri-environmental policy switchings: an agent-based analysis of the German region Hohenlohe". In: Janssen, M.A. (Ed.), Complexity and Ecosystem Management: The Theory and Practice of Multi-Agent Systems. Edward Elgar, Cheltenham, U.K.; Northampton, MA, USA, pp. 127–157.

Barabasi, A.-L., Albert, R. (1999). "Emergence of scaling in random networks". Science 286, 509–512.

Barreteau, O., Bousquet, F. (2000). "SHADOC: a multi-agent model to tackle viability of irrigated systems". Annals of Operations Research 94, 139–162.

Barreteau, O., Bousquet, F., Attonaty, J.M. (2001). "Role-playing games for opening the black box of multi-agent systems: method and lessons of its application to Senegal River Valley irrigated systems". Journal of Artificial Societies and Social Simulation 4 (2). Online: http://www.soc.surrey.ac.uk/JASSS/4/2/5.html.

Barreteau, O., Le Page, C., D'Aquino, P. (2003). "Role-playing games, models and negotiation processes". Journal of Artificial Societies and Social Simulation 6 (2). Online: http://jasss.soc.surrey.ac.uk/6/2/10.html.

Berger, T. (2001). "Agent-based spatial models applied to agriculture: a simulation tool for technology diffusion, resource use changes, and policy analysis". Agricultural Economics 25, 245–260.

Berkes, F. (1986). "Marine inshore fishery management in Turkey". In: Proceedings of the Conference on Common Property Resource Management. National Academy Press, Washington, DC, pp. 63–83.

Bodin, Ö., Norberg, J. (2005). "The role of information network topology for robust local adaptive management", Environmental Management, in press.

Börner, K., Maru, J.T., Goldstone, R.L. (2004). "The simultaneous evolution of article and author networks in PNAS", The Proceedings of the National Academy of Science, in press.

Bossel, H., Strobel, M. (1978). "Experiments with an "intelligent" world model". Futures 10 (3), 191–212.

Bousquet, F., Cambier, C., Morand, P. (1994). "Distributed artificial intelligence and object-oriented modeling of a fishery". Mathematical and Computer Modelling 20 (8), 97–107.

Bousquet, F., Bakam, I., Proton, H., Le Page, C. (1998). "Cormas common-pool resources and multi-agent systems". Lecture Notes in Artificial Intelligence 1416, 826–838.

Bousquet, F., Barretau, O., D'Aquino, P., Etienne, M., Boissau, S., Aubert, S., Le Page, C., Babin, D., Castella, J.-P. (2002). "Multi-agent systems and role games: collective learning processes for ecosystem management". In: Janssen, M.A. (Ed.), Complexity and Ecosystem Management: The Theory and Practice of Multi-Agent Systems. Edward Elgar, Cheltenham, U.K.; Northampton, MA, USA, pp. 248–285.

Bowles, S. (1998). "Endogenous preferences: the cultural consequences of markets and other economic institutions". Journal of Economic Literature 36, 75–111.

Bowles, S., Gintis, H. (2004). "The evolution of strong reciprocity: cooperation in heterogeneous populations". Theoretical Population Biology 65 (1), 17–28.

Boyd, R., Richerson, P.J. (1992). "Punishment allows the evolution of cooperation (or anything else) in sizable groups". Ethology & Sociobiology 13, 171–195.

Brandt, H., Hauert, C., Sigmund, K. (2003). "Punishment and reputation in spatial public goods games". Proceedings of the Royal Society of London Series B-Biological Sciences 270 (1519), 1099–1104.

Brenner, T. (2006). "Agent learning representation: advice on modelling economic learning", this handbook.

Bromley, D.W., Feeny, D., McKean, M., Peters, P., Gilles, J., Oakerson, R., Runge, C.F., Thomson, J. (Eds.) (1992). Making the Commons Work: Theory, Practice, and Policy. ICS Press, San Francisco, CA.

Brosig, J. (2002). "Communication and individual cooperation—an experiment". Journal of Economic Behavior and Organization 47, 275–290.

Brown, D.G., Page, S.E., Riolo, R., Zellner, M., Rand, W. (2005). "Path dependence and the validation of agent-based spatial models of land use". International Journal of Geographical Information Science 19 (2), 153–174.

Camerer, C.F. (2003). Behavioral Game Theory. Princeton University Press, Princeton, NJ.

Camerer, C., Ho, T.-H. (1999). "Experience-weighted attraction learning in normal form games". Econometrica 67 (4), 827–874.

Cardenas, J.-C., Stranlund, J., Willis, C. (2000). "Local environmental control and institutional crowding-out". World Development 28 (10), 1719–1733.

Carpenter, S.R., Brock, W., Hanson, P. (1999a). "Ecological and social dynamics in simple models of ecosystem management". Conservation Ecology 3 (2), 4. Online: http://www.consecol.org/vol3/iss2/art4.

Carpenter, S.R., Ludwig, D., Brock, W.A. (1999b). "Management of eutrophication for lakes subject to potentially irreversible change". Ecological Applications 9 (3), 751–771.

Castillo, D. (2002). "Simulating common pool resource experiments: a behavioral model of collective action", M. Phil. Thesis, Department of Information Science, University of Bergen, Norway.

Chichilnisky, G. (2000). "An axiomatic approach to choice under uncertainty with catastrophic risks". Resource and Energy Economics 22, 221–231.

Clark, C.W. (1990). Mathematical Bioeconomics: The Optimal Management of Renewable Resources. John Wiley, New York.

Cohen, P.R., Greenberg, M.L., Hart, D.M., Howe, A.E. (1989). "Trial by fire: understanding the design requirements in complex environments". AI Magazine 10 (3), 34–48.

Cole, H.S.D., Freeman, C., Jahoda, M., Pavitt, K.L.R. (Eds.) (1973). Models of Doom—A critique of the Limits to Growth. Universe Books, New York.

Colman, A.M. (1995). Game Theory and Its Applications in the Social and Biological Sciences. Butterworth-Heinemann, Oxford, UK.

Costanza, R., Ruth, M. (1998). "Using dynamic modelling to scope environmental problems and build consensus". Environmental Management 22, 183–195.

Costanza, R., Low, B.S., Ostrom, E., Wilson, J. (2001). "Ecosystems and human systems: a framework for exploring the linkages". In: Costanza, R., Low, B.S., Ostrom, E., Wilson, J. (Eds.), Institutions, Ecosystems, and Sustainability. Lewis Publishers, New York, pp. 3–20.

Couclelis, H. (1985). "Cellular worlds—a framework for modelling micro-macro dynamics". Environment and Planning A 17 (5), 585–596.

Coulson, R.N., Folse, L.J., Loh, D.K. (1987). "Artificial-intelligence and natural-resource management". Science 237, 262–267.

D'Aquino, P., Le Page, C., Bousquet, F., Bah, A. (2003). "Using self-designed role-playing games and a multi-agent system to empower a local decision-making process for land use management: the selfcormas experiment in senegal". Journal of Artificial Societies and Social Simulation 6 (3). http://jasss.soc.surrey.ac.uk/6/3/5.html.

Dasgupta, P.S., Heal, M. (1979). Economic Theory and Exhaustible Resources. Cambridge University Press, Cambridge.

Dasgupta, P., Mäler, K.-G. (2003). "The economics of non-convex ecosystems: introduction". Environmental and Resource Economics 26 (4), 499–525.

Davis, D.D., Holt, C.A. (1993). Experimental Economics. Princeton University Press, Princeton, NJ.

Deadman, P.J. (1999). "Modelling individual behaviour and group performance in an intelligent agent-based simulation of the tragedy of the commons". Journal of Environmental Management 56, 159–172.

Deadman, P.J., Gimblett, R.H. (1994). "A role for goal-oriented autonomous agents in modeling people-environment interactions in forest recreation". Mathematical and Computer Modelling 20 (8), 121–133.

Deadman, P.J., Schlager, E., Gimblett, R.H. (2000). "Simulating common pool resource management experiments with adaptive agents employing alternate communication routines". Journal of Artificial Societies and Social Simulation 3 (2). Online: http://jasss.soc.surrey.ac.uk/JAstrophys.Space.Sci.S.html.

Deffuant, G., Huet, S., Bousset, J.P., Henriot, J., Amon, G., Weisbuch, G. (2002). "Agent based simulation of organic farming conversion in Allier Département". In: Janssen, M.A. (Ed.), Complexity and Ecosystem Management: The Theory and Practice of Multi-Agent Systems. Edward Elgar, Cheltenham, U.K.; Northampton, MA, pp. 158–187.

Dibble, C. (2006). "Agent-based computational laboratories", this handbook.

Dietz, T., Ostrom, E., Stern, P. (2003). "The struggle to govern the commons". Science 302, 1907–1912. Special issue, December 12.

Dodds, P.S., Muhamad, R., Watts, D.J. (2003). "An experimental study of search in global social networks". Science 301, 827–829.

Dreyfus-Leon, M.J. (1999). "Individual-based modeling of fishermen search behaviour with neural networks and reinforcement learning". Ecological Modelling 120, 287–297.

Dreyfus-Leon, M., Kleiber, P. (2001). "A spatial individual behaviour-based model approach of the yellow tuna fishery in the eastern Pacific Ocean". Ecological Modelling 146, 47–56.

Duffy, J. (2006). "Agent-based models and human-subject experiments", this handbook.

Durlauf, S.N. (2003). "Complexity and empirical economics", Santa Fe Working Paper 03-02-014.

Erev, I., Roth, A.E. (1998). "Predicting how people play games: reinforcement learning in experimental games with unique, mixed strategy equilibria". American Economic Review 88 (4), 848–868.

Etienne, M., Le Page, C., Cohen, M. (2003). "A step-by-step approach to building land management scenarios based on multiple viewpoints on multi-agent system simulations". Journal of Artificial Societies and Social Simulation 6 (2). http://jasss.soc.surrey.ac.uk/6/2/2.html.

Evans, T.P., Kelley, H. (2004). "Multiscale analysis of a household level agent-based model of land-cover change". Journal of Environmental Management 72 (1–2), 57–72.

Farolfi, S., Le Page, C., Tidball, M., Bommel, P. (2002). "Management of livestock effluent in Réunion: use of a multi-agent system to analyse the economic behaviour of players". In: Agent-Based Simulation 3, Passau, Germany. April 7–9.

Flache, A., Hegselmann, R. (2001). "Do irregular grids make a difference? Relaxing the spatial regularity assumption in cellular models of social dynamics". Journal of Artificial Societies and Social Simulation 4 (4). http://www.soc.surrey.ac.uk/JAstrophys.Space.Sci.S/4/4/6.html.

Ford, A. (1999). Modeling the environment: an introduction to system dynamics modeling of environmental systems. Island Press, Andrew Ford.

Forrester, J.W. (1971). World Dynamics. Wright-Allen Press, Cambridge.

Frank, S.A. (1998). Foundation of Social Evolution. Princeton University Press, Princeton, NJ.

Gibson, C., McKean, M., Ostrom, E. (Eds.) (2000a). People and Forests: Communities, Institutions, and Governance. MIT Press, Cambridge, MA.

Gibson, C., Ostrom, E., Ahn, T.K. (2000b). "The concept of scale and the human dimensions of global environmental change". Ecological Economics 32, 217–239.

Gibson, C.C., Williams, J.T., Ostrom, E. (2005). "The importance of rule enforcement to local-level forest management". World Development 33 (2), 273–284.

Gigerenzer, G., Selten, R. (Eds.) (2001). Bounded Rationality: The Adaptive Toolbox. MIT Press, Cambridge, MA.

Gigerenzer, G., Todd, P.M., The ABC Research (1999). Simple Heuristics That Make Us Smart. Oxford University Press, New York.

Gintis, H. (2000). "Beyond homo economicus: evidence from experimental economics". Ecological Economics 35 (3), 311–322.

Goldstone, R.L., Ashpole, B.C. (2004). "Human foraging behavior in a virtual environment". Psychonomic Bulletin & Review 11, 508–514.

Gordon, H.S. (1954). "The economic theory of a common property resource: the fishery". Journal of Political Economy 62, 124–142.

Gotts, N.M., Polhill, J.G., Law, A.N.R. (2003). "Agent-based simulation in the study of social dilemmas". Artificial Intelligence Review 19 (1), 3–92.

Grimm, V. (1999). "Ten years of individual-based modelling in ecology: what have we learned and what could we learn in the future?". Ecological Modeling 115 (2–3), 129–148.

Hardin, G. (1968). "The tragedy of the commons". Science 162, 1243–1248.

Hare, M.P., Pahl-Wostl, C. (2002). "Stakeholder categorisation in processes of participatory integrated assessment". Integrated Assessment 3, 50–62.

Hauert, C., De Monte, S., Hofbauer, J., Sigmund, K. (2002). "Volunteering as Red Queen mechanism for cooperation in public goods games". Science 296 (5570), 1129–1132.

Hauert, Ch., Szabo, G. (2003). "Prisoner's dilemma and public goods games in different geometries: compulsory versus voluntary interactions". Complexity 9 (4), 31–38.

Henry, C. (1974). "Investment decisions under uncertainty: the irreversibility effects". American Economic Review 64, 1006–1012.

Hoffmann, M., Kelley, H., Evans, T. (2002). "Simulating land-cover change in south-central Indiana: an agent-based model of deforestation and afforestation". In: Janssen, M.A. (Ed.), Complexity and Ecosystem Management: The Theory and Practice of Multi-Agent Systems. Edward Elgar, Cheltenham, U.K.; Northampton, MA, pp. 218–247.

Holland, J.H. (1992a). "Complex adaptive systems". Daedalus 121, 17–30.

Holland, J.H. (1992b). "Adaptation in Natural and Artificial Systems". MIT Press, Cambridge.

Holling, C.S. (1978). Adaptive Environmental Assessment and Management. John Wiley, London.

Huston, M., DeAngelis, D., Post, W. (1988). "New computer models unify ecological theory". BioScience 38 (1), 682–691.

Isaac, R.M., Walker, J.M. (1988). "Group size effects in public goods provision: the voluntary contribution mechanism". Quarterly Journal of Economics 103, 179–200.

Isaac, R.M., Walker, J.M., Thomas, S.H. (1984). "Divergent evidence on free riding: an experimental examination of possible explanations". Public Choice 43, 113–149.

Isaac, R.M., McCue, K.F., Plott, C.R. (1985). "Public goods provision in an experimental environment". Journal of Public Economics 26, 51–74.

Isaac, R.M., Walker, J.M., Williams, A.W. (1994). "Group size and the voluntary provision of public goods: experimental evidence utilizing large groups". Journal of Public Economics 54 (1), 1–36.

Iwasaki, A., Imura, S., Oda, S.H., Hatono, I., Ueda, K. (2003). "Does reinforcement learning simulate threshold public goods games?: a comparison with subject experiments". IEICE Transactions on Information and Systems E 86D (8), 1335–1343.

Jager, W., Janssen, M.A. (2002). "Using artificial agents to understand laboratory experiments of common-pool resources with real agents". In: Janssen, M.A. (Ed.), Complexity and Ecosystem Management: The Theory and Practice of Multi-Agent Systems. Edward Elgar, Cheltenham, U.K.; Northampton, MA, pp. 75–102.

Jager, W., Janssen, M.A., De Vries, H.J.M., De Greef, J., Vlek, C.A.J. (2000). "Behaviour in commons dilemmas: Homo economicus and Homo psychologicus in an ecological-economic model". Ecological Economics 35 (3), 357–379.

Jager, W., Janssen, M.A., Vlek, C.A.J. (2002). "How uncertainty stimulates over-harvesting in a resource dilemma: three process explanations". Journal of Environmental Psychology 22, 247–263.

Janssen, M.A. (2001). "An explorative integrated model to assess lake eutrophication". Ecological Modelling 140, 111–124.

Janssen, M.A. (Ed.) (2002a). Complexity and Ecosystem Management: The Theory and Practice of Multi-Agent Systems. Edward Elgar, Cheltenham, U.K.; Northampton, MA.

Janssen, M.A. (2002b). "Modeling Human Dimensions of Global Environmental Change". In: Munn, T., Timmerman, P. (Eds.), Social and Economic Dimensions of Global Environmental Change. In: Encyclopedia of Global Environmental Change, vol. 5. John Wiley and Sons Ltd, London, UK.

Janssen, M.A. (2005). "Evolution of institutional rules: an immune system perspective". Complexity 11 (1), 16–23.

Janssen, M.A., de Vries, H.J.M. (1998). "The battle of perspectives: a multi-agent model with adaptive responses to climate change". Ecological Economics 26 (1), 43–65.

Janssen, M.A., Carpenter, S.R. (1999). "Managing the resilience of Lakes: A multi-agent modeling approach". Conservation Ecology 3 (2), 15. Online: http://www.consecol.org/vol3/iss2/art15.

Janssen, M.A., de Vries, H.J.M. (1999). "Global modelling: managing uncertainty, complexity and incomplete information". In: van Dijkum, C., de Tombe, D., van Kuijk, E. (Eds.), Validation of Simulation Models. SISWO, Amsterdam, pp. 45–69.

Janssen, M.A., Ahn, T.K. (2005). "Adaptation vs. anticipation in public good games", in review.

Janssen, M.A., Ostrom, E. (2005). "Adoption of a new regulation for the governance of common-pool resources by a heterogeneous population". In: Baland, J.M., Bardhan, P., Bowles, S. (Eds.), Inequality, Cooperation and Environmental Sustainability. Princeton University Press, Princeton, NJ, in press.

Janssen, M.A., Walker, B.H., Langridge, J., Abel, N. (2000). "An adaptive agent model for analysing co-evolution of management and policies in a complex rangelands system". Ecological Modelling 131, 249–268.

Janssen, M.A., Anderies, J.M., Walker, B.H. (2004). "Robust strategies for managing rangelands with multiple stable attractors". Journal of Environmental Economics and Management 47, 140–162.

Kahneman, D., Tversky, A. (1979). "Prospect theory—analysis of decision under risk". Econometrica 47 (2), 263–291.

Kameda, T., Nakanishi, D. (2002). "Cost-benefit analysis of social/cultural learning in a non-stationary uncertain environment: an evolutionary simulation and an experiment with human subjects". Evolution and Human Behavior 23, 373–393.

Kameda, T., Nakanishi, D. (2003). "Does social/cultural learning increase human adaptability?: Rogers's question revisited". Evolution and Human Behavior 24, 242–260.

Kameda, T., Takezawa, M., Hastie, R. (2003). "The logic of social sharing: an evolutionary game analysis of adaptive norm development". Personality and Social Psychology Review 7 (1), 2–19.

Keser, C., Gardner, R. (1999). "Strategic behavior of experienced subjects in a common pool resource game". International Journal of Game Theory 28 (2), 241–252.

Kollman, K., Page, S.E. (2006). "Computational methods and models of politics", this handbook.

Kreps, D.M., Milgrom, P., Roberts, J., Wilson, R. (1982). "Rational cooperation in the finitely repeated prisoner's dilemma". Journal of Economic Theory 27, 245–252.

Lam, W.F. (1998). Governing Irrigation Systems in Nepal: Institutions, Infrastructure, and Collective Action. ICS Press, Oakland, CA.

Lansing, J.S. (1991). Priests and Programmers: Technologies of Power in the Engineered Landscape of Bali. Princeton University Press, Princeton, NJ.

Lansing, J.S. (2000). "Anti-chaos, common property and the emergence of cooperation". In: Kohler, T.A., Gumerman, G.J. (Eds.), Dynamics in Human and Primate Societies. Oxford University Press, Oxford, pp. 207–224.

Lansing, S.J., Kremer, J.N. (1993). "Emergent properties of Balinese water temple networks: coadaptation on a rugged fitness landscape". American Anthropologist 95, 97–114.

Lansing, J.S., Miller, J.H. (2003). "Cooperation in Balinese rice farming", SFI Working Paper 03-05-030, Santa Fe, NM.

Lau, S.-H.P., Mui, V.-L. (2003). "Achieving intertemporal efficiency and symmetry through intratemporal asymmetry: (eventual) turn taking in a class of repeated mixed-interest games", Working Paper, University of Hong Kong, School of Economics and Finance.

Ludwig, D., Hilborn, R., Walters, C. (1993). "Uncertainty, resource exploitation, and conservation: lessons from history". Science 260, 17–18.

Mäler, K.G. (1974). Environmental Economics. Johns Hopkins University Press, Baltimore, MD.

Marwell, G., Ames, R.E. (1979). "Experiments on the provision of public goods I: resources, interest, group size, and the free rider problem". American Journal of Sociology 84, 1335–1360.

Marwell, G., Ames, R.E. (1980). "Experiments on the provision of public goods II: provision points, stakes, experience and the free rider problem". American Journal of Sociology 85, 926–937.

Marwell, G., Ames, R.E. (1981). "Economists free ride, does anyone else". Journal of Public Economics 15, 295–310.

Meadows, D.H., Meadows, D.L., Randers, J., Behrens III, W.W. (1972). The Limits to Growth. Universe Books, New York.

Meadows, D.L., Behrens III, W.W., Meadows, D.H., Naill, R.F., Randers, J., Zahn, E.K.O. (1974). Dynamics of Growth in a Finite World. Wright-Allen Press, Cambridge, UK.

Mosler, H.-J., Brucks, W. (2002). "Integrating resource dilemma findings in a simulation model". European Journal of Social Psychology 33 (1), 119–133.

National Research Council (1986). Proceedings of the Conference on Common Property Resource Management. National Academy Press, Washington, DC.

National Research Council (2002). The Drama of the Commons." Committee on the Human Dimensions of Global Change. E. Ostrom, T. Dietz, N. Dolšak, P. Stern, S. Stonich and E. Weber, (Eds.) (National Academy Press, Washington, DC).

Nordhaus, W.D. (1973). "World dynamics: measurement without data". The Economic Journal 83, 1156–1183.

Nowak, M.A., May, R.M. (1992). "Evolutionary games and spatial chaos". Nature 359 (6398), 826–829.

Ostrom, E. (1990). Governing the Commons. Cambridge University Press, New York.

Ostrom, E. (1992). Crafting Institutions for Self-Governing Irrigation Systems. ICS Press, San Francisco, CA.

Ostrom, E. (1996). "Incentives, rules of the game, and development". In: Proceedings of the Annual World Bank Conference on Development Economics 1995. The World Bank, Washington, DC, pp. 207–234.

Ostrom, E. (1998). "A behavioral approach to the rational choice theory of collective action". American Political Science Review 92 (1), 1–22.

Ostrom, E., Ahn, T.K. (Eds.) (2003). Foundations of Social Capital. Edward Elgar, Cheltenham, UK.

Ostrom, E., Gardner, R., Walker, J. (1994). Rules, Games and Common-Pool Resources. University of Michigan Press, Ann Arbor.

Ostrom, E., Walker, J.M. (Eds.) (2003). Trust and Reciprocity: Interdisciplinary Lessons from Experimental Research. Russell Sage Foundation, New York.

Pahl-Wostl, C. (2002). "Towards sustainability in the water sector: the importance of human actors and processes of social learning". Aquatic Sciences 64 (4), 394–411.

Parker, D.C., Meretsky, V. (2004). "Measuring pattern outcomes in an agent-based model of edge-effect externalities using spatial metrics". Agriculture, Ecosystems, and Environment 101 (2–3), 233–250.

Parker, D.C., Manson, S., Janssen, M.A., Hoffmann, M., Deadman, P. (2003). "Multi-agent systems for the simulation of land-use and land-cover change: a review". Annals of the Association of American Geographers 93 (2), 313–337.

Peterson, G.D., Carpenter, S., Brock, W.A. (2003). "Model uncertainty and the management of multi-state ecosystems: a rational route to collapse". Ecology 84 (6), 1403–1411.

Pitt, M.A., Myung, I.J. (2002). "When a good fit can be bad". Trends in Cognitive Sciences 6 (10), 421–425.

Purnomo, H., Yasmi, Y., Prabhu, R., Yuliani, L., Priyadi, H., Vanclay, J.K. (2003). "Multi-agent simulation of alternative scenarios of collaborative forest management". Small-scale Forest Economics, Management and Policy 2 (2), 277–292.

Rieskamp, J., Busemeyer, J., Laine, T. (2003). "How do people learn to allocate resources? Comparing two learning theories". Journal of Experimental Psychology: Learning, Memory and Cognition 29 (6), 1066–1081.

Rouchier, J., Bousquet, F., Requier-Desjardins, M., Antona, M. (2001). "A multi-agent model for describing transhumance in North Cameroon: comparison of different rationality to develop a routine". Journal of Economic Dynamics & Control 25, 527–559.

Ruttan, V.W. (2003). Social Science Knowledge and Economic Development. University of Michigan Press, Ann Arbor.

Sally, D. (1995). "Conversation and cooperation in social dilemmas: a meta-analysis of experiments from 1958 to 1992". Rationality and Society 7, 58–92.

Salmon, T.C. (2001). "An evaluation of econometric models of adaptive learning". Econometrica 69 (6), 1597–1628.

Scheffer, M., Carpenter, S., Foley, J., Folke, C., Walker, B. (2001). "Catastrophic regime shifts in ecosystems". Nature 413, 591–596.

Schlager, E. (2004). "Common-pool resource theory". In: Durant, R.F., Fiorino, D.J., O'Leary, R. (Eds.), Environmental Governance Reconsidered. MIT Press, Cambridge, pp. 145–176.

Selten, R., Mitzkewitz, M., Uhlich, G.R. (1997). "Duopoly strategies programmed by experienced players". Econometrica 65, 517–555.

Sugden, R. (1989). "Spontaneous order". Journal of Economic Perspectives 3 (4), 85–97.

Tang, S.Y. (1992). Institutions and Collective Action: Self-Governance in Irrigation. ICS Press, San Francisco, CA.

Thébaud, O., Locatelli, B. (2001). "Modelling the emergence of resource-sharing conventions: an agent-based approach". Journal of Artificial Societies and Social Simulation 4 (2). Online: http://www.soc.surrey.ac.uk/JAstrophys.Space.Sci.S/4/2/3.html.

Thompson, M., Ellis, R., Wildavsky, A. (1990). Cultural Theory. Westview Press, Boulder, CO.

Tierney, J. (2000). "A tale of two fisheries". New York Times Magazine (August 27), 38–43.

Valente, T.W. (1995). Network Models of the Diffusion of Innovations. Hampton Press, Cresskill, NJ.

Vitousek, P.M., Mooney, H.A., Lubchenco, J., Melillo, J.M. (1997). "Human domination of Earth's ecosystems". Science 277, 494–499.

Vriend, N.J. (2006). "ACE models of endogenous interactions", this handbook.

Watts, D.J., Strogatz, S.H. (1998). "Collective dynamics of "small-world" networks". Nature 393, 440–442.

Weisbuch, G., Duchateau-Nguyen, G. (1998). "Societies, cultures and fisheries from a modeling perspective". Journal of Artificial Societies and Social Simulation 1 (2). Online: http://www.soc.surrey.ac.uk/JAstrophys.Space.Sci.S/1/2/2.html.

Wilcox, N.T. (2003). "Heterogeneity and Learning Principles", Manuscript June 2003, Department of Economics, University of Houston.
Wilhite, A.W. (2006). "Economic activity on fixed networks", this handbook.
Young, H.P. (2006). "Social dynamics: theory and applications", this handbook.

Chapter 31

COMPUTATIONAL LABORATORIES FOR SPATIAL AGENT-BASED MODELS

CATHERINE DIBBLE

Department of Geography, University of Maryland, College Park, MD 20742, USA
e-mail: cdibble@umd.edu; url: http://myprofile.cos.com/cdible

Contents

Handbook of Computational Economics, Volume 2. Edited by Leigh Tesfatsion and Kenneth L. Judd
© 2006 Elsevier B.V. All rights reserved
DOI: 10.1016/S1574-0021(05)02031-9

Abstract

An agent-based model is a virtual world comprising distributed heterogeneous agents who interact over time. In a *spatial* agent-based model the agents are situated in a spatial environment and are typically assumed to be able to move in various ways across this environment. Some kinds of social or organizational systems may also be modeled as spatial environments, where agents move from one group or department to another and where communications or mobility among groups may be structured according to implicit or explicit channels or transactions costs.

This chapter focuses on the potential usefulness of computational laboratories for spatial agent-based modeling. Speaking broadly, a *computational laboratory* is any computational framework permitting the exploration of the behaviors of complex systems through systematic and replicable simulation experiments. By that definition, most of the research discussed in this handbook would be considered to be work with computational laboratories. A narrower definition of computational laboratory (or comp lab for short) refers specifically to specialized software tools to support the full range of agent-based modeling and complementary tasks. These tasks include model development, model evaluation through controlled experimentation, and both the descriptive and normative analysis of model outcomes.

The objective of this chapter is to explore how comp lab tools and activities facilitate the systematic exploration of spatial agent-based models embodying complex social processes critical for social welfare. Examples include the spatial and temporal coordination of human activities, the diffusion of new ideas or of infectious diseases, and the emergence and ecological dynamics of innovative ideas or of deadly new diseases.

Keywords

agent-based simulation, computational laboratory, computational social science, computational economics, spatial economics, spatial social science, spatial networks, small-world networks, scale-free networks, synthetic landscape, inference

JEL classification: C63, C73, C88, C99, D43, I10, O33, Z13

1. Introduction

1.1. Overview of chapter

"Research has been likened to warfare against the unknown. ... The attacker will have a great advantage if he can bring to bear a new technical weapon."
[Beveridge (1957), page 176]

An agent-based model is a virtual world comprising distributed heterogeneous agents who interact over time. In a *spatial* agent-based model the agents are situated in a spatial environment and are typically assumed to be able to move in various ways across this environment. Some kinds of social or organizational systems may also be modeled as spatial environments, where agents move from one group or department to another and where communications or mobility among groups may be structured according to implicit or explicit channels or transactions costs.

This chapter focuses on the potential usefulness of computational laboratories for spatial agent-based modeling. Speaking broadly, a *computational laboratory* is any computational framework permitting the exploration of the behaviors of complex systems through systematic and replicable simulation experiments. By that definition, most of the research discussed in this handbook would be considered to be work with computational laboratories. A narrower definition of computational laboratory (or comp lab for short) refers specifically to specialized software tools to support the full range of agent-based modeling and complementary tasks. These tasks include model development, model evaluation through controlled experimentation, and both the descriptive and normative analysis of model outcomes.

The objective of this chapter is to explore how comp lab tools and activities facilitate the systematic exploration of spatial agent-based models embodying complex social processes critical for social welfare. Examples include the spatial and temporal coordination of human activities, the diffusion of new ideas or of infectious diseases, and the emergence and ecological dynamics of innovative ideas or of deadly new diseases.

Consider a thought experiment to help motivate the usefulness of comp labs as complements to spatial agent-based models: Imagine that top decision-makers have asked you to apply an agent-based research model to avert a global pandemic, where the livelihoods and perhaps the lives of millions of people may depend upon the timeliness and quality of your results [Osterholm (2005), Aldhous and Tomlin (2005)]. They need your answers within six months. Preliminary results even before then could provide crucial leverage for averting disaster, yet misleading results may do more harm than good.

Which comp lab tools would you wish you had available to assist with development, testing, and refinement of your model? Which simulations would you run first to explore the problem? How would you calibrate, test, apply, evaluate, and perhaps generalize your model and your results within six months? How would you adapt your model or your inference as the crisis begins to unfold, or as preliminary feedback from the success or failure of your advice begins to arrive? Which analytical tools would you most wish you had, given reasonable yet finite computational power and limited time for analysis of simulation results as they accumulate?

Comp labs provide the tools researchers need to perform such tasks. At the simplest level, a good agent-based model is capable of generating the phenomenon we seek to study. Yet generating a phenomenon is far from sufficient for effective agent-based research. What matters most is what we can *learn* from our models, and how much we can trust their results.

This chapter provides an overview of the comp lab capabilities most likely to be useful for spatial agent-based models, and explores the various ways they could be used effectively. This exploration is explicitly normative and does not presume to represent current practices in Agent-based Computational Economics (ACE).

Although this chapter specifically addresses comp lab tools for working with spatial agent-based models, many of the comp lab principles and tools discussed apply to aspatial models as well. Similarly, spatial landscapes may be interpreted quite broadly as anything that structures local context and interactions among a model's agents.

This chapter orients newcomers to comp labs by discussing and illustrating basic components and capabilities of comp labs for research with spatial agent-based models. The remainder of Section 1 highlights research challenges posed by richly structured distributed dynamic systems for standard economic modeling, and briefly summarizes how comp labs might aid researchers in addressing these challenges. Sections 2–4 examine three main categories of tools, such as comp lab support for controlling and testing models, for modeling agents, and for creating empirical or synthetic social and spatial landscapes. Subsequent Sections 5–7 address finer points and more sophisticated methods for inference and for effective analysis of robustness and risk. Concluding remarks are provided in Section 8.

1.2. Challenges posed by spatial systems

> [N]ew tools ... have removed crucial technical barriers and transformed a once inhospitable field into fertile ground for theorists.
>
> [Fujita et al. (1999), page 2]

Local (micro) interactions among distributed dynamic agents generate global (macro) structures; diverse examples include market prices, market failures, organizational behavior, social norms, and regional settlement patterns. These dynamic spatial processes defy top-down modeling or deductive analytical inference due to the complex exogenous and endogenous boundary conditions arising from their micro-level interactions. Local interactions may be either spatial or aspatial; in general, the term refers to interactions among distributed subsets of agents.

Realistic geographic landscapes may generate conditions that violate one or more assumptions underlying the First and Second Welfare Theorems. The First Welfare Theorem (efficiency) roughly states that if markets exist for all valued goods and services, if no firm or consumer can influence prices, if prices adjust perfectly so that all markets clear, and if all (price-taking) firms and consumers correctly anticipate these prices, then the market outcomes will be Pareto Optimal. The Second Welfare Theorem (equity) roughly states that if the First Welfare Theorem applies and if there are no externalities of consumption or of production, then any Pareto Optimal outcome may be reached, given appropriate transfers of wealth [Mas-Colell et al. (1995), page 308].

Yet uneven spatial distributions of goods and people across a geographic landscape may lead to conditions that violate these assumptions. For example:

- There may be too few local buyers and sellers to create local markets for goods, especially when there are high transportation costs.
- Small numbers of buyers or sellers may lead to thin markets where one side or both no longer acts as a price taker.
- Even with modern transportation and telecommunication systems, spatial distance continues to impose significant transactions costs such as imperfect information and severe coordination problems that affect market transactions.
- Geographic landscapes generate local environments where externalities of consumption or production are often the norm rather than the exception.

As Tesfatsion (2006a) demonstrates with respect to the implicit Walrasian Auctioneer assumed in competitive market models, tractable theoretical models often naively assume agent coordination or sophistication that may in fact not be feasible given the agents' contexts, information, or incentives.

The complexity that arises from interacting agents becomes even more interesting once we consider *strategic* interactions. Schelling's *Micromotives and Macrobehavior* (Schelling, 1978) summarizes the essential challenges for modeling strategic interactions among distributed agents:

> What we typically have is a mode of *contingent behavior*—behavior that depends on what others are doing. (Page 17)

> [P]eople locate themselves voluntarily in some pattern that does not possess evident advantages even for the people who by their own choices form the pattern. (Page 12)

> How well each does for himself in adapting to his social environment is not the same thing as how satisfactory a social environment they collectively create for themselves. (Page 19)

Economic theory and game theory begin to provide formal theoretical frameworks for emergent macro effects of non-strategic and strategic micro-level interactions among agents. Yet it is nearly impossible to extend the fundamental theoretical results to realistically distributed systems of heterogeneous, dynamic, adaptive, and mobile agents when researchers are limited to thought experiments or top-down, equation-based computational models. Well equipped comp labs for spatial agent-based models can greatly extend our ability to explore beyond the bounds of purely analytical inference to establish new theoretical and applied results for important and interesting richly structured systems.

1.3. Addressing spatial system challenges with comp labs

A prototypical *spatial agent-based model* consists of a full specification for the following aspects:

- One or more classes of agents, and the types of interactions they may have with one another and possibly also with their environment.
- The nature of the spatial, social, or organizational environments within which these agents may or may not move around and which may structure their encounters.
- A specification of initial conditions for the simulation, generally including the initial locations of agents within their environment.
- A schedule of activities for the simulation, including a means for determining when each simulation should end.
- Means for observing and recording key data about the simulation's behavior.

In principle, the conceptual specification of a spatial model exists independently of any given *implementation* of the model in a particular computer language, simulation platform, or comp lab. Ideally, important models will be implemented in more than one computer language, model platform, or comp lab. In practice, implementation details such as the order in which agents take turns, nuances of their interaction structures, or the specific random number generators used often affect the model's behavior. So in practice the term "agent-based model"—whether spatial or aspatial—almost always refers to a specific implementation of the conceptual model. Essentially, for now, an agent-based model's implementation *is* its complete specification.

Tesfatsion (2006a) provides an excellent introduction to agents and an "ACE Trading World" that exemplifies a typical fully specified aspatial agent-based model. She includes pseudo-code outlines for the public and private data for each agent and its behavioral methods, and for the initial conditions, agent activities, and stopping rule for each simulation. The ACE Trading World has three types of cognitive agents: bean producers, hash producers, and consumer-shareholders who purchase beans and hash to consume at each simulation step [Tesfatsion (2006a), Tables 1–4]. It is an interesting exploration of the operation of a simple market once agents are required to engage in explicit procurement rather than trading indirectly via a mythical Walrasian auctioneer.

Yet the ACE Trading World is strictly aspatial; each agent has perfect information about the prices posted by all other agents, and there are no transaction costs or spatial locations of the agents to structure their information or their interactions with one another. This is wise, as its behavior is already complex. Even models that seek to understand the effects of spatial or other interaction structures should be able to run aspatial control simulations where the same set of agents interacts in a null space, such as a perfectly mixed soup, in order to distinguish the effects of agent or other model specifications from the effects of their interaction structure. Thus, when simulations with the same populations of agents with the same random number seeds are run on richly structured spatial or organizational landscapes, the effects due to landscape structure can be thoroughly isolated from the effects due to other aspects of the model or of their interactions.

1.3.1. Richly structured spatial or organizational network landscapes

Extending the ACE Trading World [Tesfatsion (2006a)] even to simple spatial landscapes raises interesting questions. For example, imagine a network landscape of local villages, where each village is aspatial, per the original model, and links such as roads connect villages to one another in various patterns. This is likely to introduce several kinds of information costs (effort, noise) and transaction costs (shipping, time delay, tariffs). For now, consider simply Samuelson's [Samuelson (1952)] simple iceberg model of shipping costs, where $x\%$ of the goods melt per mile.

If shipping costs are prohibitive even for the nearest neighbors, then we simply have islands, each of which operates as a separate ACE Trading World. Even so, it may nevertheless be interesting to explore the effects of population sizes and relative proportions of its three types of agents, per Tesfatsion's (Tesfatsion, 2000, 2001) exploration of the effects of market power in labor markets. Alternatively, if shipping costs are zero and we have assumed perfect information and no transaction costs despite distance, then the distribution of agents across villages makes no difference and it functions as one global trading world.

In all other situations, imperfectly linked local markets for identical goods are distinguished only by their locations relative to each potential consumer. The landscape's network characteristics and its distribution of agents may have tremendously interesting effects on the adjustment dynamics and potential equilibria of local markets. We have not even begun to discuss related extensions such as information costs, local resource constraints, heterogeneous distribution of resources or production conditions, local externalities of consumption or production, or migration of agents from one node to another. ACE researchers have barely begun to explore such extensions, although see Wilhite (2001, 2006) and Dibble (2001b) for early work along these lines.

Networks are especially relevant for economics because almost all economic exchanges are mediated by transportation or communication networks of some kind. The structure of such networks is generally fixed within the time frame considered for most ACE models, although it can be even more interesting to consider the long-run co-evolution of economic processes, population distributions, and network infrastructure.

Such questions have been difficult to address in part because we have not had good tools to generate synthetic network landscapes and population distributions in order to explore their effects. While extensions to network landscapes will not be deeply explored within this chapter, the objective here is to motivate the importance of landscapes and other interaction structures for ACE research, as a key example of potentially useful capabilities provided by a well-equipped comp lab to support spatial modeling.

2. A well-equipped comp lab for spatial agent-based modeling

In contrast, the real world is a single time-series realization arising from a poorly understood data generating process. Even if an ACE model were to accurately embody this real-world data generating process, it might be impossible to verify this accuracy using standard statistical procedures. For example, an empirically observed outcome might be a low-probability event lying in a relatively small peak of the outcome distribution for this true data-generating process, or in a thin tail of this distribution.

[Tesfatsion (2006a), page 845]

In the real world, we almost never have an opportunity to rewind the historical tape to replay and explore the different outcomes that may result from chance events [Fontana and Buss (1994)]. In econometrics, we understand that each empirical observation contains some proportion of variation due to explanatory variables, inextricably entwined with an unknown but ideally well-behaved proportion of noise assigned to its error term and ascribed to chance or imperfect observation. Each implementation of an agent-based model is, by itself, a means to simulate one time-series realization at a time. With an agent-based comp lab, we have perfect control over both treatments and stochastic sources of variation. Thus we have the capability to simulate *exact* replicates of each treatment, to fully explore the effects of stochastic variation.

In my research on spatial systems, I have found the following three types of comp lab tools to be especially useful:

1. tools to facilitate implementation, testing, calibration, and basic operation of a spatial agent-based simulation model, including its landscapes, agent populations, initial conditions and spatial distributions, and model-specific rules and schedules;
2. basic tools to generate, control, and observe multiple realizations of the model, including separable realizations of landscape characteristics, agent characteristics, initial conditions and distributions, and stochastic events during the simulation's execution; and
3. advanced tools to provide especially effective control, search, optimization, and evaluation within an especially large or complex space of potential scenarios and associated stochastic realizations for each scenario of characteristics and initial conditions.

Multi-purpose spatial agent-based modeling platforms and comp labs are generally implemented in object-oriented programming languages. In an object-oriented language, each type of agent is defined by a *class*, which acts as a blueprint to define the basic private and public data fields and behavioral methods that each agent created with this class will possess. This class approach to the construction of agents offers two important advantages.

First, each agent instantiated from a class is *encapsulated* as its own separate entity, with private data and methods that may be accessed only by asking the agent for its answer or by telling it to do something that it knows how to do. Encapsulation seems

intuitively obvious to social scientists. Moreover, an important advantage of agent encapsulation from a modeling perspective is that it supports modular programming. That
is, agents only need to know what they can ask of each other. Any agent may alter its
internal characteristics or methods without disrupting the public characteristics of its
methods.

Second, classes can *inherit* characteristics from other classes, which provides tremendous advantages for developing agent-based simulation models and complementary
laboratory tools. For example, we may define a *base class* of ruminant livestock, which
we can use as the parent class from which we create *child classes* for sheep, goats, cows,
camels, and llamas. Each child class inherits all capabilities of its base class, and may
then redefine inherited methods or add new data and methods to the base class. When
used wisely, encapsulation and inheritance enhance conceptual clarity and economical
software design, development, and modifications.

A well-equipped comp lab provides a rich set of classes for cognitive and other
agents, each provided with diverse capabilities to support use directly in models or as
base classes for model-specific extensions. The laboratory should also provide at least
one "landscape" class to provide structure for agent interactions, whether this is an aspatial institution, an organizational structure that may or may not include some metric
for distances among teams, or a fully spatial landscape.

Even laboratories with sophisticated classes to generate spatial landscapes should
always provide an aspatial randomly-mixed null landscape. This serves as a control to
test for artifacts of the model unrelated to the structure of interactions among agents.

"Docking" refers to the practice of comparing results from matching simulation runs
for different implementations of a given conceptual model. Docking can be an especially
important approach to identify, isolate, and control for subtle differences that may be
introduced even by apparently congruent implementations. See Axtell et al. (1995) or
Axelrod (1997) for an interesting discussion of their experience docking their respective
simulation models.

In this spirit, a comp lab's aspatial landscape can also be useful for docking spatial
models with aspatial mathematical models of corresponding processes. For example, a
new agent-based model of an infectious disease epidemic may be docked and calibrated
against classical aspatial mathematical models or highly simplified spatial mathematical
models for a particular population of agents. The spatial agent-based model can then
be used with greater confidence to explore the unique effects of more realistic spatial
structures on epidemic dynamics for the same disease as it unfolds within the same
population of agents.

Finally, spatial comp labs that are well equipped to support both applied and theoretical work may also include tools to calibrate synthetic landscapes according to empirical
characteristics, or to directly import various types of empirical landscapes from Geographic Information Systems (GIS) or satellite remote sensing observations [Dibble
and Feldman (2004)].

In order to simulate synthetic initial conditions, synthetic landscapes, stochastic
events, and stochastic choices by cognitive agents, well equipped comp labs should

provide classes to start and seed multiple, fully separable, ultra long-period (i.e. Mersenne Twister) random number series for a wide variety of distributions (e.g. uniform, Gaussian, fair or weighted coin flip, or roulette wheels that assign probability distributions derived from histograms, which are important for genetic algorithms). The long period before repeating random number patterns is essential for serious inference with any stochastic spatial agent-based model, in order to prevent spurious artifacts where observed cycles or patterns are driven merely by repetition in one or more of the model's random number series.

Time in simulation models may be absolute, relative, or both. These correspond, respectively, to agent actions that are triggered by a simulation clock (e.g. via simulation 'steps'), by other endogenous events or agent actions within the simulation, or by relative time elapsed since some endogenous triggering event. Simple examples of each would include aging, contracting an infectious disease, and becoming ill with the disease after some incubation period beyond infection.

Scheduling tools are important, not only for cognitive agents within each simulation, but also for other simulation agents (trees may grow, toxins may diffuse, water may accumulate), and especially for meta-activities such as data collection and other forms of simulation monitoring such as those related to stopping the simulation. Stopping rules may also be absolute, relative, or both. For example, a simulation may be set to stop after a certain number of steps have elapsed, after a persistent condition has been reached, or following a set delay after a specific event.

Ideally, each comp lab should have at least one fully-constructed proto-model, no matter how trivial, of a fully-implemented spatial agent-based simulation model on a simple landscape. Such proto-models serve several important purposes. For example, they provide simple working examples to show that the comp lab itself was correctly installed. They also provide a simple model from which researchers may learn, and a simple foundation that researchers may modify to create their own models.

Finally, at least one and ideally two important classes control simulations. First, a "main" class is generally responsible for setting up and running each simulation. It reads in the parameters and treatments for that simulation, sets up the landscape, agents, and initial conditions of the simulation, starts the simulation, and supervises data collection, visualization (if any), and stopping conditions. One or more secondary classes can supervise multiple simulations by allowing researchers to specify parameters and treatments for large batches of simulations.

2.1. Generating, controlling, and observing many simulations for each model

The secondary classes mentioned above provide batch-control tools to specify fixed parameters, to specify lists of values for each of the parameters chosen for parameter sweeping for sensitivity analysis, or to specify levels of treatment variables in order to explore model behavior. For stochastic models, it is especially important to sweep across one or more sets of random number seeds for each of the separable random number series to be used by the model, in order to generate statistically significant realizations for each scenario. It is important to explore the variability of stochastic outcomes for each scenario's specific combination of model parameters and treatment variables.

Some of these parameters chosen for sweeping, including random number seeds, may be used to generate specific realizations of synthetic landscapes or other interaction structures, as discussed in greater detail in Section 4 of this chapter. Other parameters or series of random number seeds may in turn be used to generate synthetic agent populations and to control their initial conditions and stochastic decisions or events.

For example, one random number seed may control the initial distributions of agent characteristics and endowments. Another may be responsible for allocating agents to initial locations within a spatial landscape or related interaction structure such as an organization. Others may control various stochastic aspects of agent decisions or of landscape events as each simulation unfolds.

2.2. Advanced tools for effective search, control, optimization, and testing

An especially helpful tool for any comp lab is a supervisory genetic algorithm, simulated annealing, or other automated search and optimization heuristic to help discover combinations of scenarios and random number seeds that lead to particularly interesting outcomes. For example, see Section 7 of this chapter for a discussion of the ways in which a comp lab supervisory genetic algorithm can be used to support inference, optimization, and analysis of risks.

In turn, complementary analytical tools for network analysis, and analytical measures such as spatial statistics, can help to support generalization from specific spatial landscapes or populations to broader classes. Such analytical measures may characterize combinations of initial conditions, distributions, or outcomes, to relate common characteristics of each across multiple simulation outcomes.

Finally, spatial comp labs may also be used in conjunction with familiar econometric and statistical tools through systematic analysis of output when highly stochastic models generate especially large numbers of simulation outcomes. This can be especially helpful to support analysis of risk or resilience that may be associated with particular interventions such as for controlling epidemics or similarly normative modeling objectives.

These are classifications for comp lab tools that have been especially useful in my research with spatial agent-based simulations on richly structured organizational and spatial landscapes. As with agent-based simulation models, even general-purpose comp labs differ widely in their strengths and capabilities. However, this superset of capabilities that have proven useful for spatial agent-based modeling may provide helpful existence proofs and inspiration for evaluating the strengths and limitations of particular comp labs.

2.3. *Principles of comp lab engineering*

Eventually, spatial agent-based models and comp labs may become so powerful and well equipped that serious researchers devote entire careers simply to studying the behavior of a well established and fully implemented model, or of model variants fully supported by the comp lab's existing classes. (This is one way to introduce students to comp lab research.) For now, even the simplest spatial agent-based modeling project generally involves the design and programming implementation of at least one new model-specific child class for agents, landscapes, or both. Thus, I highly recommend that comp lab researchers carefully study the O'Reilly *Extreme Programming Pocket Guide* [Chromatic (2003)]. This graceful little book (81 pages) is as much about the clear communication and coordination of model specifications as about programming, so it is at least as important for researchers who hire programmers as it is for those who program models themselves.

Ideally, a comp lab provides a rich hierarchy of *well-factored* base classes, where the accumulation of a rich library of classes for agents, spatial landscapes or other interaction structures and related comp lab tools provides researchers with powerful research leverage. Factoring classes is similar to factoring numbers into primes; it refers to the clean division of class functionality into unique and irreducible units. To consider an example closer to the hearts of most researchers, factoring classes in an agent-based model is similar to factoring sections of a research paper to reduce unnecessary repetition.

3. Comp Lab support for heterogeneous, mobile, cognitive agents

3.1. *Hierarchies of Agent Classes*

Here "agent" refers broadly to bundled data and behavioral methods representing an entity constituting part of a computationally constructed world. Examples of possible agents include individuals (e.g., consumers, workers), social groupings (e.g., families, firms, government agencies), institutions (e.g., markets, regulatory systems), biological entities (e.g., crops, livestock, forests), and physical entities (e.g., infrastructure, weather, and geographical regions). Thus, agents can range from active data-gathering decision-makers with sophisticated learning capabilities to passive world features with no cognitive functioning. Moreover, agents can be composed of other agents, thus permitting hierarchical constructions. For example, a firm might be composed of workers and managers.

[Tesfatsion (2006a), pages 835–836]

One of the most important distinctions between a spatial agent-based simulation model and a comp lab is the laboratory's provision of a powerful set of base classes for agents, for other model components such as landscapes (see Section 4 below), and for comp lab tools to support visualization, data collection, analysis, search, optimization, and control for simulation models.

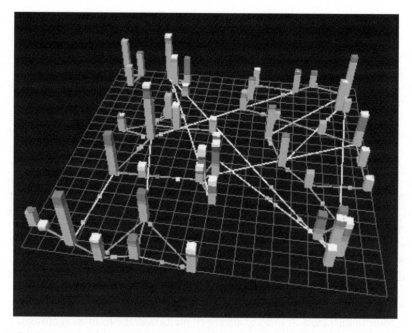

Figure 1. Synthetic or empirically derived organizational or geographic network landscapes, where individual agents travel between team or city nodes and bar charts summarize the current status of each node's population.

For example, the GeoGraph Comp Lab [Dibble and Feldman (2004)] in use by my research group at the University of Maryland provides two base classes for agents, from which model agents may inherit specific geographic capabilities that correspond to classes of GeoGraph landscapes.

- **GeoAgent** is a network-enabled agent. It may either teleport from node to node or may be restricted to follow specific types of links within the landscape. It can evaluate nodes within a network-specific neighborhood, and can compute shortest paths from one node to another along multiple links. It is written to utilize the GeoGraph Node3D class, which is a network enabled node class used with GeoGraph network landscapes for modeling organizational structures or geographical landscapes such as networks of cities. Most of the simulations extend this class, including the epidemic model illustrated in Figure 1.
- **FreeAgent** is a free-roaming agent. This class provides the basis for 'flocking agents' such as villagers or wildlife on synthetic fractal terrain or empirical digital elevation models of natural landscapes, illustrated in Figure 2.

As a second layer in our hierarchy of agent classes, we have developed two child classes, each of which serves as an agent class or base class for one of our primary research lines:

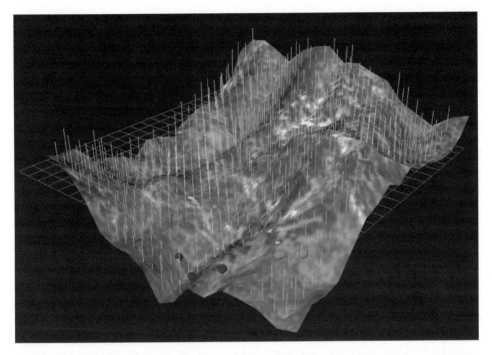

Figure 2. A synthetic three-dimensional fractal terrain landscape with parameterized renewable green "tree" agents and small flocks of "deforestation" round agents, shown toward the front. This could instead use empirically derived geographic terrain and vegetation, imported from a Geographic Information System or from Remote Sensing data.

- **EconAgent** is a **GeoAgent** that knows how to collect information about its world in order to select from among its list of alternatives the one that provides sufficient (for satisficing) or optimal satisfaction of its objective function.
- **EpiAgent** is a **GeoAgent** that knows how to become infected with or immune to a disease, and how to progress through various stages of incubation, sickness, and death or recovery if it becomes infected. For many diseases, an EpiAgent becomes infectious for some duration that may overlap other stages, during which the agent "knows" how to transmit the disease to the landscape (e.g. via doorknobs or keyboards) or directly to other agents (e.g. via "sneezing").

For example, our EconAgent class could be used to implement Schelling's segregation game [Schelling (1978)] directly, without further modification. We simply create instances for a simulation population of $n + m$ agents, tell each of n agents that it is type "Blue" and each of m agents that it is type "Green," and tell each what minimum percentage of neighbors of its own type it considers to be satisfactory.

In general, we develop a new child class only when we need to add new data fields or new capabilities (methods) to an agent. We simply use the class directly to create individual "instances" of agents for each simulation if all we need to do is to provide each individual model agent created from the class with values for its variables. In our case, the objective function for an EconAgent may be provided to the agent as a parameter rather than "hard-coding" each equation into a new class that differs only according to that equation. We create separate child classes only when their objective functions need to be defined according to radically different sets of variables.

3.2. *Cognitive agent learning, adaptation, and evolution*

Cognition refers to the methods agents use to make decisions about their behavior. Learning refers to their ability to modify their cognitive methods over time. Adaptation is generally distinguished from learning by being passive and biological rather than active and cognitive, although these two terms are often confused and used interchangeably. Alternatively, adaptation may refer to an agent selecting an alternative strategy that was already known to it, without requiring any cognitive effort to develop new methods. Evolution refers to the improvement of subsequent generations of agents as a result of natural selection (e.g. via survival and reproduction in proportion to relative fitness of the agents).

In general, learning may be modeled simply as imitation of the behavioral rules used by more successful agents. Alternatively, learning models such as genetic-based machine learning [Holland (1992), Goldberg (1989), Dibble (2001a)] may apply "fitness selection," "cross-over" and "mutation" operations to sets of competing behavioral rules in an attempt to evolve better-performing rules. Evolutionary models may not involve learning within individual agents, but may instead simply select for the agents who employ the most successful strategies. For example, evolution may select for firms that are able to compete most profitably in a given environment. Yet such models in principle provide an excellent demonstration of the importance of learning as opposed to evolution, as individuals or firms that cannot learn or adapt to changing circumstances are likely to die or go out of business when conditions change.

For more detailed discussions of models of learning, adaptation, and evolution, see the handbook chapters by Brenner (2006), Duffy (2006), and Young (2006).

4. Comp lab spatial and organizational landscapes

Sound generalizations based on scientific experiments require controlled conditions and sufficient experimental trials in order to distinguish fully their incidental effects from their systematic effects. A well-equipped agent-based comp lab provides such controls over the characteristics of agent populations for each model. Yet agents are only half of the story for realistically structured systems we wish to study.

Each agent's opportunities and constraints for interaction are determined not only by the characteristics of its own position in an organizational structure, or by its geographic location, but also by its structural *situation*; its access to other positions or locations, each with its current complement of agents and other characteristics. Historically, spatial and even social situations have been determined primarily by geographic distance, with the relative ease of access modified by natural features such as rivers, mountains, or coastlines. More recently, opportunities for social and economic interaction are driven by networks of transportation or communication *spatial technologies* [Couclelis (1994)] that shrivel time and cost surfaces unevenly at all scales [Tobler (1999)].

Many of the fundamental open questions at the frontiers of theoretical and applied economics and related social science research are driven by the analytical intractability of studying dynamic interactions among distributed, heterogeneous, mobile agents embedded or mobile within richly structured spatial and social networks. Formal theoretical analysis of the behavior of aggregate systems of such agents becomes intractable almost immediately. Agent-based comp labs can help theorists to explore the behavior of these spatially distributed socio-economic systems. Spatial structure is central to the dynamics of spatial processes such as the diffusion of innovations or of infectious diseases within a population of mobile individuals.

Section 4.1 introduces comp lab generation of synthetic landscapes. Section 4.2 briefly summarizes the original work on aspatial small-worlds that inspired the extensions by Wilhite (2001, 2006), Dibble (2001b), and Dibble and Feldman (2004) to spatial small-world synthetic landscapes. Section 4.3 introduces the contraction factor, distance decay, and positive feedback extensions that provide the conceptual foundation for generating geographically interesting spatial small-worlds for use in comp lab experiments. Finally, Section 4.4 summarizes typical comp lab options for generating richly-structured synthetic landscapes for controlled experiments.

4.1. Introduction to comp lab generation of synthetic landscapes

Ideally, we should be able to study the effects of exogenous landscape structure by exploring the ways in which selected local and global network characteristics affect the micro and macro evolution of systems of agents. Similarly, we should be able to study the effects of endogenous network structure by studying the co-evolution of agents and networks, especially the effects of positive feedback and of both micro and macro path dependence [Tesfatsion (1997)]. Systematic exploration of either is problematic when we are limited to observations and analysis of real-world geographies. For example, real-world network landscapes that have dissimilar characteristics may be inhabited by agents whose economic and social conditions are too different for meaningful comparison.

Similarly, a real-world landscape limits the generality of our results by offering only a single observation of an interaction structure and associated population distributions.

In contrast, parameterized families of synthetic landscapes can be coupled with parameterized families of synthetic population distributions to offer essential control for comp lab experiments, leading to far deeper and more generalizable understanding of the relationships between network structures and distributed dynamic processes.

In order for comp labs to reach their full potential as tools for theorists modeling distributed systems, we need to be able to generate parameterized families of richly structured synthetic landscapes that vary in the characteristics that we seek to study, yet that remain congruent in their other characteristics. For example, DeCanio et al. (2000, 2001) evaluate the effects of richly structured synthetic organizational networks on the efficiency of distributed processes among a collection of workers. Wilhite (2001) considers a trading economy modeled as a ring landscape divided into contiguous regions, then adds one or two random aspatial shortcuts to each landscape to explore the effects of network structure on local commodity markets.

Section 4 extends such approaches by addressing comp lab tools for controlled synthesis of landscapes and other interaction structures, ranging from simple fully-mixed aspatial random soups to richly structured network landscapes that structure opportunities for interactions among agents.

Our GeoGraph Comp Lab has been explicitly designed for use in controlling experimental conditions for spatial agent-based modeling through its ability to generate richly structured parameterized families of synthetic landscapes. These landscapes are useful for building and testing formal models grounded in interesting spatial structures, homogeneous or heterogeneous distributed mobile agents, and context-specific behaviors. To the best of our knowledge, this is the first and remains the only general purpose research comp lab for building bottom-up models that have large numbers of heterogeneous, spatially distributed, mobile individuals on richly structured synthetic network and terrain landscapes.

4.2. Aspatial small-world and scale-free networks

The goal before us is to understand complexity. To achieve that, we must move beyond structure and topology and start focusing on the dynamics that take place along the links. *Networks* are only the skeleton of complexity, the highways for the various processes that make our world hum.

[Barabási (2002)]

New formalizations of network structures have begun to revolutionize the study of everything from human social networks [Watts (1999)] to the Internet [Albert et al. (1999)], the error and attack tolerance of networks [Albert et al. (2000)], and metabolic networks within a cell [Jeong et al. (2000)]. *Small-world networks* are networks characterized by a high degree of local structure, which nevertheless have surprisingly short average path lengths (e.g. "six degrees of separation") due to the importance of random shortcuts [Watts and Strogatz (1998)]. *Scale-free networks* have a distribution of links per node that is exponential rather than normal or uniform, implying that almost all nodes have very few connections while a few "hub" nodes are extremely well connected [Barabasi and Albert (1999)]. See Strogatz (2001) for an excellent review.

Yet Barabási was right about the limitations of these network formulations. Each addresses merely the structural analysis of a static network, with limited capability to model dynamic processes among heterogeneous mobile individuals. Similarly, each network formulation has been purely aspatial, in the sense that it has structure but not yet spatial relationships or corresponding weights for the links; rather, each link has a uniform "distance" of one, and nodes have no natural location. Finally, small-worlds and scale-free networks represent only two dramatically distinct families of networks; until our GeoGraph Comp Lab [Dibble and Feldman (2004)], there had not yet been a generalization to the synthesis and use of realistically hybrid spatial networks.

The original *Nature* paper on small-world networks [Watts and Strogatz (1998)] reported the synthesis and analysis of a particular parameterized class of irregular networks. Each ring of n ($= 1000$) nodes was initially configured with links to each node's k ($= 4$) nearest neighbors on either side. A small-world network was created from each k-connected ring by randomly rewiring each link in the network with a very small probability p. All networks in the paper were aspatial, where each link has its distance normalized to one, and the length of any given path is defined by simply counting the number of links it contains.

Two characteristics were measured for each small-world network. First, the Characteristic Path Length ($L(p)$) measured the average shortest-path distance between each pair of nodes in a network. Second, the Cluster Coefficient ($C(p)$) measured the number of links for each node that are still attached only to one of its k nearest neighbors [Watts and Strogatz (1998)].

When compared across small-worlds, $L(p)$ falls precipitously and then levels off as p increases from 0 to 1. $C(p)$ falls extremely gradually for p close to 0, and only begins to fall precipitously as p converges to 1. Thus, the $L(p)$ and $C(p)$ curves leave a large lens-shaped gap for small values of p, for their example of 1000-node rings. This gap corresponds to the network's small-world characteristics; where the $L(p)$ is low and it is relatively easy for signals to traverse the network, yet $C(p)$ is high as almost all links in the world remain local rather than shortcuts [Watts and Strogatz (1998)].

Watts (1999) defines the *range* of a link to be the second-shortest path available between the two nodes. For example, the range of a shortcut connecting nodes separated by three base links would be three. Intuitively, small-world characteristics arise when the rewired links provide dramatically advantageous shortcuts by spanning especially large ranges of the base network.

Despite Watts's claims to the contrary [Watts (1999)], the configuration of the base network does have an important effect on a network's small-world characteristics for any given n and p. To see this, consider the maximum range for alternative configurations of a network of n nodes, where each node is initially connected only to its nearest neighbors. For a ring landscape, the maximum range is $n/2$. For a square grid landscape, the maximum range is $2n^{1/2}$. For $n = 100$, this corresponds to 50 versus 20. For $n = 10\,000$, this corresponds to 5000 versus 200. The larger the network, the more dramatic the small-world characteristics are on the ring landscape. This is true for aspatial networks, where each shortcut link has unit distance no matter how large its range.

To extend this analysis to spatial networks, consider the small-world characteristics of a grid lattice where each link has Euclidean distance. Without loss of generality, we can normalize to unit distance for each (orthogonal) base link. In such networks, maximum range remains as defined above, yet the shortcut links that correspond to each maximum range now have distances of n/π and $2^{1/2}n^{1/2}$, respectively. Small-world characteristics still exist for each, yet they are considerably less dramatic. For example, in unpublished small-world simulations conducted on Berkeley's Cray T3E super computer with $n = 1000$ for a spatial (Euclidean) grid, we found that $C(p)$ falls only linearly with respect to p.

Yet, although small-world effects are interesting and important, the truly profound innovation in Watts and Strogatz (1998) is the synthesis and study of parameterized families of irregular networks. In addition, small-world effects do seem to exist in everyday geographic landscapes, so it makes sense instead to turn the question around: what drives the small-world characteristics of a network, and how best can this be modeled in organizational networks or in spatial networks for geographic landscapes?

4.3. Spatial small-worlds, contraction factors, and modeling globalization

In synthetic landscapes such as these GeoGraph spatial small-world networks, we can control structure as we improve shortcut technologies, or we can control technologies as we change structure. So we can explore separately the effects of changes in technology from changes in structure, in order to study the specific effects of each on geographic systems and processes. This is an important scientific advantage. Unlike real-world landscapes, GeoGraph's ability to synthesize stochastic families of spatial small-world networks allows us to control geographic structure to compare effects of different spatial technology regimes across landscapes that have equivalent numbers and arrangements of spatial technology shortcuts.

The driving force behind a network's small-world properties is the ratio between the length and the range of its small-world shortcuts. In large aspatial ring networks, the maximum of this ratio is high because $1 : (n/2)$ is high. In square grids, the maximum of this ratio is low because $(2^{1/2}n^{1/2}) : (2n^{1/2})$ simplifies to $0.71 : 1$, which is quite low. Yet real-world geographic landscapes do exhibit small-world properties, primarily due to the technological advantage of their shortcuts.

To model this, we generalize our synthesis of small-world networks and unify both aspatial and spatial small-worlds by introducing a *contraction factor* multiplier for the length (weight, time, cost, etc.) of each small-world shortcut. Let C denote the value of this contraction factor, which may be any real number between 0 and 1. Let x denote the uncontracted length of a small-world shortcut, and x' denote its contracted length. Then $x' = C \cdot x$.

The simplest such model would simply choose a contraction factor $C \in [0, 1]$ and apply it to each small-world shortcut generated for the network. More complicated models might apply different values of the contraction factor to different shortcuts, or perhaps even assign the value of the contraction factor as a linear or non-linear function of properties of the shortcut itself. In principle, contraction factors could also have values greater than one, which would still represent a shortcut in many networks, merely a less effective shortcut than its corresponding aspatial or Euclidean value.

Contraction factors model improvements in spatial technologies as shortcuts become faster and cheaper over time. In geographic landscapes, the most natural interpretation of a contraction factor's value is its relative technological advantage in speed or cost with respect to the base technology. So a synthetic landscape that has one uniform contraction factor could be interpreted as a landscape spanned by two spatial technologies, one for the base and one for the shortcuts. Alternatively, the base could be interpreted as an isotropic plane, with a single network of spatial technology shortcuts super-imposed. The application of several different contraction factors to various sets of shortcuts would be interpreted as a selection of complementary or competing spatial technologies. Finally, the application of non-linear contraction factors could be interpreted as corresponding to various economic pricing schemes such as are often used to separate shipping costs into fixed and variable components according to the nature of the cargo.

4.3.1. Distance decay

Distance decay is the usual geographic term reflecting a diminished effect or degree of interaction with respect to greater distance. In principle, this generalization could be used to alter the probability of assigning a shortcut's destination node either to nodes that tend to be closer or to nodes that tend to be farther away. For example, given a particular origin node for the small-world shortcut, its corresponding destination node could be interpreted to be either more or less likely to be chosen, according to some function of its distance from the origin node.

4.3.2. Positive feedback

Similarly, define the degree of a node to be the number of links of any type attached to it. Then we may also define the probability of selecting a particular shortcut destination node according to its respective degree relative to the degrees of other nodes in the landscape. Again, we usually think in terms of positive feedback with respect to degree, but this is fully generalizable and could just as easily be modeled as negative feedback that would make a node less likely to be chosen as a destination if it were already well connected. Refinements of this principle could also pay attention to the type of links attached to a particular node, so that nodes are either more or less likely to be selected as shortcut destinations depending upon the degree to which they are or are not already well connected to a particular type of small-world shortcuts.

4.3.3. Addition of new links

The net addition of new links could obviously affect the outcome of a particular model. The original small-world paper by Watts and Strogatz (1998) held the number of links constant by rewiring edge links rather than adding new links as shortcuts. For real-world landscapes, the base geography would generally be affected in different ways by the addition of new links, depending upon the scale of the model and upon the interpretation of the various types of spatial technologies. This last extension is important to note, yet it is not essential to the distinction between spatial and aspatial small-worlds.

4.4. Extensions and calibration of synthetic spatial small-world networks

Section 4.3 presented a general conceptual model for the synthesis of spatial small-world networks that may also incorporate spatial analogs for the characteristics of scale-free networks. Yet this is only the simplest beginning. Each could be further generalized or calibrated, depending upon the modeling task at hand. Different contraction factors can be applied to different sets of shortcuts in order to model disparate spatial technology networks. Variable or non-linear contraction factors may be calibrated to represent more realistic technological and economic relationships among the various spatial technologies.

In turn, distance decay or expansion, as well as positive or negative feedback with respect to various types of node degree, may be tailored to actual or theoretical properties of specific organizational or geographic networks. Parameters for each may be tuned until the characteristics of the synthetic spatial small-worlds correspond to the characteristics of existing real-world networks suitable for each model. Finally, the spatial small-world extensions discussed above may be applied to either one or both nodes for each shortcut.

The following lists indicate GeoGraph agent-based comp lab options for modeling landscapes, initial population distributions, and agent travel or relocation decisions:

A. Network landscapes (usually spatial, but may be aspatial)

Nodes may be distributed:
- as a circle,
- as a square grid,
- randomly,
- from data (e.g. geographic coordinates read from a file).

Base links may be distributed:
- between immediate neighbors on the circle (i.e, as its circumference),
- between orthogonal immediate neighbors on the square grid,
- as radial dendrites from a core node to peripheral nodes on square grid,
- from network data read from a file (with optional attributes).

Base links may be weighted:
- 1 for all links (a binary/aspatial network, with no distance or weights),
- Euclidean distance for each link (determined by node coordinates),
- from data, providing distances or costs for each link (read from the link file).

Shortcut links may be distributed:

- stochastically according to small-world logic (between randomly selected nodes),
- stochastically according to scale-free logic (to a node according to its link count),
- stochastically according to Dibble (2001b) and Dibble and Feldman (2004) spatial small-world logic, where both nodes are selected stochastically according to:
  - distance (with positive or negative weighting for distance decay),
  - degree (with positive or negative weighting for node's # of links).

B. Initial population distributions

Agents may be distributed:
- entirely to one node (whether there is one node or many in the landscape),
- uniformly across nodes (population must be an integer multiple of the # of nodes),
- stochastically across nodes, with variability ranging from 0 (1 node) to 1 (uniform),
- from data, providing integer populations for each node.

C. Simple models of agent travel patterns

In a locational game, each agent may decide at each turn where it would prefer to be, which may or may not lead to a decision to relocate. In a simulation of an epidemic, an agent may decide whether to travel to another node based on endogenous perceptions of local risks or on a stochastic model parameter such as travelProbability. In turn, evaluations of potential destinations could be modeled as one of the following:
- random node—randomly choose any node in the landscape,
- random neighbor—randomly choose any node that is one link away from current,
- random base neighbor—randomly choose one node that is one base link away,
- local or global characteristics of a node—such as its current residents or neighbors,
- gravity model—choose nodes in the landscape according to a probability distribution across k destination nodes that is proportional to:

$$\text{gravityWeight} = \left(\text{jPop}^{\text{tau2}} \cdot \text{kPop}^{\text{tau1}}\right) / \text{distance}^{\text{rho}}$$

where:
gravityWeight = weight for the number of trips from node j to node k
j, k = nodeIDs for the from and to nodes, respectively
jPop = population of the origin node
kPop = population of the (potential) destination node
tau2 = scaling power for the origin node
tau1 = scaling power for the destination node
rho = distanceDecay

Note: tau2 and jPop can be ignored, as these will be the same for any given node. We only need to find the probability of a given destination node. Origin probability already scales with respect to jPop via travelProbability · jPop.
Here, a simple gravity model simplifies to:

gravityWeight $= $ kPop/distance^{distanceDecay}
where: distanceDecay defaults to 2.0

When we assume that node populations remain constant, this means that each node calculates a roulette wheel of proportional probabilities for each of the $n - 1$ other nodes in the landscape, where all probabilities sum to 1. Any agent who travels from that node thus uses that roulette wheel to decide where to go. The roulette wheel remains constant for each node during each simulation. When node populations fluctuate significantly during a simulation, each node would need to recompute its roulette wheel of population-weighted probabilities for each of the $n - 1$ other nodes in the landscape.

5. Examples: games, diffusion, innovation, and globalization

This section introduces several spatial processes and related practical applications in order to illustrate the kinds of problems that may be explored via comp labs for spatial agent-based models.

Locational games and coordination problems include many familiar ACE examples such as the segregation tipping game, audience seating, and cafeteria selection first introduced by Schelling (1978). These also include the El Farol spatio-temporal bar-coordination problem, and the Standing Ovation Problem used by Miller and Page (2004) to teach agent-based modeling.

Diffusion processes become especially interesting when the diffusion occurs among mobile heterogeneous agents interacting on richly structured landscapes. Understanding diffusion dynamics can be especially important to encourage the diffusion of important information or to inhibit the diffusion of deadly infectious diseases.

Ecological innovation refers to the degree to which diffusion of heterogeneous ideas or viruses may encourage or inhibit opportunities for their recombination within agents to create new ideas, inventions, or deadly diseases.

Finally, increasing population densities and improvements in transportation and communication technologies facilitate globalization processes by profoundly altering the ease, frequency, and range of spatial interactions. In turn, such changes affect locational choices, spatio-temporal coordination, diffusion processes, and ecological innovation at all scales.

5.1. Locational games and spatio-temporal coordination problems

Consider a class of models where agents play a locational game on the nodes of a network landscape. This is modeled as a game rather than as an individual optimization problem because the payoffs for each agent's locational choice are an endogenous function of the locational choices of the other agents. Persistent configurations reflect the Nash equilibrium [Nash (1950, 1951)] aspect of settlement patterns: each agent's objective score is affected by the locations of other agents, so each agent's location (its strategy) is best subject to where everyone else has decided to locate (their strategies).

A Nash equilibrium need not be unique, and Nash equilibria may have very different degrees of stability with respect to small perturbations or errors in one or more of the strategies played. In non-zero-sum games such as these, some equilibria will generally have very different average payoffs than others. Mutually beneficial equilibria may evolve over time in repeated games, even when there exist no formal or even informal mechanisms to support cooperation among the agents. Analogs to many of these questions become especially interesting when considering the independent, localized actions of non-cooperative agents acting in space, with varying degrees of imperfect (local) versus perfect (global) information and coordination mechanisms.

If it were possible to logically derive all such results with respect to locational choices of individuals via spatial analysis or game theory, then we would solve such puzzles using only formal analysis, and there would be no need for simulation models. Simulation models are useful for modeling locational games precisely because of the degree of complexity introduced by the non-linear and widely divergent payoffs that arise from individual agent contexts, embedded in each unique spatial situation that may emerge.

Yet any persistent spatial configuration that emerges when agents are free to move is in effect a *generalized Nash equilibrium (gNE)*; given the configuration of agents in the landscape, individual agents may continue to make marginal moves among nodes between which they are indifferent, yet the spatial configuration generally remains unchanged [Dibble (2001b)]. The term "generalized" contrasts with a pure locational Nash equilibrium, in which no agent would move once the equilibrium was reached. In a generalized locational Nash equilibrium, the overall characteristics of the configuration remain unchanged and agents who move do so only on the margin. In other words, they are sufficiently happy with their locations that they would move only to approximately equivalent positions, and they would not move at all if we applied even a modest epsilon moving cost. Thus, we could formalize the notion of a gNE_ε that applies a moving cost of ε to induce a pure locational Nash equilibrium. Simulations here do not impose ε but such models could be used to study persistent configurations.

Similarly, we may define a *distributed Nash equilibrium (dNE)* according to the degree that local neighborhoods overlap by some percentage of each landscape's spatial diameter; a *range* treatment variable [Dibble (2001b)]. As *range* converges to 0, strategic interactions among agents converge to normal, isolated games among strictly local sets of agents. As *range* converges to 1, this becomes simply one global game involving all of the agents in the landscape. But for intermediate values of *range*, where neighborhoods for each local game overlap for some strategic positions or some players, we introduce the potential for tremendously interesting and empirically important percolation dynamics as strategic interactions from one semi-isolated local game ripple through the landscape to disturb or encourage equilibria in neighboring games.

5.2. *Diffusion of ideas, information, or infectious diseases*

Mathematical models of diffusion and percolation among static populations are well established. See for example Nowak and May (2000), and Stauffer and Aharony (1992). The new science of networks (see Barabási (2002) or Strogatz (2001)) continues to offer important breakthroughs on the immunization of complex networks [Pastor-Satorras and Vespignani (2002)] and halting viruses in scale-free networks [Dezsó and Barabási (2002)]. Yet each of these models is limited to static social networks where the pattern of encounters between agents has been fixed *a priori* and remains static throughout the analysis.

Consider exploration of the fundamental characteristics of diffusion among populations of mobile, heterogeneous agents where the pattern of encounters is dynamic throughout the simulation and where the chance of transmission—whether of a virus or of an idea—is dependent upon the characteristics of each agent involved in each encounter. Encounters among agents are structured by two types of networks: social networks determine friendships, yet spatial networks determine the geographic distribution of social agents. For example, I may be able to catch an idea via email, but I am unlikely to catch a cold via email from a friend who is currently living far away.

5.3. *Innovation and ecological emergence of new ideas, inventions, or diseases*

Even in the most sophisticated models, diffusion is treated as though there is a single element to be traced, and as though its effect upon each individual is independent of any competing or complementary elements that may be diffusing or have diffused in the past among members of the population in question. Yet the diffusion of complementary or competing infectious disease strains or ideas may make all the difference. Simply setting up multiple diffusions among a population is not especially difficult. What has been missing is some way to model the cumulative effects of multiple exposures (e.g. for anthrax or even for SARS) and the internal evolutionary effects of the competition or complementarity of multiple strains within each individual. What happens when otherwise relatively benign disease strains or ideas combine within affected individuals to evolve into an especially virulent strain?

This fundamental scientific question could have practical relevance such as:

- Globalization increases the range and frequency of interactions among distributed mobile agents, thus providing ideal conditions for exposure to multiple disease strains. Moreover, globalization facilitates the emergence of new diseases as strains from different species in distant parts of the world encounter one another and recombine to form novel and potentially lethal strains such as H5N1 Avian Influenza.
- During volatile social conditions, conditions favoring civil unrest are likely to be fostered by the diffusion of multiple competing or complementary rumors and ideas. Understanding their dynamics both among and within agents is important for understanding how best to respond to their emergent effects such as riots, looting, sniping and related resistance, or genocide against unpopular civilian factions.

Sufficiently deep understanding of these models may lead not only to effective response but perhaps also to effective control or prevention, as peacekeeping teams diffuse competing information to calm the situation.

Research domains such as multi-scale diffusion of competing and complementary infectious diseases, behavioral norms, and social, economic, political, or technological ideas provide examples of multi-disciplinary research on fundamental ecological mechanisms and the dynamics of richly structured systems of interacting agents. Comp lab research for these domains benefits from our ability to simulate the full multi-scale range of dynamic processes, from the adaptive mechanisms within agents such as the internal genetic algorithms introduced in Dibble (2001a) and in Brenner (2006) and Duffy (2006) to the richly structured organizational and geographic landscapes introduced here and in Dibble (2001b), Dibble and Feldman (2004), and Wilhite (2006).

5.4.   Globalization processes and the effects of new technologies

Finally, consider a model of globalization where decreases in costs and other barriers to long-distance communication, exchange, travel, and migration facilitate increased ranges and frequencies of many types of spatial interactions among geographically separated agents. In the long run, reductions in the costs of spatial interaction generally lead to corresponding locational, socio-economic, institutional, and infrastructure adjustments as well, as agents adapt to the new costs of interaction.

Dibble (2001b) presents a simple example of a model of this type, which makes use of the GeoGraph Comp Lab spatial small-world landscapes described in Dibble and Feldman (2004). First, decreasing contraction factors model technological improvements or falling fuel prices, which reduce the impedance of distance along selected network shortcuts. Second, agents respond to the new contraction factors immediately via a change in their analysis of their current locations, by implicitly increasing their interaction range. In turn, such increases in their scales of interaction may result in direct or indirect incentives to relocate, as other nodes become more attractive either directly through their improved relative accessibility or indirectly through the relocations of other agents as disturbances ripple through the landscape.

6.   Exploration and analysis of spatial system behaviors

Always the more beautiful answer who asks the more beautiful question.
                                                                    (e.e. cummings, i: six non-lectures)

There is a fine art to designing any research model, not merely agent-based. There is of course the obvious necessary condition that it be capable of generating—either deductively or via simulation—the phenomenon of interest. See Epstein and Axtell (1996) and Epstein (1999, 2006). Yet generative models are necessary but not sufficient for the effective conduct of agent-based research [Epstein (2006)]. Undue focus on the model itself provides insufficient guidance for asking meaningful questions of our models, and for undertaking related refinements and further exploration. What matters most is understanding when a simulation model is required in order to generate insights that are not available in other ways, to be clear about what we can *learn* from the model, what is truly new about its results, and how much we can trust what we learn.

6.1. Parsimony and predictive accuracy

Predictive accuracy concerns a model's fit to the population, whereas postdictive accuracy concerns a model's fit to a sample.

(Gauch, 2003, page 280)

Parsimonious modeling means selecting the simplest possible model capable of generating a phenomenon of interest. Although Gauch (2003) addresses the importance of parsimony for statistical modeling of empirical data, his distinctions between predictive and postdictive accuracy and between signal and noise provide compelling arguments for the importance of parsimony in agent-based modeling as well.

As with econometric models, a highly complicated agent-based model that has many types of agents and a large number of parameters provides additional degrees of freedom that allow it to adjust to stochastic noise and thus to fit too closely to sample data. The costs of developing, calibrating, and running complicated agent-based models can be especially prohibitive. Yet complicated models risk overfitting to sample data, which provides merely *postdictive* accuracy that is least valuable for generalization beyond the sample data. In contrast, parsimonious models are more useful to the extent that they can generate crucial *predictive* accuracy regarding the full population of potential outcomes for whichever spatial processes we seek to understand.

Parsimonious spatial agent-based modeling provides two further advantages as well. First, parsimonious models are generally far easier, faster, and less expensive to develop, test, calibrate, and run. Second, systematic exploration of the interactions among key parameters affecting initial conditions or model behavior can be challenging due to the combinatorial explosion of parameter interactions even for simple models. Thorough exploration of model behavior quickly becomes prohibitive for highly complicated simulation models, as such models suffer exponentially from the effects of combinatorial explosion among their parameters, with the additional burden that each simulation generally takes far longer to run.

6.2. Preliminary thought experiments

Theories help experimentalist[s] to design incisive experiments, and experiments yield results that guide the thinking of theoreticians. They coevolve. The indispensability of experiments in scientific research and the surprises experiments constantly throw up suggest that nature has many emergent characteristics in store. ... Emergent characters mostly belong to the *structural* aspect of systems and stem mainly from the organization of their constituents. ... Emergence is closely associated with microexplanations of macrophenomena.

[Auyang (1998), pages 175–176]

As first mentioned in the introduction to this chapter, Schelling's *Micromotives and Macrobehavior* [Schelling (1978)] provides compelling examples of incisive questions about the behavior of distributed agent systems, where each question is framed sufficiently clearly to be answerable, of necessity, purely via thought experiments. Ideally, framing research questions for agent-based comp lab research does begin with questions answerable by thought experiments. Indeed, testing results from such a simulation model against logically derived results from thought experiments can be one of the most powerful methods both for aligning the simulation model with extant theory and for checking the implementation and reasonable behavior of the model. Both approaches are highly recommended. Yet neither is sufficient to establish new insights.

Thought experiments can save years of modeling and guide researchers toward essential questions that cannot be answered in any other way. Nevertheless, to establish new results, research with an agent-based model must extend to unknown territory, where macrophenomena emerge beyond what could be predicted by a careful thought experiment applied to knowledge of initial micro conditions. If you know the values for all of your explanatory variables, can you predict the values of your dependent variable?

That's appropriate for early calibration and testing for a new model. Yet there is no need for simulation modeling if true emergence or surprises are never possible. Finally, can you tell from thinking in depth about your model that you are likely to find trustworthy treasure out there, for reasonable costs, risks, and opportunity costs of the research?

In order to be worthy of study, an emergent property needs to be more than merely something that is not programmed into the individual agents; it must meet the stronger standard that it arise from interactions among agents in a way that could not easily be predicted simply by knowing the micro specifications or objectives of the agents. For example, if you program agents to seek high concentrations of sugar in the landscape, their congregation at such places once the simulation runs is easily predicted and would not be considered an emergent property of the model.

6.3. Scaling agent-based simulation models

Well designed general purpose simulation modeling tools should be able to represent any spatial or temporal scale, depending for visual clarity only upon suitable cartographic generalization in the representation of the landscape and of its agents. For example, each GeoGraph node or agent can be scaled visually from the tiniest dots to a fully detailed graphic image. Similarly, nodes in a network landscape may be interpreted, and represented, as anything from tables in a café to world cities or even planets. Agents for each landscape may be scaled in proportion to the geographic scale, enlarged to facilitate visualization of the model's behavior, or reduced to avoid visual clutter.

The maximum number of nodes and agents for an agent-based simulation model depends upon the fidelity of the respective node and agent classes. Specifically, it depends upon the CPU time and memory requirements for the behavior and visualization of each agent and for each of the other components of the model. Interactive display of the landscape and its agents generally places a greater burden on the computer and thus limits the number of nodes and agents by approximately one order of magnitude, compared with running the equivalent simulation with visualization of real-time data charts but with the landscape graphics hidden.

The demographic and geographic resolution of an agent-based simulation model may be confused informally with scale, yet resolution refers in each case to the number of simulated units per unit in the real world. For example, to study diffusion processes in a true population of 1 000 000 people, we could run models that have resolutions of 1000, 10 000, or 1 000 000 agents.

Although CPU time and memory requirements may determine the maximum number of nodes or agents for simulations on any given computer, it could be a grave mistake to assume that more of either is necessarily desirable. Higher resolution should be used only when it turns out to be important to the behavior of the model. Unnecessary demographic or spatial resolutions that extend the duration of each simulation impose an opportunity cost by limiting the number of research questions, scenarios, and stochastic replicates that can be explored. Sufficient lower bounds for the resolution may be specific to each model or to each research question. These can be established by comparing simulation outcomes from controlled simulations that are identical except for their levels of resolution.

6.4. Visualization and data collection

In our own laboratory work, we typically develop and debug each model using a 2-dimensional or 3-dimensional graphical user interface with a landscape and population of agents comfortable for visualization. After we are thoroughly comfortable with the model and have tested it extensively, we can turn off the visual landscape display and scale up the numbers of nodes and especially the numbers of agents for batch-mode experiments, if that turns out to be important scientifically for the model's results. Depending upon the model and upon the level of abstraction and resolution appropriate for rigorous results, very large numbers of agents can be available but are not necessarily required.

For batch-mode experiments, each simulation logs at least one record—and often several detailed files—to a text file for subsequent analysis. Log files can be inspected visually, but are best read into a more powerful database management system such as the Statistical Analysis System (SAS *www.sas.com*). SAS's macro capabilities are especially effective for reading tens of thousands of log files at a time, and SAS's plotting, regression, data management, and data filtering capabilities support statistical inference, quality control, and exploration of anomalies and other surprises.

6.5.   Practical advice for implementation and testing

"This problem, too, will look simple after it is solved."

(Charles Francis Kettering)

The ACE web site provides links to currently available comp lab platforms [Tesfatsion (2006b)]. Look for the comp lab that has the best comparative advantage for your purposes. In particular, look for class hierarchies that best support the agents, interaction structures, and laboratory tools you plan to employ. In many cases, existing demonstration models and prototypes may provide classes for types of agents that can be modified to develop early proof-of-concept models.

A comp lab development platform that is widely used serves an important role as standardized laboratory equipment, which provides scientific advantages for publication, evaluation, and replication of results. So far, Swarm (*www.swarm.org*), RePast (*repast.sourceforge.net*), and AnyLogic (*www.xjtek.com*) have played key roles in this regard. Agent-based comp lab research is still quite new, however, so it is important to balance the advantages of standardized equipment against important comparative advantages due to specialized or extended comp lab platforms such as the Trade Network Game (TNG) and SimBioSys [McFadzean and Tesfatsion (1999), McFadzean et al. (2001)] or GeoGraphs [Dibble and Feldman (2004)].

6.5.1.   Testing model components

The most exciting phrase to hear in science, the one that heralds new discoveries, is not 'Eureka!' (I found it!) but 'That's funny...'

(Isaac Asimov)

Test *everything*. Put proto-agents and each model agent through its paces one at a time, to test their responses under controlled conditions. Then test agents and agent interactions again within the smallest possible controlled groups to test whatever interactions with other agents may be part of the model. Test their landscape or other interaction structure. Test the agents' ability to gather local or global info, to make appropriate choices, to move about within the structure, and, if relevant, to endogenously modify their landscape or interaction structure.

One of the essential yet often overlooked practices in comp lab work is to have a careful look at the raw data. Of course this is essential for superficial quality control: Did every simulation run correctly? Did anything go wrong, break down, turn up missing, or behave pathologically?

Yet examinations of raw data serve a far deeper scientific purpose than mere quality control. Although we may expect scientific surprises and insights to occur as a result of analytical procedures such as statistical analyses, they may also occur at the level of the raw data. Consequently, this basic step can be central to the scientific process of observation, insight, and understanding. Do the outcomes make sense? When they don't make sense, are we sufficiently alert to their "that's funny" intimations, however inconvenient they may be for our preconceived immediate purpose?

7. Genetic algorithm inference, optimization, and risk analysis

Miller (1998) proposed to use a supervisory genetic algorithm to perform what he called
"active nonlinear tests" (ANTs) by using the genetic algorithm to challenge each simulation model by seeking outcomes that provide exceptions or counter-examples to its
usual results. This section briefly discusses a generalization of Miller's ANTs to the
broader problem of providing effective search and optimization across both treatments
and outcomes for a model.

7.1. Exploring model behavior

Systematic analysis of model behavior may involve millions of simulation runs, each
controlled by sweeping across discrete lists of values for sensitive model parameters,
for each treatment variable of interest, and for seeds to control one or more random
number series for stochastic simulations. For example, consider even a very simple
model that has four parameters, each with three levels to evaluate for sensitivity, and two
treatment variables, each with five levels to evaluate for an experiment. This requires
$3 \times 3 \times 3 \times 3 \times 5 \times 5 = 2025$ simulation runs, even for a deterministic model where a
single simulation is sufficient to evaluate each combination.

When stochastic behavior, synthetic landscapes, synthetic agent populations, and
stochastic initial conditions are involved, even minimal evaluation of representative
outcomes for each vector of parameters and treatment variables may require multiple seed values for one or more separate random number series. For example, in our
GeoGraph framework, even a basic evaluation of epidemic outcomes requires analysis of combinations of three sets of random number seeds. For synthetic landscapes
such as globalization networks, one random number seed determines landscape details
(geoSeed). Another random number seed determines stochastic initial conditions such
as population distributions and the locations of initial cases of the disease (iniSeed).
A third controls all stochastic actions such as who travels where and who infects whom
(actSeed).

Such controls enable us to replicate experiments to systematically evaluate the effects
of stochastic events under controlled conditions. Yet even ten histories for each of the
three random number seeds would require running $10 \times 10 \times 10 = 1000$ stochastic
replications for each of the 2025 distinct combinations of parameter and treatment levels
in the example above, for a total of 2 025 000 simulations just for one simple experiment.

Of far greater importance scientifically, the standard focus on exploring model behavior via combinatorial sweeping across regularly spaced parameter values is a blind
search for significant outcomes. As illustrated in Figure 3, regularly spaced parameter
values may be entirely unrelated to the truly important parameter values where model
behavior may reach significant extrema.

Ideally, we would like to be able to search for interesting behavior in the outcome
space rather than sweeping blindly in parameter space. As illustrated in Figure 4, a supervisory genetic algorithm allows us to do precisely that, and with far greater efficiency

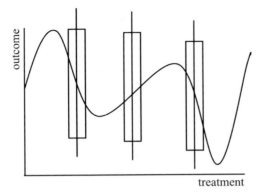

Figure 3. Running only a few stochastic replicates of each treatment level can result in variances so large that the signal becomes lost in the noise. Similarly, selecting treatment levels blindly via random or regular spacing may completely miss important local and global extrema.

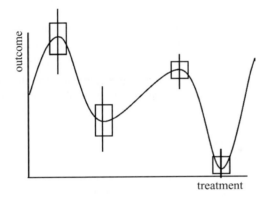

Figure 4. In contrast, an ideal experimental design runs enough stochastic replicates for reliable inference. Similarly, data-driven experimental designs may provide guidance for identification of key values for treatment variables and for basins of attraction leading to common outcomes.

than brute force combinatorial sweeping of parameter spaces. To do so, the genetic algorithm can be set up to search across combinations of key parameters for extreme values of single or multiple combinations of outcome variables, based on results from one or more stochastic replications of the scenario that is associated with each combination of key parameters. In addition, the greater economy in searching for key scenarios releases computational resources that may in turn be used to simulate sufficient stochastic replications for each to be able to distinguish statistically significant differences among scenario outcomes.

7.2. *Inference and discovery of key exceptions*

Using supervisory genetic algorithms to discover highly effective treatments or to search for exceptional or surprising simulation outcomes has the potential to profoundly enhance our ability to make the most effective use of limited computational and analytical resources. It permits us to discover and test incisive empirical insights, effective normative designs or interventions, and surprising heuristic insights. Once such treatments or outcomes have been identified by the genetic algorithm, subsequent ordinary batches of simulations can be carefully targeted in order to evaluate the accuracy, uncertainty, risk, and inference power of results obtained from any well-specified agent-based simulation model.

Finally, a supervisory genetic algorithm can be used to thoroughly explore the robustness with respect to risk of promising designs or interventions. When used to discover effective designs or interventions, the genetic algorithm searches across combinations of scenarios or intervention parameters for those that perform best across the population of simulations that is run to evaluate each string. In contrast, when the genetic algorithm is used to evaluate the stochastic risks associated with each intervention that corresponds to specific values for the treatment variables: it holds constant the model's sensitive parameters and treatment variables, and instead searches across random number seeds for "Murphy's Law" worst-case combinations of stochastic events, where everything that could go wrong does go wrong. Some interventions may be far more resistant to worst case outcomes, which may be crucial to evaluate when stakes are high.

Figure 5 illustrates a supervisory GA where fitness for each GA string of model parameters is determined by the outcomes of large numbers of agent-based simulations based upon those parameters.

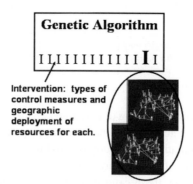

Figure 5. A supervisory Genetic Algorithm evolves populations of strings of simulation parameters by evaluating combinations of simulation parameters according to the results of one or more simulation runs based on those parameters.

8. Opportunities, challenges, and resources

Most of the comp lab issues discussed in this chapter have addressed support for relatively abstract theoretical research with spatial agent-based models. Yet comp lab models and tools such as supervisory genetic algorithms for exploration, optimization, and risk analysis can potentially support policy-relevant computational spatial social science. Spatial agent-based models are beginning to be used to provide decision-support for complex emergencies such as controlling the spread of infectious diseases.

In many cases, research on abstract landscapes provides sufficient insight to support real-world decisions. For this, synthetic landscapes such as those introduced in Section 4 provide powerful scientific leverage. Comp labs would benefit from corresponding tools for populating agent-based models with initial distributions of carefully calibrated synthetic demographic populations.

Nevertheless, one of the most important methodological challenges facing comp labs for spatial agent-based models is to provide easy-to-use tools for importing real-world geographic landscapes from Geographic Information Systems (GIS) or satellite remote sensing data. In turn, closer interoperability between comp labs and GIS would provide spatial agent-based modeling researchers with access to the powerful tools for spatial analysis, visualization, and mapping that are incorporated in modern GIS.

A complementary methodological frontier, for both spatial and aspatial agent-based modeling, would provide comp lab tools to streamline the art of developing families of models ranging from highly abstract parsimonious theoretical models to highly calibrated models for policy and testing against empirical data.

We may also cross the ultimate boundary from *modeling* cognitive agents in our comp lab models to *incorporating* live human cognitive agents in our spatial agent-based models. This blurs the distinction between experimental economics with humans under controlled conditions in a laboratory versus experimental economics with humans under controlled conditions interacting within a virtual spatial environment in a comp lab [Macmillan (1996)].

Finally, as hinted at in the thought experiment on pandemics in Section 1, we may begin to combine policy-relevant comp lab simulations and inference with near real-time collection and relevance filtering of real-world surveillance data. This would permit us to improve our models in general and, more importantly, to learn how to signal when it is appropriate to begin, modify, or conclude a specific intervention. Pure comp lab experiments with spatial agent-based models on geographic landscapes may pave the way for new and effective uses of near real-time remote sensing satellite data or social systems sensing data [Gelernter (1992)] as it arrives.

For example, comp lab simulations may be used to identify sensitive empirical indicators and corresponding critical thresholds for phase transitions in complex dynamic processes such as pandemics of infectious diseases, civil violence, or business cycles. When is an epidemic in danger of flaring into a full global pandemic? When and where should interventions to control the outbreak begin? What are the early warning signs that an outbreak of disease or civil violence or a downturn in the business cycle has turned the corner toward successful containment or recovery?

To return to our original thought experiment, global pandemics of infectious diseases have been infrequent events that create considerable disruption and are extraordinarily difficult to study, much less to control or to repeat in order to explore the effects of chance events. Spatial agent-based computational laboratories allow us to learn from virtual experience by creating and studying millions of simulated pandemics under controlled conditions, to evaluate risks and to explore effective methods for their prevention and control.

In turn, as illustrated by Section 5, pandemics are merely one example of broad classes of complex social and environmental spatial dynamic processes. Effective spatial agent-based models and fully equipped computational laboratories provide opportunities to learn from far more extensive and better controlled virtual experience than could ever be generated by real-world systems: to understand the fundamental driving forces within such systems, and to discover and evaluate wiser designs, more effective interventions, and the risks or resilience associated with each.

Acknowledgements

For their thoughtful recommendations on earlier drafts I thank Leigh Tesfatsion, Allen Wilhite, and three anonymous reviewers. My thanks to Stephen Wendel for his research expertise and insightful comments. For financial support I thank the Office of Naval Research, the Environmental Protection Agency, and the National Institutes of Health, National Institute of General Medical Sciences.

References

Albert, R., Jeong, H., Barabasi, A.L. (1999). "Internet—diameter of the world-wide web". Nature 401 (6749), 130–131.

Albert, R., Jeong, H., Barabási, A.-L. (2000). "Error and attack tolerance of complex networks". Nature 406, 378–382.

Aldhous, P., Tomlin, S. (2005). "Avian flu: are we ready?". Nature 435 (7041), 399.

Axelrod, R. (1997). The Complexity of Cooperation: Agent-Based Models of Competition and Collaboration. Princeton University Press, Princeton.

Axtell, R., Axelrod, R., Epstein, J.M., Cohen, M.D. (1995). "Aligning simulation models: a case study and results", Santa Fe Institute working paper 95-07-065.

Auyang, S.Y. (1998). Foundations of Complex-System Theories in Economics, Evolutionary Biology, and Statistical Physics. Cambridge University Press, Cambridge, UK.

Barabási, A.-L. (2002). Linked: The New Science of Networks. Perseus Publishing, New York.

Barabasi, A.-L., Albert, R. (1999). "Emergence of scaling in random networks". Science 286, 509–512.

Beveridge, W.I.B. (1957). "The Art of Scientific Investigation", 3rd edn. Vintage Books, New York.

Brenner, T. (2006). "Agent learning representation: advice on modelling economic learning", this handbook.

Chromatic (2003). Extreme Programming Pocket Guide. O'Reilly Media, Sebastopol, CA.

Couclelis, H. (1994). "Spatial technologies". Environment and Planning B—Planning & Design 21 (2), 142–143.

DeCanio, S.J., Dibble, C., Amir-Atefi, K. (2000). "Organizational structure for the adoption of innovations". Management Science 46 (10), 1285–1329.

DeCanio, S.J., Dibble, C., Amir-Atefi, K. (2001). "Organizational structure and the behavior of firms: implications for integrated assessment". Climatic Change 48, 487–514.

Dezsó, Z., Barabási, A.-L. (2002). "Halting viruses in scale-free networks". Physical Review E 65 (5), 4.

Dibble, C. (2001a). "Beyond data: handling spatial and analytical contexts with genetics based machine learning". In: Krzanowski, R., Raper, J. (Eds.), Spatial Evolutionary Modeling. Oxford University Press, Oxford. Chapter 3.

Dibble, C. (2001b). "Theory in a complex world: geograph computational laboratories", unpublished doctoral dissertation, University of California.

Dibble, C., Feldman, P.G. (2004). "The GeoGraph 3D comp lab: network and terrain landscapes for RePast". Journal of Artificial Societies and Social Simulation 7 (1). http://jasss.soc.surrey.ac.uk/7/1/7.Html.

Duffy, J. (2006). "Agent-based models and human-subject experiments", this handbook.

Epstein, J. (1999). "Learning to be thoughtless: social norms and individual computation", Brookings Institution, Center on Social and Economic Dynamics, working paper no. 6.

Epstein, J. (2006). "Remarks on the foundations of agent-based generative social science", this handbook.

Epstein, J., Axtell, R. (1996). Growing Artificial Societies: Social Science from the Bottom Up. Brookings Institution, MIT Press, Washington, DC.

Fontana, W., Buss, L.W. (1994). "What Would be Conserved if The Tape Were Played Twice?". In: Cowan, G., Pines, D., Meltzer, D. (Eds.), Complexity: Metaphors, Models, and Reality. Addison-Wesley, New York, pp. 223–236.

Fujita, M., Krugman, P., Venebles, A.J. (1999). The Spatial Economy. The MIT Press, Cambridge, MA.

Gauch, H.G. (2003). Scientific Method in Practice. Cambridge University Press, Cambridge, UK.

Gelernter, D. (1992). Mirror Worlds: Or the Day Software Puts the Universe in a Shoebox: How It Will Happen and What It Will Mean. Oxford University Press, New York.

Goldberg, D.E. (1989). Genetic Algorithms in Search, Optimization, and Machine Learning. Addison-Wesley, Reading, MA.

Holland, J.H. (1992). Adaptation in Natural and Artificial Systems, 2nd edn. The MIT Press, Cambridge, MA.

Jeong, H., Tombor, B., Albert, R., Oltval, Z.N., Barabasi, A.L. (2000). "The large-scale organization of metabolic networks". Nature 407 (6804), 651–654.

Macmillan, B. (1996). "Fun and games: serious toys for city modelling in a GIS environment". In: Longley, P., Batty, M. (Eds.), Spatial Analysis: Modelling in a GIS Environment. John Wiley & Sons, New York, pp. 153–165.

Mas-Colell, A., Whinston, M.D., Green, J.R. (1995). Microeconomic Theory. Oxford University Press, New York.

McFadzean, D., Tesfatsion, L. (1999). "A C++ platform for the evolution of trade networks". Computational Economics 14, 109–134.

McFadzean, D., Stewart, D., Tesfatsion, L. (2001). "A Comp Lab for evolutionary trade networks". IEEE Transactions on Evolutionary Computation 5 (5), 546–560.

Miller, J.H. (1998). "Active nonlinear tests (ANTs) of complex simulation models". Management Science 44 (6), 820–830.

Miller, J.H., Page, S.E. (2004). "The standing ovation problem". Complexity 9 (5), 8–16.

Nash, J. (1950). "Equilibrium points in *n*-person games". Proceedings of the National Academy of Sciences, USA 36 (1), 48–49.

Nash, J. (1951). "Non-cooperative games". Annals of Mathematics 54 (2), 286–295.

Nowak, M.A., May, R.M. (2000). Virus Dynamics Mathematical Principles of Immunology and Virology. Oxford University Press, New York.

Osterholm, M.T. (2005). "Preparing for the next pandemic". Foreign Affairs (July/August).

Pastor-Satorras, R., Vespignani, A. (2002). "Immunization of complex networks". Physical Review E 65, 1–4. article no. 036104.

Samuelson, P. (1952). "The transfer problem and transport costs". Economic Journal 64, 264–289.

Schelling, T.C. (1978). Micromotives and Macrobehavior, 1st edn. Fels Lectures on Public Policy Analysis. W.W. Norton, New York.

Stauffer, D., Aharony, A. (1992). Introduction to Percolation Theory. Taylor and Francis, London.

Strogatz, S.H. (2001). "Exploring complex networks". Nature 410, 268–276.

Tesfatsion, L. (1997). "A trade network game with endogenous partner selection". In: Amman, H.M., Rustem, B., Whinston, A.B. (Eds.), Computational Approaches to Economic Problems. Kluwer Academic Publishers.

Tesfatsion, L. (2000). "Concentration, capacity, and market power in an evolutionary labor market". In: Evolution at Work for the New Millenium, Proceedings of the 2000 Congress on Evolutionary Computation, vol. II. IEEE, Inc., New Jersey, pp. 1033–1040.

Tesfatsion, L. (2001). "Structure, behavior, and market power in an evolutionary labor market with adaptive search". Journal of Economic Dynamics and Control 25 (3–4), 419–457.

Tesfatsion, L. (2006a). "Agent-based computational economics: a constructive approach to economic theory", this handbook.

Tesfatsion, L. (2006b). "Agent-based computational economics (ACE) demos web site", web page, available at http://www.econ.iastate.edu/tesfatsi/acedemos.htm.

Tobler, W. (1999). "The world is shriveling as it shrinks", ESRI User Conference.

Watts, D.J. (1999). Small Worlds: The Dynamics of Networks between Order and Randomness. Princeton University Press, Princeton, NJ.

Watts, D.J., Strogatz, S.H. (1998). "Collective dynamics of 'small-world' networks". Nature 393, 440–442.

Wilhite, A.W. (2001). "Bilateral trade and small-world networks". Computational Economics 18 (1), 49–64.

Wilhite, A.W. (2006). "Economic activity on fixed networks", this handbook.

Young, H.P. (2006). "Social dynamics: theory and applications", this handbook.

PART 2

PERSPECTIVES ON THE ACE METHODOLOGY

Chapter 32

OUT-OF-EQUILIBRIUM ECONOMICS AND AGENT-BASED MODELING

W. BRIAN ARTHUR[1]

Contents

[1] W. Brian Arthur is External Professor, Santa Fe Institute, and Institute Scholar, IIASA, Laxenburg, Austria. Website: www.santafe.edu/arthur. I thank Robert Axelrod, David Colander, Geoffrey Hodgson, Roger Koppl, Gregory Nemet, and Martin Shubik for comments on this paper. Parts of the material here appeared in an earlier essay in *Science* (Arthur, 1999).

Handbook of Computational Economics, Volume 2. Edited by Leigh Tesfatsion and Kenneth L. Judd
DOI: 10.1016/S1574-0021(05)02032-0

Abstract

Standard neoclassical economics asks what agents' actions, strategies, or expectations are in equilibrium with (consistent with) the outcome or pattern these behaviors aggregatively create. Agent-based computational economics enables us to ask a wider question: how agents' actions, strategies, or expectations might react to—might endogenously change with—the patterns they create. In other words, it enables us to examine how the economy behaves out of equilibrium, when it is not at a steady state.

This out-of-equilibrium approach is not a minor adjunct to standard economic theory; it is economics done in a more general way. When examined out of equilibrium, economic patterns sometimes simplify into a simple, homogeneous equilibrium of standard economics; but just as often they show perpetually novel and complex behavior. The static equilibrium approach suffers two characteristic indeterminacies: it cannot easily resolve among multiple equilibria; nor can it easily model individuals' choices of expectations. Both problems are ones of formation (of an equilibrium and of an "ecology" of expectations, respectively), and when analyzed in formation—that is, out of equilibrium—these anomalies disappear.

Keywords

agent-based, out-of-equilibrium economics, evolutionary economics, indeterminacy, complexity

JEL classification: B41, C63, C65

Over the last twenty years a different way of doing economics has been slowly emerging. It goes by several labels: complexity economics, computational modeling, agent-based modeling, adaptive economics, research on artificial economies, generative social science—each of these with its own peculiarities, its own followers, and its own nuances. Whatever the label, what is happening, I believe, is more than just the accumulation of computer-based or agent-based studies. It is a movement in economics.[1]

Why this movement? One answer all its practitioners agree on is that agent-based modeling came along in the 1980s because at that time economists got desktop workstations. For the first time we could not just study equilibria but ask how they form. Agent-based modeling is about how patterns in the economy form (I like Joshua Epstein's term *generative explanation* for this (Epstein, 2006)), and usually such formation is too complicated to be handled analytically—hence the resort to computer simulation. This is fine. But does it mean agent-based computational economics is merely an adjunct to conventional economics that adds something about pattern formation? And if it relies mainly on simulating economic processes on the computer, isn't this a retreat from theory? What does this way of doing economics really provide?

In this overview essay I want to argue that this movement is not a minor adjunct to neoclassical economics; it is something more than this. It is a shift from looking at economic problems at equilibrium to looking at such problems out of equilibrium, a shift to a more general economics—an out-of-equilibrium economics.

Before I begin, a caveat to the reader. This essay is a line of reasoning about the nature of agent-based economics; it makes no attempt to review the agent-based computation literature, nor does it give instructions on how to carry out agent-based computation. Both topics have been well covered elsewhere.

I will start not by discussing agent-based modeling, but the economy itself.

1. Beyond equilibrium

Economic agents—banks, consumers, firms, investors—continually adjust their market moves, buying decisions, prices, and forecasts to the situation these moves or decisions or prices or forecasts together create. To put this another way, individual behaviors collectively create an aggregate outcome; and they react to this outcome. There is nothing new in saying this. Economists have seen the economy this way at least since Adam Smith. Behavior creates pattern; and pattern in turn influences behavior.

It might be natural in such a setting for economic theorists to study the unfolding of patterns that economic agents create. But this obviously is complicated. And therefore to seek analytical solutions, historically economics chose to simplify its questions.

---

[1] The progression of the subject can be seen by comparing the volumes: Anderson et al. (1988); Arthur et al. (1997b); Blume and Durlauf (2005); and this volume of Tesfatsion and Judd (2006). For other commentaries on this approach see: Lane (1993a, 1993b); the introduction to Arthur et al. (1997a); Colander (2000); and Tesfatsion (2006).

It asked instead what behavior caused an outcome or pattern that leads to no incentive to change that behavior. In other words, it asked what patterns in the economy would look like if they were at equilibrium—were consistent with the micro-behavior (actions, strategies, expectations) that creates them. Thus, for example, general equilibrium theory asks: What prices and quantities of goods produced and consumed are *consistent with*—would pose no incentives for change to—the overall pattern of prices and quantities in the economy's markets? Game theory asks: What strategies, moves, or allocations are consistent with—would be the best course of action for an agent (under some criterion)—given the strategies, moves, allocations his rivals might choose? Rational expectations economics asks: What forecasts (or expectations) are consistent with—are on average validated by—the outcomes these forecasts and expectations together create? Partial-equilibrium economics—say in international trade theory—asks: what local behaviors would produce larger patterns that would support (be consistent with) those local behaviors.

This equilibrium approach lends itself to expression in equation form. And because an equilibrium by definition is a pattern that doesn't change, in equation form it can studied for its structure, its implications, and the conditions under which it obtains. Of course the simplicity that makes such analytical examination possible has a price. To ensure tractability we usually have to assume homogeneous (or identical) agents, or at most two or three classes of agents. We have to assume that human behavior— a notoriously complicated affair—can be captured by simple mathematical functions. We have to assume agent behavior that is intelligent but has no incentive to change; hence we must assume that agents and their peers deduce their way into exhausting all information they might find useful, so they have no incentive to change. Still, as a strategy of advancement of analysis, this equilibrium approach has been enormously successful. As it evolved into the neoclassical structure we know today, it has built a degree of understanding that is the envy of other social sciences.

I believe that economics is currently pushing beyond this equilibrium paradigm. It is natural to ask how agents' behavior might not just be *consistent with* the aggregate pattern it creates, but how actions, strategies, or expectations might in general react to— might *endogenously change with*—the patterns they create. In other words, it is natural to ask how the economy behaves when it is not at a steady state—when it is *out of equilibrium*. At this more general level, we can surmise that economic patterns might settle down over sufficient time to a simple, homogeneous equilibrium. Or, that they might not: they might show ever-changing, perpetually novel behavior. We might also surmise they might show new phenomena that do not appear in steady state.

By its very nature this approach calls for detailed instructions on how individual behavior adjusts as the situation unfolds; therefore it is algorithmic. And since there is considerable scope for learning or reacting in different ways, this approach sees no reason to treat adjustments in behavior as identical. Agents must therefore be separately considered; hence the approach is based on individual agents. Consideration of economic patterns out of equilibrium therefore naturally introduces algorithmic updating and heterogeneity of agents. On both these counts it is best handled by computation.

One possible objection to doing economics this way is that because the approach is computational, it does not constitute theory. But this statement is too facile. If working out the implications of a set of assumptions is theory, then whether this is done by hand or by computer does not matter. Both methods yield theory. But certainly there is a difference in style. Equation-based methods call for equation-based dissection of the results—and equation-based discovery of telling implications—and this dissection and analysis can be accomplished rigorously. Of course often the rigor is specious. Implications match reality only as well as the chosen assumptions and chosen functional forms do; and functional forms are always abstractions of reality—often gross ones when closely examined—so there is plenty of scope for rigorous deduction based upon faulty assumptions. Computer-based modeling is different but parallel in these regards. It calls for statistical dissection of the phenomena discovered, and in many computer-based models it may be difficult to discern phenomena through the thicket of events. There is also scope for unrealistic assumptions and for needless complication. And doing computer-based economics well is not necessarily easier than doing analytical economics well. Good work here shows an eye for elegance of experiment for the telling, simple, computational model that demonstrates a phenomenon clearly; and for extracting a phenomenon from the jumble of other data that obscure it.

The two styles can of course be mixed. If a phenomenon shows up computationally, often it can be reproduced in a simpler analytical model. If it shows up analytically, it can be probed computationally. Properly carried out, computation does not replace theory. It allows more realistic assumptions and accommodates out-of-equilibrium behavior. It thereby extends theory. It is also good to remember—and I want to emphasize this—that exploring the economy out of equilibrium does not *require* computation. That could be done in principle by analytical methods, as it has in some particular cases, especially those involving learning mechanisms (Samuelson, 1997; Fudenberg and Levine, 1998; Brock and Hommes, 1998). But for most agent-based situations analytical formulations are highly complicated, hence the resort to computation.

A different objection is that because out-of-equilibrium studies require detailed modeling of how individual behavior adjusts (and how agents interact), they encourage behavioral assumptions that are *ad hoc*. The point has some merit: assumptions are sometimes adopted for convenience. But we need to remember that the standard assumptions of "rational behavior" themselves are highly stylized versions of reality. If modeling agent adjustments forces us to study and think rigorously about *actual* human behavior, this is actually a strength.

Out-of-equilibrium studies of course do not answer all possible questions. They do not tell us usually about the formation of tastes, or of technologies, or of structure. David Lane (1993a, 1993b) notes that such studies "offer only very limited scope to the emergence of new structures—and, so far, none at all to the emergence of higher-level entities." What emerges is pattern, not hierarchical structure.

One thing noticeable about agent-based studies is that they are nearly always evolutionary in approach. Why should this be? I said earlier that an assumption common to most studies is that agents differ in the way they react to aggregate patterns; they have different circumstances, different histories, different psychologies. That is, agents are adaptive and heterogeneous. On first thought, this might seem to yield at most a trivial extension to standard homogeneous theory. But consider. If heterogeneous agents (or heterogeneous strategies or expectations) adjust continually to the overall situation they together create, then they adapt within an "ecology" they together create. And in so adapting, they change that ecology. So providing we use "evolution" in the broadest sense of the word, which I interpret as elements adapting their state to the situation they together create, we see that in this sense evolution emerges naturally from the very construction of such modeling. It need not be added as an adjunct. (Of course in any particular case we would need to define precisely what we mean by "elements," "adapting," "states," and "situation.") Because out-of-equilibrium economics is by its nature evolutionary, it resembles modern evolutionary biology more than it does 19th century physics.

Agent-based, non-steady-state economics is also a generalization of equilibrium economics. Out-of-equilibrium systems may converge to or display patterns that are consistent—that call for no further adjustments. If so, standard equilibrium behavior becomes a special case. It follows that out-of-equilibrium economics is not in competition with equilibrium theory. It is merely economics done in a more general, generative way.

I have made a large claim so far, namely that a new form of economics is a-birthing— a generative or out-of-equilibrium economics. If the reader accepts this, a natural question to ask is what it delivers. What novel phenomena do we see when we do economics out of equilibrium? Are there questions that equilibrium economics can not answer, but that this more general form of economics can? In Kuhnian language, are there anomalies that this new paradigm resolves?

The answer to this last question is yes. In the remainder of this essay I want to look at two characteristic anomalies—two indeterminacies, to be precise—in equilibrium economics and show that these disappear under the new approach. Along the way, I want to point to some characteristic phenomena that arise in the new approach. I will base the discussion mainly on a study by Lindgren and on three topics I have been heavily involved with, because these address directly the points I want to make (and because I am most familiar with them). There are certainly other studies that widen the scope of agent-based economics beyond the discussion here.[2] These also, I believe, corroborate the arguments I will make here.

---

[2] For some early studies see: Bak et al. (1993); Durlauf (1993); Lindgren (1992); Marimon et al. (1990); Sargent (1994); and Schelling (1978). See also Young (1998). The earliest agent-based studies I know of were by Miller (1988), and Marks (1989). From the most recently available collection (Arthur et al., 1997a), the reader might consult the papers of Blume (1997), Durlauf (1997), Kirman (1997), Kollman et al. (1997), Ioannides (1997), Lane and Maxfield (1997), and Tesfatsion (1997). The forthcoming collection of Blume and Durlauf (2005) and this volume contain more recent work. For the literature on network interactions, see Wilhite (2006, this volume).

2. Perpetual novelty

Let me begin with a phenomenon, one often we see in this sort of economics. That is the absence of any equilibrium, or more positively, the presence of ever-changing, perpetually novel behavior. For an example, consider the classic study of Kristian Lindgren (1992). Lindgren sets up a computerized tournament where strategies compete in randomly chosen pairs to play a repeated prisoner's dilemma game. The elements in his study are therefore strategies rather than human agents. Strategies that do well replicate and mutate. Ones that lose eventually die. Strategies can "deepen" by using deeper memory of their past moves and their opponent's. A strategy's success of course depends on the current population of strategies, and so the adaptive elements here— strategies—react to, or change with, the competitive world they together create.

In his computerized tournament Lindgren discovered that the simple strategies in use at the start went unchallenged for some time. Tit-for-tat and other simple strategies dominated at the beginning. But then other, deeper strategies emerged that were able to exploit the mixture of these simple ones. In time, yet deeper strategies emerged to take advantage of those, and so on. If strategies got "too smart"—that is, too complicated— sometimes simple ones could exploit these. In this computer world of strategies, Lindgren found periods with very large numbers of diverse strategies in the population, and periods with few strategies. And he found periods dominated by simple strategies, and periods dominated by deep strategies. But nothing ever settled down. In Lindgren's world the set of strategies in use evolved and kept evolving in a world of perpetual novelty. This is unfamiliar to us in standard economics. Yet there is a realism about such dynamics with its unpredictable, emergent, and complicated sets of strategies. Chess play at the grand master level evolves over decades and never settles down. Lindgren's system is simple, yet it leads to a dynamic of endless unfolding and evolution.

When, in general, do we see perpetually novel behavior in the economy? There is no precise rule, but broadly speaking perpetual novelty arises in two circumstances. One is where there is frustration (to use a physics term) in the system. Roughly this means that it is not possible to satisfy the needs of all the agents (or elements) at the same time and that these jostle continually to have their needs fulfilled. The other is where exploration is allowed and learning can deepen indefinitely—can see better and better into the system it is trying to understand. In this case collective behaviors can explore into constantly new realms, sometimes mutually complicate, sometimes simplify, but not settle down.

3. Equilibrium indeterminacy and the selection process

In the Lindgren case, the situation shows no equilibrium; it is always in perpetual novelty. In other cases equilibrium is possible, but there may be more than one natural pattern of consistency: there may be multiple equilibria. This situation arises naturally in the presence of positive feedbacks or increasing returns—or more technically, under non-convexity. Here multiple equilibria are the norm. At first sight this does not seem to pose any major difficulty to equilibrium economics. Instead of a unique equilibrium there are several. But there *is* a difficulty. Equilibrium economics can identify consistent patterns, but can not tell us how one comes to be chosen. Standard economics therefore runs up against an indeterminacy.

This indeterminacy has been an embarrassment to economics over the years. "Multiple equilibria," wrote Schumpeter (1954), "are not necessarily useless, but from the standpoint of any exact science the existence of a uniquely determined equilibrium is, of course, of the utmost importance, even if proof has to be purchased at the price of very restrictive assumptions; without any possibility of proving the existence of uniquely determined equilibria—or at all events, of a small number of possible equilibria—at however high a level of abstraction, a field of phenomena is really a chaos that is not under analytical control." Faced with this potential "chaos," different subfields of economics took different approaches. Some—especially within game theory in the 1960s and '70s—added restrictive (and somewhat artificial) assumptions until only a single solution remained. Others, contrary to Schumpeter, accepted the chaos. They statically determined the possible equilibria in a problem and left the choice of equilibrium open and therefore indeterminate. An example is the international trade theory of Helpman and Krugman (1985) which allowed increasing returns and settled for multiple static, but indeterminate, equilibria.

A more natural approach, I believe, is to tackle the issue generatively (Arthur 1989, 1994a, 1994b): to see the problem not as one of equilibrium *selection* but as one of equilibrium *formation*. Economic activity is quantized by events that are too small to foresee, and these small "random" events—who sits next to whom on an airplane, who tenders an offer when, who adopts what product when—can over time cumulate and become magnified by positive feedbacks to determine which solution was reached. This suggests that situations with multiple equilibria can best be modeled by looking at what happens over time—what happens in formation. That is, they are best modeled not as static deterministic problems, but as dynamic processes with random events, with natural positive feedbacks or nonlinearities. With this strategy the situation can then be "observed" theoretically as its corresponding process unfolds again and again to "select" or determine an outcome. Sometimes one equilibrium will emerge, sometimes (under identical conditions) another. It is impossible to know in advance which of the candidate outcomes will emerge in any given unfolding of the process, but it is possible to study the probability that a particular solution emerges under a certain set of initial conditions. In this way the selection problem can be handled by modeling the situation in formation, by translating it into a dynamic process with random events. With an out-of-equilibrium approach, the anomaly disappears.

In this sense a whole realm of economics—increasing returns problems—requires an out-of-equilibrium approach. This realm, by the way, is not small. Increasing returns arise in economic geography, finance, economics of markets, economic development, economics of technology, and economics of poverty; and the literature in these areas is becoming large. Interestingly, in most of the important cases the work has been analytical, not computational. The reason is that most increasing returns problems lend themselves to sufficient homogeneity of agents to be handled by analysis.

Whatever their topic of focus, increasing returns studies tend to show common properties: a multiplicity of potential "solutions"; the outcome actually reached is not predictable in advance; it is "selected" by small events; it tends to be locked in; it is not necessarily the most efficient; it is subject to the historical path taken; and while the problem may be symmetrical, the outcome is usually asymmetrical. These properties have counterparts in a different science that emphasizes the formation of pattern: solid-state physics. What economists call multiple equilibria, non-predictability, lock-in, inefficiency, historical path dependence, and asymmetry, physicists call multiple meta-stable states, unpredictability, phase- or mode-locking, high-energy ground states, non-ergodicity, and symmetry breaking. Some of these properties can be identified by static analysis (multiplicity, possible non-efficiency, non-predictability, and lock-in). But to see how they come about, and to see symmetry breaking, selection, and path-dependence in action, requires looking at the situation as the solution forms—out of equilibrium.

4. Expectational indeterminacy and inductive behavior

Multiple equilibria cause one type of indeterminacy in static economics. Expectations can cause another, and this also requires out-of-equilibrium resolution. Let me explain.

All economic actions are taken on the expectation of some outcome. And in many situations this outcome is determined collectively—it depends upon the results of other people's actions. Thus an entrepreneur may have to decide on whether to invest in a new semiconductor fabrication plant today, based upon what he forecasts supply in the market to be like in two years' time. And his competitors may have to make similar decisions. But the collective result of their choices today will determine the aggregate supply (and hence prices and profits) in two years' time.

In cases like this, agents attempt to forecast what the outcome will be; but their actions based on their forecasts determine this outcome. So the situation is self-referential: agents are trying to form expectations about an outcome that is a function of their expectations. Or, to collapse this further, their choices of expectation depend on their choices of expectation. Without some additional conditions imposed, there is no logical or deductive way to settle this self-referential choice. This is a fundamental indeterminacy in static economics.

It is tempting to dismiss this as a minor anomaly, but the situation that causes it pervades economics: it occurs anywhere agents' decisions affect other agents.[3] It confronts economics with a lacuna—how expectations might logically be formed in multi-agent situations. And it is the main reason economists feel uneasy about problems with expectations.

---

[3] For some history and commentary on this indeterminacy see Koppl and Rosser (2002).

Static economic theory, of course, *does* deal with problems where multi-agent expectations must be considered; it has evolved a theoretical method—a sort of analytical workaround—to do this: the rational expectations approach. Rational expectations asks, within a given economic problem, what expectational model (if everyone adopted it) would lead to actions that would on average validate that expectational model. If such a model existed, agents' expectations would be on average upheld, and this would solve the problem of selecting suitable expectations.

Actually, this last assertion came too fast. To be rigorously exact, if such a model existed it would demonstrate at least one set of expectations consistent with the outcome. Whether this translates into a *theory* of expectations formation matched by reality is another question, one that leaves even supporters of this approach uncomfortable. To suppose that this solution to a given problem would be reached in a one-off non-repeated problem, we would need to assume that agents can somehow deduce in advance what model will work, that everyone "knows" this model will be used, and everyone knows that everyone knows this model will be used, ad infinitum. (This is the common knowledge assumption.) And we would further require a unique solution; otherwise agents might coordinate on different expectations.

The net effect is that unless there is good reason for agents to coordinate somehow on a single set of expectations, rational expectations become theoretically singular: they resemble a pencil balanced on its point—logically possible but in reality unlikely. The situation worsens when agents differ. They must now form expectations of an outcome that is a function of expectations they are not privy to. Whether behaviorally or theoretically, barring some obvious coordinating set of expectations, the indeterminacy can not be avoided. Deductive equilibrium economics therefore faces an anomaly.

As a theory of expectations formation, rational expectations begin to look better if the situation is repeated over time, because we might suppose that agents "learn" their way over time into on-average correct expectations. In this case rational expectations would at least form a solution to which expectations converge. But it is possible to construct repeated situations in economics where rational expectations are not a guide— where in fact they *must* fail. Consider the El Farol bar problem (Arthur, 1994a, 1994b). One hundred people must decide independently each week whether to show up at their favorite bar (El Farol in Santa Fe, say). The rule is that if a person predicts that more that 60 (say) will attend, she will avoid the crowds and stay home; if she predicts fewer than 60 she will go. We see at once the self reference I mentioned above: agents attend based on their predictions of how many agents will attend.

Will rational expectations work here? Suppose for a moment they do. Suppose that a rational expectations prediction machine exists and all agents possess a copy of it. Such a machine would take a given history of attendance (say, ten weeks back) and map it into a forecast of the coming week's attendance, and by definition it would on average predict correctly. Suppose now this machine predicts one week that 74 will attend. But, knowing this nobody shows up, negating that forecast. Suppose the next week it predicts 44. Then 100 people go, negating that forecast as well. In El Farol, expectations that are shared in common negate themselves. Therefore forecasts that are on average consistent with the outcome they predict do not exist and can not be statically deduced. As a theory of expectations formation, rational expectations fails here. The indeterminacy is also manifest in this case. Any attempt to deduce a reasonable theory of expectations that applies to all is quickly confounded.[4]

The anomaly resolves itself in this case (and in general) if we take a generative approach and observe expectations in formation. To do this we can assume agents start each with a variety of expectational models or forecasting hypotheses, none of them necessarily "correct." We can assume these expectations are subjectively arrived at and therefore differ. We can also assume agents act as statisticians: they test their forecasting models, retain the ones that work, and discard the others. This is inductive behavior. It assumes no a-priori "solution" but sets out merely to learn what works. Such an approach applies out of equilibrium (expectations need not be consistent with their outcome) as well as in equilibrium; and it applies generally to multi-agent problems where expectations are involved. (See Holland et al. (1986), and Sargent (1994).)

Putting this into practice in the case of El Farol means assuming that agents individually form a number of predictive hypotheses or models, and each week act on their currently most accurate one. (Call this their active predictor.) In this way beliefs or hypotheses compete for use in an ecology these beliefs create. Computer simulation then shows that the mean attendance quickly converges to 60. In fact, the predictors self-organize into an equilibrium pattern or "ecology" in which, on average, 40% of the active predictors are forecasting above 60 and 60% below 60. And while the population of active predictors splits into this 60/40 average ratio, it keeps changing in membership forever. There is a strong equilibrium here, but it emerges ecologically and is not the outcome of deductive reasoning.

My point in this discussion is not just that it is possible to construct problems that confound rational expectations. It is this: In multi-agent situations the formation of expectations introduces a fundamental indeterminacy into equilibrium economics; but if we allow expectations to form out of equilibrium in an inductive, agent-based way, the indeterminacy disappears. Expectation formation then becomes a natural process.

If we apply this generative approach to standard problems, do expectations indeed usually converge to the rational expectations norm? The answer is mixed: sometimes they do and sometimes they don't, depending on whether there is a strong attractor to the rational expectations norm or not. Interestingly both answers can obtain in the same problem. Different parameter sets can show different behaviors. In one set (or phase or regime) simple equilibrium behavior might reign; in another complex, non-converging pattern-forming behavior might obtain. My guess is that such phases will turn out to be common in agent-based models.

Consider as an example the Santa Fe artificial stock market (Palmer et al., 1994; Arthur et al., 1997a). The model is essentially a heterogeneous-agent version of the

---

[4] This El Farol situation of preferring to be in the minority occurs in the economy anywhere pre-committed decisions have to be made under diminishing returns (to the numbers committing). In its minority game formulation, the problem is much studied among physicists (see Challet et al., 2004; and Coolen, 2005).

classic Lucas equilibrium model (Lucas, 1978). In it heterogeneous agents, or artificial investors, form a market within the computer where a single stock is traded. Each monitors the stock price and submits bids and offers which jointly determine tomorrow's price. Agents form (differing) multiple hypotheses of what moves the market price, act on the most accurate, and learn by creating new hypotheses and discarding poorly performing one. We found two regimes: if agents update their hypotheses at a slow rate, the diversity of expectations collapses into a homogeneous rational expectations regime. The reason is simple: if a majority of investors believes something close to the rational expectations forecast it becomes a strong attractor; others lose by deviating from these expectations and slowly learn their way to them. But if the rate of updating of hypotheses is tuned higher, the market undergoes a phase transition into a "complex regime." Here it displays several properties seen in real markets. It develops a rich "psychology" of divergent beliefs that do not converge over time. Expectational rules such as "If the market is trending up, predict a 2% price rise" appear randomly in the population of hypotheses and become temporarily mutually reinforcing. (If enough investors act on these, the price will indeed go up.) In this way sub-populations of mutually reinforcing expectations arise, and fall away again. This is not quite perpetual novelty. But it is a phenomenon common to such studies: patterns that are self-reinforcing arise, lock-in for some time (much as clouds do in meteorology), and disappear.

We also see another phenomenon, again common to out-of-equilibrium studies: avalanches of change of varying sizes. These arise because individual out-of-equilibrium behavior adjusts from time to time, which changes the aggregate, which in turn may call for further behavioral changes among agents. As a result in such systems cascades of change—some small and some large—can ripple through the system. In artificial markets this phenomenon shows up as agents changing their expectations (perhaps by exploring new ones) which changes the market slightly, and which may cause other agents to also change their expectations. Changes in beliefs then ripple through the market in avalanches of all sizes, causing random periods of high and low price volatility. This phenomenon shows up in actual financial market data but not in equilibrium models. One interesting question is whether such avalanches show properties associated with phase boundaries in physics, namely power laws where the size of the avalanche is inversely proportional to its frequency. Systems that display this behavior may be technically *critical*: they may lie precisely between ordered and chaotic behavior. We might conjecture that in certain economic situations behavior ensures that the outcome remains poised in this region—technically that self-organized criticality (Bak et al., 1988) arises.

5. Conclusion

After two centuries of studying equilibria—patterns of consistency that call for no further behavioral adjustments—economists are beginning to study the emergence of equilibria and the general unfolding of patterns in the economy. That is, we are starting to study the economy out of equilibrium. This way of doing economics calls for an algorithmic approach. And it invites a deeper approach to agents' reactions to change, and a recognition that these may differ—and therefore that agents are naturally heterogeneous. This form of economics is naturally evolutionary. It is not in competition with equilibrium theory, nor is it a minor adjunct to the standard economic theory. It is economics done in a more general, out-of-equilibrium way. Within this, standard equilibrium behavior becomes a special case.

When viewed out of equilibrium, the economy reveals itself not as deterministic, predictable and mechanistic; but as process-dependent, organic and evolving. Economic patterns sometimes simplify into a simple, homogeneous equilibrium of standard economics. But often they do not. Often they are ever-changing, showing perpetually novel behavior.

One test of a different fundamental approach is whether it can handle certain difficulties—anomalies—that have stymied the old one. Certainly this is the case with out-of-equilibrium economics. Within the static approach, both the problem of equilibrium selection and of choice of expectations are in general indeterminate. These two indeterminacies should not be surprising, because both problems are in essence ones of formation—of coming into being—that can not be resolved by static analysis. Both have been the source of considerable discomfort in economics. But when analyzed out of equilibrium they fall into their proper setting, and the difficulties they cause dissolve and disappear.

References

Anderson, P.K.J., Arrow, K.J., Arrow, K., Pines, D. (Eds.) (1988). The Economy as an Evolving Complex System. Addison-Wesley, Reading, MA.

Arthur, W.B. (1989). "Competing technologies, increasing returns and lock-in by historical events". Economic Journal 99, 106–131.

Arthur, W.B. (1994a). Increasing Returns and Path Dependence in the Economy. University of Michigan Press, Ann Arbor.

Arthur, W.B. (1994b). "Bounded rationality and inductive behavior (the El Farol problem)". American Economic Review Papers and Proceedings 84, 406–411.

Arthur, W.B. (1999). "Complexity and the Economy". Science 284, 107–109.

Arthur, W.B., Holland, J.H., LeBaron, B., Palmer, R., Tayler, P. (1997a). "Asset pricing under endogenous expectations in an artificial stock market". In: Arthur, W.B., Durlauf, S.N., Lane, D.A. (Eds.), The Economy as an Evolving Complex System II. Addison-Wesley, Reading, MA, pp. 15–44.

Arthur, W.B., Durlauf, S.N., Lane, D.A. (Eds.) (1997b). The Economy as an Evolving Complex System II. Addison-Wesley, Reading, MA.

Bak, P., Tang, C., Wiesenfeld, K. (1988). "Self-organized criticality". Physical Review A 38, 364.

Bak, P., Chen, K., Scheinkman, J., Woodford, M. (1993). "Aggregate fluctuations from independent sectoral shocks". Ricerche Economiche 47 (3).

Blume, L.E. (1997). "Population games". In: The Economy as an Evolving Complex System II. Addison-Wesley, Reading, MA, pp. 425–460.

Blume, L.E., Durlauf, S.N. (Eds.) (2005). The Economy as an Evolving Complex System III. Oxford University Press.

Brock, W.A., Hommes, C.H. (1998). "Heterogeneous beliefs and routes to chaos in a simple asset pricing model". Journal of Economic Dynamics and Control 22, 1235–1274.

Challet, D., Marsili, M., Zhang, Y.-C. (2004). Minority Games. Oxford University Press.

Colander, D. (Ed.) (2000). The Complexity Vision and the Teaching of Economics. Edward Elgar, Cheltenham, UK.

Coolen, A.C.C. (2005). The Mathematical Theory of Minority Games. Oxford University Press.

Durlauf, S.N. (1993). "Nonergodic economic growth". Review of Economic Studies 60, 349–366.

Durlauf, S.N. (1997). "Statistical mechanics approaches to socioeconomic behavior". In: The Economy as an Evolving Complex System II. Addison-Wesley, Reading, MA, pp. 81–104. Journal of Economic Growth 1 (1997) 75.

Epstein, J.M. (2006). "Remarks on the foundations of agent-based generative social science", this handbook.

Fudenberg, D., Levine, D. (1998). The Theory of Learning in Games. MIT Press.

Helpman, E., Krugman, P.R. (1985). Market Structure and Foreign Trade. MIT Press, Cambridge, MA.

Holland, J.H., Holyoak, K., Nisbett, R., Thagard, P. (1986). Induction. MIT Press.

Ioannides, Y.M. (1997). "The evolution of trading structures". In: The Economy as an Evolving Complex System II. Addison-Wesley, Reading, MA, pp. 129–167.

Kirman, A. (1997). "The economy as an interactive system". In: The Economy as an Evolving Complex System II. Addison-Wesley, Reading, MA, pp. 491–531.

Kollman, K., Miller, J., Page, S. (1997). "Computational political economy". In: The Economy as an Evolving Complex System II. Addison-Wesley, Reading, MA, pp. 461–490.

Koppl, R., Rosser, J.B. (2002). "All that I have to say has already crossed your mind". Metroeconomica 53, 339–360.

Lane, D.A. (1993a). "Artificial worlds and economics, part I". Journal of Evolutionary Economics 3 (2), 89–107.

Lane, D.A. (1993b). "Artificial worlds and economics, part II". Journal of Evolutionary Economics 3 (3), 177–197.

Lane, D.A., Maxfield, R. (1997). "Foresight, complexity and strategy". In: The Economy as an Evolving Complex System II. Addison-Wesley, Reading, MA, pp. 169–198.

Lindgren, K. (1992). "Evolutionary phenomena in simple dynamics". In: Langton, C.G., Taylor, C., Farmer, J.D., Rasmussen, S. (Eds.), Artificial Life II. Addison-Wesley, Reading, MA, pp. 295–312.

Lucas, R.E. (1978). "Asset prices in an exchange economy". Econometrica 46, 1429.

Marimon, R., McGrattan, E., Sargent, T.J. (1990). J. Econ. Dynamics and Control 14, 329.

Marks, R.E. (1989). "Breeding hybrid strategies: optimal behavior for oligopolists". In: Schaffer, J.D. (Ed.), Proceedings of the Third International Conference on Genetic Algorithms. Morgan Kaufmann, George Mason University, pp. 198–207.

Miller, J.H. (1988). "The evolution of automata in the repeated prisoner's dilemma", Ph.D. dissertation, University of Michigan, Ann Arbor.

Palmer, R.G., Arthur, W.B., Holland, J.H., LeBaron, B., Tayler, P. (1994). "Artificial economic life: a simple model of a stockmarket". Physica D 75, 264–274.

Samuelson, L. (1997). Evolutionary Games and Equilibrium Selection. MIT Press, Cambridge, MA.

Sargent, T.J. (1994). Bounded Rationality in Macroeconomics. Clarendon Press, Oxford.

Schumpeter, J. (1954). A History of Economic Analysis. Oxford University Press, New York.

Schelling, T. (1978). Micromotives and Macrobehavior. Norton, New York.

Tesfatsion, L. (1997). "How economists can get ALife". In: The Economy as an Evolving Complex System II. Addison-Wesley, Reading, MA, pp. 533–564.

Tesfatsion, L. (2006). "Agent-based computational economics: a constructive approach to economic theory", this handbook.

Tesfatsion, L., Judd, K. (Eds.) (2006). Agent-Based Computational Economics. Handbook of Computational Economics, vol. 2. Elsevier, North-Holland.

Wilhite, A.W. (2006). "Economic activity on fixed networks", this handbook.

Young, H.P. (1998). Individual Strategy and Social Structure. Princeton University Press, Princeton, NJ.

Chapter 33

AGENT-BASED MODELING AS A BRIDGE BETWEEN DISCIPLINES

ROBERT AXELROD[1]

Gerald R. Ford School of Public Policy, University of Michigan, USA

I dedicate this chapter to William Hamilton, an outstanding collaborator and a wonderful human being. Bill Hamilton literally gave his life for science. In 2000, despite the risks, he went to the jungles of central Africa to gather evidence needed to test a theory about the origin of AIDS. He contracted a virulent form of malaria that proved fatal.

Contents

[1] Acknowledgements: For their help I thank Ross Hammond, Kenneth L. Judd, Leigh Tesfatsion, Robert Marks and Tarah M. Wheeler. For financial support I thank the National Science Foundation, the Intel Corporation, and the University of Michigan LS&A College Enrichment Fund. For permission to quote William Hamilton [Hamilton, W.D. (2002). "The evolution of sex". In: Narrow Roads of Gene Land The Collected Papers of W.D. Hamilton, vol. 2. Oxford University Press, Oxford, pp. 117–132, 561–566, and 601–615] I thank Oxford University Press.

Handbook of Computational Economics, Volume 2. Edited by Leigh Tesfatsion and Kenneth L. Judd
© 2006 Elsevier B.V. All rights reserved
DOI: 10.1016/S1574-0021(05)02033-2

Abstract

Using the author's own experiences, this chapter shows how agent-based modeling (ABM) can address research questions common to many disciplines, facilitate inter-disciplinary collaboration, provide a useful multidisciplinary tool when the math is intractable, and reveal unity across disciplines. While ABM can be a hard sell, convergence within the agent-based community can enhance the interdisciplinary value of the methodology.

Keywords

interdisciplinary research, agent-based models, evolutionary biology, prisoner's dilemma

JEL classification: A12, C63, C73

1. Introduction

This chapter describes some of my experiences with agent-based modeling (ABM) as a bridge between disciplines. I offer these experiences to provide concrete examples of how agent-based modeling can help overcome the somewhat arbitrary boundaries between disciplines. I do not claim that my experiences are typical, or that my style would work well for others.

Although I am occasionally mistaken for an economist, my PhD is in political science. In graduate school, I took the micro-macro sequence designed to socialize the economic doctoral students into their discipline. I distinctly remember an occasion when the professor—a future Nobel Prize winner—was presenting a formal model of consumer behavior. A student remarked, "But that's not how people behave." The professor replied simply, "You're right," and without another word, turned back to the blackboard and continued his presentation of the model. We all got the idea.

I have undertaken ABM projects that both draw on and contribute to economics. Although I often work alone, or with a graduate student, I have also collaborated on ABM projects with political scientists, evolutionary biologists, computer scientists, and economists. This chapter draws on those experiences.

This chapter is organized in terms of five propositions, followed by some suggestions. First, here are the propositions and the research projects that I will use to illustrate them.

1. *ABM can address certain problems that are fundamental to many disciplines.* To illustrate how agent-based modeling can address a fundamental problem, I will use my computer tournaments for the iterated Prisoner's Dilemma that addressed the question of what it takes for egoists to cooperate with each other. I will describe how computer tournaments originated from a link between game theory and artificial intelligence, how the entries drew on the strategic understanding of theorists from many disciplines, and how the results had a wide range of applications in the social sciences and beyond.

2. *ABM facilitates interdisciplinary collaboration.* An informative example is the interdisciplinary collaboration between a political scientist and an evolutionary biologist, namely myself and William Hamilton. Using Hamilton's published memoirs, I will be able to compare and contrast his perspective with mine on how our relationship got started, and what happened along the way.

3. *ABM provides a useful multidisciplinary tool when the math is intractable.* My second collaboration with William Hamilton began when he told me about his explanation for one of the most important evolutionary puzzles: why do almost all large animals and plants reproduce sexually even at the cost of allowing only half the adults to have offspring? Hamilton had a highly original explanation, but had been unable to demonstrate its plausibility. I showed Bill how agent-based modeling could easily simulate the evolutionary effects of a dozen or more genes. Together we were able to build an agent-based model that demonstrated that Bill's

theory was indeed a biologically plausible explanation for the origin and maintenance of sexual reproduction.

4. *ABM can reveal unity across disciplines*. My example of this point is an agent-
   based model I designed based on the principle that when possible, agents will
   tend to align themselves into groups that are self-organized and minimize the
   "stress" each agent faces in its relationships with the each of the others. Scott Bennett, then a graduate student in political science, and I developed, operationalized
   and validated this model with alignments among the seventeen European nations
   that participated in World War II. Two economists, Will Mitchell and Robert E.
   Thomas, at my university's Business School and their graduate student, Erhard
   Bruderer, heard me present this theory, and immediately suggested we work together to apply it to a specific example of computing business alliances. We found
   that the agent-based model about military alignments could also successfully predict strategic alignments of computer companies.

5. *ABM can be a hard sell*. Since most formal theorists equate models with mathematical models, it is not surprising that some of them are hard to convince about
   the appropriateness and value of an agent-based simulation. This point is demonstrated by the kind of objections that Bill Hamilton and I met when we tried to
   publish what we thought were compelling results from our simulation of his evolutionary theory.

This chapter concludes with some suggestions for enhancing the interdisciplinary value
of agent-based modeling.

From my perspective, agent-based modeling is not only a valuable technique for exploring models that are not mathematically tractable; it is also a wonderful way to study
problems that bridge disciplinary boundaries.

2. ABM can address fundamental problems seen in many disciplines

Agent-based modeling has proven helpful in exploring issues that arise in two or more
disciplines. Examples of such issues are path dependency, the effects of adaptive versus
rational behavior, the consequences of heterogeneity among agents, the design of institutional mechanisms to achieve specific goals in a population of autonomous agents, the
effects of network structure, cooperation among egoists, provision of collective goods,
the diffusion of innovation, and the tradeoff between exploiting current best practice
and exploring for new knowledge.

My own experience includes work on the possibility of cooperation among egoists.
My work on computer tournaments for the iterated Prisoner's Dilemma, for example,
drew upon strategic ideas from the different disciplines of the entrants, including economics, political science, psychology, sociology, and mathematics. Simulation results
and my related mathematical theorems then proved applicable to an even wider range of
disciplines, as illustrated in some of my own subsequent work and that of many others.

But where did the idea for a computer tournament come from? In retrospect, I realize that it came from my interest in artificial intelligence that started while I was in high school, and an interest in game theory that started in college. In high school, a just-published article I came across fascinated me with its description of a checker playing program that learned to improve its own play (Samuel, 1959). Afterwards, I followed the development of computer chess through the 1960s, and as well as the computer chess tournaments that began in 1970.

In college, I was a math major with a growing interest in international politics and especially the risk of nuclear war. While studying a then-standard text (Luce and Raiffa, 1957), I came across the iterated Dilemma Prisoner's. To me, the Prisoner's Dilemma seemed to capture the essence of the tension between doing what is good for the individual (a selfish defection) and what is good for everyone (a cooperative choice). In graduate school, while pursuing a PhD in political science, I read the intriguing research on how human subjects played the game, and how game theorists were still arguing with each other about the best way to play the game.

The literature on the iterated Prisoner's Dilemma left me somewhat frustrated because there was no clear answer to the question of how to avoid conflict, or even how an individual (or country) should play the game for itself.[2] Apparently, my frustration stayed with me because I started thinking about the problem again a dozen years later. This time I came up with the tournament idea as a means of studying these questions.

I somehow put two and two together, and realized that a good way to find a successful strategy for the iterated Prisoner's Dilemma was to hold a tournament and see what strategy would win. While I could not have articulated it then, my interest in finding out how sophisticated individuals would play to maximize their own score was probably based on the implicit belief that one would then be able to learn about the conditions under which even egoistic players would choose to cooperate.

I solicited entries from both game theorists and amateurs. Using computer chess programs as a guide, I expected the most successful strategy would have to take into account a wide variety of considerations and hence be very complicated. I was surprised when

---

[2] I learned about the "solution" by backwards induction that says it pays both players to defect on the last move, hence on the next to last move, and so forth right to the beginning of the game. To me, the foresight required for a long backwards induction does not seem very realistic. I doubted that even if someone understood this logic, he or she would expect the other player to understand it, and hence the fully rational reasoning might not apply to real people. In fact, in my first computer tournament, it was common knowledge that the game would be exactly 200 moves, and I provided the entrants with an excerpt from Luce and Raiffa (1957) on backward induction in the finite iterated Prisoner's Dilemma. Although I did not realize it at the time, this design provided a test of what sophisticated and well informed researchers would expect of each other. In the event, the strategy that always defected was not entered, and three of the entrants submitted strategies that automatically defected on the last three moves, apparently because they predicted that others would do backwards induction for only *two* moves. In any case, reasoning by backwards indication does not apply when the players do not know when the iterated game will end, as was true for the second round of the tournament.

Tit for Tat, the simplest of all the submitted strategies, and one of the simplest *possible* strategies, won the tournament.[3]

Since entries came from professors of economics, political science, psychology, sociology, and mathematics, the tournament itself illustrates how ABM can provide the means to bridge disciplines. These were mostly people who had published treatments of the iterated Prisoner's Dilemma in their own disciplinary journals. The tournament provided a way for their strategic ideas to be evaluated in the common setting, namely the rich environment that they would provide for each other. Among the most interesting results was that Tit for Tat, a strategy that could never score better than the other guy it was playing with, nonetheless won both tournaments. Wanting to reach people in many fields, I published the results in an interdisciplinary journal, the *Journal of Conflict Resolution* (Axelrod, 1980a, 1980b).

Seeing that Tit for Tat was quite robust, I used my math background to formulate and test a series of theorems about the conditions under which cooperation based upon reciprocity can emerge in a population of egoists, and then resist invasion by mutant strategies. This time I aimed for my major reference group by publishing the theorems in a disciplinary journal, *The American Political Science Review* (Axelrod, 1981).

What happened next was quite fortuitous. Following my usual practice of scanning a wide range of journals, I saw a review in a sociology journal of a fascinating study based on soldiers' diaries from World War I. The book focused on the "live and let live" system that spontaneously arose between the two sides fighting each other in the trenches. Upon reading the book, I realized that this example, in all its richness, was an apt illustration of my theory about when and how cooperation among egoists can emerge. What made the example so useful was that it showed cooperation where you might least expect it, between opposite sides in the midst of a brutal war. Yet, when viewed from the perspective I was proposing, the cooperation in trench warfare made perfect sense. When I came across this wonderful case, I thought I just might be able to write a book that could speak to a wide audience.[4]

I had no trouble finding illustrations from a wide range of fields. For instance, in economics, issues of cooperation among egoists arose in battles over barriers to trade, attainment of microcredit for those without tangible assets, strategic alliances between businesses, and the possibilities for tacit cooperation in a duopoly.

Seeing that the results of my computer tournaments, and the related theorems that I had provided, could address a very wide range of problems, I started to think about writing a book. When I discovered that people with little or no social science training were able to understand the basic theory and the trench warfare example, I decided to

---

[3] See Axelrod (1984). Now that I have better understanding of the effects of errors in perception and implementation, I would recommend adding a little generosity or contrition to a strategy of strict reciprocity. See Wu and Axelrod (1995).

[4] The readers of *The Evolution of Cooperation* often found the trench warfare case to be the most persuasive part of the book. I am still pondering why a single case study can be more persuasive than quantitative analysis, proofs of theorems, or a host of diverse illustrations.

try it. It took me over a year to transform and extend four of my journal articles and some new research into a book that had a chance of being read with interest by scholars and graduate students in different disciplines, and perhaps even by undergraduates and some members of the educated public. Based on its sales and citations, *The Evolution of Cooperation* succeeded beyond my hopes. From my perspective, agent-based modeling, as exemplified by the computer tournaments for the iterated Prisoner's Dilemma, demonstrated its ability to illuminate fundamental questions of interest far beyond any single discipline such as economics or political science.

One conclusion I drew from this and similar experiences was that following my own interests regardless of where they led could occasionally be not only fun, but also productive. I also realized that three of the fields that have been especially helpful to me—evolutionary biology, artificial intelligence, and game theory—I had studied on my own. I now suggest to graduate students that they should never let coursework interfere with their education.

3. ABM facilitates interdisciplinary collaboration

I did not feel the need for a collaborator to conduct and analyze the tournaments. Nor did I feel the need for a collaborator to prove some general theorems about how co-operation based on reciprocity could get started and could resist invasion.[5] However, when I thought about the potential implications for evolutionary biology, I knew I was in over my head. I wrote to an entrant in one of my tournaments who happened to be a well-known evolutionary biologist, Oxford professor Richard Dawkins. He pointed me to another evolutionary biologist who happened to be at my own university, William Hamilton. I already knew of Hamilton's very influential theory of inclusive fitness.[6] So I gave him a call.

In his memoirs, Bill describes his reactions to this phone call.[7]

One day in the Museum of Zoology at Ann Arbor there came a phone call from a stranger asking what I knew about evolutionarily stable strategies and for some guidance to relevant literature. (p. 118)

Now on the phone to me was someone out of political science who seemed to have just the sort of idea I needed. A live games theorist was here on my own campus! Nervously, and rather the way a naturalist might hope to see his first mountain lion in the woods, I had long yearned for and dreaded an encounter with a games

---

[5] See Axelrod (1981).

[6] Dawkins himself had written a lucid exposition of Hamilton's theory of inclusive fitness in a book entitled *The Selfish Gene* (Dawkins 1976, 1989). Once you read this book, you will see why your genes can be considered "selfish" and how your selfish genes use you to get themselves reproduced—but not necessarily in ways that are to *your* advantage. Spooky.

[7] All quotes are from William D. Hamilton (2002).

theorist. How did they think? What were their dens full of? Axelrod on the phone sounded nice and, very surprising to me, he was more than a bit biological in his manner of thinking. I sensed at once a possibility that the real games theorists might be going to turn out to be a kind of kindred to us [biologists]. (p. 120)

Had Bill known of my long-standing interest in evolutionary theory, he might not have been quite so surprised that my thinking was more than a bit biological. For example, in high school I wrote a computer simulation to study hypothetical life forms and environments.[8] This early interest in evolution was nurtured during college by a summer at the University of Chicago's Committee on Mathematical Biology.

That first phone call led to a lunch where he proposed that we work together.

Soon after the lunch again I proposed that the work seemed so interesting biologically we might try writing it up for a joint paper in *Science*; [Axelrod's] contribution would be the basic ideas plus the description of his tournaments, and mine to add a natural scientist's style and some biological illustrations. (p. 122)

I was delighted to accept Bill's invitation to collaborate. Despite coming from different disciplines, Bill and I shared not only mathematical training, but also a desire to get at the heart of things. Bill had even published some work on the Prisoner's Dilemma, although he was hoping to get away from that when I dragged him back.

Bill's proposed division of labor turned out to be a reasonable description of how the collaboration developed. I gradually realized, however, just how much was included by Bill's modest formulation of adding "a natural scientist's style and some biological illustrations." Bill's naturalist's style included having at his fingertips an astonishing knowledge of species from bacteria to primates. His knowledge would be equivalent to an economist knowing much of what there is to know about hundreds, if not thousands, of companies of every type from GM and Microsoft to a self-employed sidewalk vendor.

His experience as a naturalist often gave him the capacity to check out the plausibility of an idea with pertinent examples right off the top of his head. It also helped him to generate surprising new ideas.

Bill's disciplinary training as an evolutionary biologist and a naturalist proved essential to making our theoretical work compelling to biologists. He was able to identify and exploit pertinent biological examples so that biologists could see what we were talking about. While not all of his proposed applications have been borne out, he was able to demonstrate the potential relevance of agent-based computer tournaments for the major

---

[8] The recognition I received for this work from the Westinghouse (now Intel) Science Talent Search contributed to my readiness ever since to follow my own instincts and not worry about what was in the mainstream of any particular discipline. The simulation had agents who responded to their environment, but was not an agent-based model because the agents neither interacted with each other, nor changed over time. In 1960–61, Northwestern University gave me some time on their one and only machine, an IBM 650 the size of four refrigerators. It had only 20k memory—about a millionth of my current laptop's memory.

biological puzzle of why individuals cooperate with unrelated others.[9] Second, he was able to explain what our contribution added to what was already understood about evolution. Specifically, he showed how our modeling work provides a solid foundation for many of the insights about altruism formulated years earlier by Rabert Trivers (1971). Bill was also able to show how our model could be used by other evolutionary biologists to formulate and test new hypotheses about animal behavior,[10] as well as explore dozens of variants of the simple iterated Prisoner's Dilemma.[11]

At the beginning, Bill and I took a while to get used to each other's style. For example, when I asked Bill a question he sometimes thought long and hard before saying a word. His face took on a blank look, his gaze was in the distance, and I could almost hear the wheels spinning inside his head for the longest time. I learned to be patient. When he finally spoke, it would be either a deep insight, or casual remark on a totally different subject.

Here is how Bill saw us working together.

> That brilliant cartoonist of the journal *American Scientist,* Sidney Harris, has a picture where a mathematician covers the blackboard with an outpouring of his formal demonstration. ... [I]t starts top left on the blackboard and ends bottom right with a triumphant 'QED'. Halfway down, though, one sees a gap in the stream where is written in plain English: 'Then a miracle occurs', after which the mathematical argument goes on. Chalk still in his hand, the author of this *quod est demonstrandum* now stands back and watches with a cold dislike an elderly mathematician who peers at the words in the gap and says: 'But I think you need to be a bit more explicit-here in step two.' I easily imagine myself to be that enthusiast with the chalk and I also think of many castings for the elderly critic. Yet how easy it is to imagine a third figure-Bob-in the background of this picture, saying cheerfully: 'But maybe he has something all the same, maybe that piece can be fixed up. What if...' (p. 123)

I shared Bill's surprise at how well we worked together. As he put it,

> I would have thought it a leg-pull at the time if someone had told me of a future when I would find it more rewarding to talk 'patterns' to political scientists rather than to fellow biologists. (p. 126)

Perhaps the most important thing we shared was our aesthetic sense.

---

[9] Bill was already well known for his rigorous treatment of how evolution might cause an individual to be altruistic toward a close relative (Hamilton, 1964). Because Hamilton showed how to treat the unit of selection as the gene rather than the individual to the gene, this work has been called "the only true advance since Darwin in our understanding of natural selection" (Trivers, 2000).

[10] For early confirmations in bats, fish and primates, as well as early extensions of the iterated Prisoner's Dilemma framework, see the sources cited in Axelrod and Dion (1988). Recently, even viruses have been found to play the Prisoner's Dilemma (Turner and Chao, 1999).

[11] For early developments of the theoretical framework, see Axelrod and Dion (1988). For a twenty year retrospective, see Hoffmann (2000).

[A]n intuitive understanding between us was immediate. Both of us always liked to be always understanding new things and to be listening more than talking; both of us had little inclination for the social manoeuvring, all the 'who-should-bow-lowest' stuff, which so often wastes time and adrenalin as new social intercourse starts. Bob is the more logical, but beyond this what we certainly share strongly is a sense for a hard-to-define aesthetic grace that may lurk in a proposition, that which makes one want to believe it before any proof and in the midst a confusion and even antagonism of details. Such grace in an idea seems often to mean that it is right. Rather as I have a quasi-professional artist as my maternal grandmother, Bob has one closer to him-his father. Such forebears perhaps give to both of us the streak that judges claims not in isolation but rather by the shapes that may come to be formed from their interlock, rather as brush strokes in a painting, shapeless or even misplaced considered individually, are overlooked as they join to create a whole... (p. 122)

I see a further connection between art and modeling. My father painted to express how he saw the world that day, highlighting what was important to him by leaving out what was not. Likewise, I see my modeling, especially my agent-based modeling, as an expression of how I see some social dynamic, highlighting what I regard as important, and leaving out everything else.

Our differing disciplinary backgrounds would show up in surprising ways, such our reactions to visiting the church where Shakespeare is buried. I pondered the social science question of why Shakespeare might have wanted others to read a mediocre poem on his gravestone, and Bill pondered the biological puzzle of why a very rare plant was growing on the fence outside the church.

Anyway, between us and with surprisingly little difficulty we pushed our paper into *Science*.[12] Once published it drew so much interest that it won us the Newcomb-Cleveland Prize as *Science's* supposed best paper for its year, 1981. (p. 123, 124)

4. ABM provides a useful multidisciplinary tool when the math is intractable

Agent-based modeling can also be useful for discovering regularities that might suggest theorems that can then be proved. For example, my finding that Tit for Tat did well playing with a wide variety of other strategies, led me to expect that something very general could be proved about the conditions under which Tit for Tat could withstand "invasion" by *any* other strategy. And so it turned out.[13]

---

[12] Axelrod and Hamilton (1981).

[13] See Proposition 2 in (Axelrod 1984, pp. 207–209). Taylor (1976) had already proved that Tit for Tat could resist invasion by several specific strategies, but the success of Tit for Tat with a wide range other strategies in the tournaments suggested to me that it was worthwhile to seek a theorem that would apply to *all* other strategies. By viewing Tit for Tat as a two-state finite automaton, I was able to prove such a general result.

A second collaboration with Bill Hamilton demonstrates another valuable characteristic of agent-based modeling: its ability to analyze problems by simulation when mathematical analysis is impossible.

When Bill took a very prestigious position at Oxford, we still kept in touch. We shared our on-going thinking. One day, about five or six years after our first collaboration was finished, Bill told me about a truly amazing theory he was developing. The theory proposed an answer to one of biology's largest unresolved puzzles: why have most large animals and plants evolved to reproduce sexually? The reason this is such a puzzle is that sexual reproduction has a huge cost: only half the population has offspring. What might be the advantage of sexual reproduction that is so great that it can overcome this two-fold cost compared to asexual reproduction?

There was already a serious contender whose leading advocate was the Russian geneticist Alexei Kondrashov. Kondrashov's explanation was based on the possibility that sexual reproduction might be helpful for bearing the cumulative burden of many generations of deleterious mutations. Bill's theory was completely different. Put simply, he thought of sexual reproduction as an adaptation to resist parasites.[14] This struck me as a totally bizarre, but intriguing idea.[15]

Bill explained to me that there was a serious problem with convincing others that his theory could, in fact, account for the two-for-one burden of sexual reproduction. The problem was that the equations that described the process were totally intractable when the genetic markers had more than more than two or three loci. Yet, the whole idea relies on there being many loci so that it would not be trivial for the parasites to match them. When I heard this, I responded to Bill with something like, "No problem. I know a method to simulate the evolution of populations with a lot of genetic markers. The method is called the Genetic Algorithm, and I've already used it to simulate a population of individuals each of whom has seventy genes."[16]

I explained to Bill that a computer scientist, John Holland, had been inspired by the success of biological evolution in finding "solutions" to difficult problems by means of competition among an evolving population of agents.[17] Based on the evolutionary analogue, including the possibility for sexual reproduction, Holland developed the Genetic Algorithm as an artificial intelligence technique. I could simply turn this technique

[14] Bill liked this formulation of mine, and we used it as the title of our paper.

[15] Bill's reasoning was that parasites are ubiquitous, and their short life spans give them the advantage of being able to adapt quickly to an ever-changing host population. If the host population reproduced *asexually*, a line of parasites that had evolved to mimic the genetic markers on the cells of one host would automatically be well adapted to mimic the genetic markers of its offspring. On the other hand, if the hosts reproduced sexually, their offspring would not be virtual carbon copies of either of their parents, and thus would not be as vulnerable to a line of parasites that had become adapted to match the genetic loci of one parent or the other.

[16] I used this evolutionary technique to avoid having to run new tournaments indefinitely. See Axelrod (1987). I had earlier developed a technique now known as replicator dynamics, to study an interacting population with many different types of individuals, but without any mutation to introduce new types (Axelrod, 1980b, and Axelrod, 1984, pp. 48–54).

[17] See Holland (1975, 1992), and Riolo (1992).

around and help Bill simulate biological evolution, with or without sex. Since Bill was used to thinking in terms of heterogeneous populations of autonomous individuals, he readily grasped the idea of agent-based modeling. He also grasped without difficulty that an agent-based simulation was capable of demonstrating that certain assumptions are sufficient to generate certain results, even if the same results could not be proven mathematically.[18]

So, working with a computer science graduate student, Reiko Tanese, we built an agent-based model with two co-evolving populations: hosts with long life spans, and parasites with short life spans. If a parasite interacted with a host of similar marker genes, it killed the host and reproduced. In the simulation, the parasite population would tend to evolve to concentrate in the region of the "genetic space" where there were many hosts. Thus, successful hosts tended to suffer from increasing numbers of deadly parasites, reducing the numbers of those hosts. Meanwhile, other types of hosts with very different genetic markers might thrive. Then the process would repeat itself as the population of parasites tracked the ever-changing population of hosts. The system would always be out of equilibrium.[19]

Bill was pleased with the results of our agent-based simulations. He felt that

> the notion I had started with, that even against sex's full halving inefficiency the problem could be solved by looking at the need of a population to manoeuvre against its many rapidly evolving parasites, with these differentiating resistance tendencies at many host loci (the more the better), had been vindicated. (p. 561)

> Returning to the story of the work, once Reiko under Bob's guidance had done the program, I experimented with it by e-mailing her or Bob with requests for chosen runs. At one point I visited the University of Michigan at Ann Arbor and worked for a fortnight intensively on modifications to the program with Reiko-this came after a bad patch of misunderstandings and unpromising runs that had caused us all to become somewhat pessimistic. (p. 606)

It seems to me that agent-based modeling is quite vulnerable to misunderstanding, even among the collaborators themselves. In our case the problem arose while we were exploring different ways to model host-parasite interaction. At one point Bill sent an e-mail from Oxford asking Reiko and me to undo our recent changes and try something else that he described. It wasn't until a month or so later that Bill noticed the unpromising runs might be caused by our simulation program not doing quite what he had in mind. We eventually traced the problem to a misunderstanding between us about

---

[18] Not proven by humans at least. Epstein, in this volume, points out that the premises of simulations can themselves be regarded as mathematical statements, and results as deductions derived from those statements.

[19] Agent-based models are convenient for studying out-of-equilibrium dynamics. Real economies may be perpetually out of equilibrium, for instance if there is continual innovation (Nelson and Winter, 1982). Systems far from equilibrium are notoriously difficult to analyze mathematically, and perhaps for that reason are often downplayed in neoclassical economics. Agent-based modeling allows the analysis systems that are far from equilibrium.

whether Bill's request to remove our recent changes referred to the previous day's work, or the previous week's work.[20]

> Daily Reiko sprinkled me and Bob, like tender house plants, with her floppy disks bearing her updated codes... (p. 607)

> Our model had achieved results that others had stated impossible with the tools we were allowing ourselves. Many of the dragons that had oppressed individual-advantage models in the past seemed to us to be slain. ...[O]ur explicit modeling of a large number of loci in a Red Queen situation[21] certainly was [new] and the increase of stability of sex that came with the growth of numbers of loci made the most dramatic feature in our results. (p. 602)

> It is the paper that I regard as containing the second most important of all my contributions to evolution theory.[22] That second joint paper of 1990 (actually mainly written some three or so years before) was to be the first model where sex proved itself able to beat any asex competitor immediately and under very widely plausible assumptions. (p. 560)

5. ABM can reveal unity across disciplines

So far, I have described my experiences of using agent-based modeling to bridge disciplines by addressing fundamental problems, by facilitating collaboration, and by avoiding intractable mathematics. Finally, I want to discuss an example of how an agent-based model designed for a specific problem in one discipline can sometimes be applied directly to an apparently quite different problem in another discipline.

My own specialty in political science is international security affairs. I wanted to predict alignments in war. I did not want to beg the question by taking into account any alliances the countries might have already formed. The problem is exemplified by the mutual hatred on the eve of World War II between Germany, Britain, and the Soviet

---

[20] While a mathematical proof can usually be checked for accuracy without great difficulty, the same can not be said for an agent-based simulation program. The frequency of this problem became evident when I was part of a team that tried to replicate the results from the published description of the eight agent-based models (Axtell et al., 1996). We found that in most cases it was not easy. In one case, it took us about four months to track the problem to an inconsistency between the published account and the actual code used to implement it. Results from macro-economic models are also notoriously difficult to replicate from published descriptions, even when the identical data set is used.

[21] Bill is referring here to the character in *Alice Through the Looking Glass* who says, "It takes all the running you can do, to keep in the same place."

[22] Hamilton et al. (1990). Bill regarded his most important paper to be the one that presented his formal theory of inclusive fitness (Hamilton, 1964). As mentioned earlier, Dawkins (1976, 1989) provides a lucid exposition of Hamilton's theory of inclusive fitness.

Union. If they all hated each other, what would predict their alignment into just two opposing sides when the war came?

The model began by assigning countries at random to one of two sides, and giving each country, one at a time, the opportunity to change sides if it would reduce the "stress" of its being aligned with countries they were repelled from and/or *not* aligned with countries they were attracted to. Naturally, the felt stress would also have taken into account the relative importance of each of the other countries. Scott Bennett, a political science graduate student, and I operationalized the pairwise propensities by combining five previously identified factors causing attraction or repulsion. These factors included things like shared religion and border disputes. We operationalized the importance of each country by the magnitude of its relative strength at the time. We then simulated the process using the seventeen European countries that became involved in World War II. No matter which of the 65 536 different alignments we started with, the agents always organized themselves into one of just two alignments. One of these two is almost exactly what happened in World War II.[23]

Around this time, I was invited to present my latest research at Michigan's Business School. After my talk, two economists from the school, Will Mitchell and Robert E. Thomas, came up to Scott and myself. They told us that our work reminded them of the business coalitions that often form to compete over whose preferred standard will dominate an industry. They said they had in mind the specific case in which eight computer companies joined one of the two coalitions that competed over which version of the UNIX operating system would prevail. We decided to see if we could account for the specific alignment of companies in the UNIX case. We used exactly the same theory, and simply adapted the measures of pairwise propensity and relative size so they made sense for the UNIX case. For example, we assumed that a company would find it more stressful to align with a company that was largely in the same market as it was, compared to a company that was mainly in a completely different market. We were delighted to find that the agent-based model of military alignments was also successful at predicting the pattern of strategic alignments among the eight computer companies involved in the UNIX case.[24]

6. ABM can be a hard sell

As noted earlier, my collaboration with Bill Hamilton on cooperation in biological systems was accepted for publication with little problem. Just the opposite was true of our

---

[23] See Axelrod and Bennett (1993). The one mistaken prediction was that Portugal with its fascist government would side with Germany and Italy, but it actually stayed with its long-term ally, Britain. The other alignment was essentially a pro-vs.-anti Communist alignment. On another point, economists sometimes ask me why the agents in this model might not keep switching sides forever. The short answer is that the pairwise propensities are symmetric, so "stress" provides a Lyapunov function.

[24] See Axelrod et al. (1995).

second collaboration. Our simulation of Bill's theory that sexual reproduction could be an adaptation to resist parasites had a hard time getting published.

First, we tried *Nature*, a leading scientific journal closely followed by biologists of all types. The referees had many complaints, chiefly about the robustness of our results. So, we did many more runs under a broad range of parameters to show that the explanation worked under a wide range of realistic conditions. We thought our second try had nailed our point.

> Nevertheless when the revised paper went back to the referees with these new experiments included, but with no change to our centralizing of the Homo-like life history, we found all our new points left uncommented and the manuscript rejected by the referees even more curtly than before. Two of them indeed dug out new objections they hadn't thought of [the] first time and claimed to see no substantial changes in the rest... (p. 608)

After our revised version was rejected at *Nature*, we submitted our paper to *Science*, another leading scientific journal widely read by biologists. We were also rejected by *Science*, which left us a little dejected.

> Failing with these I sent it in preliminary way to an editor of the Royal Society journals to see if they would be interested, but the comments I received were as discouraging as the rest. It particularly shamed me to have to tell Bob that even the society that supported me in general believed me to be over the hill on this topic... (p. 609)

> One of the puzzles about the dislike, even contempt, the work ... seemed to arouse in my evolutionary peers is that it was as if we had been unable to explain what we were thinking. ...And yet while one referee praised our style, another described the paper as written very badly; because neither said anything good about the ideas or content I presume that even the one that liked the writing found it a kind of eloquent twittering. (p. 601, 602)

> [T]he only intelligible claim in [one review] was that we had not reported on any simulations outside the range we had studied in detail. ... If one criticized every paper studying some feature of one-locus population genetics, for example, on grounds that it hadn't yet probed into even just possible two-locus complications (or hadn't reported having done so), a substantial fraction of the literature of population genetics would have stayed unpublished. (p. 613).

> Our statement that we had tested the model much more widely than we covered in the states we reported evidently wasn't believed, as also was the case with our description of the model. Several referees said this wasn't adequate; and yet it was quite as thoroughly described as models usually are in papers whose results rely on simulation. ... [In fact] a subsequent team (Richard Ladle and Rufus Johnstone, later joined by Olivia Judson) reproduced and extended our model purely [from] the paper's specification. Ladle and Johnstone did not even tell me they were working on this until our major results had been verified. (p. 610)

Bill was surprised by the difficulties we were having.

The above record of rejections probably actually isn't long compared with some that much more revolutionary yet valid papers have received from journals. What, for example, about the attempts of Alfred Wegener to publish on continental drift, or Ignaz Semmelweiss to publish on puerperal fever, or Richard Altmann on the symbiotic origin of the mitochondrion? On the other hand, at the time we were submitting neither Bob nor I was an unknown scientist and neither of us had a reputation for mistaken or trivial ideas. The number of suspicious and hostile referees we found had come, therefore, as a considerable surprise. (p. 609)

...my efforts to remould [our simulation] to appease the latest whims of referees ...never worked: the referees always had new objections; dislike for our solution seemed to be unbounded. (p. 562).

Nevertheless, we were dogged. We kept revising the paper to take into account, as best we could, the reviewers' criticisms. Finally, the fifth version was successful at the *Proceedings of the National Academy of Sciences, USA*. At last, two reviewers saw the point of our paper, and one was even enthusiastic.

Why was our agent-based model (Hamilton et al., 1990) such a hard sell? It was not because our model was less realistic than analytic models of evolution that had already been published, or our work did not break new ground, or that the problem was not important. So what was it? Bill thought about it this way:

Simulation in itself admittedly isn't understanding and various previous papers, including some of my own..., had already drawn attention to the kinds of possibilities we were now testing. The simpler analytical discussions and models, however, including again my own, all had had severe snags and none showed any chance to be general. Besides treating many loci and many parasites at once-obviously much closer to the real situation (and the importance of our studying truly many loci, not just three or four, cannot be overstated)-we had brought in a variable life history that I consider to be much more realistic than is typical in most evolutionary modelling... (p. 603)

Nor could anyone pretend that this theme of evolution of sex was a narrow one nor of specialist interest only: from Erasmus Darwin to the present time, sex has repeatedly been saluted as one of biology's supreme problems, perhaps its very greatest. Hence Bob Axelrod and I at first believed that our model, with its realism and its dramatic success under conditions others had deemed impossible for it, was virtually sure to be acceptable to one of the major general scientific journals such as *Science* or *Nature*. (p. 604, 605)

We suspected that part of the problem was that the reviewers were threatened by our application of Bill's theory to the case of human-like organisms—organisms similar to the reviewers themselves. It must not have been easy for them to accept that their own sexuality derived from the selective pressure of parasites.

Since we wanted to demonstrate that his theory could explain sexual reproduction in humans, Bill thought it was important that we include the salient characteristics of human reproduction. For instance, he wanted to include the fact that humans are not fertile for the first dozen or so years of their life. I, however, wanted our model to be as simple as possible to make it easier to understand and appreciate. This was the only significant disagreement we ever had. Since it was Bill's theory and Bill's audience, I deferred to his preferences in this regard. So one reason our model might have been so hard to sell is that it included some realistic details that may have obscured the logic of the simulation. On the other hand, Bill was probably right that had we *not* included these details, the reviewers would complain that we had not demonstrated the theory could account for sexual reproduction in humans. Sometimes you just can't win.[25]

Agent-based modeling is not alone in suffering from the inevitable trade-off between realism and clarity. Analytic models of economic, political, and social phenomena must deal with the same tradeoff.

There are at least two factors, however, which make it harder to sell an agent-based model than a model that can be analyzed mathematically. The first problem is that most reviewers (and potential readers) of theoretical work are familiar with the logic of deductive mathematics, but not with logic of agent-based modeling. Indeed, they often demand that the results of an agent-based model must be as general as the results of an analytic model. This point is illustrated by neoclassical economic models that rigorously demonstrate that (under certain assumptions) raising the minimum wage will lower total employment. Now suppose that an agent-based model demonstrates the same effect under less restrictive assumptions about the uniformity of the labor market, but much greater specificity about the value of the parameters describing the situation. A mathematically inclined reader is likely to want to know how robust the results are, and agent-based modeling may not be able to provide a definitive answer to that question.

A typical mathematical result might take the form "For all $A > 0$ and all $B > 0$, $f(A, B) > 0$" where f is some given function. An agent-based model typically needs to assume specific values for certain parameters in order for the simulation to run. The simulation might be run many times, with a range of positive values for A and B, and get the same result each time. But the reviewer can always say, "but have you tried $A = 1/9$, or $B = 10\,000\,000$? And if it works for those values, what about $A = B^2$ where B is some integer multiple of pi?" In general, there is always a question of the robustness of the results of a simulation, unless the simulation results suggest a theorem that can be proved analytically.

Even if the reviewer is satisfied with the range of parameter values that have been tested, he or she might think up some new variations of the model to inquire about.

---

[25] We might have tried another tactic. We could have first introduced a minimal version of the model to highlight the essential mechanisms to demonstrate that Bill's theory could, in principle, explain how sexual reproduction could overcome its two-fold cost. We could then have provided a more realistic and detailed simulation to show the theory also applied to situations characteristic of human life spans. Unfortunately, the journals we aimed for had such strict page limits that we were not able to write our paper this way.

Demands to check new variants of the model as well as new parametric values in the original model can make the review process seem almost endless. What is worse is that a reviewer with a not-so-legitimate problem with the submission can always use "insufficient" checks for robustness as a cover for a negative review.

Years later, Bill noticed that other researchers doing work related to his theory of sexual reproduction met with the same problem we did. Bill put a positive spin on it.

> [I]nsinuations of unreliability [i.e. insufficient checks for robustness] so extremely similar to those being directed at my work with Bob and Reiko ... tended to reassure me that our rejection didn't necessarily mean that... I'd completely lost my marbles. (p. 614)

7. Convergence within the ABM community can enhance the interdisciplinary value of ABM

In closing, I have three suggestions to facilitate interdisciplinary work with agent-based modeling.[26]

First, the agent-based modeling community should converge on standards for testing the robustness of an agent-based model. My own experience suggests that the lack of such standards can make agent-based modeling a hard sell. Just as the social sciences have converged on 0.05 as the minimal standard of statistical significance, the agent-based modeling community should converge on standards appropriate to the kinds of simulations we do.[27]

Second, the agent-based modeling community should converge on its tools. Just as there is a convergence on regression as one of the standard tools of statistics in the social sciences, there should be convergence on the basic tools for agent-based modeling. This is already underway. For instance, in models with a two-dimensional space, there is already something close to a consensus that unless there is a stated reason not to, the borders of the space should wrap around, e.g. making the top row adjacent to the bottom row. On the other hand, there is less consensus on whether the default assumption about whether a given cell should have four neighbors (the cells to the north, south, east and west) or eight neighbors (those four plus the diagonal cells).[28] Greater standardization of programming tools would also be helpful.[29]

---

[26] For my suggestions on how to actually do agent-based modeling, see Axelrod (1997a).

[27] For example, one might halve and double the base values of each parameter to see if the results hold up across this wide range. John Miller has proposed another possibility (Miller, 1998). He suggests searching for the largest and smallest values of each parameter that will maintain the central result. In other words, we should report what extreme values cause for the model to "break."

[28] These are called the Von Neumann neighborhood and the Moore neighborhood, respectively.

[29] This is easier said than done. An early attempt called Swarm has had limited success. With object oriented programming and sharable languages like Java, the prospects are better at least for shared libraries of commonly used procedures. Repast is a good example.

Finally, the agent-based community should converge on a set of fundamental concepts and results. Just as the content of a microeconomics course at any given level has become largely standardized, it would be helpful if the same would become possible for courses in agent-based modeling. Textbooks are one way in which this convergence could be promoted. Before then, however, candidates for the shared set of fundamentals could take the form of a topics or even specific readings that anyone interested in the field could be expected to know. An example of a strong candidate for inclusion is Schelling's well-known model of residential mobility that demonstrates how an emergent property like segregation can occur even if everyone is quite tolerant (Schelling, 1978).

Agent-based modelers actually know quite a bit about the possibilities for convergence in a heterogeneous population of autonomous agents—such as themselves.[30] Fortunately, the bottom-up form of convergence is already underway, but we need to be wary of convergence taking place only within rather than across disciplines.[31] As a step in this direction, Axelrod and Tesfatsion (2006) have developed a Guide to Newcomers to Agent-Based Modeling.[32] Perhaps we are approaching the time when it becomes possible to develop a more or less authoritative statement of proposed core readings and best practices. This volume itself is a major step in that direction, thereby facilitating the potential of agent-based modeling to serve as a bridge between disciplines.

References

Axelrod, R. (1980a). "Effective choice in the prisoner's dilemma". Journal of Conflict Resolution 24, 3–25. Included in revised form as part of Chapter 2 and Appendix A of Axelrod (1984).

Axelrod, R. (1980b). "More effective choice in the prisoner's dilemma". Journal of Conflict Resolution 24, 379–403. Included in revised form as part of Chapter 2 and Appendix A of Axelrod (1984).

Axelrod, R. (1981). "Emergence of cooperation among egoists". American Political Science Review 75, 306–318. Included in revised form as Chapter 3 and Appendix B of Axelrod (1984).

Axelrod, R. (1984). The Evolution of Cooperation. Basic Books, NY.

Axelrod, R. (1986). "An evolutionary approach to norms". American Political Science Review 80, 1095–1111. Included with an introduction in Axelrod (1997c).

Axelrod, R. (1987). "The evolution of strategies in the iterated prisoner's dilemma". In: Davis, L. (Ed.), Genetic Algorithms and Simulated Annealing. Pitman, London, pp. 32–41. Included with an introduction in Axelrod (1997c).

Axelrod , R. (1997a). "Advancing the art of simulation in the social sciences". In: Conte, R., Hegselmann, R., Terna, P. (Eds.), Simulating Social Phenomena. Springer, Berlin, pp. 21–40. Included with an introduction in Axelrod (1997c). An updated version of this paper is in The Japanese Journal of Management Information, Special Issue: Agent-Based Modeling, vol. 12, No. 3, Dec. 2003. This article is among the papers available at http://www-personal.umich.edu/~axe/.

[30] My two cents worth are models of the emergence of norms (Axelrod, 1986) and the dissemination of culture (Axelrod, 1997b).

[31] For an agent-based model of local convergence and global polarization, see Axelrod (1997b).

[32] The Guide is an Appendix to this volume, and is also available at http://www.econ.iastate.edu/tesfatsi/abmread.htm.

Axelrod, R. (1997b). "The dissemination of culture: a model with local convergence and global polarization". Journal of Conflict Resolution 41, 203–226.

Axelrod, R. (1997c). The Complexity of Cooperation: Agent-Based Models of Competition and Collaboration. Princeton University Press, Princeton, NJ. Some of the chapters in this book are available at http://www-personal.umich.edu/~axe/.

Axelrod, R., Hamilton, W.D. (1981). "The evolution of cooperation". Science 211, 1390–1396. Reprinted in modified form as Chapter 5 of Axelrod (1984).

Axelrod, R., Dion, D. (1988). "The further evolution of cooperation". Science 242, 1385–1390.

Axelrod, R., Bennett, S. (1993). "A landscape theory of aggregation". British Journal of Political Science 23, 211–233. Included with an introduction in Axelrod (1997c).

Axelrod, R., Tesfatsion, L. (2006). "A guide for newcomers to agent-based modeling", Appendix to this volume.

Axelrod, R., Mitchell, W., Thomas, R.E., Bennett, D.S., Bruderer, E. (1995). "Coalition formation in standard-setting alliances". Management Science 41, 1493–1508. Reprinted with introduction in Axelrod (1997c).

Axtell, R., Axelrod, R., Epstein, J., Cohen, M.D. (1996). "Aligning simulation models: a case study and results". Computational and Mathematical Organization Theory 1, 123–141.

Dawkins, R. (1976). The Selfish Gene. Oxford University Press, Oxford.

Dawkins, R. (1989). "The Selfish Gene", 2nd edn. Oxford University Press, Oxford.

Hamilton, W.D. (1964). "The genetical evolution of social behaviour I and II". Journal of Theoretical Biology 7, 1–52.

Hamilton, W.D. (2002). "The evolution of sex". In: Narrow Roads of Gene Land, The Collected Papers of W.D. Hamilton, vol. 2. Oxford University Press, Oxford, pp. 117–132, 561–566, and 601–615.

Hamilton, W.D., Axelrod, R., Tanese, R. (1990). "Sexual reproduction as an adaptation to resist parasites". Proceedings of the National Academy of Sciences USA 87, 3566–3573.

Hoffmann, R. (2000). "Twenty years on: the evolution of cooperation revisited". Journal of Artificial Societies and Social Simulation 3 (2). Available at http://www.soc.surrey.ac.uk/JASSS./3/2/forum/1.html.

Holland, J.H. (1975). Adaptation in Natural and Artificial Systems: An Introductory Analysis With Applications to Biology, Control, and Artificial Intelligence. University of Michigan Press, Ann Arbor, MI. Reissued MIT Press, Cambridge, MA, 1992.

Holland, J.H. (1992). "Genetic algorithms". Scientific American (July), 44ff.

Luce, R.D., Raiffa, H. (1957). Games and Decisions, Introduction and Critical Survey. Wiley, York New.

Miller, J.H. (1998). "Active nonlinear tests (ANTs) of complex simulations models". Management Science 44, 820–830.

Nelson, R., Winter, S.G. (1982). An Evolutionary Theory of Economic Change. Harvard University Press, Cambridge.

Riolo, R.L. (1992). "Survival of the fittest bits". Scientific American (July), 89ff.

Samuel, A. (1959). "Some studies in machine learning using the game of checkers". IBM Journal of Research and Development 3 (3), 210–229.

Schelling, T. (1978). Micromotives and Macro Behavior. Norton, NY.

Taylor, M. (1976). Anarchy and Cooperation. Wiley, New York.

Trivers, R. (1971). "The evolution of reciprocal altruism". Quarterly Journal of Biology 46, 35–57.

Trivers, R. (2000). "Obituary: William Donald Hamilton (1936–2000)". Nature 404, 828.

Turner, P.E., Chao, L. (1999). "Prisoner's dilemma in an RNA virus". Nature 398, 367–368.

Wu, J., Axelrod, R. (1995). "How to cope with noise in the iterated prisoner's dilemma". Journal of Conflict Resolution 39, 183–189. Reprinted with an introduction in Axelrod (1997c).

Chapter 34

REMARKS ON THE FOUNDATIONS OF AGENT-BASED GENERATIVE SOCIAL SCIENCE

JOSHUA M. EPSTEIN[*,†]

The Brookings Institution, 1755 Massachusetts Avenue, NW, Washington, DC 20036, USA
url: http://www.brookings.edu/scholars/jepstein.htm

Contents

[*] Joshua M. Epstein is a Senior Fellow in Economic Studies at The Brookings Institution, a member of The Brookings-Johns Hopkins Center on Social and Economic Dynamics and an External Faculty member of The Santa Fe Institute.

[†] For thoughtful comments on this chapter, the author thanks Claudio Cioffi-Revilla, Samuel D. Epstein, Carol Graham, Ross Hammond, Kislaya Prasad, Brian Skyrms, Leigh Tesfatsion, and Peyton Young. For assistance in preparing the manuscript for publication, he thanks Danielle Feher.

Handbook of Computational Economics, Volume 2. Edited by Leigh Tesfatsion and Kenneth L. Judd
© 2006 Elsevier B.V. *All rights reserved*
DOI: 10.1016/S1574-0021(05)02034-4

Abstract

This chapter treats a variety of epistemological issues surrounding generative explanation in the social sciences, and discusses the role of agent-based computational models in generative social science.

Keywords

generative social science, agent-based modeling, philosophy of social science

JEL classification: A12, B41, C63, C65

1. Generative explanation

The scientific enterprise is, first and foremost, *explanatory*. While agent-based modeling can change the social sciences in a variety of ways, in my view its central contribution is to facilitate *generative* explanation [see Epstein (1999)]. To the generativist, explaining macroscopic social regularities, such as norms, spatial patterns, contagion dynamics, or institutions requires that one answer the following question:

> *How could the autonomous local interactions of heterogeneous boundedly rational agents generate the given regularity?*

Accordingly, to explain macroscopic social patterns, we generate—or "grow"—them in agent models. This represents a departure from prevailing practice. It is fair to say that, overwhelmingly, game theory, mathematical economics, and rational choice political science are concerned with equilibria. In these quarters, "explaining an observed social pattern" is essentially understood to mean "demonstrating that it is the Nash equilibrium (or a distinguished Nash equilibrium) of some game."

By contrast, to the generativist, it does *not* suffice to demonstrate that, if a society of rational (*homo economicus*) agents were placed in the pattern, no individual would unilaterally depart—the Nash equilibrium condition. Rather, to explain a pattern, one must show how a population of cognitively plausible agents, interacting under plausible rules, could actually arrive at the pattern on time scales of interest. The motto, in short, is [Epstein (1999)]: *If you didn't grow it, you didn't explain it.* Or, in the notation of first-order logic:

$$\forall x(\neg Gx \supset \neg Ex). \tag{1}$$

To explain a macroscopic regularity x is to furnish a suitable microspecification that suffices to generate it.[1] The core request is hardly outlandish: To explain a macro-x, please show how it could arise in a plausible society. Demonstrate how a set of recognizable— heterogeneous, autonomous, boundedly rational, locally interacting—agents could actually get there in reasonable time. The agent-based computational model is a new, and especially powerful, instrument for constructing such demonstrations of generative sufficiency.

2. Features of agent-based models

As reviewed in Epstein and Axtell (1996) and Epstein (1999), key features of agent-based models typically include the following:[2]

---

[1] In slightly more detail, if we let $M = \{i: i \text{ is a microspecification}\}$ and let $G(i, x)$ denote the proposition that i generates x, then the proposition Gx can be expressed as $\exists i\, G(i, x)$. Then, longhand, the motto becomes: $\forall x(\neg \exists i\, G(i, x) \supset \neg Ex).$

[2] I do not claim that every agent-based model exhibits all these features. My point is that the explanatory *disiderata* enumerated (heterogeneity, local interactions, bounded rationality, etc.) are easily arranged in agent-based models.

- *Heterogeneity*. Representative agent methods—common in macroeconomics—are not used in agent-based models. Nor are agents aggregated into a few homogeneous pools. Rather, every individual is explicitly represented. And these individuals may differ from one another in myriad ways: by wealth, preferences, memories, decision rules, social network, locations, genetics, culture, and so forth, some or all of which may adapt or change endogenously over time.
- *Autonomy*. There is no central, or "top down," control over individual behavior in agent-based models. Of course, there will generally be feedback between macrostructures and microstructures, as where newborn agents are conditioned by social norms or institutions that have taken shape endogenously through earlier agent interactions. In this sense, micro and macro will, in general, co-evolve. But as a matter of model specification, no central controllers (e.g., Walrasian auctioneers) or higher authorities are posited *ab initio*.
- *Explicit space*. Events typically transpire on an explicit space, which may be a landscape of renewable resources, as in Epstein and Axtell (1996), an *n*-dimensional lattice, a dynamic social network, or any number of other structures. The main *desideratum* is that the notion of "local" be well-posed.
- *Local interactions*. Typically, agents interact with neighbors in this space (and perhaps with sites in their vicinity). Uniform mixing (mass action kinetics) is generically not the rule. Relatedly, many agent-based models, following Herbert Simon, also assume:
- *Bounded rationality*. There are two components of this: bounded information and bounded computing power. Agents have neither global information nor infinite computational capacity. Although they are typically purposive, they are not global optimizers; they use simple rules based on local information.
- *Non-equilibrium dynamics*. Non-equilibrium dynamics are of central concern to agent modelers, as are large-scale transitions, "tipping phenomena," and the emergence of macroscopic regularity from decentralized local interaction. These are sharply distinguished from equilibrium existence theorems and comparative statics, as is discussed below.

3. Recent expansion

The literature of agent-based models has grown to include a number of good collections (e.g., The Sackler Colloquium, *Proceedings of the National Academy of Sciences, 2002*), special issues of scholarly journals (*Computational Economics, 2001, The Journal of Economic Dynamics and Control, 2004*), numerous individual articles in academic journals (such as *Computational and Mathematical Organization Theory*), the science journals (*Nature, Science*), and books [e.g., Epstein and Axtell (1996), Axelrod (1997), Cederman (1997)]. New journals (e.g., *The Journal of Artificial Societies and Social Simulation*) are emerging, computational platforms are competing (e.g., Ascape, Repast, Swarm, Mason). International societies for agent-based modeling are being formed. Courses on agent-based modeling are being offered at major universities. Conferences in the U.S., Europe, and Asia are frequent, and agent-based modeling is receiving considerable attention in the press. The landscape is very different than it was a decade ago.

4. Epistemological issues

Einstein wrote that, "Science without epistemology is—in so far as it is thinkable at all—primitive and muddled." [Pais (1982)]. Given the rapid expansion of agent-based modeling, it is an appropriate juncture at which to sort out and address certain epistemological issues surrounding the approach. In particular, and without claiming comprehensiveness, the following issues strike me as fundamentally important, and in need of clarification, both within the agent modeling community and among its detractors.

(1) Generative sufficiency vs. explanatory necessity.

(2) Generative agent-based models vs. explicit mathematical models.

(3) Generative explanation vs. deductive explanation.

(4) Generative explanation vs. inductive explanation.

(5) Generality of agent models.

I will attempt to address these and a variety of related issues. At several points, there will be a need to distinguish claims from their converses. The first example of this follows.

4.1. Generative sufficiency

The generativist *motto* (1) cited above was:

$$\forall x (\neg Gx \supset \neg Ex).$$

If you didn't grow it, you didn't explain it. It is important to note that we reject the converse claim. Merely to generate is not necessarily to explain (at least not well). A microspecification might generate a macroscopic regularity of interest in a patently absurd—and hence non-explanatory—way. For instance, it might be that Artificial Anasazi [Axtell et al. (2002)] arrive in the observed (true Anasazi) settlement pattern stumbling around backward and blindfolded. But one would not adopt that picture of individual behavior as explanatory. In summary, *generative sufficiency is a necessary, but not sufficient condition for explanation.*

Of course, in principle, there may be competing microspecifications with equal generative sufficiency, none of which can be ruled out so easily. The mapping from the set of microspecifications to the macroscopic *explanandum* might be many-to-one. In that case, further work is required to adjudicate among the competitors.

For example, if the competing models differ in their rules of individual behavior, appropriate laboratory psychology experiments may be in order to determine the more plausible empirically. In my own experience, given a macroscopic *explanandum*, it is challenging to devise *any* rules that suffice to generate it. In principle, however, the search could be mechanized. One would metrize the set of macroscopic patterns, so that the distance from a generated pattern to the target pattern (the pattern to be explained) could be computed. The "fitter" a microspecification, the smaller the distance from its generated macrostructure to the empirical target. Given this definition of fitness, one would then encode the space of permissible micro-rules and search it mechanically—with a genetic algorithm, for example (as in Crutchfield and Mitchell, 1995).

In any event, the first point is that the motto (1) is a criterion for explanatory candidacy. There may be multiple candidates and, as in any other science, selection among them will involve further considerations.[3]

4.2. The indictment: no equations, not deductive, not general

Plato observed that the doctors would make the best murderers. Likewise, in their heart of hearts, leading practitioners of any approach know themselves to be its most capable detractors. I think it is healthy for experienced proponents of any approach to explicitly formulate its most damaging critique and, if possible, address it. In that spirit, it seems to me that among skeptics toward agent modeling, the central indictment is tripartite: First, that in contrast to mathematical "hard" science, there are no equations for agent-based models. Second, that agent models are not deductive;[4] and third, that they are *ad hoc*, not general. I will argue that the first two claims are false and that, at this stage in the field's development, the third is unimportant.

4.3. Equations exist

The oft-claimed distinction between computational agent models, and equation-based models is illusory. Every agent model is, after all, a computer program (typically coded in a structured or object-oriented programming language). As such, each is clearly Turing computable (computable by a Turing machine). But, for every Turing machine, there is a unique corresponding and equivalent partial recursive function [see Hodel (1995)].

This is precisely the function class constructible from the zero function, the successor function, and the "pick out" or projection function (the three so-called initial functions) by finite applications of composition (substitution), bounded minimization, and—the really distinctive manipulation—*primitive recursion*. This, as the defining formula (Figure 1) suggests, can be thought of as a kind of generalized induction.

[See Hamilton (1988), Boolos and Jeffrey (1989), Epstein and Carnielli (1989), or Hodel (1995) for a technical definition of this class of functions.] So, in principle, one

---

[3] As noted, empirical plausibility is one such. Theoretical economy is another. In generative linguistics, for example, S.D. Epstein and N. Hornstein (Epstein and Hornstein, 1999) convincingly argue that minimalism should be central in selecting among competing theories. See pp. ix–xviii.

[4] Not everyone who asserts that computational agent modeling is non-deductive necessarily regards it as a defect. See, for example, Axelrod (1997).

$$h(\vec{x}, 0) = f(\vec{x})$$
$$h(\vec{x}, n + 1) = g(\vec{x}, n, h(\vec{x}, n))$$

Figure 1. Scheme for primitive recursion.

could cast any agent-based computational model as an explicit set of mathematical formulas (recursive functions). In practice, these formulas might be extremely complex and difficult to interpret. But, speaking technically, they surely exist. Indeed, one might have called the approach "recursive social science," "effectively computable social science," "constructive social science," or any number of other equivalent things. The use of "generative" was inspired by Chomsky's usage [Chomsky (1965)]. In any case, the issue is not whether equivalent equations exist, but which representation (equations or programs) is most illuminating.

To all but the most adept practitioners, the recursive function representation would be quite unrecognizable as a model of social interaction, while the equivalent agent model is immediately intelligible as such. However, at the dawn of the calculus, the same would doubtless have been true of differential equations. It is worth noting that recursive function theory is still very young, having developed only in the 1930s. And, it is virtually unknown in the social sciences. It is the mathematical formalism directly isomorphic [see Jeffrey (1991)] to computer programs, and over time, we may come to feel as comfortable with it as we now do with differential equations. Moreover, it is worth noting that various agent-based models have, in fact, been revealingly mathematized using other, more familiar, techniques. [See Dorofeenko and Shorish (2002), Pollicot and Weiss (2001), Young (1998).]

In sum, the first element of the indictment, that agent models are "just simulations" for which no equations exist, is simply false. Moreover, even if equivalent equations are not in hand, computational agent models have the advantage that they can be run thousands of times to produce large quantities of clean data. These can then be analyzed to produce a robust statistical portrait of model performance over the parameter ranges (and rule variations) of interest.

This critique, moreover, betrays a certain naiveté about contemporary equation-based modeling in many areas of applied science, such as climate modeling. The mathematical models of interest are huge systems of nonlinear reaction diffusion equations. In practice, they are not solved analytically, but are approximated computationally. So, the opposition of analytically soluble mathematical models on the one hand, and computational models on the other, while conceptually enticing, is quite artificial in practice.

4.4. Agent models deduce

Another misconception is that the explicit equation-based approach is deductive, whereas the agent-based computational approach is not. This, too, is incorrect. Every realization of an agent model is a *strict deduction*. There are a number of ways to establish this. Perhaps the most direct is to note that it follows from the previous point.

Every program can be expressed in recursive functions. But recursive functions are computed deterministically from initial values. They are mechanically (effectively) computable—in principle by hand with pencil and paper. Given the nth (including the initial) state of the system, the $(n + 1)$st state is computable in a strictly mechanical and deterministic way by recursion. Since this mechanical procedure is obviously deductive, so is each realization of an agent model.

A more sweeping equivalence can be established, in fact. It can be shown that Turing machines, recursive functions, and first-order logic itself (the system of deduction *par excellence*) are all strictly intertranslatable [see Hodel (1995)]. So, in a rigorous sense, every state generated in an agent model is literally a theorem. Since, accepting our motto, to explain is to generate (but not conversely), and to generate a state is to deduce it as a theorem, we are led to assert that to explain a pattern is to show it to be theorematic.

A third, slightly less rigorous way to think of it is this. Every agent program begins in some configuration x—a set of initial (agent) states analogous to axioms—and then repeatedly updates by rules of the form; if x then y. But, $\{x, x \supset y\}$ is just *modus ponens*, so the model as a whole is ultimately one massive inference in a Hilbert-type deductive system. To "grow" a pattern p (and to explain a pattern p) is thus to show that it is one of these terminal y's—in effect, that it is theorematic, very much as in the classic hypothetico-deductive picture of scientific explanation.

4.5. What about randomness?

If every run is a strict deduction, what about stochasticity, a common feature of many agent models? Stochastic realizations are also strict deductions. In a computer, random numbers are in fact produced by strictly deterministic pseudo-random number generators. For example, the famous linear congruential method [Knuth (1998)] to generate a series of pseudo-random numbers is as follows:

Define: m, the modulus ($m > 0$); a, the multiplier ($0 \leq a \leq m$); c, the increment ($0 \leq c \leq m$), and $x(0)$, the seed, or staring value ($0 \leq x(0) \leq m$). Then, the (recursion) scheme for generating the pseudo-random sequence is given in Figure 2, for $n \geq 0$:

This determinism is why, when we save the seed and re-run the program, we get exactly the same run again.

$$x(n + 1) = (ax(n) + c \bmod m)$$

Figure 2. Linear congruential method.

4.6. What types of propositions are deduced?

In principle, the only objects we ever technically deduce are *propositions*. When we deduce the Fundamental Theorem of Calculus, we deduce the proposition: "The definite integral of a continuous real-valued function on an interval is equal to the difference of an anti-derivative's values at the interval's endpoints." The result is normally expressed in mathematical notation, but, in principle, it is a proposition statable in English.[5] In turn, we explain an empirical regularity when that regularity is rendered as a proposition and that proposition is deduced from premises we accept. For example, we *explain* Galileo's leaning Tower of Pisa observation (i.e., that objects of unequal masses dropped from the same height land simultaneously) by strictly deducing, from Newton's Second Law and the Law of Universal Gravitation, the following proposition: "The acceleration of a freely falling body near the surface of the earth is independent of its mass."

Well, if agent models explain by generating, and thus deducing, and if, as I have just argued, the only deducible objects are propositions, the question arises: what sorts of propositions are deduced when agent models explain? In many important cases, the answer is: a normal form.

4.7. Social science as the satisfaction of normal forms

We explain a pattern when the pattern is expressed as a proposition and the proposition is deduced from premises we accept. Seen in this light, many of the macroscopic patterns we, as social scientists, are trying to explain are expressible as large disjunctive normal forms, DNFs. In general a DNF, δ has the logical form below

$$\delta = \bigvee_{i=1}^{n} \bigwedge_{j=1}^{m} \phi_{ij}$$

where ϕ_{ij} is a statement form [see Hamilton (1988)]. Clearly, this discussion applies to arbitrarily large, but *finite,* populations.

---

[5] In principal, it can be further broken down into statements about limits of sums, and so forth. As a completely worked out simple example, consider the mathematical equation

$$\lim_{x \to 2} x^2 = 4. \tag{2}$$

It asserts: "The limit of the square of x, as x approaches two, is four." In further detail, it is the following claim:

$$\forall (\varepsilon > 0) \exists (\delta > 0)[0 < |x - 2| < \delta \Rightarrow |x^2 - 4| < \varepsilon]. \tag{3}$$

In English, "For every number epsilon greater than zero, there exists a number delta greater than zero such that if the absolute value of the difference between x and 2 is strictly between zero and delta, then the absolute value of the difference between the square of x and four is less than epsilon." The fact that it is easier to manipulate and compute with mathematical symbols than with words may say something interesting about human psychology, but it does not demonstrate any limit on the precision or expressive power of English.

Example 1. Distributions

Suppose, then, that we are trying to explain a skewed wealth distribution observed in some finite population of agents. For simplicity's sake, imagine three agents: A, B, and C. And suppose we observe that 6 indivisible wealth units (the country's GNP) are distributed as 3 : 2 : 1. That is the empirical target; and our model will be deemed a success if it grows that distribution, *regardless of who has what*. What that means is that the successful model will generate any one of the six conjunctions in the following DNF, shown in braces (where A3 means "Agent A has 3 units," and so forth):

> {
> $(A1 \wedge B2 \wedge C3) \vee$
> $(A1 \wedge B3 \wedge C2) \vee$
> $(A2 \wedge B1 \wedge C3) \vee$
> $(A2 \wedge B3 \wedge C1) \vee$
> $(A3 \wedge B1 \wedge C2) \vee$
> $(A3 \wedge B2 \wedge C1)$
> }

The model succeeds if it grows any one of these conjuncts, that is, a conjunction whose truth makes the DNF true.

Example 2. Spatial patterns

Likewise, suppose we are trying to model segregation in a population composed of two white and two black agents (W1, W2, B1, B2) arranged on a line with four positions: 1, 2, 3, 4. The model works if it generates two contiguous agents of the same color, followed by two contiguous agents of the other color. As above, we don't care who is where so long as we get segregation on the line. The truth of any of the eight conjunctions of the following DNF will therefore suffice (here W12 denotes the proposition: "white agent 1 occupies position 2"):

> {
> $(W11 \wedge W22 \wedge B13 \wedge B24) \vee$
> $(W11 \wedge W22 \wedge B23 \wedge B14) \vee$
> $(W21 \wedge W12 \wedge B13 \wedge B24) \vee$
> $(W21 \wedge W12 \wedge B23 \wedge B14) \vee$
> $(B11 \wedge B22 \wedge W13 \wedge W24) \vee$
> $(B11 \wedge B22 \wedge W23 \wedge W14) \vee$

$(B21 \wedge B12 \wedge W13 \wedge W24) \vee$

$(B21 \wedge B12 \wedge W23 \wedge W14)$

}.

Again, success in generating "segregation" consists in generating any one of these conjunctions. That suffices to make the DNF true. While this exposition has been couched in terms of wealth distributions and distributions of spatial position, it obviously generalizes to distributions of myriad sorts (e.g., size and power), and with straightforward modification, to sequences of patterns over time. A dynamic sequence of patterns would, in fact, be a Conjunctive Normal Form (CNF), each term of which is a DNF of the sort just discussed.[6]

4.8. Generative implies deductive, but not conversely: nonconstructive existence

A generative explanation is a deductive one. Generative implies deductive. The converse, however, does not apply. It is possible to deduce without generating. Not all deductive argument has the constructive character of agent-based modeling. Nonconstructive existence proofs are clear examples. Often, these take the form of *reductio ad absurdum*[7] arguments, which work as follows.

Suppose we wish to prove the existence of an x with some property (e.g., that it is an equilibrium). We take as an axiom the so-called Law of the Excluded Middle (LEM), implying that either x exists or x does not exist. Symbolically:

$$\exists x \vee \neg \exists x.$$

One of those *must* be true. Next, we assume that x does not exist and derive a contradiction. That is, we show that

$$\neg \exists x \supset [p \wedge \neg p].$$

Since contradictions are always False, this has the form:

$$\neg \exists x \supset F.$$

But this implication can be True only if the antecedent, $\neg \exists x$, is False. From this it follows from the LEM that $\exists x$ is True and *voila*: the x in question must exist!

But we have failed to exhibit x, or specify any algorithm that would generate it, patently violating our generative motto (1). We have failed to show that x is generable at all, much less that it is generable on time scales of interest. But, the existence argument is nonetheless deductive.

---

[6] The general problem of satisfying an n-term CNF is NP-Complete. Garey and Johnson (1979). Based on this observation, it is tempting to conjecture that nonequilibrium social science—suitably cast as CNF satisfaction—is computationally hard in a rigorous sense.

[7] Reduction to an absurdity.

Now, there are deductive and nonconstructive existence proofs that do not use *reductio ad absurdum*. One of my favorites is the beautiful and startling index theoretic proof that, in regular economies, the number of equilibria must be an odd integer [see Mas-Colell et al. (1995), Epstein (1997)]. This proof gives no clue how to compute the equilibria. Like *reductio*, it fails to show the equilibria to be generable at all, much less on time scales of interest. But, the existence argument is nonetheless deductive.

Hence, if we insist that explanation requires generability, we are led to the position that deductive arguments can be non-explanatory. *Generative explanation is deductive, but deduction is not necessarily explanatory.*

We have addressed the first two points of the indictment: that there are no equations, and that agent modeling is not deductive. The third issue was the generality of agent models. I would like to approach this topic by a seemingly circuitous route, extending the preceding points on existence and generability into the areas of incompleteness and computational complexity.

4.9. Incompleteness (attainability at all) and complexity (attainability on time scales of interest) in social science

As background, in mathematical logic, there is a fundamental distinction between a statement's being *true* and its being *provable*. I believe that in mathematical social science there is an analogous and equally fundamental distinction between a state of the system (e.g., a strategy distribution) being an *equilibrium* and its being *attainable (generable)*. I would like to discuss, therefore, the parallel between the following two questions: (1) Is every true statement provable? and (2) Is every equilibrium state attainable?

In general, we are interested in the distinction between *satisfaction* of some criterion (like being true, or being an equilibrium) and *generability* (like being provable through repeated application of inference rules, or being attainable through repeated application of agent behavioral rules).

Now, mathematico-logical systems in which every truth is provable are called *complete*.[8] The great mathematician David Hilbert, and most mathematicians at the turn of the Twentieth Century, had assumed that all mathematical systems of interest were complete, that all truths statable in those systems were also provable in them (i.e., were deducible from the system's axioms via the system's inference rules). A major objective of the so-called Hilbert Programme for mathematics was to prove precisely this. It came as a tremendous shock when, in 1931, Kurt Godel proved precisely the opposite: *all sufficiently rich*[9] *mathematical systems are incomplete.* In all such systems, there are true statements that are unprovable! Indeed, he showed that there were true statements that

---

[8] Sometimes the terms *adequate* or *analytical* are used.

[9] For a punctilious characterization of precisely those formal systems to which the theorem applies, see Smullyan (1992).

were neither provable nor refutable in the relevant systems—they were *undecidable*.[10] [See Godel (1931), Smullyan (1992), Hamilton (1988)].

Now, truth is a special criterion that a logical formula may *satisfy*. For example, given an arbitrary formula of the sentential calculus, its truth (i.e., its tautologicity) can be evaluated mechanically, using truth tables. Provability, by contrast, is a special type of *generability*. A formula is provable if, beginning with a distinguished set of "starting statements" called *axioms*, it can be ground out—attained, if you will–by repeated application of the system's rule(s) of inference.

Equilibrium (Nash equilibrium, for example) is strictly analogous to truth: it too is a criterion that a state (a strategy distribution) may satisfy. And the Nash "equilibrium-ness" of a strategy configuration (just like the truth of a sentential calculus formula) can be checked mechanically.

I venture to say that most contemporary social scientists—analogous to the Hilbertians of the 1920s—assume that if a social configuration is a Nash equilibrium, then it must also be attainable. In short, the implicit assumption in contemporary social science is that these systems are *complete*.

However, we are finding that this is not the case. Epstein and Hammond (2002) offer a simple agent-based game almost all of whose equilibria are unattainable outright. More mathematically sophisticated examples of incompleteness include Prasad's result, based on the unsolvability of Hilbert's 10th problem:

> For n-player games with polynomial utility functions and natural number strategy sets the problem of finding an equilibrium is not computable. There does not exist an algorithm which will decide, for any such game, whether it has an equilibrium or not... When the class of games is specified by a finite set of players, whose choice sets are natural numbers, and payoffs are given by polynomial functions, the problem of devising a procedure which computes Nash equilibria is unsolvable. [Prasad (1997)]

Other examples of uncomputable (existent) equilibria include Foster and Young (2001), Lewis (1985, 1992a, 1992b), and Nachbar (1997). Some equilibria are unattainable outright.

A separate issue in principle, but one of great practical significance, is whether attainable equilibria can be attained on time scales of interest to humans. Here, too, we are finding models in which the waiting time to (attainable) equilibria scales exponentially in some core variable. In the agent-based model of economic classes of Axtell et al. (2001), we find that the waiting time to equilibrium is exponential in both the number of agents and the memory length per agent, and is astronomical when the first exceeds 100 and the latter 10. Likewise, the number of time steps (rounds of play) required to reach the attainable equilibria of the Epstein and Hammond (2002) model was shown to grow exponentially in the number of agents.

---

[10] Importantly, he did so *constructively*, displaying a (self-referential) true statement that is *undecidable*; that is, neither it nor its negation are theorems of the relevant system.

One wonders how the core concerns and history of economics would have developed if, instead of being inspired by continuum physics and the work of Lagrange and Hamilton [see Mirowski (1989)]—blissfully unconcerned as it is with effective computability—it had been founded on Turing. Finitistic issues of computability, learnability, attainment of equilibrium (rather than mere existence), problem complexity, and undecidability, would then have been central from the start. Their foundational importance is only now being recognized. As Duncan Foley summarizes,

> The theory of computability and computational complexity suggest that there are two inherent limitations to the rational choice paradigm. One limitation stems from the possibility that the agent's problem is in fact undecidable, so that no computational procedure exists which for all inputs will give her the needed answer in finite time. A second limitation is posed by computational complexity in that even if her problem is decidable, the computational cost of solving it may in many situations be so large as to overwhelm any possible gains from the optimal choice of action. [See Albin (1998).]

For fundamental statements, see Simon (1982, 1987), Hahn (1991), and Arrow (1987). Of course, beyond these *formal* limits on canonical rationality, there is the body of evidence from psychology and laboratory behavioral economics that *homo sapiens* just doesn't behave (in his decision-making) like *homo economicus*.

Now, the mere fact that an idealization (e.g., *homo economicus*) is not accurate in detail is not grounds for its dismissal. To say that a theory should be dismissed because it is "wrong" is vulgar. Theories are idealizations. There are no frictionless planes, ideal gases, or point masses. But these are useful idealizations in physics. However, in social science, it is appropriate to ask whether the idealization of individual rationality in fact illuminates more than it obscures. By empirical lights, that is quite clearly in doubt.

This brings us to the issue of generality. The entire rational choice *project*, if you will, is challenged by (1) incompleteness and outright uncomputability, by (2) computational complexity (even of computable equilibria), and by (3) powerful psychological evidence of framing effects and myriad other systematic human departures from canonical rationality. Yet, the social science theory that enjoys the greatest formal generality[11] (and mathematical elegance) is precisely the rational choice theory.

4.10. Generality is quantification over sets

Now, generality has to do with quantification. Universal gravitation says that *for any two masses* whatsoever, the attractive gravitational force is inversely proportional to the square of the separation distance. Mechanics quantifies over the set of all masses. Axiomatic general equilibrium theory quantifies over the set of all consumers in the

---

[11] Here, I mean generality in the theory's formal statement, not in its range of successful empirical application.

economy, positing constrained utility maximization *for every agent* in the system. Rational choice theory likewise posits expected utility maximization for all actors.

Clearly, agent modelers do not quantify over sets this big. There is a great deal of experimentation with tags, imitation, evolution, learning, bounded rationality, and zero-intelligence traders, for example. In many cases, however, the experiment is motivated by responsiveness to data. Empirically successful (generatively sufficient) behavioral rules for the Artificial Anasazi of 900 A.D. probably *should not* look much like the agent rules in the Axtell–Epstein (Axtell and Epstein, 1999) model of U.S. retirement norms, which in turn may have little relation to the rules governing agents in Axtell's (Axtell, 1999) model of firms, or the Epstein et al. (2004) model of smallpox response, or the zero-intelligence traders of Farmer et al. (2003). Yet, despite their diversity, these models are impressive empirically. If reasonable fidelity to data requires us to be *ad hoc* (i.e., to quantify over smaller sets), with different rules for different settings, then that is the price of empirical progress.

4.11. Truth and beauty

All of this said, the real reason some mathematical social scientists don't like computational agent-based modeling is not that the approach is empirically weak (in notable areas, it's empirically stronger than the neoclassical approach). It's that it isn't beautiful. When theorists, such as Frank Hahn, lament the demise of "pure theory" in favor of computer simulation [Hahn (1991)], they are grieving the loss of mathematical beauty. I would argue that reports of its death are premature. Let us face this aesthetic issue squarely.

On the topic of mathematical beauty, none have written more eloquently than Bertrand Russell (1957):

> Mathematics, rightly viewed, possesses not only truth, but supreme beauty—a beauty cold and austere, like that of sculpture, without appeal to any part of our weaker nature, without the gorgeous trappings of painting or music, yet sublimely pure, and capable of a stern perfection such as only the greatest art can show.

Later, in the same essay, Russell writes:

> In the most beautiful work, a chain of argument is presented in which every link is important on its own account, in which there is an air of ease and lucidity throughout, and *the premises achieve more than would have been thought possible, by means which appear natural and inevitable.* (emphasis added)

Hahn (1991) defines "pure theory" as "the activity of deducing implications from a small number of fundamental axioms." And when he writes that "with surprising frequency this leads to beauty (Arrow's Theorem, The Core, etc.)," it is clear that it is Russell's beauty he has in mind.

Generality (mathematical unification) for its own sake satisfies this fine impulse to beauty and has proven to be highly productive scientifically. Physics is highly general, and so is mathematical equilibrium theory. And, as Mirowski (1989) has documented, "physics envy" was quite explicitly central to its development. This is entirely understandable. Any scientist who doesn't have physics envy is an idiot. I am not advocating that we abandon the quest for elegant generality in favor of a case by case narrative (i.e., purely historical) approach. By comparison to a beautiful (Newton-like) generalization, actual history is just this particular apple bobbling down this particular hill. To me, the mathematical theory of evolution is more beautiful than any particular tiger. One of the most miraculous results of our own evolution is that our search for beauty can lead to truth. But there are different kinds of beauty. An analogy to music history may be apposite.

Just as the German classical composers had the dominant 7th and circle of fifths as harmonic propulsion, so the neoclassical economists have utility maximization to propel their analyses. And it is a style of "composition" subscribed to by an entire school of academic thought. We agent modelers are not of this school. We don't have the Germanic dominant 7th of utility maximization to propel every analysis forward—more like the French impressionists, we must in each case be inventive to solve the problem of social motion, devising unique agent rules model by model. If that makes us *ad hoc*, then so was Debussy, and we are in good artistic company.

Schelling's (Schelling, 1971) segregation model is important not because it's right in all details (which it doesn't purport to be), and it's beautiful not because it's visually appealing (which it happens to be). It's important because—even though highly idealized—it offers a powerful and counter-intuitive insight. And it's beautiful because it does so with startling Russellian parsimony. The mathematics of chaos is beautiful not because of all the pretty fractal pictures it generates, useful as these are in stimulating popular interest. What's beautiful in Russell's sense is the startlingly compact yet sweepingly general Li–Yorke (Li and Yorke, 1975) theorem that "period three implies chaos." And when an agent-based model is beautiful in this deep sense, it has nothing to do with the phantasmagorical "eye candy"—Russell's gorgeous trappings—of animated dot worlds. Rather, its beauty resides in the far-reaching generative power of its simple micro-rules, seemingly remote from the elaborate macro patterns they produce. Precisely as Russell would have it: *"the premises achieve more than would have been thought possible, by means which appear natural and inevitable."*

The musical parallels are again irresistible. To be sure, Bach's final work, *The Art of the Fugue*, is gorgeous music, but to Bach, the game was to explore the generative power of a single fugue theme. Bach wrote nineteen stunningly diverse fugues based on this single theme, this "premise," if you will.[12] In Bach's hands, it certainly "achieves more than would have been thought possible." While its musical beauty is clear, the *intellectual* beauty lies not in the sound, but in its silent unified structure. Perhaps the best agent models unfold as "social fugues" in which the apparent complexity is in fact generated by a few simple individual rules.

---

[12] Bach died before completing this work, and doubtless could have composed countless further fugues.

In any case, and whatever one's aesthetic leanings, agent modelers are in good scientific company trading away a certain degree of generality for fidelity to data. The issue of induction arises in this connection.

4.12. Induction over theorem distributions

As noted earlier, one powerful mode of agent-based modeling is to run large numbers of stochastic realizations (each with its own random seed), collect clean data, and build up a robust statistical portrait of model output. One goal of such exercises is to understand one's model when closed form analytical expressions are not in hand (though these exist in principle, as discussed). A second aim of such exercises is to explain observed statistical regularities, such as the distribution of firm sizes in the U.S. economy [Axtell (1999, 2001)]. In either case, one builds up a large sample of model realizations. But, as emphasized earlier, *each realization is a strict deduction*. So, while I have no objection to calling such activity inductive, it is *induction over a sample distribution of theorems*, in fact. And it has quite a different flavor from "inductive" survey research, where one collects real-world data and estimates it by techniques of aggregate regression.

5. Summary

A number of uses of agent-based models have not been touched on here. These include purely exploratory applications and those related to mechanism design, among others [see Epstein (1999)]. My focus has been on computational agent models as instruments in the generative explanation of macroscopic social structures. In that connection, the main epistemological points treated are as follows:

(1) We distinguish the generative motto from its converse. The position is:

$$\forall x(\neg Gx \supset \neg Ex).$$

If you didn't grow it, you didn't explain it. But not conversely. A microspecification that generates the *explanandum* is a candidate explanation. Generative sufficiency is explanatorily necessary, but not explanatorily sufficient. There may be more than one explanatory candidate, as in any science where theories compete.

(2) For every agent model, there exist unique equivalent equations. One can express any Turing Machine (and hence any agent model) in partial recursive functions. Many agent models have been revealingly mathematized in other ways, as stochastic dynamical systems, for example.

(3) Every realization of an agent model is a strict deduction. So, $(Gx \supset Dx)$, but not conversely, as in non-constructive (*reductio ad absurdum*) existence proofs. One can have $(Dx \wedge \neg Gx)$ and hence, by (1), $(Dx \wedge \neg Ex)$. Not all deduction is explanatory.

(4) We often generate, and hence deduce, conjuncts satisfying Disjunctive Normal Forms, as when we grow distributions or spatial settlement patterns in finite agent populations.

(5) We carefully distinguish between existence and attainability in principle. And we furthermore carefully distinguish between asymptotic attainability and attainability on time scales of interest. In short, we are attentive to questions of incompleteness (á la Godel) and of computational complexity (as in problems whose time complexity is exponential in key variables). These considerations, when combined with powerful psychological evidence, cast severe doubt on the rational choice picture as the most productive idealization of human decision-making, and serve only to enforce the bounded rationality picture insisted on by Simon (1982).

(6) Generality, while a commendable impulse, is not of paramount concern to agent-based modelers at this point. Responsiveness to data often requires that we *quantify over smaller sets* than physics or neoclassical economics. If that is *ad hocism*, I readily choose it over what Simon (1987) rightly indicts as an empirically oblivious *a priorism* in economics.

(7) Empirical agent-based modeling can be seen as induction over a sample of realizations, each one of which is a strict deduction, or theorem, and comparison of the generated distribution to statistical data. This differs from inductive survey research where we assemble data and fit it by aggregate regression, for example.

6. Conclusion

As to the core indictment that agent models are non-mathematical, non-deductive, and *ad hoc*, the first two are false, and the third, I argue, is unimportant. Generative explanation is mathematical in principle; recursive functions could be provided. *Ipso facto*, generative explanation is deductive. Granted, agent models typically quantify over smaller sets than rational choice models and, as such, are less general. But, in many cases, they are more responsive to data, and in years to come, may achieve greater generality and unification. After all, a fully unified field theory has eluded even that most enviable of fields, physics.

References

Albin, P.S. (Ed.) (1998). Barriers and Bounds to Rationality: Essays on Economic Complexity and Dynamics in Interactive Systems. Princeton University Press, Princeton.

Arrow, K.J. (1987). "Rationality of self and others in an economic system". In: Hogarth, R.M., Reder, M.W. (Eds.), Rational Choice: The Contrast Between Economics and Psychology. University of Chicago Press, Chicago.

Axelrod, R. (1997). "Advancing the art of simulation in the social sciences". Complexity 3, 193–199.

Axtell, R. (1999). "The emergence of firms in a population of agents: local increasing returns, unstable Nash equilibria, and power law size distributions", Santa Fe Institute working paper 99-03-019.

Axtell, R.L. (2001). "Zipf distribution of U.S. firm sizes". Science 93, 1818–1820.

Axtell, R.L., Epstein, J.M. (1999). "Coordination in transient social networks: an agent-based computational model of the timing of retirement". In: Aaron, H. (Ed.), Behavioral Dimensions of Retirement Economics. Brookings Institution Press, Washington, DC.

Axtell, R.L., Epstein, J.M., Young, H.P. (2001). "The emergence of economic classes in an agent-based bargaining model". In: Durlauf, S., Young, H.P. (Eds.), Social Dynamics. MIT Press, Cambridge, MA.

Axtell, R.L., Epstein, J.M., Dean, J.S., Gumerman, G.J., Swedlund, A.C., Harburger, J., Chakravarty, S., Hammond, R., Parker, J., Parker, M. (2002). "Population growth and collapse in a multiagent model of the Kayenta Anasazi in Long House Valley". Proceedings of the National Academy of Sciences 99 (3), 7275–7279.

Berry, B.J.L., Kiel, L.D., Elliott, E. (Eds.) (2002). Adaptive agents, intelligence, and emergent human organization: capturing complexity through agent-based modeling. Proceedings of the National Academy of Sciences 99 (3). Results from the Arthur M. Sackler Colloquium of the National Academy of Sciences held October 4–6, 2001.

Boolos, G.S., Jeffrey, R.C. (1989). Computability and Logic, 3rd edn. Cambridge University Press, Cambridge.

Cederman, L.-E. (1997). Emergent Actors in World Politics: How States and Nations Develop and Dissolve. Princeton University Press, Princeton.

Chomsky, N. (1965). Aspects of the Theory of Syntax. MIT Press, Cambridge, MA.

Crutchfield, J.P., Mitchell, M. (1995). "The evolution of emergent computation". Proceedings of the National Academy of Sciences 92, 10740–10746.

Dorofeenko, V., Shorish, J. (2002). "Dynamical modeling of the demographic prisoner's dilemma". In: Economic Series 124. Institute for Advanced Studies, Vienna.

Epstein, J.M. (1997). Nonlinear Dynamics, Mathematical Biology, and Social Science. Addison-Wesley, Menlo Park.

Epstein, J.M. (1999). "Agent-based computational models and generative social science". Complexity 4 (5), 41–57.

Epstein, J.M., Axtell, R. (1996). Growing Artificial Societies: Social Science from the Bottom Up. MIT Press, Cambridge, MA.

Epstein, J.M., Hammond, R.A. (2002). "Non-explanatory equilibria: an extremely simple game with (mostly) unattainable fixed points". Complexity 7 (4).

Epstein, J.M., Cummings, D.A.T., Chakravarty, S., Singha, R.M., Burke, D.S. (2004). Toward a Containment Strategy for Smallpox Bioterror: An Individual-Based Computational Approach. Brookings Institution Press, Washington, DC.

Epstein, R.L., Carnielli, W.A. (1989). Computability: Computable Functions, Logic, and the Foundations of Mathematics. Wadsworth & Brooks, Belmont, CA.

Epstein, S.D., Hornstein, N. (Eds.) (1999). Working Minimalism. MIT Press, Cambridge, MA.

Farmer, J.D., Patelli, P., Zovko, I. (2003). "The predictive power of zero intelligence in financial markets", Santa Fe Institute working paper 03-09-051.

Foster, D.P., Young, H.P. (2001). "On the impossibility of predicting the behavior of rational agents". Proceedings of the National Academy of Sciences 98 (22), 12848–12853.

Garey, M.R., Johnson, D.S. (1979). Computers and Intractability: A Guide to the Theory of NP-Completeness. W.H. Freeman and Company.

Godel, K. (1931). "Uber formal unentscheidbare Satze der Principia Mathematica und verwadter Systeme I". Monatshefte fur Mathematik und Physik 38, 173–198. For the English version: "On formally undecidable propositions of the I Principia Mathematica and related systems" (1986). In: Feferman, S. (Ed.), Kurt Godel Collected Works, Vol. 1 (Oxford University Press, Oxford), 145–199.

Hahn, F. (1991). "The next hundred years". Economic Journal 101 (404), 47–50.

Hamilton, A.G. (1988). Logic for Mathematicians. Cambridge University Press, Cambridge.

Hodel, R.E. (1995). An Introduction to Mathematical Logic. PWS Publishing Company, Boston.

Jeffrey, R. (1991). Formal Logic: Its Scope and Limits, 3rd edn. McGraw-Hill, Inc., New York.

Knuth, D.E. (1998). The Art of Computer Programming, 3rd edn, Seminumerical Algorithms, vol. 2. Addison-Wesley, Boston.

Lewis, A.A. (1992a). "Some aspects of effectively constructive mathematics that are relevant to the foundations of Neoclassical mathematical economics and the theory of games". Mathematical Social Sciences 24, 209–235.

Lewis, A.A. (1992b). "On Turing degrees of Walrasian models and a general impossibility result in the theory of decision making". Mathematical Social Sciences 24 (2–3), 141–171.

Lewis, A.A. (1985). "On effectively computable realizations of choice functions". Mathematical Social Sciences 10, 43–80.

Li, T.Y., Yorke, J.A. (1975). "Period three implies chaos". American Mathematical Monthly 82, 985.

Mas-Colell, A., Whinston, M.D., Green, J.R. (1995). Microeconomic Theory. Oxford University Press, Oxford.

Mirowski, P. (1989). More Heat Than Light: Economics as Social Physics, Physics as Nature's Economics. Cambridge University Press, Cambridge.

Nachbar, J.H. (1997). "Prediction, optimization, and learning in games". Econometrica 65, 275–309.

Pais, A. (1982). Subtle is the Lord: The Science and the Life of Albert Einstein. Oxford University Press, Oxford.

Pollicot, M., Weiss, H. (2001). "The dynamics of Schelling-type segregation models and a nonlinear graph Laplacian variational problem". Advances in Applied Mathematics 27, 17–40.

Prasad, K. (1997). "On the compatability of Nash equilibria". Journal of Economic Dynamics and Control 21, 943–953.

Russell, B. (1957). Mysticism and Logic. Doubleday Anchor Books, New York.

Schelling, T.C. (1971). "Dynamic models of segregation". Journal of Mathematical Sociology 1, 143–186.

Simon, H.A. (1982). Models of Bounded Rationality. MIT Press Cambridge, MA.

Simon, H.A. (1987). "Rationality in psychology and economics". In: Hogarth, R.M., Reder, M.W. (Eds.), Rational Choice: The Contrast Between Economics and Psychology. University of Chicago Press, Chicago.

Smullyan, R.M. (1992). Godel's Incompleteness Theorems. Oxford Press, New York.

Young, H.P. (1998). Individual Strategy and Social Structure: An Evolutionary Theory of Institutions. Princeton University Press, Princeton.

Chapter 35

COORDINATION ISSUES IN LONG-RUN GROWTH

PETER HOWITT[*]

Department of Economics, Brown University, Providence, RI 02912, USA
e-mail: Peter_Howitt@brown.edu; url: http://www.econ.brown.edu/fac/Peter_Howitt

Contents

[*] For helpful suggestions I thank, without implicating, Rob Axtell, David Laidler, Richard Lipsey, Malcolm Rutherford, Leigh Tesfatsion and three anonymous referees.

Handbook of Computational Economics, Volume 2. Edited by Leigh Tesfatsion and Kenneth L. Judd
DOI: 10.1016/S1574-0021(05)02035-6

Abstract

Economic growth depends not only on how people make decisions but also upon how their decisions are coordinated. Because of this, aggregate outcomes can diverge from individual intentions. I illustrate this with reference to the modern literature on economic growth, and also with reference to an older literature on the stability of full-employment equilibrium. Agent-based computational methods are ideally suited for studying the aspects of growth most affected by coordination issues.

Keywords

growth, coordination, innovation, stability, agent-based systems

JEL classification: E00, O33, O40

1. Introduction

Economic growth, like most economic phenomena, depends on the incentives that people face when making decisions. Measured in per-capita terms, growth cannot be sustained indefinitely unless some combination of capital, skills and knowledge grows without bound. So we cannot understand long-term growth without some understanding of what induces people to invest in capital, skills and knowledge. Reduced-form AK theories focus on the intertemporal choices by households that underlie capital accumulation. Innovation-based growth theories of the sort that Philippe Aghion and I have been working on for some time[1] focus on the R&D decisions of profit-seeking business firms that lead to the innovations that raise the stock of disembodied technological knowledge. Human-capital based theories focus on the time-allocation decisions of households investing in education and training. In all cases, changes that impinge on the incentives of the decision makers affect an economy's long-run growth rate.

Some writers have gone so far as to make incentives the *sine qua non* of growth economics. Thus Easterly (2001, p. 289) states that "Prosperity happens when all the players in the development game have the right incentives," and quotes approvingly (p. xii) from Steven Landsburg that "People respond to incentives; all the rest is commentary." To Lucas (2002, p. 17) what matters above all is the incentives facing household decision makers:

> For income growth to occur in a society, a large fraction of people must experience changes in the possible lives they imagine for themselves and their children, and these new visions of possible futures must have enough force to lead them to change the way they behave, the number of children they have, and the hopes they invest in these children: the way they allocate their time.

My purpose in this essay is to take issue with this exclusive focus on incentives and the logic of choice. Not to deny that incentives matter for economic growth but to assert that much else matters also, and that much of what also matters is ideally suited for study by computational methods.

Economies are large complex systems that can be studied at different levels. Macroeconomic issues, which involve the functioning of the system as a whole, need to be studied at a coarser level than microeconomic issues involving the behavior of just one market or just a small group of individuals, households or business firms. A clear understanding of the entire system would be obscured by focusing on a detailed analysis of these constituent working parts, just as a clear understanding of ocean tides would be obscured by focusing on the molecules of water in the ocean, or a clear view of a pointillist painting would be obscured by examining each dot one at a time. The system as a whole is not a macrocosm of its individual parts and the parts are not microcosms of the whole. Instead, as Schelling (1978) has argued forcefully, macro behavior can

---

[1] Aghion and Howitt (1998a).

depart radically from what the individual units are trying to accomplish. So when you stand back the details become hard to see but patterns emerge that were not visible from up close.

Thus my primary objection to the agenda laid out by Lucas and others is that it is likely to involve a fallacy of composition. Incentives and decision-making are properties of the constituent parts of an economy, whereas economic growth is a property of the system as a whole. If the economy functioned as a macrocosm of its parts then focusing on incentives would yield a clear picture of the growth process. But I believe it is not. What matters at the macro level is not just how individual transactors formulate their plans but also the nature of their interactions with each other and with their environment. In short, an economy's growth performance often depends not so much on how people make their decisions as it does on how those decisions are coordinated, or in some cases how the decisions become uncoordinated.

One of the virtues of the ACE approach to economics, as outlined by Tesfatsion (2006), is that it forces one to make explicit the mechanisms through which individual actions are coordinated, for better or worse. That is, in order to make a model "dynamically complete," in Tesfatsion's terminology, one has to specify what will happen from any given set of initial conditions, including those in which different people are acting on the basis of inconsistent beliefs and hence in which aggregate outcomes will necessarily diverge from individual intentions. Another virtue of the ACE approach is that it provides a method for discovering a system's "emergent properties," i.e. those properties that are not inherent in the individual components. Thus it seems ideally suited for studying those aspects of the growth process that go beyond the Lucas agenda.[2]

2. The representative agent model and its limitations[3]

The idea that the economy as a whole can behave very differently from what the individual transactors are trying to accomplish is hardly original. Indeed one of the oldest themes of economic theory is that things are not as they seem to the individual. The classical economists delighted in pointing out how the unconstrained pursuit of maximal profit by competing sellers would end up minimizing their profit. Smith's attack on mercantilism was based on the idea that although the accumulation of precious metals would make an individual wealthy it would not do the same for a nation. Keynes argued that the unemployment rate was determined not by individual labor-supply decisions but by what was happening in product markets and in the financial system. The first textbooks promoting the Keynesian revolution highlighted the paradox of thrift, according to which the attempt by individual households to save more could end up reducing the

---

[2] Work that has used the ACE approach for studying technological change, the ultimate mainspring of long-run growth, is surveyed by Dawid (2006).

[3] The limitations of the representative agent model have been examined extensively by Kirman (1992).

economy's overall level of saving. One of Friedman's central arguments in promoting Monetarism was that people who favor a policy of cheap money don't realize that in the long run this will cause higher interest rates. Thus what happens to profits, wealth, unemployment, saving or interest rates depends not so much on individual choices and intentions as on how those choices and intentions are coordinated. Focusing on the incentives faced by individuals trying to influence the variable would produce the wrong answer. A broader perspective is needed.

But by the start of the 21st Century, the education of a macroeconomist no longer included any warnings against the fallacy of composition. On the contrary, the very foundations of modern macroeconomics, as practiced in academic research and taught to graduate students, is the belief that macro variables are best understood by focusing on the details of decision-making by individual households and firms. In such theories, macroeconomic variables such as interest rates, wage rates and unemployment rates reflect intertemporal substitution and time-allocation decisions on the part of a representative household, whose behavior is indeed a small-scale replica of the system as a whole. High unemployment reflects a disincentive to work, low saving a disincentive to abstain from current consumption, and high interest rates a high rate of individual time preference or a low elasticity of intertemporal substitution in consumption. The fallacy of division that this approach entails is just the dual of the fallacy of composition. In effect, these twin fallacies play an even bigger role in a macroeconomist's education than they did a generation ago; the difference is that instead of being taught as pitfalls to be avoided they are now presented as paradigms to be emulated.

How this transformation in economics took place is a long story that I cannot begin to unravel here. The transformation is clearly related to the rational-expectations revolution started by Lucas's celebrated *Journal of Economic Theory* paper (Lucas, 1972), which provided a micro-foundation for a macro theory that claimed to reconcile the long-run neutrality of money with short-run non-neutrality. When rational expectations was adopted by the advocates of Keynesian economics as well as by its critics, the gap between micro and macro became not bridged but papered over. For the very idea that individual actions could have unforeseen consequences does not sit easily with the idea that everyone acts rationally, guided by an accurate model of how the overall economy works. Moreover, the very terminology of "rational" expectations draws one's attention to individual thought processes, obscuring the fact that the achievement of rational expectations is really a collective process requiring the coordination of what must initially have been non-rational expectations.

But clearly there is more to this transformation than rational expectations. The history of the development of Keynesian macroeconomics from the end of World War II was one of providing a choice-theoretic underpinning to the behavioral functions that comprise the IS-LM system. The representative household and firm played as much a part in this pre-rational-expectations theoretical development as they have since 1972. It seems that in seeking to provide a bridge between micro and macro, economists have been driven by a reductionist imperative to bring everything down to the level of individual choices and by an "irrational passion for dispassionate rationality."[4] Conventional acceptance of these attitudes makes it easy to dismiss as *ad hoc* or poorly grounded any theory that starts with behavioral rules not explicitly derived from rational foundations. Adherence to this standard makes it necessary to use something like the representative agent just to keep manageable a model of the whole economy that focuses sharply on the constituent parts. It also makes it necessary to assume away most of the coordination problems that would get in the way of rational expectations by blurring the link between individual choices and their consequences.

To be sure, not all macroeconomists accept this representative-agent view of short-run macroeconomics, and much progress has been made recently in studying the coordination problems that might impede the formation of rational expectations (see for example Sargent, 1993 or Evans and Honkapohja, 2001). But there is still a widespread belief that the importance of coordination problems is limited to short-run theory, like the price-stickiness that can keep the economy away from its natural rate of unemployment in the short run or the informational imperfections that permit a short-run Phillips curve to be exploited by policy-makers. It is generally regarded as uncontroversial to model long-run phenomena like economic growth by assuming that aggregate variables are chosen rationally by some representative agent, whose incentives are therefore all that really matter for understanding the economy's performance.

Economics being an empirical science, the first question to ask of the agenda that Lucas and others have laid out is whether there is a prima facie case for believing that overall economic performance reflects the intentions of the individual decision makers. Is it really true that, to a first approximation, rich nations are those whose citizens have a lot of education, save a large fraction of their incomes and work long hours? More to the point, is it really true that nations that grow rapidly are those in which there is high investment in physical capital, education and R&D?

The evidence from the recent "development accounting" literature is not all that convincing. Although Mankiw et al. (1992) tried to argue that 75 percent or more of the cross-country variation in per-capita GDP was accounted for by a simple Solow–Swan model in which the main variables were investment rates in physical capital and enrollment rates in education, the vast literature spawned by this provocative article has shown that these rates are themselves endogenous to income levels and also highly correlated with productivity. Thus it seems that countries with high investment and enrollment rates tend to be rich to a large extent just because they are also nations in which more output can be produced from any given amount of physical capital and education. Klenow and Rodríguez-Clare (1997) estimate that more than 60 percent of the cross-country variation of per-worker GDP is attributable to productivity rather than to the accumulation of physical and human capital.

When it comes to accounting for differences in growth rates, which is after all the primary objective of growth theory, the evidence for the incentive agenda is even less

---

[4] The phrase, which I first heard from David Laidler, is commonly attributed to J.M. Clark.

convincing. According to Klenow and Rodríguez-Clare, over 90 percent of the cross-country variation in growth rates of per-worker GDP is attributable to differences in productivity-growth rates rather than to differences in investment rates or enrollment rates. Thus it seems that almost everything to be explained by the theory lies in the Solow residual, which Abramowitz once called nothing more than a measure of our ignorance.

This is part of the evidence that inclines me towards innovation-based growth theory, since most of the effects of innovation work through productivity-growth rates. So is it really countries that spend a large proportion of their GDP on R&D that have the fastest productivity-growth rates? Coe and Helpman (1995) and Coe et al. (1997) have examined the cross-country relationships between growth rates and R&D intensities (the fraction of GDP spent on R&D) and found that there is indeed a powerful relationship, but what matters to an individual country is not so much its own R&D intensity as that of its major trading partners. This mirrors at the country level the result that one typically finds at the industry level (see for example Zachariadis, 2003). That is, the research efforts undertaken by firms in one country or one industry aimed at enhancing their own productivity end up enhancing productivity in other countries and industries. Presumably this reflects a process of technology spillover, or what is sometimes called "technology transfer." So here again, the behavior of a variable (one country's productivity or one industry's productivity) is an unintended consequence of the incentives faced at the individual level, a consequence that involves the channels through which individual transactors interact rather than the manner in which they decide to act.

3. Externalities and unintended side effects

As I have already observed, the professional consensus in macroeconomics seems to be that coordination issues are more important for short-run theory than for the theory of long-run growth. This is a legacy of the neoclassical synthesis, according to which sticky prices and informational imperfections are just transitory impediments to the smooth coordination of rational choices. More generally it reflects what Clower and Howitt (1998) have called the "classical stability hypothesis," to the effect that in the long run the economy will converge to a coordinated state. Yet there are sound theoretical reasons for thinking that the process of economic growth brings with it a set of forces that widen the gap between individual intentions and aggregate outcomes rather than the reverse, and reasons for thinking that the growth process often exacerbates the impediments to smooth coordination rather than the reverse. The present section of the paper and the next elaborate on this point.

One reason why the growth process can widen the intention-output gap is the central role that externalities play in the process. The ultimate mainspring of growth is technological change, which is known to involve significant external effects: the empirical work on technology spillovers referred to above corroborates a plausible theoretical presumption that the ideas generated by R&D are hard to appropriate. Thus as Arrow

(1969) argued, innovation tends to go under-rewarded because it confers much of its benefits on third parties. To complicate matters, Schumpeter's notion of creative destruction, which Aghion and I have developed in our work, involves a negative spillover that tends to give people too strong an incentive to perform R&D. That is, the firm performing R&D takes into account the prospective rents that would be created by a new product or process but does not take into account the rents that would be destroyed through obsolescence by the same innovation.

Externalities are hard to ignore in growth theory not just because of these substantive reasons but also because of the technical difficulties of coping with increasing returns to scale. That increasing returns is involved in one form or another once technology becomes endogenous has been recognized at least since Allyn Young (1928). In modern innovation-based theory increasing returns takes the form of a setup cost of research, which is independent of the size of the market to be served by the resulting innovations. Producing the first unit of a new product takes so much resource input for the original innovation and so much for the variable production cost. Producing each subsequent unit requires only the variable cost. Average cost is thus decreasing with the amount produced.

Indeed the upsurge of endogenous growth theory in the past two decades can arguably be attributed not so much to the new substantive ideas that it has produced as to the progress it has made in dealing with the technicalities of increasing returns. In particular, we know that a competitive equilibrium without externalities generally fails to exist in a world with ubiquitous decreasing cost. You need to introduce some combination of either pecuniary externalities (imperfect competition) or direct non-pecuniary externalities. What endogenous growth theory did was to borrow techniques for dealing with these externalities from other areas of economics (the Dixit–Stiglitz–Ethier model for dealing with imperfect competition and the concept of symmetric anonymous Nash equilibrium for dealing with non-pecuniary externalities) in order to develop manageable models of ideas that have been common among economic historians and specialists in the economics of technology for several generations.

How the growth theories that have been developed on these grounds can generate aggregate outcomes that contradict individual intentions is illustrated by a central result of Aghion et al. (2001) concerning the effects of intellectual property protection on an economy's overall level of R&D and hence on its overall rate of technological progress. Weaker patent protection reduces the direct incentive for a firm in any given situation to perform R&D. Yet it can actually raise the aggregate level of R&D and hence raise the overall rate of technological progress. It does this through a "composition effect," which works as follows. Innovation takes place at the greatest rate in those industries where the leading firms are neck-and-neck; that is, where they produce using similar technologies. This is because profits are lowest in such industries and hence the incentive to escape competition by innovating is strongest. If patent laws were weakened, a firm with any given technological lead over its rivals would have its incentive to innovate blunted, but the steady-state distribution of lead sizes would also be changed; specifically, more firms would find themselves in the R&D-intensive situation of neck-and-neck competition because of a rival's success in imitating their technological capability. As a result, it can be shown theoretically that under a wide variety of circumstances there is a point up to which weaker patent laws will raise the economy's overall growth rate, even though the incentive for a firm in any given situation goes in the opposite direction.

Likewise, as Mokyr (1990) has argued, nations that experience the most rapid growth are not necessarily those in which people have the strongest incentive to develop new technologies but those which have developed the greatest tolerance for, and capacity to adjust to, the many negative side-effects of economic growth. Those negative side-effects are almost always the result of obsolescence—the destructive side of creative destruction. Because of obsolescence, technological change is a game with losers as well as winners. From the handloom weavers of early 19th century Britain to the former giants of mainframe computing in the late 20th century, many people's skills, capital equipment and technological knowledge have been devalued and rendered obsolete by the same inventions that have created fortunes for others. The conflict between winners and losers from new technologies is a recurrent theme in economic history, and the difficulty of mediating the conflict affects society's willingness to foster and tolerate economic growth.

Thus for example, ever since the introduction of machinery into manufacturing processes in the early part of the industrial revolution, people have been worried that economic growth could cause technological unemployment. Mainstream professional economists have tended to regard such popular concerns as fallacious, with a few notorious exceptions like Ricardo's (Ricardo, 1821) chapter "On Machinery". The classical stability hypothesis leads one to believe that the unemployment created by any one technological innovation should be short-lived; those rendered unemployed will eventually find employment elsewhere. But this is not true if we look at an increase in the rate at which new technologies are being introduced rather than at a single innovation. As Aghion and Howitt (1994) have argued, a faster pace of job-destroying innovations will raise the flow into unemployment in any given situation, and can thereby increase the steady-state (natural?) rate of unemployment.

Unemployment is more of a social problem in some countries than others. In the United States, for example, where wages are more flexible and employment regulations less restrictive, technologically induced unemployment is likely to be less of a social problem than in many European countries. But this just tends to exacerbate another common side-effect of rapid technological progress, namely rising wage-inequality. As many have pointed out, the last quarter of the 20th Century was a period of rapidly rising inequality, especially in the United States. Although public opinion often blames globalization for this rise in inequality, the culprit to which academic research points more often is skill-biased technological change. In short, the same phenomenon that caused high unemployment levels in Europe by destroying jobs seems to have caused high wage-inequality in the US by enriching those who can work with new technologies and driving those whose jobs are destroyed into less remunerative jobs.

To some extent this side effect is one that can be dealt with by more investment in education—by raising the number of people able to work profitably with new technologies instead of being displaced by new technologies. In principle this should help not just those whose skills are enhanced by more education but also those who remain relatively less skilled, whose wages should be lifted by their increasing relative scarcity. But recent theoretical research suggests at least two problems with this approach. One is that not all of the increase in inequality is explained by an increasing educational premium. Instead, roughly half of the overall increase is attributable to a rise in residual inequality, the inequality that is unexplained by education, experience or any other observable individual characteristic.

Aghion et al. (2002), have argued that this is because whether or not someone is able to work with new technologies is often a matter of pure luck rather than of education levels. The luck factor is always there in the wage distribution; indeed we know that income inequality between identical twins tends to be about as large as within the whole population. But it was greatly leveraged by the IT revolution, not only because this was a general purpose technology that hastened the pace of technical change, and hence further raised the wages of those lucky enough to have just the right skills, but also because of the nature of IT. That is, because of the generality of computer technology and the associated reduction in communication costs, many of those lucky enough to be able to work on the leading edge of technology today have skills that can easily be marketed throughout the entire economy, rather than in just one sector, and they receive a compensation that is correspondingly enhanced. There is nothing that increased investment in human capital can do to counteract this particular side effect of economic growth.

The other problem that has been raised by theoretical research is the "market-size effect" that Acemoglu (2002) has explained. That is, because the cost of R&D takes the form of a setup cost, researchers tend to direct their efforts towards enhancing the productivity of factors that are relatively abundant in the economy rather than those that are relatively scarce; although the cost of either type of effort might be the same, the payoff is larger from enhancing a factor that is more widely used. Acemoglu shows how this can produce a positive feedback loop, whereby more education induces even more innovations that enhance the relative productivity of educated workers and hence increase their relative wage, which in turn induces even more people to become educated. This is just fine for those who are capable of joining in, but for the old and less able the situation is one of increasing relative poverty, one that would just be exacerbated by policies raising the incentive to acquire education.

Societies that are willing to cope with and possibly mitigate high unemployment and/or high inequality are thus likely to be those that put up the fewest impediments to the introduction and adoption of new technologies, and hence to be those that have the highest long-run growth rates. Of course incentives matter in this story, but not those that we would be led to examine by simple representative-agent models. What promotes growth in these stories is not the willingness of households to accumulate physical or human capital or the willingness of firms to engage in R&D but rather the willingness of politicians to permit side effects to persist or to devise institutions like unemployment insurance, redistributive schemes, relocation subsidies, etc., that alleviate the side effects. In short, economic growth is at least as much about mediating social conflict as it is about the individual virtues of thrift, study and hard work.

4. Uncertainty and the classical stability hypothesis

The main reason for thinking that the growth process can exacerbate coordination problems is the fundamental uncertainty of technological progress. Technological innovation is a destabilizing force that is constantly disrupting established patterns of economic activity, much like the disturbance term in a time-series process. But the path that technology follows is a highly non-stationary one which, while it may exhibit some aggregate patterns, is virtually unpredictable in its details. Thus from the point of view of the individual decision maker, an innovation is not something that simply alters the initial condition in some well understood dynamic game, but one that destroys the value of previous information and starts an adaptive learning process all over again. The more rapid the pace of innovation the more chaotic the process becomes, the less confidence people are able to place in history as a guide to the future, and therefore the more likely their individual plans are to be thwarted by unsuspected macro forces.

The unpredictability of technological progress is a major theme in the writing of Nathan Rosenberg, who has pointed out how technologies that were developed for one purpose very often had their major impact on something their discoverer was unaware of. Bell Labs, for example, where scientists invented the laser, was reluctant to patent it because in their opinion it had no conceivable industrial uses in the telephone industry (Rosenberg, 1994, p. 223). Thomas Watson Sr., the founder of IBM, at first regarded the computer as a highly specialized scientific instrument with no potential commercial uses (Rosenberg, 1994, p. 220). Technological developments in the sewing machine industry ended up having a major effect on automobiles, which had not yet been invented at the time of the discoveries (Rosenberg, 1963).

Writers like Brian Arthur (1989) have observed that because of this fundamental uncertainty, the pace and direction of innovation are necessarily guided by short-term considerations, even though they can lead society down irreversible paths whose long-run consequences are of great import, especially when there are "network externalities" involved. That is, the course of technological progress, rather than reflecting the intentions of those individuals that create it, is a social process driven by the largely unforeseen consequences of individual decisions. If these aggregate consequences are unforeseen at the level of the individuals involved then surely we have little chance ourselves of understanding them unless we look at them from a different level, presumably from the level of the system as a whole.

The disruptiveness of technological change is something that writers like Freeman and Perez (1988) and David (1990) have analyzed extensively. They argue that major technological changes come in waves, driven by what are now commonly called general purpose technologies (GPTs); that is, new technologies that are used throughout the economy, have a profound effect on the way economic life is organized, and give rise to a wave of complementary innovations. In the long run our standard of living has been greatly enhanced by the succession of GPTs introduced since before the first Industrial Revolution, including such things as the steam engine, electric power, and the computer.[5] However, the period during which a new GPT is being introduced can be a period of wrenching adjustment, not just at the level of the individual firm but for the economy as a whole.

There are many aspects to this adjustment cost that have been studied in the literature. Helpman and Trajtenberg (1998) emphasize the lost output that can occur because a GPT never arrives fully developed but instead requires the subsequent invention of a set of complementary components. During the period when the components are being developed, the new GPT will not yet be used to its full effect. Meanwhile the labor that is drawn into developing new components will be drawn out of producing final output. The result can be a fall in the overall level of output. Others have pointed out a variety of additional channels through which the cost of adjusting to a new GPT can show up at the macroeconomic level. Greenwood and Yorukoglu (1997) argue that real resources are used up in learning to operate the new GPT. Aghion and Howitt (1998b) point out that the process of reallocating labor from sectors using older technologies to those using the new GPT may involve a rise in unemployment, for the same reason that any large reallocation of labor often entails unemployment in a less than frictionless economic system. Howitt (1998) calibrates to U.S. data a Schumpeterian model with capital-embodied technological change, and shows numerically that the speedup in the rate of innovation induced by a new GPT can reduce the rate of output growth by increasing the rate of induced capital obsolescence, both human and physical. In this calibration, the introduction of a new GPT that raises the productivity of R&D by 50 percent until overall productivity has doubled will reduce the level of per-capita GDP below the path it would otherwise have followed for a period of about two decades, before eventually resulting in a level of GDP twice as high as it would otherwise have been.

A full account of how an economy copes with these adjustments is something that goes beyond incentives, and involves the institutional mechanisms that determine the extent to which the economy is a self-regulating mechanism. This is because the more often an economy is disturbed by major shocks that require people to learn new patterns of behavior, the harder it is for the "invisible hand" to keep it near a harmonious state of smoothly coordinated plans and actions. That is, the more unlikely it is that the classical stability hypothesis implicit in the neoclassical synthesis will be valid.

The self-regulating mechanisms of a modern free-market economy like that of any OECD country are obviously very powerful and robust, because they manage to coordinate the activities of millions of independent transactors, at least most of the time. At the microeconomic level, surpluses and shortages are relatively rare, small and short-lived. At the macro level the system seems to maintain itself within five or ten percent of a

---

[5] Carlaw et al. (2005) develop a comprehensive analysis of economic growth based on general purpose technologies.

full-employment growth path, except for a few dramatic exceptions such as the Great Depression. But surely there are limits to the power of any regulatory mechanism, not matter how skillfully designed or how far evolved, to cope with unusually large and frequent shocks.[6] One of the big challenges that economic growth poses to economic theory is to understand how the regulatory mechanisms of a modern economy work, what their limitations are, and what kinds of collective interventions might be needed to help them cope with circumstances that challenge their efficacy.

All of these questions remain largely unanswered. Almost all of modern economic theory proceeds by assuming that they do not need to be addressed, for it starts from the unexamined premise that observed prices and quantities are generated by a system in equilibrium. In micro theory the convention is to assume that Nash equilibrium prevails in static contexts, or that some form of subgame perfect equilibrium prevails in dynamic settings. In either case, everyone's actions generally depend on expectations of everyone else's and the assumption is that at every node of the tree there are no surprises, in the sense that everyone does what everyone had expected they would do if this state of the world were to prevail. In macro theory the analogous convention is to assume that the economy is always in a rational-expectations equilibrium, where again there are no surprises given the state of the world. It is now widely understood that to assume rational expectations is to assume not just that people are efficient users of information but also that their expectations are perfectly coordinated. My actions in any state of the world will depend on my expectations in that state. For everyone to have anticipated those actions correctly their expectations must have been consistent with mine. How people could acquire a mutually consistent set of expectations is something that we typically don't ask. We just assume they have them.

There have been attempts, in both micro and macro theory to examine the disequilibrium foundations of those equilibrium notions. For example there was a literature on the stability of general equilibrium that flourished in the 1950s and 1960s. But nothing in that literature in any way establishes a presumption of stability. All that can be shown is that there are hypothetical sufficient conditions for stability, such as universal gross substitutability. When theorists discovered what a messy subject they had on their hands they just dropped it, although they had hardly begun to deal with expectations. In fact, most of the literature analyzes only nonmonetary economies in which no one has to trade until the auctioneer has succeeded in arriving at an equilibrium, that is, economies in which effective demand, unemployment, bankruptcy, debt-deflation, endogenous money supply, and so forth have no meaning.

There is also a macroeconomic literature on the stability of full-employment equilibrium, going back to the famously neglected chapter 19 of Keynes's *General Theory*. Thus Tobin (1947, 1975) and Patinkin (1948) both supported Keynes's view that adverse distributional and expectational effects were likely to make it difficult for an economy to converge upon full employment through the unaided market forces of wage

---

[6] Cf. Leijonhufvud (1973).

and price adjustment. In recent years it has come to be recognized that the stability of a rational-expectations equilibrium depends on the convergence of a self-referential learning process in which peoples' attempts to learn about a system lead them to take actions that effectively change the system itself. Several years ago (Howitt, 1992) I argued that whether or not this process would converge would depend on the nature of the monetary policies being pursued, and in particular that convergence would require the monetary authority to obey what has subsequently come to be called the Taylor Principle of making the nominal interest rate rise more than point-for-point when inflation increases. This has been shown by a subsequent literature (recently summarized by Evans and Honkapohja, 2001; and Woodford, 2003) to be a valid proposition about the stability of equilibrium under a wide variety of different assumptions.

But all of this work is in its infancy and none of it has reached the position of accepted wisdom, judged by the fact that it has not filtered down to introductory economics textbooks, which are filled with stories of perfectly coordinated individual choices and have nothing to say about how those choices come to be coordinated. Thus it appears that the long-run wealth of a nation depends to a large extent on the convergence properties of a regulatory mechanism about which we as economists know very little.

Moreover, there are good reasons for thinking that policies and institutions that raise the pace of technological progress make it less likely that the mechanism will converge. This is not just because of the increased frequency and amplitude of the shocks with which the system must cope, and not just because of the dangers of financial bubbles and crashes that seem inevitably to be associated with major technological developments,[7] but also because the process of economic growth brings with it a deeper coordination problem that has not yet been addressed in the endogenous growth literature, one which lies at the heart of the growth process.

A particular form of this problem is what motivated Harrod (1939, 1948) and Domar (1946, 1947) to make the contributions that originally gave rise to the modern literature on economic growth. This "Harrod–Domar" problem is the problem of how to ensure enough effective demand so that the increased productive potential created by economic growth will be fully utilized, rather than becoming excess capacity and causing unemployment. It is a question of coordinating the expectations of investors with the yet unarticulated future demands of savers. As long as the marginal propensity to consume is less than unity, business firms will somehow have to see it in their interests to increase their investment outlays each year, and by just the right amount. Harrod rightly perceived that this brought into question the stability of equilibrium. Under his assumptions, any time entrepreneurs found they had overestimated the growth of final sales, they would scale back their collective investment outlays, and the subsequent multiplier effects of this cutback would cause actual sales to fall even more than anticipated. A vicious circle would be created, whereby shortfalls in investment demand would feed on themselves in cumulative fashion.

---

[7] On this, see Minsky (1992) and Nabar (2004).

One response to this problem is to invoke the classical stability hypothesis—to say that if entrepreneurial expectations don't respond appropriately, then sooner or later wages will have to fall, and the problem will go away. But this response begs the further questions of whether recovery will really be promoted by a debt deflation that will drive many firms out of existence, possibly bringing down with them some of the financial intermediaries whose services will be needed to finance adjustment, whether it will be possible for central banks preoccupied with exchange rates, and controlling a shrinking fraction of the means of payment, to avoid a monetary contraction once prices start falling, and what will counteract the destabilizing expectational and distributional effects upon which Keynes rested his instability case in the *General Theory*.

As Fazzari (1985) and Sen (1960) have made clear, the Harrod–Domar problem is a particularly intractable one because it involves a positive feedback loop between expectations and outcomes. That is, under the assumptions of the model if entrepreneurs are overly pessimistic in their growth expectations—expecting a rate of growth less than the economy's equilibrium (in Harrod's terms "warranted") rate of growth—then the simple investment multiplier of the Keynesian–Cross model implies they will experience an actual rate of growth even less than they were expecting. In other words, the interactions involved in the multiplier process are such that entrepreneurs will be receiving the wrong signal. Instead of learning that they were too pessimistic they will learn that they were too optimistic. Any sensible attempt to correct this expectational error will lead them to reduce their expectations by even more, thus leading the economy even further from its equilibrium.

I know of no modern attempt to resolve this Harrod–Domar problem. The literature starting with my 1992 contribution and recently summarized by Woodford would seem to imply that as long as the monetary authority obeys the Taylor Principle the economy should be able to converge to its rational-expectations equilibrium. But my own recent, as yet unpublished, research shows that this is not the case, that when the economy's capacity output is growing then this principle is still necessary but no longer sufficient for stability of equilibrium. Instead the monetary authority must generally also react with sufficient vigour to changes in the level of output, not just to the rate of inflation.

Moreover, the aggregate stability problems that Harrod raised constitute the tip of an iceberg, because adjustment to technological change requires far more than the right level of overall investment demand. We know that Engel curves are not straight lines through the origin. As incomes grow, marginal expenditures are devoted to new and different goods. Full adjustment in a multi-good economy requires entrepreneurs to create the sort of productive capacity and the sort of jobs, in many cases to create entirely new goods and markets, that will enable them ultimately to satisfy the yet unknown wants that people will have when their incomes are higher. Until people have that increased income, or at least enough of a prospect of increased income that they are induced to run down their liquid assets even faster, how are they to make their demands effective, especially if technological change has made them unemployed?

Entrepreneurs not only have to anticipate demands that have not yet been articulated, they have to anticipate the decisions that other entrepreneurs are making, because paying the setup cost of hiring people and capital and developing a market to produce and sell any particular range of goods will only pay off if that range is compatible with the standards, techniques, and strategies that others are developing. And of course these decisions have to be coordinated somehow with those of the unemployed and young workers trying to choose occupations, find sectors, and acquire skills to anticipate the job opportunities of the future.

More generally, in order to accomplish the social objective of exploiting an increased productive potential each year, new trading relationships have to be established that involve literally millions of people. How are these arrangements going to be made when none of the transactors can possibly have a detailed understanding of what is going on, none of them is in direct communication with all the others, and all of them are guided by purely private interests? What signals are going to induce business firms collectively to provide the kind of capital equipment, job opportunities, products, processes and markets that will profitably absorb the potential increases in purchasing power wrought by technological change? How much time, bankruptcy, mismatch and unemployment will it take? Or will adjustment ever be complete without some form of collective guidance, and if so what kind?

5. Looking ahead

I conclude by elaborating on what I said in the introduction, and what should by now be apparent, namely that the coordination issues raised by economic growth are ideally suited for investigation by computational methods. Indeed the computer has already been used by various authors to address some of these questions, mostly by writers in the evolutionary tradition pioneered by Nelson and Winter (1982),[8] but there is much more to be done.

One reason for turning to the computer is that when aggregate outcomes differ from individual intentions it is typically because of a complex set of interactions that are hard to characterize in analytical terms. To illustrate, the above-mentioned result of Aghion et al. (2001) to the effect that weaker intellectual property protection would, up to some point, raise aggregate R&D even though it would always have a negative effect on the R&D of a firm in any given situation depended on how the steady-state cross-industry distribution of technology gaps between leading and lagging firms reacted to parameter changes. Except in very special cases the behavior of this distribution was just too complicated for us to sign the comparative-static effect analytically. But the parameter space was simple enough that we were able to demonstrate numerically with reasonable certainty that the effect was always present. And this model was an extremely simple one, with exactly two firms in each industry and all industries ex-ante identical. We really need to examine richer models to test the robustness of such results. The

---

[8] A good sample of this literature can be found in the book by Dosi et al. (1988).

complex web of externalities that growth theory has uncovered makes it highly unlikely that as we go to even richer models we will be able to dispense with the computer for the purpose of discovering robust comparative-static effects.

Another reason for going to the computer in growth theory is to get an idea of the likely size of different effects. Thus in Howitt (1998) I was able to state analytically under what conditions there would be a downturn in overall economic activity following the introduction of a new GPT. But it was only through computational calibration methods that I was able to argue that this is an effect likely to last for many years rather than just a few weeks. These results would have to be replicated in much richer models before they could become generally accepted as true. Again there is no way to do this without computational methods.

The biggest challenge posed by all of these coordination problems is to characterize the mechanisms that keep a modern economic system reasonably near a fully coordinated state most of the time, and hence to deal with the generalized Harrod–Domar problem. We can deal analytically with the stability properties of two-dimensional, sometimes even three-dimensional systems, but beyond this we are lost without the computer.

In addition to the issue of dimensionality, no study of the coordination properties of an economic system will be fully satisfactory if it does not come to grips with the elementary fact that most transactions in actual economies are coordinated not by some unspecified agent like the Walrasian auctioneer but by an easily identified set of agents; namely, specialist trading enterprises. Economic transactions do not take place on a do-it-yourself basis but always involve such agents as grocers, department stores, realtors, car dealers, legal firms, accounting firms, and so forth. These are specialist traders that reduce the costs of search, bargaining and exchange, by using their expertise and by setting up trading facilities that enable non-specialists to trade on a regular basis. Collectively they coordinate the exchange process, for better or worse, by setting prices, holding buffer-stock inventories, announcing times of business, entering into implicit or explicit contracts with customers and suppliers, and taking care of logistical problems that arise in delivery, inspection, payment, and other aspects of the transaction process. When there are imbalances between demand and supply, specialist traders typically are responsible for making whatever adjustments are needed to ensure that non-specialists can continue their activities with minimal interruption. Those that do the job poorly do not survive competition.

The job that these trading specialists perform is the "procurement process" that Tesfatsion (2006) argues ACE modeling is ideally designed to study. Howitt and Clower (2000) show how the ACE approach can be used to study the formation and performance of a network of such specialists. In that paper Clower and I imagined a world with a large number of people who could potentially benefit from trading with one another but who lacked the information and the organizational infrastructure necessary to realize those benefits. We asked what would happen if some of the people from time to time were inspired to set up a trading facility, or "shop" that others could use, from which the shopkeeper might also profit by charging different buying and selling prices.

We realized early on that the only sensible approach to modeling how a coordination network might evolve from such a foundation was to write a computer program. For we did not want to impose on people any beliefs or information that implied some kind of prior coordination. Instead we wanted coordination to emerge from the basic assumptions of the model. Thus we needed a model that specified what would happen from any conceivable initial position, no matter what sorts of expectations people started with and no matter how incompatible their plans were to begin with. In short, our model had to constitute a multi-agent system that would generate observed outcomes from any given initial position. This to me is the essential characteristic of ACE methodology that distinguishes it from other uses of the computer in economic theory; in other uses computer programs approximate the behavior of a model, whereas with the ACE approach the program is the model. Since we were going to create a program anyway it seemed sensible to run it on the computer and study its behavior directly rather than seek what would at best be a partial and not very helpful analytical characterization of its properties.

What Clower and I discovered was that even though no one in the world we were describing ever possessed a reliable model of the overall system in which they were participating, nevertheless their interactions often resulted eventually in the emergence of a stable set of shops, each with a stable set of customers and suppliers, and everyone engaging in a pattern of exchange that can be described as a general (Nash) equilibrium in prices and quantities. Moreover, what we found was that whenever such a stable pattern emerged it took on a monetary structure. That is, one of the commodities traded would emerge as a universal medium of exchange, used in every single transaction in the economy, even by people that had no direct use for the commodity and were not capable of producing it.

The fact that this particular application of ACE methodology is capable of growing[9] a coordination network which is sometimes capable of leading people into an equilibrium pattern of exchange, at least in the very simple setting that we postulated, and is also capable of growing some of the ancillary institutions of real-world economic systems, such as monetary exchange, gives me hope that the methodology will some day be capable of shedding light on the big coordination issues raised by economic growth.

References

Acemoglu, D. (2002). "Technical change, inequality and the labor market". Journal of Economic Literature 40, 7–72.
Aghion, P., Howitt, P. (1994). "Growth and unemployment". Review of Economic Studies 61, 477–494.
Aghion, P., Howitt, P. (1998a). Endogenous Growth Theory. MIT Press, Cambridge, MA.
Aghion, P., Howitt, P. (1998b). "On the macroeconomic effects of major technological change". In: Helpman, E. (Ed.), General Purpose Technologies and Economic Growth. MIT Press, Cambridge, MA, pp. 121–144.

---

[9] Epstein (2006) elaborates on the use of ACE methodology to explain real-world institutions and behavioral patterns by "growing" them on the computer.

Aghion, P., Harris, C., Howitt, P., Vickers, J. (2001). "Competition, imitation and growth with step-by-step innovation". Review of Economic Studies 68, 467–492.

Aghion, P., Howitt, P., Violante, G.L. (2002). "General purpose technology and wage inequality". Journal of Economic Growth 7, 315–345.

Arrow, K.J. (1969). "Classificatory notes on the production and transmission of technological knowledge". American Economic Review Papers and Proceedings 59, 29–35.

Arthur, W.B. (1989). "Competing technologies, increasing returns, and lock-in by historical events". Economic Journal 99, 116–131.

Carlaw, K.I., Lipsey, R.G., Bekar, C. (2005). Economic Transformations: General Purpose Technologies and Sustained Economic Growth. Oxford University Press, Oxford.

Clower, R., Howitt, P. (1998). "Keynes and the classics: An end of century view". In: Ahiakpor, J.C.W. (Ed.), Keynes and the Classics Reconsidered. Kluwer, Boston, pp. 163–178.

Coe, D.T., Helpman, E. (1995). "International R&D spillovers". European Economic Review 39, 859–887.

Coe, D.T., Helpman, E., Hoffmaister, A.W. (1997). "North-south R&D spillovers". Economic Journal 107, 134–149.

David, P. (1990). "The dynamo and the computer: An historical perspective on the modern productivity paradox". American Economic Review Papers and Proceedings 80, 355–361.

Dawid, H. (2006). "Agent-based models of innovation and technological change", this handbook.

Domar, E.D. (1946). "Capital expansion, rate of growth and employment". Econometrica 14, 137–147.

Domar, E.D. (1947). "Expansion and employment". American Economic Review 37, 34–55.

Dosi, G., Freeman, C., Nelson, R., Silverberg, G., Soete, L. (Eds.) (1988). Technical Change and Economic Theory. Pinter Publishers, London.

Easterly, W. (2001). The Elusive Quest for Growth: Economists' Adventures and Misadventures in the Tropics. MIT Press, Cambridge, MA.

Epstein, J.M. (2006). "Remarks on the foundations of agent-based generative social science", this handbook.

Evans, G., Honkapohja, S. (2001). Learning and Expectations in Macroeconomics. Princeton University Press, Princeton, NJ.

Fazzari, S.M. (1985). "Keynes, Harrod and the rational expectations revolution". Journal of Post Keynesian Economics 8, 66–80.

Freeman, C., Perez, C. (1988). "Structural crises of adjustment, business cycles and investment behaviour". In: Dosi, G., Freeman, C., Nelson, R., Silverberg, G., Soete, L. (Eds.), Technical Change and Economic Theory. Pinter Publishers, London, pp. 38–66.

Greenwood, J., Yorukoglu, M. (1997). "1974". Carnegie-Rochester Conference Series on Public Policy 46, 49–95.

Harrod, R.F. (1939). "An essay in dynamic theory". Economic Journal 49, 14–33.

Harrod, R.F. (1948). Towards a Dynamic Economics. Macmillan, London.

Helpman, E., Trajtenberg, M. (1998). "A time to sow and a time to reap: Growth based on general purpose technologies". In: Helpman, E. (Ed.), General Purpose Technologies and Economic Growth. MIT Press, Cambridge, MA, pp. 55–83.

Howitt, P. (1992). "Interest rate control and nonconvergence to rational expectations". Journal of Political Economy 100, 776–800.

Howitt, P. (1998). "Measurement, obsolescence, and general purpose technologies". In: Helpman, E. (Ed.), General Purpose Technologies and Economic Growth. MIT Press, Cambridge, MA, pp. 219–251.

Howitt, P., Clower, R. (2000). "The emergence of economic organization". Journal of Economic Behavior and Organization 41, 55–84.

Kirman, A. (1992). "Whom or what does the representative individual represent?". Journal of Economic Perspectives 6, 117–136.

Klenow, P.J., Rodríguez-Clare, A. (1997). "The neoclassical revival in growth economics: Has it gone too far". In: Bernanke, B., Rotemberg, J. (Eds.), NBER Macroeconomics Annual. MIT Press, Cambridge, MA, pp. 73–103.

Leijonhufvud, A. (1973). "Effective demand failures". Swedish Journal of Economics 75, 27–48, now Scandinavian Journal of Economics.

Lucas Jr., R.E. (1972). "Expectations and the neutrality of money". Journal of Economic Theory 4, 103–124.

Lucas Jr, R.E. (2002). Lectures on Economic Growth. Harvard University Press, Cambridge, MA.

Mankiw, N.G., Romer, D., Weil, D.N. (1992). "A contribution to the empirics of economic growth". Quarterly Journal of Economics 107, 407–437.

Minsky, H.P. (1992). "The financial instability hypothesis", unpublished (The Jerome Levy Economics Institute, Bard College, New York).

Mokyr, J. (1990). The Lever of Riches. Oxford University Press, Oxford.

Nabar, M. (2004). "Technology-driven booms and crashes, productivity growth and volatility", unpublished (Brown University, Providence, RI).

Nelson, R., Winter, S. (1982). An Evolutionary Theory of Economic Change. Harvard University Press, Cambridge, MA.

Patinkin, D. (1948). "Price flexibility and full employment". American Economic Review 38, 543–564.

Ricardo, D. (1821). The Principles of Political Economy and Taxation, 3rd edn. Everyman's Library, New York.

Rosenberg, N. (1963). "Technological change in the machine tool industry, 1840–1910". Journal of Economic History 23, 414–443.

Rosenberg, N. (1994). Exploring the Black Box: Technology, Economics, and History. Cambridge University Press, Cambridge, UK.

Sargent, T.J. (1993). Bounded Rationality in Macroeconomics. Clarendon Press, Oxford.

Schelling, T.C. (1978). Micromotives and Macrobehavior. Norton, New York.

Sen, A. (1960). "Introduction". In: Sen, A. (Ed.), Growth Economics. Penguin, Harmondsworth, UK, pp. 9–40.

Tesfatsion, L. (2006). "Agent-based computational economics: A constructive approach to economic theory", this handbook.

Tobin, J. (1947). "Money wage rates and employment". In: Harris, S.E. (Ed.), The New Economics. Albert A. Knopf, New York, pp. 572–587.

Tobin, J. (1975). "Keynesian models of recession and depression". American Economic Review Papers and Proceedings 65, 195–202.

Woodford, M. (2003). Interest and Prices: Foundations of a Theory of Monetary Policy. Princeton University Press, Princeton, NJ.

Young, A.A. (1928). "Increasing returns and economic progress". Economic Journal 38, 527–542.

Zachariadis, M. (2003). "R&D, innovation, and technological progress: A test of the Schumpeterian framework without scale effects". Canadian Journal of Economics 36, 566–586.

Chapter 36

AGENT-BASED MACRO

AXEL LEIJONHUFVUD

UCLA, USA

University of Trento, Trento, Italy
e-mail: axel@economia.unitn.it

Contents

Handbook of Computational Economics, Volume 2. Edited by Leigh Tesfatsion and Kenneth L. Judd
© 2006 Elsevier B.V. All rights reserved
DOI: 10.1016/S1574-0021(05)02036-8

Abstract

Acceptance of computer modeling and experimentation has spread slowly at best in economics in large part because agent-based models often seem foreign to the neoclassical core of economics, as that core is understood today. But in its beginnings neoclassical economics was not built from choice theory, did not represent decisions as solutions to constrained optimization problems, made no strong assumptions about the rationality of agents, and did not view the world as always in equilibrium. Agent-based economics can tap into this older neoclassical economics of adaptive behavior and ongoing market processes while circumventing the technical obstacles which forced the forerunners to adopt the "static" method.

Agent-based process analysis will finally make it possible to tackle the central problem of macroeconomics, namely, the self-regulating capabilities of a capitalistic economy. Keynes challenged the presumption that flexibility of all prices guaranteed the stability of general equilibrium, arguing that effective demand failures meant that Say's Law did not hold. When supply did not create its own demand, stabilization policy in the form of aggregate demand management was required to restore full employment. In modern general equilibrium based macroeconomics, in contrast, Say's Law always holds, only "frictions" stand in the way of full employment, and stabilization policy lacks any tenable rationalization.

Agent-based computational methods provide the only way in which the self-regulatory capabilities of complex dynamic models can be explored so as to advance our understanding of the adaptive dynamics of actual economies.

Keywords

adaptive behavior, market processes, effective demand failure, stability of equilibrium, Say's Law, natural rate of unemployment, Marshall, Keynes

JEL classification: B13, B22, C62, E12

The first responsibility of a macroeconomist, surely, is to work towards an understanding of major economic disasters, of how to avoid them and of what to do when, unavoidably, they occur. Macroeconomics originally emerged as a distinct subdiscipline because the Great Depression was not well explained as a manifestation of efficient allocation theory. Disasters keep happening. The last fifteen years have seen the great break in the astonishing growth of Japan, the crises that forced Britain and Sweden to devalue, the Mexican 'tequila' crisis and its repercussions elsewhere, the East Asian and Russian crisis, and the Argentinian default crisis, for example. In the same period, macroeconomics has been reabsorbed into the theory of efficient resource allocation. Many people in the field see this development as having healed an unhealthy rift in the fabric of general economic theory. But this modern macroeconomics fails to throw light on disasters.

An economy is an evolving, complex, adaptive dynamic system. Much progress has been made in the study of such systems in a wide variety of fields, such as medicine and brain research, ecology and biology, in recent years. To people from one of these fields who come to take an interest in ours, economists must seem in the grips of an entirely alien and certainly unpromising methodology. In these other fields, computer modeling and experimentation is accepted without much question as valuable tools. It was possible, already 15 years ago, to hope that economists would find them valuable as well [Leijonhufvud (1993)]. But the intervening years have not witnessed a stampede into agent-based economics.

In fact, macroeconomists are more apt than most to be suspicious, if not outright hostile, to the agent-based approach. The apparent threat of cognitive loss is perhaps steeper in macro than in other areas. Each generation of scholars inherits a knowledge base of theory, of empirically confirmed "facts" and of investigative techniques. Inherent in this base are directions for future work—which problems are interesting and which ones not, what facts are puzzling and which ones can be taken for granted, what methods of investigation are approved and not approved, and so forth. The macroeconomics of the last quarter century, from Lucas through Prescott to Woodford, has been very strongly wedded to stochastic intertemporal general equilibrium theory. It is the well-developed knowledge base with which the last couple of generations of macroresearchers have been equipped. Acquiring it required a large investment. But then recruits to this research program are confident that their technical equipment is the best in the business.

Agent-based economics, in contrast, is in its technical infancy. The tendency, moreover, is to use it to tackle analytically intractable problems, thus making limited use of the treasured skills of modern macroeconomists. ACE models can claim to handle multitudes of heterogenous agents, which intertemporal general equilibrium models do not, but these simple agents, heterogenous though they be, have one thing in common, namely, "bounded rationality"—which runs afoul of how the neoclassical tradition is most often understood. It is also difficult to impose some analytical discipline or empirical constraint on complex dynamic behavior that systems of such agents tend to exhibit—and thus difficult to prevent such models from deteriorating into some species of computer games. There is also some guilt by association: complex simulation models have a bad track record in economics (Rosser, 1999, pp. 171–175).

The allegiance to modern macroeconomics is also very much fortified by a strong sense of tradition, of carrying on an economics that was 'always' built on 'rational choice', on 'optimizing behavior', on equilibrium, a tradition that you stray from at your peril. But this sense of tradition is in large measure based on a misreading (or, more likely perhaps, a lack of reading) of the history of our subject. What is today commonly thought of as neoclassical economics is really the hypertrophy of optimizing choice theory—the branch of neoclassicism which at one stage in the development of economics happened to be the most easily formalized. There is an earlier tradition of neoclassical economics, in some respects a more interesting one, which could not be adequately formalized and therefore gradually fell into neglect. This tradition could be revived with agent-based methods. It would be worth doing.

1. Two traditions

The British Classical writers, including Marx, sought to deduce how society would develop and the income distribution among classes change with time. The theory was inherently dynamic, driven by basic behavior propositions that were really verbal differential equations of the type "population will grow as long as real wages are above subsistence" or "capitalists will accumulate as long as profits are positive." But no one could handle systems of differential equations, of course. The best that could be done "rigorously" was to deduce the properties of the long-run equilibrium where these *laws of motion* ceased to operate, i.e., the stationary state of the Dismal Science.

The early neoclassicals shared this general outlook. Micro-behavior was thought of as adaptive. People sought to maximize utility or profit, but these were propositions about motivation, not performance. Certain agents in certain roles in certain social settings would be more calculating and better at calculating than others but in general no ambitious claims were made about the 'rationality' of people. Agents were capable of learning and most would be fairly efficient in situations with which they had a lot of experience. Since they were not super-rational, individuals would rely on a framework of institutions constraining the behavior of others so as to make the utility-relevant outcome of effort reasonably predictable. What people would learn from interacting with others would also depend on the institutions governing their transactions. Some countries (Western countries, of course) would do better than others.

The modern theory focuses on the principles of efficient resource allocation. Its core is choice theory, formalized in terms of constrained optimization. When used to explain observed behavior, constrained optimization models attribute *substantive rationality* to agents. Thus, in this theory utility or profit maximization is a statement about actual performance not just motivation. For this to be the case, decision-makers must be assumed to know their *true* opportunity sets in all their dimensions. Applying this behavior description to all agents implies that all choices made must be consistent. The theory does not leave room for failures to realize the relevant optima. Consistency of plans is the definition of equilibrium in this younger tradition. Set in a temporal context, substantive optimization requires that agents know all future prices (among other things) in drawing up their plans. Thus all choices have to be reconciled *before* anyone's choice can be made. Intertemporal general equilibrium theory may be 'rigorous' but it pays little attention to the sequencing of decisions in time.

In this theory, the 'rationality' of agents knows no bounds. Consequently, they have no very obvious need of institutions. Why they should use money or organize production in firms become riddles, not easily answerable within competitive general equilibrium theory.

2. The ambivalence of neoclassical economics

How the earlier neoclassicism which dominated until the 1930's or 1940's metamorphosed into the modern version is a long and complex story not to be attempted here [cf. Leijonhufvud (2004a)]. What needs to be noted is that neoclassical economics is not one coherent tradition. There is a strong conceptual tension between the older and the modern versions. The older neoclassical economics has a strong affinity to complex systems theory that general equilibrium theory entirely lacks.

Central concepts of complex systems theory, which have caused some excitement in other fields, are old themes in economics. *Emergent order* we have known about since Adam. The troubles with *top-down* control we have known about since Lu and Fritz. *Parallel processing* is what methodological individualism should have committed us to long ago.

Complex systems are generally hierarchical, often with multiple layers. Each system consists of interrelated components or modules that are systems in themselves. The components are simpler than the system of which they are parts. In general, they also have to work on a different time-scale (faster) than the higher-level system [Leijonhufvud (1995)].

All these statements fit naturally into the analytical mode of the older neoclassical tradition. They do not fit into the intertemporal general equilibrium framework of modern macroeconomics. (And the practitioners of modern macro tend to view references to these matters as irritating, wooly-headed talk.) The representative agent that has been made to do such heavy duty in Real Business Cycle theory is a case in point. This mythical figure is not a component, simpler than the system of which he is part. Although the poor man may suffer from multiplicity of equilibria, his 'rationality' is fully adequate to the complexity of the entire system. It is trite to note that the representative agent model leaves no room for supply and demand or "market forces." But the reason why this is thought to be adequate is of some interest, namely, that interactions at modular interfaces are considered inessential in this theory.

Agent-based economics should be used to revive the older tradition. So far the agent-based models that have gotten the most favorable—or at least most tolerant—reception by the profession at large have tended to tackle problems neglected by the mainstream, such as the work by Kollman et al. (1997) on Tiebout's 'voting with your feet', and the work by Axtell (2001) on the size-distribution of firms. These serve the cause by showing that agent-based economics can solve problems for which economists previously have not had the requisite tools. But it is not with new problems but with the *oldest* that agent-based methods can help us the most. We need to work on the traditional *core* of economics—supply and demand interactions in markets—for, to put it bluntly, economists don't know much about how markets work.[1]

3. Tapping into the older tradition

If the older neoclassical economics made more sense than today's, why did it decline and why did the "modern" take over? The answer, in brief, is that the older tradition in its time came to face insuperable technical obstacles while optimal choice theory did point a way forward to the solution of many problems and ambiguities in received theory. The story is a perfect illustration of both the negative and the positive side of Robert Lucas's (Lucas, 1987, p. 272) thesis that "purely technical developments that enlarge our ability to construct analogue economies" are one of the main forces driving the evolution of economics.

Alfred Marshall is the right representative of the older neoclassicism for the purposes of agent-based economics. Over the last half-century or more, Marshall's influence has steadily declined while that of Walras has been in the ascendance. Marshall's reputation has suffered at the hands of people who read him as a sloppy Slutsky or a Walras unable to attain anything more than a partial equilibrium. But this is judging him by a standard that is conceptually quite alien to his theory. Marshall did not build from choice theory, did not represent decisions as solutions to constrained optimization problems, and made no strong assumptions about the 'rationality' of decision-makers.

Recall that Marshall drew his supply-and-demand diagrams with quantity on the horizontal and price on the vertical axis. He was a conventional man and convention dictated that the independent variable go on the horizontal and the dependent on the vertical axis. (Convention dictates so still, but respect for conventions is not what it used to be.) Marshall started from supply prices and demand prices as functions of quantities. His $p^s(q)$ and $p^d(q)$ schedules are *not* loci of optimal points but indicate minimum and maximum prices, respectively, at which the decision-maker would be disposed to transact.

The "quantity-into-price" constructions [Hicks (1956)] do not state correspondences between price and most preferred quantity. They provide, rather, routines of adaptation in a constantly changing market environment. We may refer to them as "Marshall's *laws of motion*":

For the consumer:

[1] In all fairness, experimentalists and market designers have made important contributions to the understanding of market processes. But macroeconomics is still mired in unclear notions of "flexibility" or the lack of it.

If demand price exceeds the market price, buy more; in the opposite case, buy less.

For the producer:

If market price is above supply price, increase production; in the opposite case, cut back.

To which we should add the requisite rules for the middleman/market maker:

If demand exceeds supply, raise prices to both consumers and producers; in the opposite case, lower prices.

And a second rule for the producer:

If quasi-rents are positive, add to capacity; in the opposite case, let it depreciate.

These behavior rules fall short of the 'substantive rationality' attributed to agents in general equilibrium models. But gradient rules of this sort qualify at least for a measure of 'procedural rationality' [Simon (1976)] in settings where continuity and convexity can be taken for granted.

The combination of these 'laws of motion' makes an almost prototypical agent-based model. As with most such models, the combination of several differential or difference equations makes a non-linear dynamical system that may not be at all well behaved. Certainly, it was well beyond what could be handled with analytical methods in Marshall's time. He improvised his "static method" to tame the potentially unruly dynamics—but he did not trust it very far, although he seems to have thought that what he called the 'continuity principle' (*Natura non facit saltum*) gave some considerable assurance that it would work.

The static method was to take each of the 'laws of motion' separately, rank them in rough order from the speediest to the slowest, and then for each of them find the conditions under which the 'law' would cease to operate, assuming that all processes slower than the one under investigation could be treated as (approximately) constant. This amounts, of course, to assuming that each process will always converge to a well-defined point-attractor, an assumption for which there can be no general warrant, since when all these 'laws of motion' are operating on more or less the same time-scale, the system might well go, for example, to a complex attractor.

4. Taking supply and demand seriously

A simple market model of this general type will help point out a number of items for the agenda of agent-based theory. The first lesson is that the 'laws of motion' are not enough. One must also specify some minimal institutional structure within which they can be shown to operate. A fish market was the favored vehicle for generations of Marshallian pedagogues. It may serve here as well.

We assume a fishing fleet operating out of a port city. Each night, T, the boats go out and return in the morning. The entire catch of the fleet, q_T, is brought to the local fish auction house and sold at auction.

Let lower case t denote clocktime and let capital T denote dates. The adjustment speed of price is assumed qualitatively faster than that of output. Price finds the market clearing level within each market day; output finds its equilibrium over a sequence of days. Assume a stationary demand function:

$$q^d = D(p). \tag{1}$$

The catch landed on day T, q_T, is auctioned off:

$$p_{t+1} = f[D(p_t) - q_T] + p_t;$$
$$p_{t+2} = f[D(p_{t+1}) - q_T] + p_{t+1}; \tag{2}$$

etc.

By assumption, the algorithm (2) will converge on:

$$p_T^* = p^*(q_T), \quad \text{the market clearing price for day } T. \tag{3}$$

The expected size of the catch for any one boat depends simply on the amount of labor input during the night. The j-th boatowner's supply price is given by his marginal cost schedule:

$$p_j^s = s_j(q_j). \tag{4}$$

He compares his supply price for the catch most recently landed to the market price received and adjusts his rate of production accordingly:

$$q_{T+1,j} = h_j[s_j(q_{T,j}) - p_T^*] + q_{T,j}, \dots \text{ etc.} \tag{5}$$

Industry output (the catch of the fleet) evolves according to:

$$q_T = \Sigma q_{T,j} \tag{6}$$

and the condition for short-run equilibrium is (temporary) stationarity of output:

$$\Delta q_T = 0. \tag{7}$$

Equation (7) presumes, without explicit rationale, that the dynamic system will go to a simple point attractor. This attractor defines one point on Marshall's industry supply schedule. To get the rest of it, one has repeatedly to shift the demand function (1) and let the feedback loops (2) and (5) run to find the successive short-period equilibria.

The model has the virtue of portraying a market process with distinct laws of motion for both price and for output. It shows a rivalrous competitive process free of the infinitely elastic demand nonsense of 'perfect competition'. In several other ways, however, it is contrived to simplify matters that are seldom so simple. Here the market is a market *place* where well-defined sets of buyers and sellers meet for a limited time at defined intervals. The price must clear the market at each meeting and the meaning of market clearance is reasonably well-defined since inventory carry-over is ruled out (no frozen fish in Marshall's time!). However, the *tâtonnement* process in (2) is neither Marshallian nor realistic. Marshall would have assumed a double auction and argued that the final price would normally end up the same as in (3) above.[2]

In a normal, ongoing market, transactors are not all brought together in a single location and at the same time. Without centralization and synchronization, the supply-equal-demand condition "cannot be used to determine price, in Walras's or Marshall's manner" (Hicks, 1989, p. 11). But this also means that Marshall's "static method" will not work after his manner. Instead, ongoing markets require market makers who announce their prices and maintain inventories to handle customers arriving at irregular intervals. Virtually all manufactured goods are produced under increasing returns, not the diminishing returns of Marshall's fishermen and corn farmers. In markets where the producer operates under increasing returns, he often becomes the market maker and has to set a price based on speculation on what volume of sales he may achieve. The gradient climbing of Marshall's law of motion is then obviously inapplicable and a different algorithm has to be found to represent the producer's strategy.[3]

Combining the laws of motion for price and output makes a non-linear market process. Marshall tamed it by his ranking of adjustment speeds and corresponding hierarchy of equilibria. Agent-based modeling has no need for these conceptual crutches. When they are abandoned, however, one has to explain why markets normally do not fluctuate as much as the old laws of motion would suggest. The basic reason is simple. Consider again the fish market. The demand side is made up of middlemen—wholesalers and perhaps some retailers. They would have learned that the housewives, who are the ultimate buyers, will readily change their menus in response to rather small variations in the price of fish. Intertemporal substitution would keep short-period price fluctuations quite constrained. Similarly, fishermen will learn not to respond immediately to every little tick in the market price. Thus, the short-period demand price and supply functions will be much less elastic than the steady-state ones deduced from static utility and production functions. Agent-based methods should enable us to show the coevolution of the strategies of consumers, middlemen and producers that normally keep the tendencies of such systems to oscillate under pretty tight control. The theory should show the tendencies to be present although suppressed, rather than assume them away, for in certain situations the control will break down and make them boil to the surface. Under conditions of high inflation, for example, they show up in the extreme volatility of relative prices (Heymann and Leijonhufvud, 1995, pp. 169–182).

Marshall's adaptive theory avoids the perfect coordination trap which prevents modern optimization/equilibrium theory from helping us understand macroeconomic disasters. However, his 'static method', with its hierarchy of market day, short period and

---

[2] Much experimental evidence would nowadays support him on this point. But then the double-auction experiments are most often set up so as to conform to the assumptions of the fish-market discussed in the text.

[3] When sales occur in discrete quantities at discrete intervals, the monitoring of demand conditions becomes a non-trivial problem. How long a run of observations is needed to determine whether demand has changed?

long period equilibria, was a set of logical crutches that allowed him to hobble onward a piece with the theory of a complex dynamic economy. We can abandon Marshall's crutches. When that is done, a large, interesting and do-able agenda, of which the items above are only a sample, opens up for agent-based economics.

All this, however, deals with the microfoundations of an agent-based macro. It remains to consider an agenda for macroeconomics proper. The main item concerns the stability properties of the macrosystem—a topic that general equilibrium theorists gave up on some decades ago.

5. Keynes and all that

Prior to Keynes's *General Theory*, economists were quite generally convinced that, if only all agents in an economy obeyed Marshall's "laws of motion", that economy must most surely home in on a full employment equilibrium. Most particularly, of course, this would have to include the willingness of workers to let wages "flex" in the face of unemployment. It was generally accepted that the adjustment process would involve "frictions" of various sorts, but the overall stability of general equilibrium was not in doubt. This view of the matter is the one that we have returned to in the last thirty years or so.

The Great Depression persuaded Keynes that these beliefs must be wrong and that received theory, therefore, stood in need of a fundamental reappraisal. Keynes was a Marshallian and his reappraisal came to involve two departures from that tradition. The first was an argument directed against Marshall's "continuity principle". *Natura non facit saltum* did not hold for investment expectations. These were not solidly founded and could, therefore, shift both abruptly and drastically.

The second departure was more far-reaching. Keynes rejected the proposition that "Supply creates its own Demand" which apparently went under the label of "Say's Law" in Cambridge oral tradition [Clower (2004)]. Say's Law was taken to mean that any excess supply somewhere in the system would be balanced by an excess demand elsewhere. It was conjectured that Say's Law guaranteed the stability of full employment equilibrium as long as all prices (including wages) responded appropriately to excess demands and supplies in the respective markets. Keynes had come to realize that this conjecture was not generally true. (He thought, in fact, that it was always false, but in that he himself was mistaken.)

The problem was that excess supplies might not be balanced by *effective* excess demands, that is, by excess demands that would trigger the 'laws of motion' and cause market participants to change prices and activity levels. The *General Theory* stressed two such *effective demand failures*. The first concerns the coordination of consumption and production over time. An increase in savings creates an immediate excess supply of present goods but does not by itself signal an excess demand for consumption goods in the future. Thus, argued Keynes, "investment causes saving" (by changing income) "but saving does not cause investment"—two propositions that make no sense within si-multaneous equation models but that could be rendered meaningful within the modular architecture of a process model written in an object-oriented program.

The second effective demand failure can occur because the offer of labor services is not in itself an effective demand for consumer goods. In a monetary economy, "goods buy money and money buys goods, but goods do not buy goods" [Clower (1967)]. When labor is thrown out of work, consumption declines and the recessionary impulse is am-plified.

The two effective demand failures interact. When a negative shock to long-term ex-pectations reduces investment, the intention of savers is to accumulate more 'bonds' than the business sector intends to issue. If then the Central Bank's policy or ruling opinion on the stock market prevents the interest rate from falling sufficiently, output and real income will fall until saving no longer exceeds investment. There is then no growing market pressure for a correction of the interest rate. At that point, however, we have unemployment at wage rates which would be consistent with full employment had only saving and investment been brought into equality by a decline in the rate of interest rather than by falling output.

The resulting state of the economy, therefore, is one where one price (the interest rate) is inconsistent with general equilibrium, but excess demand in that market is zero so there is no automatic tendency for that price to change. At the same time, a second price (the money wage) *is* consistent with general equilibrium, but there is excess supply (unemployment) in that market that tends to drive it away from that level. Declining money wages would not cure the situation in Keynes's view. If wages and prices were very flexible downwards, a Wicksellian deflation would wreck the financial system and make matters far worse.

Keynes called this state of the economy an "equilibrium" with "involuntary unem-ployment." Semantic confusion has been unending ever since. His unemployment state will qualify as a Marshallian (short-period) equilibrium in the sense that the time-derivatives of output and employment are zero, but it obviously cannot be a Walrasian equilibrium. Similarly, the notion of "involuntariness" makes no sense within a choice-theoretical framework. What Keynes meant by it was essentially that this unemployment had emerged without any *intentional* interference with the laws of motion in labor markets. Economists have long been used to the *invisible hand* bringing about a coordi-nated state that was not part of anyone's intention. Keynes's involuntary unemployment should be understood in the same way as a different and less favorable *emergent prop-erty* of money-using market systems.

6. Decline and fall

When Say's Law fails to hold, so that Supply does *not* create its own Demand, a readily understandable case can be made for stabilization policy, in the sense made familiar in the Keynesian era, namely, aggregate demand management. Keynes certainly thought that effective demand failures were ever present and Keynesian economics has probably been overly addicted to aggregate demand management.

The *natural rate of unemployment* (NAIRU) postulate of Phelps and Friedman served in effect to reinstate Say's Law in macroeconomics. It was predicated on the old notion that departures of observed from equilibrium unemployment must be due to lags in the adjustment of wages. This was accepted also by confessed Keynesians since they had long ago left behind Keynes's worries about troubles in financial markets coming in the way of saving-investment coordination. With full employment saving equalling investment, all that is needed for full employment is wage flexibility. As macromodels incorporating the postulate conquered the field, it gradually became clear that they could not provide any rationale for aggregate demand policies. When Supply creates its own Demand, macropolicy—if any—has to be supply-side policy.

Marshall was well aware that his static method falsified the dynamics of the processes on which his theory focused and frequently expressed his doubts about how far the method could be trusted even when dealing just with the isolated market. Keynes, for lack of any feasible alternative, tried to use Marshall's method to tame the adaptive dynamics of the multidimensional macrosystem. In so doing, he was in effect trying to "talk" his way through the analytically completely intractable dynamics of a system of multiple markets with 'laws of motion' operating at different speeds, with some agents hampered by liquidity constraints, with volatile investment expectations and sluggish interest rate expectations, and so on. This was operating far, far beyond the limits of what could reasonably be expected of Marshall's method. Keynes was a very clever man and he managed to make it work after a fashion. But it is hardly surprising that the effort left a legacy of never-ending controversy over "what Keynes meant" and whether what he meant made sense. Nor is it surprising, in retrospect, that his theory could not survive when forced into the even tighter straitjacket of Walrasian general equilibrium.

7. Conclusion

The issues could not be of more importance. If NAIRU-based macrotheories are correct, aggregate demand has had nothing to do with the differences in performance between, say, the United States, the European Union countries and Japan in the 1990's. It has all been a matter of flexibility in the labor market, lower taxes, and government staying out of the way of business. If Keynes was at least partly right—and he certainly was not completely right—it is not so surprising that a country that manages to invest a lot and save hardly at all outperforms those where the opposite is more nearly the case. And the two views of the world differ on a host of other issues as well [Leijonhufvud (2004b)].

Keynes's theory of how a monetary market economy can fail to coordinate activities "automatically" was flawed. But what we have on the other side is little more than blind belief in the stability of general equilibrium.[4] The matter cannot in all intellectual

---

[4] Cf. Clower and Howitt (1996) and their discussion of the status of the "Classical Stability Postulate."

decency be left there. Agent-based methods provide the *only* way in which we can explore the self-regulatory capabilities of complex dynamic models and thus advance our understanding of the adaptive dynamics of actual economies.

References

Axtell, R. (2001). "Zipf distribution of U.S. firm sizes". Science 293, 1818–1820.

Clower, R.W. (1967). "A reconsideration of the microfoundations of monetary theory". Western Economic Journal 6, 1–9. Reprinted in: Walker, D.A. (Ed.), Money and Markets: Essays by Robert W. Clower, Cambridge University Press, Cambridge, 1984.

Clower, R.W. (2004). "Trashing J.B. Say: the story of a mare's next". In: Velupillai, K.V. (Ed.), Macroeconomic Theory and Economic Policy: Essays in Honour of Jean-Paul Fitoussi. Routledge, London, pp. 88–97.

Clower, R.W., Howitt, P. (1996). "Taking markets seriously: groundwork for a post-walrasian macroeconomics". In: Colander, D. (Ed.), Beyond Microfoundations: Post Walrasian Macroeconomics. Cambridge University Press, Cambridge, pp. 21–37.

Heymann, D., Leijonhufvud, A. (1995). High Inflation. Oxford University Press, Oxford.

Hicks, J.R. (1956). A Revision of Demand Theory. Clarendon Press, Oxford.

Hicks, J.R. (1989). A Market Theory of Money. Clarendon Press, Oxford.

Kollman, K., Miller, J., Page, S. (1997). "Political institutions and sorting in a Tiebout model". American Economic Review 87, 977–992.

Leijonhufvud, A. (1993). "Towards a Not-Too-Rational Macroeconomics". Southern Economic Journal 60 (1), 1–13.

Leijonhufvud, A. (1995). "Adaptive behavior, market processes and the computable approach". Revue Économique 46 (6), 1497–1510.

Leijonhufvud, A. (2004a). "The metamorphosis of neoclassical economics". In: Bellet, M., Gloria-Palermo, S., Zouache, A. (Eds.), Evolution of the Market Process: Austrian and Swedish Economics. Routledge, London.

Leijonhufvud, A. (2004b). "The long swings in economic understanding". In: Velupillai, K.V. (Ed.), Macroeconomic Theory and Economic Policy: Essays in Honour of Jean-Paul Fitoussi. Routledge, London, pp. 115–127.

Lucas, R.E. Jr. (1987). "Methods and problems in business cycle theory". In: Lucas, R.E. Jr. (Ed.), Studies in Business-Cycle Theory. The MIT Press, Cambridge, MA, pp. 271–296.

Rosser, J.B. Jr. (1999). "On the complexities of complex economic dynamics". Journal of Economic Perspectives 13 (4), 169–192.

Simon, H.A. (1976). "From substantive to procedural rationality". In: Latsis, S.J. (Ed.), Method and Appraisal in Economics. Cambridge University Press, Cambridge.

Chapter 37

SOME FUN, THIRTY-FIVE YEARS AGO

THOMAS C. SCHELLING[*]

Department of Economics and School of Public Affairs, University of Maryland, USA

Contents

[*] Emeritus.

Handbook of Computational Economics, Volume 2. Edited by Leigh Tesfatsion and Kenneth L. Judd
DOI: 10.1016/S1574-0021(05)02037-X

Abstract

A pencil-and-paper experiment with spacial segregation leads to some general phenomena of spatial organization.

Keywords

segregation, integration, neighbor, neighborhood, majority, minority

JEL classification: C630

Sometime in the 1960s I wanted to teach my classes how people's interactions could lead to results that were neither intended nor expected. I had in mind associations or spatial patterns reflecting preferences about whom to associate with in neighborhoods, clubs, classes, or ballparks, or at dining tables. Whether racial or linguistic differences or differences in age or income and wealth were what I had in mind, I'm not sure now. I spent a summer at RAND and took advantage of RAND's library to thumb through a few decades of sociological journals, looking for illustrative material that I could assign to my students. I found nothing I could use, and decided I'd have to work something out for myself.

One afternoon, settling into an airplane seat, I had nothing to read. To amuse myself I experimented with pencil and paper. I made a line of x's and o's that I somehow randomized, and postulated that every x wanted at least half its neighbors to be x's and similarly with o's. Those that weren't satisfied would move to where they were satisfied. This was tedious because I had no eraser, but I persuaded myself that the results could prove interesting.

At home I took advantage of my son's coin collection. He had quantities of pennies, both copper and the gray zinc one's we had all used during the war. I spread them out in a line, either in random order or any haphazard way, gave the coppers and the zincs their own preferences about neighbors, and moved the discontents—starting at the left and moving steadily to the right—to where they might inject themselves between two others in the line and be content. The results astonished me. But as I reflected, and as I experimented, the results became plausible and ultimately obvious.

Just to remind you, a line of randomly distributed coppers and zincs that looks like this,

$$0+000++0+00++00+++0++0++00++00++00++0+0+00+++0++00000+++000+00++$$
$$0+0++0,$$

when each wants at least four out of the eight nearest neighbors to be one's own type, becomes after two "rounds" of moving:

$$00000000++++++++++++++0000000000+++++++++++++++0000000000000000$$
$$++++++.$$

I experimented with different sizes of "neighborhoods"—the six, eight, or ten surrounding coins, different preferences—half like oneself, one-quarter like oneself, and different majority–minority ratios, and got results that fascinated me.

A one-dimensional line couldn't take me very far. But in two dimensions it wasn't clear how to intrude a copper or a zinc into the midst of coppers and zincs. I mentioned this problem to Herb Scarf, who suggested I put my pennies on a checkerboard leaving enough blank spaces to make search and satisfaction possible.

So I made a 16 × 16 checkerboard, located zincs and coppers at random with about a fifth of the spaces blank, got my twelve-year-old to sit across from me at the coffee table, and moved discontented zincs and coppers to where their demands for like or unlike neighbors were met. We quickly found out it didn't matter much in what order we selected the discontents to move—from middle outward, from out inward, from left to right or diagonally. We kept getting the same kind of results. The dynamics were sufficiently intriguing to keep my twelve-year-old engaged.

I found things I hadn't expected. Usually, once found, they appeared obvious. If zincs and coppers were majority and minority, or if zincs and coppers had greater and lesser demands for like neighbors, the sizes of eventual clusters and the densities of the different clusters varied accordingly.

And when we postulated that zincs and coppers had positive desires for unlike neighbors, especially if they were minority and majority, we got results that appeared weird until we saw what was happening. (The minority, desired as neighbors, had to become "rationed" among the majority.)

I had an interesting experience with computers at that time. I knew nothing about what computers could do, or how they did it, but I knew that RAND had people who did. I approached RAND and asked to be in touch with somebody who could program what I'd been doing. Somebody was put in touch with me. I quickly learned something crucial: programmer and experimenter must work closely, the former understanding what the latter wants, the latter understanding how programs work. Three thousand miles apart we didn't work that way. For me the results were perplexing. I eventually caught on that I had individuals counting themselves as their own "neighbors", had individuals on edges of the board or in corners miscounting how many neighbors they had, and in other ways had inadequately stipulated exactly how the zincs and coppers were to respond.

I later got James Vaupel to program things in Basic, but he was about to leave for the summer and I needed to know how to reprogram myself. We met on a Sunday, with sandwiches and beer, and in about five hours he taught me how to program with whatever parameters I wanted. He left the next day, but I was prepared.

Incidentally, the person at RAND who did the programming for me was John Casti. Thirty years later—I had never met him—he mentioned, in the course of a presentation that I attended, that his experience with my neighborhood patterning had initiated him into a career in simulation.

I published, along with the "checkerboard" model, a purely analytical model that I called the "bounded neighborhood" model [Schelling (1971)]. That model postulated a finite location that a person was either in or not in, positions within the neighborhood not being of concern. (It could be a model of membership or enrollment or participation, not necessarily location.) I thought the results I got from that model were as interesting as those from the checkerboard, but nobody else appeared to think so. I also explored the nature of a collective "tipping point" in a chapter in Tony Pascal's book, published about a year later, with a purely analytical model [Pascal (1972)]. It got little attention. In that "bounded neighborhood" model it became clear that an important phenomenon can be that a too-tolerant majority can overwhelm a minority and bring about segregation.

I've never been sure why my little simulation got so much attention after so many years. I discovered twenty-five years later that I'd been some kind of pioneer. It must be some limitation of my scientific imagination that I'd no idea I was doing something generic, something with promise beyond my neighborhood application.

I've had one experience that others may have had, in publishing a much abbreviated version of that model in a book [Schelling (1978)], believing that the full treatment in the Journal of Mathematical Sociology [Schelling (1971)] might be more than readers of the book would need. References to my model are usually to the version in the book, not to the original. I've seen no reference, for example, to the results I got when I postulated a strong preference for neighbors of opposite type. If one is interested in the "neighborhood" effects of differences other than in color or race, especially with individuals of one type much scarcer than individuals of the other type, the "integrationist" preferences become highly plausible. (I put "neighborhood" in quotation marks because residence is not the only interpretation.)

Another interesting result in the original, but not in the book version, a result that somewhat surprised me until I saw how it worked—an advantage of doing it manually instead of on a computer—is that if one subjects all the actors to a fairly strict limit on movement the results are usually that everyone becomes satisfied with less travel and more integration. For example—the linear case is adequate to illustrate—if we impose on all the +'s and 0's a restriction that no one may move more than five spaces, moving to the best available position if satisfaction cannot be achieved within five spaces, the original random line we used above becomes, in one round,

00000++++++000000+++++++++000000++++++00000+++++0000000000+++++++
++000,

All except two of the three on the right are satisfied, on average individuals traveled less than half the distance, and this is much more "integrated." The total number of unlike neighbors in this "restricted travel" version is twice that of the original equilibrium. And in the original, 30 of the 70 individuals ended up with no neighbors at all of opposite type; in this case of restricted movement, only 5.

This restricted-movement example is one of several results that may be unanticipated but become obvious with a little experience. Analytically one might say that restricting movement is a substitute for collaboration or anticipation. Unrestricted—and in the absence of collaboration or anticipation—an individual 0 will move to the nearest cluster of 4 or more 0's, passing numerous lonely 0's in what may be a long journey. Sufficiently restricted, the lonely 0 may be able only to join the nearest lonely 0, far from satisfactory; but the next lonely 0 looking for company can now join the two, making it three, and shortly a fourth will arrive and a fifth. (Increasing the "price" of travel may reduce the "cost" of travel.) By moving, individuals both add and subtract externalities where they leave, and add and subtract where they settle.

A similar principle is observed if the 0's are a minority and the +'s a majority. I remember being so confident that the smaller the minority relative to the majority, the smaller would be the minority clusters, that I wrote that before I tried it. When I tried it, it didn't work; the opposite occurred: the minority clusters became absolutely larger as the minority itself became smaller. What I had originally thought to be so obvious I needn't bother to demonstrate it turned out, upon demonstration, to be just as obviously the opposite.

Now that computers can display all the movement in "real time" there is, I suppose, little advantage in doing this kind of thing manually, but when I was doing it computers could compute but not display, and I often got computer results I could make little sense of until I worked it by hand.

References

Pascal, A.H. (Ed.) (1972). Radical Discrimination in Economic Life. Lexington Books D.C. Heath and Company, Lexingtom, MA.

Schelling, T.C. (1971). "Dynamic models of segregation". Journal of Mathematical Sociology 1. Abbreviated version appeared as "Models of segregation", in The American Economic Review, vol. LIX, No. 2, May 1969.

Schelling, T.C. (1978). Micromotives and Macrobehavior. W.W. Norton & Co, New York.

PART 3

GUIDELINE FOR NEWCOMERS TO
AGENT-BASED MODELING

Appendix A

A GUIDE FOR NEWCOMERS TO AGENT-BASED MODELING IN THE SOCIAL SCIENCES[*]

ROBERT AXELROD

Gerald R. Ford School of Public Policy, University of Michigan, Ann Arbor, MI, USA
e-mail: axe@umich.edu; url: http://www-personal.umich.edu/~axe/

LEIGH TESFATSION

Department of Economics, Iowa State University, Ames, IA, USA
e-mail: tesfatsi@iastate.edu; url: http://www.econ.iastate.edu/tesfatsi/

Contents

[*] The authors thank Stephanie Forrest, Ross Hammond, Ken Judd, Tom Lairson, Irene Lee, Bob Marks, John Miller, Scott Page, and Rick Riolo for helpful advice. The first author thanks the NSF (Grant 0240852) and the LS&A Enrichment Fund of the University of Michigan for financial support.

Handbook of Computational Economics, Volume 2. Edited by Leigh Tesfatsion and Kenneth L. Judd
DOI: 10.1016/S1574-0021(05)02044-7

Abstract

This guide provides pointers to introductory readings, software, and other materials to help newcomers become acquainted with agent-based modeling in the social sciences.

Keywords

agent-based modeling, complexity, emergence, collective behavior, evolution, learning, norms, markets, institutional design, networks

JEL classification: A2, A12, B4, C63

1. Purpose of the guide

The purpose of this guide is to suggest a short list of introductory readings to help new-comers become acquainted with *agent-based modeling (ABM)*. Our primary intended audience is graduate students and advanced undergraduate students in the social sciences. Teachers of ABM might also find this guide of use.

Unlike established methodologies such as statistics and mathematics, ABM has not yet developed a widely shared understanding of what a newcomer should learn. For decades, concepts such as the level of significance in statistics and the derivative in mathematics have been common knowledge that newcomers could be expected to learn. We hope that our selected readings will promote a shared understanding of ABM in the social sciences, not only among newcomers to ABM but also among researchers who already use ABM.

As a clarifying note on terminology, although this guide is directed specifically to social scientists, researchers in a wide range of disciplines are now using ABM to study complex systems. When specialized to computational economic modeling, ABM re-duces to *Agent-based Computational Economics (ACE)*.

For the convenience of readers, a parallel on-line guide for newcomers to ABM is available at *http://www.econ.iastate.edu/tesfatsi/abmread.htm* that includes links to our suggested readings, as well as demonstration software, as availability permits.

2. Agent-based modeling and the social sciences[1]

The social sciences seek to understand not only how individuals behave but also how the interaction of many individuals leads to large-scale outcomes. Understanding a po-litical or economic system requires more than an understanding of the individuals that comprise the system. It also requires understanding how the individuals interact with each other, and how the results can be more than the sum of the parts.

ABM is well suited for this social science objective. It is a method for studying systems exhibiting the following two properties: (1) the system is composed of interact-ing agents; and (2) the system exhibits *emergent* properties, that is, properties arising from the interactions of the agents that cannot be deduced simply by aggregating the properties of the agents. When the interaction of the agents is contingent on past experi-ence, and especially when the agents continually adapt to that experience, mathematical analysis is typically very limited in its ability to derive the dynamic consequences. In this case, ABM might be the only practical method of analysis.

---

[1] For more detailed discussions of many of the points raised in this section, see Robert Axelrod, *Complexity of Cooperation* (1997, Princeton University Press, Princeton, NJ), especially pp. 206–221, and Leigh Tesfatsion, "Agent-Based Computational Economics: A Constructive Approach to Economic Theory", in this Handbook.

ABM begins with assumptions about agents and their interactions and then uses computer simulation to generate "histories" that can reveal the dynamic consequences of these assumptions. Thus, ABM researchers can investigate how large-scale effects arise from the micro-processes of interactions among many agents. These agents can represent people (say consumers, sellers, or voters), but they can also represent social groupings such as families, firms, communities, government agencies and nations.

Simulation in general, and ABM in particular, is a third way of doing science in addition to deduction and induction. Scientists use deduction to derive theorems from assumptions, and induction to find patterns in empirical data. Simulation, like deduction, starts with a set of explicit assumptions. But unlike deduction, simulation does not prove theorems with generality. Instead, simulation generates data suitable for analysis by induction. Nevertheless, unlike typical induction, the simulated data come from a rigorously specified set of assumptions regarding an actual or proposed system of interest rather than direct measurements of the real world. Consequently, simulation differs from standard deduction and induction in both its implementation and its goals. Simulation permits increased understanding of systems through controlled computational experiments.

The specific goals pursued by ABM researchers take four forms: empirical, normative, heuristic, and methodological. The goal of *empirical understanding* asks: Why have particular large-scale regularities evolved and persisted, even when there is little top-down control? Examples of such regularities include standing ovations, trade networks, socially accepted monies, mutual cooperation based on reciprocity, and social norms. ABM researchers seek causal explanations grounded in the repeated interactions of agents operating in specified environments. In particular, they ask whether particular types of observed global regularities can be reliably generated from particular types of agent-based models.

A second goal is *normative understanding*: How can agent-based models be used as laboratories for the discovery of good designs? ABM researchers pursuing this objective are interested in evaluating whether designs proposed for social policies, institutions, or processes will result in socially desirable system performance over time. Examples include design of auction systems, voting rules, and law enforcement. The general approach is akin to filling a bucket with water to determine if it leaks. An agent-based world is constructed that captures the salient aspects of a social system operating under the design. The world is then populated with privately motivated agents with learning capabilities and allowed to develop over time. The key issue is the extent to which the resulting world outcomes are efficient, fair, and orderly, despite attempts by these privately motivated agents to gain individual advantage through strategic behavior.

A third goal is *heuristic*: How can greater insight be attained about the fundamental causal mechanisms in social systems? Even if the assumptions used to model a social system are simple, the consequences can be far from obvious if the system is composed of many interacting agents. The large-scale effects of interacting agents are often surprising because it can be hard to anticipate the full consequences of even simple forms of interaction. For example, one of the earliest and most elegant agent-based models—the city segregation (or "tipping") model developed by Thomas Schelling (see Section 4.1 below)—demonstrates how residential segregation can emerge from individual choices even when everyone is fairly tolerant.

A fourth goal is *methodological advancement*: How best to provide ABM researchers with the methods and tools they need to undertake the rigorous study of social systems through controlled computational experiments? ABM researchers are exploring a variety of ways to address this objective ranging from careful consideration of methodological principles to the practical development of programming and visualization tools.

In summary, ABM applied to social processes uses concepts and tools from social science and computer science. It represents a methodological approach that could ultimately permit two important developments: (1) the rigorous testing, refinement, and extension of existing theories that have proved to be difficult to formulate and evaluate using standard statistical and mathematical tools; and (2) a deeper understanding of fundamental causal mechanisms in multi-agent systems whose study is currently separated by artificial disciplinary boundaries.

3. Selection criteria

We decided at the outset to offer a short list of readings rather than make any attempt at comprehensiveness. We based our selections on two criteria: (i) the educational value of the reading for newcomers to ABM in the social sciences; and (ii) the accessibility of the reading. The specific choice of topics and readings is our own. We recognize that our selections are personal and necessarily somewhat arbitrary.

4. Suggested readings

4.1. Complexity and ABM

Vicsek, Tamas (2002), "Complexity: The Bigger Picture", *Nature*, Vol. 418, p. 131.
In this short essay, Vicsek describes how computer simulation fits into the scientific enterprise. The goal is to "capture the principal laws behind the exciting variety of new phenomena that become apparent when the many units of a complex system interact."

Callahan, Paul, "What is the Game of Life?"
Accessible online at *http://www.math.com/students/wonders/life/life.html*, this interactive website explains and demonstrates a delightful "game" invented by John Conway in 1970. Although the Game of Life is not an agent-based model, it is a fascinating illustration of how just three simple behavioral rules can lead to extremely complicated outcomes.

Schelling, Thomas C. (1978), *Micromotives and Macrobehavior*, **Norton, New York, pp. 137–157.**
This classic work demonstrates what can happen when behavior in the aggregate is more than the simple summation of individual behaviors. The highlighted pages present an agent-based model that shows how a high degree of residential segregation can emerge from the location choices of fairly tolerant individuals.

4.2. Emergence of collective behavior

Granovetter, Mark (1978), "Threshold Models of Collective Behavior", *American Journal of Sociology*, **Vol. 83, pp. 1420–1442.**
Threshold models are a class of mathematically tractable models that do not require ABM to determine the global behavior that will emerge from individual choices. In a threshold model, the key specification is each agent's *threshold* for each of its possible actions, i.e., the proportion of other agents who must take a particular action before the given agent will prefer to take this action. Granovetter develops a threshold model in which each agent has the same two alternative actions and the thresholds for these actions differ across agents. For a given frequency distribution of thresholds, the model calculates the equilibrium number of agents taking each action. One suggested application is to civil violence, in which each agent must decide whether or not to join a riot. It is interesting to compare Granovetter's threshold model outcomes to the richer outcomes obtained for an agent-based model of civil violence in the following article by Joshua Epstein.

Epstein, Joshua M. (2002), "Modeling Civil Violence: An Agent-Based Computational Approach", *Proceedings of the National Academy of Sciences, USA*, **Vol. 99, pp. 7243–7250.**
Epstein uses a spatial agent-based model to explore civil violence. A central authority uses "cops" to arrest (remove) actively rebelling citizens from the society for a specified jail term. In each time step, each agent (cop or citizen) randomly moves to a new unoccupied site within its limited vision. A rebelling citizen's estimated arrest probability is assumed to fall as the ratio of actively rebelling citizens to cops that the citizen perceives in its vicinity increases. Each citizen in each time step decides whether to actively rebel or not depending on this perceived ratio. Epstein shows how the complex dynamics resulting from these simple assumptions can generate empirically interesting macroscopic regularities that are difficult to analyze using more standard modeling approaches.

Cederman, Lars-Erik (2003), "Modeling the Size of Wars", *American Political Science Review*, **Vol. 97, pp. 135–150.**
Power-law distributions, scaling laws and self-organized criticality are features of many frequency distributions, from word usage to avalanches, and from firms to cities. A set of events is said to behave in accordance with a *power law distribution* if large events

are rarer than small events, and specifically if the frequency of an event is *inversely* proportional to its size. An example is the distribution of the sizes of wars. Cederman uses an agent-based model of war and state formation in the context of technological change to account for this observed regularity. His paper is a good example of how a fairly complicated model and its implications can be clearly presented, with details left to an appendix.

Miller, John, and Scott E. Page (2004), "The Standing Ovation Problem", *Complexity*, Vol. 9, No. 5, May/June, pp. 8–16.
Miller and Page use audience ovation to introduce many key ABM themes, in particular the emergence of collective behavior, and to provide specific modeling suggestions suitable for implementation by newcomers to the field. As a public performance draws to a close, and audience members begin to applaud and some even tentatively to stand, will a standing ovation ensue or not? This is the famous *Standing Ovation Problem (SOP)* inspired by the seminal work of Thomas Schelling on the relationship between micro decisions and macro behaviors (see Section 4.1 above). Miller and Page use the SOP to illustrate how complex social dynamics can arise from the interactions among simple personal choices, in this case to stand or not. They argue (p. 9) that the success of the SOP as an expository device is that it forces modelers "to confront the core methodological issue in complex adaptive social systems, namely, how does one model a system of thoughtful, interacting agents in time and space."

4.3. Evolution

Dawkins, Richard (1989), *The Selfish Gene*, New Edition, Oxford University Press, Oxford, UK, pp. 1–45.
If you are going to read only one book on evolution, this delightful and insightful book is a good choice. You will be amazed at the implications of the inclusive fitness perspective.

Sigmund, Karl (1993), *Games of Life: Explorations in Ecology, Evolution, and Behavior*, Oxford University Press, Oxford, UK, pp. 155–206.
Writing in a lively and engaging style, Sigmund provides a non-technical introduction to models of evolution. Topics include population ecology and chaos, random drift and chain reactions, population genetics, evolutionary game theory, and the evolution of cooperation based on reciprocity. The highlighted pages cover the latter two topics, of most relevance to social scientists.

4.4. Learning

Clark, Andy (1998), *Being There: Putting Brain, Body, and World Together Again*, The MIT Press, Cambridge, MA, pp. 179–192.
This delightfully written book addresses foundational questions about how people (and

robots) can make sense of the confusing world in which they live. The highlighted pages apply this perspective to markets.

Holland, John H. (1992), "Genetic Algorithms", *Scientific American*, Vol. 267, July, pp. 66–72.
The genetic algorithm is a search technique inspired by the evolutionary effectiveness of mutation and differential reproduction. The algorithm provides a convenient way to model agents of limited rationality that adapt and/or evolve over time. Each agent might be responding to a fixed environment, or to an ever-changing social environment consisting of many agents who are continually adapting to each other. The article by Rick Riolo in the same issue shows how to incorporate a genetic algorithm in one's own agent-based model.

Vriend, Nicolaas (2000), "An Illustration of the Essential Difference Between Individual and Social Learning, and its Consequence for Computational Analyses", *Journal of Economic Dynamics and Control*, Vol. 24, pp. 1–19.
Vriend focuses on the importance of the *level* of learning for computational agents. An agent is said to employ *individual-level learning* when it learns from its own past experiences, and to employ *population-level learning* when it learns from other agents, e.g., through mimicry of their observed behaviors. Using a simple market model for concrete illustration, Vriend demonstrates that substantially different outcomes can result when profit-seeking firms use individual-level genetic algorithm learning versus population-level genetic algorithm learning.

4.5. Norms

Hofstadter, Douglas (1983), "Computer Tournaments of the Prisoner's Dilemma Suggest How Cooperation Evolves", *Scientific American*, May, pp. 18–26.
Hofstadter explains Robert Axelrod's computer tournaments, which explored the evolution of cooperation in the iterated Prisoner's Dilemma. For the original work, including agent-based models, formal theorems, and many real-world applications, see Robert Axelrod, *Evolution of Cooperation* (1984, NY: Basic Books).

Axelrod, Robert (1986), "An Evolutionary Approach to Norms", *American Political Science Review*, Vol. 80, pp. 1095–1111.
This article develops an agent-based model with a simple form of learning using the genetic algorithm to explore what can happen when many agents adapt to each other's behavior over time. Agents can be more or less bold (say by cheating), and more or less vengeful (say by reporting cheaters). The model shows the conditions under which a collective action problem can be solved by a self-sustaining metanorm: punish those who do not enforce the norm because others might punish you for *not* doing so.

Nowak, Martin A., Karen M. Page, and Karl Sigmund (2000), "Fairness Versus Reason in the Ultimatum Game", *Science,* **Vol. 289, September 8, pp. 1773–1775.**
The authors consider the *Ultimatum Game* in which two players are offered a chance to win a certain sum of money. One player, the proposer, gets to offer a portion of the sum to the other player, retaining the rest. The second player gets to accept or reject the offer, with rejection resulting in no money for either player. The rational solution, according to game theory, is for the proposer to offer as little as possible and for the other player to accept. When humans play the game, however, the most frequent offer is an equal ("fair") share. The authors employ evolutionary dynamics to explain how this "irrational" anchoring on fair shares might have evolved among humans in part through a rational concern for reputation. Specifically, accepting low offers, if generally known and remembered, increases the chances of receiving low offers in subsequent encounters; and making low offers becomes irrational if low offers are not accepted.

Epstein, Joshua M. (2001), "Learning to be Thoughtless: Social Norms and Individual Competition", *Computational Economics,* **Vol. 18, pp. 9–24.**
Epstein uses an agent-based model to study experimentally an important observed aspect of social norm evolution: namely, that the amount of time an individual devotes to thinking about a behavior tends to be inversely related to the strength of the social norms that relate to this behavior. In the limit, once a behavioral norm is firmly entrenched in a society, individuals tend to conform to the norm without explicit thought. Epstein's innovative model permits agents to learn how to behave (what behavioral norm to adopt), but it also permits agents to learn how much to think about how to behave.

4.6. Markets

Albin, Peter, and Duncan K. Foley (1992), "Decentralized, Dispersed Exchange Without an Auctioneer: A Simulation Study", *Journal of Economic Behavior and Organization,* **Vol. 18, pp. 27–51**.
Albin and Foley simulate pure exchange among geographically dispersed utility-seeking traders with endowments of two distinct types of goods, and with bounds to rationality and calculation. Exchange is entirely decentralized. The authors show that this decentralized exchange process achieves a substantial improvement in trader welfare relative to randomly allocated goods.

Gode, D.K., and S. Sunder (1993), "Allocative Efficiency of Markets with Zero Intelligence Traders: Market as a Partial Substitute for Individual Rationality", *Journal of Political Economy,* **Vol. 101, pp. 119–137.**
Gode and Sunder report on continuous double-auction experiments with computational traders. They find that high market efficiency is generally attained even when the traders randomly select bids and offers from within their budget sets as long as these "zero intelligence" traders abide by certain protocols restricting the order of executed trades. The authors conclude that the high market efficiency typically observed in continuous

double-auction experiments with human subjects is due to the structure of the auction and not to learning. Their seminal work has highlighted an important issue now being actively pursued by many other researchers: what are the relative roles of learning and institutional arrangements in the determination of economic, social, and political outcomes?

LeBaron, Blake (2002), "Building the Santa Fe Artificial Stock Market", Working Paper, Brandeis University, June, http://www.econ.iastate.edu/tesfatsi/blake.sfisum.pdf
LeBaron provides an insider's look at the construction of the Santa Fe Artificial Stock Market model. He considers the many design questions that went into building the model from the perspective of a decade of experience with agent-based financial markets. He also provides an assessment of the model's overall strengths and weaknesses.

4.7. Institutional design

Kollman, Ken, John H. Miller, and Scott E. Page (1997), "Political Institutions and Sorting in a Tiebout Model", *American Economic Review***, Vol. 87, pp. 977–992.**
The authors develop an agent-based model to explore how social outcomes are affected by the political institutions used to aggregate individual choices on local public goods issues, such as whether or not to finance a community swimming pool. Examples of such political institutions are referenda, two-party competition, and proportional representation. For each tested political institution, assumed to be commonly in use across all jurisdictions, citizens "vote with their feet" in each time period regarding which jurisdiction they wish to inhabit. The policy positions resulting in any given jurisdiction depend on the preferences of the citizens located within that jurisdiction, in a manner determined by the political institution in force. Citizens can continue to relocate in response to changing local policy positions, and local policy positions can continue to change in response to citizen relocations. The authors find that social efficiency is highest under political institutions such as two-party competition or proportional representation that initially induce citizens to undertake a suitable degree of experimentation among alternative jurisdictions.

Lansing, Stephen, and James N. Kremer (1993), "Emergent Properties of Balinese Water Temple Networks: Coadaptation on a Rugged Fitness Landscape", *American Anthropologist***, Vol. 95, pp. 97–114.**
Over hundreds of years, Balinese farmers have developed an intricate hierarchical network of "water temples" dedicated to agricultural deities in parallel with physical transformations of their island deliberately undertaken to make it more suitable for growing irrigated rice. The water temple network plays an instrumental role in the coordination of activities related to rice production. Representatives of different water temple congregations meet regularly to decide cropping patterns, planting times, and water usage, thus helping to synchronize harvests and control pest populations. Lansing and Kremer

develop an ecological simulation model to illuminate the system-level effects of the water temple network, both social and ecological. Their anthropological study illustrates many important ABM concepts, including emergent properties, fitness landscapes, co-adaptation, and the effects of different institutional designs.

Simon, Herbert (1982), "The Architecture of Complexity", pp. 193–230 in *The Sciences of the Artificial*, Second Edition, The MIT Press, Cambridge, MA.
Simon informally defines a "complex system" to be a system made up of a large number of parts that interact in a non-simple way. He considers a number of complex systems encountered in the behavioral sciences, from families to formal organizations, and describes features that are common in a wide variety of such systems. His central theme (p. 196) is that "complexity frequently takes the form of hierarchy and that hierarchic systems have some common properties independent of their specific content." He discusses the design advantages of nearly decomposable subsystems with a hierarchical organization of their parts. He also conjectures that complex systems evolve from simple systems much more rapidly if there are stable intermediate forms along the way, hence evolution favors hierarchic over non-hierarchic systems.

4.8. Networks

Wilhite, Allen (2001), "Bilateral Trade and 'Small-World' Networks", *Computational Economics*, Vol. 18, No. 1, pp. 49-64.
Wilhite develops an agent-based computational model of a bilateral exchange economy. He uses this model to explore the consequences of restricting trade to different types of networks, including a "small-world network" with both local connectivity and global reach. His key finding is that small-world networks provide most of the market-efficiency advantages of completely connected networks while retaining almost all of the transaction cost economies of locally connected networks.

Kirman, Alan P., and Nicolaas J. Vriend (2001), "Evolving Market Structure: An ACE Model of Price Dispersion and Loyalty", *Journal of Economic Dynamics and Control*, Vol. 25, Nos. 3–4, pp. 459–502.
Social scientists typically study the implications of *given* interaction networks, e.g., friendship or trade networks. An important aspect of many social systems, however, is how agents come to *form* interaction networks. Kirman and Vriend address this issue in the context of an agent-based computational model capturing salient structural aspects of the actual wholesale fish market in Marseilles, France. Two features characterizing this actual market are: (a) loyalty relationships (persistent trade partnerships) between particular buyers and sellers; and (b) persistent price dispersion unexplainable by observable characteristics of the fish. The simulation results show that loyalty relationships can indeed emerge naturally between particular buyer-seller pairs as the buyers and sellers co-evolve their trading rules over time. Buyers learn to become loyal to particular sellers while, at the same time, sellers learn to offer higher payoffs (lower

prices and more reliable supplies) to their more loyal buyers. Moreover, this evolving trade network supports persistent price dispersion over time.

4.9. Modeling techniques

Macy, Michael W., and Robert Willer (2002), "From Factors to Actors: Computational Sociology and Agent-Based Modeling", *Annual Review of Sociology*, Vol. 28, pp. 143–166.
While written for sociologists, this review article should be of value to all agent-based modelers. It places ABM in its historical context, explains its meaning and goals, provides many good examples, and offers useful advice to those who want to try it for themselves. Other articles with explicit modeling advice include LeBaron (2002) and Miller and Page (2004) cited above.

5. What to do next

- Browse the comprehensive **website** at *http://www.econ.iastate.edu/tesfatsi/ace.htm* to find agent-based researchers in your neck of the woods, links to specific topics in ABM, course syllabi, demonstration software, and much more.
- Use the chapters in this **handbook** to help you explore specific topics.
- Explore the **journals** that publish a good deal of ABM: *Journal of Artificial Societies and Social Simulation (on-line); Computational Economics; Journal of Economic Behavior and Organization; Games and Economic Behavior; Journal of Economic Dynamics and Control*; and *Complexity*. For weekly news items, including upcoming conferences, see the *Complexity Digest* (online).[2]
- Master the **mathematical and statistical tools** that are commonly used in ABM by studying basic mathematical analysis (especially probability theory and nonlinear dynamics), game theory, and elementary statistics (e.g., hypothesis testing and regression).
- Learn a **programming language** so that you can try your hand at building and running your own agent-based models. For younger beginners, we recommend StarLogo.[3] For older beginners, we recommend a language with object-oriented capabilities such as Java, C++, or C#,[4] supplemented with an agent-based toolkit

---

[2] See *http://www.econ.iastate.edu/tesfatsi/publish.htm* for links to these journals as well as to many other journals and book publishers that support the publication of ABM-related work.

[3] StarLogo is a programmable modeling environment for exploring the workings of decentralized systems that has been specifically designed to be user-friendly for K-12 students. Extensive support materials for StarLogo can be found at *http://education.mit.edu/starlogo/*.

[4] ABM is increasingly being implemented using languages with object-oriented programming (OOP) capabilities, such as Java, C++, and C#. A good introduction to OOP is Matt Weisfeld, *The Object-Oriented Thought Process* (2000, SAMS Publishing, Division of Macmillan, Indianapolis, Indiana). This book is de-

(see below). Another possibility is Matlab, which is steadily increasing its ABM capabilities.

- Explore the **agent-based toolkits** that are available to assist agent-based modelers with common tasks such as constructing agents and displaying output in the form of tables, charts, graphs, and movies.[5] For example, *Repast* is specifically designed for agent-based modeling in the social sciences and supports model development in many different programming languages and on virtually all modern computing platforms.[6] Another possibility is *NetLogo*, a cross-platform multi-agent programming environment.[7] Both Repast and NetLogo are actively maintained and freely available, and their relative ease of use has attracted growing communities of users.

- Explore **special journal issues** devoted to agent-based modeling and related themes. These include: *American Behavioral Scientist* (Vol. 42, August 1999); *Science* (Vol. 284, April 1999); *Journal of Economic Dynamics and Control* (Vol. 25, Nos. 3–4, 2001), *Computational Economics* (Vol. 18, No. 1, 2001); and the *Proceedings of the National Academy of Sciences, USA* (Vol. 99, Supplement 3, 2002).[8]

- For a wonderful **introduction to computational aspects of complex systems**, including fractals, chaos, cellular automata, neural networks, and a helpful glossary of terms, we highly recommend Gary William Flake, *The Computational Beauty of Nature* (1998, MIT Press, Cambridge, MA).[9]

---

signed to help newcomers learn OOP guidelines for solid class design and master the major OOP concepts of inheritance, composition, interfaces, and abstract classes. The author motivates and illustrates his points by taking readers step by step through simple concrete examples.

[5] See *http://www.econ.iastate.edu/tesfatsi/acecode.htm* for annotated pointers to a wide variety of programming languages and agent-based toolkits currently being used for ABM.

[6] See *http://www.econ.iastate.edu/tesfatsi/repastsg.htm* for detailed information about Repast.

[7] See *http://ccl.northwestern.edu/netlogo* for detailed information about NetLogo.

[8] See *http://www.econ.iastate.edu/tesfatsi/avolumes.htm* for an annotated list of special ABM-related journal issues together with volumes of ABM-related readings.

[9] See *http://mitpress.mit.edu/books/FLAOH/cbnhtml/* for detailed information and supporting materials for Flake's book.

AUTHOR INDEX

n indicates citation in a footnote.

SUBJECT INDEX

HANDBOOKS IN ECONOMICS

1. HANDBOOK OF MATHEMATICAL ECONOMICS (in 4 volumes)
   Volumes 1, 2 and 3 edited by Kenneth J. Arrow and Michael D. Intriligator
   Volume 4 edited by Werner Hildenbrand and Hugo Sonnenschein

2. HANDBOOK OF ECONOMETRICS (in 6 volumes)
   Volumes 1, 2 and 3 edited by Zvi Griliches and Michael D. Intriligator
   Volume 4 edited by Robert F. Engle and Daniel L. McFadden
   Volume 5 edited by James J. Heckman and Edward Leamer
   Volume 6 is in preparation (editors James J. Heckman and Edward Leamer)

3. HANDBOOK OF INTERNATIONAL ECONOMICS (in 3 volumes)
   Volumes 1 and 2 edited by Ronald W. Jones and Peter B. Kenen
   Volume 3 edited by Gene M. Grossman and Kenneth Rogoff

4. HANDBOOK OF PUBLIC ECONOMICS (in 4 volumes)
   Edited by Alan J. Auerbach and Martin Feldstein

5. HANDBOOK OF LABOR ECONOMICS (in 5 volumes)
   Volumes 1 and 2 edited by Orley C. Ashenfelter and Richard Layard
   Volumes 3A, 3B and 3C edited by Orley C. Ashenfelter and David Card

6. HANDBOOK OF NATURAL RESOURCE AND ENERGY ECONOMICS
   (in 3 volumes). Edited by Allen V. Kneese and James L. Sweeney

7. HANDBOOK OF REGIONAL AND URBAN ECONOMICS (in 4 volumes)
   Volume 1 edited by Peter Nijkamp
   Volume 2 edited by Edwin S. Mills
   Volume 3 edited by Paul C. Cheshire and Edwin S. Mills
   Volume 4 edited by J. Vernon Henderson and Jacques-François Thisse

8. HANDBOOK OF MONETARY ECONOMICS (in 2 volumes)
   Edited by Benjamin Friedman and Frank Hahn

9. HANDBOOK OF DEVELOPMENT ECONOMICS (in 4 volumes)
   Volumes 1 and 2 edited by Hollis B. Chenery and T.N. Srinivasan
   Volumes 3A and 3B edited by Jere Behrman and T.N. Srinivasan

10. HANDBOOK OF INDUSTRIAL ORGANIZATION (in 3 volumes)
    Volumes 1 and 2 edited by Richard Schmalensee and Robert R. Willig
    Volume 3 is in preparation (editors Mark Armstrong and Robert H. Porter)

11. HANDBOOK OF GAME THEORY with Economic Applications (in 3 volumes)
    Edited by Robert J. Aumann and Sergiu Hart

All published volumes available

FORTHCOMING TITLES

HANDBOOK OF EXPERIMENTAL ECONOMICS RESULTS
Editors Charles Plott and Vernon L. Smith

HANDBOOK OF THE ECONOMICS OF GIVING, ALTRUISM AND RECIPROCITY
Editors Serge-Christophe Kolm and Jean Mercier Ythier

HANDBOOK ON THE ECONOMICS OF ART AND CULTURE
Editors Victor Ginsburgh and David Throsby

HANDBOOK OF LAW AND ECONOMICS
Editors A. Mitchell Polinsky and Steven Shavell

HANDBOOK OF ECONOMIC FORECASTING
Editors Graham Elliott, Clive W.J. Granger and Allan Timmermann

HANDBOOK OF THE ECONOMICS OF EDUCATION
Editors Eric Hanushek and Finis Welch

HANDBOOK OF ECONOMICS OF TECHNOLOGICAL CHANGE
Editors Bronwyn H. Hall and Nathan Rosenberg